21.00

The Psychology
of Sex Differences

ELEANOR EMMONS MACCOBY

AND

CAROL NAGY JACKLIN

STANFORD UNIVERSITY PRESS

STANFORD, CALIFORNIA

Stanford University Press
Stanford, California
© 1974 by the Board of Trustees of the
Leland Stanford Junior University
Printed in the United States of America
ISBN 0-8047-0859-2
Original edition 1974
Last figure below indicates year of this printing:
85 84 83 82 81 80 79 78 77 76

Dedicated to equity, affection,
and greater understanding
   Among women
   Among men
   Between men and women

Preface

In this book we have assembled a large body of evidence concerning how the sexes differ, and how they do not differ, in many aspects of psychological functioning. We do not deal with sexual behavior per se, but rather are concerned with intellectual performance and social behaviors that are not specifically sexual but have been thought to be differentiated by sex. Our objective is to sift the evidence to determine which of the many beliefs about sex differences have a solid basis in fact and which do not. In addition, we discuss the major theories of how psychological sex differentiation comes about. Throughout we are interested in *development*—in the way sex differentiation appears (or, occasionally, disappears) in the course of the life cycle. The book is a sequel to the earlier volume *The Development of Sex Differences* (Maccoby, ed., 1966), but whereas that book was composed of contributed chapters by different authors, this one attempts a more uniform treatment and a more comprehensive coverage of the various behavioral topics taken up. Like the earlier book, it includes summary tables of data and an annotated bibliography; it does not reprint entries included in the 1966 volume, but lists primarily research published since that date.

The preparation of this book has involved the devoted labors of many people. The effort to make the bibliography as complete and accurate as possible required untold hours of searching the literature, writing abstracts, checking references, and writing to authors for clarification or amplification of published materials. Mary Clare Jacobson and Chris Cozzens worked assiduously on these tasks. Mary Anderson rendered invaluable service in the early stages of the library search. Sharon Nash did a complete editing of the annotated bibliography, rewriting many entries for clarity and uniformity of style, with considerable checking back to original documents. Our most especial thanks go to Greg Buckle, who became the bibliography's gatekeeper for accuracy, and with a fierce integrity worked to keep the rest of us from overinterpreting the data or ignoring the nuances of findings. Much of this bibliographical work was underwritten by Ford Foundation grant 72-429, and we are most grateful for this support.

The preparation of a manuscript of this kind, with its many tables and references, imposes especially heavy demands upon a secretarial staff. We can only say that without the extraordinarily careful and sustained work of Ruth Prehn, Jo Denham, and Susanne Taylor, the manuscript would never have come into being.

A number of people read portions of the manuscript at various stages of preparation and gave us their critical comments. Especially helpful was the commentary by William Kessen, who served as the publisher's primary reader and gave us our first feedback on the book as a whole. On the basis of his suggestions we revised the chapter organization and rewrote several sections extensively. We believe that his critique resulted in a manuscript that was considerably more coherent than the first draft, and we are grateful to him.

We are painfully aware that despite all the efforts of ourselves and our co-workers, our coverage of the existing body of research and interpretive writing on sex differences is not complete. The ever-present problem of publication lag has meant that work completed during the past year could not be included in our summaries. We can only apologize to those whose contributions have been missed, and hope that the main themes that have emerged from our study do rest on a body of evidence sufficient to allow them to stand the test of time and replication.

Contents

Tables

The Psychology of Sex Differences

Introduction

Questions about the psychological nature of man and woman are currently under intense debate. Do the sexes differ in their emotional reactions to people and events? Do they differ in the vigor with which they attack the life problems confronting them? Do they have equal potential for acquiring the knowledge and skills necessary for a variety of occupations? If psychological differences do exist, on the average, are the differences great enough to impose any limits on, or indicate any especially promising directions for, the kinds of lives that individuals of the two sexes may reasonably be expected to lead? And, perhaps most important, where the differences do exist, how did they come about? Are they inevitable, or are they the product of arbitrary social stereotypes that could be changed if society itself changes?

In this book we address all these questions, but we have proceeded on the assumption that before we can attempt to understand the "why" and "how" of psychological sex differentiation, we must have as accurate and detailed a knowledge as possible concerning the nature of existing differences and the changes these differences undergo at successive ages. In Chapters 2–7 we attempt to establish precisely what the differences are that need to be explained. We then turn to the three major psychological theories that purport to explain them. These theories (in highly encapsulated form) are that psychological sex differentiation occurs:

1. Through imitation: children choose same-sex models (particularly the same-sex parent) and use these models more than opposite-sex models for patterning their own behavior. This selective modeling need not be deliberate on the child's part, of course.

2. Through praise or discouragement: parents (and others) reward and praise boys for what they conceive to be "boylike" behavior and actively discourage boys when they engage in activities that seem feminine; similarly, girls receive positive reinforcement for "feminine" behavior, negative reinforcement for "masculine" behavior.

3. Through self-socialization: the child first develops a concept of what

it is to be male or female, and then, once he has a clear understanding of his own sex identity, he attempts to fit his own behavior to his concept of what behavior is sex-appropriate.

Of course, the third process calls upon the other two. A child's conception of what is appropriate behavior for a male or female will depend both upon what he sees males and females doing and upon the approval or disapproval that these actions elicit differentially from others. Both of these kinds of events constitute information the child can draw upon in building his concept of sex-appropriate behavior, but in theory 3 neither modeling nor reinforcement is thought to operate in any automatic way to produce sex-typed behavior.

In Chapter 8, then, we assemble the evidence concerning whether, at what ages, and under what circumstances, children imitate same-sex models (theory 1), and ask whether selective imitation precedes or follows the development of behavioral sex-differentiation and a sex-typed self-concept. In Chapter 9, we examine the available information on how the two sexes are socialized, to see what kinds of differential rewards and punishments are known to occur (theory 2) and to determine how well the socialization pattern fits the developing behavioral differences and similarities charted in Chapters 2–7. In Chapter 10 we discuss theory 3, and also consider in what way all three processes, acting jointly, might function in such a way as to account for the phenomena documented in the earlier chapters.

In the explanatory chapters, *psychological* processes are stressed, but this is not to deny the impact of biology. An individual's sex is obviously both a biological and a social fact. If biological sex turns out to be linked with psychological functioning, the study of this linkage should help to deepen our understanding of a more basic matter: the way in which biological "predispositions" interact with the impact of social experience to shape the psychological makeup of the person. Few psychologists now believe that all newborn human individuals are alike in their potential reactions to the experiences they will have. A few brave students of human development have attempted to identify temperamental "types" or individual styles of thought and action that appear to be pervasive and stable, that affect the individual's response to experience, and that may have a biological basis. But so far, the biological base cannot be inferred with confidence. Of course, it is very difficult to know whether a psychological sex difference has a biological origin; but since sex itself *is* a biological variable, there is hope that something can be discovered concerning the role that sex hormones and other genetically sex-linked aspects of the body's functioning play in influencing an individual's reactions to his environment. It will be just as important to know what functions are *not* affected as to identify those that are.

The writers are neither geneticists nor biologists, and are therefore not equipped to undertake an in-depth account of these factors. But wherever we are familiar with genetic or biochemical information bearing upon sex differentiation in a particular sphere of behavior, we have made reference to that information. For example, the influence of sex hormones on aggression and dominance is discussed in Chapter 7; and the question whether there is any sex linkage in the genetic control of intellectual abilities is discussed in Chapters 3 and 4.

Sexual behavior per se may of course be the sphere of behavior most affected by the biology of sex. The reader should be forewarned, however, that this book does not deal with sexual behavior in the usual sense of that term. Sexual behavior is a topic widely written about, and we leave it to the sexologists. Our concern is with other aspects of psychological sex differentiation, although of course we will be interested in whether this differentiation in any degree reflects the roles the two sexes play in sexual encounters.

THE NATURE OF THE EVIDENCE

A number of the physical differences between the sexes are obvious and universal. The psychological differences are not. The folklore that has grown up about them is often vague and inconsistent. We believe there is a great deal of myth in the popular views about sex differences. There is also some substance. In Chapters 2–7, we hope to be able to identify the generalizations that may be relied upon with some confidence. Our primary method will be a detailed examination of the findings of research in which the social behavior, intellectual abilities, or motivations of the two sexes have been systematically studied.

There are some distinct limitations on what can be learned from the published body of research. In the next few pages we shall discuss briefly some of the methodological problems we have encountered in attempting to summarize and interpret the available data. Readers who do not have a technical interest in such issues are invited to turn to p. 8.

A first problem has to do with the incompleteness of the information upon which we must rely. Some information is lost owing to the selection that occurs in the publication process itself. We invite the reader to imagine a situation in which all psychological researchers routinely divide their subjects into two groups at random, and perform their data analyses separately for the two halves of the sample. Whenever a difference in findings emerges between the two groups (and this would of course sometimes happen by chance even when no difference exists that would replicate with further samples), our imaginary researcher tests the difference for significance, and any significant differences are included in the published report of the study. If we are not told that the original subdivision has been made at random, we might misspend a great deal of time attempting to explain the differences.

In a sense, this book is dedicated to testing the null hypothesis that sex differences are of this same order: that assigning cases to groups by sex is no more meaningful, for purposes of understanding the behavior of the subjects, than assigning them at random.

Let us hasten to add that we do not believe the null hypothesis for all aspects of psychological sex differences. The problem is to sift the differences that are "real" from those that are not. Let us also emphasize that we do not believe that a sex difference, to be real, must be replicable on all populations. As an example, consider the greater vulnerability of the male fetus and infant to damage by pathological prenatal or perinatal conditions. Any behavioral anomalies resulting from such damage would be more frequent in boys. However, improvements in prenatal medical care, and in the care of mothers and infants at the time of delivery, should reduce the sex difference, or conceivably eliminate it. The underlying fact, that males are more vulnerable, would continue to be true, but would only manifest itself under certain conditions. Similarly, behavioral sex differences that are the outcome of differential socialization practices could be expected to exist only in some cultures, but where they occur they are nonetheless real.

We emphasize the null hypothesis because of the way most data on sex differences find their way into the psychological literature. Researchers frequently match their experimental and control groups by sex, to guard in advance against the possibility that sex may turn out to be related to the behavior under investigation. Having so designed the study, they are then in a position to analyze by sex—and frequently do so only to confirm that this variable can be ruled out for further analysis. If the analysis yields insignificant results, the researcher usually breathes a sigh of relief and sees fit not to report his negative findings in print. If sex differences do emerge, they are often regarded as a nuisance, and the researcher may settle upon a strategy of reporting them only if he must do so in reporting significant interactions in which sex is one of the factors. There are some exceptions: when there is controversy concerning what sex differences may be expected, then the researcher may report his mean differences as of some interest in their own right. More often, the problem lies in the failure to report findings of *no* difference.

There are instances in which there has been direct pressure to keep findings out of the published literature when they do not agree with the accepted view of some process or relationship. In one instance we know of, an established figure had built a considerable theory about sex differences around the findings from a test he had employed. When a young researcher later failed to find a sex difference on the test and wrote to the senior person about her findings, she was told there must be something wrong with either her method or her sampling—that her results were "just wrong"; she then omitted reference to her contrary findings in the published report of the study.

Of course, not all negative findings are equally worthy of attention. In some cases, measures are unreliable, and any sex differences that might exist go undetected. However, when measures do demonstrate some power (in the sense of being reliable and sensitive to experimental treatment or of showing other group differences) but still do not distinguish between the sexes, there is more reason to include them in a tally as genuinely negative findings. We are aware, of course, that no amount of negative evidence "proves" that no sex difference exists. In the pages that follow we have sometimes used the phrase "There is no sex difference with respect to . . ."; this is simply a way of saying, "No sex difference has been shown." It is always possible that the wrong techniques of measurement have been used, or that the problem has been wrongly defined, and that sex-difference effects will emerge in future work with different methods.

Although negative findings probably constitute the most frequent omissions from the literature, there are some instances in which positive findings are omitted as well. We have been told of instances in which editors have insisted on the omission of significant sex-difference findings from papers on verbal memory, for example. We sympathize with the editors' problem of conserving journal space, and recognize that the deleted findings may not be central to the primary message of a study, but such rulings do hamper our efforts to discover whether the rate of significant sex differences for a given behavior is different from chance. On the whole, we believe that the omission of negative findings is considerably more frequent than the omission of positive findings, though we cannot be sure.

The reader will no doubt find that the best evidence for the sexes' not differing in some respect is to be found at the two extremities of the hypothetical distribution of differences—that is, when there are as many studies showing relatively high scores for boys as there are showing high scores for girls. A more interesting case occurs when the distribution is lopsided —when beyond the many studies showing no difference there are many others demonstrating a difference that is always (or almost always) in one direction. We take this kind of result to mean that there is something "real" about the difference but that there are triggering factors in the eliciting conditions for the behavior; we attempt in these cases to deduce what the factors are that must be present for the sex difference to appear.

It is regrettable that so few research studies have been deliberately directed toward the discovery of these factors. It continues to be true that most of the findings reported are accidental, or at least incidental to other scientific concerns. We expect that as the reader joins us in an effort to "explain" the differences that do turn out to be consistent, he will come to feel, as we do, that the time has come for research focusing directly upon manipulation of the conditions that ought to elicit differential behavior from the two sexes.

However that may be, we shall return now to the importance of the null hypothesis—to point with some alarm to the tendency for isolated positive findings to sweep through the literature, while findings of no difference, or even later findings showing opposite results, are ignored. Studies with nonreplicable positive findings are reprinted in books of readings, cited in textbooks, and used to buttress theories about the nature of the development of sex typing. It is easy to understand how this happens, for it is an extraordinarily time-consuming task to comb through the masses of published data for all the instances—positive and negative—that bear upon an issue. It is our hope that the present volume will serve as a resource and will save researchers at least part of this burdensome but necessary task.

In our review of the literature, we have encountered some peculiarities of *interpretation* of data, distortions that occur frequently enough to deserve comment here. Writers sometimes refer to studies that included subjects of only one sex as if they had demonstrated a sex difference. This occurs when a within-sex correlation suggests a hypothesis about between-sex differences. As an example: R. Q. Bell, reporting on an all-male sample, said that activity level was high in newborn boys who had suffered some degree of birth complications, compared with those who had not. He speculated that, since boys more often suffer birth complications, this might explain a higher neonatal activity level among boys. This was later reported by others as an instance in which boys had been found to have a higher activity level than girls, although Bell had not in fact studied girls.

In other instances, though the correlation for one sex is significantly different from zero, the correlation for the other is not. These facts are then interpreted as if there were a significant difference *between the correlations*. There are instances in which the correlations for the two sexes are only a few points apart, but one reaches the .05 level of statistical significance and the other does not. For example, a study might find that the correlation between the amount of mother-child interaction in infancy and the child's later IQ was .40 for boys, .30 for girls. Let us suppose that for the sample size used in this hypothetical study, only the correlation for boys is statistically significant. In the published report of the study, the authors might choose to include in their tables only those correlations that reached significance. The information available to the reader, then, would be that there was a significant correlation for boys but not for girls. He might be tempted to assume that the girls' correlation must have been zero, and might proceed to spin out a theory about how different causal factors affect intellectual development in the two sexes. But with our hypothetical sample size, a correlation of .40 is not significantly different from one of .30. We have found a number of instances in which correlational data have been misinterpreted in this way. In analysis of variance terms, to support conclusions about differential effects it is necessary to show that the *interaction* is significant, not just that there is a significant main effect within one sex but not the other.

Different patterns of findings *within* each sex have sometimes been mistaken for sex differences. A case in point is the comparison of verbal and physical aggression. Sears et al. (1965)[a] found that among a sample of preschool girls verbal aggression was more frequent than physical aggression. Among boys the reverse was true. Although there was no ambiguity about the presentation of the original findings, they were later interpreted as showing that girls were higher than boys in verbal aggression. In fact, boys showed *more of both kinds of aggression* than girls showed.

We can only caution the reader against these pitfalls, and hope that the text will help to correct such misinterpretations where we have detected them.

A basic problem with the research on sex differences is that it is almost always impossible for observers to be blind to the sex of the subjects. Stereotypes about what kind of behavior is to be expected from the two sexes run very deep, and even when sex differences are incidental to the main focus of a study, the observers must almost inevitably be biased to some extent. There are a number of instances in which a commonly believed sex difference is confirmed when ratings by parents, teachers, or other observers are used, but is not confirmed when simple frequency counts of relatively unambiguous categories of behavior are tallied in the course of direct observation.

Rater bias does not always take the form of "seeing" stereotypic behavior with greater frequency than it actually occurs. As Meyer and Sobieszek have shown (1972), there are instances in which a rater is more likely to notice a bit of behavior if it runs *counter* to his stereotype. In this case, it stands out more against the rater's adaptation level. It is our judgment that behavior observation, though not free from bias, is less influenced by the observer's expectations than rating scales are, and we have therefore placed somewhat more reliance on observational data in our text discussions. And although it would be desirable to do more research under conditions where the observer does not know the subject's sex, this can usually be managed only under highly contrived, artificial conditions; under normal conditions, the very fact that the subject's sex is known to others around him is part of the network of phenomena surrounding the sex-typed social behavior that is under study, and to change this would be to distort the behavior. Perhaps all that can be done is to make greater efforts to evaluate the degree of observer bias, so that it can be allowed for in the interpretation of findings.

ORGANIZATION AND TREATMENT OF THE MATERIAL

The present book is a sequel to the volume *The Development of Sex Differences* (Maccoby 1966b[R]). Like that book, this one focuses upon the development of sex differences through childhood and adolescence, although more work with adults is included in the present volume. The text of the earlier book consisted of six contributed chapters covering selected issues and reflecting the diverse viewpoints of different authors. The present book attempts to be more comprehensive in its topical coverage and, having uniform authorship throughout, reflects a more consistent point of view. It includes a revised and updated version of the earlier chapter on sex differences in intellectual functioning (Chapter 3), but with that one exception the chapters in the present volume are not meant to supersede those in the old one. The earlier chapters are, in our opinion, still highly relevant discussions of some of the theoretical issues in this field, and we expect teachers and researchers will find that joint use of the two books presents a fuller picture than the present book alone can offer.

The 1966 book included an annotated bibliography and a set of summary tables on selected topics. The present volume includes an annotated bibliography of studies published since the 1966 book (or not included in that book) but does not reprint the entries annotated earlier. The summary tables in the present book are now integrated in context in the topical chapters (those in the 1966 volume were collected in a single grouping). The organization of topics in the topical summaries is somewhat different from that in the earlier summaries; and studies annotated for the previous book are included in the present summary tables where they are relevant to new topics. Studies have been included in the new Annotated Bibliography only if they included subjects of both sexes; within-sex experiments and within-sex correlational analyses are cited in the text when they appear to shed light on some of the between-sex comparisons, but are listed only in the References Cited section (pp. 377–91).

The system that we have used for references in the body of the text is as follows: when a work is cited, the author's name is given, along with the year in which the study was published. The reader will find most of these references (all of those not furnished with a superscript R) listed alphabetically in the Annotated Bibliography, pp. 395–627. Works cited that bear the superscript letter R after the year will be found in the References Cited section. This section has been reserved for studies cited in the text but not included in the Annotated Bibliography; *some* of these studies (those indicated, in the References Cited section, by an asterisk) appear in Roberta M. Oetzel's Annotated Bibliography in the 1966 volume (pp. 223–321), where they are annotated much in the manner of the present Annotated

Bibliography. (All text-table references bearing the superscript R are given in the Annotated Bibliography in the 1966 volume, as well as in the References Cited section in the present volume.)

In making up the summary tables, we have listed a study as showing a sex difference if the statistical test yielded a probability value of .05 or less. The difference is listed as a "trend" if the p value is between .10 and .05. Otherwise it is listed as "no difference." Readers who wish to make their own sign tests might have preferred to have the direction of difference indicated even when it did not reach the .10 level, but such directional information would not have been interpretable without standard deviations; furthermore, many publications, while reporting p values, do not give either means or standard deviations, and our tables would have become more complex and less complete. We recognize, of course, that readers will not be satisfied merely to count studies as if they were all of equal value, and we have accordingly reported sample sizes in the summary tables, so that the reader can have some basis for assigning weights to different studies. In addition, in reporting the work on tested intellectual abilities, we have made separate tabulations of the large-sample studies showing not only the direction of the sex differences but the magnitude of the differences in z-score units. But large samples, too, must be interpreted with care; although such studies have a firmer data base, they are also capable of showing a sex difference to be significant even though it is very small, relative to a distribution.

Some difficult decisions had to be made concerning how to describe, in an economical way, the samples that had been used in the studies listed in text tables. The large bulk of the psychological work covered here has been done with white, middle-class American children and adults, studied in nursery schools, public schools, and colleges (this of course reflects no choosing on our part, but rather the population usually selected for research studies). In order to save space, we decided not to include a sample description (other than age) when it was a "standard" sample in the above sense. We did believe, however, that the reader would want to be informed when the sample deviated from this pattern—when the subjects came from, say, a different country, an ethnic American subculture, a parochial school, or a homogeneously low-income group of families. A number of the studies included in our summary tables are taken from the growing body of data on Head Start and Follow-Through children—children from low-income families who are usually, though not always, from black, Spanish-American, or American Indian backgrounds. We have designated these varying sample characteristics in the summary tables without wishing to be in any way invidious, but in the belief that there is something to be learned by determining whether a sex difference is, or is not, found across a variety of cultural settings.

There are some instances in which the literature contains several reports from a given body of data. This is especially likely to be true in large-scale longitudinal studies. Sometimes different reports have provided data for overlapping samples, with the data for a subgroup of subjects being later incorporated into a different report on a larger sample. It is not always clear when this has been done; in the instances where we are aware of it, we have included only one report for a given sample of children on a given measure at a given age, and have tried to choose the most comprehensive report when more than one source was available.

In this book, like the previous one, we have listed studies in the summary tables in order corresponding to the age of the subjects. We have done this in an effort to trace developmental patterns. In a few instances, sex differences are shown to be a transitional phenomenon—at an early point, the sexes are similar, after which they briefly diverge and then resemble one another closely once again. This can happen when one sex develops faster with respect to a particular behavioral domain; it can also happen when the two sexes take different developmental paths to reach the same mature level of proficiency. Such patterns are particularly important for students of development, even though developmental "paths" are difficult to trace in view of the changes in the nature of measures that can be appropriately used at widely differing ages.

We have not prepared summary tables (or corresponding text) on all the topics that have been included in the studies in the Annotated Bibliography. In the discussion of cognitive styles, for example, we have focused upon the dimensions where sex differences had been shown or alleged, and concerning which a body of research aimed at explaining such differences was available; we have not prepared summary tables on category breadth, focusing vs. scanning strategies, tolerance for ambiguity, or a number of other topics that may be of interest to some readers. (Data relevant to these topics may be found in the Annotated Bibliography, however, and it is our hope that readers with special interests will thereby be assisted in producing summaries in addition to those we have undertaken in the text proper.)

We have attempted to be thorough in our review of the literature. We began by reviewing all issues from January 1966 to spring 1973 in a selected set of journals in which findings of psychological sex differences are most frequently reported. We then followed leads from the reference lists of papers in these journals, and used the *Psychological Abstracts* and relevant books and review chapters as guides to still other bodies of data.

In an attempt to improve our coverage, we wrote to a number of authors whose published reports indicated that sex had been a variable in a study design but for which no analysis of sex differences was reported. In response we received many helpful letters and supplementary tables of data, and we have incorporated this additional information into our summaries in numerous instances. We have also run statistical tests in instances where authors did not report them, but for which sufficient information was given to do so; these results too have been included in our report. Even so we are aware that gaps remain. Furthermore, we have tried to acknowledge our indebtedness to the writings of others whenever we are aware of it, but it is to be expected that some of the conclusions that emerge from our review will have been anticipated, without our knowledge, in the wisdom of earlier writers, and we trust we shall be forgiven if we fail to acknowledge this specifically in every case.

Writing a book about sex differences almost forces an author into being a "trait" psychologist. The very process of arranging researches under topical headings tempts the reader—and the writer—into believing that all the items listed are indices of the trait that is named in the table title. In our discussion, we shall attempt to resist this temptation. We are aware that behavior is situation-specific. Indeed, one of our objectives is to identify the situations in which a given sex difference in behavior may be expected to occur, and the situations in which it may not. The "trait" labels that have been used in our summary-table titles have been dictated, to a large extent, by the topics that have been selected for research on sex differences—by the kind of trait psychology, in other words, that is implicit in the work that psychologists do. The summaries provide some insights into whether clusters of behavior that psychologists have included under the same label do in fact cohere, in the sense of yielding consistent findings.

We are constrained by the data in another way: there are certain restricted aspects of behavior that have been extensively studied; at the same time, many broad areas have received little research attention. The recent history of psychology and its focus of interests are reflected in our summary tables. An initial classic study, using an ingenious technique or posing an interesting issue, will be followed up by a large number of studies, some parametric, some introducing experimental refinements to shed light on interpretations of earlier findings. Thus there are masses of studies on the effects of modeled behavior on acquisition and performance; on attachment as revealed in Ainsworth's Strange Situation; and on social influence in an Asch-like situation; etc. The reader may feel that it represents overkill to summarize 21 studies on the Prisoner's Dilemma, for example, and that the usual performance of the two sexes could have been documented sufficiently with a subset of the evidence. But we have decided to present all the evidence available to us, chiefly because there was no reasonable basis for selecting some studies and excluding others (and to select would have been to run the risk of bias), but also because there are some areas (and the Prisoner's Dilemma is a good case in point) in which an early study reported a sex difference that was not replicated in many subsequent attempts. As noted above, it is our impression that there is a substantial primacy effect in beliefs about scientific truths—that it takes a great deal of evidence to refute an original erroneous impression. We have therefore reported the literature as it exists, with all its peculiarities of distribution. But the very process of scanning the topics that have been heavily researched, and noting the gaps, should assist the reader in identifying areas where further work is needed.

In dealing with the traditional topic "sex typing" or "masculinity and femininity," we encountered an organizational problem. The term "sex typing" sometimes refers to the process whereby social pressures are brought to bear upon the individual to make him or her conform to the social definitions of appropriate behavior for his or her sex. This aspect of sex typing has been dealt with in the chapter on differential socialization of boys and girls. But there is another meaning of the term "sex typing." Tests of "masculinity" and "femininity" are made up of items on which the two sexes are known to differ. In this sense, Chapters 2–7 are all focused on sex typing, since each asks how the sexes differ. Once this is known, it is easy to define the individual as "masculine" or "feminine" according to whether he or she shares the characteristics usually displayed by males or females. This meaning of the term "sex typing" renders it entirely redundant with the topic "sex differences."

However, the term "sex typing" can have narrower meanings. In one usage, a "masculine" man or a "feminine" woman is simply one who is sexually attractive to members of the opposite sex. Another meaning has to do with an individual's adopting interests and behavior related to the roles that his sex would normally play in the society in which the individual is growing up. Our treatment of this topic is to be found primarily in Chapter 8. From still another point of view, sex typing deals with the individual's adoption of a sex identity. In childhood, a boy usually comes to understand that he is and always will be a boy, comes to feel that he *wants* to be a boy, and is motivated to behave according to his conception of what boylike behavior is. In rare cases, of course, an individual resists adopting the appropriate sex identity, and the result may be transsexuality. The present volume deals only very tangentially with abnormalities of sex-identity development. This is a complex and specialized matter that is beyond the scope of our work. The reader is referred to the recent volume *Man and Woman, Boy and Girl*, by Money and Ehrhardt (1972)[x], for an extensive treatment of this issue. Our own discussion of the normal course of development of sex identity will be found chiefly in Chapters 8 and 9.

We cannot close this introduction without saying a word about the authors' own biases. We are both feminists (of different vintages, and one perhaps more militant than the other!), and although we have tried to be objective about the value-laden topics discussed in this book, we know that we cannot have succeeded entirely. We doubt, in fact, that complete objectivity is possible for anyone engaged in such an enterprise, whether male or female. If our own interpretations bear the marks of feminist bias, this will be detected soon enough by hawk-eyed readers with points of view different from ours. We expect to be challenged. We can promise the reader only that we have attempted to set forth the reasoning behind our positions as clearly as possible, so that future argument will not be diverted into irrelevancies.

PART ONE

Intellect and Achievement

The intellectual functioning of human beings has been studied from several widely divergent points of view. A large body of work deals with the processes whereby the individual comes to have the intellectual skills he does possess—how he learns, and in what way he stores the products of previous learnings in memory in such a way that previous experience can be made use of in solving new tasks. A second approach to intellect involves the assessment of "abilities," and the identification of patterns or clusters among these abilities. It might be expected that there would be a clear relationship between learning and abilities. That is, the person who learns easily should accumulate a fund of knowledge and skills that would emerge in the form of a high score on an abilities test, and if a person's learning experiences have been focused primarily in a particular subject-matter area, then his abilities should be stronger in this area than in others. In fact, however, there has been a discontinuity between studies of learning and studies of ability patterns. Studies of learning have dealt primarily with the learning process itself, and only tangentially with individual differences in how learning takes place or what is most easily learned. Studies of abilities have been focally concerned with individual differences, but only marginally with perceptual, mediational, or mnemonic processes that may underlie these differences. Indeed, assessment of an individual's abilities leaves open the question whether his achievements are a result of past learning, inherent capacity, motivation and interests, or some interweaving of these factors.

In Chapter 2, we compare males and females with respect to the basic psychological processes that are involved in intellectual functioning: perception, learning, and memory. In Chapter 3 we turn to tested abilities, and consider whether the sexes differ with respect to the profile, or pattern, of abilities that they normally display. Intellectual achievement, however, clearly depends not only upon the strategies a person can employ in perceiving, learning, and memory and upon the pattern of abilities he has devel-

oped to date, but also upon his motivation for achieving in the intellectual sphere. In Chapter 4 we take up the question of whether the two sexes have different degrees of interest in achievement for its own sake, and whether they normally try to achieve in different spheres, or work for different kinds of goals.

CHAPTER TWO

Perception, Learning, and Memory

PERCEPTION

It is alleged that the sexes differ in their perceptions. For example, Garai and Scheinfeld say: "One might postulate a 'visual stimulus hunger' of the boys and an 'auditory stimulus hunger' of the girls. From the foregoing studies we may conclude that boys tend to be showing an inherently greater interest in objects and visual patterns, while girls are congenitally more interested in people and facial features" (1968, p. 193)[R].

The statement implies two things: that boys perceive more through *looking*, girls through *listening*; and that girls are more interested in social stimuli of all kinds, whereas boys are more interested in "things." It would seem that the two tendencies should sometimes reinforce each other, sometimes cancel each other. For example, faces are perceived visually, but they are also social, so that boys and girls might be equally interested in them for different reasons. If the two tendencies do exist, they ought to show themselves more clearly in cases where they coincide, such as human voices or a variety of nonhuman visual patterns.

If the two sexes did begin life with different perceptual biases, this might have far-reaching effects upon their development, and would help to explain certain differences in aptitudes or interests that can be detected at a later point. Garai and Scheinfeld suggest (*ibid.*) that "a difference in sense modality between the sexes, ... if corroborated ... would provide an explanation for the apparent tendency of girls to develop superior verbal skills, as well as for that of boys to excel in spatial perception."

Some of the research that Garai and Scheinfeld use as a basis for their position has been done with very young infants. It may seem far-fetched to suggest that the perceptual tendencies an infant shows during the first few days of life would have any bearing upon the way he behaves several years later. But in fact, such relationships have been shown. For example, R. Bell and his colleagues (1971) have found that a newborn infant's sensitivity to touch predicts certain aspects of his play behavior when he is observed at the age of 2½. Similarly, J. Kagan (1971) reports that infants who spend only a short time looking at visual displays when they are four months old tend to be "flighty" in their play patterns two years later; that is, they shift the focus of their activity rapidly from one place, or one toy, to another. The links between infant perception and childhood behavior that have been uncovered by Bell and Kagan were found in both sexes. They suggest that if the two sexes did have different patterns of perception in infancy, this fact might indeed be important in explaining sex differences at later ages.

Is there any physiological reason why infant boys and girls should perceive differently? Conel (1941, 1947)[R] has shown that the visual system is neurologically somewhat more mature (i.e. more myelinated) in early infancy than the auditory system. If girls mature at a more rapid rate than boys, there may be a period of time during which both sexes have fairly mature visual systems, but the girls have progressed farther than the boys in the development of those portions of the neural system that are relevant to hearing. During such a period, the girls ought to be more responsive to sounds.

The hypothesis is intriguing, but in fact it is not known that the relevant portions of the nervous system do develop at different rates in the two sexes. It *is* known that girls are skeletally somewhat more mature at birth, as measured by the hardening of the wrist bones. However, their advantage in this respect is short-lived; boys are somewhat ahead in skeletal development by the end of the first year and continue to be so to about the age of 8 (Flory 1936[R]). In any case, the initially greater skeletal development of girls may not mean much for perception—the maturation of different physiological systems proceeds at different rates, and skeletal maturation does not seem to be a good index to the maturation of other parts of the body. Behavioral measures of maturation, such as the age of first sitting up, the age of beginning to crawl and walk, and the age of achieving each of the developmental stages in the use of the hand and the fingers for prehension, do not show a sex difference (Bayley 1936[R]; Table 3.1 of this book). If there were a general sex difference in the rate of maturation of the nervous system, the infant developmental scales would show it. Of course, direct measures of the nervous system itself would be the most conclusive sort of evidence. Conel (1939, 1941, 1947, 1951, 1955, 1959, 1963)[R] has produced the definitive work on the myelination of different parts of the nervous system at successive ages, but he has not had enough cases at each age to permit meaningful analysis by sex. Thus it is simply not known whether there is any sex difference in the rate of maturation of the specific parts of the brain that control vision, audition, and the other sensory systems.

Assuming for the moment that the auditory system does develop somewhat faster in girls, it might be expected that their advantage in auditory perception would be brief, and that boys would show as much responsiveness to sounds as soon as their neural growth had caught up. Another possibility (suggested by Sherman 1971[R]) is that a modality preference is established early and maintained subsequently, so that boys come to rely on vision during the time when audition is not fully functional, and continue to rely upon it even after the time when they would be physiologically able to make greater use of audition.

All this is speculation, however, for it does not rest on a solid foundation of neurological knowledge. Before we attempt to explain perceptual sex differences in these terms, it would obviously be wise to determine as precisely as possible what phenomena need to be explained. In the sections that follow, sex differences (and similarities) in chemical, tactile, auditory, and visual perception are discussed and charted. When information about each of these sense modalities is in hand, it will then be possible to address more clearly the question of modality *preferences*, which calls for comparisons among modalities as well as between sexes. Finally, we shall examine responsiveness to social as compared with nonsocial stimuli in the modalities for which information is available.

Taste and Smell—The Chemical Senses

There is good reason to expect sex differences in the chemical senses. Changes in estrogen levels during the normal fluctuations of these hormones in women are associated with changes in the acuity of the sense of smell. With increased estrogens after puberty (Le Magnen 1952, reported in Money and Ehrhardt 1972[R]) and during the menstrual cycle (Schneider and Wolf 1955[R]), women become considerably more sensitive to odors. Furthermore, olfactory sensitivity in animals has been linked to sexual behavior, which of course in its turn is functionally related to levels of sex hormones. These facts would strongly suggest that there ought to be sex differences in smell sensitivity, at least during certain portions of the life cycle or certain portions of women's monthly cycles. However, there are almost no relevant data. Two studies of responsiveness to several odors among newborns found no sex difference (Lipsitt and Jacklin 1971, Self et al. 1972). Although these infants were not assayed for sex hormones, recent work has found sex differences in both androgens and estrogens in the newborn, with the male infants, surprisingly, having higher levels of *both* kinds of hormones.* It is not known how androgens affect smell sensitivity, or how their effects might interact with varying levels of estrogens; thus it is not clear whether the neonatal hormone patterns might be expected to produce any sex differences in smell sensitivity or not. It would

* C. H. Doering, Department of Psychiatry, Stanford University, personal communication, 1973.

be especially interesting to know about smell thresholds at later points in
the life cycle, when the hormonal patterns of the two sexes are more
strongly differentiated, but this information is not available to date.

With respect to taste sensitivity, there is a report (Nisbett and Gurwitz
1970) showing that newborn girls increase their sucking rate for sweet
solutions while newborn boys do not. Of course this simple fact does not
reveal whether male infants cannot discriminate between sweet and neutral solutions, or whether they discriminate but do not especially like the
sweet taste. With adult subjects who can report their taste thresholds,
women prove to be more sensitive to bitter tastes (Kaplan and Fischer
1964[R]). In rats, estrogen injections increased saccharin preference (Zucker
1969[R]). Thus the evidence, though sparse, indicates that females are more
sensitive to at least some tastes.

The Sense of Touch

Infant girls are thought to be more sensitive to touch, and this is seen as
an important precondition for later sex differences: "They [females] also
have a greater reactivity to physical stimuli, as evidenced by their lower
tactile and pain thresholds, their greater irritability during physical examinations, and their higher skin conductance. The idea that this early
sensitivity is a necessary precondition for empathy and imagination is supported by studies of older girls and women" (Bardwick 1971[R], p. 102).

Tactile sensitivity in infants has been measured in a number of ways.
Bell and his colleagues (R. Bell et al. 1971) have used an "aesthesiometer,"
which is a series of nylon filaments graded in diameter. Starting with the
thinnest filament, each filament is applied with gently increasing pressure
to the heel of a sleeping infant until the filament bends. If the infant has
not given a reflex withdrawal of the foot, the next-thicker filament is applied, and so on until the filament is reached that will reliably elicit a
foot-withdrawal response. Other measures used to measure tactile sensitivity include a jet of air applied to the infant's abdomen (with air pressure
being increased gradually to the point where a general body movement
occurs), brushing the infant lightly on the mouth, and touching him with
a cold disk.

An important initial question is whether these procedures measure anything that is a stable characteristic of an individual child. Bell reports that
aesthesiometer measures showed reasonably good test-retest reliability
when two measures were taken hours apart during the first four days of
life. Bernstein and Jacklin (1973), using the same method of measurement,
tested infants at age 3½ months and again one week later, and found that
there was considerable intrapersonal stability over this time period, although the 3½-month measures did not correlate with tactile sensitivity
measures that had been taken by Stanton with the same infants on their

TABLE 2.1
Tactile Sensitivity

Study	Age and N	Difference	Comment
R. Bell et al. 1971	Newborns (75)	Girls	Tactile sensitivity (aesthesiometer; breast-fed infants)
		None	Tactile sensitivity (bottle-fed infants)
R. Bell & Costello 1964	Newborns (21)	Girls	More movement after removal of a covering blanket
	Newborns (17)	Girls	Lower threshold, stimulation of abdomen by air jet
		None	Air jet to cheek
Birns 1965	Newborns (30)	None	Motor response to cold disk
Lipsitt & Levy [R] 1959	Newborns (36)	Girls	Lower threshold to electroactual threshold (1 or 2 studies)
Stanton[R] 1972	Newborns (40)	None	Tactile sensitivity (aesthesiometer)
	Newborns (24)	None	Tactile sensitivity (second- and later-borns)
Turkewitz et al. 1967	Newborns (51)	None	Head turning to touch of brush on mouth
G. Weller & Bell 1965	Newborns (40)	Girls	Higher skin conductance (more sensitive)
Yang & Douthitt 1974	Newborns (43)	None	Air jet to abdomen
Bernstein & Jacklin 1973	3½ mos (38)	None	Tactile sensitivity (aesthesiometer)

second day of life. The measures do appear to be sufficiently reliable for a short time period that they should be capable of revealing sex differences if they exist. As Table 2.1 shows, there are eight studies of tactile sensitivity with neonates. Three of these have found a sex difference, with the girls having lower touch thresholds (being more sensitive) in each of the three cases. But five studies show the two sexes to be much alike, and the Bernstein and Jacklin study with infants of 3½ months also failed to find a sex difference.

The discrepancies among studies are so far unexplained. They do not appear to be a function of the measures used, since studies using the same method have sometimes found a sex difference, sometimes not. They do not seem to be a function of infant state; however, state has not always been measured or held constant. They also do not appear to be a function of whether the sample included firstborns. Rosenblith[*] has suggested that birth weight may account for some of the sex differences when they are found. A "chubbiness ratio" (a ratio of weight to length) has sometimes been used as an index of body conformation in newborns, and surprisingly, lean babies are relatively insensitive (R. Bell and Costello 1964). However,

[*] J. F. Rosenblith, Brown University, personal communication, 1973.

it is difficult to see how chubbiness could account for the fact that girls are more sensitive to touch in some samples of babies but not in others. It may be true that in some samples girls are chubbier, and hence more sensitive, whereas in other populations, with different diets and different maternal care, the sex difference in chubbiness does not appear. At the moment, however, there seems to be no good reason why the relation between chubbiness and sex should vary from one group to another.

The evidence is weak, but if we assume for the moment that newborn girls are indeed more sensitive, we may then ask: What would the implications of this fact be? If being sensitive to touch were equivalent with finding touch pleasant, an implication might be that girls would be easier to soothe by holding, swaddling, or stroking.

The possibility that girl infants are easier to soothe than boys was suggested by Moss (1967). In attempting to explain a negative relationship at age 3 months between infant crying and maternal handling that was found for boys only, he speculated: "Mothers of the more irritable boys may have learned that they could not be successful in quieting boys, whereas the girls were more uniformly responsive to (quieted by) maternal handling."

The matter of what will quiet an infant has received little systematic study. Sternglanz (1972)[R] waited for newborns to cry, and then wrapped them in a blanket with either a synthetic fur surface or a soft, smooth cotton-fabric surface touching their bodies (with temperature, infant orientation, and movement held constant). The fur was a more effective quieter, but the sexes did not differ in "quietability" with either type of surface. A similar procedure was used by Bernstein and Jacklin (1973), working with infants aged 3½ months. The crying infant was wrapped loosely in a synthetic fur blanket and brought to the shoulder, and an observer noted how quickly (or whether) the infant stopped crying. Although there was great variation among infants in how easily they could be soothed, these variations were not related to sex. Thus it has not been demonstrated that infant girls' greater tactile sensitivity (if indeed *this* is a reliable phenomenon) makes them more susceptible to tactile soothing. From a commonsense standpoint, being highly sensitive to touch could mean that touch is either more irritating or more soothing than for insensitive persons. It is not intuitively obvious which way the effect should go.

As mentioned above, R. Bell et al. (1971) have explored whether neonatal tactile-sensitive measures would predict behavior later in childhood. They found that high tactile threshold (low sensitivity) in infancy was related in both sexes to vigorous attack on barriers and sustained goal orientations at age 2½. Conversely, low threshold (high sensitivity) was related in both sexes to lethargic and briefly sustained goal behavior. Thus behavior at birth predicts much the same things in both sexes at preschool age; but the study does not reveal whether tactile threshold is itself a stable characteristic of individuals over several years' time.

We are unable to find any research in which measures of tactile sensitivity have been used as a basis for predicting behavioral characteristics in adolescence or adulthood. We are therefore unable to support Bardwick's contention that tactile sensitivity is a "necessary precondition for empathy and imagination," although of course later research may demonstrate that this is so.

Much of the work on tactile thresholds in older children and adults was done many years ago when there was less interest in sex differences. We have been able to locate only one study on sex differences in tactile sensitivity beyond infancy. Ghent (1961) found that girls aged 6, 7, and 9 were more sensitive on their nondominant than their dominant thumbs; no such difference emerged for boys. No direct comparison between sexes was made.

It is important to distinguish between sensitivity and tolerance, particularly where pain is concerned. It is possible for a person to be highly sensitive to painful stimuli (in the sense of being able to detect the first beginnings of pain at a low intensity of the stimulus) while at the same time being able to tolerate fairly high levels of painful stimulation. In a large-scale study (using over 40,000 adult subjects) Woodrow et al. (1972)[R] tested tolerance for pressure on the Achilles tendon. The mean tolerance for men was 28.7 pounds per square inch, for women 15.9 pounds. Thus men showed considerably greater tolerance for pain. Pain threshold was not measured in this study, however, and evidence is sparse concerning sex differences in either pain or touch thresholds among adults. Citing a review by Notermans and Tophoff (1967)[R], Woodrow et al. note that previous work on pain thresholds has found either no sex difference or greater sensitivity in women. No studies have found greater sensitivity in men. There has been considerable work on perceiving through touch (haptic perception), and a number of these studies permit sex comparisons. In some cases the subject is required to feel an object behind a screen and either recognize it or learn to distinguish it from other touched objects. In other instances he must match a touched object, or a length measured with the hands, to an object or length presented visually. Studies of tactile perception are summarized in Table 2.2. Out of 11 studies, 9 find no sex difference. The two that do report a difference both show girls as having finer discrimination using the sense of touch.

If a sex difference exists in touch sensitivity and in the ability to make fine discriminations by the use of this sense, our survey has revealed only hints of it. The reader, of course, can set his own criteria for the level of proof he is willing to accept, but a conservative reading of the evidence is that no such difference has been demonstrated.

TABLE 2.2
Tactile Perception

Study	Age and N	Difference	Comment
DeLeon et al. 1970	3-4 (48)	None	Correct response in haptic or haptic-visual shape discrimination
Podell 1966	3-11 (112)	None	Perceived orientation of figures traced on forehead
Abravanel 1968	3-14 (200)	Girls	Greater accuracy at 4 yrs and 12-14 yrs in moving unseen machines along rod to equal a seen distance, and at 7, 8, and 9 yrs matching visual length of tactile stimulus applied to forearm
Butter & Zung 1970	5-8 (144)	None	Recognition errors in visual stimuli varying in size, shape, and orientation after Ss saw, felt, or saw and felt stimuli
A. Siegel & Vance 1970	5, 6, 8 (64)	None	Haptic oddity discrimination in size, form, and texture
Gliner 1967	5, 8 (160)	Girls	Tendency to get more smooth-textured discrimination correct ($p < .1$)
Gliner et al. 1969	5, 8 (160)	None	Transfer trials (after redundant stimuli) in which stimulus shape or texture was the basis for haptic discrimination
Jackson 1973	6, 8, 10 (120)	None	Shape recognition tactual (tactual-visual)
Schiff & Dytell 1971	7-19 (293)	None	Number of letters identified after tactual presentation (hearing and deaf Ss)
Natsoulas 1966	18-21 (96)	None	Correct identification of drawings of letters or angles traced on heads
P. Wilson & Russell 1966	18-21 (60)	None	Estimation of how high Ss lifted weights when blindfolded

Audition

What is meant by saying that a person is "responsive" to sounds? The implication may be that he hears well—that he can make finer discriminations between similar sounds than many other people can. Or it may be that he is sufficiently interested in sounds so that he will attend to them more focally than to other available stimuli, and perhaps therefore remember them better. Especially in infancy, it is difficult to distinguish between these implications. An infant is presented with a sound, and he is observed, to see whether (and how soon) he responds. In some research, his heartbeat is monitored, and a sudden deceleration of the heartbeat is taken to indicate that he is attending to the sound. Similarly, a sudden cessation or acceleration of arm movements, or a turning of the head and eyes toward the source of sound, is used as an indicator of his having heard the stimulus and being interested in it. When children are old enough to talk and to follow an experimenter's instructions, it is possible to ask them whether two sounds are the same or different, and to find out what they remember from a set of simultaneously present stimuli.

TABLE 2.3
Audition

Study	Age and N	Difference	Comment
Birns 1965	Newborns (30)	None	Intensity of motor response to loud and soft tones
Brackbill et al. 1966	Newborns (24)	None	Crying, motor, or cardiac response to music, voice, heartbeat, metronome, or silence
F. Horowitz 1973	Newborns (44)	None	Response decrement bell and rattle and orientation to animate auditory stimuli
Porges et al. 1973	Newborns (24)	None	Cardiac response to tone
Simner 1971	Newborns (94)	Girls	Longer cry to tape of newborn crying (trend, $p < .1$)
	Newborns (155)	None	Duration of cry to tape of newborn crying (3 experiments)
Bernstein & Jacklin 1973	3½ mos (38)	Girls	Alerting to social and nonsocial sounds (sign test), 1 of 2 samples t test
Brotsky & Kagan 1971	4, 8, 13 mos (70)	None	Cardiac deceleration to male voice
J. Kagan 1969	4, 8, 13 mos (150)	None	Vocalizations or cardiac deceleration to male voices
S. Cohen 1973	5, 8 mos (96)	None	Fixation of mother or stranger when each speaks with congruous or incongruous taped voice
J. Kagan & Lewis 1965	6 mos (32)	Boys	Greater cardiac deceleration to tone
		Girls	Greater cardiac deceleration to music and more vocalizations to each of 5 stimuli (sign test); when all 5 pooled, n.s.
		None	Arm movements to tone, music, and voice
	13 mos (30)	None	Cardiac deceleration to tone, music, and voices
J. Kagan 1971	8, 13 mos (180)	None	Vocalization, orientation to speaker, activity level, cardiac deceleration to male voice tapes
Templin[R] 1957	3-8 (480)	None	Sound discrimination, ages 3-7
		Girls	Sound discrimination, age 8
Kimura 1967	5	Girls	Right ear effect on dichotic listening task
	6-8 (142)	None	Right ear effect (low-middle SES)
J. Hall & Ware 1968	5-7 (86)	None	Identifying spoken words
Knox & Kimura 1970	5-8 (80)	Boys	Correct identification of nonverbal and animal sounds
Gardner 1973	6, 8, 11, 14, 18, 19 (100)	None	Previously heard matching musical passages
Bryden 1972	11 (40)	None	Auditory oddity discrimination
Corah & Boffa 1970	18-21 (40)	Women	Rated sound as producing more discomfort
		None	Galvanic skin response
Slobin 1968	18-21 (46)	None	Matching English antonym pairs with Thai and Kanarese antonym pairs

Table 2.3 summarizes studies on audition in which the sexes have been compared. A variety of response measures and auditory stimuli have been used. Despite the alleged "hunger" of girls for auditory stimuli, the evidence for a sex difference in responsiveness to auditory stimulation is not impressive.

Newborns of the two sexes are very similar in the speed and duration of responses to a variety of auditory cues. Among older infants, the results seem to depend somewhat upon what measures are used to assess the infant's response. J. Kagan and Lewis (1965), for example, working with a group of 6-month-old infants, found no sex difference in arm movements to a variety of sounds; when cardiac deceleration was used, boys were more responsive to some sounds, girls to others; when vocalizations were taken as a measure, girls were more responsive. However, at age 8 months there were no sex differences with any of the measures used (J. Kagan 1971). In the Bernstein and Jacklin study, sounds were presented at random intervals over speakers placed on each side of the infant's head. Observers noted whether the infant alerted to the sound. In the first of two testing sessions, girls showed more alerting when the responses were summed across stimuli. But in the second session, there was no sex difference. In another study with somewhat older infants, the two sexes were similar in the degree to which they looked toward the mother or a stranger when either one began to speak (S. Cohen 1973).

There is a suggestion in these results that there may be a greater responsiveness to sounds among girls using some measures, but the difference, if it exists, appears to occur in a very narrow age span. The bulk of the evidence over the period from birth to 13 months shows that the sexes are highly similar in their attentiveness to auditory stimulation.

Among children old enough to talk about what they hear, the findings also indicate sex similarity. Some measures test essentially how "sharp" the person's sense of hearing is (e.g. Templin 1975 [R], Bryden 1972), and here the sexes do not differ. Other studies might be more aptly described as measuring what the individual has paid attention to (e.g. identifying previously heard sounds). Here too, there is not any consistent sex difference.

There is reason to believe that the processing of speech sounds in adults is localized to some degree in the left hemisphere of the brain. Kimura (1967) has used a dichotic listening procedure (presentation of different sounds to the two different ears) to determine whether the degree of lateralization is different for boys and girls. Kimura has presented evidence that girls lateralize for speech sounds at a somewhat earlier age than boys; however, this fact of course does not imply that either sex hears more acutely or is more interested in sounds.

In a series of studies on selective listening (Maccoby 1969[R]), two dif-

ferent messages were presented simultaneously by two voices. The subject
was asked either to select one voice or to report what both voices had said.
In these studies, the data were scanned initially for sex differences. None
were apparent, and sex was therefore not included in the analysis and reports. On the basis of this informal evidence, it would appear that neither
sex is more skillful at selecting from among a variety of auditory stimuli,
or at processing several such stimuli at one time. In sum, the case for a
greater "hunger" for auditory stimulation among girls has not been proved.

Vision

Vision is the sense modality in which the most extensive research has
been done. In recent years there has been a proliferation of studies with
infants. Usually records are made of infants' eye movements in response
to a variety of visual displays. It is a common procedure to show a stimulus
(or pair of stimuli) briefly, then another stimulus, and so on through a
series of trials, sometimes including the same stimuli several times in the
series. A number of scores can be used to assess the degree of an infant's
interest in a particular stimulus: one is the length of time he looks at it
upon first presentation; another is the decrement in looking-time over a
series of presentations (habituation). Habituation, of course, may be taken
as a measure of speed of learning, or of memory (or retention), as well
as of degree of interest in the stimulus. Furthermore, the various measures
of an infant's interest sometimes yield different answers to the question of
which children are showing the most interest in which kinds of stimuli.
It frequently happens that the child who looks longest at a stimulus when
it is first presented turns away from it more quickly on later presentation
(habituates faster) than the child who gives it only a brief glance on first
presentation. We have charted the results of habituation measures (Table
2.4) separately from other measures of response to visual stimuli, in order
to permit analysis of whether sex differences appear on one kind of measure but not on others. As Table 2.4 shows, there are no sex differences in
habituation to visual stimuli during the first few days of life. Thereafter,
the results are inconsistent. Boys are found to habituate more rapidly than
girls in three studies, but the difference is in the opposite direction for one
study, and no difference is found in three others. Taken jointly, the results
tend slightly in the direction of boys habituating more quickly than girls,
but whether this signifies a lower level of interest in visual cues or a greater
ability to process them quickly can only be determined by examining the
findings of studies that use other measures.

In the tables that follow, the studies have been divided by age. The newborn period is unambiguously free of demonstrated sex differences (see
Table 2.5) in response to visual stimuli, whether visual response is measured by fixation time, cardiac response, sucking, or EEG.

TABLE 2.4
Habituation to Visual Stimuli

Study	Age and N	Difference	Comment
Friedman 1972	Newborns (40)	None	Habituation of fixation to checkerboard
Friedman et al. 1970	Newborns (40)	Boys	Decrement in fixation to low-redundant stimuli (2x2 checkerboard)
		Girls	Decrement in fixation to high-redundant stimuli (12x12 checkerboard)
Friedman et al. 1973	Newborns (26)	None	Habituation of fixation to checkerboard
Haith 1966	Newborns (41)	None	Habituation of nonnurturative sucking to light panel
Horowitz 1973	Newborns (44)	None	Response decrement to light, orientation to inanimate and animate stimuli
Greenberg 1971	2, 2½, 3 mos (36)	Boys	More rapid habituation (longitudinal)
R. Caron & Caron 1969	3 mos (96)	Girls	Faster habituation rate (geometric designs and checkerboard patterns)
McCall et al.[R] 1973	3-4 mos (120)	None	Habituation to discrepant stimuli
Cohen et al. 1971	4 mos (64)	Boys	Habituation of fixation to geometric patterns
Pancratz & Cohen 1970	4-5 mos (32)	Boys	Habituation of fixation to geometric shapes
J. Kagan & Lewis 1965	6 mos (32)	None	Habituation of fixation to blinking lights
	13 mos (30)	Boys	More rapid habituation to blinking lights
Shipman 1971	3-4 yrs (1,194)	None	Habituation or recovery to redundant and varied pictures (low SES)

During the year following birth, the results are more variable. For most samples and most stimuli, sex differences are not found. When a difference is found, it favors one sex nearly as often as the other (Table 2.6), with a slight balance in favor of boys.

From the first birthday to adulthood, the very large majority of studies report no sex difference in visual perception (see Table 2.7).

There is an exception to the general picture of sex similarity in response to visual displays. Table 2.8 shows charted studies on afterimages and illusions. No sex trends may be seen in susceptibility to illusions in childhood, but in adulthood there are some intriguing findings. Brownfield (1965) reports that men have longer afterimages. In two studies out of three, men are found to be more susceptible to the autokinetic effect in studies of apparent motion (McKitrick 1965, shorter latency). There still is not a large enough body of evidence to establish these differences firmly, but if the phenomena prove to be replicable, they may be related to proficiency in spatial visualization, which tends to be an area of male strength from adolescence onward (see Chapter 3).

Preference for Auditory vs. Visual Stimulation

If a review of the evidence on responsiveness to auditory and visual stimulation had shown that the sexes differed in their responses to either kind of stimulus, it would then have been of some interest to explore whether the sex differentiation involves different sensory thresholds (dif-

TABLE 2.5
Vision in Newborns

Study	Age and N	Difference	Comment
Friedman 1972	Newborns (40)	None	Fixation to novel checkerboard
Friedman et al. 1970	Newborns (40)	None	Fixation to checkerboard
Friedman et al. 1973	Newborns (26)	None	Fixation to checkerboard
Friedman & Carpenter 1971	Newborns (96)	None	Fixation to checkerboard
Haith 1966	Newborns (41)	None	Nonnurturant sucking to light panel
Jones-Molfese 1972	Newborns (40)	None	Fixation to black squares against a white background
Korner 1970	Newborns (32)	None	Frequency and duration of visual pursuit to swinging object
Lodge et al. 1969	Newborns (20)	None	ERG and EEG responses to orange or white light
Miranda 1970	Newborns (54)	None	Fixation to stimuli: faces and geometric designs

TABLE 2.6
Vision in First Year of Life

Study	Age and N	Difference	Comment
Giacoman 1971	1 mo (32)	Girls Boys	Greater visual pursuit, first observation period Greater pursuit, second observation period
Fitzgerald 1968	1-2 mos (30)	None	Diameter of pupil and pupillary activity to photos of own mother or unfamiliar female face, checkerboard or triangles
Greenberg & O'Donnell 1972	1-2 mos (72)	Girls None	Fixated longer on checkerboard Fixation to dots or stripes
J. Weizmann et al. 1971	1-2 mos (32)	Boys	Fixation to stabile (1 of 2 groups)

(continued)

TABLE 2.6 *(cont.)*

Study	Age and N	Difference	Comment
Greenberg 1971	2, 2½, 3 mos (36)	Girls	Longer fixation, 2x2 checkerboard (2 mos only) (longitudinal)
		None	Complex checkerboard (longitudinal)
Greenberg & Weizmann 1971	2-3 mos (24)	Girls	Longer fixations to more complex checkerboard patterns (24x24; 8x8 over the 2x2)
McKenzie[R] 1972	2-5 mos (40)	None	Fixation time on cubes at 4 distances, with real size or retinal size constant by group
	2½, 3, 4 mos (40)	None	Fixation times on 2- and 3-dimensional objects of different sizes
Watson 1966	2, 3, 4, 6 mos (48)	None	Sensitivity to orientation of 3 faces (mother's, E's, cloth mask), measured by smiling; sensitivity to orientation of schematic face, measured by fixation time
	2, 4 mos (32)	None	Fixation time on cube varying in real size, retinal size, and distance
D. Collins et al. 1972	2, 4 mos (48)	None	Limb movement and sucking to flashing light
	2, 4, 6 mos (24)	Boys	Fixation time on *small* illuminated checkerboard ($p < .05$) and total fixation time, summed across stimuli
		Girls	Fixation time on *large* illuminated checkerboard ($p < .05$)
		None	Fixation times for horizontal or vertical patterns
Moss & Robson 1968	3 mos (54)	Boys	Longer fixation to geometric shapes and faces
L. Cohen 1972	3-4 mos (36)	None	Latency to fixate and length of fixation to varying checkerboards
McCall et al.[R] 1973	3-4 mos (120)	None	Fixation to discrepant stimuli
Fagan 1972	3-4 mos (52)	None	Fixation to novel, or unfamiliar, relative to familiar photos of faces
	4-6 mos (34)	None	Fixation to novel relative to familiar photos of faces
	4-6 mos (36)	None	Fixation to line drawings of faces; and to novel relative to familiar line drawings of faces
	5-6 mos (72)	None	Fixation to photos of faces; and to novel relative to familiar photos of faces
	5-6 mos (56)	None	Fixation to masks; and to novel relative to familiar masks
	5-6 mos (24)	None	Preference for photos of faces over plain gray forms, measured by fixation time
	5-6 mos (16)	None	Fixation to novel relative to familiar masks
Fagan 1971	3-8 mos (24)	None	Fixation times to novel black and white patterns relative to familiar ones
K. Nelson 1971	3-9 mos (80)	None	Visual tracking and reversals of model train

(continued)

TABLE 2.6 *(cont.)*

Study	Age and N	Difference	Comment
Lewis 1969	3, 6, 9, 13 mos (120)	Boys	Longer fixation on male faces at 3, 6, 9 mos
		None	Fixation time at 13 mos
		Girls	Vocalized more to each visual stimulus at each age; smiled differentially to stimuli, whereas boys did not
Bernstein & Jacklin 1973	3½ mos (38)	None	Fixation and smiles to faces and scrambled faces
L. Cohen et al. 1971	4 mos (64)	Girls	Higher fixation to geometric patterns
J. Kagan et al. 1966	4 mos (34)	Boys	Longer first and total fixations to face masks
McCall & Kagan 1967	4 mos (36)	None	Fixation time, vocalization time, smiling frequency, and cardiac deceleration to geometric shapes
McCall & Kagan 1970	4 mos (72)	None	Fixation time to geometric shapes
Pancratz & Cohen 1970	4-5 mos (32)	None	Fixation to colored geometric stimuli (novel and familiar)
Brotsky & Kagan 1971	4, 8, 13 mos (79)	None	Cardiac deceleration to outlines of faces, 3D doll models (longitudinal)
J. Kagan 1969	4, 8, 13 mos (150)	None	Vocalization to clay masks of faces (scrambled, normal, and missing features; longitudinal)
J. Kagan 1971	4, 8, 13 mos (180)	None	Vocalization, fixation smiles, activity level, and cardiac deceleration to 2- and 3-dimensional faces and human forms (longitudinal)
Meyers & Cantor 1966	5 mos (24)	Boys	Cardiac deceleration to pictures of ball, clown, bear, and doll
Wilcox & Clayton 1968	5 mos (10)	None	Fixation to color movies of a woman's face
S. Cohen 1973	5, 8 mos (96)	None	Fixations to mother or stranger
J. Kagan & Lewis 1965	6 mos (32)	Boys	More vocalizations to light patterns
		Girls	Fixation to pictures of faces and designs, 3 of 5 episodes (no difference, all episodes combined)
		None	Arm movements, vocalizations and cardiac deceleration to faces and designs; fixation time, arm movements, and cardiac deceleration to light patterns
	13 mos (30)	None	Fixation to light patterns (trials 1-9)
		Girls	Fixation to light patterns (trials 9-12)
Lewis et al. 1966	6 mos (64)	None	Fixation and cardiac responses to light matrix
Meyers & Cantor 1967	6 mos (44)	Boys	Greater cardiac change to new stimuli
		None	Fixation time
Rubenstein 1967 ·	6 mos (44)	None	Looking at and manipulating stimuli
Parry 1972	10-12 mos (48)	None	Fixation time to wooden dishes with 1 or 4 black dots

ferent acuity of the sense organs or their attendant cerebral projection areas), or whether it is true that the sexes simply differed in their interest in the two kinds of stimulus inputs. However, no differences were documented in either modality. Of course, comparing the audition experiments with the vision experiments taken as a whole is an insensitive method for testing the hypothesis. It involves comparing not only different stimuli but different subjects and different response measures.

It would be preferable to compare responses to visual and auditory stimulation within the same group of subjects. Although of course sights and sounds are measured in different units and cannot be directly compared, it is at least possible to use the same response measure, and to look for an interaction of sex with stimulus modality. That is, if boys are more attentive than girls to visual displays in a given experiment, and girls are more attentive than boys to sounds—the same measure of attentiveness being used in each case—this would constitute support for the hypothesis that the sexes differ in modality preference.

J. Kagan (1971) has used this approach, presenting infants with a variety of sounds and visual stimuli, and using cardiac deceleration and vocalization as measures of the infant's attention to each kind of stimulus. With these measures, he did not find sex differences in attention to either kind of stimulus, and therefore of course no interaction of sex with modality.

Watson (1969) used a similar design, but used the infant's rate of conditioning to either auditory or visual reinforcement as an index of modality preference. In the initial study, 10-week-old girls showed conditioned fixation with auditory reinforcement (or auditory plus visual), but not with visual reinforcement alone. Boys, in contrast, conditioned with visual reinforcement. This experiment has been one of the pieces of evidence most often cited in support of the view that the sexes have different modality preferences. In two follow-up studies, however (Ramey and Watson 1972[R], Dorman et al. 1971), these effects were not replicated. Dorman et al. found better conditioning of visual fixation with visual reinforcement for both sexes. Ramey and Watson found no conditioning in either sex with auditory reinforcement. Conditioning was successful (at least for boys) with visual reinforcement, but a between-sex analysis was not made. Other studies addressing the audiovisual difference have been made with older subjects. Bryden (1972) presented patterns, two at a time, to 11-year-old subjects, and asked them to judge whether the two were the same or different. On some trials, one of the patterns was visual-sequential (a series of flashing lights) and the other auditory (a series of tones); on other trials two visual patterns were compared—a visual-sequential pattern, and a visual-spatial pattern made up of dots. There were no sex differences in performance on visual-auditory matches, or on visual-spatial vs. visual-sequential patterns,

TABLE 2.7
Vision, Second Year to Adulthood

Study	Age and N	Difference	Comment
Roberts & Black 1972	1 (40)	None	Visual regard of series of 16 toys
J. Kagan 1971	2 (180)	None	Fixation, smiles, verbalizing, cardiac deceleration to colored slides of people and object
Lewis et al. 1971a	2 (60)	None	Fixation, cardiac response, arm movement, smiling, pointing, and vocalizing to human forms varying in incongruity
DeLeon et al. 1970	3-4 (48)	None	Latency of errors in shape discrimination
Heider 1971	3-4 (71)	None	Choice of basic or nonbasic colors
Kraynak & Raskin 1971	3-4 (64)	None	Matching animal or geometric stimuli
C. Dodd & Lewis 1969	3½ (52)	None	Fixation, smiling, pointing, and surprise at pictures of family and designs
Clapp & Eichorn 1965	4-5 (24)	None	Response to tachistoscopic presentation of geometric figures, drawings
Wolff 1972	4-7 (97)	Girls	Matching to standard (reach criterion faster; trend, $p < .1$)
Gaines 1972	5-6 (47)	Boys Girls	Fewer errors at midchroma. Fewer errors, color perception at high and low chroma
Hecox & Hagan 1971	5-7 (52)	None	Proportion estimations by moving lever in matching task
Butter & Zung 1970	5-8 (144)	None	Matching shapes from cutouts
Gliner et al. 1969	5, 8 (160)	None	Same/different shape judgments or transfer trials in discrimination task in which stimulus shape or texture was used
Jackson 1973	6, 8, 10 (120)	None	Shape recognition visual (or visual-tactile)
Kaess 1971a	6, 8, 10 (54)	None	Shape identification of rectangular forms in different orientation
Bosco 1972	6, 8, 11 (180)	None	Processing speed of tachistoscopically presented geometric figures (high and low SES)
Wohlwill 1965	6, 9, 13, 16 (96)	None	Relative distance perception
P. Katz et al. 1971	6, 11 (300)	None	Similarity judgments of visual nonsense items
Keenan 1972	7, 9, 11 (48)	None	Tachistoscopic presentation, English letters, Hebrew letters, or binary patterns
Kaess 1971b	7, 9, 11, 18 (80)	None	Comparing rectangles to standard forms
Gummerman & Gray 1972	7, 9, 11 18-21 (48)	None	Verbal report of letter position in tachistoscopic presentation

(continued)

TABLE 2.7 *(cont.)*

Study	Age and N	Difference	Comment
L. Miller 1971	7, 11, 20 (72)	None	Visual-target letter-selection task
Baltes & Wender 1971	9, 11, 13, 15 (120)	None	Preference of random dots and random-shape patterns (German)
Saltzstein et al. 1972	12 (63)	Boys	Fewer errors judging lengths of paper strips (group testing)
Weber 1965	16-25 (72)	Men	Better identification of steady-interval flashing light from set with varying intervals
Iverson & Schwab 1967	18-21 (80)	None	Fusion judgments of faces shown stereoscopically
Koen 1966	18-21 (72)	None	Time to match photos of same individual
W. Lambert & Levy 1972	18-21 (40)	None	Rate of using fully available visual stimuli

TABLE 2.8
Visual Afterimages and Illusions: Observational Studies

Study	Age and N	Difference	Comment
A. Hill & Burke 1971	4-20 (97)	None	Judging relative sizes of triangles under framed (illusion) and no-frame conditions (normal, retardates)
Hartmann et al. 1972	6, 7, 8, 9 (50)	None	Mueller-Lyer Illusion
Gough & Delcourt 1969	8-16 (1,065)	None	Geometric illusion (Swiss and American)
Spitz et al. 1970	9, 15, 35 (112)	None	Poggendorff and Oppel-Kundt (filled space) illusions.
Brownfield 1965	18-20 (30)	Men	Longer duration of afterimages
Bogo et al. 1970	18-21 (97)	None	Autokinetic effect
McKitrick 1965	18-21 (200)	Men	Shorter latency to perceive autokinesis

indicating that stimuli in the two modalities were as easy to deal with for one sex as the other.

An experiment by Mendelsohn and Griswold (1967) can also be interpreted as reflecting modality salience. Subjects memorized a list of 25 words presented visually, while listening to 25 different words being played on a tape recorder. The subjects then attempted to solve 30 anagrams, 10 of which had appeared on the visual list, 10 on the auditory. There were no sex differences in anagram solutions of words from either the visual or auditory list, indicating that in a situation of conflicting information from two sensory channels, the sexes did not differ in frequency of noticing and remembering the items that came in auditory, as compared with visual, form.

The simple fact appears to be that the two sexes are very similar in their interest in, and utilization of, information that comes to them via hearing and vision. Indeed, unless a child has a hearing defect or impaired vision, it is difficult to see why any consistent modality preference should develop. Of course, for some purposes, visual cues may be more useful than auditory ones, or vice versa. In learning a language, for example, it is more useful to hear other speakers of the language than to watch their lips moving. Reliance upon auditory vs. visual information should vary from one situation to another, then, but there seems to be little reason to expect that some persons should be more attuned to one sensory channel than the other in many situations. Rosner (1973)[R], however, has recently identified individual differences among first- and second-grade children in the competent use of information contained in visual vs. auditory stimulus patterns, and has found that the "visual" children do better in arithmetic, the "auditory" children in reading. He does not report whether there are sex differences in the perceptual orientations he has identified. Judging from our Tables 2.3–2.8, it is doubtful whether they will be found. Furthermore, as will be seen in Chapter 3, sex differences in reading and arithmetic achievement are minimal during the early school years. It remains an intriguing possibility, however, that modality preferences during the early school years might feed into the development of different subject-matter skills at a later time. At present it has not been demonstrated that either sex is more "visual" or more "auditory" than the other.

Orientation to Social vs. Nonsocial Stimuli

Much of the research on perception in infancy has involved presenting infants with various representations of the human face. It has been argued that, from an ethological standpoint, the human face should be a particularly salient stimulus for the human infant. Face stimuli that have been used include line drawings, three-dimensional clay masks (in color or black-and-white), photographs of real faces, or in some instances the actual human face itself, either held immobile or shown smiling and talking. Distorted representations of the face have also been used, with features missing or scrambled. In some studies, faces have been compared with nonsocial stimuli such as a checkerboard, geometric forms, random shapes, or familiar objects.

As we have seen, sex differences are not found among newborns in their attention to any of the many visual stimuli, both social and nonsocial, that have been presented to them. There is more variation in the findings of studies with infants following the neonatal period through the remainder

TABLE 2.9
Response to Social or Nonsocial Visual Stimuli in First Year

Study	Age and N	Difference	Comment
Greenberg & O'Donnell 1972	1-2 mos (72)	Girls	Nonsocial: fixation
Weizmann et al. 1971	1-2 mos (32)	Boys	Nonsocial: fixation
Greenberg 1971	2 mos (36)	Girls	Nonsocial: fixation
Greenberg & Weizmann 1971	2-3 mos (24)	Girls	Nonsocial: fixation
McKenzie[R] 1972	2, 4, 6 mos (24)	Boys Girls	Nonsocial: fixation to small checkerboard Nonsocial: fixation to large checkerboard
Moss & Robson 1968	3 mos (54)	Boys	Social and nonsocial: fixation
Lewis 1969	3, 6, 9 mos (120)	Boys Girls	Social: fixation Social: vocalization
L. Cohen et al. 1971	4 mos (64)	Girls	Nonsocial: fixation
J. Kagan et al. 1966	4 mos (34)	Boys	Social: fixation
J. Kagan & Lewis 1965	6 mos (32)	Boys	Nonsocial: vocalization
	13 mos (30)	Girls	Nonsocial: fixation

of the first year. Can some of this variation be accounted for by whether the stimuli are social? Using Table 2.6 as a starting point, we have first selected the studies where a significant sex difference was found on at least one measure, and then charted them according to whether the stimuli were social or nonsocial. Table 2.9 displays the result of this procedure.

As noted earlier, the majority of studies done in this age range found no sex differences. When significant differences were found, they sometimes favored one sex, sometimes the other. The direction of the difference does not appear to be accounted for by whether or not social stimuli were used. When nonsocial stimuli are used, boys and girls are about equally likely to come out with a higher average attention score. With social stimuli, boys somewhat more often have higher scores, but a sign test does not reach significance and the conservative conclusion is that the sexes do not differ in their interest in visual social stimuli. No social preference is revealed for either sex in responses to visual stimuli at later ages (see Table 2.7), or for social versus nonsocial sounds (see Table 2.3).

There are instances in which boys and girls show a different pattern of preferences among visual stimuli, without a significant between-sex difference. A frequently cited finding by Lewis et al. (1966) is a case in point: girls (aged 6 months) looked significantly longer at faces than they did at nonhuman patterns, whereas boys distributed their attention fairly evenly across all the stimuli presented to them. However, it was not reported that girls looked at faces significantly longer than boys, though the experiment is sometimes cited as though girls had indeed shown a greater interest in social stimuli.

When social and nonsocial stimuli are compared, they obviously differ from one another with respect to many characteristics other than their social quality. Complexity (specifically, amount of contour) has been found to be an important determiner of the amount of attention an infant gives to a stimulus: if an infant looks longer at a face than, say, a line drawing of a triangle, this may simply occur because the face is more complex. The same problem exists in comparing the human voice with tones or other nonhuman sounds (J. Kagan and Lewis 1965).

Bernstein and Jacklin (1973) compared the attentiveness of 3½-month-old infants to social and nonsocial stimuli that had been equated for other stimulus parameters. The visual social stimuli were normal faces; the nonsocial stimuli were mosaics assembled from fairly small segments of the normal faces and equated with them for contour, intensity, chroma, and filled area. The auditory social stimuli were taped words ("hello" and "baby") spoken by either a female or male voice, and the nonsocial sounds were non-speech-sounding noises, equated with the words for fundamental frequency, intensity, complexity, and contour of the sound wave. Visual interest was measured in terms of fixation time, interest in auditory cues in terms of whether the infant alerted at the presentation of the sound. Both boys and girls preferred social to nonsocial pictures and sounds, but there was no difference between them in the degree of preference.

Thus, with careful control of some of the stimulus dimensions that usually are allowed to vary, the same conclusion must be reached as before: there is no evidence that girls are more interested in social, boys in nonsocial stimulation.

Summary: Perception

There is reason to believe that females may be both more sensitive and more variable in their response to taste and smell cues, but the research base is very thin and generalizations are really not warranted at this time. The work on touch sensitivity also presents an inconclusive picture: most studies find no sex differences among newborns, but those that do show girls to be more sensitive. It is not known whether any initial differences in touch sensitivity continue after the first few days or weeks of life. Even if they do not, the early differences may be important, in the sense that at least for one sample of children they have been found to be predictive of other behavioral characteristics at a later time. These continuities need further exploration.

Boys and girls have been found to be remarkably similar in responsiveness to visual and auditory cues. The view that one sex is oriented more toward auditory stimuli and the other toward visual cannot be supported by existing evidence. The same is true when social and nonsocial stimuli are compared: neither sex consistently shows more interest in social stimuli (i.e. faces and voices) than the other.

If there are sex differences in vision and audition, the research methods used so far have not revealed them. It is possible that the approach to these matters has been too reductionist; perhaps differences, if they exist, involve the sequential and organizational properties of perception, so that experimental presentation of stimuli one at a time, isolated from their context, may have been a self-defeating strategy. However, the more important truth may be that the sexes really are very much alike in the amount and kind of information they are capable of extracting from the milieu of stimulation in which they must function.

Perceptual Motor Abilities

Summaries of early work on sex differences (e.g. Anastasi 1958[R]) conclude that boys show greater speed and coordination of gross bodily movements, whereas girls excel in manual dexterity. More recent work has not tested for individual differences in gross bodily movement, so nothing new is to be added to the earlier conclusion except to note that physical strength may be involved in the sex difference.

Manual dexterity has been studied in recent years, using a variety of different tasks. It appears that the rubric "manual dexterity" is too broad to encompass the results. Table 2.10 lists the recent studies. When speed measures are used, girls tend to score higher (Laosa and Brophy 1972, Droege 1967, Very 1967, Backman 1972, Strutl et al. 1973). Backman reports the performance of the two sexes at high school age on a speeded test of visual-motor coordination and finds girls' performance to be approximately 5 percent better than that of boys. In the Droege study, high school girls score about 8 percent higher than high school boys, on the average, on finger dexterity, and 9 to 10 percent higher on tests of motor coordination. It is worth noting, however, that whereas girls have somewhat better *finger* dexterity, there is no sex difference in *manual* dexterity —a finding that underlines the importance of the distinction between large-muscle and small-muscle movements, or fine vs. relatively gross movements.

Are there sex differences, possibly due to a difference in willingness to tolerate repetitive tasks, involved in the findings on perceptual motor tests? Cantor approached this issue by varying the interest of tasks for 6-year-olds. One group saw colored slides of high interest, another saw one geometric figure repeatedly (on successive trials), and reaction times were measured. No sex differences were found in reaction times (as measured

TABLE 2.10
Perceptual Motor Abilities

Study	Age and N	Difference	Comments
Anyan & Quillian 1971	1-8 (605)	None	Figure copying
Beiswenger 1971	2-4 (48)	None	Motor responses to visual and auditory stimuli
Eckert 1970	3-4 (22)	None	9 visual-motor tasks
Birch 1971	3-6 (35)	None	In coordination of vocal and manual responses – latencies and accuracy measures
Hamilton 1973	3, 4, 7 10 (72)	None	Ability to form imitative facial expressions
Strayer & Ames 1972	4-5 (40)	None	Form board, errors or response latencies
Laosa & Brophy 1972	5-7 (93)	Girls	Perceptual speed subtest of Primary Mental Ability test
Davol et al. 1965	5-8 (64)	None	Rotary pursuit board
Cantor 1968	6 (60)	None	Reaction time to visual stimuli
A. Siegel & McBurney 1970	6-13 (96)	None	Matching handgrip to line and length or verbal numbers
Smothergill 1973	6, 7, 9, 10, 18-21 (60)	None	Visual or proprioceptive localization of spatial targets
Strutl et al. 1973	6, 9, 12 (54)	Girls	Speed of card sorting
Kubose 1972	7 (60)	None	Response and movement time in lever-pull task
Arnold 1970	7-8 (96)	None	Simultaneous verbal and motor tasks
McManis 1965	10-13 (96)	None	Accuracy in pursuit rotor (normals, retardates)
Droege 1967	14-17 (20,541)	Girls None	Clerical and form perception, motor coordination, finger dexterity Manual dexterity
Backman 1972	17 (2,925)	Girls	Perceptual speed and accuracy (Project Talent Test Battery)
Koen 1966	18-21 (72)	None	Ability to form imitative facial expressions
Very 1967	18-21 (355)	Women	Perceptual speed and accuracy: visual motor velocity, number comparisons

by start speeds and "travel" speeds). However, nonbored girls reacted more quickly than bored girls, whereas the reverse was true for boys. These findings do not help to clarify previously found sex differences in perceptual motor performance, but they do indicate that task interest should be taken into account when examining sex differences.

LEARNING AND MEMORY

Students of the learning process have concerned themselves primarily with general laws that apply to all learners. In considering the possibility that there may be sex differences in learning, we are entering the ill-charted realm of individual differences in learning abilities and learning styles. What can be meant by the question of whether people differ in the way they learn? A first meaning has to do with a generalized capacity to learn. Are there some people who learn more readily than others, regardless of the nature of the material to be learned or the nature of the incentive offered for learning? If a high level of such a generalized learning capacity were a stable characteristic of some persons, it would clearly enter into our measures of general intelligence, and as such it is treated in Chapter 3. However, there are other ways in which the learning performance of individuals might differ. For example, people probably differ considerably in their motivations for learning. Perhaps some people learn primarily to please others, whereas others may be more intrinsically motivated, attempting to meet some standard of excellence that they impose on themselves. It has been alleged that girls are especially likely to work in order to win the approval of others, and hence it is possible they might learn best under social reinforcement, whereas boys might learn better with some other sort of incentive. (See Chapter 4 for a more detailed discussion of this issue.)

People may also differ in the preestablished biases they bring to a learning situation. Stevenson notes (1970, p. 919)[R]: "Even young children enter the experimental situation with strong response biases and stimulus preferences which, if in accord with correct response, lead to rapid learning and otherwise interfere with performance."

When experimenters speak of response biases, they usually mean something very specific, such as a tendency to choose the right-hand member of a horizontal grouping. Such a bias could presumably stem from handedness, from previous experience with directionality, or both. Seligman (1970)[R] has recently summarized evidence for a more intriguing kind of bias—a "preparedness" on the part of the organism for associating only certain kinds of cues with certain kinds of responses. It has been found, for example (Garcia and Koelling 1966[R]), that rats can associate flashing lights or noises with shock, and can use them as avoidance cues. But they cannot use taste cues in this way. They can associate tastes with becoming ill several hours later, and will learn to avoid tastes that have had a delayed association with illness, but they cannot form such an association between illness and lights or noises. Seligman stressed species differences in preparedness to make certain associations. It is conceivable that there might be sex-linked, within-species differences as well in preparedness for certain specific learnings. If this were so, the two sexes would differ not in any overall learning ability but in their readiness to learn associations that are especially relevant to their sex. It will be reasonable to examine the learning literature with this possibility in mind.

Flavell (1970)[R] has noted that children of different ages differ in the strategies they employ in learning and remembering a list or set of objects. A subject may improve his memory by verbal rehearsal of the names of the things to be remembered or by grouping (e.g. noting that several items are all fruits). Other subjects have discovered the value of tying unrelated sets of items together in a "story" invented for the occasion. Flavell shows that even when a child knows how to use a strategy of this kind, he may not make use of it spontaneously; however, once he does use it, his performance is improved. The superior performance of older subjects on recall tasks is at least in part a function of their having acquired a varied repertoire of strategies, good judgment about which strategy to use, and whatever motivation or skill it takes to put to use the strategies that they "know." As far as individual differences are concerned, it would clearly be possible for some persons to progress more rapidly than others through the developmental sequence of strategy acquisition and use; furthermore, different persons could come to rely upon different strategies. And finally, persons could differ in the associative richness (based on breadth of experience) that they brought to bear in weaving relevant stories in aid of recall. The sexes might differ with respect to any of these processes that support the retrieval of learned and "stored" material.

A distinction has sometimes been made between different "kinds" of learning. That is, it is thought that a person can learn either by simple rote association, based on repetition (as in the traditional methods of learning the multiplication tables), or with "understanding"—that is, with greater involvement of higher cognitive processes. White (1965)[R] has elaborated this distinction, arguing that young children learn primarily by association, whereas older children learn more "cognitively," and that the second phase calls for the inhibition of the first. He cites a number of developmental changes in learning as evidence, including the facts that younger children are more susceptible to simple conditioning, more susceptible to position and order effects in a series of learning trials, and less likely to combine separately learned elements by the use of inference. Stevenson also notes a developmental change in the nature of the learning process: "Young children seem to be more dependent upon the characteristics of the external situation than are older children. Older subjects are more likely to respond in terms of their own hypotheses and expectations" (1970, p. 919)[R].

It has been alleged that the sexes differ in the developmental level of the learning processes they employ. Feldstone (1969), using White's distinction, has suggested that girls may be using a developmentally more "primitive" method of learning than boys, at least when the response to be acquired is an inhibitory one. Broverman and his colleagues (1968)[R] have argued that females are superior to males in "simple overlearned repetitive behavior," whereas males excel in "complex behaviors requiring problem-solving, delay, or reversal of usual habits."

The Broverman hypothesis will be taken up later, in the section on intellectual abilities (Chapter 3) and in Chapter 7, where his theory of the possible biological foundations for different intellectual processes is discussed. At present, the theory will be referred to only as it bears specifically upon learning.

In the following pages, we chart studies that have compared the sexes on a variety of different learning tasks. The tables are arranged roughly in order from the simpler, more associative learning processes to those that are more obviously complex. Let us say at the outset, however, that we do not find the distinction between simple and complex learning processes a convincing one. As Rescorla (1967, 1969)[R] has pointed out, even in "simple" conditioning with animals, the subjects appear to be engaged in a complex computation of the probabilities of certain contingencies rather than a simple cumulative building of associative connections between stimuli and responses. A similar case has been made for discrimination learning. It seems difficult to keep organisms, particularly human ones, from engaging in "higher mental processes" even on simple tasks, and we suspect this generalization applies even to females. But let us see what the relevant research reveals.

Conditioning

Broverman et al. included conditioning in their list of "female" abilities. The belief that women condition more easily than men probably stems from early work on eyelid conditioning (see Spence and Spence 1966[R] for a review of this work). We shall return to this work shortly. But let us review the rather sparse evidence on sex differences in conditioning during childhood.

We have referred earlier to the work of Watson and his colleagues. They attempted to condition visual fixation in 10-week-old infants. In Watson's original report, although boys and girls did not differ in ease of conditioning, they did differ in the nature of the reinforcement that seemed most effective. However, these findings were not replicated in two subsequent studies. A number of other researchers have used conditioning procedures with infants; among those who have analyzed their findings according to the sex of the subjects, sex differences have not been found. For example, in a series of studies with a variety of reinforcements with newborns, 3-month-old infants, and 5-month-old infants, Papousek (1967) has not found sex differences in the acquisition of a conditioned head-turning response. At 3 months, Banikiotes et al. (1972), Rheingold et al. (1967), Haugan and McIntire (1972), and R. Caron et al. (1971) also found no sex differences.

The same situation prevails in studies with older children. Cantor and Whitely (1969) conditioned high- or low-force target-striking in 4- to 5-year-olds. Moffatt (1972) conditioned an avoidance response in children of 6 years; Walls and DiVesta (1970) also used children of 6 years and conditioned a verbal response. None of these experiments showed sex difference. The exception is an experiment by Werden and Ross (1972), who reported that boys aged 4–6 acquired a conditioned eyelid response more readily than girls of the same age.

A number of studies have conditioned verbal responses in children and adults. The results are straightforward and consistent with the findings of studies using other responses: there are no sex differences (Birnie and Whitely 1973, Slaby 1973, J. Grusec 1966, Sarason and Ganzer 1962, Insko and Cialdini 1969, Greenbaum 1966, Koenig 1966, Weiss et al. 1971, Doctor 1969, and Yelen 1969).

The one exception to the generally negative picture is in classical eyelid conditioning in adults. Here women do condition more readily. In their review of this literature, Spence and Spence note that more highly anxious subjects (as measured by the Manifest Anxiety Scale) usually show more rapid eyelid conditioning, using a standard conditioning procedure. However, when a "masked" conditioning procedure is used (where the conditioning is a byproduct of procedures ostensibly designed to measure something else), anxiety no longer affects the readiness to acquire the conditioned response. Under "masked" conditions, the sex difference also disappears. The implication is plain that women's somewhat higher level of manifest anxiety (see Chapter 5) may be responsible for the sex difference in eyelid conditioning under the normal procedure, although a direct causal link has not been established. In conditioning studies in which levels of anxiety have been experimentally varied (Stone and Hokanson 1969, Buss and Buss 1966[R]), no sex differences were found. In any case, it seems clear that "conditionability" per se is not the factor differentiating the sexes.

Conditioning has been thought of as a rather automatic process, in which stimuli become connected with responses with a minimum of involvement of the subject's higher mental processes. As noted above, conditioning is probably more complex than this; at the least, it may call for the subject's deliberately holding his higher mental processes in abeyance. Whatever abilities are called for at various ages, the two sexes seem to possess them in approximately equal degrees.

Paired-Associates Learning

A widely used method for studying learning is the paired-associates method. The subject is usually given pairs of words, or pairs of words and symbols, and asked to associate them so that when the first member of the pair is given, he can produce the second. Matching of names to faces is a real-life example of paired-associates learning. It is an area of learning in which there is some reason to expect a sex difference, since the material to be learned is usually at least partly verbal. Furthermore, it is simple associative learning (if any learning can properly be described as such), and according to the Broverman hypothesis should fall into the category of "female" skills. Table 2.11 summarizes the studies of paired-associates learning that have compared the performance of male and female subjects. The studies are remarkably consistent in finding no sex difference.

It is clear that "simple associative learning," whether in the form of conditioning or paired-associates learning, is not a function characterizing one sex more than the other. We now turn to learning that involves some degree of delay or inhibition of a competing response, where a sex difference has also been alleged. The ability to extract a stimulus from a salient context, or to restructure the elements of a problem during problem solving, will be taken up in Chapter 3, as will the ability to postpone gratification (wait for a delayed reward). In the present section we take up discrimination learning, oddity learning, studies of delayed and partial reinforcement, and the restriction of responses to the low-amplitude range.

Discrimination Learning

The subject's task in a discrimination-learning experiment seems quite simple. He is asked to choose the correct stimulus from an array, or to say whether two stimuli are the same or different. However, Stevenson (1970, p. 868)[R] points out some hidden complexities: "It is assumed that he [the subject] is capable of attending to the relevant stimuli, of inhibiting attention to irrelevant cues, of discriminating the differences among the stimuli, of remembering the stimulus chosen, of being appropriately influenced by the consequences of his response, of being motivated to persist in trying to be correct, and of not elaborating the problem so that it becomes more difficult than it actually is."

Inhibition is involved in discrimination learning: the subject must either inhibit attention to irrelevant cues, avoid responding to these cues once noticed, or both. Suppose a subject is asked to press a button whenever a stimulus with a characteristic appears on a screen before him, but is asked

TABLE 2.11
Paired-Associates Learning

Study	Age and N	Difference	Comment
H. Reese 1972	2-6 (48)	None	Paired associates in slide presentation
H. Reese 1970	3-5 (71)	None	Original learning or relearning of paired associates
Hoving et al. 1972	5-11 (72)	None	Learning, relearning, or errors in paired associates
Gahagan & Gahagan 1968	6-7 (54)	None	Verbal paired associates
Hoving & Choi 1972	6-8 (40)	None	Learning or relearning paired association
Fraunfelker 1971	6, 8 (80)	None	Trigram and color paired associates
Shultz et al. 1973	6, 10 (160)	None	Stimuli with or without specific labels (low, middle SES)
P. Katz et al. 1971	6, 11 (240)	None	Learning verbal labels of stimuli
H. Stevenson et al. 1968a	8-12 (475)	None	Paired associates with abstract words as response stimuli
H. Stevenson & Odom 1965	9, 11 (318)	None	Trigram and word paired associates
S. Shapiro 1966	10, 11, 13, 14 (80)	None	Aurally presented paired associates
Carroll & Penney 1966	11 (56)	None	Competition of words in paired associates task
McCullers 1967	11 (144)	None	Paired associates with varying interference
H. Stevenson et al. 1968a	12-14 (256)	Girls	Paired associates with abstract forms as response stimuli (high IQ subsample only; no difference, middle and low IQ subsamples)
		None	Paired associates with abstract words as response stimuli
H. Stevenson et al. 1970	14 (96)	None	Paired associates under different testing conditions (educable retardates)
Pallak et al. 1967	18-21 (39)	None	Retention of paired associates

not to press for similar patterns that are different with respect to some critical attribute. During the early stages of learning, the subject will press indiscriminately. Then, quite often, he will solve the problem abruptly, shifting from a chance level of responding to 100 percent correct. He must now inhibit the tendency to respond to attributes of the stimuli that do not distinguish the correct from the incorrect instances.

Discrimination learning studies are summarized in Table 2.12. Studies using oddity problems are shown in Table 2.13. Oddity problems are a

TABLE 2.12

Discrimination Learning

Study	Age and N	Difference	Comment
Reppucci 1971	2 (48)	None	2-choice discrimination learning
J. Turnure 1971	3-4 (40)	None	Discrimination learning under distraction and no-distraction conditions
Campione 1971	3-5 (64)	None	Discrimination transfer under high or low redundancy conditions
Friedrichs et al. 1971	3-5 (50)	None	8 discrimination-learning tasks
Campione & Beaton 1972	3-6 (100)	None	Successive or simultaneous discrimination-learning task (2 experiments)
L. Brown 1969	4-5 (64)	None	2-choice discrimination task with different reward levels
Berman et al. 1970	4, 6 (16)	None	Win-stay, lose-shift principle in discrimination task
Mitler & Harris 1969	5-9 (77)	None	Errors to criterion in discrimination task
Elkind et al. 1967	5-11 (120)	None	2-choice discrimination task
Scholnick 1971	5, 7 (96)	None	Discrimination learning with differing verbalization training
Rieber 1969	5, 7, 9 (120)	None	2-choice discrimination of 3-dimensional objects
W. Siegel & Van Cara 1971	5, 7, 9 (108)	None	3-part successive discrimination tasks to different reinforcement conditions
Harter et al. 1971a	6-7 (210)	None	2-choice size-discrimination task (normal, retardates)
Harter & Zigler 1972	6-7 (80)	None	2-choice discrimination task with different rates of stimulus presentation (normal, retardates)
Odom & Mumbauer 1971	6-19 (277)	None	Errors to criterion on discrimination task
Pishkin 1972	6, 7, 9	Girls	Made fewer errors with right or right-wrong cues in discrimination
	8 (144)	Girls	Fewer errors on concept identification task
Achenbach & Zigler 1968	7-9 (40)	None	Large-small discrimination
Spence 1966	7-9 (96)	None	Verbal discrimination task with varied feedback
Scholnick & Osler 1969	8 (192)	None	Discrimination learning with or without pretraining (low, middle SES)
Cairns 1967	9 (40)	None	Acquisition or extinction of Wisconsin Card-Sorting Test
McCullers & Martin 1971	9 (72)	None	Discrimination task with varied feedback

(continued)

TABLE 2.12 *(cont.)*

Study	Age and N	Difference	Comment
Ratcliff & Tindall 1970	9 (72)	Boys	2-choice discrimination with loud tone for incorrect responses
		None	2-choice discrimination, 2 other feedback conditions
F. Horowitz & Armentrout 1965	9-11 (48)	Boys	Trend ($p < .1$) improved over trials of simultaneous or successive discrimination tasks
Achenbach 1969	10-11 (514)	None	Discrimination-learning tasks with cues provided
Pishkin et al. 1967	10-18 (270)	Girls	Wisconsin Card-Sorting Task in several conditions
H. Stevenson et al. 1968a	12-14 (256)	Girls	Discrimination-learning tasks (with IQ subsample)
H. Stevenson et al. 1970	14 (96)	None	Shape-discrimination task (educable retardates)
Laughlin & McGlynn 1967	18-21 (192)	Women	Shorter time to solution in a visual discrimination problem

variant of discrimination learning in which the subject must choose the odd stimulus from a set of three or more—the stimulus that is unlike the others with respect to one or more attributes. As may be seen from the tables, no pattern of sex differences has been shown.

In some studies of discrimination learning, the subject's task is made more complex by changing the rules in midstream. Stimuli that were once correct are now called incorrect. These rule changes provide a direct test of the Broverman hypothesis that females have especial difficulty in tasks calling for the inhibition of an already learned habit in favor of a new habit. In some instances, the new rules are a direct reversal of the old ones—if all

TABLE 2.13
Oddity Problems

Study	Age and N	Difference	Comment
Friedrichs et al. 1971	3-5 (50)	None	Oddity discrimination
Saravo et al. 1970	3-7 (144)	Girls	Faster on learned oddity-pretraining task
Levin & Maurer 1969	4-6 (82)	None	Oddity or matching problems
Gaines 1969	4-7 (30)	None	Error rate of oddity problem
S. Hill 1965	4, 6, 9, 12 (114)	None	Oddity problem with 2 kinds of training
J. Turnure 1970	5-7 (90)	None	Oddity problem with and without distractions

TABLE 2.14
Reversal and Nonreversal Shifts

Study	Age and N	Difference	Comment
Campione & Beaton 1972	3-6 (176)	None	Intra- and extradimensional shifts
Beilin & Kagan 1969	4 (78)	None	Reversal shifts
Kendler et al. 1972	4-5 (80)	None	Pre- or post-reversal shift discrimination
Schell 1971	4-5 (72)	None	Reversal shifts
Dickerson et al. 1970	5 (96)	None	Reversal or extradimensional shifts
Heal 1966	5 (24)	None	Reversal shift performance with and without overtraining
Crowne et al. 1968	10-11 (63)	None	Intra- and extradimensional shifts

large stimuli were formerly correct, all small stimuli are now correct. In other instances, the new rules call for attending to an entirely different attribute of the stimulus. Table 2.14 summarizes the findings on reversal and nonreversal shifts. There is no indication of sex difference in performance on these tasks. Of course, many additional studies have been done with shift problems in which experimental and control groups have been equated for sex but in which the final report does not include an analysis of sex differences. This omission, we suspect, usually reflects the fact that there were no differences to report. In fact, one experimenter has written to us: "We routinely counterbalance for sex in our experiments, and at least initially look for differences associated with sex. In every instance we have failed to find such differences."

Delay of Reinforcement, Partial Reinforcement

Increasing the time interval between a response and its reinforcement increases the probability that other responses will interfere with learning the correct response. Such interfering responses must be inhibited during the delay period. Similarly, reinforcing only a portion of the correct responses probably makes it more likely that other responses will occur and compete with the correct response. Studies of delayed reinforcement are summarized in Table 2.15, studies of partial reinforcement in Table 2.16. In neither case are sex differences evident.

Incidental Learning

While a subject is learning the material that he has been instructed to concentrate on, he may or may not also be noticing and remembering other

TABLE 2.15
Delay of Reinforcement

Study	Age and N	Difference	Comment
Loughlin & Daehler 1973	2-4 (51)	None	Delayed reaction with and without filled delay
Ferraro et al. 1971	4, 5, 6, 8, 10 (40)	None	Panel-pressing matching task with varying delays
S. Goldstein & Siegel 1971	8 (48)	None	Empty or filled delay in discrimination task
S. Goldstein & Siegel 1972	8-9 (84)	None	Immediate reinforcement or empty or filled delay

things that occur at the same time. Some experiments are deliberately set up so that "incidental" stimuli will be available that are either redundant or entirely irrelevant to the stimuli that are clearly task-relevant. In other instances, the subject does not have a specific task, but there are nevertheless some events that may be considered more incidental than others. For example, in a standard fictional film, some events are part of the plot and of the development of the motivations of the central characters as they relate to the plot; other events, such as the striking of a clock in the distance or the color of the clothes worn by one of the characters, have little to do with the story, and remembering these events may be classed as incidental learning.

Incidental learning may or may not reflect absence of inhibition on the part of the learner. As Hagen (1967)[8] has shown, when one increases the

TABLE 2.16
Partial Reinforcement

Study	Age and N	Difference	Comment
Hamilton 1970	3-4 (28)	None	In extinction after direct or vicarious reinforcement in marble task
Hamilton 1972	4 (24)	None	Discrimination learning in partial and continuous reinforcement
Ryan & Voorhoeve 1966	5 (120)	None	Partial or continuous reinforcement in lever-pulling task
Stabler & Johnson 1970	5 (64)	Girls	Longer to extinguish in partial reinforcement
Bresnahan & Blum 1971	6 (60)	None	Partial or continuous reinforcement in concept-acquisition problem
Warren & Cairns 1972	7 (100)	None	Partial or continuous reinforcement in discrimination learning
Nakamura 1966	9 (32)	Boys	Longer to extinguish in low-reward condition in dissonance reduction

TABLE 2.17
Incidental Learning

Study	Age and N	Difference	Comment
Wheeler & Dusek 1973	5, 8, 10 (144)	None	Incidental learning in memory task
A. Siegel & Stevenson 1966	7-14 (96)	None	Incidental learning in discrimination tasks
Hale et al. 1968	8-12 (444)	Girls	Incidental learning in film observation
	18-21 (275)	None	
H. Stevenson et al. 1968a	8-12 (475)	Girls	Incidental learning in film observation
	12-14 (256)	Girls	Incidental learning in film observation
Hawkins 1973	8, 10, 12, 14 (306)	None	Incidental learning in film-watching task
A. Siegel 1968	8, 14 (96)	None	Incidental learning in discrimination task
Dusek & Hill 1970	9-10 (72)	Girls	More response patterns in 3-choice probability task
Hagen & Hyntsman 1971	9, 11 (21)	None	Incidental learning of pictures (retardates)
Druker & Hagen 1969	9, 11, 13 (240)	None	Incidental learning scored by matching (black working class)
H. Stevenson et al. 1970	14 (96)	Girls	Recalling details from films (in individually tested subsample only; educable retardates)

difficulty of the task to the point where the subject cannot process all the available information, a negative correlation is found between the amount of irrelevant detail a subject remembers and the amount learned on the central task. In other words, it is necessary to inhibit attention to irrelevant information in order to cope with the information-processing demands of a difficult task. Under most conditions, however, the correlations between task-relevant and incidental learning are zero or positive. That is, it is possible to attend to (and remember) both task-relevant and task-irrelevant materials, and the most skillful subject can often do both well. Under such conditions, inhibition is not required, and incidental learning may simply be taken as a measure of ability to encode and remember a wide range of stimulus inputs simultaneously.

Table 2.17 summarizes the studies of incidental learning. Two studies show an advantage for girls, both being film studies in which there was no loss of plot-relevant content as a result of remembering incidental material. We therefore take these studies to reflect breadth of memory. However, the major conclusion from the table is that the sexes do not differ in their ability to process incidental information, or to inhibit attention to it when necessary.

Learned Low-Amplitude Responding

Feldstone (1969) has used an ingenious method for charting the acquisition of a learned inhibition. The experimental subjects are reinforced for low-amplitude responding (turning a crank slowly, squeezing a dynamometer weakly), and over a series of trials the experimental group comes to respond with lower amplitude than a control group. In most instances, Feldstone finds no sex differences in the speed of acquistion of this inhibitory behavior, although when sex differences do appear, they show acquisition to be faster in girls. Feldstone, however, is especially interested in testing the White model that there are two kinds of learning processes: a simple, fast-acting associative process, and a more complex cognitive learning process, the latter being developmentally more mature. Feldstone examines his acquistion curves for evidence that these two processes occur successively. For example, if for a given group of subjects the experimental and control groups diverge at a fairly early point in a series of trials, then converge, then diverge again, he would interpret the first divergence as an instance of simple associative learning which was then briefly interfered with by the second "cognitive" learning process, which "took over" at the second divergence. In one group (the older girls) there was only one divergence. The question is whether this divergence means that the girls learned to inhibit on the basis of simple associative learning and failed to switch to a more cognitive process, or whether they turned to the more advanced process immediately without using the less mature learning style at all. Feldstone sought to determine which interpretation was correct by interviewing his subjects to find out whether they were able to verbalize the reinforcement contingencies, and whether their verbal reports corresponded with their behavior. If the correspondence was high, he thought this would indicate the mature, type 2 learning processes. The older girls showed a high degree of understanding of the contingencies, and a high degree of correspondence between their verbalizations and their behavior, but Feldstone nevertheless concluded that their performance probably represented the immature, type 1 kind of learning, and that their cognitive behavior was probably not regulating their motor behavior. We find this conclusion mysterious.

Obviously there are great difficulties in interpreting the trial-by-trial differences between an experimental and a control group. Feldstone suggests no statistical test for identifying the number of convergences and divergences. The work is provocative, but in our view it has not succeeded in demonstrating the operation of two learning processes, much less a sex

TABLE 2.18
Probability Learning

Study	Age and N	Difference	Comment
Wittig & Weir 1971	4-5 (80)	Boys	More response patterns in 4 alternative probability tasks
		None	2 alternative probability tasks
Gruen et al. 1970	6, 9 (121)	None	3-choice probability task (lower and middle SES)
Deffenbacher & Hamm 1972	7-8 (96)	None	Probability learning in 2-digit-number tasks
	13-15 (96)	None	
	19-20 (96)	None	
Endo 1968	8 (96)	None	2-choice probability task
Lewis 1965	8 (150)	None	2-choice probability task
H. Stevenson et al. 1968a	8-12 (475)	None	3-choice probability task
	12-14 (256)	None	3-choice probability task
Weinberg & Rabinowitz 1970	12-19 (48)	Boys	More maximizing strategy
		Girls	More matching strategy
Rosenhan & Messick 1966	18-21 (116)	None	2-choice probability of smiling or angry faces
F. Todd & Hammond 1965	18-21 (72)	None	Multiple-cue probability task

difference with respect to these processes. The main conclusion from his work would appear to be that the sexes are much alike in acquiring an inhibitory response, with girls possibly having a slight advantage.

Probability Learning

Some learning studies are set up so that there is no response the subject can make that is correct 100 percent of the time. If he has before him a set of three buttons to press, for example, the buttons might be programmed so that one will yield reinforcement 50 percent of the time and the other two 25 percent of the time. The subject's task is to determine how to maximize his own reward. In working on such a task, most subjects do not behave as though there were any simple increase in the strength of the tendency to push each button depending on the number of reinforcements it has delivered. Rather, they attempt to discover what the sequential pattern of reinforcement is, and adopt a problem-solving strategy to guess the "system." In this sense, it is a task that calls upon higher cognitive processes rather than simple associative learning. As may be seen in Table

2.18, the large majority of studies that have analyzed their findings by sex of subject have found no sex differences.

We have reviewed the research on a number of different traditional learning problems. Some are thought of as fairly simple associative forms of learning; others involve the delay or inhibition of an initial response tendency. There is no evidence of sex difference in either kind of task. From the learning literature alone, then, we found no basis for Broverman's contention that there is a linkage between sex and proficiency on one type of task as compared with the other.

Learning Through Imitation

We turn now to the question of whether girls are more "social," and whether this has any bearing upon their learning or memory. We have already seen, in the section on perception, that both sexes are interested in social stimuli and that neither sex has a consistently higher level of interest, although there was a tendency for boys to show somewhat more interest during the first year of life. Chapter 4, achievement motivation, takes up the question of whether girls are more motivated to work for social approval, and summarizes the evidence on the responsiveness of the two sexes to social reinforcement. Chapter 5 considers whether girls are more social in the sense of spending more time interacting with others, or in the sense of being more "empathic"—more sensitive to the needs and emotional states of others. In the present chapter we consider the literature on learning through modeling. In so doing, we have made a rather arbitrary distinction. There are some experiments in which imitation might be said to be incidental. That is, the subject is exposed to a model and is then observed at a later time to see whether he imitates the model, although he has not been instructed to imitate. This is the procedure in many studies of the effects of films, where a group of children are shown an aggressive film, for example, and then observed on a playground to determine the level of aggression as compared to a baseline. In other experiments, the model explicitly shows the subject how something is to be done—solves a puzzle, pronounces a word, etc.—and the model's actions are a good (or perhaps the only) source of the information the subject needs to solve the problem set for him. It is this second kind of modeling study that is charted here. Studies of spontaneous imitation are reviewed in Chapter 7, under "conformity." Table 2.19, then, includes the research on what might be called "instructed" or "learning-set" imitation. It is reasonable to suppose that if either sex were more "social"—more oriented toward people than impersonal objects or abstract ideas—members of that sex would find it especially easy to learn through modeling.

There has been an enormous amount of work on observational learning. The large majority of studies summarized in Table 2.19 find no sex differ-

TABLE 2.19
Learning Through Modeling

Study	Age and N	Difference	Comment
J. Grusec & Mischel 1966	3-4 (28)	None	Reproduction of models; neutral and aversive behavior
Bandura & Menlove 1968	3-5 (48)	None	Change in dog avoidance after model interacted with dog
Friedrichs et al. 1971	3-5 (50)	None	Puzzle-completion task modeled
McDavid 1959	3-5 (32)	Boys	Imitated model's choice of door in search for candy, without knowledge of model's success
Mehrabian 1970	3-5 (127)	None	Imitation of sentences
Liebert & Swenson 1971a	4 (48)	Girls	Higher recall of items model chose
Masters & Driscoll 1971	4 (48)	Boys	Toy arrangement
	4 (40)	None	Toy arrangement
Osser et al. 1969	4-5 (32)	None	Imitation of sentences read by model
Liebert & Fernandez 1970	4-6 (48)	None	Matching model's responses to stimulus items
Hetherington[R] 1965	4-11 (216)	Girls	Imitation of parents' aesthetic preferences
B. Coates & Hartup 1969	4, 5, 7, 8 (72)	None	Number of accurate reproductions of filmed model's behavior
Kuhn 1972	4, 6, 8 (87)	None	Object-sorting task after watching an adult model
Bruning 1965	5 (144)	None	Lever-movement response
Rickard et al. 1970	5 (40)	None	Imitation of animal names after hearing varying number of animal names
Staub 1971c	5 (75)	Boys	Helping child in distress after role-playing practice coupled with positive comments from E (trend, $p < .1$)
		Girls	Helping child in distress following role-playing practice
Elliott & Vasta 1970	5-7 (48)	None	Sharing behavior after exposure to altruistic model
Yando & Zigler 1971	5-6, 9-10 (192)	None	Imitation of model's designs (normals, retardates)
Presbie & Coiteux 1971	6 (64)	None	Imitation of sharing (vs. stingy) behavior
Thelen et al. 1972	6-8 (60)	None	Imitation of filmed model's button-pressing responses

(continued)

TABLE 2.19 *(cont.)*

Study	Age and N	Difference	Comment
Liebert et al. 1969a	7 (48)	None	Imitation of self-reward patterns in bowling game
Rosenthal et al. 1972	7 (80)	Boys	More imitation of model's clustering of stimulus objects
Zimmerman 1972	7 (36)	Boys	Asked more questions in retraining after modeling
Akamatsu & Thelen 1971	7-8 (48)	None	Button pressing after model was rewarded or not rewarded
W. Mischel & Liebert 1967	7-8 (56)	None	Imitation of self-reward patterns
Bandura & Kupers 1964	7-9 (160)	None	Imitation of model's self-reinforcing behavior in bowling game
M. Harris & Hassemer 1972	7-9 (48)	None	Sentence modeling (two-thirds bilingual)
Hildebrandt et al. 1973	7-9 (96)	None	Self-reward in bowling game after exposure to lenient or stringent models
J. Grusec 1971	7-11 (88)	None	Donating behavior after exposure to altruistic model
Cheyne 1971	8 (30)	None	Word choices after observing model receive varying reinforcements
Rosenthal & White 1972	8 (112)	None	Word association arrays
Rosenhan et al. 1968	8-9 (72)	None	Imitation of self-reward
Stouwie et al. 1970	8-9 (156)	None	Self-reward after watching adult model's self-reward
Debus 1970	8-10 (100)	None	Latency and error scores after viewing reflective and/or impulsive models
Bandura & Whalen 1966	8-11 (160)	None	Modeled self-reinforcement
Lamal 1971	8, 10, 12 (72)	None	Performance on "20 questions" type of problems after observing model
Hanlon 1971	9 (52)	None	Imitation of taped British accent
W. Mischel & Liebert 1966	9 (54)	None	Self-reward in bowling game
Zimmerman & Bell 1972	9-12 (84)	None	Modeled rule learning
Thelen 1970	10-12 (38)	None	Self-blame statements after exposure
Bandura & Jeffery 1973	18-21 (88)	None	Complex motor configuration after observing filmed model
Gerst 1971	18-21 (72)	None	Complex motor responses after exposure to a filmed model

(continued)

TABLE 2.19 *(cont.)*

Study	Age and *N*	Difference	Comment
E. Jones et al. 1968	18-21 (140)	None	Recall of model's problem solving
Larsen et al. 1972	18-21 (79)	Men	Shocked victim more (intensity, duration) after exposure to model who ended up shocking the victim at maximum level
		None	Total voltage administered
Yelen 1969	18-21 (96)	Women	Imitation of peer-partner's rating of nonsense syllables on semantic scale

ences. Among the studies that do, males are approximately as likely as females to obtain higher scores. We have not charted studies according to the sex of the model. A number of reports in the literature indicate that a child's imitation of a model may depend on whether the model is of the same sex. As we shall see later in reviewing the work on spontaneous imitation, some kinds of behavior are thought to be more appropriate for a model of a given sex; for example, children of both sexes are more likely to copy aggression if it is displayed by a male rather than a female model. But we have not been able to detect any overall tendency for subjects to learn more successfully from a same-sex or opposite-sex model, and this conclusion applies to both spontaneous imitation and explicit learning-set imitation.

Memory

The distinction between learning and memory is an arbitrary one. What is remembered must have been learned. What has been learned can usually only be determined through asking persons to recall or recognize the learned material. However, traditional "memory" research has differed somewhat from the work on "learning" in its methods and phrasing of questions to be answered. We have taken the easy way out of the difficult decisions over whether individual studies should be classified under learning or memory, and simply listed under memory the studies the authors labeled in this way.

We do not regard memory as a "capacity" but as a set of processes. Individuals (and groups) differ in their skill in using these processes. Furthermore, there can be differences among individuals or groups in *what* is remembered. That is, in a subject-matter area where an individual already has a good deal of information and where his interest is high, he has a substantial body of related material with which to associate new, incoming information; furthermore, he is motivated to employ whatever strategies he knows how to use, such as active rehearsal of the new material, in order to ensure that it will be available for later retrieval. If there are sex dif-

TABLE 2.20
Verbal Memory

Study	Age and N	Difference	Comment
J. Hall & Halperin 1972	2½ (23)	None	Recognition of previously heard word list
Sitkei & Meyers 1969	3-4 (100)	Girls	Sentences presented aurally (for black, middle SES subsample only)
J. Hall & Ware 1968	5-7 (86)	None	Recognition of previously heard words
Weener 1971	5-8 (90)	None	Recall of 5-word strings with 4-month follow-up
Cramer 1972	6, 7, 10, 11, (96)	None	Recall of list of 12 words (3 instruction conditions)
Cole et al. 1971	6, 8, 13 (120)	None	Number of object names recalled
	6, 9, 11, 14 (82)	None	Number of words recalled
Shepard & Ascher 1973	6, 11, 18-21 (96)	Girls	Higher total number of words recalled
Amster & Wiegand 1972	7, 11 (64)	Girls	Higher overall recall for words used in sorting tasks
H. Stevenson et al. 1968a	8-12 (475)	None	Answering questions about orally presented story
	12-14 (256)	Girls	Answering questions about orally presented story (high- and low-IQ subsamples; no difference, middle-IQ subsample)
Felzen & Anisfeld 1970	8, 11 (80)	Girls	Shorter latency in recognizing unfamiliar words in recall task
		None	Errors
Finley & Frenkel 1972	9, 12 (48)	Girls	Tachistoscopic presentation, girls recalling more words
Kossuth et al. 1971	11 (80)	Girls	Better recall and more word clustering
H. Stevenson et al. 1970	14 (96)	None	Answering questions about story heard (educable retardates)
Sarason & Harmatz 1965	15 (144)	None	Sexual learning task
Tulving & Pearlstone 1966	15-17 (929)	Girls	Immediate recall and cued recall of category name tests
Backman 1972	17 (2,925)	Girls	Verbal memory: Project Talent Test battery
DeFazio 1973	18-21 (44)	None	Repeating strings of words
Milburn et al. 1970	18-21 (134)	Women	Words recalled
Laurence & Trotter 1971	23, 75 (72)	None	Words recalled per trial

TABLE 2.21
Memory for Objects and Digits

Study	Age and N	Difference	Comment
Fagan 1972	3-6 mos (266)	None	Fixation times to novel relative to familiar stimuli (6 experiments)
Fagan 1971	3-8 mos (24)	None	Fixation times to novel relative to familiar stimuli and to less familiar relative to more familiar stimuli
C. Allen 1931	1 (100)	None	Toy hidden under 1 of 3 boxes – delayed response task
Sitkei & Meyers 1969	3-4 (100)	Boys	Object memory (for lower SES white subsample only)
		Girls	Recall of sequences of letters (for middle SES black subsample only)
		None	Visual Sequence Memory; ITPA Vocal Sequencing
Friedrichs et al. 1971	3-5 (50)	None	Serial recall of line drawings of common objects
L. Horowitz et al. 1969	3-5 (108)	None	Pictures of objects (3 experiments)
Hagen et al. 1973	4-7 (48)	None	Serial recall of pictures of animals
Rothbart 1971	5 (56)	None	Recall of toys seen in playroom
McCarver & Ellis 1972	5-6 (60)	None	Digit span, short-term, memory of location of drawings of objects
Mathews & Fozard 1970	5-8, 11-12 (128)	None	Recency judgments on picture pairs
Flavell et al. 1966	5, 7, 10 (60)	None	Serial recall of pictures of familiar objects
McCarver 1972	5, 7, 10, 18-21 (160)	None	Serial position, probe-type, short-term memory
Steele & Horowitz 1973	6 (72)	None	Recall of line drawing
Moynahan 1973	6, 8, 10 (144)	None	Recall of line drawings of common objects (categorized, noncategorized)
B. Ross & Youniss 1969	6, 10 (64)	None	Recognition of pictures under 2 delay periods
G. Harris & Burke 1972	7, 9, 11 (90)	None	Recall of grouped or ungrouped digits
Keenan 1972	7, 9, 11 (38)	None	Recall of sequences of English letters, Hebrew letters, binary patterns (tachistoscopic presentation)
Sabo & Hagen 1972	8, 10, 12 (240)	None	Short-term memory of location of pictures

(continued)

TABLE 2.21 *(cont.)*

Study	Age and *N*	Difference	Comment
Spitz et al. 1972	8, 17 (60)	None	Digit recall
	9, 13, 20 (90)	None	Digit recall
	14-17 (44)	None	Digit recall
	Adults (22)	None	Digit recall
Hagen & Huntsman 1971	9, 11 (21)	None	Short-term memory of location of pictures (retardates)
Druker & Hagen 1969	9, 11, 13 (240)	Boys None	Better recall of location of drawings. Matching previously seen line drawings of animals and household objects
Anders et al. 1972	19-21 (10)	None	Latencies of response to short digit lists
Blum et al. 1972	64, 84 (54)	None	Wechsler-Bellevue: Digits Forward, Digits Backward (longitudinal); annual rate of decline over the 20-year period

ferences in interests, areas of knowledge, and abilities, then, we would expect these to be reflected in memory. The specific areas of strength of the two sexes are discussed in later chapters (see especially Chapter 3). In the present section we anticipate the distinctions made there, and summarize the studies that deal with memory for verbal content in Table 2.20, those using objects or digits in Table 2.21, and those calling for memory of a combination of verbal and nonverbal materials in Table 2.22.

Girls show somewhat better memory for verbal content. More than half the studies have found no sex differences, but when differences are found, girls have higher scores in every case. The superiority of girls in verbal memory is especially clear after about the age of 7. By contrast, sex differences are seldom found for objects or digits. The one study with children older than preschool age showing a sex difference finds boys better at recalling designs, a task that probably relates to the area of visual-spatial skills in which boys of this age frequently excel. The studies that used tasks calling for memory of both verbal and nonverbal materials present a mixed picture, but on the whole do not show superiority of either sex. In a study of recall of a model's performance, J. Grusec (1972) found that boys remembered more performed than verbalized material, whereas girls recalled both equally well.

To summarize, verbal content in a memory task may give some advantage to girls, but it clearly cannot be said that either sex has a superior memory capacity, or a superior set of skills in the storage and retrieval of information, when a variety of content is considered. Nor does existing evidence point to a difference in choice of mnemonic strategies.

TABLE 2.22
Memory for Words and Objects

Study	Age and N	Difference	Comment
Sitkei & Meyers 1969	3-4 (100)	Boys	Picture memory (for lower SES black subsample only)
		None	Paired pictures
Ward & Legant 1971	3-4 (20)	None	Pictures with and without verbal labels
	4 (29)	None	Pictures and color stimuli, with and without verbal labels
Appel et al. 1972	4 (20)	None	Memory task for pictures and names
	7 (40)	Girls	Remembered more names of pictures
	11 (40)	None	Pictures and names
Rothbart 1971	5 (56)	None	Recall of names of zoo animals in picture
McCarver & Ellis 1972	5-6 (60)	None	Recall of location of previously labeled and non-labeled drawings
Wheeler & Dusek 1973	5, 8, 10 (144)	Boys	Matching previously seen line drawings (8-year-old sample only)
		Girls	Better recall of location of previously labeled and nonlabeled line drawings
G. Davies 1972	8-9 (100)	None	Names or pictures of objects
Koen 1966	18-21 (72)	Men	Recalled pictures seen if no labeling was allowed
		Women	Recalled picture seen if verbal labels or acting out was used

Social Memory

In an early study, Witryol and Kaess (1957)[R] reported that women college students were better able than men to remember the names associated with photographs of faces, and better able to remember the names of people they had met briefly. Primarily on the basis of this study, it has been thought that females have superior "social memory." Garai and Scheinfeld say (1968, p. 206)[R]: "The greater facility in the recall of names and faces by girls may be the result of their greater interest in people, while the better retention of information by boys appears to be related to their greater interest in objects, which is manifest in infancy."

In the earlier portion of this chapter, we were not able to find evidence that infant boys are more interested in objects, or infant girls in people. But of course this would not preclude the development of differences in social interests at a later time that could be reflected in social memory.

To our knowledge, there has been no attempt to replicate the Witryol and Kaess study directly. An indirect replication (Messick and Damarin

TABLE 2.23
Social Memory

Study	Age and N	Difference	Comment
Leifer et al. 1971	4, 7, 10 (60)	None	Memory of characters in fairy tale
G. Leventhal & Anderson 1970	5 (144)	None	Recall of own and fictitious partner's performance scores in game
Zussman & Reimer 1973	9, 10 (64)	None	Memory of what characters said in puppet show
Isen 1970	18-21 (30)	None	Recall and recognition of confederate's behavior
A. Lott et al. 1970b	18-21 (52)	None	Association of nonsense syllables with names of liked, disliked, and neutrally regarded acquaintances

1964[R]) found no sex differences. We have charted in Table 2.23 the studies that test for recall of material appearing to have some social content, and no sex difference emerges. However, the evidence is scanty, and the research has not been focused on the social-nonsocial distinction. It would be useful to have more information on the recall of names and faces in naturalistic situations. Meanwhile, the existing evidence on social memory is consistent with what has been found with respect to perception of social cues and learning through modeling: the two sexes seem to be equally oriented toward social stimuli, and equally able to recall them, at least through the college years. We have no doubt that certain adult occupations call for special skill in identifying people and recalling their names. The receptionist, bank clerk, head waiter, insurance salesman, nurse, doctor, and teacher all find it advantageous to know the names of the people with whom they deal. Most people in these occupations develop the relevant memory skills with practice. If women, more often than men, have jobs requiring these skills, it is to be expected that a sex difference in "social memory" might emerge during the post-college years. If so, it would appear that the social skills of adult women are not rooted in any childhood patterns that have emerged so far. But this issue will be reexamined in the chapters that follow.

To summarize: beginning in early infancy, the two sexes show a remarkable degree of similarity in the basic intellectual processes of perception, learning, and memory. Although the possibility remains open that females are more sensitive in the modalities of touch and smell, we found no evidence to support the contention that boys are more oriented toward vision, girls toward hearing. Hence we do not see differences in sensitivity to these two kinds of stimulation as being the foundation of any sex differences in language acquisition, or in the processing of visual-spatial materials.

The allegation that girls learn best by rote processes, boys by some more advanced form of reasoning, is clearly not supported by the evidence. If learning tasks are classified in terms of whether they call primarily upon the formation of simple associations or upon higher-level processes (such as the inhibition of previously acquired responses), there is no trend whatever in the direction of girls excelling on some classes of learning tasks and boys on others. Nor have we been able to find evidence for the widely held belief that girls are more skillful at perceiving, learning, and remembering materials that have a "social" content. However, most studies of perception, learning, and memory do not vary systematically the nature of the content to be learned. The present chapter has shown clearly that there is no difference in *how* the two sexes learn. Whether there is a difference in *what* they find easier to learn is a different question. Whether either sex is in any sense readier to respond to certain kinds of inputs from the environment is a question that will continue to be examined in Chapters 3–7, where the acquistion of specific classes of behavior by the two sexes is reviewed.

CHAPTER THREE

Intellectual Abilities and Cognitive Styles

To anyone accustomed to thinking in terms of the theories and concepts of developmental psychology, the factor-analytic studies of "abilities" have an alien ring. They address themselves to few developmental issues. An exception is the question of whether separable "abilities" become more differentiated or more integrated as intellectual development proceeds through childhood and adolescence. But this question is only tangentially linked to theories concerning the changes in information-processing strategies which are a primary concern of current developmental psychology. The ability factors that emerge from factor-analytic studies do not always make sense in terms of these processes and their developmental changes. For example, the distinction between "verbal" and "quantitative" skills poses problems. Numbers are frequently expressed in words. In what sense, then, are mathematical skills also not verbal? If the distinction has to do with the manipulation of symbols, words as well as numerals and conventional mathematical notations are symbols. There does not seem to be a clear distinction between solving a verbal syllogism and solving a mathematical problem that is couched in "if-then" terms. It would appear that complex manipulation of symbols can occur with the use of either mathematical symbols or verbal symbols. Individual differences in intellectual abilities in adolescence and adulthood should have to do with processes that are not specific to either sphere, but that ought to be better understood by reference to processes such as those described by Piaget in his analysis of "formal operations." If one thinks in these terms, it does not come as a surprise that verbal and mathematical skills are usually quite strongly correlated, or that quantitative ability has sometimes not emerged as a distinct factor in factor-analytic work (Flanagan 1961). It *does* come as a surprise if two groups of people differ in one direction on "verbal" ability and in the opposite direction on mathematical ability.

Similarly, the distinction between "spatial" abilities and other abilities is puzzling. It is widely alleged (e.g. Bruner et al. 1966[R], pp. 21ff) that young children tend to use "ikonic" (pictorial) representations in organizing, storing, and retrieving the products of their experience. With development such representations are presumably superseded, to a considerable degree, by nonpictorial symbols, including both quantitative and nonquantitative words. As the person develops, he presumably begins to solve even spatial problems (such as the representation of three-dimensional space in a two-dimensional perspective drawing) in nonpictorial ways, with increasing use of verbal symbols. A developmental psychologist might be tempted to suppose, then, that "spatial visualizing" might emerge as a factor in intellectual abilities in early and middle childhood, but that it would merge with other factors with approaching maturity; or if it continued as a distinct factor, it would represent a lower level of intellectual maturity. Such an assumption would not be warranted by the findings of the factor-analytic studies. Spatial ability does not become less distinct as a factor with increasing age, but probably more so. Little is known concerning the role that spatial-visual imagery plays in mature, complex thought, but it now seems possible that ikonic representation does not give way to other "more advanced" forms of thought, but rather can be retained and utilized as part of the most advanced levels of information processing.

Developmental psychology has focused on a single ladder of intellectual development, describing individuals in terms of the height they have reached on this ladder. Factor-analytic studies suggest that there are diverging paths of development—that there may be different "types" of advanced thought.

In comparing the intellectual development of groups of individuals (e.g. social classes, firstborns vs. later-borns, ethnic groups, males vs. females), one can ask two questions: (1) Do they differ in their rate of progress, and in the level ultimately reached, on a unidimensional developmental ladder? (2) Does one group have a higher representation than the other among certain "types"? (Are there distinct ability profiles?) The two questions can be combined, if one thinks in terms of distinct developmental progressions for different abilities, into the question: Do the groups differ in the height they reach (or their rate of progress) on the separate ability ladders? Our analysis will be primarily focused on the last question. We will not have a free choice of the content of these different ladders. We will be constrained by the nature of the tests that have been given and the clusters of abilities that have emerged from them in the course of the psychometric work that has been done.

It has been customary in the testing field to distinguish between tests of achievement and tests of ability. Achievement tests are normally focused on a range of subject matter on which training has been given. Tests of ability have been designed primarily to predict individuals' future success on particular kinds of tasks. Achievement tests are likely to emphasize *knowledge*, then, whereas ability tests include items intended to reveal how quickly a person can learn something new. In practice, the distinction becomes blurred. The products of past learning form the basis for new learning. The same processes that enabled the person to amass knowledge in past learning situations can be utilized to acquire new information. "Achievement" quite often takes the form of having learned *how to learn*, rather than merely storing learned information. Thus, although we recognize that the distinction has been a useful one for certain purposes, it is not particularly useful for our present purposes, and we will analyze the two kinds of data jointly.

This chapter, more than others in this book, takes the form of a sequel to a chapter called "Sex Differences in Intellectual Functioning," which appeared in the 1966 *Development of Sex Differences*. The tables included in this chapter summarize the research that has been done since the previous summaries were prepared (plus a few items omitted from those summaries), and although the previous summaries have not been repeated here, they will be referred to where relevant to the discussion.

GENERAL INTELLECTUAL ABILITIES

It is still a reliable generalization that the sexes do not differ consistently in tests of total (or composite) abilities through most of the age range studied. As Table 3.1 shows, girls do appear to have a slight advantage on tests given under the age of 7: out of 18 such studies, 8 found girls to have higher scores, whereas only 1 (with kibbutz children under the age of 2) found higher scores for boys. There is some question, of course, whether tests given during the first year of life may be considered tests of "intellectual" ability in any meaningful sense. By necessity they must rely upon perceptual performance and motor skills, and they do not predict later intellectual achievements, so it is difficult to interpret any group differences that occur at this age. Tests from age 2 to 7 do come closer to measuring abilities that will be involved in later intelligence, and when there is a sex difference in this age range, it favors girls. It is tempting to view this early superiority of girls, when it is found, as reflecting a differential rate of maturation in the two sexes, but there are two reasons to be cautious about such an interpretation. First, Bayley (1956)[B] has shown that the rate of intellectual development is not positively related to indexes of physical growth (indeed, that the correlations tend to be negative), so that if intellectual development is a function of physical maturation, it would have to be maturation of a different system than that reflected in height or bone development. A second issue is that of cultural differences. The higher scores of girls tend to be found in studies of "disadvantaged" children. The one instance of higher scores in boys comes from a special subculture: Israeli kibbutzim. Unless rates of maturation are affected differently in the two sexes by cultural conditions, the cultural effects would

TABLE 3.1
General Intellectual Abilities

Study	Age and *N*	Difference	Comment
Leiderman et al. 1973	0-2, 3-5 mos (64)	None	Bayley Scales of Mental and Motor Development (premature, full-term)
Kohen-Raz 1968	1, 3, 4, 8, 10, 12, 15, 18, 24, 27 mos (207)	None	Bayley Scales (Israeli sample)
	6 mos (32)	Boys	Bayley Mental Scale (Israeli infants reared in kibbutzim and institutions
		None	Bayley Motor Scale
	6 mos (18)	None	Bayley Scales (Israeli infants reared in private homes)
R. Wilson & Harpring 1972	3, 6, 9, 12 18, 24 mos (261 pairs of twins)	Girls	Bayley Motor Scale (at 9 mos only); Bayley Mental Scale (at 18 mos only)
T. Moore 1967	6, 18 mos (76)	None	Griffiths's Scale of Development (longitudinal)
	3, 5, 8 (76)	None	Stanford-Binet (longitudinal)
Goffeney et al. 1971	8 mos (626)	Girls	Bayley Scales – fine motor
		None	Bayley Scales – mental, gross motor
	7 yrs (626)	None	WISC, Bender-Gestalt
Ireton et al. 1970	8 mos (536)	None	Bayley Scale
Willerman et al. 1970	8 mos (3,037)	Girls	Bayley Motor Scale
		None	Bayley Scale
	4 yrs (3,037)	Girls	Stanford-Binet (longitudinal)
Beckwith 1971	8, 10 mos (24)	None	Cattell, Gesell
D. Stayton et al. 1971	9-12 mos (25)	None	Griffiths's Scale of Development
Clarke-Stewart 1973	10-12, 17-18 mos (36)	None	Bayley Scales (longitudinal)
Lewis et al. 1968	3 (57)	Girls	Stanford-Binet
Dickie 1968	3-4 (50)	None	Stanford-Binet (black sample)
Shipman 1971	3-4 (1,474)	Girls	Caldwell Preschool Inventory (black and white disadvantaged sample)
Zigler 1968	3-4 (52)	None	Stanford-Binet
McDavid 1959	3-5 (26)	None	Stanford-Binet Form L

(continued)

TABLE 3.1 *(cont.)*

Study	Age and N	Difference	Comment
Klaus & Gray 1968	3, 4, 5, 6, 7 (88)	None	Stanford-Binet, WISC (low SES black; longitudinal)
	6 (80)	None	Metropolitan and Gates Reading Readiness tests
	6, 7 (80)	None	Metropolitan Achievement Test (longitudinal)
	7 (30)	None	Stanford Achievement Test
Quay 1972	4 (50)	None	Stanford-Binet (black disadvantaged sample)
Radin 1973	4 (52)	None	Stanford-Binet
Massari et al. 1969	5 (33)	None	Stanford-Binet
Winitz 1959	5 (150)	Girls	WISC Performance Scale IQs
F. Brown 1944	5-6 (432)	None	Stanford-Binet Form L (multiracial sample)
Kaufman 1971	5-6 (103)	None	Large-Thorndike Intelligence Tests
SRI 1972	5, 7 (7,301)	Girls	Wide Range Achievement Test
Dykstra & Tinney 1969	6 (3,283)	Girls	Pintner-Cunningham Primary test of intelligence
G. Prescott 1955	6 (800)	Girls	Metropolitan Readiness Test Score
Goldschmid 1967	6-7 (81)	None	Pintner-Cunningham or Otis
V. C. Crandall & Lacey 1972	6-12 (50)	None	Stanford-Binet
Sundberg & Ballinger 1968	6-13 (807)	None	Goodenough Draw-a-Man Test (Nepalese sample)
Havighurst & Hilkevitch 1944	6-15 (670)	None	Arthur Point Performance Scale (Indian sample)
Schubert & Cropley 1972	6-15 (211)	None	WISC (Canadian, Indian, and white subsamples)
V. C. Crandall 1969	7-12 (41)	None	Stanford-Binet
Parsley et al. 1963	7-13 (5,020)	None	5 tests in 4 achievement areas
Eska & Black 1971	8 (100)	None	Otis-Lennon Mental Ability Test
Solkoff 1972	8-11 (224)	Boys	WISC – Coding WISC – Picture Completion and Object Assembly

(continued)

TABLE 3.1 *(cont.)*

Study	Age and *N*	Difference	Comment
Faterson & Witkin 1970	8-13 (53)	Girls	Articulation of Body Concepts (longitudinal)
	10, 14, 17 (60)	Girls	ABC at 14 yrs only (longitudinal)
Curry & Dickson 1971	8, 11 (16)	None	Stanford-Binet
Dreyer et al. 1971	9-16 (22)	None	Sophistication of body concept on Draw-a-Person Test (longitudinal)
Lekarczyk & Hill 1969	10-11 (114)	Girls	Kuhlmann Anderson, Forms E and F; Stanford Achievement Test
Achenbach 1970	10-13 (1,085)	Girls	Higher IQ, all ages
S. Stayton 1970a	16 (112)	None	Stanford-Binet (retardate sample) Science Research Associates Test of Educational Ability (normal sample)
Bayley 1957	16, 18, 21 (33)	None	Gains in intelligence (longitudinal)
Wyer 1967	18 (2,000)	None	ACT
Rosenberg & Sutton-Smith 1966	18-20 (600)	Women	Total score—ACE
Baltes et al. 1971	21-70 (280)	None	General Intelligence factor score (Primary Mental Abilities Test, Test of Behavioral Rigidity)
E. Lane 1973	27-46 (22)	None	Average IQ increase from second to eighth grades
Kangas & Bradway 1971	39-44 (48)	Men	Larger gains in IQ over a 38-year period

seem to weaken the maturational interpretation and point to environmental reasons for whatever sex difference is found.

A major issue in determining whether a given study finds a sex difference, of course, is the nature of the items included on the test. Some tests, such as the Stanford Binet, have been standardized in such a way as to minimize sex differences; other tests, such as the Thurstone Primary Mental Abilities Test, have not. Since boys are better at some kinds of tasks and girls at others (see below), the sexes can be made to differ in either direction, or to be the same, depending on the mix of items included in a test. The majority of studies of general ability with subjects over the age of 6 seem to have used well-balanced tests: they find no sex differences. The studies showing higher scores for girls seem to have used tests that rely heavily on verbal skills. If the scores obtained by boys and girls in a particular study are determined by the weighting given to certain specific abilities, then any sex difference that emerges is of little general interest. We shall turn shortly to an analysis of sex differences in specific abilities. But first we shall discuss an issue with respect to general intelligence: the question of its heritability, and whether heritability is equivalent in the two sexes.

Do the Sexes Differ in Heritability?

Bayley and Schaefer[R], in their 1964 monograph on development of mental abilities in relation to certain aspects of the behavior of the mothers in their longitudinal studies, say: "The impact of the environment (maternal behavior) on infant boys is persistent: both their behavior and their intellectual functioning tend to become fixed by the third year and to persist at least through 18 years. The girls' intellectual functioning, on the other hand, appears to be more genetically determined."

The suggestion is, then, that the path of development is somehow more fixed by biology for girls than it is for boys. The argument is partly based on the evidence concerning genetic factors from Skodak and Skeels' study of adopted children. In their reanalysis of these data, Bayley and Schaefer show that the IQs of girls are significantly correlated with the IQs of their natural mothers (from whom they have been separated since birth), whereas the IQs of boys are not significantly related to those of their natural mothers. The Bayley and Schaefer hypothesis is also an inference, based on evidence that the male of the species is more affected by environmental variations than the female. Bayley and Schaefer's data showed higher correlation between maternal behavior and the social and intellectual characteristics of boys than girls.

Before we continue with analysis of the evidence relevant to the Bayley-Schaefer hypothesis, it should be noted that although it was originally stated in the context of the inheritance of intelligence, the hypothesis applies to the heritability of other characteristics as well. Because most of the evidence we draw upon comes from studies of mental abilities, we include the discussion of heritability in the present chapter, and broaden the discussion to cover nonintellectual aspects of behavior whenever they bear upon the general issue of sex differences in heritability.

We discuss later (in the section on variability, p. 119) the matter of greater male vulnerability. We take it as demonstrated that there are certain kinds of powerful environmental insults—perhaps especially those that occur prenatally or paranatally—that affect the male more than the female. What relation does this fact have to the role of genetic control over the growing individual? Is it a reasonable inference that if one sex is more affected by certain aspects of the environment, the other must be more susceptible to genetic influence? Let us consider the case of twins. If one twin is subjected to a powerful environmental hazard while the other is not, then the twins should become more unlike than they would otherwise be. The degree of unlikeness produced by the environmental effects would be at least as great for fraternal as for identical twins. Thus the greater genetic similarity between identical twins would be gradually outweighed by the cumulative impact of environmental events for any group of twins that are highly vulnerable to such events. Heritability coefficients, as these are normally computed, would go down. Thus the argument seems persuasive that if boys are more vulnerable, they ought to show less heritability, at least when heritability is measured through twin resemblances.

We shall first examine the direct evidence that can be found concerning heritability in the two sexes, and then shall return to the issue of the relationship between heritability and environmental effects. The scarcity of data is a handicap. There are many studies of heritability, of course, and most of them include subjects of both sexes, but either the data are not analyzed by sex, or sex differences in heritability are reported only if they are positive, not if they fail to appear.

First we take studies of heritability in animals; here the amount of heritability is usually determined by relating similarities among individuals to their degree of genetic similarity. This can be carefully controlled by the use of back-crosses and other selective breeding programs. The heritability of activity level has been studied separately by sex in fruit flies and mice (Connolly 1966[R], DeFries et al. 1966[R]); Thompson (1953)[R] studied the heritability of food drive, emotionality, and exploration in mice. Dominance, aggression, and sexual behavior have been studied in chickens (Craig and Baruth 1965[R], Guhl et al. 1960[R], Wood-Gush 1960[R]). In none of these studies was heritability greater for one sex than the other. An interesting exception is a study of alcohol consumption in rats. Eriksson (1968)[R] found that females had a higher heritability for alcohol consumption than males, and linked this to a sex difference in alcohol elimination. However, the general conclusion is that when both sexes are studied in a variety of animal behaviors, there is no sex difference in heritability.

In humans, the constraints on experimentation mean that the available evidence will be less direct than that for animals. There are two main kinds of evidence: parent-child correlations and twin studies.

Parent-child correlations of mental abilities. Parent-child resemblances in IQ have been the major focus of study, with very little research being available on parent-child similarities in attributes other than intelligence. And even in the IQ studies, the data are often incomplete. Sometimes IQ scores from the parental generation are available only for mothers, not fathers. More of a problem is the fact that the parental data are sometimes *estimates*, based on education, occupation, or some other indirect index. Sometimes the measures of the parent or the child represent an incomplete coverage of the domain of mental abilities—for example, only verbal tests may have been given. This turns out to be important, for there is now some reason to believe that certain components of mental abilities may be more heritable than others. Most studies of parent-child resemblances deal with total IQ scores, and there might be more useful information if subscores were available as well. Total IQ scores may mask some parent-child resemblances that exist for some components but not others.

A final problem in the studies of parent-child resemblance has to do with the ages at which the measures are taken. Usually there is a child's score, obtained when the child is young, and this is correlated with the parent's score, obtained from an adult. Since IQ tests measure different things at different developmental stages, parent-child resemblances may be attenuated by the age differences. If a genetic substratum is accounting for some of the variance in the two distributions, this fact might be more apparent if both parent and child were measured at the same age. Obviously, it is only very extended longitudinal studies that will yield data of this kind.

The earliest report from a longitudinal study is by Conrad and Jones in 1940[R], in which estimated IQs of mother and father were correlated with measured IQs of children. In this report, boys' and girls' scores showed similar degrees of relationships with their parents' IQs, although the girls' correlations were somewhat higher. Honzik (1963)[R] and Bayley and Schaefer (1964)[R] later reported data from the Berkeley longitudinal samples. Bayley and Schaefer, using estimated IQs for the mother (estimated on the basis of a mother interview) report correlations ranging from .48 to .55 between the IQs of girls and their mothers; for boys, the comparable relationships are .34 to .48. No test was reported for the significance of the difference between these correlations. With the sample sizes involved (15 boys and 16 girls), it would not appear to be significant. Here is an instance, then, in which girls tend to show slightly more heritability than boys, but not significantly so. Honzik, working with larger numbers of families from the Berkeley Guidance Study, used estimated IQs for the parents, and she reports a tendency for boys' correlations with parental IQs to be higher than girls'; however, the significance of this difference was not tested.

The Fels longitudinal study also provides us with some interesting data on parent-child resemblance. Kagan and Moss (1959)[R] report relationships between child IQs and the IQs of their parents measured during the parents' adulthood. The parent-child resemblances were of the same magnitude for boys and girls. More recently, McCall et al. (1973)[R] have reported on families in which the parents were themselves subjects in the Fels longitudinal study as children; now that their children are also being tested, it is possible to study parent-child resemblances between IQ scores taken at the same age. The changing patterns of correlation depending upon the age of measurement are of interest in themselves; for our present purposes, however, the main point is that there are no sex differences in the degree of correlation between parents and children, regardless of whether the measures of parent IQ are taken in childhood or adulthood. One sex difference has been reported by both McCall and Honzik: for both sexes, children's scores show little resemblance to parental scores when the children are very young; as they grow older, the correlation increases. Girls reach the point of maximum correlation with parental scores at an earlier age than boys do, a fact that Honzik attributes to the more rapid maturation of girls. In any case, the bulk of the evidence indicates that the ultimate level of resemblance in IQ does not differ for the two sexes.

As mentioned above, the Bayley and Schaefer reanalysis of an earlier study of adopted children revealed a higher relationship for girls than boys between the child's IQ and that of its natural mother. There is now reason to believe that this sex difference will not replicate on other samples of children. Although the data are not yet published, the scores of a group of adopted children on the Ravens Progressive Matrices test have been related to the educational level attained by the children's natural mothers.[*] The correlations are virtually identical for the two sexes.

Later in this chapter, the studies comparing parents and children with respect to their spatial abilities are reviewed. It will be shown that children's spatial abilities are moderately related to those of the cross-sex parent. For our present purposes, the main point of interest is that the degree of correlation with the cross-sex parent does not appear to differ by sex, so that even if the attribute is sex-linked, this does not mean it is more genetically controlled in one sex than the other.

It would be very useful indeed to have parent-child correlation data, separately by sex, for psychological measures other than IQ. Our conclusions from the existing data can only be tentative, but the existing studies of parent-child resemblance would seem to indicate no sex difference in heritability.

Twin studies. Two questions are usually addressed by twin studies. One is whether male identical twins are more similar to each other than female identical twins. The other rests on a comparison between identical and fraternal twins of a given sex. Let us consider first the work with identical twins only. Lyon (1961)[R] has suggested that female monozygotic twins have somewhat more room to differ from one another than do male monozygotic twins, because females have two X chromosomes and only one of these will become apparent in the phenotypes—which one being a matter of chance. More recent work on this subject indicates that which X is activated is random within each cell, so that an individual female has a mosaic pattern of X activation throughout her body. Female identical twins, then, can be somewhat more unlike than male identicals with respect to any characteristic carried on the X chromosome but not so unlike as fraternals. To the extent that the X chromosome is implicated in a wide range of

_____

* Personal communication from S. Scarr-Salapatek, University of Minnesota, 1973.

physical and psychological attributes, then, female identical twins should show less congruence than male identical twins. Vandenberg (1962)[R] has found that this seems to be true on a range of physiological measures, and also on the verbal subtest of the Primary Mental Abilities test. Similarly, Humphreys* finds somewhat less congruence in monozygotic girl twins from the Project Talent sample on spatial tests, although it is not clear whether the difference between male twin congruence and female twin congruence is statistically significant.

The second approach with twins is to compare the correlations between identical twins with the correlations between fraternal twins. If there is no genetic contribution to a particular ability, one would expect the two kinds of twins to be equally correlated. Heritability can be computed by first finding the correlation between identical twins, then finding the correlation between fraternal twins, and expressing these two numbers as a ratio. Humphreys has done this for a variety of IQ subtests, and finds that for girls, correlations between identical twins and those between fraternal twins are somewhat more similar than for boys. Thus, girls show somewhat less heritability by this measure. The difference between the sexes is greatest for spatial abilities. That is, this ability seems to be a more genetically controlled attribute in boys than it is in girls. Again, the statistical significance of the sex differences has not been reported.

In summary, on the narrow range of attributes that have been studied, we find that the sexes show similar degrees of genetic control on the basis of parent-child resemblance, but that boys may show somewhat more genetic control if data from twin studies are used.

Heredity and Environment

There is a dilemma: we noted initially the greater vulnerability of male infants and children, and the fact that Bayley and Schaefer reported a greater relationship between maternal behavior and the child's intellectual development for boys than for girls. If it were generally true that males were more susceptible to environmental influence than females, there appears every reason to expect that heritability ought to be greater for girls. Instead, heritability is either very similar for the two sexes or on some measures higher for boys. How is it possible for one sex to show both more heritability and more susceptibility to environmental influence?

Perhaps the dilemma is not real. That is, it may be based upon false assumptions or incomplete information. Having examined what is known about heritability, let us return to the issue of whether one sex is really more susceptible to environmental influence than the other. It would be a formidable task to review all the socialization studies to see whether the correlations between parent behaviors and child characteristics are gen-

* L. G. Humphreys, personal communication, University of Illinois, 1972.

erally higher for boys than for girls. We have, however, reviewed a selected set of studies (Bayley and Schaefer 1964[R]; the Fels longitudinal study, reported in Kagan and Moss 1962[R]; Honzik 1967[R]; Bing 1963[R]; Hetherington 1967[R]; R. Sears et al. 1965[R]) with this question in mind.

Taken as a whole, these studies do not indicate that either sex is generally more susceptible to home influence. There is the further question of whether the other major sources of environmental influence—school, peer group, climate, ecological factors such as crowding, or an unlimited list of other possibilities—affect the two sexes to different degrees. For the present, it may be taken as a reasonably strong hypothesis that they do not; at least, we know of no evidence that they do.

There is still, however, the substantial evidence for the greater vulnerability of the male infant, referred to earlier. How can it be that this vulnerability exists and is not reflected in lowered heritability figures for males? Two possible resolutions to the problem come to mind. The first is that some of the prenatal and paranatal defects that are found more commonly in boys are genetic. This is not a new suggestion. Potentially injurious genetic attributes tend to be recessive. (Indeed, if they were not, they would not survive in the gene pool unless they simultaneously controlled characteristics needed for survival along with their injurious side effects.) Whenever such attributes are sex-linked (that is, carried on the X chromosome), the female has the protection of a second X chromosome, and the chances of a dangerous recessive trait being present in both her X chromosomes are small. When the male gets the recessive trait with his single X chromosome, there is no available suppressor for it, and it does whatever developmental damage it is capable of doing. If the problem is genetic in this sense, then of course it will affect both members of an identical twin pair, more so than in the case of fraternal twins.

The case of prenatal or paranatal problems that are *not* genetic is different, but it would appear to have the same outcome. That is, suppose a mother contracts rubella at the third or fourth month of pregnancy. It will presumably affect both her unborn twins. And it ought to affect identical twins in more precisely the same way than fraternals, since the nature of the effects seems to depend in a very detailed way upon the point a fetus has reached in its development when the disease strikes. Incidentally, it may be that girls' somewhat faster rate of prenatal development reduces their period of maximum vulnerability and helps to account for the lower rate of intrauterine damage among female fetuses. But to return to the matter of effects of such hazards as rubella upon twins: fraternal twins may develop at somewhat different rates, whereas identicals do not (except for those attributes that are affected by crowding in the placenta). Hence, the effects of the disease would be more similar for identicals than fraternals. Hence, also, the measures of heritability that involve comparing identical with fraternal twins would continue to reveal high heritability figures, even in the face of an environmental factor with a severe impact. Thus, the fact that males are more vulnerable to certain sorts of damage is not incompatible with the fact that they show somewhat greater heritability in twin studies. We need not accept the proposition that if one sex is more vulnerable, then the other must by definition show more heritability.

Our survey has led us to agree with the often-cited generalization that boys are more vulnerable than girls to certain physiological stressors. However, we think it is fallacious to infer that because male bodies are more vulnerable, males must therefore also be more capable of learning from experience—more susceptible to environmental feedback of all sorts. It is a great leap from the evidence of more frequent male stillbirths to an expectation that boys ought to be more affected than girls by their parents' socialization practices. A brief review of the relevant studies has led to the conclusion that, although the sex difference in physical vulnerability does exist, a sex difference in the effects of learning and teaching environments probably does not. As to the question of genetic control of behavior, the twin studies point to somewhat greater effects of heredity for boys than girls, but studies of parent-child resemblance do not bear this out. On the whole, to the extent that biology is destiny, it would appear that it is about equally so for the two sexes.

SPECIFIC ABILITIES

Verbal Abilities

Female superiority on verbal tasks has been one of the more solidly established generalizations in the field of sex differences. Recent research continues to support the generalization to a degree. It is true that whenever a sex difference is found, it is usually girls and women who obtain higher scores, but the two sexes perform very similarly on a number of verbal tasks in a number of sample populations. In particular, it may be that some of our earlier views concerning the course of development of sex differences in verbal skills should be reconsidered.

It has been thought that sex differences begin very early—from the time of the utterance of the first word or even earlier, in babbling, and diminish as the boys "catch up." A source of this generalization is the 1954[R] McCarthy summary of studies of language development. The differences reported in that study tended to be small, and many, as McCarthy noted, were not significant even on large samples. However, when there was a difference it almost always favored girls, and the many studies taken together added up to a significant trend.

The same was true generally in the studies done between the McCarthy study and our 1966 review, although the study with the largest sample (Templin 1957[R]) found no sex differences between the ages of 3 and 6. Conclusions concerning the first few years of life, however, are still

TABLE 3.2
Spontaneous Vocal and Verbal Behavior

Study	Age and N	Difference	Comment
S. J. Jones & Moss 1971	2 wks, 3 mos (28)	None	Vocalizations in each of 5 states: active and passive awake, drowsy, active and passive asleep
Lewis & Freedle 1972	3 mos (40)	Girls None	Respond vocally to mother behavior / Vocalization frequency (home observation)
Rheingold et al. 1967	3 mos (21)	None	Vocalization to E
J. Kagan 1969	4, 8, 13 mos (150)	None	Mean vocalization time to clay faces and verbal stimuli
L. Yarrow et al. 1971	5 mos (41)	None	Frequency of positive vocalization (home observation)
Lewis 1969	6 mos (64)	Girls	Vocalization to mother during free play
Rheingold & Eckerman 1969	9-10 mos (24)	None	Spontaneous verbal behavior
B. Dodd 1972	9-12 mos (15)	None	Spontaneous utterances: number, range, length
Clarke-Stewart 1973	9-18 mos (36)	None	Vocalizations to mother, total number of vocalizations (home observation; longitudinal)
Rheingold & Samuels 1969	10 mos (20)	None	Frequency of spontaneous vocalizations (mother present)
H. Ross et al. 1972	11-12 mos (8m, 4f)	None	Number of vocalizations during experimental session
Roberts & Black 1972	18-22 mos (40)	None	Mother's reports of language production
P. Smith & Connolly 1972	2-4 (40)	Girls	Talked more frequently to other children; made more play noises
R. Bell et al. 1971	2½ (74)	Girls	Teachers rated as higher in speech development
Halverson & Waldrop 1970	2½ (42)	Girls	Talking to mother
Mueller 1972	3-5 (48)	Boys	Verbalizations in free play with same-sex peer
Hartig & Kanfer 1973	3-7 (261)	None	Verbalization of instructions to self in resistance-to-temptation task
Kohlberg et al. 1968	4-5 (34)	None	Egocentric speech recorded while S performed various tasks (Americans, Norwegians)
Szal 1972	4-5 (60)	Boys None	Spontaneous verbalizations (competitive) in cooperative-competitive games / Spontaneous verbalizations (cooperative, uncooperative)
Wolff & Wolff 1972	4-5 (55)	None	Verbal output, verbal skill (teacher rating)
B. Coates & Hartup 1969	4-5, 7-8 (72)	Girls	Appropriate verbalizations during movie

(continued)

TABLE 3.2 *(cont.)*

Study	Age and N	Difference	Comment
Kohlberg et al. 1968	4-10 (112)	None	Percentage of egocentric speech while constructing sticker designs with adult
Shrader & Leventhal 1968	6-17 (599)	None	Parents' reports of speech problems
Greenglass 1971b	9-10, 13-14 (132)	Girls	Requests for information or evaluation from mother (Canadian sample, ages 9-10 only)
		None	Requests for information or evaluation from mother (Italian sample)
Sarason & Winkel 1966	18-21 (48)	None	Incomplete sentences, sentence corrections, or serial repetition of words
		Women	Emitted fewer "ah's"

based upon very early work. There has been almost no work with children under 2½ or 3 of a normative sort, involving large and unspecialized samples of children, since the 1930's and 1940's. Work in the field of language development has been very intensive during the past 15 years, and understanding of this development has been greatly enhanced, but the work has tended to be focused upon very small and rather highly selected groups of children; it does not reveal whether there has been a change in the relative standing of the two sexes at these early ages with respect to articulation, length of utterance, or early vocabulary. Recent, relatively small-scale studies seem to indicate that the presumed advantage of girls in the first two years of life is tenuous. Lewis and Freedle (1972) did find such an advantage at age 3 months, in terms of the frequency with which the infant responds vocally, rather than in some other way, to stimulation by the mother. T. Moore (1967) found that girls had higher "speech quotients" at age 18 months, though not earlier or later. Clarke-Stewart (1973) found girls to be ahead in both comprehension and vocabulary at 17 months. However, 8 other studies made with infants and children up to the age of approximately 2 find no difference (see Tables 3.2 and 3.3).

In Table 3.2 we have charted studies of spontaneous vocalizing and speaking, most of which involve fairly small samples. After the age of 2, when speech is beginning to be acquired, no trends are apparent in the amount of spontaneous talking that the two sexes do in the course of their daily activities. Table 3.3 summarizes a very large number of studies conducted in testing situations using a variety of standardized stimulus materials. Here, beginning at age 2½, several large-sample studies appear. McCarthy and Kirk (1963) tested children ranging from 2½ to 9 to obtain norms for the Illinois Test of Psycholinguistic Abilities. They found no consistently significant sex differences in overall linguistic ability. The only consistent trend across age levels was that boys were better at "visual de-

TABLE 3.3
Tested Verbal Abilities

Study	Age and *N*	Difference	Comment
T. Moore 1967	6, 18 mos (76)	Girls	Speech quotients higher at 18 mos (longitudinal)
		None	Amount of vocalization at 6 mos; vocal communicativeness at 18 mos
	3, 5, 8 yrs (76)	None	Vocabulary, verbal behavior (longitudinal)
Clarke-Stewart 1973	17 mos (36)	Girls	Language competence
Lewis et al. 1971a	2 (60)	None	Vocalization to human forms
Reppucci 1971	2 (48)	None	Vocabulary naming and recognition
Rhine et al. 1967	2-5 (50)	None	Picture vocabulary
McCarthy & Kirk 1963	2½-9, at 6-mos intervals (700)	Boys	Visual Decoding (at 4½, 8½, 9 yrs only) Motor encoding (at 5½, 9 yrs only)
		Girls	Battery of Illinois Test of Psycholinguistic Abilities (at 7½ yrs only) Auditory Decoding (at 3½, 7 yrs only) Visual-Motor Association (at 3½, 8 yrs only) Auditory-Vocal Sequencing (at 7½ yrs only) Visual-Motor Sequencing (at 7 yrs only) Auditory-Vocal Association (at 5, 6 yrs only)
		None	Vocal Encoding, auditory-vocal automatic
Herriot 1969	3 (24)	None	Understanding tenses
Dickie 1968	3-4 (50)	None	Expressive Vocabulary Inventory, Peabody Picture Vocabulary Test (PPVT), Vocal Encoding and Auditory-Vocal Association subtests of the Illinois Test of Psycholinguistic Abilities (black sample)
Sitkei & Meyers 1969	3-4 (100)	Girls	Action-Agent Divergent (lower and middle SES black subsample only); ITPA Vocal Encoding (lower SES black subsample only)
		None	PPVT, Action-Agent Convergent, Picture Description, Orpet Utility, Monroe Language Classification (lower and middle SES black and white samples)
Shipman 1971	3-4 (1,000-1,400)	None	ETS: Matched Pictures Language Comprehension Task I, Story Sequence I, PPVT, Mimicry of Meaningful Words
		Girls	Mimicry of Nonsense Words
T. Williams & Fleming 1969	3-4 (36)	None	PPVT and verbal and visual associative tasks
H. Brown 1971	3-5 (96)	None	Choice of pictures after hearing descriptive sentences
Friedrichs et al. 1971	3-5 (50)	None	Carrying out simple and complex verbal instructions

(continued)

TABLE 3.3 *(cont.)*

Study	Age and N	Difference	Comment
Mehrabian 1970	3-5 (127)	None	Picture vocabulary, comprehension, and judgment of grammaticalness of sentences
Shipman[R] 1972	3-5 (820)	Girls	ETS: Matched Pictures Language Comprehension Task II, Story Sequence II
Parisi 1971	3-6 (144)	None	Syntactic comprehension
Klaus & Gray 1968	3, 4, 5, 6, 7 (88)	None	PPVT (low SES black sample; longitudinal)
	5 (88)	Boys	Greater number of words used in descriptions of pictures
	5, 6, 7 (88)	None	ITPA, total scores (longitudinal)
	6 (88)	None	Metropolitan and Gates Reading Readiness Tests
Matheny 1973	3-8 (44)	Girls	Templin-Darley Articulation Test
Jeruchimowicz et al. 1971	4 (79)	None	PPVT, Expressive Language task (black sample)
Radin 1973	4 (52)	None	PPVT (lower SES)
Shure et al. 1971	4 (62)	None	PPVT (black sample)
W. C. Ward 1969	4 (55)	None	Fluency (Uses, Patterns, and Instances tests)
Ali & Costello 1971	4-5 (108)	None	Standard and modified PPVT (disadvantaged black sample)
A. Harrison & Nadelman 1972	4-5 (50)	None	PPVT
Osser et al. 1969	4-5 (32)	None	Verbal imitation and comprehension
Suppes & Feldman 1971	4-6 (64)	None	Response to verbal commands testing comprehension of logical connectives
James & Miller 1973	4-7 (32)	None	Identification, explanation, and conversion of meaningful and anomalous sentences
Masters 1969b	4-9 (72)	None	Word-association and word-definition tests
Brimer 1969	5 (867)	None	Orally administered English Picture Vocabulary Test 1
	5-8 (3,240)	Boys	Higher on orally administered vocabulary tests at each age level except 5 yrs
	6-8 (2,373)	Boys	EPVT 1
	7-11 (5,084)	Boys	EPVT 2
Winitz 1959	5 (150)	Girls	Mean length verbal response, fluency (1 of 4 measures)
		None	Vocabulary, articulation, WISC verbal scale

(continued)

TABLE 3.3 *(cont.)*

Study	Age and N	Difference	Comment
McCarver & Ellis 1972	5-6 (60)	None	PPVT
Milgram et al. 1971	5-7 (99)	None	Verbal reproduction of story heard (half of sample disadvantaged)
Saltz & Soller 1972	5-6, 8-9, 11-12 (72)	None	Matching pictures to concept words
SRI 1972	5, 7 (7,111)	Girls	Language ability
	5, 7 (13,155)	Girls	Reading knowledge
Cowan et al. 1967	5, 7, 9, 11 (96)	None	Mean length of response to picture
Routh & Tweney 1972	5, 10 (60)	None	Verbal free association
F. Darley & Winitz 1961	6 (150)	None	WISC Verbal Scale IQ
Sharan (Singer) & Weller 1971	6 (357)	Girls	More descriptive categorization and grouping in verbal responses to object-sorting task
O. Davis 1967	6-7 (238)	None	Reading achievement test
Dykstra & Tinney 1969	6-7 (3,283)	Boys	Orally administered vocabulary test (at age 6 only); spelling test (at age 7 only)
		Girls	5 measures of reading readiness; several subtests of 2 verbal achievement tests
Gahagan & Gahagan 1968	6-7 (54)	None	Number of verbs produced in a stimulus response language task
Lesser et al. 1965	6-7 (320)	None	Total verbal ability (some sex differences in ethnic subgroup)
France 1973	6-9 (252)	Boys	PPVT administered by taped voices of students (multiracial sample)
Graves & Koziol 1971	6-9 (67)	None	Plural noun formations
Braun & Klassen 1971	6, 9, 11 (216)	Girls	Higher frequency of noun, relative clause, and object transformations (German-, French-, and English-speaking samples)
		None	29 other linguistic indexes (e. g. number of subordinate clauses, redundancies, etc.)
Bandura & Harris 1966	7 (100)	None	Frequency of passive or mean number of prepositional phrases
J. Kagan et al. 1964	7-8 (135)	Boys	Higher verbal fluency scores
Penk 1971	7-11 (100)	Girls	Fewer mediational faults in word association task
Gates 1961	7-13 (13,114)	Girls	Speed of reading, level-of-comprehension, reading vocabulary

(continued)

TABLE 3.3 *(cont.)*

Study	Age and *N*	Difference	Comment
Parsley et al. 1963	7-13 (5,020)	None	Reading vocabulary, reading comprehension
M. Harris & Hassemer 1972	7, 9 (96)	None	Length and complexity of sentences in composed stories
Lipton & Overton 1971	7, 9, 11, 13 (80)	None	Anagrams task
Zern 1971	7, 9, 12 (69)	None	In time or error scores on questions requiring several mental steps of negation
Eska & Black 1971	8 (100)	None	Response latency and mean length of stories in picture description task
Eisenberg et al. 1968	8-10 (64)	Girls	Better understood on tapes by teachers
Corah 1965	8-11 (60)	Boys	Vocabulary IQ
Hoemann 1972	8-11 (80)	None	Communication of information of a task or game rules
H. Stevenson et al. 1968a	8-12 (475)	Girls	Anagrams task
	12-14 (256)	Girls	Anagrams task (low IQ sample)
		None	Anagrams task (middle, high IQ samples)
H. Stevenson et al. 1968b	8-14 (529)	Girls	More words generated from a single word
Palmer & Masling 1969	8, 9, 15, 16 (48)	None	Vocabulary for skin color (black and white subsamples)
B. Cohen & Klein 1968	8, 10, 12 (240)	None	Verbal communication skill
Hopkins & Bibelheimer 1971	8, 10, 12, 13 (354)	None	Language IQ: California Test of Mental Maturity (longitudinal)
Cotler & Palmer 1971	9-11 (120)	Girls	Fewer errors in reading
Nakamura & Finck 1973	9-12 (204)	Boys	Fewer errors on easy similes
		Girls	Fewer errors on hard similes
Moran & Swartz 1970	9-17 (280)	None	Free association test scored for types of responses (3 longitudinal samples)
Penney 1965	9-11 (108)	None	PPVT
Preston 1962	9, 11 (2,391)	Boys	Reading comprehension and reading speed at age 11 (German sample)
		Girls	Reading comprehension and reading speed (American sample); reading speed at age 9 (German sample)
		None	Reading comprehension at age 9 (German sample)
H. Stevenson & Odom 1965	9, 11 (318)	None	Anagrams task

(continued)

TABLE 3.3 *(cont.)*

Study	Age and *N*	Difference	Comment
Shepard 1970	9, 11, 13 (137)	Girls	More syntagmatic responses in a word association task (at 9, 11 yrs only); more complex word definitions
		None	Number of simple functional word definitions
T. Baldwin et al. 1971	10 (96)	None	Verbal communication of pictures to another child (black and white)
Herder 1971	10 (143)	None	Descriptions of abstract and face stimuli (black and white)
Achenbach 1969	11 (164)	None	WISC—information
		Girls	WISC—vocabulary
Cicirelli 1967	11 (609)	None	Reading achievement
		Girls	Higher in language achievement
Kellaghan & MacNamara 1972	11 (500)	None	Drumcondra verbal test (Irish)
Weinberg & Rabinowitz 1970	12-19 (48)	None	Vocabulary scores of WISC
Svensson 1971	13 (8,905)	Girls	Verbal achievement
		None	Verbal intelligence (Swedish)
	13 (7,694)	Girls	Verbal achievement
		None	Verbal intelligence (Swedish)
H. Stevenson et al. 1970	14 (96)	Girls	Anagrams task, 1 of 2 testing conditions (educable retarded)
Flanagan et al. Project Talent 1961	14, 17 (4,545)	Boys	Vocabulary
		Girls	Disguised words, English language; reading comprehension
Walberg 1969	16-17 (1,050)	Girls	Verbal factors in IQ, scientific processes, and understanding science (physics students)
	16-17 (450)	Girls	Henmon-Nelson Intelligence Test, Form B
Backman 1972	17 (2,925)	Girls	English language (Project Talent Test battery)
Monday et al. 1966-67	18 (238,145)	Women	ACT English scores
Rosenberg & Sutton-Smith 1966	18-20 (600)	None	Linguistic scale ACE
Bieri et al. 1958	18-21 (76)	None	SAT verbal
DeFazio 1973	18-21 (44)	None	Verbal fluency, advanced vocabulary test
Feather 1968	18-21 (60)	None	Anagrams task
Feather 1969b	18-21 (167)	None	Anagrams test
Koen 1966	18-21 (72)	None	Verbal communication of information about photography
Laughlin et al. 1969	18-21 (528)	None	Synonyms and Antonyms

(continued)

TABLE 3.3 *(cont.)*

Study	Age and *N*	Difference	Comment
Marks 1968	18-21 (760)	None	SAT verbal, Advanced Vocabulary Test
Mendelsohn & Griswold 1966	18-21 (223)	None	Vocabulary Test of the Institute of Educational Research
Mendelsohn & Griswold 1967	18-21 (181)	None	Anagrams task
Sarason & Minard 1962	18-21 (96)	None	Vocabulary subtest of WAIS
Very 1967	18-21 (355)	Women	Moore-Castore Vocabulary, Moore-Castore Paragraph Reading, English Placement Vocabulary
Rosenberg & Sutton-Smith 1964	19 (377)	Women	Linguistic scale ACE
Rosenberg & Sutton-Smith 1969	19 (1,013)	Women	Linguistic scale ACE
Sutton-Smith et al. 1968	19 (1,055)	None	ACE verbal
Bayley & Oden 1955	29, 41 (1,102)	Men	Overall score on Concept Mastery Test (at 41 yrs only), Analogies subtest score (longitudinal study of gifted sample and spouses)
		None	Synonyms and antonyms subtest score
	29 (168)	None	Overall score on Concept Mastery Test (gifted sample)
	41 (227)	None	Overall score on Concept Mastery Test (gifted sample)
Blum et al. 1972	64, 84 (54)	Women	Wechsler-Bellevue: similarities; Stanford-Binet: vocabulary (at 84 yrs only; longitudinal)
		None	Annual rate of decline over 20-year period

coding"—pointing at named objects when the stimulus was visual. Girls tended to be somewhat better at *productive* naming. A set of 13 other recent studies involving children of preschool age have found no sex differences on a variety of verbal tasks. A major exception is the work done by the Educational Testing Service (Shipman 1971) with children from impoverished families. Here, girls are clearly ahead on a number of language measures, though not on all measures used. Another large-scale study of disadvantaged preschoolers (Stanford Research Institute 1972) also finds girls ahead on language measures.

As we move into the next age range, the early school years, there are again few differences. Brimer (1969), who gave receptive vocabulary tests to very large samples in England, found, in fact, higher average scores for boys at each age from 6 through 11. Most studies in America, however, including the ITPA norming sample mentioned above, detect no consistent sex differences, and these include tasks involving productive "fluency" as well as tests of understanding. The primary exception is found in the work of the Stanford Research Institute, with very large samples of disadvantaged children in Follow-Through programs from kindergarten through the second grade. Here the girls clearly test higher in a variety of language skills, including reading, vocabulary, and the understanding of relational terms. Johnson (1973–74)[R] suggests there are sex-specific cross-cultural differences in the reading of English. Males have fewer reading problems in England. This may explain the difference in direction of sex difference of Brimer's work.

It is at about age 10 or 11 that girls begin to come into their own in verbal performance. From this age through the high school and college years we find them outscoring boys at a variety of verbal skills. Sex differences are not found in every study; the findings seem to depend in part on whether tests of general knowledge are called verbal tests—boys tend to do at least as well as girls on such tests and, in the Project Talent sample, substantially better. But in tests of verbal power, girls above age 11 frequently do better, and in some studies the difference is fairly large in absolute terms.

Table 3.4 shows the studies with the largest samples, and gives the magnitude of the sex differences found, as well as their direction. Since units of measurement are not comparable from one study to another, the magnitude of the mean sex difference has been expressed in standard deviation units. The female advantage on verbal tests ranges from about .1 to nearly .5 SD, with the usual difference being about .25 SD. One longitudinal study (Droege 1967) that followed a large group of high school students from the ninth to the twelfth grade found that the superiority of girls on verbal tasks increased through this period. This study is especially interesting, since its longitudinal design permitted a control for differential dropout. We think it important to be clear that the measures reported cover much more than spelling, punctuation, and talkativeness. Included as well are considerably higher-level skills, such as comprehension of complex written text, quick understanding of complex logical relations expressed in verbal terms, and in some instances verbal creativity of the sort measured by Guilford's tests of divergent thinking.

We suggest that there are distinct phases in the development of verbal skills in the two sexes through the growth cycle. One occurs very early—before the age of 3. We emphasize that the studies documenting sex differences at this age are very old. More recent studies tend not to show superiority for girls in spontaneous vocalization or in picture vocabulary after the understanding of speech has begun. Whether a sex difference would still be found with large samples on age of beginning to speak, age of first combining words into sentences, or mean length of utterance, we do not know. If girls do have an early advantage with respect to these aspects of language development, it is short-lived. At about 3 the boys catch up, and in most population groups the two sexes perform very similarly until adolescence. When there are differences, they favor girls; these exceptions tend to occur in populations of underprivileged children, where girls maintain an advantage to a later age. It is possible that boys' greater vulnerability to hazards of all sorts, including those prevailing prenatally, means that the poorer the prenatal and postnatal nutrition and medical care prevailing in a population, the greater the sex difference in early performance will be and the higher the age to which the difference will persist, owing to the presence of larger numbers of low-scoring boys who have suffered some sort of systemic damage in the population most at risk. We shall return shortly to the matter of variability and its possible causes; but now let us simply note that for large unselected populations the situation seems to be one of very little sex difference in verbal skills from about 3 to 11, with a new phase of differentiation occurring at adolescence.

Quantitative Ability

The earliest measures of some aspect of quantitative ability begin at about age 3 with measures of number conservation, soon followed by enumeration. As Table 3.5 shows, there appear to be no sex differences in performance on these tasks during the preschool years, or in mastery of numerical operations and concepts during the early school years, except in disadvantaged populations. Here again the data from the large studies conducted with Head Start and Follow-Through children show the girls to be ahead. The majority of studies on more representative samples show no sex differences up to adolescence, but when differences are found in the age range 9–13, they tend to favor boys. After this age, boys move ahead, and the sex differences become somewhat more consistent from one study to another, though there is great variation in the degree of male advantage reported. Table 3.6 shows the magnitude of the sex differences (in standard score units) in the studies with large samples. It may be seen that Flanagan et al. (1961, Project Talent) find that boys' math scores are .66 SD better than girls' at the twelfth grade, whereas Droege (1967), also using thousands of cases, finds no significant sex difference in high school, and a large Swedish study finds a difference of less than .2 SD. It is not possible at this point to estimate how large the sex difference in quantitative performance is likely to be in any given population.

It is frequently suggested that boys' superiority in math during the high school years simply reflects their greater interest in this area (perhaps based on greater expectations that they will need to use math for their later careers). It is true that boys tend to take more math courses when they have a choice. Is their better performance in math tests due to the fact that their interests have led them to take more courses, rather than due to any difference in aptitude? Project Talent analyzed math scores in the senior

TABLE 3.4

Sex Differences in Verbal Ability: Magnitude and Variability

Study	Age	Sample size		Mean scores		Size of mean difference*	Sex scoring higher	Standard deviation		More variable sex
		Boys	Girls	Boys	Girls			Boys	Girls	
Shipman ETS (1971):										
Peabody PVT (receptive)	3-4	1,198		25.9	26.8	-.07	F	13.10	12.58	M
SRI (1972):										
Reading	5	4,838	4,831	32.57	36.15	-.23	F	14.99	15.37	F
	7	1,768	1,718	55.01	62.09	-.26	F	26.17	26.39	F
Language	5	1,842	1,762	12.09	12.53	-.13	F	3.36	3.26	M
	7	1,774	1,723	18.36	19.69	-.18	F	7.16	7.28	F
Gates (1961): †										
Reading speed	7	938	888	7.37	8.43	-.19	F	5.11	5.73	F
Vocabulary	7	938	888	9.41	11.26	-.26	F	7.18	6.99	M
Comprehension	7	938	888	7.05	8.66	-.26	F	6.06	5.97	M
Reading speed	10	1,027	933	19.63	20.94	-.15	F	8.69	8.25	M
Vocabulary	10	1,027	933	26.36	28.16	-.18	F	10.63	9.04	M
Comprehension	10	1,027	933	22.60	23.64	-.12	F	9.20	7.43	M
Reading speed	13	846	811	20.07	21.49	-.18	F	7.84	7.62	M
Vocabulary	13	846	811	37.15	39.60	-.21	F	11.90	10.72	M
Comprehension	13	846	811	30.49	31.33	-.10	F	8.21	7.22	M
Brimer (1969) (England)	8	584	605	17.60	15.98	.22	M	7.48	6.65	M
	9	639	546	22.36	19.34	.37	M	7.96	8.00	F
	10	616	537	26.80	23.60	.40	M	7.84	8.05	F
	11	537	515	29.20	26.88	.30	M	6.91	8.29	F

(continued)

TABLE 3.4 *(cont.)*

Study	Age	Sample size		Mean scores		Size of mean difference*	Sex scoring higher	Standard deviation		More variable sex
		Boys	Girls	Boys	Girls			Boys	Girls	
Svensson (1971) (Sweden):										
School I – 1961	13	2,950	2,878	87.54	89.61	-.12	F	16.79	16.36	M
School II – 1961	13	1,499	1,578	88.69	90.18	-.09	F	16.78	15.99	M
School I – 1966	13	731	769	114.58	123.32	-.30	F	29.22	27.97	M
School II – 1966	13	3,097	3,047	54.61	58.36	-.23	F	15.77	15.50	M
Droege (1967); GATB (verbal subscore)	14	3,398	3,680	93.20	95.55	-.19	F	11.97	12.16	F
	15	3,348	3,491	96.60	100.03	-.26	F	12.83	13.47	F
	16	3,229	3,395	98.70	102.93	-.29	F	13.57	14.11	F
	17	3,028	3,139	100.19	103.38	-.21	F	14.22	14.80	F

*The difference between the means has been divided by the weighted mean of the standard deviations of the two sex distributions; that is, the difference is expressed as a standard score.

†We are reporting three of the seven ages studied.

TABLE 3.5
Quantitative Ability

Study	Age and N	Difference	Comment
Potter & Levy 1968	41 mos (29)	None	Enumeration (point once and only once at each member of a set)
	47 mos (29)	Girls	Enumeration
Shipman 1971	3-4 (1,395)	Girls	Enumeration, low SES sample
Farnham-Diggory 1970	4-9 (282)	None	Mathematical synthesis tasks
SRI 1972	5, 7 (6,607)	Girls	Quantitative scores (New York Alpha)
Ginsburg & Rapoport 1967	6, 11 (76)	None	Estimating proportions
Parsley et al. 1963	7-13 (5,020)	None	Arithmetic Fundamentals and Reasoning Tests
B. Ross 1966	7, 9, 11, 13, 15 (80)	None	3 tests of probability estimating
D. Pedersen et al. 1968	8 (24)	None	WISC arithmetic subtest
Hopkins & Bibelheimer 1971	8, 10, 12, 13 (354)	None	Nonlanguage IQ: California Test of Mental Maturity (longitudinal)
L. Siegel 1968	9, 11 (192)	None	Digit-processing tasks
T. Hilton & Berglund 1971	10, 12, 14, 16 (1,320)	Boys	STEP math test, at 12, 14, 16 yrs only; SCAT quantitative test, at 16 yrs only (longitudinal sample of college-bound students)
	10, 12, 14, 16 (539)	Boys	STEP math test, at 16 yrs only; SCAT quantitative test, at 16 yrs only
		Girls	SCAT quantitative, at 10 yrs only (longitudinal sample of vocational students)
Cicirelli 1967	11 (609)	None	California Arithmetic Test
Keating & Stanley 1972	12-13 (396)	Boys	SAT math, Math Level I Achievement Test (gifted sample)
Svensson 1971	13 (8,905)	Boys	Math achievement, math reasoning (Swedish)
	13 (6,144)	Boys	Math achievement, math reasoning (Swedish elementary school sample)
Droege 1967	14, 17 (7,078)	Boys	General Aptitude Test Battery (GATB): Numerical Aptitude (longitudinal)
	15, 17 (6,839)	Boys	GATB: Numerical Aptitude (at 15 yrs only, longitudinal)
	16, 17 (6,624)	None	GATB: Numerical Aptitude (longitudinal)
	17 (6,167)	Boys	GATB: Numerical Aptitude

(continued)

TABLE 3.5 *(cont.)*

Study	Age and N	Difference	Comment
Flanagan et al. 1961	14, 17 (4,545)	Boys	Mathematics ability
Walberg 1969	16-17 (1,050)	Boys	Physics achievement (physics students)
Backman 1972	17 (2,925)	Boys	Mathematics (Project Talent battery)
Monday et al. 1966-67	18 (238,145)	Men	Math subscore of ACT
Rosenberg & Sutton-Smith 1964	19 (377)	None	Quantitative score, ACE
Rosenberg & Sutton-Smith 1969	19 (1,013)	Men	Quantitative score, ACE
Sutton-Smith et al. 1968	19 (1,055)	None	Quantitative score, ACE
Rosenberg & Sutton-Smith 1966	18-20 (600)	Men	Quantitative score, ACE
Bieri et al. 1958	18-21 (76)	Men	SAT Quantitative
Jacobson et al. 1970	18-21 (276)	None	Digit symbol test of WAIS
Sarason & Minard 1962	18-21 (96)	None	Digit symbol subtest of WAIS
Very 1967	18-21 (355)	Men	Arithmetic Reasoning, Division, Mathematical Aptitude, General Reasoning, Moore-Castore Arithmetic, Moore-Castore Algebra
		None	Addition, Subtraction, Arithmetic Computation, Number Arrangement, Ship Destination

year of high school, after equating the two sexes on the number of math courses taken. The boys still emerged with substantially higher average scores, a finding that suggests it is not merely the amount of training the two sexes have received that is responsible for the difference in their performance at this age.

During adolescence, boys' superiority in math tends to be accompanied by better mastery of scientific subject matter and greater interest in science. The two disciplines are of course closely linked in that science relies heavily upon math in formulating its problems and finding their solutions. One may ask whether male superiority in science is a derivative of greater math abilities or whether both are a function of a third factor. In this connection, some findings of the Harvard Project Physics (Walberg 1969) are interesting. Physics achievement tests were given to a large sample of high school students. On the portions of the test calling for visual-spatial skills, the male physics students did better; on verbal test items, female physics

TABLE 3.6

Large-Sample Studies of Quantitative Ability: Magnitude of Sex Differences and Within-Sex Variability

Study	Age	Sample size		Mean scores		Size of mean difference*	Sex scoring higher	Standard deviation		More variable sex
		Boys	Girls	Boys	Girls			Boys	Girls	
SRI (1972)	5	1,799	1,724	25.46	27.40	-.12	F	7.93	7.35	M
	7	1,596	1,488	38.44	40.58	-.16	F	13.28	12.16	M
Svensson (1971) (Sweden):										
School I – 1961	13	2,950	2,878	41.53	39.85	.17	M	9.72	9.07	M
School II – 1961	13	1,499	1,578	41.72	40.02	.17	M	9.73	9.34	M
School I – 1966	13	731	769	35.14	34.09	.08	M	13.02	12.71	M
School II – 1966	13	3,097	3,047	37.26	35.02	.16	M	13.67	12.80	M
Droege (1967); GATB (numerical subscore)	14	3,398	3,680	97.70	100.19	.18	F	13.57	13.81	F
	15	3,348	3,491	99.37	101.74	.16	F	14.15	14.32	F
	16	3,229	3,395	102.76	103.08	.02	F	15.26	15.15	M
	17	3,028	3,139	106.54	105.70	.05	M	14.36	14.60	F
Project Talent; Flanagan et al. (1961)	14	1,152	990	7.14	5.81	.36	M	3.92	3.33	M
	17	1,153	1,250	11.58	7.86	.64	M	6.25	5.34	M
ACT 1966 norm manual (math subscore); Monday et al. (1966-67)	18	133,882	104,263	21.10	18.0	.47	M	6.3	6.2	M

*The difference between the means has been divided by the weighted mean of the standard deviations of the two sex distributions; that is, the difference is expressed as a standard score.

students obtained higher scores. It would appear that verbal and spatial factors account for some of the variance in science achievement.

Factor analysis of mathematical aptitude tests suggests that a similar situation exists in mathematics. Mathematical ability is not a unitary factor (see Smith 1964[R] and Werdelin 1958[R] for reviews). Moreover, a space factor emerges as an element in mathematical skills for boys but not for girls (Werdelin 1961[R], Mellone 1944[R]). Evidently there are different ways to attack mathematical problems, and individuals differ in the cognitive skills they characteristically bring to bear on such problems. In a letter, Steven Vandenberg[*] tells us: "Rumor has it that Karl Pearson did everything by algebra and Fisher thought geometrically, and that that was the reason why they were not on speaking terms even though they had offices in the same place." It is evident that more needs to be understood about such differences in "mathematical styles" before we can hope to understand sex differences in mathematical ability.

Spatial Ability and Disembedding

Spatial ability, even more than verbal or quantitative ability, is difficult to define. Should it include, for example, skill in auditory localization? Accurate maintenance of size-distance constancy? Tactual recognition of objects as they change orientation in space? Spatial ability first emerged as a distinct factor in the early work of Thurstone. His Primary Mental Abilities test had a Spatial subtest, including the Flags test. In this test, each item has a standard American flag, and a set of four from which the subject must choose those that are the same figure rotated in the plane of the page; false choices are mirror-reversals. A later version of the PMA includes items in which the subject is given a set of segments of figures and is asked to identify which segments would fit together to form the standard, if rotated in two-dimensional space. Other spatial tests have involved such stimuli as (1) drawings of systems of gears, with the subject being asked to determine what motion in one part of the system would be produced by a given motion in another part of the system, and (2) a two-dimensional representation of a three-dimensional pile of blocks, with the subject's task being to estimate accurately the number of surfaces visible from a different perspective than his own. The Block Design subtest of the WISC has been used as a measure of spatial ability, as have mazes and form boards.

In our earlier review (Maccoby 1966a[R]), following Witkin's interpretation, we listed the Embedded Figures Test and the Rod and Frame Test under "Field Dependence"—a cognitive style variable that was thought to reflect analytic ability. Both these tests require the subject to separate

[*] Steven Vandenberg, University of Colorado, 1974.

TABLE 3.7
Spatial (Visual, Nonanalytic) Ability

Study	Age and N	Difference	Comment
Shipman 1971	3-4 (1,460)	Girls	Reproduction of geometric forms
	3-4 (1,411)	None	Identifying matching geometric shapes
	3-4 (1,129)	None	Seguin Form Board
Kraynak & Raskin 1971	3-4 (64)	None	Matching 2- and 3-dimensional geometric stimuli
Kubzansky et al. 1971	3-6 (64)	None	Size constancy with 2- and 3-dimensional stimuli
Fishbein et al. 1972	3-9 (120)	None	Matching photos to room from different orientations
Strayer & Ames 1972	4-5 (40)	None	Latencies or number of errors on form board, copying geometric shapes
G. Burton 1973	4-7 (111)	None	Linear patterning tasks
Caldwell & Hall 1970	4-5, 7-8 (144)	None	Match forms to standard under different orientations
Brainerd & Huevel 1974	5-6 (120)	None	Choosing 2-dimensional drawings to represent 3-dimensional objects
Cronin 1967	5-6 (216)	None	Discrimination of triangles and mirror image reversals of them
Hecox & Hagan 1971	5-7 (52)	None	Proportion estimations matching a standard
Farnham-Diggory 1970	5-9 (332)	Girls	Maplike synthesis (1 of 2 experiments)
Conners et al. 1967	5, 6, 9, 12 (80)	None	Identification of geometric figures by touch
Coryell 1973	5, 7, 9 (90)	None	Matching pictures to room objects in different orientations
Kershner 1971	6 (160)	None	Reproducing spatial relations of cars and houses
A. Long & Looft 1972	6-12 (144)	None	Distinguishing right from left, east from west, top from bottom
Smothergill 1973	6-7, 9-10, 18-21 (60)	None	Localization of spatial target
Kaess 1971a	6, 8, 10 (54)	None	Shape identification under different orientation
Wohlwill 1965	6, 9, 13, 16 (96)	None	Perception of relative distance in third dimension
Ruble & Nakamura 1972	7-10 (56)	None	Assembling puzzles

(continued)

TABLE 3.7 *(cont.)*

Study	Age and N	Difference	Comment
Kaess 1971b	7, 9, 11, 18 (80)	None	Form constancy with rotated shapes
Keogh 1971	8-9 (135)	Boys None	Reproduced patterns by walking more accurately Copying geometric patterns
Nash 1973	11 (105)	None	Differential Aptitudes Test (DAT): Space Relations
	14 (102)	Boys	DAT
Stafford 1961	13-17 & adults (232)	Boys & men	Identical Blocks Test
Droege 1967	14-17 (26,708)	Boys	Spatial aptitude (General Aptitude Test Battery)
Flanagan et al. 1961	14, 17 (4,545)	Boys	2- and 3-dimensional visual spatialization (Project Talent Test Battery)
Backman 1972	17 (2,925)	Boys	Visual Reasoning (Project Talent Test Battery)
Brissett & Nowicki 1973	18-21 (80)	None	Angle-matching task
Kidd & Cherymisin 1965	18-21 (100)	Men	Reversal rate test
Very 1967	18-21 (355)	Men	Cards, cubes, spatial orientation, spatial relationships
A. Davies 1965	20-59 (540)	Men	Maze performance
	60-79 (540)	None	Maze performance

an element from its background, ignoring the latter, and in this sense it is analytic. However, the EFT loads heavily on a spatial factor when it is included in a battery with other visual-spatial tests (e.g. Goodenough and Karp 1961[R]). Sherman (1967)[R] has argued that it is the spatial component of these tests, rather than their analytic component, that is responsible for sex differences in performance on them. Another issue is whether sex differences in spatial ability are confined to the visual modality. With these questions in mind, we discuss separately the few studies that deal with nonvisual spatial skills, and have divided the visual-spatial tasks into two groups: those that appear to call for analytic processes as well, and those that do not.

In our earlier review (Maccoby 1966) we noted that visual-spatial ability, as measured by the spatial subtests of the Differential Aptitudes Test and the Primary Mental Abilities Test, and by mazes, form boards, and block-counting, showed an advantage for boys beginning at about age 6–8.

We have located few recent studies in which these tests have been used. These and studies using a variety of measures that would appear to have a spatial component are charted in Table 3.7. On the whole, they show no sex differences until adolescence, though Keogh (1971), using a sample of moderate size, does report higher scores for boys at age 8–9. Two studies (Droege 1967, Flanagan et al. 1961) have given space-factor tests to large samples of high school students. They both find that boys' superiority on this factor increases through high school, and that the boys' scores exceed the girls' by at least .40 standard score units, on the average, by the end of this time.

Table 3.8 shows studies using versions of the Embedded Figures Test, the Rod and Frame Test, the Body Adjustment Test, and Block Design.

The original Gottschaldt and Witkin Embedded Figures tests have been modified for use with younger subjects, and children's forms (CEFT, PEFT) have been given to children of preschool age by several researchers (Reppucci 1971, Shipman 1971, Sitkei and Meyers 1969, and S. Coates 1972, 1973). In only one of these (Coates) was a sex difference found, and this was in favor of girls. An unpublished study with French kindergarten children* found higher scores for boys on an EFT adapted for this age level. On balance, however, the EFT studies do not show a sex difference for ages 3–5, and the same is true for the early school years. Beginning at about age 8 and continuing into adulthood, studies become inconsistent. A substantial number of studies find no sex difference, but when differences are found, they show higher scores for boys and men into adulthood, with a suggestion that the differences may disappear in old age (D. Schwartz and Karp 1967). Some of the inconsistencies in Table 3.8 may possibly be accounted for by the inclusion of studies with populations from nonindustrial cultures. This issue will be discussed below. Meanwhile, it should simply be noted that not all the inconsistencies can be accounted for by variations in any obvious sample characteristics.

Tables 3.7 and 3.8 have shown that visual-spatial tasks that involve disembedding, and those that do not, have a similar developmental course. The male advantage emerges in early adolescence and is maintained in adulthood for both kinds of tasks. Thus there is no indication, if one considers simply the timetable for change, that the disembedding process contributes anything to the sex difference, beyond what would be produced by the visual-spatial component of the embedded figures tasks or the Rod and Frame test. However, comparison of the two tables does not provide a definitive answer to whether there is such a contribution. What is needed is tasks that are not visual-spatial but that do involve disembedding (or "decontextualization," as it is sometimes called). Witkin and his colleagues

---

* E. Vurpillot, Laboratoire de Psychologie Expérimentale et Comparée de Paris–Sorbonne, personal communication, 1972.

TABLE 3.8
Spatial (Visual-Analytic) Ability

Study	Age and N	Difference	Comment
Reppucci 1971	2 (48)	None	Preschool Embedded Figures Test (PEFT)
Shipman 1971	3-4 (1,288)	None	PEFT
Sitkei & Meyers 1969	3-4 (100)	None	Design discrimination
S. Coates 1972	3-5 (247)	Girls	PEFT
S. Coates 1973	4-5 (53)	Girls	PEFT; trend, $p < .1$
Mumbauer & Miller 1970	4-5 (64)	None	Children's Embedded Figures Test (CEFT)
Bigelow 1971	5-10 (160)	None	CEFT
D. Goodenough & Eagle 1963	5, 8 (96)	None	PEFT
Curry & Dickson 1971	5, 8, 11 (24)	None	Visual Closure Subtest of ITPA
Hartmann et al. 1972	6-9 (50)	None	Mueller-Lyer Illusion
V. C. Crandall & Lacey 1972	6-12 (50)	None	EFT
V. J. Crandall & Sinkeldam 1964	6-12 (50)	None	Embedded Figures Test (EFT), time measures
Schubert & Cropley 1972	6-15 (211)	None	Block Design subtest of WISC
J. Kagan et al. 1964	7 (180)	None	Hidden Figures Test (HFT)
Keogh & Ryan 1971	7 (44)	Boys	Rod and Frame Test (RFT); pattern walking test
		None	CEFT; pattern drawing test
Ruble & Nakamura 1972	7-10 (56)	None	Gerard rod-and-frame test
Wapner 1968	7-16 (192)	Boys	Apparent Vertical and Apparent Body Axis Position
Stouwie et al. 1970	8-9 (156)	None	EFT, time measures
Corah 1965	8-11 (60)	None	CEFT
	Adults (120)	Men	Solutions faster

(continued)

TABLE 3.8 *(cont.)*

Study	Age and N	Difference	Comment
Witkin et al. 1967	8, 13 (47)	Boys	RFT (longitudinal)
	8, 10-13, 15, 17-21 (515)	Boys None	RFT, EFT Body Adjustment Test (BAT)
	10, 14, 17 (51)	None	RFT (longitudinal)
Bergan et al. 1971	9 (48)	Boys	Block Design, WISC
Immergluck & Mearini 1969	9 11, 13 (120)	Girls None	EFT EFT
MacArthur 1967	9-15 (167)	None	EFT (Eskimo sample)
Saarni 1973	10-15 (64)	Boys	RFT
Berry 1966	10–adult (122)	None	Kohs Blocks, Morrisby Shapes, EFT (Eskimo sample)
Nash 1973	11 (105)	None	Group Embedded Figures Test (GEFT)
	14 (102)	Boys	GEFT
Okonji 1969	12 (33)	Boys	CEFT (rural Nigerian sample)
	21-27 (25)	Men None	RFT (Univ. of Nigeria sample) EFT
	Adults (65)	Men None	CEFT (rural Nigerian sample) RFT
Weinberg & Rabinowitz 1970	12-19 (48)	None	Block Design, WISC
Fiebert 1967	12, 15, 18 (90)	Boys	RFT, CEFT (deaf sample)
J. Silverman et al. 1973	14-17 (16)	None	RFT (patients with behavior disorders)
	13-20 (15)	Boys	RFT (siblings of above sample)
	18-22 (30)	Men	RFT
F. Gross 1959	17-25 (110)	Men	RFT
Stuart et al. 1965	17-25 (64)	None	EFT
Green 1955	17-40 (60)	Men None	RFT (2 of 3 series) Tilting Room Test (2 of 4 series) EFT
D. Schwartz & Karp 1967	17, 30-39 58-82 (120)	Men None	RFT, EFT, BAT RFT, EFT, BAT

(continued)

TABLE 3.8 *(cont.)*

Study	Age and N	Difference	Comment
Bieri 1960	18-21 (60)	None	EFT
Bieri et al. 1958	18-21 (110)	Men	EFT
Bogo et al. 1970	18-21 (97)	Men	RFT (portable)
A. Goldstein & Chance 1965	18-21 (26)	Men None	EFT, faster discovery times, first 10 items Discovery times, last 10 items
Kato 1965	18-21 (60)	Men	RFT
Morf et al. 1971	18-21 (82)	None Men	RFT, trials 1-8 RFT, trials 9-16
Morf & Howitt 1970	18-21 (44)	None	RFT
Oltman 1968	18-21 (163)	None	RFT (standard and portable)
Sarason & Minard 1962	18-21 (96)	Men	Block Design subtest of WISC
Vaught 1965	18-21 (180)	Men	RFT
Willoughby 1967	18-21 (76)	None	HFT (Hidden Figures Test)
Gerace & Caldwell 1971	25 (40)	Men	Ames distorted room (portable model)
Blum et al. 1972	64, 84 (54)	None	Block Design (Wechsler-Bellevue)

(1968) have devised a battery of such tests for blind subjects, and used them with 20 congenitally blind and 20 sighted subjects aged 12–18. They found:

Tactual block design test	No sex difference
Tactual embedded figures test	No sex difference
Auditory embedded figures	No sex difference
Tactile matchstick problem	Girls superior

Witkin notes that the last result is the opposite of the sex differences usually obtained on the visual form of this task.

In this one small-sample study, then, it would appear that girls' difficulty with disembedding may be specific to visual-spatial tasks. Or, to put a somewhat different interpretation on the matter, it may be that, as Sherman has suggested, their poorer performance on visual "field independence" tasks may simply be a reflection of their lesser visual-spatial ability and have nothing to do with "decontextualization." It is risky to pin this conclusion to a single study, however, and we must look further for work in which nonvisual disembedding has been studied.

One may interpret the studies of selective listening as measures of auditory disembedding. In these studies, a subject is asked to listen to one voice and ignore another. If he is unable to separate the desired message from its auditory context, he will make intrusive errors. That is, he will interpolate words spoken by the undesired voice into his report of the content spoken by the target voice. In a series of studies of selective listening with children ranging in age from 5 to 15 (Maccoby 1969[R]), no sex differences have been found. Thus the male advantage in visual decontextualization does not appear to generalize to the auditory modality.

It is difficult to distinguish disembedding from other forms of "analytic" responding. The matchstick problems referred to above are a good case in point. These tasks were used by Guilford (1957)[R]. In these problems the subject is given a figure made out of matchsticks in the form of a lattice; he is asked to remove (or change the position of) a specified number of matches, to form a specified new figure. The test is similar to the Embedded Figures Test in that the subject must free himself from the binding organizational properties of the initial configuration and discover new organizational properties inherent in portions of the figure. Performance on the visual form of this task is substantially correlated with the EFT (Guilford 1957[R]; Witkin et al. 1962[R]). In Guilford's work, this test is also correlated with others, such as the Dunker insight problems, which call for the subject's breaking a preestablished set. Guilford identifies a factor contributing to performance on a variety of such tests as the "adaptive flexibility" factor.

The nonvisual measures of disembedding frequently involve restructuring, or set-breaking, and therefore relate to the larger issue of analytic abilities, as well as to the narrower issue of perceptual "field independence." Set-breaking, in its turn, is related to the ability to inhibit an initial dominant response while exploring alternative solutions. We therefore turn now to studies of these kinds of "analytic abilities," and will return to the issue of visual-spatial vs. other measures in the course of discussing these studies.

Analytic Abilities

The factor-analytic literature on the dimensions of perceptual and intellectual abilities is voluminous, and we cannot hope to do justice to it here. For our present purposes, the important point is that a number of workers have identified some aspect of set-breaking, or restructuring, as an important dimension of problem-solving ability; furthermore, it has frequently been reported that males perform better than females on tests calling for this ability. For example, as we noted in Chapter 2, Broverman et al. (1968)[R] distinguish "simple, overlearned, repetitive" behaviors (at which females are alleged to be superior) from tasks that involve inhibition of initial response tendencies, mediation of higher mental processes, and production of novel solutions (at which males are alleged to be superior). We have already seen (Chapter 2) that no superiority of males is found in learning tasks that involve inhibition of already learned responses. However, it is conceivable that differences that do not emerge in learning tasks might be found in measures of "abilities." Parlee (1972)[R] has presented some cogent evidence in opposition to the Broverman classification of sex-linked abilities, and our own review in this chapter and Chapter 2 certainly supports the Parlee position. However, the point of interest here is whether males are in fact better at tasks that call for the inhibition of previously learned (or initially probable) response tendencies.

The Stroop color-word test would appear to provide a measure of at least one aspect of this ability. In this test, the subject is given a set of color names, printed in the wrong-color ink. The subject must "read" the page by giving, for each word, the color of the ink, suppressing his strongly established tendencies to read the printed word. In one version of the test, the subject's performance on this task is contrasted with his performance when he needs only to name small color blocks that are the same size as printed words but that do not give conflicting color names. Podell and Phillips (1959)[R], in factor-analyzing the Stroop test along with Witkin's field-independence measures, found that performance on the Stroop was factorially quite independent of the visual-spatial field-independence tests. In the original report by Stroop concerning this test (1935)[R], data are presented separately by sex for three successive samples of college students. It is shown that the sexes are very similar on this task, with no sex difference in the effects of introducing conflicting stimuli for which the response must be inhibited. Thus the Stroop test provides an instance of a set-breaking task (one requiring inhibition of a dominant response) in which no sex difference is found.

Another approach to the measurement of inhibition of initial response tendencies is found in the studies of reflectivity-impulsivity, initiated by Kagan, and usually employing the Matching Familiar Figures test (MFF). The subject must select a match for a standard figure from a set very much like it, but where some of the figures differ in small details from the standard. An "impulsive" child makes errors because he decides too soon that there are no differences, without systematically checking each picture, in all its details, against the standard. J. Kagan et al. (1964), in an early report using this measure, did not find sex differences on either response latency or errors. The work done since that time supports this conclusion (see

TABLE 3.9
Impulsivity, Lack of Inhibition

Study	Age and N	Difference	Comment
W. Mischel & Underwood 1973	2-5 (80)	Boys	Wait shorter time for less preferred reward
Baumrind & Black 1967	3-4 (103)	None	Observer ratings: impulsiveness, impetuousness
Shipman 1971	3-4 (1,399)	None	Matching Familiar Figures (MFF) test (low SES, largely black sample)
	3-4 (1,458)	None	Delay of gratification (low SES, largely black sample)
Friedrichs et al. 1971	3-5 (50)	None	Motor inhibition task
Klaus & Gray 1968	3-7 (80)	None	Delay of gratification (low SES black; longitudinal)
	5 (80)	None	MFF
A. Harrison & Nadelman 1972	4-5 (50)	Boys	MFF, shorter response times, higher error rate; faster responses on 2 motor inhibition tests
Massari et al. 1969	5 (33)	None	Motor inhibition tests
W. C. Ward 1968b	5 (87)	Boys	More errors on impulsivity measure (estimating relative numbers of dots)
		None	Latency to most difficult items on dot test; 4 other impulsivity measures
Meichenbaum & Goodman 1969	5-6 (30)	Girls	MFF, shorter latency
Loo & Wenar 1971	5-6 (40)	Boys	Teacher ratings: impulsivity, low "inhibiting control"
		None	Motor inhibition tests
Sharan (Singer) & Weller 1971	6 (357)	Boys	Faster performance, motor inhibition test (draw a line slowly; Israeli sample)
Yando & Kagan 1968	6 (160)	None	MFF
Wallach & Martin 1970	6, 7, 11 (283)	None	Motoric expansiveness: amount of page used in line drawing (low, middle SES)
	9	Girls	More expansive (middle SES sample only)
J. Kagan et al. 1964	7 (69)	Boys	Shorter latency, Design Recall Test (DRT)
		None	Speed of performance, Draw-a-Line-Slowly Test; DRT, errors
	8 (66)	Boys	DRT, shorter latency
		Girls	DRT, more errors (1 of 2 measures); faster performance, Draw-a-Line-Slowly Test
	8-9 (113)	None	MFF, latency and errors
J. Grusec 1968	8 (40)	None	Delay of gratification

(continued)

TABLE 3.9 *(cont.)*

Study	Age and *N*	Difference	Comment
S. Goldstein & Siegel 1972	8-9 (84)	None	Effect of delayed or immediate reward
Ault et al. 1972	8-10 (29)	None	MFF, latency and errors
Debus 1970	8-10 (320)	None	MFF, latency and errors
Kopfstein 1973	9 (60)	None	MFF, latency and errors
Bandura & Mischel 1965	9-10 (120)	None	Delay of gratification immediately and 1 month later
W. Mischel & Grusec 1967	9-10 (96)	None	Delay of gratification
Achenbach 1969	10 (40)	None	MFF, latency and errors
Strickland 1972	11-13 (300)	None	Delay of gratification (black and white samples)
Staub 1972	12 (144)	Boys	Choice; immediate gratification
Zytkoskee et al. 1971	14-17 (132)	None	Delay of gratification (biracial sample)
Brissett & Nowicki 1973	18-21 (80)	None	Persistence in no-solution task
Marks 1967	18-21 (722)	None	Degree of stimulus ambiguity S will attempt to interpret (time to reach decision)
Marks 1968	18-21 (760)	None	Self-report: quick, intuitive behavior; lack of forethought

Table 3.9). Some studies report boys as more impulsive; some find girls more impulsive. The majority, working with children ranging in age from 3½ to 11, find no difference. Thus, on this measure, the sexes are much alike in their ability to inhibit an early, impulsive response and engage in whatever "higher mediating processes" are required (in this case, a systematic search) to find the correct answer.

Mischel has developed another approach to the question of whether a person can inhibit a dominant response. In this work, the person is offered a choice between taking a small immediate reward and waiting for a larger reward at a later time. It has been shown that impulsive children—that is, those who choose the immediate rewards—score lower on the average on tests of intellectual ability (Metzner and Mischel 1962[R]). As may be seen in Table 3.9, there is some evidence that boys are more impulsive on this measure during the preschool years, but the sexes do not differ consistently at later ages.

We do not find support, then, for the Broverman contention that girls are less able than boys to inhibit an initial response tendency while engaging in systematic problem solving. Nevertheless, there may be some sex differences in specific elements of the problem-solving processes that do not rely on any generalized ability in response inhibition. We discuss first some studies on "restructuring." There has been little recent work on insight in problem solving, and we must go back to the period before 1966 for evidence on this issue. Luchins (1942)[R] devised a set of problems that presumably tested a subject's ability to break away from a maladaptive set. The problems involved the measurement of liquids with jars of different capacities. One problem might be, for example, "How can you bring from the river exactly six quarts of water, when you have only a four-quart and a nine-quart pail to measure with?" An initial set of such problems calls for a fairly indirect, cumbersome solution. The next problems can be solved by the same indirect method, but there is also a simpler, more direct method. And, finally, a problem is given in which only the more direct method leads to the solution. Luchins reported that male subjects were more successful on these problems than female subjects. Guetzkow (1951)[R] used the same procedure, and distinguished *susceptibility to set* from the *ability to break set*. He found that the two sexes were alike in the degree to which they carried over into the second set of problems the cumbersome approach that had been successful in the first set. But male subjects were more able to break away from this set and use a different approach when the first approach no longer succeeded. Guetzkow also used the Dunker two-string problem and found male superiority in restructuring for this problem as well. It is worth noting that Guetzkow found success in restructuring on his two tasks to be correlated with performance on embedded figures tests but not related to measures of verbal fluency.

Sweeney (1953)[R] used a wider variety of problems (with college-age subjects), some calling for restructuring and some not. He found:

Verbal "trick" problems (requiring breaking set)	No sex difference
Tool problems (verbal, adapted from Dunker)	Men superior
Verbal posers (including verbal form of a Luchins-jar problem)	Men superior
Figural problems (including matchsticks) calling for breaking set	Men superior (trend in one study; significant in second study)
"Extension problems" (no set-breaking required)	No sex difference

Three of Sweeney's set-breaking tests were verbal; one of them did not yield a sex difference, two did. In attempting to solve the "verbal posers," some subjects reported that they employed visual imagery, and the question is whether visual-spatial ability contributes to the solution of these problems even though they are stated in verbal terms. However, an independent measure of spatial visualization did not correlate more strongly with the tests requiring restructuring than it did with those involving no restructuring, and the correlations were generally low, so that Sweeney concluded that restructuring and spatial visualization were independent elements in the solution of these problems.

Nakamura (1958)[R] used the Sweeney tests and several other tests, and found that his male subjects (again, of college age) did better on both the tests requiring restructuring and those not requiring restructuring, with no greater superiority on the one than the other. His study, then, is negative evidence for the hypothesis that restructuring per se primarily distinguishes the problem-solving ability of the two sexes. He did find that, although the women in his sample were more conforming than the men (on an Asch-type study of social influence), their conformity did not account for the differences in problem solving; when conformity was held constant statistically, the sex difference remained.

Cunningham (1965)[R] used the Luchins jars, and also a verbal restructuring test ("alphabet mazes") involving the formation and then breaking of a set for a given problem-solving strategy. Cunningham's subjects were younger (ages 7–12). The boys in his study did better than the girls on breaking set in the Luchins-jar problem, but not on alphabet mazes.

A well-known task calling for breaking set in a verbal context is the game of Anagrams. The subject must spell as many words as he can from a set of letters; once he has spelled one word, he must break up the configuration formed by that word in order to rearrange the letters into a new word. Podell and Phillips (1959)[R], working only with male subjects, included such a task in the battery they factor-analyzed and found that the loadings for the anagrams task were either close to zero (one sample) or negative (another sample) on the visual-spatial factor defined by mazes, block design, and an Embedded Figures Test. Similarly, Guilford found that a test calling for discovery of camouflaged words was not related to his "adaptive flexibility" factor. The implication of these findings is that there is no reason to expect the sex difference on visual-spatial disembedding tasks to be replicated with verbal tasks. There are a number of studies in which the sexes have been compared with respect to their skill at anagrams (see Table 3.10). Although not all studies find a sex difference, those that do report superiority for girls. It would appear that set-breaking is not a process that generalizes across tasks, and girls appear to find it relatively easy to restructure when the thing to be restructured is a word.

The term "analytic style" has been used with still another meaning. In a widely used procedure (Sigel's sorting task), the subject is shown three objects, or pictures of three objects, and asked to say which two "go together." He may group on any basis he chooses. There are three common types of groupings: *relational* (putting together objects that have a functional relationship to one another, such as an apple and a paring knife); *inferential* (putting together objects that belong to the same more inclu-

TABLE 3.10
Anagrams

Study	Age and N	Difference	Comment
Lipton & Overton 1971	7, 9, 11, 13 (80)	None	Anagrams task
H. Stevenson et al. 1968a	8-12 (475)	Girls	Anagrams task
	12-14 (256)	Girls	Anagrams task (low IQ sample)
		None	Anagrams task (middle, high IQ samples)
H. Stevenson et al. 1968b	8-14 (529)	Girls	Anagrams task
H. Stevenson & Odom 1965	9, 11 (318)	None	Anagrams task
H. Stevenson et al. 1970	14 (96)	Girls	Anagrams task, 1 of 2 testing conditions (educable retardates)
Feather 1968	18-21 (60)	None	Anagrams task
Feather 1969b	18-21 (167)	None	Anagrams task
Mendelsohn & Griswold 1967	18-21 (181)	None	Anagrams task

sive class, such as apple and banana because they are both fruit); and *descriptive-analytic*. The last type of grouping is based upon similarity with respect to some selected detail; for example, a chair and a dog might be grouped together because they both have four legs. This grouping has been termed "analytic" because it involves responding to a part of an object rather than to the whole, and ignoring attributes of the objects not relevant to the basis for grouping. In a set of five studies with children ranging from age 3 to age 16, no sex differences in the use of analytic-descriptive groupings have been found (A. Davis 1971, Kuhn 1972, Shipman 1971, K. White 1971, and Sharan and Weller 1971). In only one study (Stanes 1973), with first-graders, was a sex difference found, with boys giving more analytic responses.

To recapitulate: it is well known that males tend to score higher than females on tests of "field independence" (embedded figures; Rod and Frame test). It has been alleged that field independence forms part of a larger cluster of abilities, sometimes called analytic abilities. A field-independent individual is alleged to be skilled in a large range of tasks that require ignoring a task-irrelevant context or focusing upon only selected elements of a stimulus display. Field independence has also been thought to imply an ability to restructure a problem-solving situation—to inhibit a well-established response in the interests of breaking away from an unproductive set and taking a fresh approach to a problem. In our review we have found the following:

1. Boys and men do perform better than girls and women on tests of field independence in many studies, but by no means all; the sex difference does not emerge consistently until approximately the beginning of adolescence. The development of sex differences in field independence parallels that in nonanalytic spatial abilities.

2. The sex difference in field independence is quite narrowly confined to visual-spatial tasks. In other tasks that call for ignoring an irrelevant context or for focusing upon an element rather than a whole gestalt, sex differences are not found. Specifically, the sexes are essentially alike on tests of selective listening (when potentially interfering messages must be ignored) and in tactual tasks requiring disembedding.

3. There is no reliable tendency for either sex to be generally more able to inhibit a dominant response while exploring potentially more successful solutions (Stroop 1935[R], measure of the reflective-impulsive dimension).

4. The use of an "analytic style" in grouping (grouping on the basis of isolated features of objects) is not more common in one sex than the other.

5. The results on set-breaking, or restructuring, are equivocal. On some verbal tasks calling for restructuring (e.g. anagrams) females do very well, and it is tempting to conclude that males are superior only on set-breaking tasks that are visual-spatial. Such a conclusion would be oversimplified, however. Judging from early studies, men appear to have an advantage on most of the Dunker and Luchins-jar kinds of problems, whether the problems are stated verbally or not. There are enough instances, however, in which the sexes do not differ on tasks that seem to call for restructuring that we cannot feel confident that set-breaking per se is the factor distinguishing the performance of the sexes. There is an elusive element in the sex differences on restructuring that we do not feel has been adequately identified.

Concept Mastery and Reasoning

Studies of concept formation overlap with studies of verbal and quantitative ability. Piagetian studies of conservation of number, mass, volume, etc., for example, are sometimes used as measures of readiness for math training in the early school years. And a number of concept-formation tasks are verbal in the sense that they require the child to know the meaning of relational terms such as "more," "longest," etc. The concept-formation tasks that focus specifically on the subject's speed of learning a concept, or the conditions governing the rate of learning, have been summarized in the learning section of Chapter 2. Table 3.11 shows studies that assess subjects' level of performance on Piagetian tasks, including conservation, transitivity, seriation, class inclusion, and other grouping problems.

As Table 3.11 shows, the research on Piagetian tasks is remarkably consistent in finding similar performance in the two sexes. The majority of studies have been done on conservation tasks, most of which are appro-

TABLE 3.11
Conceptual Level

Study	Age and N	Difference	Comment
K. Nelson 1971	3-9 mos (180)	None	Object constancy (visual tracking task)
D. Miller et al. 1970	6, 8, 10, 12, 14, 18 mos (84)	None	Object constancy (visual tracking task)
LeCompte & Gratch 1972	9, 12, 18 mos (36)	None	Object transformation tasks
Clarke-Stewart 1973	12-14 mos (36)	None	Uzgiris-Hunt Series: object permanence, schema development, object relations
Denney 1972b	2-4 (108)	None	Groupings of cardboard figures
Denney 1972a	2, 4, 6, 8, 12, 16 (96)	None	Groupings of colored blocks
A. Caron 1966	3-4 (192)	Girls	Far transposition
Shipman 1971	3-4 (1,274)	None	Numerical correspondence
Friedrichs et al. 1971	3-5 (50)	None	Object sorting
L. Siegel 1971	3-5 (77)	None	Equivalence, conservation, ordination, seriation
Lloyd 1971	3-8 (80)	Boys	Conservation of number with bricks (Yoruba sample)
		None	Conservation of number with candies
L. Siegel 1972	3-9 (415)	None	Seriation
Rothenberg 1969	4-5 (210)	None	Conservation of number
Brainerd 1972	4-6 (155)	None	Conservation of number
King 1971	4-6 (47)	None	Conservation of length
Pratoomraj & Johnson 1966	4-7 (128)	None	Conservation of substance
Kuhn 1972	4, 6, 8 (87)	None	Object classification
Curcio et al. 1972	5-6 (67)	None	Conservation tasks
Kaufman 1971	5-6 (103)	Girls	Battery of 13 Piagetian tasks
Moynahan & Glick 1972	5-6 (96)	Boys	Conservation of length, number, weight, and continuous quantity
Peters 1970	5-6 (131)	None	Conservation of number, difference, and area object-sorting task

(continued)

TABLE 3.11 *(cont.)*

Study	Age and N	Difference	Comment
Rothenberg & Orost 1969	5-6 (20)	None	Conservation of number
Roll 1970	5-7 (87)	None	Conservation of number (Colombian sample)
Roodin & Gruen 1970	5-7 (72)	None	Transitivity judgments
Wei et al. 1971	5, 7 (80)	None	4 Piagetian classification tasks
Gruen & Vore 1972	5, 6, 8, 10 (40)	None	Conservation of number, continuous quantity, and weight
P. Miller 1973	5, 8 (100)	None	Conservation of liquid
Youniss & Murray 1970	5, 8 (64)	None	Transitivity judgments of stick lengths
Snow & Rabinovitch 1969	5-13 (97)	None	Conjunctive and disjunctive card sorting
Figurelli & Keller 1972	6 (48)	None	Conservation (black sample)
Murray 1972	6 (108)	None	Conservation tasks
Goldschmid 1968	6-7 (81)	Boys	10 conservation tasks
Noithman & Gruen 1970	6-7 8-9 (60)	None Boys	Equivalence and identity conservation Equivalence and identity conservation
Hooper 1969	6-8 (108)	Boys	Identity and equivalence conservation
Wasik & Wasik 1971	6-9 (117)	None	8 conservation tasks (white and black low SES)
Gelman & Weinberg 1972	6, 7, 8, 11 (80)	None	Liquid conservation and compensation
Furth et al. 1970	6, 8-12 7 (300)	None Girls	Match conjunctive and disjunctive symbols to pictures Match conjunctive and disjunctive symbols to pictures
Brainerd 1973	7-8 (120)	Girls None	Conservation (Canadian sample) Transitivity and class inclusion (Canadian and American samples); conservation (American sample)
	5, 6, 7 (180)	None	Transitivity, conservation, class inclusion (Canadian sample)
Cathcart 1971	7-8 (120)	None	Modes of rationalization for conservation
Brainerd 1971	8, 11, 14 (72)	None	Conservation of density and volume
Elkind et al. 1970	9, 14 (120)	None	Multiple classification

(continued)

TABLE 3.11 *(cont.)*

Study	Age and N	Difference	Comment
Saarni 1973	10-15 (64)	None	Specific gravity, chemical combination
Tisher 1971	12-14 (232)	None	"Formal" vs. "concrete" operational level: solution of scientific problems
Sullivan et al. 1970	12, 14, 17 (120)	None	Hunt and Halverson's Conceptual Level Questionnaire
A. Graves 1972	33 (120)	Men None	Conservation of volume Conservation of mass and weight (black and white minimally educated)

priate for preadolescent subjects. The majority of studies of more complex operations, made with preadolescent and adolescent subjects, have also found no sex differences.

The tests of "formal operations," made with these older subjects, bear a close resemblance to tests of reasoning growing out of psychological systems other than Piaget's. Many reasoning tests, like Piaget's assessments of formal operations, involve asking the subject to formulate and test hypotheses, using evidence to confirm or contradict them. Thus both inductive and deductive reasoning are involved. Studies of reasoning, using a variety of measures, are reported in Table 3.12. Included are studies using tasks that call for serial information processing.

Up to adolescence, studies are consistent in showing an absence of sex differences. In adolescence, the bulk of the evidence continues to show no differences, with certain exceptions. For example, Leskow and Smock (1970) gave three groups of subjects (ages 12, 15, and 18) sets of four numbers and asked them to make up as many license plates with these numbers as they could, using any system they chose. The systems used were analyzed; some of the subjects approached the problem in an unsystematic way that led to the repetition of particular combinations of numbers. Others operated by holding constant a systematic series of numbers. For example, a subject might use one of the numbers in first position, and vary the others; then put another in first position; then hold constant the first two numbers jointly, etc. There were no sex differences in the employment of such strategies. One strategy involved treating the numbers as subsets in mathematical groupings, and there was a trend ($p < .10$) for boys to do this more often. We have been unable to locate studies made since 1966 in which standardized reasoning tests have been given to subjects of high school age or older. The evidence from earlier work is that the sexes do not differ on such measures as the reasoning subtest of the

TABLE 3.12
Reasoning

Study	Age and N	Difference	Comment
Sitkei & Meyers 1969	3-4 (100)	Girls	Pre-Raven Matrices (white low SES sample only)
Goldberg 1966	3-5 (32)	None	Probability judgments
C. Davies 1965	3-9 (112)	Girls None	Probability judgments (age 7 only) Probability judgments (at other ages)
A. Siegel & Kresh 1971	4-8 (80)	None	Matrix completion (black and white)
Daehler 1972	4-7 (192)	None	Inference: 2-trial concept identification task
	8 (42)	None	Inference: 2-trial concept identification task
Scholnick 1971	5-7 (96)	None	Inferences about cue relevance from positive, negative, and mixed information
Lehman 1972	5, 7, 9 (60)	None	Use of relevant vs. irrelevant information in task performance
Jacobs & Vandeventer 1971	6 (61)	None	Double-classification matrices
Beilin 1966	6-7 (236)	None	Use of infralogical strategies in quasi-conservation task
Lesser et al. 1965	6-7 (320)	None	Reasoning subtest of Hunter College aptitude scales for gifted children
Greenberger et al. 1971	6-8 (113)	None	Problem-solving flexibility
McKinney 1973	7 (60)	None	Strategy in problem solving
Shantz 1967a	7, 9, 11 (72)	None	Raven's Progressive Matrices Test; multiple relations test
Eimas 1970	7, 9, 11, 13 (192)	None	Quality of questions asked in matrix solution
B. Ross 1966	7, 9, 11, 13, 15 (140)	Boys None	Predictions in concept probability task: "uneven odds" choice situations "Sure thing" and "even odds" choice situations (deaf and hearing samples)
Calhoun 1972	8-9 (12,350)	Boys	Raven's Progressive Matrices (abbreviated form)
Lamal 1971	8, 10, 12 (72)	None	Use of modeled hypothesis-scanning or constraint-seeking in problem solving
Laughlin et al. 1969	8, 10, 12 (216)	None	20 questions: number and quality of questions
Dusek & Hill 1970	9-10 (72)	Boys Girls	Correct responses, 3-choice probability learning task Variety of response patterns and use of win-stay and lose-shift strategies

(continued)

TABLE 3.12 *(cont.)*

Study	Age and N	Difference	Comment
Roberge & Paulus 1971	9, 11, 13, 15 (263)	None	Paulus Conditional Reasoning Test (if-then problems); Paulus-Roberge Class Reasoning Test
Zern 1971	7, 9-12 (69)	None	Latency and error scores on verbal problems involving multiple negation and decoding numbers to "odd" and "even"
Nuessle 1972	10 (40)	None	Concept identification task: use of consistent hypotheses, efficient use of feedback
		Boys	Shorter time taken to complete problems
H. Stevenson et al. 1968a	12-14 (256)	Boys	Concept of probability tasks (high IQ Ss)
		None	Concept of probability tasks (average and retarded Ss)
	8-12 (475)	None	Concept of probability tasks
Pecan & Schvaneveldt 1970	12-15, 35-45 (40)	Boys & Men	Probability learning
Weinberg & Rabinowitz 1970	12-19 (48)	Boys	Probability task: used maximizing strategy to a greater extent
Leskow & Smock 1970	12, 15, 18 (96)	None	Permutation problems: number of new permutations; use of "holding constant" strategy, trend ($p < .1$); transformation with subgroups
Ziv 1972	13 (240)	None	Raven Matrix
Frederiksen & Evans 1974	18 (395)	Women	Number of acceptable hypotheses, Formulating Hypotheses Test
		None	Average judged quality and average scale value of hypotheses
Very 1967	18-21 (355)	Women	Logical Reasoning
		None	Deductive Reasoning, Letter Concepts, Inductive Reasoning, Picture Concepts, Letter Reasoning

Primary Mental Abilities test. The two studies with this age group listed in Table 3.12 show an advantage for females, but taking these studies in combination with earlier work, the overall picture remains one of little or no sex difference.

Creativity

In the most common meaning of the word, a "creative" person is one who produces something unique. An inventor who produces a new machine or a scientist who develops and proves a new theory is creative, just as the writer, musician, or graphic artist is when he produces a new work in his own expressive medium. Persons of great talent are, of course, rare, but there are lesser degrees of talent that may be seen in people with widely varying life styles. Creative people have been asked to introspect and describe the nature of the thought processes that go on during periods of artistic or scientific productivity. Wallach and Kogan (1965, p. 289)[R] conclude, after analyzing many such introspections, that the creative process involves "first, the production of associative content that is abundant and that is unique; second, the presence in the associator of a playful, permissive task attitude."

A number of researchers have attempted to measure the fluency and uniqueness of associative content. Guilford has done so in his work on divergent thinking. One of the best known of Guilford's measures is the "Uses" test, in which the subject is asked to list as many uses as possible for a familiar object (such as a brick). Torrance builds tests around the same view of the nature of creativity. He uses, for example, an "Asks" test, in which the subject is given a picture and is asked to write out all the questions he would need to have answered in order to understand the events in the picture. In another Torrance task, the subject is again presented with a picture, but this time is asked to guess at all the possible reasons why the pictured events might be occurring.

It is a far cry from the composer busy at his piano to the subject writing down answers to such test items; yet it is true that creative artists do score better on at least some such tests than matched groups of people who do not give evidence of creativity in their daily lives. (See Wallach 1970[R] for a review of evidence on the validation of creativity tests.)

It is well known that men are much more heavily represented than women in the ranks of outstanding creative artists, writers, and scientists. The question is whether this results from a greater male ability, on the average, to engage in creative thinking, or whether there is something about women's life situations that reduces the likelihood of their achieving creatively even though a creative style of thought is found among them as often as among men.

We have already encountered some work comparing the sexes on some aspects of creative thought. The Piagetian logical reasoning tasks used for testing at the level of formal operations (Table 3.11) and certain other measures of reasoning listed in Table 3.12 call for a form of problem solving in which the person must generate hypotheses to explain a phenomenon, and then either produce or use evidence to assess the truth value of the hypotheses. An important part of the process is, of course, the ability to think of a variety of alternative possibilities, which may then be tested. This aspect of intellectual performance was also discussed in the section on restructuring. No consistent sex differences emerged on the Piagetian tasks or on the other tests of reasoning; the evidence was equivocal on restructuring. We turn now to studies focused more directly on the "production of associative content that is abundant and unique."

TABLE 3.13
Divergent Thinking — Verbal Creativity

Study	Age and N	Difference	Comment
R. Bell et al. 1971	2½ (74)	None	Verbal originality (teacher rating)
R. Gross & Marsh 1970	3-6, 10, 15 (170)	None	Productivity and richness of thinking in construction of designs from geometric forms (black and white samples)
W. C. Ward 1969	4 (55)	None	Total number (fluency) and uniqueness of ideas (Uses, Patterns, and Instances tests)
Lichtenwalner & Maxwell 1969	4-6 (68)	None	Number of different verbal responses to styro-foam objects (Starkweather test)
W. C. Ward 1968a	4-6 (87)	None	Fluency and originality of ideas (Uses, Patterns, and Instances tests)
Cropley & Feuring 1971	6 (69)	None	Torrance Product Improvement Test: flexibility and originality; effects of creativity training
Torrance 1965	6-11 (555)	Boys	Product Improvement Task: originality, at 8 (1 of 2 conditions), 9 (1 of 2 conditions), and 11 yrs (1 of 2 conditions) only
		Boys	Fluency, at 8 yrs only
		Girls	Fluency, flexibility, at 10 yrs only
Ogletree 1971	8-11 (1,165)	Girls	Verbal battery of the Torrance Tests of Creative Thinking (English, German, Scottish samples)
Torrance & Aliotti 1969	10 (118)	Girls	Verbal originality, elaboration, and flexibility scores of Torrance Test (forms A and B)
Klausmeier & Wiersma 1964	10-12 (320)	Girls	Object Uses, flexibility; Plot Titles, fluency; Plot Questions; Expressional Fluency; Object Improvement
		None	Object Uses, fluency; Word Uses, flexibility; Plot Titles, cleverness; Sentence Improvement, metaphor, onomatopoeia
Cicirelli 1967	11 (609)	Girls	Verbal elaboration score of Minnesota Tests of Creative Thinking
		None	Combined verbal fluency-flexibility-originality score
Torrance 1965	11 (50)	Girls	Ask and Guess test: asking questions, causal hypotheses
		None	Consequential hypotheses
	12-13 (75)	Boys	Consequences Test, flexibility
		None	Consequences Test, fluency; Ask-and-Guess Test, Unusual Uses Test, Product Improvement Task (gifted sample)
Dewing 1970	12 (394)	None	Minnesota Tests of Creative Thinking: alternate uses of tin cans, alternate uses of bricks (number and uniqueness of verbal responses)
		None	Imaginative composition on "The Lion Who Couldn't Roar"
Raina 1969	13-15 (180)	Boys	Torrance Test total verbal score (India)

(continued)

TABLE 3.13 *(cont.)*

Study	Age and N	Difference	Comment
Frederiksen & Evans 1974	18 (395)	Men	Number of remote consequences (Guilford's Consequences test)
		Women	Number of obvious consequences
Abney 1970	18-21 (50)	Women	Remote Associations Test (RAT) (honors group)
	18-21 (118)	None	RAT (high, average GPAs)
Bieri et al. 1958	18-21 (111)	None	Bricks Test
Gall & Mendelsohn 1967	18-21 (120)	None	Baseline number of solutions, RAT
		Women	Number of solutions following opportunity to free-associate about missed items (no difference in 2 other conditions)
Keillor 1971	18-21 (22)	Women	RAT
Mendelsohn & Griswold 1966	18-21 (223)	None	RAT
Ohnmacht & McMorris 1971	18-21 (74)	Women	RAT

In most work on creativity, two measures are used: the *number* of different ideas produced and the *uniqueness* of the ideas produced. In Guilford's "Uses" test, for example, the response that a brick may be used "to build houses with" would be included as one item in a child's score for the number of uses offered but would not receive weight for uniqueness, since most other children would also mention this item. However, the response "You could write on the sidewalk with it" would contribute to both a number and a uniqueness score.

It should be noted that these tests tend to be verbal by their very nature; some writers (e.g. Bhavnani and Hutt 1972[R]) have equated them with measures of verbal fluency. We feel that a distinction should be made between sheer fluency of verbal output (which may be measured by mean length of utterance, length of papers turned in at school, amount of talking that occurs in social situations, etc.) and the number of different hypotheses or approaches generated in a test of creative thinking. We have summarized the measures of sheer fluency under verbal abilities, and have included in Table 3.13 the measures that might more properly be called measures of "ideational variety" or "hypothesis availability." Nevertheless, it is important to distinguish those measures of creativity that are entirely verbal from those that are not, and we have charted them separately.

As Table 3.13 shows, on verbal tests of creative ability no sex differences are found in the preschool and earliest school years, but from about the age of 7 girls show an advantage in a majority of studies. On nonverbal measures (Table 3.14), no clear trend toward superiority of either sex can be discerned. In general, then, it may be said that tests of creativity reflect the already documented difference between the sexes in verbal skills; clearly, girls and women are at least as able as boys and men to generate a variety of hypotheses and produce unusual ideas. Thus the underrepresentation of women in the ranks of the outstanding creative figures of earlier and present times would not appear to arise from any general deficiency in "the production of associative content that is abundant and unique."

Moral Judgments

We have included moral judgments with intellectual abilities because we believe, with Kohlberg (1964)[R], that these judgments are linked to the person's level of cognitive development while not being identical with it. Moral judgments are distinguished from moral behavior (as measured, for example, in tests of resistance to temptation). Studies with behavioral measures are included in Chapter 6. As Table 3.15 shows, the development of the two sexes with respect to the Kohlberg stages of moral reasoning appears to be quite similar. The finding of Saltzstein et al. (1972) is worth noting, in view of the fact that Turiel has also found* that girls tend to be overrepresented at stage 3—the level of "good boy" or "good girl" morality. The level just below stage 3 involves an orientation toward punishment; the level just above is "law and order" morality. It appears likely that both these levels have a greater element of aggression, and a greater orientation toward power, than stage 3. If so, a greater concentration of girls in stage 3, and of boys in the neighboring classes, would be understandable. However, three studies (Selman 1971a, Keasey 1972, and Weisbroth 1970) find no sex differences in levels of moral judgment, so perhaps an attempt at explanation is superfluous.

So far, we have been giving a descriptive account of the incidence and magnitude of sex differences on a variety of intellectual tasks. Before turning to a discussion of the "why" of these differences, there is one more descriptive issue to be taken up. This is the question of whether one sex is more variable than the other (whether the distributions of scores are different), even in the cases where mean values are the same.

VARIABILITY

The problem of differential variability was raised initially in Terman's work when he identified more boys as gifted (Terman et al. 1925[R]). The excess of boys having IQs over 140 was found on a test where there were no sex differences in the means of large samples; hence it appeared that

* E. Turiel, Harvard University, personal communication, 1973.

TABLE 3.14
Nonverbal Measures of Creativity

Study	Age and N	Difference	Comment
Baumrind & Black 1967	3-4 (103)	None	Observer ratings: imaginativeness, originality of work
Emmerich 1971	4-5 (415)	Boys Girls	Fantasy activity during free play Classroom observations, early fall and late fall: artistic activity during free play (black and white low SES)
	4-5 (596)	Boys Girls	Fantasy activity during free play Classroom observations, early fall and spring: artistic activity during free play (black and white low SES)
Torrance 1965	6-11 (320)	Boys	Picture Construction Test: originality, at 8 yrs (1 of 2 conditions) only; elaboration, at 10 yrs (1 of 2 conditions) only
		Girls	Picture Construction Test: originality, at 6 yrs only; elaboration, at 8, 9 (1 of 2 conditions) 10 (1 of 2 conditions), and 11 yrs (1 of 2 conditions) only
		Boys	Incomplete Figures Test: closure, at 8 yrs (1 of 2 conditions) only
		Girls	Incomplete Figures Test: originality, at 8 yrs only; elaboration, at 10 (1 of 2 conditions) and 11 yrs only; closure, at 11 yrs (1 of 2 conditions) only
	11 (50)	Boys Girls None	Parallel Lines Test: originality Elaboration Flexibility and fluency
	12-13 (75)	Boys	Torrance Tests, figural scores (gifted sample)
Ogletree 1971	8-11 (972)	Girls	Figural battery of the Torrance Tests of Creative Thinking (English, German samples)
	8-11 (193)	None	Figural battery, Torrance Tests (Scottish sample)
Torrance & Aliotti 1969	10 (118)	Boys	Figural flexibility (1 of 2 forms) and originality scores (Torrance Tests)
		Girls None	Figural elaboration scores Figural fluency scores
Cicirelli 1967	11 (609)	None	Torrance Tests, figural scores
Dewing 1970	12 (394)	None	Minnesota Tests of Creative Thinking: Circles, Squares (number and uniqueness of responses)
		None	Teacher and peer ratings
Raina 1969	13-15 (180)	Boys	Torrance Tests, figural scores (India)
Mendelsohn & Griswold 1966	18-21 (223)	Women	Barron-Welsh Art Scale of creative potential

TABLE 3.15
Moral Judgment

Study	Age and N	Difference	Comment
Rhine et al. 1967	2-5 (50)	None	Identifying pictured actions as "good" or "bad"
Irwin & Moore 1971	3-5 (65)	None	"Justice" score, choosing just vs. unjust story endings
Wasserman 1971	4 (180)	Boys	Choice of humanitarian values, trend ($p < .1$) (multiracial lower SES sample)
		Girls	Choice of humanitarian values (multiracial, middle SES sample)
Jensen & Hughston 1971	4-5 (72)	None	Moral judgments
Hebble 1971	6-11 (944)	None	Judgments of "badness" of storied characters, stories varying in intent of actors and severity of physical consequences
Gutkin 1972	6, 8, 10 (72)	None	Moral judgments based on intent of actors in stories
Chandler et al. 1973	7 (80)	None	Judgments: videotaped and verbally presented moral dilemmas, varied as to intent and consequences
Jensen & Rytting 1972	7 (25)	None	Causal explanation: accidents related or unrelated to misdeeds
Lepper 1973	7 (129)	None	Attitudes toward moral offenses
Selman 1971a	8-10 (60)	None	Kohlberg's moral judgment stages
Luria & Rebelsky 1969	10-13 (80)	None	Projective: how deviant child felt before confession and the consequences of his confession
Dlugokinski & Firestone 1973	10, 13 (164)	Girls	Baldwin's test of moral understanding
Aronfreed 1961	11 (122)	Boys	More "internal" responses (projective story completion device)
Keasey 1972	11 (155)	None	Kohlberg's moral judgment stages
Turiel 1973	11, 14 17 (210)	Girls Boys None	Higher moral maturity Higher moral maturity Moral knowledge test
Saltzstein et al. 1972	12 (63)	Girls Boys	Representation at Kohlberg stage 3 Representation at both lowest and highest stages
LeFurgy & Woloshin 1969	12-13 (53)	Girls	More realistic moral judgments
McMichael & Grinder 1966	12-13 (98)	None	Responses of remorse, confession, and restitution to transgression stories (Japanese-American, Hawaiian, Caucasian Ss)
	12-13 (23)	Girls	Confession and restitution (Japanese-American rural sample)

(continued)

TABLE 3.15 *(cont.)*

Study	Age and *N*	Difference	Comment
Sullivan et al. 1970	12, 14, 17 (120)	None	Kohlberg's moral judgment stages
Porteus & Johnson 1965	14 (235)	Girls	Guilt in response to deviation stories; cognitive level of moral judgments
Coombs 1967	18-21 (369)	Men	Considered property crimes more serious than women did
		Women	Considered abortion a more serious crime than men did
Gorsuch & Smith 1972	18-21 (1,030)	Women	More severe in ratings on Crissman's moral behavior scale
Hass & Linder 1972	18-21 (150)	None	Judgment of guilt in bigamy trial
Rettig 1966	18-21 (160)	None	Predictions of moral behavior from stories
Shaw & Skolnick 1971	18-21 (116)	None	Attribution of responsibility to fictitious male
Walster 1966	18-21 (88)	Women	Judged fictitious male more responsible for seriously injuring a person than demolishing own car
Weisbroth 1970	21-39 (78)	None	Kohlberg's moral judgment stages

boys must be more variable, including more of both unusually high scorers and unusually low scorers. As Miles and Terman noted in the 1954 edition of the Carmichael *Manual,* the method of selection of cases for the Terman study made interpretation of the sex ratios difficult. The initial identification of high-scoring children was made by asking teachers to nominate children they considered to be especially bright; some additional children volunteered for the testing. We know that girls tend to underestimate their own intellectual abilities more than boys do, and so there is danger of sex bias in testing self-selected groups. Both Miles (1954)[R] and Terman and Tyler (1954)[R] reviewed a number of studies to find out whether there was a concentration of either sex among the very high scorers on tests of mental abilities. They concluded that there appeared to be no consistent tendency toward a higher incidence of gifted boys, and that the sex ratios in the gifted range depended on the content of the test.

What about variability in specific abilities? Considering the mean sex differences reported earlier on verbal, spatial, and mathematical tests, it should come as no surprise that there would be a higher incidence of very high-scoring boys on tests emphasizing content in which boys, as a group, do better. Presumably, if one looked for the exceptionally high scorers on verbal tests, one would find more girls. Of course, such results do not necessarily mean that one sex is more variable than the other—the two distributions could have equal standard deviations, with the distribution of one sex simply being displaced upward, yielding more cases above any arbitrary cutting-off point.

We shall first examine what information is available since the work of Miles, and Terman and Tyler, to see whether the new evidence points to a sex difference in variability. If it does, we will then consider the shape of the distributions, to determine whether any difference in variability is determined by one sex having more exceptionally low scores, or exceptionally high scores, or both.

In Tables 3.4 and 3.6, we showed data from studies with large samples, for which information is available on variability as well as on mean scores. Beginning with verbal ability, it may be seen that studies of younger children do not show one sex to be consistently more variable than the other. At ages 3–4 (Shipman 1971) girls are more variable on two tests, boys on a third. In the Stanford Research Institute work (ages 5–7) girls tend to be more variable, and this is also the case in the work by Brimer (1969), in England, with children aged 8–11. Gates (1961) finds a fairly consistent picture of greater male variability over the age range 7–13, and this is also true in the work of Svensson in Sweden (1971, with 13-year-olds) and that of ACT norms based on tests with subjects of college age. Droege's work (1967), however, with subjects aged 14–17, consistently finds greater variability among girls, and Project Talent (Flanagan et al. 1961) presents a mixed picture depending on the age of measurement during the high school period. The differences found in variability are not large in an absolute sense. Taken together, the studies do not provide firm support for the hypothesis that males are more variable, although the trend is in this direction for subjects of 12 years or older.

There are fewer studies of quantitative ability that report measures of variability; here there is a fairly consistent trend in the direction of greater male variability, the exception being the work of Droege. In some cases, the difference in variability is substantial, male variability being up to 15 percent and 16 percent greater (Svensson, and Flanagan et al. 1961). We have not tabled the data for spatial ability, since there are only two studies (Droege, and Flanagan et al.) for which variability data are available. Both of these studies had subjects of high school age; both found greater variability among boys, and the difference in standard deviations was of the order of 7 to 8 percent.

In summary, we do find some evidence for greater male variability in numerical and spatial abilities but not consistently in verbal ability. The question is, when differences in variability are found, what does this imply in terms of the incidence of exceptionally high or low scores among the two sexes? Considering first the lower end of the ability scale, studies consistently indicate that more boys than girls suffer from learning deficits.

The greater vulnerability of the male child to anomalies of prenatal development, birth injury, and childhood disease is well known. For documentation, the reader is referred to review papers by Singer et al. (1968)[R], Bentzen (1963)[R], Bledsoe (1961), Garai and Scheinfeld (1968)[R], and Lapouse and Monk (1964). These reviews document a greater incidence among boys of a variety of developmental problems, ranging in severity from enuresis to mental retardation and autism. The incidence rates for the two sexes are substantially different. For example, stuttering is three to four times as common among boys, and reading disabilities are from three to ten times more common for boys, depending on how the disability is defined and what population is studied. The greater vulnerability of boys to this variety of problems, of course, affects the incidence of very low scores on tests of mental abilities. In school systems, children with exceptionally low scores tend to be siphoned off into classes for the educationally handicapped, and these classes may or may not be included in psychometric work. When they are included, or when the cut-off score for taking a child out of the normal classroom is very low, it may be expected that there will be more boys than girls with extremely low scores in a sampling of schoolchildren.

As noted in Table 3.4, Gates found greater variability in reading scores among boys from grades 2 through 7. After examining the distributions of these scores, he reports (1961, p. 432): "The distribution of scores on tests of reading ability shows that a relatively large proportion of boys obtained the lowest scores, without a corresponding increase in the number obtaining top scores." Gates notes that boys outnumbered girls among the lowest scorers by about 2 to 1 in the lower grades, with the ratio decreasing thereafter.

The situation is quite different with respect to mathematical ability. Work by Stanley et al. (1972)[R] on mathematically and scientifically precocious youth is relevant here. In one report (Keating 1972[R]), data are reported for 396 seventh- and eighth-graders who entered a science and math competition. Some of the children were nominated by their teachers as being especially talented, and some volunteered—the competition was well publicized. The subjects took the mathematics portion of the Scholastic Aptitude Test and the Mathematics Achievement Test Level I. The standard deviations of the boys' scores were higher than the girls', and considerably more boys scored at the top of the range. As noted elsewhere (Chapter 4), girls tend to have less confidence in their academic ability than boys, so that some girls with good mathematical skills might not have chosen to enter the competition. However, it seems unlikely that the girls who did enter would have less ability than the ones who did not. If the girls who entered include a reasonable representation of the best female math students, then this study, along with the previously reported work on retardation, indicates that the greater male variability in math scores reflects greater representation of males at both the high and low ends of the distribution. To our knowledge, no search for persons with outstanding spatial talents has been made, so we can only surmise that the situation would be similar in this domain as well.

In the verbal domain, the higher average scores of girls are not consistently accompanied by higher standard deviations; in fact, in some instances (e.g. Gates), the boys' scores are more variable and have a higher instance of low scores. In cases where girls earn higher mean scores but the standard deviations are similar for the two sexes, it would appear that the girls' distribution is simply displaced upward without changing its conformation; that is, there are more very high scorers and fewer very low scorers among the girls.

BIOLOGICAL AND ENVIRONMENTAL INFLUENCES

So far in this chapter, we have summarized the differences and similarities between human males and females in their intellectual functioning, as far as these are known. We have said little so far about the "why" of what has been discovered. There have been efforts to explain the sex differences in specific ability domains by reference to both genetic and experiential factors. We turn first to a review of the genetic argument and evidence, and then consider to what extent specific abilities appear to be a product of direct training or cultural factors. As we noted earlier, spatial ability enters into a variety of kinds of intellectual performance, including mathematics. When we discuss "explanations" of the sex difference in spatial ability, then, the explanations may be taken to apply to other kinds of performance, to the degree that spatial thinking is involved in them.

Genetic Factors in Specific Abilities

Until recently, most research on genetic factors in intellectual performance has been concerned with measures of general intelligence. When it comes to the inheritance of specific abilities, especially those that may be sex-linked, the genetics become more complex, and relatively little research is directly relevant. Vandenberg (1968)[R], in summarizing data from twin studies, reports that both spatial and verbal ability have high levels of heritability, with spatial ability seeming to be less influenced by educational and cultural factors than verbal ability. The fact that spatial ability appears to be both highly heritable and different in mean level for the two sexes has suggested a genetic sex linkage. Four studies (Stafford 1961, Corah 1965, Hartlage 1970[R], and Bock and Kolakowski 1973[R]) have now shown a pattern of cross-sex correlations between parents and children in spatial abilities. That is, boys' scores are correlated with their mothers' scores but not their fathers', and girls' scores are correlated with their fathers' scores and to a lesser degree with their mothers'. Stafford's hypothesis is that at least one important genetic determiner for spatial ability is sex-linked, being carried on the X chromosome and being recessive. Girls, with two X chromosomes, would have a relatively low chance of receiving two recessives, which would have to be the case for the trait to be manifest. Among boys, whenever the recessive trait was present, it would be manifest, since there would be no dominant X-linked character to suppress it. Since boys always receive their only X from their mothers, they would inherit the recessive trait through the mother, whether she expressed it phenotypically or not. Girls could only manifest the trait if they inherited a recessive from mother and father, but their phenotypical similarity would be greater to their fathers, since whenever he possessed the trait, it would be manifest, whereas the mother might carry it without its being expressed. It is possible to work out fairly precise predictions concerning what the correlations should be between children and their cross-sex or same-sex parents, and the correlations obtained in the four studies conform quite closely to these predictions. Bock and Kolakowski carry the argument one step further, using curve-fitting to test the hypothesis that spatial ability has two major components, only one of which is genetically sex-linked, and again, the predictions are quite accurate.

It appears likely, then, that there is at least some degree of sex-linked genetic control over spatial ability. Verbal ability also shows a significant degree of heritability (though not so high as for spatial ability).* However, there is no evidence of sex linkage in the inherited component of verbal abilities.

To say that there is a genetic component in spatial ability does *not* imply that this ability is something, like male genitals, that men have and women do not. With respect to a spatial gene that is sex-linked and recessive, some women will of course have two space-recessives, and their genetic potential for spatial ability will be the same as that of men who have a single recessive space gene on the X chromosome. The *proportion* of persons so endowed will be different for the two sexes—Bock and Kolakowski estimate that the ratio may be approximately 2 to 1, with 50 percent of men and 25 percent of women showing the trait phenotypically. But it should be noted that spatial ability, like all other human abilities, is genetically multidetermined. As noted above, Bock and Kolakowski hypothesize two specific determiners (only one of which is sex-linked), and there may very well be more. Furthermore, there are probably determiners of spatial performance that are not specific to this domain. Spatial ability is usually positively correlated with other kinds of cognitive per-

---

* L. G. Humphreys, University of Illinois, personal communication, 1972.

formance in which the sexes do not differ, or in which females are superior. Insofar as these other kinds of abilities have genetic components, they
are not sex-linked, and any contribution they make to performance on spatial tasks will be impartial as to sex. All this is to say that a person may
have a good genetic potential for the acquisition of spatial skills without
having the X-linked space gene, and further, that both sexes do manifest
the X-linked space gene, though in different proportions.

There is more than one way to attack almost any intellectual task. It is
likely that problems such as the Luchins-jar problem may be tackled in one
way by people with high spatial potential and in another way by people
with a different pattern of abilities. Even more important, however, is the
role of experience and training. To say that an ability has a genetic component is not to say that it is impervious to training. Obviously, a genetic
potential has little meaning in the absence of the experiences and practice
to actualize the potential. We shall return to this issue later.

Assuming that there is a genetically sex-linked component in spatial
ability, in what way does it organize the body's functioning so as to produce the behavioral differences? One possibility is that the sex hormones
are involved in the control system, but this is not the only way in which
sex-linked traits are manifest. The development of secondary sex characteristics at puberty is determined both by prenatal programming (that
occurs under the influence of testosterone) and by increasing levels of
sex-appropriate hormones at puberty. On the other hand, certain sex-
linked traits (e.g. color blindness) are not responsive to changes in the
levels of sex hormones during the life cycle. What evidence do we have
that the sex linkage of spatial ability operates through the hormonal system?

Hormones and spatial ability. Broverman et al. (1968)[a] have offered a
theory concerning the relationship of sex hormones to intellectual performance. As noted earlier, they use a twofold classification of tasks: set A
involves "simple, overlearned, repetitive" behaviors at which females are
alleged to be superior; set B involves inhibition of initial response tendencies, and more complex information processing that calls for the reorganization of stimulus elements. As shown earlier in this chapter, this does
not appear to be a useful classification for encapsulating sex differences.
There is no consistent sex difference in tasks calling for inhibition of
previously learned responses; boys excel at spatial tasks that do not call
for the reorganization of stimulus elements (restructuring) as well as for
those that do, and spatial tasks as a whole do not appear to call for any
higher order of information processing than the verbal tasks at which
girls characteristically excel. The differences in mathematical abilities do
not fall easily into this classification—that is, higher mathematics is not
simply a matter of the reorganization of stimulus elements. Furthermore,

in the analysis of findings on sex differences in learning (see Chapter 2), no evidence emerged supporting the Broverman classification of functions; in fact, the evidence was inconsistent with this formulation.

However, we may consider the Broverman theory of hormonal effects apart from the validity of the classification of tasks. Briefly, the argument rests on the sympathetic and parasympathetic nervous systems and the balance in their functions: adrenergic (sympathetic) activating processes are alleged to support and stimulate the intellectual functions involved in set A types of tasks, whereas cholinergic inhibitory neural processes facilitate performance on set B types of tasks. As Parlee points out (1972)[R], both the sympathetic and parasympathetic nervous systems use acetylcholine as a transmitter substance; hence effects of varying amounts of sex hormones on the amounts of this substance available for neural transmission do not bear upon the issue of sympathetic-parasympathetic balance. There is a further problem in equating the sympathetic-parasympathetic balance with the balance between set A and set B tasks; as Parlee points out, the evidence summarized by the Broverman group of work prior to their own work does not establish any such connection. However, for present purposes the point is that the Broverman group did develop a hypothesis that they then tested with new data. The hypothesis (in simplified form) is that large amounts of either estrogens or androgens will tip the neural balance toward activating, rather than inhibiting, functions (toward set A tasks and away from set B tasks); however, estrogens are more powerful, so the balance is tipped further in females than in males.

In one experiment, Klaiber et al. (1971)[R] tested a group of normal adult male subjects on a simple "overlearned" task (serial subtraction). They then gave injections of testosterone to the experimental group, and of saline solution to the control group. Both groups declined in their performance on the task in the post-test, but the control group declined significantly more. The decline in the experimental group is troublesome for the hypothesis, but the authors suggest that the injection of testosterone prevented as great a decline as would normally have occurred as a result of the normal diurnal variation in testosterone levels: "The results suggest that infused testosterone positively affects performance of a repetitive mental task." It is unfortunate that this study used no tasks involving inhibition or restructuring, which presumably would be interfered with by testosterone. In another study by this group of investigators, however (Klaiber et al. 1967[R]), both kinds of tasks were used. The study is correlational rather than experimental. Male college students did some simple repetitive tasks (speed of reading repeated color names, speed of naming repeated pictured objects), and also were given two tests calling for restructuring: the WAIS Block Design subtest and the Embedded Figures Test. Measures were also taken of urinary 17-ketosteroids, and ratings were made of pubic hair growth, height, weight, and chest and biceps circumference. Both 17-KS scores and masculine physical characteristics (large chest and biceps, plentiful pubic hair) were found to be positively correlated with performance on the simple repetitive tasks and negatively correlated with the restructuring tasks. The correlations were not large in an absolute sense, but many were significant and they were consistent in direction.

The work cited so far has been done entirely with male subjects and with male hormones or their derivations. A finding that male hormones "feminize" performance among men hardly helps to explain sex differences, unless it can be shown that female hormones do so even more strongly. An interesting study by Petersen (1973) with subjects from the Fels longtitudinal sample does include female subjects, but still does not fill the gap. Measures were made of the degree of body "androgenization" in both boys and girls at three age levels: 13, 16, and 17 or 18. Scores were also available on spatial ability (measured by the PMA space test and the Block Design subtest of the Wechsler) and on "fluency" (measured by the Digit Symbol subtest of the Wechsler and the Word Fluency subtest of the Primary Mental Abilities test). The results for fluency are ambiguous, partly because it did not prove to be a coherent dimension. For spatial ability, however, the results show that at age 17 or 18 boys with a more masculine body type tended to have lower spatial scores. At age 13 this correlation was not present, and only marginally so at age 16. Among girls, the more androgenized body types (narrow hips, wide shoulders, solid muscles, small breasts) were associated with *higher* spatial scores, although the correlations were lower than for boys.

At first glance, the results with the female subjects seem anomalous: why should high body androgenization be associated with low spatial scores in boys (as the Broverman theory would imply) but with *high* spatial scores in girls? A possible explanation is that the endocrine picture among girls with masculine body types is one of low estrogen rather than (or in addition to) high androgen. From the Petersen data it is difficult to tell, and the puzzle probably will not be unraveled until direct measures of both male and female hormones have been made with subjects of both sexes and two types of tasks related to their performance: the tasks on which males normally excel and those showing female advantage.

To date, evidence does appear to be accumulating that, among males, highly "masculine" characteristics, either of physique or personality, are associated with *low* spatial scores. An additional item of evidence for this generalization was discussed in our 1966 review, in reference to a study of children who were relatively more skillful on spatial tasks than on verbal or quantitative tasks (Ferguson and Maccoby 1966). The boys with high spatial scores were rated by their peers as less "masculine" than boys with low scores; that is, 11-year-old peers rated high-score boys as unlikely to have those characteristics, such as fighting ability, that they thought most distinguished boys from girls.

Granted, for the moment, that spatial ability in boys is negatively related to various indexes of androgen level, where does this leave us in our attempt to explain sex differences in spatial ability? Clearly, if androgen were an important negative factor in this ability, it would be expected that boys, who have more androgen, would have lower spatial skills than girls. The Broverman case rests on the thesis that, although both male and female hormones are inimical to spatial ability, estrogens are more so than androgens. There is simply no evidence either to support or refute this latter claim. The negative effects of androgen are mysterious indeed when one considers the age curves for hormonal and intellectual development. Boys experience their greatest rise in spatial ability—and their greatest rate of divergence from girls' scores—from the beginning of adolescence until late adolescence, precisely when their androgen levels are rising most steeply. If androgens exercise a negative influence upon spatial ability, then there must be other powerful forces operating in an opposite direction to stimulate spatial development in adolescence and to more than neutralize the effects of the increasing androgens. It seems possible that the two sets of phenomena may actually be physiologically unrelated, even though both are sex-linked and occur at the same time.

We have one final note concerning hormonal effects on intellectual development: an early report of Ehrhardt and Money (1967)[R] found that fetally androgenized girls had unusually high IQs. The average IQ of the ten girls studied was 125, which the authors believed was higher than might be expected from socioeconomic predictors of their probable level, though no figures were presented on this point and there was no matched control group. Dalton, working with a group of English children whose mothers had received large amounts of progesterone (a female hormone) during pregnancy, found that both the male and female offspring of these mothers scored significantly higher than matched controls on general aptitude tests (Dalton 1968[R]). It seemed possible, then, that unusual amounts of either male or female hormone, present prenatally, might be a positive factor for intellectual development. However, a more recent study by Ehrhardt and Baker (1973)[R] found that fetally androgenized girls had higher-than-average IQs (see Chapter 5); but so did their normal sisters, who were the control group. Thus, the most likely explanation of the previous findings appears to be that there is a selective factor such that children who receive unusual dosages of hormones during prenatal life are more often found in families with a high likelihood of the children's having high IQs.

Brain lateralization. Another hypothesis concerns the way genetic factors may operate to affect intellectual functioning in the two sexes, one having to do with sex differences in cerebral dominance. It has been known for some time that the cerebral functions relevant to the perception and production of speech tend to be localized in the left hemisphere of the brain, those relevant to spatial perception and perception of nonverbal sounds in the right hemisphere. Kimura (1963)[R], using a dichotic listening technique, found that this localization had developed by the age of 4 among boys and girls of above-average IQ from professional homes, but that among less-advantaged children (Kimura 1967) left-hemisphere dominance had developed by age 5 among girls, and not till later among boys. Furthermore, it has been shown that boys with reading difficulties lag even further behind girls in the establishment of hemisphere dominance. The reader is referred to a summary of the work on sex differences in cerebral dominance by Buffery and Gray (1972)[R] for detailed documentation. The question of whether spatial abilities are more specifically localized in the right hemisphere for one sex than the other is not yet settled. Knox and Kimura (1970) and Kimura (1969) found greater localization among males for certain spatial tasks, with the sex difference being apparent as young as age 5. Buffery (1971)[R], however, found girls to be more fully lateralized on a spatial task, and more advanced in the development of handedness, beginning at ages 3–4. The Buffery and Gray thesis is that the earlier and stronger development of lateralization in females facilitates their verbal development, but that spatial skills call for a more bilateral cerebral representation and hence is facilitated in men, in whom laterality is not so strong or developed so early.

There is another, and somewhat contradictory, view about cerebral dominance. Sperry and his colleagues, working with patients in whom the functional connections between the two hemispheres of the brain have been severed, have argued that the localization of verbal functions in the left hemisphere and spatial functions in the right tends to be weaker in women. Levy-Agresti and Sperry (1968)[R] believe that strong cerebral dominance facilitates performance for spatial tasks, and they report that left-handed men (in whom cerebral lateralization is weak) are similar to women in obtaining low scores in spatial abilities. Thus Levy and Sperry believe that male superiority in spatial tasks stems from *greater* specialization of the two hemispheres among men than among women, whereas Buffery and Gray's position is that it results from a *lesser* degree of specialization. The issue is yet to be resolved. It may be, as Buffery and Gray suggest, that the findings on which the Levy-Sperry hypothesis is based apply to epilectic patients but not normals.

Some puzzling questions arise from the work on cerebral lateralization in the two sexes. One is that the "packages" of skills localized in each hemisphere do not correspond in detail to the known sex differences in abilities. Levy-Agresti (1968)[R], for example, has described the left hemisphere as being verbal, sequentially detailed, analytic, and computer-like.

Although girls are superior in a variety of verbal tasks, the rest of the description does not fit them better than boys. A theory that purports to account for female superiority on verbal tasks and inferiority on spatial tasks, in terms of stronger or earlier lateralization of the left hemisphere, would have to expect that the other functions controlled by this hemisphere would also be superior in girls.

A second problem has to do with timing, and whether the girl's early left-hemisphere dominance orients her toward the use of verbal means of problem solving. Sherman (1967)[R] suggests that girls develop verbally earlier than boys and that this operates to eliminate the need for the development of nonverbal (particularly spatial) thought. Do girls, as Sherman claims, have a head start in verbal development and do boys start out higher in spatial thinking? Do boys eventually catch up in verbal development and thereafter begin to equalize their ability to use alternative modes of thought? The developmental pattern, as we have seen, is quite different, with no sex differences found in verbal vs. spatial thought in the years boys are lagging behind girls in lateralization, whereas sex differences in modes of thought appear at an age when boys have caught up and become as lateralized as they ever will be. Perhaps Sherman is right that there is an early "bent twig" period during which a person establishes certain modes of problem solving, and continues, with the aid of sex-typed activities, to emphasize these modes after the original reason for doing so has disappeared.

We have reservations concerning this idea, because we believe that far-reaching, qualitative changes in intellectual processes occur with development; that large transformations in modes of thought do occur in middle childhood, after lateralization is virtually complete; and that the chances are slim that early habitual reliance on one kind of data will survive these transformations. However, the issue is an empirical one. To determine whether early language development in any way shuts off development of spatial ability, what appears to be needed is examination *within sex* of the relationship between the rate of early language development and later spatial skills. If boys who talk late have better spatial ability in later childhood than boys who talk early, this would be good evidence for the inhibiting effects of early left-hemisphere functioning on right-hemisphere functions. In the absence of this kind of data, the question remains open whether there is a critical period when the degree of lateralization is especially important for the future.

Effects of Training

All the abilities discussed in this chapter improve with age, from early childhood to adulthood. Our educational institutions are dedicated to the proposition that these changes are not entirely (or even primarily) a result of simple maturation—that verbal, mathematical, spatial, and conceptual skills can be taught, and indeed if they are not taught, they will probably not be learned to an adequate level of proficiency. This is not to say that success in teaching is independent of a child's already-developed readiness to learn a given task, or that success in training does not depend upon genetic factors (including those controlling maturation) and previous learning. However, if any group of children have not acquired certain intellectual skills that other children of their age possess, there is a reasonable presumption that at least part of the problem lies in deficiencies in the teaching they have received.

Witkin et al. have argued that training plays only a limited role in performance on the tests used to measure field dependence. It has been noted above that these talks have a large spatial component, and therefore the Witkin case is relevant to the "trainability" of spatial ability. The Witkin group trained subjects in estimating the upright in the Tilting-Rod-Tilting-Chair situation. The subjects improved, but their improvement did not generalize to performance on the standard Rod and Frame Test, or to the Embedded Figures Test. They also found that a group of dancers, who have extensive training in sensitivity to cues of body position, obtained higher-than-average scores on the Body Adjustment Test, but not on other measures of field dependence. They interpret this finding as follows (Witkin et al. 1962[R], p. 372):

These results suggest that no fundamental change in mode of field approach, in the sense of alteration of the subject's characteristic way of perceiving, occurred in consequence of training. Our observations of subjects during training tended to confirm this impression. We noted that subjects who improved their scores in the test on which they receive training accomplished this apparently by the acquisition of special techniques or "tricks" useful in correcting the immediate impression of the upright.

Recent work on training in spatial tasks has not added a great deal to our understanding of the issues raised by Witkin et al. Subjects can benefit from direct training on spatial tasks (Kato 1965; female subjects only, A. Goldstein and Chance 1965), though in an earlier study with fewer practice trials, subjects showed no improvement (Elliott and McMichael 1963[R]). Engineering practice (Blade and Watson 1955[R]) and programmed instruction techniques (Brinkmann 1966[R]) have been shown to enhance spatial visualization performance. However, these studies have not investigated how widely the training generalized, or how long the effects of training lasted. More important for our present purposes, it has not been demonstrated that male and female subjects respond differentially to training. It is reasonable to expect that if the deficit in spatial ability of females results from lack of training, they should begin to catch up with males after additional training; if there were a difference in underlying "ability," however, males might profit more from training than females. At present, the issue is simply unresolved. Goldstein and Chance (1965) did find that, with an extended series of Embedded Figures items permitting extended practice, women improved more; male college students scored better on early trials but there was no sex difference on later trials. If this finding replicates, it will be strong evidence that sex differences in spatial ability are (in large degree) a product of differential training. However, we cannot consider that the issue is resolved on the basis of this single piece of evidence.

What conclusions can be drawn if training on a specific task does not generalize widely to other kinds of performance in the same ability domain? The lack of generalization is probably the rule rather than the exception in the effects of instruction. Math teachers know that different arithmetical operations must be trained individually even though individuals may differ in their general readiness to learn various numerical skills. The point is that lack of generalization does not imply the absence of an underlying "ability."

Furthermore, a generalized "ability" may itself be a product of previous learning. The question whether a given kind of intellectual proficiency (e.g. high math ability) is an additive product of many elements acquired piece by piece, or whether it is related to larger structures that develop in a necessary sequence and are resistant to the immediate impact of specific training, is a widely debated issue, and we cannot contribute much to it here. However, even if one takes the structuralist position, one can argue that there is a heavy impact of experience upon the development of structures. We assume that field independence (which we translate as visual spatial ability), as well as other abilities, is a fairly stable characteristic of an individual upon which any specific training procedures may have only a limited effect, though there are undoubtedly cumulative effects of continued training. Beyond this, we think it likely (as Witkin also does) that early opportunities to learn, and affective aspects of the child's milieu, do have an impact upon the developmental course of these abilities. We turn to a brief consideration of variations in milieu.

Cultural Factors

Cross-cultural work on intellectual abilities (especially as it relates to sex differences) seems to have focused upon the field-dependence field-independence dimension. In their excellent review chapter on cognitive styles, Kagan and Kogan (1970, pp. 1337–40)[a] have summarized the work of Berry, Dawson, and others on field-dependence in people being reared in contrasting cultures. A first point to note is that when "traditional" (nonacculturated) groups are compared with "transitional" people from the same genetic background who are adopting more modern life styles, the "transitionals" have higher spatial scores. The probable role of formal education is evident here.

Taking their lead from Witkin, Dawson (1967)[R] and Berry (1966) have investigated the hypothesis that field-dependence will be more marked in cultures in which there is emphasis upon conformity, reliance upon authority, and restriction of the autonomy of the individual; field-independence, on the other hand, they expect to be more characteristic among individuals growing up in an atmosphere where independence is respected and encouraged. And within cultures, the hypothesis continues, the degree of difference in field-dependence between the sexes should be a function of the degree of sex-role differentiation—the degree to which females are restricted and males allowed independence.

A first point to be noted is that in Berry's work the Embedded Figures Test correlated substantially with three other visual-spatial tests that were also used, and the cluster of measures showed similar cultural and between-sex effects. Hence we can discuss this work in terms of visual-spatial ability rather than field-dependence per se.

Comparisons between African cultural groups that differ in the degree of maternal dominance over children (the Temne vs. the Mende in Sierra Leone, Dawson 1967[R]) have shown that adult males obtain higher scores on spatial tests in the cultures where young children are allowed more autonomy. (Female subjects were not included in this study.) Comparisons between a restrictive African culture and a permissive Eskimo culture have yielded the same relation to adult spatial abilities. Furthermore, when children of both sexes are allowed considerable independence (Eskimo), no sex difference has been found in spatial ability (Berry 1966, MacArthur 1967), whereas substantial sex differences are found when males exercise strong authoritarian control over females (the Temne, as reported by Berry 1966).

Kagan and Kogan point out that it is possible that the lack of sex differences in spatial ability among the Eskimo might result from a specialized gene pool, representing the adaptation of this human subgroup to the special requirements of life in the arctic environment. This possibility cannot be ruled out; we note only that the cross-cultural evidence available to date is consistent with the hypothesis that child-rearing practices, and the social roles assigned the two sexes, affect the degree to which the sexes differ in spatial ability.

Personality mediators. As we have seen above, cultures that allow independence to children tend to produce adults with higher spatial scores than cultures that use more restrictive socialization practices. It would appear that, within cultures, it ought to be true, as Witkin suggested, that the more passive, dependent individuals would have lower scores on spatial tests, with the more assertive, autonomous individuals having higher scores. The direct evidence for this relationship is equivocal. V. J. Crandall and Sinkeldam (1964) observed the free play of children ranging in age from 6 to 12, and recorded instances of dependent behavior toward adults (seeking help, affection, recognition, or approval). Girls who were dependent in this sense had lower-than-average scores on the Embedded Figures Test. However, when IQ was held constant, the correlation dropped to an insignificant level.

Konstadt and Forman (1965)[R], on the other hand, obtained more positive results. They first obtained field-dependence scores for a group of fourth-grade children. Then they observed the children as they worked on another task under conditions of either experimenter approval or experimenter disapproval. The field-independent children were relatively unaffected by the experimenter's attitude, whereas the field-dependent children performed better under approval and worse under disapproval conditions. Thus, if sensitivity to an adult's approval is taken as an index of dependency, the hypothesis is confirmed.

In the earlier review (Maccoby 1966a[R]) it was noted that there were some puzzling findings in which correlations between spatial ability and personality measures ran in opposite directions for the two sexes. Specifically, there was evidence that high spatial ability was associated with "masculine" traits in women, but with *low* masculinity in men. We noted above some evidence relating high body androgenization to low spatial ability among men (p. 122ff). Kagan and Kogan review other evidence on this issue in detail, concluding that the evidence does continue to support the generalization that spatial ability is associated with cross-sex typing, although the relationship appears to be stronger in women than in men. Recently, additional findings have appeared showing very different patterns of correlations between personality variables and measures of intellectual performance for the two sexes. For example, (1) S. Coates (1972) reports a correlation of .41 between aggression and IQ in preschool girls, and a correlation of −.74 for boys; (2) a sense of personal potency (internal locus of control) is positively related to scores on the Embedded Figures Test for girls aged 6–12, but not related among boys of the same age (V. C. Crandall and Lacey 1972); and (3) intellectual achievement striving is positively related to activity level among girls, negatively related among boys (Battle and Lacey 1972). However, a large-scale study with Head Start children (aged 3–6) (Ward 1973[R]) has shown that impulsivity (as measured by low scores on the Motor Inhibition Test) is a negative factor for intellectual performances in *both* sexes. On the whole, the recent correlation evidence supports the earlier contention that different personality constellations are associated with good intellectual performance in the two sexes, and the more bold, assertive girls continue to show greater intellectual abilities and interests than other girls. Evidence is insufficient to reveal whether these personality attributes are more strongly related to spatial than other abilities.

The 1966 Maccoby paper attempted to explain some portion of the sex differences in intellectual performance in terms of sex differences in personality structure. Some of the points made were as follows:

1. For both sexes, independence (autonomy) is positively associated with good intellectual performance, particularly on tests on spatial ability or field-independence. Girls' poorer performance on these tests may stem from greater dependency.

2. Tasks calling for internal serial processing are especially vulnerable to distraction; girls may do poorly on these tasks because they are more oriented toward external, interpersonal cues, and hence more distracted by them.

3. Activity is involved in those intellectual tasks that require restructuring or breaking set. Boys have a higher average activity level, which may give them an advantage on such tasks.

4. Aggression and impulsivity are related to poor intellectual performance in boys but not in girls. It was suggested that a curvilinear relationship may exist between performance on an intellectual task and a dimension running from passive-inhibited to bold-impulsive, such that the midpoint of the dimension is optimal for intellectual performance in both sexes. Boys, being more often at the impulsive end of the scale, profit intellectually from becoming less impulsive; girls, being more often at the passive, timid end of the scale, profit from becoming more bold.

These arguments have not stood up well under the impact of new evidence appearing in the intervening years. As will be seen later, there is now good reason to doubt that girls are more "dependent," in almost any sense of the word, than boys. Hence point 1 is not supported. Point 2 suffers from two weaknesses: there is no evidence (as we have seen in the present chapter) that the sexes differ on tasks calling for serial internal processing; furthermore, girls are not more oriented toward interpersonal cues (see Chapter 5).

With respect to point 3, it is by no means demonstrated that boys do excel on tasks calling for restructuring or breaking set, so that perhaps there is nothing to explain. If there were, activity level is a poor candidate for a personality mediator. We shall see later that the sexes do not differ generally with respect to activity level. There are certain specific stimulus situations under which boys do show elevated activity levels, but these are not the situations that normally prevail while children are performing intellectual tasks; furthermore, high activity level appears to be a *negative* factor among boys for intellectual performance, so that if boys were given ability tests when under high activity arousal, it is doubtful whether this would improve their performance in comparison to girls, even on tasks calling for restructuring.

As for point 4, it is true that different personality factors do seem to promote intellectual competence in the two sexes, but this is not well explained by reference to a dimension running from passivity to impulsiveness. The sexes do not differ in most measures of impulsiveness devised so far, although Mischel does find that boys of preschool age have more difficulty waiting for a delayed reward. The sexes *do* differ with respect to aggressiveness, and on some measures girls are more timid or anxious; perhaps a dimension running from timidity at one end to aggressiveness at the other will be a better candidate for the curvilinear model.

The earlier argument began by assuming the existence of certain sex differences in intellectual performance that have not turned out to be consistently present; it then attempted to explain these on the basis of personality differences that have also proved to be more myth than reality. In view of this, the senior author can do little more than beg the reader's indulgence for previous sins. However, the studies on personality correlates of intellectual performance have continued to suggest that intellectual development in girls is fostered by their being assertive and active, and having a sense that they can control, by their own actions, the events that affect their lives. These factors appear to be less important in the intellectual development of boys—perhaps because they are already sufficiently assertive and have a sufficient sense of personal control over events, so that other issues (e.g. how well they can control aggressive impulses) become more important in how successfully they can exploit their intellectual potential.

CHAPTER FOUR

Achievement Motivation and Self-Concept

We have reviewed what is known about the aptitudes and academic achievement of the two sexes, as these are shown in a variety of standardized tests. However, to have an "aptitude" for learning a particular kind of material, or even to have a good store of already acquired knowledge and problem-solving skill in a given area, is not the same as to do well in school classes or a job, or to seek out opportunities in which one's aptitudes and knowledge may be put to work. Willingness to work, interest in improving one's level of skills, responsiveness to the demands of others to acquire new skills, are all obviously involved.

It has been alleged that the sexes differ in their motivations to achieve. Here is an illustrative assertion: "Girls have different orientations toward intellectual tasks than do boys. Little girls want to please; they work for love and approval; if bright, they underestimate their competence. Little boys show more task involvement, more confidence" (Hoffman 1972[R], p. 130).

Several hypotheses are implied in these assertions. We shall first state the hypotheses concerning sex differences in achievement motivation that have been put forward in these and other writings, and attempt to evaluate each of them in the light of existing evidence. The hypotheses are as follows:

1. Males have a greater need for achievement and are more oriented to achievement for its own sake.

2. Males show greater task involvement and persistence.

3. Males show more curiosity, and engage in more exploratory behavior.

4. Females are motivated to achieve primarily in areas related to interpersonal relations (e.g. to be especially attractive to others; to associate with high-status others, especially men; to have achieving children), whereas males strive to achieve in non-person-oriented areas including intellectual endeavors.

5. Female efforts to achieve are primarily motivated by the desire to please others, so that regardless of the area of achievement (whether in-

tellectual, social, etc.) they care primarily about praise and approval for their performance, whereas males are more motivated by the intrinsic interest of the task.

6. Females have low self-confidence about many tasks. This is sometimes thought to be part of a generalized lack of self-esteem.

We begin with hypothesis 1. One might expect that the simplest, most direct manifestation of a lack-of-achievement motivation would be low achievement. If one takes academic achievement as the criterion, hypothesis 1 is faulted at the outset. It is well known that girls get better grades throughout their school years (see Maccoby 1966b[R], Oetzel summary on pp. 323–51). Table 4.1 shows recent evidence on school performance and interest in school, and supports the earlier conclusion. Girls are more interested in school-related skills from an early age (Baumrind and Black 1967, Barnard 1966), and are less likely to drop out of school before completing high school (Fitzsimmons et al. 1969). Interestingly enough, boys' poorer performance in school does not seem to be a function of any greater feeling of distrust or lack of rapport toward the teacher. In a study of Solomon and Alli (1972), boys showed a more positive perception of the teacher than the girls did (particularly in the early grades) when reacting to taped teacher-child interactions. We will present some evidence later that teachers tend to have more interactions, and longer conversations, with boys in their classrooms. We suggest that boys' poorer school performance is not due to lesser interest in their performance on the part of teachers, or to any greater tendency on the boys' part to dislike the teachers.

We have seen that girls do not obtain higher aptitude or achievement test scores (see Chapter 3), taking all the subject-matter areas together. Hence their better grades must reflect some combination of greater effort, greater interest, and better work habits. Evidently, these school-related motivations are not what is meant when assertions are made about girls' low achievement motivation. Let us turn to research focused more directly on this motivation.

NEED FOR ACHIEVEMENT

The classic work on need for achievement was done some time ago by McClelland and his colleagues. Most of their work was done with male subjects, but they did study women as well, and summarized their findings on sex differences as follows: "1. Women get higher N Ach scores than men under neutral conditions (2 studies). 2. Women do not show an increase in N Ach scores as a result of achievement-involving instructions (3 studies). 3. Women's N Ach scores seem as valid as men's, in that they relate to performance in the same way" (McClelland et al. 1953[R], p. 178). Need for achievement was measured projectively, through a scoring of achievement themes in stories told in response to pictures in the Thematic

TABLE 4.1
School Performance

Study	Age and N	Difference	Comment
R. Bell et al. 1971	2½ (74)	None	Interest in attending nursery school (teacher rating)
Baumrind & Black 1967	3-4 (103)	Girls	Higher interest in preschool skills (observer ratings)
Solomon & Ali 1972	5, 7, 9, 11, 13, 15, 17, 21-25 (294)	Boys & Men	More positive perception of teachers from taped teacher-child interaction
Yando et al. 1971	8 (144)	None	"Classroom achievement" (teacher rating)
Barnard 1966	10 (220)	Girls	Higher positive semantic differential for concepts related to school
C. Johnson & Gormly 1972	10 (113)	Girls	Course grade in mathematics
Achenbach 1970	10-13 (1,085)	Girls	Higher grades, all ages
Buck & Austrin 1971	14-16 (100)	None	Display of positive classroom behavior (teacher rating; black sample)
Monday et al. 1966-67	14-17 (225,402)	Girls	Higher high school grades
Fitzsimmons et al. 1969	15-17 (270)	Girls	Lower dropout rate
Wyer 1967	18 (2,000)	None	First-term freshman grades
Constantinople 1967	18, 21 (353)	None	Perceived instrumentality of college

Apperception Test (TAT). The "achievement arousal" treatment involved having the subjects work on an anagrams task, after being told that the task reflected not only an individual's intelligence but his capacity to organize material and to evaluate situations quickly and accurately—"in short, his capacity to be a leader." After such an "arousal" session, male subjects increased the achievement themes in their TAT responses, but women did not.

It was initially thought that women must have less achievement motivation, since they did not respond to an achievement-arousal condition. However, it may make a difference how the arousal is done—what other motivations it taps. With this question in mind, Field (reported in McClelland et al., p. 179) used a "social" arousal, which involved first of all a discussion concerning the importance of social acceptance by a group as the most important determiner of satisfaction with life, and the claim that the best predictor of social acceptance in a wide range of social situations was acceptance in the present situation. Subjects were then given social acceptance scores that presumably reflected their acceptance by the other members of the group.

In response to this arousal, men's n Ach scores went up somewhat (not significantly), but women's increased considerably more sharply (and significantly). This finding has been a primary basis for the popularity of hypothesis 4 above; it has been assumed that the higher scores for women were due to the emphasis of the Field arousal on social acceptability (an area in which women presumably want to achieve), whereas the previous results with the standard achievement arousal reflected men's interest in intellectual achievement. It should be pointed out that the emphasis on "leadership" introduces a competitive element, and it is difficult to be sure whether the greater increase in women's scores after the Field arousal resulted from omitting the competitive theme, adding the social acceptance theme, or both.

A complication in the measurement of n Ach comes from the use of projective measures, which assume a relationship between projective responses and the subject's own motivations or behavior. It is not uncommon for boys to be given a boys' form of a projective test, in which the central character presented in the story or picture is a male; the girls' form, on the other hand, uses female characters. If girls give fewer achievement themes under these conditions, is this due to their own low-achievement motivation or to their assumption that other girls and women are not achievers? It has been found (Veroff et al. 1953[R], Monahan et al. 1974) that *subjects of both sexes* give fewer achievement themes (and report more negative events) when responding to a story or picture about a female, suggesting that girls' usually lower n Ach scores may not reflect their own motivations but rather their concepts (which they share with men) concerning the usual characteristics of women and girls.

To illustrate the magnitude of this effect, Table 4.2 reproduces mean n Ach scores from groups of high school students.

It should be noted that the achievement-oriented arousal (followed by

TABLE 4.2
*Mean Need-Achievement Scores Under Neutral
and Achievement-Oriented Conditions*

| | Mean n Ach score on picture test | | | |
| | Neutral condition | | Achievement-oriented condition | |
Subjects	Male pictures	Female pictures	Male pictures	Female pictures
Male	1.94	1.72	4.93	1.57
Female	5.76	1.77	5.21	1.92

SOURCE: McClelland et al. 1953[R], pp. 167, 172.

an n Ach test with male pictures) succeeded in bringing the male n Ach scores only up to the level where the female scores already were without arousal. Similar results were obtained in the Field work: women subjects had higher n Ach scores than men under the relaxed conditions, although not so high as relaxed-condition scores obtained in other studies; "social" arousal raised their scores to approximately their usual level, but did not increase the male scores from an initially very low level.

Perhaps a more accurate way of summarizing this early work on achievement motivation would be as follows: when n Ach is measured projectively with male pictures, females in high school and college show a high level of achievement imagery whether given an "arousal" treatment or not; men show a high level only when aroused by reference to assessment of their intelligence and leadership ability. There may be a clue here to boys' lower grades in school—it appears that it takes stronger efforts to motivate them. But the results certainly do not indicate a generally low level of achievement motivation in girls, or that they are motivated only by appeals to their social acceptability. The fact that neither sex shows as much achievement motivation with female pictures is difficult to interpret. We simply do not know whether this reflects the subjects' own motivation to a greater extent for female than male subjects.

Recent work on achievement motivation is summarized in Table 4.3. In studies done with younger children, competition is not stressed. These studies measure achievement motivation from teachers' ratings or observers' reports of the child's efforts to improve some aspect of his performance in relation to an implicit or explicit standard. For example, if a child looks at his own drawing, says "That's not right," and erases what he has done and tries again, the incident is coded as an instance of achievement striving. In three of the four studies with children under six, girls were found to exhibit more "autonomous achievement striving" than boys.

At later ages, there is a shift to questionnaire and projective methods of measurement. The evidence is thin and inconsistent. There were four studies summarized in the 1966 book (Oetzel, pp. 344–45)—one with children and the other three with adults—all using projective measures. Three showed no sex differences. The fourth (McClelland et al., described above) found higher achievement imagery among women under neutral conditions and an increase among men under an intellectual-competitive arousal. More recently, Ramirez et al. (1971) report greater achievement imagery among boys on a projective test in a mixed sample of Mexican American and Anglo adolescents. This study used different forms for the two sexes, presenting own-sex stimulus pictures to each subject, and thus raising the problems of interpretation noted above. Lunneborg and Rosenwood (1972), with a sizable sample of college students, followed up a suggestion by Bardwick, who had found a remarkably low level of achievement-

TABLE 4.3
Achievement Striving

Study	Age and N	Difference	Comment
Baumrind & Black 1967	3-4 (103)	None	Observer ratings: stretches to meet vs. retreats from performance demands; sets easy vs. hard goals to achieve; hazards failure vs. avoids difficult tasks
Wyer 1968	3-6 (70)	None	Preference for easy or difficult games
Klaus & Gray 1968	3-7 (80)	None	Choice of achievement or nonachievement endings to short stories (low SES black; longitudinal)
Callard 1968	4 (80)	Girls	Chose to resume more challenging tasks
Radin 1973	4 (52)	None	Academic motivation (teacher and psychologist ratings)
S. Coates 1973	4-5 (53)	Girls	Autonomous achievement strivings (teacher ratings: Beller Scale)
Emmerich 1971	4-5 (596)	Girls	Classroom observations, early fall and spring: autonomous achievement strivings (black and white, low SES)
	4-5 (415)	None	Classroom observations, early fall and late fall: autonomous achievement strivings (black and white, low SES)
Hatfield et al. 1967	4-5 (40)	None	Observer ratings of child's achievement standards
Lansky & McKay 1969	5-6 (36)	Girls	Autonomous achievement strivings (teacher ratings: Beller Scale)
Masters & Christy 1973	7 (32)	None	Self-reward for easy and difficult tasks
Bandura & Perloff 1968	7-10 (80)	None	Self-imposed performance standards
Battle 1965	12-14 (74)	None	Importance of doing well in math
Battle 1966	12-14 (500)	Boys	Rated importance of doing well in math higher; higher minimal standards of performance (English)
		Girls	Rated importance of doing well in English higher
		None	Minimal standards of performance (Math)
Ramirez et al. 1971	12-17 (600)	Boys	Need achievement, scored from Ss' stories about school-related pictures (Mexican-American, white)
Kimball 1973	13	None	"Fear of success" imagery
	17 (187)	Boys	Less "fear of success" imagery in projective stories (Canadian)
Strickland 1971	14 (120)	Boys	Level of aspiration, Rotter Board (black and white middle SES)
		None	Level of aspiration, Rotter Board (black and white low SES)
Sampson & Hancock 1967	15-17 (251)	None	Need for achievement as measured by Edwards Personal Preference Schedule
Lunneborg & Rosenwood 1972	18-21 (465)	None	Achievement themes in answer to "What makes you happy," "sad?"

oriented responses to the questions "What makes you happy? What makes you sad? What makes you angry?" among a pilot group of college women. Lunneborg and Rosenwood used the same questions with college subjects of both sexes. Points were given toward an achievement score if the individual said, for example, that "success," "a rewarding career," or "getting through school" would bring happiness, or that "doing badly on a test," "inability to explain," or "losing something I should have had a chance at" would make him (her) sad. Although there was a slight trend in the direction of men's giving more achievement responses, the difference was not significant (e.g. 33 percent of men as against 30 percent of women gave "happy" achievement imagery).

Some of the most interesting recent work has focused on the "motive to avoid success" (Horner 1968[R], 1970). Horner argues that traditional measures of achievement motivation do not reflect the conflict situation that particularly affects women, namely that they feel it is acceptable (indeed, expected) to do well at school, but that it is at the same time unladylike to "beat" men at almost any task. This conflict produces a situation in which women want to succeed, but not too much. Horner devised an ingenious method for identifying this conflict. She asked subjects to write stories about highly successful members of their own sex, and scored the stories for all the unpleasant things that were described about ensuing events or the personal characteristics of the successful person. She found that 65 percent of college women described unpleasant events and attributes in discussing successful women, whereas only 10 percent of college men gave such descriptions of successful men. More recently, a more complete design has been used, with adolescent subjects of both sexes being asked to write stories about both successful boys and successful girls (Monahan et al. 1974). *Both* sexes gave more negative responses to stories about successful girls—in fact, boys were even more negative about female success than girls were. Subjects of the two sexes were equally positive about male success.

The work on the fear of success is new and the results are not consistent. Alper (1973)[R] found as much success imagery as failure imagery in women. One study (Kimball 1973) has not found a sex difference in the fear-of-success motive at age 13. A number of other studies (as yet unpublished) have come to our attention in which sex differences in fear of success have also failed to appear. We do not yet know what the age changes may be in the development of the conflict over success, or how the conflict finds expression (if it does) in behavior. But the studies do underline the possibility that a sex difference in "achievement motivation" will be found only (or primarily) in situations in which achievement is assessed in comparative terms. In our culture, achievement tends to be defined in just these terms. All achievements can in principle be rank-ordered, but it may be a mistake to suppose that all achievement is motivated by a concern for rank order.

A recent study by Martin (1973) illustrates nicely how introducing competition into a task has a different effect upon the achievement striving of the two sexes. Martin worked with second-grade children in a beanbag toss game. The subject aimed for one of a series of target areas marked on the floor with each toss. The more distant the target, the more points gained if the toss was successful. Each child played this game alone in one session, and in another session as a member of a same-sex pair taking turns. The rules of the competitive session were that the child with the highest number of points got *all* the points earned by both scorers—or "winner take all." Boys became slightly more conservative in their target choices under competitive conditions, but girls became *much* more conservative, choosing to aim for very near targets. Their aspirations were much lower than those of boys in the competitive condition, but not otherwise. It is true that girls were not as accurate as boys, on the average, in their beanbag throws, so that their conservative behavior under competition may have simply reflected a realistic judgment that this was the only way they were likely to win; however, they were competing against other girls, no more competent than they, and their actual success was not different under the two conditions, so that their loss of self-confidence (if this is indeed what occurred) is not, after all, especially realistic. We shall return to the relation between self-confidence and achievement motivation below.

Is there any inconsistency between the hypothesis that boys are more willing to try to achieve under competitive conditions, and the fact that girls get better grades in school? We think not. We would argue that grades are not generally seen as competitive by children. Grading on the normal curve is not common in the lower grades, and even when it is done, it is probably not well understood by the children. They would not normally believe that an individual's obtaining a high grade on a test would in any way affect anyone else's chances of getting a high grade. It is reasonable, then, that even girls who find overt competition distasteful can work comfortably toward some standard of excellence in the academic sphere. We do not doubt that many girls want to be the "best" in the class, but the competition is indirect, compared for example to sports, and does not involve directly injuring or defeating another specific individual.

RISK TAKING

In a number of the tasks used to measure achievement strivings, a child's willingness to take risks is involved. If he chooses to aspire to a difficult task, he runs an increasing risk of not winning anything at all—or even of losing what he has already won. Slovic (1966) has devised an ingenious task to measure risk taking. The child has a series of nine switches that may be pulled. All except one, when pulled, yield a spoonful of M&M's. One, however, is the "disaster" switch, and when this is pulled, the child loses all the candies previously accumulated. The location of the disaster switch is varied randomly among the nine, so there is no way the child can determine where it is. All he knows is that if he has already pulled several switches, all of which were positively loaded, the chances that the next pull will be a "disaster" have been increased. The subject can pull as many switches as he chooses, and quit with his winnings at any time. Through the age range 11–16, Slovic found boys continuing their play longer (taking more risks), with the result that their total winnings were less than those of girls. He did not find sex differences among children aged 6–10, however. Kopfstein (1973), using the Slovic procedure with 9-year-old children, also found no sex differences. We do not know whether there is a consistent but age-specific tendency for boys to take more risks—replication is needed in the 11–16 age range. In any case, it is evident that the outcome of level-of-aspiration studies may be greatly affected by the degree and kind of risk they involve.

TASK ORIENTATION VERSUS PERSON ORIENTATION

As noted above, one hypothesis about sex differences in achievement motivation is that both sexes are motivated to achieve, but they are oriented toward different *kinds* of achievement, boys being primarily interested in achieving on tasks that deal with inanimate objects or impersonal ideas, and girls on tasks that involve interaction with people. Another related hypothesis is that when the two sexes are working on a task, boys tend to be intrinsically interested in the task itself, whereas girls work primarily for the praise and approval of others (or to avoid their disapproval). As Garai and Scheinfeld put it (1968, p. 270)[8]: "From early childhood on, males appear to have greater achievement needs directed toward successful task accomplishment, while females exhibit greater affiliative or social needs directed toward successful relations with the people in their environment."

Two aspects of task orientation have been studied fairly extensively: task persistence and curiosity (exploration). These studies almost always involve nonsocial tasks, i.e. the child's involvement with objects and materials. The research relevant to these two topics is summarized in Tables 4.4 and 4.5.

In some of the studies reported in Table 4.4, children were assigned tasks by the experimenter, and scores were based either on the child's initial persistence or on his willingness to return to an unfinished task in order to finish it. It could be argued that task persistence in such a situation may have reflected the child's interest in pleasing the experimenter and his docility toward the experimenter's instructions as much as his intrinsic

TABLE 4.4
Task Persistence and Involvement

Study	Age and N	Difference	Comment
J. Kagan 1971	8, 13, 27 mos (180)	None	Number of activity changes, duration of each play activity
Rheingold & Eckerman 1969	9-10 mos (24)	None	Duration of manipulation of toys and other objects
Clarke-Stewart 1973	9-18 mos	Boys	Duration of object involvement (longitudinal)
	10-13 mos	None	Number of prolonged involvements with objects (home observation, longitudinal sample)
	16-17 mos (36)	Boys	Number of prolonged involvements with objects (home observation, longitudinal sample)
Rheingold & Samuels 1969	10 mos (20)	None	Duration of time touched toys or objects
J. Brooks & Lewis 1972	11-15 mos (17 opp.-sex twin pairs)	None	Amount of sustained play or number of toy changes
Wenar 1972	12-15 mos (26)	None	Home observations of initiating and sustaining activities
Jacklin et al. 1973	13 mos (80)	None	Number of toy changes and amount of sustained play
Maccoby & Feldman 1972	2 (64)	None	Duration of longest manipulation of one toy before shifting to another (longitudinal)
	2½ (35)	None	
	3 (38)	None	
Weinraub & Lewis 1973	2 (18)	None	Time spent in sustained play
R. Bell et al. 1971	2½ (74)	None	Interest in obtaining bells, bell-pull situation (teacher rating)
F. Pedersen & Bell 1970	2½ (55)	Girls None	Longer times in single activity before changing / Persistence to secure object
Baumrind & Black 1967	3-4 (103)	None	Observer ratings: perseverance in the face of adversity; gives his best vs. expends little effort; does not vs. does become pleasurably involved in tasks
Zunich[R] 1964	3-4 (40)	Girls	Greater number of attempts to solve puzzle box alone
		None	Did not attempt to solve puzzle
Friedrichs et al. 1971	3-5 (50)	None	Time Ss voluntarily pushed pegs down with Experimenter present
Stodolsky 1971	3-5 (16)	Girls	Longer activity segments, fewer activity changes (lower SES black)
	3-5 (19)	None	Same measures as above (middle SES black and white)
	4-6 (38)	None	Same measures as above (middle SES black and white)

(continued)

TABLE 4.4 *(cont.)*

Study	Age and *N*	Difference	Comment
Wyer 1968	3-6 (70)	None	Perseverance on easy or difficult tasks
Bee et al. 1969	4-5 (114 & mothers)	None	Frequency of toy shifts
Emmerich 1971	4-5 (596)	Girls	Task orientation: behavior observation in nursery school
W. Mischel et al. 1968	7-9 (60)	None	Amount of time worked on maze and number of mazes completed
Stouwie et al. 1970	8-9 (156)	None	Number of seconds attempting to solve difficult EFT
Nakumura & Finck 1973	9-12 (251)	None	Task orientation (questionnaire)
McManis 1965	10-13 (96)	Boys	More persistent in continuing-pursuit rotor task (normal, retardates)
Maehr & Stallings 1972	13 (154)	Girls	Volunteered to repeat task (astronaut aptitude test)
Berger & Johansson 1968	18-21 (144)	None	Number of trials on probability-learning type of task before S expressed desire to quit
Rotter & Mulry 1965	18-21 (120)	None	Number of trials until subjects stopped a matching task with no correct matches

interest in the task. But other studies in the table involved measures of the child's persistence on tasks he had chosen for himself. In both cases, there is no evidence of a sex difference in persistence in the manipulation of objects. The question of whether girls show more "social task persistence" in the sense of sustained interaction with others will be discussed in detail in Chapter 6; anticipating that discussion, in brief it may simply be noted here that girls are not more task-persistent in social tasks.

Research on curiosity and exploration yields inconsistent results. In the 1966 summary, three studies of children aged 3–6 reported greater curiosity in boys, and one study with children aged 9–11 reported no difference. The more recent work shows that under age 3, the sexes are quite similar in their willingness to explore a novel environment. In the age range 3–6, there is a clear trend for boys to show more curiosity and exploratory behavior, although there are several studies finding no difference at this age. For later childhood, the amount of research is limited; some studies show higher scores for boys, some for girls, and some no difference. It appears, then, that there is a tendency for boys to do more exploring and show more interest in novelty, but that this is true only for a fairly narrow age range —the preschool and kindergarten years. The reader may recall that this is the age at which boys were found to be more "impulsive," in the sense that

TABLE 4.5
Curiosity and Exploration

Study	Age and N	Difference	Comment
Rubenstein 1967	6 mos (44)	None	Exploratory visual behavior
Rheingold & Samuels 1969	10 mos (20)	None	Exploratory behavior (mother present)
H. Ross et al. 1972	11-12 mos (8m, 4f)	None	Exploration: novel toy and room
Finley & Layne 1969	1-3 (96)	None	Visual exploration (Indian, white)
Marvin 1971	2 (16)	Girls	"Strange situation": manipulatory exploration; visual exploration (mother-absent episodes only)
		None	Locomotor exploration
	3 (16)	None	Locomotor, manipulatory, and visual exploration
	4 (16)	Boys	Manipulatory exploration; visual exploration (Mo's first departure)
		None	Locomotor exploration
Baumrind & Black 1967	3-4 (103)	Boys	Observer ratings: exploration of environment
		None	Observer ratings: curiosity, enjoyment of new learning experiences
L. Harris 1965	3-4 (32)	Girls	Choice of novel vs. familiar toy
	4-5 (32)	None	Choice of novel vs. familiar toy
Hutt 1970	3-4 (59)	Boys	Exploration in presence of novel toy
		None	Number of manipulations of novel toy, first day
Shipman 1971	3-4 (1,445)	Boys	Choice of unknown (concealed) toy over known (visible) toy
Daehler 1970	4-6 (160)	Boys	Investigatory responses in discrimination task
Yando et al. 1971	8 (144)	Girls	Curiosity: choice of unknown vs. known picture (black)
		None	Curiosity (white)
Maw & Maw 1965	10-11 (914)	Boys	Questionnaire of activity preferences; selection of "outgoing, investigatory activities," 3 studies
Walberg 1969	16-17 (450)	Girls	Greater preference for new, different activities (high school physics students)

they were less able than girls to wait for a delayed, more attractive reward (compared to accepting a smaller immediate reward; see Chapter 3). This is also the age at which sex differences in activity level have most frequently been detected. The relatively uninhibited behavior of the male preschooler, then, has fairly wide implications and affects some aspects of what might be called achievement behavior. It is an open question, however, whether interest in novel stimuli of the sort implied in the boy's free-ranging activity from age 3 to 6 may properly be considered part of what is usually meant by "task orientation." Apart from this rather narrow age period, the sexes are seen in Tables 4.4 and 4.5 to be much alike in their degree of task orientation and task persistence. We do not see any evidence that would lead to the conclusion that boys are any more intrinsically interested in tasks than girls are.

Emmerich (1971 and personal communications) provides some interesting insights into task orientation in young children. Working with large groups of children in Head Start classes, with repeated behavior observations over a year's time, he obtained large numbers of behavioral measures and factor-analyzed them. He identified three dimensions, one of which he labeled *task orientation* vs. *person orientation*. The cluster of behaviors that characterized the task-oriented children, according to Emmerich, represents "autonomous achievement strivings in which social responses are subordinated to individualized, task-oriented goals." Task-oriented children are quite capable of being social, he says. However, they direct more of their social responses to adults; that is, they are likely to ask them for information and task-related help. "By contrast, the second cluster reflects affiliative tendencies toward peers in which task requirements and individual achievements are subordinated to interaction processes and goals." In Emmerich's sample of preschool-aged children, girls were more often found at the task-oriented end of this dimension. Emmerich notes, however, that there are some developmental trends complicating the picture. The younger, more immature children tend not to be either very task-oriented or very person-oriented—they are more withdrawn and inactive. The oldest, most mature children tend to be *both* person-oriented and task-oriented. It is only in the middle range of age and competency that the dimension becomes bipolar and differentiates the sexes. It is as though there is a point in development where the child cannot take on both kinds of tasks simultaneously; at this point (at least in Emmerich's sample) girls tend to concentrate on task-related activities (including using adults as resources for help in these activities), whereas boys concentrate on social interaction with peers. But with increasing competence, both sexes can handle both kinds of activities. Thus sex differences, when they appear, should be age-specific and transitory. Table 4.4 would certainly sustain the view that any sex differences in task involvement are transitory. However, the table does not point to any particular age where a sex difference emerges across different populations and different measures.

"Person orientation" can be considered independently of whether it is differentiated from "task orientation." As Emmerich has pointed out, they may occur together. Is there any solid evidence that girls are more "person-oriented"? Elsewhere (Chapter 6) we review the research on sensitivity to the cues signifying the needs and emotional states of others and do not find that girls are more "empathic" than boys in this sense. Another approach to the issue is to ask whether, and how, an individual's behavior is affected by the presence of other people. We show (in Chapter 6) that a boy's activity level tends to change when he is with a play group, as compared to when he is alone, while there is no such change for girls. Ryan and Strawbridge (1969) report an experiment involving lever pulling, where boys pulled the lever faster when they were alternating on the task with another boy than when the other boy was merely standing and watching; there was no such effect for girls. McManis (1965) found that boys persist longer at a pursuit-rotor task when another boy is present than when only the experimenter is watching the performance; again, no such effect was found for girls.

Horner (1970), working with college-age subjects, found that men performed better on a task when being observed by peers, whereas for women observation by a peer made no difference in performance. Meddock et al. (1971), on the other hand, found that the effect of presence or absence of an *adult* experimenter during a child's performance on a marble-dropping task did not differ for boy and girl subjects. Thus, it appears that boys are more "person-oriented" only in the sense that they are more influenced by the presence and actions of a *peer*; neither sex seems to be more person-oriented in the sense of being more influenced by the presence or actions of an adult.

This latter possibility can be approached in a different way. Many studies of learning have compared the effectiveness of different reinforcement conditions. In some studies, social reinforcement has been contrasted with material rewards (e.g. candy); in others, positive reinforcement for correct responses has been compared with negative reinforcement for incorrect responses; in still other studies, verbal feedback from the experimenter has been compared with nonverbal (e.g. buzzer), to signal whether a response was correct. And still another design is to compare reinforcement from a liked vs. disliked person. Presumably, a person-oriented subject would find social reinforcement more effective than nonsocial; it is difficult to predict whether positive vs. negative reactions would have a greater impact on such a person, but it is reasonable to expect that verbal feedback would be more effective than nonverbal (nonhuman) information feedback, and that performance would be more affected (for a person-oriented subject) by whether the person delivering the reinforcement is liked or disliked. Table 4.5 shows a large number of studies in which these various comparisons of reinforcement conditions have been made. Of course, many of the studies had positive results in showing that one reinforcement condition was more effective than another across all subjects; but Table 4.6 documents a remarkable unanimity with respect to sex: girls are no more affected than

TABLE 4.6
Sensitivity to Social Reinforcement

Study	Age and N	Difference	Comment
Quay 1971	3-5 (100)	None	Praise or candy in giving Stanford-Binet (black)
K. Hill & Watts 1971	4 (48)	None	Change of preference in response to social reinforcement or nonreinforcement (2-choice learning task)
Meddock et al. 1971	4-5 (64)	None	Supportive or unresponsive E (marble-dropping task)
Spence 1972	4-5 (200)	None	Nonverbal or verbal reward or punishment in picture discrimination task
Crowder & Hohle 1970	5 (64)	None	Praise or information feedback in time estimation task
R. Brooks et al. 1969	5-6 (80)	None	Positive words stated with positive or neutral inflection (marble task)
	5-6 (168)	None	Positive or negative words stated with positive, neutral, or negative inflection (marble task)
Unikel et al. 1969	5-6 (144)	None	Tangible, social, or no reward (discrimination-learning task, low SES)
Yando & Zigler 1971	5-6, 9-10 (192)	None	Imitation of designs projected on screen or drawn by E (normal, retardates)
J. Todd & Nakamura 1970	5-7 (54)	None	Marble sorting in response to positive vs. negative tone of voice, social vs. nonsocial feedback
	6-7 (48)	None	Bead sorting in response to social vs. nonsocial feedback
H. Leventhal & Fischer 1970	5-9 (96)	None	Positive or no reinforcement from E: hole preference, marble insertion rate in marble game
Unruh et al. 1971	6-8 (144)	Boys	Tendency to play marble game longer with social reinforcement
S. Allen et al. 1971	6-7, 10-11 (192)	None	2-choice discrimination task under approval, disapproval, or silence
Spear & Spear 1972	6-7 10-11 (192)	None	Praise, criticism, or silence in discrimination task
Berkowitz et al. 1965	7 (240)	None	Persistence in marble task with intermittent verbal praise
Zimmerman 1972	7 (36)	None	Question-asking training, using praise and no-praise (Mexican-American)
Patterson 1965	7-9 (60)	None	Social disapproval from father or mother in marble game
Babad 1972	8 (40)	Girls	More responsive to deprivation of social reinforcement
Pawlicki 1972	8 (170)	Boys	Contingency and supportiveness of comments influencing performance (marble game)
Zigler & Balla 1972	8, 11 (50)	None	Persistence in marble game with verbal or nonverbal reinforcement (normal, retardates)

(continued)

TABLE 4.6 *(cont.)*

Study	Age and N	Difference	Comment
Montanelli & Hill 1969	10 (108)	None	Change in achievement expectancies or response rates after praise, criticism, or no reaction
McManis 1965	10-13 (96)	None	Performance on pursuit-rotor task under 4 verbal-incentive conditions: neutral, reproof, praise, or competition (normal, retardates)
A. Lott & Lott 1969	14 (100)	None	Performance in visual discrimination task when reinforced by photo of liked, neutrally-regarded, or disliked peer or by card printed with the word "right"
Deci 1972	18-21 (96)	Men	Trend ($p < .07$): spent less time in puzzle task after no verbal reinforcement
		None	Time spent working on puzzle after receipt of verbal reinforcement

boys by social (as compared with nonsocial) reinforcement; and they are not more sensitive to the affective overtones of the feedback provided by an experimenter. Furthermore, neither sex is more influenced by information about the correctness of a response, as distinct from praise. Thus, once more, the hypothesis that boys are task-oriented and girls are person-oriented is not supported.

In previous discussions of this issue, evidence for a linkage between social motives and academic achievement has been sought in correlations between measures of affiliation needs and achievement scores. P. S. Sears (1963)[a] found a significant correlation of .31 between need affiliation (as measured by the TAT) and a composite academic achievement score among fifth- and sixth-grade girls. The correlation for boys was not significant and is not reported; we do not know whether it was significantly different from the girls' correlation, and thus it is not clear whether the finding embodies a sex difference. We have not located other evidence concerning the relationship between social motives and academic performance in the two sexes, and it must remain an open question whether this linkage is stronger in one sex than in the other.

The hypotheses with which this chapter began have not stood up well to the test of accumulated evidence. Males do not appear to have generally greater achievement motivation, although they may show more arousal of this motivation under directly competitive conditions. The task-orientation vs. person-orientation distinction seems to be a poor one from the standpoint of understanding achievement motivation in the two sexes. Boys' greater responsiveness to competitive conditions, and their greater output of energy on a task in the presence of peers, suggest a high degree of person orientation in boys, just as the effectiveness of the "social acceptability" arousal suggests person orientation in girls.

It can hardly be doubted that male adolescents and college students have somewhat different life goals, on the average, than females of the same age. Both have a certain awareness of the kinds of occupations they may realistically hope to enter. Looft (1971), presenting his findings from a study of the vocational aspirations of the two sexes, discusses this point in the following terms: "That girls learn very early the societal expectation for them was perhaps captured most poignantly by the expression of that single girl who initially said she wished to be a doctor when she grew up; when asked what occupation she *really* expected to hold in adulthood, she resignedly replied, 'I'll probably have to be something else, maybe a store lady.' "

So far the impact (if any) of the differences in ultimate occupational goals has not been adequately described; the fact remains that during the long, formative years of schooling, the two sexes have much the same tasks before them and much the same orientation toward achieving on these particular tasks. Do girls' realistic appraisals of their own vocational chances in the present adult society have an impact upon their achievement motivations—and if so, at what point? To understand why this question is difficult to answer, we must return for a moment to the question of the way achievement motivation is measured and what it means. The n Ach measures have been validated in the sense (1) that a correlation has been found between the amount of TAT achievement imagery and performance on selected tasks and (2) that the score is responsive to achievement-oriented "arousal" conditions. It would be unwise, however, to equate the projective measure with the subject's own real-life achievement motivation. Subjects may differ in how thoroughly they project themselves into the storied characters; furthermore the stimulus pictures must necessarily constitute a very limited representation of real-life situations in which achievement strivings might occur. We have not been able to document a sex difference in achievement motivation, as measured in n Ach tests, but it still remains true that in adulthood the achievements of women, in terms of the kind of "success" the world values, are less than those of men. Although the work achievements of the average man spending his life in an average eight-to-four or nine-to-five job may not be especially impressive, a high proportion of the very high achievers in business, science, and the arts are men. We turn now to studies of self-concept, to see whether these post school differences can be traced to any differences in the self-confidence or self-definition of the two sexes.

SELF-CONCEPT

As we have seen, there is some evidence that boys' achievement motivation may be sustained or even stimulated by competitive conditions, whereas girls react in an opposite way. If girls are indeed more vulnerable to competition, is this linked in any way to lack of confidence in their own abilities? Do they suffer from any generalized lack of self-esteem that affects their motivation to achieve a standard of excellence in the tasks they undertake? We shall begin with the question of generalized self-esteem.

When either men or women are asked to rate qualities they associate with an ideal male, they rate them higher than qualities they associate with an ideal female (Rosenkrantz et al. 1968[R]). Both men and women, describing people who succeed in academic settings, depict painful and embarrassing things happening to successful women, good things happening to successful men (Monahan et al. 1974). Both men and women, and high school boys and girls, devalue work labeled as done by women over the same work labeled as normally done by men (H. Mischel 1974[R]). Surely women, knowing that they belong to a sex that is devalued in these and other ways and sharing these values, must have a poor opinion of themselves. We would expect to be able to conclude, with Bardwick, that "women have lower self-esteem than men" (1971, p. 155)[R].

Much research has dealt directly with the question of how people feel about themselves. This question has been approached directly through questionnaires and self-administered scales. It has also been approached indirectly through projective measures, such as the one developed by Brown,* in which the experimenter takes a Polaroid snapshot of the subject child and then asks each subject how the child shown in his own picture feels about his appearance, his academic abilities, his skill in sports, etc. Other studies use ratings made by teachers or other observers, reporting the degree of self-confidence the child seems to display. The majority of studies summarized in Table 4.7 have used self-ratings on standardized self-esteem scales. In such studies, sex differences are seldom found; in the studies that do report a difference, it is as often girls as boys who receive higher average scores. It will be shown in Chapter 5 that girls are somewhat more willing than boys to disclose their weaknesses. Boys obtain higher scores on "lie" scales and "defensiveness" scales that are designed to measure the degree to which an individual disguises his actual evaluation of himself and attempts to present an entirely favorable picture of himself to the researcher. If boys are presenting a more glowing picture of themselves in self-concept inventories than they really feel to be justified, then their scores should actually be somewhat lower than those reported in Table 4.7, and the sex difference would shift in favor of girls' having higher self-esteem.

Studies in which children's self-esteem or self-confidence has been rated by others have had mixed results. Parent ratings of sons do not differ from their ratings of daughters in this respect (Shrader and Leventhal 1968). Teachers sometimes rate girls as having higher self-esteem, even though

* B. R. Brown, Department of Psychology, Cornell University.

TABLE 4.7
Self-Esteem

Study	Age and N	Difference	Comment
Baumrind & Black 1967	3-4 (103)	None	Observer ratings: valuing of self
Shipman 1971	3-4 (1,371)	None	Self-esteem—preschool form of Children's Self-Social Constructs Test (black and white subsample)
Goldschmid 1968	6-7 (81)	None	Ratings of actual and ideal self
Klaus & Gray 1968	6-7 (80)	None	Self-Concept Scale (low SES black; longitudinal)
B. Long et al. 1967	6-13 (312)	None	Self-esteem on Children's Self-Social Constructs Test
Shrader & Leventhal 1968	6-17 (599)	None	Parents' reports of child's self-feelings
Carpenter & Busse 1969	6, 10 (80)	Boys None	Higher self-concept (black subsample) Self-concept (white subsample)
Lepper 1973	7 (129)	None	Negative or positive self-ratings
S. Harris & Braun 1971	7-8 (60)	None	Piers-Harris Self-Concept Test (black)
Herbert et al. 1969	9 (40)	Boys None	Higher self-esteem ratings on Sears Self-Concept Inventory Bledsoe-Garrison Self-Concept Inventory
Bledsoe 1961	9-12 (197)	Girls	Attributed more assets, fewer liabilities to self (elementary form of mental health analysis)
Amatora 1955	9-13 (1,000)	Girls	Higher self-esteem (teacher ratings)
Bledsoe 1967	9, 11 (271)	Girls	More positive self-concepts (adjective checklist)
Coopersmith 1967	10-11 (1,748)	Girls None	Higher self-esteem (teacher ratings) Self-reports of self-esteem
Lekarczyk & Hill 1969	10-11 (114)	None	Revised Coopersmith Self-Esteem Inventory
Coopersmith 1959	10-12 (87)	Girls None	Higher teacher ratings of self-esteem Self-esteem inventory
Carlson 1965	11, 17 (49)	None	Level or stability of self-esteem (longitudinal)
Nawas 1971	18 (125) 26 (125)	Women Men	Ego sufficiency and complexity scores (projective test; longitudinal) Ego sufficiency and complexity scores
Jacobson et al. 1969	18-21 (276)	None	Self-esteem as measured by discrepancy between level of aspiration and expectancy of success
Koenig 1966	18-21 (40)	None	Positive or negative statements about academic self
Nisbett & Gordon 1967	18-21 (152)	None	2 measures of self-esteem

(continued)

TABLE 4.7 *(cont.)*

Study	Age and N	Difference	Comment
Sarason & Koenig 1965	18-21 (48)	Women	More positive self-references (academic self-description)
		None	General description of self
Sarason & Winkel 1966	18-21 (48)	Men	Fewer negative self-references
		None	Positive or ambiguous references
I. Silverman et al. 1970	18-21 (98)	None	Percentage of favorable adjectives checked about self (Gough and Heilbrun's Adjective Checklist)
P. Skolnick 1971	18-21 (114)	None	Level of self-esteem as assessed by questionnaire and self-rating on semantic differential after receiving positive or negative evaluation from confederate
Zander et al. 1972	18-21 (88)	Men	Higher pride-in-self ratings
Bortner & Hultsch 1972	20-88 (1,292)	None	Rating of present status with respect to rating of past status; rating of future status with respect to rating of present status
Kaplan 1973	21 & over (500)	Men	Lower self-derogation scores (subsample of white Ss without a college education)
		Women	Lower self-derogation scores (subsample of black Ss with a high school education or better)
		None	Self-derogation on rating scale (black, white)
Goldrich 1967	25-40 (80)	Women	More optimistic about future professional life, future interpersonal relations, and future self-evaluations
Schaie & Strother 1968	70-88 (50)	None	Burgess Scale of happiness, self-ratings of accomplishments (retired academic and professional workers)

the same boys and girls do not differ when asked to rate themselves (Coopersmith 1959, 1967).

The similarity of the two sexes in self-esteem is remarkably uniform across age levels through college age. We have been able to locate only two studies using post-college subjects. In a study of graduate students, Goldrich (1967) found higher feelings of optimism in women aged 25 to 40, both about their future careers and about their lives in general. In a study of retired professionals, no differences were found in self-ratings or happiness ratings. There are a few discordant notes in the self-esteem picture for women, however. In preliminary inspection of data, to be reported later, on the most recent follow-up of Terman's sample of gifted children, P. S. Sears and M. H. Odom (personal communication, 1974) find that in later middle age women who were gifted as children feel more bitterness and disappointment about their lives than do men who were similarly gifted in childhood. The men, by and large, have had considerably more "successful" lives in terms of personal achievements outside the domestic sphere, and the women tend to look back with some regret on what they now see as missed opportunities. There are two other much smaller-scale longitudinal studies in which measures of self-esteem have been taken. Nawas (1971) reports that among a group studied at age 18 and again at 26, women subjects showed a decrease in ego-sufficiency and complexity scores, whereas men increased in these respects. Engel (1959), working with adolescents, did not find a decrease in self-esteem for either sex over a two-year period. In a study with young adults, Bortner and Hultsch (1972) determined their subjects' current level of self-satisfaction, and then asked them to look back to a period five years earlier and recall how happy they had been with their accomplishments and adjustment to life at that time; the sexes were similar in their self-views, and neither sex reported a loss in self-satisfaction over this time span. Clearly, we do not yet have a consistent picture of how the sexes compare in their self-satisfaction through the adult years. Much must depend on their early-developed talents, on the quality of their marriages, and on the nature of their adult occupations, as well as on wide-impact societal changes (such as depression, war, and technological "progress") that affect the quality of life differently for different generations and different sexes.

So far the work we have summarized on self-concept indicates that when males and females are asked to rate themselves on a series of characteristics, they have equally positive (or negative) self-images, on the whole. One might conclude from this that the two sexes would approach a variety of tasks with equal confidence, but this inference does not prove to be warranted. For example, Carey (1958) found that male college students had a more positive attitude toward problem solving than did female college students. Although almost all the work on self-concept up to college age involves self-ratings, an additional measure of self-esteem has been used with college students. Subjects are asked to participate in a task (or sometimes *imagine* performing a task); they are then asked to predict how well they will do, or following the performance, to describe their satisfaction or pride in their performance. The tasks are sometimes contrived so that a subject's performance is clearly inferior or superior, in terms of some stated norm. Studies asking for confidence measures are summarized in Table 4.8. Clearly, college men are more likely than college women to expect to do well, and to judge their own performance favorably once they have finished their work. Some of the tasks involved are ones in which men characteristically *do* do better (such as work with geometric figures); but many are not. Anagrams are a case in point. Also, women get at least as good grades as men, and often better; yet, when asked what grades they think they will get at the next grading period, men are optimistic in the sense that they think they will do at least as well, and perhaps better, than they have been doing, whereas women are more likely to predict that they will do less well than their past performance would indicate (V. C. Crandall 1969).

There are several possible reasons why women, even though they feel generally as comfortable as men about their own value and competence in the life situations in which they find themselves, should nevertheless express less self-confidence about how they will perform on tasks they are about to undertake. The simplest explanation is that they are more hesitant about bragging, so that though they really feel self-confident they do not say so. However, the confidence measures shown in Table 4.8 are all private (paper and pencil), so no overt bragging is involved. It is difficult to see why reluctance to report favorable things about themselves should affect their task confidence more than their answers to a self-esteem questionnaire.

An obvious possibility is that women do not define themselves in terms of success on these kinds of tasks, and are willing to accept a wider range

TABLE 4.8
Confidence in Task Performance

Study	Age and N	Difference	Comment
V. C. Crandall 1969	7-12 (41)	Boys	Expectancy of success on 6 tasks
	18-22 (380)	Men	Expected grades in relation to past academic record
	18-26 (41)	Men	Expectancy of success on task requiring recall and reproduction of geometric patterns
Montanelli & Hill 1969	10 (108)	Boys	Higher initial expectancy of task success (marble-dropping game)
Battle 1966	12-14 (500)	None	Certainty of reaching minimal goals of school performance in math
Rychlak & Lerner 1965	18-20 (40)	Men	Higher initial expectancy of success on manual dexterity task
Feather 1967b	18-21 (76)	None	Estimate of probability of success on task described as involving luck or skill
Feather 1968	18-21 (60)	Men	Confidence in predicting own performance on anagrams task
Feather 1969b	18-21 (167)	Men	Confidence in predicting own performance, anagrams
Feather & Simon 1971	18-21 (128)	None	Confidence in predicting own performance, anagrams
Jacobson et al. 1970	18-21 (276)	Men	Expectancy of success on the Digit Symbol Test
Julian et al. 1968	18-21 (240)	Men	Confidence in own judgments of timing of light flashes, Asch-type social-influence situation
G. Leventhal & Lane 1970	18-21 (61)	Men	Agree in judging own performance superior when performance is contrived to be superior to partner's
		None	In S's judgments when performance is contrived to be inferior to partner's
S. Schwartz & Clausen 1970	18-21 (179)	Men	Express less uncertainty about what to do in helping with a simulated seizure

of performance as being consistent with a favorable self-image. There is evidence that women are more acceptant of others, despite any weaknesses they may have (Berger 1955[R], Zuckerman et al. 1956[R]), and they may have a similarly more tolerant attitude toward their own performance. Another way of putting this is to say that their aspirations are lower. We have reservations about this hypothesis, in view of the work on achievement motivation discussed above. Girls *do* seem to apply high standards to their own work in the intellectual-academic sphere. Nevertheless, there may be some differences in what aspects of life are deemed important that permit women to feel successful privately, even though they are not seen to be so in the eyes of the world.

TABLE 4.9

Internal Locus of Control

Study	Age and N	Difference	Comment
V. C. Crandall & Lacey 1972	6-12 (50)	None	Intellectual Achievement Responsibility (IAR) Scale
MacMillan & Keogh 1971b	8 (120)	None	Placing blame for interruption of task (normal and retarded subsample)
Walls & Cox 1971	8-9 (80)	None	Internal-External (I-E) Locus of Control Scale (non-disadvantaged)
		Boys	Internal locus (disadvantaged)
V. C. Crandall et al. 1965b	8-10 11, 13, 15, 17 (923)	None Girls	IAR Scale Internal locus (IAR Scale)
O. Solomon et al. 1969	9, 11 (262)	Girls	Acceptance of responsibility for achievement efforts and internal responsibility score (white subsample only)
Dweck & Reppucci 1973	10 (40)	None	Internal locus (IAR Scale)
MacMillan & Keogh 1971a	11 (60)	None	Placing blame for interruption of task
M. Buck & Austrin 1971	14-16 (100)	Girls None	Internal locus (IAR Scale) (adequate-achiever subsample, black) IAR Scale (underachiever subsample, black)
Zytkoskee et al. 1971	14-17 (132)	None	Bialer Locus of Control Scale (black and white)
Benton et al. 1969	18-21 (80)	Men	More self-attribution of responsibility for scores in task (in 1 of 4 conditions only)
Branningan & Tolor 1971	18-21 (333)	Men	Internal score on Rotter I-E Scale
Feather 1969b	18-21 (167)	Men	Internal attribution of performance on anagrams task
Levy et al. 1972	18-21 (110)	None	Rotter I-E Control Scale
Pallak et al. 1967	18-21 (39)	None	Perceived choice in leaving boring task

Another possible reason why women may lack confidence in their performance on a forthcoming task is that they feel less in a position to bring about the ends they strive for—are less in control of their own fates. In recent years, measures have been developed for the "locus of control," and individuals may be characterized on whether they normally feel that the events affecting them are the result of luck or chance (externalizers), or whether they feel that they can control their lives through their own actions (internalizers). As may be seen from Table 4.9, the sexes do not differ consistently on these scales through the grade school and high school years, but in college there is a trend for women to be externalizers. That is, they believe their achievements are often due to factors other than their own skills and hard work.

The greater power of the male to control his own destiny is part of the cultural stereotype of maleness, and is inherent in the images of the two sexes portrayed on television and in print. For example, in a recent study of stories in elementary school textbooks, Jacklin and Mischel (1973[R]) found that when good things happened to a male character in a story, they were presented as resulting from his own actions. Good things happening to a female character (of which there were considerable fewer) were at the initiative of others, or simply grew out of the situation in which the girl character found herself. It is not surprising, then, that young women should be externalizers, by reason of cultural shaping if for no other reason. What is surprising is that the sex difference in this scale does not emerge earlier in life.

In fact, a greater sense of personal strength and potency does emerge among males during the grade school years, if one takes a broader definition than merely the locus-of-control measures. Table 4.10 summarizes a series of studies in which children have been asked to assess their own strength, dominance, or power. Boys and men clearly see themselves as higher on these dimensions. The work on the actual occurrence of dominant behavior of the two sexes is described elsewhere (Chapter 7). For our present purposes, the point of interest is how the sexes perceive themselves, rather than how they actually behave. Omark et al. (1973), using peer ratings to determine a "toughness" hierarchy in a large number of classrooms in several societies, found that boys overestimated their own position in this hierarchy more often than girls did. A boy's position in the dominance hierarchy is a salient aspect of life to him. A girl is normally less concerned about it. But having less feeling of dominance and power might clearly affect a girl's self-confidence in undertaking a task, particularly if she thought she might have to defend her problem solutions in any way.

A boy's tendency to look on the bright side of his own abilities is not confined to the dominance sphere, however. Even with respect to social sensitivity—a presumedly feminine trait—young men seem not to "hear"

TABLE 4.10
Self-Concept: Strength and Potency

Study	Age and N	Difference	Comment
B. Long et al. 1968	6-13 (312)	Boys	Rated self higher on power scale
Fleming & Anttonen 1971	7 (1,087)	Boys	Potency scale on semantic differential self-concept measure
Goss 1968	8 11, 14, 17 (192)	None Boys	Self-ratings of physical strength Self-ratings of physical strength (multiracial)
McDonald 1968	17 (528)	Boys	Described self as higher on dominance (black and white)
Benton et al. 1969	18-21 (80)	Men	Expressed greater feeling of power in contrived role and rated same-sex partner as more powerful
Kurtz 1971	18-21 (40)	Men	Higher potency score on Body Attitude Scale
Cameron 1970b	Adults (317)	Men	Judged self as more powerful and wealthy

comments to the effect that they are insensitive, and their self-ratings of sensitivity are scarcely affected by negative feedback (Eagly and Whitehead 1972), whereas they do react with improved self-ratings to positive information about their social sensitivity. Young women are responsive to both kinds of information. If this male selective filter operates across a fairly wide range of behaviors, it might help to explain men's greater feeling of potency.

So far, we have found that there is no overall difference between the sexes in self-esteem, but there is a "male cluster" among college students made up of greater self-confidence when undertaking new tasks, and a greater sense of potency, specifically including the feeling that one is in a position to determine the outcomes of sequences of events that one participates in. Is there a "female cluster"? Table 4.11 suggests that there may be one, although the area is amorphous. A number of the studies cited here have used the Carlson adjective checklist. The subject is asked to choose ten adjectives that he believes describe himself, and to circle the five that are *most* descriptive. These five are then weighted more heavily in computing a subject's overall score. The adjectives are scored as either personal or social. Such characteristics as *ambitious, energetic, fair-minded, optimistic,* and *practical* are scored as "personal," while *attractive, cooperative, frank, leader, sympathetic* are coded as "social." There are five studies listed in Table 4.11 that used the Carlson method for scoring individuals on the personal and social dimensions; in four out of five of these, women subjects in late adolescence and adulthood rated themselves higher on the

TABLE 4.11
Social Self-Concept

Study	Age and N	Difference	Comment
Walker 1967	8-11 (450)	None	Socialness ratings by self and teacher
P. Katz & Zigler 1967	10 13 16 (120)	Girls Boys None	Social self rated higher Social self rated higher Ss' ratings of social self
Carlson 1965	11 17 (49)	None Girls	Self-description of social orientation Described self as more socially oriented (longitudinal)
Smart & Smart 1970	11-12 18 (267)	Girls None	More socially oriented Social orientation (Asian Indian)
McDonald 1968	17 (528)	Girls	Higher love scores on the Interpersonal checklist: described self as higher (black and white)
Carlson 1971	18-21 (76)	Women	Defined self in social terms
Carlson & Levy 1970	18-21 (202)	None	Social-personal orientation on adjective checklist (black)
Carlson & Levy 1968	18-45 (133)	Women	Defined self in terms of social experiences

social, lower on the personal, adjectives than did men of the same age. These studies reveal something about how the two sexes define themselves; but since the Carlson adjectives are all couched in positive, socially desirable terms, it is not possible to differentiate positive from negative self-images with this scale. Consistent with the Carlson studies is Walberg's finding that girl high school physics students say they have more social interests than their male counterparts. Women consider themselves socially more competent, less shy, more attractive or acceptable to others than men do. The study by McDonald (1968) does report that women believe they feel, and display, more love toward others than men do, but aside from this, our information on the social self is more a matter of definition than of self-esteem. If women do indeed invest themselves more heavily in affiliative relations with other people, it does not follow that they must have higher social self-concepts; indeed, they would be more vulnerable to self-doubt in this very area. It is also true that men's greater involvement with status and power need not imply greater general self-confidence. If they choose to compete for status, they open themselves to many opportunities for failure. There must be numerous bruised egos that are the casualties of competitive encounters. Therefore, although the two sexes may have chosen somewhat different arenas for ego investment, there is no reason to expect any overall difference in self-satisfaction, and indeed, as we have seen, none is found. However, there is some reason to believe that each sex does have a higher sense of self-worth in the area of more central ego involvement.

There is an aspect of the manifestations of self-concepts that is intriguing but hardly explored vis-à-vis sex differences: namely, ego defenses. It has been widely asserted that the "machismo" concept of the male ego is one that leads to the adoption of a variety of defenses: denial of feminine attributes, exaggeration of supermasculine behavior, etc. It seems likely that the young boy's horror of being seen playing with girls is part of this system of ego defense. We have seen that boys exaggerate their own dominance (Omark et al. 1973); also that males are less likely to take in negative feedback about their own performance (Eagly and Whitehead 1972). It is commonly believed that women are more willing to talk about themselves and their frailties—in other words, that they are less defensive about the public presentation of self—but the case is not well documented. Rivenbark (1971) does find that boys do not disclose their thoughts and personal feelings to parents and peers as readily as girls; Williams and Byars (1968) also report that boys are more defensive about whatever level of self-esteem they report than girls are; Bogo et al. (1970) find that boys defend their egos more by turning against a real or presumed external frustrating object, whereas girls engage in more self-blame. All this seems to indicate that girls are more willing to admit weakness, but there is contrary evidence in a study by Hundleby and Cattell (1968)[R], in which girls less often admitted to common frailties than did boys. It is a reasonable hypothesis, based on informal observation, that women defend their egos through dissociation—lack of commitment. They seem less likely to say "I believe" or "I want," and more likely to attribute ideas to others and say "Wouldn't you like to . . ." If an idea or proposal proves unpopular, then the initiator is in a position to dissociate herself from it. We have seen no solid evidence, however, on whether this is actually a form of self-protection more often used by women than men, so it remains hypothesis.

Before closing the discussion of self-esteem and self-definition, we would like to comment on the alleged "narcissism" of females. It is widely believed that women are more concerned than men about having an attractive appearance. Douvan and Adelson (1966)[R] and Coleman (1961)[R] have found this to be the case in adolescent samples. In our review of recent research, we have encountered very little additional evidence for or against this view, except for the isolated fact that girls and women are somewhat more likely to want orthodontic treatment (Lewit and Virolainen 1968). The popular stereotype pictures girls as spending more time in front of the mirror, taking more interest in clothes, daydreaming about being admired, etc. We have learned to be wary of stereotypes, since so many have not stood the test of careful observation. Also, this particular stereotype, if it is valid, probably reflects a sex difference that may be changing rapidly, under the impact of the unisex movement. Men now go to hair stylists and even occasionally suffer the indignities of curlers or driers to achieve the effects they want. Men's clothing styles are much more varied, more colorful, more showy than in the recent past. Still, there is some evidence to support the view that girls continue to be more interested in physical attractiveness than men and boys. Witness the fact that parents, teachers, and peers are more likely to describe girls as concerned about their looks; girls' fantasies and information also reflect this interest (Wagman 1967, Nelsen and Rosenbaum 1972).

However, lest we think of boys as being indifferent to other people's reactions, we must remember the boys' tendency to "show off." Whiting and Pope (1974), in their observations of children in a variety of cultures, recorded "attempts to call attention to oneself by boasting, or by performing either praiseworthy or blameworthy acts with the intent of becoming the focus of another person's attention." They found that boys more frequently engaged in this behavior, and that the sex difference was stronger at ages 7–11 than ages 3–6. In competitive sports, although overt "grandstanding" is frowned upon, there is certainly a large element of self-display. Of course, narcissism is defined as *self*-admiration. In private moments, is a girl more likely to admire herself in the mirror than a boy is to admire his own muscles and daydream self-admiringly about his triumphs? We do not know. We suspect that both sexes are narcissistic, but in somewhat different ways. It is the boy with the most status and power (as well as a reasonable amount of good looks) who can interest the most attractive girls. Traditionally it has been the most beautiful, alluring girl who can interest the highest-status boys. When a girl dresses in an eye-catching manner, or expends a great deal of time on her hair and makeup, she is making a statement to boys about her interest in them, as well as seeking admiration for herself. Similarly when a boy "shows off" to girls, he is signaling to them that he has status and potency; at the same time, he is certainly not free of narcissism. As we have seen, boys tend to believe that their status is greater than it is. We suggest that both sexes admire themselves at the same time that they seek admiration from others and that narcissism is a universal human frailty that is not selective as to sex, though the sexes may admire themselves for somewhat different qualities.

In sum, we have seen that the sexes are quite similar with respect to the aspects of achievement motivation for which evidence is available. They show similar degrees of task persistence. Their achievement efforts are directed toward similar goals; that is, there is no evidence that one sex works more than the other because of intrinsic interest in a task rather than for praise and approval. The two sexes give similar achievement imagery on projective tests under "arousal" conditions. There is some reason to believe that boys' achievement motivation needs to be sustained or stimulated by competitive, ego-challenging conditions, whereas girls throughout the school years seem to maintain their achievement motivation more easily without such stimulation; indeed, at certain ages they may be motivated to avoid competition.

We return to the question of why it is, if males and females have equally good intellectual potential and the two sexes are similar in their achievement motivation throughout the school years, that female achievement in other spheres than the domestic one should drop off so sharply in the years after they have finished their formal schooling. Are there any signs that can be detected earlier than this that would give us grounds for predicting a greater drop-off in women? We investigated the issue of whether there are any differences in self-concept during the school years that might constitute a basis for what happens later. We found that on most measures of self-esteem girls and women show at least as much satisfaction with themselves as do boys and men. During the college years some sex differentiation does occur. At this time, women have less confidence than men in their ability to perform well on a variety of tasks assigned to them; they have less sense of being able to control the events that affect them, and they tend to define themselves more in social terms.

Can women's lesser sense of "internal control" at college age be responsible for lack of achievement during the ensuing years? A first approach to answering this question would be to determine whether "locus of control" measures have been shown to be related to achievement. The answer complicates the picture: among children and young adults high scores on internal locus of control are positively related to school achievement in boys and men, but are unrelated, or only slightly related, in girls and women (Nowicki and Roundtree 1971, Clifford and Cleary 1972[R]). In other words, girls maintain a high level of achievement motivation during the school years whether they have a sense of personal potency or not, whereas boys require this sense for strong achievement motivation. If having a sense of personal control over important events in one's own life is irrelevant to girls' achievement in school, is it irrelevant to achievement after school? Possibly it becomes more relevant during these later years. School is a relatively structured situation, where the tasks to be accomplished are already established. Schools do offer students certain choices, but on the whole, there is an established regimen of courses to be taken and assignments to be completed. Once these tasks are laid out, the two sexes appear to be equally motivated by intrinsic interest in them. But in the post-school world perhaps it is necessary for the individual to seize more initiative in organizing the sequence of actions and events that lead to achievement, and in this situation it may be that a sense of personal potency does make a difference in the achievements of women as well as of men.

However, this is speculation. Whether or not any aspect of the self-concept of the two sexes proves to affect post-college achievement, there are many other factors that differentiate the lives of the two sexes at this point that clearly have an impact. First and foremost are the demands of the domestic duties which have traditionally fallen to women. The struggles of women who have tried to become writers in the face of the daily-life demands normally placed upon women are poignantly described by Virginia Woolf in *A Room of One's Own* (1929)[8]. Until very recently, women have seldom been allowed to be by themselves to do their own work. If a girl does not marry immediately, she is more likely than a boy to live in her parents' home, and more likely to be financially supported by her parents; boys are expected to support themselves (and later their families), which of course acts as a spur to vocational achievement. We should not forget that for many of the greatest creative geniuses (e.g. Mozart) their art was the means of earning a living, and they produced abundantly, partly because of the need to support large families and partly because they had jobs that demanded a large output of creative work. Women have seldom had this kind of pressure. Beyond this, most high-level achievement, we believe, comes as the culmination of a long period of training (perhaps including apprenticeship, as in the case of some of the great Italian painters) and ordered steps of promotion. Until recently many of the training opportunities, as well as later steps in the career ladder, have been either closed to women or considerably less open to women than to men.

We do not deny the possibility that there are certain sparks of genius (e.g. potential for mathematical insights) that may occur more frequently among men than women. But until some of the situational factors that have hindered women's nondomestic achievements come to bear more equally upon the two sexes, it is impossible to know whether the initial potential for creative genius is equal in the two sexes or not.

PART TWO

Social Behavior

We have seen that charting the domain of intellectual abilities is not a simple matter. Visual-spatial processes may or may not be involved in the solution of mathematical problems. Verbal processes mediate what are usually classified as nonverbal skills. Even so, the task of organizing the evidence on sex differences in intellectual performance was somewhat simplified by the existence of a body of empirical factor-analytic work, as well as some theorizing, on the "structure" of intellect. This work may not mesh nicely with some of the current thinking about the nature of the cognitive operations that are involved in information processing, but it does nevertheless provide some sort of rationale for topical arrangement of a report on sex differences.

The difficulties of organization are infinitely greater in social behavior. The factorial structure of social behavior has not been clearly delineated —perhaps cannot be. Empirical clusterings change with age, and very probably with the settings in which behavior is observed. The social behaviors that correlate with one another, and that seem to be linked in the sense that they are responsive to similar arousal or eliciting conditions, do not correspond well with the clusters that would be expected on the basis of traditional motivational theories (see Sears et al. 1965^{a}). It is sometimes argued that the reason for this disappointing outcome is that we cannot observe motives, only behavior. With this caveat in mind, many social and developmental psychologists have turned to a strategy of identifying a class of behaviors that appears to be behaviorally definable, then searching for the situational or motivational conditions governing the occurrence of these behaviors. The strategy has not always succeeded in avoiding the quicksands of imputing motives to human actions, however. A researcher may set out to study "altruism," for example, or more narrowly "helping behavior," but he will hesitate to classify a person's action in helping someone as altruism if he knows that the actor was attempting to win the con-

fidence of the other person for purposes of future exploitation. Such an action would be referred to the student of Machiavellianism.

We shall attempt, here, to restrict our classifications to the behavioral level, while recognizing that assumptions about needs and motives will influence our decisions about what behaviors "go together" in many instances. We must also deal with the problem of "levels" of explanation. Suppose it should prove true that children of one sex are more likely than those of the other to cry when the mother or father leaves them alone. Are these children more "attached" to the parent or more frightened of being alone? Or do they show more intense attachment behavior because they become frightened more easily? We have encountered frequent instances in which sex differences at an overt level of behavior are attributed to dispositions that are thought to underlie them.

In the chapters that follow, we have attempted first to lay a groundwork by exploring any differences in "temperament" between the sexes (Chapter 5). In Chapter 6 we take up the approach-avoidance dimension of social behavior—the tendency of the individual to seek, or to avoid, contact with other human beings. Included here are the studies of attachment, affiliation, "sociability," empathy, interest in others, nurturance, and altruism, the last two on the grounds that being helpful to another both expresses an attraction and strengthens an affiliative bond. Chapter 7 addresses roughly the cluster of behaviors that deal with power relationships among people—aggression, competition, dominance, compliance, and conformity.

A theme that runs through all three of these chapters on social behavior is the question whether females are in any sense more "passive" than males. Before taking up the specific topics to be discussed, let us first consider what the term passivity means and how it relates to each of the subject-matter areas covered in Chapters 5–7. Some years ago, Helene Deutsch stated the then-current psychoanalytic position as follows (Psychology of Women, 1944, pp. 220ff)[R]: "If the sexual 'passivity' of the female is generally regarded as typical, it still remains to be seen to what extent other non-sexual manifestations of women's life are patterned after this behavior. The theory I have long supported—according to which femininity is largely associated with passivity and masochism—has been confirmed in the course of years by clinical experience. . . . While fully recognizing that women's position is subjected to external influence, I venture to say that the fundamental identities 'feminine passive' and 'masculine active' assert themselves in all known cultures and races."

What precisely is implied in the assertion that females are more passive than males? In some instances the term refers explicitly to the amount of

bodily movement. In other instances the term is seen as reflecting the ac-
tions and postures of the two sexes during sexual intercourse: the female
is receptive, the male is intrusive; the male is said to be the actor, the
female is acted upon. The passivity of the female is thought to show itself
in a variety of somewhat more attenuated forms, however, allegedly in-
cluding:

1. Submissiveness. The female is thought to invite, or allow, the male to
dominate her. In interactions between the sexes, the male is more likely
to initiate interactions, the female to respond.

2. Lack of aggression. The female withdraws from attack rather than
launching a counterattack, and does not initiate aggressive interactions as
frequently as the male.

3. Dependency. The female is more likely to ask for help, or to cling to
others in the face of threat or challenge, while the male engages in active
problem solving with or without the mediation of others.

4. By extension, the female finds security in the company of others and
is therefore more "social" than the male—more oriented toward social
stimulation, more responsive to social reinforcement or the danger of losing
social approval, more likely to seek proximity to others rather than working
or playing independently.

If the female does indeed submit to dominance attempts, withdraw from
threats, and cling to others under stress, this might mean that the female
is basically more timid, more easily frightened, than the male. Fear is an
arousal state, and although it may be confusing to link it with passivity,
the possibility exists that females show immobilization and other "passive"
behavior primarily when they are afraid. We begin Chapter 5 by discussing
activity level and other manifestations of "arousal" states; we then take up
the evidence on the relative timidity of the two sexes.

CHAPTER FIVE

Temperament: Activity Level and Emotionality

ACTIVITY LEVEL

Activity level can be measured in a variety of ways. The traditional method involves the use of a "stabilimeter," which records a shift of weight on different parts of the floor of an animal's cage, or in different portions of an infant's crib or playpen. A method more widely used in recent years involves an observer's recording, either from films or live as the child moves about his environment, of the distance covered per unit time or the number and vigor (or extension) of bodily movements of predetermined kinds. We shall first summarize the animal studies that have been done using measures of these kinds, and then turn to the studies of human children.

Female rats in an activity cage are considerably more active than males (Brody 1942[R]). Most studies have also shown that normal female rats and mice are more active than males in an open-field situation (Gray and Levine 1964[R], Furchgott and Lazar 1969[R], Barrett and Ray 1970[R])—they cross more segments of the floor per unit time. An exception is the work of Wild and Hughes (1972)[R], who did not find a sex difference among rats' activity in exploring a novel space. Administration of male hormones to females neonatally reduces their open-field activity at a later age (Gray et al. 1965[R]). Thus, in the rat, sex differences in activity run counter to what might have been expected, and female sex hormones are associated with high activity levels, male with low.

What about animals closer to man? Harlow reported (1962)[R] that young males engaged in more rough-and-tumble play, whereas females tended to withdraw to the periphery of the play group. Subsequent work (Young et al. 1964[R]) indicates that infant female monkeys, whose mothers have been given injections of male hormones just before the infant's birth, are masculine in a number of respects, including certain aspects of play behavior. Specifically, they engage in more mutual threats and more rough-and-tumble play, and thus they are similar to the normal males that Harlow described. But activity level per se was not measured in these studies. In a recent study with monkeys, Jensen and his colleagues (Jensen et al. 1968[R]) did measure activity. They found that monkey mothers push their male infants away earlier than they do their female infants—perhaps because male infants bite their mothers more and hence are less comfortable to hold (Mitchell 1968[R]). But despite the greater separation from their mothers' bodies, the male infants in the Jensen study were not more active, although the experimenters expected they would be. Preston et al. (1970)[R], working with 7-month-old patas monkeys, also did not find a sex difference in movement in the cage prior to, during, or following separation from the mother.

Sackett (1971)[R], in a study of the effects of early social deprivation on later behavior, tested monkeys at the ages of 4 and 7 years. For our present purposes, the groups of interest are the two control groups—the animals that spent their infancy in a wild (natural) environment, and those born in captivity that were raised with live mothers and peers—in short, those animals that experienced no early social deprivation and that showed normal patterns of social behavior and exploration in adulthood. Among these animals, there were no sex differences in the activity level, as measured by the amount of time spent moving about a test cage. (Females were more active among the socially deprived animals, a fact that Sackett interprets as an indication of greater male vulnerability to depriving environments.)

Mitchell and Brandt (1970)[R], however, observed mother-infant pairs of rhesus monkeys in one side of a cage with another mother-infant pair in the other side; the two pairs were separated by a transparent panel, so they could see but not touch one another. Male infants in this situation climbed longer, ran-jumped more than female infants, and interacted more with the other infant (as far as this was possible) by play-imitating and threatening the other infant. The presence of another infant does appear to stimulate a male monkey infant to greater activity than a female, as part of the rough-and-tumble pattern, but there does not appear to be any general sex difference in activity level apart from this particular eliciting condition.

We turn now to studies of human infants and children. The measurement of activity level in the newborn infant must, of necessity, be a limited affair. In one sense, the infant who spends more time awake is more active than the one with long sleep cycles, so that time spent awake could be considered an index of activity. Other possible indicators are amount of diffuse, spontaneous body movement, breathing rate, height of lifting the head when placed in a prone position, frequency of "startle" response, and amount of body movement in response to specific stimuli. The difficulty regarding these measures as indicators of some underlying quality of the individual that may be labeled "activity level" is that (1) the behaviors are not positively intercorrelated, and (2) most are not stable for individual infants even across brief periods of time. For example, the newborn infant who most frequently shows a startle response also tends to have a relatively *low* level of spontaneous body movement (Wolff 1959[R]). Gordon and Bell (1961)[R] also report that the relationships between activity measures taken within an hour or two of one another show very low, nonsignificant correlations.

Considering prediction over much longer periods of time (R. Bell et al. 1971), we find that newborn boys who appear to be the most active, in the sense that they react most quickly and vigorously when a bottle is removed from their mouths, and who have high breathing rates, tend to be the same children who, as young preschoolers, are passive in the sense that they stand quietly watching other children play rather than becoming involved in active group games. For girls, the predictions are complex: girls who lift their heads relatively high during the first week of life tend to be easily awakened, easily upset, and active as preschoolers; on the other hand, the newborn girls who show a good deal of spontaneous motor movement upon blanket removal show *low* levels of gross body movements as preschoolers. Those neonatal measures that do show some stability in the first few days of life do, in other words, predict certain behaviors several years later, but they do not predict the *same* behavioral qualities; indeed, in a number of instances, the neonatal measures that might be interpreted as indicating a high activity level are associated with later *low* activity levels.

Bell (1960)[R], in reporting a study of a group of male infants, noted that a high neonatal activity level appeared to reflect birth traumas, at least in a number of cases, and he speculated that since boys more often suffer from birth complications, there would probably be a higher proportion of hyperactives among them. When groups of male and female infants are compared, then, the results may depend upon whether or not the samples include children who have undergone complications of pregnancy or delivery of varying degrees of severity. A number of research reports do not describe their selection criteria in detail. Variations in findings of sex differences from one study to another, then, may be partly a function of the proportion of the subjects having birth complications. Some birth traumas have relatively transitory effects; others are long-lasting. Thus sex differences reported from measures taken very early in life are particularly likely to depend upon the number of infants in the research sample with some complications at delivery.

For all the above reasons, we do not regard the available measurements of the behavior of young infants as reliable indicators of any characteristic that can be placed along the activity-passivity dimension, and we have not included the studies of infants under 2 months in Table 5.1. We shall merely mention the possibility that young male infants spend more time awake, although the evidence is not consistent. Based on observations of a group of infants at age 3 weeks and again at 3 months, Moss (1967) reports that the girls slept for a larger proportion of the observation time;

this finding is consistent with a more recent study by Sander and Cassel (1973)[R], who studied a group of 16 infants during their first month of life. The infants were placed in a monitoring crib which recorded movements and permitted distinguishing sleeping from waking states. This study too found that boys sleep significantly less than girls. However, an attempted replication by Moss and Robson (1970) with infants who were observed at 1 month and again at 3 months did not find differential sleep-wake cycles for the two sexes. Results on sex differences in the frequency of startle responses among newborns are similarly ambiguous. Korner (1969) found a tendency ($p < .10$) for boys to startle more frequently while either sleeping or wakeful, but Ashton (1971) found no sex differences in startle reactions. Measures of hand-mouth contacting among newborns may or may not be thought of as legitimate indicators of activity level; in any case, they have not consistently found the behavior to be more frequent in one sex than the other (Korner et al. 1968, Korner 1973, Nisbett and Gurwitz 1970).

Before we review studies of children beyond early infancy, we must consider once again the matter of stability. In a short-term longitudinal study, Maccoby and Feldman (1972) found that activity scores of children aged 2 in an unfamiliar room did not correlate with the activity scores of the same children in a highly similar situation at age 2½ and 3; Escalona and Heider (1959)[R] also found early activity scores to be poor predictors of later behavior; J. Kagan (1971) reports low stability of activity scores for a group of children studied longitudinally at age 8 months, 13 months, and 27 months. Some stability was reported (for boys, but not for girls) by Battle and Lacey (1972) on ratings of "hyperactivity." These ratings were made on the basis of the Fels longitudinal data, for age periods 0–3, 3–6, and 6–10. "Hyperactivity" included impulsive, uninhibited, and uncontrolled behavior, as well as a high frequency of vigorous motor activity. For boys there were significant correlations of hyperactivity scores for adjacent age periods ($r = .42$ and $.44$), but ages 0–3 and 6–10 were not significantly correlated. An earlier report on the Fels sample (Kagan and Moss 1962[R]) indicated temporal stability (after age 3) for a score called "behavioral disorganization"—again, stability was found for boys but not for girls. Behavioral disorganization referred primarily to episodes of loss of emotional control, and would seem to overlap with the "impulsive, uninhibited, and uncontrolled" aspect of Battle and Lacey's hyperactivity score. We do not know, then, whether the stability reported for boys in the hyperactivity score reflects stability of the "impulsive, uncontrolled" component or the vigorous motor activity component. The latter component would be more comparable to the measures of activity level in the other longitudinal studies.

Walker (1967) found reasonable stability over a one-year period of the

TABLE 5.1
Activity Level

Study	Age and N	Difference	Comment
Lewis et al. 1971b	3 mos (22)	None	Activity changes in response to visual and auditory stimuli
C. Turnure 1971	3, 6, 9 mos (33)	Girls	More limb movement upon presentation of slightly and grossly distorted voice (at 3 mos only); more limb movement in response to mother's normal voice (at 9 mos only)
	3, 6, 9 mos (15)	None	Limb movement in response to mother's and unfamiliar person's voices
L. Yarrow et al. 1971	5 mos (41)	None	Focused exploration of environment (home observation)
J. Kagan & Lewis 1965	6 mos (32)	None	Arm movements in response to a variety of visual and auditory stimuli
	13 mos (30)	None	Number of rectangles traversed during free play period in playroom
J. Kagan 1971	8 mos	None	Number of squares crossed during free play period in playroom
	13 mos	None	Number of squares crossed, playroom
	27 mos (180)	None	Number of squares crossed per unit time (longitudinal)
Rheingold & Eckerman 1969	9-10 mos (24)	None	Locomotor activity in playroom
Clarke-Stewart 1973	9-18 mos (36)	None	Activity level (home observation; longitudinal)
Rheingold & Samuels 1969	10 mos (20)	None	Locomotor activity in observation room with mother present
Goldberg & Lewis 1969	13 mos (64)	Boys	Banging with toys, vigor of play
Messer & Lewis 1972	13 mos (25)	Girls	Number of squares traversed in playroom (low SES sample)
Maccoby & Jacklin 1973	13-14 mos (40)	Boys	Number of squares crossed, playroom, before and after loud noise
	13-14 mos (40)	None	Number of squares crossed before and after loud noise
W. Bronson 1971	15 mos (40)	None	Overall rating of motor activity
Feldman & Ingham 1973	1 (56)	None	Number of squares crossed (Ainsworth "Strange Situation")
Finley & Layne 1969	1-3 (96)	Boys	Number of squares crossed (American and Mexican samples)
Lewis et al. 1971a	2 (60)	None	Arm movements upon presentation of pictures of the human form

(continued)

TABLE 5.1 *(cont.)*

Study	Age and N	Difference	Comment
Maccoby & Feldman 1972	2 (64)	Boys	Number of squares crossed in presence or absence of mother and/or stranger
	2½ (35)	None	Number of squares crossed
	3 (38)	Boys	Number of squares crossed, mo-ch episode
		None	Number of squares crossed, ch-str, mo-ch-str, ch alone episodes
R. Bell et al. 1971	2½ (74)	None	Vigor in play (teacher rating)
Feldman & Ingham 1973	2½ (79)	None	Number of squares crossed ("Strange Situation")
F. Pedersen & Bell 1970	2½ (55)	Boys	Activity recorder, walking
		Girls	"Passive motion" in glider or swing
		None	Tricycle riding, running, rate of tearing down barrier, force exerted to secure object, restless movement
Marvin 1971	2-4 (48)	None	Locomotor exploration
P. Smith & Connolly 1972	2-4 (40)	Boys	Higher overall activity level (observations, indoor and outdoor free play)
Zern & Taylor 1973	2-4 (41)	None	Rhythmic, repetitive body movements, observation in nursery school
Baumrind & Black 1967	3-4 (103)	Boys	Observer ratings of energy levels, and exploration of environment
Shipman 1971	3-4 (1,470)	Boys	Vigor of crank turning
		None	Running speed
J. Schwartz & Wynn 1971	3-5 (108)	None	Motility: observation, first day of nursery school
J. Schwartz 1972	4 (57)	None	Motility: observation in experimental room, alone or with peer
Bee et al. 1969	4-5 (114)	None	Frequency of movement in waiting room from one quadrant to another
Hatfield et al. 1967	4-5 (40)	None	Ratings of activity in laboratory setting
Wolff & Wolff 1972	4-5 (55)	None	Teacher's ratings of gross or fine motor movements
Loo & Wenar 1971	5-6 (40)	Boys	Teacher ratings: activity
		None	Actometer scores (classroom)
Pulaski 1970	5-7 (64)	Boys	Motility during play sessions
J. Kagan et al. 1964	7-8 (76)	None	Restless movement during test-taking at school
Ault et al. 1972	8-10 (29)	Boys	Teacher ratings of hyperactivity (irrelevant talk or play)

(continued)

TABLE 5.1 *(cont.)*

Study	Age and *N*	Difference	Comment
Walker 1967	8-11 (450)	Boys	Teacher rating "energetic"
	8-11 (406)	Boys	Self-appraisal "energetic"
Achenbach 1969	10 11 (159)	Boys None	Teacher ratings, amount of physical activity
Marks 1968	18-21 (760)	None	Self-report scale, activity level

trait "energetic," as rated independently by two successive teachers of a large group of children in the third to sixth grades of school. The stabilities were comparable for the two sexes, and ranged from .37 to .61 (.51 for all grades and both sexes combined).

In general, high or low activity level does not appear to be a consistent characteristic of individual children from one time to another during the preschool years. This fact would lead us to expect that sex differences, if any are found during this period, may be specific to certain ages.

As may be seen in Table 5.1, during the first year of life, results are quite consistent in showing no sex differences in activity level. From the first birthday on, although many studies continue to show no sex differences, those that do find boys to be more active. The only kind of highly mobile behavior that is reported to be more frequent for girls than boys is "passive motion" in a swing or glider (F. Pedersen and Bell 1970).

It is possible that the sex difference in activity level is age-specific, but we cannot be sure from the evidence in Table 5.1. Most studies have been made with children of preschool age. The studies that deal with older children usually shift to new methods—they rely on teacher ratings, rather than systematic behavioral observations. The problems with these methods are seen in the study by Loo and Wenar (1971)—actometers that recorded the amount of gross motor movement a child engaged in did not show boys being more active than girls, whereas teachers reported concerning the same group of children that the boys were more active. Were the teachers simply reflecting sex stereotypes? Or were they reacting to some qualitative difference in the behavior of the two sexes that did not show up in actometer scores? We do not know, but can only point out that with an age-related shift from one kind of measurement to the other, it is not possible to know whether the sex differences in activity level are age-specific or not.

Within a given study, sex differences in activity level are likely to be found with respect to some aspects of behavior but not others. For example, in the Pedersen-Bell report on a group of 2½-year-old children, the two sexes were found to be equally vigorous in tearing down a barrier to obtain a desired object; furthermore, boys and girls did equal amounts of running, tricycle riding, and fidgeting during story time. Boys did do more walking, however, and activity recorders strapped to their backs (which recorded large muscle movements) yielded higher scores.

Evidently there are some situations that elicit high-energy or highly mobile behavior, especially from boys; or, perhaps conversely, there are certain situations that tend to reduce the activity of girls and not boys. Two hypotheses have been considered. The first is that under conditions of stress, girls tend to freeze more than boys do. As a test of this hypothesis, two experiments were done with 13-month-old children (Maccoby and Jacklin 1973). The children were placed on the floor of a room, with their mothers nearby, and the taped sound of a loud, angry male voice was used as a source of moderate stress. In Experiment I, boys remained in one place longer than girls after the onset of the voice—a finding directly contrary to the hypothesis that girls are more likely to become immobile under stress. In Experiment II, the intensity of the sound stimulus was varied. The outcome was that with an intense stimulus both boys and girls moved quickly from the point on the floor where they had been placed (usually moving to the mother); with moderate levels of sound, girls tended (but this time not significantly) to move more quickly than boys. The findings of Experiment II suggest that in the first experiment the girls moved more quickly because they were more frightened—they reacted as they would have to an intensely noxious sound—whereas the boys reacted as they would to a sound that was only moderately intense. Clearly, these results cannot be generalized to other forms of stress; but the experiments provide no support for the hypothesis that it is especially in stressful situations that boys are more active than girls. Other evidence is consistent with this conclusion. As will be seen below, in the studies of attachment in which a child is introduced into a strange room and left alone with a stranger (e.g. Maccoby and Feldman 1972), children of both sexes show reduced activity levels when the stranger enters, but they do so to a similar degree— the girls are not more immobilized than the boys by the strangeness of the environment and the people in it.

A second hypothesis (Maccoby and Jacklin 1971[R]) is that a young male is especially likely to be stimulated to high-energy, high-motoric activity by the presence of other young (or slightly older) males. Halverson and Waldrop (1973) report a further analysis of the actometer data shown in Table 5.1 (Pedersen and Bell 1970) for the NIMH longitudinal sample. They subdivided the records according to whether the children were playing alone or in groups, and found that there was no sex difference in the amount of gross bodily activity when children were playing alone, but that when playing in groups, the girls were approximately as active as they would be while playing alone, while the boys' activity increased markedly. Although Halverson and Waldrop did not have information on the sex of the playmates who made up the play groups, nursery school play groups at this age tend to be sex-segregated, so the findings are consistent with the hypothesis that it was the presence of other young boys that triggered the increased male activity. If this hypothesis proves to be correct, it would help to explain why sex differences tend to appear most frequently after the age of 2, when children begin to interact more frequently with other children. Furthermore, it may account for the great variability in findings from study to study, since the results should depend on the nature of the social situation in which the observations were taken.

To summarize: the studies reviewed have shown a tendency for boys to be more active than girls, but not consistently so for all ages and experimental conditions. During the first year of life, the evidence indicates no sex differences. From this age onward, studies vary greatly as to whether a sex difference is found, but when it is, boys are more active. There appear to be certain eliciting conditions in which boys are more active, and others in which the two sexes are much alike. Very seldom has a greater level of activity among girls been observed. It is well to remember that activity levels have not been studied in situations that might provide elicitors that are especially salient to women and girls. It is clearly possible that there may be a constitutional contribution to the male's tendency to put out more energy, or respond with more movement, to certain stimulating conditions. On the other hand, it is not accurate to describe him as generally more active.

EMOTIONAL UPSETS, FRUSTRATION REACTIONS

In earliest childhood, it is difficult to put a name to a child's state of emotional distress. There have been many efforts to distinguish fear from rage on the basis of physiological indicators. Whatever the success of these efforts with a battery of devices for measuring autonomic reactions, the parent or other observer of the child must usually attempt to infer the nature of the child's emotional state from its sounds and movement, and from the situation that gave rise to the disturbance. Initially, the primary signal of the child's distress is that he cries—sometimes vigorously, with reddened face and thrashing limbs, sometimes in a more subdued fashion. A first index, then, to the frequency of episodes of emotional disturbance in the two sexes is the frequency of crying. As Table 5.2 shows, most of the available information on crying deals with the first year of life. During this time, the two sexes are much alike in the frequency and duration of crying. In Chapter 6, studies of attachment behavior are reported, and some

TABLE 5.2
Crying

Study	Age and N	Difference	Comment
Korner & Thoman 1972	Newborns (40)	None	Crying time
Moss 1967	3 wks, 3 mos (29)	Boys	Less time asleep, more time fussing; higher irritability level (longitudinal)
G. Bronson 1970	1-15 mos	None	Percentage of time infants cried during examination
	4-36 mos (60)	None	Crying in response to novelty (longitudinal)
G. Bronson 1972	3 mos (32)	None	Rating on persistence-of-crying scale
Lewis 1969	3, 6, 9, 13 mos (120)	None	Fret-cry during experimental sessions
R. Caron et al. 1971	3½ mos (98)	None	Crying during conditioning
L. Yarrow et al. 1971	5 mos (41)	None	Frequency of fussing and crying (home observation)
Fourr[R] 1974	6 mos (57)	Boys	Fuss-cry to fear stimuli
Clarke-Stewart 1973	9-18 mos (36)	None	"Irritability" (home observation; longitudinal)
Rheingold & Samuels 1969	10 mos (20)	None	Frequency of fussing (mother present)
B. Coates et al. 1972	10, 14 mos (23)	None	Amount of crying before, during, and after separation from mother (2 longitudinal samples)
	14, 18 mos (23)	None	
S. Bell & Ainsworth 1972	1st yr (26)	None	Frequency and duration of crying (home observation; longitudinal)
Goldberg & Lewis 1969	13 mos (64)	Girls	Crying when placed behind barrier
Jacklin et al. 1973	13-14 mos (40)	Girls	Crying behind barrier, if placed near mother in earlier experimental condition
		None	Crying behind barrier, if placed across room from mother in earlier condition
Maccoby & Jacklin 1973	13-14 mos (80)	None	Crying following loud voice (2 trials, 40 in each trial)
Kaminski 1973	1 (48)	None	Frequency of fusses or cries in presence or absence of mother and/or stranger
Feldman & Ingham 1973	1, 2½ (135)	Boys	Crying in "Strange Situation" (in several but not all of the episodes; 2 experiments)
Maccoby & Feldman 1972	2 (64)	None	Crying: child alone or in presence of stranger after separation from mother (longitudinal)
	2½ (35)	None	
	3 (38)	None	

(continued)

TABLE 5.2 *(cont.)*

Study	Age and N	Difference	Comment
Marvin 1971	2-4 (48)	None	Frequency of crying, "Strange Situation"
Dawe[R] 1934	2-5 (40)	Girls	Crying during quarrel with other child
Landreth[R] 1941	2½-5 (32)	Boys None	Crying at home (incident sampling record) Crying at nursery school

of this work has recorded the child's crying when the mother or father leaves the room as an index of attachment. Working with a sample of Australian children, Feldman (1974)[R] found *boys* (aged 1 year) more likely to cry with separation; Marvin (1971) obtained the same result with 2-year-olds, as did Shirley and Poyntz (1941)[R] in an earlier study. On the whole, however, the reactions of the two sexes to separation are quite similar (see Table 6.1).

Early work by Landreth (1941)[R] included records of the frequency of crying among boys and girls of preschool age. The report included 32 children, ranging in age from just under 3 to 5 years of age, and involved observations in the home as well as at school. Boys cried more frequently at home, and the author suggested that this might reflect a greater tendency on the part of boys to become irked with routines and parental restrictions on their activities. The frequency of crying at nursery school was similar for the two sexes in this sample, but the situations that led to crying were different: girls were more likely to cry because of accidental injury, boys from frustration over dealing with a recalcitrant inanimate object or during conflict with an adult. In other words, when boys cried, this was usually part of a frustration reaction, but for girls this was less likely to be the case.

Frustration reactions have not been widely studied, but the work that does exist suggests there may well be a sex difference in these reactions, at least at certain ages. It is not always clear just what should be included as frustration reactions. In Chapter 3 we discussed the studies involving the Matching Familiar Figures test, in which the child must muster the patience to examine a set of highly similar alternatives in detail, rather than quickly make a choice that gets the search process over with (even though speed results in many errors). This test is regarded as a measure of "impulsivity," which is in a sense the inability to tolerate the frustration involved in continued problem-solving efforts. We saw that there was no consistent sex difference in this kind of frustration tolerance. On the other hand, there was a tendency for boys of preschool age to have more difficulty "postponing gratification" on Mischel's test (see p. 101). Furthermore, quick outbursts of temper in frustrating situations may also be more characteristic of boys. Many years ago, F. Goodenough (1931)[R] published a carefully documented study based on diaries kept by parents of 45 young children ranging in age from 7 months to 7 years. For one month, the parents were asked to record each instance of an outburst of anger on the child's part, and to note what events immediately preceded and followed each outburst. Whereas the frequency of anger outbursts was quite similar for the two sexes up to age 18 months, there was a dramatic divergence thereafter: the frequency of outbursts declined to a low level among girls, and declined only slightly among boys, so that during the age range 2½ to 5, boys became angry at least twice as frequently as girls.

Consistent with this early work are the findings of some current (unpublished) work by Van Lieshout (1974)[R]. Sixty-four Dutch children were observed at age 18 months, and again at 24 months. During free play in an observation room, displays of negative emotion were rare. When an attractive toy was taken from the child, however, and placed in a plastic box where it could be seen but not obtained without considerable effort, an appreciable percentage of children at 18 months cried or showed other signs of being emotionally upset. At age 2, the number of girls becoming upset at this instigation had declined considerably, while boys continued to be upset with about the same frequency that had prevailed among them at age 18 months. (The sex difference at 24 months in frequency of "negative emotion" was significant at the <.01 level.) We have seen several instances (e.g. Feldman and Ingham 1973, Marvin 1971, F. Goodenough 1931[R], Landreth 1941[R], Van Lieshout 1974[R]) in which boys have shown more negative reactions (including crying) in a situation where they were frustrated. We could add to this list the finding by Maccoby and Feldman (1972) that boys, when left alone by their mothers in a strange room, were more likely than girls to beat or kick angrily upon the door through which the mother had departed, accompanying this activity with loud crying. However, there are some reports in which *girls* have cried more when subjected to frustrating situations. In a widely cited study by Goldberg and Lewis (1969), a child of 13 months is placed behind a barrier, from which he can see desirable toys (and also see his mother, who is seated in the room) but is prevented by the wooden gate or fence from reaching them. Goldberg and Lewis found that girls cried more than boys when placed behind this barrier, while boys more often manipulated the catches at the ends of the barrier, in an apparent effort to get out of their confined position. Maccoby and Jacklin (1973) repeated some aspects of this study; that is, they also used 13-month-old children, and placed them behind a barrier that separated them from the mother and the toys. But this episode was preceded by several events, including a fear-producing stimulus, and a session in which the mother and child played together with the toys on the floor of the experimental room. They compared two groups of children: (1) those who had been close to their mothers at the time of the earlier introduction of the fear stimulus, and (2) those who had been stationed across the room from her. In group 1, the girls cried more than the boys when placed behind the barrier; in group 2, there was no sex difference in crying. In neither group was there any indication that boys were making more efforts to get out from behind the barrier. We cannot tell, in these studies, whether the greater incidence of crying by the girls reflected greater frustration over separation from the toys, greater fear of separation from their mothers, or a choice of crying (instead of pulling at the barrier) as a means of extricating themselves. Possibly vigorous reactions to frustration become channeled into strongly motivated coping behavior rather than crying if the child has the necessary skills and opportunity.

Is it true that boys, when facing impediments, will characteristically make a more vigorous attack upon the barrier instead of crying for help? Pedersen and Bell (1970) studied this question in two situations with children of 2½ years. One test involved showing the child that it was necessary to tear down a paper barrier to reach some attractive toys. The vigor and persistence with which the children attacked this barrier were recorded. In a second task, a row of bells rested upon a table, and had to be picked up individually to be rung. Several of the bells were stuck to the table, and equipped with devices that would measure the strength of the pull exerted to detach them. On both of these measures, boys and girls were quite similar in the vigor of their reactions to the impediments to their actions. Both engaged in vigorous "coping" behavior. In a similar kind of behavioral test, Block (1971)[R] equipped a sliding door in such a way that it would become stuck after being only slightly opened, and the strength and duration of pressure exerted to open it further were measured. The experimenter would approach with an armful of books, and ask the child to open the door. In this situation, boys pushed more intensely (and for a longer time) on the stuck door. There was no sex difference, however, in the children's skill in finding an alternative route to the next room once it became clear that the door would not open.

In summary, what can be said about frustration reactions in young boys and girls? The tendency to show an outburst of negative emotion would appear to be greater in boys after the age of 18 months (see F. Goodenough 1913[R], Van Lieshout 1974[R], Maccoby and Feldman 1972, Landreth 1941[R]). In some cases this takes the form of undirected emotional reactions —what Kagan and Moss (1962)[R] called "behavioral disorganization." In other cases anger is focused upon the frustrating person or object and becomes aggression (see Chapter 7). If boys are more aroused by frustration, does this mean that they attack barriers more energetically, and thus cope more successfully with certain kinds of impediments? The answer to this question is equivocal. The work by Goldberg and Lewis (1969), and that by Block, would suggest that they do. That by Pedersen and Bell, and by Maccoby and Feldman, found the two sexes to be similar in the degree to which they focused their frustration responses toward removing the obstacle.

It is worth noting that the age of the subjects appears to make a considerable difference in the outcome of some of the research cited in this section. The Goodenough and Van Lieshout findings suggest that, if sex differences are found at the age of 2 or later, it is not that boys are increasing in their emotional volatility as they grow older, but that girls are decreasing in the frequency and intensity of their emotional reactions at a faster rate than boys. Why should this be so? Are girls acquiring skills more rapidly that permit them to deal with frustrations before they become too great? Are boys, for some reason, more frequently placed in situations that frustrate them? It is tempting to speculate that girls may be acquiring language faster and that this skill may serve them in good stead in overcoming frustration. But as we saw in Chapter 3, the girls' advantage in language development is slight and, in many samples of children, not demonstrable at all. Furthermore, Brackett (1934)[R] showed many years ago that the amount of crying a child does in nursery school is not related to the level of his verbal productivity. In other words, crying is not outgrown when and because a child acquires sufficient language to express his needs in other ways. As we shall see in later chapters, there is evidence that cooperative behavior in children does not depend upon their verbal skills, and angry, aggressive behavior (more common in boys) frequently takes verbal as well as nonverbal forms. We do not believe that language development is a good candidate to explain why the frequency of negative emotional responses to frustration declines faster in girls than in boys, but are at a loss to suggest an alternative.

FEAR, TIMIDITY, AND ANXIETY

We will not review the animal work on this subject in detail, partly because the parallels to human beings seem quite weak. Concerning rodents, for example, Gray (1971, p. 94)[R] says:

In general, the differences between male and female rodents conform to this pattern: as Maudsley Reactive rat is to Maudsley Nonreactive ... so male is to female. Thus male rats have been reported to defecate more and ambulate less in the Open Field, to emerge into a novel environment more slowly, and explore it less readily, and to freeze more in response to a novel sound. ... Ulcer formation as the result of psychological conflict is also more severe in the male than the female rat.

Gray has argued that these sex differences in fear that are found in rodents are reversed in man. But the human evidence cited is either self-report studies (reviewed below) or clinical evidence from doctors' reports of psychiatric symptoms. Fidell (1973)[2] has shown that the same symptoms tend to be diagnosed differently in male and female patients. In cases of ambiguous symptoms (equally ambiguous for the two sexes of patients), doctors more often consider a patient's illness to be psychosomatic if the patient is a woman. Hence we must hesitate to rely upon this source of evidence for information about the prevalence of anxiety states (and their attendant somatic disorders) in the two sexes. We turn now to a search for other sources of information.

The classic work on children's fears was done many years ago by Jersild. In one study involving over 130 families, Jersild and Holmes (1935) asked parents to keep a diary for 21 days, recording all the instances in which their young children showed fear, and giving a detailed description of the situation that appeared to have been frightening to the child. These reports were made for children ranging in age from early infancy through the age of 6. Boys and girls were remarkably similar in the frequency and intensity of fears reported, as well as in the nature of the situations that aroused their fears. Jersild and his co-workers then undertook an experimental study in which they presented children aged 2 through 6 with situations that (judging from parental reports) might be expected to be frightening to at least some children. These situations involved asking the children to approach a snake; approach a large dog; walk across a board elevated several feet above the floor; go into a dark passage to retrieve a ball; obtain a toy from a chair adjacent to a strangely dressed, immobile, and heavily veiled stranger; walk across a slightly elevated runway which tipped when stepped upon; remain alone in an unfamiliar room; and investigate the source of a loud, unexpected noise. There were no differences in the percentages of each sex displaying fear to any of the stimulus situations. However, the intensity of the fear response was higher for girls than it was for boys.

The more recent studies in which children's fear reactions have been directly observed, or in which parents have been asked to make records of their children's emotional reactions, have found few sex differences. Although girls may show a slightly earlier age of onset of stranger fear (Robson et al. 1969), this is not found in all studies (e.g. Bronson 1972) and there is no consistent difference in stranger reactions after the first year. Although Maccoby and Jacklin found in one study that girls of 13 months responded more quickly to a loud sound than boys did, the sex difference did not replicate on a second sample of children. Blayney (1973) did not find a sex difference when testing 4-year-old children's willingness to cross a narrow, elevated plank—a finding consistent with the earlier observation by Jersild. Bandura and Menlove (1968) screened all the children in a large nursery school and identified 32 girls and 16 boys who, by behavioral test, were afraid of dogs. Unfortunately, the recent observational studies have not included a wide range of eliciting conditions, so that it cannot be determined whether some of the sex differences that emerged as especially striking in the Jersild work (stepping on the tipping board, fear of the strange person) would be replicated in present-day groups of children. It would appear that the sexes do not differ in their readiness to enter quickly into nursery school activities when they are first introduced to this new environment (Baumrind and Black 1967, J. Schwartz and Wynn 1971). On the whole, recent observational work does not reveal any consistent tendency for one sex to be more timid than the other. However, there are indications that there may be some specific elicitors that arouse fears more readily in girls than in boys. See Table 5.3.

After children are old enough to read and write, research on fearfulness is done almost entirely with self-reports. Here, as in the case of teacher ratings, a sex difference is sometimes found and sometimes not, but when there is a difference, it is in the direction of greater reported fearfulness among girls. Bandura, in his research on the cure of snake phobias, has on several occasions advertised in local newspapers for subjects who are afraid of snakes and would like to be subjects in a desensitization experiment. The large majority of people responding to such ads have been women (see Bandura et al. 1969[R]). In a few instances, these women were found with behavioral tests to be fully as able to approach and handle snakes as unselected adults who did not describe themselves as being afraid of snakes. And upon discovering that they could actually handle snakes, these subjects were pleased and relieved, feeling that they could now comfortably go on camping trips and enter other situations they had avoided before because of their preconceived snake phobias. Of course, a large number of volunteer subjects *did* prove, behaviorally, to be extremely avoidant of snakes, just as they had thought. However, Bandura and his colleagues have found that their subjects could be fairly readily desensitized to the objects of their fear, so it is difficult to see these fears as in any sense "built in."

How can we distinguish self-attribution of fearfulness from fearfulness itself? This question becomes even more pressing in our efforts to understand the results of studies of anxiety. Whereas studies of fears in early childhood tend to focus on fears of specific objects, work with older subjects shifts to a focus on more generalized anxiety states, and these are usually assessed through self-reports. General "manifest anxiety" scales have been devised for adults and adapted for children (TASC, the Test Anxiety Scale for Children; and GASC, the General Anxiety Scale for Children). In a 1960 summary of their work, Sarason and his colleagues conclude that "the most consistent sex difference we have found is that girls get higher scores than boys on both the TASC and the GASC. The difference between boys and girls on the GASC is greater than on the TASC. This pattern of differences was obtained both in England and America"

TABLE 5.3
Fear and Timidity

Study	Age and N	Difference	Comment
Jersild & Holmes 1935	0-6 (153)	None	Parent report: 21-day diary record of children's fears
Bronson 1972	4, 6½, 9 mos (32)	None	E rating of S's responses to encounter with male stranger
Robson et al. 1969	8, 9½ mos (45)	Girls	Earlier age of onset of fear of strangers
		None	Fear-of-stranger ratings during home visits (longitudinal)
Jacklin & Bonneville[R] 1974	9½ mos (20)	None	Responses to noisy toys, hesitancy to touch buzzing toy, latency to leave mother for attractive toy (2 trials)
Maccoby & Jacklin 1973	13-14 mos (40)	Girls	Shorter latency to move following loud noise
	13-14 mos (40)	None	Latency to move following loud voice
Schaffer & Parry 1972	1 (12)	None	Approach to strange object with flashing lights and bleeps
Kaminski 1973	1 (48)	None	Hesitancy to touch whirring toy
Vernon et al. 1967	2-5 (32)	None	Anxiety following hospitalization, mother questionnaire
Jersild & Holmes 1935	2-6 (105)	Girls	Fear in response to 8 experimentally pre- sented, potentially fearful situations
Baumrind & Black 1967	3-4 (103)	None	Observer ratings: apprehensiveness, at ease vs. ill at ease at nursery school
J. Schwartz & Wynn 1971	3-5 (108)	None	Emotional reaction, first day of nursery school
Blayney 1973	4 (29)	None	Timidity, crossing narrow elevated board mounted on springs
Jersild & Holmes 1935	5-12 (398)	None	Children's reports (in individual interviews) of their fears
Shrader & Leventhal 1968	6-17 (599)	None	Frequency of fears, depression (parent reports)
Yando et al. 1971	8 (144)	Girls	More fearful in interaction with adults (E's rating)
		None	Fearfulness in interaction with adults (class- room teacher's rating)
Walker 1967	8-11 (450)	Girls	Teacher rating, fearfulness
	8-11 (406)	Girls	Self-appraisal, fearfulness
Hannah et al. 1965	18-19 (1,958)	Women	Higher total fear scores (self-rated Fear Survey Schedule)
W. Mischel et al. 1969	18-21 (51)	None	Unpleasantness ratings of hypothetical high and low intensity shocks

(Sarason et al. 1960[R], p. 250). A similar pattern emerged in the Oetzel bibliography (Maccoby 1966b[R]), and it is again apparent in the evidence that has been collected since then. Table 5.4 lists studies in which general anxiety scales have been used, and Table 5.5 includes those on test anxiety. The greater general anxiety of girls and women is fairly consistent across studies. Measures of test anxiety frequently find no sex difference, but when there is a difference, girls score higher.

The first question we must ask about these studies is whether the scales measure "real" fear states of any sort. The anxiety scales have not been validated against behavioral observations. They have been validated primarily by comparison with teacher ratings, and the correlations are low. For example, the overall correlation of the TASC with teacher ratings of children's test anxiety is .20. Secondarily, the value of the anxiety scales has been proved through their correlation, in predicted ways, with academic performance. This has been an entirely reasonable way to proceed from the standpoint of the purposes of the developers, who were primarily interested in the role anxiety plays in taking tests and motivating, or interfering with, school-related tasks. For our purposes, however, the procedure leaves the question open as to whether girls' higher anxiety scores do reflect genuinely greater fear. Sarason discusses this question in detail (Sarason et al. 1960[R], chap. 9). He notes that boys score higher than girls on the lie scale, although two studies have found no sex differences on the lie scale (Cowen et al. 1965, Cowen and Danset 1962). In later work (Sarason et al. 1964[R], K. Hill and Sarason 1966, Lekarcyzk and Hill 1969), it has also been shown that boys are more "defensive"—that is, less willing to admit to weaknesses of various sorts. For example, when asked "Do you sometimes dream about things you don't like to talk about?" or "When one of your friends won't play with you, do you feel badly?" a boy is more likely to say no. On the assumption that these are fairly universal feelings a denial is interpreted as defensiveness.

Sarason suggests the possibility that girls score higher on self-report anxiety scales simply because they are more willing than boys to admit that they feel anxious. It should be noted that Sarason has shown that even though some children may minimize their own anxious feelings when completing an anxiety scale, this does not invalidate the scale for purposes of understanding school-related fears and their effects. This has been demonstrated by showing that Anxiety scores still correlate significantly (and negatively) with academic performance, even when Lie Scale and Defensiveness Scale scores are held constant. However, the sex differences in anxiety scores might still be a function of boys' greater defensiveness. It would be possible to analyze for sex differences after having co-varied out the scores on the Lie and Defensiveness scales, but to our knowledge this has not yet been done, so the issue remains in doubt.

TABLE 5.4
General Anxiety Score

Study	Age and N	Difference	Comment
Goldschmid 1968	6-7 (81)	None	Children's Manifest Anxiety Scale (CMAS)
Holloway 1958	8 (121)	None	CMAS
Cowen & Danset 1962	9 (132)	Girls	CMAS (French sample)
Cowen et al. 1965	9 (169)	Girls	CMAS
Iwawaki et al. 1967	9 (155)	None	CMAS (Japanese sample)
B. Lott & Lott 1968	9-10 (233)	None	CMAS (white, black)
Barton 1971	9-10 (64)	Girls	Modified form of State-Trait Anxiety Inventory
Grams et al. 1965	9-11 (110)	Girls None	General Anxiety Scale for Children (GASC) CMAS
Palermo 1959	9-11 (470)	Girls	CMAS (white, black)
Penney 1965	9-11 (108)	Girls	CMAS
L'Abate 1960	9-13 (96)	None	CMAS
Hafner & Kaplan 1959	10 (188)	None	CMAS
Baltes & Nesselroade 1972	12-16 (1,249)	Girls	Tense, Cattell's High School Personality Questionnaire (longitudinal)
Templer et al. 1971	13-85 (2,559)	Girls & women None	Death anxiety scores (students, parents of students, upper middle SES apartment dwellers) Death anxiety scores (hospital aides, psychiatric patients)
Hannah et al. 1965	18-19 (1,958)	Women	Higher neuroticism scores (Maudsley Personality Inventory)
Benton et al. 1969	18-21 (80)	Women	Self-report of tension following experiment requiring S to doubt confederate's statements (in high-deceptive-rate condition only)
Kidd & Cherymisin 1965	18-21 (100)	None	Taylor MAS, short version
MacDonald 1970	18-21 (149)	Women None	Self-report, anxiety while waiting for shock; first-borns more likely to drop out of experiment Later-borns, drop out of experiment
Mendelsohn & Griswold 1967	18-21 (181)	Women	Anxiety scale, MMPI
Vassiliou et al. 1967	Adults (400)	Women	Greek translation, Taylor Manifest Anxiety Scale

TABLE 5.5
Test Anxiety

Study	Age and N	Difference	Comment
K. Hill & Sarason 1966	6, 8, 10 (323)	Girls	At ages 8 and 10, higher on Test Anxiety Scale for Children (TASC) (longitudinal)
	9, 11 (347)	Girls	At age 11, higher on TASC (longitudinal)
Feld & Lewis 1969	7 (7,355)	Girls None	TASC (white sample) TASC (black sample)
Solkoff 1972	8-11 (224)	None	TASC
Lekarczyk & Hill 1969	10-11 (114)	Girls	TASC
Entwisle & Greenberger 1972b	14 (566)	Girls	Test Anxiety Questionnaire (black, white)
Sampson & Hancock 1967	15-17 (251)	None	Text Anxiety Scale (Mandler-Sarason)

K. Hill and Sarason suggest (1966, p. 65) that the content of existing anxiety scales may be such as to touch more closely upon the particular anxieties that affect boys, and hence arouse their defensiveness most. Our reading of the General Anxiety Scale for Children leads us to a different conclusion. Some of the items are: "Do you get scared when you have to walk home alone at night?" and "When you are home alone and someone knocks on the door, do you get a worried feeling?" Girls are almost universally warned about the danger of sexual molestation. Sometimes the warnings are vague—girls must avoid strange men, not be out alone at night, lest "something terrible" should happen. We suggest that fears built up in this way would generalize to such settings as a visit to the doctor (usually male), or take the form of a generalized fear of the dark. We count 10 items out of the 45-item GASC that we believe might be weighted toward eliciting fears of these sorts, thus inviting higher scores from girls. There is another set of items (fear of mice, snakes, sharp objects, lightning, being bitten by animals) that could be considered weighted in the same direction if one took a Freudian view of the symbolic meaning of these stimuli. We see very few items in the scale that relate to the boy's special fear of appearing cowardly in the eyes of his age-mate, his fear of public humiliation or failure, etc. Therefore we suggest that girls' higher scores on existing anxiety scales might be just as much a function of the content of the scales as of girls' greater readiness to disclose anxious feelings. Perhaps both factors make a difference.

Where does this leave us, in relation to the question of whether girls are "really" more anxious than boys? It might be possible to reverse the usual sex difference by changing the content of test items. However, the very fact that girls do appear more ready to admit their fears is important. A person who says to himself "I am afraid of snakes" probably really *is* more afraid (in the behavioral sense) than the person who is afraid but denies it to himself. That is, the admission allows the person to act in accordance with his fears and avoid snakes, so that the self-attribution becomes the reality. If this is so, it is less serious that we have so little information on the actual behavior of the two sexes in potentially fear-producing situations.

When one is faced with difficulties in interpreting psychological data, it is always tempting to turn to what seems to be the more objective realm of physiological measures. There have been a number of attempts to relate physiological measures, particularly skin conductance, to scores on the Taylor Manifest Anxiety Scale. They have been largely unsuccessful (Rossi 1959[R], Raphelson 1957[R], Silverman 1957[R], McDonnell and Carpenter 1960[R]). As we have seen, the difficulty may be that the anxiety scales are not measuring "true" anxiety, but even if they were, it might be difficult to obtain a relationship with physiological measures. Lacey (1967)[R], in a review of the work on physiological measures of response to stress (the stress usually being experimentally induced), concludes that no one physiological measure can be related to stress, and that the psychophysiologist's best hope is to look at response *patterns* rather than any individual score. Duffy (1962)[R] discusses sex differences in physiological measures of arousal, and there do seem to be some sex differences. But the relationship of these to fear states has so far not been shown, and we do not have an answer from physiological measures as to whether one sex is more timid or fearful than the other. We would not be surprised if the answer turns out to depend on the stimulus situation. That is, the two sexes may be afraid of somewhat different things, on the average. For the present, however, we can only summarize the state of our knowledge on fear and timidity as follows:

1. Observational studies do not usually show a sex difference in timidity.

2. Teacher ratings and self-reports show girls to be more timid and anxious than boys.

3. Since boys are less willing to admit to fears or anxious feelings (have higher scores on Lie and Defensiveness scales), the sex differences on anxiety scales may be due to this factor.

4. Physiological measures of fear states have not so far clarified differences on psychological measures within and between the sexes.

What are the implications of the findings reported above for the issue of whether girls and women are "passive"? In the studies that reported boys as being more active than girls, it would not be accurate to say that the girls were inactive. In some research, the measure of activity is the amount of space crossed per unit time. When boys were doing somewhat more moving from place to place in a play room, girls were typically settling down to concentrated play with a toy. They did not sit passively doing nothing or stare into space. When teachers rated boys as more "energetic" or "hyperactive," they may have meant that boys made larger or more forceful movements, but there is no implication that girls were unoccupied. In a similar vein, if a boy responds to frustration with an outburst of temper while a girl does not, this may or may not imply that the girl is being "passive" in the sense of giving up and allowing her activities to be impeded by the barrier; perhaps she simply attempts to cope with the obstacle somewhat more calmly. In most studies using behavioral observation, fearfulness is not more common in one sex than the other; when fear is present, it does not appear to immobilize girls more than boys.

So far, then, "feminine-passive" does not appear to be the "fundamental identity" that Deutsch thought it was. It is possible that girls' self-attribution of fearfulness does impose restrictions on their adventurousness in exploring new situations. But it is equally possible that a boy's tendency to lose his temper interferes with constructive, active coping behavior (produces a state of disorganization) that is just as severe an impediment to ongoing activity as timidity would be. Although some provocative (though inconsistent) indications of temperamental differences between the sexes have emerged in the preceding pages, the dimensions have not been defined in such a way as to yield a clear picture of what these dimensions are or what their consequences may be.

Social Approach-Avoidance

DEPENDENCY

Dependency is one of the two most extensively studied behaviors that are presumed to be sex-typed (the other being aggression). Although W. Mischel (1970, p. 6)[R] indicates that the evidence is not so consistent for dependency as it is for aggression, he does read the existing research as indicating that there is "greater dependency, social passivity, and conformity in females than in males." What is meant when it is alleged that girls are more "dependent" than boys? R. Sears et al. (1965, p. 27)[R] define dependency as "an action system in which another person's nurturant, helping, and caretaking activities are the rewarding environmental events." There are a number of different kinds of actions that a child may engage in in order to obtain "nurturant, helping, and caretaking" activities from another person. Simply remaining near the other person, or touching and clinging to this person, would be examples of dependent supplications. So would noncontact forms of calling attention. So would seeking help, consolation, reassurance, or protection. And even getting attention from another person by being annoying—nagging, whining, disruptive actions— can be interpreted as instances of dependency. All these were indexes of dependency used by Sears and his colleagues (1957, 1965)[R] in their efforts to trace the aspects of family interaction that established dependent behavior in children. A subsidiary interest in this research was to determine whether the sexes differed in the strength of their dependency motivation, or in the frequency of any or all of the behavioral manifestations of this motivation.

Before discussing sex differences in this sphere of behavior, it may be well to underline the currently well-known fact that dependency in the above senses of the word does not represent an identifiable cluster in the social behavior of young children. Sears et al. (1965)[R] reported this lack of clustering among the relevant behaviors. Maccoby and Masters (1970)[R] noted that proximity seeking and attention seeking are part of different clusters which have distinct courses of development and are responsive to different antecedent conditions. They also indicated that the tendency for a child to orient toward adults is relatively independent of the tendency to orient toward age-mates. Two recent studies (R. Bell et al. 1971, Emmerich 1971) have factor-analyzed a large number of measures of young children's behavior, and have identified coherent patterns, but have not found any pattern that can be identified with the hypothesized "dependency" cluster. To complicate the picture, Bell et al. note that the factorial structure of behavior, although largely similar for the two sexes, is different in some rather important respects, so that a given form of "dependent" behavior (e.g. asking for help) might have a different meaning for boys than for girls, depending upon the other behaviors with which it was integrated and the situations in which it tended to occur. Despite these complications, some similar themes emerge from the two studies. Bell et al., studying 2½-year-olds from predominantly white middle-class backgrounds, found that children who showed assertive behavior in response to a barrier and who had good cognitive (especially verbal) skills tended to be oriented toward adults, but "were not dependent in the usual sense." The tendency to orient toward adults was relatively independent of the tendency to orient toward peers. Emmerich worked with a very different sample—disadvantaged children, many of whom were black—with ages ranging from 4 to 5 years. As noted in Chapter 4, "task orientation" (that is, the tendency to persist autonomously in goal-directed efforts) among these children was associated with adult orientation and cognitive interests. Orientation toward other children, on the other hand, was factorially quite distinct and was associated with a good deal of gross motor behavior out-of-doors and with social thematic play (make-believe games).

In view of these findings from cluster analysis, it would be surprising if one sex were to emerge as more "dependent" in all the initial meanings of the word. We may find, for example, that the two sexes are equally sociable, but that one is more oriented toward peers and the other toward adults; or we may find that proximity seeking is more common in one sex, attention seeking in the other. Or it may turn out that the sexes are much alike on the average on all the measures, with a great deal of variation within each sex along the dimensions that have been found to describe stable, consistent individual differences.

In the summaries that follow, sex differences are discussed separately under four categories: (1) proximity seeking, touching, and resistance to separation in relation to child's parents or other adult caretakers; (2) proximity seeking, touching, and resistance to separation in relation to age-mates; (3) social responsiveness, social interests, and social skills in relation to parents or other adults (attention seeking is included here); and (4) social responsiveness, social interests, and social skills in relation to age-mates, or with age of target unspecified. There will be very little information under topic (2).

In a number of earlier studies, global measures of dependency were used, in which instances of help seeking, attention getting, proximity seeking, and touching were combined into a single "dependency" score. In other studies, although distinctions have been made between the various components, scores do not reflect whether the behavior is directed toward adults or age-mates. These studies are not included in the tables, but will be discussed in the text where they seem most appropriate.

Some of the sex differences in other types of behavior have been attributed to a presumed tendency for girls to remain closer to the mother, and cling to her more often, in early childhood. For example, Garai and Scheinfeld say (1966, p. 199)[R]: "The earlier speech development and greater verbal fluency of girls appear to be related to the earlier maturation of their speech organs, their innate tendency toward more sedentary pursuits, *their closer contact with mothers* and their greater interest in people." Table 6.1 presents a summary of the research in which measures have been taken of the physical proximity a child maintains with its mother, and the amount of touching or clinging that has been observed. A few studies with measures of proximity and clinging to fathers are also included. These kinds of behavior are, of course, seen much more commonly in young children than in older ones. It is something of a problem to know whether there are any behaviors in later life that ought to be included here. Our own theoretical bias is no doubt reflected in our decision: we regard early childhood proximity seeking and clinging as the child's response to uncertainty or anxiety about some aspect of the situation he is in, and an indication of the fact that certain crucial individuals in his life are able to reassure him with their close presence. Thus, if a child of 9 or 10 has a bad dream and goes to his parents' room and asks to get in bed with them, this we would see as an instance of perseveration of a pattern established early in life which is seldom manifest at this age; if the same child pesters his father to take him to a ball game, however, we would not regard this as part of the "proximity seeking" behavioral cluster, even though the child is, in a sense, trying to be near his father. With this rather vague criterion in mind, we have included in Table 6.1 only studies of infants and preschoolers, with one exception where the parallel in the behavior of older children seemed very clear.

The studies summarized in Table 6.1 represent a fairly wide range of observation situations and measures. Most commonly, children under age 3 have been observed in a structured situation in which the mother and child have come to a toy-stocked observation room, and the child has been observed in interaction with his mother and the toys, with or without an experimental manipulation of some aspect of the situation. In a few studies, the child's tendency to approach the mother or cling to her has been observed in the home. From age 3 on, a wider range of measurement situations and methods have been used, including records of the child's readi-

TABLE 6.1
Touching and Proximity to Parent, Resistance to Separation from Parent

Study	Age and N	Difference	Comment
Fleener & Cairns 1970	3-19 mos (64)	None	Protest over mother or stranger leaving room
Beckwith 1972	7-9 mos 8-11 mos (24)	None Girls	Percentage of mother initiations to which infant responds with smile, vocalization, or approach (longitudinal)
F. Pedersen & Robson 1969	8, 9½ mos (45)	None	Age of onset and intensity of infant's greeting behavior upon father's return (home observation)
Corter et al. 1972	9-10 mos (10)	Boys	Shorter latency: child follows mother out of room (no toys present)
	9-10 mos (26)	Boys	Shorter latency: child follows mother out of room (1 or 6 toys present)
Rheingold & Eckerman 1969	9-10 mos (24)	None	Child leaves mother to explore adjoining room
Clarke-Stewart 1973	9-18 mos (36)	None	Attachment to mother (home and laboratory observations); "physical" attachment to mother (home observation; longitudinal)
Rheingold & Samuels 1969	10 mos (20)	None	Touching mother during play session in observation room
B. Coates et al. 1972	10, 14 mos (23)	None	Look at mother, vocalize to mother, proximity to mother, touch mother before or after separation
Littenberg et al. 1971	11 mos (24)	None	Vocalize, fret, cry, follow when mother leaves room
J. Brooks & Lewis 1972	11-15 mos (17 opp.-sex twin pairs)	Girls None	Look at mother, remain in proximity to mother Touching mother
Ainsworth et al.[R] 1971	12 mos (56)	None	Proximity to mother, reaction to separation from mother
Goldberg & Lewis 1969	13 mos (64)	Girls	Return to mother after removal from lap. Touch mother, proximity to mother
Messer & Lewis 1972	13 mos (25)	Girls	Return to mother after removal from lap, touch mother
		None	Vocalize to mother, look at mother (low SES sample)
Maccoby & Jacklin 1973	13-14 mos (40)	Boys None	"Trips" to mother Proximity to mother; touching mother; looks to mother
	13-14 mos (40)	None	Proximity to mother; touching mother; looks to mother; "trips" to mother
W. Bronson 1971	15 mos (40)	Girls	Amount of time near mother, structured observation (1 of 3 episodes)
Ban & Lewis 1971	1 (20)	None	Look, touch, proximity, or vocalize to mother or father

(continued)

TABLE 6.1 *(cont.)*

Study	Age and N	Difference	Comment
Feldman & Ingham 1973	1 (19)	Boys	Cry when mother leaves room (Ainsworth "Strange Situation," 1 of 2 episodes)
		None	Proximity to mother
	1 (19)	None	Cry when father leaves room, proximity to father
	2½ (39)	None	Cry when mother leaves room, proximity to mother ("Strange Situation")
	2½ (28)	Boys	Cry when father leaves room ("Strange Situation," 1 of 2 episodes)
		None	Proximity to father
Finley & Layne 1969	1-3 (96)	None	Proximity to mother, contact with mother (American and Mayan Indian samples)
Rheingold & Eckerman 1970	1-5 (48)	None	Distance child roams from mother
Weinraub & Lewis 1973	2 (18)	None	Look, touch, proximity, or vocalize to mother or father
Maccoby & Feldman 1972	2 (64)	None	Proximity to mother, protest over separation from mother (longitudinal) ("Strange Situation")
	2 (20)	None	Proximity to mother, protest over separation in "Strange Situation" (Israeli sample)
	2½ (35)	None	
	3 (38)	None	
Marvin 1971	2 (16)	Boys	"Strange Situation": contact-maintaining behavior (1 of 2 measures), crying following mother's departure; less proximity-avoiding behavior (significant for mother-reunion episodes only)
		None	Proximity-seeking behavior, looks at mother, searches for mother following her departure
	3 (16)	None	"Strange Situation": contact-maintaining behavior, proximity-avoiding behavior, looks at mother, crying, searches for mother following her departure
	4 (16)	Girls	"Strange Situation": contact-maintaining behavior (1 of 2 measures), proximity-seeking behavior, crying following first reunion with mother
		None	Proximity-avoiding behavior, looks at mother, searches for mother following her departure
Blurton-Jones & Leach 1972	2-4 (73)	None	Cry when mother leaves room
Shirley & Poyntz[R] 1941	2-8 (199)	Boys	Upset when separated from mother

(continued)

TABLE 6.1 *(cont.)*

Study	Age and *N*	Difference	Comment
J. Schwartz & Wynn 1971	3-5 (108)	None	Reaction to separation from mother, first day of nursery school
Blayney 1973	4 (29)	None	Reaches for, touches father while on elevated balance beam
Wohlford et al. 1971	4-6 (66)	None	Father-absent lower-class black Ss. Extent of child's involving adult doll in doll play; mother ratings of dependency (clinging)
Guardo & Meisels 1971	8-15 (431)	Girls	Place self-referent silhouette close to parent silhouette while latter praises
		None	Placement of self silhouette while parent silhouette reproves
Ferguson & Maccoby 1966	10 (126)	Girls	Seek parent (or other older people) when sick, alone, or afraid (self-administered scales)

ness to separate from the mother when brought to nursery school. In all, 32 studies report observational data on proximity, touching, or resistance to separation in relation to the mother (or rarely, the father). As Table 6.1 shows, the large majority of these studies find no sex differences. Several studies found no differences for some measures, and differences favoring one sex or the other on other measures. For example, in Maccoby and Jacklin's first study (1973) with children 13 months of age, boys made more "trips" to the mother, but there was no sex difference in the degree of closeness to the mother that the children maintained. In all, there are seven instances in which at least one measure shows greater proximity-seeking behavior in boys, and eight in which there are higher scores for girls. As noted in Chapter 5, higher scores tend to be found for boys in measures of resistance to separation. In several studies, boys cry more when the mother or father leaves the room; and at the early age of 9–10 months, they are more likely to crawl quickly after the mother if she moves into an adjacent room (Corter et al. 1972). In the few instances in which girls obtain higher scores, they tend simply to remain nearer to the mother. However, the number of studies finding no difference in proximity outnumber the "girls higher" studies by more than three to one, and hence the picture as a whole is quite clearly one of sex similarity rather than sex difference.

Two reports of studies that were carried out in field situations by anthropologists (Munroe and Munroe 1971, Nerlove et al. 1971[R]) show records sampling how far away from home children aged 3–8 were found during their free time, when they had a choice of where to play. In two different cultures in Kenya, boys customarily played at a greater distance from home. It is difficult to know how to interpret these findings. The behavior does not seem precisely similar to remaining close to the mother when the two are in the same room. Do girls stay closer to home because they want to be able to run to the mother for security in case any threatening situation arises? Have they been given more warnings than boys about the dangers of the outdoor environment? Are the kind of settings they are allowed or expected to participate in located closer to home? We do not know; meanwhile, it would be premature to classify this behavior as "proximity seeking" in the same sense as the behavior in the studies summarized in Table 6.1.

What about children's seeking of security through proximity and clinging to adults other than their primary caretakers? There is evidence that "dependency" (in the proximity-seeking sense) generalizes to nonfamily adults. Rosenthal (1967)[R] has found that instances of remaining near an adult woman experimenter increase with the introduction of fear-producing stimuli (e.g. the taped sound of another child crying). Feldman and Ingham (1973) have similarly found that a child increases proximity to a briefly acquainted baby-sitter upon the entrance of a complete stranger to a strange room. Do girls transfer this security-seeking behavior toward surrogates more readily than boys? A difficulty in answering this question lies in the nature of the measurements available. As Table 6.2 shows, there are eight observational studies of the interaction of children with nonfamily adults (Heathers, Bell et al., Feldman and Ingham, Emmerich, Serbin et al., Zunich, Maccoby and Feldman). Five of these find no sex difference in proximity or clinging. The Feldman and Ingham study with one-year-olds shows boys more likely to remain near a strange adult. The Zunich study, showing higher scores for girls, involved presenting children with a very difficult puzzle—too difficult for them to solve. Their behavior while attempting to cope with this situation was observed. Boys more often showed destructive and emotional responses, more often rationalized their failure, and more often sought help; girls more often sought information relevant to the problem, tried to solve it alone, and *sought contact* with the Experimenter. Their contact seeking, in this case, was part of a pattern of active coping, and would appear to have a somewhat different meaning than the escape from threat that is usually implied in clinging or proximity seeking. In observational studies, then, the picture is one of no established sex difference in proximity seeking to nonfamily adults.

In two of the three studies in which *ratings* have been used, however (Beller and Turner 1962[R], Hattwick 1937[R], Lansky and McKay 1969), girls have been rated more likely to remain close to a nursery school teacher than boys. In our earlier review (Maccoby 1966b[R]) studies using more global measures of "dependency" were summarized, and it was noted that observational studies seldom found sex differences, whereas rating studies fre-

TABLE 6.2
Touching and Proximity to Nonfamily Adult

Study	Age and N	Difference	Comment
Feldman & Ingham 1973	1 (19)	None	Proximity to female stranger when accompanied by mother in "Strange Situation"
	1 (19)	Boys	Proximity to female stranger when accompanied by father in "Strange Situation"
	1 (18)	Boys	Proximity to female stranger when accompanied by adult female acquaintance in "Strange Situation"
		None	Proximity to adult female acquaintance
	2½ (67)	None	Proximity to female stranger when accompanied by mother or father in "Strange Situation"
	2½ (12)	None	Proximity to female stranger when accompanied by adult female acquaintance in "Strange Situation"
	2½ (12)	None	Proximity to female stranger when accompanied by adult female acquaintance in "Strange Situation"; proximity to female acquaintance
Heathers[R] 1955	2 (20)	None	Observation: cling to teacher
	4-5 (20)	None	Cling to teacher (observation)
Maccoby & Feldman 1972	2 (64)	None	Proximity to stranger ("Strange Situation"; longitudinal)
	2½ (35)	None	
	3 (38)	None	
Hattwick[R] 1937	2-4 (579)	Girls	Stay near nursery school teacher (teacher rating)
R. Bell et al. 1971	2½ (74)	None	Frequency of contact with teachers (teacher rating)
Zunich[R] 1964	3-4 (40)	Girls	Seeking contact with adult during puzzle task
Beller & Turner[R] 1962	3-5 (190)	Girls	Seeking physical contact and nearness to teacher (observer rating)
Serbin et al. 1973	3-5 (225 pupils, 15 teachers)	Girls	More often within arm's reach of teacher (nursery school observation)
Emmerich 1971	4-5 (596)	None	"Attachment" to adults in nursery school (observation: remaining near, following, imitating)
Lansky & McKay 1969	5-6 (36)	None	"Dependency," Beller Scales (teacher rating)
B. Long & Henderson 1970	6 (192)	Girls	Projective measure: place "self" figure closer to "teacher" figure
Yando et al. 1971	8 (144)	None	Child positioning self in relation to E

quently reported that girls were more dependent. We can only reiterate now the warning that, although any measurement (including behavior observation) embodies the danger of observer bias, it would appear that ratings are especially susceptible to this problem, particularly where sex differences are concerned. The fact that ratings can be made reliably (in the sense that two raters agree) does not rule out the possibility that the two observers share culturally imposed biases that would lead them to perceive girls as being, on the average, more "clingy" than boys. When rating studies and observational studies conflict, then, in the picture of sex differences they present, we believe it is reasonable to rely more heavily upon the observational ones. In so doing, we conclude that children of both sexes do to some extent transfer to relatively unfamiliar adults their tendencies to seek comfort or security through proximity or clinging, but that there is no consistent tendency for girls to make this transfer any more readily than boys.

It is rare for children to use other children as "security" sources in the same way that they use their parents or surrogate adult caretakers. Harlow (1962)[R] has noted that infant monkeys raised without mothers but in contact with age-mates will cling to these age-mates for comfort in the same way that a normally reared infant clings to its mother. But when an infant monkey has had access both to his mother and to age-mates in early life, it will cling to the mother when frightened but will *not* cling to a favorite playmate, even when the playmate is the only other social object present (Patterson et al. 1974[R]). Though little work has been done on the tendency of human children to cling to one another in fear-producing situations, there is reason to believe that mutual comfort giving is fairly rare, except among children reared together under conditions of maternal deprivation (see Freud and Dann 1951[R]). Infants and young children find other infants and other young children interesting social objects, but the interest appears to be of a different sort, and to serve different functions, than the proximity seeking and physical contacting directed toward adults. The only study we found that reports specifically concerning proximity seeking to other children in a nursery school setting is Emmerich's (1971), in which the tendency to "tag along" after other children, and imitate them, was recorded as "attachment to other children." *Boys* showed this behavior more frequently than girls in the Emmerich sample.

Among adults, of course, any tendency to seek the company of others, or to cling to them, under stressful conditions, is likely to be expressed toward age-mates. The original Schachter work (1959)[R] on affiliation, in which subjects waited for a painful experience (shock) and had a choice of whether to wait alone or in the company of others, included only female subjects, and focused upon individual differences that were related to birth order. Recent work by MacDonald (1970), using a similar anticipation of shock situation and subjects of both sexes, has revealed no sex differences in the tendency to seek closeness to age-mates under this particular stressful condition.

So far, we have discussed separately the child's proximity seeking directed toward the mother, toward other children, and toward nonfamily adults. There is an important body of research that reports physical contact without regard to the identity of the target. R. Sears et al. (1965)[x] recorded touching and holding, and also simply "being near" an adult or child during periods of free play in a nursery school. They found no significant sex differences in such behavior. Whiting and Pope (1974) describe the sex differences that were found in the "Six Cultures" study. Time-sampled observations were made of a group of children in each of six "villages" as the children went about their daily activities. Many of the observations were made when the children were in their own homes or outdoors near their homes (in the "yard," if there was one). Half the children were in the age range 3–6, the other half 7–11. The intent was to obtain multiple observations on 12 girls and 12 boys in each culture, although in two of the societies the sample size fell short of this goal. One of the behaviors recorded was "nonaggressive touching and holding"; this category was scored when the child touched another person, regardless of this person's age, sex, or relationship to the child. In five of the six cultures, girls tended to touch or hold others more frequently than boys, although the sex difference was not significant within any culture. When the six societies were combined, the sex difference was significant, but only in the 3–6 age range, when the behavior was most common. There is some suggestive evidence here, then, that young girls more often make physical contact with a variety of other persons; it is important to be cautious, however, concerning any implications of cross-cultural universality, in view of the small samples and the fact that (perhaps in consequence of the small samples) none of the within-culture differences was significant. Assuming for the moment, however, that the observed differences would be replicated with observations of additional children in these cultures, many interesting questions arise as to the nature of the settings in which the observations took place. In several of these societies, boys are assigned chores (such as the herding of animals) that take them farther away from the house than girls' chores do. Although such chores are normally assigned to older boys, the chances are that boys of 6 or younger may sometimes be allowed to go along; in any case, we do know that boys in several of these cultures are normally found farther away from the house than are girls at any given moment of the day. Their opportunities to seek physical contact with family members is, then, somewhat reduced in comparison to girls'. In most of the studies summarized in Tables 6.1 and 6.2, settings were standardized for the two sexes. This may have been done at the sacrifice of a certain amount of real-life validity, if the sexes differ in the frequency with which they would normally be in settings similar to the ones in which measurements have been taken. In any case, it makes a difference in how results may be interpreted if behavior varies with settings rather than with the use children make of a given setting. In view of the negative outcome of our review of the other studies on proximity seeking (some of which were done in nonindustrial cultures), we regard the Whiting and Pope report as an indication that further cross-cultural observations are needed, and that there may indeed be some cultural settings in which sex differences will consistently emerge; but the fact remains that in the large majority of situations studied so far, they have not emerged.

To summarize so far: the tendency to seek close contact with attachment objects or their surrogates does not appear to be differentiated by sex during the childhood years when this kind of behavior is most apparent; at least, there are no consistent sex differences in the cultural settings where most of the research has been done. Clinging to parents or other caretakers, or remaining near them under conditions of uncertainty or anxiety, is a characteristic of human children that may be observed in all cultures. The ethological view is that this behavior has evolved as a relatively high-potential behavior in young children because of its survival value (Bowlby 1969^R). From this standpoint there would be no reason why one sex should display the behavior more frequently than the other, unless (a) young children of one sex were more frequently subjected to stressful conditions; or (b) one sex tended to become more frightened with a given degree of objective threat. The sexes were compared in Chapter 5 with respect to their timidity; for the present it need only be said that in the variety of relatively novel situations in which young children have been placed in psychological studies, the two sexes have been remarkably similar in their tendency to seek comfort through proximity to the mother or other familiar adult.

As children grow older, they less and less often seek comfort or protection through closeness to an adult. Their social behavior is more oriented around age-mates, and the functional meaning of proximity changes. That is, if two friends stand quite close together while talking, we suggest that this is not so likely to reflect security needs as is the case with children's proximity seeking toward adults. There is a body of work in which the social interactions of pairs of school-aged children and adults have been studied, and where the focus is on how far from one another the participants in an interaction stand, and whether they face one another directly or turn somewhat away while talking. As Table 6.3 shows, in one study out of five, girls and women stood closer together than boys and men, and in two out of three instances, they faced each other more directly. Furthermore, when projective measures were used—the subject being asked to

TABLE 6.3
Proximity and Orientation Toward Friends

Study	Age and *N*	Difference	Comment
Langlois et al. 1973[R]	3-5 (32)	Girls	Touch partner, same-sex or mixed-sex pairs (black sample)
		None	Stand close to partner
B. Long & Henderson 1970	6 (192)	None	Projective: distance between placement of "self" symbol and symbols representing other children
Aiello & Jones 1971	6-8 (210 same-sex pairs)	Girls	Stand closer together on playground (white subsample)
		None	Black, Puerto Rican subsamples
		Boys	Face each other more directly (all 3 sub-samples combined)
S. Jones & Aiello 1973	6, 8 10 (96 same-sex dyads)	None	Interpersonal distance in conversation
		Girls	Face each other more directly (black, white)
Meisels & Guardo 1969	8-15 (431)	Girls	Closer placement of silhouette "self" to figure described as "best friend"; farther placement of "self" from "stranger," "someone neither liked nor disliked," "someone disliked very much," "someone feared," "strangers," and "feared peers"
		None	Distance between "self" and "friends," "self" and "someone liked very much," and "self" and "an acquaintance"
Guardo 1969	11 (60)	Girls	Closer placement of silhouette "self" and figure described as "best friend," someone you like very much; farther placement, "someone you're afraid of"
S. Jones[R] 1971	Adolescent & adult (220 same-sex dyads)	Girls & women	Face each other more directly during interaction
		None	Interpersonal distance
Dosey & Meisels 1969	18-21 (186)	Women	More affected by sex of other
		None	Closeness of approach to same- or opposite-sex other
Levinger & Moreland 1969	18-21 (96)	None	Placement of figure representing self in relation to silhouettes representing "good friend," "stranger," "dissimilar stranger," and "similar stranger"
Little 1968	18-21 (432)	Women	Doll figures placed close together when discussing pleasant topic, far apart when discussing unpleasant topic (multinational sample)
Argyle & Dean 1965	22-26 (24)	None	Eye contact with confederate during discussion
F. Willis 1966	Adults (755)	Men	Stand close to "friends" (not good friends) during conversation
		Women	Stand close to good friends

place dolls or paper cutouts in relation to one another—girls more often adjusted their placement according to how well acquainted the actors were or how well they liked one another, whereas boys were relatively uninfluenced by these factors in making their placements. In the F. Willis study (1966), the actual proximity of female pairs was similarly sensitive to the degree of friendship between them.

These results are consistent enough to be interesting. They do not appear to reflect any greater general tendency for girls to be "proximity seekers" (see also preceding summaries). It may be that the findings can be interpreted in the light of other aspects of social interests and social behavior, to which we now turn.

It has been alleged that girls are more interested in social stimuli of all kinds, more responsive to the nuances of relationships implied by social cues, and more sensitive to the reactions of others toward one another and toward themselves. Garai and Scheinfeld (1968)[R], for example, say: "In psychological development, from earliest infancy on, males exhibit a greater interest in objects and their manipulation, whereas females show a greater interest in people and a greater capacity for the establishment of interpersonal relations."

As shown in Chapter 2, we were unable to detect any superiority among girls in sensitivity to, or interest in, social cues. That is, there was no sex differentiation in the tendency to fixate faces as compared with nonsocial visual stimuli, or to orient toward voices rather than matched nonsocial sounds. Social responsiveness toward a variety of live people also appears to be undifferentiated by sex during the first two years of life, although there may be some differences in the rate at which certain social responses appear. We see in Table 6.4, for example, that although there appear to be no sex differences in reactions to strange observers at age 3 months (Zelazo) at about 8 or 9 months of age girls show stranger fear while boys do not (Beckwith, Robson et al.). The Robson study is longitudinal, and the authors note that girls developed stranger fear at an earlier age than the boys, on the average. However, in the age range 9–17 months, Clarke-Stewart finds no sex difference in stranger reactions; it may be that the difference detected by Beckwith and Robson et al. simply reflects a sex difference in maturation rate, with boys catching up very shortly after the initial onset of stranger fear in girls at about 8 months. There are slight indications that girls may, in fact, soon begin to be more receptive toward adult strangers—W. Bronson (1971) reports that the girls in her study were most likely to approach a silent and unresponsive stranger than were the boys. Also Maccoby and Feldman (1972) found a somewhat greater incidence of friendly interaction with the stranger among the girls in their longitudinal study (although the difference was not significant at any single age, the direction was consistent at three successive ages). However,

TABLE 6.4
Positive Social Behavior Toward Nonfamily Adult

Study	Age and N	Difference	Comment
Zelazo 1971	3 mos (20)	None	Base rate, smiling at unresponsive E: number of contingently stimulated and elicited smiles during conditioning
G. Bronson 1972	3, 4, 6, 9 mos (32)	None	Response to male stranger (facial expression, vocalizations, gross body movements; Caucasian and Oriental subsamples; longitudinal)
Beckwith 1972	7-11 mos (24)	Boys	Responsiveness to stranger (Rheingold scale)
Robson et al. 1969	8, 9½ mos (45)	Boys	Unsolicited approach to stranger (Boys older at onset of stranger-fear; longitudinal)
Clarke-Stewart 1973	11-13 mos (36)	None	Positive social responsiveness to female stranger (laboratory observation)
W. Bronson 1971	15 mos (40)	Girls	More positive response to silent adult stranger
		None	Reaction to responsive stranger
Feldman & Ingham 1973	1 (56)	None	Positive interaction with female stranger (Ainsworth "Strange Situation")
	1 (18)	None	Positive interaction with female acquaintance ("Strange Situation")
	2½ (79)	None	Positive interaction with female stranger ("Strange Situation")
	2½ (12)	None	Positive interaction with female acquaintance ("Strange Situation")
Maccoby & Feldman 1972	2 (64)	None	Positive interaction with adult stranger ("Strange Situation"; longitudinal)
	2½ (35)	None	
	3 (38)	None	
Fagot & Patterson 1969	3 (36)	None	Help teacher
Baumrind & Black 1967	3-4 (103)	None	Observer ratings: affection toward nursery school staff
M. Yarrow et al. 1971	3-5 (118)	None	Bids for adult attention
Kohlberg & Zigler[R] 1967	3-8 (72)	None	Seeking praise, permission, help, or attention from E during joint task
Ashear & Snortum 1971	3-5, 7, 10, 13 (90)	Girls	Eye contact with female E during interview
R. Sears et al.[R] 1965	4 (40)	None	Seek positive attention from teacher or other adult (behavior observation)

(continued)

TABLE 6.4 *(cont.)*

Study	Age and N	Difference	Comment
Emmerich 1971	4-5 (415)	None	Classroom observations, early fall and late fall: adult orientation (black and white low SES)
	4-5 (596)	None	Classroom observations, early fall and spring: affiliation with adults, adult orientation (black and white low SES)
Yando et al. 1971	8 (144)	Boys	Display more positive attention-seeking behavior (teacher rating, white sample only)
		Girls	Display less negative attention-seeking behavior (teacher rating, white sample only)
		None	Display of positive and negative attention-seeking behaviors (E rating, black and white samples)

the bulk of the evidence is that the two sexes are very similar with respect to the amount of friendly interaction with nonfamily adults, including nursery school teachers.

As noted earlier, the amount of friendly interaction with age-mates tends to be factorially quite distinct from proximity seeking or other kinds of interaction with adults. As Table 6.5 shows, the weight of the observational evidence is in the direction of boys being more "sociable" than girls, in the sense that they engage in more positive social interaction with age-mates.

It is difficult to know precisely what to include under this heading—does rough-and-tumble play, for example, qualify as positive social interaction? Such play is frequently exuberantly happy in its affective tone; it can quickly turn into fighting, however, and it is sometimes difficult to distinguish playful rough-and-tumble from aggression. If such play were to be included here, the balance would be even more heavily shifted toward greater "sociability" in boys. Whiting and Pope (1974), for example, report a greater frequency of rough-and-tumble play among boys aged 3–6 in four out of six of the societies they studied, and in five out of the six societies at ages 7–11. The fact that girls less frequently engage in such play, however, does not account for the fact that they emerge as less "sociable" with peers in the studies reported in Table 6.5, since there are many opportunities for girls to interact extensively with age-mates in other kinds of activities and they do not appear to have done so to a degree comparable to the social interactions of boys.

Table 6.6 summarizes the studies in which the tendencies to like and want to be near other people have been measured. We have just seen that boys tend to be more "affiliative" in the sense that they appear to engage

TABLE 6.5
Positive Social Interaction with Peers

Study	Age and N	Difference	Comment
Clark et al. 1969	2-4 (40)	Boys	Have a few close friends, and more children with whom S never plays
		None	Mean number of companions per time interval
McIntyre 1972	2-4 (27)	Boys	Rate of social interaction with peers and adults, observations in nursery school
Anderson 1937	2-6 (128)	Boys	"Integrative" behaviors (i. e. behaviors that show common purpose by work or action) in same-sex or mixed-sex pairs
R. Bell et al. 1971	2½ (74)	None	Friendliness with peers (teacher rating)
Charlesworth & Hartup 1967	3 (37)	Boys	Give affection, acceptance, or submissive types of reinforcements to peers; higher number of different peers reinforced
		None	Give positive attention and approval
	4 (33)	None	Same measures as above
Baumrind & Black 1967	3-4 (103)	Boys	Observer ratings: takes initiative in making friends
		None	Observer ratings: helps (vs. does not help) other children adapt
Barnes 1971	3-5 (42)	None	Frequency of parallel, associative, or cooperative play
Feshbach 1972	4 (104)	None	Child's use of positive reinforcement in teaching task to 3-year-old
Feshbach & Devor 1969	4 (102)	None	Child's use of positive reinforcement in teaching task to 3-year-old
J. Schwartz 1972	4 (57)	None	Time spent looking at or talking to close friend or unfamiliar peer
Emmerich 1971	4-5 (415)	Boys	Classroom observations, early fall and late fall: peer orientation (black and white low SES)
	4-5 (596)	Boys	Classroom observations, early fall and spring: affiliation with peers, peer orientation (black and white low SES)
Anderson 1939	5 (38)	None	"Integrative" behaviors in same-sex or mixed-sex pairs
Feshbach 1969	6 (126)	None	Approach behavior toward same-sex newcomer (2-person groups)
Waldrop 1972	7½ (62)	Boys	Play with group of same-sex peers
		Girls	Play with only one same-sex peer
Walker 1967	8-11 (450)	None	Teacher rating: "socialness"
Benton 1971	9-12 (96)	Boys	More positive evaluation of disliked peer after bargaining over selection of toys
		None	Evaluation of friend or neutrally regarded peer after bargaining session
Hollander & Marcia 1970	10 (52)	Boys	More peer-oriented (vs. self-oriented; questionnaire)

(continued)

TABLE 6.5 *(cont.)*

Study	Age and N	Difference	Comment
Feshbach & Sones 1971	12-13 (87)	Boys	Established pairs of same-sex "close friends": shorter latency to speak to a third person (newcomer), higher frequency of incorporating newcomer's ideas, more favorable post-experimental rating of newcomer
		None	Frequency of direct verbal rejection of newcomer's ideas

in more social interaction with age-mates. Girls, on the other hand, are more likely to report that they like the people with whom they interact, even when the other person has not behaved in a rewarding way. A complication in interpreting the two kinds of studies is that the studies of interaction have been observational ones done at early ages, whereas the studies of liking and affiliative feelings are almost always based on self-reports, and have been done with older subjects. Do the different trends appearing in Tables 6.5 and 6.6 reflect an age change, or is it true that girls feel more attraction for others while boys overtly engage in more social interaction?

Our male informants suggest that for much of the interaction that occurs in boys' play groups, liking and disliking one's playmates is essentially irrelevant. The game is the thing. Often there is no choice of who the other participants will be, but if there is, the choice will be made on the basis of game skills. Is it the case that girls are more likely to choose their companions on the basis of personal attraction?

The only information available that is relevant to this question is the size and composition of play groups. Clark et al. (1969), observing children aged 3–4, found that although there was no sex difference in the size of play groups, boys' social relationships tended to be somewhat more intense in that they played consistently with the same other children, and there were certain other children with whom an individual boy would never play. Girls, by contrast, distributed their interactions across a larger number of playmates. R. Bell et al. (1971), reporting on the amount and kind of peer interaction in their longitudinal sample, did not find a sex difference at preschool age, but when these children had reached the age of 7 (Waldrop and Halverson 1973[R]) their patterns of playmate choices had shifted dramatically. Girls were focusing their play in intensive relations with one or two "best friends," while boys played in larger groups of children. We do not know just when the tendency for girls to develop "chumships" and for boys to form "gangs" emerges. Laosa and Brophy (1972) observed these different social patterns for the two sexes among a group of children aged 5–7. Omark et al. (1973) observed it in American, Swiss, and African children in a cross-cultural study discussed in detail in the next chapter.

TABLE 6.6
Self-Report of Liking for Others and Rating of Others

Study	Age and N	Difference	Comment
B. Long et al. 1967	6-13 (312)	Girls	Prefer to do activities in group rather than alone
Mallick & McCandless 1966	8-9 (60)	Girls	Express less initial dislike for confederate who has frustrated them
		None	Dislike of confederate after either (1) opportunity to aggress, or (2) rational explanation of confederate conduct
Walker 1967	8-11 (406)	None	Self-appraisal: "socialness"
Benton 1971	9-12 (96)	Boys	Pairs of nonfriends evaluated each other more favorably
		None	Evaluation of partner, pairs of friends or acquaintances
Ramirez et al. 1971	12-17 (600)	None	Affiliation, projective measure from School Situation Picture Stories Test (Mexican American and Anglo-American Ss)
Rabbie & Howitz 1969	15 (112)	None	Evaluation of own and other group members after rewards were given to only 1 group (Dutch sample)
Benton et al. 1969	18-21 (80)	Women	Less satisfaction at catching same-sex partner in lie
Byrne et al. 1970	18-21 (88)	None	Evaluation of opposite-sex peer after spending 30 minutes with peer (Interpersonal Judgment Scale)
Gallo et al. 1969	18-21 (160)	None	Evaluation of partner's personality (Prisoner's Dilemma game)
Insko et al. 1973	18-21 (300)	None	Liking for same- or opposite-sex stranger after learning some of stranger's attitudes (Interpersonal Judgment Scale)
E. Jones et al. 1968	18-21 (140)	Women	Predicted higher performance for female stimulus person
		None	Ratings of female stimulus person's intelligence
A. Lott et al. 1970c	18-21 (50)	Women	Described liked person in more laudatory terms (adjective checklist)
Lunneborg & Rosenwood 1972	18-21 (465)	Women	Frequent affiliation themes in answer to "What makes you happy?"
Mascaro & Groves 1973	18-21 (33)	None	Attraction to stranger after being informed about stranger's attitudes (Interpersonal Judgment Scale)
Novak & Lerner 1968	18-21 (96)	Men	Rate same-sex partner higher in adjustment and attractiveness
	18-21 (86)	None	Willingness to interact with same-sex partner
Rosenfeld 1966	18-21 (92)	Women	Liking of same-sex partner after contrived interaction
Sampson & Hancock 1967	15-17 (251)	None	Need for affiliation, Edwards Personal Preference Schedule

(continued)

TABLE 6.6 *(cont.)*

Study	Age and N	Difference	Comment
Sarason & Winkel 1966	18-21 (48)	None	Positive, negative, or ambiguous references to others
C. Smith et al. 1967	18-21 (119)	None	Ratings of friendship potential: persons of varying sex, race, and beliefs
Steiner and Rogers[R] 1963	18-21 (100)	Women	Acceptance of peer with conflicting opinion
Touhey 1972	18-21 (250)	Women	Attraction to date selected by computer-dating program (Interpersonal Judgment Scale)
Wagman 1967	18-21 (206)	Women	Higher frequency of affiliative daydreams
Wilson & Insko 1968	18-21 (158)	None	Ratings of confederate on positive and negative personality traits (Prisoner's Dilemma game)
Craig & Lowery 1969	22 (56)	Women	Express more liking for confederate whom they observe being shocked (questionnaire)

Is it accurate to describe girls' friendships as more exclusive, or "deep"? We saw earlier (Table 6.3) that the distance a girl places herself from another person is likely to be a function of how well she knows the person, and that this is less true among boys and men. It is not true, however, that girls are generally more unfriendly to strangers of their own age (see Table 6.6). Studying a large group of Swedish elementary school children, Schaller (1973)[R] inquired about children's reactions to a newcomer to the class. Girls, on the whole, expressed more friendly attitudes toward the hypothetical newcomer. Feshbach and Sones (1971), on the other hand, experimentally formed two-person cohesive groups of junior high school children, and found that boy pairs accepted a newcoming third party more quickly than did girls. It is widely believed that girls establish a considerable degree of intimacy with their best friends, disclosing secrets and otherwise revealing themselves to a friend to a degree that a boy might be unlikely to do. If this were true, it would be understandable that girls would attempt to protect the intimacy of their friendships and be reluctant to accept others into the inner circle, although they might be "friendly" toward newcomers to a classroom. The work on self-disclosure is summarized in Table 6.7. There is little work with subjects under college age. The only study concerned with self-disclosure to age-mates found girls to be more likely than boys to tell secrets to friends. At the adult level, however, a sex difference does not emerge. It is particularly interesting that self-disclosure to one's spouse among married couples seems to be similar for husbands and wives, according to their own reports.

It would appear that there is a qualitative difference in the friendship patterns of the two sexes during childhood and adolescence (reflected in

TABLE 6.7
Self-Disclosure and Trust in Others

Study	Age and N	Difference	Comment
Rivenbark 1971	9, 11, 13, 15, 17 (149)	Girls	Disclosed more to peers
Vondracek & Vondracek 1971	11 (80)	None	Degree of intimacy of self-disclosure to E
Hochreich & Rotler 1970	18-21 (4,605)	None	Interpersonal Trust Scale
Jourard & Friedman 1970	18-21 (48)	Men None	More self-disclosure to male E Self-disclosure, tape-recorded with no E present
	18-21 (64)	None	Time spent in self-disclosure (male E present)
Levinger & Senn 1967	Adults (64)	None	Pleasant and unpleasant feelings described to spouses (self-report)

the size of groupings), but so far we have not been able to identify what lies behind these differences. By definition, girls' friendship patterns are more intimate, by simple virtue of the fact that they are smaller. Yet it is not clearly demonstrated that this "exclusiveness" implies greater hostility to newcomers, or greater self-disclosure, although both these elements may be present.

Another approach would be to inquire whether having only one or two "best friends" implies that a child is especially vulnerable to social pressure from these friends. Is it true that girls attach more weight to peer values and associations than boys do? What happens, for example, when a child must choose between what his peers want him to do and what he himself believes to be right or necessary? What if he must choose between peer values and those of adults (particularly his parents)? The rather limited evidence on this point suggests that it is boys, rather than girls, who are more susceptible to peer influence. In a study by Hollander and Marcia (1970), for example, children were asked to identify classmates in terms such as this: "This is a classmate who goes along with what the other children are doing," "This is a classmate who does what grown-ups think is right," "This is a classmate who does things independently." The subjects also were asked to complete a "dilemmas questionnaire," in which they chose, for example, whether they would go to a camp where their friends were going, even if the activities were not as interesting as those in another camp where they wouldn't know the other campers. On these measures, boys were more "peer-oriented" than girls. That is, more often than girls they chose peer associations and peer values when these conflicted with their own interests and values or with those of adults. This was true of the boys' self-reports about their own probable choices, and also true in their classmates' description of them.

Most of the peer relationships discussed so far refer to same-sex groupings. There is little information concerning the cross-sex attitudes and frequency of spontaneous interaction, although these no doubt change markedly with time. As early as the age of 4, there is evidence that children are more interested in other children of their own sex. That is, R. Sears et al. (1965)[n] found that boys of this age more often attempted to attract the attention of other boys, whereas girls directed their attention-getting attempts toward other girls. No doubt this is relevant to the spontaneous sex segregation of play groups that can be observed during the preschool years. H. Reese (1966) has shown that in the fifth grade, girls like boys better than boys like girls (and we suspect this is even more true at younger ages). At about the age of 10, however, the situation begins to shift: during the fifth-grade year, girls' evaluation of boys remains stable but boys become more favorably disposed toward girls. In grades 6 and 7, the attitudes of both boys and girls toward one another become more favorable, but the boys change at a faster rate. Presumably these attitude changes have some behavioral manifestations, with some spontaneous social groupings becoming less sex-segregated. But the shift in orientation toward the opposite sex does not imply that either sex is becoming more "sociable" than the other.

A picture has emerged, through the last several pages, of boys being more gregarious in terms of the number of peers with whom they interact and of dependence upon the peer group for values and interesting activities. This picture is distant indeed from the view of female personality as involving "greater interest in people, and greater capacity for the establishment of interpersonal relations," unless one regards girls' *intense* (i.e. "best friend") relationships as revealing more such capacity than the more dispersed social relations of boys.

What of the stereotype that girls are more sensitive to the nuances of interpersonal relationships—more "tuned in" to what other people are thinking and feeling—than boys? "Empathy" is a difficult quality to measure. Children's understanding of the motives, feelings, and social relationships of others has usually been studied in two ways: (1) by presenting stories or pictures (or both) that describe social situations, and asking the child to identify how the subjects of the storied incidents feel, what they mean to do, etc.; (2) by experimentally varying the social cues (e.g. tones of voice, supportive vs. neutral statements, friendliness vs. coldness) available to children, and determining the effects of such variation on their behavior.

Table 6.8 summarizes studies using these and related techniques. From these studies, no clear tendency emerges for girls to be more sensitive to social cues. The majority of studies show no differences, and the remainder

TABLE 6.8
Sensitivity to Social Cues: Empathy

Study	Age and N	Difference	Comment
Simner 1971	Newborns (94)	Girls	Cried longer in response to tape of newborn crying (trend, $p < .1$)
	Newborns (155)	None	Duration of cry in response to tape of new-born crying (3 experiments)
Borke 1971	3-8 (20)	None	Skill in identifying others' feelings (selection of faces to match story characters)
Hamilton 1973	3-4, 7, 10 (72)	None	Correct recognition of facial expressions
R. Burton et al. 1966	4 (112)	Boys	Effect of continuous vs. interrupted attention from E on resistance to deviation in marble-dropping task
Shure et al. 1971	4 (62)	None	Preschool interpersonal problem-solving test: alternative solutions to interpersonal problems
Cantor 1971	4-5 (40)	None	Happiness ratings of ambiguous faces
Feshbach & Feshbach 1969	4-5 (48)	Girls	Empathy scores based on response to series of slide sequence (trend, $p < .06$)
	6-7 (40)	None	Empathy scores: response to series of slide sequences
Meddock et al. 1971	4-5 (64)	None	Responsiveness to whether E was supportive or unresponsive in marble-dropping task
Gitter et al. 1971	4-6 (80)	None	Identifying emotions portrayed in pictures (after training) (black, white)
Savitsky & Izard 1970	4-8 (50)	None	Matching photos on basis of facial emotion
J. Todd & Nakamura 1970	5-7 (54)	None	Responsiveness to positive vs. negative tone of voice in marble-sorting task
Solomon & Ali 1972	5-25 (294)	Girls & women	Sensitivity to tone of voice (pleasant, indifferent, displeased) of taped evaluative statements
Whiteman 1967	5-6, 8-9 (42)	None	Understanding of motivations of story characters (black, Puerto Rican)
K. Rubin 1972	5, 7, 9, 11 (80)	None	Egocentrism score, description of nonsense cues to visually separated E
Feshbach & Roe 1968	6 (46)	Girls	Empathy scores: responses to slide sequences utilizing same-sex characters
Madsen & London 1966	7-11 (42)	None	Dramatic acting test (ability to take different roles)
Babad 1972	8 (40)	Girls	Sensitivity to satiation or deprivation of social reinforcement (discrimination task)
Hebda et al. 1972	8 (31)	None	Perception of aggressiveness in faces or expectation of retaliation after hypothetical aggressive act
Pawlicki 1972	8 (170)	Boys	Sensitivity to supportiveness of E's comments (marble-dropping game)

(continued)

TABLE 6.8 *(cont.)*

Study	Age and N	Difference	Comment
Rothenberg 1970	8, 10 (108)	None	Sensitivity to others' emotions (judgments of recorded stories)
Nakamura & Finck 1973	9-12 (251)	None	Sensitivity to social stimuli and/or to potential evaluation by others (questionnaire)
De Jung & Meyer[R] 1963	10-11 (408)	None	Accuracy of guessing how others rate self
Kohn & Fiedler[R] 1961	14, 18, 21 (120)	Men	Make more distinctions among familiar people when rating them on personality dimensions
R. Buck et al. 1972	18-21 (38)	Women	Identification of emotions of televised faces
I. Hilton et al. 1969	18-21 (44)	None	Predictions of behavior in hypothetical situation
Isen 1970	18-21 (30)	None	Attention to confederate's behavior (measured by recall and recognition)
Marlatt 1970	18-21 (96)	None	Effect on discussion of personal problems of interviewer reacting positively, negatively, or neutrally
Craig & Lowery 1969	22 (56)	Women	Rate watching confederates receive shock as more painful
Ekman & Friesen 1971	Children & adults (319)	None	Selection of faces to match emotions of characters in stories (New Guinea sample)

are nearly evenly divided as to whether boys or girls emerge as more skillful in interpreting, or more sensitive in responding to, social cues. A valuable clue to understanding these results is provided by Feshbach and Roe (1968). They showed first-graders pictures designed to embody four different affective situations: happiness, sadness, fear, and anger. Two sets of the same situations were prepared, one set using a female stimulus person, the other a male. The children were asked to report their own feelings upon viewing the pictures, and then to tell how they thought the central character in the picture felt. With the boy as the central character in a scene, boys were more accurate than girls in identifying the probable feelings of the character; on the other hand, when a girl was the central character, girls were more accurate. It is not clear from these results whether children felt more confidence in their judgments about the meaning of a situation when a same-sex person was involved or whether they took more interest in it—both are possible. Although the study standardized the situations in which boy and girl characters appeared, it is probable that the results would be even more dramatic if female central characters were involved in "girlish" activities and boys in "boyish" activities. A child's skill in using social cues probably depends to some extent on his familiarity with the situation in which the people he is evaluating find themselves, as well as upon his feeling of personal identity with them. We might expect, then, that children will be more "empathic" with other children than they are with adults, and more empathic with other children of their own sex especially when the activities involved are sex-typed, so that the observing child is more likely to be familiar with them. A visitor to England, attending his first cricket game, will find it hard to judge whether a particular player on the field is feeling glad or sorry when another player throws or hits the ball in a particular way, although he might be very skillful in making such judgments at an American ball game. What Table 6.6 suggests is that neither sex has greater ability to judge the reactions and intentions of others in any generalized sense, but when activities are sex-typed, so that one sex is likely to know more about a given situation than the other, that sex will have better-developed social judgments. Most men, as well as most women, are in the company of others during a large portion of their waking hours and must learn to take others' reactions into account. It is true that some occupations call for a higher level of social judgment skills than others; it may be that women's usual occupations call for this skill more than men's, although to our knowledge this has not been demonstrated. It would be reasonable to expect, for example, that people with recent experience as parents or nursery school teachers would be more adept at anticipating when a child in their care was about to become emotionally upset than would people inexperienced in child care. Since women are more likely to have daily or even hourly contact with young children, they may be expected, on the average, to have better-developed empathic reactions with young children. On the other hand, because of their greater work experience, men may be better able to "read" the reactions of people at various levels of an organizational hierarchy.

The summaries of earlier research presented in *The Development of Sex Differences* (1966) indicated that women and girls showed more interest than boys in social activities and that their tastes in books and TV programs were more oriented toward the gentler aspects of interpersonal relations and less toward aggression, "action," and science than was true for boys; furthermore, girls developed an interest in the opposite sex at an earlier age, and were more concerned about their personal appearance and attractiveness. To our knowledge nothing in the more recent research contradicts these conclusions. The danger is simply in overgeneralizing from them. Such findings do not warrant any conclusion that girls have a greater "capacity" for social responsiveness. In fact, it is our opinion that the social judgment skills of men and boys have been seriously underrated.

NURTURING OTHERS, MATERNAL BEHAVIOR, AND HELP GIVING

Some time ago, H. A. Murray (1938)[8] used the term "nurturance" to describe the giving of aid and comfort to others; in Murray's terms, nurturant behavior often took the form of a response to "succorance" (bids for help and comfort) from others who were younger, weaker, or for some other reason in a dependent position vis-à-vis the nurturant person. There can be no doubt that women throughout the world and throughout human history are perceived as the more nurturant sex, and are far more likely than men to perform the tasks that involve intimate care-taking of the young, the sick, and the infirm. There is currently considerable interest in this aspect of women's lives, and many questions are being raised concerning whether the assignment of such duties as care of children needs to be a sex-linked thing. To what extend could, or should, boys and men be involved in the care of children? Are there any biological predeterminers that make child-care roles more compatible with "natural" inclinations for one sex than the other?

As a starting point, we shall examine the nurturant behavior of mammals lower than man. If "instinctive" patterns are found in lower animals, we do not think that this implies in any sense that they must be carried over to man. However, we do believe that, since man is a mammal, any biologically based elements in nurturant behavior that man *does* have may represent continuities with those found in subhuman mammals, and we may learn something from tracing their evolutionary history. Furthermore, there have been some rather loose analogies comparing the care of infants in man with that in other mammalian species, and before we consider the validity of such analogies, it is well to be as informed as possible concerning the nature of the behavior in lower animals, its determinants, and its variability.

Let us consider first the role of hormones in animal maternal behavior. A first question is whether the hormones associated with pregnancy and parturition "prime" the female in some way for taking care of the young. Rosenblatt (1969)[R] reports that when blood plasma is taken from female rats that have recently given birth and is administered to virgin females, the latency is reduced for the recipients to show such maternal behavior as retrieving, nest-building, and licking pups. Normally, a virgin female will show such behavior without hormonal treatment when given pups, but the delay in the appearance of the behavior is two or three times as long as when the treatment with maternal plasma has been given. Rosenblatt also finds a gradual increase, during pregnancy, in a female rat's maternal responsiveness to foster pups—an increase that does not occur if she has been ovariectomized. Thus the increase in responsiveness that occurs during pregnancy has a hormonal basis. Moltz et al. (1970)[R] report that virgin female rats will show maternal behavior more quickly and more consistently if they have received a combination of female hormones than if they have not. This, too, points to hormonal control of maternal behavior. It should be noted, however, that the hormonal impetus to maternal behavior gradually declines during the postparturition period. This is shown by continually supplying a postparturient female with young litters; when this is done, her "mothering" behavior diminishes, and the change cannot be attributed to the changes in the appearance of the pups. It is true that young pups are more effective elicitors of maternal behavior than older ones, but when this factor is held constant, there is still a temporal decline in maternal motivation (Rosenblatt 1969[R]).

The hormonal impetus to maternal behavior in rats is superimposed upon a base level of responsiveness that is greater than zero and is *not* hormonally controlled. Both virgin females and males will show maternal behavior toward pups after about five days if a fresh litter of newborns is given to them each day. And this is true even if they have been deprived of the glands that produce sex hormones. A female that has just given birth to pups, of course, is responsive immediately. Rosenblatt has shown (1969)[R] that the stimulation from the pups during the first few days following parturition is crucial in establishing and maintaining maternal responsiveness; if a mother is separated from her pups just after delivery, for a period of two to four days, she will not effectively rear a substitute litter. A similar period of separation at a somewhat later point in time, after maternal behavior has become established, is not so disruptive, and a new litter will normally be effectively cared for. The effect of contact with young is further illustrated in a study by Moltz et al. (1970)[R] in which it was found that ovariectomy and Caesarian section did not interfere with maternal behavior in rats that had borne and cared for previous litters, but it did disrupt maternal behaviors in animals bearing their first litter.

In Rosenblatt's studies, male rats behaved much like virgin females in their responsiveness to pups: such items of "maternal" behavior as licking, crouching over the young, and retrieving them did appear, but only after several days of exposure to the pups. The males did differ in that they were less likely than virgin females to build nests. Rosenberg et al. (1971)[R] have reported that male rats tend to be more aggressive toward pups, and are likely to kill the first litters that are given to them. After several fresh litters have been supplied, however, the male's aggression diminishes and nurturant behavior ultimately appears.

Little is known concerning the possible hormonal basis of maternal behavior in species higher than rodents. To our knowledge, no work has been done relating maternal behavior in apes or humans to the amounts of hormones present in their bodies that are associated with pregnancy and childbirth. A study by Ehrhardt and Baker (1973)[R] does discuss the relevance of *masculinizing* hormones for later "maternal" behavior for girls. A group of girls showing the "adrenogenital syndrome" at birth were studied. These girls received excess androgens prenatally owing to a genetic defect affecting the prenatal functioning of the adrenal cortex, and were born with masculinized genitalia which were subsequently surgically corrected (during the first two years of life). Despite being normal females with respect to internal body structures, and indistinguishable from normal girls externally after surgery, these girls showed a number of "masculine" behavior traits. For our present purpose the point of interest is that they were reported to be less interested in playing with dolls, and less interested in caring for younger children, than a control group composed of their own normal sisters. Unfortunately the source of information is mothers' reports, and the mothers, of course, knew the medical history of the children and hence may not have been unbiased reporters. The magnitude of the differences, however, was striking. If further more objective measures bear out the original findings, this study will indicate that, although the effects of female hormones on maternal behavior are not known in humans, the effects of *male* hormones may be to suppress such behavior.

Whether or not there is a hormonal component underlying maternal responsiveness in humans, it seems that contact with a young infant may be important in maintaining, or activating, this behavior. In saying this, we mean something more than the obvious fact that a person cannot be maternal unless there is an appropriate object to be maternal toward. We mean that it might be true in humans, as it has been shown to be in lower mammals, that there is a critical period immediately following the birth of an infant during which it is important for the mother to have contact with her infant, and that if she does not, at a later time the infant will not elicit as complete maternal behavior from her as it would otherwise do. Investigating this possibility, Leifer et al. (1972)[R] studied maternal responsiveness to premature infants from whom the mothers had been separated during a 3–12-week period when the newborn was hospitalized. The mother-infant pairs were observed after the infant had been discharged from the hospital and returned to the mother's care, and they were compared with full-term infants and their mothers who had not been separated. At one week and four weeks after the infants had left the hospital, observations were made; full-term infants were more often held close to the mother's body, touched affectionately, and smiled at than premature infants from whom the mother had been separated. Of course, it is possible that the mothers were more concerned over the fragility of premature babies, and therefore hesitated to handle them, so the differences in handling cannot confidently be attributed to separation. More crucial information is potentially available from another comparison in the Leifer et al. study. There were two groups of mothers of premature infants. One group had an opportunity to touch and handle their infants during the hospitalization period, and the other group followed the more usual hospital procedure of viewing their infants through a window. Unfortunately the amount and frequency of contact with the infants among the "touch" group were minimal. Even so, there were indications that the mothers in the "touch" group were showing stronger attachment behavior toward their infants than the no-touch group several months after the infants were brought home (Leifer 1970[R]). These findings are consistent with the hypothesis that early contact is important in establishing some aspects of the mother-infant attachment bond in human beings.

It should be noted that in the Leifer et al. study (1972)[R], no group of *fathers* was studied, so we do not know whether contact with a young infant is similarly important in establishing his attachment to a child.

What about the potential of the male for nurturing the young of a species? We noted above that the rat male's initial response to newborns frequently is to attack them, so that it is only after this response has been extinguished that nurturant behavior appears. A similar situation appears to exist in rhesus monkeys. Chamove et al. (1967)[R] used 15 male-female pairs of preadolescent monkeys, aged 18–30 months. An infant monkey, 20–40 days old, was introduced as a stimulus to the juvenile pair. The young females showed four times as much positive behavior toward the infant (including ventral contact, grooming, and play) as did the males; the males exhibited ten times as much hostility toward the infants. In view of this difference in the reactions of the two sexes to an infant, it is understandable that if both sexes of older animals are available, it will normally be a female who "adopts" an orphan. However, Harlow (1962)[R] has reported that if only a male is available, an infant caged with him will persist in its attempts to achieve ventral contact despite repeated rebuffs, and that eventually the male will permit the contact and spend a good deal of time holding the infant close to his body.

The Harlow work, and the work by Chamove et al., has been done with animals raised in captivity, and their behavior may not be typical of animals growing up in the social conditions of a free-living troupe. DeVore (1963[R], Hall and DeVore 1965[R]) studied free-living troupes of cynocephalus baboons in Kenya. In this species, males play a protective role for the troupe as a whole but, aside from this, take little interest in infants. Occasional exceptions occur among high-status males, who may approach a mother with a young infant and attempt to hold or examine the infant briefly, but juvenile males and young adult males who are nondominant were not seen to make such approaches. Juvenile females, by contrast, frequently approached newborns, looked at them intently, touched them, and would hold them if the mother permitted. At a later time, when the infants had moved away from their mothers and formed a play group, they would climb on the adult males and tease them, and the males would permit this up to a point, but did not themselves engage in play or care-taking with the young.

It is well to be aware, however, of how much variability there is in the role of the male among species that are fairly closely related. In another variety of baboon, the hamadryas, for example, the male is much more involved with infants than is the cynocephalus male. Kummer observed these animals in Ethiopia, and reports (1968, p. 301)[R]:

Typical of the hamadryas organization is the high frequency of child care behavior by subadult and young adult males. In the initial unit, the one-year-old female flees into her male's arms when another baboon threatens her, and rides on his back across passages in the sleeping cliff, which she cannot negotiate because of her small size. Such "maternal" tendencies are already prominent in the young subadult hamadryas males. They sometimes pick up a black infant, and hug and carry it at a safe distance from the mother and her leader. The same tendency is later shown by young adult males before they have any females of their own. Five young juveniles of both sexes that we trapped at one cliff and released near another were all caught and mothered in the described way, each by another young adult male. Thus the "maternal" behavior of the male toward his first consort is a continuation of similar behavior at an earlier age. "Child care" motivations in the male are one important root for the formation of the one-male units in hamadryas.

The last point is important. Lest we be tempted to think of the male participation in child care among the male hamadryas as an evolutionary precursor of female liberation, it should be noted that the male hamadryas baboon keeps his females in total subjugation—he isolates them from the rest of the troupe by "herding" them and attacks them if they do not follow him closely at all times. Also, of course, it is still the female who does most of the nurturing of the young.

For our present purposes, the important points to be derived from the behavior of mammalian species other than man are as follows:

1. "Maternal" behavior is to some degree hormonally controlled. Hormonal factors are more powerful during the period immediately following the birth of young, and in untreated animals they diminish strongly toward the end of the "infancy" period.

2. The hormones associated with pregnancy, childbirth, and lactation are not necessary for the appearance of parental behavior. With sufficient exposure to newborns, virgin females and males will show parental behavior, but the behavior is not so readily aroused as it is in a female that has been hormonally "primed."

3. In the males of some species, aggression interferes with responsiveness to the young.

4. Among subhuman primates, there is great variability from one species to another in the degree of male participation in caring for the young.

5. The child-care functions that the two sexes will perform in adulthood are anticipated in the behavior of preadolescents and young subadults. That is, in species in which the adult males do not participate in care of the young, juvenile males do not show positive social interest in infants

(and may even attack them), whereas juvenile females do show such interest; in species in which the adult males are involved in child care, juvenile males show more positive interest in infants.

In view of point 5, it becomes especially important to try to discover whether there is a reliable sex difference among human juveniles in the tendency to be responsive toward infants. We turn now to studies of nurturance in homo sapiens.

Existing research has seldom focused on a child's offering of nurturance to an infant or a younger child—that is, on behavior that might be considered a precursor to later child care. To our knowledge children have not been offered a live baby, or a live kitten or puppy, to care for under conditions where their reactions might be systematically observed. It would be interesting indeed to know whether young boys and girls differ in their response to younger and more helpless beings. Certainly the folklore is that a boy frequently becomes intensely attached to his dog; there is no evidence that either sex is more strongly attracted to *young* animals, as distinct from full-grown ones. The fact that girls more frequently play with dolls from an early age has been taken as evidence of their greater tendency to show spontaneous nurturance. However, considering that girls are more often given dolls, it may be that their nurturant behavior is more frequently *elicited* without there being any underlying difference in "potential" for the behavior. As we noted above, Ehrhardt and Baker (1973)[n] did find that fetally androgenized girls were less interested in dolls than were their normal sisters (according to the mother's report), which suggests a biological component in this behavior.

Parenthetically, in studies of interest in dolls, it might be well to determine to what extent the play with dolls is actually nurturant. It is true that dolls are hugged and tucked into bed, which are nurturant actions by any definition; however, they are also scolded, spanked, subjected to surgical operations, and (in the personal experience of one of the authors) even scalped. If girls choose dolls as a vehicle for acting out a variety of fantasies, this is not in itself evidence that the fantasies are more nurturant than those of boys, although they may be.

What about the potential of adult men and women for nurturant behavior toward animals, infants, and children? This is a topic that is only just beginning to be studied. Extrapolating from what is known about animals much lower than man, it would appear possible that the hormones associated with pregnancy, childbirth, and lactation may contribute to a "readiness" to care for a young infant on the part of a woman who has just given birth. The animal studies also suggest, however, that contact with infants is a major factor in developing attachment and care-taking behavior in the juvenile and adult members of a species, and this is true for both individuals that have given birth and individuals (male or female) that have not.

Even with little experience with infants, however, the human male may have more potential for nurturant reactions than he has been given credit for. In a recent study by S. L. Bem (1974), college students were given the opportunity to interact with an eight-week-old kitten. During one part of the procedure, they were instructed to play with the kitten; during another part of the procedure, kitten play was one of several activities from which the subjects could choose. There was no significant difference between men and women subjects, on the average, in their interest in the kitten, amount of contact with it, and their enjoyment of playing with it.

Recent observations by Parke and O'Leary (1974)[R] bear on the level of interest among adult men in newborn infants. In this study, observations were made in hospital wards. In some instances, the situation involved both the mother and father being present together. The newborn infant was brought in by a nurse, who asked which parent wanted to hold the infant. Records were made of which parent initially took the child, and of the amount of nurturant interaction (looking, touching, rocking, holding, smiling) with the infant that each parent engaged in during the father's visit. With the exception of smiling, fathers engaged in *more* nurturant interaction with the infants than did mothers, when both parents were present. The study also involved observations of fathers alone with their newborn infants (that is, with the mother not being present) and of mothers when the fathers were not present. Here, too, the fathers engaged in as much or more nurturant behavior, by comparison with the mothers. It is of especial interest that Parke used two samples of families. The first was a well-educated group many of whom were especially interested in natural childbirth—half the fathers in this initial sample had attended classes on natural childbirth and many were present at the child's delivery. The second sample was taken in a working-class hospital serving a racially mixed population, and none of the fathers in this group were present at the infant's birth. It is striking that the two groups of fathers, from such diverse backgrounds, should both have shown such high levels of "mothering" behavior toward their newborn infants. The widespread belief that men tend to be uninterested in very young infants, becoming interested only as the children acquire more fully differentiated "personalities," has not been supported by the Parke work. Clearly, detailed information is needed through the growth phases following the newborn period, before it will become clear what truth, if any, there is in the popular belief.

HELPING AND SHARING

We have been discussing nurturant, "maternal" behavior directed toward infants, or other individuals younger and more helpless than the subject. There is a body of research on "altruism" that deals with helpful, supportive behavior that a person may direct toward a variety of other persons, including age-mates. Whiting and Pope (1974), in their observational study of children in six cultures, report the frequency of *offering help*. This category included offering food, toys, or tools, or offering to contribute one's own labor to the joint completion of a task that another person was engaged in. The observers also recorded *offering emotional support*, in the form of consolation, encouragement, physical contact-comfort, or reassurance. Whiting and Pope do not report the ages of the targets of these behaviors—presumably helpful and supportive efforts were sometimes directed at younger children (in which case they would reflect nurturance in the sense discussed above), sometimes toward age-mates, and sometimes toward adults. The authors report that in the age range 3–6, although there is a tendency for girls to show more help-giving behavior than boys, the tendency is not consistent over the six cultures studied, the differences are not large, and they are not significant within any culture or when the cultures are combined. During the ages 7–11, however, girls emerge strongly as the more helpful sex. Offering help is more common among girls in five of the six societies at this age, and the overall sex difference is significant ($p < .01$). The giving of emotional support shows even stronger results: girls aged 7–11 give more in all six of the cultures studied, and the difference for the combined data is significant at the .001 level.

It should be noted that the giving of help by girls in the six cultures studied by Whiting and Pope was accompanied by a form of dominance called "suggesting responsibly." This category included instances in which a child would attempt to control another child in the interests of that other child's well-being or safety. (Warning another child not to go near a dangerous cliff and insisting that the child come in to a meal would be cases in point.) It would appear that girls, in a variety of cultures, are more likely than boys to adopt the role of being responsible for the welfare and conduct of others. It is reasonable to suppose that this stems from the more frequent assignment of girls to baby-sitting responsibilities (Whiting and Pope 1974, Barry et al. 1959[R]).

Aside from the Whiting and Pope report, research is rare that involves observations of young children's giving of comfort and assistance to one another in naturalistic situations. Hartup and Keller (1960)[R], observing children aged 3–5, found no sex difference in giving affection to other children, giving praise or help, or giving reassurance and comfort. It is worth noting that the children who most often gave help and affection to others were the same children who most often *asked* for help and affection from others—in other words, helpful behavior was part of a reciprocal system. The nurturance-giving children, however, were significantly *unlikely* to engage in the more passive forms of proximity seeking—that is, simply remaining close to others. Help giving, then, is distinctly not a passive process, even though it is associated with forms of seeking positive social contact that have sometimes been labeled "dependency."

R. Sears et al. (1965)[R] did time-sampled observations of the free play of 40 four-year-olds, and reported the frequency with which children behaved nurturantly. Their definition was "voluntarily guiding or assisting another with the intent of being helpful or performing a service," and included offering comfort to another child who was upset as well as offering task-oriented help. They found such behavior to be rather rare among children of this age, and the frequency did not differ significantly between the sexes. In the same study, projective doll-play measures of nurturance were also obtained. In this procedure, a child was presented with a one-story roofless dollhouse and a family of five dolls: a mother, father, boy, girl, and baby. The child was invited to act out domestic scenes or "stories" of his own invention. Again, helpful behavior by one member of the doll family toward another was a fairly infrequent occurrence; however, girls more frequently than boys showed the dolls engaging in such behavior.

Recent research on altruistic behavior has involved setting up experimental situations in which there are opportunities for the subject to go to the assistance of someone who appears to be in distress. These studies (along with the naturalistic ones on help giving) are charted in Table 6.9. Many of the experimental studies are done with college students or adults. It may be seen that there is no consistent tendency for one sex to offer help more readily than the other. In those studies where a sex difference does appear, there is reason to believe, at least in some instances, that situational elements make helping easier for one sex than the other. For example, in the Gaertner and Bickerman study, the subject was required to phone a garage mechanic to get help for the person in distress. A garage mechanic could be expected to be male. Presumably, women, on the average, are more reluctant to initiate interaction with a strange man than a male subject would be.

The major exception to the no-difference trend in Table 6.9 is the cross-cultural work of Whiting and Pope. Either girls are more consistently trained to be help givers in other cultures than our own, or the major experimental studies of help giving have not sampled the situations in which female helpfulness would be most apparent. Despite the cross-cultural findings, the conclusion reached from our examination of findings on helping behavior is that a person's helpfulness is not consistently related to his sex.

The same is true of other manifestations of altruism. Tables 6.10 and 6.11 chart the studies in which subjects are given the opportunity to donate to charity, and those in which the willingness to share toys, candy, or other valued items is measured. The large majority of these studies show no sex differences. Where a difference is found, the direction somewhat more frequently favors girls and women, but the number of no-difference findings requires us to conclude that no trend toward greater female altruism has been shown.

TABLE 6.9

Helping Behavior

Study	Age and N	Difference	Comment
Hartup & Keller[R] 1960	3-5 (41)	None	Giving help, praise, reassurance, affection to age-mate
Whiting & Pope 1974	3-6 7-11 (134)	None Girls	Offers help, gives support (overall 6 cultures) Same measure
R. Sears et al.[R] 1965	4 (40)	None	Guiding or assisting another
Staub 1971a	5 (64)	None	Helping other child in distress
Staub 1971c	5 (75)	Girls None	Helping child in distress (1 of 4 groups) Helping adult pick up paper clips
Staub 1970	5, 6, 7 9, 11 (232)	None	Helping child in distress
Dlugokinski & Firestone 1973	10, 13 (164)	None	Amount of money donated to charity
I. W. Silverman 1967	11 (199)	None	Minutes volunteered for later experiment
Staub 1971b	12 (40)	None	Responses to distress cues from adjoining room
Nemeth 1970	15-17 (120)	None	Completing survey or getting other to complete survey
Aronson & Cope 1968	18-21 (80)	None	Number of phone calls made as a favor
Bickman 1972	18-21 (423) 18-21 (300) 18-21 (298)	None None None	Helping behavior in response to phone call Helping behavior in response to letter Helping behavior in response to person present
J. Darley & Latané 1968	18-21 (72)	None	Speed in reporting fictitious epileptic seizure
Gruder & Cook 1971	18-21 (104)	None	Number of questionnaires stapled as a favor
Isen 1970	18-21 (30)	None	Helpfulness to confederate carrying armload of items
S. Schwartz & Clausen 1970	18-21 (179)	None None Men Women None	Speed of helping victim believed to be having a seizure Response to tape-recorded cries of victim with 4 other bystanders present Responded more quickly when one of 4 bystanders is medically competent Responded more quickly when no other bystanders are present Number of Ss who did not respond (all 3 conditions combined)

(continued)

TABLE 6.9 *(cont.)*

Study	Age and N	Difference	Comment
Thalhofer 1971	18-21 (192)	Women	Offering time or money to help fictitious boy (1 of 2 conditions)
Gaertner & Bickerman 1971	Adults (1,109)	Men	Made phone calls to a garage when asked to over the phone by a confederate (black and white sample)
Piliavin et al. 1969	Adults (4,450)	Men	First to help in staged collapse on subway train
Wispé & Freshley 1971	Adults (176)	Men None	Helped pick up dropped groceries (black sample) Picking up dropped groceries (white sample)

TABLE 6.10
Donating to Charities

Study	Age and N	Difference	Comment
Staub 1971c	5 (75)	Boys	Donating candy to needy children (1 of 4 groups)
Bryan et al. 1971	7-8 (96)	None	Donating rewards to charity
B. Moore et al. 1973	7-8 (42)	None Girls	Mean pennies contributed Median penny contributions higher
J. Grusec 1971	7, 11 (88)	None	Donating rewards to charity
J. Grusec 1972	7, 11 (100)	None	Donating marbles to poor children
J. Grusec & Skubiski 1970	8, 10 (80)	None	Marbles to poor children
Rosenhan & White 1967	9-10 (130)	None	Gift certificates to charity box
G. White 1972	9-10 (210)	Girls None	2 days later, donation of gift certificates Immediate donating behavior
Fouts 1972	10-11 (40)	None	Donating pennies to charity
Dlugokinski & Firestone 1973	10, 13 (164)	Girls	Donate more money to charity (trend, $p < .1$)
Regan 1971	18-21 (81)	None	Donating behavior

In summary, our survey of research on attachment, affiliation, and positive interactions of all kinds has shown surprisingly little sex differentiation. To be sure, we have woefully little information on some topics (such as nurturance), and on other topics (such as empathy) we must remain dissatisfied with the way the disposition in question has been measured. Nevertheless, the picture that has emerged is one of high "sociability" in both sexes. There may be a qualitative difference in the nature of the social relationships most sought by the two sexes. The fact that boys travel in

TABLE 6.11
Sharing Behavior

Study	Age and N	Difference	Comment
Masters 1968	3-5 (40)	None	Token sharing with partners
I. Lane & Coon 1972	4-5 (80)	None	Rewards to self and partner
Masters 1971	4-5 (120)	None	Tokens to absent partner
Masters 1972a	4-5 (80)	None	Token sharing after model absent
G. Leventhal & Anderson 1970	5 (144)	Boys	Took more rewards than girls did when told performance was superior to fictitious same-sex partner
		None	When told performance was same or inferior to fictitious same-sex partner
Dreman & Greenbaum 1973	5-6 (120)	None	Candy sharing to known and unknown recipients (Israeli sample)
Elliott & Vasta 1970	5-7 (48)	None	Sharing candy or pennies after observing models
Presbie & Coiteux 1971	6 (64)	None	Sharing marbles after observing models
Hapkiewicz & Roden 1971	7 (60)	Boys	Shared viewing time of peep show with same-sex partner
Slaby 1973	8-9 (66)	None	Pennies shared
M. Harris 1970	9-10 (168)	None	Sharing game winnings
Kahn 1972	18-21 (120)	Women	Shared more money in an underpay condition
		None	Amount of money shared in the equal and overpay conditions
I. Lane & Missé 1971	18-21 (128)	Women	Shared more of game rewards
G. Leventhal & Lane 1970	18-21 (61)	Women	Shared monetary reward more equally

larger groups whereas girls more often establish close friendships in twos (or sometimes threes) probably has considerable significance. We suspect that the size of social groups has a great deal to do with dominance patterns. Large groups cannot so easily function without a dominance hierarchy as can small groups; is the small size of girls' social groups in part a reflection of their reluctance to enter into dominance hierarchies and compete for positions in such hierarchies? This question takes us squarely into the area of power relationships in social groupings, the topic to which we now turn.

CHAPTER SEVEN

Power Relationships

In the history of humankind, group efforts to seize territory, possessions, or governments by force have been the province of men. So have efforts to resist the incursions of others. Societies are rare indeed that have placed women in the front ranks of their armies. Forceful person-to-person power struggles (duels, jousting, boxing), whether for blood or "sport," have also been almost exclusively male endeavors. Why should this be so? In the present chapter, we shall ask whether it is all forms of power assertion or only the directly aggressive ones that characterize the male. We shall be concerned with the developmental course that power relations take within and between the sexes as children progress through childhood and adolescence. Especially interesting is the question of the female response to male aggression—is the female submissive, compliant, yielding? In asking these questions, it will be necessary to consider both biological and social factors that may affect sex differentiation.

AGGRESSION

The word "aggression" refers to a loose cluster of actions and motives that are not necessarily related to one another. The central theme is the intent of one individual to hurt another. But attempts to hurt may reflect either the desire to hurt for its own sake or the desire to control another person (for other ends) through arousing fear. Modes of expressing hostile feelings vary greatly—in some instances, the intent to hurt never gets beyond the stage of vindictive daydreams; in others the expression is overt but highly disguised; direct physical attack is rare among adults, though sharp words and other kinds of hostile actions are ubiquitous. Most important of all, a person who is known for a readiness to fight under some circumstances will be meek and gentle under others, and this is true among animals as well as among human beings. For example, Kuo (1967)[1] has studied chow dogs, and reports that they will attack cats in one setting and interact with them in a friendly fashion in others. So even the presence of a consistent "stimulus" does not yield consistent behavior.

Defn:

Given this variability, there is no reason to expect that any one group of individuals will be consistently more "aggressive" than another. It is surprising, then, to find that males do appear to be the more aggressive sex, not just under a restricted set of conditions but in a wide variety of settings and using a wide variety of behavioral indexes. This generalization was documented some years ago by Terman and Tyler (1954)[R] in their review of the research of the 1930's and 1940's. A similar picture emerged from the 1966 summary by Oetzel (Maccoby 1966b[R]). More recent studies (plus several omitted from the earlier listing) are shown in Table 7.1. The major fact highlighted by the table is that males are consistently found to be more aggressive than females. Even the exceptions, when examined in detail, prove not to be strong. For example, Blurton Jones (1972) reports that his sample of 25 children appears to be atypical, and when an associate (Burke) did further observations on a larger sample, including the original Blurton Jones group of 25 children, the usual higher level of aggression in boys was found.

The behavioral sex difference is found in a variety of cultures. For example, the cross-cultural work reported by Whiting and Pope (1974) involved time-sampled behavior observations in seven cultures. (Only six of the cultures are included in their tables, and the seventh is discussed in the text.) Two age cohorts were observed in each culture: children from 3 to 6, and another group from 6 to 10. In all the cultures studied, direct physical assault of one child upon another was rare, and the data base was insufficient to test for sex differences. However, boys engaged in more "mock fighting" (rough-and-tumble play); they exchanged more verbal insults; and a boy was more likely than a girl to counterattack if aggressed against in either verbal or physical form.

Omark, Omark, and Edelman (1973)* have reported extensive time-sampled observations in three societies: the United States, Switzerland, and Ethiopia. In each culture, children were observed on the school playground. Aggression was defined as pushing or hitting without smiling; a greater incidence of this behavior was found among boys in all three societies.

The bulk of the psychological research done on aggression with subjects beyond the preschool years has involved standardized eliciting situations. Modeling studies are numerous; the subjects observe models performing a variety of actions, some aggressive and some nonaggressive, and the subjects' subsequent behavior is observed. Studies measuring aggression follow-

---

* The work by Omark et al. forms part of a larger cross-cultural project initiated by Daniel G. Freedman (1971)[R]. A report of the project, "The Development of Social Hierarchies," was presented at the meetings of the World Health Organization, Stockholm, 1971.

following models

ing exposure to a model have been included in Table 7.1. Boys consistently exhibit more aggression following exposure to a model; this conclusion applies to both directly imitative and nonimitative aggression (see Table 7.1). Another large body of research involves giving the subject the opportunity to administer shocks to an age-mate. The situation is presented as *shock* one in which the subject is helping teach something to the target person and is administering the shock as punishment for wrong responses. (The "victim" is a confederate who does not receive real shocks—a fact that the subject learns after the experimental session is over.) The subject may choose the duration and intensity of shocks to be administered. The findings of a number of studies are consistent in showing male subjects to be more likely than females to administer high levels of shock and to hold the shock button down longer.

It is possible that the sexes differ in aggressiveness not only quantitatively but qualitatively. E. Goodenough (1957) noted this possibility in reporting the comments of parents whom she interviewed. The parents were asked to describe their children's personalities. Goodenough discussed their comments as follows (p. 302):

Parents' comments about aggression or activity in their children seem to imply in boys a force barely held under control, "dynamic," "a bomb shell," "bold," "belligerent." These mothers felt that the cup was running over: "a great deal of unnecessary energy," "so much energy he doesn't know what to do," "so much energy he can't use it all up." Differentiation in this category is significant largely because of the abundant physical energy ascribed to boys, and because aggression seems closely associated with physical force. Parents of girls seem more likely to equate aggressiveness with the personal reaction of anxiety and confusion, rather than with a release of uncontrollable gross motor energy.

We saw in Chapter 5 that boys were likely to be more active than girls in precisely those situations where aggression may also be observed—namely, during play with other boys. It seems quite possible, then, that aggression and activity may be linked in boys in much the way that parents believe it is, although whether intense activity arises from the arousal of aggressive impulses or vice versa, we do not know. It would be interesting indeed to know whether aggression and activity level co-vary more among boys than among girls, but for the present the question must remain open.

There have been a number of suggestions in previous writings on sex differences to the effect that the two sexes may be equally aggressive in the sense of their underlying motivation to hurt others, but that the two sexes characteristically show their aggression in different ways. The hypothesis takes two different forms:

1. The two sexes are reinforced for different forms of aggression. Girls are allowed to show hostility in subtle ("catty") ways, but not physical

TABLE 7.1
Aggression

Study	Age and N	Difference	Comment
Observational Studies			
F. Pedersen & Bell 1970	2-3 (55)	Boys	Observation of aggressive behavior in indoor free play with peers
McIntyre 1972	2-4 (27)	Boys None	Physical aggression, classroom observation Verbal aggression
P. Smith & Connolly 1972	2-4 (40)	Boys None	Rough-and-tumble play, play noises Aggression
Blurton Jones 1972	2, 3-4 (25)	Boys Girls None	Wrestling and hitting (during rough-and-tumble play when the slide was not available) Rough-and-tumble at age 2 (no difference in older age group) Aggressive play
Berk 1971	2-5 (72)	None	Offensive-combative response to interference with desired activity
Vernon et al. 1967	2-5 (32)	None	Observer ratings of aggression while child goes through standard hospital admission procedures
Fagot & Patterson 1969	3 (36)	None	"Throw rocks, hit with an object, push" (nursery school observation)
Baumrind & Black 1967	3-4 (103)	None	Becomes hostile (vs. does not become hostile) when hurt or frustrated (observer ratings)
Serbin et al. 1973	3-5 (225)	Boys	Frequency of aggressive responses, observation of free play in nursery school
Whiting & Pope 1974	3-10 (57)	None	Rough-and-tumble play (Kenya)
	3-11 (134)	Boys None	Behavior observation in 6 cultures: counteraggression in response to aggressive instigation by other (in 7-11-year-old age group only), rough-and-tumble play, verbal aggression Number of physical assaults (trend: boys, but n. s.)
Langlois et al.[R] 1973	3, 5 (32)	Boys	Hit with objects, 2-child play session (black suburban sample; first 2 sessions only)
Emmerich 1971	4-5 (415)	None	Defiance-hostility, classroom observations, early fall and late fall (black and white low SES)
	4-5 (596)	None	Defiance-hostility, classroom observations, early fall and spring (black and white low SES)
Hatfield et al. 1967	4-5 (40)	Boys None	Verbal and fantasy aggression during mother-child interaction (trend, $p < .1$); physical aggression Direct, indirect aggression to mother
Omark et al. 1973	4-8 (450)	Boys	Playground observation, frequency of hitting or pushing without smiling (American sample)
	5-9 (250)	Boys	Playground observations (Swiss sample)
	8-10 (250)	Boys	Playground observations (Ethiopian sample)

(continued)

TABLE 7.1 *(cont.)*

Study	Age and *N*	Difference	Comment
		Experimental Studies	
Rosekrans & Hartup 1967	3-5 (36)	None	Aggression toward toys, following modeled aggression
Feshbach 1972	4 (104)	Boys	Negative reinforcement administered by preschool-aged "teacher" to younger child (black, white; low, middle SES)
Feshbach & Devor 1969	4 (102)	None	Negative reinforcement administered to younger child
Larder 1962	4 (15)	Boys	Percent of trials, choice of aggressive toy
C. Madsen 1968	4-5 (40)	Boys	Imitation of filmed aggression, nonimitative verbal aggression
		Girls	Nonimitative physical aggression directed at Bobo doll
		None	Imitative verbal aggression
Parton & Geshuri 1971	4-5 (112)	Boys	Imitation of videotaped aggressive responses toward toys and dolls
Rau et al. 1970	4-10 (79)	Boys	Emotionally disturbed children; aggression toward mother and toys, observation session
M. Martin et al. 1971	5-7 (100)	Boys	Total and imitative aggression toward doll after observing male model
J. Nelson et al. 1969	5-7 (96)	Boys	Aggression toward objects, nonaggressive modeling
		None	Aggression toward objects after aggressive modeling
D. Hicks 1968	5-8 (84)	Boys	Imitative aggression with toys after exposure to filmed male model and hearing male E evaluate model's acting
Liebert & Baron 1972	5-6, 8-9 (136)	Boys	Aggressive play with knife, gun, and doll (observations following exposure to films)
		None	Willingness to hurt unseen peer
J. Grusec 1973	5, 10 (60)	None	Aggression to Bobo doll after exposure to female model and hearing female E evaluate model's behavior
N. Feshbach 1969	6 (126)	Boys	Session 1, aggressive responses to Bobo doll
		None	Session 1, direct, indirect aggression to partner
		Girls	Session 2, indirect aggression to newcomer, first 4 minutes
		None	Session 2, indirect aggression to newcomer, last 12 minutes; direct aggression to newcomer; direct and indirect aggression displayed by newcomer
Bandura et al. 1966	6-8 (72)	Boys	Imitation of model performing aggressive and non-aggressive behaviors
Hapkiewicz & Roden 1971	7 (60)	Boys	Aggression toward peers after viewing aggressive cartoon, nonaggressive cartoon, or no cartoon
J. Grusec 1972	8-9 (54)	Boys	Imitative aggressive responses (trend, $p < .1$)
		None	Nonimitative aggressive responses

(continued)

TABLE 7.1 *(cont.)*

Study	Age and N	Difference	Comment
Mallick & McCandless 1966	8-9 (48)	None	Number of "shocks" administered to same-sex confederate
	8-9 (60)	None	Impede confederate's progress on task
	8-9 (60)	None	Impede confederate's progress on task
Slaby 1973	8-9 (60)	Boys	Delivering "punches" to unseen peer by pressing button
M. Moore 1966	8, 10, 12, 14, 16, 18 (180)	Boys	Amount of violence perceived, simultaneous stereoscopic exposure to violent and nonviolent scenes
Shortell & Biller 1970	11 (48)	Boys	Deliver a higher intensity of noise to unseen peer
Ditrichs et al. 1967	12-13 (150)	Boys	Constructed more sentences using hostile verbs, following vicarious reinforcement
Titley & Viney 1969	17 (40)	Boys	Shock delivered to confederate
Buss 1966	18-21 (240)	Men	Intensity of shock to confederate
Epstein 1965	18-21 (40)	Men	Intensity of shock to confederate "learner"
Knott & Drost 1970	18-21 (80)	Men	Shocks to confederate after receiving shock: "masculine" men higher than "feminine" men, "masculine" women, and "feminine" women
Larsen et al. 1972	18-21 (213)	Men	Intensity and duration of shocks to male victim, following aggressive modeling (no difference in total voltage administered)
		None	Duration of shocks, maximum and total voltage administered: control, female learner, conformity, high model conditions
D. Leventhal et al. 1968	18-21 (80)	None	Shocks given to male confederate
Paolino 1964	18-21 (84)	Men	Intensity and frequency of aggressive episodes in dreams
Shomer et al. 1966	18-21 (64)	Men	More threats to partner, in effort to achieve cooperative game strategy
Shuck et al. 1971	18-21 (40)	Men	Intensity of shock given to confederate
Taylor & Epstein 1967	18-21 (24)	Women	Increase in intensity of shocks with increased provocation from opponent
		None	Intensity of shocks given to confederate
Youssef 1968	18-21 (120)	Men	Intensity of shocks delivered to confederate
Hokanson & Edelman 1966	18-24 (28)	None	Shock to confederate following shock to S

(continued)

TABLE 7.1 *(cont.)*

Study	Age and *N*	Difference	Comment
Deaux 1971	Adults (123)	None	Speed of honking at driver blocking intersection
Doob & Gross 1968	Adults (74)	Men	Speed of honking at slow driver at intersection

Ratings, Questionnaires, Projective Measures

Study	Age and *N*	Difference	Comment
Vernon et al. 1967	2-5 (32)	None	Aggression toward authority (mother questionnaire following child's release from hospital)
Manosevitz et al. 1973	3-5 (222)	Boys	Number of fights (parent report)
Santrock 1970	4-6 (60)	Boys	Doll play aggression (disadvantaged black sample, half father absent)
		None	Aggression (mother interview)
Wohlford et al. 1971	4-6 (66)	Boys	Intensity and frequency of aggression in doll play (black, low SES, father absent)
		None	Frequency of intense aggression, mother interview
Klaus & Gray 1968	6 (88)	None	Peer nominations (low SES black sample)
Semler et al. 1967	8 (567)	Boys	Peer ratings, aggressive behavior items
Semler & Eron 1967	8 (863)	Boys	Peer ratings, aggressive behavior items
Walker 1967	8-11 (450)	Boys	Teacher rating, aggressiveness
	8-11 (406)	Boys	Self-appraisal, aggressiveness
Ferguson & Maccoby 1966	10 (126)	Boys	Self-report, antisocial aggression
Devi 1967	16-24 (220)	Men	Asian-Indian students; self-reports, overtly aggressive reactions to frustrating situations
		None	Self-reports, suppressive aggressive reactions to frustrating situations
Barclay 1970	18-21 (55)	Men	Aggressive TAT imagery following arousal by hostile female E
Brissett & Nowicki 1973	18-21 (80)	Men	Self-rating, Child and Waterhouse Frustration Reaction Inventory
Harmatz 1967	18-21 (50)	Women	Pre-test, hostility scale
		None	Post-test, hostility scale, following verbal conditioning
Pytkowicz et al. 1967	18-21 (120)	Men	Aggressive content, attitude questionnaire. Increase in hostility following insult
		None	Sarason Hostility Scale (change in scores after being insulted)
Wagman 1967	18-21 (206)	Men	Higher frequency of aggressive and hostile daydreams
Youssef 1968	18-21 (120)	Men	Hostility Scale (Cook-Medley's, Siegel's)
Zillmann & Cantor	18-21 (40)	None	S's ratings of the humorous content and novelty of aggressive jokes and cartoons

ways. Physical aggression is thought appropriate for boys, whereas catti-
ness is not. Behavioral differentiation follows different socialization pressures for the two sexes in these two directions.

2. Aggression in general is less acceptable for girls, and is more actively
discouraged in them, by either direct punishment, withdrawal of affection,
or simply cognitive training that "that isn't the way girls act." Girls then
build up greater anxieties about aggression, and greater inhibitions against
displaying it; the result is that their aggressive impulses find expression in
displaced, attenuated, or disguised forms.

In both forms of this hypothesis, then, it is argued that the sexes do not
differ in "real" aggression but only in behavioral forms or modes of showing aggression. S. Feshbach (1970, pp. 192–93)[R] states the position as follows: "These data [on acceptance of newcomers; see below] along with
evidence that girls are higher in pro-social forms of aggression and also
have more conflict over aggression and greater aggression anxiety than
males suggest that the difference between boys and girls in aggression does
not lie in the strength of aggressive drive, but in the mode of behavior by
which aggression is manifested. The evidence is compelling that boys are
more physically aggressive than girls, yet a different pattern of results is
obtained when more indirect, non-physical forms of aggression are evaluated."

This point of view has been based on several pieces of evidence. First,
some studies (e.g. Bandura et al. 1961[R]) indicated that, although there
was a greater incidence of direct, physical aggression among boys, there
was no sex difference in verbal aggression. However, other reports have
not sustained this generalization. R. Sears et al. (1965)[R] found that boys
displayed both more physical and more verbal aggression than girls during
free play with peers in the nursery school. Hatfield et al. (1967), reporting
on the same sample of children, presented data on observations of mother-
child interaction. Physical aggression was rare, though somewhat more
common for boys than girls ($p < .10$). The sex difference in verbal aggression was greater, with boys having a significantly higher rate. Whiting and
Pope (1974) report that, in seven cultures, both verbal and physical aggression was more common among boys. McIntyre (1972), on the other
hand, found boys to be more aggressive only with respect to physical, not
verbal, forms of behavior. In free play among children, it is often the case
that fights are preceded or accompanied by verbal taunts, threats, or insults
(see Whiting and Pope). At least in some situations, then, the two types
of aggressive behavior may be expected to co-vary, rather than being alternative "outlets." However, this is by no means a universal finding. McIntyre,
for example, found verbal and physical aggression to be positively correlated for girls, negatively for boys! For the present, the most that can be

said is that if there is a sex difference in the forms aggression takes, the verbal-physical distinction does not accurately describe the difference.

A second piece of evidence for the "different modes" hypothesis is a study by Feshbach (1969) with first-graders, which has been widely cited as showing that girls are less accepting (more hostile) toward a newcomer than boys. In this study, children were first formed into two-person (same sex) "clubs," with badges and attractive equipment to promote cohesion. Then at a subsequent meeting a third child was introduced into the group; in some instances, the newcomer was of the same sex as the original pair, in others, of opposite sex. Responses to the newcomer that were coded as Direct Aggression included Physical Aggression, Verbal Aggression, and Expressive Aggression (sneering, threatening gestures). Ignoring, Avoiding, Refusals, and Excluding were coded as Indirect Aggression. The results were as follows:

| | Average total response in 16 minutes | | | |
| | By boy pairs toward: | | By girl pairs toward: | |
Type of aggression	Boy newcomer	Girl newcomer	Boy newcomer	Girl newcomer
Direct	1.3	.5	.4	.6
Indirect	1.7	1.4	2.4	2.2

Boys were somewhat more directly aggressive toward a newcomer than were girls, but this was confined to male targets, and the difference was not significant. The girls did show a significantly higher rate of ignoring, avoiding, and excluding during the first four minutes of the interaction, but this was temporary, and the interactions "warmed up," with sex differences becoming insignificant. As in all indirect measures of aggression, there is room for argument about whether the initial lack of acceptance by girls toward a newcomer is properly called "aggression." As will be discussed more fully below, girls normally congregate in smaller groups than boys. Their initial exclusiveness, then, may be related to their normal social patterns and have little relation to aggression. There is no evidence in the Feshbach work that the girls' initial avoidance or ignoring represented efforts to hurt or derogate the newcomers; on the other hand, it *may* have involved this quality. The fact that the sex difference was transitory, however, and the fact that boys showed somewhat more direct aggression toward a male newcomer (and the fact that boys, as newcomers, significantly more often displayed aggression toward the established pair) would not permit us to conclude that there is more hostility involved in "breaking into" an established group of girls than into one of boys.

There is a third kind of evidence that has led to the conclusion that sex differences in aggression are more apparent than real. This is the work on modeling. As Table 7.1 shows, boys normally do more spontaneous copying of modeled aggression than do girls. Bandura (1965)[R], however, showed that if children were offered a reward for performing as many of the model's aggressive responses as they could remember, sex differences were greatly reduced (though not eliminated), and it became apparent that girls had noticed and remembered more of the modeled aggression than they displayed in their spontaneous behavior. Mischel (1970, p. 42)[R] discusses this experiment in the following terms: "Boys and girls may be similar in their knowledge of aggressive responses, but they usually differ in their willingness to perform such responses. These differences presumably reflect differences in the sex-determined response consequences that boys and girls obtained and observed for such behavior in the past, and that they therefore expect in the future." The term "disinhibition" is used by Bandura in discussing the findings, and both Mischel and Bandura suggest that girls would show very nearly as much aggression as boys if they were not inhibited by fear based upon negative socialization experiences.

A first point to note in interpreting the Bandura results is that, although he has shown a large part of the sex difference in imitative aggression to be found in performance rather than acquisition, there probably are some differences in acquisition as well. Girls do not notice and retain the details of modeled aggression to the same extent that boys do. In the Bandura experiment, even under the incentive conditions, girls recalled less. In an early study of memory for film content, Maccoby and Wilson (1957)[R] found that girls recalled less of the aggressive content. In the work by M. Moore (1966), children in the age range 8–16 were shown pairs of pictures in a stereoscope, one picture showing a violent scene, the other a nonviolent one. Boys more often reported seeing the violent scene. Kagan and Moss (1962)[R] found that, in tachistoscopic presentation of aggressive scenes, girls required longer exposure times than boys to recognize the picture. Thus, whether as a result of anxiety and "perceptual defense" or not, it would appear that girls do not add aggressive actions to their repertoires of potential behaviors as readily as boys do through observing aggressive events.

Nevertheless, it is clear that girls do have a great deal of information about aggression that they never put into practice. The question is whether their failure to perform aggressive actions is to be attributed to anxiety-based inhibition that has been developed as a result of negative socialization pressure in the past. This is an extraordinarily difficult hypothesis to either falsify or confirm. There is reason to believe that girls do experience (or, at least, report) more anxiety about aggression than boys. R. Sears (1961)[R] developed a self-report scale on aggression anxiety, and found that girls obtained higher scores. Rothaus and Worchel (1964)[R] found evidence of greater aggression anxiety in women's TAT responses. However, we do not know whether these anxiety differences are present as early in life as sex differences in aggression may be detected. As will be documented in Chapter 9, young boys receive as much punishment for aggression as girls, or more, and on the basis of punishment alone, they would be expected to have as much fear of performing aggressive acts. Even if a difference in anxiety about aggression could be documented for the early years, the existence of more anxiety among girls need not be taken as the only, or even the major, reason why they are not so greatly influenced by aggressive models. The vast majority of actions that individuals observe being performed by others in their presence are not imitated at (or near) the time they are observed. In some instances the observer would be afraid of the consequences if he did imitate, but there are other much more common reasons. The observed action may be incompatible with the ongoing, organized stream of the observer's own actions and motives; it may not be consonant with the observer's self-concept; the observer may have a different, habitual response already established for the situation; or the observer may simply lack any motivation that would make imitation rewarding. The Bandura study has demonstrated that girls may know nearly as much as boys about how to go about hurting others; it has *not* shown that the major reason they do not make behavioral use of this knowledge is fear of the consequences, although of course such fear may be present in many instances.

To our minds the attempt to interpret sex differences in aggression in terms of anxiety-induced displacement or attenuation of aggressive responses is equally unsatisfactory. As we noted earlier, high levels of anxiety about displaying aggression should lead to attenuation of the response. Surely, one form of attenuation would be to convert hostile feelings into mock fighting—to act out, "in play," aggressive impulses that would be unacceptable in "real" form. Yet one of the best established sex differences is the much greater incidence of mock fighting (rough-and-tumble play) among boys. Boys, rather than girls, seem to express aggression in attenuated form. Another similar instance may be found in aggressive fantasies, which are presumably "safe" forms of aggression, and are nevertheless consistently reported more frequently among boys. What about displacement of aggression to safe objects—teasing of animals, bullying of younger children? We have little evidence on this point. Titley and Viney (1969) did investigate the question of whether "helplessness" in a victim increased or decreased aggression (in the form of shocks) displayed toward him. They found that males delivered more intense shocks to a victim who appeared to be physically disabled than they did to a normal victim; for female subjects, the reverse was true. A related finding by Aronson and Cope (1968) is that men who overheard someone being harshly treated developed a dislike for the victim, while women felt positively emotionally drawn to the victim of another's attack. Thus, if either sex could be said to be "displacing" aggression toward safe targets, it was the men, not the women, who were doing so. Of course, it could be argued that girls and women have such deep, strong anxiety about aggression that it operates to suppress (to some extent) initial perception of aggressive events, aggressive fantasies, aggressive behavior toward any target no matter how helpless, and even the mildest, most attenuated forms of aggression (horseplay, practical jokes). But if this is so, it becomes impossible to distinguish strong aggressive tendencies accompanied by strong inhibition from weak aggressive tendencies. We would like to urge serious consideration of the possibility that the two sexes are not equal in initial aggressive response tendencies. Whether the early sex differences in aggressive tendencies have a biological base, or spring from greater social encouragement of this behavior in boys, is a question to which we return below.

An interesting feature of the research on aggression is the sex difference in targets, or victims, of aggression. In three of the experiments in which subjects of college age were asked to administer shocks to learners (Buss 1966, Taylor and Epstein 1967, Youseff 1968), the sex of the victim was systematically varied. In all three, women "learners" were given milder shocks, and fewer of them, than male "learners." In another study with 11-year-olds (Shortell and Biller 1970), subjects used a loud noise as "punishment" for another child and, again, girls were given less punishment than boys. Patterson et al. (1967)[R], in their observational study of aggression in two nursery schools, found that girls were less frequently aggressed against. This study showed that there was a positive correlation between being a victim and being an aggressor; thus victimhood is part of being involved in dyadic aggressive interchanges that are more characteristic of boys than girls.

The tacit assumption that girls will not be aggressed against is further revealed in a study by Sandidge and Friedland (1973). Children aged 9–10 from relatively impoverished homes were shown cartoons of a child (either a boy or a girl) speaking aggressively to another child of the same or opposite sex. The subjects were asked to respond as they believed the other child would. The responses of boy and girl subjects were very similar: both gave more aggressive responses (that is, retaliated more strongly) if the cartoon aggressor was a boy. An interesting sidelight on this study is that subjects of both sexes responded more aggressively if they were answering for a girl. This finding would be consistent with the interpretation that, since girls are not supposed to be attacked, when they *are* attacked, they are seen as justified in retaliating as strongly as possible.

In a study by Langlois et al. (1973)[R], children were brought in pairs to a playroom stocked with toys, and their interactions recorded. Some of the subjects were observed in same-sex pairs, others in mixed-sex pairs. At age 3, there was little sex difference in aggression, though both boys and girls aggressed somewhat more often (not significantly so) against a female playmate. At age 5, however, the situation was clear: boys were more aggressive, but only toward a male playmate. This applied both to hitting the other child directly and hitting with an object. Thus, the differentiation of targets did not occur in this sample until age 5, but it did occur.

The single exception in the "victim" data comes from one study of honking at other drivers at an intersection. Deaux (1971) placed either a man or woman driver in a car at an intersection. When the light turned green, the driver deliberately stalled his (or her) car and did not move forward through the intersection. Observers recorded how soon other drivers began to honk. Other drivers honked more quickly at a woman driver than at a man driver. This work suggests that the prohibition against aggression toward women does not extend to a mild form of aggression toward an unfamiliar person with whom one is not in a face-to-face encounter. Another interpretation is that others feel freer to try to influence the behavior of an unknown woman than that of an unknown man—that is, that women are seen as more proper objects of dominance attempts. This issue will be taken up later in the section on dominance.

Although the studies are few, the results are quite consistent: girls and women are less often the objects, as well as the agents, of aggressive action. This same phenomenon has been observed among monkeys and apes.

Males aggress primarily against each other, and seldom against females. One may speculate about the biological utility of this. For the survival of a bisexual species, it is more important for a higher proportion of females than males to survive to maturity; hence a low level of aggression toward them by the more powerful male would have value from an evolutionary standpoint. Pointing to biological utility, however, does not explain behavior. We still need to know what the process is that leads to a lower level of victimizing females.

There may be a clue in the work of Cairns (1972)[R]. Working with mice, Cairns first isolated male mice (a treatment shown to increase aggressiveness when they are subsequently placed with a partner), and then used drugs to vary the "state" of the cage-mate with whom they were placed. If placed with a placebo-treated male cage-mate, the isolated animal would attack. But if the cage-mate was sedated, attacks against him were much less frequent. Cairns's observations were that aggressive interchanges did not occur full-blown, but that there were preliminary exploratory "probes" by one animal of the other; if one animal nosed or licked the other vigorously and the other reacted with equal vigor, the first animal would then respond with increased vigor, and so on in a circular escalating process until violent fighting ensued. This cycle could be interrupted simply by nonreactivity of one of the partners.

Patterson et al. (1967)[R], too, found evidence of an escalation process, though the role of a victim's passivity is ambiguous. They charted the reactions of the victim to each initiation of aggression by another child and then coded them as either positively or negatively "reinforcing" to the aggressor:

Positively reinforcing. Target does not respond, withdraws, gives up toy, cries, assumes defensive posture (e.g. covers head), protests verbally.

Negatively reinforcing. Target tells teacher, recovers the property that aggressor took, retaliates (e.g. hits back).

They found first of all that most aggressive acts were positively reinforced in a nursery school setting. Furthermore, when a child was positively reinforced for an act of aggression, he was likely, subsequently, to repeat the same action toward the same victim. If he was negatively reinforced, the likelihood of a repetition decreased. Thus we see a process of conditioning of aggressive behavior at work.

If one considers these results jointly with those of Cairns, an interesting dilemma appears: Patterson et al. indicate that a "passive" response by the victim (i.e. nonresponse or withdrawal) supports the aggressive tendencies of the aggressor, making him more likely to attack this same victim again. Cairns, on the other hand, finds that if the victim is experimentally made passive so that he does not respond to an attack, the aggressor does not continue his attack. Is it possible that one kind of response by the victim governs the immediate continuation of the encounter, and another governs the probability of recurrence of the behavior on future occasions?* However this question may be answered, it would appear that a victim's crying or showing other signs of distress will stimulate the aggressor to continue the attack; but under some circumstances, so will resistance. Perhaps the only way for the victim to turn off an attack is either to "play dead" or to counterattack with enough force to drive the attacker away.

When it comes to explaining sex differences, however, the findings of Cairns and those of Patterson et al. leave many unsolved puzzles. Girls do not "play dead," nor do they counterattack. Patterson et al. considered the possibility that girls were less often victims of aggression because they did not positively reinforce aggression when it was directed toward them. However, the findings were that girls were no more and no less likely than boys to cry or yield in response to an aggressive attack. Thus they were less frequent victims despite the fact that they provided the same contingencies for aggressors' behavior.

Whiting and Pope (1974) also found that girls do not provide more positive reinforcement for aggression—that is, they are no more likely to withdraw or yield when attacked. Whiting and Pope do report that boy victims are more likely than girls to retaliate actively against an aggressor —to provide negative reinforcement. It appears, then, that boys are more

* This question was raised in a personal communication from Gerald Patterson.

frequently selected as the victims of aggression despite the fact that the consequences to the aggressor are more likely to be aversive.

Another possibility considered by Patterson et al. (1967)[3] was that individual differences in frequency of aggression and of being victimized might be accounted for by vigor, or activity level. It seemed reasonable that the more active, vigorous children might get into more social encounters of all kinds than less active ones, and the Cairns work underscores the importance of the reactivity of the victim in producing escalation of initial encounters into fights. Patterson et al. measured activity level in three ways: the amount of distance covered per unit time; the vigor of physical activity; and the vigor of verbal activity (high vigor-screaming, loud crying, or shouting). Surprisingly, the correlations between aggressiveness and the first two measures were low and insignificant (.23 and .10, respectively). Only the correlation between aggression and verbal vigor was significant (.66). Thus the hypothesis that general activity level is related to the aggressor-victim cycle received only weak support. The authors say (p. 35):

The highly aggressive child seemed to be interacting at a high rate. Initially, this was thought to reflect little more than the general activity level of the child. However, upon closer examination, it would seem likely that amount of social interaction is more than just a function of activity level. The child who interacts at a high level with his peers is not only an active child but he is also an individual who has been conditioned to be highly responsive to peer-dispensed reinforcers.

The reader will note the assumption by Patterson et al. that a child who is highly responsive to peer-dispersed reinforcers must be so because of prior conditioning. They may be right, but the possibility of biological factors should not be overlooked. If prior conditioning is the key, we must ask why boys, rather than girls, should have been more thoroughly conditioned to this particular variety of social responsiveness. In any case, the work of Patterson et al. is relevant to the question of sex differences in that it focuses attention upon the nature of the reactivity of children to one another during social interaction. They report that certain children in their study, when they were aggressive, seemed, for some reason not clear from the data, to obtain more reinforcement from other children than the average child's aggression receives. (Whether this means that some children find a given set of reactions to an attack more exciting, or that some children's attacks produce stronger reactions, we do not know.)

It was shown in the preceding chapter that, although boys and girls do not consistently differ in general activity level, boys tend to be more active in the company of their peers and seem to engage in interaction with a larger number of peers. We suggest that when a young boy makes a tentative "probe" of another boy, he is more likely to get an exciting reaction than if the probe is directed toward a girl. What precisely makes a reaction exciting, or why some children produce more excitement in others so that an interaction is prolonged and escalated, we do not know. Evidently, classifying the responses of the other into "positive" and "negative" reinforcers does not capture the behavioral quality that is important for sex differences, although it *is* important for the acquisition of aggressive behavior when children's behavior is charted without regard to sex. Exciting reactions to initial approaches are no doubt a central feature of rough-and-tumble play, a form of "mock aggression" that is consistently more common among male than female play groups. Detailed observations are needed, perhaps drawing upon the methods of ethology, to provide further insights into the nature of "exciting reactions." It will be especially important to take note of signs of submission or distress on the part of the victim, and the effect these have upon the aggressor. This may be an aspect of interaction wherein the sexes differ, but there is no evidence to date on whether this is the case. G. R. Patterson reports (personal communication) that when a victim cries, the aggressor is likely to hit again. Thus, if girls did cry more when attacked (which they probably don't), this would not explain their being under-chosen as victims. There must be something else that they do or fail to do when attacked that interrupts the circular process, but exactly what it is has not yet been identified.

One suggestion: perhaps girls are more skilled at eliciting responses from others that are incompatible with aggression. Could it be that they inspire affection or sympathy? Or make the attacker feel guilty? Or divert the attention of the aggressor from themselves? Clearly, the continuation of an aggressive sequence can only be understood if consideration is given to the alternative forms of response that are available to the parties to a quarrel; it would also be useful to know the conditions that govern an aggressor's or victim's turning to these alternatives.

So far, we have argued that the higher level of male aggression probably cannot be accounted for by learned fear of aggression among girls, or by any tendency for girls to reinforce the aggression of boys. It is time to consider whether the sex difference in aggression has a biological foundation. We contend that it does. This is not to say that aggression is unlearned. As can be seen from the work of Bandura (1973)[R] and Patterson et al. (1967)[R], there is clear evidence that aggression *is* learned. But the learning process calls for a form of reactivity that is not well understood, and with respect to which the sexes may have different degrees of preparedness. Let us outline the reasons why biological sex differences appear to be involved in aggression: (1) Males are more aggressive than females in all human societies for which evidence is available. (2) The sex differences are found early in life, at a time when there is no evidence that differential socialization pressures have been brought to bear by adults to "shape" aggression differently in the two sexes (see Chapter 9). (3) Similar sex differences are found in man and subhuman primates. (4) Aggression is related to levels of sex hormones, and can be changed by experimental administrations of these hormones.

Let us provide some documentation for the fourth point. We shall not attempt to summarize the extensive body of research that has accumulated in recent years concerning the relationships between sex hormones and behavior. The reader will find several existing reviews useful for more complete coverage of these issues: Hutt 1972[R], Hamburg and Van Lawick–Goodall 1973[R], Lunde 1973[R], Levine 1971[R], Money and Ehrhardt 1972[R]. We shall simply present here some of the well-established generalizations with a few selected references.

1. Male hormones (androgens) function during prenatal development to masculinize the growing individual. Genetic females exposed to abnormally high (for females) levels of androgens prenatally are masculinized both physically and behaviorally, including elevated levels of threat behavior and rough-and-tumble play.

Young, Goy, and Phoenix (1964)[R] demonstrated this fact experimentally by administering testosterone to pregnant monkeys; the female offspring of these animals not only had masculinized genitalia but showed malelike play patterns, including elevated levels of rough-and-tumble play. There are a few parallel cases in human development, in which genetic females receive excess amounts of male hormones prenatally. (This can result from abnormal activity of the fetus's adrenal glands as well as from maternal injection of masculinizing hormones during pregnancy.) The most thorough study of girls of this kind has recently been reported by Ehrhardt and Baker (1973)[R]. They studied 17 fetally androgenized girls, and compared them with their 11 normal sisters. As we noted in Chapter 5, the androgenized girls underwent surgical correction of their masculinized external genitalia, following which they could not be distinguished physically from normal girls. Their behavior, however, continued to be masculinized, by comparison with their sisters, in the following ways: they much more often preferred to play with boys; they took little interest in weddings, dolls, or live babies, and preferred outdoor sports. Initiation of fighting was somewhat more common among these girls, but not significantly so by comparison with their normal sisters. A cautionary note is needed about this work: the initial abnormality of the experimental subjects was caused by a prenatal malfunctioning of the adrenal gland. The subjects all required continued treatment with cortisone, through childhood, to correct the adrenal deficiency. The cortisone treatment was designed to bring their cortisone concentrations to a normal level, and, hence, after treatment, this level should not be different between them and their normal controls; however, there may be side effects of artificial restoration of a deficient hormone level that have not yet been detected and may have led to some of the behavioral characteristics of the treated girls. Furthermore, as we noted earlier, the behavioral evidence comes from mother interviews. Although we do not doubt that mothers are in a better position than anyone else to know many details of their children's interests, preferences, and habitual activities, the mothers' expectations for the girls' behavior and their own responses to them might have been influenced by prior knowledge of their daughters' medical problems.

It is primarily in their consistency with the animal experimental work on early-administered hormones that the findings with human subjects become especially compelling. Specifically with respect to aggression, it has been shown that administration of testosterone to infant female rodents increases their fighting in adulthood (Edwards 1969[R]), whereas neonatal administration of the female hormone estradiol *reduces* adult fighting (Bronson and Desjardins 1968[R]).

These studies and many others with animals indicate that sex hormones present before birth or just at the time of birth sensitize or "program" the individual so as to affect behavior in childhood and adulthood. This is true in spite of the fact that the sexes are not very different in their levels of sex hormones from birth until puberty. The primary effect of prenatal androgens is frequently referred to as the production of a "male brain." Although accurate, this terminology may be misleading, in that it may imply to the lay reader that the major effects are upon intellectual functioning. Actually, what is meant is that the brain's functions (or, more specifically, the functions of the hypothalamus) in controlling the production of hormones are "set" in a different way for the two sexes early in development, and that this setting depends on the amount of testosterone present at a crucial period of prenatal growth. The timing of the crucial period varies between species. In any case, it now appears to be demonstrated that the amounts of sex hormones present prenatally and perinatally affect two things: the amount of certain behavior (including fighting, rough-and-tumble play, and threat behavior) during childhood, and the way sex hormones produced at adolescence and adulthood will affect the individual. Thus, administration of androgens in adulthood to a fetally untreated female will not fully masculinize her sexual behavior; but it will do so if she was also subjected to the influence of unusually high (for a female) levels of male hormone prenatally (Levine 1966[R]).

2. Male hormones increase aggressive behavior when they are administered postnatally even without prenatal sensitization. A study by Joslyn (1973)[R] illustrates the kinds of effects that can be produced. The subjects were three male and three female rhesus monkeys that were separated from their mothers at 3–4 months of age. Beginning at age 6½ months, regular injections of testosterone were begun for the three females, and continued to the age of 14½ months. The males were untreated. There were

three time periods during which the animals were placed together for 30 minutes a day in an observation cage and their social behavior recorded. The three time periods were ages 5–9½ months, ages 13½–16 months, and ages 25–27½ months. The main focus of the study was on social dominance, a topic that will be discussed more fully below. Aggressive responses were studied as part of the establishment of dominance relations. The findings were that initially, before the testosterone treatment of the females began, the males were dominant and showed more aggression than the females. After the onset of testosterone treatment, the frequency of aggression by the females increased; it was approximately equal to that of the males by the end of the first observation period (age 9 months). During the early portion of the second observation period, two of the females attacked and subdued the two most dominant males. These two females continued to be dominant throughout the second observation period (after hormone treatment had been discontinued) and also maintained their dominance through the third observation period, almost a year after the cessation of hormonal treatment. At this time, aggression was infrequent within the group, and there was an increased frequency of social play, but the amount of rough-and-tumble play among the males was considerably reduced by comparison with normal males, as was their sexual behavior. The androgen treatment of the females did not significantly increase the incidence of rough-and-tumble play among them or the incidence of malelike sexual behavior; it only reduced these behaviors in their untreated male cage-mates! During androgen treatment, the females developed a more luxuriant growth of hair, and gained weight to the point that they outweighed the males, but the weight difference disappeared after the termination of the treatment. The female who gained the most weight was the one who did *not* attack the males and move up the status hierarchy during the second observation period. However, after the cessation of treatment, when she had lost some weight, she then began to dominate the two initially dominant males. Thus the ability of one animal to subdue another in a fight was not solely a matter of their relative weights, although this was undoubtedly involved.

The reader will recall that the male animals in this experiment were untreated. What has been shown in the studies cited so far is that dosages of male hormones will increase fighting (or rough-and-tumble) in females. Will dosages of androgens elevate the already higher levels of these behaviors in males? There is little research relevant to this question. Ehrhardt did find that fetally androgenized *boys* were not behaviorally very different from their normal brothers, suggesting that there may be a certain minimum level of prenatal male hormone needed to masculinize an individual's behavior, and that once this level has been reached, further amounts will have little effect. However, the data from a species far distant from man

—chickens—suggest a different conclusion. Andrew (1972)[R] administered varying amounts of testosterone to chicks, and measured the frequency of their attacks upon the experimenter's hand. The treated males were more aggressive than untreated males. Among females, however, although the testosterone did bring about comb growth, there was no increase in attack behavior as a result of hormone treatment. It is an open question whether, among human beings, variations in the amount of testosterone present prenatally are associated with individual differences in aggressive behavior during the growth cycle.

3. More aggressive males tend to have higher current levels of androgens. Rose et al. (1971)[R] have measured the plasma testosterone levels of the members of a monkey troupe, and found higher androgen levels among the dominant animals. Although little is known about the relation between adult androgen levels and behavior among human males, a study by Kreuz and Rose (1972)[R] is suggestive. Plasma testosterone measures were taken from blood samples of a group of 21 young men in prison. Verbal aggression and fighting in prison did not correlate with blood scores, but the men with higher testosterone levels had committed more violent and aggressive crimes during adolescence.

It is important to be cautious in interpreting the "effects" of testosterone levels from correlations. Rose et al. (1972)[R] have shown that if males low on the dominance hierarchy among their male cage-mates are placed with females whom they can dominate and with whom they can have an active sex life, their testosterone levels rise markedly and remain high. After an animal is defeated in a fight, however, his testosterone level goes down and remains low. Thus hormone levels constitute an open system. A testosterone level is not something that an individual "has" independently of experience, even though in a stable social situation a given individual's score is quite stable. At the present state of our knowledge, it would appear that a high testosterone level can be both a cause and a result of aggressive behavior.

So far we have been discussing the effects of male hormones (particularly testosterone) upon behavior in the two sexes. What about female hormones? Here our knowledge is meager indeed, but what is known is sufficient to make clear that the action of female hormones is by no means simply opposite to that of male hormones. For example, in a study with rats, Bronson and Desjardins (1968)[R] found that neonatal administration of estradiol decreased the later aggressiveness of males, but *increased* this behavior in females. Levine and Mullins (1964)[R], also working with rats, found that neonatal dosages of estradiol interfered with adult sexual behavior in both sexes—it did not make the females more "female," but less so. Thus it would appear that estrogens "mimic" androgens in females but not in males. The anti-androgenic effects in males are further indicated in the research of Work and Rogers (1972)[R]. They identified a stable dominance hierarchy among six male rats, and then administered an estrogen to each of the three animals highest in the hierarchy. On the seventh day of treatment, a new stable hierarchy emerged, with the three treated rats now occupying the lowest three status positions in the hierarchy. Following the termination of treatment, the original hierarchy gradually reappeared. The effect of estrogens upon human beings, or even upon animals close to man, remains essentially unexplored.

We have been presenting a fairly detailed case for a biological contribution to the sex difference in aggression. It seemed incumbent upon us to establish this case as explicitly as possible, since many readers will no doubt address the issue initially with an assumption that any psychological difference between human groups is entirely a result of differences in experience and training. It is time to restore some balance to the discussion. We have been emphasizing male aggression to the point of allowing females to be thought of, by implication, as either angelic or weak. Women share with men the human capacity to heap all sorts of injury upon their fellows. And in almost every group that has been observed, there are some women who are fully as aggressive as the men. Furthermore, an individual's aggressive behavior is strengthened, weakened, redirected, or altered in form by his or her unique pattern of experiences. All we mean to argue is that there is a sex-linked differential readiness to respond in aggressive ways to the relevant experiences.

The aggressiveness of the male has been thought to express itself in a number of ways other than in interpersonal hostility. Competition and dominance, for example, are both thought to have an aggressive element. Indeed, as has been seen above, in some of the animal research, aggression has been studied in the context of the establishment and maintenance of dominance hierarchies. We now examine competition, dominance, and compliance to see whether we can determine how close the similarity is between aggression and these behaviors with respect to sex differentiation.

COOPERATION AND COMPETITION

There is little doubt that the human male is more interested in competitive sports than the human female. Although the two sexes may be said to compete equally for grades during their school years, much academic achievement striving does not appear, to the individual concerned, to involve defeating another person. That is, as we have pointed out earlier, it is possible for a student to strive to improve upon his record of grade performance or to compare himself with an objective standard of achievement without feeling subjectively that he is striving to be better than someone else, and without being competitive in the narrower sense of the word. The old-fashioned spelling bee is a thing of the past in most classrooms, and defining academic success in competitive terms is quite deliberately avoided by many teachers. Still, children do rank-order themselves and others with respect to a variety of skills. The degree of competitive motivation that is involved in academic achievement striving is something that can vary widely from one achieving student to another. As we have seen in Chapter 4, girls work hard for grades, but especially during adolescence they frequently try to avoid the implication of being "better" than boys.

In the daily activities of adult life, men more frequently than women find themselves in open competition with others for jobs, promotions, contracts, clients, etc. In the traditional occupations of women, competitive pressures are notably less. It would be interesting to know whether the competitive interests and behavior of the male are merely a derivative of the social roles assigned to him, or whether there is a built-in element, linked to the patterns of aggression and dominance that have already been identified. But before this question is addressed, let us review the results of the research on competitiveness, as compared with cooperativeness, in the two sexes.

Much of the work with children has involved experimental procedures developed by Madsen and his colleagues. The procedure used by Szal (1972) with nursery school children, for example, used the Madsen marble-pull game. This game involves a marble holder that will slide back and forth across a table. Two children play, each standing at one end of the table holding a string attached to one end of the marble holder. If one child pulls while the other releases his string, the marble holder can be pulled over to one end of the table, where the marble will drop into a player's cup. If both players pull at once, the marble holder comes apart, and the marble rolls into a trough and is not "won" by either player. The players are told that the objective of the game is for both players to get as many marbles as they can. Subjects in the Szal study included boy-boy pairs, girl-girl pairs, and mixed-sex pairs. In this situation, the boy-boy pairs obtained few marbles; each player seemed unwilling to let the other player gain a point, and the marble holder was frequently pulled apart. Girl-girl pairs, by contrast, usually arrived quite quickly at a turn-taking strategy. The experimenters expected that in mixed-sex pairs the boys might dominate the play, getting most of the marbles while the girl yielded, but this did not happen. The two sexes were quite similar in the number of marbles obtained, and girls became more competitive, boys more cooperative, than they were when playing against a same-sex partner.

There are few other studies of competition in young children that have been designed to test for sex differences. The Nelson-Madsen study (1969), also done with four-year-olds, involved a two-person "cooperation board" in which the object was to pull strings in such a way that a pointer would move across a target. Cooperation between the two players was necessary for the pointer to be moved to the desired places. The payoff arrangements were varied, in one case involving joint rewards, in the other individual rewards (each player having his own target spot). The time taken to achieve the necessary degree of cooperation and the amount of turn-taking were not significantly related to the sex composition of the pairs, but the experiment was not designed with such a test in mind and the sex groupings were uneven, with only seven boy-boy pairs being included in the study.

Other studies reporting cooperative and competitive behavior among subjects of varying ages have not yielded consistent results where sex differences are concerned. About half the studies find no sex differences. Among those that do, boys are most frequently found to be more competitive, although there is a reversal in a Mexican-American subsample in one of the Madsen studies (S. Kagan and Madsen 1972a). On the whole, it may be said that boys tend to be more competitive, but the behavior is evidently subject to situational and cultural variations to a considerable degree.

With older children and adults, cooperation has been studied most frequently through the use of the Prisoner's Dilemma game. In this game, two players must simultaneously choose A or B (see diagram).

Player 1

		A	B
Player 2	A	5,5 AA	10,1 BA
	B	1,10 AB	1,1 BB

The payoff arrangements are such that if both choose A, both get a moderate reward. If both choose B, both get a minimal reward. If Player 1 chooses B while Player 2 chooses A, 1 gets a large reward while 2 gets a small one, and the reverse situation applies if it is Player 2 who chooses B while Player 1 continues with an A (cooperative) choice. An illustrative set of rewards is shown above. The nature of the payoff matrix can, of course, be varied, as can the nature and amount of communication between the two players. An early study by Rapoport and Chammah (1965) reported male pairs as being more cooperative on this game than female pairs (although there was no difference in number of cooperative choices between the members of a male-female pair). Since that time a large number of studies have used variants of the Prisoner's Dilemma game, and, as may be seen from Table 7.3, the results of the studies taken as a whole are remarkably consistent in finding little or no sex difference.

The picture that emerges from Tables 7.2 and 7.3 is not entirely consistent with the view that males are the more competitive sex, although in Table 7.2 there is a trend in this direction. Clearly, the issue must be raised whether these studies of "competition" really are studying anything reflecting the behavior that is labeled "competitive" on the sports field or among

TABLE 7.2
Competition (Contrasted with Cooperation)

Study	Age and N	Difference	Comment
Lapidus 1972	3-4 (30)	None	Taking marbles out-of-turn while playing marble-pull game with mother
L. Nelson & Madsen 1969	4 (72)	None	Cooperation board, group and limited reward conditions: solution time, turn-taking (white, black)
Hatfield et al. 1967	4-5 (40)	None	Direct, indirect aggression to mother (observer ratings of mother-child interaction)
Szal 1972	4-5 (40)	Boys	Low cooperation, Madsen (boy-boy pairs vs. girl-girl pairs)
S. Kagan & Madsen 1971	4-5, 7-9 (320)	None	Performance on cooperation board after receiving either cooperative, competitive, neutral, or no instructions (Anglo-American, Mexican-American, and Mexican samples)
S. Kagan & Madsen 1972b	5-6, 8-10 (96)	Boys None	Rivalrous in choice of division of marbles with age-mate, 1 out of 4 conditions (American sample) Number of rivalrous choices (Mexican sample)
Stingle 1973	5, 8, 11 (126)	None Boys None	Age 5, 8, cooperation task Age 11, competitive behavior on cooperation task: time per trial Age 11, number and type of rewards achieved
Shapira & Madsen 1969	6-10 (80)	Boys None	Cooperation board, competition was adaptive (urban sample only) Cooperation board, cooperation was adaptive (Israeli sample, half urban and half kibbutz)
S. Kagan & Madsen 1972a	7-9 (128) 7-9 (64) 7-11 (160)	None None Boy-boy pairs Girl-girl pairs None	Frequency of taking partner's present, frequency of letting partner keep present (circle matrix board, Mexican and American samples) Willingness to block partner from obtaining prize (circle matrix board, Mexican and American samples) Open box requiring simultaneous use of 4 hands more slowly (Mexican sample, trial I) Open box more slowly (American sample, trial I) Trials II-V (both samples)
M. Madsen & Shapira 1970	7-9 (144) 7-9 (156)	None None	Group vs. individual reward: difference in performance between conditions on cooperation board (multiracial sample) Cooperation board, individual reward condition (Mexican and multiracial American sample)
A. Miller & Thomas 1972	7-11 (96)	None	Cooperative board, group and individual rewards (Indian and Canadian samples)
Shears & Behrens 1969	8, 9 (316)	Boys	Higher frequency of "exploitative" behavior when in most powerful position in 4-player game requiring the formation of alliances

(continued)

TABLE 7.2 *(cont.)*

Study	Age and N	Difference	Comment
Marwell et al. 1971	18-21 (186)	Women	Frequency of taking from other player's winnings (in 2 out of 5 experiments)
		None	Number of pairs of Ss who reached state of steady cooperation
Shomer et al. 1966	18-21 (64)	Women	Slower to achieve cooperative state in non-zero-sum game

junior executives who covet the same higher job. In these real-life situations, competition is the path to real individual gains. In most of the Madsen studies, competition is maladaptive. The same is true of most versions of the Prisoner's Dilemma game. Players must develop a cooperative strategy, and come to trust one another, if both are to maximize their individual gains; furthermore, each is in a position to prevent the other from succeeding by using a noncooperative strategy. Madsen's point is, of course, that people in modern Western cultures are so thoroughly trained to be competitive that they continue to be so even in situations that are carefully arranged so that cooperation would be more individually functional. A "cooperative choice" in the Madsen games may reflect either enlightened self-interest, a player's altruistic interest in gratifying his partner, or both. Procedural variations are needed to distinguish these motives from one another, and to distinguish both of them from actions designed to diminish the rewards to one's partner, apart from gains or losses to oneself. McClintock and his colleagues (1972, 1973)[R] have devised a set of problems that will yield the necessary distinctions. First, the subject is offered a simple choice between two peanuts (or candies, or marbles) and one. The subject, of course, chooses the larger number. Then the subject is asked to choose for himself and another person simultaneously: in option A, when the subject chooses three peanuts, the other person receives four; in option B, when the subject chooses two peanuts, the other person receives one. If the subject chooses three for himself, the other player gets more than he does; the only way he can "beat" the other player is to accept a smaller reward for himself. The choices can be varied in such a way that the player can increase the other's reward without either sacrifice or gain to himself, etc. Using a series of such choices, McClintock can distinguish pure competitive motivation (that is, the desire to "defeat" the other) from self-interest and generosity. At the time of this writing, McClintock had not completed the work, using same-sex and mixed-sex pairs, that will make it possible to contrast the sexes on the three motivations. When these results are in hand, they should help to resolve the discrepancies among previous studies as to whether boys or girls were shown to be more competitive. They may

TABLE 7.3
Cooperation: Prisoner's Dilemma Game

Study	Age and N	Difference	Comment
Ware 1969	6, 9, 12 (216)	Girls None	Cooperation in same-sex dyads Cooperation in mixed-sex dyads
Tedeschi et al. 1969a	8, 9 (96)	Girls	More cooperative choices, fewer jointly competitive choices, more trusting, more forgiving
		None	Number of jointly cooperative choices, trustworthiness, repentance
Lindskold et al. 1970	10, 11 (144)	Boys	Cooperative choices, simulated same-sex partner
Oskamp & Kleinke 1970	14-17 (100)	Boys	Cooperative choices, same-sex pairs
Bedell & Sistrunk 1973	18-21 (90)	Men	Male-male dyads and mixed-sex dyads made more cooperative responses and rewarded partners more than female-female dyads
Crowne 1966	18-21 (76)	Men None	Cooperative choices; same-sex pairs, Ss having entrepreneurial fathers Ss having bureaucratic fathers
Gallo et al. 1969	18-21 (160)	None	Cooperative choices, same-sex pairs
Gallo & Sheposh 1971	18-21 (200)	None	Cooperative choices, same-sex pairs
Grant & Sermat 1969	18-21 (48)	None	Cooperative choices, simulated same-sex and opposite-sex partners
Horai & Tedeschi 1969	18-21 (90)	None	Cooperative choices, simulated partner
Kahn et al. 1971	18-21 (40)	None	Cooperative choices, same-sex pairs
	18-21 (80)	Men	Cooperative choices (cooperative response optimal)
		Women	Cooperative choices (competitive response optimal)
		None	Cooperative choices, mixed-sex pairs
Kershenbaum & Komorita 1970	18-21 (96)	None	First competitive response, same-sex pairs, with cooperative instructions and controlled feedback
Komorita 1965	18-21 (72)	Women	Cooperative choices: simulated same-sex partner whose responses made competition optimal
	18-21 (40)	Men	Cooperative choices, simulated same-sex partner whose responses made cooperation optimal
Komorita & Mechling 1967	18-21 (64)	None	Cooperative choices following betrayal by partner; same-sex pairs

(continued)

TABLE 7.3 *(cont.)*

Study	Age and N	Difference	Comment
McNeel et al. 1972	18-21 (144)	Mixed-sex pairs	More cooperative responses in modified Prisoner's Dilemma game than either male-male or female-female pairs
		Like-sex pairs	Cooperative choices
R. Miller 1967	18-21 (120)	None	Modified Prisoner's Dilemma, same-sex pairs
Pilisuk et al. 1968	18-21 (176)	None	Cooperative responses (modified Prisoner's Dilemma game)
Pruitt 1967	18-21 (100)	None	Cooperative choices, same-sex pairs (standard-modified versions)
Rapoport & Chammah 1965	18-21 (420)	Men	Cooperative choices on later trials, same-sex pairs
		None	Cooperative choices in mixed-sex pairs
Speer 1972	Adult married couples (120)	None	Cooperative choices
Swingle 1970	18-21 (60)	None	Percentage of exploitative responses in non-zero-sum game
Tedeschi et al. 1968b	18-21 (64)	Women	Cooperative choices, first 10 trials of a 100-trial game with a simulated partner
		None	Cooperative choices, overall
Voissem & Sistrunk 1971	18-21 (96)	None	Cooperative choices, with or without communication, same-sex pairs

also yield results more consistent with known sex differences in interest in competitive games and occupations. In future work, it will not be surprising if "competitiveness" is found to serve a complex cluster of motivations. A track star may be primarily interested in setting a new world's record; he measures his own performance against an abstract record. Another runner, however, may be trying to win a particular race, judging his own performance by comparison with that of the other runners. In either case, he may not care particularly about humiliating the other runners. In other sports, the damage to the egos of other players is an important part of the victor's pleasure in winning. Some sports, which seem to the spectator to be viciously aggressive, may have more the quality of rough horseplay to the participants, and a game may be followed by a convivial beer party including both teams (this is not uncommon in soccer games, for example). On the other hand, real hatred can develop during a game, hatred that continues outside the sports arena and leads to continual brawls and individual acts of revenge. Much depends, of course, on the nature of the prize that is offered for winning.

Team sports are intensely competitive between teams, but call for close cooperation within the team and a considerable degree of subordination of the individual player's desire to star. Internal team discipline is often maintained through a tough dominance hierarchy that is not especially friendly (Fiedler 1954[R]), but the result is more effective cooperation and subordination of the individual. In one-to-one sports, however (tennis, boxing), the individual can both compete intensely against the opponent and "show off" individually. In other words, competition involves varying degrees of aggression and varying degrees of simultaneous cooperation. In view of what is known about sex differences in aggression, we would expect men to be more competitive than women in those situations in which aggression toward the opponent plays an especially strong role. However, it is quite possible that males are both more competitive *and* more cooperative (via a dominance hierarchy) in those situations calling for both qualities.

It should be stressed that the intensity of competition depends on the identity of the opponent. In a recent study (Peplau 1973[R]), dating couples of college students competed under two conditions: against each other, or as a team competing against another couple. The task was a verbal skill task (anagrams). Girls who had traditional attitudes about women's roles, and who feared success (in Horner's terms), performed considerably less well when competing against their boy friends than when joining them to compete against others. For women with more "liberated" attitudes, the identity of the competitor made little difference in performance. Evidently, many women feel that to compete against a man with whom they are emotionally involved will make them less attractive. It would seem that competition, for them, implies that they are either aggressing against, or attempting to dominate, the opponent; for other women in this situation, either competition does not have this implication or they are not afraid of being seen as dominant.

The contrasting behavior of men in these two competitive situations is interesting. There was one group of men who, in an independent measurement, gave "threatened" or hostile responses to stories of achievement by women. These men *increased* their performance when competing against their girl friends, by comparison with their performance in team competition. Men who did not feel threatened by female achievement, on the other hand, performed better in the team competition situation (J. Pleck, cited in Peplau 1973[R]). It would appear the implications of competition are very different for some couples than for others: for some men, competition with a woman is seen as a challenge to male dominance, whereas for others it is not. We now turn to dominance within and between the sexes.

DOMINANCE

Like competition, efforts by one individual to dominate another can serve a number of motives. In some cases, one individual is attempting to use

another as an instrument to achieve his own ends, regardless of the consequences for the other person. In other instances, dominance attempts are
part of an individual's efforts to assume leadership so as to organize a group
to strive cooperatively for a mutually rewarding goal. Sometimes, the dominating individual may simply want the perquisites that go with leadership. On some occasions, dominant behavior would be more accurately
called "counterdominance"—in the sense that it represents a refusal to
be guided or controlled by another—and is thus a means whereby the
individual defends his right to his own freedom of action. Finally, there
are instances in which dominant behavior seems primarily intended to
humiliate another, and in such cases it is hardly distinguishable from aggression. Table 7.4 details the recent studies of dominance.

The writing about dominance in the two sexes has been much influenced
by ethological work with primates. (The reader is referred to *Primate
Behavior*, 1965, edited by DeVore[R], for documentation of some major generalizations below.) In primate troupes, as well as among lower mammals,
it has been clearly shown that a fairly stable dominance hierarchy exists
among the males of certain groups, although these hierarchies are more
stable in some species than others. Among chimpanzees, for example, a
stable "pecking order" among the males is not always identified (Reynolds
and Reynolds 1965[R]), though some troupes do show it; among baboons a
dominance hierarchy has always been found.

In observational work, a dominant animal is defined as one whose threats
result in withdrawal by other animals; who prevails in conflicts over females, food, sleeping places, etc.; toward whom submissive gestures are
made; and who is likely to be followed by other members of the group
when he moves away from the group. The adult male dominance hierarchy
evolves out of both real fights and playful rough-and-tumble encounters
among juveniles. In adulthood, although threatening, chasing, and harass-
ment occur fairly frequently among the males of a primate troupe, serious
fighting is fairly rare, and occurs primarily when a long-established dominance hierarchy is being threatened. It is thought that the dominance
hierarchy has functional importance in that it reduces the necessity for
constant fighting. A wounded animal easily falls victim to predators, and
thus it is important for survival that fighting should be rare after the males
acquire their large teeth (or horns, or whatever fighting equipment the
species provides) and can inflict real injury on one another.

In some primate troupes, coalitions among males have been observed,
and in some instances the dominant male functions in the leadership role
only so long as his "lieutenant" is present. DeVore notes (1965[R], pp. 61–62):
"A male's dominance status was a combination of his individual fighting
ability and his ability to enlist the support of other males."

Dominance hierarchies among female primates exist, but they are less well documented than the male ones. There is reason to believe that the female hierarchies are less stable. A female's status tends to change when she is in estrus, and to reflect the status of her male consort while she is in the mating phase of her cycle. At other times, she resumes her place in the female hierarchy. Perhaps because of these movements in and out of the female hierarchy, there tends to be rather frequent aggression among the females, but this is mild in degree and does not result in disabling damage being inflicted, hence it is not dangerous to the survival of the troupe. However, there are certain females who do succeed in exercising unchallenged dominance toward other females over long periods of time.

During the time when they are establishing their dominance hierarchy, juvenile males tend to withdraw from the company of females and congregate in groups of five, six, or more. Males at this age generally do not attempt to dominate adult females, and they avoid dominance attempts from them. In adulthood, the males generally dominate the females, although there is some overlap in the two status hierarchies in some species. In others, there is not. A record of the dominant interactions of pairs of individuals in a troupe of chimpanzees is reported by Jane Goodall (1965)[x] as follows:

	Adult male	Adult female	Adolescent male	Adolescent female	Juvenile
Adult male dominates	16	11	14	8	7
Adult female dominates	0	6	3	5	—

Beginning with the assumption that human beings ought to be similar to lower primates in the biological origins of dominance behavior and in the social functions this behavior serves, Omark et al. (two 1973 papers) have looked for similar patterns of social behavior among human children. They have worked in several cultures, using behavior observation of children aged 4–10 in free play, and a "hierarchy test," in which they asked each child to rate each pair of children in the classroom group in terms of "which is tougher." The child included himself in the comparative ratings. In order to make sure that the children understood what was meant by "tough," the subjects were asked to give another word for "tough"; if the subject had difficulty expressing the concept verbally, he was asked to "do something tough," whereupon he would usually double up a fist and make a threatening gesture. Younger subjects were given pictures of class members as aids to memory while they were making their ratings, and responded orally in an individual session; older children worked with paper-and-pencil forms. The stability of a dominance hierarchy within a classroom group was determined by the amount of agreement (a) between the two members of a pair and (b) among the class as a whole, concerning the relative toughness of the class members.

The major findings from these studies are as follows:

1. Beginning at about first grade, boys congregate in larger groups than girls. Girls play together in twos or threes, boys in "swarms."

2. The play groups are very largely sex-segregated, but a few girls are found in the largest boys' play groups, and these tend to be the girls who are at the top of the girls' toughness hierarchy.

3. There is more rough-and-tumble play among the boys.

4. Boys are rated as tougher than girls as early as nursery school age, though there is some overlap, with the toughest girls being tougher than the least tough boys.

5. There are dominance hierarchies for both sexes, but the boys' hierarchy tends to be more stable (that is, more agreed upon) than the girls' hierarchy. Highest agreement is reached on boy-girl pairs, where other children, and the two participants themselves, usually agree that the boy is tougher.

Omark et al., then, have shown a remarkable degree of consistency between the dominance relations found among certain primates and those found among young human beings, when dominance is defined as toughness. The matter of definition is important. The fact that males are the more aggressive sex has been amply documented (see Table 7.1). If toughness is merely a synonym for aggression, the Omark work does not add a great deal to what is already known, other than to show that there is a stable rank-order of aggressiveness *within,* as well as between, the sexes. Is it true that the position an individual establishes in the toughness hierarchy, largely through his fighting ability, forms the basis for a more generalized dominance status, so that the toughest child also dominates others in situations where aggression is not especially relevant? As a test of this question, Omark and Edelman (1973) set pairs of children (American sample, nursery school through third grade) to work on a "Draw a picture together" task, in which each child was given a crayon of distinctive color and the pair were asked to make a joint picture. Dominance could be measured by seeing which child's color established the main outline of the resulting picture, and which child's color occupied more of the available space (territorial dominance). In mixed-sex pairs, boys dominated girls at every grade except kindergarten. In same-sex pairs, the consonance with the toughness hierarchy was not clearly established. Although it was true that outline dominance was achieved by a somewhat higher proportion of tough children (as determined by the "hierarchy test") at each grade, the relationship was significant only in two grades out of five. Thus there is some tendency for toughness scores to predict dominance in cooperative situations, but the point is not fully established.

In the cross-cultural report of Whiting and Pope (1974), a useful distinction is made between "egoistic dominance" and "suggesting responsibly." If an older child warns a younger one to stay away from the fire,

TABLE 7.4

Dominance

Study	Age and N	Difference	Comment
Parten 1933a	2-4 (34)	None	Directing group activities
Anderson 1937	2-6 (65)	Girls None	More dominance behavior in same-sex pairs Dominance behavior in mixed-sex pairs
Baumrind & Black 1967	3-4 (103)	None	Not easily (vs. easily) intimidated or bullied, bullies (vs. avoids forcing will on) other children, permits self to be dominated vs. will not submit (observer ratings)
Sutton-Smith & Savasta 1972	3-4 (17)	Boys None	Engage in more attempts to influence other children's behavior Number of attempts to influence adult's behavior (nursery school observation)
Gellert 1962	3-5 (55)	None	Teachers' rank orderings of children's dominance
Whiting & Pope 1974	3-11 (134)	Boys None Girls None	"Egoistic dominance" (attempt to control other for own ends) at ages 3-6 "Egoistic dominance" at ages 7-11 "Prosocial dominance" (offer responsible suggestions) at ages 3-6 "Prosocial dominance" at ages 7-11
Emmerich 1971	4-5 (415)	None	Classroom observations, early fall and late fall: submissiveness vs. dominance (black and white low SES)
	4-5 (596)	None Boys	Classroom observations, early fall and spring: submissiveness vs. dominance, attempts to control peers Attempts to control adults (black and white low SES)
Szal 1972	4-5 (60)	None	Number of commands, marble-pull game (same- and mixed-sex pairs)
Omark et al. 1973	4-8 (450)	Boys	Position in "toughness" hierarchy, peer ratings (American sample)
	5-9 (250)	Boys	Toughness (Swiss sample)
	8-10 (250)	Boys	Toughness (Ethiopian sample)
Omark & Edelman 1973	4-8 (436)	Boys	Dominate in the "Draw a Picture Together" test at ages 4, 6, 7, and 8; no difference at age 5 (mixed-sex pairs)
Anderson 1939	5 (38)	Boys None	More dominance behavior in same-sex pairs Dominance behavior in mixed-sex pairs
Feshbach 1969	6 (126)	None	Number of orders given to same-sex partner, or to same- or opposite-sex newcomer
C. Harrison et al. 1971	6-11 (649)	None	Teacher's report: child chosen as a leader by peers

(continued)

TABLE 7.4 *(cont.)*

Study	Age and N	Difference	Comment
Zander & van Egmond 1958	7, 10 (418)	Boys	In mixed-sex, 4-person groups: influence attempts (both successful and unsuccessful), demands
		None	Suggestions, evaluations of others
Bee 1964	9 (36)	Boys	Speak first in problem-solving interaction with parents
Braginsky 1970	10 (225)	None	Children's Machiavellianism Scale
	10 (96)	None	Success in persuading other child to eat bitter crackers; strategies of persuasion employed
Christie 1970b	11 (72)	None	Children's version of Christie's Likert-type Mach Scale
Nachamie 1969	11 (72)	None	Kiddie Machiavellianism Scale, success in bluffing in a dice game
Baltes & Nesselroade 1972	12-16 (1,249)	Boys	"Dominance," Cattell's personality questionnaire
Sharma 1969	18-20 (293)	None	Asian Indians: self-ratings, dominance-deference scale
Arkoff et al. 1962	18-21 (252)	Men	Caucasian American and Japanese samples, self-ratings on dominance-deference scale
		None	Japanese-American sample
Christie 1970a	18-21 (1,596)	Men	Scores on Machiavellianism Scales, Likert-type and forced-choice versions, (white sample)
	18-21 (148)	Men	Scores on Likert-type Mach Scale (black sample) Scores on forced-choice version of Mach Scale (trend, $p < .1$)
Denmark & Diggory 1966	18-21 (308)	None	Fraternity and sorority members' reports of their leaders' use of authoritarian practices
	18-21 (19)	None	Fraternity and sorority leaders' reports of their leadership styles
Gardiner 1968	18-21 (199)	None	Thai sample: self-ratings, dominance-deference scale
Markel et al. 1972	18-21 (72)	Men	Greater speaking intensity when addressing female E
		None	Speaking intensity when addressing male E
Strongman & Champness 1968	18-21 5M, 5F	None	Eye contact, directed gaze, speech with gaze upon introduction to new acquaintance

for example, this is a form of dominance, but it is quite different in quality from the behavior of the child who attempts to make another child run an errand for him. In each of the seven cultures studied, girls were more likely to attempt to control the behavior of another person in the interests of some social value or in the interests of that other person's welfare. Boys, on the other hand, showed more "egoistic dominance" in five of the six societies reported.

In the Whiting and Pope work the age ranges are broad, and we do not have a clear picture of the starting age for the greater frequency of male dominance attempts in the various cultures studied. It should also be noted that the target of "egoistic dominance" was not specified—we do not know whether boys were issuing dominant directives primarily to one another, to girls, or to adults. Since boys congregate primarily in all-male play groups, it would appear likely that most of their dominance attempts are directed toward one another. If this were true, it would be consistent with the observations of primate groups.

Although the evidence is scanty, it would also appear that boys make more attempts to dominate adults than do girls. The studies by Berk (1971), Emmerich (1971), and Bee (1964) all indicate that boys take more initiative vis-à-vis adults, in the sense of trying to establish the form that the interaction will take, and hence more often run into conflict with what the adult wants done (Berk). See Table 7.4.

Although the Omark and Edelman (1973) work indicates that boys dominate girls in the sense that both know which is tougher, it is not clear whether this implies that boys issue directives to girls any more frequently than the other way around. Feshbach (1969) found that pairs of girls slightly more frequently issued directives to a boy newcomer than did pairs of boys to a girl newcomer, but the frequency of this behavior toward a stranger was low and the sex difference was not significant. Szal (1972) did not find that either sex succeeded in dominating the other in the Madsen marble-pull game. Thus the existence of a dominance hierarchy in the Omark and Edelman sense does not imply a unidirectional flow of controlling acts from one sex to the other. See Table 7.4.

These findings suggest that perhaps being tougher does not imply a generalized dominance among human children. If dominance is thought of as successful efforts by one person to control or manipulate the behavior of another, it is clear that there are many ways to do this other than through physical force or the threat of it. The work of Christie and his colleagues (1970a,b) on Machiavellianism makes this point. An individual may be accommodating and even submissive as part of a plan to influence another's behavior; if he succeeds, he has, in one sense, succeeded in dominating the other. A "Mach" scale has been devised, to measure the extent to which an individual uses exploitative and manipulative behavior in interpersonal relations. High scores on this scale have been shown to be related to success in bargaining with others for desired outcomes. Much of the work on Machiavellianism has not looked for sex differences. In the adult studies that do analyze for sex differences, men have generally proved to be more Machiavellian than women (Christie 1970a, p. 32). However, using a children's form of the Mach test, Nachamie (1969) did not find a sex difference. Braginsky (1970) also adapted the Mach scale for use with children; she compared the scores of 10-year-old boys and girls on this scale, and also observed the performance of the children toward one another in a situation calling for Machiavellian behavior. On the children's form of the

Mach test, the sexes did not differ, although there was a good deal of variation among children within each sex in their willingness to take a manipulative stance toward others. In the behavioral test, the subject child was offered money for every unpleasant-tasting cracker (soaked in quinine solution and then dried) that he could get another child to eat. Boys and girls were equally successful in "dominating" other children in the sense of being able to persuade them to eat the bitter crackers. High-Mach boys were more directly coercive in their methods, and told more direct lies to their victims; high-Mach girls were more indirect and were more likely simply to omit unpleasant truths. However, these results were reversed in the low-Mach groups: low-Mach girls were coercive, low-Mach boys were indirect. Thus there were no overall sex differences in the strategies employed to influence the other children. This study, then, does not reflect a greater dominance by one sex than the other, or even, surprisingly, the use of different strategies of persuasion, at the age of 10.

What can be said concerning dominance relations between the sexes during adolescence and adulthood? Many studies have been made of leadership in small adult groups; but because most of the groups studied have been homogeneous as regards sex, cross-sex dominance patterns have not been revealed. However, some of the major findings of leadership studies may be relevant to cross-sex dominance. Leadership studies have shown that very few individuals seem to be endowed with a general personal quality of leadership such that they can assume leadership in different groups having different objectives. Other things being equal, dominance in a group will be exercised by the person whose formal status assigns him to leadership (e.g. the ranking officer in a military group). When a group is first formed, and where no formal statuses have been assigned (as in the case of a jury beginning its deliberations), the group will usually choose its formal leader on the basis of preexisting status indicators such as education, occupation, age, and sex. But expertise in the subject-matter areas related to the group's objectives is also important in dominance patterns in informal groups, and this is a major factor that limits the ability of an individual to transfer his leadership status to a new group.

Collins and Raven (1968)[R] summarize research on dominance within groups; they make the point that, whereas among animals there seems to be a simple rank-ordering of power that generalizes across situations, this is less true in groupings of human children, and becomes progressively less true the older the members of the group and the more complex the social setting in which they function. This warns us that it is unwise to infer, from having identified some similarities between dominance in children's play groups and dominance among groups of subhuman primates, that dominance patterns among human adults can be easily described in the same terms.

On the issue of dominance relationships between the sexes in adulthood, perhaps the studies of marriage partners are the most relevant. Here, it becomes difficult indeed to identify the dominant partner, at least in American families. Parsons (1955)[R] attempted to describe family influence patterns in terms of the differentiation of two kinds of leadership: "instrumental" leadership, directed toward the organization and completion of joint tasks, and normally exercised by the husband; and "expressive" leadership, aimed at creating, restoring, and maintaining bonds of emotional solidarity among family members, a form of leadership (Parsons thought) normally assumed by the wife. Later work did not find, however, that the roles actually assumed by the members of functioning families correspond to this description (see Leik 1963[R], Burke 1972[R]). In a large number of families, power over decision making seems to be either exercised jointly or divided according to the individual competencies of the members, and husband and wife influence one another in a variety of direct and indirect ways, with no one person being consistently "in charge." Collins and Raven say (p. 160): "In the analysis of husband-wife interaction, the power structure shows even greater variability and multidimensionality [than in other groups], with dominance varying according to task domain, and changing with time." They point out that wives become relatively more dominant (or more equal in dominance) the longer the marriage continues (see also Wolfe 1959[R]).

In many interactions between adult men and women outside marriage, dominance relations are dictated by formal status, as in the case of the male employer and his female secretary. Judging from the work on leadership, it would be likely that, even when formal status requirements are not present, a man's generally higher status would lead him to adopt a dominant role, and a woman to accept or even encourage this, in the early stages of group formation. An item of evidence is that men are chosen as jury foremen much more frequently than their numbers alone would warrant (Strodtbeck and Mann 1956[R]). With continued association, the relative competence of the individual group members in skills that are important to the group's objectives should weigh more heavily, so that whenever a woman group member possesses these skills, her dominance should increase, if lack of formal status does not prevent it. An interesting illustration of how stereotyped sex roles affect initial group formation, but do not necessarily hold up with increased acquaintance among the individuals involved in a continuing relationship, is found in the work of Leik (1963)[R]. When Leik formed strangers into simulated families, the men and women involved took up traditional role relationships toward one another (the man taking instrumental leadership, the woman assuming "expressive" functions). In actual families, however, this role differentiation did not occur.

It becomes important to know how stable the dominance patterns are that have been established on the basis of preexisting status considerations. If leadership is initially assumed by someone who has less relevant knowledge or skill than someone else in the group, how easily does the dominance pattern shift? This issue has been the subject of research by Cohen and Roper (1973)[R] with interracial groups of schoolchildren. They have found that it is necessary not only that the black children in such a group should *have* greater knowledge, but that both the black and white children in the group should be explicitly aware that they do, before the black children will assume (or be allowed) leadership. It is likely that a similar situation prevails between the sexes, although the matter has not yet been studied systematically.

A final point should be made concerning the relation of aggression and dominance. Dominance among groups of primates or young boys is largely achieved by fighting or threats, although we should remember that, even among apes, the ability to maintain coalitions with other animals is important. In human groups, particularly as humans move from childhood into adulthood, they begin to outgrow their reliance upon aggression as the chief means for achieving dominance. When children identify other children who, they say, can "get them to do things," the characteristics of these "influential" children often include "toughness," particularly when the influential child is a boy. Girls stress, in addition, however, that they can be influenced by someone who is polite and pleasant (Gold 1958[R]). In an early study of disturbed, aggressive children from deprived environments (Polansky et al. 1950[R]), the children whose behavior was imitated by others, and who directly influenced other children, tended to be good athletes, physically strong, and independent of social pressure from others. In a study of normal adolescents, however (Marks 1957[R]), male clique leaders were boys who were interested in social activities, were popular, and were "acceptable," though athletic prowess was important. A boy's popularity or prestige at this age seems to be much less based upon fighting prowess than it once was, at least among middle-class children. Among girls in the Marks study, leadership was exercised by girls who were attractive, popular, and style-setters, but also by girls who had either strong scientific interests or athletic skills. Leadership qualities, then, have become quite diverse, and adolescents who are able to dominate other adolescents, in the sense of achieving leadership status, can no longer simply be described as tough. By college age, there is some reason to believe that male leaders employ more authoritarian methods of leadership and control within their own groups than women do within their groups (Denmark and Diggory 1966), and athletic ability still plays a role in some groups (though not in many others); but maintaining a leadership position depends above all on being effective in achieving the group's goals. This is increasingly true as individuals go into adult social groups of greater complexity.

Effective leadership does call for toughness of a certain kind, but inter-personal aggression is usually not needed; indeed, it is detrimental to many aspects of group functioning and must be strictly controlled if a group is to stay together and function effectively. Dominance in adulthood (in the sense of influencing others) may be exercised by nonaggressive Machia-vellian means (flattery, bribery, deception), or it may depend upon sub-ject-matter competency and supportiveness toward other group members.

It is true that dominance in some adult human relationships still depends upon brute force. A report from the *Manchester Guardian* on wife-beating in midsummer 1973 provides an illustration:

One day, for instance, he came home from work and it was five o'clock and he said "Why aren't the children in bed?" and I said it was too early and he beat me and said "None of your lip." So I put them to bed and he said "Hit him," meaning my son and I did. Then he said "Hit him again, he's not crying loud enough." I wouldn't, and he hit me and broke my nose and laid my face open so that I needed stitches in it. I ran out on him and went to the police and tried to take him to court, but I still had to live at home, and in the end he forced me to withdraw the summons.

The report of the *Guardian* revealed that this was not an isolated instance, and that brutality of husbands to wives occurred in a range of social classes (the above report comes from a family with a good income). The reader will note that this kind of violent imposition of one person's will upon another can occur among members of the same sex; the potentialities for it are greater, however, between the sexes because of their unequal strength. Although incidents of this kind exist as an ugly aspect of marital relations in an unknown number of cases—an aspect that tends to be unseen, or deliberately ignored and denied, by outsiders—there can be little doubt that direct force is rare in most modern marriages. Male behavior such as that described above would be considered pathological in any human (or animal!) society and, if widespread, would endanger a species. But the question is, how much does the *potentiality* for direct force affect the rela-tionship between normal adult men and women? We have seen, in the section on aggression, that there is a consistent prohibition against the expression of aggression by men toward women. It may be that there is a reciprocal restraint on the part of women, which operates to protect them from the aggressive potential of men, and takes the form of their seldom producing the behavior that will stimulate male aggression, and turning off an aggressive sequence once it has begun (perhaps simply by refusing to respond to a provocation with a counterprovocation), so that the cir-cular escalating process described by Cairns (1972, pp. 71–81)[8] does not occur. The above account describes the relationship between human males and females as an ethologist would see it, with emphasis on cross-species similarities. There are important differences between the human condition and that of animals, however. We shall discuss more fully below the social conditions that we believe limit the use of aggression as an instrument of dominance between the sexes; for the present, let us simply say that we believe any man-woman pair usually forms a coalition in which, in the interests of maintaining the mutually rewarding aspects of the relationship, aggression is deliberately minimized. When this has happened, it is by no means clear that one sex usually succeeds in dominating the other. We have seen that males tend to be the more dominant sex in the sense of directing more dominance attempts toward one another, toward authority figures, and perhaps toward females as well; it does not follow that females are submissive. It is possible, in fact, that dominance-submission is not a single continuum. We shall now consider the evidence on submission (compliance, conformity), and we shall then return later to the role of aggression in the maintenance of hierarchical relationships between the sexes.

COMPLIANCE, SUBMISSION, SUGGESTIBILITY

Among animals, as we have seen, males direct more of their dominance attempts toward one another, although they do dominate females when conflicts occur. Among human children, partly because of the sex segregation of play groups, it is again true that the higher rate of dominance attempts by males is largely a within-sex matter. Whereas everyone agrees that boys are "tougher," it is not clear that in direct encounters between the two sexes boys use more direct power assertion or that girls submit to it. It is necessary to examine directly the evidence on compliance and submission.

As may be seen in Table 7.5, there is considerable evidence that young girls (of preschool age or younger) are more likely than boys to comply with an adult's directions. Minton et al. (1971) made home observations of instances in which children of 2½ did something that called for maternal intervention, and noted the outcome of such interventions. A higher number of incidents occurred with boys; when they did occur, girls more often complied immediately with the mother's first directive to stop or change the behavior. With boys it was more often necessary to repeat the direction, or increase pressure, to get compliance. A similar situation was observed by Serbin et al. (1973) in interactions between nursery school teachers and their pupils. Hertzig et al. (1968), recording lower and middle SES children's behavior while taking an intelligence test, found that in the lower SES group, girls were more likely to make a serious, sustained effort to follow the tester's directions, the boys to ignore or forget them. Studies are not completely consistent in their findings, however: Landauer et al. (1970) compared children's willingness to obey when asked by their own mothers (as compared with other children's mothers) to pick up a

TABLE 7.5
Compliance with Adult Requests and Demands

Study	Age and N	Difference	Comment
D. Stayton et al. 1971	9-12 mos (25)	None	Compliance to mother's verbal commands
Minton et al. 1971	27 mos (90)	Girls	Comply immediately with mother's suggestion or command
F. Pedersen & Bell 1970	2-3 (55)	Girls	Conform to adult models during rest period: lie down
R. Bell et al. 1971	2½ (74)	Girls	Teacher ratings: cooperate with teacher's suggestions to change activities
Hertzig et al. 1968	3 (116)	None	Attempt to follow instructions during administration of IQ test (middle SES U.S. sample)
	3 (60)	Girls	Attempt to follow instructions (low SES Puerto Rican sample)
Baumrind & Black 1967	3-4 (103)	None	Observer ratings: disrespectful vs. courteous demeanor with adults, provokes vs. avoids conflict with adults, responsible vs. irresponsible about following nursery school rules, conforming vs. willing to risk adult disapproval
Landauer et al. 1970	3-4 (33)	None	Obedience to own mother's or other mother's command
Serbin et al. 1973	3-5 (225)	Girls	Ignore teacher's requests less often
Blayney 1973	4 (29)	None	Agree to follow father's instructions
Hatfield et al. 1967	4-5 (40)	Girls	Observer ratings: obedience to mother during experimental session (trend, $p < .1$)
London & Cooper 1969	5-16 (240)	None	Hypnotic susceptibility
Sgan 1967	6 (72)	Girls	Change preference to agree with E's preference (low SES sample)
		None	Middle SES sample
C. Madsen & London 1966	7-11 (42)	None	Hypnotic susceptibility
Bronfenbrenner 1970	12 (353)	Girls	In conflict situation choose more alternatives acceptable to adults

large number of objects. Children complied more readily with the requests of a strange mother than with those of their own mothers, but there were no sex differences in compliance. In studies of "resistance to temptation" (see Table 7.6), children are instructed by an adult experimenter not to touch an attractive toy while the experimenter is out of the room. In two studies with American children (Stouwie 1971, 1972), girls obeyed for a longer time, although in a study with Brazilian children (Baggio and Rodrigues 1971) no sex difference was found. On the whole, the bulk of evidence favors the girls being more "obedient" to adults in the early years.

The situation is different with respect to compliance to pressure from age-mates. In the Whiting and Pope (1974) work, time-sampled behavioral

TABLE 7.6
Resistance to Temptation

Study	Age and N	Difference	Comment
Hartig & Kanfer 1973	3-7 (261)	None	Comply with E's request not to look at attractive toys, and other instructions
R. Burton 1971	4 (60)	Boys	Cheat less in beanbag game, rules established by adult E
Mumbauer & Gray 1970	5 (96)	None	Comply with adult-established rule during E's absence, beanbag game
W. D. Ward & Furchak 1968	5-7 (24)	Girls	Comply with E's request not to touch attractive toys, temptation situation
Slaby & Parke 1971	5-8 (132)	Girls	Comply with E's request not to touch toy; 1 experimental group (2 of 3 measures)
		None	Comply with E's request not to touch toy; 5 experimental groups
Parke 1967	6, 7 (80)	Girls	Comply with E's request not to touch toy
Biaggio & Rodrigues 1971	7 (39)	None	Brazilian sample: conform to E's prohibition against touching toy
Stouwie 1971	7-8 (120)	Girls	Conform to E's instruction not to touch toy: longer latency, less time spent playing with toy
Stouwie 1972	7-8 (112)	Girls	Less time spent playing with forbidden toy
		None	Latency to touch forbidden toy
Rosenkoetter 1973	8-12 (48)	None	Compliance with adult command in temptation situation after exposure to deviant or nondeviant model
Keasey 1971a	11 (108)	Boys	Complied in resistance to temptation situation
Jacobson et al. 1970	18-21 (276)	Boys	Not cheating on test, temptation situation

observations were analyzed for the occurrence of "dominance instigations" from others directed at the subject child, as well as for the subject child's responses. Although dominance instigations by peers and by adults were not separated, most of the time-samples occurred while the children were not under direct adult supervision, but were in either child play groups or child work groups. Most of the dominance instigations, then, must have come from peers. In none of the six cultures studied did girls prove to be significantly more compliant when others attempted to dominate them; the trend was in this direction for three of the cultures, but boys showed a higher incidence of compliance in two cultures. Overall, then, neither sex was more compliant.

Another form of compliance to peer pressure may be seen in the so-called Asch situation, in which the subject must make a judgment in a perceptually ambiguous situation (e.g. degree of autokinetic movement) when his own judgments differ considerably from those of a group of peers and all the judgments are public. In this situation, some subjects adjust their judgments to those of the group members; others do not. The majority of studies show no sex difference in this situation. When differences are found, it is more often girls and women who are more "suggestible," although there are three studies in which males are more susceptible to social influence. On the other hand, the reader will recall that in a study by Hollander and Marcia (1970; discussed in Chapter 6, p. 210) ten-year-olds were asked to nominate the members of the class who "go along with what the other children are doing." On this measure, as well as by self-report, boys were more conforming to peer group values.

Studies on the effects of persuasive communication have a more consistent outcome. In pioneering work by Janis (Hovland and Janis 1959[R]) female subjects were found to be more "persuasible." Since this original work, an enormous literature on attitude change has developed. Following are some generalizations that have emerged: an individual is more likely to change his views following a persuasive communication if he is either uninvolved or uninformed concerning the issue the communication deals with; individuals with generally low self-esteem are more persuasible, which may be only another way of saying that people who *believe* they are poorly informed about an issue will change their minds readily, whether or not they actually are less well informed than others. Sex differences in persuasibility, then, ought to depend upon the nature of the issue under consideration, and how interested and informed the two sexes are concerning it. We did see in Chapter 4 that women of college age lack confidence in their performance on a variety of new tasks; it would be reasonable to expect, then, that there might be a general tendency for women to be more subject to social influence in a variety of situations. On the other hand, women did not prove to have a generally lower sense of self-esteem, and on those grounds no overall difference in susceptibility to social influences would be expected. In any case, as Table 7.7 shows, none is found.

In the relatively impersonal situation that is involved in persuasive communications, neither sex is more suggestible than the other. In face-to-face encounters, when an individual must openly disagree with the opinions of others, as is the case in the Asch situation, women somewhat more often conform to others' judgments, but inconsistency of the findings and the frequency of sex similarity are striking. So far we have not been able to find a common theme in the studies that find a sex difference as compared with those that do not. Perhaps there is a clue in the study by Sitrunk and McDavid (1971): men complied with group judgments when the subject matter was "feminine"—that is, when they would have reason to lack confidence in their own judgment. The Asch situation frequently involves judgments of the lengths of lines. Since this is a visual-spatial task, do women lack confidence in their ability to be accurate and hence defer to others on only this type of task? Most of the studies in which women are

TABLE 7.7

Conformity, Compliance with Peers, Susceptibility to Influence

Study	Age and N	Difference	Comment
Baumrind & Black 1967	3-4 (103)	None	Observer ratings: submits to group consensus vs. takes independent stand, suggestible vs. has mind of own
Whiting & Pope 1974	3-11 (134)	None	Withdrawal from aggressive instigations, compliance with prosocial and egotistically dominant instigations (6 cultures)
Samorajczyk 1969	6 (60)	None	Barber Suggestibility Scale
V. Allen & Newtson 1972	6, 9, 12, 15 (366)	None	Asch-type conformity to adult and peer pressure; 3 types of stimuli
Bishop & Beckman 1971	7-11 (144)	None	Conformity to confederates' judgments of line length
Costanzo & Shaw 1966	7-9, 11-13 15-17, 19-21 (96)	None	Conformity to confederates' judgments of line length
H. Hamm & Hoving 1969	7, 10	Girls	Conformity to partners' judgments, auto-kinetic effect
	13 (192)	None	Conformity to partners' judgments, auto-kinetic effect
N. Hamm 1970	7, 10, 13 (216)	Girls	Conformity to peers' judgments (1 of 3 tasks)
Mock & Tuddenham 1971	9-11 (280)	Girls	Conformity to same-sex peers' visual-spatial judgments (white, black)
Sistrunk et al. 1971	9-10, 13-14 17-18, 20-21 (80)	Girls	Conformity to other's judgments of line length, Brazilian sample, ages 9-10, 20-21
		Boys	Brazilian sample, ages 13-14, 17-18
		None	American sample
Carrigan & Julian 1966	11 (96)	Girls	Match own story choice to "popular" choice
N. Dodge & Muench 1969	11 (122)	None	Conformity to peers' perceptual judgments
Bronfenbrenner 1970	12 (353)	Boys	In conflict situations, choose more antisocial alternatives urged by peers (Soviet Russian sample)
LeFurgy & Woloshin 1969	12-13 (53)	None	Conformity to same-sex peers' moral judgments
Schneider 1970	12-13 (96)	None	Judgments of area of geometric figures (white, black)
Landsbaum & Willis 1971	13-14, 18-21 (64)	None	Length judgments of lines, Asch-type social influence situation
Gerard et al. 1968	14-17 (154)	Girls	Conformity to group judgments in Asch situation
Wyer 1966	14-17 (80)	None	Conformity to fictitious group norms, quantitative judgments

(continued)

TABLE 7.7 *(cont.)*

Study	Age and N	Difference	Comment
Sistrunk & McDavid 1971	14-21 (270)	Girls & women	Conformity to masculine opinion items (3 of 4 experiments)
		Men	Conformity to feminine opinion items (2 of 4 experiments)
		Boys & men	Conformity to neutral opinion items (1 of 4 experiments)
Sampson & Hancock 1967	15-17 (251)	Boys	Conformity to fictitious group norms
Sistrunk 1971	16-17 (32)	Girls	Conformity to fictitious group response (black sample)
	16-17 (32)	None	White sample
Stricker et al. 1970	16-18 (190)	None	Conformity to fictitious group norm; conformity to group judgment in Asch situation
Beloff 1958	18-21 (60)	None	Change in response set (Thurston-Chave War Scale) after exposure to simulated group report
T. Cook et al. 1970	18-21 (63)	Women	Accept legitimacy of experimental deception
Dean et al. 1971	18-21 (161)	None	Attitude change following persuasive communication
Dillehay & Jernigan 1970	18-21 (90)	None	Influence of biased questionnaire on recommendations of severity of punishment
Eagly & Telaak 1972	18-21 (118)	None	Attitude change after exposure to discrepant communication
Endler 1966	18-21 (120)	Women	Agreement with contrived consensus following positive or negative reinforcement for agreement or disagreement
Endler & Hoy 1967	18-21 (120)	None	Conformity to simulated group opinion
Frager 1970	18-21 (139)	None	Conformity to peer judgments, Asch situation (Japanese sample)
Glinski et al. 1970	18-21 (56)	None	Conformity to majority opinion in social influence situation
Greenbaum 1966	18-21 (100)	None	Attitude change after speaking in defense of counterattitudinal topic
Hollander et al. 1965	18-21 (112)	Women	Conform to inaccurate perceptual judgments of same-sex others
Insko 1965	18-21 (70)	None	Influence of telephone caller's approval or disapproval on S's opinion
Insko & Cialdini 1969	18-21 (152)	None	Responses to opinion statements after positive or negative reinforcement
Julian et al. 1968	18-21 (240)	Women	Conform to erroneous judgments of same-sex others
Linder et al. 1967	18-21 (53)	None	Attitude change following writing essay taking position opposed to S's own

(continued)

TABLE 7.7 *(cont.)*

Study	Age and N	Difference	Comment
Marquis 1973	18-21 (52)	None	Attitude change after exposure to persuasive communication
Nisbett & Gordon 1967	18-21 (152)	None	Effect of persuasive communication
Osterhouse & Brock 1970	18-21 (160)	None	Acceptance of discrepant communication
Rosenkrantz & Crockett 1965	18-21 (176)	None	Charges in S's recorded impressions of a confederate after hearing others' impressions
Rule & Rehill 1970	18-21 (90)	None	Attitude change following persuasive communication
I. Silverman 1968	18-21 (403)	None	Effect of persuasive communication
I. Silverman et al. 1970	18-21 (98)	None	Responsiveness to implicit demands or persuasibility
R. Willis & Willis 1970	18-21 (96)	None	Conformity to partner's judgments of aesthetic value
Worchel & Brehm 1970	18-21 (73)	None	Attitude change following persuasive speech
Wyer 1967	18 (128)	None	Conformity to fictitious group norms, quantitative judgments

more likely than men to yield to group pressure do indeed involve spatial stimuli; however, there are numerous instances in which spatial stimuli have been used and the sexes have not differed in conformity. All that can be said at this point is that the results are inconsistent, and that when Asch experiments are considered in conjunction with other conformity studies, neither sex shows an overall tendency to be more susceptible to social influence from peers.

Another indicator of readiness to be influenced by others is spontaneous imitation. As we have seen in Chapter 2, in the section on modeling, there is no sex difference in the ability to learn from a model when given the instructions to use the model's behavior as a guide for one's own performance. However, spontaneous imitation may indicate something deeper in the way of a person's reliance upon others, or lack of confidence in himself. Table 7.8 summarizes the studies in which the occurrence of imitation has been tabulated, and where task instructions did not specifically call for imitation. There appears to be no generalized sex difference in imitation. Any differences that occur are usually related to the nature of the modeled behavior. We saw earlier, in Table 7.1, that when the model behaves aggressively, boys are more likely to imitate; girls imitate more when the model is showing affectionate behavior; and for many modeled behaviors, there is no sex difference.

TABLE 7.8
Sex Differences in Spontaneous Imitation

Study	Age and N	Difference	Comment
F. Pedersen & Bell 1970	2-3 (55)	Girls	Copy posture, follow game, with adult model
Fryrear & Thelen 1969	3-4 (60)	Girls	Imitation of filmed female model's affectionate behavior Imitation of filmed male model's affectionate behavior (trend, $p < .1$)
Bandura & Huston 1961	3-5 (48)	None	Imitation of novel action displayed by female model
W. Mischel & Grusec 1966	3-5 (56)	None	Imitation of novel aversive and neutral behaviors
S. Ross 1971	3-5 (48)	None	Imitation of peer-modeled storekeeper mannerisms
Yarrow & Scott 1972	3-5 (118)	None	Imitation of neutral, nurturant, and nonnurturant responses
Hamilton 1973	3-4, 7, 10 (72)	None	Spontaneous imitation of facial expressions to happy and sad films
Dubanoski & Parton 1971	4 (90)	None	Imitation of object manipulation after viewing filmed model
C. Madsen 1968	4-5 (40)	None	Imitation of toy rejection
Masters 1972a	4-5 (80)	None	Imitation of neutral behaviors displayed by male and female models
Hetherington & Frankie 1967	4-6 (160)	None	Imitation of parent's novel responses
Rosenblith[R] 1961	5 (80)	Girls	Tend to imitate model's color choice ($p < .1$)
Portuges & Feshbach 1972	8-10 (96)	Girls	Imitation of incidental gestures and remarks of filmed female teacher

We have seen, then, that girls are not generally more compliant, conforming, or suggestible than boys across all subject matters and sources of influence. They do not change their minds more readily following persuasive communications; they do not usually yield more to group pressure in the Asch-type experiments. When play is observed, girls are not more often seen to yield when age-mates attempt to coerce them. One consistent sex difference has been uncovered in our analysis of compliant behavior, however: girls do tend to conform more readily than boys to directives from parents and teachers. This fact has implications for the demands that continue to be made on girls. Whiting and Pope (1974) note that boys in several of the societies they studied showed a higher frequency of self-initiated acts; they comment that this probably reflects the fact that girls are more frequently interrupted in their activities by the demands of others. Not surprisingly, a person who wants a service done is more likely to choose as a target for his new request someone who has responded positively to previous requests.

The possibility should not be overlooked that girls' greater readiness to comply with adult requests stems from the way the requests are delivered. If adults make a demand upon a girl with a greater sense that they have the *right* to make the demand, and a greater confidence that it will be obeyed, there may be some subtle expression of assurance in the manner of delivery that increases the chance of success.

Considering the findings on dominance and compliance jointly, the conclusion seems to be that boys are more dominant than girls, in the sense that they more frequently attempt to dominate others, but their dominance attempts are *primarily directed toward one another*. Girls are more compliant, but *primarily toward adults*. It is possible that girls form a coalition with the more dominant adults as a means of coping with the greater aggressiveness of boys, whose dominance they do not accept. Perhaps this complex interplay of forces is one of the reasons for the spontaneous sex segregation of children's friendship and play groups. This suggests that it is girls who avoid playing with boys; there is every reason to believe, however, that spontaneous sex segregation occurs at least as often at the initiation of boys.

In adulthood, new forces come into play. If we ask whether, in a dating couple or a married pair, it is usually the man or the woman who is more likely to accommodate to the wishes of the other, we are asking a question that probably has no general answer. It seems evident that an individual's susceptibility to being influenced by another person or group will depend crucially upon two things: (1) the importance to the individual of maintaining the relationship involved; and (2) his freedom to leave the relationship if it ceases to be satisfying. There is no reason to expect a sex difference with respect to these factors over all the situations in which the sexes encounter one another, and the evidence to date suggests that no overall pattern of dominance and submission exists between the two sexes. Within certain prescribed social arrangements, however—notably, marriage—there may well be an imbalance. Traditionally, maintaining a marriage has been more important to a woman, because she has fewer alternatives for economic support, cannot so easily find sexual satisfaction outside the marriage (because of the sexual double standard), and because the rearing of children, although important to both, is usually more central to her life than her husband's. Under these conditions, a woman would be more likely to accept her partner's dominance within a marriage than vice versa. However, the more important fact is that both partners to a long-standing man-woman relationship derive benefits and satisfactions from the relationship and both are reluctant to give it up. This fact imposes strict limits on the degree to which either party can dominate the other in any coercive sense.

SUMMARY

The evidence is strong that males are the more aggressive sex. In this chapter, we have considered the widely held view that the two sexes are actually equivalent in aggressive motivation but that girls are conditioned to be afraid of displaying their aggressive tendencies openly, showing them instead in attenuated forms. We have argued that this position is a weak one, inconsistent with much that is known about the nature and development of aggression in the two sexes. We have argued that the male is, for biological reasons, in a greater state of readiness to learn and display aggressive behavior, basing the argument in part on studies of the relationship between sex hormones and aggression. The evidence for greater male aggressiveness is unequivocal; a different picture emerges from the research on competitiveness and dominance, although these behaviors have been assumed to be directly linked to aggression. Male competition in real-life settings frequently takes the form of groups competing against groups (as in team sports), an activity that involves within-group cooperation as well as between-group competition, so that cooperative behavior is frequently not the antithesis of competitiveness. Most research on competition has been conducted in contrived situations that fail to take account of this fact and that do not correspond well with the naturalistic conditions under which competitiveness is most intense; hence, the failure to find consistent sex differences in existing studies of competition has not closed the issue. Studies of dominance have revealed a greater tendency among males to attempt to dominate one another, and during childhood a boy's aggressiveness has a considerable bearing upon his ability to dominate other boys. There is little evidence, however, on whether boys successfully dominate girls during childhood. Their unstructured encounters are relatively few, since the sexes usually segregate themselves during play. In adolescence and adulthood, aggression declines as the means for achieving dominance (or leadership). As the power to influence others comes to depend more and more upon competencies and mutual affection and attraction, rather than simple power assertion by force, equality of the sexes in power-bargaining encounters becomes possible. The relation of the outcome to the social-institutional settings in which the encounters occur will be taken up in the final chapter.

PART THREE

On the Origins of Psychological Sex Differences

In the preceding chapters, we have presented and summarized a large body of evidence concerning how the sexes differ psychologically, and how psychological sex differentiation changes with age. We have discussed possible explanations of specific differences at a number of points. For example, hormones and brain lateralization were explored in connection with sex differences in spatial ability; and in the analysis of aggressive behavior, studies of hormonal effects were reviewed, and parallels were drawn between sex differentiation in human beings and that in the lower animals, with the implication that cross-species biological factors were at work. So far, however, the social shaping of sex-typical behavior has only been lightly touched upon, and it is to these processes that we now turn.

We believe social shaping to be of the utmost importance in children's acquisition of sex typical behavior. We also believe this acquisition is related to certain sex-linked biological predispositions, but to say so is not to deny the importance of social learning. The question is: what form does social shaping take? Given that adults and other children have expectations concerning how a boy or girl ought to behave, how are these expectations conveyed and how precisely do they operate to influence the child's behavior? Obviously one means of communication to the child is for the adults responsible for his care to deliver rewards and punishments to the child, contingent on whether his behavior is sex-appropriate. Another means is by example: if it can be shown that children imitate people of the same sex as themselves, then the demonstration of appropriate behavior by the same-sex models should be a powerful source of influence upon the nature of the sex-typed behavior that children adopt. We have chosen to take up the second topic first, because we believe that the answer to the question of whether children do in fact consistently imitate same-sex models determines how much weight we must place upon alternative explanations. We begin Chapter 8 with a brief résumé of the evidence on the age at which children show sex-typing in the narrower sense: how early they come to prefer the toys and activities that are stereotypically "masculine" or "feminine." We then turn to the question of whether the early development of this kind of sex typing can be attributed to the imitation of same-sex models. In Chapter 9, we take up the direct socialization pressures brought to bear upon children, and attempt to determine what the differences are in the way boys and girls are treated. We ask whether differential parental behavior reflects (1) direct attempts to shape children toward what is thought to be sex-appropriate behavior; (2) the fact that children of the two sexes have different initial behavior tendencies that result in their eliciting different behavior from their parents; (3) parents' views about what the two sexes are like (rather than what they should be like); or (4) simple transfer into the family situation of behavior that the two parents have learned previously in their relationships with people of the same or opposite sex. The four processes are not, of course, mutually exclusive, but they might produce quite different outcomes in the way of parental actions toward sons or daughters.

Chapter 10 summarizes the major findings of the survey of factual evidence detailed in Chapters 2–9, listing what appears to be "myth" and what "reality" among the widely believed generalizations about sex differences. It also summarizes the weaknesses of the two most popular theories concerning the origins of psychological sex differentiation, and considers alternatives to them.

CHAPTER EIGHT

Sex Typing and the Role of Modeling

In the narrower sense, sex-typed behavior refers to "role behavior appropriate to a child's ascribed gender" (R. Sears et al. 1965[R], p. 171). It is difficult to determine what behaviors are, and what are not, linked to sex roles. The mere existence of a behavioral sex difference does not constitute evidence of such linkage. For example, it may eventually be substantiated that infant girls are more sensitive to touch and pain than infant boys; if this were so, however, it would not necessarily be the case that an infant girl would be thought "unfeminine" if she were relatively insensitive to touch and pain. In a similar vein, spatial ability is not central to the usual concepts of masculinity and femininity, although it does differentiate the sexes. But there are some aspects of behavior that are clearly labeled "masculine" or "feminine." In the present chapter, we begin by tracing the differentiation of the sexes with respect to such behavior.

SEX-TYPED INTERESTS AND ACTIVITY PREFERENCES

By what age do children's interests and activities become differentiated into "masculine" and "feminine" patterns? Is this a gradual process, with more differentiation occurring year by year, or are there certain crucial points in development where fairly radical changes may be seen in the degree of sex typing that children's interests show?

We begin with studies of toy preferences. A number of studies have been done with children just over a year old in which a child is brought with its mother to a play room stocked with toys. The child is allowed to explore, and records are made of the amount of time spent with each toy. There is evidence that boys and girls do make somewhat different choices even at this early age, but the toy attributes responsible for the choices are obscure. W. Bronson (1971) found that girls spend more time with a stuffed animal, and Goldberg and Lewis (1969), who obtained the same result, thought that girls might be especially interested in any toy with a face (as a manifestation of their greater social interests). This hypothesis, however, is not consistent with later findings. Jacklin et al. (1973) found that the two sexes spent equal amounts of time with stuffed animals, but that the boys preferred toy robots—which also had faces. Furthermore, Kaminski (1973) found that boys of 13 months played with dolls more than did the girls; she suggested that this might reflect the fact that more girls than boys had dolls at home, so that dolls were more novel, and hence more interesting, to boys. In any case, "faceness" is evidently not the factor that accounts for early sex differences in toy preference. Another possibility is that it is the soft tactual quality of stuffed animals that attracted the girls in the Bronson and Goldberg and Lewis studies. Kaminski, however, provided several toy trucks for 13-month-olds (along with a variety of other toys), one truck being covered in rabbit fur, one in aluminum foil; the girls did not prefer the furry surface, nor did the boys prefer the metallic one, so it is doubtful that it is the tactual quality of the surface that is important. Nor is the "manipulability" of the toy related to sex differences in preference. In the Kaminski study, the most manipulable toys were the most attractive to children of both sexes and there were no sex differences in their use. The same was true in two studies by Jacklin et al. Goldberg and Lewis found boys to be more interested in door knobs, floor tiles, and electric outlets, girls in blocks and pegboards; both sexes manipulated the objects of their choice, and there seemed to be no relationship to the number of moving parts. It would be interesting to be able to find developmental links between the early toy preferences and the choices of more clearly "masculine" and "feminine" toys that may be discerned from age 2 onward, but the elements that differentially attract one-year-old boys and girls are not well enough understood to permit identifying the continuities that may exist. The point is of some interest, because it is possible that societies begin to label as "masculine" those toys that differentially attract boys even if there is no relationship of the toy to a masculine role. For example, blocks are thought of as "boyish" toys even though they are not related to adult male occupations in the sense that a fireman's hat or a toy truck is. In a similar vein, there is no obvious reason why preschool girls should be spending more time in painting, drawing, cutting paper, or manipulating play dough (since few modern mothers make bread, and professional artists are frequently male). If these activities become labeled as more appropriate for one sex, then, it seems possible that it is because children of one sex choose to do them rather than vice versa. However, by preschool age, differentiation may be seen that does clearly relate to adult sex-typed activities: girls sew, string beads, play at housekeeping; boys play with guns, toy trucks, tractors, and fire engines, and do carpentry. Based on adult judgments of what activities are feminine and what masculine, a number of investigators have used picture tests for preferences in toys or activities. Clear tendencies for girls to choose stereotypically feminine activities, boys masculine ones, have been found as early as such tests have been used (R. Sears et al. 1965[R]), with 4-year-olds. In developing their "area usage" test for sex typing, Sears and his colleagues also found that 4-year-old boys spent more time in the portion of a large nursery school play room where blocks, wheel toys, and carpenter tools were to be found, whereas girls spent more time in the area having the dress-up clothes, the cooking equipment, and the doll houses. That other aspects of sex typing are also developing in the preschool years is indicated by the responses of children aged 4–6 to questions about whether they will be "mommies or daddies" when they grow up (S. Thompson and Bentler 1973). With only a single exception, all the children in this study answered this question sex-appropriately. Furthermore, very few thought they could be the opposite-sex parent if they wished. Although Emmerich (1971), agreeing with Kohlberg's (1966)[R] earlier contention, finds that children of 4–6 do not have well-developed "sex constancy" (i. e. they believe that it is possible for a pictured person's sex to change with a change in dress and hair style), it would appear that they do have a fairly clear, stable concept of their own sexual identity and the fact that this implies certain adult functions that are not arbitrary or subject to change. Table 8.1 shows the evolution of sex-typed interests as children grow older. The early tendency of boys to engage in more large-muscle or "gross motor" activity appears later in the form of greater interest in both organized and informal sports. The games that girls prefer during the elementary school years (jacks, jump rope) are not so clearly related to their artistic and manipulative activities of the preschool years, but the dress-up theme can of course be seen in their greater interest in, and knowledge about, styles and appearance during adolescence (Nelsen and Rosenbaum 1972).

Given that boys show "masculine" and girls "feminine" interests from the preschool years onward, can it be said that one sex is more fully sex-typed than the other? Does either sex have more inhibitions about performing activities normally associated with the opposite sex?

Efforts to measure the degree of sex typing of the two sexes have frequently involved use of the "It" test (Brown 1956[R]). This is a projective test in which a cut-out doll, referred to as "It," is offered the opportunity to choose among a variety of sex-typed activities. Commonly, girls have It engage in feminine activities, and boys choose masculine activities for It. Early reports indicated that, with this measure, boys appeared to develop sex-typed choices at an earlier age, and that in fact there might be a decline in sex typing among girls between the ages of 5 and 10. However, these results were called into question by the possibility that the It doll in widest use objectively resembled a boy more than a girl (N. Thompson and McCandless 1970), so that girls were making realistic choices for the sex that they perceived the doll to be, rather than making choices projectively for themselves. Not all studies, however, showed a "masculine bias"

TABLE 8.1
Toy and Activity Preferences

Study	Age and N	Difference	Comment
J. Brooks & Lewis 1974	11-15 mos (17 pairs of twins)	None	Stuffed animals, pull-toys
Kaminski 1973	12 mos (48)	None	Baby doll, young child doll, pick-up trucks, ring stack toy, merry-go-round
		Boys	Both dolls (combined score)
Goldberg & Lewis 1969	13 mos (64)	Boys	Play with "non-toys."* Bang with toys rather than manipulate them
		Girls	Play with blocks, pegboard, stuffed dog, and inflated plastic cat; manipulation of combinations of toys
		None	Play with pail, toy lawnmower, mallet, wooden bug (pull-toy), quoits
Messer & Lewis 1972	13 mos (25)	None	Blocks, pail, toy lawnmower, stuffed dog, inflated plastic cat, mallet, pegboard, quoits, wooden bug, non-toys; bang with toys (low SES sample)
Jacklin et al. 1973	13-14 mos (40)	Boys	Amount of time playing with robots
		None	Amount of time spent manipulating toys; play with stuffed ("cuddly") animals, toy work bench, toy ferris wheel
W. Bronson 1971	15 mos (40)	Girls	Play with small toy dog
Bridges 1927	2-3 (10)	Boys	Most frequent activities: building with large bricks, fitting cylinders into holes, color pairing, naming objects in postcards, cube construction
		Girls	Most frequent activities: fitting cylinders into holes, threading beads, writing on blackboard, fastening buttons
F. Pedersen & Bell 1970	2-3 (55)	Boys	Manipulate physical objects (e. g. blocks, toys); gross motor activity
		Girls	Play with clay or dough; play on swing or glider
		None	Ride tricycles
Clark et al. 1969	2-4 (40)	Boys	Play with blocks and push-toy; drink milk
		Girls	Play with dolls; paint, cut, glue, crayon, sew
		None	Play with toy cars and trucks, puzzles, old car parts, plasticine, sand, clay, and musical instruments; play house; saw and hammer; climb up and play in balcony
Parten 1933b	2-4 (34)	Boys	Trains, kiddie cars, blocks; play with boys
		Girls	Swings, paper, beads, painting; play with girls
		None	Play house (doll play excluded)

*Non-toys include structured features of a room, such as doorknobs, floor tiles, and electric outlets.

(continued)

TABLE 8.1 *(cont.)*

Study	Age and N	Difference	Comment
Fagot & Patterson 1969	3 (36)	Boys	Blocks, transportation toys
		Girls	Painting, artwork
		None	Puzzles, tinkertoys, marbles, beads, design board; hammering; engaging in musical activities; playing with live or toy animals; dressing up in costumes; using tools; playing on swing, teeter-totter, or slide
Rabban[R] 1950	3 (60)	None	Choices among masculine and feminine toys
	4-8 (240)	Boys	Guns, steamrollers, trucks, racing cars, fire engines, cement mixers, soldiers, knives
		Girls	High chair, buggy, crib, beads, dishes, purse, doll, bathinette
Moyer & Von Haller 1956	3-5 (87)	None	Time playing with blocks, number of structures built
Vance & McCall[R] 1934	3-6 (32)	Boys	Woodwork, large blocks, equipment requiring large muscle activity
		Girls	Housekeeping materials; materials for "passive play"
Farrell 1957	3-7 (376)	Boys	Play with blocks
Whiting & Pope 1974	3-11 (134)	Boys	Feed and pasture animals
		Girls	Domestic chores, food preparation
J. Schwartz 1972	4 (57)	Boys	Frequency of firing toy gun
R. Sears et al.[R] 1965	4 (40)	Boys	Choice of masculine toys and pictured activities
		Girls	Choice of feminine toys and pictured activities
Emmerich 1971	4-5 (415)	Boys	Gross motor activity, fantasy activity
		Girls	Artistic activity
		None	Cognitive and fine manipulative activity (early-fall, late-fall observation sessions)
	4-5 (596)	Boys	Gross motor activity, fantasy activity
		Girls	Artistic, cognitive, and fine manipulative activity (early-fall, late-spring observation sessions)
Fauls & Smith 1956	4-5 (38)	Boys	Choice of pictured "masculine" activity
		Girls	Choice of pictured "feminine" activities
Wohlford et al. 1971	4-6 (66)	Boys	Masculine choices, picture activities test
		Girls	Feminine choices, picture activities test
DeLucia 1972	5-6 (24)	Boys	Picture preference test: prefer wheel toys, tool set, airplane, Erector set, football
		Girls	Prefer cosmetics, doll buggy, doll wardrobe, broom set, dish cabinet
Farwell 1930	5-7 (271)	Boys	Prefer building with blocks
		Girls	Prefer sewing
		None	Preference for modeling and painting materials

(continued)

TABLE 8.1 *(cont.)*

Study	Age and N	Difference	Comment
Laosa & Brophy 1972	5-7 (93)	Boys	Masculine choices, measures of sex-role orientation, preference and adoption
		Girls	Feminine choices, same measures as above
W. D. Ward 1969a	5-8 (32)	Boys	Preference for masculine toys, pairs of pictured toys
		Girls	Preference for feminine toys, pairs of pictured toys
DeLucia[R] 1963	5-9 (226)	Boys	Masculine choices, picture toy preference test
		Girls	Feminine choices, picture toy preference test
Liebert et al. 1971	6-8 (40)	Boys	Prefer toys said to be "boys' toys"
		Girls	Prefer toys said to be "girls' toys"
Looft 1971	6-8 (66)	Boys	Name larger range of occupations in answer to "What would you like to be?" Order of preference: football player, policeman, doctor, dentist, priest, scientist, pilot, astronaut
		Girls	Occupational preferences in order: teacher, nurse, housewife, mother, stewardess, salesgirl
Ables 1972	7-12 (128)	Boys	Wish for material possessions and money
		Girls	Wish for another person
		None	Wish for pets, activities, specific skills or attributes, or for some identity
Rosenberg & Sutton-Smith (1960)	9-11 (187)	Boys	Prefer games: forceful physical contact, dramatization of conflict between male roles, propulsion of objects through space, complex team games
		Girls	Prefer games: dramatization of "static activity," verbal games, ritualistic non-competitive games, choral and rhythmic games, and games with central role for 1 player
Maw & Maw 1965	10-11 (914)	Boys	Self-report: choose outgoing investigatory activities
Honzik[R] 1951	11-13 (468)	Boys	In constructing "scene from exciting movie," use blocks, vehicles, persons in uniform
		Girls	Use persons in ordinary dress and furniture
Nelsen & Rosenbaum 1972	12-17 (1,916)	Boys	Know more terms related to money, autos, motorbikes
		Girls	Know more terms related to clothes, style, appearance, boys, popularity
T. Hilton & Berglund 1971	12, 14, 16 (1,859)	Boys	Read scientific books and magazines at ages 14 and 16; indicate more interest in math courses at ages 14 and 16; talk about science with friends and parents at ages 14 and 16
Walberg 1969	16-17 (1,050)	Boys	Cosmological activities, tinkering
		Girls	Participation in nature study, application of science to everyday life

(continued)

TABLE 8.1 *(cont.)*

Study	Age and *N*	Difference	Comment
Monday et al. 1966-67	18 (238,000)	Men	Prefer engineering, agriculture, technology
		Women	Prefer social, religious, educational fields
Thomas 1971	18-21 (60)	None	Student activism, political participation
Constantinople 1967	18, 20 (353)	Men	Achieving academic distinction, preparing for a career that requires postgraduate study
		Women	Important college goals: acquiring an appreciation of ideas, establishing own values, developing relationship with opposite sex, finding a spouse, developing ability to get along with different kinds of people, preparing for a career beginning immediately after college
		None	Learning how to learn from books and teachers, contributing in a meaningful manner to some campus group, becoming self-confident, achieving personal independence, gaining many friends

of this sort (see Kohlberg 1966[R], Hartup and Zook 1960, Brown 1962[R], Lansky and McKay 1969). There followed a series of studies in which the original It doll was replaced by a "concealed It" (a cut-out in an envelope) or a "blank It" (a card replacing the doll), or in which the subject makes choices directly for himself rather than for a projective figure of any sort. The reader is referred to Fling and Manosevitz (1972) for a brief review and list of references to these studies, which yielded conflicting results. With the masculine bias of the test eliminated, Fling and Manosevitz find that among children of 3–4 years, both boys and girls make sex-typed choices, but neither sex is significantly more likely to make sex-appropriate choices than the other, though there was a nonsignificant trend in this study for boys to be more sex-typed.

Other kinds of measures have been used in the attempt to discover whether one sex is more clearly sex-typed than the other. R. Sears and his colleagues (1965)[R] asked 4-year-old children to carry out a "pretend" telephone conversation with their mothers; each child was asked, in turn, to pretend to be the "mommy" or the "daddy" talking to a child, and was then asked to pretend to be either a boy or girl talking to a parent. Some children refused to adopt the role of an opposite-sex child or parent, others did so easily. However, no sex difference was found in the willingness of boys and girls to adopt an opposite-sex role.

Hartup, Moore, and Sager (1963)[R] did find a sex difference in willingness to engage in cross-sex activities. They offered children of nursery school age two toys: one a rather unattractive sex-neutral toy, and the other an attractive toy that was clearly suitable for the other sex. They found that boys were more likely to avoid the sex-inappropriate toy than were girls. The boys' avoidance of feminine toys was especially marked when an experimenter was present, suggesting that the boys expected adult disapproval for playing with girlish things. The girls, on the other hand, showed interest in boys' toys whether an adult was present or not. S. Ross (1971) found that among 3-5-year-olds playing shopkeeper, boys were more concerned than girls that their customers in the play store (a same-sex peer) choose a sex-appropriate toy. In Chapter 9 we shall discuss the evidence for differential pressure being brought to bear on the two sexes for sex-appropriate behavior. For the present, the point of interest is that in this particular respect, existing research using behavioral (rather than projective) measures indicates that boys of preschool age are more fully sex-typed than girls.

Working with children aged 4–7, W. D. Ward (1968) found that boys made more sex-appropriate toy choices than did girls; Pulaski (1970), putting children aged 5 and 6 into a play room with a variety of toys available, found that boys played consistently with masculine toys while girls were more likely to choose some boyish and some girlish toys. Wolf (1973) allowed children aged 5–9 to observe a model playing with a toy inappropriate for the subject's sex, and found that following such exposure, girls were more willing to play with a sex-inappropriate toy than were boys. And, finally, a study by Ferguson and Maccoby (1966), involving measures of sex-role acceptance, found that at the age of 10 boys preferred the activities associated with their own sex role more than did girls. There is some evidence that the greater preference by males for the activities associated with their own sex continues into college age. S. Bem (personal communication, 1974) found that men choose masculine activities over feminine ones even when they would be paid more for performing feminine activities. This result is especially striking, considering that when choosing among sex-appropriate tasks, men choose so as to maximize monetary reward considerably more than women do. But their desire for money notwithstanding, they avoid stereotypically female tasks, whereas women's choices of activities are more sex-neutral. Recent research, then, is consistent with earlier work (DeLucia 1963[R], Hartup and Zook 1960, Rabban 1950[R]) in showing that (a) at nursery school age, both sexes are sex-typed, and (b) starting at approximately the age of 4, boys become increasingly more sex-typed than girls, in that they are more likely to avoid sex-inappropriate activities, and more likely to accept (prefer) the activities associated with their own sex role.

In earlier chapters, we have seen that the behavior of young boys and girls is differentiated along sex lines in some respects but not in others. Some of the stereotyped views about how the sexes differ, such as the greater aggressiveness of boys, have been borne out. Some, such as the belief that girls are generally more dependent or sociable, have not. We have now seen that preschool boys and girls do differ, on the average, in a number of their preferences for activities and toys; furthermore, it is true that children tend to choose same-sex playmates, although there is great variation in these matters among children of the same sex. In presenting the evidence on sex differences, we have touched upon some of the reasons why differential development might occur, including some aspects of genetic involvement and hormonal influences. We now turn to some of the social processes that have been thought to underlie sex differences.

HYPOTHESES CONCERNING THE ROLE OF MODELING

The major summarizing papers and chapters on sex typing (Kagan 1964[R], R. Sears et al. 1965[R], Kohlberg 1966[R], Mussen 1969[R], Mischel 1970[R]) all emphasize the role of imitation and identification in the acquisition of the child's sex-typed behavior. Although treatments and emphases differ considerably, certain major themes may be found in the arguments presented.

1. *Differential reinforcement alone would not account for the rate and breadth of sex-role acquisition; imitation must be involved.* "Gender roles are very broad and very subtle. It would be difficult to imagine that any kind of direct tuition could provide for the learning of such elaborate behavioral, attitudinal and manneristic patterns as are subsumed under the rubrics of masculinity and femininity. Furthermore, these qualities are absorbed quite early and are highly resistant to modification" (R. Sears et al. 1965[R], p. 171). Bandura and Walters describe how children in other cultures acquire sex-role activities: the girls stay with their mothers, watching and imitating the mothers' domestic activities; the boys accompany the fathers and are given child-size tools so that they can copy their fathers' work activities. The parents offer very little direct tuition. The authors say (1963[R], p. 48):

While playing with toys that stimulate imitation of adults, children frequently reproduce not only the appropriate adult-role behavior patterns but also characteristic or idiosyncratic parental patterns of response, including attitudes, mannerisms, gestures, and even voice inflections, which the parents have certainly never attempted directly to teach. . . . Children frequently acquire, in the course of imitative role-playing, numerous classes of inter-related responses *in toto*, apparently without proceeding through a gradual and laborious process of response differentiation and extinction or requiring a lengthy period of discrimination training.

2. *Because parents are (a) highly available, (b) nurturant, and (c) powerful, they are the models most likely to be copied in the acquisition of sex-*

typed behavior, particularly in the preschool years (see especially Mischel 1970[R], pp. 28–37). Some writers stress the hypothesis that the child's love, admiration, and respect for his parents cause him to take one or both parents as "ego ideal," and to establish enduring motivation to emulate them.

3. *Children are more frequently exposed to models of their own sex than to cross-sex models.* Therefore, through imitating whatever model happens to be available, they will tend to acquire more sex-appropriate than sex-inappropriate behavior. Since children of both sexes initially spend more time with the mother than the father, both will initially acquire feminine behavior; at a later age, boys will begin to be in the presence of male models for an increasing proportion of their time, and hence will increasingly acquire masculine behavior.

4. *Same-sex models will be imitated more than opposite-sex ones because the child tends to imitate models whom he perceives as similar to himself.* Mischel (1970)[R] amplifies this point as follows (p. 38):

From the viewpoint of social learning theory, the greater attentiveness to same-sex models, especially when they are displaying appropriately sex-typed behavior, probably reflects that people generally are reinforced throughout their histories more for learning the sex-typed behaviors of same-sex models than those of cross-sex models. It certainly seems likely that children are much more frequently rewarded for watching and imitating same-sex models (rather than cross-sex models), especially when the models display sex-typed behaviors. Boys do not learn baseball by watching girls and girls do not learn about fashions from observing boys.

We should note that points 1 and 2 above would not jointly be sufficient to explain the acquisition of sex-typed behavior through modeling. It has been clearly demonstrated that children will imitate the more dominant powerful figure when more than one model is available; furthermore, children will choose to imitate a more nurturant model, other things being equal (Bandura and Huston 1961, Hetherington 1965[R], and Hetherington and Frankie 1967). Within a given family, then, if the mother is the more nurturant figure, children of both sexes should imitate her for this reason; if the father is the dominant figure, children of both sexes should imitate him for this reason. These processes would not make boys masculine and girls feminine. Freud, in his discussions of the psychosexual development of the two sexes, stumbled over this issue and attempted to solve it by simply saying that the boy identifies with the aggressor, whereas the girl's identification with her mother is "anaclitic"—that is, based upon nurturance and dependency. This "solution" is merely a restatement of the problem. It does not provide a reason why the power of a model, or the nurturance of a model, should affect the two sexes differentially. It simply asserts that this is the case.

It was noted above that the "model availability" hypothesis (point 3) leads to the assumption that a boy's first primary model is his mother, and that he must shift his identification at some point from his mother to his father and to other male models in order to become masculine. This same point is stressed by writers who emphasize the role of nurturance in early identification. The first and strongest attachment figure for both sexes is likely to be the mother. Because of this attachment, children of both sexes are alleged to form an initial identification with the mother, and in the case of the boy, this identification must be disrupted and replaced if the child is to be adequately sex-typed, whereas the girl may simply continue identification with her initial model. Hence, the development of sex typing of girls is thought to be simpler, more consistent, and capable of consolidation at an earlier age than that of boys. The most recent exponent of this position is Lynn (1969, especially p. 23)[R]. The view that boys must shift from one primary model to another has been thought to imply two things: (1) that in the early preschool years, a boy will resemble his mother more than his father, with father-son similarity appearing at age 4 or later—the precise age depending upon the mechanism that is thought to bring about the shift from one model to the other; (2) that the boy may make his shift in choice of model with respect to some attributes and not others; he may continue to identify with his mother with respect to aspects of his behavior and personality that are not directly linked to sex typing, while adopting his father's behavior where masculinity is an issue. Another possibility, particularly if the father is not a strong identification figure, is that the boy will be like his mother with respect to "latent" aspects of sex typing but masculine with respect to the more obvious, or superficial, aspects of his sex identity, and may show signs of conflict over his sex role.

Kohlberg (1966)[R] argues that if age-related shifts do occur in any aspect of a boy's or girl's "identification" with the mother or the father, these shifts can hardly be attributed to characteristics of the model such as their nurturance or power: "The power theories of identification cannot account for . . . age shifts in terms of family structure variables as such, because the family's power structure does not change regularly according to the age of the child." Kohlberg's statement alerts us to the fact that if there is a shift at a particular age in any aspect of sex-role adoption, it is necessary to consider not only whether there has been a corresponding shift in the availability of the appropriate-sex model, but whether there has been a shift in the nurturance or power assertion directed by each parent to the same-sex child. Kohlberg believes that no such age-related shift occurs in the internal dynamics of family relationships, but the question is an empirical one.

To recapitulate: the fact that observational learning occurs is not in doubt. It is also clear enough that children learn many items in their behavioral repertoires through imitation of their parents. The problem is why children of the two sexes should learn *different things*—sex-typed things.

Two explanations have been offered: (1) that the same-sex model is more available, and (2) that children select same-sex models, among those that are available, on the basis of perceived similarity between themselves and the model.

Let us first consider the issue of model availability.

AVAILABILITY OF SAME-SEX MODELS

The identity (and sex) of the individuals with whom the child spends most time is highly culture-bound. Among the Rajput in India, for example (Minturn and Hitchcock 1963[R]), women are confined to a courtyard; children also spend most of their time in the courtyard when they are very young, while they are still dependent upon the care-taking of their mothers and other female relatives; but as soon as they are old enough to escape from the courtyard, they can go to the fields with their fathers, and spend time with men and older boys at the men's sleeping platform. Although girls can leave the courtyard before they officially go into purdah when they are married, they have less freedom of movement and are less likely to go to the men's platform or accompany men during their work in the fields. The view that both sexes of children initially have primarily female models available, but that with increasing age each sex is exposed more and more to same-sex models, seems to fit this culture very well.

The matter is by no means as clear in most segments of American society. Children of both sexes tend to be primarily in the care of female adults during the preschool years. Mothers may make a special effort to see to it that their children have same-sex playmates—or the children may *choose* same-sex playmates—but this would hardly provide an explanation of sex typing, since other children would presumably have been exposed to the same kind of primarily female modeling as the subject child. Fathers do not normally take their children to work with them; hence there is no opportunity to give their sons any greater exposure to the world of masculine work. When the children are quite young, their primary exposure to their father comes when the father is at home after work and on weekends. It is an open question whether a young boy sees more of his father at home than does the young girl. F. Pedersen and Robson (1969) report that when the father is at home he spends as much time playing with a 9-month-old daughter as he does with a son of the same age. There is little evidence of how the situation develops during the years from 2 through 5. Is a father more likely to take a son with him on an errand? Ask him to help with masculine chores? Chat with him and take an interest in his activities and concerns? It may be that this is the case, and in one study (R. Sears et al. 1965[R] and personal communications) fathers of kindergarten-aged children did say in an interview that they spent more time with sons than daughters. However, as will be shown later, there are special elements of tension between father and son, and of attraction between father and daughter, that might imply at least as much interaction (at least *supportive* interaction) between fathers and girls. It has not been demonstrated that fathers are more "available" as models to their sons than their daughters during the preschool years; indeed, we do not consider it likely that there is any substantial difference in availability in the sense of sheer amounts of time the child spends in the father's presence. At later ages, of course, fathers will no doubt be more likely to take their sons to ball games and into primarily male settings, but this differentiation occurs, we suggest, *after* the child has already developed sex-typed interests, and may be a result rather than a cause of this development.

Parents, of course, are not the only sex-typed models. What about the differential availability of other same-sex models to boys and girls? Children spend enormous amounts of time watching television, but both sexes see the same models until such time as they select different programs on the basis of their previously developed sex-typed interests. In school, it is frequently the case that the teachers are women and the principals are men, but these two kinds of models are equally available to children of the two sexes. Older siblings of the two sexes are equally available as models to young boys and girls. The fact that children play primarily with same-sex peers does not appear to be a function of which peer is *available*, but which sex peer is *chosen*—again, an outcome, rather than a cause, of sex-typed interests. It seems reasonable to assume, then, that at least in most segments of American culture, models of the two sexes are available to boys and girls to a similar degree. There are settings where models of only one sex are primarily available, but young children of both sexes tend to be exposed to such settings equally often.

Regardless of the *relative* frequency of exposure to male and female models, both boys and girls do have *frequent* exposure to models of both sexes, though not in all settings. American children seldom have the opportunity to see their fathers at work, and therefore their initial concepts of the adult world of work, and the different roles played in it by men and women, are likely to come from other sources, such as television. Such sources may provide more stereotypic views about these roles than the child would acquire if he did have more direct exposure to the work of his parents or other personally known models. Nevertheless, we are suggesting that models of both sexes are plentifully available to both boys and girls, and that children can learn from their actions what behavior is considered appropriate for each sex.

SELECTION OF SAME-SEX MODELS

When models of both sexes are available, do girls more often attend to, and/or imitate, the female model, and boys the male model? There is some evidence that in adulthood such selection does occur. In an early study, Maccoby et al. (1958)[R] monitored the eye movements of college-aged subjects as they viewed two standard Hollywood films. In the scenes in which both the male and female leads were on screen (and no other characters were present), male viewers spent proportionally more time watching the male leading character while female viewers spent proportionally more time looking at the female lead. Less direct evidence of model selection is found in a study (Maccoby and Wilson 1957[R]) that tested children of junior high school age on their recollection of the details of the actions, and stimuli to actions, of various filmed characters. Boys remembered more detail from the aggressive incidents depicted in the film, *provided that the agent of the action was a boy rather than a girl*; similarly, the girls recalled more of the social and romantic content, provided that the agent of the action was a female character in the film. Mischel (1970, p. 39)[R] summarizes a series of studies, all done with adults or children aged 12 or older, in which some models were objectively more similar to the viewer than others, or a perception of similarity was induced by telling the viewer that a given model shared some of his tastes and attributes whereas another model did not. In these studies it was repeatedly demonstrated that viewers are more likely to match some aspect of their behavior to a model's if that model is perceived as similar to themselves. We may extrapolate from these findings to the probability that an adolescent or adult will imitate a same-sex model rather than an opposite-sex model whenever the fact of shared sex is relevant to the situation. Mischel adds the proviso that imitation is more likely to occur when learners have little information—when their own past experience provides little guidance to what behavior is appropriate.

The subjects in the experiments cited above were old enough to be fairly sophisticated about perceiving similarities between themselves and others. What about younger children? Are they likely to take note of the fact that another person is of the same sex as themselves, and govern their imitation accordingly? Kohlberg (1966)[R] argues that selective imitation on this basis ought not to occur until children have established a fairly stable concept of their own sex. He says that such a concept depends, in part, upon the achievement of "gender constancy"—the understanding that a person's sex is not changed by changing clothes or hair styles, but remains as a constant attribute of the person throughout life.

Some work in progress by R. G. Slaby and his colleagues at the University of Washington (personal communication, 1974) bears upon the relationship between gender constancy and model selection. Using subjects aged 3–5 years, Slaby assessed gender constancy through questioning the children concerning whether they believed they could be a different sex if they wished to, etc. Each child then viewed a split-screen videotape.

One side of the screen showed a man, the other a woman, both engaged in the same activities; the child could see only one side of the screen at any given moment—which side was a matter of the subject's choice. Although there were no overall sex differences in choice of model, the children who measured high on gender constancy watched the same-sex model more than the children who did not show gender constancy. This finding is consistent with Kohlberg's contention, for although Slaby did not study imitation, selective attention to a model's actions would presumably facilitate later imitation of the model.

We have seen that some aspects of sex typing (such as the preference for same-sex playmates and certain sex-typed toys) occur at ages 3 and 4; but Kohlberg argues that a more general tendency to group all males together and "identify" along sex lines does not occur till later. In discussing age changes in the development of sex identity, Kohlberg says:

[A boy's] preference for same-sex peers is established before his preference for same-sex parent figures. The cognitive-developmental theory suggests two reasons for this discrepancy. The first is that the boy's classification of adult males in the common category "we males" is a more cognitively advanced achievement, and therefore comes later than his classification of other boys in that category. It is not until about age five-six, when the child begins to sort objects predominantly on the basis of similar attributes, that he forms groupings which include same-sex figures of diverse ages. The second consideration is that the boy's affectional tie to his mother is deep, and it takes time before the boy's self-conceptual or sex-role identity considerations can lead him to subordinate it to the development of a tie to the father.

If Kohlberg is right that the tendency to imitate selectively the same-sex parent, or other same-sex adults, does not occur earlier than age 5 or 6, then assumptions concerning such modeling would obviously be a weak explanation of any sex typing in behavior that occurs before this time.

To evaluate the Kohlberg position on age changes, as well as the positions of the previously cited social learning theorists concerning the importance of modeling, information is needed concerning the occurrence of same-sex imitation and the ages at which it may be demonstrated to occur. There are two approaches to this issue, one indirect and the other direct. If it can be demonstrated that children show clear and detailed resemblances to the same-sex parent, this fact would be consistent with the hypothesis that the child has imitated that parent. Clearly, the existence of the resemblances would not constitute proof of modeling—a resemblance might have come about through differential reinforcement or even sex-linked inheritance. However, the likelihood of a modeling explanation is increased if the matched behavior is of the sort—such as speech inflections—that is seldom subject to direct socialization pressure from parents. Furthermore, if parent-child resemblances are weak or absent, a modeling explanation of the acquisition of sex-typed behavior is jeopardized. We first present what little evidence is available on parent-child resemblance, and then turn to direct studies of imitation of same-sex and cross-sex models.

PARENT-CHILD SIMILARITIES

Before the studies and their findings are discussed, a word about method may be useful. Parent-child similarities can be studied in terms of mean level of a given attribute. For example, the number of hours spent in outdoor sports could be recorded for a set of fathers, mothers, sons, and daughters. The fathers would no doubt be found to spend more time in such activity than the mothers. And the boys would probably be spending more time in sports than the girls. The boys' mean scores for the total number of hours spent, then, would be more similar to the fathers' than to the mothers' mean scores, and girls' more similar to the mothers' than to the fathers'. These facts reveal little, however, about whether the tendency to be interested in sports is a product of modeling the behavior of the same-sex parent. Boys and men might both be more interested in sports for some biological reason, such as greater physical strength or a higher metabolism rate; or boys might simply have accepted sports as part of the cultural definition of masculinity, regardless of the behavior of their own fathers. What is needed is a determination of whether it is the boys whose *own* fathers are most active in sports who become especially interested in sports, and the sons of the more sedentary, cerebral fathers who are also sedentary and cerebral. In short, within-sex correlations are needed.

Studies reporting within-family correlations find, in general, that children are not notably similar to their own parents. Furthermore, when there is a correlation between parent and child scores, the correlations are not stronger between same-sexed parent and child. An early study by Lazowick (1955)[R] involved having college students and their parents rate a set of concepts on the semantic differential. The concepts to be rated included "myself," "man," "woman," and "family." All the correlations between parent and child scores were low. Daughters were no more like their mothers than they were like their fathers. Sons were slightly more like their fathers than their mothers, but they were no more like their own fathers than they were like a randomly selected set of other people's fathers.

Roff (1950)[R] summarized the research that had been done prior to 1950 on parent-child similarity in social and political attitudes and on personality traits as measured by personality inventories. Most of the studies were done with adolescents or young adults and their parents. His conclusion from the survey was as follows: "For any particular variable, there is either no difference or little difference between father-son, mother-son, father-daughter, and mother-daughter correlations." In other words, for aspects of beliefs and personality that are not specifically related to sex typing, there is little evidence that people tend to resemble the same-sex parent, at least by the time they have reached young adulthood. More recent work by Troll et al. (1969)[R] reveals a number of correlations between college students and their parents with respect to values and personality traits, but, again, no consistent tendency was found for students to resemble the same-sex parent more than the opposite-sex parent.

What has been found with respect to more clearly sex-typed attributes? In a study by Rosenberg and Sutton-Smith (1968)[R], college women from 2-child families were given the Gough Femininity scale. The scale was also administered to the subjects' mothers, fathers, brothers, and sisters. Correlations were computed for all the within-family pairs. The male siblings' scores correlated to a small degree with the parents' scores, but equally with mothers' and fathers' scores. The girls' scores—those of the college girls who were the primary subjects and their sisters—did not correlate significantly with the femininity scores of either parent. The work of Troll et al. yields a consistent result: correlations between generations with respect to stereotypic sex-role behavior are near zero and nonsignificant.

Perhaps it is true that by the time the children have reached adolescence, their sex-typed behavior is subject to so much peer pressure that daughters of especially feminine mothers are no longer especially feminine, and that a boy's masculinity is not clearly related to his father's masculinity. But perhaps the within-family similarities could be detected at an earlier age, when the children's mothers and fathers were the children's primary models. Again, the existing studies do not support the hypothesis of parent-child similarities. Hetherington (1965)[R] reports that the femininity of girls aged 3–6 is unrelated to their mothers' femininity. In a similar vein, Mussen and Rutherford (1963)[R] found that the femininity of first-grade girls, as measured in the It test, was unrelated to the femininity of their mothers' activities and interests, and that boys' masculinity scores were unrelated to either their fathers' masculinity or their mothers' interests. Boys whose mothers especially enjoyed cooking and sewing did not choose feminine activities of this sort for the It doll. Thus there is no evidence in this study either that the young boy is acquiring his masculine behavior and interests through modeling from his father, or that he is being hindered in his sex-role development by modeling feminine behavior from his mother.

The findings of Fling and Manosevitz (1972) point to a similar conclusion. Mothers' and fathers' It test scores were not significantly related to the It scores of their preschool sons or daughters.

IMITATION OF SAME-SEX MODEL

Perhaps the problem is that the measurements are too indirect. The measures in the studies of parent-child similarity we have discussed up till now are either projective measures or paper-and-pencil personality in-

ventories of uncertain validity for comparing the behavior of two generations. Perhaps to determine whether girls acquire their sex-typed characteristics by copying their mothers, and boys by copying their fathers, it
would be more satisfactory to obtain direct observations of the phenomenon by putting children in a position to imitate their parents and seeing
whether they do so. More specifically, the question is whether, when offered the opportunity to imitate one parent rather than (or more frequently than) the other, the child chooses the same-sex parent as primary
model. Ideally, studies are needed in which children have been observed
with their own parents, and their imitations recorded. Hetherington (1965)[R]
has done three such studies. The first involved children ranging in age
from 4 to 11. The children saw each of the parents express aesthetic preferences, and subsequently had an opportunity to make aesthetic choices
of their own from the same stimulus materials. Hetherington was interested primarily in the relationship between parental dominance (and other
parental characteristics) and childrens' imitations. She obtained powerful
results with respect to these objectives. For present purposes, however,
the important finding is that at every age level the subjects failed to show
any consistent tendency to imitate the same-sex parent. In a second experiment with children aged 4–5, selective imitation of the same-sex parent was
found, significant for girls and of borderline significance $(p < .10)$ for
boys. In a third study, with subjects ranging in age from 3 to 6, prefer-
ential imitation of the same-sex parent did not occur.

Most of the research on imitation does not involve the child with his
own parents, but exposes the child to unfamiliar models—either peers or
adults—or, in some cases, makes use of doll play. Hartup (1962), for example, used doll play incidents in which a mother doll would perform one
action and a father doll another; the subject was then given a child doll
and asked to show which one of the two actions the child doll would perform. With this technique, Hartup found that children of nursery school
age imitated the same-sex parent. Kohlberg and Zigler (1967)[R] used a
similar technique with children aged 4, 5, and 7, but in their analysis combined imitation of same-sex parent doll with measures of attachment to
same-sex parent (e.g. "Whom does the boy doll want to put him to bed
and say goodnight?"). The combined score was called "parent orientation,"
and the subjects did show, on the average, greater orientation toward the
same-sex parent. The contribution of imitation (as distinct from attachment) to this score is not known. These same children did *not* show sex-
typed imitation when they could either copy the paper cut-out done by a
male or female experimenter or make one of their own design.

We have located over 20 studies in which children were exposed to models of both sexes, and their imitation of same-sex vs. cross-sex models compared. The studies are show in Table 8.2. An entry of "No" in the table

means that there was no significant interaction between sex of child and sex of model. A significant interaction could be of two kinds: selective imitation of same-sex models by each sex, or selective imitation of cross-sex models. The table specifies, whenever an interaction exists, which kind it is. In instances in which subjects of both sexes chose primarily one sex of model (i.e. when there was a main effect for sex of model) the table entry is "No."

Table 8.2 indicates that there is little consistent tendency for children of preschool or grade school age to select same-sex models. The studies in which children copied indiscriminately from male or female models included imitation of affection from filmed models, imitation of aggression, imitation of toy choices, aesthetic preferences, self-reinforcement, and a variety of relatively novel actions. The studies that do report a same-sex model choice tend to have subjects over the age of 5, so there may be an age trend; however, other factors are present in these studies that make any conclusions about age trends risky. For example, in the two Wolf studies, the models were of the same age as the subjects and were shown playing with toys that would be inappropriate for the subject's sex. In the first experiment, male subjects saw a model (either a boy or a girl) playing with an oven with a kettle on it, and girls saw the model playing with a truck with a tire on it. The subject later had an opportunity to choose between these two toys to play with. In the second experiment, the sex-typed toys were a doll and a fire engine. A boy was found to be more likely to play with the toy stove or the doll if he had previously seen a boy playing with these toys; seeing a girl play with these toys did not serve to encourage a boy in sex-inappropriate play. The same was true, in mirror image, for girls, who in general played more freely with boys' toys than boys did with girls' toys, but who were even more likely to do so after viewing another girl play with the truck or the fire engine. Thus it appears to be true that when a child already has built up inhibitions against playing with a given toy, a same-sex peer can symbolically "give permission," or make the situation seem safe, to play with the normally forbidden toy. But the Wolf studies do not indicate that the initial preference for same-sex toys was acquired through selective imitation of same-sex models. On the whole, it simply cannot be said that young children spontaneously imitate people of their own sex more than people of the opposite sex. This is true of imitations of parents as well as of models who are unfamiliar to the child.

Table 8.2 does not show findings separately for boys and girls, and hence does not permit us to evaluate the hypothesis that boys initially tend to imitate their mothers and then switch to their fathers as a primary model. In fact, however, the studies give little support for such a hypothesis. There are a number of studies in which both boys and girls imitate male models

TABLE 8.2
Imitation of Same-Sex or Cross-Sex Models

Study	Age and N	Interaction	Comment
Fryrear & Thelen 1969	3-4 (60)	No	Imitation of filmed M and F model's affectionate behavior
Bandura et al.[R] 1963a	3-5 (96)	No	Imitation of aggressive behavior from live and filmed adult models
Bandura et al.[R] 1963b	3-5 (72)	No	Imitation of novel responses of M or F E who either controlled or consumed resources
Hartup 1962	3-5 (63)	Same-sex	Imitation of action of Mo or Fa doll
McDavid 1959	3-5 (32)	No	Imitation of adult M or F model's choice of door for candy search (S had no knowledge of model's success)
D. Hicks[R] 1965	3-6 (60)	No	Imitation of aggressive responses from filmed adult and peer models
Kohlberg & Zigler[R] 1967	3-8 (72)	No	Imitation of M and F E's paper cutouts
Leifer[R] 1966	3, 5, 7 (108)	No	Imitation of filmed preadolescent model's novel actions and choice of sex-neutral toys
Cook & Smothergill 1973	4 (154)	Same-sex	Imitation of M and F model's picture choices
Hetherington[R] 1965	4-5 (72)	No	Imitation of parents' aesthetic preferences
	6-8 (72)	No	Imitation of aesthetic preference of Mo or Fa
	9-11 (72)	No	Imitation of aesthetic preference of Mo and Fa
Masters 1972a	4-5 (80)	No	Imitation of neutral stylistic behaviors
Hetherington & Frankie 1967	4-6 (160)	Same-sex (n.s. for boys)	Imitation of novel game behaviors of Mo and Fa
DuHamel & Biller	5 (63)	Same-sex	Imitation of child doll of Mo and Fa doll's judgments of traits of human figures
Rickard et al. 1970	5 (40)	No	Forced imitation, 5-word strings
Rosenblith[R] 1959	5 (120)	No	Imitation of adult M or F E's color choice
W. D. Ward 1969a	5-6 (16)	No	Imitation of M or F placing bets in a game of chance
	7-8 (16)	Same-sex	Same as above

Note: M and F designate male and female models other than the parents. Mo and Fa designate mother and father.

(continued)

TABLE 8.2 *(cont.)*

Study	Age and N	Interaction	Comment
Wolf 1973	5-9 (140)	Same-sex	Imitation of televised M or F peer model, duration of play with sex-inappropriate toy
	7-11 (60)	Same-sex	Imitation of live peer model playing with sex-inappropriate toys
Bandura & Barab[R] 1971	6-7 (16)	No	Imitation of modeled motor responses (sample includes 4 retardates)
Bandura & Kupers 1964	7-9 (160)	No	Imitation of standard-setting and self-reinforcement in bowling game

more (Bandura et al. 1963a,b[R], Hicks 1965[R], Rosenblith 1959[R] and 1961[R]). In two of these studies, the response to be imitated is aggression, and Bandura has suggested that a response is more likely to be imitated (by a child of either sex) if it is displayed by a model for whom the behavior seems appropriate to the child. But over the range of behaviors represented in the studies in Table 8.2, it is not true that both sexes of children initially prefer female models; there is simply little selection on the basis of the model's sex.

It should be noted in addition that if boys initially imitated their mothers and then switched, girls should be more fully sex-typed than boys, at least during the preschool years. As was shown at the beginning of this chapter, the opposite is the case.

Earlier in this chapter, we noted the fact that research to date has not demonstrated the existence of within-sex parent-child similarities on any of the dimensions that have been measured. Roff's (1950)[R] early summary of the work on social and political attitudes did reveal that adolescent children have attitudes that are related to those of their parents, but that children's attitudes are no more closely related to those of the same-sex than the cross-sex parent. These findings are reasonable in the light of the research on imitation: children do imitate models, but they do not systematically imitate a same-sex model. Hence, they ought to resemble both their parents, not particularly the same-sex one. When it comes to measures of sex typing, the results are puzzling. Children's scores on sex typing are not correlated with those of the same-sex parent. In the light of the fact that we know children do imitate their parents with respect to many things, we should expect them to resemble both parents with respect to sex-typed behavior as well, even though they do not imitate the same-sex parent more than the opposite-sex parent. Why should they resemble neither parent? Clearly, the methods used to measure sex typing are relevant here. Assume, for example, that a little girl is copying behavior from both parents; every time she copies feminine behavior from her mother she achieves a point toward a score that might produce a positive correlation with her mother's femininity score ; but whenever she copies a bit of masculine behavior from her father, she not only reduces her own femininity score but moves toward obtaining a negative correlation with her mother's femininity score. If bisexual modeling is what is actually going on in the home, then zero-order correlations between the parent and child M-F scores would be the result.

Unfortunately, this solution to the problem is too glib. Children do not develop androgenously. As has been shown above, the results of many studies are quite unequivocal on this score: by age 4, children on the average prefer toys and activities that are considered by the adult society to be sex-appropriate. Children of each sex prefer to play with other children of their own sex, although this is more pronounced for boys. These preferences can be demonstrated projectively with the It test, and they can also be demonstrated in straightforward choices that the child makes on his own behalf in toy preference tests; in addition, the preferences may be observed in the child's behavior when his activities are time-sampled and enumerated during the free play periods at nursery school. The children are clearly sex-typed; but their degree of sex typing is unrelated to that of the same-sex parent; furthermore, in experimental situations when children have choices of models, they do not consistently select same-sex models. It would appear, then, that their sex typing does not originate through modeling.

Before this conclusion is accepted, there are some other possibilities that must be considered. Perhaps the problem is that when "masculinity" or "femininity" is measured in an adult, different things are measured than when the presumably similar characteristics are measured in childhood. A mother's M-F score reflects interests, activities, and attributes that her daughter may not even perceive, much less be able to copy. Perhaps little girls *are* learning their sex-typed behavior by imitating their mothers, but perhaps they are imitating behaviors that are not normally included in the measures of the mother's femininity. For example, most of the toy preference tests rely heavily upon dolls as indicators of feminine interest. The toy preference test used by R. Sears et al. (1965)[R], modeled after Rabban's test, included a baby doll, a doll crib, a doll bathinette, a doll feeding chair, and a doll buggy. The only feminine items not related to dolls were a set of dishes and two purses. The masculine toys offered for choice were more varied. Perhaps a girl who gets a highly feminine score is imitating her mother's care-taking with younger siblings. But the mother's femininity score does not include items that would reveal whether she is frequently engaged in this activity or not. If same-sex imitation were at work, we would expect to find that when a girl saw her mother taking care of a baby, the girl would spend a good deal of time playing with dolls. The boy, on the other hand, should be less affected by whether he sees his mother caring for a baby, since the mother is not his primary model. We have not been able to find published data bearing upon this matter. Sears has provided us with doll-play data from the 1965 study *Identification and Child-Rearing*. In this study, girls showed significantly more nurturant responses to the baby doll than did the boys. Sears' new analysis (personal communication, 1974) involves separating the children who have younger siblings from those who do not, to see whether the child's responses to the baby doll are influenced by opportunities to see the mother take care of a younger child. When the sample is subdivided by both sex and ordinal position, the number of cases in each group is small, and the results are only suggestive, but they are interesting nonetheless: girls tend to be nurturant to the baby doll whether they have younger siblings or not; boys tend to show nurturance *only* when they have younger siblings. Thus it is boys, rather than girls, who seem to be copying the behavior they have observed in their mothers!

On the basis of this rather fragmentary evidence, we are inclined to believe that our earlier conclusion was justified: that early sex typing is not a function of a child's having selectively observed, and selectively learned, the behavior of same-sex, rather than opposite-sex, models. Furthermore, it would appear that the lack of parent-child similarity in sex typing is not just a function of the fact that the wrong things are being measured in the two generations. It has been noted before (R. Sears et al. 1965[R], p. 186) that masculine and feminine behavior at age 4 is a qualitatively very different thing from masculinity and femininity in adulthood. When a little girl shows flirtatious behavior toward her father, this behavior is not a carbon copy of what she sees her mother doing. What the little girl sees might be the father coming home from the office, a quick kiss or brief hug between the mother and father, the mother flashing some smiles at her husband as she gets dinner, the exchange of conversation such as "How was your day, honey?" etc. This is not the kind of behavior fathers are referring to (see p. 329) when they say that their daughters are "little flirts," "soft and cuddly," etc. If the daughters are imitating their mothers, the match is not close, and the model's behavior has been filtered through childish eyes and the imitative actions are a function of a childish body and a childish level of behavior organization. This brings us to a very central point about imitation. The developmental psycholinguists have shown us that when a child is asked to repeat a grammatically complex sentence, the child will simplify it. In many instances the child reprocesses the sentence so that most of the meaning is retained, but uses a structure that expresses the child's level of grammatical competence. It would not be surprising if this same kind of process goes on in social behavior. If the little girl perceives that her mother is being affectionate toward the father, and sets out to copy this behavior, the behavioral output will have to be constrained by the child's already developed behavioral capabilities, at least to a degree, and the result will be childlike affection-showing. We recognize that it is hazardous to suggest that a child will sometimes copy the "meaning" of an action rather than the action itself; it is extraordinarily difficult to be operational about the "meaning" of action. And, in any case, the possibility of transformational imitation does not seem to help in understanding the issue before us. If a young child were imitating the meaning of the same-sex parent's behavior, then it ought to be true that the little girls who are most feminine in a childish way have mothers who are especially feminine in an adult way, and we have seen that this does not appear to be true.

Our analysis of the arguments concerning the role of modeling in sex typing and our review of the research on selective imitation have led us to a conclusion that is very difficult to accept, namely that modeling plays a minor role in the development of sex-typed behavior. This conclusion seems to fly in the face of common sense and to conflict with many striking observations of sex-typed role playing on the part of children. For example, here is an excerpt taken from Minturn and Hitchcock's report of the play of Rajput children in India (1963, p. 334)[B]:

Both sexes have their own type of fantasy play which is modeled on adult work. The little girls play at cooking and the boys at farming. One child in the sample was particularly fond of playing at cooking. She had a set of toy dishes, and she would build herself a hearth out of three stones and go through the exact motions of making bread. She used either mud or potsherds for her bread, rubbed oil in the frying pan, patted the breads, fried them on the fire underneath the pot to let them puff, took them out, flattened them, and stacked them on a dish beside her. It was an exact copy of the motions that an adult woman goes through in making bread. When she finished she washed the dishes and stacked them, and washed the floor in the place where she had cooked.

When the boys play at farming, they sometimes make rather elaborate imitations of fields, and then irrigate them. More often the play is somewhat simpler, as in the following observation: A group of boys were playing at sowing. They had long sticks and were pretending to plow. They said, "Let's grow wheat." Some of the boys started scattering dust like seed. They were following boys who were "plowing" the ground with sticks. They said "burr," "burr," "burr," which is what the men say to the cattle. They leveled the ground with a stick by rolling it along the ground.

In the face of observations of this kind, how can we possibly say that modeling is not of crucial importance in the acquisition of sex-typed behavior? We must note that Rajput culture is highly sex-segregated, because of the custom of purdah for women; it is possible that in this culture girls are primarily exposed to female models and boys to male models, and that their play reflects this fact. We are inclined to doubt, however, that the matter of model availability is the primary explanation. American children, too, display sex-typed imitations of adult work when they play. But when they are offered models of the two sexes in controlled experimental situations, their imitations are usually indiscriminate as to sex. Clearly, the discrepancy between acquisition and performance that Bandura and Walters (1963)[R] and Mischel (1970)[R] have espoused so vigorously must be involved. Note that someone *had given the little Rajput girl a set of dishes.* Having the dishes in her hands, she knew what to do with them, on the basis of previous observational learning. We suspect that if someone had given such a set of dishes to a small Rajput boy, he too would be quite capable of displaying the detailed motions involved in making bread.

What are the reasons, then, a child might not perform actions that he has in fact learned how to do through observational learning? A first reason is the one we have just suggested: the necessary eliciting conditions do not occur. A second is that the child has reason to believe the action is inappropriate for him. He knows there are many actions permitted to an adult that are not permitted to a child; e.g. adults may handle sharp objects, drive cars, etc., whereas a child may not, and a child must wait for a considerable time to put into practice many of the actions that are in one sense already in his repertoire (Maccoby 1959[R]). In a similar vein, he comes to know that certain actions are appropriate for a person of his own sex, and others are not. This factor, we believe, is paramount. To be as explicit as possible, we suggest that (a) the modeling process is crucial in the acquisition of a wide repertoire of potential behaviors, but this repertoire is not sex-typed to any important degree; (b) knowledge of what behavior is appropriate is crucial in the selection of what items will be used in performance out of the repertoire of potential actions.

There is a reservation to point (a): the repertoire itself might become sex-typed if the person does in fact come to seek exposure to, or selectively attend to, same-sex models. If a girl decides to take sewing lessons, she is likely to go to a woman teacher, and thus add to her repertoire some specific female-role skills that a boy will not possess because he did not expose himself to this modeling. Furthermore, it is possible that when both sexes of models are available for a particular skill that a child wishes to acquire, the child will normally choose to copy whichever model might be expected, on the basis of sex, to be more proficient in the activity. But this is a shaky assumption. Cooking, for example, is a female activity; yet if offered the choice to imitate a housewife cooking dinner or a male chef cooking at a restaurant, the chances are that children of both sexes would copy the latter. The prestige of model can override the sex-appropriateness of the activity. In any case, if children do operate on the assumption that one sex is likely to be a better model for certain kinds of skills, we suggest that selective imitation based on such assumptions is a relatively late development; we saw little evidence of it in the studies of imitation in children under 10, though most of the studies cited were not designed with this particular issue in mind. In any case, seeking out a same-sex model implies that the seeker has already developed sex-typed interests; hence, such selection cannot be an explanation of the development of such interests.

Like other writers on the subject, we have stressed the distinction between acquisition and performance, and have argued that, at least in early childhood, *acquisition* of behavior through modeling is not sex-typed. The sex typing of behavior that may be observed at these ages is then held to be a function of performance factors. What are these factors? Two general classes have been proposed: Mischel's position is that the reinforcement history of the individual, and his observations of the reinforcements delivered to models, will determine which actions a child selects out of his repertoire for performance. Sex typing, then, according to this view, would be a product of direct reinforcement (to self or others) for sex-appropriate behavior. The alternative point of view is Kohlberg's: that it is the child's growing understanding of his own sexual identity, coupled with his growing understanding of the content of the sex roles prescribed by the culture around him, that determine the child's behavioral choices. In this view, sex typing is dependent upon certain aspects of cognitive growth. A child's inferences concerning what behavior is sex-appropriate are partly based, of course, upon the instances of differential reward and punishment, and in this sense Kohlberg's theory is not distinct from Mischel's. But in the cognitive-developmental view, differential reinforcement is only one of the sources of information a child uses to construct the concept of sex-appropriate behavior that he uses to guide himself.

It becomes important to know as precisely as possible what different patterns of reinforcement contingencies *are* experienced (directly or vicariously) by the two sexes. It is to this topic that we now turn.

CHAPTER NINE

Differential Socialization of Boys and Girls

A scene from the early musical "Carousel" epitomizes (in somewhat caricatured form) some of the feelings that parents have about bringing up sons as opposed to daughters. A young man discovers he is to be a father. He rhapsodizes about what kind of son he expects to have. The boy will be tall and tough as a tree, and no one will dare to boss him around; it will be all right for his mother to teach him manners but she mustn't make a sissy out of him. He'll be good at wrestling and will be able to herd cattle, run a riverboat, drive spikes, etc. Then the prospective father realizes, with a start, that the child may be a girl. The music changes to a gentle theme. She will have ribbons in her hair; she will be sweet and petite (just like her mother), and suitors will flock around her. There's a slightly discordant note, introduced for comic relief from sentimentality, when the expectant father brags that she'll be half again as bright as girls are meant to be; but then he returns to the main theme: she must be protected, and he must find enough money to raise her in a setting where she will meet the right kind of man to marry.

Despite recent changes in social attitudes, this rendition no doubt still contains more than a kernel of truth about the way mothers and fathers feel about the two sexes. It is widely assumed that these parental attitudes and feelings must translate themselves into differential behavior on the part of parents toward sons and daughters. Parents, it is thought, must bring to bear direct or indirect pressure to make their children fit sex stereotypes. The theory that sex typing in children's behavior is brought about through direct "shaping" by socialization agents is probably the most pervasive point of view in writings on the subject. Even theories that stress modeling tend, as shown in Chapter 8, to depend upon prior occurrence of differential socialization, so that children of the two sexes are motivated to select different models. The role of direct socialization appears to be crucial, then, not only in its own right but also in establishing the foundation upon which later self-socialization is based. The objective of the present chapter is to determine whether, and in what ways, boys and girls are treated differently by parents and other socializing agents. In addition, we shall consider the following questions: To what extent is the differential treatment consistent with the characteristic behavioral differences between children of the two sexes? Are there any aspects of family dynamics that transcend the simple preference among parents that their boys shall be masculine and their girls feminine, and that lead to differential treatment of boys and girls?

A search of the literature for studies of differential socialization reveals an interesting phenomenon. Most work on sex-role socialization has been done within sex, not between sex. Most researchers have been interested in the question of what makes some boys more masculine than others, or some girls more feminine than others. Tables of correlations are presented, for a given sex, showing the relationship between socialization practices and some measure of masculinity or femininity; the correlations are shown separately for boys and girls. There is an assumption underlying this practice, only sometimes made explicit, that if we know what makes some boys more masculine than others, we will automatically have discovered what makes most boys more masculine than most girls.

There are some pitfalls in this assumption. For example, Sears et al. (1965)[R] found that parental punitiveness feminized both boys and girls. Then, according to the usual assumption, it might be inferred parents must be more punitive toward girls, on the average, and this must be one factor that makes girls more feminine than boys. In fact, as we shall see, parents are probably more punitive toward boys. We must recognize the possibility that boys are more "masculine" than girls (in some sense of this term) *despite* what their parents are doing, not because of it. We do not mean to imply that there are different laws of learning, or different laws of human behavior, for the two sexes. However, it does seem clear that if we want to understand the role of differential socialization, there is no substitute for direct comparisons between the parents of boys and the parents of girls; inferences from within-sex correlations are simply not sufficient.

A second trend that emerges when one reviews the studies of parent-child interaction and its effects is that the large majority of the studies deal with children under school age. We suspect this age bias stems from several implicit assumptions. A major one is the assumption that the influence of the parents declines when the child enters school, while that of teachers and age-mates increases. Beyond this, there is the assumption that the impact of external socialization agents is greatest in the younger years because of changes in the psychological dynamics of the child. The young child is sometimes thought to be more pliable because he is more dependent—he needs the attention and affection of his parents more than an older child does and is therefore more willing to conform to their demands. A second reason for emphasizing the importance of early socialization is, of course, the concept of identification and its consequences: once a child has "identified" with his parents, he spontaneously accepts their values and, to a major degree, thereafter socializes himself (primarily by imitation). A related view, that of the cognitive-developmental theorist, is that once the child has achieved a fairly stable self-concept (including a stable sex identity) he will select models accordingly, and socialization will become a more and more autonomous process. A Skinnerian view, on the contrary, would argue that there is no reason why external contingencies should not continue to shape and reshape the individual; this view would not point to any developmental change in the relevance of external socialization forces. Unfortunately, the existing body of research, concentrating as it does upon the early years, does not provide a basis for an appraisal of these contrasting points of view.

In the sections that follow, a set of hypotheses will be set forth concerning possible processes that might underlie differential treatment of children of the two sexes; then findings of existing studies will be summarized; and finally the hypotheses will be evaluated in the light of this evidence.

HYPOTHESES

Hypothesis 1. Parents treat children of the two sexes so as to shape them toward the behavior deemed appropriate for their sex. This hypothesis leads to the prediction, for example, that boys would be rewarded for being tough and competitive, girls for being compliant and nurturant, and that each sex would receive negative reactions for sex-inappropriate behavior. It need not be true, of course, that this parental behavior is deliberate; it may be quite unintended from a subjective point of view. Furthermore, in the case of sex-typed behavior that is deemed undesirable by the parent, it may simply be opposed with less vigor in the sex for which it is consistent with a sex-role stereotype. That is, there may be differential withholding of negative reinforcement as well as differential reward.

Hypothesis 2. Because of innate differences in characteristics manifested early in life, *boys and girls stimulate their parents differently and hence elicit different treatment from them.* Furthermore, the same parental behavior may produce a different response in a boy than a girl, again because of innate sex-linked characteristics. In short, the child "shapes" the parent rather than vice versa, and a circular pattern of interaction becomes established based upon an individual child's demands and the parent's discovery of what works with that child. The nature of the child's demands, and the nature of the parental actions that will be effective, will differ initially to some degree for the two sexes.

Hypothesis 3. Parents base their behavior toward a child on their conception of what a child of a given sex is likely to be like. Whether innate temperamental differences exist or not, many parents believe they do, and parents govern their socialization practices accordingly. This adaptation may take one or more of three forms:

3a. Parents devote special attention to training children to overcome what they believe to be their natural weaknesses. If parents believe, for example, that boys are naturally more aggressive than girls, they may make stronger efforts to control and counteract aggressive behavior in sons than daughters. With girls, their efforts might be more directed toward helping them to overcome their assumed natural timidity.

3b. Parents accept as inevitable, and do not attempt to change, any behavior they believe to be "natural" for a given sex.

3c. Parents have a perceptual adaptation level that is different for the two sexes. *They tend to notice, and react to, whatever behavior is seen as unusual for a child of a given sex.*

Hypothesis 4. A parent's behavior toward a child will depend, in some degree, upon whether the child is of the same sex as himself. We suggest three possible mechanisms underlying cross-sex and same-sex parent-child relationships:

4a. Each parent expects and wants to be a model for the same-sex child. He will be especially interested in teaching that child the "lore" that goes along with being a person of their shared sex.

4b. Each parent transfers to his children some of the behavior he is accustomed to displaying toward adults of the two sexes. In some cases this amounts to outright sexual attraction and seduction of the opposite-sex child. In addition to cross-sex attraction, there are cases on record of a homosexual parent who seduces a same-sex child. Most commonly, of course, there are simply discreet elements of flirtation with the opposite-sex child, and elements of rivalry with the same-sex child. Dominance-submission relationships, as well as sexual ones, may generalize to children. If a woman is accustomed to taking a submissive stance toward her husband and other adult men, the hypothesis says that she will be more likely to behave submissively toward a son than a daughter. Clearly there are instances in which the role demands of parenthood (especially motherhood) are not consistent with habitual male-female interaction patterns. It would be reasonable to expect that the simple generalization of a parent's own habitual behavior toward adult males or females would be more likely to occur with older, rather than younger, sons and daughters.

4c. Parents will tend to identify more strongly with a same-sex child. Specifically, the parent will see more similarities between himself and a same-sex child, and will have stronger empathetic reactions to that child's emotional states. A given parent's relation to a same-sex child will depend, then, to some degree on the parent's self-attitudes. A parent with low self-esteem will be frequently made anxious by the things a same-sex child does; this parent will be preoccupied with the things the child might do wrong or the ways he might get into trouble, and will tend to assume that other people are reacting negatively to the child. A self-confident parent will have confidence in a same-sex child. Rothbart (1971) suggests that this "counteridentification" of parent with the same-sex child is particularly strong for firstborn children, and rather weak with later-borns.

All four of the kinds of processes we have hypothesized may be at work in the interactions in a given family. Sometimes the processes are not entirely compatible with one another. We now turn to an examination of what is known about parental behavior toward children of the two sexes, to see to what extent these themes may be detected and how they are orchestrated and balanced when they create conflicting pressures within a family.

Total Parent-Child Interaction

The amount of interaction between the parent and the young child does not consistently depend on the sex of the child. Among studies that do report a sex difference, there are more studies that find greater interaction with boys, but the majority report no difference (see Table 9.1). Some of the studies cited report interaction in terms of the amount of time the parent spends in specific activities with the child; others use scores based on detailed time-sampling of specific behaviors, such as touching or eye contact with the child; the conclusion reached by the study, however, does not seem to depend in any systematic way upon the nature of the measure used.

Most of the studies, of course, report interaction between the *mother* and the child. The studies that do report father data are inconsistent. Gewirtz and Gewirtz (1968) find that Israeli fathers tend to stay longer with infant sons than daughters when they visit their children in the children's house. Consistent with this, though at a later age, is the R. Sears et al. (1965)[R] finding (from father interviews) that fathers have more interaction with sons than daughters of kindergarten age. (Note that this is the same sample of children as that reported by Hatfield et al. 1967.) F. Pedersen and Robson (1969), however, did not find a sex difference in the amount of time fathers spent caring for, and playing with, their 8-9-month-old infants, and in Tasch's study (1952)[R], fathers who were interviewed said they had been more involved in the care-taking of their daughters than their sons.

Turning to more specific classes of parental behavior, we do find a consistent trend for parents to elicit "gross motor behavior" more from their sons than from daughters (see Table 9.2). This parental behavior takes several forms. Lewis (1972) reports that mothers are more likely to respond to a son's large-muscle movements than to those of a daughter; Moss (1967) and L. Yarrow et al. (1971) report that parents "stress the musculature" of male infants—meaning, presumably, that they are more likely

TABLE 9.1

Total Interaction (Social Stimulation)

Study	Age and N	Difference	Comment
Parke et al. 1972	0-2 days (19)	Boys None	Mother and Father touch infant Mother and Father hold, kiss, feed, rock, explore infant
Tasch[R] 1952	0-17 yrs (85)	Girls	Father participation in daily care (father interview)
Thoman et al. 1972	2 days (40)	Firstborn boys Later-born girls	Time spent breast-feeding
Leiderman et al. 1973	1, 4 wks postdischarge (66)	None	Mother holds infant (full-term and premature samples)
Moss 1967	3 wks (29) 3 mos (25)	Boys None None	Mother attends infant Mother holds, feeds, looks at infant Mother holds, feeds, attends, looks at infant (longitudinal)
Lewis 1972	3 mos (32)	Boys None	Time mother holds infant Mother touches, looks, smiles, rocks, plays with infant; total time of interaction; ratio of mother-child interaction to infant action
Gewirtz & Gewirtz 1968	4 mos (8m, 4f) 8 mos (8m, 4f)	Boys None Boys Boys	Amount of time spent feeding Duration of mother's visits to children's house (kibbutz) Time spent feeding Duration of father's visits to children's house
L. Yarrow et al. 1971	5 mos (41 & primary caretakers)	Boys None	Variety and level of social stimulation from caretaker (black sample) Caretaker proximity
Beckwith 1972	7-11 mos (24 adoptive mo-inf. pairs)	None	Mother touching
Clarke-Stewart 1973	9-18 mos (36)	None	Total amount of mother-child-interaction; amount of social stimulation from mother; mother's response to infant's distress and demand behaviors; mother's response to infant's social signals (home observation; longitudinal)
F. Pedersen & Robson 1969	9½ mos (45)	None	Father caretaking, emotional involvement, time spent in play, level of play stimulation (assessed by interviewing mother; firstborn)
Minton et al. 1971	27 mos (90)	Boys	Total mother-child interactions

(continued)

TABLE 9.1 *(cont.)*

Study	Age and N	Difference	Comment
Biber et al. 1972	4 (225)	Girls	Amount of teacher's instructional contact with child (videos of class-room)
Radin 1973	4 (52)	None	Total mother-child interaction (behavior observation during mother interview; multiracial, low SES)
Bee et al. 1969	4-5 (114)	Both	Maternal interaction during child's problem solving (boys, white middle SES; girls, black and white lower SES)
Hatfield et al. 1967	4-5 (40)	None	Mother involvement and attentiveness during structural mother-child interaction
Sears et al.[R] 1965	4-5 (40)	Boys	Amount of father interaction (father interview)
Rothbart 1971	5 (56)	Girls	Mother's "anxious intrusions" during supervision of child's performance on 5 tasks

TABLE 9.2
Stimulation of Gross Motor Behavior

Study	Age and N	Difference	Comment
Tasch[R] 1952	0-5 yrs 6-17 yrs (160)	None Boys	Father interview: report of father-child rough-and-tumble play
Moss 1967	3 wks (29)	Boys	Mother stimulates, arouses; stresses musculature
	3 mos (25)	None	Mother stimulates, arouses; stresses musculature (longitudinal sample)
Lewis 1972	3 mos (32)	Boys	Mother "responds proximally" (touch-hold) to gross motor movement of infant
L. Yarrow et al. 1971	5 mos (41 & primary caretakers)	Boys	Caretaker encourages gross motor responses (black sample)

to handle them roughly and pull their arms and legs vigorously. In an interview conducted by Tasch (1952)[R] with fathers of children of a wide range of ages, the fathers reported engaging in more rough-and-tumble play with their sons than with their daughters. The form of the motor stimulation undoubtedly changes drastically with the age of the child, but the continuing theme appears to be that girls are treated as though they were more fragile than boys. F. Pedersen and Robson (1969) report that

TABLE 9.3
Verbal Interaction and Stimulation

Study	Age and N	Difference	Comment
Parke et al. 1972	0-2 days (19)	None	Mother and father vocalizations to infant
Thoman et al. 1972	2 days (40)	Girls	Mother talks to infant during breast-feeding (firstborns)
		None	Later-borns
		Girls	Mother talks to infant during nonfeeding activities (trend, $p < .1$)
Leiderman et al. 1973	1, 4 wks postdischarge (66)	None	Mother laughs and talks to infant (longitudinal)
Moss 1967	3 wks (29)	None	Mother imitates and talks to infant
	3 mos (25)	None	Mother imitates and talks to infant (longitudinal)
Lewis 1972	3 mos (32)	Girls	Mother vocalizes to infant
Lewis & Freedle 1972	3 mos (40)	Boys	Mother responds to infant vocalization
		Girls	Mother vocalizes to infant
J. Kagan 1971	4 mos (180)	Girls	Distinctive vocalizations from mother (upper-middle SES only)
		None	General vocalizations from mother
L. Yarrow et al. 1971	5 mos (41)	None	Mother's contingent response to infant vocalization
Goldberg & Lewis 1969	6 mos (64)	Girls	Mother talks to infant during experimental session
Beckwith 1972	7-9, 8-11 mos (24 adoptive *mo*-inf pairs)	None	Mother vocalizes to infant
Phillips 1973	8, 18, 28 mos (57)	None	Mother's verbalizations to child
Clarke-Stewart 1973	9-18 mos (36)	None	Verbal stimulation by mother, home observation (longitudinal)
Minton et al. 1971	2 (90)	None	Mother reasons with child, questions child
Halverson & Waldrop 1970	2½ (42)	Girls	Number of mother's statements and words to child while administering tasks
Lapidus 1972	3-4 (30)	None	Mother's verbalizations to child while teaching cooperation game
Serbin et al. 1973	3-5 (225 & 15 teachers)	Boys	Teacher holds extended conversation with child
Blayney 1973	4 (29)	None	Father's verbalizations to child while child performs on elevated balance beam
Bee et al. 1969	4-5 (114)	Both	Mother gives information to child in waiting room (boys, black and white lower SES; girls, white middle SES)
		None	Mother asks question, makes suggestion to child in waiting room

(continued)

TABLE 9.3 *(cont.)*

Study	Age and N	Difference	Comment
Hatfield et al. 1967	4-5 (40)	None	Mother reasons with child (observation)
Rothbart 1971	5 (56)	Girls	Mother questions child ($p < .1$)
		None	Amount of information mother gives to child about tasks; amount of time mother spends in conversation or explanation; complexity of mother's explanations
Greenglass 1971a	9-10, 13-14 (132)	None	Mother's communication during joint problem solving (Canadians and Italian-Canadians)
M. Hoffman & Saltzstein 1967	12 (270 & available mothers & fathers)	Girls	Both parents' use of induction, father's more pronounced (child report, middle SES)
		None	Mother's and father's use of induction (parent report)
	12 (174)	Girls	Father's use of induction (child report, low SES)
		None	Mother's use of induction (child report)

fathers are more apprehensive about the physical well-being of infant daughters than infant sons at the age of 9 months; Minton et al. (1971) detect a similar trend somewhat later, at age 27 months, when mothers express more worry about physical danger to daughters than sons. However, few studies have measured either roughness of handling or fears about injury to the child, so it is too early to say whether this is a consistently sex-typed aspect of parental beliefs and behavior.

Amount of Verbal Interaction

As noted in Chapter 3, recent evidence does not clearly indicate that girls undergo more rapid verbal development in the first few years of life. Earlier evidence did point to such a conclusion, however, and it has sometimes been assumed that a female head start in verbal ability might be a function of girls' receiving more verbal stimulation or reinforcement from their caretakers. As may be seen from Table 9.3, the evidence on this subject is inconsistent. The majority of studies show no difference in the amount or kind of parental vocalizations to sons as compared with daughters. In a number of instances when differences are found, it is only for a portion of the sample. For example, Thoman reports mothers talking more to daughters when the child is a firstborn, but not for later-born infants. Kagan finds that well-educated mothers use more distinctive vocalizations (that is, vocalizations when in face-to-face orientation to an infant and unaccompanied by any other form of stimulation) with daughters than with sons, but this difference is not found among mothers with less education, and there is no difference in the total amount of maternal vocalization directed by mothers toward infants of the two sexes. Furthermore, although well-educated mothers are somewhat more likely to respond to a female infant's vocalization within 10 seconds, less-well-educated mothers are somewhat more likely to respond to a *son's* vocalizations within this short time. The significance of these differences was not tested. Bee also found, with older children, that whether a mother vocalizes more to a son or daughter is a function of the social class of the families. J. Kagan (1971, p. 106) makes the point that it is probably the direct and immediate interaction with an infant, accompanied by eye contact, that serves to build the child's vocalizations. It may be that much of the evidence summarized in Table 9.3 is not sufficiently refined to reflect important interactional properties of this kind that might be differential for boys and girls. But on the basis of existing evidence, it can only be said that results are highly variable across sample subgroups, and that the bulk of the evidence does not add up to any clear trend for mothers to provide more verbal stimulation to daughters than sons. A number of studies found no sex differences, and those that did are inconsistent in the direction of the difference found.

Parental Warmth

Perhaps the most widely studied dimension of parent-child relationships is the warmth-hostility or warmth-rejection dimension. In the early 1950's, in an interview study with mothers of 5-year-old children (R. Sears et al. 1957[R]), the mothers were asked to recall how much time they had spent playing with the child when it was an infant, and how much they had cuddled it. The current level of affectional interaction with the child was also assessed. Summary ratings of "mother's warmth to infant" and "mother's warmth to child currently" were made; the mothers of daughters recalled somewhat warmer interaction with their infants than did mothers of sons, but no difference in the amount of warmth to the two sexes was reported at the age of 5. Since that time there have been many observational studies as well as additional interview studies, and the work has even been extended to subhuman primates. Observations of rhesus monkey mothers and their infants (Mitchell and Brandt 1972[R], Mitchell 1968[R]) have revealed that mother monkeys embrace and clasp an infant more if it is a female. After about the age of 3 months, there is an increase in the amount of rejection and threat behavior the mother shows to male infants, but not to females. Mothers bit the male infants more frequently than the female infants (sometimes in response to being bitten). On the other hand, mixed with threats toward male infants were seemingly contradictory bits of behavior: the mothers occasionally played with their male infants, but almost never with their female infants; and the mothers of the males more often lip-smacked to their male infants (a conciliatory gesture), presented sexually to them, and were more often seen submitting to rough treatment from them. Similar differential treatment of infant males and females by adult male monkeys of some species has been reported (see Mitchell and Brandt 1972[R] for a review). It is difficult to know what precisely it is about an infant's appearance or behavior that permits a monkey mother to "recognize" its sex, but it is evident that infants of the two sexes do stimulate their mothers differently and establish a different pattern of relationships with them. The interactions become more differentiated with the infant's increasing age, and one result is a higher level of nonpunitive physical contact between a mother and a female infant.

With human infants, however, no clear-cut pattern of differential treatment emerges from the nine observational studies now available (see Table 9.4). Six of these report no difference in the amount of affectional contact between mother and infant in the first two years. Leiderman et al. (1973), working with a group of infants some of whom were premature, found that during the first week after the infants were discharged from the hospital, mothers did tend to hold daughters in a ventral-ventral position more often; however, the total amount of holding and other affectionate contact did not differ for male and female infants. When these mother-infant pairs were observed one month postdischarge, the girls were still receiving more ventral-ventral holding, but now the boys received more total affectionate touching. Lewis (1972) found that among a group of 3-month-old infants, the boys were held more; Goldberg and Lewis (1969), however, report concerning a group of 6-month-old infants that the girls were more frequently touched than the boys. At nursery school age, Radin (1973) finds mothers showing more affection to daughters; but three studies (Baumrind 1971, Hatfield et al. 1967, and Allaman et al. 1972) find no differences in maternal affection. In these studies, observations of parental behavior are available, as well as interview data in some instances. Both Baumrind and Hatfield et al. do report tendencies for fathers to show somewhat more hostility toward sons at this age, but the trends do not reach statistical significance.

When children themselves, at older ages, are questioned on how much affection they have received from their parents, girls are likely to report receiving more affection (Siegelman 1965, Hoffman and Saltzstein 1967, Droppleman and Schaefer 1963[R], Bronfenbrenner 1960[R]). Since observational studies of parent behavior when the children are younger do not usually report differential parental warmth to children of the two sexes, the differences reported by the children themselves may either reflect selective perceptions on the children's part or indicate that differentiation in parental warmth to the two sexes does develop but only some time after the children reach school age.

TABLE 9.4
Warmth, Nurturance, and Acceptance

Study	Age and N	Difference	Comment
Allaman et al. 1972	0-6 yrs (95)	None	Mother affectionateness (observation)
	0-10 yrs (65)	None	Mother affectionateness, intensity of contact (observation)
Sears et al.[R] 1957	"infancy" (379)	Girls	More warmth by mother to infant (mother recall)
	5 yrs (379)	None	Warmth to child (mother interview)
Leiderman et al. 1973	1, 4 wks post-discharge (66)	Boys	Mother affectionately touches infant (4 wks)
		Girls	Mother and infant in ventral contact (observation; 1, 4 wks)
		None	Mother holds, smiles, touches infant affectionately (1 wk); mother holds, smiles at infant (4 wks)
Moss 1967	3 wks (29)	None	Mother smiles, rocks, gives affectionate contact
	3 mos (25)	None	Mother smiles, rocks, gives affectionate contact (longitudinal)
Lewis 1972	3 mos (32)	Boys	Mother holds infant
		None	Mother rocks, touches, smiles at infant
Kagan 1971	4 mos (180)	None	Physical affection from mother
L. Yarrow et al. 1971	5 mos (41 & primary caretakers)	None	Expression of positive affection by caretaker (black sample)
Goldberg & Lewis 1969	6 mos (64)	Girls	Mother touches infant (observation)
Clarke-Stewart 1973	9 mos (36)	None	Mother's positive attitude toward child (interview)
	9-18 mos	None	Physical contact with mother (home observation; longitudinal); mother's positive attitude toward child (observer rating)
	18 mos	Boys	More positive attitude toward child (questionnaire)
D. Stayton et al. 1971	9-12 mos (25)	None	Mother's acceptance (vs. rejection) (observer ratings)
Baumrind 1971	3-4 (293 parents)	None	Mother is rejecting, father is rejecting (observer ratings)
Baumrind & Black 1967	3-4 (95 parents)	None	Warmth: presence of loving relationship, demonstrativeness, approval, empathy, sympathy (mother and father interviews)
Sears et al.[R] 1953	3-5 (40)	None	Mother's nurturance when child is upset or mother busy; father's nurturance (mother interview)
		Boys	Mother's bedtime nurturance

(continued)

TABLE 9.4 *(cont.)*

Study	Age and N	Difference	Comment
Serbin et al. 1973	3-5 (225 & 15 teachers)	None	Teacher hugs child in response to dependent behavior
		Boys	Teacher hugs child in response to appropriate participation in classroom activities
Kagan & Lemkin[R] 1960	3-6 (67)	Girls	Child perceives father as affectionate
Blayney 1973	4 (29)	None	Father expresses affection or approval to child
Hilton 1967	4 (60 & mothers)	None	Number of overt expressions of love and/or support while child attempts series of puzzles
Radin 1973	4 (52)	Girls	Mother's nurturance (observation; trend, $p < .1$)
Hatfield et al. 1967	4-5 (40)	None	Mother's warmth toward child, mother's responsiveness to child (observer ratings)
Sears et al.[R] 1965	4-5 (40)	Girls	Father's satisfaction with child's socialization (father interview)
Laosa & Brophy 1972	5-7 (93)	Boys	Mother and father equally nurturant (child questionnaire)
		Girls	Mother more nurturant than father (child questionnaire)
Siegelman 1965	9-11 (212)	Girls	More affective reward, less expressive rejection from father (child questionnaire)
		None	Nurturance, instrumental and affiliative companionship from father; affective reward, expressive rejection, nurturance, instrumental and affiliative companionship from mother
Armentrout & Burger 1972	9, 10, 12 (635)	None	Parental acceptance, child report (working-class sample)
	11, 13	Girls	Greater parental acceptance, child report (working-class sample)
Cox 1970	11-13 (100)	Girls	Perceive fathers as more loving, less rejecting
		None	Perception of maternal love and rejection
Droppleman & Schaefer[R] 1963	12 (165)	Girls	More love and nurturance from both parents (child interview)
M. Hoffman & Saltzstein 1967	12 (270 & available mothers & fathers)	Girls	More affection from mother, father; child report (middle SES)
		None	Parental affection (mother and father interviews)
	12 (174)	Girls	More affection from mother, father; child report (lower SES)
T. Miller 1971	13 (35)	Girls	More empathy, genuineness, and positive regard from mother (inner city black; mother questionnaire)
	13 (99)	None	Empathy, genuineness, and positive regard from mother (white suburban sample; mother questionnaire)

(continued)

TABLE 9.4 *(cont.)*

Study	Age and *N*	Difference	Comment
Bronfenbrenner[R] 1960	15 (192)	Girls	Tendency for more affection, especially from father (child questionnaire)
Wyer 1965	18 (889)	Women	Acceptance by mother (mother ratings of child)
		None	Father's acceptance (father ratings of child)

Restrictiveness

Another child-rearing dimension of some importance is the restrictiveness (vs. autonomy-granting) dimension. Mitchell (1968)[R] found that mother rhesus monkeys restrained their female infants more than their male infants. In a number of factor analyses of the behavior of human parents, the restrictiveness dimension has emerged as relatively distinct from the warmth-hostility dimension. Furthermore, those who assume that there is a sex difference with respect to the amount of independent or exploratory behavior children show attribute the difference sometimes to parental tendencies to allow children of one sex more freedom than is allowed to the other. In the early study by Sears et al. (1957)[R], sex differences were not found in this area of parental behavior. Mothers placed similar limits on boys and girls with respect to how far away from the house they were allowed to go. The mother checked on the child's whereabouts equally often when the child was out of sight, and allowed no more freedom to one sex than to the other when it came to making noise or being rough with household objects. Similarly, mothers held similar expectations for daughters and sons with respect to the kind of self-help they should be capable of: demands were similar for being able to dress themselves, take care of their own clothes, and wait on themselves at the table. Nakamura and Rogers (1969) have made a useful distinction between what they call "assertive autonomy" and "practical autonomy." The former refers to a child's acts of independence that do not have labor-saving value for the mother; the latter, by contrast, involves the child's being helpful to the mother by waiting on himself. As we have noted above, the Sears study found no sex differences in granting autonomy of either kind. The bulk of more recent studies have had similar results (see Table 9.5). The studies that have identified any differential treatment of boys and girls have more often found greater independence-granting to girls than boys. For example, in Radin's (1973) recent work with parents of 4-year-old children, both interview data and direct observations of parent-child interaction have been collected. Scores are summarized into an overall restrictiveness

TABLE 9.5

Restrictions, Low Encouragement of Independence

Study	Age and N	Difference	Comment
White House Conference[R] 1936	0-12 mos (4,100)	None	Restriction of play area (mother interview)
Allaman et al. 1972	0-80 mos (95)	None	Mother restrictiveness; coerciveness of mother's suggestions (home observation)
	0-10 yrs (65)	None	Same measures as above
Tasch[R] 1952	0-17 yrs (160)	Girls	Father concerned about child's safety (father interview)
Beckwith 1972	7-11 mos (24 adoptive mo-inf pairs)	Boys	Mother's restrictiveness, particularly mother with only high school education
F. Pedersen & Robson 1969	8, 9½ mos (45)	Girls	Father apprehensive over infant's well-being (mother interview)
D. Stayton et al. 1971	9-12 mos (25)	None	Maternal control over child (home observation)
Clarke-Stewart 1973	9-18 mos (36)	None	Mother's restrictiveness and directiveness (home observation, longitudinal sample)
Minton et al. 1971	27 mos (90)	Boys	Mother gives "simple" prohibition to child (trend, $p < .09$)
		Girls	Mother concerned about physical danger to child; gives "directive" prohibition (home observation)
Block 1972	3 (90)	Boys	Father: "I have firm rules for my child"
		None	Mother: "I have firm rules for my child"
		Boys	Father does not encourage child to be independent of him
		None	Mother: "I encourage my child to be independent of me"
Nakamura & Rogers 1969	3 (39)	Boys	Low expectations for "assertive autonomy" by father
		None	Low expectations for "assertive autonomy" by mother
		Girls	Low expectations for "practical autonomy" by mother
		None	Low expectations for "practical autonomy" by father
Baumrind 1971	3-4 (293 parents)	Boys	More firm enforcement for father and trend ($p < .1$) of more firm enforcement from mother
		None	Mother's and father's encouragement of independence and individuality, directiveness; father values conformity, father authoritarianism (home observation)
	3-4 (415 parents)	None	Mother and father: firm enforcement, authoritarianism, early maturity demands, value of conformity, promotion of nonconformity (parent interviews)

(continued)

TABLE 9.5 *(cont.)*

Study	Age and N	Difference	Comment
Baumrind & Black 1967	3-4 (95)	Boys	Father's restrictions on child's initiative (no difference—mother)
		Girls	Mother's demands for obedience, strictures about neatness (no difference—father)
		None	Mother and father: maturity expectations (permissiveness for exploration, rewarding of self-sufficiency), strictness (care of family property, aggression toward other children, television, responsibilities about orderliness), encouragement of independence (contact with other adults, introduction to new experiences) (parent interviews)
Blayney 1973	4 (29)	None	Father's protectiveness, restrictiveness (observation)
Callard 1968	4 (80)	Girls	Lateness of age recommended by mother for independence granting
Newson & Newson 1968	4 (700)	None	Level of restrictions and demands vis-à-vis bedtime, table behavior, neatness, physical mobility (mother interview)
Radin 1973	4 (52)	Boys	Mother's restrictiveness (observation of mother-child interaction during mother interview; low SES, multiracial sample)
Bee et al. 1969	4-5 (114)	None	Mother's use of control statements
Hatfield et al. 1967	4-5 (40)	Boys	Mother restricts, punishes independence; directiveness ($p < .1$)
		Girls	Mother's concern over water play (structured observation)
		None	Mother's pressure, reward for independence; pressure for obedience; concern over neatness, orderliness
Rothbart 1971	5 (56)	Girls	"Anxious intrusions" by mother while child performs task (structured observation)
Sears et al.[R] 1957	5 (379)	None	Level of restrictions and demands; neatness, TV watching, household tasks, bedtime, table manners, physical mobility (mother interview)
J. Gordon & Smith[R] 1965	6-7 (48)	None	Maternal strictness (mother interview)
Armentrout & Burger 1972	9-13 (635)	Boys	Greater parental psychological control (child's report)
		None	Firmness of parental control (child report, lower-middle SES)
Thomas 1971	18-21 (60 parent-child pairs)	Women	Low "permissiveness" (parent and S interview, politically conservative sample)
		None	Permissiveness (liberal sample)

scale. Radin finds (personal communication) that mothers are significantly more restrictive with boys than with girls. Baumrind (1971) finds that both mothers and fathers use firmer enforcement with sons than with daughters —that is, once a direction has been given, they are more likely to follow it up to make sure that a boy has complied with it. Baumrind also finds, however, that boys and girls are given equal encouragement for "independent individuality." In the Hatfield et al. (1967) study, mothers were more likely to restrict the independent movements of sons—and more likely to punish independence—than of daughters. When it came to the kinds of independence that were helpful to the mother, mothers did exert pressure for the child to be independent, and rewarded independence, but sons and daughters were treated equally in these respects.

The Newson and Newson study in England (1968) found no sex differences in the range of movement inside and outside the home that was allowed to the child at age 4, or in the demands the mother made for the child to do things by himself rather than asking for help. Their study is a longitudinal one, and they have collected socialization data at successive points in the child's development. At the time of this writing, the data for age 7 are being analyzed. At this age, for the first time in the Newsons' study of this large group of families, a substantial difference has begun to emerge in the treatment of sons and daughters. Daughters are receiving more of what the Newsons call "chaperonage." For example, mothers are much more likely to meet a daughter after school and escort her home. Although the chaperonage difference is very clear, this does not imply that girls are restricted with respect to all aspects of independent behavior. Girls are allowed to make as many decisions as boys about where they wish to go and what they wish to do. It is only that their whereabouts must be known and that they are more often in the company of an adult. Probably the greater chaperonage of girls stems directly from the greater danger of molestation—a danger that, although often elaborated in maternal fantasies, is also quite real. Possibly there is also some anticipation of whatever chaperonage the parents will deem suitable when their daughters reach adolescence. It is interesting that this particular difference in the socialization of boys and girls occurs so late. During the preschool years, of course, both of the sexes are watched and accompanied and their whereabouts are carefully monitored, so that in a sense the issue does not yet arise.

To summarize: during the preschool years, there is a trend in some measures toward greater restriction of boys, but the findings from study to study are not consistent, and the bulk of the evidence is that there is little or no difference in the socialization of boys and girls when it comes to independence-granting.

Reactions to the Child's Dependency

The term "dependency weaning" has sometimes been used to describe the process whereby a parent who has consistently given help or affection whenever the child wanted it begins to detach the child by ignoring such demands, guiding the child into more independent actions, or sometimes actively pushing the child away. Do parents begin dependency weaning at an earlier age if the child is a son? Do they become more irritated over a son's dependency demands? Mischel (1970[R], p. 49) says: "In regard to dependency, the average difference between the sexes . . . seems consistent with the widely assumed greater permissiveness for dependency by females as opposed to males in our culture." There is evidence that reward for dependency is indeed associated with high (or increased) levels of dependent behavior in children (see Maccoby and Masters 1970[R], pp. 141–42). But as Mischel notes, the prevalent view that the amount of reward by socializing agents for this behavior is a function of the child's sex is usually an *assumption*—little evidence is cited from direct observation or parent interviews concerning how parents do in fact handle dependency bids from sons as compared with daughters. Table 9.6 summarizes studies that do report data on this subject.

There are four observational studies cited. Two of these (Clarke-Stewart 1973, Baumrind 1971) report no difference in the way parents respond to dependency supplications from sons and daughters. In the Serbin et al. (1973) study, children and their teachers were observed in nursery school. Boys and girls equally often solicited help from their teachers, but teachers responded to a higher proportion of boys' solicitations. The teachers' response to children's seeking of proximity, on the other hand, was not differentiated as to sex. The girls more frequently sought proximity, but the probability of a teacher response, once a child did seek proximity, was similar for boys and girls. (We do not know to what extent male teachers would make similar differentiations.) In the Hatfield et al. study (1967), boys were more frequently punished by their mothers for dependency bids, but, as noted in the previous section, they were also more frequently punished for *independent* behavior. It appears, then, that these maternal reactions are part of the more general picture of greater punitiveness to boys (discussed below); they do not appear to reflect any specific shaping of dependent, as distinct from independent, behavior.

Two of the studies cited in Table 9.6 involve the use of tapes of a child's voice, identified to some parents as the voice of a boy, and to others as the voice of a girl. The parent was asked to say what his reaction would be if his own son (or daughter for those hearing the girl's voice) said the things that had been taped. Some of the remarks made by the child's voice

TABLE 9.6
Reward (Permissiveness) for Dependency

Study	Age and N	Difference	Comment
Clarke-Stewart 1973	9-18 mos (36)	None	Mother's responsiveness to infant's social signals (home observation; longitudinal)
Block 1972	3 (90)	Girls	Father feels it important to comfort child when upset (questionnaire; trend, $p < .1$)
		None	Importance to mother of comforting child when upset (questionnaire)
Baumrind 1971	3-4 (293 parents)	None	Mother and father discourage emotional dependency and infantile behavior (home observation)
	3-4 (415 parents)	None	Mother and father discourage infantile behavior (parent questionnaire)
Rothbart & Maccoby[R] 1966	3-4 (98 mothers, 32 fathers)	Boys	Mother's permissiveness and positive attention to comfort seeking (mother's written response to tape of child's voice)
		Girls	Father's permissiveness and positive attention to comfort seeking (father's written response to taped voice)
		None	Mother's and father's response to help seeking
Serbin et al. 1973	3-4 (225 children, 15 teachers)	Boys	Rate of teacher response to child's solicitation of attention
		None	Rate of teacher response to child's proximity seeking
Baumrind & Black 1967	4 (95)	Boys	Mother rewards dependency (interview)
		None	Father rewards dependency (interview)
Hatfield et al. 1967	4-5 (40)	Girls	Less punishment of dependency (observation; trend, $p < .1$)
		None	Mother rewards dependency
Sears et al.[R] 1957	5 (379)	None	Reward, permissiveness, punishment for dependency (mother interview)
Lambert et al. 1971	6 (73)	Girls	Parental compliance to comfort-seeking requests
		None	Parental compliance to requests for help (mother's and father's response to tape of child's voice)
Levitin & Chananie 1972	6-7 (40 teachers)	None	Teacher's approval of dependent behavior in hypothetical boy or girl (questionnaire)

represented dependency supplications—demands for help or nurturance. The Rothbart and Maccoby (1966)[R] study found that mothers were more permissive toward such demands from boys, and fathers from girls. In the Lambert et al. (1971) study, both French-Canadian and English-Canadian mothers and fathers, when hearing a child's demand for comfort for a minor injury, were more likely to say they would withhold comfort if they believed the child to be a boy. There was no significant difference, by sex of child, in the tendency to give help of other kinds when demanded by the child.

Interview studies have also produced mixed results. In the Baumrind and Black study (1967), mothers of boys were more likely to report that they responded positively to the child's dependency than were mothers of girls. In the Sears et al. study (1957)[R], mothers were asked about their handling of the child's help seeking, attention seeking, and clinging. Mothers of boys and mothers of girls were highly similar in their permissiveness for such behavior, and in the amount of reward and punishment they reported administering for it. In the Block study (1972), fathers reported feeling that it was more important to give comfort to a girl when she was upset than to do so for a boy, but mothers made no such distinction.

Recent work by Osofsky and Oldfield (1971)[R] shows clearly that when a girl behaved dependently, her parents changed their behavior toward her. A structured observation situation was arranged including two tasks, one of which required the child (age 4–6) to seek the parent's help, while the other permitted independent functioning. During the time when the daughter was behaving dependently, both mothers and fathers talked to her more and became more controlling; perhaps more interesting is the fact that fathers, but not mothers, reacted positively to their daughters' increased dependency. It would be interesting to see this same procedure repeated with male subjects. Judging from the Rothbart and Maccoby (1966)[R] findings, it is possible that mothers would react more positively to the dependency bids of sons than daughters. But this remains to be seen. For our present purposes, the salient point is that the Osofsky and Oldfield study did not include subjects of both sexes, so no comparison can be made between the treatment of sons and daughters.

Considering the evidence as a whole, there has been no clear demonstration that one sex received more reinforcement for dependency than the other. As further evidence accumulates, it appears likely that the answer to the initial question will depend upon a much more fine-grained analysis of child behavior—that "dependency" is much too broad a category. If any sex differences do emerge, it appears that the degree and even the direction of such differences may depend both upon the sex of the *parent* and upon what particular aspect of dependency is involved. A good hypothesis is that instrumental dependency (help seeking in pursuit of some goal other than affectional contact itself) will not be rewarded more in girls; in fact, the reverse may be the case (see Serbin et al. 1973). Possibly a supportive, positive response to a child's display of feelings of all sorts, including a positive response to clinging (whether it is activated by fear or love), is an aspect of socialization that will eventually be more evident in parental responses to girls. At present, however, the evidence does not exist to support such a generalization. It is well to remember that there is very little difference between the sexes in the frequency or intensity with which dependent behavior occurs (see Chapter 4); hence, it should not be surprising that patterns of differential reinforcement have not become apparent.

Reactions to the Child's Aggression

It is commonly asserted that parents are more likely to permit or encourage aggression in boys than in girls, and that this is one of the reasons boys are more aggressive. Frequently cited in support of this view is the early report by Sears, Maccoby, and Levin (1957)[R] that mothers of boys said they allowed their children to show more aggression toward neighborhood children (particularly in self-defense) than did mothers of daughters. Furthermore, mothers of boys reported themselves as being more permissive than mothers of girls when a child was aggressive toward its parents, although the two sexes received approximately equal amounts of punishment for such behavior. More recent research calls for reevaluation of the question of differential parental reinforcement of aggression in the two sexes.

Lambert et al. (1971), in their study of French-Canadian and English-Canadian parents, found that both mothers and fathers reacted more harshly to a show of temper from a boy than to the identical behavior from a girl (see Table 9.7). Minton et al. (1971), observing 2-year-olds and their mothers at home, found that boys were more likely to be reprimanded for aggression toward the mother than were the girls. The observational study by Serbin et al. (1973) in nursery school classrooms showed not only that boys were more likely to commit an aggressive or destructive act, but that, once such an act had occurred, the probability of the teacher's responding to it was greater if the actor was a boy. The nature of the teacher's response also differed for the two sexes. When girls were aggressive, the teacher usually "softly reprimanded" them. When boys were aggressive, the teacher's response was more often a loud reprimand, restraint, or talking to the child and giving directions concerning desired behavior.

In a study of 40 preschoolers and their families, involving both behavior observation and parent interviews, Sears et al. (1965)[R] found no sex differences in the permissiveness of the parents toward a child's display of aggression toward the parents. Nor did the amount of punishment for such behavior differ by sex of child. Surprisingly, the parents in this study also said they did not press their sons, more than their daughters, to hit back when attacked by a neighbor child. In a similar vein, with a much larger sample studied in England through mother interviews, the Newsons (1968) found no differences between the mothers of sons and the mothers of daughters in their reactions to the children's aggression. Parents of boys

TABLE 9.7

Permissiveness (Reward) for Aggression (or Competitiveness)

Study	Age and N	Difference	Comment
Tasch[R] 1952	0-17 (85)	Boys	Father expects more aggressiveness; worried if unaggressive
		None	Father worries over disobedience (father interview)
D. Stayton et al. 1971	9-12 mos (25)	None	Frequency of discipline-oriented physical interventions by mother (home observation)
Minton et al. 1971	27 mos (90)	Girls	Less often reprimanded for aggression toward mother (home observation)
Block 1972	3 (90)	Boys	Mother and father believe competitive games are beneficial (questionnaire)
		Girls	Father allows anger toward himself (questionnaire)
Baumrind & Black 1967	3-4 (95)	Boys	Mother tolerates verbal protest, believes in less control of parent-directed verbal and/or physical aggression (interview)
		None	Father's tolerance of verbal protest, belief in control of parent-directed verbal and/or physical aggression (interview)
Lapidus 1972	3-4 (30)	Boys	Mother makes self-deprecatory statements during game
		None	Mother lets child win, encourages cooperation (observation)
Rothbart & Maccoby[R] 1966	3-4 (98 mothers, 32 fathers)	None	Mother's and father's reaction to other-directed aggression (written response to tape of child's voice)
		Boys	Mother permits aggression toward herself
		Girls	Father permits aggression toward himself
Sears et al.[R] 1953	3-5 (40)	None	Mother's responsiveness to aggression (interview)
Serbin et al. 1973	3-5 (225 pupils, 15 teachers)	Girls	Lower likelihood of teacher response to child's aggressive or destructive ($p < .08$) behavior; fewer loud reprimands for disruptive act
J. Gordon & Smith[R] 1965	3-4, 6-7 (48)	None	Permissiveness for aggression (mother interview)
Newson & Newson 1968	4 (700)	None	Mother does not intervene in children's quarrels; encourages, permits aggression toward parents (English sample)
Sears et al.[R] 1965 and pers. communication	4-5 (40)	None	Permissiveness of aggression toward parents Demands aggression toward peers (parent interview and observation)
Sears et al.[R] 1957	5 (379)	Boys	Mother more permissive of aggression toward parents and peers; mother's encouragement to fight back if attacked (interview)
		None	Punishment for aggression

(continued)

TABLE 9.7 *(cont.)*

Study	Age and *N*	Difference	Comment
Lambert et al. 1971	6 (73)	Girls	Parental acceptance of show of anger (parent response to taped hypothetical situations, English-Canadian and French-Canadian samples)
		None	Parental acceptance of insolence
		Boys	Mother's acceptance of insolence (French-Canadian sample only)
		Girls	Father's acceptance of insolence (French-Canadian sample only)
		None	Parent's reaction to argument between child and baby, and between child and baby after child is hurt
		Boys	Mother sides more with child in argument between child and guest (French-Canadian sample only)
		Girls	Father sides more with child in argument between child and guest
Levitin & Chananie 1972	6-7 (40 teachers)	None	Teacher approval of aggressive behavior in hypothetical boy or girl (questionnaire)

and girls were equally likely to say that they allowed their children to settle their own quarrels with neighbor children or siblings; equally likely to tell a boy or girl to hit back when attacked; and equally unwilling to permit a child to be insolent or "cheeky" toward the parents. In the Baumrind and Black (1967) study, however, the mothers of boys did say, during interviews, that they were more tolerant of resistive behavior (protests, aggression toward the parents) than did the mothers of girls.

Taken together, the series of studies summarized in Table 9.7 certainly does not present a consistent picture of greater permissiveness toward boys' aggressive behavior. The observational studies of parents' reactions to their children's aggression have all been done in the home or in a contrived experimental situation where other children are not present; thus information is available from these studies only on socialization pressures directed toward the child when he is aggressive toward the parents or toward siblings. Only interview data are available concerning what a parent does when children fight with other children outside the home. Observations are needed of the way that parents, when they supervise a play group, handle aggressive behavior among children. And data concerning father reactions would be especially useful; it may be that fathers, but not mothers, encourage their sons to fight. Still, it is in the area of aggression more than any other sphere of behavior that we find evidence for cross-sex effects, with fathers being especially severe toward boys. Rothbart and Maccoby (1966)[8] found that mothers were more willing to accept angry behavior toward themselves from sons than from daughters, whereas fathers reacted in the reverse manner, being more permissive of aggression from daughters than from sons. Lambert et al. (1971) replicated this cross-sex effect, finding that fathers would accept "insolence" from daughters more readily than from sons, and that if a child got into an argument with a guest, the father would tend to take his daughter's side but take the guest's side against a son. Mothers, on the contrary, accepted insolence more readily from sons, and sided with their sons against the guest, but not with their daughters. Block (1972) found that fathers of boys were more likely than fathers of girls to say: "I don't allow my child to get angry with me."

The Sears et al. (1965)[R] and Newson (1968) findings concerning parents' attitudes about allowing a child to fight with other children are puzzling, especially in view of Tasch's report (1952)[R] that fathers, during an interview, say that they tend to worry if a son is unaggressive (unwilling to defend himself), whereas they feel little such concern over an unaggressive daughter. Some of the inconsistency in the data no doubt stems from different understandings of what is implied by "aggression." At least in middle-class families, with which most of the research has been done, parents attempt to train children of both sexes to solve their interpersonal problems through reasoning and negotiation rather than physical force; especially as children grow older, they are unlikely to draw much parental approval for physical fighting. At the same time, parents do not want their children to be the victims of other children's aggressions, and many do value a kind of competitive toughness in their children, which presumably parents prefer to see expressed in sports and in forms of dominance behavior short of physical force.

Is competitive toughness more encouraged in boys than in girls? It seems a good hypothesis that this would be so. Observational work on parental encouragement of competitive behavior is very scarce. Lapidus (1972) did observe mother-son pairs and mother-daughter pairs while the mother was teaching a cooperative marble game to her nursery-school-age child (see Chapter 6 for details of the procedure). The game was designed in such a way that individual players could earn "points" only if the other player allowed him to. The hypothesis of the study was that mothers would let their sons win, thus encouraging them in competitive behavior, whereas they would insist on taking turns with their daughters. The results did not sustain the hypothesis. Although boys did get somewhat more points than girls in competition with their mothers, the difference was not significant. Mothers quite uniformly encouraged cooperative behavior with both sons and daughters. Mothers did not explicitly allow boys to take marbles out of turn more often than girls, or show approval when they won a point. The only significant sex difference was that mothers were more likely to make self-deprecatory comments to sons than to daughters. For example, a mother would occasionally say to a son: "I don't play this game very well," or "I must be doing something wrong." Such remarks were very seldom made to daughters. Preliminary data from a study by Williams (1973)[R] on fathers' encouragement of a son's or daughter's competitive behavior suggest that fathers too do not differentiate in this respect.

This kind of study does not reveal whether the parents are encouraging their children's competitiveness toward other children; it is quite possible that a mother would encourage cooperative behavior when the child is interacting with her, but do so less consistently when it came to cooperative or competitive behavior with age-mates. A more critical problem is that the Madsen marble game is designed so that competitive behavior is self-defeating; in many real-life situations, rewards are a scarce commodity that can be obtained only by defeating another person. Parental encouragement of competitiveness needs to be studied in relation to such situations. The primary implication of the Lapidus study is that in a situation where cooperativeness is a productive strategy, mothers are as likely to try to teach this strategy to a son as to a daughter.

Encouragement of Sex-typed Activities

To what extent do parents actively support the development of sex-typed activities and interests in the two sexes? Although quantitative reports are not available, it would appear obvious that when Christmas or birthdays approach, parents are likely to buy dolls or toy cookstoves for their daughters and trucks or electric trains for their sons. Whether these choices occur because the parents are responding to already developed preferences expressed by the children, or whether their purchases precede and guide the development of such preferences, we do not know—it is likely that the influence works in both directions. Parental sex-typing pressures need to be studied in the earliest portions of children's lives, and little such observation has been done. In two recent experiments (Jacklin et al. 1973), a variety of toys was available in a playroom, and records were made of mothers' choices of toys to offer to their 13- and 14-month-old children during a free-play session. The toys included stuffed animals, robots, a toy workbench, and a musical ferris wheel. There was no evidence that the mother chose different toys to offer to a son, as compared with a daughter. The children's toy choices differed by sex, but the mothers' did not. However, the available toys did not include some of the most highly sex-typed ones, and we do not doubt that many parental toy choices are sex-typed, and that children are actively discouraged from playing with sex-inappropriate toys. When parents buy sex-typed toys for their children, this of course can have a long-term effect, since the toys remain part of the child's daily environment for a considerable period.

It is interesting to consider whether boys have been more heavily conditioned than girls to avoid opposite-sex interests and activities. Intuitively, it seems that a boy would be subject to more disapproval for being a "sissy" than a girl would for being a tomboy. As reported earlier, Hartup, Moore, and Sager (1963)[n] found boys were more likely to avoid the sex-inappropriate toys than were girls. The fact that boys' avoidance of feminine toys was especially marked when an experimenter was present suggested that the boys had previously been subjected to more socialization pressure than were the girls to adopt appropriately sex-typed activities. Direct evidence on the relevant parent behavior is available from two studies.

Lansky (1967) presented parents of preschool children with hypothetical situations in which a boy or girl chose either a masculine or feminine activity. When a girl chose a boyish activity, neither mothers nor fathers seemed especially concerned. When a boy chose girlish activities, however, both parents reacted quite negatively, and this was especially true of fathers. Fathers were also somewhat more likely to show positive reactions when a boy chose boyish activities than when a girl chose feminine ones. But the primary sex differences were found in negative parental reactions to cross-sex activity choices by boys. Similar results have been obtained by Fling and Manosevitz (1972). They studied families with nursery-school-age children, asking the parents to make "It test" choices for their children and, in an interview, inquiring about parental guidance of the children toward or away from certain sex-typed activities. Parents were asked how strongly they would object to their children's engaging in any of the activities they had omitted in their choices for It. Scores were derived that represented the extent of their discouragement of a child's sex-inappropriate activities. Both mothers and fathers chose more sex-appropriate activities for their sons in the It test than they did for girls. Both parents much more strongly discouraged sex-inappropriate behavior in sons than daughters. Positive encouragement for sex-appropriate activities was not so clearly biased toward heavier pressure on the boys; mothers of girls encouraged their daughters somewhat more than their sons in this respect. On the whole, the results of the two studies clearly sustain the Hartup and Moore interpretation of their findings: more social pressure against inappropriate sex typing is directed at boys than at girls.

Fathers' emotional reactions can be powerful, as illustrated by the comment made by a father who was asked in an interview whether he would be disturbed by indications of "femininity" in his son: "Yes, I would be, very very much. Terrifically disturbed—couldn't tell you the extent of my disturbance. I can't *bear* female characteristics in a man. I abhor them" (E. Goodenough 1957, p. 310). In view of the strength of these feelings, it is not surprising to find fathers playing an active role in guiding their sons away from "sissy" behavior. In addition, however, a father's reactions are important in developing the femininity of his daughter. There are certain subtle ways in which he shows interest in and appreciation of his daughter's femininity. Some clues to this are to be found in comments by fathers reported by Goodenough. She asked parents to describe their children's personalities. Most of the children being described were 2 or 3 years old. The parents began by describing the things that seemed most salient to them in their children's personalities. Then they were asked: "Is your child more masculine or more feminine in personality? Give some examples of what you mean." Here are some of the things that fathers said about their little daughters: "A bit of a flirt, arch and playful with people, a pretended coyness." "Soft and cuddly and loving. She cuddles and flatters in subtle ways." "I notice her coyness and flirting, 'come up and see me sometime' approach. She loves to cuddle. She's going to be sexy—I get my wife annoyed when I say this." Ten out of 20 fathers of girls described their daughters in similar terms.

These comments no doubt reflect to some degree what the little girls' behavior was really like; but they also reflect the fathers' perceptions. The point of interest here is that the fathers appeared to enjoy being flirted with by their daughters; furthermore, the mothers in the Goodenough study reported instances in which their husbands had put pressure on them to dress their daughters in dresses rather than pants, to keep their hair long, etc., when the mother would not have considered it especially important for their daughters to look dainty and feminine at this young age. Fathers appear to want their daughters to fit their image of a sexually attractive female person, within the limits of what is appropriate for a child, and they play the masculine role vis-à-vis their daughters as well as their wives. This may or may not generate rivalry between mother and daughter, but there can be little doubt that it is a potent force in the girl's development of whatever behavior is defined as "feminine" by her father.

Parental Responses to Children's Sexuality

In most cultures, there is a double standard of adult sexual morality. Women are expected to be modest and, to some degree, chaste. Men are allowed (or even expected) to have a more active sex life and engage in more sexual exploration. In encounters between the sexes, men are expected to take the initiative. These cultural definitions of the role to be played by the two sexes are central to the meaning of "masculinity" and "femininity" in any culture where the definitions exist. It might certainly be expected that the treatment of children would reflect them. We do not know precisely how early in a child's life the socialization for his adult role in courtship and sex might be expected to begin, but it would not be surprising if, even in early childhood, parents emphasized the importance of modesty more with daughters, and were less permissive toward them in dealing with overt displays of sexual activity and interest.

This is an area of socialization, of course, in which direct observation of parent-child interaction yields little information. For the most part the child's sexual behavior occurs either when the child is alone (and is revealed only when the mother "catches" him), when he is with other children and adults are not present, or in the intimacy of bathtime and bedtime. We must rely upon parental reports of such instances and their outcomes for our information on how sexual behavior is socialized.

Three interview studies have obtained data on socialization as it is directed toward childhood sexuality. The first is the Sears, Maccoby, and Levin study of a group of 379 families in the Greater Boston area (1957)[R]. The second is the small-sample study by Sears et al. (1965)[R] done in a suburban community in California. The third is the study of 700 English families living in or near Nottingham, conducted by the Newsons (1968). In each of these studies, detailed information was obtained concerning the parents' reactions to their children's masturbation and to any instances of sex play with other children. Parents were also asked what kind of information they gave their children on sexual matters, and whether children were allowed to be seen, or to see other family members, in the nude. In both England and the United States, working-class parents were considerably less permissive toward children's sexuality than were middle-class parents. But in none of the studies did any difference whatever emerge in the treatment of boys and girls. Parents were equally severe in their reactions to masturbation, whether it occurred in a son or daughter; they were equally likely, or unlikely, to allow the child to be seen in the nude by other family members; they were equally likely to give the child information about sex; and they reacted similarly to instances of sex play with neighbor children, regardless of the sexes of the children involved.

It is possible, of course, that there are counteracting tendencies involved here. According to the Sears hypotheses, discussed below, both parents ought to be made more anxious by sexuality in a boy, and hence they should insist more firmly on his being modest. On the other hand, since modesty is going to be more important for a girl later in life, they ought to begin training her more consistently for this behavior than they would a son. If both factors are at work, they might cancel one another and yield what has been found—no difference in the training of the two sexes. In any case, no positive evidence has emerged that parents are engaging in specific sexual socialization that prepares children differentially for "double standards" of adult sexual life. Of course, the sex information that is given to both boys and girls—that babies grow inside the mother and that the father plants the "seed" for the baby—fosters the development of the children's sex-role concepts, but this development does not stem from differential treatment of the two sexes with respect to information-giving.

Physical Punishment and Other Negative Sanctions

There are some fairly clear differences in the amount and kind of discipline directed at boys and girls. As Table 9.8 shows, with few exceptions

TABLE 9.8
Physical Punishment (Power Assertion)

Study	Age and N	Difference	Comment
Tasch[R] 1952	0-17 (85)	Boys	Use of physical punishment (father interview)
Minton et al. 1971	2 (90)	Boys	Maternal use of physical punishment (home observation; trend, $p < .1$)
Block 1972	3 (90)	Boys	Father believes "physical punishment is best way of discipline" (trend, $p < .1$)
		None	Mother believes "physical punishment is best way of discipline"
		Boys	Mother does not "find it difficult to punish child"
		None	Father "finds it difficult to punish child"
J. Kagan & Lemkin[R] 1960	3-6 (67)	Girls	Child perceives father as punitive
J. Gordon & Smith[R] 1965	3-4, 6-7 (48)	None	Physical punishment (mother interview)
Baumrind & Black 1967	4 (95)	Boys	Physical punishment by father (father interview)
		None	Physical punishment by mother (mother interview)
Newson & Newson 1968	4 (700)	Boys	Mother's use of physical punishment (mother interview)
Sears et al.[R] 1957	5 (379)	Boys	Use of physical punishment (mother interview)
Simpson[R] 1935	5-9 (500)	Boys	Father spanking (child interviews)
		Girls	Mother spanking (child interviews)
		Girls	Father spanking (child's stories to pictures)
Siegelman 1965	9-11 (212)	Boys	Physical punishment by mother and father (child report)
Zussman 1973	10 (44)	None	Parental use of power assertive techniques (mother, child report)
M. Hoffman & Saltzstein 1967	12 (270 + available mothers & fathers)	Boys	Power assertion from mother and father (child report, middle SES sample)
		None	Parental use of power assertion (mother and father interviews)
	12 (174)	None	Power assertion from mother and father (child report, lower SES sample)
Bronfenbrenner[R] 1960	15 (192)	Boys	Physical punishment received from both father and mother (child report)

boys receive more physical punishment than girls do. This finding is consistent over a wide range of ages, and is found in both interview and observational studies. Boys also appear to receive more of what M. Hoffman and Saltzstein (1967) have called "simple power assertion"; this may take the form of physical punishment, but there are other forms of direct coercion, such as picking the child up and moving him from an undesired activity toward a desired one. Feshbach (1972) tabulated aversive maternal behaviors of all sorts in a mother-child interaction session in which the mother was attempting to teach her 4-year-old child to solve a puzzle. The sample included middle- and lower-class mother-child pairs, and each of these social-class groups was composed of two racial groups. Boys received more "negative reinforcement" in each middle-class racial group. Minton et al. (1971), observing 27-month-olds with their mothers at home, report that the boys receive somewhat more physical punishment, and that when they do something disapproved (or seem about to do so) their mothers are more likely to prohibit the action by simply saying "No!" With girls, prohibitions are softened or deflected with suggestions of something else the girl might do instead. In a large-scale study done in England, the Newsons (1968) found very few differences indeed in parental treatment of boys and girls up to 4 years old. An exception occurred with respect to physical punishment: boys were "smacked," as the English say, more frequently than girls, and this is consistent with the findings of the earlier American study by Sears, Maccoby, and Levin.

Why do boys receive more physical punishment? The work of Taylor and Epstein with college students (1967) is interesting in relation to this question. They tested the willingness of subjects to administer shocks to other college students who were behaving in a deliberately uncooperative, irritating way. Both male and female subjects showed much greater reluctance to shock a confederate they thought was a girl. There seemed to be a deep-seated prohibition against inflicting physical pain on girls. Consistent with this is Block's (1972) finding that mothers report they find it more difficult to punish their daughters than their sons. We may speculate about why this reluctance to hurt girls exists: is it because they are believed to feel pain more intensely? Because they are physically weaker and less able to defend themselves against attack? Because they are potential child-bearers? It would be interesting to know how cross-culturally universal the prohibition is, and under what conditions it breaks down.

There is another explanation for the more frequent spanking of boys. Perhaps they simply "need" it more! Minton et al. (1971) have done a sequential analysis in which they find that mothers tend to escalate their pressures according to the demands of the situation. The mother begins a sequence with a simple command to the child to do something or to stop doing something. If the child complies, the sequence ends there. If the child does not comply, the mother raises her voice, or forces compliance by physically moving the child out of harm's way, or spanks (this latter rarely). As noted in Chapter 6, Minton et al. find that girls obey the first command more frequently than boys, and hence the later escalating steps tend not to occur for girls. Furthermore, one instance of compliance or noncompliance affects subsequent episodes. In the Minton study, if a child did not obey one command from the parents, the next time an issue came

TABLE 9.9
Nonphysical Discipline

Study	Age and N	Difference	Comment
Minton et al. 1971	27 mos (90)	Boys	Mother's simple prohibitions (observation; trend, $p < .09$)
		Girls	Mother's directive prohibitive
		None	Mother totally prohibitive
Fagot & Patterson 1969	3 (36)	None	Criticism by female nursery school teachers (observation)
Baumrind 1971	3-4 (293 parents)	None	Mother's and father's willingness to express anger or displeasure to child; father authoritarianism (home observation)
	3-4 (415 parents)	None	Mother's and father's anger with child, mother and father authoritarianism (questionnaire)
Baumrind & Black 1967	3-4 (95)	Boys	Mother uses deprivation of privileges (mother interview)
		None	Father uses deprivation of privileges (father interview)
		Girls	Mother uses withdrawal of love (mother interview)
		None	Father uses withdrawal of love (father interview)
		None	Frightening the child (mother, father interview)
Serbin et al. 1973	3-5 (225 pupils, 15 teachers)	Boys	Teacher uses loud reprimands
		None	Teacher uses soft reprimands
Feshbach 1972	4 (104)	Boys	Mother uses negative reinforcement in teaching child to solve puzzle (black and white, middle SES sample)
		None	Black and white, low SES sample
Bee et al. 1969	4-5 (114)	Boys	Mother expresses disapproval of child's action in waiting room (black and white, lower SES)
		None	Mother gives negative feedback during problem-solving interaction (white middle SES)
Sears et al.[R] 1965	4-5 (40)	Boys	Severity of toilet training and child's reaction (mother questionnaire)
Rothbart 1971	5 (56)	None	Mother criticizes, says child is incorrect during problem solving
Sears et al.[R] 1957	5 (379)	Girls	Mother's withdrawal of love (mother interview)
Davis 1967	6-7 (238)	Boys	Negative comments from teacher (child interview)
Hermans et al. 1972	9-10 (40)	None	Mother and father give negative task-oriented or negative person-oriented reinforcement while child performs 4 tasks (Dutch)

(continued)

TABLE 9.9 *(cont.)*

Study	Age and N	Difference	Comment
Armentrout & Burger 1972	9-13 (635)	Boys	Parental psychological control (child report, lower-middle SES)
Zussman 1973	10 (44)	Boys	Parental use of love-withdrawal techniques (mother, child report)
		Girls	Parental use of teaching techniques (reasoning, discussion, role-taking; mother report)
		None	Parental use of teaching techniques (child report)
W. Meyer & Thompson 1956	11 (78)	Boys	Frequency of teacher disapprovals (classroom observation); receive teacher disapproval (peer nomination, 2 of 3 classrooms)
M. Hoffman & Saltzstein 1967	12 (444)	Girls	Father uses induction (child report, both middle and low SES)
		Girls	Mother uses induction (child report, middle SES only)
		None	Mother and father use love withdrawal (child report, both subsamples)
	12 (129 mothers)	None	Mother uses induction, love withdrawal (interview with middle SES mothers)
	12 (75 fathers)	None	Father uses induction, love withdrawal (interview with middle SES fathers)

up and the parent made a new demand, the parent was likely to move to coercive methods more quickly than he would if his previous demand had had a more satisfactory outcome. Thus a series of episodes in which a child has taken a restrictive posture has cumulative impact, involving increasing amounts of scolding and punishment. Minton et al. (1971) observed children and their mothers in an experimental situation two weeks after their observations in the home; they report that the children who had been punished at home remained a greater distance away from their mothers in the experimental room. Thus parent avoidance may enter into the developing circular process and make it more difficult for the parent to influence the child with the gentler pressures that he might otherwise use.

The observations by Serbin et al. (1973) of teachers and children in a nursery school setting also point to a circular process. Boys more often than girls ignore a teacher's direction. Boys also receive more negative control: they receive more reprimands of all sorts, especially loud reprimands, and they are more likely to be physically restrained (see Table 9.9). But perhaps the most interesting feature of the analysis is that when the frequency of the child's resistive behavior is controlled for, there is still a greater incidence of negative control (per instance of resistive child behavior) directed toward boys. It appears quite possible that this greater tendency of teachers to scold or restrain boys when they do something that calls for teacher intervention may be a product (as in the Minton study) of a history of interactions in which weaker forms of intervention were ineffective.

Praise, Reward, and Positive Feedback

Table 9.10 presents the studies in which the amount of praise, reward, or other positive feedback to the child has been studied. The picture is a mixed one. A number of studies found no sex differences, but those that did usually report that boys receive more positive feedback than girls. Several studies have reported that boys receive both more positive and more negative feedback than girls. In the Serbin et al. (1973) study, nursery school teachers were shown, as noted above, to use more negative feedback with boys, but, as Table 9.10 shows, they also used more praise and longer conversations in response to an action of the child's, and Table 9.4 shows that they hug the boys more often. At an older age, W. Meyer and Thompson (1956) found that boys received both more praise and more disapproval from teachers during class than did girls. Bee et al. (1969) found that lower-class mothers gave their sons more positive feedback during a problem-solving task than they did their daughters, but at the same time they expressed more disapproval of boys' actions while mother and child were in a room waiting for a session to begin. It is clear enough, first of all, that positive and negative feedback are not to be thought of as opposite ends of a single continuum. But beyond this perhaps obvious point, it is more interesting for our present purposes that boys seem to be more often the objects of this dual input system than girls. As we noted on p. 307, it is not clear that parents and teachers have any greater total amount of interaction of all kinds with boys than with girls. The present findings do point to the possibility that parents have more of a certain kind of interaction with boys—how shall this relationship be described? As evaluative? As a relationship of surveillance? Perhaps the fact is that the data on total interaction deal more with the first two years of a child's life, whereas the data on positive and negative discipline tend to come from studies of nursery-school-age children or older. In some situations, boys appear to be more attention-getting, either because they do more things calling for adult response or because parents and teachers see them as having more interesting qualities or potential.

Achievement Pressure

We saw in Chapter 4 that there was little consistent sex difference in the achievement orientation of the two sexes, although there was a tendency for girls to maintain a higher level of interest in academic achievement through the school years. It would be interesting to know whether either sex is subject to more parental pressure for school achievement. The evidence is scanty. Table 9.11 shows observational studies in which mea-

TABLE 9.10
Praise and Reward (Positive Feedback)

Study	Age and N	Difference	Comment
Fagot & Patterson 1969	3 (36)	None	Total reinforcement by female teachers (observation)
Charlesworth & Hartup 1967	3-4 (70)	Boys	Reinforcement from same-age boys (observation)
		Girls	Reinforcement from same-age girls
Serbin et al. 1973	3-4 (225 children, 15 teachers)	Boys	Amount of praise by teacher for participation in appropriate classroom activities
Baumrind & Black 1967	4 (95)	Boys	Father's use of tangible reward (father interview)
		None	Mother's use of tangible reward (mother interview)
Biber et al. 1972	4 (225)	Girls	Teacher gives positive reinforcement during instruction: Montessori and "enrichment" preschools
		None	Positive reinforcement from teacher in "structured academic" preschools
Blayney 1973	4 (29)	Girls	Father demands that child assume self-direction (1 of 3 experimental phases)
		None	Father requests child to assume self-direction
			Father presents child with challenging situation
Feshbach 1972	4 (104)	None	Mother gives positive reinforcement while teaching puzzle to child (black and white, low and middle SES sample)
Hamilton 1972	4 (24)	Girls	Amount of social reinforcement received from adults in nursery school (observation; trend, $p < .1$)
Bee et al. 1969	4-5 (114)	Both	Mother gives positive feedback during problem solving (boys, black and white lower SES; girls, white middle SES)
		None	Mother gives child approval in waiting room situation
Rothbart 1971	5 (56)	None	Amount of praise, number of times mother says child is correct during problem solving
Sears et al.[R] 1957	5 (379)	Girls	Mother's praise (mother interview)
Hermans et al. 1972	9-10 (40)	None	Mother and father give positive task-oriented or positive person-oriented reinforcement while child performs 4 tasks (Dutch)
Meyer & Thompson 1956	11 (78)	Boys	Receive teacher praise (observation: 1 of 3 classrooms)
		None	Receive teacher approval (peer nomination)

TABLE 9.11
Achievement Demands, Pressure.

Study	Age and N	Difference	Comment
Allaman et al. 1972	0-6 yrs (95)	None	Amount of praise or criticism for intellectual performance; standards held by mother and father for intellectual performance
Tasch[R] 1952	0-17 yrs & older (160 & 85 fathers)	Boys	Father's expectation for child to go to college (father interview)
Minton et al. 1971	27 mos (90)	Girls	Mother's pressure for competence (home observation, upper-middle SES only)
Baumrind 1971	3-4 (293 parents)	None	Parents' expectation of household help (home observation)
Callard 1968	4 (80)	None	Achievement-inducing scale (parent questionnaire)
I. Hilton 1967	4 (60)	None	While children attempted to solve a series of puzzles: amount of direct help and number of task-oriented suggestions, critical or supportive statements (observation)
Hatfield et al. 1967	4-5 (40)	Boys	Mother's pressure for achievement (observation)
Rothbart 1971	5 (56)	None	Maternal pressure for success on memory task; mother's expectations of child's performance on picture and puzzle tasks
		Girls	Mother's "anxious intrusions" into child's task performance
Sears et al.[R] 1957	5 (379)	Boys	Mother expects child to go to college
Greenglass 1971a	9-10, 13-14 (132)	None	Mother's demands during joint problem solving (observation)
Buck & Austrin 1971	14-16 (100)	Girls	Mother's concern with child's intellectual achievements, high expectancy levels, high minimal academic standards (black sample)
T. Hilton & Berglund 1971	14-16 (1,859)	Boys	Mother wants college-prep child to continue education beyond high school (child questionnaire)
		Boys	Father wants college-prep child to continue education beyond high school (significant for age 16 only; child questionnaire)
		None	Vocational sample, same measures as above

sures have been taken of the amount of pressure a mother puts on a young child for competent task performance; there is no consistent tendency for either sex to be singled out for such pressure. When it comes to expectations for the child to go to college, however, it is clear that parents more often hold such an expectation for sons than daughters. Whether the belief that a son will, and should, go to college is accompanied by greater pressure on him to prepare himself academically is something that existing studies do not reveal. One problem in interpreting data is that when parents are asked such questions as "How important is it to you for your child to do well in school?" or "How concerned are you about your child's grades?" the parent may answer in terms of worry over the child's doing poorly, rather than in terms of insisting that the child shall be an outstanding student. More information is needed concerning such things as parents' reactions to report cards, and the extent to which they monitor the homework of sons and daughters during grade school and especially high school years.

EVALUATION OF HYPOTHESES

Sex-typed Shaping

Having summarized the research on differential socialization, we return to the hypotheses with which this chapter began. The first issue is whether parents (and other socializing agents) treat children of the two sexes so as to shape them toward behavior deemed appropriate for their own sex. Do parents reward sex-appropriate behavior and punish or otherwise negatively sanction inappropriate behavior? The question of what kind of behavior is considered by parents to be sex-appropriate perhaps deserves brief discussion here. Traditionally this concept encompasses a wide range. In previous centuries not only the way a person dressed, but also the kind of work he could engage in, the places he could go, and the kind of recreational activities he engaged in were almost completely determined by his sex. This has changed radically in recent years, but the rate of change varies among cultural groups, and, for many parents, "ladylike" behavior still implies many constraints on bodily movements (such as the requirement to sit in a modest position), the maintenance of an appealing quality in her social approaches, particularly toward men, and many assumptions concerning appropriate activity and the kind of life a girl will lead when she is grown. The definitions of masculine behavior, of course, also vary enormously among parents, with a core of culturally agreed-upon features. The way a parent goes about socializing a child with respect to the sex typing of behavior must depend on his own definitions and values. In some cases the parent may rather deliberately attempt to prepare the child for a role the child is expected to play as an adult; in other instances, the parent's reaction to something the child does will not depend upon the parent's conception of the ultimate consequences of the behavior for the child's adult sex role, but will represent an immediate response to something that is seen as sex-inappropriate for the child at the time the behavior occurs. In other words, not all sex-typing socialization is *anticipatory* socialization.

It is widely assumed that parents do a great deal during the child's early life to define for the child what sex-appropriate behavior is, and to guide the child directly toward the adoption of this behavior. Our survey of the research on socialization of the two sexes has revealed surprisingly little differentiation in parent behavior according to the sex of the child. However, there are some areas where differential "shaping" does appear to occur. First, there is the obvious matter of dressing the two sexes differently. We hypothesize that parents are uncomfortable if others misidentify their children. If a child's sex is not clearly discernible from body build or hair style, parents may be expected to add an item of dress that will convey the necessary information.

There is evidence that parents encourage their children to develop sex-typed interests, in part through providing sex-typed toys for them. Even more strongly, they *discourage* their children—particularly their sons—from engaging in activities they consider appropriate only for the opposite sex. We may ask why it is that parents are more upset when a boy wants to wear lipstick or put on high heels than they are when a girl wants to paint a false moustache on her face or wear cowboy boots. Although the dynamics underlying this parental reaction are not clear, it would appear that feminine behavior in a boy is likely to be interpreted as a sign of possible homosexual tendencies, and, as such, it is a danger signal to parents and triggers powerful anxieties in them—perhaps especially in fathers. Following an analysis of parental sex anxiety in relation to the parent's care-taking interactions with infant sons and daughters, Sears comments, "Sex anxiety is essentially heterosexual in females, but is essentially homosexual in males" (Sears 1965[R], p. 159). Both parents, in other words, are likely to find their own sex anxieties more stimulated by the sexual qualities of a son than by those of a daughter, and hence will avoid too intimate physical contact with him. Furthermore, if the Sears interpretation holds, it is easy to see why a father would react more strongly against any possible signs of homosexuality in a son than in a daughter. It is less easy to see why a mother should do so. Perhaps we are simply dealing here with a realistic parental appraisal of the fact that homosexuality is considerably more common among males than females; if the likelihood of later development of this widely disvalued behavior is in fact greater for boys, then it becomes especially important for parents to nip early signs of it in the bud.

Whatever the underlying determiners, we have seen that in the area of sex-typed behavior as narrowly defined, parents do press their children toward the adoption of sex-appropriate behavior. There are other aspects of the children's behavior that the parents do not regard as relevant to masculinity or femininity, and they do not socialize differentially for these behaviors, even though the sexes may actually differ with respect to them. Even more interesting, however, are the behaviors that parents do consider relevant to masculinity and femininity but that they do not appear to treat differently in boys and girls. An interesting case in point is aggression. We have not found that parents reward boys more for aggressive or competitive behavior, or punish girls more for these behaviors. To some degree, the reverse may be true: boys receive more punishment for aggression. One might argue that punishment will actually serve to stimulate the child's aggressiveness by providing aggressive models, but even though this may be true, it involves a different mechanism of learning than what is normally meant by a "shaping" process. There is evidence that parents believe boys naturally are more aggressive than girls, on the average. They usually do not value the behavior in either sex, and one of the primary concerns of parents and children of preschool-aged children is to help them control their tempers and teach them socially acceptable ways of getting what they want, without grabbing, hitting, or pulling, and without being destructive toward valued objects. The frequency of temper outbursts and fights does decrease dramatically between the ages of 3 and 6. Since a low level of aggressiveness is actually desired by parents for both boys and girls, positive reinforcement for it will be rare. Although it is undoubtedly true that parents—especially fathers—are worried about a boy who is notably unaggressive, seeing it as a sign of his being a "sissy," the situation is different than in the case of the boy's putting on lipstick. In the latter case, there is a clear action on the part of the child that can serve as a signal for the parent's counteraction. In the case of a child's failure to fight, there is seldom a clear occasion calling for the parent's intervention, even though he may be worried about the total character pattern he sees his child developing. If parents want their sons to be tough in a fight, we might expect, at the least, that they would punish them less severely for fighting; we have not found this to be true, but the data are by no means adequate to provide a totally convincing picture. Studies often report the *frequency* with which a child is punished for fighting, without reporting the frequency of fighting itself. It may be that boys are punished equally often, or more often, than girls for this behavior, but that there are also more boy fights that go unpunished. And, of course, parents may be transmitting a mixed message to their sons in the midst of their discipline, so that the boy really understands his parents to be saying, "You are not supposed to fight, but I'm glad you did." On the basis of existing information on parent-child interaction, all that can be said is that there is no evidence that parents are systematically reinforcing sons, more than daughters, for aggressive behavior.

The same picture of lack of differential socialization emerges with respect to other aspects of behavior that are thought to be relevant for the development of sex typing. For example, parental reactions to the child's displays of sexual behavior or sexual curiosity might be expected to be different for boys and girls, considering the different standards that exist in most cultures for adult male and female sexual conduct. Yet in the three available studies—all interview studies—no tendencies have been found for girls to be more reinforced for modesty or punished more for sexual exploration.

With respect to allowing the child autonomy—encouraging independent, exploratory behavior or, on the contrary, restricting such behavior—we again find very little difference in the treatment of boys and girls, although the tendency is for parents (or at least mothers) to restrict boys somewhat more. Parental treatment of young children's dependency is also not clearly differentiated by sex. In the relatively few studies that report parental reactions to children's clinging, proximity seeking, separation resistance, and demands for attention, positive and negative parental reactions seem to be about evenly distributed to boys and girls.

Of course, "shaping" a child toward a particular form of behavior may take more than one form. In the usual meaning of the term, parental reactions would have to be contingent on particular actions by the child. That is, in the development of dependent behavior, for example, it is reinforcement of the child specifically for approaching the parent, or clinging to him, or crying when he attempts to leave, that ought to increase the behavior. It is precisely these kinds of contingencies that do *not* appear to be different for the two sexes with respect to a wide range of behaviors that are normally thought to be relevant to sex typing. However, there might be differences in more global aspects of child rearing that would have similar effects, even if the contingencies are less explicit. If it were true that mothers held and caressed their daughters more than their sons, for example, or interacted with them more frequently, this might have the effect of increasing the child's orientation and proximity seeking toward the mother. Here again, the evidence does not point to differential socialization. The total amount of interaction between mother and child is similar for the two sexes, as is the amount of expressed affection and "warmth," so that neither the global reinforcement conditions nor the specifically contingent ones are such as to differentiate the dependency behavior of young boys and girls. The only global difference in child rearing that might affect the child's dependency is the more frequent physical punishment and other negative sanctions administered to boys. These might cause the boy to distance himself from his caretaker, and thus to score lower on certain measures of dependency. However, there is evidence that punishment sometimes increases a child's anxiety, which in turn can lead directly to contact seeking and proximity seeking, so it is by no means clear that differential punishment would differentiate the sexes in the direction consistent with our concepts of masculinity and femininity. And in any case, a generally punitive home atmosphere could hardly be regarded as an instance of "shaping" behavior in the sense that is implied in hypothesis 1. We must summarize our analysis of this hypothesis with the conclusion that we have been able to find very little evidence to support it, in relation to behaviors other than sex typing as very narrowly defined (e.g. toy preference). The reinforcement contingencies for the two sexes appear to be remarkably similar.

Different Eliciting Qualities of Boys and Girls

The second hypothesis was that boys and girls begin life with different behavioral tendencies that are biologically based: that because of their different initial behaviors they stimulate their parents differently, and thus initiate a different sort of circular process that becomes established as a habitual mode of interaction between parent and child. An example of such a presumed situation may be found in Moss (1967). Moss noted that at age 3 weeks, the more an infant cried, the more a mother interacted with it, and his inference was, reasonably enough, that the infant was controlling the mother—that its cry was a signal to the mother and the rate of her response was closely related to the frequency of her receiving this signal. At age 3 months, however, Moss found that the infant's irritability continued to be positively related to the amount of mother-infant interaction for girls only ($r = .54$ for girls), but *negatively* for boys ($r = -.47$, $p < .10$ for this sample size). His hypothesis is that female infants may be more readily quieted than male infants, so that when a female infant cries and the mother goes to it and picks it up, the mother's nurturant behavior is reinforced by the cessation of the infant's crying; if boys, on the other hand, continue to cry while the mother attempts to minister to them, her nurturant behavior is *not* reinforced and she may become more and more reluctant to pick up her crying child. As we have seen in Chapter 2, it is doubtful that girls are more easily quieted than boys. The Moss hypothesis, however, serves as an example of a kind of differential parent behavior that *could* occur in response to preexisting behavioral sex differences. Are there any instances among the studies summarized above where a similar interpretation would be reasonable?

As noted above, there is some evidence that boys are more "resistive" than girls. In the Minton et al. study with 2-year-olds (1971) and the Serbin et al. (1973) study with 3–4-year-olds, boys did not comply as readily as girls to directions from the mother or a teacher. The Minton study showed that it was following noncompliance on the part of the child that mothers tended to move to somewhat more coercive methods to obtain compliance. In the Serbin study, controlling and sanctioning behavior of all sorts by the teacher was more frequent toward boys, but it is difficult to say whether this was a consequence or a cause of the boys' greater tendency to ignore the teacher's directions, since detailed sequential analysis was not reported.

In any case, the boy's greater resistiveness to directions, and his lesser susceptibility to milder forms of pressure, may be part of the explanation of the fact that parents use more punishment with boys. The finding of greater punishment administered to sons is, then, compatible with hypothesis 2—more compatible, we think, than it is with hypothesis 1. But there may be other explanations, as we shall see below.

Our major finding, however—that parents treat boys and girls much alike—would suggest that there are probably not very many initial biologically based behavioral differences, at least not many that are strong enough to elicit clear differential reactions from caretakers.

Parents' Conceptions of What the Two Sexes Are Like

Parents and teachers, of course, operate on the basis of certain stereotypes about children's characters. Having labeled a child "shy" or "rambunctious," they then govern their own actions accordingly. Do they characteristically label the two sexes differently? And if so, what implications does this have for the way they socialize their children?

Few studies have asked parents directly how they believe the two sexes do in fact differ, apart from what behavior the parent would prefer to see in a boy or girl. Lambert et al. (1971) worked with French-Canadian and English-Canadian parents, using a modification of the "Perception" and "Expectation" scales originally used by Rothbart and Maccoby (1966)[R].[*] In the Perception scale, parents were given a series of 40 items such as "more helpful around the house," "more likely to be rough and boisterous at play," "more likely to act scared," and were asked to check whether they believed a boy or girl would be more likely to engage in the behavior described. A box was provided where the parent could check if he believed that neither sex was more likely than the other to show the behavior. In the Expectation scale, the parent was asked how important he thought it was for a child of each sex to have each behavioral characteristic. A five-point scale was provided, ranging from "very important *not* to" to "very important to," with the central point being "unimportant," and the parents rated each item separately for boys and girls.

The finding of greatest interest for our present purposes was that these groups of parents thought the typical behavior of boys and girls was different on many items, but their values concerning how the two sexes ought to behave were quite similar. Boys were described as being more likely to be rough at play, be noisy, defend themselves, defy punishment, be physically active, be competitive, do dangerous things, and enjoy mechanical things. Girls were described as being more likely to be helpful around the house, be neat and clean, be quiet and reserved, be sensitive to the

---

[*] The authors are grateful to W. Lambert and J. Hammers for making the data available for an item-by-item analysis.

feelings of others, be well mannered, be a tattletale, cry or get upset, and be easily frightened. But when asked which of these characteristics they thought it was important for boys and girls to have (or *not* to have) parents said they thought it was important for *both* boys and girls to be neat and clean, to be helpful around the house, to be able to take care of themselves, not to be easily angered, not to do dangerous things, not to cry, and to be thoughtful and considerate of others. Surprisingly, it was also thought important for both boys and girls to defend themselves from attack, and to be competitive. There were unexpectedly few differences in the values held for the behavior of sons and daughters. Similar results were obtained by W. Smith (1971)[R] working with 48 pairs of American black parents. On the whole, these studies indicate that parents are trying to socialize children of both sexes toward the same major goals, but that they believe they are starting from different points, with each sex having a different set of "natural" assets and liabilities.

A similar conclusion can be reached from the Levitin and Chananie (1972) study with first- and second-grade teachers, although this study focuses on a narrower range of behaviors. In this study, teachers were given a description of a hypothetical child who might be in their classroom: "Tom (Alice) is sometimes disobedient to the teacher and often aggressive with other children in his (her) class." The teachers were then asked whether they approved of the child's behavior, how much they thought they would like this child, and how typical they thought the behavior was of other boys (girls) of the same age. Aggressive behavior was more often thought to be typical of boys, but it was disapproved (and equally so) in both sexes. Dependent behavior was not thought to be especially typical in either sex, and although a dependent girl was somewhat better liked than a dependent boy, the difference was not significant. The aggression findings again point to an area of behavior where adults believe that a sex difference exists but they do not value it more (or depreciate it less) in the sex for which it it believed typical.

When parents consider a kind of behavior "natural" for a given sex, and the behavior is undesired, do they direct stronger socialization efforts toward the behavior, or do they assume that there is little they can do to change it and hence reconcile themselves to the behavior? Unfortunately we do not have a sufficiently detailed listing of parents' beliefs concerning behavioral sex typing, or sufficiently detailed descriptions of usual parental reactions to these same behaviors, to answer the question. For example, the Smith (1971)[R] and Lambert et al. (1971) studies indicate that parents believe girls cry more easily, and that they think it is important for children not to cry frequently. But we do not know how widely this finding applies to other samples of parents, or whether parents react more harshly or more sympathetically to this behavior in a girl. We can make a rough assessment with respect to two categories of behavior: dependency and aggression. We have seen earlier that these behaviors are treated quite similarly in boys and girls. If the findings of Lambert et al. and Smith replicate on other populations, this would mean that although aggression is seen as typical for boys, and is undesired, parents neither direct more intense socialization toward boys because aggression is seen as a greater "danger" in them, nor ignore the behavior more often because it is seen as "natural." The same situation applies to the treatment of dependency in girls.

Earlier, we mentioned another possible effect of a parent's believing that a particular behavior is more typical of one sex than the other: perhaps the probability of a child's behavior being *noticed* is a function of the probability level the parent unconsciously assigns to it. This was called the "perceptual adaptation level" hypothesis. Let us consider some of the implications of this hypothesis. Many (perhaps most) of the actions a child performs do not call for any parental response at all. Only when the child's action is defined by the parent as naughty, or dangerous, or especially nice, does it call for the parent to react with positive or negative sanctions. In the case of aggression, there are many ambiguous actions that a child performs concerning which the parent has some latitude. The parent could see a given action either as exuberant horseplay or as the beginning of a fight. The way he defines an action by a particular child will depend on his range of expectations for that child. If the parent is adapted to a rather high continuous level of exuberant horseplay, only the rare especially vigorous action, or the one that makes another child cry, will be seen as aggressive. If the parent expects this particular child to be normally quiet and gentle, however, any vigorous social action will be noticed, and any mild protest from another child may cause the action to be defined as aggressive. Because parents have different levels of expectation for the two sexes, the hypothesis says, parents will be more likely to define a given ambiguous action as aggressive if performed by a girl than if by a boy.

J. Meyer and Sobieszek (1972) made a study bearing on the issue. They showed video tapes of behavior sequences of young children at play to adult viewers of both sexes. The children on the film were dressed in play clothes that would be appropriate for either sex, and their appearance was not sex-typed. A given child was identified as a boy for some observers, and as a girl for others. After viewing a tape, the adult viewer was asked to rate the child on a series of sex-typed traits, saying how "independent," "aggressive," "confident," "cooperative," "shy," and "affectionate," among other traits, the child on the tape had seemed. One possible outcome of the study might have been, of course, that raters would tend to see children as conforming to the raters' stereotypes, so that boys would be seen as more aggressive and girls as more cooperative or shy. In fact, however, the reverse was true, at least for the subsample of subjects who had previous experience with children. If a child behaved in a vigorous, uninhibited way on the screen, the behavior was more likely to be labeled aggressive if the actor was thought to be a girl than if the same actor was thought to be a boy. In other words, behaviors were especially noticed if they ran counter to sex-role stereotypes.

A mechanism has been identified whereby parents will notice and punish sex-inappropriate behavior. But, unfortunately, the explanation cuts two ways, and does not help to explain why a parent should reward sex-appropriate behavior. As noted above, many parents see girls as naturally more cooperative, more tractable, more sociable than boys, and on the whole they see these as attractive traits; but they also see girls as more timid and more likely to cry, and many parents do not especially like these aspects of "feminine" personality. Similarly for boys: parents generally see boys as naturally stronger and more self-reliant than girls, and they may like this about boys; but at the same time they see them as more aggressive and less obedient. Particularly when aggression is directed by a boy toward his parents, it is not seen as praiseworthy; neither is his disobedience.

The principle of perceptual adaptation level predicts that when a girl behaves in a cooperative, helpful manner, this will either tend to go unnoticed or draw only moderate approval because that is the way a girl is expected to act. When a boy behaves in this manner, however, his mother will react with pleased surprise and reinforce him vigorously. As the principle works out, then, punishment from parents will tend to support existing sex stereotypes—each sex will be punished more for behavior seen as unusual, or wrong, for his sex. *Positive* reinforcement, however, will run counter to sex stereotypes. Each sex will be rewarded for desirable behavior when it is seen as relatively unusual for his sex. Hence, the perceptual-adaptation-level theory does not seem so promising as it might have seemed at first glance as a basis for explaining the role of parental socialization in children's sex differentiation.

Cross-Sex and Same-Sex Effects

At the beginning of this chapter, it was suggseted that a parent's reaction to a child might depend on whether the child was the same sex as the parent. This would mean that, in some respects, fathers would tend to react to daughters as mothers do to sons. We suggested that parents might show rivalry with a same-sex child, and flirtation, submissiveness, or dominance with an opposite-sex child, depending upon the parent's usual relationship with opposite-sex adults.

Most of the research summarized in the present chapter involves observations or interviews with mothers. Hence, cross-sex or same-sex effects can rarely be assessed. However, the studies that have obtained data concerning both maternal and paternal behavior have revealed some extremely interesting cross-sex effects, particularly in the area of aggressive behavior

directed by a child toward an adult. Fathers appeared to be more tolerant
of aggression from a daughter, mothers from a son. Why should this be so?
In Chapter 6, we saw that there is some reason to believe that boys are
more likely to be aggressive when interacting with other boys than they
are with other persons. Young males appear to challenge one another, and
to react with counterthreat when challenged by another male. Perhaps a
father, at least on some occasions, is reacting to a son simply as another
male—reacting as though a threat to his dominance were involved when
his son is angry toward him, whereas he feels no such threat when challenged by a girl. Most women, on the other hand, are accustomed to moderating their reaction to male threat; frequently, they would have a good
deal to lose, in terms of actual or potential status derived from men, if they
reacted with open counterthreat, although of course the more subtle forms
of resistance and retaliation have long been a woman's game. When a
woman is challenged by another woman, however (and this does not happen as often as male–male threat), the challenge may be more safely re-
sisted in an open way. If a woman's experience in this regard is transferred
in any degree to the family arena, a mother would be more likely, then,
to take direct countermeasures against a daughter's aggression than a son's.

With respect to dependency, one study (Rothbart and Maccoby 1966[R])
found cross-sex effects, with mothers being more supportive of dependency
behavior in sons and fathers in daughters; this finding, however, was not
replicated in the Lambert et al. (1971) study, where mothers and fathers
both treated the two sexes similarly when asked for help, and gave girls
more positive response when asked for comfort. Until further information
is available that will help to identify the conditions under which cross-sex
effects occur, it is fruitless to speculate about their meaning for intrafamily
dynamics. It is worth noting, however, that when cross-sex effects *do* occur,
they present a problem for simple reinforcement theory. If fathers react
repressively to a boy's aggression and mothers do likewise toward girls
while being permissive toward a son's aggression, the two parents are
working against one another in terms of sex-typing pressure. One parent
is differentiating between boys and girls in a sex-typed direction, the other
in the opposite direction. When the two parents are behaving inconsistently
with respect to reinforcing a particular kind of behavior in a child, the
analogy to a Skinnerian "shaping" process becomes unclear. Is the situation
analogous to an intermittent schedule of reinforcement—one that produces
a strong habit that is resistant to extinction? If so, then a strong habit is being produced in both sexes. Although the identity of the parent who is
punishing and the identity of the parent giving positive reinforcement differ for boys and girls, intermittent reinforcement is occurring for both sexes.
Thus the situation does not produce an explanation of the fact that a given
behavior develops more strongly in one sex than in the other.

Of course, in early childhood children of both sexes spend more time with the mother. And when they enter school, they are usually under the supervision of a female teacher. Thus, if cross-sex indulgence and same-sex severity are the rule, boys should have an easier time in both the home and school settings. We suspect, however, that the sheer amount of time spent in the presence of a particular socializing agent may not be the most important index of that agent's influence and that fathers may be very effective despite their fewer hours at home. Furthermore, any tendency for mothers and teachers to be more indulgent toward boys for any given bit of behavior is tempered by their belief that boys are more mischievous and more difficult to socialize. We cannot conclude that either sex is dealt with more leniently, on the whole.

Overview

Our survey of data has revealed a remarkable degree of uniformity in the socialization of the two sexes. In many instances, however, the evidence has been quite limited and the data have not been adequate for testing our initial hypotheses. Particularly handicapping has been the lack of information about fathers; it may be that fathers differentiate between the sexes to a much greater degree than do mothers, from whom most of our information comes. It is also possible that we would have obtained a more differentiated picture if more research on working-class families had been available. In any case, existing evidence has not revealed any consistent process of "shaping" boys and girls toward a number of behaviors that are normally part of our sex stereotypes.

Some unanticipated themes have emerged, however. Boys seem to have more intense socialization experiences than girls. They receive more pressure against engaging in sex-inappropriate behavior, whereas the activities that girls are not supposed to engage in are much less clearly defined and less firmly enforced. Boys receive more punishment, but probably also more praise and encouragement. Adults respond as if they find boys more interesting, and more attention-provoking, than girls. The simplest hypothesis to explain this fact would be that boys are more active, thus providing more stimulation to observers. But we have seen in Chapter 5 that there is not a reliable sex difference in total activity level, so that the issue becomes one of whether boys' actions are qualitatively, rather than quantitatively, more attention-getting. Other possible explanations come to mind: perhaps boys are valued more; or perhaps their greater strength and aggressiveness make it more important that they be adequately socialized. Whatever the explanation, the different amounts of socialization pressure that boys and girls receive surely have consequences for the development of their personalities.

CHAPTER TEN

Summary and Commentary

In Chapters 2–7 we set out to discover which of the widely held beliefs about sex differences are myth, which are supported by evidence, and which are still untested. We shall now summarize some of the answers that have emerged, and shall then return to the question, raised in Chapters 8 and 9, of how the patterns of similarity and difference are to be explained. Finally, we shall consider the social implications of what has been learned.

SUMMARY OF OUR FINDINGS

Unfounded Beliefs About Sex Differences

1. *That girls are more "social" than boys.* The findings: First, the two sexes are equally interested in social (as compared with nonsocial) stimuli, and are equally proficient at learning through imitation of models. Second, in childhood, girls are no more dependent than boys on their caretakers, and boys are no more willing to remain alone. Furthermore, girls are not more motivated to achieve for social rewards. The two sexes are equally responsive to social reinforcement, and neither sex consistently learns better for this form of reward than for other forms. Third, girls do not spend more time interacting with playmates; in fact, the opposite is true, at least at certain ages. Fourth, the two sexes appear to be equally "empathic," in the sense of understanding the emotional reactions of others; however, the measures of this ability have so far been narrow.

Any differences that exist in the "sociability" of the two sexes are more of kind than of degree. Boys are highly oriented toward a peer group and congregate in larger groups; girls associate in pairs or small groups of age-mates, and may be somewhat more oriented toward adults, although the evidence for this is weak.

2. *That girls are more "suggestible" than boys.* The findings: First, boys and girls are equally likely to imitate others spontaneously. Second, the two sexes are equally susceptible to persuasive communications, and in face-to-face social-influence situations (Asch-type experiments), sex dif-

ferences are usually not found. When they are, girls are somewhat more likely to adapt their own judgments to those of the group, although there are studies with reverse findings. Boys, on the other hand, appear to be more likely to accept peer-group values when these conflict with their own.

3. *That girls have lower self-esteem.* The findings: The sexes are highly similar in their overall self-satisfaction and self-confidence throughout childhood and adolescence; there is little information about adulthood, but what exists does not show a sex difference. However, there are some qualitative differences in the areas of functioning where the two sexes have greatest self-confidence: girls rate themselves higher in the area of social competence; boys more often see themselves as strong, powerful, dominant, "potent."

Through most of the school years, the two sexes are equally likely to believe they can influence their own fates, rather than being the victims of chance or fate. During the college years (but not earlier or later), men have a greater sense of control over their own fate, and greater confidence in their probable performance on a variety of school-related tasks that they undertake. However, this does not imply a generally lower level of self-esteem among women of this age.

4. *That girls are better at rote learning and simple repetitive tasks, boys at tasks that require higher-level cognitive processing and the inhibition of previously learned responses.* The findings: Neither sex is more susceptible to simple conditioning, or excels in simple paired-associates or other forms of "rote" learning. Boys and girls are equally proficient at discrimination learning, reversal shifts, and probability learning, all of which have been interpreted as calling for some inhibition of "available" responses. Boys are somewhat more impulsive (that is, lacking in inhibition) during the preschool years, but the sexes do not differ thereafter in the ability to wait for a delayed reward, to inhibit early (wrong) responses on the Matching Familiar Figures test (MFF) or on other measures of impulsivity.

5. *That boys are more "analytic."* The findings: The sexes do not differ on tests of analytic cognitive style. Boys do not excel at tasks that call for "decontextualization," or disembedding, except when the task is visual-spatial; boys' superiority on the latter tasks seems to be accounted for by spatial ability (see below), and no sex differences in analytic ability are implied. Boys and girls are equally likely to respond to task-irrelevant aspects of a situation, so that neither sex excels in analyzing and selecting only those elements needed for the task.

6. *That girls are more affected by heredity, boys by environment.* The findings: Male identical twins are more alike than female identical twins, but the two sexes show equivalent amount of resemblance to their parents.

Boys are more susceptible to damage by a variety of noxious environmental agents, both prenatally and postnatally, but this does not imply that they are generally more influenced by environmental factors. The correlations between parental socialization techniques and child behavior are higher for boys in some studies, higher for girls in others. Furthermore, the two sexes learn with equal facility in a wide variety of learning situations; if learning is the primary means whereby environmental effects come about, sex equivalence is indicated.

7. *That girls lack achievement motivation.* The findings: In the pioneering studies of achievement motivation, girls scored higher than boys in achievement imagery under "neutral" conditions. Boys need to be challenged by appeals to ego or competitive motivation to bring their achievement imagery up to the level of girls'. Boys' achievement motivation does appear to be more responsive to competitive arousal than girls', but this does not imply a generally higher level. In fact, observational studies of achievement strivings either have found no sex difference or have found girls to be superior.

8. *That girls are auditory, boys visual.* The findings: The majority of studies report no differences in response to sounds by infants of the two sexes. At most ages boys and girls are equally adept at discriminating speech sounds. No sex difference is found in memory for sounds previously heard.

Among newborn infants, no study shows a sex difference in fixation to visual stimuli. During the first year of life, results are variable, but neither sex emerges as more responsive to visual stimuli. From infancy to adulthood, the sexes are highly similar in interest in visual stimuli, ability to discriminate among them, identification of shapes, distance perception, and a variety of other measures of visual perception.

Sex Differences That Are Fairly Well Established

1. *That girls have greater verbal ability than boys.* It is probably true that girls' verbal abilities mature somewhat more rapidly in early life, although there are a number of recent studies in which no sex difference has been found. During the period from preschool to early adolescence, the sexes are very similar in their verbal abilities. At about age 11, the sexes begin to diverge, with female superiority increasing through high school and possibly beyond. Girls score higher on tasks involving both receptive and productive language, and on "high-level" verbal tasks (analogies, comprehension of difficult written material, creative writing) as well as upon the "lower-level" measures (fluency). The magnitude of the female advantage varies, being most commonly about one-quarter of a standard deviation.

2. *That boys excel in visual-spatial ability.* Male superiority on visual-spatial tasks is fairly consistently found in adolescence and adulthood, but not in childhood. The male advantage on spatial tests increases through

the high school years up to a level of about .40 of a standard deviation.
The sex difference is approximately equal on analytic and nonanalytic spatial measures.

3. *That boys excel in mathematical ability.* The two sexes are similar in
their early acquisition of quantitative concepts, and their mastery of arithmetic during the grade-school years. Beginning at about age 12–13, boys'
mathematical skills increase faster than girls'. The greater rate of improvement appears to be not entirely a function of the number of math courses
taken, although the question has not been extensively studied. The magnitude of the sex differences varies greatly from one population to another,
and is probably not so great as the difference in spatial ability. Both visual-
spatial and verbal processes are sometimes involved in the solution of
mathematical problems; some math problems can probably be solved in
either way, while others cannot, a fact that may help to explain the variation in degree of sex difference from one measure to another.

4. *That males are more aggressive.* The sex difference in aggression has
been observed in all cultures in which the relevant behavior has been observed. Boys are more aggressive both physically and verbally. They show
the attenuated forms of aggression (mock-fighting, aggressive fantasies)
as well as the direct forms more frequently than girls. The sex difference
is found as early as social play begins—at age 2 or 2½. Although the aggressiveness of both sexes declines with age, boys and men remain more aggressive through the college years. Little information is available for older
adults. The primary victims of male aggression are other males—from early
ages, girls are chosen less often as victims.

Open Questions: Too Little Evidence, or Findings Ambiguous

1. *Tactile sensitivity.* Most studies of tactile sensitivity in infancy, and
of the ability to perceive by touch at later ages, do not find sex differences. When differences are found, girls are more sensitive, but such findings are rare enough that we cannot have confidence that the difference
is a meaningful one. Additional work is needed with some of the standard
psychophysical measurements of tactile sensitivity, over a range of ages.
Most of the existing studies in which the data are analyzed by sex have
been done with newborns.

2. *Fear, timidity, and anxiety.* Observational studies of fearful behavior
usually do not find sex differences. Teacher ratings and self-reports, however, usually find girls to be more timid or more anxious. In the case of
self-reports, the problem is to know whether the results reflect "real" differences or only differences in the willingness to report anxious feelings.
Of course, the very willingness to assert that one is afraid may lead to
fearful behavior, so the distinction may not turn out to be important. However, it would be desirable to have measures other than self-report (which
make up the great bulk of the data from early school age on) as a way of

clarifying the meaning of the girls' greater self-attribution of fears and anxiety.

3. *Activity level.* Sex differences in activity level do not appear in infancy. They begin to be seen when children reach the age of social play. During the preschool years, when sex differences are found they are in the direction of boys' being more active. However, there are many instances in which sex differences have not been found. Some, but not all, of the variance among studies can be accounted for by whether the measurement situation was social. That is, boys appear to be especially stimulated to bursts of high activity by the presence of other boys. But the exact nature of the situational control over activity level remains to be established. Activity level is responsive to a number of motivational states—fear, anger, curiosity—and is therefore not a promising variable for identifying stable individual or group differences. More detailed observations are needed on the vigor and qualitative nature of play.

4. *Competitiveness.* When sex differences are found, they usually show boys to be more competitive, but there are many studies finding sex similarity. Madsen and his colleagues find sex differences to be considerably weaker than differences between cultures and, in a number of studies, entirely absent. Almost all the research on competition has involved situations in which competition is maladaptive. In the Prisoner's Dilemma game, for example, the sexes are equally cooperative, but this is in a situation in which cooperation is to the long-run advantage of both players and the issue is one of developing mutual trust. It appears probable that in situations in which competitiveness produces increased individual rewards, males would be more competitive, but this is a guess based on commonsense considerations, such as the male interest in competitive sports, not upon research in controlled settings. The age of the subject and the identity of the opponent no doubt make a difference—there is evidence that young women hesitate to compete against their boyfriends.

5. *Dominance.* Dominance appears to be more of an issue within boys' groups than girls' groups. Boys make more dominance attempts (both successful and unsuccessful) toward one another than do girls. They also more often attempt to dominate adults. The dominance relations between the sexes are complex: in childhood, the sex segregation of play groups means that neither sex frequently attempts to dominate the other. In experimental situations in which the sexes are combined, the evidence is ambiguous on whether either sex is more successful in influencing the behavior of the other. Among adult mixed pairs or groups, formal leadership tends to go to males in the initial phases of interaction, but the direction of influence becomes more sex-equal the longer the relationship lasts, with "division of authority" occurring along lines of individual competencies and division of labor.

6. *Compliance.* In childhood, girls tend to be more compliant to the de-

mands and directions of adults. This compliance does not extend, however, to willingness to accept directions from, or be influenced by, age-mates. Boys are especially concerned with maintaining their status in the peer group, and are probably therefore more vulnerable to pressures and challenges from this group, although this has not been well established. As we have seen in the discussion of dominance, it is not clear that in mixed-sex interactions either sex is consistently more willing to comply with the wishes of the other.

7. *Nurturance and "maternal" behavior.* There is very little evidence concerning the tendencies of boys and girls to be nurturant or helpful toward younger children or animals. Cross-cultural work does indicate that girls between the ages of 6 and 10 are more often seen behaving nurturantly. Within our own society, the rare studies that report nurturant behavior are observational studies of free play among nursery school children; sex differences are not found in these studies, but the setting normally does not include children much younger than the subjects being observed, and it may be that the relevant elicitors are simply not present. Female hormones play a role in maternal behavior in lower animals, and the same may be true in human beings, but there is no direct evidence that this is the case. There is very little information on the responses of adult men to infants and children, so it is not possible to say whether adult women are more disposed to behave maternally than men are to behave paternally. If there is a sex difference in the tendency to behave nurturantly, it does not generalize to a greater female tendency to behave altruistically over varying situations. The studies of people's willingness to help others in distress have sometimes shown men more helpful, sometimes women, depending on the identity of the person needing help and the kind of help that is needed. The overall finding on altruism is one of sex similarity.

In Chapters 5 and 6, we raised the question of whether the female is more passive than the male. The answer is complex, but mainly negative. The two sexes are highly similar in their willingness to explore a novel environment, when they are both given freedom to do so. Both are highly responsive to social situations of all kinds, and although some individuals tend to withdraw from social interaction and simply watch from the sidelines, such persons are no more likely to be female than male. Girls' greater compliance with adult demands is just as likely to take an active as a passive form; running errands and performing services for others are active processes. Young boys seem more likely than girls to put out energy in the form of bursts of strenuous physical activity, but the girls are not sitting idly by while the boys act; they are simply playing more quietly. And their play is fully as organized and planful (possibly more so), and has as much the quality of actively imposing their own design upon their surroundings as does boys' play. It is true that boys and men are more aggressive, but this does not mean that females are the passive victims of aggression—they do not yield or withdraw when aggressed against any more frequently than males do, at least during the phases of childhood for which observations are available. With respect to dominance, we have noted the curious fact that while males are more dominant, females are not especially submissive, at least not to the dominance attempts of boys and girls their own age. In sum, the term "passive" does not accurately describe the most common female personality attributes.

Returning to one of the major conclusions of our survey of sex differences, there are many popular beliefs about the psychological characteristics of the two sexes that have proved to have little or no basis in fact. How is it possible that people continue to believe, for example, that girls are more "social" than boys, when careful observation and measurement in a variety of situations show no sex difference? Of course it is possible that we have not studied those particular situations that contribute most to the popular beliefs. But if this is the problem, it means that the alleged sex difference exists only in a limited range of situations, and the sweeping generalizations embodied in popular beliefs are not warranted.

However, a more likely explanation for the perpetuation of "myths," we believe, is the fact that stereotypes are such powerful things. An ancient truth is worth restating here: if a generalization about a group of people is believed, whenever a member of that group behaves in the expected way the observer notes it and his belief is confirmed and strengthened; when a member of the group behaves in a way that is not consistent with the observer's expectations, the instance is likely to pass unnoticed, and the observer's generalized belief is protected from disconfirmation. We believe that this well-documented process occurs continually in relation to the expected and perceived behavior of males and females, and results in the perpetuation of myths that would otherwise die out under the impact of negative evidence. However, not all unconfirmed beliefs about the two sexes are of this sort. It is necessary to reconsider the nature of the evidence that permits us to conclude what is myth and what is (at least potentially) reality.

HOW MUCH CONFIDENCE CAN BE PLACED IN THESE CONCLUSIONS?

Having gone through the often tedious process of summarizing and analyzing existing research, we must ask ourselves about the adequacy of this method as a way of knowing the truth about sex differences. We have tallied studies—the number showing higher scores for boys, the number favoring girls, and the number showing no difference—knowing, of course, that the studies differ widely in the rigor of their design and procedures, the number of subjects used, the definition of variables, etc. It is not uncommon to find a "box score" in which the majority of studies find no difference, but where the studies that do find a difference favor one sex by a considerable margin (say, two or three to one). We have interpreted such an outcome as a weak trend in the direction indicated by the largest number of studies, but recognize that it is quite possible that the minority of studies might turn out to have more than a kernel of truth. With stereotypes and biases being as common as they are in the field of sex differences, it is quite possible that the majority of studies were all distorted in the same direction. We think it equally likely, however, that the appearance of a sex difference often depends upon detailed aspects of the situation in which behavior was studied—details that have so far gone unrecognized, but that interact with the more obvious aspects of a situation to change the way in which it is perceived.

We have repeatedly encountered the problem that so-called "objective" measures of behavior yield different results than ratings or self-reports. Ratings are notoriously subject to shifting anchor points. For example, if a parent is asked, "How often does your daughter cry?," the parent may answer "Not very often," meaning "Not very often *for a girl*." The same frequency of behavior might have been rated "quite often" for a son, from whom the behavior was less expected. Ratings, then, if they are made against different subjective standards, should minimize sex differences where they exist. Where they do not exist, ratings might produce them, but in the opposite direction from stereotypical behavior. It is puzzling that ratings so frequently yield sex differences in the stereotypical direction. For example, in one study, teachers rated each child in their class on activity level; the boys received higher average ratings; but "actometer" recordings for the same group of children did not show the boys to be engaging in more body movement. Obviously, the possibility exists that teachers are noticing and remembering primarily the behavior that fits their stereotypes. There is another possibility, however: that teachers are analyzing clusters or patterns of behavior that a simple single-attribute measurement such as an actometer score does not capture. If this is so, however, and the teachers are reporting something real about sex differences, the cluster that they are attending to should not be named "activity level," for the label implies that the behavior is simpler than it is.

The problems of shifting anchor points for ratings, selective perceptions of raters, and unclear definitions of what is being rated are not the only problems that beset the student of sex differences. It matters how large a "chunk" of behavior is chosen for analysis. This point has been nicely illustrated in work by Raush (1965)[R], in which he compared the social interactions of a group of clinically diagnosed "hyperaggressive" boys with a group of normals. The sequences of aggressive behavior were monitored. The two groups of boys were similar in the frequency and kind of response the victim first made. They were also similar in the aggressor's response to the victim's response. It was only in the fourth and fifth actions in the sequence that the groups diverged—the "hyperactives" continued to respond intensely; the normals "let it go" without continuing the sequence. It may be that sex differences, too, emerge at only certain points in a sequence, and the results of a study will depend upon how detailed and continuous the measurements are. Often, of course, an experimental situation is arranged in such a way that only single responses are recorded, and then summed across trials. Such a procedure makes it nearly impossible to detect either sequences or other patterning of behavior.

We have found a number of instances in which sex differences are situation-specific. For example, although boys and girls do not differ in their attachment to their parents in early childhood (that is, their tendency to remain close to them, interact with them, and resist separation from them), or in the amount of positive interaction with nonfamily adults, boys do interact more with same-sex age-mates. Unfortunately, many studies tally social behavior without specifying the "target" of this behavior. Similarly, studies of "nurturance" behavior (rare in the first place) have usually not identified the beneficiary of the behavior. Clearly, if a child brings a glass of water to his mother, the behavior is subject to different interpretations than if he does the same helpful act for a younger sibling. Furthermore, it makes a difference who is watching. We suspect, for example, that a man may behave more dominantly toward his girl friend and she more submissively when other men are present than they would do in private. It is possible, too, that marriage partners are especially likely to become more equal in dominance with time if there are children—that it is the need to maintain a united front before the children and to support one another's disciplinary moves that is a primary factor producing a change in the dominance relations of a married pair. These situational subtleties have gone largely unnoticed in existing research; we have had no choice but to report the data that researchers have obtained, but we think findings will be much clearer when these distinctions begin to be introduced.

We have attempted to understand the relationship of sex differences to age; we have wanted to know at what age a particular difference first manifests itself, whether it is temporary, whether it increases or decreases with development. We have been able to make only a tantalizing beginning to a genuinely developmental analysis. It is reasonably clear that differences in "temperament" and in social behavior emerge much earlier than differences in specific intellectual abilities. Furthermore, there are a few instances in our review where a difference was evident only briefly, during a limited age period. This appears to be true, for example, on certain measures of "impulsivity," where boys are more impulsive only during the preschool years. On the whole, however, our efforts to understand developmental change have been frustrated by two things: (1) the fact that certain ages are overrepresented, others underrepresented, in research on a given topic; and (2) the fact that the methods of measuring a given attribute change so drastically with age that cross-age comparison becomes virtually impossible. Newborn infants in the first two or three days of life, nursery school children, and college students are the groups most frequently studied. In addition, extensive data are available for school-age children on attributes that are clearly relevant to school success (e.g. intellectual aptitudes and achievement scores), with much less information available on social behavior. Very little is known about age changes during adulthood with respect to either cognitive or social measures.

The problem of changing measures over ages is a ubiquitous one in developmental psychology. One can learn something about a young child's attachments and fears by tallying the frequency with which he literally hides behind his mother's skirts; to attempt to do so with an adult would be absurd. One may measure quantitative skill in a preschooler by finding how accurately he can count, and of a fifth- or sixth-grader by asking him to do percentages; but by college age, subjects must be asked to solve differential equations before stable individual differences can be identified. There are great shifts with age not only in *what* is measured but in *how* measurement is done. Behavioral observation is fairly frequent with young children. From the time children become literate through adulthood, however, observational studies in naturalistic settings are very rare, and scores are based either on questionnaires or other self-reports, or on experimental situations using a deliberately restricted set of eliciting conditions and behavioral measures.

It is to be expected that results of experiments may yield quite different results than "real life" observations. It is possible, for example, that if a girl is put into a foot race, she will be as competitive and active as a male. But she might be much less likely to enter such a race spontaneously, and naturalistic observation would show her to be less frequently engaged in competitive behavior, whereas the foot race "experiment" would not. The conclusions of both kinds of studies are correct, but they have rather different implications. The shift from naturalistic observation in early childhood to experimental studies at later ages may mean that sex differences in self-selection of activities have had a better chance of being detected in the early years, rather than that there has been any decline in the importance of motivation and interest with growth.

In a certain sense it is reasonable to make the shift from observational data to questionnaires or self-reports. If one is sampling behavior in a nursery school, it may be meaningful to record simply that a child moved across the room. If one looked out the window at a college student walking down the sidewalk just before the bell rang, however, what is meaningful to record about his behavior? The fact that he was walking? The fact that he was going to class? The fact that he was taking a course in psychology? The fact that his attendance at this class was part of his four-year program to obtain a bachelor's degree? Elements of an adult's behavior are usually part of a nested set of organized action sequences (i.e. "plans"). Judging by the data we collect about people at different ages, researchers implicitly assume that a young child's behavior is less so. This is probably correct, although there are probably many more nested sequences in children's behavior than have been detected with the usual techniques of time sampling and frequency tallies of individual behavior elements. If plans of varying duration and complexity do assume more and more control of behavior as the individual develops, it would be reasonable to ask about the plans, rather than to spend so much time enumerating specific responses, as is done for young children. However, the value of observational data surely does not decline to zero with increasing age. We can point out here only that, reasonable though the shift in methods may be, it makes the meaning of measured age changes quite ambiguous. We hope there will be an increase in observational work in naturalistic settings with subjects beyond nursery school age, so that a few more cross-age comparisons will be possible.

One interesting age trend emerged in our survey that is probably *not* a reflection of changes in methods of measurement: this is the tendency for young women of college age to lack confidence in their ability to do well on a new task, and their sense that they have less control over their own fates than men do. These trends are not seen among older or younger women. Age 18–22 is the period of their lives when many young adults are marrying or forming some other kind of relatively enduring sexual liaison. In the dating and mating game, women traditionally are expected to take less initiative than men. Perhaps it is at this period of their lives more than any other that individuals define themselves in terms of their "masculinity" and "femininity," and when greater sex differences may therefore appear than at earlier or later ages, with respect to any attribute considered central to this definition.

This brings us to a related point: that sex differences may be greater among certain subgroups of men and women than among others. In a recent paper, "On Predicting Some of the People Some of the Time," Bem and Allen (1974)[R] suggest that an individual's behavior is likely to be stable across situations and across time with respect to only those attributes that are central to his self-definition. If the individual thinks of himself as a "friendly" person, and considers it important to be as friendly as possible, then he should be consistently friendly in many situations, partly because he will continually monitor his own behavior to take note of how friendly he is being and will correct his own behavior if he is not behaving in ways that are consistent with his self-definition. For other individuals, however, friendliness is not a defining attribute; self-monitoring activity will not be directed toward maintaining consistency with respect to friendly behavior, and hence such behavior will vary greatly depending on the situation in which the person finds himself. In this vein, it is reasonable to believe that "masculinity" and "femininity" are essential self-defining attributes for some people but not for others. If the studies summarized in previous chapters of this book had been based on selected subsamples of subjects, including only those women who consider it important to be feminine and those men for whom masculinity is central to their self-concept, the chances are that greater sex differences would have been reported and the findings would have been much more consistent than we have found them to be. The variations in findings from one study to another probably reflect, in part, the relative concentration of people of this type in the subject population, as well as subtle variations in experimental situations that would signal to the subjects whether the tasks they were called on to perform had any relevance to masculinity or femininity.

ON THE ETIOLOGY OF PSYCHOLOGICAL SEX DIFFERENCES

In previous chapters we have discussed three kinds of factors that affect the development of sex differences: genetic factors, "shaping" of boylike and girl-like behavior by parents and other socializing agents, and the child's spontaneous learning of behavior appropriate for his sex through imitation. Anyone who would hope to explain acquisition of sex-typed behavior through one or two of these processes alone would be doomed to disappointment. Not only do the three kinds of processes exert their own direct influence, but they interact with one another.

Biological factors have been most clearly implicated in sex differences in aggression and visual-spatial ability. We have argued that the male's greater aggression has a biological component, citing in support the fact that (1) the sex difference manifests itself in similar ways in man and subhuman primates; (2) it is cross-culturally universal; and (3) levels of aggression are responsive to sex hormones. We have also found, surprisingly, that there is no good evidence that adults reinforce boys' aggression more than girls' aggression; in fact, the contrary may be true. Here, however, there are questions about the adequacy of our information. Direct observational studies of parental reactions to aggression have been carried out in settings in which only the responses to a child's aggression *toward the parents* (or sometimes toward siblings) could be observed. When it comes to permissiveness for fighting among unrelated children, we must rely on parent interviews. Parents *say* they encourage daughters to defend themselves as much as they do sons, and that they attempt to teach non-aggression to the same degree to both sexes. Serbin et al. (1973) found that in the case of aggressive or destructive behavior by one child toward another child in nursery school, teachers were more likely to intervene (and perhaps scold the guilty child) if the aggressor was a boy. It is possible that mothers react in an opposite way when they are supervising groups of children in neighborhoods and parks. We doubt it, but we do not know. Meanwhile, the available evidence is that adults do not generally accept or approve aggression in either sex. Either their reaction is equally negative for the two sexes, or they react somewhat more strongly to boys' aggression, on the grounds that boys are stronger and more given to fighting and therefore must be kept under closer control. Although strong negative reactions by parents and teachers may actually be "reinforcing" to some children, this is not usually what is meant when it is alleged that parents shape the aggressive behavior of the two sexes differently. What is usually meant is that they allow, accept, or encourage the behavior more in boys, and this we have not found to be true. The negative evidence on differential socialization has strengthened the case for biological origins of the sex differences in aggression. This does not mean that we believe aggressive behavior is unlearned. There is plentiful evidence that it *is* learned. We argue only that boys are more biologically prepared to learn it.

Does the male predisposition toward aggression extend to other behavior, such as dominance, competitiveness, and activity level? Probably yes, to some degree, but the case is not strong. Among subhuman primates, dominance is achieved largely through aggression, and an individual's position in the dominance hierarchy is related to levels of sex hormones. However, there is no direct evidence that dominance among adult human groups is linked either to sex hormones or to aggressiveness. The fact that "dominance" in most human groups is called "leadership" provides a clue to the fact that adult human beings influence one another by persuasion, charisma, mutual affection, and bargaining, as well as by force or threats thereof. To the extent that dominance is *not* exercised by coercion, the biological male aggressiveness is probably not implicated in it.

The case for biological control of visual-spatial ability rests primarily with genetic studies. There is evidence of a recessive sex-linked gene that contributes an element to high spatial ability. Present estimates are that approximately 50 percent of men and 25 percent of women show this element phenotypically, although of course more women than this are "carriers." This sex-linked element is not the only genetic element affecting spatial ability, and the others appear not to be sex-linked. There is so far little evidence for sex linkage of any of the genetic determiners of other specific abilities such as mathematical or verbal ability. The existence of a sex-linked genetic determiner of spatial ability does not imply that visual-spatial skills are unlearned. The specific skills involved in the manifestation of this ability improve with practice. Furthermore, cross-cultural work indicates that the sex difference can be either large or small, or may even disappear, depending upon cultural conditions affecting the rearing of the two sexes. Where women are subjugated, their visual-spatial skills are poor relative to those of men. Where both sexes are allowed independence early in life, both sexes have good visual-spatial skills.

Our review of the socialization pressures directed at the two sexes revealed a surprising degree of similarity in the rearing of boys and girls. The two sexes appear to be treated with equal affection, at least in the first five years of life (the period for which most information is available); they are equally allowed and encouraged to be independent, equally discouraged from dependent behavior; as noted above, there is even, surprisingly, no evidence of distinctive parental reaction to aggressive behavior in the two sexes. There *are* differences, however. Boys are handled and played with somewhat more roughly. They also receive more physical punishment. In several studies boys were found to receive both more praise and more criticism from their caretakers—socialization pressure, in other words, was somewhat more intense for boys—but the evidence on this point is inconsistent. The area of greatest differentiation is in very specifically sex-typed behavior. Parents show considerably more concern over a boy's being a "sissy" than over a girl's being a tomboy. This is especially true of fathers, who seem to take the lead in actively discouraging any interest a son might have in feminine toys, activities, or attire.

Is the direct socialization pressure from parents sufficient to account for known sex differences? For some behaviors, probably so. In some areas, clearly not. Aggression is a case of the second kind. Also, we see nothing in the socialization of the two sexes that would produce different patterns of intellectual abilities. In the area of sex typing as narrowly defined, there is clear parental pressure, particularly on boys; nevertheless, children seem to adopt sex-typed patterns of play and interests for which they have never been reinforced, and avoid sex-inappropriate activities for which they have never been punished. Observations of parental behavior may not have been detailed enough to pick up the more subtle pressures exerted, but it is our impression that parents are fairly permissive where many aspects of sex typing are concerned, and that direct "shaping" by parents does not, in most instances, account for the details of the behavior that is acquired. Parents seem to treat a child in accordance with their knowledge of his individual temperament, interests, and abilities, rather than in terms of sex-role stereotypes. We suspect that others who do not know the child well as an individual are more likely to react to him according to their stereotyped views of what a child of a given sex is likely to be like. Although this conclusion runs counter to common sense, it appears possible that relative strangers exert more stereotyping pressure on children than their own parents do. In any case, we believe that socialization pressures, whether by parents or others, do not by any means tell the whole story of the origins of sex differences.

How then does psychological sex differentiation come about? The psychoanalytic theory of identification would have it that the child identifies with the same-sex parent and learns the details of a sex role through imitation of this parent. Social-learning theory also emphasizes imitation, but argues that children are more often reinforced when they imitate a same-sex than an opposite-sex model, so that they acquire a generalized tendency to imitate not only the same-sex parent but other same-sex models as well. The distinction between acquisition and performance of a given item of behavior is stressed. A child may learn how to do something by watching an opposite-sex model, but may seldom do it because he learns (through observation or otherwise) that such action would probably be punished if performed by a person of his own sex.

We have found several reasons to be dissatisfied with these theories. The first is that children have not been shown to resemble closely the same-sex parent in their behavior. In fact, the rather meager evidence suggests that a boy resembles other children's fathers as much as he does his own, at least with respect to most of the behaviors and attributes measured so far. The same applies to girls' resemblance to their mothers. When people believe they see parent-child resemblance, we suspect they are often noticing physical resemblance rather than behavioral resemblance.

A second problem is that when offered an opportunity to imitate either a male or female model, children (at least those under age 6 or 7) do not characteristically select the model whose sex matches their own; their choices are fairly random in this regard. Yet their behavior is clearly sex-typed at a much earlier age than the age at which choice of same-sex models begins to occur. A final problem is that children's sex-typed behavior does not closely resemble that of adult models. Boys select an all-male play group, but they do not observe their fathers avoiding the company of females. Boys choose to play with trucks and cars, even though they may have seen their mothers driving the family car more frequently than their fathers; girls play hopscotch and jacks (highly sex-typed games), although these games are totally absent from their mother's observable behavior.

To recapitulate briefly: we have been discussing the biological factors and the learning processes that have been alleged to underlie the development of behavioral sex differences. It is tempting to try to classify the differential behaviors as being either innate or learned, but we have seen that this is a distinction that does not bear close scrutiny. We have noted that a genetically controlled characteristic may take the form of a greater *readiness to learn* a particular kind of behavior, and hence is not distinct from learned behavior. Furthermore, if one sex is more biologically predisposed than the other to perform certain actions, it would be reasonable to expect that this fact would be reflected in popular beliefs about the sexes, so that innate tendencies help to produce the cultural lore that the child learns. Thus he adapts himself, through learning, to a social stereotype that has a basis in biological reality. (Of course, not all social stereotypes about the sexes have such a basis.) It is reasonable, then, to talk about the process of acquisition of sex-typed behavior—the *learning* of sex-typed behavior—as a process built upon biological foundations that are sex-differentiated to some degree.

So far we have discussed two learning processes that have been presumed to account for the development of socially defined sex-appropriate behavior. The first emphasizes direct parental reinforcement. We have seen that, although differential reinforcement of boys and girls may account for some sex typing as narrowly defined (e.g. the fact that boys avoid wearing dresses and playing with dolls), there are large areas of sex-differentiated behavior where parental sanctions and encouragement seem to play only a very minor role. A second process widely believed to be crucial in differentiation is the child's identification with (and imitation of) the same-sex parent and, by generalization, other same-sex models. The weaknesses of this process in accounting for the evidence have been delineated above.

We turn now to a third kind of process—the one we entitled "self-socialization" in Chapter 1. This process has been most explicitly enunciated by Kohlberg (1966)[x]. Kohlberg stresses that sex-typed behavior is not made up of a set of independent elements acquired by imitating actions the child has seen same-sex people perform. It stems from organized rules the child has induced from what he has observed and what he has been told, and these rules are in many ways a distortion of reality. They are based upon a limited set of features that are salient and describable from a child's point of view (e.g. hair styles and dress); the child's sex-role conceptions are cartoon-like—oversimplified, exaggerated, and stereotyped. He fails to note the variations in the sex-role behavior of his real-life models. A compelling example of this is seen in the case of a 4-year-old girl who insisted that girls could become nurses but only boys could become doctors. She held to this belief tenaciously even though her own mother was a doctor. Hers was a concept clearly not based upon imitation of the most available model. It represented an induction from instances seen and heard (in fiction as well as fact), and like most childish rule inductions it did not easily take account of exceptions.

The child's problem in behaving in ways appropriate to his sex is twofold: he not only must have some conception of what boylike and girl-like behavior is, but also must have a clear conception of his own sex identity so that he knows which kind of behavior to adopt. Kohlberg notes that neither a child's conception of his own sexual identity nor his notions of what it means to be "masculine" or "feminine" are static. Both change with intellectual growth. Initially a child might know only what his or her own sex is without understanding that his own gender is unchangeable. When sex constancy has been achieved, the child then seeks to determine what behavior is appropriate for his own sex. Early in development, he may not know precisely which other people share a sex category with him; a boy of 4 may know, for example, which other children are also boys, but he may class all adults together as "grown-ups" and fail to make consistent distinctions between men and women or to realize that men and boys are similar in the sense of all being males. When sex groupings have been understood, the child is then in a position to identify what behavior is appropriate for his sex by observing what kinds of things males, as distinct from females, do and to match his own behavior to the conceptions he has constructed.

There is a problem with the Kohlberg view: sex typing of behavior occurs much earlier than gender constancy normally develops. We do not question that the achievement of gender constancy may accelerate the process of sex typing. Indeed, R. G. Slaby* has found that those kindergartners who have come to understand that gender is constant choose to observe same-sex models (as compared with opposite-sex models), whereas other children of the same age do not. But we would like to argue that gender constancy is not necessary in order for self-socialization into sex roles to begin. Children as young as 3, we suggest, have begun to develop a rudimentary understanding of their own sex identity, even though their ability to group others according to sex is imperfect and their notion about the permanence of their own sex identity incomplete. As soon as a boy knows that he is a boy in any sense, he is likely to begin to prefer to do what he conceives to be boylike things. Of course, he will not selectively imitate male models if he does not yet know which other people around him are in the same sex category as himself. But he will nevertheless try to match his own behavior to his limited concept of what attributes are sex-appropriate.

We believe that the processes of direct reinforcement and simple imitation are clearly involved in the acquisition of sex-typed behavior, but that they are not sufficient to account for the developmental changes that occur in sex typing. The third kind of psychological process—the one stressed by cognitive-developmental theorists such as Kohlberg—must also be involved. This third process is not easy to define, but in its simplest terms it means that a child gradually develops concepts of "masculinity" and "femininity," and when he has understood what his own sex is, he attempts to match his behavior to his conception. His ideas may be drawn only very

* R. G. Slaby, University of Washington, personal communication, 1974.

minimally from observing his own parents. The generalizations he constructs do not represent acts of imitation, but are organizations of information distilled from a wide variety of sources. A child's sex-role concepts are limited in the same way the rest of his concepts are, by the level of cognitive skills he has developed. Therefore the child undergoes reasonably orderly age-related changes in the subtlety of his thought about sex typing, just as he does with respect to other topics. Consequently, his *actions* in adopting sex-typed behavior, and in treating others according to sex-role stereotypes, also change in ways that parallel his conceptual growth.

IMPLICATIONS FOR SOCIAL ISSUES

Schooling

If boys and girls, on the average, have somewhat different areas of intellectual strength and weakness, does this imply that they should be taught in different ways? There have been a number of attempts to match instructional techniques to the specific aptitudes and learning styles of specific groups of students. The reader is referred to a review paper on this subject by Glaser (1972)[R]. Glaser shows that the results of these attempts have been disappointing. To date there is no evidence that an individual learns better if an instructional program is geared to his areas of strength. That is, it has not proved especially effective to instruct people with high visual-spatial abilities through visual-spatial (rather than verbal) means. Glaser believes that one reason for the failure to find such matches is that diagnosis of special abilities has been made with tests based upon psychometric, factor-analytic definitions of what these abilities are. He argues that instructional techniques must be adapted to the individual's repertoire of *learning processes*, not to "abilities" as psychometrically defined. Now it is just in the area of learning processes that sex differences have not been found. We have found the two sexes to be equally adept at paired-associates learning, discrimination learning, complex problem solving, adoption of useful strategies in memorizing, etc. Taking the Glaser position, then, there would be no grounds for separate instructional programs for the two sexes. It should be added that Glaser does not advocate working primarily with the skills that a child already has, and sidestepping the areas of weakness. He argues, rather, that the educator should focus directly upon teaching the strategies (processes) that are missing from a child's repertoire. This means that if a child seems to have a poor level of visual-spatial skills, one should *not* attempt to teach him exclusively by verbal means, but should attempt to improve his visual-spatial skills.

Schools are already coping with some of the educational handicaps wherein the sexes differ. There are special remedial classes for poor readers, and boys are considerably overrepresented in such classes. However, special remedial instruction in visual-spatial skills is not normally offered in the schools. If such skills do prove to be important in higher education or adult occupations, it might well be the case that many students, especially girls, would profit from such remedial instruction.

Sex differences in the social-emotional sphere have implications for the classroom, too, bearing not so much upon teaching strategies as upon the nature of the organization of classroom activities that may be optimal for the two sexes. We have seen that boys stimulate one another to increased activity and mock fighting. We also found, however (Chapter 4), that boys perform better on certain experimental tasks in the presence of other boys, so the possibility clearly exists that the competitive spirit among boys may feed into improved academic performance under certain circumstances. Little is known concerning the cross-sex effects of boys and girls upon each other's performance in the classroom. Do boys "show off" for girls or primarily for each other? Does the desire to impress the other sex take pro-academic or anti-academic forms? Does the presence of girls have a "gentling" effect on boys? Do boys stimulate girls to greater competitive striving? We cannot rely on our intuition for the answers to these questions, and, to our knowledge, data are not yet available. All we can say is that the sex mix in the classroom undoubtedly makes a difference in the motivation of students, and it would be worthwhile to consider how these motivations could be constructively utilized. Instructional techniques and classroom organization are not, of course, the only educational issues related to sex. There is the problem of admissions quotas. If girls are, on the average, less skilled in visual-spatial tasks, does this mean that fewer of them should be admitted to graduate schools in engineering, architecture, and art? Should fewer men be admitted to training in languages, linguistic science, and creative writing, on the grounds that girls, with their greater verbal skills, are more likely to profit from advanced training? Here we must emphasize once again the overlap in the sex distributions. There are many girls with high-level visual-spatial skills. It is by no means self-evident that visual-spatial skill is the intellectual ability that is most needed by engineers, but even if it were, and even if the elusive sex-linked recessive gene carried the major part of the variance in these skills (which it probably does not), current estimates are that at least 25 percent of women have it, as compared with approximately 50 percent of men. This is more than enough women to fill our engineering schools, if women's talents were developed through the requisite early training and interests. Women are now considerably underrepresented in engineering in terms of any criterion by which potential talent can be measured. We have no wish to push women toward careers that do not attract them. At the same time, we believe it would be a grievous injustice to establish formal or informal quotas that would exclude any women with the requisite talents and interests. We are discussing quotas that exclude women because, historically, women have been excluded from training for high-status careers more frequently than men, but of course the argument applies in both directions. After a certain amount of positive recruiting of qualified women to redress historical imbalances, the reasonable approach would appear to be to assess an applicant on the basis of his or her measurable talents, not on the basis of probabilities based on sex.

Dominance, Leadership, and Vocational Success

We have seen that the greater aggressiveness of the male is one of the best established, and most pervasive, of all psychological sex differences. We have also seen reason to believe there is a biological component underlying this difference. It has been alleged (see, for example, Goldberg 1973[R]) that aggression is the primary means whereby human beings dominate one another, so that in cross-sex encounters it will be true that (with rare exceptions) men will dominate women, and will therefore come to occupy the positions in society in which status and authority are vested. In this view, the implications of male aggressiveness go very deep. In a business setting, for example, it would be the man who would be (and *should* be) the foreman, the supervisor, the chairman of the board. Leadership would also properly be assumed by men in politics, in the professions, and within the family.

We believe it is true that males have occupied the high-status positions in the large majority of human social groupings through the history of man. We do not think this is a historical accident. We doubt, however, that dominance and leadership are inevitably linked to aggression.

Aggression may be the primary means by which apes and little boys dominate one another (although even here the ability to maintain alliances is important). However, aggression is certainly not the method most usually employed for leadership among mature human beings. Perhaps it once was. But the day of the iron-fisted tycoon appears to be waning. Business leadership is now exercised (especially at the highest levels in the management of conglomerates) by negotiation and attempts to reach agreement among managerial groups; leaders must be supportive toward the people with whom they work, and more skilled in guiding a group toward consensus than in imposing their own wills. We must leave it to the reader's judgment to estimate how often the "killer instinct" is involved in achieving success in the business or political world. Clearly, it sometimes is, and in these cases there will be a smaller number of women than men who will have the temperament for it. We wish only to suggest that it is entirely possible to achieve status by other means, and that the sexes have a more equal chance at success by these alternative routes. We believe we see a shift toward more nonaggressive leadership styles in high-level management, but at the moment this is speculation.

In small face-to-face groups and within families, it may be that similar shifts have occurred. We do not know whether wife beating was ever the norm. Certainly in earlier times husbands had formal control over their wives' lives and fortunes to a degree that would be highly unusual now, and although physical force may not have been frequently used in maintaining this control, the possibility of its use as a last resort no doubt helped to support male authority. Nowadays, marriages are maintained to a much greater degree by mutual consent. Expanding the argument presented at the close of Chapter 7, we would like to suggest the following generalizations concerning the role of aggression in dominance and submission:

1. Aggression is a relatively primitive means of exerting influence over others. It entails risks and costs for the aggressor as well as the victim, and will normally be superseded by alternative forms of interaction as individuals acquire the skills needed for these more mature approaches.

2. Dominance of one individual over another can be maintained by aggression only to the degree that the dominee is not free to leave the relationship (i.e. to the degree that the individual needs the relationship and has no good alternatives). This, indeed, is one of the reasons why aggression is of limited effectiveness (see point 1 above).

2a. Young children have few alternatives to the same-sex play group. A boy cannot easily escape the aggression-maintained hierarchy of the male play group unless he is willing to be solitary or to play with girls.

2b. As children grow older, a variety of social groups become available, and hence aggression declines in importance as a means by which the leaders of these groups maintain their dominance.

2c. The amount of aggression displayed by adult men toward women in the maintenance of dominance depends, in part, on the degree to which the social system gives women a "way out" in marriage. In modern times, divorce is always an alternative, albeit not an attractive one in many cases. In some traditional societies, a woman can return to her parents' home to escape the brutality of a mate, or she may claim the protection of her brothers. All societies provide women and girls some protection against the aggression of men.

Social restraints on the expression of aggression by men toward women go a long way to create equality of bargaining power between them, but they do not necessarily equalize this power. Other aspects of the social system determine whether "institutionalized" dominance relations exist. The evidence is that the formal role structure of a society may determine the initial dominance-submission relations of men and women toward one another when they first become acquainted. But dominance within long-standing relationships has surprisingly little relationship to formal role structure. It is doubtful whether most long-standing relationships between individual human beings can be described in terms of a single "dominance-submission" dimension. One member of a pair will usually be more influential with respect to certain kinds of decisions, the other member with respect to others. The dominance relationship within a pair or social group fluctuates, depending on changes in coalitions and patterns of interpersonal loyalty or antagonism. What matters is the individual competencies, motivations, and commitments of the parties to a relationship, and their mutual affection.

These considerations imply that there is nothing inevitable about male achievement of all available leadership positions. As women acquire the relevant competencies, and as these competencies become known to themselves and others, groups will less and less be formed on the initial assumption that the male members will have more of the needed skills. Leadership roles should thus gradually become more equitably distributed. There will no doubt continue to be groups in which physical strength, or aggression-based dominance, will be the means of seizing leadership, or in which these traits are needed in a leader if the group is to achieve its goals. In such cases, we would expect leadership to gravitate to males. But in groups where leadership is achieved and held through skill in setting achievable goals, in planning, organizing, persuading, conciliating, and conveying enthusiasms, we see no reason for a sex bias.

Apart from leadership, we may ask whether the characteristics of men and women suit them particularly for certain occupations. We have already seen that intellectual aptitudes are similarly distributed by sex, at least enough so as to rule out reserving certain occupations for one sex or the other on the basis of ability patterns. Clearly, there are some occupations that call for great physical strength, and men can be expected to predominate in them. Some women, however, are strong enough to do any task, and if one looks at work assignments across the world, it is surprising how often women's work matches or exceeds men's work in strenuous physical exertion: thus we often find women carrying huge burdens on their heads, hoeing weeds for hours on end, and so on. In any case, physical exertion is not a prominent requirement of most jobs these days, and there are fewer and fewer jobs that must be assigned to men simply because men alone have the strength to perform them.

What about the male pattern of aggression and dominance attempts—are there occupations to which these contribute positively? Undoubtedly there are some, although it is difficult to know precisely what they are. It was once thought that a salesman needed to be "aggressive," but it is now known that a softer approach can be equally or sometimes more effective. A salesman does need to convey a sense of confidence in himself and his product, but the ability to do this is by no means a special province of the male.

Perhaps the traditional assignment of certain jobs to men and others to women has come about not so much because men are in jobs that call for aggressiveness as because women, being slower to anger, are less likely to protest onerous assignments. We have seen that girls are more likely than boys to comply with demands that adults make upon them; although it has not been demonstrated, it appears likely that in adulthood as well they will "take orders" from authority figures with less coercion. To put the matter bluntly, they are easier to exploit.

Childbearing and Child Care

We saw in Chapter 5 that, among lower animals, the hormones associated with pregnancy and childbirth produce a state of "readiness" to care for the young. It is not known whether there are similar biochemical elements in human responsiveness to young infants.

Hormonal priming or not, it is obvious that when a woman is breast-feeding her infant, this increases the likelihood of her being the infant's primary caretaker. It probably also imposes some constraints on the nature of the outside occupational duties she can undertake, although this issue is complex. In traditional agricultural societies, women who were breast-feeding frequently took their infants with them to the fields, and their assignment to certain other kinds of "heavy" labor was scarcely impeded. On the other hand, it is possible that some occupations (e.g. coal mining) became largely male because a breast-feeding woman could not take her infant to the work site. If some of the traditional division of labor between the sexes was indeed initially based upon the biological fact of breast-feeding, it is well to remember that these occupational distinctions grew up in a time when a woman would bear and nurse a very large number of children, so that she would be involved in this especially demanding form of care-taking for a high proportion of her adult life. During a time when families are small, breast-feeding briefer, and the woman's life span much longer, many of the traditional occupational constraints need no longer apply, even if they were at one time truly relevant. Furthermore, in societies where women's labor is needed, it has been found possible to organize nurseries near places of work, so that nursing mothers can be brought into occupations previously reserved for men.

Cross-cultural work has indicated that girls are more likely than boys to engage spontaneously in care-taking behavior toward younger children, but it is not known whether this stems entirely from their more intensive training as babysitters or whether they also have a greater readiness to acquire this behavior with appropriate training. Whether a boy can as easily learn to care for children depends in part upon whether his aggressive tendencies interfere.

We did see, in our review of the animal literature, that in rodents and some monkeys there is an initial tendency for males to attack the young, a tendency that must be weakened before "maternal" behavior develops in a male. That the same tendencies may exist in higher species is suggested by an incident recently observed in the course of a field study of free-living chimpanzees. David Hamburg* saw an adult male chimpanzee, in a fit of violent rage, seize an infant from the arms of its mother, swing it around by the feet, and dash its head against a rock; the mother attempted to retrieve it and was herself severely beaten. Of course, such incidents are very rare. In fact, this is the only incident of its kinds that has been witnessed over many years of observing this species; but the potentiality of its occurring must be one of the reasons why primate mothers keep their infants away from males as much as possible. To balance the picture, we should recall that there are subspecies of apes in which males play a considerable part in caring for infants. There are also instances (described in Chapter 5) in which male primates have "adopted" younger animals and cared for them effectively. Among humankind, is the danger of male aggression toward infants one of the reasons why child care has been assigned so exclusively to women? We do not know. Studies of battered children indicate that mothers are at least as likely as fathers to brutalize their children.

Of course, the vast majority of men and women are not notably aggressive toward children. Whether they are positively nurturant or merely indifferent seemingly depends in large measure on how much contact they have with children and how much responsibility they have for child care. C. E. Baldwin, using observations of children in six cultures (Whiting and Pope 1974), found that boys who had been involved in caring for younger siblings were less aggressive in their daily encounters with age-mates than boys who had not had such responsibilities. It would appear, then, that aggression is largely incompatible with child care, and that the process of caring for children moderates aggressive tendencies.

The role of dominance in child rearing is an important issue that has seldom been discussed. We have seen that boys are more likely than girls to try to dominate the adults with whom they deal. There is some reason to believe that women yield to these attempts from boys more readily than men do. Men, on the other hand, yield to the blandishments of small girls. Both men and women take a tougher stance toward children of their own sex. Thoughtful people differ in whether they value strictness toward chil-

* Professor of biological sciences and psychiatry, Stanford University, personal communication, 1974.

dren, and in how important they believe it is for adults to maintain "control" over children's behavior. In any case, when boys need control, men can probably provide it more effectively than women; when boys need support for independent action, they are more likely to get it from women. The reverse situation probably applies for girls: closer control from their mothers, indulgence and/or encouragement in adultlike behavior from their fathers. The major implication of these considerations would appear to be that a healthy balance of forces is best maintained when adults of both sexes are involved in the care of childen of both sexes.

Is Biology Destiny?

We have seen that the sexes are psychologically much alike in many respects. We have also seen that some of the ways in which they do differ probably have a biological basis, whereas others do not. It has been argued (Goldberg 1973[R]) that where a biological basis exists, it behooves societies to socialize children in such a way as to emphasize and exaggerate the difference. That is, since males are more aggressive, girls should be carefully trained in nonaggression throughout childhood; otherwise they will be doomed to failure and disappointment as adults in their encounters with men. By extension, if women's greater propensity for nurturance has a biological basis, it would follow that men should not be trained in nurturance, leaving all nurturant activity to the sex biologically better suited for it.

The curious fact is, however, that social pressures to shape individuals toward their "natural" sex roles sometimes boomerang. Traits that may be functional for one aspect of a sex role may be dysfunctional for other aspects. A man who adopts the "machismo" image may gain prestige with his peers, or enhance his short-term attractiveness to women, at the expense of his effectiveness as a husband and father. A similar problem exists for the highly "feminine" woman. Effective care-taking of the young, for example, involves a good deal of assertiveness; people are more likely to be helpful toward others when they have had ego-enhancing experiences that make them feel competent in coping with problem situations (Moore et al. 1973). Training a girl to be "feminine" in the traditional nonassertive, "helpless," and self-deprecatory sense may actually make her a worse mother. Consistent with this possibility is a recent finding of E. Cohen (1973)[R] that schoolteachers who wanted to be promoted to principal had a more child-centered view of education, and more maternally warm feelings toward their pupils, than teachers who lacked this ambition. Of course, we need more information on the possible side effects of attempting to change the definitions of "masculine" and "feminine" that are used as yardsticks in the rearing of boys and girls. But it is by no means obvious that attempts to foster sex-typed behavior (as traditionally defined) in boys and girls serve to make them better men and women. Indeed, in some spheres of adult life such attempts appear to be positively handicapping. We suggest that societies have the option of minimizing, rather than maximizing, sex differences through their socialization practices. A society could, for example, devote its energies more toward moderating male aggression than toward preparing women to submit to male aggression, or toward encouraging rather than discouraging male nurturance activities. In our view, social institutions and social practices are not merely reflections of the biologically inevitable. A variety of social institutions are viable within the framework set by biology. It is up to human beings to select those that foster the life styles they most value.

References Cited

References Cited

Works cited in the text (or in the summary tables) that bear the superscript letter R are listed here. Works not bearing the superscript are listed in the Annotated Bibliography, pp. 395–627. The distinction is explained in the Introduction, p. 8.

Works designated by an asterisk in the following list appear in Roberta M. Oetzel's Annotated Bibliography in Eleanor E. Maccoby, ed., *The Development of Sex Differences* (Stanford, 1966), pp. 224–321, where they are annotated much in the manner of the present Annotated Bibliography.

Ainsworth, M. D. S., Bell, S. M. V., and Stayton, D. J. Individual differences in strange-situation behavior of one-year-olds. In H. R. Schaffer, ed., *Origin of human social relations*. London: Academic Press. 1971.

Alper, T. G. Role orientation in women. *J. Personality*, 1973, *41*, 9–31.

Anastasi, A. *Differential psychology*. 3d ed. New York: Macmillan, 1958.

Andrew, R. J. Changes in search behavior in male and female chicks, following different doses of testosterone. *Animal Behaviour*, 1972, *20*, 741–50.

*Bandura, A. Influence of models' reinforcement contingencies on the acquisition of imitative responses. *J. Personality & Social Psychology*, 1965, *1*, 589–95.

Bandura, A. *Aggression: a social learning analysis*. Englewood Cliffs, N.J.: Prentice-Hall, 1973.

Bandura, A., and Barab, P. G. Conditions governing nonreinforced imitation. *Developmental Psychology*, 1971, 5, 244–55.

Bandura, A., and Barab, P. G. Processes governing disinhibitory effects through symbolic modeling. *J. Abnormal Psychology*, 1973, 82, 1–9.

Bandura, A., and Walters, R. *Social learning and personality development*. New York: Holt, Rinehart & Winston, 1963.

*Bandura, A., Ross, D., and Ross, S. A. Transmission of aggression through imitation of aggresive models. *J. Abnormal & Social Psychology*, 1961. 63, 575–82.

*Bandura, A., Ross, D., and Ross, S. A. Imitation of film-mediated aggressive models. *J. Abnormal & Social Psychology*, 1963a, 66, 3–11.

Bandura, A., Ross, D., and Ross, S. A. A comparative test of the status envy, social power, and secondary reinforcement theories of identificatory learning. *J. Abnormal & Social Psychology*, 1963b, 67, 527–34.

Bandura, A., Blanchard, E. B., and Ritter, B. Relative efficacy of desensitization and modeling approaches for inducing behavioral, affective and attitudinal changes. *J. Personality & Social Psychology*, 1969, 13(3), 173–99.

Bandura, A., Jeffery, R. W., and Wright, C. L. Efficacy of participant modeling as a function of response induction aids. *J. Abnormal Psychology*, 1974, 83, 56–64.

Bardwick, J. M. *Psychology of Women*. New York: Harper & Row, 1971.

Barrett, R. J., and Ray, O. S. Behavior in the open field, Lashley III maze, shuttle-box, and Sidman avoidance as a function of strain, sex, and age. *Developmental Psychology*, 1970, 3, 73–77.

Barry, H., Child, I. L., and Bacon, M. K. Relation of child training to subsistence economy. *American Anthropologist*, 1959, *61*, 51–63.

Bayley, N. The development of motor abilities during the first three years. *Monographs of the Society for Research in Child Development*, 1936, *1*, 1–26.

Bayley, N. Individual patterns of development. *Child Development*, 1956, *27*, 45–74.

*Bayley, N., and Schaefer, E. S. Correlations of maternal and child behaviors with the development of mental abilities: data from the Berkeley Growth Study. *Monographs of the Society for Research in Child Development*, 1964, *29*, serial no. 97.

Bell, R. Q. Relations between behavior manifestations in the human neonate. *Child Development*, 1960, *31*, 463–77.

*Beller, E. K., and Turner, J. L. A study of dependency and aggression in early childhood. From progress report on NIMH project M-849, National Institute of Mental Health, Washington, D.C., 1962.

Bem, D. J., and Allen, A. On predicting some of the people some of the time: the search for cross-situational consistencies in behavior. *Psychological Review*, 1974, in press.

Bentzen, F. Sex ratios in learning and behavior disorders. *J. Orthopsychiatry*, 1963, *23*, 92–98.

Berger, E. M. Relationships among acceptance of self, acceptance of others and MMPI scores. *J. Counseling Psychology*, 1955, *2*, 279–84.

Bhavnani, R., and Hutt, C. Sexual differentiation in human development. In C. Ounsted and D. C. Taylor, eds., *Gender differences: their ontogeny and significance*. Baltimore: Williams & Wilkins, 1972.

*Bing, E. Effects of childrearing practices on development of differential cognitive abilities. *Child Development*, 1963, *34*, 631–48.

Blade, M. F., and Watson, W. S. Increase in spatial visualization test scores during engineering study. *Psychological Monographs*, 1955, *69* (12, whole no. 397).

Block, J. (Discussant). Longitudinal relations between newborn tactile threshold, preschool barrier behavior, and early school age imagination and verbal development. Symposium presented at the meeting of the Society for Research in Child Development, Minneapolis, 1971.

Bock, D. R., and Kolakowski, D. Further evidence of sex-linked major-gene influence on human spatial visualizing ability. *American J. Human Genetics*, 1973, *25*, 1–14.

Bowlby, J. *Attachment*. New York: Basic Books, 1969.

Brackett, C. W. Laughing and crying of preschool children. *Child Development Monographs*, 1934, *14*, 1–90.

Brinkmann, E. H. Programmed instruction as a technique for improving spatial visualization. *J. Applied Psychology*, 1966, *50*, 179–84.

Brody, E. G. Genetic basis of spontaneous activity in the albino rat. *Comparative Psychology Monographs*, 1942, *17*, serial no. 89.

*Bronfenbrenner, U. Some familial antecedents of responsibility and leadership in adolescents. In L. Petrullo and B. M. Bass, eds., *Studies in leadership*. New York: Holt, 1960.

Bronson, F. H., and Desjardins, C. Aggression in adult mice: modification by neonatal injections of gonadal hormones. *Science*, 1968, *161*, 705–6.

Broverman, D. M., Klaiber, E. L., Kobayashi, Y., and Vogel, W. Roles of activation and inhibition in sex differences in cognitive abilities. *Psychological Review*, 1968, *75*, 23–50.

Broverman, I. K., Broverman, D. M., Clarkson, F. E., Rosenkrantz, P. S., and Vogel, S. R. Sex-role stereotypes and clinical judgments of mental health. *J. Consulting & Clinical Psychology*, 1970, *34*, 1–7.

Brown, D. G. Sex-role preference in young children. *Psychological Monographs*, 1956, *70*, no. 14.

Brown, D. G. Sex-role preference in children: methodological problems. *Psychological Reports*, 1962, *11*, 477–78.

Bruner, J. S., Olver, R. R., and Greenfield, P. M. *Studies in Cognitive Growth.* New York: Wiley, 1966.

Buffery, A. W. H. Sex differences in the development of hemispheric asymmetry of function in the human brain. *Brain Research*, 1971, *31*, 364–65.

Buffery, A. W. H., and Gray, J. A. Sex differences in the development of spatial and linguistic skills. In C. Ounsted and D. C. Taylor, eds., *Gender differences: their ontogeny and significance.* Baltimore: Williams & Wilkins, 1972.

Burke, P. J. Leadership role differentiation. In C. G. McClintock, ed., *Experimental social psychology.* New York: Holt, Rinehart & Winston, 1972.

Buss, A. H., and Buss, E. H. Stimulus generalization with words connoting anxiety. *J. Personality & Social Psychology*, 1966, *4*, 707–10.

Cairns, R. B. Fighting and punishment from a developmental perspective. In J. K. Cole and D. D. Jensen, eds., *Nebraska Symposium on Motivation.* Lincoln: University of Nebraska Press, 1972.

Chamove, A., Harlow, H. F., and Mitchell, G. D. Sex differences in the infant-directed behavior of preadolescent rhesus monkeys. *Child Development*, 1967, *38*, 329–35.

Clifford, M. M., and Cleary, T. A. The relationship between children's academic performance and achievement accountability. *Child Development*, 1972, *43*, 647–55.

Cohen, E. G. Open-space schools: the opportunity to become ambitious. *Sociology of Education*, 1973, *46*, 143–61.

Cohen, E. G., and Roper, S. Modification of interracial interaction disability. *American Sociological Review*, 1973, *37*, 643–47.

*Coleman, J. S. *The adolescent society.* New York: Free Press of Glencoe, 1961.

Collins, B. E., and Raven, B. E. Group structure: attraction, coalitions, communication, and power. In G. Lindzey and E. Aronson, eds., *Handbook of social psychology*, vol. 4. Reading, Mass.: Addison-Wesley, 1968.

Conel, J. L. *The cortex of the newborn.* Cambridge: Harvard University Press, 1939.

Conel, J. L. *The cortex of the one-month infant.* Cambridge: Harvard University Press, 1941.

Conel, J. L. *The cortex of the three-month infant.* Cambridge: Harvard University Press, 1947.

Conel, J. L. *The cortex of the six-month infant.* Cambridge: Harvard University Press, 1951.

Conel, J. L. *The cortex of the fifteen-month infant.* Cambridge: Harvard University Press, 1955.

Conel, J. L. *The cortex of the twenty-four-month infant.* Cambridge: Harvard University Press, 1959.

Conel, J. L. *The cortex of the four-year child.* Cambridge: Harvard University Press, 1963.

Connolly, K. Locomotor activity in Drosophila. II. Selection for activity and inactive strains. *Animal Behavior*, 1966, *14*, 444–49.

Conrad, H. S., and Jones, H. E. A second study of familial resemblance in intelligence: environmental and genetic implications of parent-child and sibling correlations in the total sample. In G. M. Whipple, ed., *The thirty-ninth yearbook of the National Society for the Study of Education.* Bloomington, Ill.: Public School Publishing Co., 1940.

Craig, J. W., and Baruth, R. A. Inbreeding and social dominance. *Animal Behavior*, 1965, *13*, 109–13.

*Cunningham, J. D. Einstellung rigidity in children. *J. Experimental Child Psychology*, 1965, *2*, 237–47.

Dalton, K. Ante-natal progesterone and intelligence. *British J. Psychiatry*, 1968, *114*, 1377–82.

*Dawe, H. C. An analysis of two hundred quarrels of preschool children. *Child Development*, 1934, *5*, 139–57.

Dawson, J. L. M. Cultural and physiological influences upon spatial-perceptual processes in West Africa. *International J. Psychology*, 1967, *2*, 115–28, 171–85.

DeFries, J. C., Hegmann, J. P., and Weir, M. W. Open-field behavior in mice: evidence for a major gene effect mediated by the visual system. *Science*, 1966, *154*, 1577–79.

*De Jung, J. E., and Meyer, W. J. Expected reciprocity, grade trends, and correlates. *Child Development*, 1963, *34*, 127–39.

*DeLucia, L. A. The toy preference test: a measure of sex-role identification. *Child Development*, 1963, *34*, 107–17.

Deutsch, H. *The psychology of women.* New York: Grune & Stratton, 1944.

DeVore, I. Mother-infant relations in free-ranging baboons. In H. L. Rheingold, ed., *Maternal behavior in mammals.* New York: Wiley, 1963.

DeVore, I., ed. *Primate behavior: field studies of monkeys and apes.* New York: Holt, Rinehart & Winston, 1965.

Douvan, E., and Adelson, J. *The adolescent experience.* New York: Wiley, 1966.

*Droppleman, L. F., and Schaefer, E. S. Boys' and girls' reports of maternal and paternal behavior. *J. Abnormal & Social Psychology*, 1963, *67*, 648–54.

Duffy, E. *Activation and behavior.* (See esp. sex differences in measures of activation, pp. 224–28.) New York: Wiley, 1962.

Edwards, D. A. Early androgen stimulation and aggressive behavior in male and female mice. *Physiology & Behavior*, 1969, *4*, 333–38.

Ehrhardt, A. A., and Baker, S. W. Hormonal aberrations and their implications for the understanding of normal sex differentiation. Paper presented at the meetings of the Society for Research in Child Development, Philadelphia, 1973.

Ehrhardt, A. A., and Money, J. Progestin-induced hermaphroditism: IQ and psychosexual identity in a study of ten girls. *J. Sex Research*, 1967, *3*(1), 83–100.

Elliott, R., and McMichael, R. E. Effects of specific training on frame dependence. *Perceptual & Motor Skills*, 1963, *17*, 363–67.

Entwisle, D. R. To dispel fantasies about fantasy-based measures of achievement motivation. *Psychological Bulletin*, 1972, *77*, 377–91.

Eriksson, J. Genetic selection for voluntary alcoholic consumption in the albino rat. *Science*, 1968, *159*, 739–41.

Escalona, A., and Heider, G. M. *Prediction and outcome: a study in child development*. New York: Basic Books, 1959.

Feldman, S. S. Some possible antecedents of attachment behavior in two-year-old children. Unpublished manuscript, Stanford University, 1974.

Feshbach, S. Aggression. In P. H. Mussen, ed., *Carmichael's manual of child psychology*. New York: Wiley, 1970.

Fidell, L. S. Empirical verification of sex discrimination in hiring practices in psychology. *American Psychologist*, 1970, *25*, 1094–98.

Fidell, L. S. Put her down on drugs: prescribed drug usage in women. Paper presented at the meetings of the Western Psychological Association, Anaheim, California, 1973.

Fiedler, F. E. Assumed similarity measures as predictors of team effectiveness. *J. Abnormal & Social Psychology*, 1954, *49*, 381–88.

Flavell, J. H. Concept development. In P. H. Mussen, ed., *Carmichael's manual of child psychology*. New York: Wiley, 1970.

Flory, C. D. Osseous development in the hand as an index of skeletal development. *Monographs of the Society for Research in Child Development*, 1936, *1*, 96–97.

Fourr, J. S. Strength, timidity, and sleep cycles in the six-month-old infant: stability, sex differences, and relationships to newborn behaviors. Unpublished honors thesis, Stanford University, 1974.

Freedman, D. G. The development of social hierarchies. Paper presented at the World Health Organization conference, 1971. In Lennart Levi, ed., *Society, stress and disease in childhood and adolescence*, vol. 2. New York: Oxford University Press, in press.

Freud, A., and Dann, S. An experiment in group upbringing. *Psychoanalytic Studies of the Child*, 1951, *6*, 127–68. (See also in C. B. Stendler, ed., *Readings in child behavior and development*. New York: Harcourt, Brace & World, 1964.)

Furchgott, E., and Lazar, J. Maternal parity and offspring behavior in the domestic mouse. *Developmental Psychology*, 1969, *1*, 227–30.

Garai, J. E., and Scheinfeld, A. Sex differences in mental and behavioral traits. *Genetic Psychology Monographs*, 1968, *77*, 169–299.

Garcia, J., and Koelling, R. Relation of cue to consequence in avoidance learning. *Psychonomic Science*, 1966, *4*, 123–24.

Glaser, Robert. Individuals and learning: the new aptitudes. *Educational Researcher*, 1972 *1*(6), 5–13.

Gold, M. Power in the classroom. *Sociometry*, 1958, *21*, 50–60.

Goldberg, S. *The inevitability of patriarchy*. New York: Morrow, 1973.

Goodall, J. Chimpanzees of the Gombe Stream Reserve. In I. DeVore, ed., *Primate behavior*. New York: Holt, Rinehart & Winston, 1965.

Goodenough, D. R., and Karp, S. A. Field dependence and intellectual functioning. *J. Abnormal & Social Psychology*, 1961, *63*, 241–46.

Goodenough, F. L. *Anger in young children*. Minneapolis: University of Minnesota Press, 1931.

*Gordon, J. E., and Smith, E. Children's aggression, parental attitudes, and the effects of an affiliation-arousing story. *J. Personality & Social Psychology*, 1965, *1*, 654–59.

Gordon, N. S., and Bell, R. Q. Activity in the human newborn. *Psychological Report*, 1961, 9, 103–16.

Gray, J. *The psychology of fear and stress.* London: Weidenfeld & Nicolson, 1971.

Gray, J. A., and Levine, S. Effect of induced oestrus on emotional behavior in selected strains of rats. *Nature*, 1964, 201, 1198–2000.

Gray, J. A., Levine, S., and Broadhurst, P. S. Gonadal hormone injections in infancy and adult emotional behavior. *Animal Behavior*, 1965, 13, 33–45.

*Guetzkow, H. An analysis of the operation of set in problem-solving behavior. *J. General Psychology*, 1951, 45, 219–44.

Guhl, A. A., Craig, J. V., and Mueller, C.D. Selective breeding for aggressiveness in chickens. *Poultry Science*, 1960, 39, 970–80.

Guilford, J. P. A revised structure of intellect. Rep. Psychol. Lab., no. 19, University of Southern California, Los Angeles, 1957.

Hagen, J. W. The effect of distraction on selective attention. *Child Development*, 1967, 38, 685–94.

Hall, K. R. L., and DeVore, I. Baboon social behavior. In I. DeVore, ed., *Primate behavior.* New York: Holt, Rinehart & Winston, 1965.

Hamburg, D. A., and Van Lawick–Goodall, J. Factors facilitating development of aggressive behavior in chimpanzees and humans. Unpublished manuscript. Stanford University, 1973.

Hamers, J., and Lambert, W. Unpublished data, McGill University, 1973.

Harlow, H. F. The heterosexual affectional system in monkeys. *American Psychologist*, 1962, 17, 1–9.

Hartlage, L. C. Sex-linked inheritance of spatial ability. *Perceptual & Motor Skills*, 1970, 31, 610.

*Hartup, W. W., and Keller, E. D. Nurturance in preschool children and its relation to dependency. *Child Development*, 1960, 31, 681–89.

*Hartup, W. W., Moore, S. G., and Sager, G. Avoidance of inappropriate sex-typing by young children. *J. Consulting Psychology*, 1963, 27, 467–73.

*Hattwick, L. A. Sex differences in behavior of nursery school children. *Child Development*, 1937, 8, 343–55.

*Heathers, G. Emotional dependence and independence in nursery school play. *J. Genetic Psychology*, 1955, 87, 37–57.

*Hetherington, E. M. A developmental study of the effects of sex of the dominant parent on sex-role preference, identification, and imitation in children. *J. Personality & Social Psychology*, 1965, 2, 188–94.

Hetherington, E. M. The effects of familial variables on sex typing, on parent-child similarity, and on imitation in children. In J. P. Hill, ed., *Minnesota Symposia on Child Psychology*, vol. 1. Minneapolis: University of Minnesota Press, 1967.

*Hicks, D. J. Imitation and retention of film-mediated aggressive peer and adult models. *J. Personality & Social Psychology*, 1965, 2, 97–100.

Hoffman, L. W. Early childhood experiences and women's achievement motives. *J. Social Issues*, 1972, 28, 129–55.

*Honzik, M. P. Sex differences in the occurrence of materials in the play constructions of preadolescents. *Child Development*, 1951, 22, 15–35.

*Honzik, M. P. A sex difference in the age of onset of the parent-child resemblance in intelligence. *J. Educational Psychology*, 1963, 54, 231–37.

Honzik, M. P. Environmental correlates of mental growth: prediction from the family setting at 21 months. *Child Development*, 1967, 38, 337–64.

Horner, M. S. Sex differences in achievement motivation and performance in competitive and noncompetitive situations. Unpublished Ph.D. dissertation, University of Michigan, 1968.

*Hovland, C. I., and Janis, I. L., eds. *Personality and persuasibility.* New Haven: Yale University Press, 1959.

Hundleby, J. D., and Cattell, R. B. Personality structure in middle childhood and the prediction of school achievement and adjustment. *Monographs of the Society for Research in Child Development,* 1968, *33,* serial no. 121.

Hutt, C. *Males and females.* Middlesex, England: Penguin Books, 1972.

Jacklin, C. N., and Bonneville, L. The 9½-month-old infant: stability of behavior, sex differences, and longitudinal findings. Unpublished manuscript, Stanford University, 1974.

Jacklin, C. N., and Mischel, H. N. As the twig is bent—sex role stereotyping in early readers. *School Psychology Digest,* 1973, *2,* 30–37.

Jensen, G. D., Bobbitt, R. A., and Gordon, B. N. Sex differences in the development of independence of infant monkeys. *Behavior,* 1968, *30,* 1–14.

Johnson, D. D. Sex differences in reading across cultures. *Reading Research Quarterly,* 1973–74, *9,* 67–86.

Jones, S. E. A comparative proxemics analysis of dyadic interaction in selected subcultures of New York City. *J. Social Psychology,* 1971, *84,* 35–44.

Joslyn, W. D. Androgen-induced social dominance in infant female rhesus monkeys. *J. Child Psychology & Psychiatry,* 1973, *14,* 137–45.

*Kagan, J. The child's sex role classification of school objects. *Child Development,* 1964, *35,* 1051–56.

Kagan, J., and Kogan, N. Individuality and cognitive performance. In P. H. Mussen, ed., *Carmichael's manual of child psychology.* New York: Wiley, 1970.

*Kagan, J., and Lemkin, J. The child's differential perception of parental attributes. *J. Abnormal & Social Psychology,* 1960, *61,* 440–47.

Kagan, J., and Moss, H. A. Parental correlation of child's IQ and height: a cross-validation of the Berkeley Growth Study results. *Child Development,* 1959, *30,* 325–32.

*Kagan, J., and Moss, H. A. *Birth to maturity: a study in psychological development.* New York: Wiley, 1962.

Kaplan, A. R., and Fischer, R. Taste sensitivity for bitterness: some biological and clinical implications. In J. Wortis, ed., *Recent advances in biological psychiatry,* vol. 8. New York: Plenum Press, 1964.

Keating, D. P. The study of mathematically precocious youth. Paper presented at the meetings of the American Association for the Advancement of Science, Washington, D.C., 1972.

Kimura, D. Speech lateralization in young children as determined by an auditory test. *J. Comparative & Physiological Psychology,* 1963, *56,* 899–902.

Klaiber, E. L., Broverman, D. M., and Kobayashi, Y. The automatization cognitive style, androgens, and monoamine oxidase (MAO). *Psycholopharmacologia,* 1967, *11,* 320–36.

Klaiber, E. L., Broverman, D. M., Vogel, W., Abraham, G. E., and Cone, E. L. Effects of infused testosterone on mental performances and serum LH. *J. Clinical Endocrinology & Metabolism,* 1971, *32,* 341–49.

Kohlberg, L. Development of moral character and moral ideology. In M. L. Hoffman and L. W. Hoffman, eds., *Review of child development research,* vol. 1. New York: Russell Sage Foundation, 1964.

Kohlberg, L. A cognitive-developmental analysis of children's sex-role concepts and attitudes. In E. E. Maccoby, ed., *The development of sex differences*. Stanford, Calif.: Stanford University Press, 1966.

*Kohlberg, L., and Zigler, E. The impact of cognitive maturity on the development of sex-role attitudes in the years 4–8. *Genetic Psychology Monographs*, 1967, 75, 84–165.

*Kohn, A. R., and Fiedler, F. E. Age and sex differences in the perception of persons. *Sociometry*, 1961, 24, 157–64.

Konstadt, N., and Forman, E. Field dependence and external directedness. *J. Personality & Social Psychology*, 1965, 1, 490–93.

Kreuz, L. E., and Rose, R. M. Assessment of aggressive behavior and plasma testosterone in a young criminal population. *Psychosomatic Medicine*, 1972, 34, 321–32.

Kummer, H. Two variations in the social organization of baboons. In P. C. Jay, ed., *Primates—studies in adaptation and variability*. New York: Holt, Rinehart & Winston, 1968.

Kuo, Z. Y. *The dynamics of behavior development: an epigenetic view*. New York: Random House, 1967.

Lacey, J. I. Semantic response patterning and stress: some revisions of activation theory. In M. H. Appley and R. Turnbull, eds., *Psychological stress: some issues in research*. New York: Appleton-Century-Crofts, 1967.

Landreth, C. Factors associated with crying in young children in the nursery school and the home. *Child Development*, 1941, 12, 81–97.

Langlois, J. H., Gottfried, N. W., and Seay, B. The influence of sex of peer on the social behavior of preschool children. *Developmental Psychology*, 1973, 8, 93–98 (and personal communication).

*Lazowick, L. M. On the nature of identification. *J. Abnormal & Social Psychology*, 1955, 51, 175–83.

Leifer, A. D. The relationship between cognitive awareness in selected areas and differential imitation of a same-sex model. Unpublishd M.A. thesis, Stanford University, 1966.

Leifer, A. D. Effects of early, temporary mother-infant separation on later maternal behavior in humans. Unpublished Ph.D. dissertation, Stanford University, 1970.

Leifer, A. D., Leiderman, P. H., Barnett, C. R., and Williams, J. A. Effects of mother-infant separation on maternal attachment behavior. *Child Development*, 1972, 43, 1203–18.

Leik, R. K. Instrumentality and emotionality in family interaction. *Sociometry*, 1963, 26, 131–45.

Levine, S. Sex differences in the brain. *Scientific American*, 1966, 214, 84–90.

Levine, S. Sexual differentiation: the development of maleness and femaleness. *California Medicine*, 1971, 114, 12–17.

Levine, S., and Mullins, R. Estrogen administered neonatally affects adult sexual behavior in male and female rats. *Science*, 1964, 144, 185–87.

Levy-Agresti, J. Ipsilateral projection systems and minor hemisphere function in man after neocomissurotomy. *Anatomical Record*, 1968, 61, 1151.

Levi-Agresti, J., and Sperry, R. W. Differential perceptual capacities in major and minor hemispheres. Paper presented at fall meetings, National Academy of Sciences, California Institute of Technology, Pasadena. *Proceedings of the National Academy of Science*, 1968, 61.

*Lipsitt, L. P., and Levy, N. Electroactual threshold in the human neonate. *Child Development*, 1959, 30, 547–54.

Luchins, A. S. Mechanization in problem-solving—the effect of Einstellung. *Psychological Monographs*, 1942, *54*, no. 6.

Lunde, D. T. Sex hormones, mood and behavior. Paper presented at the Sixth Annual Symposium, Society of Medical Psychoanalysis, New York, 1973.

Lynn, D. B. *Parental and sex role identification: a theoretical formulation.* Berkeley, Calif.: McCutchan, 1969.

Lyon, M. F. Gene action in the X-chromosome of the mouse (*Mus musculus L.*) *Nature*, 1961, *190*, 372.

McCall, R. B., Appelbaum, M., and Hogarty, P. S. Developmental changes in mental performance. *Monographs of the Society for Research in Child Development*, 1973, *38*, serial no. 150.

McCarthy, D. Language development in children. In L. Carmichael, ed., *Manual of child psychology*, 2d ed. New York: Wiley, 1954.

*McClelland, D. C., Atkinson, J. W., Clark, R. A., and Lowell, E. L. *The achievement motive.* New York: Appleton-Century-Crofts, 1953.

McClintock, C. G. Game behavior and social motivation in interpersonal settings. In C. McClintock, ed., *Experimental social psychology.* New York: Holt, Rinehart & Winston, 1972.

McClintock, C. G., Messick, D. M., Kuhlman, D., and Campos, F. Assessing social motivation in a triple decomposed game. *J. Experimental Social Psychology*, 1973, in press.

Maccoby, E. E. Role-taking in childhood and its consequences for social learning. *Child Development*, 1959, *30*, 239–52.

Maccoby, E. E. Sex differences in intellectual functioning. In E. E. Maccoby, ed., *The development of sex differences.* Stanford, Calif.: Stanford University Press, 1966a.

Maccoby, E. E., ed. *The development of sex differences.* Stanford, Calif.: Stanford University Press, 1966b.

Maccoby, E. E. The development of stimulus selection. In J. P. Hill., ed., *Minnesota Symposium on Child Development*, 1969, *3*, 68–98.

Maccoby, E. E., and Jacklin, C. N. Sex differences and their implications for sex roles. Paper presented at the meetings of the American Psychological Association, Washington, D.C., 1971.

Maccoby, E. E., and Masters, J. C. Attachment and dependency. In P. H. Mussen, ed., *Carmichael's manual of child psychology*, vol. 2, 1970.

*Maccoby, E. E., and Wilson, W. C. Identification and observational learning from films. *J. Abnormal & Social Psychology*, 1957, *55*, 76–87.

*Maccoby, E. E., Wilson, W. C., and Burton, R. V. Differential movie-viewing behavior of male and female viewers. *J. Personality*, 1958, *26*, 259–67.

McDonnell, G. J., and Carpenter, J. A. Manifest anxiety and prestimulus conductance levels. *J. Abnormal & Social Psychology*, 1960, *60*, 437–38.

McKenzie, B. E. Visual discrimination in early infancy. Ph.D. dissertation, Monash University, Australia, 1972.

Marks, J. B. Interests and leadership among adolescents. *J. Genetic Psychology*, 1957, *91*, 163–72.

*Mellone, M. A. A factorial study of picture tests for young children. *British J. Psychology*, 1944, *35*, 9–16.

Messick, S., and Damarin, F. Cognitive styles and memory for faces. *J. Abnormal & Social Psychology*, 1964, *69*, 313–18.

Metzner, R., and Mischel, W. Achievement motivation, sex of subject, and delay behavior. Unpublished manuscript, Stanford University, 1962.

Miles, C. C. Gifted children. In L. Carmichael, ed., *Manual of child psychology*, 2d ed. New York: Wiley, 1954.

Minturn, L., and Hitchcock, J. T. The Pajputs of Khalapur, India. In B. B. Whiting, ed., *Six cultures*. New York: Wiley, 1963.

Mischel, H. Sex bias in the evaluation of professional achievements. *J. Educational Psychology*, 1974, 66, 157–66.

Mischel, W. Sex-typing and socialization. In P. H. Mussen, ed., *Carmichael's manual of child psychology*. New York: Wiley, 1970.

Mitchell, G. Attachment differences in male and female infant monkeys. *Child Development*, 1968, 39, 611–20.

Mitchell, G., and Brandt, E. M. Behavioral differences related to experience of mother and sex of infant in the rhesus monkey. *Developmental Psychology*, 1970, 3, 149.

Mitchell, G., and Brandt, E. M. Paternal behavior in primates. In F. E. Poirier, ed., *Primate socialization*. New York: Random House, 1972.

Moltz, H., Lubin, M., Leon, M., and Numan, M. Hormonal induction of maternal behavior in the ovariectomized rat. *Physiology & Behavior*, 1970, 5, 1373–77.

Money, J., and Ehrhardt, A. A. *Man and woman, boy and girl*. Baltimore: Johns Hopkins University Press, 1972.

Murray, H. A. Explorations in personality. New York: Oxford University Press, 1938.

Mussen, P. H. Early sex-role development. In D. A. Goslin, ed., *Handbook of socialization theory and research*. Chicago: Rand McNally, 1969.

*Mussen, P. H., and Rutherford, E. Parent-child relations and parental personality in relation to young children's sex-role preferences. *Child Development*, 1963, 34, 589–607.

*Nakamura, C. Y. Conformity and problem solving. *J. Abnormal & Social Psychology*, 1958, 56, 315–20.

Nerlove, S. B., Munroe, R. H., and Munroe, R. L. Effects of environmental experience on spatial ability: a replication. *J. Social Psychology*, 1971, 84, 3–10.

Notermans, S. L. H., and Tophoff, M. M. W. A. Sex differences in pain tolerance and pain apperception. *Psychiatria, Neurologia, Neurochirurgia*, 1967, 70, 23–29.

Osofsky, J. D., and Oldfield, S. Children's effects upon parental behavior: mothers' and fathers' responses to dependent and independent child behaviors (summary). *Proceedings of the 79th Annual Convention of the American Psychological Association*, Washington, D. C., 1971.

Parke, R., and O'Leary, S. Mother-father-infant interaction in the newborn period: some findings, some observations, and some unresolved issues. In K. Riegel and J. Meacham, Determinants of behavioral development, II, 1974 (in press).

Parlee, M. B. Comments on D. M. Broverman, E. L. Klaiber, Y. Kobayashi, and W. Vogel: Roles of activation and inhibition in sex differences in cognitive abilities. *Psychological Review*, 1972, 79, 180–84.

Parsons, T. The American family: its relations to personality and to the social structure. In T. Parsons and R. F. Bales, eds., *Family, socialization and interaction process*. New York: Free Press, 1955.

Patterson, G. R., Littman, R. A., and Bricker, W. Assertive behavior in children: a step toward a theory of aggression. *Monographs of the Society for Research in Child Development*, 1967, 32, serial no. 113.

Patterson, P., Bonvillian, J. D., Reynolds, P.C., and Maccoby, E. E. Mother and peer attachment under conditions of fear in rhesus monkeys. *Primates*, 1974, in press.

Peplau, A. Impact of sex-role attitudes and opposite-sex relationships on women's achievement: an experimental study of dating couples. Ph.D. dissertation, preliminary report, Harvard University, 1973.

Podell, J. E., and Phillips, L. A developmental analysis of cognition as observed in dimensions of Rorschach and objective test performance. *J. Personality*, 1959, 27, 439–63.

Polansky, N., Lippitt, R., and Redl, F. An investigation of behavioral contagion in groups. *Human Relations*, 1950, 3, 319–48.

Preston, D. G., Baker, R. P., and Seay, B. Mother-infant separation in the patus monkey. *Developmental Psychology*, 1970, 3, 298–306.

*Rabban, M. Sex-role identification in young children in two diverse social groups. *Genetic Psychology Monographs*, 1950, 42, 81–158.

Ramey, C. T., and Watson, J. S. Nonsocial reinforcement of infant's vocalizations. *Developmental Psychology*, 1972, 6, 538 (extended version of brief report).

Raphelson, A. C. The relationships among imagination: direct, verbal, and physiological measures of anxiety in an achievement stimulus. *J. Abnormal & Social Psychology*, 1957, 54, 13–18.

Raush, H. R. Interaction sequences. *J. Personality & Social Psychology*, 1965, 2, 487–99.

Rescorla, R. A. Pavlovian conditioning and its proper control procedures. *Psychological Review*, 1967, 74, 71–80.

Rescorla, R. A. Pavlovian conditioned inhibition. *Psychological Bulletin*, 1969, 72, 77–94.

Reynolds, V., and Reynolds, F. Chimpanzees of the Budongo Forest. In I. Devore, ed., *Primate behavior*. New York: Holt, Rinehart & Winston, 1965.

Roff, M. Intra-family resemblances in personality characteristics. *J. Psychology*, 1950, 30, 199–227.

Rose, R. M., Holaday, J. W., and Bernstein, I. S. Plasma testosterone, dominance rank, and aggressive behavior in male rhesus monkeys. *Nature*, 1971, 231, 366–68.

Rose, R. M., Gordon, T. P., and Bernstein, I. S. Plasma testosterone levels in the male rhesus: influences of sexual and social stimuli. *Science*, 1972, 178, 643–45.

Rosenberg, B. G., and Sutton-Smith, B. Family interaction effects on masculinity-femininity. *J. Personality & Social Psychology*, 1968, 8, 117.

Rosenberg, K. M., Denenberg, V. H., Zarrow, M. X., and Bonnie, L. F. Effects of neonatal castration and testosterone on the rat's pup-killing behavior and activity. *Physiology & Behavior*, 1971, 7, 363–68.

Rosenblatt, J. S. The development of maternal responsiveness in the rat. *American J. Orthopsychiatry*, 1969, 39 (1), 36–56.

*Rosenblith, J. F. Learning by imitation in kindergarten children. *Child Development*, 1959, 30, 69–80.

*Rosenblith, J. F. Imitative color choices in kindergarten children. *Child Development*, 1961, 32, 211–23.

Rosenkrantz, P. S., Vogel, S. R., Bee, H., Broverman, I., and Broverman, D. Sex-role stereotypes and self-concepts in college students. *J. Consulting & Clinical Psychology*, 1968, 32, 287–95.

Rosenthal, M. K. The generalization of dependency behavior from mother to stranger. *J. Child Psychology & Psychiatry*, 1967, *8*, 117–33.

Rosner, J. A. The development and validation of an individualized perceptual skills curriculum. University of Pittsburgh, Learning Research and Development Center, 1973.

Rossi, A. M. An evaluation of the manifest anxiety scale by the use of electromyography. *J. Experimental Psychology*, 1959, *58*, 64–69.

*Rothaus, P., and Worchel, P. Ego-support, communication, catharsis, and hostility. *J. Personality*, 1964, *32*, 296–312.

*Rothbart, M. K., and Maccoby, E. E. Parents' differential reactions to sons and daughters. *J. Personality & Social Psychology*, 1966, *4*, 237–43.

Sackett, G. P. Isolation rearing in monkeys: diffuse and specific effects on later behavior. Unpublished manuscript, University of Washington, 1971.

Sander, L. W., and Cassel, T. Z. An empirical approach to the study of interactive regulation in the infant-caretaking system and its role in early development. Paper presented at the meetings of the Society for Research in Child Development, Philadelphia, 1973.

*Sarason, S. B., Lighthall, F. F., Davidson, K. S., Waite, R. R., and Ruebush, B. K. *Anxiety in elementary school children*. New York: Wiley, 1960.

Sarason, S. B., Hill, D. T., and Zimbardo, P. G. A longitudinal study of the relation of test anxiety to performance on intelligence and achievement tests. *Monographs of the Society for Research in Child Development*, 1964, *29*, serial no. 98.

Schachter, S. *Psychology of affiliation*. Stanford, Calif.: Stanford University Press, 1959.

*Schaefer, E. S., and Bayley, N. Maternal behavior, child behavior, and their intercorrelations from infancy through adolescence. *Monographs of the Society for Research in Child Development*, 1963, *28*, serial no. 87.

Schaller, J. Children's attitudes to newcomers. *Goteborg Psychological Reports*, 1973, *3*, 1–6.

Schneider, R. A., and Wolf, S. Olfactory perception thresholds for citral utilizing a new type olfactorium. *J. Applied Physiology*, 1955, *8*, 337–42.

Sears, P. S. The effect of classroom conditions on the strength of achievement motive and work output on elementary school children. Cooperative Research Project no. OE 873. Stanford University, 1963.

*Sears, R. R. Relation of early socialization experiences to aggression in middle childhood. *J. Abnormal & Social Psychology*, 1961, *63*, 466–92.

Sears, R. R. Development of gender role. In F. A. Beach, ed., *Sex and behavior*. New York: Wiley, 1965.

*Sears, R. R., Whiting, J., Nowlis, V., and Sears, P. S. Some child rearing antecedents of aggression and dependency in young children. *Genetic Psychology Monographs*, 1953, *47*, 135–234.

*Sears, R. R., Maccoby, E. E., and Levin, H. *Patterns of child rearing*. Evanston, Ill.: Row, Peterson, 1957.

*Sears, R. R., Rau, L., and Alpert, R. *Identification and child rearing*. Stanford, Calif.: Stanford University Press, 1965.

Seligman, M. E. P. On the generality of the laws of learning. *Psychological Review*, 1970, *77* (5), 406–18.

Sherman, J. A. Problem of sex differences in space perception and aspects of intellectual functioning. *Psychological Review*, 1967, *74*, 290–99.

Sherman, J. A. *On the psychology of women*. Springfield, Ill.: Charles C Thomas, 1971.

Shipman, V. C. Disadvantaged children and their first school experiences. Educational Testing Service, Head Start Longitudinal Study, 1972, Report PR-72-18, Princeton, N.J.

*Shirley, M., and Poyntz, L. The influence of separation from the mother on children's emotional responses. *J. Psychology*, 1941, *12*, 251–82.

Silverman, R. E. Manifest anxiety as a measure of drive. *J. Abnormal & Social Psychology*, 1957, *55*, 94–97.

*Simpson, M. Parent preferences of young children. *Contributions to Education* (Columbia University Teachers College), no. 652, 1935.

Singer, J. E., Westphal, M., and Niswander, K. R. Sex differences in the incidence of neonatal abnormalities and abnormal performance in early childhood. *Child Development*, 1968, *39*, 103–12.

Smith, I. M. *Spatial ability*. San Diego, Calif.: Knapp, 1964.

Smith, W. D. Black parents' differential attitudes toward childhood behaviors and child-rearing practices. Unpublished first year project, Stanford University, 1971.

Spence, K. W., and Spence, J. T. Sex and anxiety differences in eyelid conditioning. *Psychological Bulletin*, 1966, *65*, 137–42.

Stanley, J. C., Fox, L. H., and Keating, D. P. *Annual report to the Spencer Foundation*, The Johns Hopkins University, October 1972.

Stanton, A. M. Hormones and behavior in newborns: biochemical factors in the development of behavioral sex differences. Unpublished manuscript, Stanford University, 1972.

*Steiner, I. D., and Rogers, E. D. Alternative responses to dissonance. *J. Abnormal & Social Psychology*, 1963, *66*, 128–36.

Sternglanz, S. B. An ethological approach to neonatal quieting. Unpublished Ph.D. dissertation, Stanford University, 1972.

Stevenson, H. W. Learning in children. In P. H. Mussen, ed., *Carmichael's manual of child psychology*. New York: Wiley, 1970.

Strodtbeck, F. L., and Mann, R. D. Sex role differentiation in jury deliberations. *Sociometry*, 1956, *19*, 3–11.

Stroop, J. R. Studies of interference in serial verbal reactions. *J. Experimental Psychology*, 1935, *6*, 643–62.

*Sweeney, E. J. Sex differences in problem solving. Unpublished Ph.D. dissertation, Stanford University, 1953.

*Tasch, R. J. The role of the father in the family. *J. Experimental Education*, 1952, *20*, 319–61.

*Templin, M. C. *Certain language skills in children—their development and interrelationships*. Institute of Child Welfare Monograph no. 26. Minneapolis: University of Minnesota Press, 1957.

*Terman, L. M., and Tyler, L. E. Psychological sex differences. In L. Carmichael, ed., *Manual of child psychology*, 2d ed. New York: Wiley, 1954.

*Terman, L. M., et al. *Genetic studies of genius*. I: *Mental and physical traits of a thousand gifted children*. Stanford, Calif.: Stanford University Press, 1925.

Thompson, W. R. The inheritance of behaviour: behavioural differences in 15 mouse strains. *Canadian J. Psychology*, 1953, 7 (4), 145–55.

Thurstone, L. L. *A factorial study of perception*. Chicago: University of Chicago Press, 1944.

Troll, L. E., Neugarten, B. L., and Kraines, R. J. Similarities in values and other personality characteristics in college students and their parents. *Merrill-Palmer Quarterly*, 1969, *15*, 323–36.

*Vance, T. F., and McCall, L. T. Children's preferences among play materials as determined by the method of paired comparisons of pictures. *Child Development*, 1934, 5, 267–77.

Vandenberg, S. G. Twin data in support of the Lyon hypothesis. *Nature*, 1962, *194*, 505–6.

Vandenberg, S. G. Primary mental abilities or general intelligence? Evidence from twin studies. In J. M. Thoday and A. S. Parkes, *Genetic and environmental influences on behavior*. New York: Plenum Press, 1968.

Van Lieshout, C. F. M. Reactions of young children to barriers placed by their mothers. Unpublished manuscript, Stanford University, 1974.

Veroff, J., Wilcox, S., and Atkinson, J. W. The achievement motive in high school and college age women. *J. Abnormal & Social Psychology*, 1953, *48*, 108–19.

Waldrop, M. F., and Halverson, C. F., Jr. Intensive and extensive peer behavior: longitudinal and cross-sectional analyses. Unpublished manuscript, Child Research Branch, National Institute of Mental Health, Washington, D. C., 1973.

Wallach, M. A. Creativity. In P. H. Mussen, ed., *Carmichael's manual of child psychology*. New York: Wiley, 1970.

Wallach, M. A., and Kogan, N. *Modes of thinking in young children*. New York: Holt, Rinehart & Winston, 1965.

Ward, W. C. Development of self-regulatory behaviors. ETS Head Start Longitudinal Study, 1973, Report PR-73-18, Educational Testing Service, Princeton, N.J.

Werdelin, I. *The mathematical ability*. Lund, Sweden: CWK Gleerup, 1958.

Werdelin, I. *Geometrical ability and the space factors in boys and girls*. Lund Studies in Psychology and Education. Lund, Sweden: CWK Gleerup, 1961.

White, S. H. Evidence for hierarchical arrangement of learning processes. In L. P. Lipsitt and C. C. Spiker, eds., *Advances in child development and behavior*, vol. 2. New York: Academic Press, 1965.

*White House Conference on Child Health and Protection, Section III. *The young child in the home. A survey of 3,000 American families*. New York: Appleton-Century, 1936.

Whiting, B. B., ed. *Six cultures*. New York: Wiley, 1963.

Wild, J. M., and Hughes, R. N. Effects of postweaning handling on locomotor and exploratory behavior in young rats. *Developmental Psychology*, 1972, 7, 76–79.

Williams, K. Father-child interaction in cooperation and competition with preschool children. Honors thesis, Stanford University, 1973.

*Witkin, H. A., Dyk, R. B., Faterson, H. F., Goodenough, D. R., and Karp, S. A. *Psychological differentiation*. New York: Wiley, 1962.

*Witryol, S. L., and Kaess, W. A. Sex differences in social memory tasks. *J. Abnormal & Social Psychology*, 1957, 54, 343–46.

Wolfe, D. M. Power and authority in the family. In D. P. Cartwright, ed., *Studies in social power*. Ann Arbor: University of Michigan Press, 1959.

Wolff, P. H. Observations on newborn infants. *Psychosomatic Medicine*, 1959, *21*, 110–18.

Wood-Gush, D. G. M. A study of sex drive of two strains of cockerels through three generations. *Animal Behavior*, 1960, *8*, 43–53.

Woodrow, R. M., Friedman, G. D., Siegelaub, A. B., and Collen, M. F. Pain tolerance: differences according to age, sex, and race. *Psychosomatic Medicine*, 1972, *34*, 548–56.

Woolf, V. *A room of one's own.* New York: Harcourt, Brace & World, 1929.

Work, M. S., and Rogers, H. Effect of estrogen on food-seeking dominance among male rats. *J. Comparative & Physiological Psychology,* 1972, 79, 414–18.

Young, W. C., Goy, R. W., and Phoenix, C. H. Hormones and sexual behavior. *Science,* 1964, *143,* 212–18.

Zucker, I. Hormonal determinants of sex differences in saccharin preference, food intake and body weight. *Physiology & Behavior,* 1969, *4,* 595–602.

Zuckerman, N., Baer, M., and Monachkin, I. Acceptance of self, parents, and people in patients and normals. *J. Clinical Psychology,* 1956, *12,* 327–32.

*Zunich, M. Children's reactions to failure. *J. Genetic Psychology,* 1964, *104,* 19–24.

Annotated Bibliography

Annotated Bibliography

Works cited in the text (or in the summary tables), excluding works
bearing the superscript letter R, are listed here. Works bearing
the superscript are listed in References Cited, pp. 377–91.
The distinction is explained in the Introduction, p. 8.

Some of the entries in this bibliography are not included
in the summary tables or treated in the corresponding text.
The nature of these entries is explained in the Introduction, p. 10.

Ables, B. The three wishes of latency age children. *Developmental Psychology*, 1972, 6,
186 (brief report and extended unpublished report).
>Subjects: $N = 128$; 7–12 yrs. Measures: Each S was asked what he would wish for if he had
>3 wishes. Results: (1) Girls more often than boys wished for another person. (2) Boys more
>often than girls wished for material possessions and money. (3) There were no sex differences
>in percentage of wishes relating to pets, activities, personal, miscellaneous, or more wishes.

Abney, C. W. A comparative study of creative thinking ability in three student groups
at the University of Arkansas as measured by the Remote Associations Test. *Dissertation
Abstracts International*, 1970, 30, 2717a.
>Subjects: $N = 168$; 18–21 yrs (college). Measures: The Remote Associations Test (RAT)
>was administered to 3 groups: honors students, students with comparable grade-point aver-
>ages (GPA), and a control group with lower GPA's. Results: In the honors group, women
>scored higher than men on the RAT.

Abravanel, E. The development of intersensory patterning with regard to selected spatial
dimensions. *Monographs of the Society for Research in Child Development*, 1968, 33.
>Subjects: $N = 200$; 3–14 yrs. Measures: (1) After handling, but not looking at, wooden bars
>of varying sizes, Ss estimated the length of each bar on a measuring tape. (2) Ss tried to
>adjust 2 unseen brass rings to equal the distance marked off on a visually perceived rod. (3)
>After touching, but not looking at, grooves of varying lengths cut into masonite, Ss estimated
>the length of each on a measuring tape. (4) Tactile stimulation was applied at 2 distinct
>points along Ss' forearms. Ss estimated the distance between the 2 points on a measuring
>tape. (5) Ss touched, but did not look at, lines of tacks of standard lengths driven into a
>wooden board. Following each presentation Ss viewed 2 lines constructed in a similar man-
>ner. Ss judged which of the 2 lines was equal in length to the standard. (6) After looking
>at, but not touching, a standard cylinder, Ss handled 2 other cylinders, 1 of which was equal
>in size to the standard. Ss' task was to pick out the matching cylinder. Results: Among 4-
>and 12-14-year-old Ss, girls showed greater accuracy on tasks 2 and 6 than boys. Among 7-,
>8-, and 9-year-old Ss, girls showed greater accuracy on task 4 than boys.

Achenbach, T. M. Cue learning, associative responding, and school performance in children. *Developmental Psychology*, 1969, 1, 717–25.
>In 3 experiments, multiple-choice analogy tests were administered in which half the items
>had incorrect alternative words with high-frequency associations as the third word of the
>analogy ("foils") whereas the correct alternative was a low-frequency associate. For the
>other half of the items, the third word of the analogy had no high-frequency associates. D
>scores equal the difference between the number of "foil" responses made by S and the num-
>ber of his "nonfoil" errors.
>EXPERIMENT I: Subjects: $N = 191$; 10 yrs. Measures: E administered a 50-item analogy
>test to all Ss. Teachers rated each S on intellectual independence and learning effectiveness.
>Two weeks later, the 10 highest and 10 lowest D scorers of each sex were individually tested
>on the Matching Familiar Figures test and on a discrimination-learning task (cues provided at
>increasing intervals after each trial began). Results: No sex differences.
>EXPERIMENT II: Subjects: $N = 159$; 10, 11 yrs. Measures: E administered a 54-item anal-

ogy test to all Ss. Teachers rated each S on learning effectiveness and physical activity. The 16 highest and 16 lowest D scorers were assigned to groups by sex, grade, D score, and type of learning task. Two versions of discrimination learning task were administered: (1) same as Experiment I with randomized cues presented, and (2) delayed cues presented with only correct responses being cued. Information and Vocabulary subjects of the Weschler Intelligence Scale for Children (WISC) were administered to each S. **Results:** Among 10-year-old Ss boys were rated more physically active than girls. No other sex differences in traits, learning task, or cognitive tests were found.

EXPERIMENT III: **Subjects:** $N = 164$; 11 yrs. **Measures:** E administered a 68-item analogy test to all Ss. Teachers rated each S on learning effectiveness and physical activity. The 24 highest and 24 lowest D scorers were assigned to groups by sex, D score, and learning condition. Learning conditions varied by delayed cue format (Experiment II) and control condition (no cue provided). Information and vocabulary subtests of the WISC and the Matching Familiar Figures test preceded the learning task. **Results:** Girls performed better than boys on the WISC vocabulary subtest.

Achenbach, T. M. Standardization of a research instrument for identifying associative responding in children. *Developmental Psychology*, 1970, 2, 283–91.
  Subjects: $N = 1,085$; 10–13 yrs. **Measures:** Ss completed a multiple-choice analogy Children's Associative Responding Test. Half of the items had an incorrect response alternative (foil) that was a frequent association to the third word of the analogy. The other half had no alternatives that were frequent associations. Associative responding was measured by foil minus nonfoil errors (D score). **Results:** (1) Among 11- and 12-year-old Ss, boys made more nonfoil errors than girls. (2) Among 10- and 11-year-old Ss, girls had higher achievement test percentiles than boys. (3) Girls had higher IQs and grade averages than boys at all ages. (4) There were no sex differences in analogy errors or foil errors at any age. (5) Among 12-year-old Ss, girls had higher D scores than boys.

Achenbach, T. M. The Children's Associative Responding Test: a two-year follow up. *Developmental Psychology*, 1971, 5, 477–83.
  Subjects: $N = 561$; 12, 13 yrs. **Measures:** Otis-Beta IQ scores, SRA achievement scores, and grade-point averages were obtained from school records. **Results:** No sex differences.

Achenbach, T. M., and Zigler, E. Cue-learning and problem learning strategies in normal and retarded children. *Child Development*, 1968, 39, 827–48.
  EXPERIMENT I: **Subjects:** $N = 120$; 7, 9 yrs (normals), 12–13, 17–18 yrs (noninstitutionalized retardates), 20–21, 25–26 yrs (institutionalized retardates). **Measures:** On each trial of a discrimination-learning task, Ss were presented with 3 squares that varied in color and size. Ss' task was to determine which of the 3 squares was "correct." Ss were assigned to 1 of 2 conditions. In the experimental condition, a light went on above the correct square after a short interval of time. As the experiment progressed, this interval became longer. The criterion of learning for Ss in this group was correct responses on 5 consecutive trials before the onset of the light. The learning criterion for Ss in the control condition (no light cue) was 5 successively correct choices within the time limit imposed on Ss in the experimental condition. **Results:** No sex differences.
  EXPERIMENT II: **Subjects:** $N = 120$; 7, 11–12 yrs (normals, noninstitutionalized retardates). **Measures:** Similar to Experiment I. **Results:** No sex differences.

Adams, W. V. Strategy differences between reflective and impulsive children. *Child Development*, 1972, 43, 1076–80.
  Subjects: $N = 80$; 6, 8 yrs. **Measures:** Impulsive and reflective Ss (as determined by the Matching Familiar Figures test) performed a 3-choice learning task using a marble game apparatus. Correct choices were randomly rewarded 33% of the time. Perseveration and 3 kinds of pattern guessing strategies were analyzed. **Results:** No sex differences.

Aiello, J. R., and Jones, S. E. Field study of the proxemic behavior of young school children in three subcultural groups. *J. Personality & Social Psychology*, 1971, 19, 351–56.
  Subjects: $N = 420$; 6–8 yrs (white, black, Puerto Rican). **Measures:** Dyadic interactions during recess periods and lunch hours were observed. Each pair of Ss engaged in verbal interaction and were relatively stationary. The distance apart (inches) and axis of orientation (directness of shoulder orientation) were measured. **Results:** (1) Among white Ss, boys stood farther apart than girls did. (2) Overall axis scores combining all cultures showed that girls were less direct in orientation than boys. However, no sex differences were found within cultures.

Akamatsu, T. J., and Thelen, M. H. The acquisition and performance of a socially neutral response as a function of vicarious reward. *Developmental Psychology*, 1971, 5, 440–45.
  Subjects: $N = 48$; 7–8 yrs. **Measures:** Ss viewed a videotaped adult male model pressing a button, with either predetermined verbal reward or no reward. They were then given the same task with the same instructions as the model, but with no reward (performance measure). Ss were asked to show everything they could remember about the way the man played, and were praised for correct responses (acquisition measure). **Results:** No sex differences.

Alderman, D. Effects of anticipating future interaction on the preference for balanced states. *J. Personality & Social Psychology*, 1969, 11, 214–19.
  Subjects: $N = 268$; 18–21 yrs (college). **Measures:** Ss rated each of 8 hypothetical situations involving themselves, another person, and an impersonal entity for experienced pleasantness or unpleasantness. **Results:** No sex differences.

Ali, F., and Costello, J. Modification of the Peabody Picture Vocabulary Test. *Developmental Psychology*, 1971, 5, 86–91.
  Subjects: $N = 108$; 4–5 yrs (black, low SES). **Measures:** Two comparable samples were given the PPVT and a modified version of the PPVT (MPPVT) that was designed to identify and modify aspects having adverse effects on disadvantaged preschoolers' performances. **Results:** No sex differences.

Allaman, J. D., Joyce, C. S., and Crandall, V. C. The antecedents of social desirability response tendencies of children and young adults. *Child Development*, 1972, 43, 1135–60.
  EXPERIMENT I: **Subjects:** $N = 95$; tested at 0–80 mos and 6–10 yrs, and their mothers and fathers. **Measures:** (1) Until Ss reached 80 months of age, semiannual home observations were made of their mothers' behavior toward them. Mothers were rated on the following bipolar scales: Affectionateness: hostility-affection; Direction of Criticism: criticism-praise; Restrictiveness: permissive-restrictive; Severity of Punishment: mild-severe; Coerciveness of Suggestions: optional-mandatory; Acceleration Attempts: retardatory-acceleratory. The amount of praise or criticism Ss received for intellectual performance was also recorded. (2) Standards held by mother and father for intellectual performance were assessed from their responses to a questionnaire. (3) When Ss were between 6 and 12 years of age, they completed the Children's Social Desirability Scale. **Results:** (1) No differences were found between mothers of boys and mothers of girls. (2) There were no sex differences in standards held by mothers or fathers for intellectual performance. (3) Younger girls (6–9½ yrs) had higher CSD scores than younger boys ($p < .05$). No sex difference was found among older Ss.
  EXPERIMENT II: **Subjects:** $N = 65$; tested at 0–40 mos, 41–80 mos, 80 mos–10 yrs, 18–26 yrs, and their mothers. **Measures:** (1) Until Ss were 10 years old, home observations were made of them and their mothers; 7 scales were used to rate mothers' behavior: Affectionateness, Direction of Criticism, Restrictiveness, Severity of Punishment, Coerciveness of Suggestions, Acceleration Attempts, and Intensity of Contact (indifference–high involvement). (2) When they were between 18 and 26 years of age, Ss were measured on the Marlowe-Crowne Social Desirability Scale. **Results:** (1) During each of the 3 age periods (0–40 mos, 41–80 mos, and 80 mos–10 yrs), no differences were found between mothers of boys and mothers of girls. (2) No sex differences were found in Ss' MC-SD scores.

Allen, C. N. Individual differences in delayed reaction of infants. *Archives of Psychology*, 1931, 19, 1–40.
  Subjects: $N = 100$; 1 yr and mothers. **Measures:** S sat on his mother's lap while a desired toy was hidden in one of 3 small boxes placed on a table before him. The table was withdrawn far enough to place the boxes out of S's reach (distraction technique). After measured time intervals of 10, 20, 30, 45, and 60 seconds, the table was pushed back toward S. Speed of reaction was recorded. **Results:** No sex differences.

Allen, M. K., and Liebert, R. M. Effects of live and symbolic deviant modeling cues on adoption of a previously learned standard. *J. Personality & Social Psychology*, 1969, 11, 253–60.
  EXPERIMENT I: **Subjects:** $N = 24$; 8–9 yrs. **Measures:** After receiving instructions from E to use a stringent self-reward standard when playing a bowling game, Ss were exposed to a lenient model. The performance measure was Ss' subsequent self-rewarding behavior. **Results:** No sex differences.
  EXPERIMENT II: **Subjects:** $N = 32$; 7–9 yrs. **Measures:** Same as Experiment I, with Ss also exposed to a stringent model. **Results:** No sex differences.

Allen, S. A., Spear, P. S., and Johnson, J. Experimenter role effects on children's task performance and perception. *Child Development*, 1970, *40*, 1–9.
Subjects: $N = 256$; 10, 11 yrs. Measures: Ss played a marble-sorting game with either a warm or cold, male or female E. After a baseline period of 1 minute, Ss were verbally reinforced by E for a period of 6 minutes. Reinforcement was delivered on a fixed-interval schedule. Measures were taken of the number of marbles Ss sorted. Difference scores were also obtained (number of marbles sorted during each minute of reinforcement minus Ss' baseline rate of responding). Afterward, Ss were asked to describe E, using 23 pairs of bipolar adjectives. Results: (1) Boys and girls did not differ in their performances in the marble-dropping task. (2) Boys perceived Es as more masculine than did girls.

Allen, S. A., Spear, P. S., and Lucke, J. R. Effects of social reinforcement on learning and retention in children. *Developmental Psychology*, 1971, *5*, 73–80.
Subjects: $N = 192$; 6–7, 10–11 yrs. Measures: Ss were given either easy or difficult 2-choice simultaneous discrimination tasks under 1 of 3 reinforcement conditions—approval, disapproval, or silence. Retention was measured 8 days later. Results: There were no sex differences in response latency, total number of trials, or total task time.

Allen, V. L., and Newtson, D. Development of conformity and independence. *J. Personality & Social Psychology*, 1972, *22*, 18–30.
Subjects: $N = 366$; 6, 9, 12, 15 yrs. Measures: Ss were assigned to 1 of 3 conditions in an Asch-type conformity experiment—unanimous group, social support, and adult pressure. 3 types of stimuli were used: visual judgments, opinion statements, and delay of gratification preferences. For each S, a mean conformity score was calculated for each of the 3 types of stimuli. Results: No main sex differences.

Amatora, M. Comparisons in personality self-evaluation. *J. Social Psychology*, 1955, *42*, 315–21.
Subjects: $N = 1,000$; 9–13 yrs. Measures: Ss rated themselves on the Child Personality Scales. Results: Girls evaluated themselves more favorably than boys did on all but 3 scales.

Ammons, R. B., and Ammons, H. S. Parent preferences in young children's doll-play. *J. Abnormal & Social Psychology*, 1949, *44*, 490–505.
Subjects: $N = 48$; 3–5 yrs. Measures: Ss were asked parental preference during free play. In the doll-play measure, E had a child doll (same sex as S) go through actions of S's daily routine. S was repeatedly asked which parent he wanted to help him or to do things with him. Mother and father dolls were equally rewarding and punishing. S was observed during free play with dolls and then questioned on preference. The session was repeated a few days later. Parents were questioned about participation in activities with the child. Results: Overall, girls showed a preference for their mothers, boys showed a preference for their fathers. When separate age analyses were done, the difference between the sexes was found to be significant only among 4-year-olds.

Amster, H., and Wiegand, V. Developmental study of sex differences in free recall. *Proceedings*, 80th Annual Convention, American Psychological Association, 1972.
Subjects: $N = 64$; 7, 11 yrs. Measures: Ss heard, saw, and repeated words from 2 36-item lists, sorting each word card without regard to meaningful grouping on first 2 sorting trials. They were given either categorizing or sequential (no meaningful grouping) sorting instructions for the third trial, and categorizing for the fourth. Free recall was tested after the first 3 trials and after the fourth. Results: (1) There were no sex differences in the first recall. (2) Girls showed higher overall recall than boys.

Anders, T. R., Fozard, J. L., and Lillyquist, T. D. Effects of age upon retrieval from short-term memory. *Developmental Psychology*, 1972, *6*, 214–17.
Subjects: $N = 10$; 19–21 yrs. Measures: Ss saw a short list of visually presented digits (containing 1, 3, 5, or 7 items) 1 at a time, with instructions to memorize. Then Ss were presented with test digits and were asked to decide whether or not each digit had appeared in the previous list. Results: No sex differences in response latency.

Anderson, H. H. Domination and integration in the social behavior of young children in an experimental play situation. *Genetic Psychology Monographs*, 1937, *19*, 341–408.
Subjects: $N = 128$; 2–6 yrs (65 of the children were from an orphanage; 34 attended nursery school, 31 did not. These 31 Ss constituted the control group). Measures: Ss were taken in same-sex or opposite-sex pairs to a testing room where they were allowed to play for 5 min-

utes. Dominance behaviors (e.g. verbal demands or forceful attempts to secure materials from partner, verbal commands or forceful attempts to direct partner's behavior, etc.) and integrative behaviors (e.g. verbal requests to secure materials or direct partner's behavior, suggestions, attempts to share or participate in partner's activity, etc.) were recorded. **Results:** (1) Girls exhibited more dominance behaviors and fewer integrative behaviors than boys. (2) Among orphanage Ss, girl-girl (GG) pairs were more dominative than boy-boy (BB) pairs (for nursery school Ss, $p < .01$; for control Ss, NS). No differences were found between boys in BG pairs and girls in GB pairs. Differences in integration scores between boys in BB pairs and girls in GG pairs or between boys in BG pairs and girls in GB pairs were also not significant. (3) No detailed analysis was made of the data from the nonorphanage sample.

Anderson, H. H. Domination and integration in the behavior of kindergarten children in an experimental play situation. *J. Experimental Education*, 1939, *8*, 123–31.
> **Subjects:** $N = 38$; 5 yrs. **Measures:** Ss in same-sex and opposite-sex pairs were observed in play for 5-minute periods. Ss were scored for dominance and integration. **Results:** (1) Boys in boy-boy (BB) pairs exhibited more dominance behaviors than girls in girl-girl (GG) pairs. Boys in BG pairs exhibited more dominance behaviors than girls in GG pairs. Girls in GB pairs exhibited more dominance behaviors than girls in GG pairs. (2) There were no differences between boys in BB pairs and boys in BG pairs, boys in BB pairs and girls in GB pairs, or boys in BG pairs and girls in GB pairs. (3) No sex differences were found in number of integrative behaviors displayed.

Anyan, W. R., Jr., and Quillian, W. W., II. The naming of primary colors by children. *Child Development*, 1971, *42*, 1629–32.
> **Subjects:** $N = 605$; 1–8 yrs. **Measures:** Ss were asked to (a) name colors presented on cards and (b) to copy several simple figures. **Results:** (1) Among 4-5-year-old Ss, girls named yellow more accurately than boys ($p < .025$). Among 5-6-year-old Ss, girls named each color more accurately than boys (red, $p < .001$; blue, $p < .001$; yellow, $p < .005$). (2) There were no sex differences in figure copying.

Appel, L. F., Cooper, R. G., McCarrell, N., Sims-Knight, J., Yussen, S. R., and Flavell, J. H. The development of the distinction between perceiving and memorizing. *Child Development*, 1972, *43*, 1365–81.
> **Subjects:** $N = 100$; 4, 7, 11 yrs. **Measures:** Ss looked at colored stimulus drawings and were asked to remember the names of pictures, under different conditions. During 1.5 minutes of each task, Ss' behavior was observed. A recall test was administered after each task. **Results:** (1) Among 7-year-old Ss, girls recalled more than boys ($p < .01$). (2) There were no sex differences among 4- and 11-year-old-Ss.

Argyle, M., and Dean, J. Eye-contact, distance, and affiliation. *Sociometry*, 1965, *28*, 289–304.
> **Subjects:** $N = 24$; 22–26 yrs (graduate students). **Measures:** Ss individually discussed TAT cards with confederates at different conversational distances. Confederates were instructed to gaze continually at Ss. The response variables were amount of eye contact and average length of each glance. **Results:** (1) No sex differences were found in amount of eye contact or length of glance. (2) Less eye contact was observed between mixed-sex confederate-S pairs; the difference was most marked at the shortest conversational distance ($p < .001$).

Arkoff, A., Meredith, G., and Iwahara, S. Dominance-deference patterning in Motherland-Japanese, Japanese-American, and Caucasian American students. *J. Social Psychology*, 1962, *58*, 61–66.
> **Subjects:** $N = 252$; 18–21 yrs (college). **Measures:** A dominance-deference scale, consisting of 10 dominance and 10 deference items, was administered. Ss were instructed to select the 10 items that best described themselves. The response measure was the number of dominance items chosen. **Results:** Among Caucasian American and Japanese Ss, men scored higher than women ($p < .01$, $p < .05$). No sex differences were found among Japanese-American Ss.

Armentrout, J. A., and Burger, G. K. Children's reports of parental child-rearing behavior at five grade levels. *Developmental Psychology*, 1972, *7*, 44–48.
> **Subjects:** $N = 635$; 9–13 yrs (low SES). **Measures:** Ss completed the revised Child's Report of Parental Behavior Inventory for each parent. **Results:** (1) Among 11- and 13-year-old Ss, girls reported greater parental acceptance than boys. (2) Boys reported greater overall parental psychological control than girls. (3) There were no sex differences in parental firmness of control.

Arnold, C. R. Role of discriminative stimuli in the formation of functional response to classes. *J. Experimental Child Psychology*, 1970, 9, 470–88.

Subjects: $N = 96$; 7–8 yrs. **Measures:** Ss learned to say animal names while pushing buttons corresponding to chemical symbols or learned responses, separately. Then Ss simultaneously performed verbal and motor responses to various stimuli. **Results:** There were no sex differences in acquisition, transfer, or effect of different training conditions.

Aronfreed, J. The nature, variety, and social patterning of moral responses to transgression. *J. Abnormal & Social Psychology*, 1961, 63, 223–40.

Subjects: $N = 122$; 11 yrs (low, middle SES). **Measures:** A projective story completion device was individually scored for the presence of a number of independently defined forms of moral response. **Results:** (1) Regardless of social status, boys emphasized external responsibility less than girls ($p < .05$), and were less dependent on an external initiation of their own moral reactions ($p < .05$ for middle SES Ss, $p < .01$ for low SES Ss). (2) Among middle SES Ss, girls showed a greater tendency than boys to display their moral reactions through expressions of remorse and promises of conformity ($p < .05$).

Aronson, E., and Cope, V. My enemy is my friend. *J. Personality & Social Psychology*, 1968, 8, 8–12.

Subjects: $N = 80$; 18–21 yrs (college). **Measures:** Ss were treated either harshly or pleasantly by an E, and were then allowed to overhear E being treated either harshly or pleasantly by his supervisor. Ss were asked if they'd be willing to make some phone calls for the supervisor. Number of phone calls made was recorded. Ss also indicated how much they enjoyed working with E. **Results:** (1) No sex differences were found in number of phone calls made. (2) Men liked E more if he was pleasantly treated by the supervisor; women liked E more if he was harshly criticized by the supervisor ($p < .005$).

Aronson, E., and Gerard, E. Beyond Parkinson's Law: the effect of excess time on subsequent performance. *J. Personality & Social Psychology*, 1966, 3, 336–39.

Subjects: $N = 32$; 18–21 yrs (college). **Measures:** Ss were allowed either too much time or a minimum of time to prepare a speech. Ss then worked at their own pace while preparing a second speech. Amount of time Ss used in preparing the second speech was recorded. **Results:** No sex differences.

Ashear, V., and Snortum, J. R. Eye contact in children as a function of age, sex, social and intellective variables. *Developmental Psychology*, 1971, 4, 479.

Subjects: $N = 90$; 3–5, 7, 10, 13 yrs. **Measures:** Ss' speech patterns and eye contact with female E were recorded during an interview about interests and aspirations. **Results:** Girls showed more eye contact with E than boys while speaking and overall (including silence). There were no sex differences in eye contact during listening.

Ashton, R. Behavioral sleep cycles in the human newborn. *Child Development*, 1971, 42, 2098–100.

Subjects: $N = 22$; 3 days (bottle-fed). **Measures:** Following feeding, Ss were observed for a period of 2–3 hours. Sleep cycles were studied. Measures were taken of the durations of the successive epochs of sleep and of the frequency of startling in these epochs. **Results:** No sex differences.

Ault, R. L., Crawford, D. E., and Jeffrey, W. E. Visual scanning strategies of reflective, impulsive, fast-accurate, and slow-inaccurate children on the Matching Familiar Figures Test. *Child Development*, 1972, 43, 1412–17.

Subjects: $N = 29$; 8–10 yrs. **Measures:** Ss were given 30 problems to solve from the Matching Familiar Figures Test (MFF), during which time their visual scanning strategies were recorded. 4 weeks later, teachers rated Ss on an attention scale, a motivation scale, and a hyperactivity scale (irrelevant talk or play). **Results:** (1) There were no sex differences in performance on the MFF. (2) There were no sex differences in teachers' ratings of Ss on the attention scale. (3) Teachers rated boys more hyperactive than girls ($p < .01$).

Axtell, B., and Cole, C. W. Repression-sensitization response mode and verbal avoidance. *J. Personality & Social Psychology*, 1971, 18, 133–37.

Subjects: $N = 96$; 18–21 yrs (college). **Measures:** After completing the Health and Opinion Questionnaire, a measure of R-S, Ss were asked to discuss themselves positively or negatively. Half of the Ss were exposed to prerecorded verbal feedback during their discussion. The response measure was the duration of S's verbalization. **Results:** No sex differences.

Babad, E. Y. Person specificity of the "social deprivation satiation effect," *Developmental Psychology*, 1972, 6, 210–13.
　Subjects: $N = 40$; 8 yrs. **Measures:** Ss were given a 10-minute treatment in which the stimulus word "good" was received either 2 times (deprivation) or 16 times (satiation), followed by a discrimination-learning task in which each correct response was reinforced with "good." **Results:** No main sex differences were found in number of correct responses. Girls performed better than boys in the deprivation condition, whereas the reverse was true among Ss in the satiation condition ($p < .05$).

Backman, M. E. Patterns of mental abilities: ethnic, socioeconomic, and sex differences. *American Educational Research Journal*, 1972, 9, 1–12.
　Subjects: $N = 2,925$; 17 yrs (participants from Project TALENT: Jewish white, non-Jewish white, black, Oriental). **Measures:** 60 information achievement and aptitude tests were administered to Ss; 6 mental ability factors were examined: Verbal Knowledge, English Language, Mathematics, Visual Reasoning, Perceptual Speed and Accuracy, and Memory. **Results:** Sex was related to both shape and level of performance patterns ($p < .001$). Girls scored higher than boys on ENG, PSA, and MEM; boys scored higher than girls on VKN, MAT, and VIS.

Baldwin, C. P., and Baldwin, A. L. Children's judgments of kindness. *Child Development*, 1970, 41, 29–47.
　Subjects: $N = 696$; 5, 7, 9, 11, 13, 18–21 yrs (college). **Measures:** Ss read pairs of stories with pictures and were asked to choose the picture in which they thought the child involved was kinder. The subjects of stories were both girls or both boys. All Ss were asked to explain their choices, and responses were coded. **Results:** (1) There were no sex differences for the adult sample. (2) On only one story boys gave more adult responses than girls did ($p < .05$).

Baldwin, T. L., McFarlane, P. T., and Garvey, C. J. Children's communication accuracy related to race and socioeconomic status. *Child Development*, 1971, 42, 345–57.
　Subjects: $N = 96$; 10 yrs (white and black, low and middle SES). **Measures:** Ss were arranged in matched sex, SES, and race pairs. One S had 7 pictures and the other had 1. The task was to verbally communicate which of the 7 pictures the 1 matched. **Results:** No sex differences.

Balint, M. Individual differences of behavior in early infancy and an objective method for recording them. *J. Genetic Psychology*, 1948, 73, 57–117.
　Subjects: $N = 100$; 1 day–9 mos. **Measures:** The number of sucks in each 10-second interval was recorded. **Results:** (1) No sex differences were found in basic frequency, restart frequency, or second frequency. (2) Quivering was observed in more girls than boys.

Baltes, P. B., and Nesselroade, J. R. Cultural change and adolescent personality development. *Developmental Psychology*, 1972, 7, 244–56.
　Subjects: $N = 1,249$; 12–16 yrs. **Measures:** Cattell's (1964) High School Personality Questionnaire was administered to Ss twice (once in 1970 and again in 1971) for assessment of ontogenetic (age-related) vs. generational (cohort-related) change in adolescent personality development. **Results:** (1) Boys were more reserved, detached, dominant, surgent, adventurous, and self-sufficient than girls. Boys had greater ego strength than girls. (2) Girls scored higher in general intellectual ability, had greater superego strength, and were more sensitive, zestful, guilt-prone, and tense than boys. (3) There were no sex differences on the lax-controlled dimension or the phlegmatic temperament–excitability dimension.

Baltes, P. B., and Wender, K. Age differences in pleasantness of visual patterns of different variability in late childhood and adolescence. *Child Development*, 1971, 42, 47–55.
　Subjects: $N = 120$; 9, 11, 13, 15 yrs (Germany). **Measures:** Ss viewed 2 sets of 70 stimuli (random dots and random shapes). As S viewed 1 set, each stimulus appeared for 3 seconds, then for 7 seconds, followed by a 10-second interval during which Ss were asked to indicate on a 9-point scale how they liked the stimulus. **Results:** No sex differences.

Baltes, P. B., Schaie, K. W., and Nardi, A. H. Age and experimental mortality in seven-year longitudinal study of cognitive behavior. *Developmental Psychology*, 1971, 5, 18–26.
　Subjects: $N = 280$; 21–70 yrs. **Measures:** The 5 subtests of the Intermediate Form of the Primary Mental Abilities Test (Verbal Meaning, Space, Reasoning, Arithmetic, and Word Fluency) and Schaie's Test of Behavioral Rigidity were administered to Ss. Estimated factor scores for 3 second-order ability factors (General Intelligence, Cognitive Flexibility, and Visuo-motor Flexibility) were analyzed for sex differences. **Results:** No sex differences were

found in General Intelligence or Cognitive Flexibility. The direction of the significant sex difference in Visuo-motor Flexibility was not specified.

Ban, P. L., and Lewis, M. Mothers and fathers, girls and boys: attachment behavior in the one-year-old. Paper presented at the meetings of the Eastern Psychological Association, New York, April 1971.

Subjects: $N = 20$; 1 yr. Measures: On 2 different occasions, Ss were observed in a free-play situation. Ss were tested once in the presence of their mothers and once in the presence of their fathers. Parents were told to respond to their children, but not to initiate any interaction; 4 attachment behaviors were recorded: time spent touching parent, time spent looking at parent, time spent vocalizing to parent, and time spent in proximity to parent. Results: (1) No main sex differences were found. (2) Boys spent more time looking at their fathers than at their mothers; no such difference was found for girls. (3) Both sexes directed more proximal behavior toward their mothers than toward their fathers ($p < .01$ for touching; $p < .001$ for proximity-seeking). (4) Both sexes spent more time vocalizing to their mothers than to their fathers ($p < .05$).

Bandura, A., and Harris, M. B. Modification of syntactic style. *J. Experimental Child Psychology*, 1966, 4, 341–52.

Subjects: $N = 100$; 7 yrs. Measures: The roles of appropriate modeling cues, reinforcement variables, and strong attentional responses in the modification of syntactic style were derived from sentences Ss composed using stimulus words scored for frequency of passives and prepositional phrases. Results: During baseline, more boys than girls produced at least 1 passive sentence. No other sex differences were found.

Bandura, A., and Huston, A. C. Identification as a process of incidental learning. *J. Abnormal & Social Psychology*, 1961, 63, 311–18.

Subjects: $N = 48$; 3–5 yrs. Measures: Ss performed diverting, 2-choice discrimination problem with a female model, who exhibited explicit, but functionless behavior. Ss experienced either a rewarding interaction or a cold, non-nurturant relationship with the model prior to the task. The measure of performance was the extent to which Ss reproduced the model's behavior. Results: No sex differences.

Bandura, A., and Jeffery, R. W. Role of symbolic coding and rehearsal processes in observational learning. *J. Personality & Social Psychology*, 1973, 26, 122–30.

Subjects: $N = 88$; 18–21 yrs (college). Measures: Ss observed a filmed model perform complex movement configurations. Observational learning and retention were measured. Results: No sex differences.

Bandura, A., and Kupers, C. J. Transmission of patterns of self-reinforcement through modeling. *J. Abnormal & Social Psychology*, 1964, 69, 1–9.

Subjects: $N = 160$; 7–9 yrs. Measures: Ss self-reinforcement patterns were assessed after exposure to either peer or adult models who exhibited either a high or a low criterion for self-reinforcement. Results: No sex-of-subject or sex-of-model effects were found.

Bandura, A., and Menlove, F. L. Factors determining vicarious extinction of avoidance behavior through symbolic modeling. *J. Personality & Social Psychology*, 1968, 8, 99–108.

Subjects: $N = 48$; 3–5 yrs. Measures: Ss were initially given a test of avoidance behavior to identify those Ss fearful of dogs. Ss were then exposed to a graduated series of films in which a model interacted nonanxiously with a dog. Following completion of the treatment series, Ss were given the same avoidance test twice (immediately afterward and approximately 1 month later). Results: No sex differences were found in the effectiveness of the treatment series.

Bandura, A., and Mischel, W. Modification of self-imposed delay of reward through exposure to live and symbolic models. *J. Personality & Social Psychology*, 1965, 2, 698–705.

Subjects: $N = 120$; 9–10 yrs. Measures: From a larger group of approximately 250, children who exhibited predominately either immediate-reward or delayed-reward patterns of behavior were assigned to 1 of 3 treatment conditions. One group of Ss was exposed to a live adult model who exhibited delay-of-reward responses counter to their predominate response patterns, while a second group of Ss was exposed to a symbolic model. Ss in a third group had no exposure to any models. Immediately afterward and again 1 month later, Ss chose between less valuable immediate rewards and more valuable delayed rewards. Results: No sex differences.

Bandura, A., and Perloff, B. Relative efficacy of self-monitored and externally imposed reinforcement systems. *J. Personality & Social Psychology*, 1968, 7, 111–16.
Subjects: $N = 80$; 7–10 yrs. Measures: Ss performed a task in which progressively higher scores could be achieved by turning a wheel on a mechanical device. After selecting their own performance standards, Ss in 1 group were instructed to reward themselves with tokens whenever they attained their self-imposed standards. For Ss in a second group, the same performance standards were externally imposed and the reinforcers were automatically delivered. Results: (1) No sex differences were found in self-imposed performance standards. (2) Boys performed more responses than girls ($p < .05$).

Bandura, A., and Whalen, C. K. The influence of antecedent reinforcement and divergent modeling cues on patterns of self-reward. *J. Personality & Social Psychology*, 1966, 3, 373–82.
Subjects: $N = 160$; 8–11 yrs. Measures: Ss were exposed to a same-sex model who either (a) adopted a high criterion for self-reward and performed the experimental task (a bowling game) at a superior level, (b) adopted a low criterion for self-reward and performed at an inferior level, or (c) adopted a moderately high criterion for self-reward and performed at a moderately high performance level. Ss then performed the game in the model's absence. Measures were taken of the performance scores for which Ss rewarded themselves. Results: (1) No sex differences were found in the number of reinforcers Ss administered to themselves for low and superior performance scores. Girls rewarded themselves with more reinforcers than boys did for moderately high performance scores ($p < .001$). (2) No sex differences were found in frequency of self-reinforcement. (3) With the exception of the superior model condition, where there was no sex difference, boys displayed a greater amount of verbal self-reinforcement than girls did.

Bandura, A., Grusec, J. E., and Menlove, F. L. Observational learning as a function of symbolization and incentive set. *Child Development*, 1966, 37, 499–506.
Subjects: $N = 72$; 6–8 yrs. Measures: Children watched a movie in which an adult male model exhibited a series of novel behavior patterns. They were randomly assigned to 1 of 3 conditions: (1) facilitative symbolization—Ss were instructed to verbalize every action of the model as it was being performed in the movie, (2) passive observation—Ss were simply instructed to pay close attention to the movie, and (3) competing symbolization—Ss were instructed to pay close attention to the movie while counting repeatedly. Half of the Ss were assigned to the incentive-set condition, in which they were told they would be asked to demonstrate what they learned in the movie, and half of the Ss were placed in the no-incentive-set condition, in which they were told they would return to class immediately following the movie. After the movie, each S was asked to demonstrate all of the model's responses they could recall. Results: Boys produced a higher number of matching responses than girls did.

Bandura, A., Grusec, J. E., and Menlove, F. L. Some social determinants of self-monitoring reinforcement systems. *J. Personality & Social Psychology*, 1967, 5, 449–55.
Subjects: $N = 128$; 7–11 yrs. Measures: Ss were initially exposed to a same-sex adult model who performed a task (bowling game) at a consistently superior level and adopted a high criterion of self-reward. Afterward, Ss either did or did not observe a peer model perform less well and adopt a lower standard of self-reward. Ss then played the bowling game alone, receiving instructions to reward themselves with tokens whenever they felt they had performed well. Results: No sex differences were found in either the number of rewards Ss administered to themselves or in the percentage of trials Ss rewarded themselves for performances below the criterion adopted by the adult model.

Banikiotes, F. G., Montgomery, A. A., and Banikiotes, P. G. Male and female auditory reinforcement of infant vocalizations. *Developmental Psychology*, 1972, 6, 476–81.
Subjects: $N = 16$; 3 mos. Measures: Infants' vocalizations were counted after baseline (nonreinforced) and conditioning stages. Each S received auditory reinforcement for vocalizations from a male in 1 conditioning stage and from a female in the other conditioning stage. Results: No sex differences.

Barclay, A. M. The effect of female aggressiveness on aggressive and sexual fantasies. *J. Projective Techniques & Personality Assessment*, 1970, 34, 19–26.
Subjects: $N = 55$; 18–21 yrs (college). Measures: After being angered by a hostile female E, Ss wrote stories to 2 male-dominant (MD) and 2 female-dominant (FD) TAT pictures. Results: (1) Men expressed more aggressive imagery than women did. More aggression was expressed toward FD pictures than toward MD pictures. (2) Men expressed more sexual

imagery than women did. (3) No sex differences were found in aggressive defensiveness imagery. More aggressive defensiveness imagery was expressed toward FD pictures than toward MD pictures. (4) As assessed by a postexperimental questionnaire, no sex differences were found in level of arousal.

Barnard, J. W. The effects of anxiety on connotative meaning. *Child Development*, 1966, *37*, 461–72.
Subjects: $N = 220$; 10 yrs. Measures: Ss who received either high or low scores on the Test Anxiety Scale for Children were asked to rate concepts related to school on the semantic differential (SD). The SD was administered under either evaluative or nonevaluative conditions. Results: Girls rated the concepts more positively than boys.

Barnes, K. E. Preschool play norms: a replication. *Developmental Psychology*, 1971, *5*, 88–103.
Subjects: $N = 42$; 3–5 yrs. Measures: Play behavior categories of unoccupied, solitary, onlooker, parallel, associative, and cooperative were scored during 10 minutes of free-play observation. Results: No sex differences.

Barthol, R. P. Individual and sex differences in cortical conductivity. *J. Personality*, 1958, *26*, 365–78.
Subjects: $N = 106$; 18–21 yrs (college). Measures: Measurements of the movement-simultaneity threshold (phi phenomenon) were correlated with measures of the kinesthetic figural aftereffect for men and women. Movement refers to a report of a single light moving back and forth; simultaneity refers to a report of 2 stimuli appearing rapidly and approximately at the same time. Results: No sex differences.

Bartol, C. R., and Pielstick, N. L. The effects of ambiguity, familiarization, age, and sex on stimulus preference. *J. Experimental Child Psychology*, 1972, *14*, 21–29.
Subjects: $N = 45$; 7, 11, 18–21 yrs (college). Measures: During the slide presentation of pairs of ambiguous-unambiguous figures, looking time was recorded. Results: (1) There were no main sex differences. (2) Among 7- and 11-year-old Ss, boys viewed ambiguous stimuli longer than girls did. (3) Among 18 to 21-year-old Ss, women viewed ambiguous stimuli longer than men did.

Barton, K. Block manipulation by children as a function of social reinforcement, anxiety, arousal, and ability pattern. *Child Development*, 1971, *42*, 817–26.
Subjects: $N = 64$; 9–10 yrs (half of the Ss were high verbal–low spatial (HV-LS) and half were high spatial–low verbal (HS-LV) on the basis of Thurstone's Primary Mental Abilities Test). Measures: Baseline Palmer Sweat Index (PSI) was established for each S. S played with blocks during either social reinforcement or no reinforcement. Number and complexity of structures were measured, as were PSI and state of anxiety (State-Trait Anxiety Inventory). Results: Girls were more anxious than boys on the questionnaire ($p < .01$) during 2 of 3 administrations.

Batchelor, T. R., and Tesser, A. Attitude base as a moderator of the attitude similarity-attraction relationship. *J. Personality & Social Psychology*, 1971, *91*, 229–36.
Subjects: $N = 406$; 18–21 yrs (college). Measures: After completing an attitude questionnaire, Ss were given information about other individuals, including each other's attitude on a topic (similar-dissimilar) and the reason given for holding this attitude. Ss then recorded their impressions of each other on a modified version of the Byrne Interpersonal Judgment Scale. Results: No sex differences.

Battle, E. S. Motivational determinants of academic task persistence. *J. Personality & Social Psychology*, 1965, *2*, 209–18.
Subjects: $N = 74$; 12–14 yrs. Measures: Ss indicated on a 10-point scale the personal importance of doing well in math. Results: No sex differences.

Battle, E. S. Motivational determinants of academic competence. *J. Personality & Social Psychology*, 1966, *4*, 634–42.
Subjects: Approximately 500; 12–14 yrs. Measures: For 2 subject areas, English and mathematics, Ss indicated (a) the lowest grade they could get and still be satisfied, (b) how certain they were that they could achieve that grade, (c) the grade they expected to receive on their next report card, and (d) the importance to them of doing well in that area. Ss also listed their favorite academic subject and the 2 school subjects they thought they were "best"

in. **Results:** (1) Boys thought it was more important to do well in mathematics than girls did ($p < .001$). (2) Boys expected to perform better in English than girls did ($p < .001$). The lowest grade that boys reported they would be satisfied with was higher than the grade girls reported ($p < .001$). Girls were more certain than boys, however, that they would achieve the grade they indicated ($p < .001$). Girls thought it was more important to do well than boys did ($p < .001$). (3) Boys chose English as their favorite subject and listed it as their "best" subject less frequently than girls did ($p < .01$, $p < .001$). No sex differences were found in the frequency with which math was chosen as the favorite subject.

Battle, E. S., and Lacey, B. A context of hyperactivity in children, over time. *Child Development*, 1972, *43*, 757–73.
Subjects: $N = 74$; 18–26 yrs. **Measures:** Observational data for Ss had been collected at 6-month intervals from birth to 6 years at home, and from 6 to 12 years at the Fels Day Camp. Interview data were available for 60 of 74 Ss at ages 12–18. 65 out of the 74 Ss were assessed in interviews at ages 18–26 concerning motivational and behavioral variables. Data were divided into 5 age periods and rated for evidence of hyperactivity. **Results:** Among 6-10-year-old Ss, boys were rated more hyperactive than girls were ($p < .05$).

Baumrind, D. Current patterns of parental authority. *Developmental Psychology Monograph*, 1971, *4*.
EXPERIMENT I: Subjects: $N = 238$; 3, 4 yrs. **Measures:** Episodes of interpersonal and social behavior were recorded while Ss engaged in activities in nursery school. In addition, each S was observed and rated while taking the Stanford-Binet. **Results:** Boys displayed more hostility to peers and more resistiveness to adult supervision than girls ($p < .01$, $p < .01$). Boys were also more domineering; girls, on the other hand, were more tractable. No sex differences were found in dominance, purposiveness, independence, or achievement orientation.
EXPERIMENT II: Subjects: $N = 293$; parents of 3- and 4-year-old children. **Measures:** Parent's behavior toward their children was recorded. **Results:** (1) Fathers were more firm with their sons than with their daughters. No differences were found between fathers of boys and fathers of girls on the following dimensions: encouragement of independence and individuality; passiveness and acceptance; rejection; encouragement of nonconformity; authoritarianism. (2) No differences were found between mothers of boys and mothers of girls on the following dimensions: firm enforcement; encouragement of independence and individuality; passiveness and acceptance; rejection; self-confident, secure, potent parental behavior. (3) No differences were found between parents of boys and parents of girls on the following dimensions; expectation of participation in household chores; enrichment of child's environment; directiveness; discouragement of emotional dependency; discouragement of infantile behavior.
EXPERIMENT III: Subjects: $N = 415$; parents of 3- and 4-year-old children. **Measures:** Parents' child-rearing attitudes and values were assessed in individual interviews. **Results:** (1) No differences were found between mothers of boys and mothers of girls or between fathers of boys and fathers of girls on the following dimensions: early maturity demands; values conformity; anger over lack of control; firm enforcement; encouragement of nonconformity; discouragement of infantile behavior; authoritarianism. (2) No differences were found between mothers of boys and mothers of girls on the following dimensions (these dimensions did not appear for fathers): impatience; consistent, articulated child-rearing philosophy.

Baumrind, D., and Black, A. E. Socialization practices associated with dimensions of competence in preschool boys and girls. *Child Development*, 1967, *38*, 291–327.
Subjects: $N = 103$; 3–4 yrs and their mothers and fathers. **Measures:** (1) Ss were observed in their classrooms by a pair of psychologists who used a 95-item Q-sort to describe each child's behavior. (2) 95 of the 103 families were visited at home. After being interviewed separately, mothers and fathers were rated on their attitudes and child-rearing practices. **Results:** (1a) On the Q-sort, boys were rated higher on "high energy level," "good sense of humor," "contentedness," "does not seek assurance that he is liked," "explores environment," and "takes initiative in making friends," while girls were rated higher on "acts too mature," "enjoys aesthetic experiences," "exploits dependent state," "interested in pre-primer skills," "guileful and manipulative," and "chatters to obtain attention." (1b) No sex differences were found on the following items: alienates vs. attracts other children; able vs. not able to form close friendships; uses vs. does not use persuasion to get what he wants; affiliative, supportive vs. negativistic; irritable vs. even-tempered; obstructive vs. helpful; becomes hostile vs. does not become hostile when hurt or frustrated; helps vs. does not help other children adapt;

impulsive vs. self-controlled; impetuous vs. deliberate; thoughtless, inconsiderate vs. thoughtful, considerate; disrespectful vs. courteous demeanor with adults; provokes vs. avoids conflict with adults; responsible vs. irresponsible about following rules; affectionate vs. unaffectionate with nursery school staff; submits to group consensus vs. takes independent stand; conforming vs. willing to risk adult disapproval; suggestible vs. has mind of own; listens vs. actively participates in discussions; an interesting, arresting child vs. uninteresting and bland; imaginative; emotionally expressive vs. bland; produces stereotyped vs. original work; curious vs. lacks curiosity; gives up vs. perseveres when adversity is encountered; stretches to meet vs. retreats from performance demands; sets easy vs. hard goals to achieve; hazards failure vs. avoids difficult tasks; withdraws vs. stands his ground when hurt or frustrated; high vs. low self-confidence; at ease vs. ill at ease at nursery school; apprehensive vs. nonapprehensive; self-abasive vs. self-valuing; indecisive vs. resolute about making decisions; does not vs. does regret wrong-doing; dependable, trustworthy vs. undependable, untrustworthy; bullies vs. avoids forcing will on other children; managerial and bossy vs. tactful and modest; permits self to be dominated vs. will not submit; not easily vs. easily intimidated or bullied; seldom vs. often spends time in withdrawn fantasy; poorly vs. well oriented in his environment; does not vs. does become pleasurably involved in tasks; gives his best vs. expends little effort; enjoys vs. avoids new learning experiences. (2a) Mothers of boys were rated higher than mothers of girls on "negative sanctions: deprivation of privileges" and "tolerance of verbal protest." Mothers of girls were rated higher than mothers of boys on "strictness regarding neatness," "demands for obedience," "negative sanctions: withdrawal of love," "control of verbal and/or physical aggression toward parent," and "maturity expectations: does not reward dependency." No differences were found between fathers of boys and fathers of girls on the above items. (2b) Fathers of boys were rated higher than fathers of girls on "negative sanctions: corporal punishment," "positive sanctions as reinforcers: tangible reward," and "directiveness: restrictions on child's initiative." No differences were found between mothers of boys and mothers of girls on the preceding items. (2c) No differences were found between mothers of boys and mothers of girls or between fathers of boys and fathers of girls on the following items: strictness in care of family property, in responsibilities about orderliness, in aggression toward other children, and in television; negative sanctions on isolation and on frightening the child; parents' feeling of control over the child; lack of internal conflict about disciplinary procedures; parent's appraisal of his/her general influence on child; consistency: follow-through in discipline; consistency: child-rearing practices; consistency of discipline: parental agreement; reason for restrictions; an absolutist ethical imperative; maturity expectation; household responsibilities; maturity expectation, rewarding of self-sufficiency, and intellectual achievement expected; independence, encouraging contact with other adults, and introducing child to new experiences; communication, attentiveness to child's communication, and expression of negative feelings to child; individual character of child perceived; warmth, presence of loving relationship, demonstrativeness, approval, absence of hostility, empathy, and sympathy; conscientiousness, keeping track of child, sacrificing own needs to those of children, and acceptance of responsibility.

Bayley, N. Data on the growth of intelligence between 16 and 21 years as measured by the Wechsler-Bellevue Scale. *J. Genetic Psychology*, 1957, *90*, 3–15.
Subjects: $N = 33$; tested at 16, 18, 21 yrs (Berkeley Growth Study). Measures: Wechsler-Bellevue Adult Intelligence Scale. Results: Both sexes showed similar increases in intelligence over the 5-year period.

Bayley, N., and Oden, M. The maintenance of intellectual ability in gifted adults. *J. Gerontology*, 1955, *10*, 91–107.
Experiment I: Subjects: $N = 768$; tested at 29, 41 yrs (Ss were taken from Terman's Study of the Gifted). Measures: At each testing, Ss were given the Concept Mastery Test. The test is composed of 2 subtests: (1) Synonyms and Antonyms and (2) Analogies. Results: At the initial testings, men scored higher on the Analogies subtest than women. At the later testing, men scored higher than women on the Analogies subtest and on both subtests combined.
Experiment II: Subjects: $N = 334$, tested at 29, 41 yrs (Ss were the spouses of the men and women in the sample above). Measures: Concept Mastery Test. Results: At the initial testing, men scored higher on the Analogies subtest than women. At the later testing, men had higher Analogies subtest and overall scores than women.
Experiment III: Subjects: $N = 168$; 29 yrs (Ss were originally part of Terman's Study). Measures: Concept Mastery Test. Results: No sex differences were found in overall scores.
Experiment IV: Subjects: $N = 227$; 41 yrs (Ss were originally part of Terman's Study). Measures: Concept Mastery Test. Results: Men had higher overall scores than women.

Beckwith, L. Relationships between attributes of mothers and their infants' IQ scores. *Child Development*, 1971, *42*, 1083–97.

Subjects: $N = 24$; tested at 8, 10 mos (adopted infants). **Measures:** S was given the Cattell Infant Intelligence Scale and motor items from the Gesell Developmental Schedules at each of 2 visits. Mother and S were observed during 1 hour of spontaneous interaction and care-taking activities. **Results:** No sex differences (even though female Ss' natural mothers were more educated).

Beckwith, L. Relationships between infants' social behavior and their mothers' behavior. *Child Development*, 1972, *43*, 397–411 (and personal communication).

Subjects: $N = 24$; tested at 7–9 mos (session 1), 8–11 mos (session 2). **Measures:** Mothers and their adopted children were observed in their homes for 2 1-hour sessions. Measures were taken of the frequency with which mothers touched and talked to their infants and of the amount of freedom they gave their infants to explore objects and places. Two infant measures were also recorded: number of social approaches to mother, and ratio of number of 30-second intervals Ss responded to mother to number of 30-second intervals in which mother initiated contact. At the end of each session, Ss' reactions to the observer were assessed in 4 standard-ized situations (Rheingold Social Responsiveness Scale). **Results:** (1) No differences were found between mothers of boys and mothers of girls in the amount they touched or talked to their infants. (2) Mothers with only a high school education treated boys particularly restric-tively. (3) No sex differences were found in number of social approaches to mother. (4) Girls were more socially responsive to their mothers in the second session than boys were ($p < .05$, one-tailed test). No difference was found in the first session. (5) Boys were more responsive to the observer on the Rheingold Social Responsiveness Scale than girls ($p < .05$).

Bedell, J., and Sistrunk, F. Power, opportunity costs, and sex in a mixed-motive game. *J. Personality & Social Psychology*, 1973, *25*, 219–26.

Subjects: $N = 90$; 18–21 yrs (college). **Measures:** Ss played the Prisoner's Dilemma game in same-sex or opposite-sex pairs. On every fifth trial, S was given the opportunity to either add or subtract 4 points from his partner's score. A third response also available ("none") did not affect the other's score. **Results:** (1) No differences were found between male and mixed-sex dyads in number of mutually cooperative responses. Both were more cooperative than female dyads ($p < .01$). (2) Both male and mixed-sex dyads showed an increase in number of mutually cooperative responses across trial blocks; female dyads showed no change ($p < .05$). (3) Following DC, CC, or DD trials, Ss in the male and mixed-sex dyads made cooperative responses more often than Ss in the female dyads. No differences were found following CD trials. (The first letter represents S's response, the second represents partner's response; C = cooperative, D = competitive.) (4) Ss in mixed-sex dyads rewarded their partners more often than Ss in the female dyads. No differences were found between male and mixed-sex dyads or between male and female dyads. (5) Ss in the mixed-sex dyads punished their partners less frequently than Ss in the female dyads. No differences were found between male and mixed-sex dyads or between male and female dyads.

Bee, H. L. Parent-child interaction and distractibility in 9-year-old children. *Merrill-Palmer Quarterly*, 1967, *13*, 175–90 (and unpublished doctoral dissertation, Stanford University, 1964).

Subjects: $N = 36$; 9 yrs and parents. **Measures:** Initially, Ss were assigned to distractible and nondistractible groups based upon the difference in their problem-solving performance under conditions of distraction and no distraction. All Ss were then observed in problem-solving interaction with their parents. **Results:** (1) No sex differences were found in the specificity of the suggestions or in the amount of positive or negative encouragement given to them by their parents. Mothers of nondistractible boys gave less negative encouragement than mothers of distractible boys did; for girls, the reverse was true ($p < .05$). (2) There were no sex differences in rate of suggestive and nonsuggestive interaction. Among parents of distractible Ss, boys' parents gave the greatest relative number of suggestions; among parents of non-distractible Ss, girls' parents gave the greatest relative number of suggestions ($p < .001$). (3) There were no sex differences in number of bids for help or attention. (4) More boys than girls spoke first in the presence of their parents (not tested for significance).

Bee, H. L., Van Egeren, L. F., Streissguth, A. P., Nyman, B. A., and Leckie, M. S. Social class differences in maternal teaching strategies and speech patterns. *Developmental Psychology*, 1969, *1*, 726–34 (and personal communication).

Subjects: $N = 114$; 4–5 yrs and their mothers (76 black and white low SES, 38 white middle

SES). **Measures:** Mothers were observed in an unstructured "waiting room" situation and in a structured problem-solving situation with the child. The waiting room response measures were mother's rates of control statements, suggestions, approval, ignoring, disapproval, questions, information statements, and attention; child's rates of acceptance, rejection, general seeking, ignoring, questions, demands, information statements, toy shifts, and space shifts. The problem-solving response measures were mother's rates of nonquestion suggestions, question suggestions, positive feedback, negative feedback, and nonverbal intrusions; mean specificity of mother's suggestions; child's rates of acceptance, rejection, and dependency bids; and total time spent on problem. **Results:** (1) No main sex-of-child effects were found. (2) Mothers of middle SES girls gave more information and positive feedback than mothers of middle SES boys; in the low SES sample, mothers of girls gave less information and positive feedback than mothers of boys. (3) Mothers of low SES boys expressed disapproval of their child's actions more often than mothers of low SES girls. No difference was found among middle SES mothers. (4) During the problem-solving session, middle SES mothers of boys and low SES mothers of girls interacted with their child to a greater extent than their SES counterparts did (overall measure).

Beilin, H. Feedback and infralogical strategies in invariant area conceptualization. *J. Experimental Child Psychology*, 1966, 3, 267–78.
Subjects: N = 236; 6, 7 yrs. **Measures:** There was an attempt to improve performance in a quasi-conservation task where high rate of error was previously reported. Translocation, iteration, and feedback training methods were used. Number of correct quasi-conservation responses and classified verbal reports was analyzed (categorized in terms of infralogical strategies used). **Results:** There were no sex differences before or after conservation performance training, or in use of infralogical strategies.

Beilin, H., and Kagan, J. Pluralization rules and the conceptualization of number. *Developmental Psychology*, 1969, 1, 697–706.
EXPERIMENT I: **Subjects:** N = 78; 4 yrs (private nursery school). **Measures:** (1) Pluralization rules were tested for nouns, possessives, and verbs. (2) Number of conceptualizations was assessed from a discrimination task using quantitative propertires. If S reached criterion in 45 trials, he was shifted to reverse concept. **Results:** (1) There were no sex differences in proportion of Ss among concept attainers and reversers. (2) There were no sex differences in trials to concept attainment. (3) Girls did better than boys did in attaining reversal criterion.
EXPERIMENT II: **Subjects:** N = 96; 4 yrs (private nursery school). **Measures:** Ss were divided into 5 training groups and a control group: 3 training groups consisted of Ss who failed both the verb pluralization and concept attainment pretests, and were trained in number conceptualization, pluralization, or both; 2 other training groups consisted of Ss who passed 1 of pretest and received training on the pretest they failed. The control Ss failed both pretests and received no training. **Results:** No sex differences.

Beiswenger, H. Linguistic and psychological factors in the speech regulation of behavior in young children. *J. Experimental Child Psychology*, 1971, 11, 63–75.
Subjects: N = 48; 2–4 yrs. **Measures:** Ss were given 2 sets of verbal commands, the first consisting of conditional and nonconditional commands to respond to a sequence of visual signals ("When the blue light comes on, get a blue marble and put it in the dish"), the second requiring mental transformation of the spatial relationship of the target ("Touch the toothbrush with the spoon"). **Results:** No sex differences.

Bell, R. Q., and Costello, N. S. Three tests for sex differences in tactile sensitivity in the newborn. *Biologica Neonatorium*, 1964, 7, 335–47.
EXPERIMENT I: **Subjects:** N = 21; 4 days (bottle-fed infants born to primiparae). **Measures:** A weighted index of observed movements was obtained before and after removal of a covering blanket. **Results:** Girls showed a higher movement index than boys after removal of the blanket ($p < .05$).
EXPERIMENT II: **Subjects:** N = 17; 3 days (bottle-fed infants born to primiparae). **Measures:** Time-sampled observations of movements of eyeballs, mouth, face, head, and hands were recorded. When all Ss reached a comparable level of arousal, several skin surfaces were stimulated by an air jet. The threshold of the flow of air was measured at the time the infant responded. Each S was tested twice in 2 testing sessions, separated by at least 16 minutes. **Results:** Girls showed lower thresholds for abdomen areas than boys.
EXPERIMENT III: **Subjects:** N = 74; 3 days (breast-fed and bottle-fed infants born to multiparae). **Measures:** Observations were made from the time immediately following feeding through to awakening. Time samples of movements (Experiment II), numbers of respirations,

number of mass movements, and number of cries after being offered a sterile nipple filled with cotton were obtained. When arousal criteria were met (Experiments I and II), tactile sensitivity was tested twice using aesthesiometer (initially near 74 hours, and retested near 87 hours). **Results:** (1) Breast-fed boys and bottle-fed girls showed highest thresholds on both initial test and retest. (2) Breast-fed boys and bottle-fed girls were leaner.

Bell, R. Q., and Darling, J. F. The prone head reaction in the human neonate: relation with sex and tactile sensitivity. *Child Development*, 1965, 36, 943–49.
    Subjects: $N = 75$; 3 days (breast- and bottle-fed, second- or later-born). **Measures:** Each S's general bodily movements and respiration were observed for 3½ hours on two occasions. During sleep, tactile sensitivity was measured with a set of nylon filaments. Prone head reaction was tested when the infant was awake (extent and duration of chin lift at the highest point during a 60-second period). **Results:** (1) On the first test, there were no sex differences in prone head reaction. Breast-fed boys and bottle-fed girls had the highest prone head reaction scores. (2) On the retest, boys' prone head reaction scores were higher than those of girls.

Bell, R. Q., Weller, G. M., and Waldrop, M. F. Newborn and preschooler: organization of behavior and relations between periods. *Monographs of the Society for Research in Child Development*, 1971, 36, series no. 142.
    Experiment I: Subjects: $N = 75$; newborns (second- or later-born). **Measures:** On 2 separate occasions, Ss were observed for a 3½-hour interfeeding period covering a complete cycle of sleep and waking. During sleep, measures were taken of number of mouth movements, number of closed-eye movements, tactile threshold, highest respiration rate, and lowest respiration rate. While the infants were awake, the following measures were obtained: degree of arousal, prone-head reaction, number of sucks preceding the first or second pause in nonnutritive sucking, average size of a suck group (the initial suck group was not included in this calculation), nonnutritive suck rate, formula consumption relative to birth rate, and latency of response and number of cries following removal of the nipple. **Results:** (1) Boys lifted their heads higher than girls on the prone head reaction test. (2) Breast-fed boy infants had higher tactile thresholds than breast-fed girl infants. No difference was found between bottle-fed boy and girl infants. (3) Families of girl infants were lower in educational and occupational level, larger in size, and had shorter intervals between births than families of boy infants.
    Experiment II: Subjects: $N = 74$; 2½ yrs (including 55 follow-up cases from Experiment I. **Measures:** Ss were rated by their nursery school teachers on the following behaviors: contact with female teacher; contact with male teacher; vigor in play; friendliness with peers (involvement); friendliness with peers (positive); negative interaction; interest in bells (Bell Pull situation); active coping, object block; active coping, peer block; seeking help, peer block; tractability (cooperativeness with teacher's suggestions to change activities); geographic orientation; speech development; gross motor coordination; interest in attending school; manipulative skill, excitability; verbal originality; rhythmic response to music; reaction to teacher contact, child upset; seeking admiration. **Results:** Girls were rated higher than boys in speech development, gross motor coordination, seeking admiration, and tractability. No other sex differences were found.

Bell, S. M., and Ainsworth, M. D. S. Infant crying and maternal responsiveness. *Child Development*, 1972, 43, 1171–90.
    Subjects: $N = 26$; 1–54 wks. **Measures:** Ss were observed in their homes at 3-week intervals. Duration and frequency of crying were recorded. **Results:** No sex differences.

Beloff, H. Two forms of social conformity: acquiescence and conventionality. *J. Abnormal & Social Psychology*, 1958, 56, 99–104.
    Subjects: $N = 60$; 18–21 yrs (college). **Measures:** Ss completed a shortened version of the Thurston-Chave War Scale. After a 3-week interval, Ss again responded to the T-C statements under simulated group conditions. (Stooges presented strongly agreeing, neutral, and strongly disagreeing positions.) Acquiescence was defined as the difference between Ss' first and second response sets with respect to the group report. From Eysenck's Inventory of Social Attitudes and Ss' preferences for pictures of teapots, 2 indexes of conventionality (defined as the degree of agreement between an individual S and the mean or modal response of the rest of the group) were obtained. **Results:** (1) There were no sex differences in acquiescence scores. (2) There were no differences in aesthetic conventionality (teapot preference). (3) On political conventionality, women's conformity scores were higher than those of men (Eysenck's Inventory).

Bem, S. L. Sex-role adaptability: one consequence of psychological androgyny. *J. Personality & Social Psychology*, 1974, in press.

EXPERIMENT I: **Subjects:** $N = 54$; 18–21 yrs (college). **Measures:** Ss described themselves on the Bem Sex-Role Inventory. The BSRI includes both a masculinity and femininity scale; the 2 scales yield logically independent scores. Among the Ss selected for the experiment, one-third of each sex were masculine, one-third feminine, and one-third androgynous. After being assigned to same-sex groups of 4, Ss were tested in an Asch-type conformity situation. The number of trials in which Ss conformed was recorded. **Results:** No sex differences.

EXPERIMENT II: **Subjects:** $N = 66$; 18–21 yrs (college). **Measures:** 3 groups of Ss were chosen on the basis of their responses to the BSRI; one-third of each sex were masculine, one-third feminine, and one-third androgynous. Ss were first asked to build something with 60 plastic disks (this activity served to equalize mood across Ss). A kitten was then brought into the room and placed in an enclosed playpen. Instructions were given to interact with the kitten (forced play period). For their third activity, Ss were given a game of skill. Finally, the kitten was again placed in the playpen. Ss were told they could do anything they liked (spontaneous play period). The room contained a number of interesting magazines, games, and puzzles. The response measures were the amount of time Ss spent in spontaneous play with the kitten, the extent to which they touched the kitten during forced play, and their self-reported enjoyment of the forced-play interaction. **Results:** (1) No overall sex differences were found. (2) Among masculine males and females, females scored higher on a combined measure of the above-listed responses.

Benton, A. A. Productivity, distributive justice and bargaining among children. *J. Personality & Social Psychology*, 1971, *18*, 68–78.

Subjects: $N = 96$; 9–12 yrs. **Measures:** Same-sex pairs of friends, nonfriends, and neutrals were formed: 1 member of each pair (choice determined randomly) passed a reading test that made toys (previously rank-ordered by each S) available for play; 5 pairs of toys were presented to each group. Ss' first choice was paired with other's fifth choice (1:5), Ss' second choice was paired with other's fourth choice (2:4), etc. Ss rated the acceptability of each of the 5 options. Ss then decided between themselves which of the 4 pairs of toys they would like to play with. (In order to avoid an easy middle choice, each S's fifth-choice toy was removed.) **Results:** (1) No sex differences were found in the acceptability of toy allocations. (2) Female pairs agreed to an equity solution (1:4, 2:3) more often than male pairs did ($p < .025$). (3) Female nonfriends made lower evaluations of one another and saw each other as less friendly than male nonfriends did ($p < .05$). No sex differences were found for friends and neutrals.

Benton, A. A., Gelber, E. R., Kelley, H. H., and Liebling, B. A. Reactions to various degrees of deceit in a mixed-motive relationship. *J. Personality & Social Psychology*, 1969, *12*, 170–80.

Subjects: $N = 80$; 18–21 yrs (college). **Measures:** Ss played a 2-person, 2-choice, mixed-motive game with simulated same-sex partners. Each trial involved the following sequence: Ss picked the top card from a deck of (40 red and 40 black) shuffled cards. After noting its color, Ss passed the card through an opening in a partition to their partners (actually E, who henceforth will be referred to as declarer). Declarer informed Ss whether or not their cards were of the same color as the card that he had picked from a similar deck of red and black cards. Ss had the option of either accepting or doubting declarer's message. Accepting declarer's message that the cards were of the same color resulted in S receiving 2 points and declarer 0. Accepting declarer's message that the cards were different resulted in S receiving 0 points and declarer 2. Doubting the declarer on trials in which declarer had given Ss correct information resulted in a mutual loss to both players. Doubting the declarer on trials in which declarer deceived Ss (in an attempt to improve his own score at Ss' expense) resulted in 1 point being added to Ss's score and 1 point being deducted from declarer's score. Depending on the treatment condition to which they were assigned, declarer lied to Ss in either 0%, 25%, 50%, or 75% of the trials when it was to his advantage to present inaccurate information to Ss. After the last trial, Ss completed a postexperimental questionnaire. **Results:** (1) As assessed by a questionnaire administered just prior to the beginning of the game, men expressed a greater feeling of power in their role than women did ($p < .05$). Women indicated a preference for the declarer role; men indicated no role preference ($p < .05$). No sex differences were found in Ss' expected trustworthiness ratings of declarer. (2) No sex differences were found in Ss' doubting behavior. (3) On the postexperimental questionnaire, (a) women indicated they were less successful in affecting the declarer's behavior than men did ($p < .05$); (b) women reported they felt less responsible ($p < .05$) for their scores than men did (in the

75% rate-of-deception condition only); no sex differences were found when the deception rate was 0%, 25%, or 50%; (c) women reported they felt more tension ($p < .01$) than men did (in the 75% rate-of-deception condition only); no sex differences were found when the deception rate was 0%, 25%, or 50%; (d) women reported less satisfaction with the relationship they established with the declarer ($p < .05$) and indicated a greater preference for a new partner than men did ($p < .05$); (e) women reported less satisfaction with catching the declarer at lying than men did ($p < .05$); when asked if they would have preferred to face the declarer during the task, women indicated less desire to do so than men did ($p < .05$); (f) men rated the declarer more potent than women did in the 0% ($p < .10$), 25% ($p < .01$) and 50% ($p < .05$) conditions.

Bergan, A., McManis, D. L., and Melchert, P. A. Effects of social and token reinforcement on WISC Block Design performance. *Perceptual & Motor Skills*, 1971, 32, 871–80.
   Subjects: $N = 48$; 9 yrs. **Measures:** Ss were given the Block Design subtest of the WISC and assigned to 1 of 3 treatment groups that were matched on the basis of total score and time score. Assignment to groups was randomly determined within each sex. 3 weeks later, Ss were retested under 1 of 3 conditions: (1) control (standard instructions), (2) social reinforcement (positive verbal statement made after each correct response), and (3) token reinforcement (chips given for each correct response). **Results:** (1) Boys exceeded girls in accuracy on each test. (2) There were no sex differences in relative improvement in accuracy under control and token reinforcement. Girls showed a greater gain in accuracy under social reinforcement than boys. (3) Boys showed a decrease in absolute percentage of time required from pretest to post-test, whereas girls showed an increase in percentage of time. (4) Boys performed with greater speed under social reinforcement than girls. No sex differences were found for other treatment groups. (5) Under social reinforcement, boys made greater gains in speed than girls did, but not under other conditions.

Berger, S., and Johansson, S. L. Effect of a model's expressed emotions on an observer's resistance to extinction. *J. Personality & Social Psychology*, 1968, 10, 53–58.
   Subjects: $N = 144$; 18–21 yrs (college). **Measures:** After observing a model guess either 25% or 100% of the answers correct in a guessing game, Ss played the game with E. Ss were always told their guesses were wrong. Performance measure was the number of trials Ss played until they expressed a desire to quit. **Results:** No sex differences.

Berk, L. E. Effects of variations in the nursery school setting on environmental constraints and children's modes of adaptation. *Child Development*, 1971, 42, 839–69.
   Subjects: $N = 72$; 2–5 yrs. **Measures:** Ss' encounters with positive and negative environmental force units (EFUs) in nursery school were observed. EFUs were defined as any actions or constraints imposed upon the child by the environment that were directed to some specifiable end that the child was aware of. **Results:** (1) Boys encountered more EFUs than girls did. (2) Boys' actions were more frequently disrupted by their teachers than were girls'. (3) A higher percentage of boys' than girls' responses to EFUs were categorized as compliant. There were no sex differences in responses categorized as offensive-combative.

Berkowitz, H., and Zigler, E. Effects of preliminary positive and negative interactions and delay conditions on children's responsiveness to social reinforcement. *J. Personality & Social Psychology*, 1965, 2, 500–505.
   Subjects: $N = 80$; 7 yrs. **Measures:** Ss received intermittent verbal praise for inserting marbles into holes. Ss played until they expressed a desire to stop or until they did not insert a marble for 30 seconds. **Results:** No sex differences were found in task persistence.

Berkowitz, H., Butterfield, E. C., and Zigler, E. The effectiveness of social reinforcers on persistence and learning tasks following positive and negative social interactions. *J. Personality & Social Psychology*, 1965, 2, 706–14.
   Subjects: $N = 240$; 7 yrs. **Measures:** (1) Ss received intermittent verbal praise for inserting marbles into holes. Ss played until they expressed a desire to stop. Ss' persistence at the task was measured. (2) Ss turned off colored lights by pushing either of 2 buttons beneath the lights. After a baseline period, Ss received verbal praise for pressing the least preferred button. The number of responses to the reinforced stimulus was recorded. **Results:** No sex differences.

Berman, P. W., Rane, N. G., and Bahow, E. Age changes in children's learning set with win-stay, lose-shift problems. *Developmental Psychology*, 1970, 2, 233–39.
   Subjects: $N = 32$; 4, 6, 8, 10 yrs. **Measures:** Ss performed 2-trial object-discrimination prob-

lems. A single stimulus presented on trial 1 was rewarded on half of the problems and not rewarded on the remaining ones. The stimulus was presented again on trial 2, paired with a new stimulus. Ss were required to respond according to a win-stay, lose-shift principle. A criterion of correct responses was set. **Results:** There were no sex differences among 4- and 6-year-old Ss (only groups tested).

Bermant, G., Starr, M., and Trowbridge, B. Are men more inclined than women to take risks? *Personnel Psychology*, in press.
Subjects: $N = 112$; 18–21 yrs (college). **Measures:** Ss were randomly placed in 24 mixed-sex discussion groups of 4–5 members each. Each S was given the short form of the Kogan-Wallach Choice Dilemmas Questionnaire. After individual tests, each problem was discussed in a group until consensus was reached. After the discussion, Ss individually solved the problems. **Results:** (1) There were no sex differences in pregroup risk taking or postgroup shift to risk. (2) Women's post-group scores were more varied than men's ($p. < .02$).

Bernstein, R. C., and Jacklin, C. N. The 3½-month-old infant: stability of behavior, sex differences, and longitudinal findings. Unpublished master's thesis, Stanford University, 1973.
     EXPERIMENT I: **Subjects:** $N = 18$; 3½ mos and mothers. **Measures:** Responses measured were: tactile threshold; prone head reaction; first fixation time, total fixation time, and number of smiles to slides of faces and scrambled faces; and number of alerts to voices and auditory controls for voices. Mothers reported the amount of time the infant slept during the day. **Results:** (1) Girls were more responsive to (combined) auditory stimuli than boys ($p < .05$). There were no sex differences in responsiveness to social versus nonsocial auditory stimuli. (2) There were no other sex differences.
     EXPERIMENT II: **Subjects:** $N = 20$; tested at birth, 3½ mos. **Measures:** Response measures at birth were prone head reaction and tickle sensitivity (pressure aesthesiometer). Response measures at 3½ months were the same as for Experiment I. **Results:** (1) At birth, boys raised their heads higher than girls ($p < .05$). (2) Mothers reported that, at 3½ months, boys slept more than girls ($p < .05$). (3) There were no other sex differences.

Berry, J. W. Temne and Eskimo perceptual skills. *International J. Psychology*, 1966, *1*, 207–29.
Subjects: $N = 366$; 10–15, 15–20, 21–30, 31–40, over 40 yrs (Temne of Sierra Leone, Eskimo, Scots). Ss in the Temne and Eskimo samples were from either traditional or transitional societies. Ss in the Scottish sample were from either a rural or an urban area. **Measures:** 4 tests of spatial skills were administered to Ss—(1) Kohs Blocks, (2) Witkin's Embedded Figures Test, (3) Morrisby Shapes, and (4) Raven Matrices. In each sample, comparisons were made between men and women from the same area (e.g. rural Scottish men were compared only with rural Scottish women). This yielded a total of 24 comparisons, 6 for each of the 4 measures. **Results:** (1) in 4 of 8 comparisons in the Temne sample, men were superior to women. (2) In 4 of 8 comparisons in the Scottish sample, men were superior to women. (3) No sex differences were found in the Eskimo sample.

Biaggio, A., and Rodrigues, A. Behavioral compliance and devaluation of the forbidden object as a function of probability of detection and severity of threat. *Developmental Psychology*, 1971, *4*, 320–23.
Subjects: $N = 39$; 7 yrs (Brazil). **Measures:** Ss were left alone for 10 minutes and instructed not to play with 1 of 4 attractive toys (always child's second preferred toy). Conditions varied as to level of threat and probability of detection: severe threat/high probability of detection, severe threat/low probability of detection, mild threat/high probability, or mild threat/low probability. **Results:** No sex differences.

Biber, H., Miller, L. B., and Dyer, J. L. Feminization in preschool. *Developmental Psychology*, 1972, *7*, 86 (brief report).
Subjects: $N = 14$ classes (size 13 to 20); 4 yrs and their female teachers. **Measures:** Videotape records of classes in 4 different types of school programs were observed. **Results:** (1) Girls received more instructional contact (requests for information by teacher and information given individually to child) than boys did. (2) Girls received more positive reinforcement for instruction (feedback for correct or adequate academic performance) than boys did in the Montessori, enrichment-type preschool programs, and in a program emphasizing attitudes as well as abilities. (3) There were no sex differences in amount of positive reinforcement in the structured academic program.

Bickman, L. Sex and helping: interaction and ingratiation. Paper presented at Symposium on Sex and Helping Behavior, 80th Annual Convention of the American Psychological Association, Hawaii, 1972.
> EXPERIMENT I: **Subjects:** $N = 200$; 18 yrs (college). **Measures:** Ss were telephoned by an E who said either he was a freshman or he was a senior. E asked the S to help him by participating in a psychology experiment. S's helping behavior was noted. Sex of E and sex of S were varied. **Results:** No sex differences.
> EXPERIMENT II: **Subjects:** $N = 223$; 18–21 yrs (college). **Measures:** Same as Experiment I, except E said he needed subjects for either a male or a female friend. **Results:** No sex differences.
> EXPERIMENT III: **Subjects:** $N = 300$; 18–21 yrs (college). **Measures:** Ss received a letter asking them to participate in an experiment. The letter was signed by a male or female E. **Results:** No sex differences.
> EXPERIMENT IV: **Subjects:** $N = 298$; 18–21 yrs (college). **Measures:** Same as Experiments I–III, except (male or female) Es asked Ss for help, face to face. **Results:** No sex differences.

Bieri, J. Parental identification, acceptance of authority and differences in cognitive behavior. *J. Abnormal & Social Psychology*, 1960, *60*, 76–79.
> **Subjects:** $N = 60$; 18–21 yrs (college). **Measures:** Embedded Figures Test. **Results:** No sex differences.

Bieri, J., Bradburn, W., and Galinsky, M. Sex differences in perceptual behavior. *J. Personality*, 1958, *26*, 1–12.
> EXPERIMENT I: **Subjects:** $N = 110$; 18–21 yrs. **Measures:** An 8-item form of the Embedded Figures Test was administered to Ss. **Results:** Men located the figures faster than women did.
> EXPERIMENT II: **Subjects:** $N = 112$; 18–21 yrs. **Measures:** (1) Ss were given the Barron-Welsh Art Scale, a measure of Ss' preference for complex, asymmetrical line drawings vs. simple, symmetrical drawings. (2) Ss were assigned an External-Construct Score based on their responses to a modified version of Kelly's Role Construct Repertory Test. **Results:** No sex differences.
> EXPERIMENT III: **Subjects:** $N = 111$; 18–21 yrs. **Measures:** Ss were asked to list possible uses of a brick (Bricks Test). **Results:** No sex differences.
> EXPERIMENT IV: **Subjects:** $N = 76$; 18–21 yrs. **Measures:** SAT. **Results:** Men had higher quantitative scores than women. No sex difference was found in verbal scores.

Bigelow, G. Field dependence–field independence in 5- to 10-year-old children. *J. Educational Research*, 1971, *64*, 397–400.
> **Subjects:** $N = 160$; 5–10 yrs. **Measures:** Children's Embedded Figures Test. **Results:** No sex differences.

Birch, D. Evidence of competition and coordination between vocal and manual responses in preschool children. *J. Experimental Child Psychology*, 1971, *12*, 10–26.
> **Subjects:** $N = 35$; 3½–6½ yrs. **Measures:** To extinguish a light, Ss were required to perform either a manual or a vocal response, or both. Start times, reach times, target times (sum of start and reach times), and voice times were recorded. **Results:** No sex differences.

Birnie, L., and Whitely, J. H. The effects of acquired meaning on children's play behavior. *Child Development*, 1973, *44*, 355–58.
> **Subjects:** $N = 32$; 5 yrs. **Measures:** E told Ss 2 activities that a boy doll did or did not like to engage in when he visited a toy farm. 1 of the activities was 1 of 4 behaviors designated as a high-probability response, the other was 1 of 2 behaviors designated as a low-probability response (probabilities were determined by two Ss' free-play activity during the pilot study). Afterward, Ss were presented with the toy doll and the toy farm and were observed for 5 minutes. The number of times Ss exhibited each of the 4 high-probability and 2 low-probability responses was recorded. **Results:** No sex differences.

Birns, B. Individual differences in human neonates' responses to stimulation. *Child Development*, 1965, *36*, 249–56.
> **Subjects:** $N = 30$ (24 girls, 6 boys); tested at 2, 3, 4, 5 days. **Measures:** Each of 4 stimuli (soft tone, loud tone, cold disk, and pacifier) was applied to Ss 3 times at each session. Intensity of response (consisting primarily of changes in body movement) was recorded. **Results:** No sex differences.

Bisett, B. The effects of age and incentive value on discrimination learning. *J. Experimental Child Psychology*, 1966, 3, 199–206.
> **Subjects:** $N = 120$; 6–7, 10–11 yrs. **Measures:** Ss' relative preferences for 8 reward objects (paper clips, metal washers, small white rocks, pennies, miniature cars, small tin birds, trinkets, and Beatle cards) were assessed. **Results:** (1) Boys' choices of reward objects differed from girls' choices ($p < .001$). (2) Girls had a preference for the pennies more than boys did ($p < .05$).

Bishop, B. R., and Beckman, L. Developmental Conformity. *Developmental Psychology*, 1971, 5, 536 (brief report).
> **Subjects:** $N = 144$; 7–11 yrs. **Measures:** Confederates gave erroneous prearranged responses about line length to naïve Ss. Number of yieldings by Ss was recorded. **Results:** No sex differences.

Blanchard, E. B., and Price, K. C. A developmental study of cognitive balance. *Developmental Psychology*, 1971, 5, 344–48.
> **Subjects:** $N = 120$; 6, 8, 13, 18 yrs. **Measures:** Nonconserving 6-year-old Ss and conserving 8-year-old Ss, 9-year-old Ss who failed and 13-year-old Ss who passed tests of formal operational thought, and 18-year-old Ss were orally presented with 8 triadic situations of the form "You (like, dislike) (name of person)"; "You (like, dislike) (different person)"; "You see that (first person) and (second person) (like, dislike) each other." Ss were asked to indicate feelings regarding each situation on 2 5-point scales anchored by good-bad, happy-sad. **Results:** No sex differences.

Blayney, G. Sex differences in father protectiveness toward their preschool children. Unpublished senior honors thesis, Stanford University, 1973.
> **Subjects:** $N = 29$; 4 yrs and fathers. **Measures:** To assess their basic level of timidity, Ss were initially tested on an elevated balance beam mounted on springs (Phase 1). Fathers were then brought to the experimental room and the beam was raised 1 foot. Ss were allowed to cross the beam if they desired (Phase 2). Next, 3 wooden blocks were placed along the beam. Both the father's and the child's reactions to this challenge were recorded (Phase 3). In the final phase of the study (Phase 4), Ss and their fathers were given the opportunity to manipulate the toy's challenge by either adding or removing blocks. Measures were taken of the following: latency to begin crossing the beam; time spent crossing the beam; time spent in the sitting and crawling positions while on the beam; child reaches for father; child touches father; father reaches for child; father touches child; father's proximity to child; number of blocks added or removed by father or child (Phase 4). A timidity rating was assigned to each child based on the time it took him to cross the beam and on whether or not a crossing was completed in both directions. In addition, all verbalizations and communicative gestures (both child's and father's) were recorded, tallied, and then classified into the following categories: *child*—(a) requests father's help; (b) agrees to follow father's instructions; (c) refuses to perform expected act; (d) seeks father's encouragement and attention; (e) rejects father's help, accepts challenge, praises self; *father*—(a) withdraws aid, demands child assume self-direction; (b) withdraws aid, requests child to assume self-direction; (c) withdraws aid, presents child with challenging situation to overcome; (d) warns child of danger, suggests that child decrease degree of challenge; (e) offers aid, encourages parental reliance; (f) expresses affection or approval; (g) criticizes or complains about child's performance; (h) submits to child's demands or requests. **Results:** No differences were found between boys and girls. During the final phase of the study, fathers of girls made more independent-encouraging commands (withdraws aid, demands child assume self-direction) than fathers of boys did. No other differences were found between fathers of boys and fathers of girls.

Bledsoe, J. C. Sex differences in mental health analysis scores of elementary pupils. *J. Consulting Psychology*, 1961, 25, 364–65.
> **Subjects:** $N = 197$, 9–12 yrs. **Measures:** Ss were given the Elementary Form of Mental Health Analysis; 5 personality "liabilities" (behavioral immaturity, emotional instability, feelings of inadequacy, physical defects, and nervous manifestations) and 5 personality "assets" (close personal relationships, interpersonal skills, social participation, satisfying work and recreation, and adequate outlook and goals) were assessed. **Results:** Girls scored higher than boys on total assets, close personal relationships, and adequate outlook and goals, and lower on total liabilities, behavioral immaturity, and feelings of inadequacy. Overall, girls' mental health scores were superior to those of boys.

Bledsoe, J. C. Self-concepts of children and their intelligence, achievement, interests, and anxiety. *Childhood Education*, 1967, *43*, 436–38.
Subjects: $N = 271$; 9, 11 yrs. Measures: A 30-item self-concept, adjective checklist was administered to Ss. Results: Girls had more positive self-concepts than boys ($p < .01$).

Block, J. H. Conceptions of sex role: some cross-cultural and longitudinal perspectives. Unpublished manuscript (to be revised and submitted to *American Psychologist*), 1972.
Subjects: $N = 90$; 3 yrs and parents. Measures: Using the Child-rearing Practices Report, parents described their child-rearing attitudes and behaviors. Results: (1) Mothers of boys scored higher on the following items than mothers of girls: I think competitive games are good for a child; I encourage my child always to control his feelings; I don't think young children should see each other naked; I teach my child punishment will "find" him when he's bad. (2) Fathers of boys scored higher on the following items than fathers of girls: I think competitive games are good for a child; I encourage my child to always do his best; I think a child must learn early not to cry; I have firm rules for my child; I don't allow my child to get angry with me; I don't want my child looked upon as different. (3) Mothers of girls scored higher on the following items than mothers of boys: I find it difficult to punish my child; I like some time to myself away from my child; I give up some of my own interests for my child. (4) Fathers of girls scored higher on the following items than fathers of boys: I encourage my child to wonder and think about life; I feel a child should have time to daydream and loaf; I encourage my child to talk about her troubles; I encourage my child to be independent of me.

Blum, J. E., Fosshage, J. L., and Jarvik, L. F. Intellectual changes and sex differences in octogenarians: a twenty-year longitudinal study of aging. *Developmental Psychology*, 1972, *7*, 178–87.
Subjects: $N = 54$; tested at 64 yrs, 84 yrs (mean). Measures: In 1947 and again in 1967, Ss were given 5 tests from the Wechsler-Bellevue Intelligence Test (Similarities, Digits Forward, Digits Backward, Digit Symbol Substitution, Block Design), a vocabulary test from the Stanford-Binet Scale (1916), and a paper-and-pencil tapping test. Results: (1) In 1947, women scored higher than men on the Digit Symbol Substitution and Tapping tests. (2) In 1967, women scored higher than men on the Vocabulary, Similarities, Tapping, and Digit Symbol Substitution tests. (3) For each of the 7 tests, no sex difference was found in annual rate of decline in performance over the 20-year period.

Blumenfield, W. S., and Remmers, H. H. Research note on high school spectator sports preference of high school students. *Perceptual & Motor Skills*, 1965, *20*, 166.
Subjects: $N = 2,000$; 14–17 yrs. Measures: Ss were asked which of 11 sports was their favorite high school spectator sport. Results: Girls chose basketball and baseball more frequently than boys did; boys chose football more frequently than girls did.

Blurton Jones, N. Categories of child-child interaction. In N. B. Jones, ed., *Ethological Studies of Child Behaviour*. London: Cambridge University Press, 1972, pp. 97–127.
Subjects: $N = 25$; 2, 3–4 yrs. Measures: Ss were observed in a playroom well equipped with toys. Frequencies of rough-and-tumble, aggressive, and social play were recorded. Results: (1) Among younger Ss, girls engaged in more rough-and-tumble play than boys did. No sex differences were found in the older sample. Most displays of rough-and-tumble play by the older girls occurred when the slide was put out; this was not so true for older boys ($p < .001$). (2) When the slide was not available, boys engaged in more wrestling and hitting during rough-and-tumble play than girls did ($p < .04$). (3) No sex differences were found in aggressive or social play. (4) Among older Ss, girls displayed more kinds of behavior toward their teacher than boys did.

Blurton Jones, N., and Leach, G. M. Behaviour of children and their mothers at separation and greeting. In N. B. Jones, ed., *Ethological Studies of Child Behaviour*. London: Cambridge University Press, 1972, pp. 217–47.
Subjects: $N = 73$; 2–4 yrs and mothers. Measures: Data on whether a child cried when his mother left him at nursery school were obtained from a variety of sources: arrival and departure records; teacher's logbook; teacher's and author's memories. Results: No sex differences.

Bogo, N., Winget, C., and Gleser, G. C. Ego defenses and perceptual styles. *Perceptual & Motor Skills*, 1970, *30*, 599–604.
Subjects: $N = 97$; 18–21 yrs (college). Measures: (1) Rod and Frame test (portable model), (2) Figure-drawing test, (3) Defense Mechanisms Inventory: a paper-and-pencil measure

assessing the relative strength of 5 different defense mechanisms, (4) Autokinetic Effect: Ss sat in a darkened room and watched a pinpoint of light. Ss' task was to trace the path of any apparent movement of the light. Measure of autokinesis was the length of the line(s) Ss produced. **Results:** (1) Men were more field-independent than women on the RFT ($p < .005$). (2) No sex differences were found in FDT scores. Women drew larger figures of both sexes than men did. (3) No sex differences were found in Autokinetic Effect Scores. Women's scores were more varied than men's ($p < .01$). (4) On the Defense Mechanisms Inventory, men demonstrated more turning against an object ($p < .01$) and less turning against self ($p < .001$) than women. No sex differences were found in reversal, principalization, or projection.

Bokander, I. Semantic description of complex and meaningful stimulus material. *Perceptual & Motor Skills*, 1966, *22*, 201–2.
> **Subjects:** $N = 29$; 18–21 yrs (college). **Measures:** Ss rated each of 7 photographs of male faces on 22 different semantic scales. **Results:** No sex differences.

Borke, H. Interpersonal perception of young children. *Developmental Psychology*, 1971, *5*, 263–69.
> **Subjects:** $N = 20$; 3–8 yrs. **Measures:** Ss heard stories about another child and indicated how the story child felt by picking a happy, sad, afraid, or angry face. 8 more stories were told in which Ss behaved toward story children in ways that might make story children feel happy, sad, or angry. Ss chose the face that best indicated each story child's feelings. **Results:** There were no sex differences in ability to identify other people's feelings.

Bortner, R. W., and Hultsch, D. F. Personal time perspective in adulthood. *Developmental Psychology*, 1972, *7*, 98–103.
> **Subjects:** $N = 1,292$; 20–88 yrs. **Measures:** After defining in their own terms the worst and best possible lives they could imagine for themselves, Ss were asked to rate their past, present, and future status with respect to these extremes. 2 scores were derived from Ss' ratings: a retrotension score (S's rating of his present status was compared with his assessment of his past status) and a protension score (S's rating of his future status was compared with his assessment of his present status). **Results:** No sex differences.

Bosco, J. The visual-information-processing speed of lower- and middle-class children. *Child Development*, 1972, *43*, 1418–22 (and personal communication).
> **Subjects:** $N = 180$; 6, 8, 11 yrs. **Measures:** Ss viewed a test stimulus (square, circle, star, or triangle) on a tachistoscope. A variable interstimulus interval was followed by presentation of a masking stimulus. Processing speed (i.e. the minimum time necessary for recognition of the stimulus) was measured. **Results:** No sex differences.

Bourne, L. E., and O'Banion, K. Conceptual role learning and chronological age. *Developmental Psychology*, 1971, *5*, 525–34.
> **Subjects:** $N = 288$; 7, 9, 11, 13, 15, 19 yrs. **Measures:** Ss solved 3 conceptual rule-learning problems (relevant attributes of concept given, rule unknown) based on 1 of 4 rules: conjunctive (and), disjunctive (and/or), conditional (if, then), or biconditional (if and only if). **Results:** Girls were superior to boys on number of trials to last error. Authors say this effect is constant over all variables (grade and type of rule), and therefore imposes no qualifications on interpretation of other variables.

Bowers, K. S., and van der Meulen, S. J. Effect of hypnotic susceptibility on creativity test performance. *J. Personality & Social Psychology*, 1970, *14*, 247–56.
> **Subjects:** $N = 60$; 18–21 yrs (college). **Measures:** 9 creativity measures were derived from Ss' responses to Guilford's Consequences Test, the Holtzman Inkblot Test, and a free association test. The 3 tasks were administered while Ss were either awake or hypnotized. A third group of Ss feigned hypnosis to a naïve E. **Results:** In every comparison, 4 of which were significant, women achieved higher creativity scores than men.

Bowers, P., and London, P. Developmental correlates of role-playing ability. *Child Development*, 1965, *36*, 499–508.
> **Subjects:** $N = 40$; 5, 7, 9, 11 yrs. **Measures:** (1) A Dramatic Acting Test was used to measure ability to portray another person. E described a situation to S and asked him to respond in ways appropriate to mother, father, friend, bully, and teacher. (2) The Children's Hypnotic Susceptibility Scale, used to measure S's ability to portray himself in an unfamiliar role, was administered without hypnotic induction or relaxation. **Results:** No sex differences.

Brackbill, Y. Cumulative effects of continuous stimulation on arousal level in infants. *Child Development*, 1971, *42*, 17–26.
Subjects: $N = 24$; 1 mo. **Measures:** S was tested on 5 consecutive days under 5 different randomly ordered conditions: no extra stimulation, continuous stimulation of 1, 2, 3, and 4 sensory modalities including auditory stimulation (tape-recorded heartbeat), visual stimulation (combination of fluorescent and incandescent bulbs), swaddling, and temperature stimulation. Heart rate, respiration regularity, motor activity, and general state were measured. **Results:** No sex differences.

Brackbill, Y., Adams, G., Crowell, D., and Gray, M. L. Arousal level in neonates and preschool children under continuous auditory stimulation. *J. Experimental Child Psychology*, 1966, *4*, 178–88.
EXPERIMENT I: **Subjects:** $N = 41$; 3 yrs. **Measures:** Ss heard 4 continuously presented auditory stimuli at nap time for an hour every day. The stimuli were no sound, paired heartbeats, beating of a metronome, and unfamiliar lullabies in a foreign language. Number of minutes until S fell asleep was recorded. **Results:** No sex differences.
EXPERIMENT II: $N = 24$; 2 days. **Measures:** Ss heard 4 consecutive 15-minute presentations of no sound, heartbeat, metronome beating, and unfamiliar lullabies in a foreign language. Amount of crying, general motor activity, heart rate, regularity of heart rate, and regularity of respiration were recorded. **Results:** No sex differences.

Braginsky, D. D. Machiavellianism and manipulative interpersonal behavior in children: two explorative studies. Unpublished doctoral dissertation, University of Connecticut, 1966.
Subjects: $N = 48$; 10 yrs. **Measures:** Ss responded to a modified version of Christie's Likert-type Machiavellianism (Mach) scale. Ss classified as either low Machs or high Machs were then paired with a middle Mach of the same sex. Their task was to persuade their middle partners to eat as many crackers strongly flavored with quinine as possible. Ss were promised a reward for every cracker they could persuade their partners to eat. **Results:** No sex differences were found in Mach scores or in the effectiveness of Ss' persuasive attempts.

Braginsky, D. D. Machiavellianism and manipulative interpersonal behavior in children. *J. Experimental Social Psychology*, 1970, *6*, 77–99.
Subjects: $N = 225$ (on the Mach test), 96 (for the behavioral measures); 10 yrs. **Measures:** The Christie Mach Scale was adapted for suitability to 10-year-old children. On the basis of Mach scores, pairs of Ss were chosen such that the subject child in each pair had either a high or a low score while his partner (the "target child") had a Mach score in the middle range. On the pretext of wanting to test the palatibility of a new "health cracker," E asked each subject child to see how many quinine-flavored crackers he could get his partner to eat, and offered to pay the subject 5¢ for every cracker his partner consumed. Tape recordings were made of the interactions during the persuasive session. **Results:** There were no sex differences on the Mach test, or in the number of crackers consumed by the targets of boy and girl Ss. High-Mach boys told more direct lies, whereas high-Mach girls more often failed to mention unpleasant truths. However, the reverse pattern was found among low-Mach children, so there was no overall sex difference in the persuasive strategies employed.

Brainerd, C. J. The development of the proportionality scheme in children and adolescents. *Developmental Psychology*, 1971, *5*, 469–76.
Subjects: $N = 72$; 8, 11, 14 yrs. **Measures:** Ss with conservation of number and length were given conservation tests of density, solid volume, and liquid volume. **Results:** No sex differences.

Brainerd, C. J. The age-stage issue in conservation acquisition. *Psychonomic Science*, 1972, *29*, 115–17 (and personal communication).
Subjects: $N = 155$; 4–6 yrs. **Measures:** Ss were pretested and post-tested on conservation of number tasks with or without intervening training. **Results:** No sex differences.

Brainerd, C. J. Order of acquisition of transitivity, conservation, and class inclusion of length and weight. *Developmental Psychology*, 1973, *8*, 105–16.
EXPERIMENT I: **Subjects:** $N = 120$; 7–8 yrs (Canada, U.S.). **Measures:** Ss were tested in 2 concept areas (length and weight) for 3 concrete-operational skills (transitivity, conservation, and class inclusion). **Results:** In the U.S. sample, there were no sex differences in correct tran-

sitivity, conservation, or class inclusion judgments of weight and length. In the Canadian sample, boys found conservation more difficult than girls did ($p < .05$).
EXPERIMENT II: **Subjects:** $N = 180$; 5, 6, 7 yrs (Canada). **Measures:** Same as Experiment I. **Results:** No sex differences.

Brainerd, C. J., and Huevel, K. V. Development of geometric imagery in five- to eight-year-olds. *Genetic Psychology Monographs*, 1974, *86*, in press.
Subjects: $N = 120$; 5, 6 yrs. **Measures:** Ss were presented with 3 3-dimensional objects (a cube, a box, and a cylinder). Ss picked from among 21 drawings the 3 that accurately represented what the objects would look like if they were "opened up." **Results:** No sex differences.

Brannigan, G. G., and Tolor, A. Sex differences in adaptive styles. *J. Genetic Psychology*, 1971, *119*, 143–49.
Subjects: $N = 333$; 18–21 yrs (college). **Measures:** Ss completed a modified version of the Future Events test (a measure of personal future-time perspective) and Rotter's Internal-External Scale (a measure of Ss' generalized expectations about how reinforcement is controlled). **Results:** (1) Women were less futuristically oriented, having more constricted scores on a greater number of items than men. (2) Women were more external in their expectancy, scoring higher than men on the Rotter scale ($p < .001$).

Braun, C., and Klassen, B. A transformational analysis of oral syntactic structures of children representing varying ethnolinguistic communities. *Child Development*, 1971, *42*, 1859–71.
Subjects: $N = 216$; 6, 9, 11 yrs (German-, French-, English-speaking). **Measures:** Ss were divided into ability groups by the Pintner-Cunningham Primary Test (grade 1) and the Pintner General Ability Test (grades 4, 6). Ss viewed a film, after which they summarized the story and answered questions. Ss viewed another soundless film that was interrupted; they were asked to tell the story of the film and to conjecture what might have happened. Linguistic indexes were measured. **Results:** Girls used more noun plus relative clause transformations and object transformations than boys did. No sex differences were found on the 29 other indexes (e.g. number of subordinate clauses, redundancies, etc.).

Bresnahan, J. L., and Blum, W. L. Chaotic reinforcement: a socioeconomic leveler. *Developmental Psychology*, 1971, *4*, 89–92.
Subjects: $N = 60$; 6 yrs (low, high SES). **Measures:** Ss were given a concept acquisition problem after either 0, 6, or 12 random reinforcement trials. **Results:** No sex differences.

Bresnahan, J. L., Ivey, S. L., and Shapiro, M. M. Developmentally defined obviousness and concept formation tasks. *Developmental Psychology*, 1969, *1*, 383–88.
Subjects: $N = 64$; 5–6 yrs (white and black, Head Start program). **Measures:** Ss were given 4 concept-formation tasks: (a) number as the relevant dimension with size as a partial cue, (b) number without size, (c) size as the relevant dimension with number as a partial cue, and (d) size without number. **Results:** No sex differences.

Bridges, K. M. B. Occupational interests of three-year-old children. *J. Genetic Psychology*, 1927, *34*, 415–23.
Subjects: $N = 6$ boys, 4 girls; 2–3 yrs. **Measures:** Ss were observed in nursery school during free-play period. **Results:** Boys' favorite activities were building with large bricks, fitting cylinders into holes, color pairing, naming objects in picture postcards, and cube construction. Girls' favorite activities were fitting cylinders into holes, threading beads, writing on the blackboards, and fastening buttons.

Brimer, M. A. Sex differences in listening comprehension. *J. Research & Development in Education*, 1969, *3*, 72–79.
Subjects: $N = 8,324$; 5–8 yrs (test 1), 7–11 yrs (test 2). **Measures:** Ss took 1 of 2 versions of the orally administered English Picture Vocabulary Test (a modification of the Peabody Picture Vocabulary Test). **Results:** Among 6-8-year-old Ss, boys scored higher than girls (test 1). No other sex differences were found.

Brissett, M., and Nowicki, S., Jr. Internal vs. external control of reinforcement and reaction to frustration. *J. Personality & Social Psychology*, 1973, *25*, 35–44.
EXPERIMENT I: **Subjects:** $N = 80$; 18–21 yrs (college). **Measures:** Ss were given the Child and Waterhouse Frustration Reaction Inventory to assess Ss' claimed reactions to frustration in terms of 7 behavioral tendencies: preoccupation, pessimism, striving, vindication, aggres-

sion, self-blame, and nondistractibility. Ss' reported reactions to frustration were classified as either generally constructive or generally unconstructive. **Results:** Men scored higher in aggression than women ($p < .05$). No sex differences were found for striving, vindication, or self-blame. No mention was made of preoccupation, pessimism, or nondistractibility. There were no sex differences in generally constructive versus unconstructive reactions to frustration.

EXPERIMENT II: **Subjects:** Same as Experiment I. **Measures:** On an angle-matching task, Ss judged which of several angles matched a standard (none actually did). The measure was the amount of time Ss took to reach a decision. **Results:** No sex differences.

EXPERIMENT III: **Measures:** Ss responded to 4 TAT cards suggesting achievement situations. Ss' stories were scored for positive, negative, and doubtful outcomes, need for achievement, achievement imagery (task and general), and imagery unrelated to achievement. **Results:** No sex differences.

Brockman, L. M., and Ricciuti, H. N. Severe protein-calorie malnutrition and cognitive development in infancy and early childhood. *Developmental Psychology*, 1971, *4*, 312–19.
    Subjects: $N = 39$; 1–3½ yrs. **Measures:** 20 protein-calorie-deficient children and 19 controls without a history of malnutrition were administered 10 sorting tasks. After 12 weeks of nutritional treatment, the tasks were readministered to the experimental Ss. Highest-level serial ordering and highest-level similar-object grouping were assessed. **Results:** (1) No sex differences were found when experimental and control Ss' scores at the initial testing were compared. (2) An analysis of the experimental Ss' data from both testings showed that girls' overall task performance was superior to that of the boys.

Bronfenbrenner, U. Reaction to social pressure from adults versus peers among Soviet day school and boarding school pupils in the perspective of an American sample. *J. Personality & Social Psychology*, 1970, *15*, 179–89.
    Subjects: $N = 353$; 12 yrs (USSR). **Measures:** Ss responded to a series of conflict situations, each of which presented Ss with the choice of engaging in either antisocial behavior being urged by peers or behavior acceptable to adults and society. **Results:** Boys chose the "antisocial" alternatives more often than girls.

Bronson, G. W. Fear of visual novelty: developmental patterns in males and females. *Developmental Psychology*, 1970, *2*, 33–40.
    Subjects: $N = 60$; tested monthly from 1 to 15 mos, at increasing intervals from ages 15 mos to 8½ yrs. **Measures:** At each testing, Ss completed various measures of mental ability and physical and motor development. A record was kept during the first 15 sessions of the percentage of time each child cried. When Ss were between 4 and 36 months of age, judgments were made as to whether or not the strangeness of the experience had made them cry. Beginning at age 10 months, and continuing until the age of 8½ years, Ss were rated on the amount of shyness they had exhibited. **Results:** No sex differences.

Bronson, G. W. Infants' reactions to unfamiliar persons and novel objects. *Monographs of the Society for Research in Child Development*, 1972, *37*.
    Subjects: $N = 32$; tested at 3, 4, 6½, 9 mos (white, Oriental). **Measures:** (1) During the first home visit at 3 months, Ss were rated on a 5-point persistency-of-crying scale ranging from "no crying, or baby quickly quieted" to "baby recurrently cried unless being held in mother's arms." Mothers were also asked to describe their infants' reactions to being bathed during the first and second months of their lives. (2) At 3 and 6½ months, mothers' behaviors toward their infants were rated on 2 5-point scales, yielding an overall measure of quality of maternal care. (3) At 3, 4, 6½, and 9 months, the frequency with which Ss smiled at their mothers was recorded. (4) At 3, 4, 6½, and 9 months, a red-patterned paper parasol was rapidly opened and closed in front of Ss. Incidences of blinking responses were recorded. (5) At 4, 6½, and 9 months, Ss' responses to an encounter with a male stranger were rated on a 5-point scale of affect ranging from "smiled with delight" to "cried." (6) At 6½ months, a large beeping object was placed near Ss. The number of infants who reached out and grabbed the object was recorded. **Results:** No sex differences.

Bronson, W. C. Exploratory behavior of 15-month-old infants in a novel situation. Paper read at the meeting of the Society for Research in Child Development, Minneapolis, 1971.
    Subjects: $N = 40$; 15 mos and mothers. **Measures:** Mother and infant entered a room containing 2 chairs, a small toy dog, and a novel object. After showing the novel object to the infant, the mother walked over to a chair, taking the infant with her. The infant was then set on the floor; if he did not spontaneously approach the object within 30 seconds, the mother began encouraging the child to do so until an approach was effected (Episode 1).

Next, a young woman who was a stranger to Ss entered the room and sat down, remaining silent for 60 seconds (Episode 2). After the minute had elapsed, she began speaking to both the mother and the infant. Moving over to the object, she continued to attend to the baby. For the remainder of the time, she responded to the infant's approaches, but did not initiate interaction (Episode 3). **Results:** (1) In Episodes 2 and 3, boys attended to the novel object more frequently than girls did ($p < .05$, $p < .001$). In Episode 1, boys spent more time near the object than girls did ($p < .01$). In Episodes 1 and 3, girls gazed at the object more than boys did ($p < .01$, $p < .01$). In Episodes 1, 2, and 3, boys pulled the stick and observed the contingent effects more frequently than girls did ($p < .05$, $p < .001$, p $< .05$). No sex differences were found in the amount of time Ss spent examining or playing with the object. (2) In Episode 1, girls attended to and spent more time near their mothers than boys did ($p < .05$, $p < .05$). (3) In Episodes 1, 2, and 3, girls attended to the toy dog more frequently than boys did (p $< .01$, $p < .01$, $p < .01$). (4) In Episode 2, girls reacted more positively to the stranger than boys did ($p < .01$). No sex differences were found in the amount of attention Ss directed toward the stranger. (5) No sex differences were found in overall ratings of motor activity and affect.

Brooks, J., and Lewis, M. Attachment behavior in thirteen-month-old, opposite-sex twins. *Child Development*, 1974, 45, 243–47.
> **Subjects:** $N = 17$ pairs of opposite-sex twins; 11–15 mos. **Measures:** Each child and mother were observed for 15 minutes in a room containing the following toys: a set of blocks, a pail, a cornpopper, a rubber dog, a stuffed cat, a set of quarts, a wooden mallet, a pegboard, and a pull toy. **Results:** (1) Girls looked at their mothers more frequently than boys did ($p < .001$). (2) Girls spent more time in proximity to their mothers than boys ($p < .02$). (3) No sex differences were found in frequency of touching mother, number of pleasant vocalizations to mother, number of toy changes, or amount of sustained play. (4) No sex differences were found in Ss' preferences for the various toys.

Brooks, R. L., Brandt, L., and Weiner, M. Differential response to two communication channels: socioeconomic class differences in response to verbal reinforcers, communicated with and without tonal inflection. *Child Development*, 1969, 40, 453–70.
> **Experiment I: Subjects:** $N = 80$; 5, 6 yrs (low, middle SES). **Measures:** Ss played a marble-dropping game in which they were free to drop marbles into either of 2 holes. Following an initial baseline period, Ss were reinforced (good-fine or right-correct) for dropping a marble into the hole they had chosen less frequently during baseline. The reinforcers were said in either a positive or neutral tone of voice. The number of reinforced responses Ss performed and the total number of marbles they dropped were recorded. **Results:** No sex differences.
>
> **Experiment II: Subjects:** $N = 168$; 5–6 yrs. **Measures:** Procedures similar to Experiment I were followed. The reinforcers E used (good-right or bad-wrong) were said in either a positive, neutral, or negative tone of voice. **Results:** No sex differences.

Brotsky, S., and Kagan, J. Stability of the orienting reflex in infants to auditory and visual stimuli as indexed by cardiac deceleration. *Child Development*, 1971, 42, 2066–70.
> **Subjects:** $N = 79$; tested at 4, 8, 13 mos. **Measures:** At 4 and 8 months of age, Ss were exposed to a series of achromatic slides. At 8 months, infants also heard 4 different recitations read by a male voice. At 13 months of age, 3 3-dimensional figures were shown to Ss, 1 at a time. Afterward, auditory stimuli (identical to the set of stimuli used at 8 months) were presented. At each session, cardiac deceleration to the first stimulus in the visual or auditory series was assessed. **Results:** No sex differences.

Brown, F. An experimental and critical study of the intelligence of Negro and White kindergarten children. *J. Genetic Psychology*, 1944, 65, 161–75.
> **Subjects:** $N = 432$; 5–6 yrs. **Measures:** Stanford-Binet Intelligence Test, Form L. **Results:** No sex differences.

Brown, H. Children's comprehension of relativized English sentences. *Child Development*, 1971, 42, 1923–36.
> **Subjects:** $N = 96$; 3–5 yrs. **Measures:** Ss heard a sentence describing 1 of 2 pictures and were asked to choose the matching picture. **Results:** No sex differences.

Brown, L. Developmental differences on the effects of stimulus novelty on discrimination learning. *Child Development*, 1969, 40, 813–22.
> **Subjects:** $N = 64$; 4–5 yrs (middle-high SES). **Measures:** Ss initially learned a constant posi-

tive–constant negative, 2-choice discrimination learning problem to criterion. Ss were then presented with 1 of 4 shift problems. For half the Ss, the positive stimulus was replaced either by a new constant positive stimulus or by a series of new positive stimuli, a different one of which appeared on each trial. For the other half of the Ss, similar replacement procedures were followed with the constant negative stimulus. **Results:** No sex differences were found in number of trials needed to reach criterion on the initial constant positive–constant negative problem or in number of correct responses made on the shift problems.

Brown, R. A. Interaction effects of social and tangible reinforcement. *J. Experimental Child Psychology*, 1971, *12*, 289–303.
Subjects: $N = 60$; 4–6 yrs. **Measures:** Ss performed a bar-pressing task under either tangible, social, or alternated tangible and social reinforcement. Difference scores were derived by subtracting Ss' base rates from their average response rates in each of the 5 experimental trial blocks. **Results:** (1) Over trials, girls showed a greater increase in performance than boys ($p < .01$). Tests for sex differences within each block of trials showed that girls responded to the reinforcement in trial blocks 3, 4, and 5 more than boys did ($p < .05$). (2) During extinction, no sex differences were found.

Brownfield, M. K. Sex and stimulus time difference in afterimage durations. *Perceptual & Motor Skills*, 1965, *21*, 446.
Subjects: $N = 30$; 18–20 yrs (college). **Measures:** In a dark room, Ss viewed a stimulus of .2 candlepower, 1 square centimeter in area. The durations of Ss' afterimages were recorded. **Results:** Men's afterimages lasted longer than women's.

Bruning, J. L. Direct and vicarious effects of a shift in magnitude of reward on performance. *J. Personality & Social Psychology*, 1965, *2*, 278–82.
Subjects: $N = 144$; 5 yrs. **Measures:** Ss received rewards each time they performed a lever movement response. In 1 condition, Ss played 2 sets of 30 trials each. In a second condition, 1 group of Ss (models) performed 30 trials while a second group of Ss (observers) watched. Observer Ss then played 30 trials by themselves. **Results:** (1) There were no main sex differences. (2) The presence of an observer facilitated the performance of female models, but inhibited the performance of male models ($p < .025$).

Bruning, J. L., and Husa, F. T. Given names and stereotyping. *Developmental Psychology*, 1972, *7*, 91 (brief report).
Subjects: $N = 60$; 5, 8, 11 yrs. **Measures:** 2 male stickfigures were presented, 1 with an active and 1 with a passive name; statement to Ss: "These are two little boys. This one's name is ———— and this one's name is ————. Which one do you think would ————?" 25 active and 25 passive behavioral statements were used. Number of correct matches of behaviors with names was recorded. **Results:** Among 11-year-old Ss, boys made more correct matches than girls.

Bryan, J. H., and Walbek, N. H. Preaching and practicing generosity: children's actions and reactions. *Child Development*, 1970, *41*, 329–53.
Experiment I: **Subjects:** $N = 91$; 8, 9 yrs. **Measures:** Ss observed a same-sex adult model win gift certificates while playing a bowling game. On winning trials, the model either did or did not always donate a proportion of his certificates to charity. On no-win trials, one-third of the Ss in each group heard the model preach generosity, and one-third heard the model preach selfishness; the remaining third heard the model make neutral comments. All Ss then played the game in the model's absence. The number of Ss who donated in each condition was recorded. **Results:** No sex differences.
Experiment II: **Subjects:** $N = 168$; 8, 9 yrs. **Measures:** Same as Experiment I, except videotapes of peer models were used instead of live adult models. After playing the bowling game, Ss evaluated the model's attractiveness. **Results:** No sex differences were found in Ss' donating behavior or their attractiveness ratings.
Experiment III: **Subjects:** $N = 132$; 8, 9 yrs (white and black). **Measures:** Same as Experiment II, with 2 exceptions: (1) the model's appeals to Ss to be either charitable or selfish were personalized, and (2) Ss were asked to comment into a microphone while playing the game. Ss were rated for the emphasis they placed upon generosity. **Results:** (1) No main sex differences were found in Ss' attractiveness ratings. (2) Among black Ss, boys preached more generosity than girls. No sex difference was found among white Ss. (3) The authors did not report whether tested for sex differences in donating behavior.

Bryan, J. H., Redfield, J., and Mader, S. Words and deeds about altruism and the subsequent reinforcement of the model. *Child Development*, 1971, *42*, 1501–8.

Subjects: $N = 96$; 7–8 yrs. Measures: Ss initially observed a videotape of an adult female model playing a bowling game. On selected trials, the model won gift certificates and either donated all of them to charity or kept them for herself. On no-win trials, the model either urged Ss to be charitable or selfish or made neutral comments. When the film ended, the model entered the experimental room where Ss were seated. Ss then played a lever-pressing game. On each trial, Ss could choose to press either a lever that yielded an M&M candy or 1 that illuminated a bright light. Half the Ss in each treatment condition were verbally reinforced by the model whenever the blue light came on. The remaining Ss received no social reinforcement. Afterward, Ss related the model's attractiveness. Results: No sex differences were found in Ss' attractiveness ratings or in the number of times they pressed the lever associated with the blue light.

Bryden, M. P. Auditory-visual and sequential-spatial matching in relation to reading ability. *Child Development*, 1972, *43*, 824–32.

Subjects: $N = 40$; 11 yrs. Measures: Ss were given a same-different matching task in which patterns were presented in 3 modes: auditory, visual-sequential, and dot patterns. Each of 20 pairs of patterns was presented once in each combination. Ss had to decide if 2 patterns were the same or different. Results: No sex differences.

Buck, M. R., and Austrin, H. R. Factors related to school achievement in an economically disadvantaged group. *Child Development*, 1971, *42*, 1813–26.

Subjects: $N = 100$; 14–16 yrs (black). Measures: Pairs of adequate achievers and underachievers were established on the basis of the Iowa Tests of Basic Skills. Ss were given Crandall's Intellectual Achievement Responsibility questionnaire. Teachers rated Ss on classroom behavior, attitudes, personality characteristics, and performance. Mothers rated their own attitudes and Ss' attitudes. Results: (1) Among adequate achievers, teachers rated girls less deviant in behavior than boys ($p < .01$). (2) Among adequate achievers, girls received higher scores on IAR total ($p < .05$) and on IAR negative ($p < .01$) than boys; i.e. girls in this group were more internal, especially for negative events. (3) There were no sex differences for total positive teacher rating. (4) Mothers of girls were more reactive concerning daughters' intellectual achievement than mothers of boys ($p < .05$). (5) Mothers of girls expressed higher expectancy levels, higher degree of satisfaction with accomplishments, and higher minimal academic standards than mothers of boys ($p < .01, p < .01, p < .05$).

Buck, R. W., Savin, V. J., Miller, R. E., and Caul, W. F. Communication of affect through facial expressions in humans. *J. Personality & Social Psychology*, 1972, *23*, 362–71.

Subjects: $N = 38$; 18–21 yrs (college). Measures: 1 subject (sender) in each pair of like-sex Ss watched slides designed to elicit affect, while the other subject (observer) viewed the sender subject's face over television. After each slide, both observer and sender Ss made judgments about the strength and pleasantness of the emotional response experienced by sender Ss. Skin conductance and heart rate were recorded. Results: (1) No sex differences were found in the physiological responses of senders. (2) Among observer Ss, women had higher heart rates than men ($p < .01$). Men had more numerous skin-conductance responses than women ($p < .05$).

Bugenthal, D. E., Kaswan, J. W., and Love, L. R. Perception of contradictory meanings conveyed by verbal and nonverbal channels. *J. Personality & Social Psychology*, 1970a, *16*, 647–55.

Subjects: $N = 160$; 5–12 yrs and parents. Measures: Ss evaluated videotaped messages that varied on 3 dimensions: vocal channel (voice), visual channel (facial expressions, etc.), and verbal channel (script). Each channel contained either positive-evaluative (friendly) or negative-evaluative (unfriendly) content. Results: Women speakers were rated more negatively than men ($p < .01$); the difference was greater for conflicting messages than for messages that were either uniformly positive or uniformly negative.

Bugenthal, D. E., Kaswan, J. W., Love, L. R., and Fox, M. N. Child versus adult perception of evaluative messages in verbal, vocal, and visual channels. *Developmental Psychology*, 1970b, *2*, 367–75.

Subjects: $N = 120$; 5–18 yrs and parents. Measures: Ss rated televised parent-child interaction scenes on a 13-point scale representing degrees of positive and negative evaluation. Scenes were either positive (friendly), neutral, or negative (unfriendly) in content, voice tone, and/ or facial expression. Results: (1) There were no sex differences in ratings of male actor scenes or female actor scenes. (2) Female actors were evaluated more favorably in positive scenes and more unfavorably in negative scenes than male actors.

Burton, G. M. Variations in the ontogeny of linear patterns among young children. Unpublished doctoral dissertation, University of Connecticut, 1973.
> **Subjects:** $N = 111$; 4–7 yrs (inner-city schools). **Measures:** 3 tasks involving linear patterns (reproduction, identification, and extension) in 3 cognitive modes (enactive, iconic, and symbolic) were used to assess patterning ability. **Results:** No sex differences.

Burton, R. V. Correspondence between behavioral and doll-play measures of conscience. *Developmental Psychology*, 1971, 5, 320–32.
> **Subjects:** $N = 60$; 4 yrs (2 studies). **Measures:** In each of 2 doll-play sessions, Ss completed 4 deviation story stems. Ss' responses were scored for the presence of the following: reparations (actions whereby the deviation is repaired), punishment (e.g. verbal censure, isolation, physical punishment, etc.), and confession (admission of the deviation). Between doll-play sessions, Ss were taught the rules of beanbag game, after which Ss were left alone for 3 minutes to play the game. The number of Ss who conformed to the rules and the number who deviated were recorded. In the second study, 2 temptation story stems were added in each doll-play session. **Results:** (1) When both samples were combined, girls were found to deviate from the rules more often than boys. (2) No sex differences were found in Ss' Session 1 or Session 2 doll-story completions. (3) No sex differences were found in changes in Ss' doll-story completions between Session 1 and Session 2.

Burton, R. V., Allinsmith, W., and Maccoby, E. E. Resistance to temptation in relation to sex of child, sex of experimenter, and withdrawal of attention. *J. Personality & Social Psychology*, 1966, 3, 253–58.
> **Subjects:** $N = 112$; 4 yrs. **Measures:** Ss were taught the rules of a beanbag game by either a same-sex or opposite-sex E. Ss then performed an intervening task, receiving either continuous or interrupted attention from E. Following E's departure, Ss played the beanbag game for attractive toys. For each act of breaking the rules, Ss were rewarded with a "hit." The number of bags Ss threw correctly before deviating from the rules was recorded. **Results:** (1) No main sex differences were found. For boys, continuous attention from E produced greater resistance to deviation than interrupted attention from E ($p < .01$). No treatment effect was found for girls. (2) Ss assigned to opposite-sex Es threw more bags before deviating from the rules than Ss who were assigned to same-sex E's ($p < .05$).

Bush, L. E., II. Individual differences multidimensional scaling of adjectives denoting feeling. *J. Personality & Social Psychology*, 1973, 25, 50–57.
> **Subjects:** $N = 762$; 18–21 yrs (white and black, college). **Measures:** Using Ss' judgments of the similarity of adjective pairs, 264 adjectives were scaled by the Individual Differences Multidimensional Scaling method (INDSCAL). **Results:** No sex differences.

Buss, A. H. Instrumentality of aggression, feedback, and frustration as determinants of physical aggression. *J. Personality & Social Psychology*, 1966, 3, 153–62.
> **Subjects:** $N = 240$; 18–21 yrs (college). **Measures:** Ss administered shocks to either same-sex or opposite-sex victims. **Results:** Men administered higher intensities of shock to victims than women did. Ss administered more intense shocks to men than women ($p < .001$).

Butter, E. J., and Zung, B. J. A developmental investigation of the effect of sensory modality on form recognition in children. *Developmental Psychology*, 1970, 3, 276 (brief report).
> **Subjects:** $N = 144$; 5–8 yrs. **Measures:** Ss could see, feel, or see and feel each stimulus form while trying to find the matching cutout on a formboard containing 58 cutouts of varying size, shape, and orientation. Number of recognition errors was recorded. **Results:** No sex differences.

Byrne, D., Clore, G. L., Jr., and Worchel, P. Effect of economic similarity-dissimilarity on interpersonal attraction. *J. Personality & Social Psychology*, 1966, 4, 220–24.
> **Subjects:** $N = 84$; 19 yrs (college). **Measures:** Using the Interpersonal Judgment Scale, Ss evaluated strangers on the basis of the strangers' responses to attitude items and to items dealing with "spending money." **Results:** No sex differences were found in attraction to stranger.

Byrne, D., Lamberth, J., and Ervin, C. R. Continuity between the experimental study of attraction and real-life computer dating. *J. Personality & Social Psychology*, 1970, 16, 157–65.
> **Subjects:** $N = 88$; 18–21 yrs (college). **Measures:** Men and women were paired on the basis of maximal or minimal similarity of responses on an attitude-personality questionnaire. After

spending 30 minutes together, Ss evaluated each other on the Interpersonal Judgment Scale. Two to three months later, further information was obtained from Ss, including whether each S's evaluation of his or her date was influenced more by physical attractiveness or by attitude similarity. **Results:** (1) No sex differences were found in Ss' responses to the IJS. (2) 18 men and 17 women indicated that their evaluations were influenced more by either physical attractiveness or attitude similarity. The remaining Ss (53) indicated either that both factors were equally important or that neither factor was important. Of the 35 Ss who selected one or the other, most of the men ($N = 14$) indicated that their evaluations were more influenced by physical attractiveness, while most women ($N = 16$) indicated that their evaluations were more influenced by attitude similarity ($p. < .001$).

Cairns, R. B. Informational properties of verbal and nonverbal events. *J. Personality & Social Psychology*, 1967, 5, 353–57.
  Subjects: $N = 40$; 9 yrs. **Measures:** Ss were given a modified version of the Wisconsin Card-Sorting Test. During the first 50 trials (acquisition phase), Ss were reinforced for choosing the correct response. During the last 20 trials (extinction phase), no reinforcement was administered. **Results:** No sex differences.

Cairns, R. B. Meaning and attention as determinants of social reinforcer effectiveness. *Child Development*, 1970, *41*, 1067–82.
  Experiment I: **Subjects:** $N = 120$; 6, 7 yrs. **Measures:** During the first phase of the experiment Ss were instructed to put cards into the "mouth" of a machine. On 16 of the 43 trials Ss received an M&M candy after responding. Depending on the condition to which they were assigned, on each trial the delivery of an M&M was either preceded or not preceded by a signal (for half the Ss, the signal was the word "right"; for the remaining Ss, the signal was a bell-light combination). After Ss completed trial 43, no M&M's were delivered. Every subsequent response was followed by a signal. The number of cards Ss put into the machine during a 5-minute period was recorded. During the second phase of the experiment, Ss were tested on a discrimination-learning problem. On each trial, Ss were presented with a red and a blue token. Selection of the "correct" color was always followed by either the word "right" or a bell-light combination. The response measure was number of times Ss chose the reinforced color. **Results:** No sex differences.
  Experiment II: **Subjects:** $N = 20$; 6, 7 yrs. **Measures:** Similar to Experiment I. **Results:** No sex differences.
  Experiment III: **Subjects:** $N = 40$; 8, 9 yrs. **Measures:** Similar to Experiment I. **Results:** No sex differences.

Caldwell, E. C., and Hall, V. C. Concept learning in discrimination tasks. *Developmental Psychology*, 1970, *2*, 41–48.
  Subjects: $N = 144$; 4–5, 7–8 yrs. **Measures:** Ss under 1 of 3 sets of instructions picked which of several transformed figures were the same as a standard form. Some Ss were allowed to rotate the standard form, others were not. **Results:** There were no sex differences in percentage of correct matches with line-to-curve transformations, rotation and reversal transformations, perspective transformations, or break-and-close transformations. Instructions to rotate affected the two sexes equally.

Calhoun, W. Stanford Research Institute, Menlo Park, California. Personal communications, 1972.
  Subjects: $N = 12,350$; 8, 9 yrs. **Measures:** Raven's Coloured Progressive Matrices (abbreviated form). **Results:** Boys scored higher than girls.

Callard, E. D. Achievement motive of four-year-olds and maternal achievement expectancies. *J. Experimental Education*, 1968, *36*, 15–23.
  Subjects: $N = 80$; 4 yrs and mothers (low, high SES). **Measures:** (1) 4 achievement tasks (bead designs, picture memory, basket throw, drawing forms) were administered to Ss. After performing each task, Ss were given the opportunity to repeat either an easy, difficult, or challenging version of the task. The number of times Ss chose to repeat a challenging task was recorded. (2) Torgoff's Parental Developmental Timetable was used to assess the age at which mothers thought it appropriate (a) to start to teach, encourage, or train a child to adopt new, more mature modes of behavior (Achievement Inducing Scale); and (b) to allow the child to engage in activities requiring autonomy and independence of action and decision (Independence-Granting Scale). A controlling score was calculated by dividing the mean age recommended on the IG scale by the mean age on the IA scale. **Results:** (1) Girls chose to resume more challenging tasks than boys did. (2) The mean age recommended by mothers of boys on

the IG scale was younger than the mean age recommended by mothers of girls. No differences were found in AI or controlling scores.

Cameron, P. The generation gap: beliefs about sexuality and self-reported sexuality. *Developmental Psychology*, 1970a, *3*, 272 (brief report).
Subjects: $N = 317$; 18–25, 40–55, 65–79 yrs. Measures: Ss responded to a questionnaire assessing their beliefs about their own and the 3 generations' sexual knowledge, desire, skill, capacity, attempts, opportunities, access, and frequency. Results: No sex differences.

Cameron, P. The generation gap: which generation is believed powerful versus generational members' self-appraisals of power. *Developmental Psychology*, 1970b, *3*, 403–4.
Subjects: $N = 317$; 18–25, 40–55, 65–79 yrs. Measures: Ss completed a questionnaire assessing their beliefs about their own wealth and power, and the differences in wealth and power among the 3 generations. Results: Men tended to judge themselves as more powerful and wealthy than women did (no statistics given).

Campione, J. C. The effects of stimulus redundancy on transfer of stimulus pretraining. *Child Development*, 1971, *42*, 551–59.
Subjects: $N = 64$, 3–5 yrs. Measures: Ss performed high- or low-redundancy tasks from a modified version of the Wisconsin General Test Apparatus. Verbal and perceptual stimulus pretraining were given; task involved discrimination-learning transfer. Results: No sex differences.

Campione, J. C., and Beaton, V. L. Transfer of training: some boundary conditions and initial theory. *J. Experimental Child Psychology*, 1972, *13*, 94–114.
Experiment IIIa: Subjects: $N = 36$; 3–6 yrs. Measures: After verbal pretraining, Ss were given a simultaneous 2-choice discrimination-learning task. Results: No sex differences.
Experiment IIIb: Subjects: $N = 48$; 3–6 yrs. Measures: Ss were divided into 2 groups. One-half were pretrained on a successive discrimination-learning problem, while the other half were pretrained on a simultaneous discrimination problem. After reaching the learning criterion, Ss in both groups were tested on a simultaneous 2-choice discrimination problem involving either an intradimensional (ID) or extradimensional (ED) shift. Results: No sex differences.
Experiment IV: Subjects: $N = 128$; 5–6 yrs. Measures: Same as Experiment IIIb. Results: No sex differences.
Experiment V: Subjects: $N = 64$; 3–6 yrs. Measures: After verbal pretraining, Ss were tested on a successive discrimination-learning task. Results: No sex differences.

Canavan, D. Field dependence in children as a function of grade, sex, and ethnic group membership. Paper received at the APA Meeting, Washington, D.C., 1969.
Subjects: $N = 1,510$; 5–11 yrs (white, black, Mexican). Measures: Man in the frame test (adaptation of Witkin's Rod-and-Frame Test). Results: When scores were adjusted to control for differences in IQ (as measured by the Full Scale WISC), boys were more field-independent than girls.

Canon, L. K. Motivational state, stimulus selection, and distractibility. *Child Development*, 1967, *38*, 489–96.
Subjects: $N = 40$; 10 yrs. Measures: (1) 10 boys and 10 girls were assigned to isolation or nonisolation conditions. Nonisolated Ss spent time with E in casual conversation prior to the task; isolated Ss waited alone for 20 minutes prior to the task. (2) All Ss worked under the influence of a social distractor involving a female voice relating a nurturant story as well as an impersonal distractor involving nonhuman sound effects. All Ss worked on 2 forms of a concept-utilization task in which they were required to select symbols out of several alternatives that identically matched a standard. Results: No sex differences.

Cantor, G. N. Effects of a "boredom" treatment on children's simple RT performance. *Psychonomic Science*, 1968, *10*, 299–300.
Subjects: $N = 60$; 6 yrs. Measures: Ss were given alternating blocks of trials on a picture-viewing and a reaction-time (RT) task. On the picture-viewing task, half of the Ss viewed different colored slides of high-interest value (nonbored group), while the remaining Ss were repeatedly exposed to the same geometric form (bored group). On the RT task, Ss had to move their finger off a start button and depress a response button upon representation of a light stimulus. Response measures were start (time from onset of light to the moment Ss removed their fingers from the start button) and travel speed (time from the moment Ss removed their fingers from the start button to the moment they depressed the response button). **Re-**

sults: (1) No sex differences were found in start speed. (2) For travel speed, boys were faster than girls ($p < .01$). Nonbored girls were faster than bored girls; bored boys were faster than nonbored boys ($p < .04$).

Cantor, G. N. Effects of context on preschool children's judgments. *J. Experimental Child Psychology*, 1971, *11*, 505–12.
    Subjects: $N = 40$; 4–5 yrs. **Measures:** Ss saw 10 slide pictures of either happy or unhappy faces and then rated ambiguous slides of an individual infant or young child on a 5-point happy-unhappy continuum. **Results:** No sex differences.

Cantor, G. N. Effects of familiarization on children's ratings of pictures of whites and blacks. *Child Development*, 1972a, *43*, 1219–29.
    Subjects: $N = 80$; 9–12 yrs. **Measures:** Ss were initially exposed to photographs of 3 black boys and 3 white boys. Ss then rated these pictures and those of 6 other boys (3 black, 3 white) on the extent to which they "would like to bring the boy home to spend time with them and their families." **Results:** Boys gave more favorable ratings to black boys than girls did ($p < .01$). No sex differences were found in Ss' ratings of white boys.

Cantor, G. N. Use of a conflict paradigm to study race awareness in children. *Child Development*, 1972b, *43*, 1437–42 (and personal communication).
    Subjects: $N = 60$; 7–8 yrs. **Measures:** Ss viewed pairs of photographs of boys in which both were black, both were white, or one was black and one was white. A story was read describing behaviors of the boys in the photographs, and Ss were asked to choose which of the 2 boys was the "good" or the "bad" boy. Response latencies and choices were measured. **Results:** Boys had greater response latencies for choosing the "good" boy ($p < .05$), whereas girls had greater latencies for choosing the "bad" boy ($p < .05$).

Cantor, G. N., and Whitely, J. H. Effects of rewarding children's high- and low-amplitude motor responses. *Psychonomic Science*, 1969, *16*, 211–12.
    Subjects: $N = 48$; 4–5 yrs. **Measures:** Ss were presented with a wooden mallet and a padded metal plate that served as a response target. On baseline trials, Ss were informed they could hit the target either "hard" or "soft." Response amplitudes were recorded. Subsequently, a series of 36 training trials were administered; half the Ss were reinforced for response amplitudes exceeding their baseline scores while the remaining Ss were reinforced for amplitudes lower in magnitude than their baseline scores. Response amplitudes were again recorded. **Results:** (1) No sex differences were found in either baseline or training response amplitudes. (2) When difference scores were computed by subtracting baseline scores from training scores, no main sex differences were found. Boys' response amplitudes decreased between baseline and the first block of 4 trials; girls showed an increase ($p < .05$).

Carey, G. L. Sex differences in problem-solving performance as a function of attitude differences. *J. Abnormal & Social Psychology*, 1958, *56*, 256–60.
    Subjects: $N = 144$; 18–21 yrs (college). **Measures:** Before and after participating in a discussion, the disguised intent of which was the promotion of a more favorable attitude toward problem solving, Ss were administered problem sets and a scale designed to measure their attitudes toward problem solving. **Results:** (1) Men had more favorable attitudes toward problem solving than women. (2) Following the discussion, women performed better on the second problem set than on the first set ($p < .02$); men showed no improvement ($p < .05$). (3) There were no sex differences in attitude score improvement following the discussion.

Carlson, R. Stability and change in the adolescent's self-image. *Child Psychology*, 1965, *36*, 659–66.
    Subjects: $N = 49$; tested at 11, 17 yrs. **Measures:** Ss were given parallel forms of a self-descriptive questionnaire at both ages. Self and ideal-self descriptions were included. Kelley's Role Construct Repertory Test was administered at age 17. **Results:** (1) There were no sex differences at the preadolescent level. (2) Among 17-year-old Ss, girls were more socially oriented than boys ($p < .02$). (3) There were no sex differences in level or stability of self-esteem.

Carlson, R. Sex differences in ego functioning: exploratory studies of agency and communion. *J. Consulting & Clinical Psychology*, 1971, *37*, 267–77.
    Experiment I: **Subjects:** $N = 76$; 18–21 yrs (college). **Measures:** Carlson's Adjective Checklist. **Results:** A greater number of women than men checked interpersonal adjectives (e.g.

friendly, persuasive) more frequently than individualistic adjectives (e.g. ambitious, ideal-
istic).

EXPERIMENT II: **Subjects:** $N = 41$; 18–21 yrs (college). **Measures:** A modified version of
Kelley's Role Construct Repertory Test. **Results:** When asked to choose from among 3 persons
(1 of whom was the self) the 2 who were most alike and different from the third, more women
than men included themselves with another person ($p < .05$).

EXPERIMENT III: **Subjects:** $N = 82$; 18–21 yrs (college). **Measures:** Ss were asked to write
a brief personality sketch of a friend. The first sentence of each sketch was scored for the
presence or absence of demographic constructs. **Results:** More men than women included
demographic constructs in their first sentence ($p < .01$).

EXPERIMENT IV: **Subjects:** $N = 48$; 18–21 yrs (college). **Measures:** Ss were asked to describe the physical-geographic environment of their childhood. Responses were classified as
either proximal (inclusion of personal memories, attention to details that only a person who
has lived in a neighborhood would know about) or distal (demographic description of the
town, its climate, size of population, SES levels, etc.). **Results:** More women than men gave
proximal responses ($p < .05$).

EXPERIMENT V: **Subjects:** $N = 55$; 18–21 yrs (college). **Measures:** Ss were asked the following questions: What sort of person do you expect to be in 15 years? What will you be
doing? How might have you changed? Ss' responses were scored on whether mention was made
of work, family, physical change, or inner psychological change. **Results:** More men than women
mentioned work ($p < .05$), whereas more women than men mentioned inner psychological
change ($p < .01$) and family ($p < .01$).

EXPERIMENT VI: **Subjects:** $N = 43$; 18–21 yrs (college). **Measures:** Ss were asked to recall
emotional incidents in their lives. Ss' responses were coded as agentic (concerned with achievement, success, separateness, or aloneness), communal (concerned with social acceptance,
togetherness, or dependence), or mixed (having both agentic and communal themes). **Results:** More men than women gave agentic responses (in reporting negative affects, $p < .05$;
overall, $p < .02$).

Carlson, R., and Levy, N. Brief method for assessing social-personal orientation. *Psychological Reports*, 1968, *23*, 911–14.
  Subjects: $N - 133$; 18–45 yrs. **Measures:** Ss completed an adjective checklist measuring social-personal orientation. **Results:** Men were more frequently personally oriented, women more
  socially oriented ($p < .001$).

Carlson, R., and Levy, N. Self, values, and affects: derivations from Tomkins' polarity
theory. *J. Personality & Social Psychology*, 1970, *16*, 338–45.
  EXPERIMENT I: **Subjects:** $N = 202$; 18–21 yrs (college, black). **Measures:** Ss completed the
  Carlson adjective checklist and were classified as either socially or personally oriented. **Results:** No sex differences.
  EXPERIMENT II: **Subjects:** $N = 80$; 18–21 yrs (college, black). **Measures:** Ss were presented with 25 pictures and asked to judge whether each picture portrayed a pleasant or unpleasant experience. **Results:** No sex differences.

Carlson, R., and Price, M. A. Generality of social schemas. *J. Personality & Social Psychology*, 1966, *3*, 589–92.
  Subjects: $N = 158$; 7–11, 25–50 yrs. **Measures:** Ss were asked to arrange 9 sets of stimulus
  figures on a felt-covered board (man, woman, child; man, woman, dog; man, child; woman,
  child; man, woman, 2 rectangles; 3 men, 3 rectangles; 3 women, 3 rectangles; 3 rectangles;
  square, circle, triangle). For each set, E recorded the order of arrangement and the distance
  between the figures. **Results:** (1) Males were more likely than females to produce a vertical
  arrangement of the square, circle, and triangle ($p < .01$). (2) Both sexes centered the like-
  sexed figure in the man, woman, dog set ($p < .02$).

Caron, A. J. Far transposition of intermediate-size in preverbal children. *J. Experimental
Child Psychology*, 1966, *3*, 296–311.
  Subjects: $N = 192$; 3–4 yrs. **Measures:** Multiple discrimination training and far transposition
  administered to preverbals to test for abstraction of middle size. **Results:** (1) Girls trained
  faster than boys. (2) Girls were superior to boys in transposition.

Caron, R. F., and Caron, A. J. Degree of stimulus complexity and habituation of visual
fixation in infants. *Psychonomic Science*, 1969, *14*, 78–79.
  Subjects: $N - 96$; 14–16 wks. **Measures:** Ss were presented with 15 20-second trials of visual
  stimuli. Geometric designs were shown on trials 1–4 and 10–12, 1 of 3 red-and-white checker-

board patterns on trials 5–9 and 13, and abstract art photos on trials 14 and 15. Fixation times were recorded. **Results:** (1) On trials 1–4 and 5–9, no sex differences were found in fixation times. The slope of the fixation curve over trials 5–9 was steeper for girls than for boys ($p <$ .025). (2) The decline in fixation time between trial 5 and trial 13 was greater for girls than for boys ($p < .005$). (3) Girls showed a greater increase in fixation time from trial 13 to trial 14 than boys ($p < .005$).

Caron, R. F., Caron, A. J., and Caldwell, R. C. Satiation of visual reinforcement in young infants. *Developmental Psychology*, 1971, 5, 279–89.
  Subjects: $N = 98$; 3½ mos. **Measures:** After a conditioning period in which head turning was continuously reinforced with abstract pictures, Ss were exposed to an interval of variable reinforcement, redundant reinforcement (repeatedly presented 4 x 4 or 24 x 24 checkerboards, or checkerboards alternating in either color, pattern, or both), and recovery (reconditioning of head turning with variable reinforcement). **Results:** (1) There were no sex differences in head-turn rate in the minute prior to onset of redundancy. (2) Girls' head turning declined faster than boys' in the minute prior to redundancy, plus 3 minutes of redundancy ($p < .001$). (3) During each minute of redundancy, the response rate of girls was lower than that of boys ($p < .01$, $p < .001$, $p < .05$). (4) There were no sex differences in recovery of the head-turn response. (5) There were no sex differences in hard crying during any of the 3 intervals.

Carpenter, T. R., and Busse, T. V. Development of self-concept in Negro and White welfare children. *Child Development*, 1969, 40, 935–39.
  Subjects: $N = 80$; 6, 10 yrs (father-absent welfare families). **Measures:** Ss were asked to rate themselves on a 5-point scale for 7 bipolar dimensions of positive-negative qualities. **Results:** Among blacks, girls had a more negative self-concept than boys. No sex difference was found in the white sample.

Carrigan, W. C., and Julian, J. W. Sex and birth-order differences in conformity as a function of need affiliation arousal. *J. Personality & Social Psychology*, 1966, 3, 479–83.
  Subjects: $N = 96$; 11 yrs. **Measures:** One group of Ss initially rated fellow classmates on a sociometric questionnaire; the remaining group of Ss did not. 4 different stories were then presented with each of 10 TAT cards. Ss' task was to pick the story that provided the best description of each TAT picture. Before responding, Ss were informed which stories had received the most votes in another class. The number of times Ss picked the popular choice was recorded. **Results:** Girls made more popular choices than boys ($p < .01$). This sex difference was greater among those Ss who completed the sociometric questionnaire than among those who did not ($p < .05$).

Carroll, W. R. Response availability and percentage of occurrence of response member in children's paired associate learning. *J. Experimental Child Psychology*, 1966, 4, 232–41.
  Subjects: $N = 80$; 10–11 yrs. **Measures:** Ss learned a paired-associates list by either the conventional anticipation method or by having the responses of the to-be-learned list presented in a vertical array next to each stimulus during the anticipation interval. Under both methods, the specific response to each stimulus word appeared on either 33% or 100% of trials. **Results:** There were no main sex differences. Girls gave more correct responses than boys on the first trial block; boys gave more correct responses on several of the later trial blocks.

Carroll, W. R., and Penney, R. Percentage of occurrence of response member, associative strength, and competition in paired associate learning in children. *J. Experimental Child Psychology*, 1966, 3, 258–66.
  Subjects: $N = 56$; 11 yrs. **Measures:** Ss were assigned either to a typical paired-associates task or to one in which the second member of the pair occurred only 33% of the time. Each S learned word pairs of high or low associative strength. One-half learned a competitional list, the other half a concompetitional. **Results:** No sex differences.

Castore, C. H., and Stafford, R. E. The effect of sex role perception on test taking performance. *J. Psychology*, 1970, 74, 175–80.
  Subjects: $N = 462$; 18 yrs (college). **Measures:** Ss were given the Identical Blocks Test and 1 of 3 forms of a spatial visualization test: (a) a neutral form entitled "Pattern Development," (b) a masculine form entitled "Drafting Aptitude Test" (the instructions to this form were read by a male E; performance on the test was related to ability in engineering, architecture, and sheet-metal work), or (c) a feminine form entitled "Fashion Design Aptitude Test" (the instructions were read by a female E; scores on the test were related to success in the fields

of fashion design, pattern-making, and dressmaking). **Results:** Men performed better than women on the Identical Blocks Test and on all 3 forms of the spatial visualization test. The magnitude of the sex differences on the spatial test did not vary among forms.

Cathcart, W. G. The relationship between primary students' rationalization of conservation and their mathematical achievement. *Child Development*, 1971, *42*, 755–65.
    Subjects: $N = 120$; 7, 8 yrs. **Measures:** An 8-item conservation test was administered to Ss. Ss were asked to provide a rationale for each of their responses. **Results:** No sex differences were found in the frequency of different modes of rationalization.

Chandler, M. J., Greenspan, S., and Barenboim, C. Judgments of intentionality in response to videotaped and verbally presented moral dilemmas: the medium is the message. *Child Development*, 1973, *44*, 315–20.
    Subjects: $N = 80$; 7 yrs. **Measures:** Ss were preesnted with 1 videotape of children and adults portraying a moral dilemma and 1 verbal account of a moral dilemma; intention and seriousness of consequence were varied. Ss were asked to judge which character was the naughtiest and which should be punished the most. **Results:** No sex differences.

Charlesworth, R., and Hartup, W. W. Positive social reinforcement in the nursery school peer group. *Child Development*, 1967, *38*, 993–1002.
    Subjects: $N = 70$; 3, 4 yrs. **Measures:** Ss were observed in their preschool over a period of 5 weeks. Measures were taken of the frequency of occurrence of the following types of positive social reinforcement: gives attention and approval to peer; gives affection, shows acceptance of peer; submissively reinforces peer. The total number of other children that each child reinforced was also recorded. **Results:** (1a) Among 3-year-olds, boys scored higher than girls on "gives affection, shows acceptance of peer" and "submissively reinforces peer'" ($p < .01$, $p < .05$). Boys also reinforced a greater number of other children than girls did ($p < .001$). Overall, girls gave less positive reinforcement ($p < .02$). (1b) Among 4-year-olds, no sex differences were found. (2) When both age groups were combined, both boys and girls were found to reinforce same-sex peers more frequently than opposite-sex peers.

Cheyne, J. A. Effects of imitation of different reinforcement combinations to a model. *J. Experimental Child Psychology*, 1971, *12*, 258–69.
    Subjects: $N = 30$; 8 yrs. **Measures:** Ss performed a word-choice task (2 response alternatives, no feedback) after observing a same-sex peer perform the same task under 3 reinforcement conditions: feedback for right and wrong choices, feedback for right only, and feedback for wrong only. Ss were then instructed to perform the model's choices, under no feedback conditions. **Results:** No sex differences.

Christie, R. Scale construction. In R. Christie and F. L. Geis, eds., *Studies in Machiavellianism*, pp. 10–34. New York: Academic Press, 1970a.
    Subjects: $N = 1,596$ (white), 148 (nonwhite); 18–21 yrs (college). **Measures:** Ss were given the Likert-type and forced-choice versions of the Machiavellianism scale. **Results:** Among white Ss, men scored higher than women on both scales. Among nonwhite Ss, men scored higher than women only on the Likert-type scale.

Christie, R. Social correlates of Machiavellianism. In R. Christie and F. L. Geis, *Studies in Machiavellianism*, pp. 314–36. New York: Academic Press, 1970b.
    Subjects: $N = 72$; 11 yrs (Puerto Rican, black, Chinese, and European ancestry). **Measures:** A children's version of Christie's Likert-type Machiavellianism Scale was administered to Ss. **Results:** No sex differences.

Cicirelli, V. G. Sibling constellation, creativity, IQ, and academic achievement. *Child Development*, 1967, *38*, 481–90.
    Subjects: $N = 609$; 11 yrs. **Measures:** The California Short-Form Test of Mental Maturity, the California Arithmetic Test, the California Language Test, the Gates Basic Reading Tests, and the Minnesota Tests of Creative Thinking, Verbal and Nonverbal Forms A were administered to Ss. An analysis of Ss' scores on the creativity tests yielded 4 factors: (a) verbal fluency-flexibility-originality, (b) verbal elaboration, (c) nonverbal fluency-flexibility-originality, and (d) nonverbal elaboration. **Results:** (1) Girls scored higher in language achievement and verbal elaboration than boys. (2) In 2-child families, girls scored higher in reading achievement than boys.

Clapp, W., and Eichorn, D. Some determinants of perceptual investigatory responses in children. *J. Experimental Child Psychology*, 1965, *2*, 371–87.

> **Subjects:** $N = 24$; 4–5 yrs. **Measures:** 32 stimuli cards were tachistoscopically exposed during 3 experiments: incongruity, redundancy (geometric figures), and redundancy (meaningful objects). The response measure was the mean number of times a card was looked at. **Results:** No sex differences.

Clark, A. H., Wyon, S. M., and Richards, M. P. M. Free play in nursery school children. *J. Child Psychology & Psychiatry*, 1969, *10*, 205–16.

> **Subjects:** $N = 40$; 2–4 yrs. **Measures:** Observations were made of Ss during their morning free play session. **Results:** (1) Boys spent more time than girls playing with blocks, drinking milk, and playing with toys on which they sat and propelled themselves. Girls spent more time than boys painting, playing with dolls, and engaging in table activities (cutting, gluing, sewing, crayoning, etc.). No sex differences were found in the amount of time Ss spent playing with cars, trucks, puzzles, old car parts, sand, plasticine, clay, or musical instruments; or in the amount of time they spent playing house, sawing and hammering, getting out/putting back toys, or climbing up and playing in the balcony. (2) No sex differences were found in average length of time between activity changes or in the amount of time Ss spent in supervised work. (3) More boys than girls exhibited the tendency to have a few close friends ($p < .01$). More children were observed with whom boys never played than girls ($p = .02$). (4) No sex differences were found in average number of companions, in the number of times Ss were observed alone or with teacher, or in the number of times they initiated contact with the teacher.

Clarke-Stewart, K. A. Interactions between mothers and their young children: characteristics and consequences. *Monographs of Society for Research in Child Development*, 1973, *38*, no. 153.

> **Subjects:** $N = 36$; tested at 9–18 mos (black and white low-SES firstborns), and their mothers. **Measures:** *The capital letters following many of the measures listed below refer to the factors on which the measures load. The 5 infant factors (Competence, C; Object Orientation, O; Early Test Talent, E; Physical Attachment, P; and Irritability, I) and 3 maternal factors (Optimal Care, 0; Effectiveness, E; and Restrictiveness, R) reported here were among the 11 factors with eigenvalues greater than 1 that emerged from factor analyses of the data.* 12 home visits were made to each mother-child pair. (1) At the initial home visit, interviews were conducted with mothers to assess their attitudes toward their children. (2) During 7 of the visits, naturalistic observations were made of a variety of infant and maternal behaviors. Infants were assessed on the following: schema development (C); attachment to mother (P); positive involvement with mother (C); number of vocalizations to mother (C); number of looks to mother (C); number of prolonged involvements with objects (O); stimulation by materials (looks at or plays with toys or other objects) (O); number and variety of objects played with (0); frequency of negative behavior (cries, fusses, whines, frets when not hurt) (I); physical attachment to mother (P); frequency of giving, offering, or taking object to mother; number of 10-second intervals spent eating or sleeping; frequency of vocalizations; number of interactions with observer; activity level. Mothers were assessed on the following: verbal stimulation (O); frequency of giving, showing, or placing toy near child (O); social stimulation (O); rejectingness (O); responsiveness to infant's distress and demand behaviors (O); responsiveness to infant's social signals (O); appropriateness (selectivity of mother's response, appropriateness for infant's age) (O); referential speech ratio (O); frequency of looking to infant (O); frequency of giving food, object, or toy to infant (O); directiveness; physical contact with infant; restrictiveness (R); frequency of nonresponsive speech; effectiveness of physical contact; effectiveness of stimulation with materials (O); effectiveness of instrumental speech (E); effectiveness of social behavior (E). Also recorded during these observation sessions were the number of times mother and child were present in the same room, the number of times they were in eye-to-eye contact, the number of times they interacted, and the number of times they played together. At 17 months, the number, functional availability, variety, and age appropriateness of the infant's toys were assessed. When the data from these sessions were analyzed, scores from the first 3 visits were summed together to yield a combined score, as were the scores from the final 3 visits. (3) The Bayley Mental and Motor Scales were given to the infants when they were 10½–12½ months old, and again when they were 17–18 months old. Infants' scores on the Motor Scale were combined with the ratings observers assigned to them on a developmental checklist to yield an overall measure of motor development. Their scores on the Mental Scale loaded on the factor Early Test Talent. (4) After a brief home observation session at 11–13 months of age, mother-infant pairs were brought to the laboratory for further testing. As they arrived, Ss were led to a

group of attractive toys, while their mothers were directed to chairs in the corner of the room. The infants were then exposed to a sequence of events consisting of varying episodes of free play, stranger intrusion, and mother absence. The episodes were arranged in an order designed to be increasingly stressful for the infant. 5 measures were assessed during this session: intensity of attachment to mother (P); positive social responsiveness to the female stranger (P); variety of toys played with (O); average length of involvement with individual toys (C); "play level." The latter 3 variables were assessed only during the mother-present free-play episodes. (5) When Ss were 12–14 months old, items for assessing cognitive development from 4 of the Uzgiris-Hunt series were administered; 3 scores were obtained: objective permanence (C); schema development (E); and object relations (E). (6) At 17 months of age, Ss completed several tests designed to assess language competence (C). (7) At the final home visit, mothers completed a questionnaire assessing their attitudes toward their children and their knowledge of child rearing and child development. **Results:** (1) During the first 3 home observation sessions, no sex differences were found on any measure (2) During the last 3 sessions in the home, girls spent more time eating and sleeping, exhibited more positive involvement with their mothers, received higher scores on the measures of language competence, exhibited fewer prolonged involvements with objects, and looked at and played with toys and other objects less frequently than boys did. (3) When all visits were taken into consideration, white boys were found to be more object-oriented than white girls; no difference was found between black boys and black girls. No sex differences were found among Ss of either race on the other 4 factors—Competence, Early Test Talent, Physical Attachment, and Irritability. (4) Among white Ss, mothers of boys scored higher than mothers of girls on 2 measures: "plays with infant" and "gives, shows, or places toy near infant"; among black Ss, the reverse was true. On the questionnaire administered at the final home session, boys' mothers expressed more positive attitudes toward their children than girls' mothers. No sex differences were found on any other measure of maternal behavior or on any of the 3 maternal factors— Optimal Care, Effectiveness, or Restrictiveness.

Clement, D. E., and Sistrunk, F. Judgments of pattern goodness and pattern preference as functions of age and pattern uncertainty. *Developmental Psychology*, 1971, 5, 389–94.
Subjects: $N = 96$; 9–10, 13–14, 17–18, 20–21 yrs. **Measures:** Ss rated dot patterns of known pattern uncertainty for "goodness" (how well formed they were) and for their own preference. **Results:** No sex differences.

Clore, G. L., and Jeffery, K. M. Emotional role playing, attitude change, and attraction toward a disabled person. *J. Personality & Social Psychology*, 1972, 23, 105–11.
Subjects: $N = 76$; 18–21 yrs (college). **Measures:** Ss in one group played the role of a person confined to a wheelchair for an hour, while Ss in a second treatment group walked behind role players, observing their experiences. Afterward, Ss responded to affective ratings and attitude scales and indicated their attraction to E (who appeared to be confined to a wheelchair). Ss also provided written descriptions of their experiences, which were analyzed for emotional content. **Results:** (1) Women described themselves as feeling weaker ($p < .01$) and more anxious ($p < .01$) than men did. (2) Women expressed a more favorable attitude toward disabled students than men did ($p < .01$). (3) No sex differences were found in attraction to E or in Ss' written descriptions of their experiences.

Coates, B. White adult behavior toward Black and White children. *Child Development,* 1972, 43, 143–54.
Subjects: $N = 48$; 18–23 yrs. **Measures:** Ss were asked to instruct a black or white male child how to perform a discrimination task. The child's responses were fixed so that each adult thought his pupil had a slow learning curve. Ss could make 5 negative-to-positive statements about the child's behavior. Ss also filled out a questionnaire on their attitudes toward the child. **Results:** When teaching the black child, men used more negative statements than women did ($p < .025$). No other sex differences were found.

Coates, B., and Hartup, W. W. Age and verbalization in observational learning. *Developmental Psychology*, 1969, 1, 556–62.
Subjects: $N = 72$; 4–5, 7–8 yrs. **Measures:** Ss observed a filmed male model perform novel behaviors. In the induced verbalization (IV) condition, Ss were told to repeat E's description of the model's action while watching the movie. In the free verbalization (FV) condition, Ss were asked to describe the model's behaviors in their own words. In the passive observation (PO) condition, no instructions related to verbalizing were given. After viewing the film, Ss were asked to demonstrate their learning of the model's actions. **Results:** While watching the

movie, girls in the IV and FV conditions emitted more accurate verbalizations than boys ($p < .05$). No sex differences were found in number of correct matching responses on the acquisition test.

Coates, B., Anderson, E. P., and Hartup, W. W. Interrelations in the attachment behavior of human infants. *Developmental Psychology*, 1972, *6*, 218–30.
Subjects: $N = 23$; tested at 10, 14 mos, and their mothers. $N = 23$; tested at 14, 18 mos, and their mothers. Measures: Mother-infant pairs were observed in a testing room with several toys. After an initial 3-minute period of nonseparation, mothers left the room for 2 minutes. A reunion phase then followed. Frequency of (a) visual orientation to mother, (b) touching mother, (c) proximity to mother, and (d) vocalizing to mother was recorded preceding and following the separation phase. Frequency of crying was recorded during all 3 periods (preseparation, separation, reunion). Results: No sex differences.

Coates, S. W. Preschool Embedded Figures Test. Consulting Psychologists Press, Inc., Palo Alto, California, 1972.
Subjects: $N = 247$; 3–5 yrs. Measures: Preschool Embedded Figures Test. Results: Girls' performance was superior to boys' ($p < .05$).

Coates, S. W. Field dependence, autonomy striving, and sex differences in preschool children. Unpublished manuscript, State University of New York, Downstate Medical Center, 1973.
Subjects: $N = 53$; 4–5 yrs. Measures: (1) S's scores on the Preschool Embedded Figures Test, the WPPSI Block Design test, and the Geometric Design test were converted to Z scores and added together to yield a composite field dependence score. (2) Each S was rated by his teacher on Beller's Autonomous Achievement Striving Scale. Results: No sex differences were found in composite field dependence scores. Teachers rated girls higher than boys in autonomous achievement striving ($p < .05$).

Cohen, B. D., and Klein, J. F. Referent communication in school age children. *Child Development*, 1968, *39*, 597–609.
Subjects: $N = 240$; 8, 10, 12 yrs. Measures: Pairs of Ss matched by age and sex were tested. One S was assigned the role of speaker, the other S was assigned the listener role. Both Ss were presented with 30 word pairs. On the speaker's list 1 word of each pair was underlined. The speaker was instructed to give the listener cues so he could identify which of the 2 words was underlined. Results: No sex differences in communication skills.

Cohen, L. B. Attention-getting and attention-holding processes of infant visual preferences. *Child Development*, 1972, *43*, 869–79.
Subjects: $N = 36$; 3–4 mos. Measures: Ss viewed red-and-white checkerboard patterns that varied in size and number of checks. Latency and fixation were measured. Results: No sex differences.

Cohen, L. B., Gelber, E. R., and Lazar, M. A. Infant habituation and generalization to differing degrees of stimulus novelty. *J. Experimental Child Psychology*, 1971, *11*, 379–89.
Subjects: $N = 64$; 4 mos. Measures: Ss were exposed to simple geometric patterns, followed by test trials of 2 exposures to the same pattern, 2 to patterns with the same form but with a novel color, 2 to a novel form but the same color, or 2 to both novel form and color. Fixation times were measured. Results: (1) Both sexes initially attended to the simple pattern at similar levels, but fixation times decreased over trial blocks for boys and not for girls. (2) During the test trials, girls had greater overall fixation time than boys ($p < .01$). (3) During the 2 trial blocks and for the first test trial, girls had greater fixation times than boys ($p < .01$, $p < .01$).

Cohen, S. E. Infant attentional behavior to face-voice incongruity. Paper presented at meeting of Society for Research in Child Development, Philadelphia, March 1973.
Subjects: $N = 96$; 5, 8 mos and mothers. Measures: With mother and a female stranger in full view, Ss were twice presented with 4 taped stimulus conditions, each emanating from a speaker held at shoulder level of a supposed person speaking: mother speaking with mother's voice, mother speaking with stranger's voice, stranger speaking with stranger's voice, and stranger speaking with mother's voice. Visual fixation behaviors were recorded. Results: There were no main sex differences. Girls looked more to the sound source under all conditions; boys deployed their attention more widely, especially when the mother was the sound source ($p < .001$).

Cole, M., Frankel, F., and Sharp, D. Development of free recall learning in children. *Developmental Psychology*, 1971, *4*, 109–23.

EXPERIMENT II: **Subjects:** $N = 120$; 6, 8, 13 yrs. **Measures:** Ss either heard and repeated the names of 20 objects or saw and named the actual objects. Ss were later tested for recall of the stimuli. **Results:** No sex differences.

EXPERIMENT III: **Subjects:** $N = 82$; 6, 9, 11, 14 yrs. **Measures:** After learning and repeating the names of 20 objects, Ss were asked to recall as many of the names as possible. **Results:** No sex differences.

Collins, D., Kessen, W., and Haith, M. Note on an attempt to replicate a relation between stimulus unpredictability and infant attention. *J. Experimental Child Psychology*, 1972, *13*, 1–8.

Subjects: $N = 48$; 2, 4 mos. **Measures:** Ss were presented with 3 patterns of flashing lights varying in complexity. Limb movement and sucking behavior were recorded. **Results:** No sex differences.

Collins, W. Learning of media content: a developmental study. *Child Development*, 1970, *41*, 1133–42.

Subjects: $N = 168$; 8, 11, 12, 14 yrs. **Measures:** Ss viewed an old situation-comedy that included both male and female family members. Afterward, Ss were tested for recall of essential and nonessential content. **Results:** (1) Girls showed better learning of essential content than boys did. (2) No sex differences were found in learning of nonessential content. (3) Difference scores (number of essential items correct minus one-half the number of correct nonessential items) were larger for girls than for boys.

Connell, D. M., and Johnson, J. E. Relationship between sex-role identification and self-esteem in early adolescents. *Developmental Psychology*, 1970, *3*, 268 (brief report).

Subjects: $N = 143$; 13 yrs. **Measures:** Gough Femininity Scale, Coopersmith Self-Esteem Inventory. **Results:** (1) Among high sex-role identification Ss, boys had greater feelings of self-esteem than girls ($p < .05$). (2) Low sex-role identification boys had lower feelings of self-esteem than girls, regardless of girls' sex-role identification level ($p < .05$).

Conners, C. K., Schuette, C., and Goldman, A. Informational analysis of intersensory communication in children of different social class. *Child Development*, 1967, *38*, 251–66.

Subjects: $N = 80$; 5, 6, 9, 12 yrs (low, middle SES). **Measures:** 27 geometric forms were constructed, which varied by orthogonal combinations of 3 levels of size, shape, and angle. Ss reached beneath a panel and felt a hidden form. Ss were asked to identify each form in a visual display. The 27 forms were presented 3 times, for a total of 81 trials. **Results:** Among 5-year-old, lower-class Ss, girls performed more poorly than boys.

Constantinople, A. Perceived instrumentality of the college as a measure of attitudes toward college. *J. Personality & Social Psychology*, 1967, *5*, 196–201.

Subjects: $N = 353$; 18, 20 yrs. **Measures:** Ss rated each of the following items on its importance to them as a goal and on the degree to which college either helped or hindered their progress toward that goal: (1) learning how to learn from books and teachers, (2) acquiring an appreciation for ideas, (3) establishing their own personal, social, and academic values, (4) developing relationships with the opposite sex, (5) contributing in a distinguished and meaningful manner to some campus group, (6) developing ability to get along with different kinds of people, (7) becoming self-confident, (8) personal independence, (9) finding a spouse, (10) achieving academic distinction, (11) having many good friends, (12) discovering their own strong points and limitations, (13) preparing for a career that begins right after graduation, and (14) preparing for a career that requires further study beyond the BA or BS. **Results:** (1) The following goals were more important to women than to men: 2, 3, 4, 6, 9, and 13. The following goals were more important to men than to women: 10 and 14. (2) Women more than men perceived college as helping in their progress toward the following goals: 1, 2, 3, 4, 7, 8, 9, and 13.

Constantinople, A. Some correlates of average level of happiness among college students. *Developmental Psychology*, 1970, *2*, 447 (brief report).

Subjects: $N = 58$; tested at 18, 21 yrs. **Measures:** At each testing, Ss completed both the Inventory of Psychosocial Development (IPD) and a 10-point bipolar scale measuring average level of happiness during the academic year. **Results:** (1) Men showed a significant increase in happiness from their freshman to their senior year; women showed a nonsignificant decrease

($p < .01$). (2) On the IPD, both sexes showed significant changes in the direction of greater maturity on the following scales: Autonomy, Identity, Shame and Doubt, and Guilt.

Cook, H., and Smothergill, D. W. Racial and sex determinants of initiative performance and knowledge in young children. *Educational Psychology*, 1973, 65, 211–15.
Subjects: $N = 154$; 4 yrs (low SES white and black). Measures: Ss observed a white or black adult model choose the picture he liked best in each of 12 picture pairs. Afterward, Ss were asked (1) to indicate their own preferences (imitative performance phase) and (2) to try to recall the model's choices (imitative knowledge phase). Results: (1) In the imitative performance phase, no main sex differences were found in the number of times Ss' choices were identical to the model's responses. Both sexes imitated same-sex models more than opposite-sex models. (2) No sex differences were found in the imitative knowledge phase. Black Ss had higher recall scores with a female model than with a male model.

Cook, T. D., Bean, J. R., Calder, B. J., Frey, R., Krovetz, M. L., and Reisman, S. R. Demand characteristics and three conceptions of the frequently deceived subject. *J. Personality & Social Psychology*, 1970, 14, 185–94.
EXPERIMENT I: Subjects: $N = 63$; 18–21 yrs (college). Measures: After participating in an experiment involving deception, Ss completed a questionnaire designed to assess their reactions to the experiment. Results: (1) Women liked the experiment more ($p < .02$), perceived the deception as more legitimate ($p < .001$), and were less annoyed by the deception ($p < .05$) than men were. (2) No sex differences were found in how truthful Ss perceived E to be, in how much they tried to figure out what the experiment was about, in how much they tried to understand and follow instructions, or in how much they considered the experiment to be scientific and valuable.
EXPERIMENT II: Subjects: $N = 113$; 18–21 yrs (college). Measures: After listening to a persuasive message, Ss evaluated the source and completed an attitude questionnaire. Results: No sex differences were found in Ss' perceptions of the source or in the extent to which Ss agreed with the source.

Coombs, C. H. Thurstone's measurement of social values revisited forty years later. *J. Personality & Social Psychology*, 1967, 6, 85–91.
Subjects: $N = 369$; 18–21 yrs (college). Measures: Ss were presented with pairs of criminal offenses, and were asked to judge which of the 2 crimes was more serious. Results: (1) Women considered abortion to be a more serious crime than men did. (2) Men judged offenses against property to be more serious crimes than women did. (3) Men were more homogeneous in their evaluations than women were.

Coopersmith, S. A method for determining two types of self-esteem. *J. Abnormal & Social Psychology*, 1959, 59, 87–94.
Subjects: $N = 87$; 10–12 yrs and their teachers. Measures: Ss completed a 50-item Self-Esteem Inventory. Teachers rated Ss on behaviors presumed to be related to self-esteem. Results: (1) No sex differences were found on the Self-Esteem Inventory. (2) Teachers rated girls more favorably than boys ($p < .001$).

Coopersmith, S. *The antecedents of self-esteem.* San Francisco: W. H. Freeman & Co., 1967.
Subjects: $N = 1,748$; 10, 11 yrs and teachers. Measures: (1) Coopersmith's Self-Esteem Inventory. (2) Teachers were asked to rate each child on a set of behaviors that were presumed to be related to self-esteem. Results: No sex differences were found in self-esteem scores. Teachers' ratings of girls were more favorable than those of boys.

Corah, N. L. Differentiation in children and their parents. *J. Personality*, 1965, 33, 300–308.
Subjects: $N = 60$; 8–11 yrs and parents. Measures: The Full-Range Vocabulary Test, Form A, and the Draw-A-Person (DAP) test were administered to Ss and their parents. IQ equivalents were derived from vocabulary scores. In addition, Ss were given the Children's Embedded Figures Test (CEFT); parents were given Witkin's Embedded Figures Test (EFT). Results: (1) Boys achieved higher vocabulary IQ scores than girls ($p < .02$); fathers achieved higher vocabulary IQ scores than mothers ($p < .05$). (2) Girls achieved higher DAP scores than boys ($p < .05$); no difference was found between mothers and fathers. (3) Fathers discovered the solutions to the EFT more quickly than mothers ($p < .001$); no difference was found between boys' and girls' CEFT scores.

Corah, N. L., and Boffa, J. Perceived control, self-observation, and response to aversive stimulation. *J. Personality & Social Psychology*, 1970, *16*, 1–4.
  Subjects: $N = 40$; 18–21 yrs (college). **Measures:** Ss rated the amount of discomfort they experienced after being exposed to aversive white noise. Galvanic skin responses were recorded. **Results:** Women rated the sounds as producing more discomfort than men did (p < .05). There were no sex differences in GSR.

Corter, C. M., Rheingold, H. L., and Eckerman, C. O. Toys delay the infant's following of his mother. *Developmental Psychology*, 1972, *6*, 138–45.
  EXPERIMENT I: **Subjects:** $N = 10$; 9–10 mos and mothers. **Measures:** After placing their children alone in a room, mothers went into an adjoining room out of the infants' sight. **Results:** Boys followed their mothers into the adjoining room more quickly than girls did.
  EXPERIMENT II: **Subjects:** $N = 26$; 9–10 mos and mothers. **Measures:** Same as Experiment I, except children were left alone with either 1 or 6 toys. **Results:** In the 1-toy group boys followed their mothers more quickly than girls did, and girls spent more time in touching the toy than boys did. No sex differences were found in the 6-toy group.

Coryell, J. Children's lateralizations of self, other, and object images. Unpublished manuscript, Boston University, 1973.
  Subjects: $N = 90$; 5, 7, 9 yrs. **Measures:** (1) A pencil was placed in S's hand. He was then shown a photograph of himself and was asked to point to the hand (in the picture) with which he had held the pencil. (2) E stood on S's left side, holding a pencil in his hand. S was then shown a photograph of E and was asked to point to the hand E had used to hold the pencil. (3) A model TV set with an antenna in one corner was placed next to S. S was then shown a photograph of a model TV set with no antenna, and was asked to point to the corner of the TV set where the antenna should be. S's responses were classified either as mirror or diagonal. **Results:** No sex differences were found in number of diagonal responses.

Costanzo, P. R., and Shaw, M. E. Conformity as a function of age level. *Child Development*, 1966, *37*, 967–75.
  Subjects: $N = 96$; 7–9, 11–13, 15–17, 19–21 yrs (college). **Measures:** 4 Ss of the same age and sex were in each experimental session. Ss were subjected to erroneous judgments in a simulated conformity situation in which they were asked to match comparison lines to standard. Each S sat in a booth containing lights that he expected to reflect the responses of other Ss. E controlled "response" lights and signaled erroneous responses in 16 of 24 trials. The number of times S's response agreed with an erroneous response was recorded. **Results:** No sex differences.

Cotler, S., and Palmer, R. J. Social reinforcement, individual difference factors, and the reading performance of elementary school children. *J. Personality & Social Psychology*, 1971, *18*, 97–104.
  Subjects: $N = 120$; 9–11 yrs. **Measures:** Ss were divided into overachievers and underachievers on the basis of scores on the Iowa Tests of Basic Skills and the Otis Lennon Mental Abilities Test. Ss also completed the Sarason Test Anxiety Scale. Ss then read paragraphs and received either positive, negative, or no reinforcement for their reading performance. Afterward, Ss listened as E read each of the paragraphs to them. This sequence of reading-reinforcement-instruction was repeated 3 times. Reading errors were recorded on the fourth reading. **Results:** (1) Overall, girls made fewer reading errors than boys ($p < .05$). (2) Girls made fewer errors in every comparison except one: among overachieving, low-test-anxiety Ss, girls made more errors than boys ($p < .05$). (3) Although errors decreased over trials for both boys and girls, the decrease was greater for boys ($p < .01$).

Cowan, P. A., Weber, J., Hoddinott, B. A., and Klein, J. Mean length of spoken response as a function of stimulus, experimenter, and subject. *Child Development*, 1967, *38*, 191–203.
  Subjects: $N = 96$; 5, 7, 9, 11 yrs (low, high SES). **Measures:** Ss were shown at least 10 pictures and asked to talk about them. E attempted to elicit a minimum of 3 responses per picture, and a total of 50 responses in all from each S. Average number of words per remark was determined. **Results:** (1) No main sex differences were found. (2) Sex differences within each age and SES group were not tested for significance.

Cowen, E. L., and Danset, A. Étude comparée des réponses d'écoliers français et américains à une échelle d'anxiété. *Revue de Psychologie Appliqué*, 1962, *12*, 263–74.
  Subjects: $N = 132$; 9 yrs (France). **Measures:** Children's Manifest Anxiety Scale. **Results:**

Girls scored higher than boys on the Anxiety Scale. No sex differences were found on the lie scale.

Cowen, E. L., Zax, M., Klein, R., Izzo, L. D., and Trost, M. A. The relation of anxiety in school children to school record, achievement and behavioral measures. *Child Development*, 1965, *36*, 685–95.
Subjects: *N* = 169; 9 yrs. Measures: Children's Manifest Anxiety Scale. Results: Girls scored higher than boys on the anxiety scale. No sex differences were found on the lie scale.

Cox, H. Intra-family comparison of loving-rejecting child-rearing practices. *Child Development*, 1970, *41*, 437–48.
Subjects: *N* = 100; 11, 12, 13 yrs and parents (98 mothers, 77 fathers). Measures: Ss and parents filled out the Roe-Siegelman Parent-Child Relationship Questionnaire. Results: (1) Girls perceived fathers as more loving than boys did. (2) Girls perceived fathers as less rejecting than boys did. (3) Girls perceived mothers as less rejecting than boys perceived fathers. (4) Girls perceived fathers as less rejecting than boys perceived mothers. (5) Mothers of girls reported themselves as more loving than fathers of boys did.

Craig, K. D. Vicarious reinforcement and noninstrumental punishment in observational learning. *J. Personality & Social Psychology*, 1967, *7*, 172–76.
Subjects: *N* = 80; 18–21 yrs (college). Measures: Ss in same-sex pairs served as either performers or observers. While the observer Ss watched, performer Ss attempted to learn a complex temporal maze task. For incorrect responses, one-half of the observers and all performers received a shock; correct responses were indicated by a green light. After performer Ss were dismissed, observer Ss attempted to master the same maze task. The number of correct choices made by observer Ss was recorded. Results: (1) There were no sex differences in number of correct choices. (2) Women who were not shocked as observers learned more rapidly and required fewer trials to criterion than women who were shocked as observers; the opposite was true for men ($p < .05$). (3) Women rated the shock as being more painful than men did (assessed by a post-experimental questionnaire).

Craig, K. D., and Lowery, H. J. Heart-rate components of conditioned vicarious autonomic responses. *J. Personality & Social Psychology*, 1969, *11*, 381–87.
Subjects: *N* = 56; 22 yrs (college). Measures: 10 colored slides of common objects were shown to a confederate. Half the Ss observed the confederate being shocked whenever certain slides were presented and were led to believe that they either would or would not have to perform the confederate's task afterward. Ss in a third condition simply observed the confederate move his arm rather than being shocked. No movement was observed by Ss in the control condition. During each slide presentation, galvanic skin responses (GSRs) and heart rate were recorded. Upon completion of the slide series, a postexperimental questionnaire was administered to Ss. Results: (1) Women had fewer vicarious and conditioned GSRs than men did ($p < .01$, $p < .01$). (2) No sex differences were found in heart rate. (3) No sex differences were found in Ss' ratings of the severity of the shocks received by the confederate. Women rated their reactions to observing the confederate as being more painful than men did ($p < .01$). Women also expressed more liking for the confederate than men did ($p < .05$).

Cramer, P. A developmental study of errors in memory. *Developmental Psychology*, 1972, *7*, 204–9.
Subjects: *N* = 96; 6–7, 10–11 yrs. Measures: Ss were instructed to remember 12 words that were read to them. As a memory aid, Ss in the experimental conditions were told to think of synonyms or rhyming words for each of the words. Afterward, Ss were presented with the 12 stimulus words along with 12 generalization stimuli (6 synonyms, 6 rhymes) and 12 control words. Ss indicated which words they had heard before. Results: (1) No main sex differences were found. (2) Among 6-7-year-old Ss in the control group, girls made more correct recognitions of presentation words, whereas boys gave more false recognition responses to both generalization stimuli and control words. (3) There were no sex differences in generalization difference scores (number of errors to synonyms minus one-half the number of errors to control words; number of errors to rhyming words minus one-half the number of errors to control words).

Cramer, P., and Bryson, J. The development of sex-related fantasy patterns. *Developmental Psychology*, 1972, *8*, 131–34.
Subjects: *N* = 89; 4–6, 8–10 yrs. Measures: Ss were asked to tell stories about 4 pictures, 2

from the Thematic Apperception Test (depicting a man clinging to a rope and a boy looking at a violin), and 2 depicting either a male or female circus performer swinging on a trapeze, and a child running across a field with a bird overhead. Using May's scoring system, the number of categories of "enhancement" and "deprivation" were identified. More positive scores signified a more feminine story pattern—stories that began with deprivation and ended with enhancement or happiness; the male pattern was the reverse. **Results:** (1) There were no sex differences among younger Ss. (2) Among older Ss, girls had more positive scores than boys did ($p < .01$). (3) There were no sex differences in younger boys' and girls' scores to any pictures except male and female circus performers. Girls gave more positive responses to that picture than boys did ($p < .02$). (4) Among older Ss, girls gave more positive responses than boys did to all but 1 picture, the male and female circus performers. The 3 pictures with more positive girls' responses were the man clinging to the rope ($p < .01$), the boy looking at a violin ($p < .02$), and the child in a field with bird overhead ($p < .05$).

Crandall, V. C. Personality characteristics and social and achievement behaviors associated with children's social desirability response tendencies. *J. Personality & Social Psychology,* 1966, 4, 477–86.
    Experiment I: **Subjects:** $N = 76$; 15 yrs. **Measures:** Children's Social Desirability Scale. **Results:** No sex differences.
    Experiment II: **Subjects:** $N = 50$; 6–11 yrs. **Measures:** Children's Social Desirability Scale. **Results:** No sex differences.

Crandall, V. C. Sex differences in expectancy of intellectual and academic reinforcement. In C. P. Smith, ed., *Achievement related motives in children,* New York: Russell Sage Foundation, 1969.
    Experiment I: **Subjects:** $N = 41$; 7–12 yrs (Fels sample). **Measures:** Ss were presented with 6 tasks, each of which was graduated into 8 levels of difficulty. The most difficult level at which each S predicted he would be able to perform when tested constituted his expectancy estimate for that task. Tasks were estimating number of blocks in constructions, brain teasers (logical relations), jigsaw puzzles (spatial relations), numerical skills, memory for objects, and mazes. **Results:** (1) Boys had higher overall expectancies and higher individual task expectancies than girls did. (2) There were no sex differences in Stanford-Binet IQ scores, Children's Social Desirability Scale scores, or Intellectual-Academic Attainment Value scores.
    Experiment II: **Subjects:** $N = 380$; 18 yrs (college). **Measures:** At entrance and at each quarter's registration, Ss listed courses they were taking and the grades they expected in each course. **Results:** (1) There were no sex differences in quarter grades actually received. (2) Men had higher quarterly grade expectancies than women did. (3) Over a 5-year period, men overestimated quarterly grade they were to receive more than women did. (4) Over a 5-year period, girls made lower grade estimates than their past grades warranted, whereas boys estimated higher than their grades warranted.
    Experiment III: **Subjects:** $N = 41$; 18–26 yrs (Fels sample). **Measures:** Ss received identical predetermined schedules of verbal reinforcement from a same-sex E on a complex task requiring storage, recall, and reproduction of different geometric patterns. Estimates of success expectancy were obtained from each S before the task and after 10 trials. **Results:** (1) First expectancy estimates of women were lower than those of men. After 10 trials, women's expectancies were still lower than those of men. (2) There were no sex differences in amount of expectancy change between first and second estimates.
    Experiment IV: **Subjects:** $N = 256$; 13 yrs. **Measures:** A digit-symbol substitution task was presented to Ss as a test of intellectual competence. After expectancy of success estimates were obtained, Ss were assigned to 1 of 6 reinforcement conditions (52 Ss were dropped from the study at this point in order that groups could be matched on initial expectancy). The 6 schedules of reinforcement were: 50% positive, 50% negative, 60% positive, 60% negative, 80% positive, and 80% negative. Performance feedback was provided to Ss via a display panel of 10 lights. Each light supposedly represented 1 of 10 schools in which the test had previously been given. After each trial, 5 lights came on in the 50% reinforcement conditions, 6 lights came on in the 60% conditions, and 8 lights came on in the 80% conditions. Ss in the 3 positive groups were informed that each light signified they had "beaten the kids at that school." In the 3 negative groups, Ss were told that the onset of any light meant "the kids at that school had beaten" them. Post-task expectancies were obtained at the end of 10 trials. **Results:** (1) No sex differences were found in expectancy change scores. (2) Each S's grades and initial expectancy scores were transformed into z scores. A discrepancy (D) score was then computed by subtracting the grade z score from the expectancy z score. More boys had positive rather than negative D scores, whereas the reverse was true for girls ($p < .001$).

Crandall, V. C., and Gozali, J. The social desirability responses of children of four religious-cultural groups. *Child Development*, 1969, *40*, 751–62.
> **Subjects:** $N = 1,474$; 9–17 yrs (U.S. non-Catholic, U.S. Catholic parochial, Norwegian State Lutheran, Norwegian Fundamentalist Lutheran). **Measures:** Children's Social Desirability Scale. **Results:** Girls gave more socially desirable responses than boys did ($p < .001$).

Crandall, V. C., and Lacey, B. W. Children's perceptions of internal-external control in intellectual-academic situations and their Embedded Figures Test performance. *Child Development*, 1972, *43*, 1123–34.
> **Subjects:** $N = 50$; 6–12 yrs. **Measures:** Ss were given 10 figures from the Embedded Figures Test, the Intellectual Achievement Responsibility scale (a measure of locus of control), and the Stanford-Binet IQ test. **Results:** No sex differences.

Crandall, V. C., Crandall, V. J., and Katkovsky, W. A children's social desirability questionnaire. *J. Consulting Psychology*, 1965a, *29*, 27–36.
> **Subjects:** $N = 956$; 8, 9, 10, 11, 13, 15, 17 yrs. **Measures:** Children's Social Desirability Questionnaire. **Results:** Girls gave more socially desirable responses than boys did ($p < .001$).

Crandall, V. C., Katkovsky, W., and Crandall, V. J. Children's beliefs in their own control of reinforcements in intellectual-academic achievement situations. *Child Development*, 1965b, *36*, 91–109.
> **Subjects:** $N = 923$; 8, 9, 10, 11, 13, 15, 17 yrs. **Measures:** Intellectual Achievement Responsibility Scale. **Results:** (1) Among 11-, 13-, 15-, and 17-year-old Ss, girls attributed more internal responsibility for failure than boys did. (2) Among 11- and 17-year-old Ss, girls attributed more internal responsibility for success than boys did. (3) Overall, older girls (ages 11, 13, 15, and 17) gave more internal responses than older boys did. (4) No differences were found between younger boys and girls.

Crandall, V. J., and Sinkeldam, C. Children's dependent and achievement behaviors in social situations and their perceptual field dependence. *J. Personality*, 1964, *32*, 1–22.
> **Subjects:** $N = 50$; 6–12 yrs (Fels Day Camp). **Measures:** Ss were given the 10 least difficult figures of the Witkins Embedded Figures Test. Total number of seconds used attempting to solve all 10 test figures was recorded. **Results:** No sex differences.

Cronin, V. Mirror-image reversal discrimination in kindergarten and first grade children. *J. Experimental Child Psychology*, 1967, *5*, 567–85.
> **Subjects:** $N = 216$; 5–6 yrs. **Measures:** Ss performed 1 of 3 discrimination tasks with triangles and their mirror-image reversals: same-different judgments with standard and mirror-image triangle pairs, judgments of which triangle of a triad was different (i.e. reversed), and matching a standard triangle to 1 of 2 others. **Results:** No sex differences.

Cropley, A. J., and Feuring, E. Training creativity in young children. *Developmental Psychology*, 1971, *4*, 105 (extended version of brief report).
> **Subjects:** $N = 69$; 6 yrs. **Measures:** Ss were given the Product Improvement Test of the Torrance Tests of Creativity (child is presented with a toy and asked how it could be changed to make it more fun to play with). Instructions were either to produce as many ideas as possible (quantity) or to produce clever and unusual ideas (quality). Half of the Ss received creativity training, the other half did not. Tests were scored for fluency (total number of suggested improvements), flexibility (number of distinct principles employed in suggestions), and originality (number of clever and unusual suggestions). **Results:** (1) There were no sex differences in flexibility or originality. (2) Among Ss given quantity instructions, boys scored higher on fluency than girls. Under quality instructions, girls surpassed boys on fluency. (3) There were no sex differences in the effects of creativity training.

Cross, J. F., and Cross, J. Age, sex, race and the perception of facial beauty. *Developmental Psychology*, 1971, *5*, 433–39.
> **Subjects:** $N = 300$; 7, 12, 17, 30–50 yrs. **Measures:** Ss rated photographic portraits of black and white males and females, ages 7, 18, and adult, on a 7-point scale of facial beauty. **Results:** Females rated female faces higher than males did ($p < .01$).

Crowder, A., and Hohle, R. H. Time estimation by young children with and without informational feedback. *J. Experimental Child Psychology*, 1970, *10*, 295–307.
> **Experiment I: Subjects:** $N = 48$; 5, 7, 9 yrs. **Measures:** Ss attempted to estimate the time

it took a hidden toy to travel along a path to a designated point, after watching E perform the same task (but with toy not hidden at destination point). Ss received either informational feedback or no feedback. **Results:** No sex differences.

EXPERIMENT II: **Subjects:** $N = 64$; 5 yrs. **Measures:** Same as Experiment I, except that the feedback procedure was modified. One group received informational feedback with no praise for correct estimates, and the other received only praise with no information about performance. **Results:** No sex differences.

Crowne, D. P. Family orientation, level of aspiration, and interpersonal bargaining. *J. Personality & Social Psychology*, 1966, *3*, 641–45.
Subjects: $N = 76$; 18–21 yrs (college). **Measures:** Ss played the Prisoner's Dilemma Game in same-sex pairs. Ss' parents were classified as to whether they were engaged in entrepreneurial occupations (farmer, small businessman, lawyer, etc.) or bureaucratic occupations (employment in a relatively large organization of complex structure). **Results:** Among Ss with entrepreneurial parents, men played more cooperatively than women did ($p < .05$). No sex differences were found among Ss with bureaucratic parents.

Crowne, D. P., Holland, C. H., and Conn, L. K. Personality factors in discrimination learning in children. *J. Personality & Social Psychology*, 1968, *10*, 420–30.
Subjects: $N = 63$; 10–11 yrs. **Measures:** After completing the Children's Social Desirability Scale, Ss were given visual discrimination learning tasks. Number of trials needed to reach criterion, time between presentation of each stimulus and S's response (impulsivity), and heart rates were recorded. **Results:** No sex differences.

Croxern, M. E., and Lytton, H. Reading disability and difficulties in finger localization and right-left discrimination. *Developmental Psychology*, 1971, *5*, 256–62.
Subjects: $N = 164$; 9, 10 yrs. **Measures:** Tactile stimulation was applied to Ss' fingers while their hands were either hidden from view or visible. On each trial, Ss reported which finger had been touched either by pointing to the correct finger on a numbered diagram of a right and left hand, by indicating its number, or by naming it. Ss were also tested on their ability to discriminate between the left and right sides of their bodies. **Results:** Girls performed better on the right-left discrimination task than boys did (for control group, $p < .02$; for experimental group, NS; for both groups combined, $p < .05$). No sex differences were found on the tactile stimulation task.

Cruse, D. B. Socially desirable responses at ages 3 through 6. *Child Development*, 1966, *37*, 909–16.
Subjects: $N = 299$; 3, 4, 5, 6 yrs. **Measures:** A social-desirability scale was administered to each S. The child was asked to endorse or reject 20 desirable and 20 undesirable items. **Results:** At ages 4 and 6, girls gave more socially desirable responses than boys did.

Curcio, F., Kattef, E., Levine, D., and Robbins, O. Compensation and susceptibility to conservation training. *Developmental Psychology*, 1972, *7*, 259–65.
Subjects: $N = 67$; 5–6 yrs. **Measures:** Ss were given the following pretests: understanding of "more" and "same," compensation of height-width dimensions, and conversation of discontinuous quantity. Conservation training was administered, followed by post-tests of discontinuous quantity conservation and transfer conservation. **Results:** No sex differences.

Curry, L., and Dickson, P. Sex differentiation by age in embedded figures test. Unpublished paper, Stanford University, 1971.
Subjects: $N = 24$; 5, 8, 11 yrs. **Measures:** The Visual Closure subtest of the Illinois Test of Psycholinguistics Abilities was used as a measure of embedded figures skill. Stanford-Binet IQ scores were collected for 8- and 11-year-old Ss. **Results:** No sex differences.

Daehler, M. W. Children's manipulation of illusory and ambiguous stimuli, discriminative performance and implications for conceptual development. *Child Development*, 1970, *41*, 224–41.
Subjects: $N = 160$; 4, 5, 6 yrs. **Measures:** 4 discrimination tasks were used as measures of investigatory activity. Problems were a length, a brightness, and 2 size-discrimination tasks. Illusory arrangements of stimuli prevented correct choices unless Ss were willing to investigate the problem further. Correct responses were reinforced with a marble and a verbal comment. **Results:** Boys performed more investigatory responses than girls did ($p < .01$).

Daehler, M. W. Developmental and experimental factors associated with inferential behavior. *J. Experimental Child Psychology*, 1972, *13*, 324–38.

> EXPERIMENT I: Subjects: $N = 192$; 4, 5, 6, 7 yrs. Measures: In 16 2-trial identification problems, Ss inferred positive instance from 4 alternatives (outline pictures of faces) appearing 2 at a time. Results: There were no sex differences in mean number of correct responses or kinds of errors.
>
> EXPERIMENT II: Subjects: $N = 42$; 8 yrs. Measures: Ss in 3 conditions inferred positive instance in 24 2-trial problems. Dimensions were varied to determine the effect on difficulty. Results: There were no sex differences in mean number of corrct responses.

Darley, F. L., and Winitz, H. Comparison of male and female kindergarten children on the WISC. *J. Genetic Psychology*, 1961, *99*, 41–49.

> Subjects: $N = 150$; 6 yrs. Measures: Wechsler Intelligence Scale for Children. Results: (1) Girls were superior to boys on the Performance Scale IQ ($p < .02$), the Similarities subtest ($p < .05$), and the Coding A subtest ($p < .01$). (2) No sex differences were found in Verbal Scale IQ or Full Scale IQ.

Darley, J. M., and Latané, B. Bystander intervention in emergencies: diffusion of responsibility. *J. Personality & Social Psychology*, 1968, *8*, 377–83.

> Subjects: $N = 72$; 18–21 yrs (college). Measures: Ss overheard a person experiencing an epileptic seizure. Ss were led to believe that another subject had also overheard the seizure. Response measure was the speed in which Ss reported the emergency. Results: No sex differences.

Davidson, H. H., and Lang, G. Children's perceptions of their teachers' feelings toward them related to self-perception, school achievement and behavior. *J. Experimental Education*, 1960, *29*, 107–18.

> Subjects: $N = 203$; 9, 10, 11 yrs. Measures: Ss completed an adjective checklist measuring their perceptions of teachers' feeling toward them. Teachers rated each pupil's academic achievement, behavior, and personality characteristics. Results: (1) Girls perceived their teachers' feeling toward them as more favorable than boys did ($p < .02$). (2) Girls were rated more favorably than boys on behavioral and personality characteristics ($p < .05$).

Davies, A. D. The perceptual maze test in a normal population. *Perceptual & Motor Skills*, 1965, *20*, 287–93.

> Subjects: $N = 540$; 20–79 yrs. Measures: Perceptual maze tests were administered to Ss. Results: Among 20-59-year-old Ss, men performed better than women ($p < .01$). Among 60-79-year-old Ss, no sex differences were found.

Davies, C. M. Development of the probability concept in children. *Child Development*, 1965, *36*, 779–88.

> Subjects: $N = 112$; 3–9 yrs. Measures: Ss played a lever-pressing marble game for prizes in which the outcomes were fixed to preclude learning the concept of probability. A verbal measure followed in which Ss judged which color marble they would be most likely to get if they chose without looking from an assortment of known proportions. Results: At age 7, girls performed better than boys on the verbal test ($p < .02$).

Davies, G. M. Quantitative and qualitative aspects of memory for picture stimuli. *J. Experimental Child Psychology*, 1972, *13*, 382–93.

> Subjects: $N = 100$; 8–9 yrs. Measures: Ss were shown names or pictures of objects and were instructed to find likenesses among alternatives. Written recall and identification accuracy were assessed twice: 5 hours and 3 days after stimulus presentation. Results: No sex differences.

Davis, A. J. Cognitive style: methodological and developmental considerations. *Child Development*, 1971, *42*, 1147–59.

> Subjects: $N = 120$; 10, 13, 16, 18–21 yrs (college). Measures: Ss were given Sigel's Cognitive Style Test, Form A. Responses were scored as Descriptive Part-Whole, Descriptive Global, Relational-Contextual, or Categorical-Inferential. Results: No sex differences.

Davis, J. H., Cohen, J. L., Hornik, J., and Rissman, A. K. Dyadic decision as a function of the frequency distributions describing the preferences of members' constituencies. *J. Personality & Social Psychology*, 1973, *26*, 178–95.

> Subjects: $N = 246$; 18–21 yrs (college). Measures: Pairs of Ss, each acting as a representative for a hypothetical constituency, discussed and reached a decision on one of the follow-

ing: the percentage of university control that should be invested with students, or the percentage of the national budget that should be spent on pollution control. **Results:** No sex differences were found in the decisions Ss reached.

Davis, O. L. Teacher behavior toward boys and girls during first grade reading instruction. *American Education Research J.*, 1967, 4, 261–70.
> **Subjects:** $N = 238$; 6, 7 yrs. **Measures:** Ss' perceptions of pupil-teacher interactions were ascertained in individual interviews. Teachers rated each pupil's motivation and readiness for reading. Observations were made of teacher-pupil interactions during reading instruction. In addition, all Ss received the Stanford Achievement Test, Primary Battery, Form X. **Results:** Ss perceived boys as receiving more negative comments from the teacher ($p < .01$) and as being poor readers ($p < .05$). No sex differences were obtained in each of the following categories: amount of praise received from teacher, amount of opportunity to read, best reader in class. (2) Teachers assessed more boys as "less motivated and ready" than girls ($p < .01$). Teachers' mean assessment of boys and girls did not differ significantly, however. (3) No differences were found in the number of times boys and girls were called on to respond by their teachers, nor did teachers react differently to boys' and girls' responses. (4) No sex differences were found on the achievement test.

Davol, S. H., Hastings, M. L., and Klein, D. A. Effect of age, sex and speed of rotation on rotary pursuit performance by young children. *Perceptual & Motor Skills*, 1965, 21, 351–57.
> **Subjects:** $N = 54$; 5–8 yrs. **Measures:** During each of 5 2-minute trials on a rotary pursuit task, Ss attempted to follow a revolving gold circle with the end of a stick. Performance measure was time on target. **Results:** No sex differences.

Dean, R. B., Austin, J. A., and Watts, W. A. Forewarning effects in persuasion. *J. Personality & Social Psychology*, 1971, 18, 210–21.
> **Subjects:** $N = 161$; 18–21 yrs (college). **Measures:** Ss were either forewarned or not forewarned about the persuasive nature of a message. After reading the message, Ss responded to an attitude questionnaire (Ss' scores were compared to a control group's scores, yielding a measure of attitude change). Ss then evaluated the message in terms of its fairness, interest, forcefulness, and persuasiveness. **Results:** No sex differences.

Deaux, K. K. Honking at the intersection: a replication and extension. *J. Social Psychology*, 1971, 84, 159–60.
> **Subjects:** $N = 123$; adult drivers. **Measures:** Ss were blocked at an intersection by either a male or a female confederate who failed to move his (her) car when the light turned green. Ss' horn-honking responses were recorded. **Results:** More drivers honked at the female confederate than at the male confederate ($p < .05$). No sex differences were found.

Debus, R. L. Effects of brief observation of model behavior on conceptual tempo of impulsive children. *Developmental Psychology*, 1970, 2, 22–32.
> **Subjects:** $N = 320$; 8–10 yrs. **Measures:** Ss were given an 8-item form of the Matching Familiar Figures test. The 100 children with the shortest response latencies and largest number of errors were asked to return. These Ss were exposed at a later testing session to same-sex 11-year-old models who exhibited reflective and/or impulsive response patterns while taking the MFF. Models were reinforced for correct choices. Immediately after the model(s) left, Ss completed a second 8-item form of the MFF; 2½ weeks later, a third form of the MFF was administered. **Results:** No sex differences were found on either the initial pretest, the immediate post-test, or the delayed post-test.

Deci, E. L. Intrinsic motivation, extrinsic reinforcement, and inequity. *J. Personality & Social Psychology*, 1972, 22, 113–20.
> **Subjects:** $N = 96$; 18–21 yrs (college). **Measures:** Ss either did or did not receive verbal reinforcement while attempting to solve a spatial puzzle. The amount of time Ss spent working on the puzzle during a free-choice period immediately afterward was recorded. **Results:** No sex differences.

DeFazio, V. J. Field articulation differences in language abilities. *J. Personality & Social Psychology*, 1973, 25, 351–56.
> **Subjects:** $N = 44$; 18–21 yrs (college). **Measures:** (1) Word Beginnings and Endings Test (Ss were asked to write as many words as possible beginning with one letter and ending with another); (2) Advanced Vocabulary Test; (3) Cloze Test (Ss were presented with 6

paragraphs. Every fifth word in each paragraph was deleted. Ss' task was to guess the identities of the deleted words); (4) Shadowing Task (Ss were asked to repeat aloud sentences or strings of words that were read to them). **Results:** No sex differences.

Deffenbacher, K. A., and Hamm, N. H. An application of Brunswik's lens model to developmental changes in probability learning. *Developmental Psychology*, 1972, *6*, 508–19.
> **Subjects:** *N* = 288; 7–8, 13–15, 19–20 yrs. **Measures:** Ss were instructed to guess what 2-digit number went best with a 2-digit number presented. Cue and criterion number were presented after Ss recorded their response. Half of the younger Ss also saw a pattern of dots close to the corresponding numerals, in order to make the task more concrete. **Results:** No sex differences.

DeLeon, J. L., Raskin, L. M., and Gruen, G. E. Sensory-modality effects of shape perception in preschool children. *Developmental Psychology*, 1970, *3*, 358–62.
> **Subjects:** *N* = 48; 3–4 yrs. **Measures:** Ss performed shape-discrimination tasks (judging which comparison form is the same as the standard) under 4 conditions: seeing stimuli, feeling stimuli, seeing and feeling stimuli, and combination (seeing and feeling standard and only feeling comparison stimuli). Correct responses were reinforced with M & M candies. Responses and response latencies were recorded. **Results:** No sex differences.

DeLucia, L. Stimulus preference and discrimination learning. In J. F. Rosenblith, W. Allinsmith, and J. P. Williams, eds., *The Causes of Behavior*. Boston: Allyn & Bacon, 1972.
> **Subjects:** *N* = 24; 5 yrs. **Measures:** Ss' relative preferences for each of 24 toys were determined by the method of paired comparisons. **Results:** No significance tests for sex differences were performed on a toy-by-toy basis. Girls' and boys' relative preferences, however, were considerably different, as is evident from the following list (boys' choices are ordered from most to least preferred, and the position of each item within girls' rank-ordering of preferences is given in parentheses): convertible (14), dump truck (19), tool set (23), airplane (20), racing car (22), erector set (19), football (24), wheelbarrow (21), banjo (5), tractor (17), wading pool (11), alphabet ball (12), blackboard (15), roller skates (14), rocking horse (8), teddy bear (16), telephone (7), jump rope (9), dish cabinet (6), sewing machine (10), broom set (4), doll wardrobe (3), doll buggy (2), cosmetics (1).

Denmark, F. L., and Diggory, J. C. Sex differences in attitudes toward leaders' display of authoritarian behavior. *Psychological Reports*, 1966, *18*, 863–72.
> **Subjects:** *N* = 327; 18–21 yrs (college fraternity and sorority members). **Measures:** Part I, Scale A: All Ss were asked to describe how the leader (president) of their fraternity or sorority behaved in concrete situations. Scale B: Ss, excluding the 19 leaders, were then asked to describe how the leader should have behaved. On both scales, Ss rated the leaders on a 19-item list of authoritarian characteristics. In Part II, Ss were asked to answer yes or no to 16 propositions about the personal characteristics "necessary for good leaders." **Results:** (1) There were no sex differences among leaders or followers in mean scores on either Scale A or Scale B. (2) On Scale A, followers considered male leaders more authoritarian on 9 characteristics and female leaders more authoritarian on 2 characteristics. The leaders themselves rated 2 items more characteristic of male leaders and 1 more characteristic of female leaders. (3) On Scale B, male leaders were considered more authoritarian on 9 characteristics and female leaders more authoritarian on 4 characteristics. (4) On Part II, more men believed good leaders should oppose those who disagree with them (item 2) and good leaders usually help you with your personal problems (item 7). More women believed a good leader will be adequate in almost all types of situations (item 16).

Denney, N. W. A developmental study of free classification in children. *Child Development*, 1972a, *43*, 221–32.
> **Subjects:** *N* = 96; 2, 4, 6, 8, 12, 16 yrs. **Measures:** Ss were given colored blocks of various shapes and were asked to arrange them under a free-grouping procedure and under a verbal-labeling (nonsense syllables) procedure. **Results:** No sex differences.

Denney, N. W. Free classification in preschool children. *Child Development*, 1972b, *43*, 1161–70.
> **Subjects:** *N* = 108; 2, 3, 4 yrs. **Measures:** Ss were asked to place 32 cardboard figures of various shapes, colors, and sizes in groups of their own choosing. **Results:** No sex differences.

Denney, N. W., and Lennon, L. Classification: a comparison of middle and old age. *Developmental Psychology*, 1972, *7*, 210–13.

Subjects: $N = 74$; 25–55, 67–95 yrs. **Measures:** Ss arranged geometric figures varying in color, size, and shape according to instructions to group things that are alike or go together. Responses were classified as graphic (design made with stimuli), similarity (common attribute shared by stimuli in each grouping), or other (neither graphic nor similarity). **Results:** No sex differences.

Desor, J. A. Toward a psychological theory of crowding. *J. Personality & Social Psychology*, 1972, *21*, 79–83.
    Subjects: $N = 70$; 18–21 yrs (college). **Measures:** Ss were presented with scaled-down rooms and human figures and asked to place as many people as possible in the rooms without over-crowding them. **Results:** No sex differences.

Devi, G. A study of sex difference in reaction to frustration situations. *Psychological Studies*, 1967, *12*, 17–27.
    Subjects: $N = 220$; 16–24 yrs (Asian Indian college). **Measures:** Ss reported what their reactions would be to each of 10 frustrating situations. **Results:** (1) Men reported more overtly aggressive reactions than women did. (2) Women reported more regressive and withdrawal reactions than men did. (3) No sex differences were found in the frequency of suppressed aggressive reactions, self-aggressive reactions, anxiety, adjustment, or rationalization.

Dewing, K. The reliability and validity of selected tests of creative thinking in a sample of seventh grade West Australian children. *British J. Educational Psychology*, 1970, *40*, 35–42.
    Subjects: $N = 394$; 12 yrs. **Measures:** (1) 2 verbal (Alternate uses: tin cans; Alternate uses: bricks) and two nonverbal (Circle, Squares) tests of creative thinking were administered to Ss. Each test was scored for fluency and originality. (2) 5 additional measures of creativity were also assessed: (a) teacher ratings of in-school creativity, (b) peer ratings of in-school creativity, (c) Torrance Creative Leisure Interests Checklist, (d) Golann Creative Motivation Scale, and (e) an imaginative composition on the topic "The Lion Who Couldn't Roar." **Results:** No sex differences.

Di Bartole, R., and Vinacke, W. E. Relationship between adult nurturance and dependency and performance of the preschool child. *Developmental Psychology*, 1969, *1*, 247–51.
    Subjects: $N = 24$; 4 yrs (low SES). **Measures:** 2 teachers independently rated Ss for dependency on Beller's scale (1957). Within each sex, Ss were divided into high- and low-dependency groups based on these scores. For 2 weeks prior to the experimental session, Ss were allowed to play with 4 jigsaw puzzles used in the experiment. Each S was individually brought into the experimental room by a female E and asked to solve a puzzle in a nurturant situation (E adopted predetermined nurturant patterns of behavior involving permissiveness, praise, affection, verbal reward, nearness, and attention). After a rest period, Ss were asked to solve the puzzle again under conditions of continued nurturance or nurturance deprivation (E avoided nurturant behaviors and left S alone). **Results:** No sex differences.

Dickerson, D. J., Wagner, J. F., and Campione, J. Discrimination shift performance of kindergarten children as a function of variation of the irrelevant shift dimension. *Developmental Psychology*, 1970, *3*, 229–35.
    Subjects: $N = 96$; 5 yrs. **Measures:** After discrimination training for color-relevance or form-relevance, Ss performed either intradimensional (ID), reversal (RV), or extradimensional (ED) shifts. Original relevant dimension remained relevant in ID shift; original irrelevant dimension became relevant in ED shift. RV Ss were assigned 2 new cues along the irrelevant dimension. **Results:** No sex differences.

Dickie, S. P. Effectiveness of structured and unstructured (traditional) methods of language training. *Monographs of the Society for Research in Child Development*, 1968, *33*, serial no. 124, 62–79.
    Subjects: $N = 50$; 3–4 yrs. **Measures:** Ss were pretested on the Peabody Picture Vocabulary Test, the Stanford-Binet IQ test, tasks of color naming, counting, block-building, the Expressive Vocabulary Inventory, and the Auditory-Vocal Association subtest of the Illinois Test of Psycholinguistic Abilities. Ss underwent 5 months of language training using structured or unstructured methods of teaching. Ss were post-tested on language tests. **Results:** No sex differences.

Dienstbier, R. A., and Munter, P. O. Cheating as a function of the labeling of natural arousal. *J. Personality & Social Psychology*, 1971, *17*, 208–13.
Subjects: $N = 105$; 18–21 yrs (college). Measures: Ss experienced failure on a vocabulary test and were then given an opportunity to improve their scores by cheating. Results: No sex differences were found in the percentage of Ss who cheated.

Dillehay, R. C., and Jernigan, L. R. The biased questionnaire as an instrument of opinion change. *J. Personality & Social Psychology*, 1970, *15*, 144–50.
Subjects: $N = 90$; 18–21 yrs (college). Measures: Ss initially responded to biased questionnaires designed to elicit either harsh or lenient opinions concerning the treatment of criminals. All Ss then responded to Likert and Thurstone scales of punishment orientation. Results: No sex differences.

Dion, K., Berscheid, E., and Walster, E. What is beautiful is good. *J. Personality & Social Psychology*, 1972, *24*, 285–90.
Subjects: $N = 60$; 18–21 yrs (college). Measures: Ss were presented with photographs of college students who varied in physical attractiveness. Ss rated each of the students on 32 personality traits and estimated which of the stimulus persons would be most likely, and least likely, to have a number of different life experiences. Ss also indicated which of the students would be most likely to engage in each of 30 different occupations. Results: No sex differences.

Ditrichs, R., Simon, S., and Greene, B. Effect of vicarious scheduling on the verbal conditioning of hostility in children. *J. Personality & Social Psychology*, 1967, *6*, 71–78.
Subjects: $N = 150$; 12–13 yrs. Measures: Ss were free to use either hostile or neutral verbs in the construction of sentences. Prior to the experiment, Ss had been vicariously reinforced for choosing hostile verbs. Results: Boys constructed more sentences using hostile verbs than girls did ($p < .05$).

Dixon, J. F., and Simmons, C. H. The impression value of verbs for children. *Child Development*, 1966, *37*, 861–66.
Subjects: $N = 100$; 9 yrs. Measures: 45 simple past-tense verbs were presented to Ss for rating in terms of "what my teacher would think of me if I used the word about myself." Each verb was rated on a 5-point scale ranging from "would not like me at all" to "would like me very much." Results: (1) Girls scaled the following verbs more positively than boys did: trusted, helped, liked, loved, found. (2) Boys scaled the following verbs more positively than girls did: looked, lost, cried. (3) Girls rated positive and negative verbs in a more extreme direction (i.e. positive verbs higher, negative verbs lower) than boys did. (4) Boys showed greater variability in rating positive and negative verbs than girls did.

Dlugokinski, E., and Firestone, I. J. Congruence among four methods of measuring other-centeredness. *Child Development*, 1973, *44*, 304–8.
Subjects: $N = 164$; 10, 13 yrs. Measures: Ss were given a value scale, a test of moral understanding (Baldwin), a peer-impact scale (S rated by peers), and a behavioral measure concerning donations of money earned as subject to UNICEF under varying appeals. Results: (1) Girls had a higher relative ranking of other-centered values than boys did ($p < .01$). (2) Girls showed higher moral understanding than boys did ($p < .05$). (3) No sex differences were found in the amount of money Ss donated.

Dmitruk, M. Incentive preference and resistance to temptation. *Child Development*, 1971, *42*, 625–28.
Subjects: $N = 302$; 5–10 yrs. Measures: Incentive preferences were assessed. Ss were offered a preferred, nonpreferred, or no object in a resistance-to-temptation situation. Results: No sex differences.

Doctor, R. M. Awareness and the effects of three combinations of reinforcement on verbal conditioning in children. *Child Development*, 1969, *40*, 529–38.
Subjects: $N = 60$; 10, 11 yrs. Measures: Ss constructed sentences from stimulus pronouns and selected verbs. Correct and incorrect responses received either positive, negative, or no reinforcement in varying combinations. E checked Ss for awareness of reinforcement contingencies. Results: No sex differences in acquisition or extinction.

Dodd, B. J. Effects of social and vocal stimulation on infant babbling. *Developmental Psychology*, 1972, *7*, 80–83.
Subjects: $N = 10$ boys, 5 girls; 9–12 mos. Measures: Ss' spontaneous vocalizations were re-

corded for a period of 15 minutes. **Results:** No sex differences were found in the number, range, or length of Ss' utterances.

Dodd, C., and Lewis, M. The magnitude of the orienting response in children as a function of changes in color and contour. *J. Experimental Child Psychology*, 1969, *8*, 296–305.
Subjects: $N = 52$; 3½ yrs. **Measures:** Ss viewed achromatic and chromatic pictures of a family and of designs (curved and straight lines). Fixation, smiling, pointing, and surprise were measured. **Results:** No sex differences.

Dodge, N., and Muench, G. A. Relation of conformity and the need for approval in children. *Developmental Psychology*, 1969, *1*, 67–68.
Subjects: $N = 122$; 11 yrs. **Measures:** Conformity to group pressure was measured in an Asch-type situation. **Results:** No sex differences.

Dodge, W. F., West, E. F., Bridgeforth, E. B., and Travis, L. B. Nocturnal enuresis in 6- to 10-year-old children. *American J. Diseases of Children*, 1970, *120*, 32–35.
Subjects: $N = 1,436$; 6–8 yrs (white, black, Hispanic). **Measures:** Mothers were interviewed about their children's bed-wetting habits. **Results:** At each age, more boys than girls were enuretic ($p < .025$).

Doob, A. N., and Gross, A. E. Status of frustrator as an inhibitor of horn-honking responses. *J. Social Psychology*, 1968, *76*, 213–18.
Subjects: $N = 74$; adult drivers. **Measures:** Ss were blocked at an intersection by a male confederate who failed to move his car when the signal turned green. Measures were taken of the duration and latency of each honk. Total number of honks was also recorded. **Results:** Men honked faster than women did ($p < 05$).

Dorman, L., Watson, J. S., and Vietze, P. Operant conditioning of visual fixation in infants under three intensities of auditory and visual reinforcement. Submitted to *Developmental Psychology*, 1971.
Subjects: $N = 48$; 14 wks. **Measures:** Visual fixation on 1 of 2 blank targets was reinforced with either visual or auditory stimuli in 1 of 3 intensity sequences: (1) low, medium high, (2) medium high, low, or (3) high, low medium. The observer, blind to the reinforced target, modality, and sequence of reinforcement, recorded the number of fixations on each target. A learning score was obtained by subtracting the number of looks at the nonrewarded side in conditioning period from the number in the base period. **Results:** No main sex differences were found.

Dosey, M. A., and Meisels, M. Personal space and self-protection. *J. Personality & Social Psychology*, 1969, *11*, 93–97.
Subjects: $N = 186$; 18–21 yrs (college). **Measures:** Ss approached members of the same and opposite sex. **Results:** There were no main effects of sex of S on approach distance. Female Ss approached closer to women than to men; the approach behavior of male Ss was not affected by sex of other ($p < .01$).

Dreman, S. B., and Greenbaum, C. W. Altruism or reciprocity; sharing behavior in Israeli kindergarten children. *Child Development*, 1973, *44*, 61–68.
Subjects: $N = 120$; 5–6 yrs (low, middle SES). **Measures:** Ss were given an odd number of candies to either share or not share with an alleged same-sex peer, who would either know or not know who gave him the candies. S thought E would not know how many he chose to share. **Results:** No main sex differences.

Dreyer, A. S., Hulac, V., and Rigler, D. Differential adjustment to pubescence and cognitive style patterns. *Developmental Psychology*, 1971, *4*, 456–62.
Subjects: $N = 22$; 9–16 yrs (longitudinal sample). **Measures:** The Draw-a-Person test was administered annually and scored on a 5-point scale of degree of sophistication of body concept. **Results:** No sex differences.

Droege, R. C. Sex differences in aptitude maturation during high school. *J. Counseling Psychology*, 1967, *14*, 407–11.
Subjects: $N = 20,541$; 14–16 yrs (retested at 17 yrs). $N = 6,167$; 17 yrs. **Measures:** General Aptitude Test Battery (U.S. Employment Service, 1958). **Results:** (1) In every comparison, boys scored higher than girls in intelligence and spatial aptitude. Girls scored higher than

boys in verbal aptitude, form perception, clerical perception, motor coordination, and finger dexterity. (2) At the initial testing, and again at 17 years, 14-year-old boys scored higher in numerical aptitude than 14-year-old girls. At the initial testing, but not at the retesting 2 years later, 15-year-old boys scored higher in numerical aptitude than 15-year-old girls. Among 17-year-olds who were tested just once, boys scored higher in numerical aptitude than girls. No differences were found among 16-year-old Ss either at the initial testing or at the retesting a year later. (3) 14-year-old boys scored higher in manual dexterity when they were retested at 17 years than 14-year-old girls did. No sex differences were found at the initial testing. Among 15-year-old Ss, girls scored higher in manual dexterity at the initial testing than boys did. No sex differences were found at the retesting 2 years later. No sex differences were found in the 16- or 17-year-old samples.

Druker, J. F., and Hagen, J. W. Developmental trends in the processing of task-relevant and task-irrelevant information. *Child Development*, 1969, *40*, 371–82.
    Subjects: $N = 240$; 9, 11, 13 yrs (black low SES). **Measures:** As the central task, Ss viewed cards of objects paired with animals. The cards were then covered, and a duplicate of one of the cards served as a cue. Ss were asked to point to the location of the covered card that matched the cue card. As the incidental task, Ss were asked to match objects with animals they had appeared with before. **Results:** (1) Boys had higher scores than girls on the central task. (2) There were no sex differences on the incidental task.

Dubanoski, R. A., and Parton, D. A. Effect of the presence of a human model on imitative behavior in children. *Developmental Psychology*, 1971, *4*, 463–68.
    Subjects: $N = 90$; 4 yrs. **Measures:** Ss saw films of either a female model manipulating (stimulus) objects, a hand manipulating objects, or objects moving with no visible means of locomotion (invisible nylon threads). Controls saw wooden puzzles assembled under the same conditions. Ss were given a free play period with the same toys plus others. Imitative responses were recorded. Then performance recall of taped manipulations was tested. **Results:** After viewing no model, boys made more imitative responses than girls did. There were no sex differences in imitation after viewing the model, or in recall scores.

DuHamel, T. R., and Biller, H. B. Parental imitation and nonimitation in young children. *Developmental Psychology*, 1969, *1*, 772.
    Subjects: $N = 63$; 5 yrs. **Measures:** Ss were presented with 3 non-sex-typed human figures and 3 dolls—a mother doll, a father doll, and a child doll of the same sex as S. Ss were asked 18 questions about the 3 figures. Each was similar in format to the following: "Which of these 3 people is nice?" Half of the questions contained familiar adjectives (e.g. nice, good, poor, happy); the other half contained unfamiliar adjectives (e.g. idealistic, smug, controversial, cynical). E informed Ss of the mother and father dolls' choices by placing the mother doll next to 1 of the figures and the father doll next to another. There were 3 options available to Ss: they could imitate either the mother or father doll (by moving the child doll to either of the parent dolls' selections), or they could imitate neither (by moving the child doll to the remaining figure). **Results:** More boys imitated the father doll; more girls imitated the mother doll ($p < .01$). When responding to questions containing familiar adjectives, more boys than girls chose not to imitate either parent doll ($p < .05$).

Duncan, C. P. Probability vs. latency of solution of an insight problem. *Psychological Reports*, 1962, *10*, 119–21.
    Subjects: $N = 1,088$; adults. **Measures:** Maier 2-string problem. **Results:** More men than women solved the problem within the specified period of time.

Dusek, J. B. Experimenter bias in performance of children at a simple motor task. *Developmental Psychology*, 1971, *4*, 55–62.
    Subjects: $N = 126$; 6–7 yrs. **Measures:** Ss performed a marble-dropping task under social reinforcement or nonreinforcement conditions, with either a neutral E, an E biased toward superior performance of girls, or an E biased toward superior performance of boys. The response measures were the base rate (number of marbles dropped in the first minute of the task) and a difference (D) score computed separately for each (number of marbles dropped in the first minute minus number of marbles dropped in each subsequent minute). **Results:** (1) Girls had a higher base rate than boys ($p < .05$). (2) No sex differences were found in D scores.

Dusek, J. B., and Hill, K. T. Probability learning as a function of sex of the subject, test anxiety, and percentage of reinforcement. *Developmental Psychology*, 1970, *3*, 195–207.
    Subjects: $N = 72$; 9, 10 yrs. **Measures:** Ss performed a 3-choice probability learning task in

which the "correct" response was reinforced 33% or 66% of the time. **Results:** (1) Boys gave a higher number of correct responses than girls ($p < .001$). (2) Girls showed more response patterns than boys ($p < .001$). (3) Boys showed more win-stay and less lose-shift responding than girls ($p < .001$, $p < .001$). Over trials, boys showed a greater decrease in lose-shift responding than girls ($p < .01$). No sex differences were found in Ss' display of low-side-shift responding.

Dweck, C. S., and Reppucci, N. D. Learned helplessness and reinforcement responsibility in children. *J. Personality & Social Psychology*, 1973, 25, 109–16.
Subjects: $N = 40$; 10 yrs. **Measures:** Ss were given the Intellectual Achievement Responsibility Questionnaire, which yielded 2 subscale scores and a total score. The I+ and I– subscales measured Ss' respective tendencies to see themselves as responsible for the positive and negative reinforcement they received in intellectual academic situations. The total I score measured Ss' acceptance of responsibility for the outcomes of their achievement efforts. **Results:** (1) No sex differences were found in total I, I+, or I– scores. (2) No sex differences were found in the number of times Ss attributed success to ability or to effort. (3) No sex differences were found in the number of times Ss attributed failure to lack of ability. Men were more likely than women to attribute failure to lack of effort.

Dykstra, R., and Tinney, R. Sex differences in reading readiness—first grade achievement and second grade achievement. *Reading & Realism*, 1969, 13, 623–28.
   Experiment I: Subjects: $N = 3,283$; tested at 6 and 7 yrs. **Measures:** The following measures of reading readiness were administered at age 6 (the beginning of first grade): Murphy-Durrell Phonemes, Murphy-Durrell Letter Names, Murphy-Durrell Learning Rate, Thurstone-Jeffery Identical Forms, Metropolitan Word Meaning, and Metropolitan Listening. Ss also completed the Pintner-Cunningham Primary, a group test of intelligence. **Results:** (1) Girls were superior to boys in intelligence, auditory discrimination (M-D Phonemes), letter knowledge (M-D Letter Names), learning rate, visual discrimination (T-J Identical Forms), and ability to follow oral directions (Metropolitan Listening). (2) Boys were superior to girls on the orally administered test of general vocabulary (Metropolitan Word Meaning).
   Experiment II: Subjects: Same as Experiment I. **Measures:** The Stanford Achievement Test, Primary Battery I, was administered to all Ss at age 6 (the end of the first grade). **Results:** Girls had higher scores on 4 of the 5 subtests (Word Reading, Paragraph Meaning, Spelling, and Work Study Skills). No sex differences were found on the orally administered vocabulary test.
   Experiment III: Subjects: Same as Experiment I. **Measures:** The Stanford Achievement Test, Primary Battery II, was administered to all Ss at age 7 (the end of the second grade). **Results:** (1) Girls were superior to boys on 6 of the 8 subtests (Word Meaning, Paragraph Meaning, Work Study Skills, Science and Social Studies Concepts, Language, and Arithmetic Computations). (2) Boys were superior to girls on the Spelling subtest. (3) No sex differences were found on the Arithmetic Concepts subtest.

Eagly, A. H., and Manis, M. Evaluation of message and communicator as a function of involvement. *J. Personality & Social Psychology*, 1966, 3, 483–85.
Subjects: $N = 124$; 14 yrs. **Measures:** Ss read 2 persuasive messages arguing that teenagers should be more strictly controlled by adults. One message was constructed to be relatively involving for boys but not for girls; the other was constructed to be relatively involving for girls but not for boys. Afterward, Ss evaluated the messages and the communicators. **Results:** (1) No main sex differences were found in Ss' evaluations of the messages. Boys responded less favorably to the boy's message than to the girl's message, while girls responded less favorably to the girl's message than to the boy's message ($p < .01$). This interaction was maintained when initial attitudes were held constant ($p < .01$). (2) No main sex differences were found in Ss' evaluations of the communicators. Boys responded less favorably to the communicator of the boy's message than to the communicator of the girl's message; girls responded less favorably to the communicator of the girl's message than to the communicator of the boy's message ($p < .05$). This interaction was not maintained when initial attitudes were held constant.

Eagly, A. H., and Telaak, K. Width of the latitude of acceptance as a determinant of attitude change. *J. Personality & Social Psychology*, 1972, 23, 388–97.
Subjects: $N = 118$; 18–21 yrs (college). **Measures:** After completing an attitude questionnaire, Ss received a persuasive communication either slightly, moderately, or strongly discrepant from their initial attitude. Ss then responded to a second attitude questionnaire. Ss were also asked to evaluate the message and the source. **Results:** No sex differences.

Eagly, A. H., and Whitehead, G. I. Effect of choice on receptivity to favorable and un-favorable evaluations of oneself. *J. Personality & Social Psychology*, 1972, 22, 223–30.
Subjects: $N = 145$; 18–21 yrs (college). **Measures:** After completing tests described as measures of social sensitivity and receiving either favorable or unfavorable feedback on their performances, Ss rated themselves on social sensitivity. Ss' ratings were scored as deviations from a control group. Ss also completed 18 items from Berger's Self-Acceptance Scale. **Results:** (1) There were no main sex differences in self-ratings of social sensitivity. Men changed more toward the favorable than the unfavorable message in their self-ratings of social sensitivity; women changed equally toward both ($p < .05$). (2) No main sex differences were found in self-acceptance.

Eckert, H. M. Visual-motor tasks at 3 and 4 years of age. *Perceptual & Motor Skills*, 1970, 31, 560.
Subjects: $N = 22$; tested at 3, 4 yrs. **Measures:** Ss performed the following visual-motor tasks: walking on the balance board, the Lowe rotor (with epicyclic pattern), 3 disk-sorting tasks (right, left, and both hands), and 4 peg-shifting tasks (right hand moving pegs away from body, left away, right hand moving pegs toward body, left toward). **Results:** No sex differences.

Edelman, M. S., and Omark, D. R. Dominance hierarchies in young children. *Social Science Information*, 1973, 12, 103–10.
Subjects: $N = $ approximately 270; 6–9 yrs. **Measures:** Ss were asked "Who is the toughest?" comparing their classmates with each other and with themselves. A "dyad of established dominance" was scored if both members agreed on who was. **Results:** (1) Boys were consistently ranked higher in toughness, with a few girls scoring in the masculine range. (2) There was a higher proportion of dyads of established dominance in boy-girl pairs than in same-sex pairs. In boy-girl pairs the boy was almost always recognized as dominant by both members. (3) There were no sex differences in accuracy of perception of the dominance relations between pairs of classmates, not including the subject.

Eimas, P. D. Information processing in problem solving as a function of developmental level and stimulus salience. *Developmental Psychology*, 1970, 2, 224–29.
Subjects: $N = 192$; 7, 9, 11, 13 yrs. $N = 48$; 18–21 yrs (college women). **Measures:** Ss were shown 8- and 16-cell matrices containing 1 of 3 types of stimuli. Instructions were to find the correct cell as quickly as possible by asking questions answerable by yes or no. Questions were analyzed to provide a measure of average amount of information obtained, categorical-ness, and focusing. **Results:** No sex differences.

Eisen, M. Characteristic self-esteem, sex and resistance to temptation. *J. Personality & Social Psychology*, 1972, 24, 68–72.
Subjects: $N = 125$; 11 yrs. **Measures:** Ss were classified as either high cheaters, low cheaters, or noncheaters, on the basis of the number of times they changed or falsified answers (in order to win a prize) in a dot-counting contest. **Results:** No sex differences.

Eisenberg, L., Berlin, C. I., Dill, A., and Frank, S. Class and race effects on the intelligibility of monosyllables. *Child Development*, 1968, 39, 1077–89.
Subjects: $N = 64$; 8–10 yrs (black and white, low and middle SES). **Measures:** 40 teachers from inner-city schools listened to tapes of Ss' speech (made in an earlier study) and recorded their perceptions of what the children said. **Results:** Girls were better understood than boys were ($p < .05$).

Ekman, P., and Friesen, W. V. Constants across cultures in the face and emotion. *J. Personality & Social Psychology*, 1971, 17, 124–29.
Subjects: $N = 319$; children and adults (Fore linguistic cultural group of the South East Highlands of New Guinea). **Measures:** After being told a story and shown a set of 3 faces, Ss were asked to select the face that showed the emotion most appropriate to the story. **Results:** No sex differences.

Elder, M. The effects of temperature and position on the sucking pressure of infants. *Child Development*, 1970, 41, 95–102.
Subjects: $N = 27$; 3–5 days. **Measures:** Infant's state was rated. Sucking strength was measured while S was supine or supported at crib temperatures of 80 or 90 degrees. **Results:** No sex differences.

Elkind, D., Van Doorninck, W., and Schwarz, C. Perceptual activity and concept attainment. *Child Development*, 1967, *38*, 1153–61.
Subjects: $N = 120$; 5–11 yrs. Measures: Ss were given a 2-choice discrimination-learning task. The stimuli used were 27 drawings of a boy, girl, or dog engaged in 1 of 3 activities (running, eating, or playing with a ball) in 1 of 3 settings (room, yard, or beach). The response measure was the number of trials Ss needed to reach the criterion of 10 successively correct responses. Results: No sex differences.

Elkind, D., Medvine, L., and Rockway, A. S. Representational level and concept production in children and adolescents. *Developmental Psychology*, 1970, *2*, 85–89.
Subjects: $N = 120$; 9, 14 yrs. Measures: Ss were asked to state 3 ways in which each of 10 stimulus pairs were alike. Stimulus pairs were either pictures, verbal labels of pictures, or mixed series of pictures and verbal labels. Results: No sex differences.

Elliott, R., and Vasta, R. The modeling of sharing: effects associated with vicarious reinforcement, symbolization, age and generalization. *J. Experimental Child Psychology*, 1970, *10*, 8–15.
Subjects: $N = 48$; 5–7 yrs. Measures: After (pretest) sharing behavior was measured (putting candy in an envelope for a poor boy), Ss saw a filmed male-peer model who exhibited sharing behavior and was either nonreinforced, tangibly reinforced with no explanation, or tangibly reinforced with explanation (all by adult female E). Controls saw no film. Post-modeling sharing was measured (candy and/or pennies put in an envelope for a poor boy). Results: There were no main sex differences in sharing after observing the model. Boys shared candy more freely than pennies, whereas girls shared pennies more freely than candy.

Ellsworth, P. C., Carlsmith, J. A., and Henson, A. The stare as a stimulus to flight in human subjects. *J. Personality & Social Psychology*, 1972, *21*, 302–11.
Subjects: $N = 216$; adults. Measures: Standing at the corner of a sidewalk, male or female Es either did or did not stare at drivers ($N = 88$) who pulled up in the near lane and stopped for a red light. When the light turned green, drivers were timed until they crossed a white line on the far side of the intersection. In a second experiment, similar procedures were followed using pedestrians ($N = 128$) as subjects. Results: No sex differences.

Emmerich, W. Continuity and stability in early social development: II. Teacher ratings. *Child Development*, 1966, *37*, 17–27.
Subjects: $N = 53$; tested at 3, 4 yrs. Measures: At the end of each semester of nursery school, Ss were rated by their teachers on 24 social-behavior scales; 3 basic factor structures emerged from factor analyses of the data: Aggression-Dominance, Dependency, and Autonomy. Results: (1) At the end of the first semester, girls scored higher than boys on the Autonomy factor; no sex difference was found at the end of the second, third, or fourth semester. (2) Girls scored consistently higher than boys on the Dependency factor (for each semester, $p < .01$). (3) No mention was made of the Aggression-Dominance factor.

Emmerich, W. The parental role: a functional-cognitive approach. *Monographs of the Society for Research in Child Development*, 1969, *34*.
Subjects: $N = 88$; parents (mean age of child 45 mos). Measures: Parents completed the Parental Role Questionnaire to assess attitudes concerning child-rearing: goal values, means-ends beliefs, means-ends capacities, and goal achievements. Results: No sex-of-parent or sex-of-child differences were found.

Emmerich, W. Structure and development of personal-social behaviors in preschool settings. Educational Testing Service—Head Start Longitudinal Study, November 1971.
Experiment I: Subjects: $N = 415$; 4–5 yrs (disadvantaged black and white). Measures: After being observed in their classrooms during free-play periods, Ss were rated on 127 unipolar scales and 18 bipolar scales. Each child was observed twice, once in the early fall and once in the late fall. Results: (1) Girls were more constructive (vs. destructive), compliant (vs. rebellious), and withdrawn, and engaged in more artistic activity. Boys were more assertive, exhibited more peer orientation, and engaged in more gross motor and fantasy activity. (2) No sex differences were found in autonomous achievement; cognitive and fine manipulative activity; adult orientation; defiance-hostility; distrustfulness; submissiveness vs. dominance; purposefulness vs. aimlessness (interpersonal cooperativeness); sociableness vs. solitariness; or loving (happiness vs. unhappiness).
Experiment II: Subjects: $N = 596$; 4–5 yrs (disadvantaged black and white). Measures: Ss were observed in their classrooms once in the early fall and once toward the end of the

school year. Since considerable overlap exists between the 2 samples, many of the early fall observations included in the data analysis in Experiment I were analyzed again in the present study. **Results:** (1) In comparison with boys, girls were more purposeful and constructive, had higher autonomous achievement scores, and engaged in more artistic, cognitive, and fine manipulative activity. (2) In comparison with girls, boys affiliated more with peers, and were more attached and more oriented to peers. Boys also engaged in more fantasy and gross motor activity and were more socially controlling with adults. (3) No sex differences were found in affiliation with adults, attachment to adults, or orientation to adults; recognition-seeking (from adults or peers); information-seeking (from adults or peers); social control of peers; assertiveness; defiance-hostility; distrustfulness; withdrawal; submissiveness vs. dominance; compliance vs. rebelliousness; sociableness vs. solitariness; dependence vs. independence; loving. (4) Overall, boys exhibited more person-oriented behavior; girls displayed more task-oriented behavior.

Emmerich, W., Goldman, K. S., and Shore, R. E. Differentiation and development of social norms. *J. Personality & Social Psychology*, 1971, *18*, 323–53.
　　Subjects: *N* = 680; 8–17 yrs. **Measures:** Ss were asked to name a friend who was a boy and a friend who was a girl. Ss were then given a set of questions asking them to indicate how frequently their parents and their named friends expected them to agree with, argue with, help and seek help from others. Ss were also asked to give their own expectations concerning their behavior. **Results:** (1) Girls indicated that their parents and friends expected them to seek help from others more frequently than boys did. No sex differences were found in the frequency with which Ss indicated that their parents and friends expected them to help others, agree with others, or argue with others. (2) Girls thought they should seek help from others more frequently than boys did; boys thought they should argue with others more frequently than girls did. No sex differences were found in the frequency with which Ss thought they should help others or agree with others. (3) Girls indicated that their parents and friends expected them to show higher standards of conduct with same-sex friends than with opposite-sex friends. A similar but weaker tendency was found among boys between the ages of 8 and 13. From age 14 on, boys indicated that their parents and friends expected them to show higher standards of conduct with their girl friends than with their boy friends. (4) Girls of all ages and boys between the ages of 8 and 13 thought they should exhibit higher standards of conduct with same-sex friends than with opposite-sex friends. Among 14- and 15-year-old boys, no trend was found. Boys aged 16–17 years thought they should exhibit higher standards of conduct with their girl friends than with their boy friends.

Endler, N. S. Conformity as a function of different reinforcement schedules. *J. Personality & Social Psychology*, 1966, *4*, 175–80.
　　Subjects: *N* = 120; 18–21 yrs (college). **Measures:** Before responding to multiple-choice stimulus items, Ss were subjected to social pressure via a Crutchfield-type conformity apparatus. On critical items, Ss were either positively or negatively reinforced for agreeing or disagreeing with the contrived group consensus. Ss in a neutral condition received no reinforcement. During a second session 2 weeks later, Ss responded to the stimulus items without social pressure or reinforcement. The number of times Ss agreed with the contrived group consensus was recorded. **Results:** Women conformed more than men did in both sessions (*p* = .05).

Endler, N. S., and Hoy, E. Conformity as related to reinforcement and social pressure. *J. Personality & Social Psychology*, 1967, *7*, 197–202.
　　Subjects: *N* = 120; 18–21 yrs (college). **Measures:** Ss responded to multiple-choice items after being informed of the choices of simulated others. The number of times Ss agreed with the unanimous group response was recorded. **Results:** No sex differences.

Endo, G. T. Social drive or arousal: a test of two theories of social isolation. *J. Experimental Child Psychology*, 1968, *6*, 61–74.
　　Subjects: *N* = 96; 8 yrs. **Measures:** Ss performed a 2-choice probability learning task (predicting which of 2 cards, in ratios of 7:3 or 3:7, would appear on the next trial) after social isolation (12 minutes alone) or nonisolation. Half of the Ss in each isolation group were verbally reinforced for correct predictions, the other half were reinforced with a buzzer and light. Total number of responses made to the more frequently occurring event were recorded, regardless of whether reinforcement occurred. **Results:** No sex differences.

Engel, M. The stability of the self-concept in adolescence. *J. Abnormal & Social Psychology*, 1959, *58*, 211–15.
　　Subjects: *N* = 104; tested at 13, 15 yrs. *N* = 68; tested at 15, 17 yrs. **Measures:** Self-concept

was assessed by a set of 100 Q-sort items, half of which had positive and half negative connotations. In responding, Ss had to place each item in 1 of 11 categories, ranging from "most like me" to "least like me." **Results:** No sex differences were found either during the initial testing in 1954 or during retesting in 1956. No sex differences were found in stability of self-concept.

Entwisle, D. R., and Greenberger, E. Adolescents' views of women's work role. *American J. Orthopsychiatry*, 1972a, *42*, 648–56.
　　Subjects: $N = 575$; 14 yrs (white, black). **Measures:** Ss' attitudes toward women's working role were assessed. **Results:** Boys' attitudes were more conservative than girls', i.e. boys felt more strongly that women should not work; rather, they should center their lives around their homes and families. Girls felt more strongly than boys that women were intellectually curious ($p < .01$).

Entwisle, D. R., and Greenberger, E. Questions about social class, internality-externality, and test anxiety. *Developmental Psychology*, 1972b, *7*, 218 (brief report and extended report).
　　Subjects: $N = 664$; 14 yrs (inner-city black, low and medium IQ; inner-city white, medium IQ; blue-collar black, low and medium IQ; blue-collar white, medium and high IQ; rural white, medium and high IQ; middle-class white, medium and high IQ; middle-class Jewish, medium and high IQ). **Measures:** All Ss completed the Intellectual Achievement Responsibility (IAR) scale. 566 of the Ss were also given a test-anxiety questionnaire. **Results:** (1) Among inner-city and rural whites of medium IQ, girls had higher IAR success scores than boys. Among middle-class whites of high IQ, boys had higher success scores than girls. (2) Girls consistently had higher test-anxiety scores than boys.

Epstein, R. Authoritarianism, displaced aggression, and social status of the target. *J. Personality & Social Psychology*, 1965, *2*, 585–89.
　　Subjects: $N = 40$; 18–21 yrs (college). **Measures:** Ss were instructed to shock a confederate whenever he made an incorrect response in a serial learning task. The intensity of the shock delivered was recorded. **Results:** Men delivered higher intensities of shock than women did ($p < .01$).

Eska, B., and Black, K. N. Conceptual tempo in young grade-school children. *Child Development*, 1971, *42*, 505–16.
　　Subjects: $N = 100$; 8 yrs. **Measures:** Ss completed the Matching Familiar Figures task and the verbal subtest of the Otis-Lennon Mental Ability Test. Ss were also presented with 6 pictures and asked to tell a story about each; measures were taken of the latency and duration of Ss' responses. **Results:** No sex differences.

Fagan, J. F., III. Infants' recognition memory for a series of visual stimuli. *J. Experimental Child Psychology*, 1971, *11*, 244–50.
　　Subjects: 12 opposite-sex twin pairs; 3–8 mos. **Measures:** Ss' fixation times to (a) novel relative to familiar stimuli, and (b) less familiar relative to more familiar stimuli, were recorded. **Results:** No sex differences.

Fagan, J. F., III. Infants' recognition memory for faces. *J. Experimental Child Psychology*, 1972, *14*, 453–76.
　　Experiment I: Subjects: $N = 17$ same-sex twin pairs; 4–6 mos. **Measures:** Ss viewed pictures of unfamiliar faces (a woman, a man, and a baby). Orientation was varied, as were lengths of familiarization. Recognition memory was assessed. **Results:** No sex differences.
　　Experiment II: Subjects: $N = 52$; 3–4 mos. **Measures:** Same as Experiment I. Masks were introduced to assess discrimination between photos and 3-dimensional representations. **Results:** No sex differences.
　　Experiment III: Subjects: $N = 72$; 5–6 mos. **Measures:** Same as Experiment I. Discrimination between male, female, and baby was assessed. **Results:** Girls responded differentially to properly oriented photos, boys did not.
　　Experiment IV: Subjects: $N = 36$; 4–6 mos. **Measures:** Same as Experiment III. Orientation was proper; line drawings were used. **Results:** No sex differences.
　　Experiment V: Subjects: $N = 56$; 5–6 mos. **Measures:** Novelty problem with masks and photos was used. Orientation varied. **Results:** There were no sex differences in discrimination of highly lifelike masks.
　　Experiment VI: Subjects: $N = 24$; 5–6 mos. **Measures:** Homogenous gray forms, equal

to photos in reflectance and outline, were paired with photos. Preference was assessed. **Results:** No sex differences.

EXPERIMENT VII: **Subjects:** $N = 16$; 5–6 mos. **Measures:** A novelty problem with masks (as in Experiment II) was contrasted with photos of a man and a woman. Ss' fixation point was watched. **Results:** No sex differences.

Fagot, B. I., and Patterson, G. R. An in vivo analysis of reinforcing contingencies for sex-role behaviors in the preschool child. *Developmental Psychology*, 1969, *1*, 563–68.

    Subjects: $N = 18$; 3 yrs (School 1). $N = 18$; 3 yrs (School 2). **Measures:** During both the fall and spring terms, observations were made of Ss, free-play activities. 28 play behaviors and 10 social consequences of these behaviors were recorded. **Results:** (1) Boys spent more time than girls (a) playing with building blocks, setting up farms and villages (School 1, both terms; School 2, fall term only); (b) playing with toy trucks, planes, boats, trains, or tractors (School 1, both terms; School 2, both terms); (c) climbing or hiding in pipes (School 1, fall term only; School 2, no difference); (d) riding trikes, cars, horses, skates, wagons, or boats (School 1, spring term only; School 2, no difference); (e) playing at the cornmeal table or sandbox outside (School 1, no difference; School 2, both terms). Girls spent more time than boys (a) painting at the easel (School 1, both terms; School 2, fall term only); (2) cutting, pasting, or drawing with crayons or chalk (School 1, both terms; School 2, both terms); (c) playing in the kitchen or large playhouse (School 1, both terms; School 2, no difference); (d) playing with the dollhouse (School 1, fall term only; School 2, no difference); (e) playing with dolls (School 1, both terms; School 2, no difference); (f) playing with clay (School 1, both terms; School 2, no difference); (g) looking at books or listening to stories (School 1, no difference; School 2, fall term only). No sex differences were found in time spent (a) playing with water, blowing bubbles; (b) playing with the design board, puzzles, tinkertoys, snakes, flannel boards or marble games; (c) stringing beads; (d) hammering; (e) playing with a steering wheel or dashboards; (f) dressing up in like-sex costumes; (g) dressing up in opposite-sex costumes; (h) using like-sex tools; (i) using opposite-sex tools; (j) singing, listening to records, or playing musical instruments; (k) playing at the science table or with dinosaurs; (l) playing with live animals or toy animals; (m) sitting and doing nothing, wandering, following the teacher around; (n) helping the teacher; (o) swinging, playing on the slide or teeter-totter, bouncing on tires; (p) throwing rocks, hitting with an object, or pushing. During the spring term, boys and girls in School 2 spent a considerable amount of time wandering. The authors noted that this accounted in part for the drop in percentage of time spent in sex-preferred activities. (2) Girls spent less time in opposite-sex behaviors than boys did. There was no sex difference in percentage of time spent in same-sex behaviors. (3) Teachers (4 women) reinforced both sexes for feminine behaviors; however, boys did not as a result become more feminine in their behavior preferences. (4) Girls were reinforced for sex-preferred behavior more frequently than boys. When neutral behaviors were included, no sex differences were found in teacher reinforcement. (5) No difference was found between boys and girls in the amount of criticism they received. (6) Ss reinforced same-sex peers more often than opposite-sex peers.

Farnham-Diggory, S. Cognitive synthesis in Negro and white children. *Monographs of the Society for Research in Child Development*, 1970, *35*.

    EXPERIMENT I: **Subjects:** $N = 192$; 6–9 yrs. **Measures:** Ss learned to associate verbalized words with pictures and with unrelated logographs. Ss were tested on decoding of logograph sentence and acting out its meaning. Ss performed a maplike test that required imitation of line drawings using pieces of string. Forms in the drawings were symbols for words; Ss were asked to construct a sentence with symbols. In the mathematical synthesis task, Ss matched different numbers of dots on card with cubes of varying sizes. **Results:** (1) Boys performed better than girls did on verbal synthesis. (2) On the maplike synthesis task, among white Ss, boys did better than girls. Among black Ss, girls did better than boys. (3) There were no sex differences in mathematical synthesis.

    EXPERIMENT II: **Subjects:** $N = 110$; 4, 5, 7–8 yrs. **Measures:** Same as Experiment I, except with verbal and motor pretraining. **Results:** There were no main sex differences. Maplike task and training affected performance of girls but not boys ($p < .05$).

    EXPERIMENT III: **Subjects:** $N = 140$; 5, 7 yrs. **Measures:** The maplike synthesis problem was given as before, except that Ss either (1) role-played the various items in the sentence before attempting the problem, (2) heard new instructions altered so as to play up their tendency to act on first word heard, or (3) attempted the problem under a perceptual shield condition in which the various steps had to be memorized (they were not always on display). The mathematical synthesis task was given with either a verbal drill on base concepts or an action drill on the various steps. **Results:** (1) Girls did better than boys on the maplike task. (2) There were no sex differences on mathematical synthesis.

Farrell, M. Sex differences in block play in early childhood education. *J. Educational Research*, 1957, *51*, 279–84.

Subjects: N = 376; 3–7 yrs. **Measures:** Teachers' observations of children's indoor play activities. **Results:** (1) A higher percentage of boys than girls played with blocks (p < .01). (2) Boys played with blocks longer than girls did (p < .01).

Farwell, L. Reactions of kindergarten, first- and second-grade children to constructive play materials. *Genetic Psychology Monographs*, 1930, *8*, 451–561.

Subjects: N = 271; 5–7 yrs. **Measures:** Ss were observed while working with modeling, building, drawing, painting, sewing, cardboard construction, and paper construction materials. **Results:** In comparison with girls, boys showed a marked preference for blocks and a lack of interest in sewing. Popular choices among both boys and girls were modeling and painting materials. A fair interest was shown by both sexes in drawing and only a slight interest in cardboard and paper construction.

Faterson, H. F., and Witkin, H. A. Longitudinal study of development of the body concept. *Developmental Psychology*, 1970, *2*, 429–38.

Subjects: N = 53; tested at 8, 13 yrs. N = 60; tested at 10, 14, 17 yrs. **Measures:** Ss first drew a person, then a person of the opposite sex. Pictures were scored on a 5-point articulation-of-body concept (ABC) scale, from "most articulated" to "most primitive and infantile." **Results:** At ages 8, 13, and 14, girls' ABC scores were higher than those of boys (p < .025, p < .025, p < .025).

Fauls, L. B., and Smith, W. D. Sex-role learning in 5-year-olds. *J. Genetic Psychology*, 1956, *89*, 105–17.

Subjects: N = 38; 4, 5 yrs. **Measures:** Ss were presented with sets of paired pictures depicting a child of the same sex and his parents. One picture in each pair showed the child performing a masculine activity; in the other picture the child was engaged in a feminine activity. Ss were asked 4 questions about each set: (1) "Which of these do you do?" (2) "Which do you like best?" (3) "Which does Mommy want the boy (girl) to do?" (4) "Which does Daddy want the boy (girl) to do?" **Results:** Boys chose the masculine activity more frequently than girls did (p < .01). (2) Both sexes perceived the parents as preferring the activity "appropriate" for the child's sex rather than the "inappropriate" activity.

Fay, T. Culture and sex differences in concepts of sex role and self. *Dissertations Abstracts International*, 1971, *31*, 6239.

Subjects: N = 45; 18–21 yrs (college: U.S., Philippines, Colombia). **Measures:** Ss rated each of 5 concepts (self, typical male, typical female, ideal male, and ideal female) on 25 semantic differential rating scales. **Results:** (1) Regardless of sex or nationality of rater, a significant difference was found between ratings of male and female stereotypes (typical and ideal). (2) Similarity between ratings or self and same-sex stereotype (whether typical or ideal) was higher for women than for men.

Feather, N. T. Level of aspiration and performance variability. *J. Personality & Social Psychology*, 1967a, *6*, 37–46.

Subjects: N = 106; 18–21 yrs (college). **Measures:** Ss were individually tested on a manual-dexterity task, which allowed E complete control over Ss' performance. Ss' scores were manipulated to be either high, medium, or low in variability. Before each of 11 trials, Ss stated both the highest and the lowest scores they expected to receive and their level of aspiration. The measures derived were (a) mean highest score expected; (b) mean lowest score expected; (c) mean goal discrepancy (difference between level of aspiration at trial $(n + 1)$ and performance at trial n); (d) mean attainment discrepancy (difference between level of aspiration at trial n and performance at trial n); (e) change in level of aspiration from trial 1 to trial 2; (f) mean change in aspiration following success; (g) mean change in aspiration following failure; and (h) number of atypical responses (number of times Ss raised their level of aspiration after failure and lowered it following success). The projective measure of n achievement, the achievement anxiety test, Radner's test of intolerance ambiguity, and Pettigrew's test of category width were also administered. **Results:** (1) No main sex differences were found. (2) Women in the high-variability condition showed a larger change in aspiration following either success or failure than women in the low-variability condition; women in the medium-variability condition fell in between these 2 extremes. No differences were found among the 3 male groups. (3) The difference between the mean change in aspiration following success and the mean change in aspiration following failure was greater for women in the low-variability condition than for women in the high-variability condition. Women in the medium-variability group again fell in between these 2 extremes. No differences were found among the 3 male groups. (4) No sex differences were found on any of the personality measures.

Feather, N. T. Valence of outcome and expectation of success in relation to task difficulty and perceived locus of control. *J. Personality & Social Psychology,* 1967b, *7,* 372–86.
> **Subjects:** $N = 76$; 18–21 yrs (college). **Measures:** Ss provided estimates of probability of success and ratings of the attractiveness of success and repulsiveness of failure for the first and last trials of a task described as involving either luck or skill. **Results:** No sex differences.

Feather, N. T. Change in confidence following success or failure as a predictor of subsequent performance. *J. Personality & Social Psychology,* 1968, *9,* 38–46.
> **Subjects:** $N = 60$; 18–21 yrs (college). **Measures:** Ss provided confidence ratings before attempting to solve each of 15 anagrams. **Results:** (1) Men had higher confidence ratings than women did ($p < .05$). (2) No sex differences were found in number of typical changes in confidence ratings (a typical change was one in which S either raised his confidence rating after a success or lowered it after a failure). (3) No sex differences were found in number of anagrams correctly solved.

Feather, N. T. Attitude and selective recall. *J. Personality & Social Psychology,* 1969a, *12,* 310–19.
> **Subjects:** $N = 138$; 18–21 yrs (college). **Measures:** One week after rating American intervention in South Vietnam on a bipolar adjective scale, Ss were asked to write arguments favoring American intervention with which they agreed or disagreed, and arguments opposing American intervention with which they agreed or disagreed. **Results:** (1) Men wrote down more arguments than women ($p < .05$). (2) No sex differences were found in initial attitudes, or in consistency of arguments with initial attitudes.

Feather, N. T. Attribution of responsibility and valence of success and failure in relation to initial confidence and task performance. *J. Personality & Social Psychology,* 1969b, *13,* 129–44.
> **Subjects:** $N = 167$; 18–21 yrs (college). **Measures:** Ss worked at a 10-item anagrams test. Before they began, Ss rated their confidence in passing the test (solve 5 or more anagrams). After they finished, Ss recorded the number of anagrams they had solved, the degree to which they felt their performance was due to ability (internal attribution) or luck (external attribution), and their degree of satisfaction with their performance. Ss also completed self-esteem and competence measures (administered prior to the anagram test) and a feeling-of-inadequacy measure (administered 1 week after the anagrams tests). **Results:** Women were lower in initial confidence ($p < .005$), higher in external attribution ($p < .01$), and higher in feelings of inadequacy ($p < .05$) than men were. No sex differences were found in self-esteem, competence, satisfaction, or performance scores.

Feather, N. T., and Simon, J. G. Attribution of responsibility and valence of outcome in relation to initial confidence and success and failure of self and other. *J. Personality & Social Psychology,* 1971, *18,* 173–88.
> **Subjects:** $N = 128$; 18–21 yrs (college). **Measures:** Like-sex pairs of Ss worked on 5 practice anagrams and then on 15 test anagrams. For both practice and test items, difficulty level was manipulated so that half of the Ss did well and half did poorly. Before beginning test items, Ss rated degree of confidence in passing for self and for other. After being informed of their test score, Ss rated the degree to which they felt their performance and that of their partner was due to luck or ability, and then rated their degree of satisfaction with their own and their partner's performance. **Results:** (1) There were no main sex differences. (2) Confidence ratings were higher for passing men than for passing women, but lower for failing men than for failing women ($p < .001$).

Feld, S. C., and Lewis, J. The assessment of achievement anxieties in children. In C. P. Smith, ed., *Achievement-related motives in children.* New York: Russell Sage Foundation, 1969.
> **Subjects:** $N = 7,355$; 7 yrs (white, black). **Measures:** Ss completed expanded forms of the Test Anxiety Scale for Children (TASC) and the Defensiveness Scale for Children, which included original and reversed questions. **Results:** (1) There were no sex differences on the Poor Self-Evaluation subscale of the TASC. On Test Anxiety, Remote School Concern, and Somatic Signs of Anxiety subscales, girls had higher scores than boys (strongest on Remote School Concern and Somatic Signs of Anxiety). (2) On total scores from the original Sarason

Test Anxiety Scale for Children, girls had higher scores than boys. (3) The overall main effects for sex were due to the white sample (there were no sex differences in the black sample).

Feldman, S. S., and Ingham, M. E. Attachment behavior: a study of the concurrent validity in two age groups. Unpublished manuscript, Stanford University, 1973.

EXPERIMENT I: Subjects: $N = 56$; 1 yr. Measures: Accompanied by either their mother, their father, or a female acquaintance, Ss were observed in the following situations: accompanying adult (AA) brings child to room with toys, then sits down (Episode 1); AA attends to child for 2 minutes, then fills out questionnaire (Episode 2); female stranger (Str) enters, sits silently for 1 minute, converses with AA for 1 minute, then plays with child (Episode 3); AA leaves, Str goes to chair (Episode 4); AA enters, Str leaves, AA plays with child (Episode 5); AA leaves, child remains alone (Episode 6); Str returns, comforts child if distressed (Episode 7); AA enters, plays with child (Episode 8). During Episodes 2, 3, 5, 6, and 7, Ss were scored for the following behaviors: manipulative play; crying; looks toward AA or Str; smiles, shows object; or speaks to AA or Str; proximity to AA or Str (this was scored only when the AA or the Str was in the chair). Activity was assessed by the number of lines Ss crossed (the room was marked off into 18-inch squares). During the reunion episodes (5 and 8), the presence or absence of the following behaviors was recorded: looks at AA; smiles, shows, or gives object to AA; talks to AA; averts looking at AA; moves toward AA; bids for comfort and physical contact; comfort derived from physical contact. Results: (1) Among those Ss accompanied by their mothers, boys exhibited less playing and more crying when left alone (Episode 6) than girls did. (2) Among those Ss accompanied by their fathers, boys exhibited more proximity to the Str, less playing, and more crying upon the stranger's return in Episode 7 than girls did. (3) Among those Ss accompanied by a female acquaintance (FA), boys exhibited more crying (Episode 2 only), more proximity to FA (Episodes 2 and 3), and less looking at FA (Episode 2 only) than girls did. (4) No other sex differences were found.

EXPERIMENT II: Subjects: $N = 79$; 2½ yrs. Measures: Identical to Experiment I. Results: (1) Among those Ss accompanied by their mother, boys exhibited more crying than girls during Episode 7, and more girls than boys looked at their mothers during Episodes 2 and 3. (2) Among those Ss accompanied by their father, boys exhibited more crying than girls when left alone (Episode 6). (3) No differences were found between boys and girls accompanied by a female acquaintance.

Feldstein, J. H., and Witryol, S. L. The incentive value of uncertainty reduction for children. *Child Development*, 1971, *42*, 793–804 (and personal communication).

Subjects: $N = 60$; 9 yrs. Measures: On each of 40 trials, Ss chose between a piece of bubble gum and a package that concealed either a charm, a piece of bubble gum, a bean, or a paper clip (each was presented on 25% of the trials). In one condition, Ss were informed of the contents of the package after every trial. Ss in other conditions experienced delays of either 10, 20, or 40 trials before becoming aware of the identity of the objects in the packages they had chosen. Results: No sex differences were found in the number of times the package was chosen.

Feldstone, C. S. Developmental studies of negatively correlated reinforcement in children. *Developmental Psychology*, 1969, *1*, 528–42.

Subjects: $N = 106$; 5–6, 8–10, 11–13 yrs (Crank Experiment II). $N = 26$; 18–27 yrs (Crank Experiment III). $N = 74$; 4–6 yrs (Grip Experiment I). $N = 32$; 11–13 yrs (Grip Experiment III). Measures: In the first series of 3 experiments, Ss were asked to turn a crank. Experimental Ss were reinforced when they turned the crank slowly. Yoked control groups were reinforced the same number of times and on the same trials, but their reinforcements were not related to how rapidly they turned the crank. In a second series of 3 experiments, strength of grip was tested. Experimental Ss were reinforced for squeezing weakly, and again yoked control groups were used. In both series, 2 of the 3 experiments were analyzed for sex of S. Results: (1) Among experimental and control Ss in Crank Experiment II, boys turned the crank faster than girls did. There were no sex differences in speed of acquiring the inhibitory response. No sex differences were found in Crank Experiment III. (2) No sex differences were found in either of the Grip experiments.

Felzen, E., and Anisfeld, M. Semantic and phonetic relations in the false recognition of words by third- and sixth-grade children. *Developmental Psychology*, 1970, *3*, 163–68.

Subjects: $N = 80$; 8, 11 yrs. Measures: On a second taped, verbal presentation of a word list, Ss indicated by saying "old" or "new" whether the word had been read on the first presentation. The second word list contained "old" words, semantically and phonetically related words, and control words. Results: (1) There were no sex differences in number of false recognition errors. (2) Boys had longer latencies of responding "new" to new words than girls did ($p < .05$).

Fenz, W. D., and Epstein, S. Manifest anxiety: unifactorial or multifactorial composition? *Perceptual & Motor Skills*, 1965, *20*, 773–80.

> **Subjects:** $N = 98$; 18–21 yrs (college). **Measures:** Ss were given a 160-item questionnaire that included the following scales: striated muscle tension, autonomic arousal, feelings of anxiety, hostility, negative attitude toward hostile expression, conflict, inhibition, and defensiveness. **Results:** Women scored higher than men on the autonomic arousal and negative attitude toward hostile expression scales. Men scored higher than women on the hostility scale.

Ferguson, L. R., and Maccoby, E. E. Interpersonal correlates of differential abilities. *Child Development*, 1966, *37*, 549–71.

> **Subjects:** $N = 126$; 10 yrs. **Measures:** Ss were selected from a larger sample of 1,200 because of performance discrepancies between 2 out of 3 abilities—verbal, number, and space. The third area of ability was at an intermediate level. Ss were matched for total intelligence. (1) The Peer Nominations Inventory was revised to include items relating to dependency, aggression, withdrawal, mastery, and sex-typing. Each S rated same-sex peers. (2) 2 self-report scales of sex-typing were administered. The Sex-Role Differentiation Scale was used to determine whether Ss made distinctions between girls' and boys' activities. The Sex-Role Acceptance Scale consisted of a series of questions in which Ss indicated their preference for one sex role or the other (Ss could also indicate that both roles were equally attractive). Ss were scored for the number of own-sex preferences they checked. (3) 2 self-report scales of dependency measured the tendency to seek help from adults (a) in difficult problem-solving situations and (b) when sick, alone, or afraid. (4) 2 self-report scales of dependency anxiety assessed derogation of dependency and anticipation of punishment for dependency. (5) 3 self-report scales measured aggression-agression anxiety, antisocial aggression, and projected aggression. (6) A task measuring susceptibility to distraction was also administered. **Results:** Girls scored higher than boys on aggression anxiety and dependency when sick, alone, or afraid. Boys scored higher than girls on antisocial aggression, derogation of dependency, and sex-role acceptance. There were no other sex differences on self-report or peer-nomination measures.

Ferraro, D. P., Francis, E. W., and Perkins, J. J. Titrating delayed matching to sample in children. *Developmental Psychology*, 1971, *5*, 488–93.

> **Subjects:** $N = 40$; 4, 5, 6, 8, 10 yrs. **Measures:** During pretraining, Ss were asked to press the 1 of 2 lighted comparison panels that matched the standard stimulus panel color. A criterion of 4 consecutive correct responses was set (2 at 0-second delay between termination of standard stimulus and onset of comparison stimuli, and 2 at 1-second delay); 60 experimental matchings followed, with 2-second delay, increasing 2 more seconds at each correct response and decreasing 2 seconds at each incorrect one. **Results:** No sex differences.

Feshbach, N. D. Sex differences in children's modes of aggressive responses toward outsiders. *Merrill-Palmer Quarterly*, 1969, *15*, 249–58.

> **Subjects:** $N = 126$; 6 yrs (middle SES). **Measures:** In the first session, same-sex pairs were encouraged to play as a cohesive unit. In the second play session, half of these groups received a same-sex newcomer. Mode and frequency of aggressive behaviors were recorded by a hidden observer. **Results:** First session: (1) No sex differences were found in direct aggressive, indirect aggressive, or approach behaviors. (2) Boys struck the Bobo doll more frequently than girls did. Second session: (1) During the first 4 minutes of the session, girls were more indirectly aggressive to the newcomer than boys were; during the last 12 minutes, no sex differences were found. (2) No sex differences were observed in the frequency of direct aggressive or approach behaviors or in the number of times a child gave an order to another child. (3) No differences were found between boy and girl newcomers in display of direct or indirect aggression.

Feshbach, N. D. Cross-cultural studies of teaching styles in four-year-olds and their mothers: some educational implications of socialization. Draft of a paper presented at the Minnesota Symposium on Child Psychology, 1972.

> **Subjects:** $N = 104$; 4 yrs and mothers (white and black, low and middle SES). **Measures:** Ss initially taught a 3-year-old how to assemble a puzzle; 1 hour later, each S's mother was asked to teach her child a similar but slightly more complex puzzle. Measures were taken of the number of times positive and negative reinforcements were administered by Ss and their mothers. **Results:** (1) Boys delivered more negative reinforcements to the younger child than girls did. No sex differences were found in number of positive reinforcements administered.

(2) Mothers of boys negatively reinforced their sons more often than their daughters (significant for middle SES sample only). No difference was found between mothers of boys and girls in number of positive reinforcements administered.

Feshbach, N. D., and Devor, G. Teaching styles in four-year-olds. *Child Development*, 1969, *40*, 183–90.
Subjects: $N = 204$; 3–4 yrs (black, white; low, middle SES). **Measures:** 4-year-old Ss initially learned how to assemble a puzzle. Afterward, they were asked to teach the task to a 3-year-old of the same or opposite sex. The number of positive and negative reinforcements administered to the 3-year-old Ss was recorded. **Results:** No sex of "teacher" or sex of "pupil" differences were found.

Feshbach, N. D., and Feshbach, S. The relation between empathy and aggression in two age groups. *Developmental Psychology*, 1969, *1*, 102–7.
Subjects: $N = 88$; 4–5, 6–7 yrs. **Measures:** Measures of empathy were obtained from Ss' responses to a series of slide sequences depicting happiness, sadness, fear, and anger. **Results:** No sex differences were found in overall scores. Among 4- and 5-year-olds, girls showed more empathy in response to the "sadness" stimulus than boys did ($p < .05$); however, no sex difference was found on the comprehension measure for sadness.

Feshbach, N. D., and Roe, K. Empathy in six- and seven-year-olds. *Child Development*, 1968, *39*, 133–45.
Subjects: $N = 46$; 6 yrs. **Measures:** Ss were presented with a sequence of slides and stories showing 4 different affective situations: happiness, sadness, fear, and anger; 2 alternate sets of the same situations were prepared, varying by sex of stimulus figure. Ss reported their feelings about the stimulus series. As an index of social comprehension, 27 Ss viewed the story-slide sequence again, and were asked to report their feelings about the central character. **Results:** (1) Empathy scores of girls observing girls were greater than corresponding scores of boys observing boys. (2) There were no sex differences in social comprehension scores, except in fear situations, where boys were more accurate than girls.

Feshbach, N. D., and Sones, G. Sex differences in adolescent reactions toward newcomers. *Developmental Psychology*, 1971, *4*, 381–86.
Subjects: $N = 87$; 12–13 yrs. **Measures:** A same-sex close-friend pair (as judged by a teacher) solved 3 social problems together. A same-sex newcomer (1 year younger) joined the pair, and 2 more social problems were solved by the triad. Latency of speaking to the newcomer, latency of newcomer speaking, frequencies of verbal rejection, and incorporation of newcomer's ideas were recorded. All Ss independently rated other 2 members on intelligence, appearance, social desirability, acceptance, and leadership. **Results:** (1) There were no sex differences in original dyads' ratings of each other. (2) Ratings of girls reflected a less favorable reaction to the newcomer than the ratings of boys did. (3) Girls took longer to speak to the newcomer than boys did. (4) Girl newcomers waited longer before speaking than boy newcomers did. (5) Initial sex differences in response to newcomer persisted after the instructions to the second problem were given. Girls took longer than boys to address the newcomer. Newcomer girls took longer than boys to address original-pair members. (6) There were no sex differences in frequency of direct verbal rejections of newcomer's ideas. (7) Girls demonstrated a lower frequency of incorporating newcomer's ideas than boys did.

Fiebert, M. Cognitive styles in the deaf. *Perceptual & Motor Skills*, 1967, *24*, 319–29.
Subjects: $N = 90$; 12, 15, 18 yrs (deaf). **Measures:** Ss were given the Rod and Frame Test, the Children's Embedded Figures Test, and the Poppelreuter Test. Ss' Paragraph Meaning scores on the Standard Achievement Test were used as a measure of reading ability. **Results:** Boys achieved higher scores than girls on each of the 3 embedded figures tests (RFT, $p < .05$; CEFT, $p < .01$; P-T, $p < .01$). No sex differences were found in Paragraph Meaning scores.

Figurelli, J. C., and Keller, H. R. The effects of training and socio-economic class upon the acquisition of conservation concepts. *Child Development*, 1972, *43*, 293–98.
Subjects: $N = 48$; 6 yrs (black). **Measures:** Ss completed the Concept Assessment Kit: Conservation once as a pretest and once after training or no training. **Results:** No sex differences.

Finley, G. E., and Frenkel, O. J. Children's tachistoscopic recognition thresholds for and recall of words which differ in connotative meaning. *Child Development*, 1972, *43*, 1098–1103.
Subjects: $N = 48$; 9, 12 yrs (white low-middle SES). **Measures:** Ss were presented with 14

stimulus words, of good or bad connotative meanings. Ss learned to recognize the words (if they did not already recognize them), and were later asked to rate and recall them. **Results:** (1) Girls rated the good words less positively and the bad words more negatively than boys did ($p < .05$). (2) Girls recalled more words than boys did ($p < .01$).

Finley, G. E., and Layne, O., Jr. Play behavior in young children. Unpublished manuscript, 1969.
Subjects: $N = 96$; 1, 2, 3 yrs (American, Mayan Indian). **Measures:** Each S was accompanied by his mother to the testing room. After setting the child down, the mother was requested not to initiate any interactions. Otherwise, she was told she could respond normally to the child's overtures. S was then observed in free play for 20 minutes with toys from both cultures present. The following measures were recorded: number of involvements with toys of less than 30 seconds duration; number of involvements with toys of more than 30 seconds duration; total number of seconds spent in prolonged involvements with toys; number of toys played with; number of squares traversed (the floor was marked off into 12 squares); number of episodes of visual exploration of toys less than 30 seconds in duration; number of episodes of visual exploration of toys more than 30 seconds in duration; total number of seconds spent in prolonged acts of visual exploration; number of looks at mother; total number of seconds spent in the 3 squares nearest mother; number of times in physical contact with mother for less than 30 seconds; number of times in physical contact with mother for more than 30 seconds; total number of seconds spent in prolonged episodes of physical contact with mother. **Results:** No main sex differences were found. Among American Ss, 3-year-old girls crossed more squares than 2-year-old girls, whereas for boys the reverse was true.

Finley, G. E., Kagan, J., and Layne, O., Jr. Development of young children's attention to normal and distorted stimuli: a cross-cultural study. *Developmental Psychology*, 1972, 6, 288–92.
Subjects: $N = 96$; 1, 2, 3 yrs (Mayan Indians, white Americans). **Measures:** Ss viewed 4 drawings of a man (normal, trunk, scrambled, free-art form) and 5 drawings of a face (normal, cyclops, blank, scrambled, free-art form). The length of Ss' first fixation to each stimulus was recorded. **Results:** No sex differences.

Fischbein, E., Pampu, I., and Manzat, I. Comparison of ratios and the chance concept in children. *Child Development*, 1970, 41, 377–89.
Subjects: $N = 60$; 5–6, 9–10, 12–13 yrs (Rumania). **Measures:** Ss were given 18 problems in which they had to choose the 1 of 2 boxes that contained a black (or white) marble. Estimates of chance could be made as Ss viewed proportion of black/white marbles before decision making. Correct answers were reinforced verbally. **Results:** No sex differences.

Fishbein, H. D., Lewis, S., and Keiffer, K. Children's understanding of spatial relations: coordination of perspectives. *Developmental Psychology*, 1972, 7, 21–33.
    EXPERIMENT I: **Subjects:** $N = 120$; 3–9 yrs. **Measures:** Ss saw either 1 or 3 toys at a time, and either 4 or 8 photographs of the toy display. During familiarization, each S was to point to the photo that corresponded to what he could see from his perspective. E then turned the toy to present each remaining view that S had on photos in front of him. In the pointing task, each S was to point to the photo that corresponded to the view E had as E walked around the display. E removed photos and asked S to turn a revolving toy display to present the specified view to E. Candy was given for correct responses; incorrect responses were corrected. **Results:** No sex differences.
    EXPERIMENT II: **Subjects:** $N = 128$; 5, 7 yrs. **Measures:** 2 tasks were given to Ss, the pointing task described in Experiment I plus a turning task in which E sat in turn on each of the 4 sides of the table. Pointing to 1 of the photographs, she asked Ss to turn the tray so that she could view the toys from the perspective depicted in the photograph. **Results:** (1) When scores from both tasks were combined, no mean sex differences were found. Among 7-year-olds, girls' overall scores were better than those of boys, whereas the reverse was true among 5-year-olds ($p < .05$). (2) Boys performed better than girls on the pointing task; girls performed better than boys on the turning task ($p < .05$).

Fitzgerald, H. E. Autonomic pupillar reflex activity during early infancy and its relation to social and nonsocial stimuli. *J. Experimental Psychology*, 1968, 6, 470–82.
Subjects: $N = 30$; 1–2 mos. **Measures:** S viewed photos of his mother's face, an unfamiliar female's face, checkerboard patterns, and a triangle. Diameter of pupil and pupillar activity were measured. **Results:** No sex differences.

Fitzsimmons, S. J., Cheever, J., Leonard, E., and Macunovich, D. School failures: now and tomorrow. *Developmental Psychology*, 1969, *1*, 134–46.

    Subjects: $N = 270$; 15–17 yrs (students with performance difficulties or dropouts). **Measures:** Ss' academic records from early elementary school through high school were studied. **Results:** More boys than girls dropped out. Boys left for alleged lack of interest in school and desire to work. Girls left for sudden, personal reasons such as marriage, pregnancy, or illness.

Flanagan, J. C., Dailey, J. T., Shaycoft, M. F., Gorham, W. A., Orr, D. B., Goldberg, I., and Neyman, C. A., Jr. Counselor's technical manual for interpreting test scores (Project Talent), Palo Alto, California, 1961.

    Subjects: $N = 4,545$; 14, 17 yrs. **Measures:** Project Talent Test Battery. **Results:** Boys scored higher than girls on the vocabulary, mathematics, and 2- and 3-dimensional visual spatialization tests. Girls scored higher than boys on the disguised words, English language, reading comprehension, and verbal memory tests. Ss' scores on the other tests were not analyzed for sex differences.

Flavell, J. H., Beach, D. R., and Chinsky, J. M. Spontaneous verbal rehearsal in a memory task as a function of age. *Child Development*, 1966, *37*, 283–99.

    Subjects: $N = 60$; 5, 7, 10 yrs. **Measures:** Each S was given 3 nonverbal, serial recall tasks: (1) Immediate recall. E pointed to series of pictures on a portable board and asked S to point to the duplicate set of pictures in the same order on another board. Sequences of 2, 3, 4, and 5 pictures were used according to age level. (2) Delayed recall. S waited 15 seconds after E pointed before beginning. (3) Point and name. Same as delayed recall procedure, except S was asked to name each picture object as E pointed to it, and name it again during the recall task. **Results:** No sex differences.

Fleener, D. E., and Cairns, R. B. Attachment behaviors in human infants: discriminative vocalization on maternal separation. *Developmental Psychology*, 1970, *2*, 215–23.

    Subjects: $N = 64$; 3–19 mos. **Measures:** Mother and unfamiliar female E alternated leaving the room for 60-second periods (thus leaving the infant alone with the other person). Frequency of crying was recorded. **Results:** No sex differences were found in total amount of crying or in the extent to which Ss cried during the absence of their mothers relative to the extent to which they cried during the absence of E.

Fleming, E. S., and Anttonen, R. G. Teacher expectancy as related to the academic and personal growth of primary-age children. *Monographs of the Society for Research in Child Development*, 1971, *36*.

    Subjects: $N = 1,087$; 7 yrs (low, middle SES). **Measures:** Teachers who were classified as having high, middle, and low opinions toward IQ tests were given 1 of 4 kinds of test information for each S: Kuhlmann-Anderson IQ scores, IQs inflated by 16 points, Primary Mental Abilities percentiles without IQ equivalents, or no intelligence test information. In October, Ss completed 3 subtests of the Stanford Achievement Test (SAT) Primary I Battery, Form W: Word Meaning, Paragraph Meaning, and Arithmetic. In February and May, Ss completed 4 subtests of the Primary II Battery, Forms W and X: Word Meaning, Paragraph Meaning, Arithmetic Computation, and Arithmetic Concepts. A semantic differential self-concept measure was administered at each testing. Grades were collected in February and June. **Results:** (1) When Ss' achievement scores in October were held constant, no sex differences were found in February or June on any of the 4 SAT subtests. (2) On the self-concept measure in February and May (with October scores held constant), boys scored higher on the Potency factor than girls did. In May (with February scores held constant), girls scored higher on the Evaluative factor than boys did. The Evaluative factor did not emerge in October. (3) In February and June, girls achieved higher grades than boys in reading, spelling, and handwriting. In June, girls achieved higher arithmetic grades than boys did; no sex difference was found in February. Overall, girls earned higher grades than boys did during each marking period.

Flick, G. L. Sinistrality revisited: a perceptual-motor approach. *Child Development*, 1966, *37*, 613–22.

    Subjects: $N = 453$; 4 yrs (black). **Measures:** Perceptual-motor functioning was measured by performance on Copy Forms (Stanford-Binet and Merrill-Palmer items) and Copy Mazes (Porteus Mazes). Hand dominance was determined by noting the preferred hand used on Copy Forms task. Eye dominance was revealed by asking S to look through a small hole in a shoe box. Stanford-Binet IQ scores were also obtained. **Results:** Girls were superior to boys on Copy Forms. No other sex differences were found.

Fling, S., and Manosevitz, M. Sex typing in nursery school children's play interests. *Developmental Psychology*, 1972, 7, 146–52.

Subjects: $N = 32$; 3–4 yrs and parents. Measures: E administered the IT Scale for Children with blank IT cards. S was asked to choose items It and S would prefer (to assess sex-role orientation and sex-role preference, respectively). S was asked whether he had pretended blank It was a boy or a girl, and was then shown Brown's It and asked to label It a boy or a girl (to assess sex labeling). E later visited S's home and asked S to show him his favorite toys, which E scored as masculine, feminine, or neuter (to assess sex-role adoption). E interviewed S's parents about the child's play interests and possible parental influences. An It test was administered in which parents indicated the It items they preferred for their child, with elaboration on omissions. Results: (1) Both boys and girls labeled standard It as boy ($p < .001$). (2) Ss labeled imaginary It as same sex ($p < .001$). (3) There were no sex differences on any of the 3 measures of sex typing (orientation, preference, adoption). Boys' scores were less variable than girls' on preference and adoption ($p < .05$, $p < .05$). (4) Boys' mothers' scores were greater than girls' mothers' scores on discouragement of sex-inappropriate interests ($p < .005$), It scores (high-sex-appropriate choices, $p < .001$), and Total (It and encouragement of sex-appropriate interests and discouragement of sex-inappropriate interests, $p < .005$). Boys' fathers' scores were greater than girls' fathers' scores on discouragement ($p < .05$), It ($p < .005$), and Total ($p < .005$). Girls' mothers' scores were greater than boys' mothers' scores on encouragement of sex-appropriate interests ($p < .01$). (5) Boys' fathers' scores were greater than boys' mothers' scores on encouragement of sex-appropriate interests ($p < .01$). Girls' mothers' scores were greater than girls' fathers' scores on the same measure ($p < .01$).

Fouts, G. T. Charity in children: the influence of "charity" stimuli and an audience. *J. Experimental Child Psychology*, 1972, 13, 303–9.

Subjects: $N = 40$; 10, 11 yrs. Measures: Ss performed a lever-pulling task, either alone or with E watching. Correct responses resulted in pennies dropping into a neutral or a "charity" box. Number of pulling responses were recorded under each condition. Results: No sex differences.

Frager, R. Conformity and anticonformity in Japan. *J. Personality & Social Psychology*, 1970, 15, 203–10.

Subjects: $N = 139$; 18–21 yrs (Japanese college). Measures: Ss judged which of 3 lines was equal in length to a fourth after exposure to the incorrect judgments of 3 confederates. E recorded the number of times Ss conformed to the inaccurate group response, and the number of times on noncritical trials Ss made the incorrect choice after confederates had made the correct choice (a measure of anticonformity). Ss also completed a Japanese values scale, measuring alienation (A) and traditionalism (T). Results: No sex differences were found in conformity or anticonformity scores. Men had higher A scores than women ($p < .02$). No sex differences were found in T scores.

France, K. Effects of "White" and of "Black" examiner voices on IQ scores of children. *Developmental Psychology*, 1973, 8, 144 (brief report).

Subjects: $N = 252$; 6–9 yrs. Measures: The Peabody Picture Vocabulary Test was administered by taped voices of black and white students reading instructions and questions. Results: Boys achieved higher scores than girls ($p < .001$).

Fraunfelker, B. S. Phonetic campatibility in paired-associate learning of first- and third-grade children. *Developmental Psychology*, 1971, 5, 211–15.

Subjects: $N = 80$; 6, 8 yrs. Measures: Ss learned 2 paired associate tasks: shape-color pairs as a warm-up task, and color-trigram (3-letter) pairs with trigrams of high and low phonetic compatibility. Response learning (number of trigrams correctly articulated and associated with correct stimulus) and retention (number of correctly articulated trigrams associated with correct stimulus at end of 12 trials) were recorded. Results: No sex differences.

Frederiksen, N., and Evans, F. R. Effects of models of creative performance on ability to formulate hypotheses. *J. Educational Psychology*, 1974, 66, 83–89.

Subjects: $N = 395$; 18 yrs (paid college volunteers). Measures: S was given findings from a research study and asked to write hypotheses that might help account for the findings. Answers were analyzed for total number of hypotheses, number of acceptable hypotheses, quality of hypotheses, value of hypotheses (independent number), and number of words per response (fluency). Other scores obtained were verbal comprehension, verbal fluency, test anxiety, and Guilford's obvious vs. remote consequences measure. Results: Women were superior to men on number of hypotheses, number of words, and number of obvious consequences. Men were superior to women on number of remote consequences.

Friedman, S. Habituation and recovery of visual response in the alert human newborn. *J. Experimental Child Psychology,* 1972, *13,* 339–49.
Subjects: $N = 40$; 1–3 days. Measures: Infants viewed a checkerboard target ($2'' \times 2''$ or $12'' \times 12''$) until habituation was demonstrated (decrement in visual fixation time). They were then exposed to either the same or a novel target to assess effect of familiarity and novelty on recovery of habituation. Results: No sex differences.

Friedman, S., and Carpenter, G. C. Visual response decrement as a function of age of human newborn. *Child Development,* 1971, *42,* 1967–73.
Subjects: $N = 96$; 1–4 days. Measures: Fixation time to a black-and-white checkerboard target was recorded. Results: No sex differences.

Friedman, S., Nagy, A. A., and Carpenter, G. C. Newborn attention: differential response decrement to visual stimuli. *J. Experimental Child Psychology,* 1970, *10,* 44–51.
Subjects: $N = 40$; 2–3 days. Measures: Ss were exposed to 1 of 2 visual stimuli, a $2'' \times 2''$ or $12'' \times 12''$ black-and-white checkerboard target. Visual fixation time was recorded. Results: There were no main sex differences. Boys showed fixation decrement to the less redundant ($2'' \times 2''$) target; girls showed fixation decrement to the more redundant ($12'' \times 12''$) target ($p < .005$).

Friedman, S., Bruno, L. A., and Vietze, P. Differential dishabituation as a function of magnitude of stimulus discrepancy and sex of the newborn infant. Paper presented at the meeting of the Society for Research in Child Development, Philadelphia, 1973.
Subjects: $N = 26$; 1–3 days. Measures: Ss were presented with 60-second exposures of 1 of 2 stimuli (either a 4-square or 144-square black-and-white checkerboard pattern). Presentation continued until evidence of decrement in looking time occurred. When Ss reached the decrement criterion, they were presented with a final 60-second exposure of either the same target stimulus to which they had shown habituation (no-discrepancy or control group) or a different target of either moderate discrepancy (a 16-square checkerboard pattern) or large discrepancy (the 144-square target for Ss who viewed the 4-square target during the habituation trials; the 4-square target for Ss who previously had viewed the 144-square target). Response measures were looking time and number of looks. Results: (1) Looking time: (a) No sex differences were found in degree of response decrement to the repeated stimulus. (b) No main sex differences were found when the mean looking time for the last 3 habituation trials was compared with looking time on the final 60-second test trial. For the moderate discrepancy group, girls showed a recovery effect, boys did not ($p < .025$). (2) Number of looks: No sex differences were reported. With introduction of the moderately discrepant stimulus, girls showed a reduction in number of looks, boys did not (significance not tested).

Friedrichs, A. G., Hertz, T. W., Moynahan, E. D., Simpson, W. E., Arnold, M. R., Christy, M. D., Cooper, C. R., and Stevenson, H. W. Interrelations among learning and performance at the preschool level. *Developmental Psychology,* 1971, *4,* 164–72.
Subjects: $N = 50$; 3–5 yrs. Measures: Ss were presented with 16 learning and performance tasks: paired associates, serial memory, oddity learning, concept formation, observational learning, incidental learning, problem solving, object sorting, social imitation, task persistence, reactivity, motor inhibition, following instructions, variability, attention, and level of aspiration. Results: (1) There were no sex differences on the learning tasks. (2) On the performance tasks there was a sex difference in level of aspiration. Boys chose taller towers to build than girls did ($p < .01$).

Fromkin, H. L. Effects of experimentally aroused feelings of indistinctiveness upon valuation of scarce and novel feelings. *J. Personality & Social Psychology,* 1970, *16,* 521–29.
Subjects: $N = 59$; 18–21 yrs (college). Measures: Ss received bogus test results that described them as either extreme, high, or low in uniqueness. Ss then received information about 4 "psychedelic" chambers, which were described as either available or unavailable to others, and as producing either novel or familiar feelings. The response measures were Ss' evaluation of each of the 4 different environments. Results: (1) No main sex differences were found. (2) On a postexperimental scale designed to measure the effectiveness of the novelty manipulation, men had higher expectations about the novelty of the experience than women.

Fry, C. L. A developmental examination of performance in a tacit coordination game situation. *J. Personality & Social Psychology*, 1967, 5, 277–81.
> **Subjects:** *N* = 84; 9, 13, 18–21 yrs (college). **Measures:** Ss played tacit coordination games with like-aged, same-sex partners. The tacit coordination game required S to anticipate the object choice of his partner. Points were awarded when both Ss made the same object choice. **Results:** No sex differences.

Fryrear, J. L., and Thelen, M. H. Effect of sex of model and sex of observer on the imitation of affectionate behavior. *Developmental Psychology*, 1969, 1, 298 (brief report).
> **Subjects:** *N* = 60; 3–4 yrs (nursery school). **Measures:** Ss observed a filmed male or female adult model display a sequence of 4 affectionate responses toward a small stuffed clown. Afterward, Ss were observed in free play with the clown and other toys. Imitative responses were recorded. **Results:** Girls imitated the female model more than boys did. No sex differences were found in the number of imitative behaviors Ss displayed after observing the male model.

Furth, H. G., Youniss, J., and Ross, B. M. Children's utilization of logical symbols: an interpretation of conceptual behavior based on Piagetian theory. *Developmental Psychology*, 1970, 3, 36–57.
> **Subjects:** *N* = 300; 6–12 yrs. **Measures:** On each trial, E put an incomplete sequence on the blackboard that was to be completed by S filling in or modifying one part of the sequence. Each sequence consisted of (1) a symbol pattern expressing 2 attribute classes (letter of the alphabet standing for a thing or shape, and a color) and a logical connective (a dot meaning "and," "v" meaning "either/or" or "both"), (2) the instance pattern (a drawing of 2 attributes), and (3) the judgment by S of whether the instance pattern was a logically correct example of the symbol pattern. **Results:** Among 7-year-old Ss, girls made more correct judgments of whether or not symbol patterns and drawings matched than boys. There were no sex differences at other ages.

Gaertner, S. L. Helping behavior and racial discrimination among liberals and conservatives. *J. Personality & Social Psychology*, 1973, 25, 335–41.
> **Subjects:** *N* = 468; adults. **Measures:** Ss received a wrong number phone call from a person in a pay telephone booth (either a black or white, male or female) whose car had broken down. Ss were asked to contact a garage for the caller (who supposedly had no more change). **Results:** (1) Men contacted the garage more frequently than women did ($p < .05$). (2) No difference was found between male and female victims in the frequency of eliciting help from Ss. More male than female victims experienced premature hanging up ($p < .01$).

Gaertner, S. L., and Bickerman, L. Effects of race on the elicitation of helping behavior: the wrong number technique. *J. Personality & Social Psychology*, 1971, 20, 218–22.
> **Subjects:** *N* = 1,109; adults (white, black). **Measures:** Ss received a wrong number phone call from a man (either black or white) in a pay telephone booth whose car had broken down. Ss were asked to contact a garage for the caller (who supposedly had no more change). **Results:** (1) Men contacted the garage more frequently than women did ($p < .05$). (2) More women than men hung up prematurely ($p < .001$).

Gahagan, G. A., and Gahagan, D. M. Paired-associate learning as partial validation of a language development program. *Child Development*, 1968, 39, 1119–31.
> **Subjects:** *N* = 54; 6–7 yrs. **Measures:** Ss were shown 8 cards; on each were pictures of 2 objects. After naming the items, Ss were asked to construct a sentence containing both words by linking them with a verb. Ss also completed the English Picture Vocabulary Test (EPVT). At the time of testing, 18 Ss had undergone language training for a period of 4 terms; the other 36 Ss had not. **Results:** No sex differences were found in EPVT scores or in number of lexically different verbs produced.

Gaines, R. The discriminability of form among young children. *J. Experimental Child Psychology*, 1969, 8, 418–31.
> **Subjects:** *N* = 30; 4–7 yrs. **Measures:** Ss performed form-oddity problems, i.e. pointing to the stimulus drawing that was different from the other 4. Stimuli varied in number of sides, form perimeter, and structure (symmetrical to asymmetrical). **Results:** No sex differences.

Gaines, R. Variables in color perception of young children. *J. Experimental Child Psychology*, 1972, 14, 196–218.
> **Subjects:** *N* = 47; 5–6 yrs. **Measures:** The effects of variations in value, chroma, and hue were studied in relation to sex, IQ, and dimensional attention; 2 measures of discrimination ability

were made on each of 54 base colors of the Munsell color matrices. **Results:** (1) There were no main sex differences. (2) Boys were more accurate in the mid-chroma range, girls were more accurate on high and low chroma stimuli ($p < .02$).

Gall, M., and Mendelsohn, G. A. Effects of facilitating techniques and subject-experimenter interaction on creative problem solving. *J. Personality & Social Psychology*, 1967, *5*, 211–16.

> **Subjects:** $N = 120$; 18–21 yrs (college). **Measures:** Ss were given the Remote Associates Test which demands the production of remote associates in the process of the solution. After attempting each of the items, Ss were allowed to continue working on the first 5 problems they had failed to solve (continued work condition), or asked to associate to the words comprising the first 5 problems they had missed (association training condition), or diverted for a time from the problems by means of a nonverbal task (incubation condition). All Ss were then given 10 minutes to work on the missed problems. **Results:** (1) No sex differences were found in mean number of solutions. (2) The association-training condition produced more solutions for women than for men ($p < .01$).

Gallo, P. S., and Sheposh, J. Effects of incentive magnitude on cooperation in the prisoner's dilemma game: a reply to Gumpert, Deutsch, and Epstein. *J. Personality & Social Psychology*, 1971, *19*, 42–46.

> **Subjects:** $N = 200$; 18–21 yrs (college). **Measures:** Same-sex pairs of Ss played the Prisoner's Dilemma game for real or imaginary dollars. **Results:** No sex differences were found in percentage of cooperative responses.

Gallo, P. S., Funk, S. G., and Levine, J. R. Reward size, method of presentation, and number of alternatives in a prisoner's dilemma game. *J. Personality & Social Psychology*, 1969, *13*, 239–44.

> **Subjects:** $N = 160$; 18–21 yrs (college). **Measures:** Like-sex pairs of Ss played either the standard Prisoner's Dilemma game or a 2-, 6-, or 11-choice nonmatrix equivalent of the game. Afterward, Ss completed a 19-item semantic differential on which they evaluated their partners. **Results:** No sex differences.

Gardiner, H. W. Dominance-deference patterning in Thai students. *J. Social Psychology*, 1968, *76*, 281–82.

> **Subjects:** $N = 199$; 18–21 yrs (college Thai). **Measures:** A dominance-deference scale, consisting of 10 dominance and 10 deference items, was administered to all Ss. Ss were instructed to select the 10 items that best described themselves. S's score was the number of dominance items chosen. **Results:** No sex differences.

Gardner, H. Children's sensitivity to painting styles. *Child Development*, 1970, *41*, 813–21.

> **Subjects:** $N = 80$; 6, 8, 11, 14 yrs. **Measures:** Ss viewed 2 paintings by 1 artist, and were then asked to select which 1 out of 4 others was painted by the same artist. **Results:** No sex differences.

Gardner, H. Children's sensitivity to musical styles. *Merrill-Palmer Quarterly*, 1973, *19*, 67–77.

> **Subjects:** $N = 100$; 6, 8, 11, 14, 18–19 yrs. **Measures:** Ss listened to 16 pairs of musical passages. Each pair consisted of 2 halves, 15 seconds in duration, separated by a 1-second bell; 8 of the pairs consisted of halves from the same piece, and the remaining 8 consisted of halves from different compositions by different composers. Ss' task was to indicate whether or not the 2 halves were from the same piece. **Results:** No sex differences.

Gates, A. I. Sex differences in reading ability. *Elementary School Journal*, 1961, *61*, 431–34.

> **Subjects:** $N = 13,114$; 7–13 yrs. **Measures:** Gates Reading Survey tests: Speed of Reading, Reading Vocabulary, and Level of Comprehension. **Results:** (1) At all ages, girls had higher scores on each of the 3 tests than boys did. (2) Among 9-, 10-, and 12-year-old Ss, boys' scores on the Speed of Reading test varied more than those of girls. Among 7- and 11-year-old Ss, girls' scores varied more than those of boys. (3) At all ages (except 7), boys' scores on the vocabulary and comprehension tests varied more than those of girls.

Geer, J. H. A test of classical conditioning model of emotion: the use of nonpainful aversive stimuli as unconditioned stimuli in a conditioning procedure. *J. Personality & Social Psychology*, 1968, *10*, 148–56.

Subjects: $N = 48$; 18–21 yrs (college). Measures: Ss were assigned to 1 of 3 experimental groups. In the forward-conditioning group, exposure to the CS (a tone of 60 decibels) preceded exposure to the UCS (color photographs of dead bodies). In the backward-conditioning group, the UCS preceded the CS. Ss in the third group experienced an essentially random relationship between CS and the UCS. Graduated skin responses to the experimental stimuli were recorded and classified into 3 categories: CS responses, pre-UCS responses, and post-UCS responses. CS responses were defined as decreases in skin resistance that began 1 and 5 seconds after tone onset. Pre-UCS responses were defined and measured as the CS responses were, except that the response's inflection began between 5 and 10 seconds after the CS's onset. Post-UCS responses were measured and defined as the preceding responses were, except that response inflection began between 1 and 6 seconds after UCS onset. Results: (1) For the last minute of the rest period prior to the experimental manipulation, there were no sex differences in number of spontaneous fluctuations of skin resistance. (2) Men had larger CS responses than women did during conditioning ($p < .01$) and extinction ($p < .05$). (3) During conditioning, no sex differences were found in pre-UCS responses. During extinction, men had larger pre-UCS responses than women did ($p < .05$). Men showed a decrease in pre-UCS responding over extinction trial blocks, while women showed an increase ($p < .05$). (4) Men had larger post-UCS responses than women did during conditioning ($p < .01$) and extinction ($p < .01$). During extinction, men showed more rapid habituation than women did ($p < .01$).

Gelfand, D. M., Hartmann, D. P., Walder, P., and Page, B. Who reports shoplifters? A field-experimental study. *J. Personality & Social Psychology*, 1973, *25*, 276–85.

Subjects: $N = 89$; 16–75 yrs. Measures: Ss observed a female confederate steal store merchandise. Results: More men than women reported the incident to a store employee ($p < .05$).

Gellert, E. The effect of changes in group composition on the dominant behavior of young children. *British J. Social & Clinical Psychology*, 1962, *1*, 168–81.

Subjects: $N = 55$; 3–5 yrs. Measures: Teachers were asked to pay special attention to dominance behaviors in their nursery school classrooms. One week later, teachers ranked the children on relative dominance. Results: No sex differences.

Gelman, R., and Weinberg, D. H. The relationship between liquid conservation and compensation. *Child Development*, 1972, *43*, 371–83.

Subjects: $N = 80$; 6, 7, 8, 11 yrs. Measures: Ss performed liquid conservation and compensation operations. Results: No sex differences.

Gerace, T. A., and Caldwell, W. E. Perceptual distortion as a function of stimulus objects, sex, naïveté, and trials using a portable model of the Ames distorted room. *Genetic Psychology Monographs*, 1971, *84*, 3–33.

Subjects: $N = 40$; 25 yrs. Measures: Using a portable model of the Ames distorted room, Ss were instructed to change the length of an adjustable rod to the size of an object in the room. The response measure was the length of the rod set by S. Results: Men were more accurate in their judgments than women ($p < .001$).

Gerard, H. B., Wilhelmy, R. A., and Conolley, E. S. Conformity and group size. *J. Personality & Social Psychology*, 1968, *8*, 79–82.

Subjects: $N = 154$; 14–17 yrs. Measures: Ss participated in an Asch experiment, judging which of 3 lines was equal in length to a standard. Girls were run in groups of 3, 5, or 7; boys were run in groups of 2, 4, 6, or 8. Results: Girls were more conforming than boys ($p < .05$).

Gerst, M. S. Symbolic coding processes in observational learning. *J. Personality & Social Psychology*, 1971, *19*, 7–17.

Subjects: $N = 72$; 18–21 yrs (college). Measures: Ss observed a filmed model perform complex motor responses. The performance measure was Ss' reproduction of the model's behavior. Results: No sex differences.

Gewirtz, H. B., and Gewirtz, J. L. Visiting and caretaking patterns for kibbutz infants: age and sex trends. *American J. Orthopsychiatry*, 1968, *38*, 427–43.

Subjects: $N = 24$; 4, 8 mos. Measures: Individual chronological logs were kept for all infants. Onset and termination of typical daily events were recorded. Results: (1) Cumulative caretaking activities were found to be of longer duration for boys than for girls. (2) Feeding took longer for boys than for girls. (3) Girls fed themselves more frequently than boys did. No difference was found in the percentage of boys and girls who were classified as "eaters." (4) The mean interval between diaper changes was shorter for boys than for girls. No sex differences were found in the frequency or duration of diaper changing. (5) No sex differences were found in "total time awake" or in its components, "time alone" (no person present in Ss' background) and "social time" (1 or more persons present in Ss' background). (6) No sex differences were found in sleeping or dressing. (7) No sex differences were found in the duration of mothers', fathers', or caretakers' visits.

Ghent, L. Developmental changes in tactual thresholds on dominant and nondominant sides. *J. Comparative & Physiological Psychology,* 1961, 54, 670–73.
Subjects: $N = 108$; 5, 6, 7, 9, 11 yrs. Measures: Tactual thresholds were determined for thumbs and upper arms. Results: (1) Among 6-, 7-, and 9-year-old girls, the nondominant thumb was more sensitive than the dominant thumb; among 6-, 7-, and 9-year-old boys, no differences in sensitivity were found ($p < .05$; $p < .01$; $p < .05$). (2) Among 11-year-old Ss, boys' nondominant thumbs were more sensitive than the dominant thumbs; no differences were found for girls. (3) No sex differences were found among 5-year-old Ss. (4) Thresholds for the upper arms did not parallel the developmental changes observed for the thumbs.

Giacoman, S. L. Hunger and motor restraint on arousal and visual attention in the infant. *Child Development,* 1971, 42, 605–14.
Subjects: $N = 32$; 5–6 wks. Measures: Ss were observed for 2 15-minute periods while lying supine in a crib. During 1 of the periods they were swaddled. At intermittent intervals, a visual stimulus (either a red plastic ring or a red ball) was held (stationary) in front of Ss for 5 seconds, after which it was slowly moved to the left and right of their line of vision. Measures were taken of fixation (the number of Ss focused on the stationary stimulus at any time during the first 5 seconds of presentation) and pursuit (the number of seconds Ss focused on the moving stimulus during the last 15 seconds of presentation). Ss were also rated for level of arousal. Results: (1) No main sex differences were found. (2) Boys had higher pursuit scores when they were swaddled during the second 15-minute observation period; girls had higher pursuit scores when they were swaddled during the first period ($p < .05$).

Ginsburg, H., and Rapoport, A. Children's estimates of proportions. *Child Development,* 1967, 38, 205–12.
Experiment I: Subjects: $N = 40$; 6, 11 yrs. Measures: Each S was given 4 problems that required estimating proportions of 2 categories of elements. Each problem used 40 black and white marbles. S estimated the proportion of each color after watching them drawn out of an opaque container, 1 at a time. Results: No sex differences.
Experiment II: Subjects: $N = 36$; 6, 11 yrs. Measures: Same as Experiment I, except 3 categories of elements were used (black, white, and yellow marbles). Results: No sex differences.

Gitter, A. G., Mostofsky, D. I., and Quincy, A. J. Race and sex differences in the child's perception of emotion. *Child Development,* 1971, 42, 2071–75.
Subjects: $N = 80$; 4–6 yrs (white, black). Measures: Ss were shown 4 cartoon-like drawings of different emotions—anger, surprise, happiness, and pain. After being trained to associate the name of each emotion with the appropriate cartoon, Ss were shown slides of black or white female models; 1 of the 4 emotions was portrayed on each slide. Ss' task was to match each slide with the appropriate cartoon. Results: No sex differences.

Glick, O. Interaction effects of sex of mother's child and child's reading performance on the mother's evaluations of the school. *J. Educational Research,* 1970, 64, 124–26.
Subjects: $N = 92$; mothers of 8-year-old children. Measures: Mothers were asked to evaluate the school their children were attending. Results: No main sex differences were found. Mothers of girls who performed above the reading criterion for third-graders on the Metropolitan Achievement Test of Reading evaluated the school more favorably than did mothers of boys who performed above the criterion. No differences were found in the evaluations of mothers whose children performed below the reading criterion.

Gliner, C. R. Tactual discrimination thresholds for shape and texture in young children. *J. Experimental Child Psychology,* 1967, 5, 536–47.
Subjects: $N = 160$; 5, 8 yrs. Measures: Ss made tactual judgments as to whether pairs of shapes (ellipses) and textures (sandpaper patches) were the same or different from each other. Textures were presented either without shape (texture condition) or on a constant shape (shaped-texture condition). Shapes were presented either untextured (shape condition) or with a

constant texture (textured-shape condition). **Results:** (1) With smoother sandpaper patches, girls performed better in the texture condition than in the shaped-texture condition; for boys, the reverse was true. In both conditions, girls more often employed successive exploration, whereas boys more often used simultaneous exploration. (2) No sex differences were found in the shape or textured-shape conditions.

Gliner, C. R., Pick, A. D., Pick, H. L., Jr., and Hales, J. J. A developmental investigation of visual and haptic preferences for shape and texture. *Monographs of the Society for Research in Child Development*, 1969, *34*.
    Experiment I: **Subjects:** $N = 160$; 5, 8 yrs. **Measures:** Ss were visually presented with a series of either pairs of shapes or pairs of textures, and were asked whether members of each pair were alike or different. Textures were presented either without shape or on a constant shape. Shapes were presented either untextured or with a constant texture. **Results:** Among 5-year-olds, boys were more sensitive than girls to differences between textures. No other sex differences were found.
    Experiment II: **Subjects:** $N = 181$; 5, 8 yrs. **Measures:** Haptic preference for shape and texture was assessed in a discrimination-learning situation. **Results:** No sex differences.
    Experiment III: **Subjects:** $N = 80$; 5, 8 yrs. **Measures:** Same as Experiment II, but discriminations were made visually rather than haptically. **Results:** No sex differences.

Glinski, R. J., Glinski, B. C., and Slatin, G. T. Nonnaivety contamination in conformity experiments: sources, effects, and implications for control. *J. Personality & Social Psychology*, 1970, *16*, 478–85.
    Subjects: $N = 56$; 18–21 yrs (college). **Measures:** After receiving the decisions of 3 other subjects of the same sex, Ss judged which of 3 girls was lying from the tone of her voice. Decisions of prior Ss either were in unanimous agreement or were characterized by a two-thirds majority. The response measure was the number of times Ss conformed to the majority opinion. **Results:** When Ss who admitted being previously informed of the true nature of the experiment were removed (all girls), no sex differences were found.

Glixman, A. F. Categorizing behavior as a function of meaning domain. *J. Personality & Social Psychology*, 1965, *2*, 370–77.
    Subjects: $N = 36$; 20–26 yrs. **Measures:** Ss categorized sets of items. **Results:** (1) Women used a greater number of categories than men did ($p < .001$). (2) No sex differences were found in the distribution of items over categories.

Goffeney, B., Henderson, N. B., and Butler, B. V. Negro-white, male-female eight-month developmental scores compared with seven-year WISC and Bender test scores. *Child Development*, 1971, *42*, 594–604.
    Subjects: $N = 626$; tested at 8 mos and 7 yrs. **Measures:** Bayley Infant Scales, Wechsler Intelligence Scale for Children, Bender-Gestalt Test. **Results:** (1) Girls' fine motor skills were superior to boys' ($p < .001$). Black boys scored the lowest, black girls the highest ($p < .05$). No sex differences were found in gross motor or mental scores. (2) No sex differences were found on the WISC or on the Bender-Gestalt Test.

Goldberg, S. Probability judgments by preschool children: task conditions and performance. *Child Development*, 1966, *37*, 157–67.
    Subjects: $N = 32$; 3–5 yrs. **Measures:** Ss made probability judgments in Piagetian or decision-making conditions. **Results:** No sex differences.

Goldberg, S., and Lewis, M. Play behavior in the year-old infant: early sex differences. *Child Development*, 1969, *40*, 21–31.
    Subjects: $N = 64$; tested at 6, 13 mos, and their mothers. **Measures:** At the initial session with their mothers present, Ss were exposed to visual and auditory stimuli. 2 maternal behaviors were recorded: number of vocalizations to infant and amount of physical contact (touching, playing, comforting) with infant. At the second session 7 months later, Ss were observed in a free-play situation. The testing room contained 9 toys: a set of blocks, a pail, a lawn mower, a stuffed dog, an inflated plastic cat, a set of quoits, a wood mallet, a pegboard, and a wooden pull toy. After their mothers placed them on the floor, Ss were assessed on the following measures: latency to return to mother; number of returns to mother; time spent touching mother; time spent vocalizing to mother; time spent looking at mother; number of looks to mother; time spent in the squares closest to and farthest from mother (the room was marked off into 12 squares); and time spent playing with each of the various toys. At the end of the free-play period, a barrier was constructed in the middle of the room. Each infant was placed on

the opposite side by his mother. Measures were taken of the number of seconds Ss cried and of the amount of time they spent at the center and at the ends of the barrier. **Results:** (1) At 6 months of age: Mothers vocalized more to girls than to boys; more mothers of girls than mothers of boys were rated high in physical contact; more girls than boys were breast-fed. (2) In the free-play situation at 13 months of age: girls returned to their mothers more quickly and more frequently than boys; girls spent more time touching mother, vocalizing to mother, and in the squares nearest mother than boys; girls exhibited a greater preference for the blocks, the cat and the dog (combined score), and the pegboard than boys: boys banged the toys more frequently than girls; boys played more vigorously than girls (observer rating). No sex differences were found on the other free-play measures or in overall toy preferences. (3) In the barrier situation, girls spent more time at the center of the barrier; boys spent more time at the two ends. Girls cried longer than boys.

Goldrich, J. M. A study in time orientation: the relation between memory for past experience and orientation to the future. *J. Personality & Social Psychology*, 1967, *6*, 216–21.
　　Subjects: $N = 80$; 25–40 yrs. **Measures:** (1) Ss' responses to the Thematic Apperception Test (cards 1, 2, 16, and 20) were scored for (a) number of stories in which the future was spontaneously mentioned, (b) prospective (future) time spans, (c) total time spans, (d) percentage of verbal output devoted to description of future events, (e) continuity of depicted events in time, (f) pleasantness of stories, and (g) degree of involvement. (2) Ss also completed a Likert-type future scale, designed to measure Ss' feelings about their future professional life, their future interpersonal relations, and their future self-evaluations. **Results:** (1) No sex differences were found in Ss' TAT scores. (2) Women were more optimistic than men on the future scale.

Goldschmid, M. L. Different types of conservation and nonconservation and their relation to age, sex, IQ, MA, and vocabulary. *Child Development*, 1967, *38*, 1229–46.
　　Subjects: $N = 81$; 6–7 yrs. **Measures:** Ss were tested on a series of 10 conservation tasks. The WISC Vocabulary subtest and either the Pintner-Cunningham or the Otis IQ test were also administered to Ss. **Results:** Boys performed better on the conservation tasks than girls did. No sex differences were found in IQ or vocabulary scores.

Goldschmid, M. L. The relation of conservation to emotional and environmental aspects of development. *Child Development*, 1968, *39*, 579–89.
　　Subjects: $N = 81$; 6–7 yrs. **Measures:** (1) The Children's Manifest Anxiety Scale was administered orally to each S. (2) Ss rated their actual and their ideal self on an adjective checklist. Teachers used the same set of adjectives to describe each child. (3) Popularity ratings were obtained by asking Ss to (1) indicate whether they liked or disliked each of their classmates, and (2) select the 3 children in their class they liked most and the 3 children they liked least. (4) The Parental Attitude Survey, a measure of parents' attitudes toward child-rearing methods, was given to mothers and fathers; 3 scores reflecting degree of dominant, ignoring, and possessive attitudes were derived for each parent. Differences between mothers' and fathers' scores were then computed. **Results:** No sex differences.

Goldstein, A. G., and Chance, J. E. Effects of practice on sex-related differences in performance on Embedded Figures. *Psychonomic Science*, 1965, *3*, 361–62.
　　Subjects: $N = 26$; 18–21 yrs (college). **Measures:** Ss were presented with 68 embedded figures. Discovery times were recorded. **Results:** On the first 10 items, women had higher discovery times than men ($p < .05$). On the last 10 items, no sex differences were found.

Goldstein, S. B., and Siegel, A. W. Observing behavior and children's discrimination learning. *Child Development*, 1971, *42*, 1608–13.
　　Subjects: $N = 48$; 8 yrs. **Measures:** Ss performed a 2-choice discrimination-learning task. Geometric figures were used as the discriminative stimuli. Response latencies and number of trials needed to reach criterion were recorded for each S. **Results:** No sex differences.

Goldstein, S. B., and Siegel, A. W. Facilitation of discrimination learning with delayed reinforcement. *Child Development*, 1972, *43*, 1004–11.
　　Subjects: $N = 84$; 8, 9 yrs. **Measures:** Ss were presented with 2 geometric figures on each trial of a discrimination-learning task. Performance measures were number of trials to criterion and number of correct responses. **Results:** No sex differences.

Golightly, C., Nelson, D., and Johnson, J. Children's dependency scale. *Developmental Psychology*, 1970, *3*, 114–18.
　　Subjects: $N = 219$; 9–11 yrs. **Measures:** The Children's Dependency Scale. **Results:** (1) Over-

all, girls had higher dependency scores than boys. (2) Girls had higher dependency scores than boys at ages 10 and 11. There were no sex differences at age 9.

Gonen, J. V., and Lansky, L. M. Masculinity, femininity, and masculinity-femininity: a phenomenological study of the MF scale of the MMPI. *Psychological Reports*, 1968, *23*, 183–94.
Subjects: $N = 94$; 18–21 yrs (college). Measures: Ss evaluated responses by a hypothetical man and woman to the MMPI MF scale's items as making the man or woman "more masculine," "less masculine," "more feminine," or "less feminine." When S placed a behavior along a continuum with masculine at one pole and feminine at the other, his conceptualization was termed bipolar. When S placed a behavior along a continuum with more masculine (or feminine) at one end and less masculine (or feminine) at the other, his conceptualization was termed unipolar. Results: Men responded with more unipolar patterns than women did ($p < .05$).

Goodenough, D. R., and Eagle, C. J. A modification of the Embedded Figures Test for use with young children. *J. Genetic Psychology*, 1963, *103*, 67–74.
Subjects: $N = 96$; 5, 8 yrs. Measures: A children's version of the Embedded Figures Test (CEFT). Results: No sex differences.

Goodenough, E. W. Interest in persons as an aspect of sex difference in the early years. *Genetic Psychology Monographs*, 1957, *55*, 287–323.
EXPERIMENT I: Subjects: $N = 80$; parents of children of 2–4 yrs. Measures: Interviews were conducted separately with mothers and fathers. Results: Girls were described as submissive more frequently than boys were ($p < .01$). No differences were found for the following traits: sensitive, emotional; obstinate; good-natured, happy; affectionate; aggressive; sense of humor. When parents gave illustrations of these traits, however, qualitative sex differences appeared.
EXPERIMENT II: Subjects: $N = 247$; 2–4 yrs. Measures: Pictures that Ss had drawn were collected and analyzed. Results: Girls included people in their drawings more frequently than boys did ($p < .01$).
EXPERIMENT III: Subjects: $N = 52$; 2–4 yrs. Measures: Verbalizations were elicited from Ss during the administration of the Mosaic Test. Results: Girls made more references to persons than boys did ($p < .01$).

Gorsuch, R. L., and Smith, R. A. Changes in college students' evaluations of moral behavior: 1969 versus 1939, 1949, and 1958. *J. Personality & Social Psychology*, 1972, *24*, 381–91.
Subjects: $N = 1,030$; 18–21 yrs (college). Measures: Ss rated each of 50 behaviors on a 10-point scale of wrongness (Crissman's moral behavior scale). Results: Women were more severe in their ratings than men were ($p < .0001$).

Goss, A. M. Paired associate learning by young children as functions of initial associative strength and percentage of occurrence of response members. *J. Experimental Child Psychology*, 1966, *4*, 398–407.
Subjects: $N = 60$; 3–4, 5–6 yrs. Measures: Ss were given a paired-associates task. The number of correct responses Ss made was recorded. Results: No sex differences.

Goss, A. M. Estimated versus actual physical strength in three ethnic groups. *Child Development*, 1968, *39*, 283–90.
Subjects: $N = 192$; 8, 11, 14, 17 yrs (black, Latin American, Anglo-American). Measures: Self-estimates of strength and estimates of the strength of mother, father, and an imagined opposite-sex partner were obtained from each S. Ss were then tested on a hand dynamometer. Results: (1) At all but the youngest age level, girls rated themselves lower than boys did on self-estimates of strength ($p < .001$). (2) There was a consistent reduction of girls' self-ratings across grades; the difference between girls' and boys' self-estimates tended to increase with age ($p < .001$). (3) On the dynamometer test, boys were consistently stronger than girls ($p < .001$). (4) Girls tended to rate imagined opposite-sex partner's strength higher than boys did ($p < .001$). (5) There were no sex differences in father-strength estimates. (6) Girls tended to estimate mothers' strength to be higher than boys did ($p < .05$).

Gough, H. G., and Delcourt, M. Developmental increments in perceptual acuity among Swiss and American school children. *Developmental Psychology*, 1969, *1*, 250–64.
Subjects: $N = 1,065$; 8–16 yrs (U.S., Switzerland). Measures: Ss were given the Perceptual

Acuity Test; 25 geometric illusion problems and 5 nonillusion problems were included. **Results:** No sex differences.

Grams, A., Hafner, A. J., and Quast, W. Child anxiety: self-estimates, parent reports, and teacher ratings. *Merrill-Palmer Quarterly*, 1965, *11*, 261–66.
Subjects: $N = 110$, 9–11 yrs. **Measures:** General Anxiety Scale for Children (GASC), Children's Manifest Anxiety Scale (CMAS). **Results:** Girls had higher scores than boys did on the GASC ($p < .01$). No sex differences were found on the CMAS.

Granger, G. W. An experimental study of color preferences. *J. General Psychology*, 1955, *32*, 3–20.
Subjects: $N = 50$; 19–36 yrs. **Measures:** 60 sets of colors, each containing approximately 7 items, were selected to represent the color spectrum with respect to hue, value, and chroma. Ss rank-ordered their preferences within each set. **Results:** No sex differences.

Grant, M. J., and Sermat, V. Status and sex of other as determinants of behavior in a mixed-motive game. *J. Personality & Social Psychology*, 1969, *12*, 151–57.
Subjects: $N = 48$; 18–21 yrs (college). **Measures:** Ss played two consecutive 30-trial games of "Chicken" (a game similar to the Prisoner's Dilemma game) with simulated partners of the same and opposite sex. On each trial, Ss predicted whether their partners would make the cooperative or the competitive choice. Information about the partners' choice was given to Ss on 4 of the 30 trials. Before beginning, Ss recorded the number of points they expected to make in each of the 2 games. **Results:** (1) Men expected to make more points than women did ($p < .05$). (2) No sex differences were found in the number of competitive responses made. Men made more competitive responses when paired first with a male and then with a female than when the order was reversed; for women, the opposite was true ($p < .01$). (3) Ss were less competitive when paired with a female than when paired with a male ($p < .05$). (4) Women were more competitive than men when paired with a male other; men were more competitive than women when paired with a female other ($p < .05$). (5) An attempt was made to distinguish submission from cooperation and exploitation from competition. For each of the first 7 trials on which Ss predicted partners would choose the competitive response, the number of men and women who chose the cooperative response (i.e. submitted) was tabulated. Similarly, for each of the first 7 trials on which Ss predicted partners would choose the cooperative response, the number of men and women who chose the competitive response (i.e. exploited) was tabulated. Women were less submissive than men ($p < .01$). Men were more exploitive than women ($p < .05$). Women were less exploited than men ($p < .05$).

Graves, A. J. Attainment of conservation of mass, weight, and volume in minimally educated adults. *Developmental Psychology*, 1972, *7*, 223 (brief report).
Subjects: $N = 120$; 33 yrs (minimally educated). **Measures:** Based on performance on the Adult Basic Learning Examination, Ss were assigned to 1 of 3 grade levels: 0–3, 4–6, and 7–8. Each S was tested for conservation of mass, weight, and volume. **Results:** (1) Men scored higher than women on conservation of volume. (2) There were no sex differences in conservation of quantity (total conservation score), conservation of mass, or conservation of weight.

Graves, M. F., and Koziol, S. Noun plural development in primary grade children. *Child Development*, 1971, *42*, 1165–73.
Subjects: $N = 67$; 6–9 yrs. **Measures:** Ss were tested on 6 types of plural noun formations. **Results:** No sex differences.

Green, A. The relation of dancing experience and personality to perception. *Psychological Monographs: General and Applied*, 1955, *69*, 399.
Subjects: $N = 60$; 17–40 yrs. **Measures:** (1) Rod-and-Frame Test, (2) Tilting-Room-Tilting-Chair test, (3) Embedded Figures Test, (4) Stabilometer. **Results:** (1) Men were more field-independent than women were on RFT series 2 ($p < .001$) and series 3 ($p < .01$). No sex differences were found on series 1. (2) Men were superior to women on series 1a ($p < .05$) and 1b ($p < .01$) of the TRTC test. No sex differences were found in series 2a or 2b. (3) No sex differences were found on the EFT. (4) Men kept the platform horizontal more often than women did. No sex differences were found in number of seconds Ss touched the surrounding guard rail in order to keep their balance.

Greenbaum, C. W. Effect of situational and personality variables on improvisation and attitude change. *J. Personality & Social Psychology*, 1966, *4*, 260–69.

Subjects: $N = 100$; 18–21 yrs (college). **Measures:** Ss were given either a choice or no choice to speak in defense of a counterattitudinal topic. After making the speech, Ss received either positive, negative, or no feedback. Attitude change was assessed immediately afterward and again 2 weeks later. **Results:** No sex differences.

Greenberg, D. J. Accelerating visual complexity levels in the human infant. *Child Development*, 1971, *42*, 905–18 (and personal communication).
> **Subjects:** $N = 36$; tested at 8, 10, 12 wks. **Measures:** Ss' fixation time to 3 checkerboard patterns of equal area was assessed. Groups viewed either a gray stimulus or various checkerboard patterns for a 4-week period. **Results:** (1) At age 8 weeks, girls maintained longer interest in the simple $2'' \times 2''$ than boys did. (2) There were no sex differences involving more complex patterns. (3) Boys habituated after an initial surge of interest in the simple pattern; girls habituated slowly but maintained interest.

Greenberg, D. J., and O'Donnell, W. J. Infancy and the optimal level of stimulation. *Child Development*, 1972, *43*, 639–45.
> **Subjects:** $N = 72$; 6, 11 wks. **Measures:** Ss viewed stimulus patterns in which equal black and white proportions were combined in checks, stripes, and dots, gradually increasing in complexity within each type. Each S saw 3 patterns of the same type. **Results:** Girls looked at checkerboards more than boys did ($p < .05$); no other sex differences were found.

Greenberg, D. J., and Weizmann, F. The measurement of visual attention in infants: a comparison of two methodologies. *J. Experimental Child Psychology*, 1971, *11*, 234–43.
> **Subjects:** $N = 24$; 2, 3 mos. **Measures:** Ss' fixation times to 3 checkerboard patterns (2x2, 8x8, 24x24) of equal area were recorded twice, once with each stimulus presented singly, and once using a paired-comparisons method of presentation. **Results:** There were no overall sex differences, but girl infants looked longer at the more complex pattern than boys did. However, post hoc comparisons qualified the sex difference: in a single-stimulus presentation, girl infants looked longer at the $24'' \times 24''$ checkerboard relative to the $8'' \times 8''$ than boys did, whereas in the paired comparison, girls looked longer at both the $24'' \times 24''$ and $8'' \times 8''$, relative to the $2'' \times 2''$, than boys did.

Greenberger, E., O'Connor, J., and Sorensen, A. Personality, cognitive, and academic correlates of problem-solving flexibility. *Developmental Psychology*, 1971, *4*, 416–24.
> **Subjects:** $N = 113$; 6–8 yrs. **Measures:** Each S was given the California Test of Mental Maturity for IQ scores, Test Anxiety Scale for Children, recall of novel information from taped stories one week later, Investigatory Activities Inventory (self-report curiosity measure), "Foolish Sayings" scale (whether or not statements made sense), teacher ratings of children's curiosity (adjective checklist, behavior profile with subscales for curiosity, achievement striving, achievement blocks), question as to "which parent best likes to answer your questions," and measure of problem-solving flexibility (giving as many reasons as possible for certain occurrences, scores for number of different categories responses fell into). **Results:** (1) There were no sex differences in problem-solving flexibility. (2) Among 6-year-old Ss, girls recalled more than boys did. There were no sex differences in recall at the other 2 age levels.

Greenglass, E. R. A cross-cultural comparison of maternal communication. *Child Development*, 1971a, *42*, 685–92.
> **Subjects:** $N = 132$ mother-child pairs; 9–10, 13–14 yrs (Italian-Canadian and Canadian). **Measures:** Mother-child pairs were required to reach a consensus in each of 3 discussion tasks. Maternal verbalizations were recorded. **Results:** No sex of child differences were found in total amount of maternal communication or in mothers' use of demands or justifications.

Greenglass, E. R. A cross-cultural study of the child's communication with his mother. *Developmental Psychology*, 1971b, *5*, 494–99.
> **Subjects:** $N = 132$; 9–10, 13–14 yrs (Italy, Canada). **Measures:** Each child's verbalizations were recorded during 3 discussion tasks in which the mother and child were required to reach consensus. **Results:** (1) There were no sex differences in the extent to which Italian children used requests for information. (2) Among 9-10-year-old Canadian Ss, girls used more requests for information or evaluation than boys did.

Greenglass, E. R. A cross-cultural study of the relationship between resistance to temptation and maternal communication. *Genetic Psychology Monographs*, 1972, *86*, 119–39.
> **Subjects:** $N = 62$; 9–10 yrs and mothers. **Measures:** Ss played a game in which it was neces-

sary to violate the rules in order to win a gold star. The number of times each S cheated was recorded. Each mother-child pair engaged in three discussion tasks. Each task required that a consensus be reached. Mothers were scored for their use of demands and justifications. **Results:** No sex differences.

Greenwald, H. J. Dissonance and relative versus absolute attractiveness of decision alternatives. *J. Personality & Social Psychology*, 1969, *11*, 328–33.
   Subjects: $N = 85$; 18–21 yrs (college). **Measures:** Ss initially rated 40 singers' acceptability on a 15-point scale; 2 weeks later, Ss were asked to evaluate the records of one of the singers. Half of the Ss were given a choice of which of 2 singers they were to evaluate, while the other Ss simply expressed their preference for 1 of 2 singers. In this latter condition, Ss were told a singer had already been selected for them by a random process. The singers Ss chose between were derived from Ss' preratings. Relative attractiveness was manipulated by presenting Ss with 2 singers they had previously rated either alike (high-conflict situation) or different (low-conflict situation). Immediately after selecting a singer (or expressing a preference for 1), Ss rerated both singers. "Spreading apart" was the increase in the chosen alternative's rating added to the decrease in the rejected alternative's ratings. **Results:** In the low-conflict condition, the decrease in spreading apart was greater for women than for men ($p < .02$).

Greenwald, H. J., and Oppenheim, D. B. Reported magnitude of self-misidentification among Negro children—artifact? *J. Personality & Social Psychology*, 1968, *8*, 49–52.
   Subjects: $N = 79$; 3–5 yrs (white, black). **Measures:** Ss were presented with a dark brown, a mulatto, and a white doll. Ss were then asked the following series of questions: Is there a doll that (a) you like to play with best? (b) you don't want to play with? (c) is a nice color? (d) is a good doll? (e) is a bad doll? (f) is not a nice color? (g) looks like a white child? (h) looks like a colored child? (i) looks like you? **Results:** No sex differences.

Gross, F. The role of set in perception of the upright. *J. Personality*, 1959, *27*, 95–103.
   Subjects: $N = 110$; 17–25 yrs. **Measures:** Rod-and-Frame Test. **Results:** Men were more field-independent than women ($p < .01$).

Gross, R. B., and Marsh, M. An instrument for measuring creativity in young children: the Gross Geometric Forms. *Developmental Psychology*, 1970, *3*, 267 (brief report).
   Subjects: $N = 170$; 3–6, 10, 15 yrs. **Measures:** For 10 trials, Ss used colored geometric forms to make "something" and were asked to name and describe their creation. Creations were scored for different form constructions and names (productivity), communicability (degree to which form constructions and names matched), and richness of thinking shown in action, color, and embellishment. **Results:** No sex differences.

Gruder, C. L., and Cook, T. D. Sex, dependency and helping. *J. Personality & Social Psychology*, 1971, *19*, 290–4.
   Subjects: $N = 104$; 18–21 yrs (college). **Measures:** Ss were requested to collate and staple copies of an 18-page questionnaire as a favor for either a male or female E who at the last moment had to change his schedule to go to a class meeting. The note that E left stated that he needed the questionnaire either in 2 hours (high-dependency condition) or next week (low-dependency condition). The number of questionnaires Ss stapled was recorded. **Results:** (1) There were no sex of S effects. (2) The female E received greater help in the high-dependency than in the low-dependency condition; the male E did not ($p < .05$).

Gruen, G. E., Ottinger, D., and Zigler, E. Level of aspiration and the probability learning of middle- and lower-class children. *Developmental Psychology*, 1970, *3*, 133–42.
   Subjects: $N = 121$; 6, 9 yrs (lower, middle SES). **Measures:** Level of aspiration was measured by each S's estimate of how many times out of 10 he could throw a beanbag into a box 6 feet away. Probability learning was measured by the number of correct knob pushes (out of 3) S made, with 1 knob reinforced 66% of the time and the other 2 knobs never reinforced. **Results:** No sex differences.

Gruen, G. E., and Vore, D. A. Development of conservation in normal and retarded children. *Developmental Psychology*, 1972, *6*, 146–57.
   Subjects: $N = 20$; 7, 10 yrs (retarded). $N = 40$; 5, 6, 8, 10 yrs (normal). **Measures:** Ss performed tasks for conservation of number, continuous quantity, and weight. **Results:** No sex differences.

Grusec, J. E. Some antecedents of self-criticism. *J. Personality & Social Psychology*, 1966, 4, 244–52.

Subjects: $N = 80$; 5–6 yrs. Measures: While playing a game with an adult female model, Ss were criticized for their performance on selected trials. The model accompanied this criticism with either withdrawal of love or withdrawal of material reward. Termination of punishment was made either contingent or noncontingent upon Ss' verbalization of the model's criticism of them. The speed with which Ss verbalized the criticism was recorded. Generalization of the model's criticism of them to a new situation and its resistance to extinction were also measured. Results: No sex differences.

Grusec, J. E. Waiting for rewards and punishments: effects of reinforcement value on choice. *J. Personality & Social Psychology*, 1968, 9, 85–89.

Subjects: $N = 40$; 8 yrs. Measures: Ss listed their preferences for immediate vs. delayed rewards and punishments. Delayed outcomes were of either equal or greater magnitude than immediate outcomes. Results: No sex differences.

Grusec, J. E. Power and the internalization of self-denial. *Child Development*, 1971, 42, 93–105.

EXPERIMENT I: Subjects: $N = 48$; 7–11 yrs. Measures: Ss experienced high or low nurturance from a model who had power or no power to administer rewards. The model played a bowling game with Ss in which the model exhibited altruism by explaining he would donate his rewards to charity. Results: No sex differences in Ss' donations to charity.

EXPERIMENT II: Subjects: $N = 40$; 7–11 yrs. Measures: Same as Experiment I, except standards of self-reward on the bowling game were enacted by the model rather than explained. Results: No sex differences.

Grusec, J. E. Demand characteristics of the modeling experiment: altruism as a function of age and aggression. *J. Personality & Social Psychology*, 1972, 22, 139–48.

EXPERIMENT I: Subjects: $N = 100$; 7, 11 yrs. Measures: Following exposure to an altruistic same-sex adult model, Ss were given the opportunity to donate marbles to charity. Results: No sex differences were found in number of marbles donated.

EXPERIMENT II: Subjects: $N = 54$; 8–9 yrs. Measures: One group of Ss observed a same-sex adult model perform a series of aggressive responses with toys. A second group of Ss simply heard a model say that aggressive behaviors were appropriate. Following the model's departure, Ss were observed with the toys and then asked to recall everything the model had either said or done. Results: There were no sex differences in number of imitative aggressive responses displayed or number of novel aggressive responses displayed. There were no sex differences in Ss' recall of the model's behavior and verbalizations.

EXPERIMENT III: Subjects: $N = 20$; 8–9 yrs. Measures: Same as Experiment II, except Ss were not observed with the toys. Results: No sex differences were found in Ss' recall of the model's behavior or verbalizations.

Grusec, J. E. Effects of co-observer evaluations on imitation: a developmental study. *Developmental Psychology*, 1973, 8, 141 (extended version of brief report).

Subjects: $N = 60$; 5, 10 yrs. Measures: Ss watched a movie of a female adult being aggressive toward a Bobo doll while hearing a female E make positive, negative, or neutral evaluations of the model's behavior. Ss were then left alone for 7 minutes in the playroom with the Bobo and other toys. Results: No sex differences were found in the number of Ss who imitated the model.

Grusec, J. E., and Brinker, D. B. Reinforcement for imitation as a social learning determinant with implications for sex-role development. *J. Personality & Social Psychology*, 1972, 21, 149–58.

EXPERIMENT I: Subjects: $N = 32$; 6, 7 yrs. Measures: Ss were shown a series of separate filmed sequences of 2 men (models A and B) performing different behaviors. After each sequence, Ss were asked to reproduce 1 of the behaviors they had seen. Half of the Ss were reinforced for imitating model A, the other half for imitating model B. The performance measure was number of trials needed by Ss to reach the criterion of 10 correct responses in succession. In the next phase of the study, a second movie of models A and B was shown and Ss' eye movements were recorded. The response measure was the number of seconds Ss spent looking at each model. Immediately afterward, Ss were asked to perform the behaviors of both models. The number of items of each model's behavior that Ss were able to recall was recorded. Results: No sex differences.

EXPERIMENT II: **Subjects:** $N = 32$; 8 yrs. **Measures:** Same as Experiment I, except new movies were made using 2 females as models and Ss' eye movements were not recorded. **Results:** (1) Girls reached the criterion of 10 correct responses in succession faster than boys did ($p < .01$). (2) No sex differences were found in Ss' recall of the model's behaviors.

EXPERIMENT III: **Subjects:** $N = 144$; 5, 7 yrs. **Measures:** Ss were shown a movie of an adult male and an adult female model, who exhibited (with the exception of 2 short sequences of nurturant and aggressive responses) mostly neutral behaviors. Afterward, Ss were rewarded for reproducing the behaviors of both models. **Results:** (1) No main sex differences were found in number of items recalled of each model's behavior. Boys remembered more of the adult male's than of the adult female's behavior, while girls remembered slightly more of the adult female's than of the adult male's behavior ($p < .001$). (2) No main sex differences were found in Ss' recall of nurturant behaviors. Girls remembered more of the female's nurturance than boys did ($p < .05$). No sex differences were found in Ss' recall of the male model's nurturance. (3) No sex differences were found in Ss' recall of aggressive behavior.

Grusec, J. E., and Mischel, W. Model's characteristics as determinants of social learning. *J. Personality & Social Psychology*, 1966, *4*, 211–15.
    Subjects: $N = 28$; 3–4 yrs. **Measures:** In the context of a game, Ss observed an adult female model display both neutral and aversive behaviors. Following the model's departure, Ss were offered attractive incentives contingent upon the reproduction of as many of the model's behaviors as they could recall. **Results:** No sex differences.

Grusec, J. E., and Skubiski, S. L. Model nurturance, demand characteristics of the modeling experiment, and altruism. *J. Personality & Social Psychology*, 1970, *14*, 352–59.
    Subjects: $N = 80$; 8, 10 yrs. **Measures:** After exposure to an altruistic same-sex model, Ss were given the opportunity to donate marbles to charity. **Results:** No sex differences were found in number of marbles donated.

Grusec, T., and Grusec, J. E. Information seeking about uncertain but unavoidable outcomes: effects of probability, valence, and intervening activity. *Developmental Psychology*, 1971, *5*, 177 (brief report).
    EXPERIMENT I: **Subjects:** $N = 48$; 11 yrs. **Measures:** Before he left for 20 minutes, E gave Ss an envelope. The envelope contained a note informing Ss whether they would later be asked to eat either some delicious or some terrible-tasting food. The speed with which they opened the envelope was recorded. **Results:** No sex differences.
    EXPERIMENT II: **Subjects:** $N = 64$, 18–21 (college). **Measures:** Same as Experiment I, except that the envelope contained information on whether Ss would later have a chance to win between $10 and $25 or whether they would be asked to receive painful shocks. **Results:** Women opened the envelope more quickly than men ($p < .05$).

Guardo, C. J. Personal space in children. *Child Development*, 1969, *40*, 143–51.
    Subjects: $N = 60$; 11 yrs. **Measures:** Ss placed a silhouette figure of themselves in relation to another figure. The other figure was described as a best friend, an acquaintance, a stranger, "someone you like very much," "someone you neither like nor dislike," "someone you dislike very much," an angry stranger, or as "someone you're afraid of." **Results:** Girls placed the silhouette figure of themselves closer to "best friend" and "someone you like very much" and farther away from "someone you're afraid of" than boys did ($p < .05$, $p < .05$, $p < .05$).

Guardo, C. J., and Bohan, J. B. Development of a sense of self-identity in children. *Child Development*, 1971, *42*, 1909–21.
    Subjects: $N = 116$; 6–9 yrs. **Measures:** Ss were asked if they could assume the identity of each of the following: a pet, a same-sex sibling or peer, and an opposite-sex sibling or peer. Ss were also asked how long they had been a boy or a girl and whether or not they would be the same person in the near future (in the higher grades) and in the remote future (when grown up). **Results:** (1) Boys more often than girls indicated they could not assume the identity of an opposite-sexed sibling or peer (significance level not reported). (2) In answer to the question regarding how long they had been a boy or a girl, boys indicated a length of time less than their chronological age more often than girls did (significance level not reported).

Guardo, C. J., and Meisels, M. Child-parent spatial patterns under praise and reproof. *Developmental Psychology*, 1971, *5*, 365 (brief report).
    Subjects: $N = 431$; 8–15 yrs. **Measures:** Ss placed self-referent paper silhouettes in spatial relation to an adult male or female silhouette, described as father or mother, praising or reproving the child. Interfigure distances were measured. **Results:** (1) In the praise condition,

girls placed silhouettes closer to parental figures than boys did ($p < .01$). (2) In the reproof condition, there were no sex differences in silhouette placement.

Guinagh, B. J. An experimental study of basic learning ability and intelligence in low socioeconomic status children. *Child Development*, 1971, *42*, 27–36.
Subjects: $N = 80$; 8 yrs (white and black, low SES). Measures: Ss were given the Raven's Progressive Matrices Test of Intelligence and a digit-span test of basic learning ability: 2 groups (low DS–low RPM and high DS–low RPM) were established; 10 from each group received experimental treatment (training for RPM), 5 received the Hawthorne Treatment (training unrelated to task), and 5 received no treatment. All Ss were post-tested on RPM. Results: No sex differences.

Gummerman, L., and Gray, C. R. Age, iconic storage and visual information processing. *J. Experimental Child Psychology*, 1972, *13*, 165–70.
Subjects: $N = 48$; 7, 9, 11, 18–21 yrs (college). Measures: Tachistoscopic presentation of a T rotated to right or left was followed by a white field or a patterned masking stimulus. Ss made a verbal report of "left" or "right" at end of each trial to indicate which side of the perpendicular bar the T appeared on. Results: No sex differences.

Gutkin, D. C. The effect of systematic story changes on intentionality in children's moral judgments. *Child Development*, 1972, *43*, 187–95.
Subjects: $N = 72$; 6, 8, 10 yrs. Measures: Ss were presented with 6 stories (3 pairs) in which a "good" or "bad" child caused high or low damage, intentionally or nonintentionally. They were then asked to make judgments comparing children in the pairs of stories. Results: No sex differences.

Guttman, R., and Kahneman, I. Sex and age differences in pattern organization in a figural-conceptual task. *Developmental Psychology*, 1971, *5*, 446–53.
Subjects: $N = 57$; 2½ yrs and parents (Jerusalem). Measures: Ss individually filled form boards with red, green, and blue / circle, square, and triangle discs. Results: Women showed higher levels of organization than men did with regard to color and "goodness of pattern" (redundancy).

Guttman, R., and Kahneman, I. Age and sex-related variation in performance on a figural-conceptual task. *Developmental Psychology*, 1972, *7*, 4–9.
Subjects: $N = 128$; 2½, 3–4, 5–6 yrs and parents. Measures: Ss filled form boards with 3 colors of disks. No time limit existed, and disks could be placed in any order with respect to color and/or location on the board. Results: (1) At each age level, a lower proportion of boys than girls used all 3 colors. (2) There were no sex differences in the order in which the colors were used. (3) At each age level, girls exceeded boys in the proportion of perfectly ordered placement patterns of disks (without regard to color). (4) Among 2½-year-old Ss, more girls than boys were in a region of the scalogram profile characterized by use of 3 colors and ordered placement. (5) Among 5-6-year-old Ss, twice as many girls as boys were in a region of the scalogram where organization of several components was at a high level.

Haber, L., and Iverson, M. A. Status maintenance in communications from dyads with high and low interpersonal comparability. *J. Personality & Social Psychology*, 1965, *1*, 596–603.
Subjects: $N = 112$; 18–21 yrs (college). Measures: Same-sex pairs of Ss composed a joint letter describing the atmosphere of their college to an outsider. Ss' letters were scored for total number of words, percentage of total number of words having an occurrence frequency of fewer than 100 times per million, total number of value-oriented statements, and percentage of negative references relating to the college. Ss' verbal scores on the College Entrance Examination Boards were also obtained. Results: Women wrote longer letters than men ($p < .05$). No other sex differences were found.

Hafner, J. A., and Kaplan, A. M. Children's manifest anxiety and intelligence. *Child Development*, 1959, *30*, 269–71.
Subjects: $N = 188$; 10 yrs. Measures: Children's Manifest Anxiety Scale. Results: No sex differences found on either the anxiety scale or the L scale.

Hagen, J. W., and Huntsman, N. J. Selective attention in mental retardates. *Developmental Psychology*, 1971, *5*, 151–60.
Subjects: $N = 21$; 9, 11 yrs (institutional retardates). Measures: Ss were shown cards with

a central and incidental picture on each. Ss' task was to remember the order in which the cards were presented. **Results:** No sex differences.

Hagen, J. W., Hargrave, S., and Ross, W. Prompting and rehearsal in short-term memory. *Child Development*, 1973, *44*, 201–4.

Subjects: $N = 48$; 4–7 yrs. **Measures:** Ss were shown cards of 1 of 7 animals. After exposure, cards were laid face down in a horizontal row, Ss were asked to show the position of the card that was the same as the cue card. In a second trial block, a verbal rehearsal strategy was taught to all Ss. The third trial block was presented 1 week later. **Results:** No sex differences in correct recall.

Haith, M. The response of the human newborn to visual movement. *J. Experimental Child Psychology*, 1966, *3*, 235–43.

Subjects: $N = 41$; 1–4 days. **Measures:** Responsiveness and habituation of responsiveness of newborns to an intermittent, moving, visual stimulus were assessed. Nonnutritive sucking rate was measured during experimental (visual stimulus present) and control situations. **Results:** No sex differences in amount of nonnutritive sucking and habituation rate.

Hale, G. A., Miller, L. K., and Stevenson, H. W. Incidental learning of film content: a development study. *Child Development*, 1968, *39*, 69–77.

Subjects: $N = 719$; 8–12, 18–21 yrs (college). **Measures:** An 8-minute dramatic skit, filmed in sound and color, was presented as a reward for participation in an earlier study for younger Ss. The film was presented to college Ss without comment. After the film, Ss answered questions about incidental aspects of the verbal and visual content of the film. **Results:** (1) Among 8-12-year-old Ss, girls answered more questions correctly than boys did. (2) There were no sex differences in adult scores.

Hall, J. W., and Halperin, M. S. The development of memory-encoding processes in young children. *Developmental Psychology*, 1972, *6*, 181 (brief report).

Subjects: $N = 23$; 2½ yrs. **Measures:** 2 lists of common words were read. Ss were asked to remember the first list. The second list, the recognition test, contained 3 words from first list, 3 unrelated words, 3 words associatively related to first list, and 3 superordinates of first-list words. Ss were asked to recognize words that appeared on both lists. **Results:** No sex differences.

Hall, J. W., and Ware, W. B. Implicit associative responses and false recognition by young children. *J. Experimental Child Psychology*, 1968, *6*, 52–60.

Subjects: $N = 86$; 5–7 yrs. **Measures:** Ss heard 16 words at 4-second intervals with instructions to repeat each word and try to remember it. After a 15-minute interval, Ss were asked to identify previously heard words from the 24-word list containing previous words, strong associates of them, and control words (which had not appeared and were not associates of previous words). False recognitions were recorded. **Results:** No sex differences.

Hall, V. W., Salvi, R., Segev, L., and Caldwell, E. Cognitive synthesis, conservation, and task analysis. *Developmental Psychology*, 1970, *2*, 423–28.

Experiment I: **Subjects:** $N = 40$; 3–4 yrs. **Measures:** Ss were assigned to 1 of 4 conditions. 3 of the groups were tested on their ability to translate logograph sentences (directing them to do something) into actions. (A logograph is a card that represents a word. Logograph sentences are constructed by overlapping 2 or 3 cards. To correctly translate each sentence, Ss must (1) remember the word each card represents and (2) respond to the sentence as a whole rather than to each word separately.) In the remaining condition, Ss were simply asked by E to perform each of the actions. The number of correct responses each S made was recorded. **Results:** No sex differences.

Experiment II: **Subjects:** $N = 20$; 6 yrs. **Measures:** Ss were asked to translate logograph sentences into actions. **Results:** No sex differences were found in number of correct responses.

Halverson, C. F. Personal communication, 1971.

Subjects: $N = 45$; 2½ yrs (nursery school). **Measures:** Data were obtained from an activity recorder worn by each S during a 2½-hour session of free play with his mother. The recorder was also worn by each child every day of a 4-week session in which he played with 4 other children (mixed-sex group). **Results:** There were no sex differences in activity level when Ss were alone. Boys were more active than girls in groups ($p < .05$).

Halverson, C. F., and Waldrop, M. F. Maternal behavior toward own and other preschool children: the problem of "ownness." *Child Development*, 1970, *41*, 839–45.

Subjects: $N = 42$; mothers of 2½-year-old children. **Measures:** Each mother was asked to administer 6 different tasks to her child and 1 other same-sexed child; 4 tasks were taken from the Stanford-Binet: from board, block stacking, bead stringing, and picture vocabulary. Mother also attempted to get the child to tell a story and to place marbles in designated holes of a box; 2 coders categorized tape-recordings of maternal verbalizations into 4 categories: (a) positive, encouraging statements, (b) negative, controlling statements, (c) total words, and (d) total statements. Coders also recorded time children spent vocalizing. **Results:** Mothers talked more with girls than with boys (in terms of both total words and total statements). Girls spent more time talking than boys did.

Halverson, C. F., and Waldrop, M. F. The relations of mechanically recorded activity level to varieties of preschool play behavior. *Child Development*, 1973, 44, 678–81.
   Subjects: $N = 58$; 2½ yrs (white, middle SES). Measures: Activity level of each S was assessed by means of mechanical recorders attached to his jacket or shirt during outdoor free play. Results: Boys were more active than girls ($p < .001$).

Hamilton, M. L. Reward and punishment in child discrimination learning. *Developmental Psychology*, 1969, 1, 735–38.
   Subjects: $N = 24$; 3–5 yrs (nursery school). Measures: Scores from a social desirability scale were used to divide Ss into 6 levels. Ss at each level were assigned to 1 of 4 experimental conditions in 2-alternative discrimination tasks. Ss were asked to play a marble game. For half the Ss, E rewarded choosing the nonpreferred hole; for the other half, E punished choosing the preferred hole. Half of Ss were informed that E's nonreaction did not consistently follow either the correct or incorrect response. Results: No sex differences.

Hamilton, M. L. Vicarious reinforcement effects on extinction. *J. Experimental Child Psychology*, 1970, 9, 108–14.
   Subjects: $N = 28$; 3–4 yrs. Measures: Ss received either direct or vicarious (watching 6-year-old male model), continuous or partial reinforcement during the acquisition stage of a marble-dropping task. During the extinction stage, Ss were instructed to play the game as long as they wanted to. A week later, extinction procedure was administered again. Results: No sex differences.

Hamilton, M. L. Response to social reinforcement rates as a function of reinforcement history. *Developmental Psychology*, 1972, 6, 180 (brief report).
   Subjects: $N = 24$; 4 yrs. Measures: Social reinforcements Ss received from adults in 12 3-minute free-play observations were recorded. Ss were divided into high- and low-reinforcement standard groups, with half of each group receiving 33% reinforcement for nonpreferred choice during the discrimination learning task and the other half receiving 100% reinforcement. Results: No sex differences.

Hamilton, M. L. Imitative behavior and expressive ability in facial expression of emotion. *Developmental Psychology*, 1973, 8, 138 (brief report and personal communication).
   Subjects: $N = 72$; 3–4, 7, 10 yrs. Measures: Ss matched pictures of facial expressions, imitated each expression, and saw films portraying happiness and sadness. Ss' happy and sad expressions during films were recorded. Results: No sex differences.

Hamm, H., and Hoving, K. L. Conformity of children in an ambiguous perceptual situation. *Child Development*, 1969, 40, 773–84.
   Subjects: $N = 192$; 7, 10, 13 yrs. Measures: An autokinetic stimulus was presented to same-sex triads for a series of 45 trials. For the first 15 trials, Ss' judgments of both latency and magnitude of perceived movement of the stimulus were made privately. For the last 30 trials, Ss made their judgments publicly. The extent to which the Ss in each triad agreed with each other's judgments was used as a measure of conformity. Results: At ages 7 and 10, girls conformed to a greater degree than boys. At age 13, no sex differences were found.

Hamm, N. H. A partial test of a social learning theory of children's conformity. *J. Experimental Child Psychology*, 1970, 9, 29–42.
   Subjects: $N = 216$; 7, 10, 13 yrs. Measures: On day 1, Ss performed perceptual discrimination judgments (judging which projected figures contained the most dots) on ambiguous, unambiguous, and partially ambiguous stimuli, with either no social influences on judgments, social influence (result of peers' judgments), or partial social influence (result of 1 peer's judgment before making own decision, and one peer result afterward). On day 2 (3 weeks later), Ss viewed filmed male and female peer models perform the same task (in competition) and be either rewarded or not. A third group of Ss saw no film. Afterward, Ss performed the task.

Results: There were no overall sex differences in conformity on day 1, but girls conformed more than boys did on the unambiguous task. No sex differences were found in change in conformity from day 1 to day 2.

Hanlon, C. C. The effects of social isolation and characteristics of the model on accent imitation in fourth grade children. *J. Experimental Child Psychology*, 1971, *11*, 322–36. **Subjects:** $N = 52$; 9 yrs. **Measures:** After either social isolation (20 minutes alone before the experimental procedure) or nonisolation (proceeding directly to the experimental situation from the classroom), American-speaking Ss learned the speaking role of either a helpless or nurturant British character in a puppet play by hearing a taped British male (if boy) or female (if girl) say lines for Ss to repeat. Accent imitation was measured by the frequency of phonetic shifts from pre-exposure reading of the script to 2 post-exposure repetitions. **Results:** No overall sex differences weer found in accent imitation, but girls imitated the model's accent more after isolation, whereas boys imitated more when taken directly from the classroom to the experimental condition.

Hannah, R., Storm, T., and Caird, W. K. Sex differences and relationship among neuroticism, extraversion, and expressed fears. *Perceptual & Motor Skills*, 1965, *20*, 1214–16. **Subjects:** $N = 1,958$; 18–19 yrs (college). **Measures:** The Maudsley Personality Inventory (MPI) and the Fear Survey Schedule (FSS) were administered to Ss. On the MPI, Ss were scored for neuroticism (N) and extraversion (E). On the FSS, Ss rated each of the 73 items for its emotion-producing effect. Ss' ratings were added together to yield a total fear (F) score. The number of items checked as "very disturbing" was also recorded. **Results:** Women received higher N and F scores and checked more items as "very disturbing" than men did.

Hapkiewicz, W. G., and Roden, A. H. The effect of aggressive cartoons on children's interpersonal play. *Child Development*, 1971, *42*, 1583–85. **Subjects:** $N = 60$; 7 yrs. **Measures:** Ss viewed an aggressive cartoon, a nonaggressive cartoon, or no cartoon. Same-sex pairs were then presented with a peep show in which sharing was necessary in order to see. Aggression (pushing, grabbing, hand over hole) and sharing were measured. **Results:** (1) Boys were more aggressive than girls. (2) Overall, boys shared more than girls. After viewing the aggressive film, boys showed a nonsignificant tendency to share less than girls.

Harmatz, M. G. Verbal conditioning and change on personality measures. *J. Personality & Social Psychology*, 1967, *5*, 175–85. **Subjects:** $N = 50$; 18–21 yrs (college). **Measures:** Ss rated positive, negative, and neutral self-references on a 9-point true-untrue scale. Ss were reinforced for placing either positive or negative self-references toward the true end of the scale. Ss were also either reinforced or not reinforced for placing either negative or positive self-references toward the false end of the scale. Before and after conditioning, Ss completed the semantic differential, the Q sort, and 5 personality scales: Test Anxiety (TA), General Anxiety (GA), Hostility (H), Lack of Protection (LP), and Defensiveness (D). **Results:** (1) No sex differences were found in Ss' ratings of positive or negative self-references. (2) For each of the personality measures, Ss' initial scores were compared with their post-conditioning scores: (a) No sex differences were found on the semantic differential. (b) No sex differences were found in TA, GA, LP, or D. (c) Mean increase in Q Sort Adjustment Scores was greater for men than for women ($p < .025$). (d) On the pretest, women scored higher on the H scale than men ($p < .005$).

Harris, G. J., and Burke, D. The effects of grouping on short-term serial recall of digits by children: developmental trends. *Child Development*, 1972, *43*, 710–16. **Subjects:** $N = 90$; 7, 9, 11 yrs. **Measures:** Ss were presented with digits that were either ungrouped, spatially grouped, or spatially and temporally grouped. Recall was measured in writing. **Results:** No sex differences.

Harris, L. The effects of relative novelty on children's choice behavior. *J. Experimental Child Psychology*, 1965, *2*, 297–305. **Subjects:** $N = 64$; 3–5 yrs. **Measures:** Ss were given 1-minute familiarization trials with 2 identical toys of different colors from each of 4 different sets of toys. Ss chose 1 of 2 toys on each trial, and on every fifth trial, Ss could chose one or both of the familiarization toys or a novel toy, either damaged or undamaged; the choice was either 1 out of 3 toys or 2 familiar toys vs. 1 novel toy. All 4 combinations of the factors of damage and kind-of-choice offered were used to measure children's preferences for novelty. **Results:** (1) There were no sex differences in toy choice alternation. (2) Among younger Ss, girls chose the novel toy more frequently than boys did; among older Ss, no sex differences were found.

Harris, L. Looks by preschoolers at the experimenter in a choice-of-toys game: effects of experimenter and age of child. *J. Experimental Child Psychology,* 1968, *6,* 493–500.
Subjects: $N = 40$; 3–5 yrs. **Measures:** Ss chose toys (locomotives, ladybugs, dump trucks, and tops) in the presence of a familiar male or female E. Looking at E was measured. **Results:** (1) The female E was looked at by all Ss more than the male E was. (2) There were no effects of sex of S.

Harris, L., Schaller, M. J., and Mitler, M. M. The effects of stimulus type on performance in a color-form sorting task with preschool, kindergarten, first-grade and third-grade children. *Child Development,* 1970, *41,* 177–91.
Subjects: $N = 100$; 5–8 yrs. **Measures:** Ss chose which of 2 pictures was more like a third (which matched in form or color). Geometric and scrambled figures were used. **Results:** No sex differences.

Harris, L. J., and Strommen, E. A. The role of front-back features in children's "front," "back," and "beside" placements of objects. *Merrill-Palmer Quarterly,* 1972, *18,* 259–71.
Subjects: $N = 80$; 4–7 yrs. **Measures:** Ss made a series of "in front," "in back," and "beside" placements of common objects. Of the 7 pairs of objects that were used, 4 pairs had front-back features and 3 pairs did not. In the object-referent condition, E placed 1 member of a pair of objects in front of the Ss and then asked them to place the other member of the pair either behind, beside, or in front of the first member. In the self-referent condition, E gave Ss an object and then asked them to place it either behind, beside, or in front of themselves. After each trial, the location and orientation of Ss' placements were recorded. **Results:** No sex differences were reported.

Harris, M. B. Reciprocity and generosity: some determinants of sharing in children. *Child Development,* 1970, *41,* 313–28.
Subjects: $N = 168$; 9, 10 yrs. **Measures:** S played a chance game with a model in which tokens were dispensed when either player was "lucky." The model always got more tokens than S. In 5 of 6 conditions the model had the opportunity to share her tokens and did so with the child or with the "charity" or refused to share. In the sixth condition there was no chance to share. Reinforcement for sharing was varied across conditions. The model and S played the game again, this time S always won more chips. The model left the room before dividing the chips. The measure of sharing was what S did with the chips. **Results:** No sex differences.

Harris, M. B., and Hassemer, W. G. Some factors affecting the complexity of children's sentences: the effects of modeling, age, sex and bilingualism. *J. Experimental Child Psychology,* 1972, *13,* 447–55.
Subjects: $N = 48$; 7, 9 yrs (two-thirds of Ss bilingual). **Measures:** Ss composed sentences about pictures before and after hearing models (speaking Spanish to half of the bilingual Ss and English to all others) compose simple and complex sentences. Scored for number of words and complexity. **Results:** No sex differences.

Harris, S., and Braun, J. R. Self-esteem and racial preference in black children. *Proceedings of the 79th Annual Convention of the APA,* 1971, *8,* 259–60.
Subjects: $N = 60$; 7–8 yrs (black). **Measures:** Ss were given a black and a white puppet and asked to choose (a) the puppet they would like to play with, (b) the puppet that is a nice puppet, (c) the puppet that is a nice color, and (d) the puppet that looks bad. Ss were also given the Piers-Harris Children's Self-Concept Test. **Results:** No sex differences.

Harrison, A., and Nadelman, L. Conceptual tempo and inhibition of movement in black preschool children. *Child Development,* 1972, *43,* 657–68.
Subjects: $N = 50$; 4, 5 yrs (black, middle SES). **Measures:** (1) Matching Familiar Figures Test, (2) Peabody Picture Vocabulary Test, (3) Draw a Line Slowly Test, (4) Walk Slowly Test. **Results:** (1) When requested to go slowly on the 2 motor-inhibition tests, girls performed more slowly and showed greater change in relationship to their normal speed than boys. (2) On the MFF test, girls exhibited longer response latencies and committed fewer errors than boys. (3) No sex differences were found on the PPVT.

Harrison, C. W., Rawls, J. R., and Rawls, D. J. Differences between leaders and nonleaders in six- to eleven-year-old children. *J. Social Psychology,* 1971, *84,* 269–72.

Subjects: $N = 649$; 6–11 yrs. **Measures:** Teachers rated how often each child in their classrooms had been chosen as leader by his peers. **Results:** No sex differences.

Harter, S. Discrimination learning set in children as a function of IQ and MA. *J. Experimental Child Psychology,* 1965, *2,* 31–43.
    Subjects: $N = 81$; 3–14 yrs (normals, retardates). **Measures:** Ss were given a series of 4-trial object-discrimination problems each day until they reached the learning criterion. **Results:** No sex differences.

Harter, S. Mental age, IQ, and motivational factors in the discrimination learning set performance of normal and retarded children. *J. Experimental Child Psychology,* 1967, *5,* 123–41.
    Subjects: $N = 160$; mental ages: 5½, 8½ yrs. **Measures:** Until they reached criterion, Ss were tested each day on a series of 4-trial object-discrimination problems. In the standard condition, E stood behind a one-way screen. In the social condition, each S was given a preliminary success experience, E and S were face to face during the discrimination task, and S's correct choices were praised by E. The number of problems to criterion was the response measure. **Results:** No sex differences.

Harter, S., and Zigler, E. Effects of rate of stimulus presentation and penalty conditions on the discrimination learning of normal and retarded children. *Developmental Psychology,* 1972, *6,* 85–91.
    Subjects: $N = 80$; 6 yrs (normal), 13–15 yrs (retarded): mental age 7 yrs. **Measures:** Ss performed a 2-choice discrimination learning problem with 2 rates of stimulus presentation and 2 reinforcement conditions (reward only or reward plus penalty). **Results:** No sex differences.

Harter, S., Brown, L., and Zigler, E. The discrimination learning of normal and retarded children as a function of penalty conditions and etiology of the retarded. *Child Development,* 1971a, *42,* 517–36.
    Subjects: $N = 210$; 6, 7 yrs (normal, cultural-familial retardates, mental retardates). **Measures:** Ss performed a 2-choice size-discrimination task. Penalty and reward conditions were varied across groups. **Results:** No sex differences.

Harter, S., Shultz, R. R., and Blum, B. Smiling in children as a function of their sense of mastery. *J. Experimental Child Psychology,* 1971b, *12,* 396–404.
    Subjects: $N = 41$; 4, 8 yrs. **Measures:** 40 items were preselected from the Peabody Picture Vocabulary Test to represent 4 levels of difficulty: very easy, moderately difficult, very difficult, and impossible. These items were then administered to Ss; Ss' spontanous smiling responses were recorded. **Results:** No main sex differences were found in the magnitude of Ss' smiling responses.

Hartig, M., and Kanfer, F. H. The role of verbal self-instructions in children's resistance to temptation. *J. Personality & Social Psychology,* 1973, *25,* 259–67.
    Subjects: $N = 261$; 3–7 yrs. **Measures:** Ss were seated with their backs to attractive toys. As E left the room for a few minutes, he instructed Ss not to look at the toys until his return. Ss were also told to verbalize either the positive consequences for nontransgression, the negative consequences for transgression, E's instructions, or a nursery rhyme. Response measures were (1) percentage of Ss who turned around within 1 minute after E left, percentage of Ss who turned around after 1 minute elapsed but before E returned, and percentage of Ss who did not turn around at all, (2) number of Ss who verbalized the self-instructions, and (3) number of Ss who denied transgressing in a postexperimental interview. **Results:** No sex differences.

Hartmann, D. P., Gelfand, D. M., Courtney, R. J., Jr., and Malouf, R. E. Successive presentation of elements of the Mueller-Lyer Figure and CA, MA, and IQ: an age extension and unsuccessful replication. *Child Development,* 1972, *43,* 1060–66.
    Subjects: $N = 50$; 6–9 yrs. **Measures:** Ss made comparative decisions about 21 variations of the Mueller-Lyer figure on a tachistoscope. **Results:** No sex differences.

Hartup, W. W. Some correlates of parental imitation in young children. *Child Development,* 1962, *33,* 85–96.
    Subjects: $N = 63$; 3–5 yrs. **Measures:** A forced-choice doll play interview was used to determine whether Ss preferred to imitate their like-sex parent more than their opposite-sex parent.

The It Scale for Children (ITSC) was also administered. **Results:** (1) Both sexes preferred to imitate the like-sex parent doll. No sex differences were found in the proportion of like-sex choices. (2) On the ITSC, boys obtained more masculine scores than girls.

Hartup, W. W., and Zook, E. A. Sex-role preferences in three- and four-year-old children. *J. Consulting Psychology*, 1960, *24*, 420–26.
  Subjects: $N = 161$; 3–4 yrs. **Measures:** It Scale for Children. **Results:** Boys received more masculine scores than girls did ($p < .001$).

Haskett, G. J. Modification of peer preferences of first-grade children. *Developmental Psychology*, 1971, *4*, 429–33.
  Subjects: $N = 106$; 6 yrs. **Measures:** Ss ranked photographs of classmates from most liked to least liked friend, and from first-best to last-best friend. They were then matched with an opposite- or same-sex peer who was neither extremely liked nor disliked. In the 3 following days, pairs either worked cooperatively on a building task, sat together but worked separately (contiguity), or sat separately and worked separately (controls). Post-treatment peer preference was measured. **Results:** (1) Almost all Ss chose as their best friend a child of the same sex; (2) no sex differences were found in change in liking for partner.

Hass, R. G., and Linder, D. E. Counterargument availability and the effects of message structure on persuasion. *J. Personality & Social Psychology*, 1972, *23*, 219–33.
  Subjects: $N = 150$; 18–21 yrs (college). **Measures:** Ss were asked to determine the guilt or innocence of a defendant on the basis of a written summary of the evidence presented at a bigamy trial. **Results:** No sex differences.

Hatfield, J. S., Ferguson, L. R., and Alpert, R. Mother-child interaction and the socialization process. *Child Development*, 1967, *38*, 365–414.
  Subjects: $N = 40$; 4–5 yrs and mothers (22–41 yrs). **Measures:** During the first half-hour session, the mother completed a questionnaire while the child played with crayons and paper. Afterward, the mother was asked to structure a telephone game in which the child was encouraged to role-play himself, a mother, a father, a deviant same-sex child, and a child of the opposite sex. During the second session, the mother was asked to have her child work with puzzles. She could help him if she wished. The child also played a fishing game in which the mother could participate. After the fishing game, the mother was asked to clean the room. Cleaning equipment was offered to both the mother and the child. **Results:** (1) Boys were rated higher than girls on verbal aggression and fantasy aggression. While playing the role of the deviant child in the telephone game, boys were more tense than girls. No sex differences were found in dependency; independence; warmth toward mother; achievement standards; disobedience; direct or indirect aggression to mother; indirectness of aggression to mother; outer-directed physical aggression; self-aggression; involvement in water play aside from fishing; tension (overall rating), activity level; willingness to adopt self-role; willingness to adopt the roles of mother, father, deviant child, and child of opposite sex; interest in adult role behavior; resistance toward adult role behavior; concern with sex appropriateness; confession (i.e. the extent to which Ss confessed to wrongdoing while playing the role of the deviant child); fixing (i.e. the extent to which Ss tried to make amends for the deviation). (2) Boys received more achievement pressure from their mothers than girls did. Mothers of girls were more concerned with water play during the fishing game than mothers of boys. No differences were found between boys' and girls' mothers in pressure for independence; restriction of independence; rewarding of independence; punishment of independence; directiveness, rewarding of dependency; punishment of dependency; warmth toward child; responsiveness to child (questionnaire situation); involvement and enjoyment (telephone game); involvement and enjoyment (fishing game); pressure for obedience; punishment of aggression; hostility toward child; rewarding of achievement; punishment of low achievement; concern with neatness and orderliness; concern with cleaning up (fishing game); pressure and reward for adult role behavior; restriction and punishment of adult role behavior; concern with sex appropriateness; use of models; use of reasoning.

Haugan, G. M., and McIntire, R. W. Comparisons of vocal imitation, tactile stimulation, and food as reinforcers for infant vocalizations. *Developmental Psychology*, 1972, *6*, 201–9.
  Subjects: $N = 24$; 3–6 mos. **Measures:** Rates of infant vocalizations were measured under 3 types of reinforcement (adult imitation, food, tactile), in 3 experimental stages (baseline, conditioning, extinction). **Results:** (1) There were no main sex differences in vocalizations before reinforcement. More boys than girls vocalized during baseline in the vocal and tactile

reinforcement groups, before reinforcement was given; more girls than boys vocalized in the food group, before reinforcement was given ($p < .05$). (2) There were no sex differences between reinforcement groups during conditioning or extinction. (3) Examination of group differences within reinforcement showed a higher vocal rate for boys than for girls in the vocal reinforcement group during conditioning and extinction ($p < .05$). (4) During extinction, girls in the tactile reinforcement group had higher vocal rates than boys ($p < .05$).

Havighurst, R. J., and Hilkevitch, R. R. The intelligence of Indian children as measured by a performance scale. *J. Abnormal & Social Psychology*, 1944, 39, 419–33.
  Subjects: $N = 670$; 6–15 yrs (Navaho, Hopi, Zuni, Zia, Pappago, and Sioux Indian tribes). **Measures:** A shortened form of the Arthur Point Performance Scale. **Results:** In 10 of 11 communities, no sex differences were found. In one community, boys scored higher than girls.

Hawkins, R. P. Learning of peripheral content in films: a developmental study. *Child Development*, 1973, 44, 214–17.
  Subjects: $N = 306$; 8, 10, 12, 14 yrs (parochial school). **Measures:** Ss viewed 1 of 2 films, a children's Western or an adult Western. Afterward, they answered questions pertaining to central or peripheral information. **Results:** (1) There were no sex differences on peripheral learning. (2) On central learning, girls did better than boys at ages 8, 10, and 14; boys did better than girls at age 12. (3) On central learning, boys did better than girls on the adult film ($p < .05$).

Heal, L. The role of cue value, cue novelty, and overtraining in the discrimination shift performance of retardates and normal children of comparable discrimination ability. *J. Experimental Child Psychology*, 1966, 4, 126–42.
  Subjects: $N = 48$; 5 yrs (normal), adult (retardate). **Measures:** Ss were given 4 2-stage discrimination-learning problems. In stage 1, 1 dimension (either form or color) was relevant whereas the other was irrelevant. In stage 2, the relevant dimension was either changed (extradimensional shift) or not changed (intradimensional reversal). The performance measure was the number of errors Ss made in both stages of problems 3 and 4. **Results:** No sex differences.

Hebble, P. W. The development of elementary school children's judgment of intent. *Child Development*, 1971, 42, 1203–15.
  Subjects: $N = 944$; 6–11 yrs. **Measures:** Ss read 4 variations of 7 stories involving good intent–light damage, good intent–heavy damage, bad intent–light damage, and bad intent–heavy damage. Ss rated the characters' "badness." **Results:** No sex differences.

Hebda, M. E., Peterson, R. A., and Miller, L. K. Aggression anxiety, perception of aggressive cues, and expected retaliation. *Developmental Psychology*, 1972, 7, 85 (brief report).
  Subjects: $N = 31$; 8 yrs. **Measures:** Ss were presented with 30 pictures of angry, neutral, and friendly male and female faces. Instructions were given to rate each stimulus on an anger-friendliness dimension and on the intensity of retaliation expected following a hypothetical act by the S. **Results:** No sex differences were found.

Hecox, K. E., and Hagen, J. W. Estimates and estimate-based inferences in young children. *J. Experimental Child Psychology*, 1971, 11, 106–23.
  Subjects: $N = 52$; 5–7 yrs. **Measures:** Ss saw visual field slides with differing proportions of red and black dots. Their task was to produce as many red and black dots on the response apparatus screen (by moving a lever to change proportions) as were projected on the display screen. **Results:** No sex differences.

Heider, E. R. "Focal" color areas and the development of color names. *Developmental Psychology*, 1971, 4, 447–55.
  Experiment I: Subjects: $N = 24$; 3 yrs. **Measures:** S made 8 free color choices from each of 2 arrays of Munsell color chips of focal colors (areas of color space previously found with adults to be most exemplary of basic color names in many languages). Each focal color was embedded in 2 array types: all brightnesses of same hue as the focal chip (maximum saturation) and all lesser saturations of the same hue and value as the focal chip. **Results:** No sex differences.
  Experiment II: Subjects: $N = 20$; 4 yrs. **Measures:** Ss were asked to match comparison chips of focal and nonfocal colors with color chips in 1 of 2 arrays differing in brightness and hue. **Results:** Girls were more accurate in overall matching than boys. There were no sex differences in relative accuracy of matching focal and nonfocal colors.

EXPERIMENT III: **Subjects:** $N = 27$; 3–4 yrs. **Measures:** Ss were asked to point to basic colors of chips when the color name was verbalized by E. Stimuli were chips of the same values, but different hues. **Results:** No sex differences.

Heilbrun, A. B., Harrell, S. N., Gillard, B. J. Perceived maternal child-rearing patterns and the effects of social nonreaction upon achievement motivation. *Child Development,* 1967, *38,* 267–81.
    Subjects: $N = 237$; 18–21 yrs (college). **Measures:** (1) Maternal child-rearing behavior was assessed by the S's impression of how his mother would answer the Parent Attitude Research Instrument; 16 scales defined perceived maternal control for males, 13 scales defined perceived maternal control for females. Ss' perception of maternal nurturance was estimated from ratings on the Parent-Child Interaction Rating Scales. (2) The achievement motivation task was a variation of a visual discrimination task in which Ss were asked to match test angles with 1 of 5 standards, none of which was actually correct. For the first trial, Ss were informed of high school students' performances, and were asked to indicate their level of aspiration under 3 reinforcement conditions (success, failure, or nonreaction). At the end of the second trial, Ss were asked to estimate their performance (without feed-back). Ss were asked to estimate their performance on the third trial; however, a third trial was never run. (3) Equal numbers of male and female Es for each of 3 reinforcement conditions were assigned; 4 child-rearing groups were high control/high nurturant (overprotected), high control/low nurturant (rejected), low control/high nuturant (accepted), and low control/low nurturant (ignored). **Results:** No main sex differences. Among Ss in the accepted and ignored groups who experienced failure on trial 1, the difference between level of aspiration prior to trial 3 and level of performance during trial 1 was greater for men than women.

Hendry, L. S., and Kessen, W. Oral behavior of newborn infants as a function of age and time since feeding. *Child Development,* 1964, *35,* 201–8.
    Subjects: $N = 19$; 1–3 days. **Measures:** Ss were observed feeding at 23 and 71 hours of age. Measures were taken of total duration and average length of contact between hand and mouth, total duration of mouthing (defined as any sucking-like movement), and total duration of contact between hand and mouth accompanied by mouthing (hand-sucking). **Results:** (1) Between 23 and 71 hours old, duration of hand-to-mouth contact and hand-sucking increased for boys but decreased for girls ($p < .05$, $p < .05$). No sex differences were found on these 2 measures at age 23 hours. (2) No sex differences were found in duration of mouthing or in average length of contact between hand and mouth.

Herbert, E. W., Gelfand, D. M., and Hartmann, D. P. Imitation and self-esteem as determinants of self-critical behavior. *Child Development,* 1969, *40,* 421–30.
    Subjects: $N = 40$; 9 yrs. **Measures:** Ss completed the P. S. Sears Self Concept Inventory and the Bledsoe-Garrison Self Concept Inventory. Ss played a bowling game with preselected scores, with or without a same-sex model (opposite-sex adult served as observer). Ss played the game by themselves, called out their own scores, and rated their own performances. **Results:** (1) When Ss were equated for self-esteem, there were no sex differences in imposing fines on self, or in self-criticism. (2) Girls had lower self-esteem ratings than boys on the Sears SCI ($p < .01$), and rated their own performance lower.

Herder, E. R. Style and accuracy of verbal communications within and between social classes. *J. Personality & Social Psychology,* 1971, *18,* 33–47.
    EXPERIMENT I: **Subjects:** $N = 143$; 10 yrs (white, low and middle SES; black, low SES). **Measures:** Ss were asked to encode (describe) abstract and face stimuli presented alongside sets of similar items, so that other children would be able to pick out the target items at a later date. Ss' statements were classified as either inferential or descriptive, referring to either all or part of the stimulus. **Results:** No sex differences.
    EXPERIMENT II: **Subjects:** $N = 141$; 10 yrs (same as Experiment I). **Measures:** Ss were recalled after several weeks to decode examples of descriptions given by each SES and sex of subject. **Results:** No sex differences.

Hermans, H. J., ter Laak, J. J., and Maes, P. C. Achievement motivation and fear of failure in family and school. *Developmental Psychology,* 1972, *6,* 520–28.
    Subjects: $N = 40$; 9–10 yrs (Dutch). **Measures:** After testing a group of 445 children, 20 boys and 20 girls were selected on the basis of their extreme scores on the achievement-motivation and debilitating-anxiety scales of the Prestatie Motivatie Test voor Kinderen (Achievement Motivation Test for Children). There were 4 groups of Ss in all: (1) high-achievement-moti-

vated—high-debilitating-anxiety; (2) high-achievement-motivated—low-debilitating-anxiety; (3) low-achievement-motivated—high-debilitating-anxiety; and (4) low-achievement-motivated—low-debilitating-anxiety. (1) Each S performed 4 tasks at home in the presence of his parents. The following parental behaviors were recorded: (a) gives specific help; (b) gives nonspecific help; (c) gives encouragement; (d) gives positive-task-oriented reinforcement; (e) gives negative-task-oriented reinforcement; (f) gives positive-person-oriented reinforcement; (g) gives negative-person-oriented reinforcement; (h) withholds reinforcement after a correct response; (i) shows signs of good mood and enthusiasm; (j) exhibits negative expressions of tension, shows signs of irritation; (k) does not react when the child shows signs of insecurity. The following behaviors were recorded for children: (a) asks parents for help; (b) refuses parental help; (c) shows signs of good mood and enthusiasm; (d) exhibits negative expressions of tension, shows signs of irritation. Prior to 2 of the tasks, parents recorded what they expected their child's performance to be. (2) Ratings of Ss' behavior in task situations were obtained from their classroom teachers. The items on which teachers made their ratings pertained to social dependence, goal setting, attention, personal responsibility, and persistence. **Results:** (1) Parents of boys exhibited more signs of good mood and enthusiasm than parents of girls ($p < .05$). No main sex differences were found on any other measure. (2) Among low-debilitating-anxiety Ss, girls received more specific help than boys did ($p < .05$). (3) High-debilitating-anxiety girls received a relatively low frequency of positive-task-oriented reinforcements in comparison with other groups ($p < .05$). (4) There were no sex differences found in teachers' ratings.

Herriot, P. The comprehension of syntax. *Child Development*, 1968, *39*, 273–82.
  Subjects: $N = 1,176$; 5–9 yrs. **Measures:** Ss were initially presented with 4 cards. On each were line drawings of either a boy and a girl or weird creatures. After E uttered a passive or an active sentence, Ss were asked to select the card that best fit the sentence. The amount of semantic content was varied by substituting nonsense words into either none, some, or all of the content word spaces of the sentence frame. **Results:** No sex differences were found in sentence comprehension, as assessed by choice of cards.

Herriot, P. The comprehension of tense in young children. *Child Development*, 1969, *40*, 103–10.
  Subjects: $N = 24$; 36–48 mos. **Measures:** E showed Ss 3 toys, in moving or resting states. For each set of actions, E asked Ss questions about which toy would move, using various tenses. Ss responded to each question to indicate their understanding of the tense employed. **Results:** No sex differences.

Hertzig, M. E., Birch, M. G., Thomas, A., and Mendez, O. A. Class and ethnic differences in the responsiveness of preschool children to cognitive demands. *Monographs of the Society for Research in Child Development*, 1968, *33*, 117.
  Subjects: $N = 176$; 3 yrs (U.S., middle SES; Puerto Rican, low SES). **Measures:** Ss were given Form L-M of the Stanford-Binet. During the administration of the test, Ss' responses to E's demands for cognitive performance were classified into 2 categories: work (Ss attempted to do what was asked of them) and nonwork (Ss failed to perform the task presented). Work responses (both verbal and nonverbal) were further classified according to whether or not they were limited to the defined requirements of the task. Verbal nonwork responses were also classified into 4 categories: (1) negation; (2) motor substitution (task-irrelevant physical activity); (3) motor requests for aid; (4) passive behavior (e.g. sitting still, staring straight ahead). **Results:** (1) Among American Ss, girls expressed passively a greater proportion of their nonverbal, non-work responses than boys ($p < .05$). No sex differences were found in other response categories, or in the proportion of (a) demands initially responded to with a work response; (b) initial work responses followed by a non-work response; (c) initial nonwork responses followed by a work response. (2) In the Puerto Rican sample, girls had a higher proportion than boys of work responses, of demands initially responded to with a work response, and of passive, nonverbal, non-work responses ($p < .05$, $p < .05$, $p < .05$). Boys had a higher proportion than girls of initial work responses followed by a non-work response, and of nonverbal, non-work responses expressed as substitution ($p < .05$, $p < .001$). No other sex differences were found.

Hess, A. L., and Bradshaw, H. L. Positiveness of self-concept and ideal self as a function of age. *J. Genetic Psychology*, 1970, *117*, 57–67.
  Subjects: $N = 175$; 16–18, 18–20, 35–50, 55–60 yrs. **Measures:** Gough's Adjective Check List. **Results:** No sex differences were found in either self-concept or ideal self.

Hetherington, E. M., and Frankie, G. Effects of parental dominance, warmth, and conflict on imitation in children. *J. Personality & Social Psychology*, 1967, 6, 119–25.
   Subjects: $N = 160$; 4–6 yrs and parents. **Measures:** At the beginning of the study, interviews were conducted with Ss' parents. On the basis of their answers to questions concerning how they would handle problem situations involving their child, each parent was rated on a 6-point warmth-hostility scale. On the basis of their behavior during the interview, parents were classified as to whether the father or mother or neither was the more dominant figure. Ss then observed each of their parents perform a variety of behaviors. The frequency of Ss' subsequent imitative behavior was recorded. **Results:** (1) No main sex differences were found. (2) Boys imitated their fathers more than their mothers; girls imitated their mothers more than their fathers ($p < .01$). (3) In mother-dominant families, both sexes imitated their mothers more than their fathers. In father-dominant families, boys imitated their fathers more than girls did; girls imitated their mothers more than boys did. (4) Parents who were rated high on warmth were imitated by both sexes more than parents rated low in warmth. Girls imitated mothers high in warmth more than boys did; boys imitated mothers low in warmth more than girls did ($p < .05$).

Hicks, B. J., and Nicholson, R. W. Need-for-approval and peer presence in goal setting. *Perceptual & Motor Skills*, 1966, 23, 1336.
   Subjects: $N = 27$; 18–21 yrs (college). **Measures:** Before each of 5 throws in a dart game, Ss were given 1 of 3 choices of distances to shoot from (6 feet, 9 feet, or 14 feet). **Results:** No sex differences were found in Ss' choices.

Hicks, D. J. Effects of observer's sanctions and adult presence on imitative aggression. *Child Development*, 1968, 39, 303–9.
   Subjects: $N = 84$; 5–8 yrs. **Measures:** Ss were divided equally by sex into 4 experimental groups and 2 control groups. All Ss viewed a 5-minute film of a male adult model exhibiting aggressive behavior to toys. An adult male E in the room made positive or negative comments about the filmed model's actions (nocomments for the control group). The Ss went to an experimental room (half being accompanied by E), where they were presented with aggressive and nonaggressive toys; 2 judges scored aggressive and nonaggressive behaviors, imitative and nonimitative, for 15 minutes. **Results:** Boys performed more imitative aggression than girls ($p < .001$).

Hicks, R. A._ Reaney, T., and Hill, L. Effects of pupil size and facial angle on preference for photographs of a young woman. *Perceptual & Motor Skills*, 1967, 24, 388–90.
   Subjects: $N = 40$; 18–21 yrs (college). **Measures:** Ss rated photographs, in which pupil size and facial angle were manipulated. **Results:** Women preferred small pupil more than men did.

Hildebrandt, D. E., Feldman, S. E., and Ditrichs, R. A. Rules, models, and self-reinforcement in children. *J. Personality & Social Psychology*, 1973, 25, 1–5.
   Subjects: $N = 96$; 7–9 yrs. **Measures:** Ss' self-reinforcement was measured on 3 separate occasions. Ss were initially instructed to reward themselves under stringent or lenient conditions while playing a pre-programmed bowling game. After completing 1 game, Ss were twice exposed to either stringent or lenient self-reinforcing models. After each interruption, Ss played 1 game in the absence of the model. **Results:** No sex differences.

Hill, A. L., and Burke, D. Apparent visual size as a function of age, intelligence, and a surrounding frame of reference for normal and mentally retarded subjects. *Developmental Psychology*, 1971, 5, 349–56.
   Subjects: $N = 97$ (normal), 4–14 yrs (normal), 9–20 yrs (retarded). **Measures:** Ss were presented with 2 illuminated triangles in an otherwise completely dark room and asked to judge whether the comparison or the standard was larger. In the illusion condition, Ss were equally distant from both stimuli; the frame of reference surrounding the comparison triangle was twice the size of the standard's frame of reference. In the distance control condition, the frame of reference surrounding the comparison triangle was identical in size to the standard's. In the constancy control condition, the frame of reference was identical to the distance control condition, except that Ss were seated closer to the comparison than to the standard triangle. The illusion control condition was identical to the illusion condition, with 1 exception—the room lights were never turned off. **Results:** No sex differences.

Hill, D. L., and Walters, R. H. Interaction of sex of subject and dependency-training procedures in a social reinforcement study. *Merrill-Palmer Quarterly*, 1969, 15, 185–98.
   Subjects: $N = 120$; 5–7 yrs. **Measures:** Ss were randomly assigned to 1 of 6 conditions, each

involving 2 successive 15-minute periods of interaction with a female E. The sessions involved either consistent dependency reinforcement (DR), DR followed by solitary play (SP), DR followed by frustration (F), consistent SP, SP followed by DR, or SP followed by F. Following these treatments, Ss played a marble-dropping game with E. Ss' task was to place marbles into either of 2 holes. Ss were reinforced by E for dropping marbles into the "correct" hole. The degree of conditionability Ss displayed was noted. **Results:** No main effects of sex were found. Among Ss who experienced solitary play followed by frustration, boys conditioned to a greater extent than girls did ($p < .05$).

Hill, K. T. Social reinforcement as a function of test anxiety and success-failure experiences. *Child Development*, 1967, 38, 723–37.
 Subjects: $N = 64$; 7 yrs. **Measures:** On the basis of their scores on the Test Anxiety Scale for Children, the Lie Scale for Children, and the Defensiveness Scale for Children, Ss were divided by sex into high and low test anxiety groups. Ss first experienced either success on an easy puzzle or failure on an unsolvable one. Ss then performed a marble-sorting task, for which half the Ss were verbally reinforced. **Results:** No main sex differences were found in number of marbles sorted. Boys decreased in responding over the entire experimental period; girls increased in responding during the latter minutes of the task after exhibiting an initial decrease in response rate ($p < .05$).

Hill, K. T., and Dusek, J. B. Children's achievement expectations as a function of social reinforcement, sex of S and test anxiety. *Child Development*, 1969, 40, 547–57.
 Subjects: $N = 96$; 8, 9 yrs. **Measures:** Selection of Ss was based on scores on the Test Anxiety Scale for Children. Ss' pretraining session involved success, failure, or nonevaluative experiences. For the experimental task (angle-matching) Ss were shown contrived graphs of other children's performances, and their achievement expectation was obtained. Ss received either social reinforcement or no reinforcement. E also obtained post-test achievement expectation from S. **Results:** (1) Girls demonstrated a greater increase in achievement expectation than boys did ($p < .05$). (2) No sex differences were found in initial achievement expectation score.

Hill, K. T., and Moely, B. E. Social reinforcement as a function of task instructions, sex of S, age of S, and baseline performance. *J. Experimental Child Psychology*, 1969, 7, 153–65.
 Subjects: $N = 192$; 6, 7, 9, 10 yrs. **Measures:** Ss performed a marble-dropping task under test or game instructions. E was neutral or supportive. **Results:** (1) No sex differences were found in baseline scores. (2) Whereas older boys (9–10 yrs) showed little change in response rate following the first minute of play, older girls showed a decrease ($p < .05$). No sex difference was found among younger Ss.

Hill, K. T., and Sarason, S. B. The relation of test anxiety and defensiveness to test and school performance over the elementary-school years. *Monographs of the Society for Research in Child Development*, 1966, 31, no. 104.
 Subjects: $N = 323$; tested at 6, 8, 10 yrs. $N = 347$; tested at 9, 11 yrs. **Measures:** At each testing, Ss completed the Test Anxiety Scale for Children (TASC), the Lie Scale for Children (LSC), and the Defensiveness Scale for Children (DSC). **Results:** At ages 8, 10, and 11, girls had higher TASC scores than boys. At ages 8, 9, 10, and 11, boys obtained higher LSC and DSC scores than girls.

Hill, K. T., and Watts, G. H. Young children's performance on a two-choice task as a function of social reinforcement, base-line preference, and response strategy. *Developmental Psychology*, 1971, 4, 487–88.
 Subjects: $N = 48$; 4 yrs. **Measures:** After an initial 25-trial baseline period, Ss performed a 2-choice learning task. Selection of the choice less preferred during baseline was either socially reinforced or not. Response strategies and change in preference were assessed. **Results:** No sex differences.

Hill, S. D. Transfer in discrimination learning. *Child Development*, 1965, 36, 749–60.
 EXPERIMENT I: **Subjects:** $N = 54$; 4, 6 yrs. **Measures:** Ss received 2 kinds of training for an oddity problem (object discrimination, or experience with double and single objects as cues but no reinforcement). They were asked to "find the candy" that was hidden under the odd of 3 objects, 2 of which were identical. **Results:** No sex differences.
 EXPERIMENT II: **Subjects:** $N = 60$; 9, 12 yrs. **Measures:** Same as Experiment 1, except color and position cues were introduced. **Results:** No sex differences.

Hilton, I. Differences in the behavior of mothers toward first- and later-born children. *J. Personality & Social Psychology*, 1967, 7, 282–90.

Subjects: $N = 60$; 4 yrs and mothers. **Measures:** Mothers' behavior toward their children was recorded while the children attempted a series of puzzles; it was recorded again later after E had informed them the children had performed either extremely well or extremely poorly on the tasks. **Results:** No differences were found between mothers of boys and mothers of girls in frequency of initiating work on the puzzle, number of task-oriented suggestions, amount of direct help, number of supportive and critical statements, or number of overt expressions of love and/or support (hugs, kisses, etc.).

Hilton, I. R., Lambert, N. W., Murphy, M. J., Epstein, R., and Samsky, J. Three experiments on variations in the conditions of judgments. *Monographs of the Society for Research in Child Development*, 1969, 34.

EXPERIMENT I: **Subjects:** $N = 44$; 18–21 yrs (college). **Measures:** In 16 situations, Ss were asked to judge the likelihood that another person would choose one alternative rather than another (Social Expectation Scale). Each S was told whether each alternative harmed or benefited the chooser (0) and whether it harmed or benefited S. Each S made 3 judgments on each situation: how many people would choose a designated alternative (with only S and the chooser knowing), how many would make that choice privately, and how many would make that choice publicly. Ss' judgment of the likelihood of another's choice involved assessment of 3 motivations: benevolence (desire to help rather than to harm), self-interest (strength of valence to benefit oneself rather than harm oneself), and intensity of a person's desire for equal outcomes. **Results:** There were no overall sex differences in Ss' judgments of the contributions of benevolence, self-interest, and equality of outcome to others' decisions on choice situation made publicly or privately. Boys judged a benevolent choice and a self-interested choice to be far more likely in public than in private; girls did not.

EXPERIMENT II: **Subjects:** $N = 45$; 18–21 yrs (college). **Measures:** Same as Experiment I. Ss were also asked to decide how many boys and girls, respectively, would make particular choices. **Results:** No overall differences by sex of S or sex of "other" making choice, but boys showed no different expectations of boys and girls, whereas girls expected other girls to be less benevolent and more self-interested than boys were.

Hilton, T. L., and Berglund, G. W. Sex differences in mathematics achievement—a longitudinal study. *Educational Testing Service Research Bulletin*, unpublished, 1971.

Subjects: $N = 1,859$; tested at 10, 12, 14, 16 yrs (academic and nonacademic high school programs). **Measures:** The Sequential Test of Educational Progress (STEP) and the School and College Ability Test (SCAT) were given to 10-year-old Ss, who were tested again at ages 12, 14, and 16. The Background and Experience Questionnaire (BEQ) was also administered to Ss at ages 12, 14, and 16. **Results:** (1) On the STEP-Math, there were no sex differences among 10-year-old Ss. In the academic group, boys had higher scores than girls at ages 12, 14, and 16. In the nonacademic group, boys had higher scores than girls at age 16. (2) On the SCAT, academic boys scored higher than girls at age 16. In nonacademic group, girls scored higher than boys at age 10, but boys scored higher than girls at age 16. (3) In both groups, boys read scientific books and magazines more frequently than girls at ages 14 and 16. (The difference in magazine reading was not significant among 14-year-old academic Ss.) (4) More boys than girls found math courses interesting at ages 14 and 16 in the academic group and at age 16 in the nonacademic group. More girls than boys found math courses boring at age 16 in the academic group. (5) More boys than girls thought math courses would be useful in earning a living at ages 14 and 16 in the academic group, and at age 16 in the nonacademic group. (6) In both groups, more boys than girls talked about science with friends and parents at ages 14 and 16. (7) Among 14- and 16-year-old academic Ss, more mothers of boys than mothers of girls felt that a student should continue his education beyond high school. (8) Among 16-year-old academic Ss, more fathers of boys than fathers of girls felt that a student should continue education beyond high school.

Himmelfarb, S. Studies in the perception of ethnic group members: accuracy, response bias, and anti-Semitism. *J. Personality & Social Psychology*, 1966, 4, 347–55.

EXPERIMENT I: **Subjects:** $N = 58$; 18–21 yrs (non-Jewish college). **Measures:** Ss identified individuals in photographs as being either Jewish or non-Jewish. **Results:** No sex differences were found in accuracy scores. Ss were more accurate in identifying males than females as either Jewish or non-Jewish ($p < .01$).

EXPERIMENT II: **Subjects:** $N = 99$; 18–21 yrs (non-Jewish college). **Measures:** Photographs of non-Jewish and Jewish individuals were presented to Ss in pairs. Ss were asked to select either the Jewish or the non-Jewish individual in the pair. **Results:** No sex differences were found in accuracy scores. Ss were more accurate in judging the identity of male photographs than in judging the identity of female photographs.

Hochreich, D. J., and Rotler, J. B. Have college students become less trusting? *J. Personality & Social Psychology*, 1970, *15*, 211–14.
  Subjects: $N = 4,605$; 18–21 yrs (college). **Measures:** Interpersonal Trust Scale. **Results:** No sex differences were found in mean scores.

Hoemann, H. W. The development of communication skills in deaf and hearing children. *Child Development*, 1972, *43*, 990–1003.
  Subjects: $N = 80$; 8, 11 yrs (deaf, normal). **Measures:** Ss were required to communicate information to peers of the same hearing group. The 3 tasks were (1) describe a variety of pictured referents, (2) describe the referents from the receiver's perspective, and (3) explain the rules of a game. Response measures for the first task were a sending score based on the percentage of messages rated as adequate, a receiving score based on the percentage of messages that resulted in correct choices by the receiver, and an overall accuracy score. The perspective task was evaluated as to which perspective the sender took and whether he communicated this information. Performance on the game task was evaluated according to rules communicated. **Results:** No sex differences.

Hoffman, L. R., and Maier, M. R. Social factors influencing problem solving in women. *J. Personality & Social Psychology*, 1966, *4*, 382–90.
  Subjects: $N = 502$; 18–21 yrs (college). **Measures:** The following problem was given to Ss twice: "A man bought a horse for $60, sold it for $70, bought it back for $80, and then sold it for $90. How much money did the man make in the horse business?" Masculine and feminine versions of 8 reasoning problems were also administered. Men answered the problems in the presence of a male E. Women responded in the presence of either a male or a female E, who either did or did not attempt to motivate them to do well on the problems. **Results:** (1) On both administrations of the horse-trading problem, more men than women solved the problem correctly under a male E. No difference was found between the performance of men under a male E and women under a female E. (2) 8 reasoning problems: (a) Under a male E, men solved more of the masculine versions of the problems than women did; when mathematical aptitude was held constant (as measured by the quantitative section of either the Graduate Record Examinations or the American Council on Education Tests of Intelligence), there were no sex differences. (b) There were no sex differences on the feminine versions of the problems. (c) No difference was found between men's performance on the feminine problems and women's performance on the masculine problems. (d) Men had higher scores than women on the quantitative sections of the aptitude tests.

Hoffman, M. L., and Saltzstein, H. D. Parent discipline and the child's moral development. *J. Personality & Social Psychology*, 1967, *5*, 45–57 (and personal communication).
  Subjects: $N = 444$; 12 yrs (low, middle SES) and parents. **Measures:** Parents' disciplinary practices were assessed in individual interviews with 270 middle SES children, 174 lower SES children, 129 middle SES mothers, and 75 middle SES fathers. A measure of parents' affection for their child was obtained from rating scales completed by each child and parent. **Results:** (1) Middle SES Ss' reports: girls viewed their mothers and fathers as expressing more affection ($p < .01$, $p < .001$) and less power assertion ($p < .05$, $p < .01$) than boys. No sex differences were reported in mothers' or fathers' use of love withdrawal techniques. (2) Middle SES parents' reports: no differences were found between boys' and girls' mothers or fathers. (3) Lower SES Ss' reports: girls reported both parents as expressing more affection than boys did ($p < .01$). Girls viewed their fathers as using more induction than boys ($p < .01$). No other sex differences were found.

Hokanson, J. E., and Edelman, R. Effects of three social responses on vascular processes. *J. Personality & Social Psychology*, 1966, *3*, 442–47.
  Subjects: $N = 28$; 18–24 yrs. **Measures:** In response to being shocked by a same-sex confederate, Ss were free to perform either an aggressive (shock), a friendly, or an ignoring counterresponse. Systolic blood-pressure levels were recorded at 20-second intervals during most of the experiment. **Results:** (1) No differences were found between men and women in their use of the available responses. (2) For the first 2 20-second intervals after making a shock counterresponse, men had lower systolic blood-pressure levels than women ($p < .05$).

Hollander, E. P., and Marcia, J. E. Parental determinants of peer orientation and self-orientation among preadolescents. *Developmental Psychology*, 1970, *2*, 292–302.

Subjects: $N = 52$; 10 yrs. **Measures:** Ss were asked a series of direct and open-ended questions designed to assess their parents' peer orientation, differential parent power (i.e. whether their mother or father was dominant in matters pertaining to them), and sibling alliance. Ss were then presented with 6 problematic situations. These required Ss to choose between peer values on the one hand and either their own or their parents' values on the other. Of the 6 items, 3 required a self vs. peer choice, and 3 a parent vs. peer choice. In the analysis of the test results, self vs. peer-orientation and parent vs. peer-orientation scores were added together to yield a measure of total peer orientation. Finally, Ss rated all other same-sex children in their class on the following items: (a) this is a classmate who does things independently; (b) this is a classmate who gets other children to do things; (c) this is a classmate who goes along with what the other children are doing; (d) this is a classmate who does what grown-ups think is right; (e) this is a classmate who gets along with other children. **Results:** (1) No sex differences were found in parents' peer orientation or in the relationship between parents' and child's peer orientation. (2) A majority of members of both sexes saw their fathers as more dominant than their mothers; however, this tendency was more pronounced for boys, since girls indicated a greater number of mother-dominant families than boys did ($p < .05$). (3) Boys were more peer- vs. self-oriented than girls. Boys also achieved higher total peer-orientation scores. (4) Peer-oriented boys and self-oriented girls were seen as "getting other children to do things"; peer-oriented girls were seen as "not getting other children to do things" ($p < .025$). (5) Boys who claimed an older sibling as an ally and girls who did not were seen as "doing what grown-ups think is right" ($p < .025$).

Hollander, E. P., Julian, J. W., and Haaland, G. A. Conformity process and prior group support. *J. Personality & Social Psychology*, 1965, *2*, 852–58.

Subjects: $N = 112$; 18–21 yrs (college). **Measures:** Ss judged which of 3 lights went off first after being informed of the (inaccurate) judgments of same-sex others. The number of trials on which Ss conformed to the inaccurate group response was recorded. **Results:** Women conformed more often than men ($p < .01$).

Holloway, H. D. Reliability of the Children's Manifest Anxiety Scale at the rural third grade level. *J. Educational Psychology*, 1958, *49*, 193–96.

Subjects: $N = 121$; 8 yrs. **Measures:** Children's Manifest Anxiety Scale. **Results:** No sex differences.

Holstein, C. B. Moral change in early adolescence and middle age: a longitudinal study. Paper presented at the meetings of the Society for Research in Child Development. Philadelphia, March–April, 1973.

Subjects: $N = 53$; tested at 13, 16 yrs, and their parents. **Measures:** At both testings, Ss were given 5 of Kohlberg's Moral Judgment Dilemmas (situations I, III, IV, VII, and VIII). At the second testing, a liberalism questionnaire was administered to assess social-political attitudes. **Results:** (1) At 13 years of age, girls were modally stage 3, whereas boys were modally stage 2. By age 16, boys were modally stage 4, whereas girls were still modally stage 3. (2) At both testings, fathers were modally stage 4 or a mixture of 4 and 5 (with no use of stage 3 thinking). Mothers' scores reflected a combination of stage 3 and stage 4 thinking. (3) Females in both age groups exhibited more liberal attitudes than males on the liberalism questionnaire.

Hooper, F. H. Piaget's conservation tasks: the logical and developmental priority of identity conservation. *J. Experimental Child Psychology*, 1969, *8*, 234–49.

Subjects: $N = 108$; 6, 7, 8 yrs. **Measures:** Ss performed Piagetian tasks of identity and equivalence conservation. **Results:** Boys conserved more than girls did across all conditions and age levels.

Hopkins, K. D., and Bibelheimer, M. Five-year stability of intelligence quotients from language and non-language group tests. *Child Development*, 1971, *42*, 645–49.

Subjects: $N = 354$; tested at 8, 10, 12, 13 yrs. **Measures:** The California Test of Mental Maturity, language and nonlanguage tests. **Results:** No sex differences.

Horai, J., and Tedeschi, J. T. Effects of credibility and magnitude of punishment on compliance to threats. *J. Personality & Social Psychology*, 1969, *12*, 164–69.

Subjects: $N = 90$; 18–21 yrs (college). **Measures:** Ss played the Prisoner's Dilemma Game with a simulated partner (SP). Intermittently, the SP threatened Ss with a loss of points (5, 10, or 20) if Ss did not perform the cooperative response on the next trial. Ss were required to reply to each threat with 1 of 3 available messages: (1) I will make the cooperative choice on the next trial, (2) I will make the competitive choice on the next trial, or (3) I do not wish to reveal my intentions on the next trial. If noncompliance occurred, the threat was enforced or unenforced depending on the condition to which Ss were assigned. **Results:** (1) Using total number of threats sent to assess compliance (thereby satisfying the criterion of 10 unsuccessful threats per game), no main sex differences were found. (2) Using the delay of first testing the veracity of the SP's message as a secondary measure of compliance, no main sex differences were found. Men delayed testing longer than women in the intermediate-punishment condition, whereas women delayed testing longer than men in the severe-punishment condition ($p < .05$). (3) No sex differences were found in Ss' use of the 3 available messages. Men lied more frequently than women did ($p < .02$). (4) No sex differences were found in the proportion of cooperative choices.

Horner, M. S. Femininity and successful achievement: basic inconsistency. In Bardwick, J. M., Douvan, E., Horner, M. S., and Gutman, D. *Feminine Personality and Conflict.* Belmont, California: Brooks Cole Publishing Company, 1970, 45–74.
　　Subjects: $N = 178$; 18–19 yrs (college). **Measures:** Men were asked to write a story based on the cue "After first-term finals, John finds himself at the top of his medical school class." The cue was changed for women: "Anne" was substituted for "John." Ss' stories were scored for fear-of-success imagery. **Results:** More women than men wrote stories that were high in fear-of-success imagery ($p < .005$).

Horowitz, F. D. American and Uruguayan infants: reliabilities, maternal drug histories, and population differences. Paper presented at the Society for Research in Child Development Conference, 1973 (and personal communication).
　　Subjects: $N = 44$; newborns (U.S. sample only). **Measures:** Observations were made of Ss for the first 10 days of life and again at 4 weeks of age. The Brazelton Neonatal Scale was also administered. **Results:** No sex differences were found in response decrements to light, rattle, bell, and pinprick; orientation to inanimate and animate visual and auditory stimuli; alertness; general tonus; motor maturity; pull-to-sit; cuddliness; defensive movements; consolability; peak of excitement; rapidity of build-up; irritability; activity level; tremulousness, startle responses; lability of skin color; lability of state; self-quieting activity; hand-mouth facility; number of smiles.

Horowitz, F. D., and Armentrout, J. Discrimination-learning, manifest anxiety, and effects of reinforcement. *Child Development*, 1965, *36*, 731–48.
　　Subjects: $N = 48$; 9–11 yrs. **Measures:** Ss were designated high or low anxiety on the Children's Manifest Anxiety Scale. Ss were given either a simultaneous discrimination task in which the object was to press a button every time a certain colored light appeared regardless of its position, or a successive discrimination task in which all these positions showed the same color, and Ss had to press a different button for every color. Ss were reinforced for correct responses by either a buzzer or a verbal "right." **Results:** No sex differences.

Horowitz, L. M., Lampel, A. K., and Takansishi, R. N. The child's memory for unitized scenes. *J. Experimental Child Psychology*, 1969, *8*, 375–88.
　　EXPERIMENT I: **Subjects:** $N = 72$; 3–5 yrs. **Measures:** Ss were initially shown a display of pictures of objects. E hid the items after Ss named them; 1 item was then removed and the remaining ones exposed. Ss' task was to name the missing object. **Results:** No sex differences.
　　EXPERIMENT II: **Subjects:** $N = 12$; 3 yrs. **Measures:** Same as Experiment I, with minor procedural changes. **Results:** No sex differences.
　　EXPERIMENT III: **Subjects:** $N = 12$; 3–5 yrs. **Measures:** Ss were shown the displays used in Experiment II and asked to describe each. Ss' descriptions were scored for (1) total number of words and (2) total number of verbs and prepositions. **Results:** No sex differences.
　　EXPERIMENT IV: **Subjects:** $N = 24$; 3–5 yrs. **Measures:** Same as Experiment II, except that Ss were asked to name each item before E hid it. **Results:** No sex differences.

Hoving, K. L., and Choi, K. Some necessary conditions for producing reinstatement effects in children. *Developmental Psychology*, 1972, 7, 214–17.
　　Subjects: $N = 40$; 6–8 yrs. **Measures:** Ss learned 10 picture pairs, and 4 weeks later received exposure to either stimulus items only, response items only, stimulus items paired with response items, original 10 stimulus items plus 10 new items, or no treatment; 8 weeks after initial learning, the same task was relearned. **Results:** No sex differences.

Hoving, K. L., Coates, L. Bertucci, M., Riccio, D. C. Reinstatement effects in children. *Developmental Psychology,* 1972, *6,* 426–29.

> **Subjects:** $N = 72$; 5–11 yrs. **Measures:** Two-thirds of the Ss in each age group learned a paired-associates task; 8 weeks later they relearned (reinstated) the same task. Pairs were repeated in a story 4 weeks after the initial learning for these reinstatement groups. One-third of the Ss received only reinstatement training (story, but no initial learning), followed 4 weeks later by formal learning of the pairs. **Results:** No sex differences.

Hurley, J. R., and Hohn, R. L. Shifts in child rearing attitudes linked with parenthood and occupation. *Developmental Psychology,* 1971, *4,* 324–28.

> **Subjects:** $N = 75$; 24–27 yrs (retested 6 years after original testing as undergraduates). **Measures:** Ss were retested on a child-rearing attitude measure consisting of items relating to manifest rejection (tendency to assume negative and punitive stance toward children), overprotection (pervasive overconcern), and achievement pressure (variety of ways in which children might be pushed toward acquisition of social skills). **Results:** No sex differences.

Hutt, C. Curiosity in young children. *Science Journal,* 1970, *6,* 68–71.

> **Subjects:** $N = 59$; preschool. **Measures:** On 6 different occasions, Ss were individually exposed to a novel toy and 5 familiar toys. The novel toy was a rectangular metal box with a lever mounted on the top. Pushing the lever in different directions sounded a bell or buzzer, lit up lights, or had no effect. Each S's behavior was cine-recorded for later analysis. **Results:** (1) More girls than boys failed to explore in the presence of the novel toy. (2) More boys than girls engaged in creative or inventive play with the new toy (creative play was defined as use of the toy in an unusual or unconventional manner for longer than 20 seconds). (3) Boys and girls did not differ in number of manipulations of the novel toy on the first day.

Immergluck, L., and Mearini, M. C. Age and sex differences in response to embedded figures and reversible figures. *J. Experimental Child Psychology,* 1969, *8,* 210–21.

> **Subjects:** $N = 120$; 9, 11, 13 yrs (Italian). **Measures:** Embedded Figures and Reversible Figures tasks. **Results:** (1) Among 9-year-old Ss, girls disembedded better than boys did. There were no sex differences at ages 11 and 13. (2) Among 9-year-old Ss, boys gave more reversal responses on the Reversible Figures test than girls did. There were no sex differences at ages 11 and 13. (3) Rate of reversal responses increased with age for girls, but not for boys.

Insko, C. Verbal reinforcement of attitude. *J. Personality & Social Psychology,* 1965, *2,* 621–23.

> **Subjects:** $N = 70$; 18–21 yrs (college). **Measures:** Ss were contacted by telephone and either positively or negatively reinforced for agreement or disagreement with a series of opinion statements relating to the creation of a special week. One week later, Ss answered a questionnaire assessing Ss' attitudes toward the creation of the special week. **Results:** No sex differences.

Insko, C. A., and Cialdini, R. B. A test of three interpretations of attitudinal verbal reinforcement. *J. Personality & Social Psychology,* 1969, *12,* 333–41.

> **Subjects:** $N = 152$; 18–21 yrs (college). **Measures:** Ss were contacted over the telephone and asked to either "strongly agree," "agree," "disagree," or "strongly disagree" with each of a series of 12 opinion statements regarding pay TV. Ss were reinforced for either pro or con statements. **Results:** No sex differences.

Insko, C. A., Thompson, V. C., Stroebe, W., Shaud, K. F., Pinner, B. E., and Layton, B. D. Implied evaluation and the similarity-attraction effect. *J. Personality & Social Psychology,* 1973, *25,* 297–308.

> **Subjects:** $N = 300$; 18–21 yrs (college). **Measures:** After examining an attitude scale completed by a same-sex or opposite-sex stranger, Ss completed the Interpersonal Judgment Scale. Liking the stranger and preference for the stranger as a co-worker were measured. Ss also provided answers to the following questions: "How rewarding would it be for you to interact with this person?" and "How much do you think this person is like you?" **Results:** No sex-of-subject effects were found. Ss preferred women as co-workers and anticipated more future rewards from interactions with female than with male strangers.

Ireton, H., Thwing, E., and Gravem, H. Infant mental development and neurological status, family socioeconomic status, and intelligence at age four. *Child Development,* 1970, *41,* 937–45.

> **Subjects:** $N = 536$; 8 mos. **Measures:** Bayley Mental Scale. **Results:** No sex differences.

Irwin, D. M., and Moore, S. G. The young child's understanding of social justice. *Developmental Psychology*, 1971, 5, 406–10.

Subjects: $N = 65$; 3–5 yrs. Measures: Ss were asked to choose just or unjust endings for 6 stories describing accidental and intentional misdeeds, 6 involving apology and restitution, and 6 involving situations in which 1 character was guilty of a transgression and another was innocent. Results: No sex differences were found in the number of times Ss chose just endings.

Irwin, M., Tripodi, T., and Bieri, J. Affective stimulus value and cognitive complexity. *J. Personality & Social Psychology*, 1967, 5, 444–48.

EXPERIMENT I: Subjects: $N = 115$; 18–21 yrs (college). Measures: Ss rated 4 liked, 4 neutral, and 4 disliked housemates on each of 10 construct dimensions (e.g. outward-decisive, etc.). Ss' responses were scored for the degree to which they differentiated among liked, disliked, and neutral others. Results: Women differentiated among neutral and disliked others more than men did ($p < .05$).

EXPERIMENT II: Subjects: $N = 80$; 18–21 yrs (college). Measures: Ss listed 2 persons of each sex they liked and 2 persons of each sex they disliked. Ss then rated each person on a different construct dimension. Ss' ratings were again scored for the degree to which they differentiated among liked and disliked others. Results: Women differentiated more among disliked others than men did ($p < .01$).

Isen, A. M. Success, failure, attention, and reaction to others: the warm glow of success. *J. Personality & Social Psychology*, 1970, 15, 294–301.

Subjects: $N = 30$; 18–21 yrs (college). Measures: After either succeeding or failing on a series of tasks, Ss were exposed to a female confederate. Performance measures were helpfulness and attentiveness to the confederate. Helping was measured by whether Ss offered to help the confederate with the armload of items she was carrying, whether they picked up the book she had dropped, and whether they offered to open a door for her. Attentiveness was measured by Ss' recall and recognition of confederate's behavior. Results: No sex differences.

Iverson, M. A., and Schwab, H. G. Ethnocentric dogmatism and binocular fusion of sexually and racially discrepant stimuli. *J. Personality & Social Psychology*, 1967, 7, 73–81.

Subjects: $N = 80$; 18–21 yrs (college). Measures: Ss (previously classified as either high or low in ethnocentric dogmatism based on their scores on the Rokeach's Dogmatism Scale E and the California Ethnocentrism Scale) viewed 3 sets of facial sketches by means of a stereoscope. The sets were pairs of (a) male with mustache–male with glasses, (b) white male–white female, and (c) black male–white male faces. Ss then selected from 3 comparison sketches the stimulus they had just viewed in the stereoscope; 2 of the comparison pictures were the same as the stereoscopic targets, while the third was a composite. Selection of the composite was recorded as an instance of binocular fusion. Results: (1) No sex differences were found in the frequency of fusion judgments. (2) When the data for each set of faces was analyzed separately, high ethnocentric-dogmatic women were found to be less inclined than other groups to select the comparison picture that fused the pair of faces in Set A (male with mustache–male with glasses). No sex differences were found in the other two sets.

Iwawaki, S., Sumida, K., Okuno, S., and Cowen, E. L. Manifest anxiety in Japanese, French, and United States children. *Child Development*, 1967, 38, 713–22.

Subjects: $N = 155$; 9 yrs (Japanese). Measures: Children's Manifest Anxiety Scale. Results: No sex differences were found on the anxiety scale. Girls scored higher than boys on the lie scale.

Jacklin, C. N., Maccoby, E. E., and Dick, A. E. Barrier behavior and toy preference: sex differences (and their absence) in the year-old child. *Child Development*, 1973, 44, 196–200.

EXPERIMENT I: Subjects: $N = 40$; 13–14 mos. Measures: In the first phase of the study, the mother placed her child on the floor either next to her chair or 2.4 meters away. Across the room were 6 toys, 3 masculine (2 robots and a Playskool workbench) and 3 feminine (2 stuffed animals and a ferris wheel decorated with pink ribbons). After playing for 5 minutes, S was brought back to his initial starting place and exposed to a loud, angry male voice (beginning of Phase II). After the fear stimulus was terminated, the child was observed for 4½ minutes. During the first 2 phases, the percentage of time S spent with each of the toys, the amount of sustained play he engaged in, and the number of toy changes he exhibited were recorded. In Phase III, each mother interacted with her child for 3 minutes. The number of times the child offered each of the toys to his mother and the number of times the mother offered each of the toys to her child were counted. In Phase IV, the child was placed behind 1 of 2 barriers located at the far corners of the room. Location (center, edge), activity (push-pull, manipulate, cling), and crying at barrier were recorded. **Results:** (1) Boys spent a greater percentage of their time with the robots than girls did ($p < .05$). No sex differences were found in percentage of time Ss spent with the cuddly or activity toys. (2) Girls who were placed near their mothers cried more than boys ($p < .05$); no sex difference was found in the far condition. (3) All other sex differences were nonsignificant.

EXPERIMENT II: **Subjects:** $N = 40$; 13–14 mos. **Measures:** Procedures were identical to the first 2 phases of Experiment I. **Results:** Boys played with the robots more than girls did ($p < .01$).

Jackson, J. P. Development of visual and tactual processing of sequentially presented shapes. *Developmental Psychology*, 1973, 8, 46–50.
> **Subjects:** $N = 120$; 6, 8, 10 yrs. **Measures:** Ss were asked to recognize shapes under cross-modal (visual to tactual, tactual to visual) or intramodal (visual to visual, or tactual to tactual) conditions. **Results:** No sex differences.

Jacobs, P. I., and Vandeventer, M. The learning and transfer of double-classification skills: a replication and extension. *J. Experimental Child Psychology*, 1971, *12*, 240–57.
> **Subjects:** $N = 61$; 6 yrs. **Measures:** Ss performed 57 double-classification tasks involving determinations of which of 4 stimuli belonged in the empty cell of 2×2 or 3×3 matrices. The 57 matrices were grouped into 12 sets based on the relationships involved. Within each set, color and shape were each paired with 1 of 9 basic relations: size, shading, elements of a set, number series, addition, added element, reversal, flip-over, and movement in a plane. **Results:** No sex differences.

Jacobson, L. I., Berger, S. E., and Millham, J. Self-esteem, sex differences, and the tendency to cheat. *Proceedings* of the 77th Annual Convention of the American Psychological Association, 1969, *4*, 353–54.
> **Subjects:** $N = 276$; 18–21 yrs (college). **Measures:** Before taking a modified version of the WAIS Digit Symbol subtest, Ss answered the following questions: "How many squares do you expect to complete?" (expectancy of success) and "How many squares would you like to complete?" (level of aspiration). Self-esteem was defined as the discrepancy between level of aspiration and expectancy of success. **Results:** No sex differences.

Jacobson, L. I., Berger, S. E., and Millham, J. Individual differences in cheating during a temptation period when confronting failure. *J. Personality & Social Psychology*, 1970, *15*, 48–56.
> **Subjects:** $N = 276$; 18–21 yrs (college). **Measures:** After being given an unrealistically high estimate of the average college student's score, Ss were presented with a modified version of the Digit Symbol test of the WAIS, and were either given or not given an opportunity to cheat. Ss also completed the Marlowe-Crown Social Desirability Scale and a self-satisfaction measure. Self-satisfaction was defined as the discrepancy between Ss' level of aspiration and Ss' expectancy of success on the Digit Symbol test. **Results:** (1) Among those Ss who were not given an opportunity to cheat, no sex differences were found in number of squares completed. Among those Ss who were given an opportunity to cheat, women completed more squares than men did ($p < .03$). However, women in the temptation condition did not complete significantly more squares than women in the control condition. (2) Men demonstrated a greater expectancy of success ($p < .001$) and a greater level of aspiration ($p < .031$) than women did. No sex differences were found in self-satisfaction scores.

Jacobson, L. I., Berger, S. E., Bergman, R. L., Millham, J., and Greeson, L. E. Effects of age, sex, systematic conceptual learning sets, and programmed social interaction on the intellectual and conceptual development of preschool children from poverty backgrounds. *Child Development*, 1971, *42*, 1399–1415.
> **Subjects:** $N = 46$; 3–4 yrs (low SES). **Measures:** Ss were trained on the Conceptual Development Program developed by the authors. The acquisition conditions were reinforcement, modeling, and feedback. The Stanford-Binet Intelligence Scale was administered to all Ss.

Results: For the first 5 concept problems, boys required fewer trial blocks to concept attainment than girls did. By the sixth problem, there were no sex differences.

James, S. L., and Miller, J. F. Children's awareness of semantic constraints in sentences. *Child Development*, 1973, *44*, 69–76.
    Subjects: $N = 32$; 4–5, 6–7 yrs. **Measures:** Ss were presented with meaningful and anomalous sentences associated with pictures of an "okay" lady and a "silly" lady. Ss were asked to identify sentences as meaningful or anomalous, to explain their choices, and to convert the sentence into whatever type it was not. **Results:** No sex differences.

Jensen, L., and Hughston, K. The effect of training children to make moral judgments that are independent of sanctions. *Developmental Psychology*, 1971, *5*, 367 (brief report).
    Subjects: $N = 72$; 4–5 yrs. **Measures:** Ss heard each 5 stories involving good and bad acts followed by punishment. Ss were then randomly assigned to either a discussion group (told a story of an act followed by punishment, discussed the goodness or badness of the act, and why sanctions occurred), a verbal discrimination group (same story, with reward given if Ss judged act correctly, ignoring sanction), or a control group (question and answer session unrelated to sanctions). Ss were post-tested 3–8 days later on judgments of situations. **Results:** No sex differences.

Jensen, L., and Rytting, M. Effects of information and relatedness on children's belief in imminent justice. *Developmental Psychology*, 1972, *7*, 93–97.
    Subjects: $N = 25$; 7 yrs. **Measures:** E told each S 6 stories, 2 in which an accident resulted directly from a misdeed, 2 in which an accident was in some way related to a misdeed, and 2 in which an accident was completely unrelated to a misdeed. E asked S, "Why did this happen?" "Would it have happened if the child had been naughty?" "Do you know if the child was naughty?" and whether the S had ever experienced the particular situation. **Results:** No sex differences.

Jersild, A. T., and Holmes, F. B. Children's fears. *Child Development Monographs*, 1935, *20*.
    EXPERIMENT I: **Subjects:** $N = 136$; 0–8 yrs. **Measures:** For a period of 21 days, parents were asked to record instances in which their child exhibited fear. **Results:** No sex differences were found in the average number of fears Ss displayed or in the nature of the situations that aroused fear in them.
    EXPERIMENT II: **Subjects:** $N = 398$; 5–12 yrs. **Measures:** Ss were asked in private interviews to describe their fears. **Results:** No sex differences.
    EXPERIMENT III: **Subjects:** $N = 105$; 2–5 yrs. **Measures:** Ss' reactions to 8 potentially fearful experimental situations were recorded. To obtain a different measure of fearfulness, Ss' nursery school teachers were asked to rate each child on a 20-point fear scale. **Results:** (1) Whereas no sex differences were found in the number of Ss who showed fear in response to the situations, girls exhibited more intense fear than boys. (2) No sex differences were found in teachers' ratings.

Jeruchimowicz, R., Costello, J., and Bagur, J. S. Knowledge of action and object words: a comparison of lower and middle class Negro preschoolers. *Child Development*, 1971, *42*, 455–64.
    Subjects: $N = 79$; 4 yrs (black, low and middle SES). **Measures:** Ss completed the Peabody Picture Vocabulary Test (Form A) and the Expressive Language task (verbal description of pictures). Responses were scored for action and object words, action and object phrases, number of words, and number of phrases. **Results:** No sex differences.

Johnson, C. D., and Gormly, J. Academic cheating: the contribution of sex, personality, and situational variables. *Developmental Psychology*, 1972, *6*, 320–25.
    Subjects: $N = 113$; 10 yrs. **Measures:** After completing a math test, Ss were allowed to correct their own papers. 2 techniques were used to determine the frequency with which Ss changed their initial answers to agree with the correct ones. Measures of n Ach and internal-external control (as assessed by the Intellectual Achievement Responsibility Questionnaire) were also obtained. **Results:** (1) No main sex differences were found in the number of Ss who cheated in n Ach, IAR, or exam scores. Girls who cheated had lower achievement motivation than

girls who did not cheat; the opposite relationship was found for boys ($p < .05$). Girls who cheated had higher IAR scores than girls who did not; a similar but not nearly so strong a relationship was found for boys ($p < .05$). (2) Girls had higher course grades than boys did ($p < .05$).

Johnson, P. J., and White, R. M., Jr. Concept of dimensionality and reversal shift performance in children. *J. Experimental Child Psychology*, 1967, 5, 223–27.
Subjects: $N = 30$; 5–7 yrs. **Measures:** Ss were presented with 6 squares varying only in brightness. Their task was to arrange the 6 items from brightest to least bright. **Results:** No sex differences.

Jones, E. E., Rock, L., Shaver, K. G., Goethals, G. R., and Ward, L. M. Pattern of performance and ability attribution: an unexpected primacy effect. *J. Personality & Social Psychology*, 1968, 10, 317–40.
Subjects: $N = 140$; 18–21 yrs (college). **Measures:** Ss were informed of a female stimulus person's (SP) performance on an initial set of 30 problems. Ss then observed a film of the SP in the act of solving a second set of problems. Before the SP attempted each problem, Ss predicted whether she would succeed or fail. Afterward, Ss rated her intelligence and recalled her performance on the initial set of problems. **Results:** (1) Men predicted a lower level of SP performance than women did ($p < .01$). (2) No sex differences were found in Ss' intelligence ratings or in Ss' recall of the SP's performance.

Jones, S. E., and Aiello, J. R. Proxemic behavior of black and white first-, third-, and fifth-grade children. *J. Personality & Social Psychology*, 1973, 25, 21–27.
Subjects: $N = 192$; 6, 8, 10 yrs (white, black). **Measures:** Observations were made of the interpersonal distance and axis orientation of same-sex pairs of children in conversation. **Results:** (1) No sex differences were found in interpersonal distance. (2) Boys were less direct in axis orientation than girls ($p < .005$).

Jones, S. J. Children's two-choice learning of predominantly alternating and repeating sequences. *J. Experimental Child Psychology*, 1970, 10, 344–62.
Subjects: $N = 122$; 3–5 yrs. **Measures:** Ss guessed which of 2 lights would come on for 100 acquisition and 100 transfer trials. During acquisition, repetition probability was set at .10 for half Ss, and at .90 for the other half. During the transfer trials, repetition probabilities were reversed for half of Ss in both probability groups. **Results:** (1) Boys made more response-repetition responses than girls did during acquisition and transfer, i.e. made the same prediction as was made on the preceding trial, regardless of outcome. (2) There were no sex differences in even-repetition responses during acquisition or transfer, i.e. making the same prediction as the preceding prediction, based on a successful preceding outcome.

Jones, S. J., and Moss, H. A. Age, state, and maternal behavior associated with infant vocalizations. *Child Development*, 1971, 42, 1039–51.
Subjects: $N = 28$; tested at 2 wks, 3 mos. **Measures:** Ss were observed in their home on 4 separate days, 2 days at the earlier testing and 2 at the later. The percentage of time infants vocalized in each of 5 states (active awake, passive awake, drowsy, active sleep, and passive sleep) was recorded. During each of the 2 awake states, measures were also taken of percentage of vocalizations in mother's presence and in her absence. **Results:** No sex differences.

Jones-Molfese, V. J. Individual differences in neonatal preferences for planometric and stereometric visual patterns. *Child Development*, 1972, 43, 1289–96.
Subjects: $N = 40$; 7–48 hrs. **Measures:** Ss viewed planometric and stereometric black squares against a white background. The stimuli were presented in pairs, within each dimensional set, for 30 seconds each. Fixation time was the measure of stimulus preference. **Results:** No sex differences.

Jourard, S. M., and Friedman, R. Experimenter-subject "distance" and self-disclosure. *J. Personality & Social Psychology*, 1970, 15, 278–82.
Experiment I: Subjects: $N = 48$; 18–21 yrs (college). **Measures:** Ss disclosed personal information to a male E who either (a) avoided eye-contact or (b) offered continuous eye-contact. Ss in a third condition spoke into a tape recorder, with E out of the room. Average time spent in self-disclosure was recorded. **Results:** (1) When E was out of the room, no sex differences were found in time spent in self-disclosure. (2) When E was present, men spent more time in self-disclosure than women did.
Experiment II: Subjects: $N = 64$; 18–21 yrs (college). **Measures:** In individual inter-

views, Ss were asked to discuss 4 intimate and 4 nonintimate topics. "Distance" between E (male) and subjects varied from E being present but silent, to E making physical contact with and making himself known to Ss. Time spent talking on each of the 8 topics was recorded. Before and after being interviewed, Ss gave their impressions of E on a 40-trait questionnaire. **Results:** No sex differences.

Julian, J. W., Regula, C. R., and Hollander, E. P. Effects of prior agreement by others on task confidence and conformity. *J. Personality & Social Psychology*, 1968, 9, 171–78.
> **Subjects:** $N = 240$; 18–21 yrs (college). **Measures:** Ss judged which of 3 lights went off first. The response measure was the number of trials Ss conformed to the erroneous judgments of 4 same-sex others (phase 2) after previously experiencing agreement on an initial set of trials with either 100%, 75%, 50%, 25%, or 0% of the group (phase 1). **Results:** (1) Women conformed more often than men did ($p < .01$). (2) Men had more confidence in their performance than women did ($p < .01$). No sex differences were found in Ss' perceptions of the difficulty of the task (which had been assessed by a questionnaire administered between phase 1 and phase 2).

Kaess, D. W. Measures of form constancy: developmental trends. *Developmental Psychology*, 1971a, 4, 296 (brief report).
> **Subjects:** $N = 54$; 6, 8, 10 yrs. **Measures:** Ss viewed sandpaper forms 105 mm high and either 145, 160, or 176 mm wide from a distance of 5 feet. Forms varied by angle of orientation. Ss were required to identify the objective shape of the form by pressing 1 of 3 buttons. **Results:** No sex differences.

Kaess, D. W. Methodological study of form constancy development. *J. Experimental Child Psychology*, 1971b, 12, 27–34.
> **Subjects:** $N = 80$; 7, 9, 11, 18 yrs. **Measures:** Ss compared widths of 3 rectangular turned forms with a comparison series of 19 similar forms. **Results:** No sex differences.

Kagan, J. Individual differences in the resolution of response uncertainty. *J. Personality & Social Psychology*, 1965, 2, 154–60.
> **Subjects:** $N = 113$; 7–8 yrs. **Measures:** Incongruous pictures were tachistoscopically presented to Ss at successively increasing exposure times. After each exposure, Ss were asked to describe the picture in detail. When Ss accurately described a picture for 3 consecutive trials, the series was terminated. Measures were taken of the latency from the presentation of the stimulus to Ss' first significant verbalization. **Results:** No sex differences.

Kagan, J. On the meaning of behavior: illustrations from the infant. *Child Development*, 1969, 40, 1121–34.
> **Subject:** $N = 150$; tested at 4, 8, 13 mos. **Measures:** At each testing, Ss were exposed to 4 3-dimensional lady faces, the features of which were either normal, scrambled, partially missing, or totally absent. The length of time Ss vocalized to each of the stimuli was recorded. At 8 months, Ss were exposed to a set of 4 taped stimuli read by a male voice. Measures were taken of cardiac deceleration vocalization rate and vocalization time. **Results:** No sex differences.

Kagan, J. *Change and continuity in infancy.* New York: Wiley, 1971 (and personal communication).
> **Subjects:** $N = 180$; tested at 4, 8, 13, 27, 48 mos (low, middle SES). **Measures:** At age 4 months, Ss were presented with 16 achromatic slides of human faces (half were photographs, half were schematic representations) and 4 3-dimensional clay faces painted flesh color. The features of the 2-D faces were either normal or scrambled; the features of the 3-D faces were either normal, scrambled, or missing. Fixation time, vocalization time, frequency of smiling, time spent crying, and heart rate were recorded; 66 of the infants were also scored for gross motor activity. During home visits, mothers' behavior toward their children was recorded. At age 8 months, identical procedures were followed, with the following 2 additions: (1) Ss heard a tape recording of 4 different recitations read with either high or low inflection by a male voice. Duration or orientation to the speaker, vocalization time, frequency of smiling, time spent crying, and heart rate were recorded. (2) Ss and their mothers were taken to a room marked off into squares. Mothers were seated in a corner of the room while the infants were placed in the middle of a set of toys. Measures were taken of the number of squares Ss traversed and the number of times they changed activities (put down one toy, picked up another). At the end of the session, mothers left the room for 2 minutes. The number of infants of each sex who cried or fretted during this period was recorded. When the infants were

13 months old, the 3-dimensional clay faces and the 4 recitations were again presented. The infants were also exposed to 7 12-inch-high male dolls. During the administration of these visual and auditory stimuli, the vocalization time, frequency of crying, time spent smiling, heart rate, and fixation time (visual episodes only) were recorded. Ss were also rated for motor activity, general alertness, positive and negative affect, and speed of habituation. The procedures at 13 months also included assessment of Ss' free-play behavior in the room marked off into squares. At age 27 months, mothers and infants were brought to a large room decorated as a living room. In the middle of the room were 10 toys arranged on a rug. Mothers were asked to remain on the couch, while infants were allowed to roam about freely. Measures were taken of locomotor movement (number of squares traversed in each of 7 5-minute time periods), amount of time spent in physical contact with mother, number of times each toy was played with, duration of each play activity, frequency of smiling, and number of verbalizations. Ss were then shown a series of colored slides accompanied by narration; 10 of the 23 slides contained discrepant information (e.g. a man wearing a dress). Fixation time, number of vocalizations, frequency of smiling, heart rate, number of times Ss turned toward their mothers and toward the examiner were recorded. Ss were then presented with 2 types of perceptual problems. The first required Ss to pick from among a set of pictures the one that was identical to a standard. The second was an embedded figures test. Measures were taken of the accuracy of Ss' responses, the length of time Ss looked at the stimulus before making their initial response, the length of time Ss looked at each stimulus before answering, the occurrence of any smiling or laughing responses, and the degree of cardiac deceleration to the first scanning of the stimulus. After Ss completed the embedded figures task, a discrimination-learning problem was administered. On each trial Ss had to decide whether to touch a red or yellow light. Ss were rewarded with an M & M only when they touched the yellow light. When Ss made 5 correct responses in succession, a series of conflict trials was initiated. These involved exposure to either a pair of red lights or a pair of yellow lights. On the final conflict trial, 2 yellow and 2 red lights were presented simultaneously, 1 light of each color on each side. The accuracy of Ss' responses and the duration of their fixations to the lights were recorded. The final measure at 27 months involved the presentation of the 3-dimensional clay faces and 4 of the male dolls. Fixation time, frequency of smiling, number of vocalizations, and heart rates were recorded. Within 2 weeks after the testing, 2 home visits were made, each of which lasted approximately 6 hours. All sequences involving a child's violation of a socialization standard set by his mother or classified a priori by the experimenters as a socialization standard were recorded, as were the mother's reactions to the child's counterreactions. During 1 of the 2 home visits, a vocabulary-recognition test and a vocabulary-naming test were administered. At 4 years of age, 30 of the Ss were given 3 different memory tasks. The first 2 tested their ability to remember pictures they had seen. The third required Ss to imitate pointing sequences demonstrated by E. **Results:** (1) At age 4 months, upper-middle-class mothers issued more distinct vocalizations to their daughters than to their sons. No sex differences were found in amount of physical affection or number of general vocalizations received. (2) At age 13 months, boys were more likely than girls to become quiet when the stimuli appeared. (3) During the free-play observation period at 27 months, girls spent more time in physical contact with their mothers than boys did (no test of significance reported). (4) During the 2 home visits, mothers were more likely to reprimand or prohibit their sons than their daughters (no test of significance reported). (5) Interviews with mothers at 27 months revealed that more girls than boys owned dolls, and more boys than girls owned guns. Sex differences in toy preference were reported.

Kagan, J., and Lemkin, J. Form, color and size in children's conceptual behavior. *Child Development*, 1961, *32*, 25–28.
   Subjects: $N = 69$; 3–8 yrs. **Measures:** Ss paired geometric stimuli that differed in form, color, or size. **Results:** Among older Ss, boys were more likely than girls to use color as a basis for similarity ($p < .05$).

Kagan, J., and Lewis, M. Studies of attention in the human infant. *Merrill-Palmer Quarterly*, 1965, *11*, 95–137.
   Experiment I: Subjects: $N = 32$; 6 mos. **Measures:** Ss were presented with: (a) filmed pictures of faces and designs (each picture was presented for 12 seconds, 5 times in 5 different orders), (b) 3 patterns of blinking lights (each pattern was presented for 30 seconds, 4 times in 4 different orders), (c) auditory stimuli consisting of an intermittent tone, modern jazz, and 3 human voices (a male, a female, and S's mother), each reading the same paragraph (each of the 5 stimuli was presented for 30 seconds 4 times in 4 different orders). Response mea-

sures for the visual episodes were fixation time (the total time during which Ss oriented their eyes toward the visual arrays), number of arm movements, frequency of vocalization, and cardiac deceleration (assessed by subtracting the heart rate during the rest period preceding each stimulation from the heart rate during the stimulation period). Response measures for the auditory episode were number of arm movements, frequency of vocalization, and cardiac deceleration. **Results:** (1) Film episode: (a) No sex differences were found in fixation time when all 5 trials were considered. When only the first 3 trials were considered, girls had longer fixation times than boys did ($p < .05$). (b) No sex differences were found in arm movements, frequency of vocalization, or cardiac deceleration. (2) Blinking lights episode: (a) No sex differences were found in fixation time, arm movements, or cardiac deceleration. (b) Boys emitted more vocalizations than girls did ($p < .05$). (3) Auditory episode: (a) No sex differences were found in arm movements. (b) Girls emitted more vocalizations than boys did to each of the 5 stimuli ($p < .05$, sign test). When all the stimuli were pooled, no significant sex difference was found. (c) Boys showed greater cardiac deceleration than girls did to the intermittent tone ($p < .05$); girls showed greater deceleration than boys did to the jazz music ($p < .05$). When the auditory episode was repeated on a new group of 6-month-old infants, no sex differences were found.

EXPERIMENT II: **Subjects:** $N = 30$; 13 mos (same as Experiment I). **Measures:** (1) Ss were presented with tape recordings of paragraphs read with or without inflection; 2 paragraphs were constructed—1 containing words and sentences that Ss most likely would be familiar with and 1 containing nonsense words. Cardiac deceleration was recorded. (2) Ss were also presented with the same 3 patterns of lights that they had been exposed to at 6 months of age. Fixation times were recorded. (3) As a final measure, Ss were brought into a room containing numerous toys. The room was marked off into 12 equal rectangles with white tape. The number of rectangles Ss traversed during a 15-minute free-play period was recorded. **Results:** (1) Auditory stimulation: For boys, the mean cardiac deceleration for trials 1 and 2 was greater than the mean deceleration for the last 2 trials, 15 and 16. For girls, the mean decelerations for the first 2 and for the last 2 trials were similar. The authors did not report whether or not this interaction was significant. Girls showed more cardiac deceleration to the low meaning–high inflection paragraph than boys ($p < .05$). (2) Blinking lights: On the last 3 trials, girls exhibited longer fixation times than boys did ($p < .05$). (3) Free play: No sex differences were found in number of rectangles traversed.

Kagan, J., Rosman, B. L., Day, D., Albert, J., and Phillips, W. Information processing in the child: significance of analytic and reflective attitudes. *Psychological Monographs: General and Applied*, 1964, 78, whole no. 578.

EXPERIMENT II: **Subjects:** $N = 180$; 7 yrs. **Measures:** Ss were given the Conceptual Style Test(CST), the Design Recall Test (DRT), and the Hidden Figures Test (HFT). Before each was administered, Ss were instructed either to delay before answering or to respond quickly. The CST was employed to assess Ss' preference for analytic conceptualizations. On each trial, Ss were presented with 3 pictures of common stimuli. After examining them, Ss were asked to pick the 2 that were alike or went together. The number of analytic responses Ss made was recorded. On each trial of the DRT, Ss were instructed to select from among an array of geometric designs the 1 that was identical to a standard. Measures were taken of the number of correct responses Ss made on the first attempt. On each trial of the HFT, Ss attempted to find a familiar object embedded in a patterned background. The response measure was the number of correct identifications Ss made on the first attempt. **Results:** No sex differences.

EXPERIMENT III: **Subjects:** $N = 135$; 7–8 yrs. **Measures:** Ss were given the CST, the Draw-a-line Slowly Test (DAL), 2 forms of the DRT, the Picture Discrimination Test (PDT), the Draw-a-face Test (DAF), and 2 verbal fluency tests. The CST was scored for number of analytic responses and mean response time. On the DAL, Ss were told to draw a straight line as slowly as possible. The time Ss took to complete the line was recorded. The DRT was administered as in Experiment II, except that Ss were told to respond neither quickly nor slowly. Measures were taken of mean response time, number of major errors, number of minor errors, and numbers of responses that were correct on the first attempt. On each trial of the PDT, Ss were asked to detect the difference between 2 similar pictures. 3 response measures were obtained: time to solution, number of incorrect solution hypotheses, and number of items for which Ss' first response was correct. On the DAF, Ss were told to draw a human face. The number of face parts included and the order in which they appeared were recorded. On the verbal fluency tasks, Ss were given 2 minutes to think of things that were round, and 2 minutes to think of things that were square. The response measure for each task was the number of appropriate items Ss named. **Results:** (1) Boys produced more analytic responses (CST), had higher verbal fluency scores, and gave more incorrect solution hypotheses (PDT) than girls. Among 8-year-olds, boys made fewer major errors on both forms of the DRT and took a longer time to draw the straight line. (2) Girls' average response latency on the CST and average latency to first response on the DRT were both higher than boys. Girls also included a greater number of face parts on the DAF. (3) No other sex differences were found.

EXPERIMENT V: **Subjects:** $N = 113$; 8, 9 yrs. **Measures:** The Matching Familiar Figures Test and 2 visual analysis (VA) tasks were administered to Ss. Both VA tasks required Ss to first learn to associate 4 nonsense syllables with each of 4 designs. Ss were then presented with cards containing the nonsense syllables and stimuli illustrating the separate components of each design. Each design that was used contained 3 component parts—the ground component was a repetitive pattern and the figural component portrayed the form into which the individual element components fell. Ss' task was to match each component part to the correct set of nonsense syllables. **Results:** (1) On the MFF test, no sex differences were found in errors or average response time. (2) On the VA tasks, boys were more likely than girls to (a) analyze the stimuli during learning (no level of significance reported) and (b) correctly label the figural, ground, and element components. No sex differences were reported in average response time or number of trials to criterion.

EXPERIMENT VIII: **Subjects:** $N = 76$; 7–8 yrs. **Measures:** Restless behavior was recorded while Ss sat at their desks. **Results:** No sex differences.

Kagan, J., Henker, B. A., Hen-Tov, A., Levine, J., and Lewis, M. Infants' differential reactions to familiar and distorted faces. *Child Development*, 1966, *37*, 519–32.

EXPERIMENT I: **Subjects:** $N = 34$; 4 mos. **Measures:** Each S was shown 4 different 3-dimensional faces (regular, scrambled, no-eyes, and blank face). Stimuli were presented individually in randomly ordered blocks, on 4 consecutive trials. A continuous record was kept of incidence and duration of S's fixation on the stimulus, smiling, and vocalizations. **Results:** Total and first fixation time scores were longer for boys than for girls on all 4 faces ($p < .05$).

EXPERIMENT II: **Subjects:** $N = 32$; 4 mos (different sample). **Measures:** Same as Experiment I, except that the order of presentation was held constant. Since earlier appearing stimuli were more likely to elicit larger decelerations, the specific order favored larger deceleartion to the scrambled face than to the regular face. Fixation time scores and continuous cardiac records were obtained. **Results:** There were no main sex effects. For girls, the cardiac deceleration was greater in response to the regular face than to the scrambled face. This was not true for boys.

Kagan, S., and Madsen, M. C. Cooperation and competition of Mexican, Mexican-American, and Anglo-American children of two ages under four instructional sets. *Developmental Psychology*, 1971, *5*, 32–39.

Subjects: $N = 320$; 4–5, 7–9 yrs (Anglo-American, Mexican-American, Mexican). **Measures:** Same-sex pairs used a circle matrix board (competition-cooperation game) under conditions of 1 of 4 sets of instructions: neutral (instructions did not stress individual or group orientation), "I" set (instructions stressed possessiveness), "we" set (no goals indicated for Ss). Number of moves, number of prizes won, and types of moves made were analyzed. **Results:** No sex differences.

Kagan, S., and Madsen, M. C. Experimental analyses of cooperation and competition of Anglo-American and Mexican children. *Developmental Psychology*, 1972*a*, *6*, 49–59.

EXPERIMENT I: **Subjects:** $N = 160$; 7–9, 10–11 yrs (U.S., Mexico). **Measures:** Same-sex pairs of Ss were instructed to open a "cooperation box." To accomplish this task, the simultaneous use of 4 hands was necessary. In the cooperation condition, E placed 2 toys in the box and told the children they each would receive 1 of the toys if they succeeded in opening the box. In the help condition, only 1 toy was placed in the box. E then indicated which child would receive the prize if the box was opened. **Results:** There were no overall sex differences in time required to open the box. On Trial 1, American boys were faster than American girls ($p < .05$) and Mexican girls were faster than Mexican boys ($p < .01$). No sex differences were found on subsequent trials.

EXPERIMENT II: **Subjects:** $N = 128$; 7–9 yrs (U.S., Mexico). **Measures:** Same-sex pairs of Ss were tested on the author's circle matrix board. After the children were seated, a present was given to 1 of them (child A). The second child (child B) was then given a marker to move. By reaching the "take" circle, B could take away A's present and either keep it for himself (competition condition) or relinquish it to E (rivalry condition). By moving his marker to the "let keep" circle, or by reaching neither the "let keep" nor the "take" circle, B allowed A to keep the present. **Results:** No sex differences were found in the frequency with which Ss chose each of the possible outcomes.

EXPERIMENT IV: **Subjects:** $N = 64$; 7–9 yrs (U.S., Mexico). **Measures:** Ss were seated on opposite sides of the circle matrix board. Each was given 1 marker. Before alternating turns, Ss were informed that a prize would be given to the child whose marker first reached the circle initially occupied by his partner's marker. Each child could choose to either block the other child's approach or move aside. No prize was awarded if neither child reached his goal. **Results:** No sex differences were found in willingness to block.

Kagan, S., and Madsen, M. C. Rivalry in Anglo-American and Mexican children of two ages. *J. Personality & Social Psychology,* 1972b, *24,* 214–20.
  Subjects: $N = 96$; 5–6, 8–10 yrs (U.S., Mexico). **Measures:** Ss distributed marbles between themselves and their same-sex partners. Condition 1 offered S the choice either of taking 3 marbles for himself and giving 3 to his partner or of taking 2 for himself and giving 1 to his partner. Condition 2 offered S the choice either of taking 3 marbles for himself and giving 3 to his partner or of taking 3 for himself and giving 1 to his partner. Condition 3 offered S the choice either of taking 3 marbles for himself and giving 4 to his partner or of taking 2 for himself and giving 1 to his partner. Condition 4 offered S the choice either of taking 2 for himself and giving 2 to his partner or of taking 3 for himself and giving 1 to his partner. In all cases, the rivalrous distribution was the choice that left fewer rewards to the partner. **Results:** (1) No main sex differences were found. (2) Among the younger Ss, boys were more rivalrous than girls in condition 3. Among the older Ss, boys were more rivalrous than girls in condition 2. (3) Among the American Ss, boys were more rivalrous than girls in condition 1. No sex differences were found in the Mexican sample. (4) Among the older American Ss in conditions 1 and 2, more boys than girls were always rivalrous, whereas more girls than boys were never rivalrous. No sex differences were found among younger American Ss or among younger or older Mexican Ss.

Kahn, A. Reactions to generosity or stinginess from an intelligent or stupid work partner: a test of equity theory in a direct exchange relationship. *J. Personality & Social Psychology,* 1972, *21,* 116–23.
  Subjects: $N = 120$; 18–21 yrs (college). **Measures:** Same-sex pairs of Ss earned money after working on 2 proofreading tasks. Each S initially received either more (overpay), less (underpay), or the same amount of money as O (S's partner) from O's distribution of their earnings from the first task. After the second task was completed, S was given the money to distribute. **Results:** (1) Men kept more money for themselves than women did when distributing earnings in the underpay condition ($p < .01$). Men felt more strongly than women that the other S kept too much money for himself ($p < .01$). (2) No sex differences were found in the equal-pay and overpay conditions. (3) Men were more concerned with the financial aspects of the study than women were (as assessed by a postexperimental questionnaire).

Kahn, A., Hottes, J., and Davis, W. L. Cooperation and optimal responding in the Prisoner's Dilemma game. *J. Personality & Social Psychology,* 1971, *17,* 267–79.
  EXPERIMENT I: **Subjects:** $N = 40$; 18–21 yrs (college). **Measures:** Ss played the Prisoner's Dilemma game in same-sex pairs. For half the Ss (the contingent group), the cooperative response led to higher earnings. For the remaining Ss (the noncontingent group), the competitive response was optimal. The number of cooperative responses made by each S was recorded. After the game, Ss were asked: "How much did you feel you influenced your partner's choices?"; "How much did you feel your partner's choices influenced your own choices?"; "How much control did you have over how many points you earned?" Ss then rated their liking for their partner on 30 bipolar adjective scales. **Results:** Women liked their partners more than men did ($p < .05$). No other sex differences were found.
  EXPERIMENT II: **Subjects:** $N = 80$; 18–21 yrs (college). **Measures:** Same as Experiment I. **Results:** No main sex difference was found in number of cooperative responses. Men were more cooperative than women in the contingent condition; women were more cooperative than men in the noncontingent condition ($p < .05$).

Kaminski, L. R. Looming effects on stranger anxiety and toy preferences in one-year-old infants. Unpublished master's thesis, Stanford University, 1973.
  Subjects: $N = 48$; 1 yr and mothers. **Measures:** Mothers and their infants were brought to a testing room marked off into 18-inch squares. In the middle of the room were 6 toys: a baby doll that could be easily cuddled, a young child doll that had movable parts, 2 pick-up trucks (the back of 1 was covered with rabbit fur, the other was covered with aluminum foil), a ring

stack toy, and a Fisher Price musical merry-go-round. Once in the room, Ss were observed in the following sequence of 3-minute episodes: (1) After placing their infants on the floor facing the toys and a folding door, mothers returned to their seats. (2) The folding door was opened, revealing either a seated female stranger (non-loom condition) or a stranger standing against the far wall who subsequently walked forward and sat down (loom condition). (3) The stranger got up, smiled at and talked to the child, and then offered him toys to play with (the musical merry-go-round was always the first toy offered). Afterward, she departed, closing the folding door behind her. (4) Mothers remained quietly seated as in episode 1. (5) Same as episode 2, except that a different female stranger was employed. (6) Same as episode 3, except that toward the end of the episode, the stranger took 2 green toy turtles out of her pockets and presented them to the child—1 with its toy wheels up and moving, the other with its wheels down and silent; (7) Same as episode 4. Measures were taken of the frequency of the following behaviors: (a) looks to the mother; (b) touches mother; (c) proximity to mother; (d) looks to the stranger; (e) touches stranger, (f) smiles at the stranger, shows or gives toy to the stranger; (g) proximity to stranger; (h) looks to the toys; (i) touches toys; (j) manipulates toys; (k) non-distress vocalizations; (l) fusses or cries; and (m) self-oral behaviors. Latencies to moving within proximity to mother and to stranger, latency to moving out of proximity of mother, latency to smile at or show or give a toy to stranger, and latency to play with the toys were also recorded. **Results:** (1) Girls looked at their mothers more than boys did ($p < .01$). (2) Girls looked at the stranger more in the non-loom condition than in the loom condition; for boys, the reverse was true ($p < .025$). (3) Boys approached the stranger more frequently than girls did ($p < .02$). Boys' proximity to the stranger greatly declined in episode 6, while girls' proximity slightly increased though it was still less than the boys' ($p < .005$). (4) No sex differences were found in toy preference during the first 2 episodes. Over all episodes, no sex differences were found in the frequency with which Ss played with any individual toy. Boys played with both dolls (combined scores) more often than girls did ($p < .05$). (5) Mothers reported boys had more friction toys and girls had more dolls.

Kanareff, V. T., and Lanzetta, J. T. The acquisition of imitative and opposition responses under two conditions of instruction-induced set. *J. Experimental Psychology*, 1958, *56*, 516–28.

> **Subjects:** $N = 48$; 18–21 yrs (college). **Measures:** Ss were asked to indicate whether the second of a pair of identical tones (in a series of 60 paired tones) was higher than the first. Before responding, Ss were provided with a simulated same-sex partner's judgment. "Partner's" choices were programmed to be correct either 20%, 50%, or 80% of the time. **Results:** No sex differences were found in number of imitative responses.

Kanareff, V. T., and Lanzetta, J. T. Effect of success-failure experiences and probability of reinforcement upon the acquisition and extinction of an imitative response. *Psychological Reports*, 1960a, 7, 151–66.

> **Subjects:** $N = 48$; 18–21 yrs (college). **Measures:** Ss predicted whether a red or green light would go on after being provided with a simulated partner's judgment. During the acquisition phase (first 80 trials) the partner's predictions were correct either 50% or 80% of the time. During extinction (the final 30 trials) 50% of partner's selections were correct. The performance measure was the number of imitative responses. **Results:** When paired with a partner who was correct 50% of the time, women imitated more than men did ($p < .01$). When paired with a partner who was correct 80% of the time, there were no sex differences in number of imitative responses.

Kanareff, V. T., and Lanzetta, J. T. Effects of task definition and probability of reinforcement upon the acquisition and extinction of imitative responses. *J. Experimental Psychology*, 1960b, *60*, 340–48.

> **Subjects:** $N = 48$; 18–21 yrs (college). **Measures:** Ss predicted whether a red or a green light would go on after being exposed to a simulated partner's judgment. The partner's choices were correct either 50% or 80% of the time. The performance measure was the number of imitative responses. **Results:** No sex differences.

Kanareff, V. T., and Lanzetta, J. T. Effects of congruent social and task reinforcement upon acquisition of imitative responses. *Psychological Reports*, 1961, 8, 47–57.

> **Subjects:** $N = 72$; 18–21 yrs (college). **Measures:** Ss predicted whether a red or a green light would go on after being provided with a simulated partner's judgment. Partner's predictions were correct either 50% or 80% of the time. After each of S's choices, E responded with

either "good" or "okay." The performance measure was the number of imitative responses. **Results:** Men imitated more often than women did ($p < .05$).

Kangas, J., and Bradway, K. Intelligence at middle age: a thirty-eight year followup. *Developmental Psychology*, 1971, 5, 333–37.
> **Subjects:** $N = 48$; 39–44 yrs (tested in 1931, 1941, 1956, 1969). **Measures:** The Stanford-Binet IQ test was administered at all 4 sessions. The Adult Intelligence Scale was administered in 1956 and 1969. **Results:** Over the 38-year period, men made greater IQ gains than women did ($p < .025$).

Kaplan, H. B. Self-derogation and social position: interaction effects of sex, race, education, and age. *International J. Social Psychiatry*, 1973 (forthcoming).
> **Subjects:** $N = 500$; over 21 yrs (white, black). **Measures:** Ss rated 10 global self-descriptive statements on a 4-point scale ranging from "strongly agree" to "strongly disagree." Ss' responses were analyzed to yield a measure of self-derogation. **Results:** (1) There were no main sex effects. (2) Among white Ss without college education, women had higher self-derogation scores than men did ($p < .01$). (3) Among black Ss with a high school education or better, women had higher self-derogation scores than men did ($p < .025$).

Kato, N. A fundamental study of rod-frame test. *Japanese Psychological Research*, 1965, 7, 61–68.
> **Subjects:** $N = 60$; 18–21 yrs (college). **Measures:** Rod and Frame Test. **Results:** Women had higher error scores than men did ($p < .05$).

Katz, J. M. Reflection-impulsivity and color-form sorting. *Child Development*, 1971, 42, 745–54.
> **Subjects:** $N = 67$; 3–5 yrs. **Measures:** Ss were given a color-form test in which a standard shape and 2 comparisons were presented; 1 comparison matched the standard in form, 1 in color. Ss were given 3 series of figures (which varied in saliency of color and form cues) and were asked to choose the comparison most like the standard. Ss were then given Matching Familiar Figures Test and were divided into impulsive and reflective groups. **Results:** On the third series of the color-form tests (color cue more salient), impulsive boys made more comparison glances than impulsive girls did ($p < .05$). Reflective girls made more comparison glances than reflective boys did.

Katz, P. A. Stimulus predifferentiation and modification of children's racial attitudes. *Child Development*, 1973, 44, 232–37.
> **Subjects:** $N = 96$; 7, 11 yrs (white, black). **Measures:** Prejudiced Ss were chosen on the basis of racial-ethnic attitude scale scores. Ss received either distinctive-labeling training with photographs of other-race faces, perceptual-differentiation training to make same-different judgments of facial pairs, or no training, i.e. they observed faces without labels. E was black or white. After training, attitude scales were readministered. **Results:** There were no main sex differences in either prejudice or perceptual judgment scores.

Katz, P. A., and Zigler, E. Self-image disparity: a developmental approach. *J. Personality & Social Psychology*, 1967, 5, 186–95.
> **Subjects:** $N = 120$; 10, 13, 16 yrs. **Measures:** Ss' ratings of their real self, ideal self, and social self were assessed by a questionnaire and an adjective checklist. **Results:** (1) There were no sex differences in Ss' real or ideal self ratings on either measure. (2) There were no sex differences in Ss' social self ratings as assessed by the questionnaire. (3) At age 10, boys' social self ratings (as assessed by the adjective checklist) were lower than girls'; at age 13, girls' social self ratings were lower than boys' ($p < .01$). At age 16, no sex differences were found.

Katz, P. A., Albert, J., and Atkins, M. Mediation and perceptual transfer in children. *Developmental Psychology*, 1971, 4, 268–76.
> EXPERIMENT I: **Subjects:** $N = 60$; 6, 11 yrs. **Measures:** Ss judged the degree of similarity of 52 pairs of random geometric forms. Ss indicated their decision by moving the lever of a perceptual similarity apparatus. **Results:** No sex differences.
> EXPERIMENT II: **Subjects:** $N = 240$; 6, 11 yrs. **Measures:** Ss in 3 verbal labeling conditions were presented with 3 nonsense forms of either high, intermediate, or low similarity. Distinctive-label Ss were taught to associate different nonsense syllables (of either 40% or 95% association value) to each of the forms. Common-label Ss were taught to associate an identical label (again high- or low-association value) to 2 forms, and a different label to the third.

Control Ss counted aloud and learned what forms looked like. Ss then made degree-of-similarity judgments for pairs of previously employed forms. Similarity responses for pairs associated with a common label were analyzed. **Results:** There were no sex differences in verbal learning of labels or perceptual judgment scores.

Kaufman, A. S. Piaget and Gesell: a psychometric analysis of texts built from their tasks. *Child Development*, 1971, *42*, 1341–60.
> **Subjects:** $N = 103$; 5–6 yrs. **Measures:** Ss were given the Gesell School Readiness Tests and the Lorge-Thorndike Intelligence Tests. Teething level was used as measure of physiological age. Ss also performed a battery of Piaget number tasks (conservation of length and number, addition and subtraction, discrimination, insertion, numeration, constructing and perceiving a straight line, sorting, class inclusion, multiple class membership, and seriation). **Results:** Girls scored higher than boys on the Piagetian tasks and on the GSRT ($p < .01$, $p < .05$).

Kaugmann, H., and Marcus, A. M. Aggression as a function of similarity between aggressor and victim. *Perceptual & Motor Skills*, 1965, *20*, 1013–20.
> **Subjects:** $N = 64$; 18–21 yrs (college). **Measures:** After reading a criminal's case history, high and low scorers on a modified version of Siegel's Manifest Hostility Scale were asked to suggest an appropriate sentence for him. **Results:** No sex differences.

Keasey, C. B. Sex differences in yielding to temptation: a function of the situation. *J. Genetic Psychology*, 1971a, *118*, 25–28.
> **Subjects:** $N = 108$; 11 yrs. **Measures:** After E explained the game and departed, Ss rolled the ball 10 times in a miniature bowling game. The score Ss earned on each roll was programmed so that the total number of pins Ss knocked over fell short of the number they needed to win a toy. Measures were taken of the number of times Ss falsified their scores, of the number of points Ss added to their scores, and of the turn on which Ss first cheated. **Results:** More girls than boys cheated. Girls cheated more frequently, added more points to their scores, and yielded to temptation earlier than boys did.

Keasey, C. B. Social participation as a factor in the moral development of preadolescents. *Developmental Psychology*, 1971b, *5*, 216–20.
> **Subjects:** $N = 144$; 10, 11 yrs. **Measures:** E administered Kohlberg's Moral Judgment Interview to each S. Teachers and peers rated Ss' leadership and popularity relative to same-sexed classmates. Ss indicated past and present membership and leadership in clubs or social organizations. Peers nominated classmates who were their best friends. **Results:** (1) Among Ss rated as leaders by their teachers, boys had higher moral judgment scores than girls did ($p < .05$). (2) Among Ss rated popular by teachers, boys had higher moral judgment scores than girls ($p < .01$).

Keasey, C. B. The lack of sex differences in the moral judgments of preadolescents. *J. Social Psychology*, 1972, *86*, 157–58.
> **Subjects:** $N = 155$; 11 yrs. **Measures:** 5 interview situations from Kohlberg's Moral Judgment Interview were administered to each S. **Results:** No sex differences.

Keating, D. P., and Stanley, J. C. Extreme measures for the exceptionally gifted in mathematics and science. Study of the Mathematically and Scientifically Precocious Youth, 1972 (correspondence from Johns Hopkins University Department of Psychology).
> EXPERIMENT I: **Subjects:** $N = 396$; 12, 13 yrs. **Measures:** Ss volunteered to participate in a contest for students exceptionally gifted in math. The quantitative section of the SAT and the Mathematics Level I Achievement Test were administered. **Results:** 20% of the boys scored above the top-scoring girl on the SAT Math section; 10% of the boys scored above the top-scoring girl on the Math Achievement Test.
> EXPERIMENT II: **Subjects:** $N = 192$ (130 boys, 62 girls); 12, 13 yrs. **Measures:** The Science section of the Sequential Tests of Education Progress was administered to Ss who were exceptionally gifted in science. **Results:** 17% of the boys scored above the top-scoring girl.

Keenan, V. Effects of Hebrew and English letters on children's perceptual set. *J. Experimental Child Psychology*, 1972, *13*, 71–84.
> **Subjects:** $N = 48$; 7, 9, 11 yrs. **Measures:** A tachistoscopic slide presentation (.2 second) was made of the alphabetic pattern of 7 randomly generated letters (Hebrew and English) and 15 binary patterns (rows of blackened or nonblackened zeros). Ss filled in response sheets to match projected patterns. Number of elements recorded in correct serial position was analyzed. **Results:** No sex differences.

Keillor, J. S. The effects of experimentally induced consciousness expansion and conscious control upon intellectual functioning. *Dissertation Abstracts International*, 1971, 31-B, p. 4339.

> **Subjects:** $N = 22$; 18–21 yrs (college). **Measures:** After listening to a description of an LSD experience, a Stelazine experience, or a visit to the Stratford Shakespeare Festival, Ss were administered the Remote Associates Test. **Results:** Girls obtained higher scores than boys.

Kellaghan, T., and MacNamara, J. Family correlates of verbal reasoning ability. *Developmental Psychology*, 1972, 7, 49–53.

> **Subjects:** $N = 500$; 11 yrs (Irish). **Measures:** Drumcondra Verbal Reasoning Test. **Results:** No sex differences.

Kellogg, R. L. A direct approach to sex-role identification of school-related objects. *Psychological Reports*, 1969, 24, 839–41.

> **Subjects:** $N = 47$; 9 yrs. **Measures:** Ss were given a list of 24 common objects and were asked to decide whether each object was more suitable for masculine or feminine use. Of the 24 items, 8 were considered more appropriate for boys, 8 were considered more appropriate for girls, and the remaining 8 were related to scholastic activities. **Results:** Of the school-related items, both sexes labeled book, blackboard, library, and chalk more appropriate for feminine use; map and pencil were labeled more appropriate for masculine use. Girls considered school to be a feminine item; boys showed no consistent tendency. Boys considered desk a masculine item; girls were equally divided in their choices.

Kempler, B. Stimulus correlates of area judgments: a psychophysical developmental study. *Developmental Psychology*, 1971, 4, 158–63.

> **Subjects:** $N = 59$; 6, 8, 10, 12 yrs. **Measures:** Ss made "large-small" judgments on each of 100 rectangles, which varied in height, width, and area. Ss were retested 1 week later. **Results:** No sex differences.

Kendler, H. H., Glasman, L. D., and Ward, J. W. Verbal-labeling and cue-training in reversal-shift behavior. *J. Experimental Child Psychology*, 1972, 13, 195–209.

> **Subejcts:** $N = 80$; 4–5 yrs. **Measures:** Ss were given a reversal-shift discrimination-learning problem. **Results:** No sex differences were found in either preshift or postshift task performance.

Kenney, J. B., and White, W. F. Sex characteristics in personality patterns of elementary school teachers. *Perceptual & Motor Skills*, 1966, 23, 17–18.

> **Subjects:** $N = 100$; adults (school teachers). **Measures:** Cattell and Stice's Sixteen Personality Factor Questionnaire, Form A. **Results:** (1) Men were more emotionally stable, independent, enthusiastic, realistic, tough-minded, adventurous, and socially responsive, and scored higher in "ego strength" than women. (2) Women were more inclined toward changeable attitudes, general emotionality, evasiveness, and neurotic fatigue, were more sober, taciturn, introspective, sensitive, shy, and restricted in their interests than men.

Keogh, B. K. Pattern copying under three conditions of an expanded spatial field. *Developmental Psychology*, 1971, 4, 25–31.

> **Subjects:** $N = 135$; 8, 9 yrs. **Measures:** Ss made pencil copies of 10 simple and complex patterns. Within a week, Ss walked these same patterns under 1 of 3 conditions: on an unmarked floor, on an unmarked linoleum mat, or on sand. **Results:** (1) No sex differences were found in the accuracy of Ss' drawings. (2) Boys walked the simple and complex patterns more accurately than girls did ($p < .01, p < .05$).

Keogh, B. K., and Ryan, S. R. Use of three measures and field organization with young children. *Perceptual & Motor Skills*, 1971, 33, 466.

> **Subjects:** $N = 44$; 7 yrs. **Measures:** Rod-and-Frame Test (portable model), Children's Embedded Figures Test, Pattern Drawing Test, and Pattern Walking Test. **Results:** (1) Boys were more field-independent than girls on the RFT ($p < .05$). (2) Boys were superior to girls on the PWT ($p < .01$). (3) No sex differences were found on either the CEFT or the PDT.

Kershenbaum, B. R., and Komorita, S. S. Temptation to defect in the Prisoner's Dilemma game. *J. Personality & Social Psychology*, 1970, 16, 110–13.

> **Subjects:** $N = 96$; 18–21 yrs (college). **Measures:** After receiving cooperative instructions, same-sex pairs of Ss played 2 Prisoner's Dilemma games simultaneously. Feedback was controlled so that Ss were never sure whether their partner had defected or not. The temptation

to defect was high or low for self and other. The main response measure was the trial on which Ss first defected. **Results:** No sex differences.

Kershner, J. R. Children's acquisition of visuo-spatial dimensionality: a conservation study. *Developmental Psychology*, 1971, 5, 454–62.
> **Subjects:** $N = 160$; 6 yrs. **Measures:** Ss were tested on their ability to remember the orientation and directional movement of elements in a previously seen field configuration. **Results:** No sex differences.

Kidd, A. H. Closure as related to manifest anxiety and rigidity. *Perceptual & Motor Skills*, 1965, *20*, 1177–81.
> **Subjects:** $N = 100$; 18–20 yrs (college). **Measures:** The Stanford-Gough Rigidity Scale and a shortened version of Taylor's Manifest Anxiety Scale were administered to Ss. Ss were also tachistoscopically presented with incomplete geometric designs (e.g. triangles with an opening along their perimeters, simple dot designs, and line drawing of angles). Immediately after exposure, Ss were asked to reproduce each figure. Ss' drawings were scored for closure (reproducing an angle smaller than the one presented, reproducing an opening taking up a smaller percentage of the perimeter than did the opening in the original figure, etc.) and elaboration (drawing more than the correct number of lines, dots, arcs, or gaps). **Results:** Men had higher elaboration scores than women ($p < .05$).

Kidd, A. H., and Cherymisin, D. G. Figure reversal as related to specific personality variables. *Perceptual & Motor Skills*, 1965, *20*, 1175–76.
> **Subjects:** $N = 100$; 18–21 yrs (college). **Measures:** Ss were given a shortened version of the Taylor Manifest Anxiety Scale, the Draw-a-Person test, the Stanford-Gough Rigidity Scale, and a reversal rate test. **Results:** Women had higher DAP scores and higher average reversal times than men.

Kimball, M. Women and success—a basic conflict? In M. Stevenson, ed., *Women in Canada*. Toronto: New Press, 1973.
> **Subjects:** $N = 187$; 13, 17 yrs (Canadian). **Measures:** (1) Ss were asked to write stories based on projective cues of the following nature: "Susan (John) finds at the end of the school year that she (he) has been named first in the class." There were 2 cues given to each S—1 contained a male name and 1 contained a female name. Ss were scored for the number of fear-of-success stories they wrote. (2) Ss were then presented with descriptions of moderately and highly successful persons. Each description of a moderately successful person was paired with that of a person highly successful in the same field. Ss answered the following questions about each set: (a) Who is happier? Why? (b) Who do you like better? Why? (c) Who would you rather be? Why? **Results:** (1) Among 17-year-olds, girls wrote more fear-of-success stories than boys did. Among 13-year-olds, no sex differences were found. (2) No sex differences were found in Ss' responses to the questions about the moderately and highly successful persons.

Kimura, D. Functional asymmetry of the brain in dichotic listening. *Cortex*, 1967, *3*, 163–78.
> **Subjects:** $N = 142$; 5–8 yrs (low-middle SES). **Measures:** 2 different digits were presented simultaneously through earphones, 1 digit to the left ear, the other to the right. Ss were asked to report all the numbers they had heard. **Results:** With the exception of the 5-year-old boys, all age-sex groups accurately reported more digits presented to the right ear than to the left ear.

Kimura, D., Spatial localization in left and right visual fields. *Canadian J. Psychology*, 1969, *23*, 445–58.
> Experiment I: **Subjects:** $N = 38$; 18–21 yrs (college). **Measures:** A stimulus field was constructed consisting of 2 squares situated to the right and left of a central point. On each trial of the experimental task, a single dot was presented in 1 of 25 positions in either the right or left square. Ss were then asked to locate the dot on a spatial map of the stimulus field. **Results:** No main sex differences were found. Men were more accurate when the dot was presented to their left visual field than when it was presented to their right visual field; women showed no difference ($p < .01$).
> Experiment II: **Subjects:** $N = 46$; 18–21 yrs (college). **Measures:** Same as Experiment I, except that the exposure time for which the dot was presented varied. **Results:** No main sex differences.
> Experiment III: **Subjects:** $N = 28$; 18–21 yrs (college). **Measures:** Each dot was presented

at increasing exposure times until Ss accurately identified it in either left or right square. The position of the dot within the square was unimportant. **Results:** No sex differences.

EXPERIMENT IV: **Subjects:** $N = 34$; 18–21 yrs (college). **Measures:** Same as Experiment I, except that the pre-exposure field consisted of a single large circle instead of 2 squares. **Results:** No sex differences.

EXPERIMENT VI: **Subjects:** $N = 20$; 18–21 yrs (college). **Measures:** Same as Experiment III except that (a) the pre-exposure field consisted of a single circle, and (b) each dot was presented just once. After every presentation, Ss were asked whether they had seen the dot or not. **Results:** No sex differences.

EXPERIMENT VII: **Subjects:** $N = 32$; 18–21 yrs (college). **Measures:** Same as Experiment VI except that the stimulus dot was presented at increasing exposure times. Ss were asked to indicate whether the dot had appeared on the left or on the right side. **Results:** No sex differences.

King, W. Learning and utilization of conjunctive and disjunctive classification rules: a developmental study. *J. Experimental Child Psychology,* 1966, *4,* 217–31.

Subjects: $N = 32$; 6, 9, 12, 18–21 yrs (college). **Measures:** Ss performed an attribute-identification task (to the criterion of 10 consecutive correct responses), and then received 6 conjunctive and disjunctive rule-learning problems. After the last problem, Ss were asked to describe the 2 different rules. **Results:** (1) On the attribute identification task, no main sex differences were found. Among 6-year-olds, boys made more errors than girls; among 12-year-olds, girls made more errors than boys ($p < .05$). (2) On the rule-learning problems, girls made fewer errors than boys ($p < .05$). The authors noted that "the significant effect for 'sex' cannot be interpreted as indicating that females perform better than males since sex was deliberately confounded with other variables."

King, W. L. A non-arbitrary behavioral criterion for conservation of illusion-distorted length in five year olds. *J. Experimental Child Psychology,* 1971, *11,* 171–81.

Subjects: $N = 47$; 4–6 yrs. **Measures:** By means of a Mueller-Lyer illusion, the apparent length of 2 unequally long sticks was perceptually reversed. After showing S a dot indicating the longer stick, each S was tested on which stick was longer (both with and without Mueller-Lyer arms) and which looked longer (with arms). If S's response was correct, S was asked to make a bridge between the 2 blocks, choosing the physically longer or shorter of the 2 sticks. **Results:** No sex differences.

Kirchner, E. P., and Vondracek, S. I. What do you want to be when you grow up? Vocational choice in children aged three to six. Paper presented at the Society for Research in Child Development Conference, Philadelphia, 1973.

Subjects: $N = 282$, 3–6 yrs (white and black, low SES). **Measures:** Ss were asked what they would like to be when they grow up. **Results:** (1) More boys than girls expressed aspirations that were classified as adult (i.e. mention of a nonoccupational status; e.g. "be a man") or as fantasy (e.g. "be Batman," "be a princess"). (2) More girls than boys expressed aspirations that were classified as parent (e.g. "be a father") or as older child (e.g. "be a Girl Scout," "be older"). (3) No sex differences were found in the number of responses that fell into the following categories: same child (lack of projection into more mature roles, e.g. "be a boy just like me"), specific occupation (e.g. "be a doctor"), nonhuman (e.g. "be a dog"), and all-adult (a category that encompasses adult, specific occupation, and parent). (4) Boys' occupational choices were more evenly distributed across occupations than those of girls (significance not tested).

Klaus, R. A., and Gray, S. W. The early training project for disadvantaged children: a report after five years. *Monographs of the Society for Research in Child Development,* 1968, *33,* Serial No. 120.

Subjects: $N = 88$; tested at 3, 4, 5, 6, 7 yrs (black, low SES). **Measures:** Ss were divided into 4 groups. Groups 1 and 2 participated in enrichment programs designed to offset some of the negative consequences of growing up in a culturally deprived environment. Specifically, the acquisition of attitudes and aptitudes relating to achievement was stressed. Groups 3 and 4 served as the control groups. Several times each year Ss were given the Peabody Picture Vocabulary Test and either the Stanford-Binet or the WISC. Other tests administered were the Matching Familiar Figures test and a social schemata measure (age 5); the Illinois Test of Psycholinguistic Abilities (ages 5, 6, and 7); the Metropolitan and the Gates Reading Readiness tests (age 6); a peer nomination measure assessing reputation (general social effectiveness, aggression, withdrawal) among peers (age 6); the Metropolitan Achievement Test and a self-concept scale (ages 6 and 7); the Stanford Achievement Test (age 7). Measures of delay of gratification and achievement motivation were administered at various unspecified times. **Results:** At 5 years of age, boys used more words in their descriptions of 3 pictures than girls did. At the same age, boys were superior to girls on certain unspecified subtests of the ITPA. No other sex differences were found.

Klausmeier, J., and Wiersma, W. Relationship of sex, grade level, and locale to performance of high IQ students on divergent thinking tests. *J. Educational Psychology*, 1964, 55, 114–19.
> **Subjects:** $N = 320$; 10–12 yrs (IQ > 115). **Measures:** 10 divergent thinking tests, 4 convergent thinking tests. **Results:** (1) On 5 of the 10 divergent thinking tests (Object Uses–Flexibility, Plot Titles–Fluency, Expressional Fluency, Plot Questions, Object Improvement), girls scored higher than boys ($p < .05$). No sex differences were found on the other 5 tests (Object Uses–Fluency, Word Uses–Flexibility, Plot Titles–Cleverness, Sentence Improvement–Metaphor, Sentence Improvement–Onomatopeia). (2) On 3 of the 4 convergent thinking tests (Current Events, Analogies, Problem Solving–Judgment), boys had higher scores than girls ($p < .05$). No sex differences were found on the fourth test (Work-Study Skills).

Klein, E. B., Gould, L. J., and Corey, M. Social desirability in children: an extension and replication. *J. Consulting & Clinical Psychology*, 1969, 33, 128.
> **Subjects:** $N = 1,008$; 7–14 yrs. **Measures:** Children's Social Desirability Scale. **Results:** At every age level (except 12 years old), girls gave more socially desirable responses than boys.

Kleinman, R. A., and Higgins, J. Sex of respondent and Rorschach M production. *J. Projective Techniques*, 1966, 30, 439–40.
> **Subjects:** $N = 92$; 18–21 yrs (college). **Measures:** Rorschach Inkblot Test. **Results:** Women produced more human movement responses (M) than men ($p < .025$).

Knott, P. D., and Drost, B. A. Sex-role identification, interpersonal aggression, and anger. *Psychological Reports*, 1970, 27, 154.
> **Subjects:** $N = 80$; 18–21 yrs (college). **Measures:** Ss were divided into 4 groups—masculine males, feminine males, masculine females, and feminine females—based on their extreme scores on the MF dimensions of the Guilford-Zimmerman Temperament Survey. After being shocked by a confederate, Ss were free to deliver shocks in return. **Results:** Masculine males delivered a greater number of shocks ($p < .05$) and more intense shocks ($p < .05$) than either feminine males, masculine females, or feminine females.

Knox, C., and Kimura, D. Cerebral Processing of nonverbal sounds in boys and girls. *Neuropsychologia*, 1970, 8, 227–37.
> Experiment I: **Subjects:** $N = 80$; 5–8 yrs. **Measures:** Different digits were simultaneously presented to Ss' left and right earphones. On each trial, Ss were asked to report what they had heard; 2 weeks later, similar procedures were followed using a variety of environmental sounds (i.e. sounds made by common objects). **Results:** Boys accurately identified more environmental sounds than girls did ($p < .05$). No sex differences were found on the digits task.
> Experiment II: **Subjects:** $N = 120$; 5–8 yrs. **Measures:** Digits, environmental sounds, and animal sounds were dichotically presented to Ss during the first session. As in Experiment I, Ss were asked to report what they had heard; 2 weeks later, Ss performed 2 additional dichotic listening tasks, both of which utilized a nonverbal method of report. **Results:** Boys correctly identified a greater number of animal sounds than girls did ($p < .05$). No sex differences were found on the other 4 tasks.
> Experiment III: **Subjects:** $N = 36$; 7, 8 yrs. **Measures:** The 2 tasks employed during the second session of Experiment II. **Results:** No sex differences.
> Experiment IV: **Subjects:** $N = 27$; 2–5 yrs. **Measures:** 18 animal sounds were individually presented to Ss through the speakers of a tape recorder. After each sound was played, Ss were asked to name or describe the animal they had heard. **Results:** Boys correctly identified more animal sounds than girls did ($p < .03$).

Koen, F. Codability of complex stimuli: three modes of representation. *J. Personality & Social Psychology*, 1966, 3, 435–41.
> **Subjects:** $N = 72$; 18–21 yrs (college). **Measures:** (1) Verbal codability: Ss were presented with 24 different photographs of the same individual. Ss were instructed to write a description of each photograph accurate to the extent that others could identify which of the 24 pictures each description applied to. Afterward, Ss' descriptions were decoded by a second group of

Ss. Performance measures were number of successful transmissions (by encoders) and number of successful identifications (by decoders). (2) Enactive codability: 2 subjects (either of the same or opposite sex) were seated across from each other at a table: 1 subject in each pair attempted to duplicate the expression of 1 of the 24 photographs. The second subject's task was to identify the picture being imitated. Ss served alternatively as senders and receivers of the expressions. The number of correct transmissions made by each pair of Ss was recorded. (3) Recognition: Ss were exposed to 2 of the 24 photographs for 2.5 seconds. Then Ss either imitated the expressions in the pictures (enactive condition), described the expressions aloud (verbal condition), or counted backward (iconic condition). Following this, Ss attempted to identify the 2 pictures they had seen. (4) Discrimination: All 24 photographs were put on display in front of Ss. Ss were then given a duplicate print of 1 of the photographs. Ss' task was to match the duplicate with the original print in the shortest possible time. Response measure was the number of seconds required by Ss to find the original print. **Results:** (1) On the recognition test, women performed better than men did in the enactive and verbal conditions ($p < .05$); no sex differences were found in the iconic condition. (2) No sex differences were found on the discriminability or codability tasks.

Koenig, K. P. Verbal behavior and personality change. *J. Personality & Social Psychology,* 1966, *3,* 223–27.

    Subjects: $N = 40$; 18–21 yrs (college). **Measures:** Ss were asked to talk about their academic work. Ss were reinforced for either positive or negative self-statements. Both before and after the interview task, Ss completed the Test Anxiety and General Anxiety scales. Pretask scores were subtracted from post-task scores to yield a difference (D) score for each S. **Results:** (1) No sex differences were found in the frequency of verbalization of positive, negative, or ambiguous self-statements. (2) No sex differences were found in D scores.

Kohen-Raz, R. Mental and motor development of kibbutz, institutionalized and home-reared infants in Israel. *Child Development,* 1968, *39,* 489–504.

    Subjects: $N = 35$; 3, 6, 12, 27 mos (reared in institutions). $N = 94$; 3, 6, 12, 18, 24, 27 mos (reared in kibbutzim). $N = 128$; 1, 3, 4, 6, 8, 10, 12, 15, 18, 27 mos (reared in private homes). **Measures:** Ss were given the Bayley Infant Scales of Mental and Motor Development. **Results:** Among 6-month-old kibbutz ($N = 22$) and institution ($N = 10$) infants, boys scored higher than girls on the Mental Scale. No other sex differences were found.

Kohlberg, L., Yaeger, J., and Hjertholm, E. Private speech: four studies and a review of theories. *Child Development,* 1968, *39,* 691–736.

    Experiment II: **Subjects:** $N = 112$; 4–10 yrs. **Measures:** Ss made sticker designs with an adult male and then with an adult female. Adults were instructed to minimally respond in a friendly fashion to Ss' verbalizations, but not to initiate conversation. Sentence-like verbal remarks made by Ss were recorded. **Results:** No sex differences were found in percentage of egocentric speech.

    Experiment IV: **Subjects:** $N = 34$; 4–5 yrs (U.S., Norway). **Measures:** Ss were individually presented with a series of 4 sensorimotor tasks (bead-stringing, easy jigsaw puzzle, tower building, hard jigsaw puzzle). Ss' verbalizations were recorded while performing the tasks. **Results:** No sex differences were found in amount of egocentric speech.

Komorita, S. S. Cooperative choice in a Prisoner's Dilemma game. *J. Personality & Social Psychology,* 1965, *2,* 741–45.

    Experiment I: **Subjects:** $N = 72$; 18–21 yrs (college). **Measures:** Ss played the Prisoner's Dilemma game with simulated same-sex partners. Conditional probabilities of cooperative and competitive responses by the simulated partner were varied so that competitive behavior was optimal in a majority of the conditions. **Results:** (1) Women were more cooperative than men ($p < .05$). (2) Women were more cooperative with more cooperative partners; no such relationship was found for men ($p < .05$).

    Experiment II: **Subjects:** $N = 40$; 18–21 yrs (college). **Measures:** Ss played the PD game with simulated same-sex partners. Partner's response always matched S's previous response. Cooperative behavior was therefore optimal. **Results:** Men were more cooperative than women ($p < .05$).

Komorita, S. S., and Mechling, J. Betrayal and reconciliation in a two-person game. *J. Personality & Social Psychology,* 1967, *6,* 349–53.

    Subjects: $N = 64$; 18–21 yrs (college). **Measures:** After receiving instructions to cooperate, Ss were led to believe they were betrayed twice by their same-sex partners in the Prisoner's Dilemma game. Response measures were the number of cooperative choices made by Ss on the first 5 trials following the initial betrayal and the number of trials needed by Ss to reach the criterion of 5 consecutive cooperative responses following the second betrayal. **Results:** No sex differences.

Kopfstein, D. Risk-taking behavior and cognitive style. *Child Development*, 1973, *44*, 190–92.

> **Subjects:** $N = 60$; 9 yrs (white, middle SES). **Measures:** Ss were given Kagan's Matching Familiar Figures task and then Slovic's "toggle-switch" risk-taking task. In the latter task Ss could lose all their prizes if they pulled 1 too many switches. A male or a female E administered the tasks. **Results:** (1) Girls took more risks than boys did in presence of male experimenter ($p < .05$). There were no sex differences in the presence of a female experimenter. (2) On the MFF, no sex differences were found in errors or response latencies.

Korner, A. F. Neonatal startles, smiles, erection, and reflex sucks as related to state, sex and individuality. *Child Development*, 1969, *40*, 1039–53.

> **Subjects:** $N = 32$; 3–5 days. **Measures:** Ss were observed for a total of 140 minutes. Most observations took place before and after feeding. Frequency of 3 spontaneous behaviors (startles, reflex smiles, and bursts of rhythmical mouthing) were recorded during each of 3 states (drowsiness, irregular sleep, and regular sleep). **Results:** No sex differences.

Korner, A. F. Visual alertness of neonates: individual differences and their correlates. *Perceptual & Motor Skills*, 1970, *31*, 499–509.

> **Subjects:** $N = 32$; 2–3 days. **Measures:** Ss were observed over a 9-hour span. Frequency and duration of alert inactivity were recorded. During this time, Ss were also exposed for 10-second periods to a moving object. Visual pursuit scores were calculated by giving Ss 1 point for each fixation, 2 points for each visual pursuit, and 3 points for each visual pursuit accompanied by a head-turning movement. **Results:** No sex differences.

Korner, A. F. Sex differences in newborns with special reference to differences in the organization of oral behavior. *J. Child Psychology & Psychiatry*, 1973, *14*, 19–29.

> **Subjects:** $N = 32$; 3–5 days. **Measures:** Films of infant's hand and mouth interactions were assessed. Categories were hand approached mouth, mouth approached hand, mouth opened when hand was closed, mouth strained after hand to maintain already established contact. **Results:** Girls engaged in more mouth-dominated approaches than boys did ($p < .01$).

Korner, A. F., and Thoman, E. B. Visual alertness in neonates as evoked by maternal care. *J. Experimental Child Psychology*, 1970, *10*, 67–78.

> **Subjects:** $N = 40$ (crying), 24 (sleeping); 2–3 days. **Measures:** Ss experienced 6 interventions, each of which entailed either contact, vestibular stimulation, or a combination of both. During each intervention, Ss were rated for level of alertness. **Results:** No sex differences.

Korner, A. F., and Thoman, E. B. The relative efficacy of contact and vestibular-proprioceptive stimulation in soothing neonates. *Child Development*, 1972, *43*, 443–53.

> **Subjects:** $N = 40$; 2 days. **Measures:** Ss experienced 6 physical interventions. Crying time was recorded during and after each intervention. **Results:** No sex differences.

Korner, A. F., Chuck, B., and Dontchos, S. Organismic determinants of spontaneous oral behavior in neonates. *Child Development*, 1968, *39*, 1145–57.

> **Subjects:** $N = 32$; 3–5 days. **Measures:** Each S was observed for 32 minutes over a 5-hour period. Measures were taken of the frequency of hand-mouth contacts, hand-face contacts, finger sucking, and mouthing. **Results:** No sex differences.

Kossuth, G. L., Carroll, W. R., and Rogers, C. A. Free recall of words and objects. *Developmental Psychology*, 1971, *4*, 480 (brief report).

> **Subjects:** $N = 80$; 11 yrs. **Measures:** Ss saw either 20 unrelated nouns or their object counterparts. Half of the Ss were required to pronounce words and name objects, the other half were not. Recall was tested immediately. **Results:** (1) Girls showed more clustering of words or objects in their recall responses than boys did. (2) Girls clustered better with objects, boys clustered better with words. (3) Girls had better overall recall than boys did.

Kranzler, G. D. Some effects of reporting Scholastic Aptitude Test scores to high school sophomores. *School Counselor*, 1970, *17*, 219–27.

> **Subjects:** $N = 154$; 15 yrs. **Measures:** Self-acceptance scale of Bill's Index of Adjustment and Values, high school form. **Results:** No sex differences.

Kravitz, H., and Boehm, J. J. Rhythmic habit patterns in infancy: their sequence, age of onset and frequency. *Child Development*, 1971, *42*, 399–413.

    Subjects: $N = 200$; newborn–1 yr. **Measures:** Rhythmic habit patterns were observed. Patterns were considered established if they lasted for more than 2 days. **Results:** (1) Boys showed more body-rocking behavior than girls did. (2) There were no sex differences in toe-sucking or head-rolling.

Kraynak, A. R., and Raskin, L. M. The influence of age and stimulus dimensionality on form perception by preschool children. *Developmental Psychology*, 1971, *4*, 389–93.

    Subjects: $N = 64$; 3–4 yrs. **Measures:** Ss performed a matching task with 2- and 3-dimensional objects: animal stimuli during pretraining, and geometric stimuli during testing. Instructions were to tap appropriate shelf when either of the comparison forms matched standard form, or to tap blank shelf when no match existed. **Results:** No sex differences.

Kreitler, H., and Kreitler, S. Children's concepts of sexuality and birth. *Child Development*, 1966, 37, 363–78.

    Subjects: $N = 185$; 4–5 yrs (Israeli-Oriental or Western origin). **Measures:** Ss were interviewed about their views on sex differences and birth. **Results:** (1) Both Oriental and Western boys were better informed than girls about location and function of sexual organs. Boys seemed to have more exact information about sexual organs of girls than girls had about sexual organs of boys. (2) More girls than boys thought that fathers' task in birth consisted of helping the mother after birth.

Kreitler, H., and Kreitler, S. Dependency of laughter on cognitive strategies. *Merrill-Palmer Quarterly*, 1970, *16*, 163–77.

    Subjects: $N = 92$; 5–6 yrs (European, Oriental). **Measures:** Ss were asked to express their opinions about 15 pictures depicting absurd situations. Ss' verbal responses and facial expressions were recorded. Classification of the verbal responses yielded 9 categories of cognitive strategies. **Results:** (1) Verbal responses of more Oriental girls than boys fell into category 1, description by enumerating various items in the situation, without pointing out the theme or the absurdity ($p < .001$). Verbal responses of more Oriental boys than girls fell into category 4, pointing out the absurdity in the depicted situation and directing criticism at it ($p < .001$). (2) Verbal responses of more European girls than boys fell into category 4 ($p < .01$). (3) The percentage of verbal answers accompanied by smiling was higher for Oriental boys than girls ($p < .05$). No sex differences were found in the European sample. (4) No sex differences were found in percentage of verbal answers accompanied by laughter.

Kubose, S. K. Motivational effects of boredom on children's response speeds. *Developmental Psychology*, 1972, *6*, 302–5.

    Subjects: $N = 60$; 7 yrs. **Measures:** Ss responded to 8- and 18-second colored picture or square stimuli with instrumental or noninstrumental lever-pulling. Response and movement times were measured. **Results:** No sex differences.

Kubzansky, P. E., Rabelsky, F., and Dorman, L. A developmental study of size constancy for two- versus three-dimensional stimuli. *Child Development*, 1971, *42*, 633–35.

    Subjects: $N = 64$; 3–6 yrs. **Measures:** Ss performed a size constancy task with 2- and 3-dimensional stimuli. **Results:** No sex differences.

Kuhn, D. Mechanisms of change in the development of cognitive structures. *Child Development*, 1972, *43*, 833–44 (and personal communication).

    Subjects: $N = 87$; 4, 6, 8 yrs. **Measures:** Ss were pretested for concept of class and classification. A week later, a modeling task was given. The stage at which the model sorted the objects was either 1 below, 1 above, 2 above, or equal to S's previously established stage of development. After the model completed her sortings, S was told it was his turn, and was asked to sort the objects and give explanations for his sortings. A second post-test was given 1 week later. S was again asked to sort the objects, recall the way the model had sorted them, recognize a sketch of the model's sorting, and tell which sketch showed the best way of sorting the objects (preference). **Results:** No sex differences.

Kurtz, R. M. Body attitude and self-esteem. *Proceedings* of the 79th Annual Convention of the APA, 1971, *8*, 467–68.

    Subjects: $N = 40$; 18–21 yrs (college). **Measures:** Ss were given the Ziller Self-Esteem Scale and the Body Attitude Scale. The latter assessed Ss' attitudes toward the outward form of their bodies on 3 dimensions: evaluative, potency, and activity. **Results:** (1) Women had higher evaluative mean scores than men ($p < .001$). (2) Men had higher potency mean scores than women ($p < .001$). High self-esteem men had higher potency mean scores than low self-esteem men; high self-esteem women had lower potency mean scores than low self-esteem women ($p < .05$). (3) Men had higher activity mean scores than women ($p < .005$).

L'Abate, L. Personality correlates of manifest anxiety in children. *J. Consulting Psychology,* 1960, *24,* 242–48.

> **Subjects:** $N = 96$; 9–13 yrs. **Measures:** Children's Manifest Anxiety Scale. **Results:** (1) No sex differences were found in anxiety or lie scores (CMAS). (2) Girls checked the following items more frequently than boys did: I am secretly afraid of a lot of things ($p < .05$); My feelings get hurt easily ($p < .001$); It is hard for me to go to sleep at night ($p < .05$); and I am afraid of the dark ($p < .001$). (3) Boys checked the following items more frequently than girls did: I wish I could be very far away from here ($p < .025$); I never get angry ($p < .05$); and I would rather win than lose in a game.

Lalljee, M., and Cook, M. Uncertainty in first encounters. *J. Personality & Social Psychology,* 1973, *26,* 137–41.

> **Subjects:** $N = 10$; 18–21 yrs (college). **Measures:** Ss discussed both anxiety-arousing and non-anxiety-arousing topics with E. The response measures were speech rate, filled pause ratios, and non-ah speech-disturbance ratios. Filled-pause ratios were calculated by summing the number of filled pauses during each minute of speech and dividing by the number of words spoken during that time. Non-ah speech-disturbance ratios were calculated by summing instances of sentence change, repetition, sentence incompletion, stutter, slip of the tongue, omission, and intruding incoherent sound, and then dividing by the number of words spoken. **Results:** (1) Filled-pause ratios were higher for men than for women. (2) No sex differences were found in speech rate or non-ah speech-disturbance ratios.

Lamal, P. A. Imitation learning of information-processing. *J. Experimental Child Psychology,* 1971, *12,* 223–27.

> **Subjects:** $N = 72$; 8, 10, 12 yrs. **Measures:** Each S tried to solve "20 questions" type problems after observing E solve a sample problem using either a hypotheses-scanning approach (testing specific hypotheses such as "Is it the apple?") or a constraint-seeking approach (more efficient strategy such as "Is it an animal?"). **Results:** No sex differences.

Lambert, W., and Levy, L. H. Sensation seeking and short-term sensory isolation. *J. Personality & Social Psychology,* 1972, *24,* 46–52.

> **Subjects:** $N = 40$; 18–21 yrs (college). **Measures:** The Sensation-Seeking Scale (SSS) was initially administered to all Ss in order to predict Ss' need for visual stimulation during a subsequent 2-hour period of sensory isolation. Ss' rate of using freely available visual stimuli during isolation was time sampled across the 2 hours. Digital skin resistance was also measured. **Results:** No sex differences were found in scores on the SSS in rate of using visual stimuli or in skin resistance. Women had higher skin resistance levels at the beginning of the 2-hour period of sensory isolation, while men had higher levels during the last hour.

Lambert, W. E., Yackley, A., and Hein, R. N. Child training values of English Canadian and French Canadian parents. *Canadian J. Behavioral Science,* 1971, *3,* 217–36.

> **Subjects:** $N = 73$; parents of 6-year-old children (French-Canadian, English-Canadian). **Measures:** (1) Parents' reactions to a tape recording of various incidents and behaviors that are frequent occurrences in a child's life were recorded and coded. (2) Parents also completed a questionnaire assessing (a) their perceptions of similarities or differences in the behavior of boys and girls and (b) their opinions as to whether sex-role differences in behavior should exist. **Results:** (1) No differences were found between boys' and girls' parents' reactions to (a) requests for help; (b) displays of insolence; (c) conflicts between a child and a baby, a child and a guest, or a child who is hurt and a baby; (d) requests to go outside and play. (2) Parents of boys were harsher than parents of girls in their reactions to anger. (3) In response to the child's request to invite a friend home, parents of girls were more restrictive than parents of boys (French-Canadian sample only). (4) In response to the child's comfort-seeking requests, parents of girls were more likely to comply than parents of boys. (5) In response to the conflict between the child and a guest, fathers of boys sided more with the guest than fathers of girls. In the FC sample, mothers of girls sided more with the guest than mothers of boys. (6) Fathers of boys responded more harshly to insolence than fathers of girls, whereas mothers of boys were less harsh than mothers of girls. This result was true only among FC parents. (7a) EC mothers were harsher in their reactions to insolence than EC fathers. No difference was found between FC mothers and fathers; (7b) EC fathers sided more with the

baby after the baby hurt the child than EC mothers did. No difference was found between FC mothers and fathers; (7c) Differences between mothers and fathers on the other items were not significant. (8) Questionnaire findings: (a) No differences were found between boys' and girls' parents' perceptions of sex-role differences in behavior. FC fathers perceived more sex-role differences in behaviors than FC mothers did. No differences were found between EC mothers and fathers. (b) Parents of boys thought sex-role differences in behavior should exist more than did parents of girls. No differences were found between mothers and fathers.

Landauer, T. L., Carlsmith, J. M., and Lepper, M. Experimental analysis of the factors determining obedience of four-year-old children to adult females. *Child Development*, 1970, *41*, 601–11.
Subjects: $N = 33$; 3–4 yrs and mothers. Measures: Each mother asked 3 Ss (1 her own child) to perform 1 of 3 obedience tasks. The latency of the first disobedience, the number of times the request was repeated, the length of time the child was obedient, and a description of the session were recorded. Results: No sex differences.

Landsbaum, J. B., and Willis, R. H. Conformity in early and late adolescence. *Developmental Psychology*, 1971, *4*, 334–37.
Subjects: $N = 64$; 13–14, 18–21 yrs (college). Measures: Systematically varied fake feedback was given to paired same-sex Ss regarding their own and partner's supposed performance on line length judgments. Ss and partners then performed a slightly different line length judgment task. After making his own response, S was allowed to see his partner's response (which was actually E's response pre-planned to disagree 50% of the time) before S made his final judgment. The number of times S changed his initial judgment to agree with partner's judgment was recorded. Results: No sex differences.

Lane, E. A. Childhood characteristics of black college graduates reared in poverty. *Developmental Psychology*, 1973, *8*, 42–45.
Subjects: $N = 22$; 27–46 yrs (black college graduates from low SES backgrounds). Measures: Group IQ tests were administered in the second grade (Kuhlman-Anderson), the sixth grade (Cleveland Classification Test), and the eighth grade (McNemar Test), with same-sex scores obtained for individually matched controls and for as many siblings as possible. Results: There were no sex differences in IQ increase from second to eighth grade.

Lane, I. M., and Coon, R. C. Reward allocation in preschool children. *Child Development*, 1972, *43*, 1382–89.
Subjects: $N = 80$; 4, 5 yrs (white, middle SES). Measures: S was told he was playing a game with a (fictitious) partner in another room. S was asked to paste gummed stickers on a special work sheet as fast as possible. S and his "partner" worked as a team, i.e. the more stickers they pasted the more rewards they would get. Time and "partner's" performance were manipulated so that S pasted many less, many more, or the same number of stickers compared with his partner. Afterward, S could distribute the rewards as he wished. Results: No sex differences.

Lane, I. M., and Missé, L. A. Equity and the distribution of rewards. *J. Personality & Social Psychology*, 1971, *20*, 1–17.
Subjects: $N = 128$; 18–21 yrs (college). Measures: Ss were given unilateral power to determine their rewards and those of 1 other person. Ss chose between a standard and an alternative distribution. Results: Men more often than women chose distributions more favorable to themselves than to other partners.

Langhorne, M. C. The effects of maze rotation on learning. *J. General Psychology*, 1948, *38*, 191–205.
Subjects: $N = 102$; 21–22 yrs. Measures: On the first day, Ss traced through a maze with a stylus until they reached the criterion of 2 consecutive, errorless trials. On the following days, the maze was successively rotated in a counterclockwise direction through the 90°, 180°, 270°, and 360° positions. Results: (1) On the first day, men averaged fewer trials, fewer errors, and less time than women did. (2) On successive days, similar gains in performance were exhibited by men and women.

Langlois, J. H., Gottfried, N. W., and Seay, B. The influence of sex of peer on the social behavior of preschool children. *Developmental Psychology*, 1973, *8*, 93–98 (and personal communication).
Subjects: $N = 32$; 3, 5 yrs (black). Measures: Same-sex and opposite-sex pairs of Ss were ob-

served in free play for 4 15-minute sessions. **Results:** First two sessions: (1) Girls talked with and touched their partners more frequently than boys did ($p < .01$; $p < .05$). (2) Boys hit their partners with objects more frequently than girls did ($p < .01$). (3) Among 3-year-old Ss, girls exhibited more nonword vocalizations than boys did; among 5-year-old Ss, the reverse was true ($p < .05$). (4) 3-year-old girls threw blocks more frequently than 3-year-old boys and 5-year-old girls did; 5-year-old boys threw blocks more frequently than any other age-sex group did ($p < .05$). Overall, boys threw blocks more frequently than girls did ($p < .01$). (5) No sex differences were found in the following behaviors (some of which had a low frequency of occurrence): hitting partner with hand and foot; moving from within to beyond or from beyond to within 1 foot of partner; being within 1 foot of partner; smiling; frowning, manipulating partner with hand; throwing, sitting on, manipulating, or embracing objects; oral contact with objects; standing; riding toy truck; touching own body or clothing. Second two sessions: (1) Girls spent more time talking with their partners and touching their own bodies and clothing than boys did ($p < .05$, $p < .05$). (2) Ss with same-sex partners displayed more hitting, more touching, less talking, and kept within 1 foot of their partners more frequently than Ss with opposite-sex partners did.

Lansky, L. M. The family structure also affects the model: sex-role attitudes in parents of preschool children. *Merrill-Palmer Quarterly*, 1967, *13*, 139–50.
> **Subjects:** $N = 196$; parents of preschool children. **Measures:** Ss completed the Sex-Role Attitude Test (SRAT); 2 forms were available, 1 for boys' parents and 1 for girls' parents. For each item, Ss judged a same-sex parent's reaction to a child's preference for 1 of 2 sex-linked objects, names, or activities. **Results:** (1) Fathers and mothers expressed more negative attitudes toward boys' than toward girls' cross-sex choices ($p < .001$, $p < .01$). (2) No differences were found in fathers' and mothers' attitudes toward boys' and girls' same-sex choices.

Lansky, L. M., and McKay, G. Independence, dependence, and manifest and latent masculinity-femininity: some complex relationships among four complex variables. *Psychological Reports*, 1969, *24*, 263–68.
> **Subjects:** $N = 36$; 5–6 yrs. **Measures:** 2 teachers independently rated Ss' overall-school behavior on the Beller's scales for dependent behavior (DEP) and independence or autonomous achievement-striving behaviors (AAS). Manifest masculinity-femininity was measured by a modified version of the IT Scale for Children (ITSC). Latent masculinity-femininity was measured by Franck's Drawing Completing Test (DCT). **Results:** (1) Boys scored higher (more masculine) on the ITSC than girls did. (2) No sex differences were found on the DCT or the DEP. (3) Girls scored higher (showed more independent, autonomous achievement-striving) on the AAS than boys did ($p < .05$).

Laosa, L. M., and Brophy, J. E. Effects of sex and birth order on sex-role development and intelligence among kindergarten children. *Developmental Psychology*, 1972, *6*, 409–15.
> **Subjects:** $N = 93$; 5–7 yrs. **Measures:** (1) Sex-role orientation: IT Scale for Children, draw-a-person task (own sex first, then sex differentiation). (2) Sex-role preference: forced- and free-choice toy preference, forced-choice game preference, occupational preference naming, peer preference naming. (3) Sex-role adoption: teacher ratings of child behaviors. (4) Other: sociometric play observations by teachers, child questionnaire of parental dominance, Primary Mental Abilities test. **Results:** (1) The sexes differed in the expected direction on all measures of sex typing: role orientation, preference, and adoption ($p < .001$, $p < .001$, $p < .001$). (2) Ss more often chose members of their own sex as playmates (interview measure and play behavior observation). (3) Girls played in pairs more often than boys did. (4) There were no sex differences in seeing fathers as dominant in decision making and competence and mothers as dominant in a limited setting. (5) Girls saw mothers as more nurturant than fathers; boys saw parents as more nearly equal.

Lapidus, D. Differential socialization of male and female preschoolers: competition versus cooperation. Psychology Honors Thesis for Dr. Eleanor Maccoby, Stanford University, 1972.
> **Subjects:** $N = 30$; 3–4 yrs and their mothers. **Measures:** Each mother-child pair played 30 trials on Madsen's marble-pull game. **Results:** (1) No differences were found between boys and girls or their mothers in (a) number of marbles obtained; (b) number of marbles taken out of turn (taking a marble out of turn was defined as winning a marble after having won a marble on the previous trial); (c) number of interaction episodes in which verbalization occurred. (2) Boys and their mothers made self-deprecatory narrative statements in more

interaction episodes than did girls and their mothers. No differences were found between boys and girls or their mothers in the frequency of the following types of verbalizations: cooperative permissive; cooperative submissive; cooperative receptive; competitive general; competitive aggressive; competitive threatening/teasing; narrative, praise of other; narrative, praise of self; narrative, suggestions/explanations. (3) Boys laughed in more interaction episodes after they had won a marble than girls did.

Lapouse, R., and Monk, M. A. Behavior deviations in a representative sample of children: variation by sex, age, race, social class, and family size. *American J. Orthopsychiatry*, 1964, *34*, 436–46.

> **Subjects:** $N = 482$; 6–12 yrs and mothers. **Measures:** Mothers were interviewed about their children's behavior and adjustment by means of a structured schedule. Reports of behavior deviations were recorded. **Results:** (1) More boys than girls were reported as displaying a high frequency of bed-wetting, masturbation, physical inactivity, and daydreaming. More girls than boys were reported as showing a high frequency of daydreaming. (2) No sex-of-child differences were found in maternal reports of deviations in speech, bedtime behavior, awaking behavior, elimination, sex behavior, eating behavior, eating habits, sleeping behavior, or body management. In addition, no differences were reported in wild behavior, overactivity, temper loss, restless behavior, tension phenomena, tics, compulsive behavior, or teachers' complaints about the child's behavior. (3) Overall, more boys than girls were reported as displaying a high incidence of behavior control problems (a category encompassing temper loss, wild behavior, overactivity, and teachers' complaints).

Larder, D. L. Effect of aggressive story content on nonverbal play behavior. *Psychological Reports*, 1962, *11*, 14.

> **Subjects:** $N = 15$; 4 yrs. **Measures:** Ss played with an aggressive toy and a nonaggressive toy. The aggressive toy was a striking doll apparatus in which a 6-inch boy hit another doll when a lever was pressed. The nonaggressive toy was a dog that came from behind swinging doors when a lever was pressed. **Results:** A greater proportion of boys' than girls' responses were aggressive ($p = .02$).

Larsen, K. S., and Minton, H. L. Attributed social power—a scale and some validity. *J. Social Psychology*, 1971, *85*, 37–39.

> **Subjects:** $N = 106$; 18–21 yrs (college). **Measures:** Ss were presented with a scale designed to measure attributed power (AP). The scale consisted of 5 power relationships: policeman-citizen, professor-student, general-private, foreman-worker, and king-subject. Ss were asked to rate each relationship on 15 7-step dichotomous power-laden adjectives (e.g. powerful-weak, restraining-noninterfering, arbitrary-reasonable, etc.). **Results:** Women attributed more power to power relationships than men did ($r = .25$, $p < .05$).

Larsen, K. S., Coleman, D., Forbes, J. and Johnson, R. Is the subject's personality or the experimental situation a better prediction of a subject's willingness to administer shock to a victim? *J. Personality & Social Psychology*, 1972, *22*, 287–95.

> **Subjects:** $N = 213$; 18–21 yrs (college). **Measures:** Willingness of Ss to shock a victim within a learning-study paradigm was assessed. Ss were assigned to 1 of 5 conditions: control, model, conformity, female learner, or high model. **Results:** (1) When exposed to a model who shocked his victim at maximal level, men shocked their victims at a higher voltage and for a longer period of time than women did ($p < .05$). No sex differences were found in total voltage administered or in Ss' estimates of the maximum voltage they had reached. (2) No sex differences were found in the control, conformity, high model, or female learner conditions.

Laughlin, P. R., and McGlynn, R. P. Cooperative versus competitive concept attainment as a function of sex and stimulus display. *J. Personality & Social Psychology*, 1967, *7*, 398–402.

> **Subjects:** $N = 192$; 18–21 yrs (college). **Measures:** Same-sex pairs of Ss performed a visual discrimination-learning task. The response measures were number of trials to solution, percentage of untenable hypotheses, and time to solution. Ss' responses were also scored for focusing and scanning strategy. **Results:** Men required more time to reach a solution than women did ($p < .05$).

Laughlin, P. R., Moss, I. L., and Miller, S. M. Information-processing in children as a function of adult model, stimulus display, school grade and sex. *J. Educational Psychology*, 1969, *60*, 188–93.

> **Subjects:** $N = 216$; 8, 10, 12 yrs. **Measures:** Ss played a modified game of "20 questions,"

attempting to determine which of 42 objects E had in mind. Performance measures were number of questions to solution, percentage of constraints (questions that referred to 2 or more objects), and average number of items included per question. **Results:** No sex differences.

Laughlin, P. R., Branch, L. G., and Johnson, H. H. Individual versus triadic performance on a unidimensional complementary task as a function of initial ability level. *J. Personality & Social Psychology*, 1969, *12*, 144–50.

    Subjects: $N = 528$; 18–21 yrs (college). **Measures:** Part 1 (Synonyms and Antonyms) of Form T of the Terman Concept Mastery Task. **Results:** No sex differences.

Laurence, M. W., and Trotter, M. Effect of acoustic factors and list organization in multi-trial free recall learning of college age and elderly adults. *Developmental Psychology*, 1971, *5*, 202–10.

    Subjects: $N = 72$; 23, 75 yrs. **Measures:** 36 words were presented to Ss on a memory drum. The 36 words included 6 homophone pairs (e.g. idol, idle), 6 pairs of acoustically similar words (e.g. jacket, jagged), and 12 acoustically and semantically unrelated words. Afterward, Ss were asked to recall as many words as possible. **Results:** No sex differences.

LeCompte, G. K., and Gratch, G. Violation of a rule as a method of diagnosing infants' levels of object concept. *Child Development*, 1972, *43*, 385–96.

    Subjects: $N = 36$; 9, 12, 18 mos. **Measures:** Ss were familiarized with a toy, which was then hidden and replaced by another toy to assess object transformation level. **Results:** No sex differences.

Lefebvre, A., and Bohn, M. J., Jr. Occupational prestige as seen by disadvantaged black children. *Developmental Psychology*, 1971, *4*, 173–77.

    Subjects: $N = 300$; 9–13 yrs (black). **Measures:** Ss ranked 12 high and low SES occupations from most admired to least admired. **Results:** Among 9-11-year-old Ss, girls ranked elementary school teachers first more often than boys did.

Leff, R. Effects of punishment intensity and consistency on the internalization of behavioral suppression in children. *Developmental Psychology*, 1969, *1*, 345–56.

    Subjects: $N = 107$; 6–8 yrs. **Measures:** Ss were asked to choose between a small, unattractive toy and a larger, attractive toy. Ss were either intermittently or continuously punished for choosing the more attractive toy. Punishment consisted of exposure to a high- or low-volume noise followed by a verbal expression of disapproval from E. **Results:** No sex differences in number of times Ss were punished.

LeFurgy, W. G., and Woloshin, G. W. Immediate and long-term effects of experimentally induced social influence in the modification of adolescents' moral judgments. *J. Personality & Social Psychology*, 1969, *12*, 104–10.

    Subjects: $N = 53$; 12–13 yrs. **Measures:** Ss were initially presented with a 10-item form of the moral realism scale, a measure designed to assess Ss' position along the moral realism–moral relativism dimension. Each of the 10 items was a story, describing a moral dilemma in which the protagonist, confronted with extenuating circumstances, had to decide whether to obey (realistic response) or disobey (relativistic response) legal or social norms. On the following day, Ss responded to 20 stories of a similar nature after being exposed to the (prerecorded) choices of same-sex confederate. Confederates' responses were consistently contrary to Ss' initial position (realistic or relativistic). Immediately following this social influence phase and again one week later, Ss were presented with a new 10-item form of the moral realism scale. Approximately 3 months later, Ss were given the original 10-item pretest. **Results:** (1) On the initial 10-item form of the moral realism scale, girls made more realistic choices than boys did ($p < .001$). (2) No sex differences were found in the difference between Ss' scores on the pretest and social influence forms of the moral realism score. (3) At each of the post-test phases, no sex differences were found in change from initial orientation.

Lehman, E. B. Selective strategies in children's attention to task-relevant information. *Child Development*, 1972, *43*, 197–209.

    EXPERIMENT I: **Subects:** $N = 60$; 5, 7, 9 yrs. **Measures:** Ss performed a haptic matching task with a standard and 2 comparison stimuli. One comparison object was identical to the standard in shape but different in texture; the other was identical in texture but different in shape. On half the trials, Ss were instructed to pick as quickly as possible the comparison that was the same shape as the standard; on the remaining trials, Ss were told to match on the basis of texture. A record was kept of the frequency with which Ss explored only the relevant dimension (i.e. either texture or shape) and of the number of times Ss felt only 1 of the 2 comparison stimuli. **Results:** No sex differences.

EXPERIMENT II: **Subjects:** $N = 30$; 5, 7, 9 yrs. **Measures:** Same as Experiment I, with the following exceptions: (1) On each trial, both comparison stimuli were identical to the standard in shape (texture), but only 1 matched the standard in texture (shape); (2) no specific instructions were given regarding which dimension was relevant. **Results:** No sex differences.

EXPERIMENT III: **Subjects:** $N = 120$; 5, 7, 9, 11 yrs. **Measures:** As in Experiments I and II, Ss performed a haptic matching task with a standard and 2 comparison stimuli (wooden crosses); 1 comparison was exactly the same size as the standard, while the other was considerably larger or smaller. Half the Ss were trained to realize that the crosses were of equal length horizontally and vertically; the other half were not. Instructions were given to match the crosses on the basis of size "in the fastest possible way." The frequency with which Ss performed only 1 hand movement (i.e. felt or spanned either 1 dimension or 1 quadrant of each cross) and the frequency with which they touched only 1 comparison stimulus were recorded. **Results:** No sex differences.

Leiderman, P. H., Leifer, A. D., Seashore, M. J., Barnett, C. R., and Grobstein, R. Mother-infant interaction: effects of early deprivation, prior experience and sex of infant. *Early Development*, 1973, *51*, 154–75.

> **Subjects:** $N = 66$ infants (premature, full-term) and their mothers; tested at time of discharge from the hospital and at 1 week, 1 mo, and 3 mos postdischarge. **Measures:** (1) Selected mother and infant behaviors were observed during caretaking in the home at 1 week postdischarge and again in the pediatrics clinic at 1 month postdischarge. During both observation sessions, mothers fed and held their infants. (2) At time of discharge and again 3 months later, the Bayley Tests of Mental and Motor Development were administered. (3) Physical growth was assessed by recording the infant's weight at discharge and again at his physical examination 1 month later. (4) Each mother's confidence in her ability to care for her infant was assessed immediately preceding her infant's discharge from the hospital and again 1 month later. A paired comparison questionnaire was used. **Results:** (1) At 1 week and at 1 month postdischarge, mothers of girls showed more ventral contact with their infants than mothers of boys ($p < .05$, $p < .05$). At 1 month but not at 1 week postdischarge, mothers of boys affectionately touched their infants more than mothers of girls ($p < .025$). At both observation sessions, no sex differences were found in the frequency of the following maternal attachment behaviors: holding, looking, talking, laughing, or smiling. (2) No sex differences were found on the Bayley Tests or on the physical growth measures. (3) No difference was found between boys' and girls' mothers in maternal self-confidence.

Leifer, A. D., Collins, W. A., Gross, B. M., Taylor, P. H., Andrews, L., and Blacknert, E. R. Developmental aspects of variables relevant to observational learning. *Child Development*, 1971, *42*, 1509–16.

> **Subjects:** $N = 60$; 4, 7, 10 yrs. **Measures:** Ss observed a filmed adaptation of a fairy tale. Afterward, they were questioned on memory and understanding of feelings and motivation attributed to male and female characters. **Results:** No sex differences.

Lekarczyk, D. T., and Hill, K. T. Self-esteem, test anxiety, stress, and verbal learning. *Developmental Psychology*, 1969, *1*, 147–54.

> **Subjects:** $N = 114$; 10, 11 yrs. **Measures:** Ss completed a revised Coopersmith's Self-Esteem Inventory, the Test Anxiety Scale for Children (TASC), the Lie Scale for Children (LSC), the Defensiveness Scale for Children (DSC), the Kuhlmann Anderson IQ test (Forms E and F), and the Stanford Achievement Test. The 5% of Ss with the highest LSC and DSC scores were eliminated from the sample. **Results:** (1) Boys scored higher than girls on the LSC and the DSC. (2) Girls had higher test anxiety, achievement, and IQ scores than boys. (3) There were no sex differences in self-esteem scores.

Lepper, M. R. Dissonance, self-perception, and honesty in children. *J. Personality & Social Psychology*, 1973, *25*, 65–74.

> **Subjects:** $N = 129$; 7 yrs. **Measures:** (1) Ss initially indicated their relative preferences for 6 attractive toys. Before leaving Ss alone for a short period of time, E told each child in the experimental condition not to play with his second-ranked toy; in the control condition, no prohibition was given. At the end of this temptation period, a second E asked Ss to rerank the 6 toys. The response was the new rank Ss assigned to the toy they had initially ranked second. (2) Half of the Ss were then given the following tasks: (a) a self-perception measure in which Ss were presented with 12 adjectives, 4 of which were chosen to fall on a dimension of honesty-

dishonesty and 8 on a more general positive-negative continuum. Ss were asked to place each adjective in 1 of 5 categories (ranging from "very much like me" to "not at all like me"); (b) an attitude-toward-moral-offenses measure in which Ss were presented with 2 brief stories of children yielding to temptation. After each story, Ss indicated how bad they thought the protagonist was and how bad they thought the protagonist felt about what he had done; (c) measure of how much they liked the first E. (3) 3 weeks later, a third E asked Ss to play a game in which they could only obtain attractive prizes by falsifying their scores. The response measure was the number of points Ss added to their scores. **Results:** No sex differences.

Lerner, M. J. Observer's evaluation of a victim: justice, guilt, and veridical perception. *J. Personality & Social Psychology*, 1971, *20*, 127–35.
> **Subjects:** $N = 61$; 18–21 yrs (college). **Measures:** Ss observed a victim receive apparently painful shocks from making incorrect responses, after which they rated the victim on 15 bipolar adjective scales. Only in 1 of 3 conditions were Ss informed that the victim was acting. **Results:** No sex differences were found in Ss' ratings.

Lerner, R. M., and Gellert, E. Body build identification, preference, and aversion in children. *Developmental Psychology*, 1969, *1*, 456–62.
> **Subjects:** $N = 45$; 5 yrs. **Measures:** E rated the body build of every student as chubby to average, average or muscular, thin to average, thin and linear. Ss were presented with same-sex photographs of chubby, average, and thin peers and were asked to indicate the pictures they most resembled, those they would most like to look like, and those they would least like to look like. Ss were also asked to name same-sex classmate who looked like stimulus picture. All tasks were administered twice. **Results:** (1) No sex differences were found in the percentage of Ss who correctly matched their own body builds. (2) A similar number of boys and girls showed an aversion to chubbiness. (3) A higher proportion of girls than boys correctly matched peers to each of the 3 body builds (level of significance not reported).

Lerner, R. M., and Schroeder, C. Kindergarten children's active vocabulary about body build. *Developmental Psychology*, 1971a, *5*, 179 (brief report).
> **Subjects:** $N = 76$; 5 yrs. **Measures:** Ss were asked questions about fat and thin children (e.g. "What does it mean to be a fat boy?" and "What would a thin boy be like?"). Ss' responses were categorized into 1 of 3 content categories (physique and physical, social, personal) or into an irrelevant-statement category. **Results:** No sex differences.

Lerner, R. M., and Schroeder, C. Physique identification, preference, and aversion in kindergarten children. *Developmental Psychology*, 1971b, *5*, 538 (brief report).
> **Subjects:** $N = 140$; 5 yrs. **Measures:** Ss were presented with same-sex figure drawings of fat, average, and thin peers, and were asked to point to the figure they most resembled, the one they most wanted to look like, and the one they least wanted to look like. **Results:** No sex differences.

Leskow, S., and Smock, C. D. Developmental changes in problem solving strategies. *Developmental Psychology*, 1970, *2*, 412–22.
> **Subjects:** $N = 96$; 12, 15, 18 yrs. **Measures:** Ss performed permutations on 4 sets of 4 stimuli, under instructions to find all possible arrangements without repetition. Performance measures were number of unrepeated permutations (NP), frequency of first-position items held constant from 1 trial to the next (IMC), and number of sequentially subgrouped transformations (GT) that were then scored on type of strategy. **Results:** No sex differences.

Lesser, G. S., Fifer, G., and Clark, D. H. Mental abilities of children from different social-class and cultural groups. *Monographs of the Society for Research in Child Development*, 1965, *30*.
> **Subjects:** $N = 320$; 6–7 yrs (Chinese, Jewish, Negro, Puerto Rican). **Measures:** Ss were given a modified version of the Hunter College Aptitude Scales for Gifted Children, which included (1) Verbal scale (picture vocabulary, word vocabulary), (2) Reasoning scale (picture analogies, picture arrangement, jump peg), (3) Numerical scale (enumeration, addition, subtraction, multiplication, division), and (4) Space scale (object completion, estimating path, jigsaw puzzles, perspective). **Results:** (1) Boys performed better than girls on the picture vocabulary and jump peg subtests and on the total Space scale. (2) Among Chinese, black, and Puerto Rican Ss, boys performed better than girls on both the Verbal and the Space scales; among Jewish Ss, the reverse was true (Verbal scale, $p < .01$; Space scale, $p < .05$).

Lessler, K. Sexual symbols, structured and unstructured. *J. Consulting Psychology*, 1962, 26, 44–49.
Subjects: $N = 120$; 9, 14, 18–21 yrs (college). **Measures:** Ss' task was to sort 20 structured and 20 unstructured (texture) symbols into 2 piles, masculine and feminine. The measure of performance was the percentage of symbols sorted in agreement with the previous ratings of 5 judges with knowledge of psychoanalytic theory. **Results:** (1) There were no sex differences in percentage of correct identifications for structured symbols. (2) Females identified more unstructured symbols consistent with the judges' ratings than males did ($p < .05$).

Leventhal, D.B., and Shemberg, K. M. Sex role adjustment and nonsanctioned aggression. *J. Experimental Research in Personality*, 1969, 3, 283–86.
Subjects: $N = 80$; 18–21 yrs (college). **Measures:** Ss were divided into 4 groups (masculine males, masculine females, feminine females, and feminine males) based on their extreme scores on the MF dimensions of the Guilford-Zimmerman Temperament Survey. Ss were instructed to teach a confederate a concept by flashing a light for each response or shocking him for each incorrect response. Ss were given ambiguous sanctions for aggressive behavior, i.e. they were informed that experiments had not yet determined whether strong or weak shocks produced faster learning. The mean intensity of the shocks Ss administered was recorded. **Results:** No sex differences were found.

Leventhal, D. B., Shemberg, K. M., and van Schoelandt, S. K. Effects of sex-role adjustment upon the expression of aggression. *J. Personality & Social Psychology*, 1968, 8, 393–96.
    Experiment I: **Subjects:** $N = 40$; 18–21 yrs (college). **Measures:** Ss were divided into 4 groups (masculine males, feminine males, masculine females, and feminine females) based on their extreme scores on the MF dimension of the Guilford-Zimmerman Temperament Survey. Ss were instructed to shock a male confederate every time he made an error. The response measure was the mean intensity of the applied shock. **Results:** There were no main effects of sex or sex-role identification. Masculine males and feminine females had higher mean aggression scores than feminine males and masculine females ($p < .0001$).
    Experiment II: **Subjects:** $N = 40$; 18–21 yrs (college). **Measures:** Ss were divided into high and low need for approval groups based on their scores on the Marlowe-Crowne Social-Desirability Scale. As in Experiment I, all Ss were told to shock a male confederate whenever he made an error. **Results:** No sex differences.

Leventhal, G. S., and Anderson, D. Self-interest and the maintenance of equity. *J. Personality & Social Psychology*, 1970, 15, 57–62.
Subjects: $N = 144$; 5 yrs. **Measures:** Ss were told their performance on a task (pasting gummed stars on a worksheet) was either superior, equal, or inferior to that of a fictitious same-sex partner. Ss were then rewarded with colorful picture seals that they were requested to divide between themselves and their partners. Ss were also asked to recall their own performance and their partners' performance scores. **Results:** (1) In the superior condition, boys took a larger number of seals for themselves than girls did. No sex differences were found in the equal or inferior condition. (2) No sex differences were found in the number of stars Ss attributed to self or to partner.

Leventhal, G. S., and Lane, D. W. Sex, age, and equity behavior. *J. Personality & Social Psychology*, 1970, 15, 312–16.
Subjects: $N = 61$; 18–21 yrs (college). **Measures:** Ss worked with a fictitious same-sex partner on a task for which their dyad received monetary reward. Ss were told their performance was either superior or inferior to that of their partner. The performance measure was Ss' allocation of the group reward. **Results:** (1) Men took a larger share of the group reward than women did ($p < .01$). (2) On a postexperimental questionnaire, women in the superior performance condition attributed a lower level of performance to themselves and judged their performance to be more similar to that of their partner than men did. No sex differences were found in the inferior performance condition.

Leventhal, G. S., and Whiteside, H. D. Equity and the use of reward to elicit high performance. *J. Personality & Social Psychology*, 1973, 25, 75–83.
Subjects: $N = 28$; 18–21 yrs (college). **Measures:** After being given information about the aptitude and examination performance of several hypothetical students, Ss assigned a midterm grade to each student. **Results:** No sex differences.

Leventhal, G. S., Michaels, J. W., and Sanford, C. Inequity and interpersonal conflict: reward allocation and secrecy about reward as methods of preventing conflict. *J. Personality & Social Psychology*, 1972, *23*, 88–102.

Subjects: $N = 44$; 18–21 yrs (college). Measures: Ss gave their opinions about the best way to divide group earnings among the members of a hypothetical group. Ss divided group rewards twice, once under the assumption that all members would know what others were receiving and once under conditions of secrecy. Afterward, Ss rated how reluctant they would be in the secrecy condition to provide group members with information about their allocation of the group rewards. Results: No sex differences.

Leventhal, H., and Fischer, K. What reinforces in a social reinforcement situation—words or expressions? *J. Personality & Social Psychology*, 1970, *14*, 83–94.

Subjects: $N = 96$; 5–9 yrs. Measures: After an initial base period, Ss received either positive reinforcement or no reinforcement for placing marbles into 1 of 2 holes. Performance measures were rate of marble insertion and hole preference. Additionally, Ss' expressive behavior was rated for anxiety, physical activity, and attentiveness. Results: No sex differences.

Levin, G. R., and Maurer, D. M. The solution process in children's matching-to-sample. *Developmental Psychology*, 1969, *1*, 679–90.

EXPERIMENT I: Subjects: $N = 19$; 5–6 yrs. Measures: Ss were given matching-to-sample problems using slides of familiar objects and animals. Response measures were choice latency and the time between observing response and choice response. Results: No sex differences.

EXPERIMENT III: Subjects: $N = 63$; 4–5 yrs. Measures: Ss were randomly assigned to "matching" or "oddity" groups. Same as Experiment I, except that slides of black and white drawings and color slides of common geometric forms were used. Color, size, and form were used separately as criteria for matching and oddity problems. Results: No sex differences.

Levinger, G., and Moreland, J. Approach-avoidance as a function of imagined shock threat and self-other similarity. *J. Personality & Social Psychology*, 1969, *12*, 245–51.

Subjects: $N = 96$; 18–21 yrs (college). Measures: Ss placed figures representing the self in relation to standing silhouette representing 4 "others" of the same sex: (a) a good friend, (b) a stranger, (c) a "similar" stranger, and (d) a "dissimilar" stranger. In 1 condition, Ss were asked to imagine both self and other waiting to receive a shock from E. Distances between Ss' placement of self and other were measured. Results: No sex differences.

Levinger, G., and Schneider, D. J. Test of the "risk is a value" hypothesis. *J. Personality & Social Psychology*, 1969, *11*, 165–69.

Subjects: $N = 250$, 18–21 yrs (college). Measures: For each of the 12 items from Kogan and Wallach's choice-dilemmas instrument, Ss indicated (a) the minimum odds of success they would want before choosing the more attractive alternative, (b) the minimum odds of success they believed their fellow students would want before choosing the more attractive alternative, and (c) the choice of odds they considered most admirable. Results: No sex differences.

Levinger, G., and Senn, D. J. Disclosure feelings in marriage. *Merrill-Palmer Quarterly*, 1967, *13*, 237–49.

Subjects: $N = 32$; married couples. Measures: Ss indicated the proportion of their pleasant and unpleasant feelings that they disclosed to their spouses. Ss also estimated what proportion of pleasant and unpleasant feelings their spouses disclosed to them. Results: No sex differences were found between husbands' and wives' reports of the proportion of feelings they disclosed to their spouses. Husbands' estimates of the proportion of unpleasant feelings their wives disclosed were higher than their wives' estimates of the proportion of unpleasant feelings their husbands disclosed ($p < .01$).

Levitin, T. E., and Chananie, J. D. Responses of female primary school teachers to sex-typed behaviors in male and female children. *Child Development*, 1972, *43*, 1309–16.

Subjects: 40 female first- and second-grade school teachers. Measures: Ss read about 2 hypothetical children who were described as either aggressive, dependent, or achieving. Ss then rated their liking for each child, their approval of his behavior, and the degree to which he was typical of children his own age and sex. Results: (1) The achieving girl was liked more than the achieving boy ($p < .05$). No sex differences were found in teachers' typicality or approval ratings. (2a) The aggressive boy and the dependent girl were seen as more typical than the aggressive girl and the dependent boy ($p < .05$). (2b) Teachers' approval ratings of the aggressive boy and the dependent girl were not significantly different from their approval ratings of the dependent boy and the aggressive girl. Overall, teachers exhibited equal approval of boys and girls. (2c) The dependent girl was liked more than the aggressive girl ($p < .05$); however, the aggressive boy was not liked more than the dependent boy (interaction, $p < .05$). Overall, boys and girls were liked equally well.

Levy, P., Lundgren, D., Ansel, M., Fell, D., Fink, B., and McGrath, J. E. Bystander effect in a demand-without-threat situation. *J. Personality & Social Psychology*, 1972, *24*, 166–71.
> **Subjects:** $N = 110$; 18–21 yrs (college). **Measures:** Ss' responses to an intrusion were recorded while Ss completed a questionnaire either alone or in the presence of 1 or 2 same-sex confederates. Intrusions were 1 or 3 nonemergency, nonthreatening demands for action by a male. The main performance measure was latency of Ss' response. Ss also completed the Rotter Internal-External Control Scale. **Results:** (1) Women had lower response latencies than men; the differences arose mainly from the alone situation. (2) No sex differences were found on the Rotter Scale.

Lewis, M. Social isolation: a parametric study of its effect on social reinforcement. *J. Experimental Child Psychology*, 1965, *2*, 205–18.
> **Subjects:** $N = 150$; 8 yrs. **Measures:** Ss were preesnted with 30 2-choice probability learning tasks after either 0, 3, 6, 9, or 12 minutes of social isolation. Correct responses were verbally reinforced, incorrect responses were not. **Results:** No sex differences.

Lewis, M. Infants' responses to facial stimuli during the first year of life. *Developmental Psychology*, 1969, *1*, 75–86.
> **Subjects:** $N = 120$; 12, 24, 36, 57 wks. **Measures:** Ss were presented with 4 variations of a male face (regular, cyclops, schematic, scrambled). Response measures were length of first fixation, smiling, vocalization, and fret/cry behavior. Only behaviors emitted during or immediately after a fixation were analyzed. **Results:** (1) At all age levels (except 57 weeks), boys looked at stimuli longer than girls did. (2) At all age levels, girls vocalized more than boys did. Girls' smiles differentiated among stimuli, boys' did not.

Lewis, M. State as an infant-environment interaction: An analysis of mother-infant behavior as a function of sex. *Merrill-Palmer Quarterly*, 1972, *18*, 95–121.
> **Subjects:** $N = 32$; 3 mos (white, black) and mothers. **Results:** (1) No sex differences were found in the frequency of the following infant behaviors: vocalizing, playing, fretting/crying, smiling, noise-making, gross motor movement. (2) Mothers of boys held their infants more and vocalized to them less than mothers of girls ($p < .05$, $p < .05$). No sex-of-infant differences were found in the following maternal behaviors: touching, looking, smiling, playing, rocking, vocalizing to others, reading/watching TV. (3) Mothers of boys were equally likely to respond in either a proximal (touch-hold) or distal (vocalize-look) modality to their infants' gross motor movements; mothers of girls responded most often in a distal modality ($p < .50$).

Lewis, M., and Freedle, R. Mother-infant dyad: the cradle of meaning. Paper presented at a Symposium on Language and Thought: Communication and Affect, Erindale College, University of Toronto, March 1972.
> **Subjects:** $N = 40$; 3 mos (black, white) and mothers. **Measures:** Mothers and infants were observed in their homes. **Results:** (1) Mothers of girls vocalized to their infants more than mothers of boys did. (2) Mothers of boys responded to vocalizations initiated by their infants more than mothers of girls did. Girls vocalized more in response to mother-initiated behaviors than boys did. (3) Boys spent more time in their mothers' laps than girls did. No sex differences were found in amount of time spent in or on crib/bed, jumper, couch/sofa, playpen, floor, infant seat, diaper-changing table or bath tub.

Lewis, M., Kagan, J., Campbell, M., and Kalafat, J. The cardiac response as a correlate of attention in infants. *Child Development*, 1966, *37*, 63–71.
> **Subjects:** $N = 64$; 6 mos. **Measures:** Fixation time and cardiac rate were measured as Ss viewed varied patterns of lights in a matrix. **Results:** No sex differences.

Lewis, M., Rausch, M., Goldberg, S., and Dodd, C. Error, response time and IQ: sex differences in cognitive style of preschool children. *Perceptual & Motor Skills*, 1968, *26*, 563–68.
> **Subjects:** $N = 57$; 3 yrs. **Measures:** Ss were shown 4 line drawings and were asked to identify which of the 4 was identical to a standard. If Ss did not initially make the correct choice, they were allowed to respond a second time. E recorded Ss' choices and the time between the

presentation of the standard and Ss' initial response. Form L-M of the Stanford-Binet Intelligence Scale was also administered to Ss. **Results:** No sex differences were found in number of errors or mean response time. Girls had higher IQs than boys ($p < .02$).

Lewis, M., Wilson, C. D., and Baumel, M. Attention distribution in the 24-month-old child: variations in complexity and incongruity of the human form. *Child Development,* 1971a, *42,* 429–38.
> **Subjects:** $N = 60$; 2 yrs. **Measures:** Ss viewed achromatic pictures of human forms varying in complexity and incongruity. Response measures were fixation time, heart rate, arm movement, smiling, pointing, and vocalizations. **Results:** No sex differences.

Lewis, M., Baumel, M., and Groch, A. Infants' attentional distribution across two modalities. Paper presented at meetings of Eastern Psychological Association, New York, 1971b.
> **Subjects:** $N = 22$; 3 mos. **Measures:** In 2 visits, 1 week apart, Ss were exposed to visual and auditory episodes separated by a test of cognitive development. Visual stimuli consisted of 3 colored lines (simple) and 20 colored lines (complex). Auditory stimuli were a C-tone (simple) and a C-chord (complex). Response measures were length of first fixation to visual episode, and heart rate and activity (stabilimeter) recorded for both auditory and visual episode. **Results:** No sex differences.

Lewit, D. W., and Virolainen, K. Conformity and independence in adolescents' motivation for orthodontic treatment. *Child Development,* 1968, *39,* 1189–1200.
> **Subjects:** $N = 129$; 13 yrs. **Measures:** Desire for Orthodontic Treatment to Children's Social Desirability Scale, Need for Peer Approval, Test Anxiety for Children Scale, Bailer's Locus of Control Scale. **Results:** Girls scored higher on the Desire for Orthodontic Treatment Scale than boys ($p < .01$).

Lichtenwalner, J. S., and Maxwell, J. W. The relationship of birth order and socioeconomic status to the creativity of preschool children. *Child Development,* 1969, *40,* 1241–47.
> **Subjects:** $N = 68$; 4–6 yrs (low, middle SES). **Measures:** The Starkweather test of creativity. **Results:** No sex differences.

Liebert, R. M., and Baron, R. A. Some immediate effects of televised violence on children's behavior. *Developmental Psychology,* 1972, *6,* 469–75.
> **Subjects:** $N = 136$; 5–6, 8–9 yrs. **Measures:** After watching 3½ minutes of "The Untouchables" or a videotaped sports sequence, Ss were given the opportunity to either help (by pressing a red button) or hurt (by pressing a green button) a child in an adjacent room. Ss were then taken to a room containing aggressive and nonaggressive toys. Ss were told they could play with any of the toys. The occurrence of each of the following aggressive responses was recorded: plays with knife, plays with gun, and assaults doll. **Results:** (1) No differences were found in the duration of boys' and girls' helping or hurting responses. (2) Boys exhibited more aggressive play responses than girls.

Liebert, R. M., and Fernandez, L. E. Imitation as a function of vicarious and direct reward. *Developmental Psychology,* 1970, *2,* 230–32.
> **Subjects:** $N = 48$; 4–6 yrs. **Measures:** After watching an adult male model choose the less popular of 2 alternatives and receive verbal reward in 1 condition or no reward in the other condition, S indicated his preference for each of 12 slide pairs. S performed the task again under instructions to match the model's responses. **Results:** No sex differences.

Liebert, R. M., and Ora, J. P. Children's adoption of self-reward patterns: incentive level and method of transmission. *Child Development,* 1968, *39,* 537–44.
> **Subjects:** $N = 72$; 8–10 yrs. **Measures:** Ss learned to play a bowling game (with preset scores) that they later had a chance to play under self-reward conditions; 1 group of Ss were shown a variety of prizes and told they could win these items if they earned enough tokens in the self-reward trial. The low-incentive group was shown a selection of dull textbooks during the length of time required for the high-incentive manipulation. The scores for which Ss took self-rewards when playing the game alone were recorded. **Results:** No sex differences.

Liebert, R. M., and Swenson, S. A. Association and abstraction as mechanisms of imitative learning. *Developmental Psychology,* 1971a, *4,* 289–94.
> **Subjects:** $N = 48$; 4 yrs. **Measures:** Ss observed a female model choose all single or all double items projected on slides (common dimension condition), or half single and half double items (no common dimension condition). Ss were then instructed to make the choices the model

had made. **Results:** (1) Girls showed better recall of the model's choices than boys ($p < .05$). (2) There were no sex differences in latency of imitative recall.

Liebert, R. M., and Swenson, S. A. Abstraction, inference, and the process of imitative learning. *Developmental Psychology*, 1971b, 5, 500–504.
  Subjects: $N = 32$; 6 yrs. **Measures:** Ss watched a model choose single items or double items from slide pictures (common dimension condition), or equal numbers of single and double items (no common dimension condition). Ss were asked to recall the model's choices when the slides were presented again, and to guess model's preferences in novel slide set. **Results:** (1) In accuracy of immediate forced recall of model's choices, boys performed better than girls in the no common dimension condition. There were no sex differences in accuracy of recall in the common dimension condition. (2) There were no sex differences on latency of imitative recall measures. (3) There were no sex differences in response latencies of predicting model's choice behavior.

Liebert, R. M., Hanratty, M., and Hill, J. H. Effects of rule structure and training method on the adoption of a self-imposed standard. *Child Development*, 1969a, 40, 93–101.
  Subjects: $N = 48$; 7 yrs. **Measures:** Before a bowling game, half the Ss received direct instructions, while the other half observed standard self-reward standards exhibited by a training agent. After learning the game, each S individually played for prizes, which were earned by acquiring self-reward tokens. The game had fixed scores for all trials. The number of tokens self-administered when S played alone was the measure recorded. **Results:** No sex differences.

Liebert, R. M., Odom, R. D., Hill, J. H., and Huff, R. L. Effects of age and rule familiarity on the production of modeled language constructions. *Developmental Psychology*, 1969b, 2, 108–12.
  Subjects: $N = 14$; 5, 8, 14 yrs. **Measures:** Ss were assigned to 1 of 2 conditions: (1) the English rule condition in which Ss were exposed to and rewarded for production of sentences containing familiar prepositional phrases, and (2) the new rule condition in which Ss were exposed to and rewarded for production of sentences containing ungrammatical prepositional phrases. All Ss were given 10 base-rate trials and 20 training trials. Difference scores were computed by doubling each S's base-rate production of relevant prepositional constructions and subtracting it from his training score. **Results:** No sex differences.

Liebert, R. M., McCall, R. B., and Hanratty, M. A. Effects of sex-typed information on children's toy preference. *J. Genetic Psychology*, 1971, 119, 133–36.
  Subjects: $N = 40$; 6–8 yrs. **Measures:** Ss were asked to indicate which of 2 toys they preferred. Before responding, Ss were told 1 of the following: (a) that both boys and girls prefer toy A, (b) that both boys and girls prefer toy B, (c) that boys prefer toy A, whereas girls prefer toy B, or (d) that girls prefer toy A, whereas boys prefer toy B. The response measure was the number of times Ss chose the toy preferred by members of their own sex. **Results:** No sex differences.

Light, C. S., Zax, M., and Gardiner, D. H. Relationship of age, sex and intelligence level to extreme response style. *J. Personality & Social Psychology*, 1965, 2, 907–9.
  Subjects: $N = 240$; 9, 13, 17 yrs. **Measures:** Ss rated each of 10 Rorschach inkblots on 15 semantic differential scales. Ss were scored for the number of extreme, intermediate, and neutral ratings made. **Results:** No sex differences.

Linder, D. E., Cooper, J., and Jones, E. E. Decision freedom as a determinant of the role of incentive magnitude in attitude change. *J. Personality & Social Psychology*, 1967, 6, 245–54.
  Subjects: $N = 53$; 18–21 yrs (college). **Measures:** After writing essays in favor of a speaker ban they were actually opposed to, Ss rated the degree to which they were either in favor of or opposed to the ban. **Results:** No sex differences.

Lindskold, S., Cullen, P., Gahagan, J., and Tedeschi, J. T. Developmental aspects of reaction to positive inducements. *Developmental Psychology*, 1970, 3, 277–84.
  Subjects: $N = 144$; 10, 11 yrs. **Measures:** The Prisoner's Dilemma game was modified so that Ss paid a simulated player, who communicated occasional promises of an extra reward if the cooperative choice was made on the next trial. The 4 manipulated variables were (1) 10%, 50%, and 90% credibility of the simulated player's promises (probability of bribe being paid as promised), (2) $5, $10, and $20 play money reward levels, (3) overall game strategies of 50% or 90% cooperative choices made by the simulated player, and (4) sex of subject. **Results:**

(1) Overall, boys were more cooperative than girls ($p < .001$). (2) Girls and boys were equally cooperative when the simulated player cooperated 50% of the time. When the simulated player was highly cooperative (90%), boys cooperated more often. Girls responded to both strategy levels the same way. (3) Girls won more often than boys ($p < .001$). (4) Neither sex won very often when the simulated player played a 50% strategy, but girls won more than boys when strategy used was 90% cooperative ($p < .004$).

Lipsitt, L. P., and Jacklin, C. N. Cardiac deceleration and its stability in human newborns. *Developmental Psychology*, 1971, 5, 535 (brief report and personal communication).
   Subjects: $N = 20$; 2 days. **Measures:** Ss' heart rates were analyzed for 10 beats before and 20 beats after 10 5-second presentations of either an odorant stimulus on 2 successive days, or a nonodorant 1 day and an odorant the next day. **Results:** No sex differences.

Lipton, C., and Overton, W. F. Anticipatory imagery and modified anagram solution: a developmental study. *Child Development*, 1971, 42, 615–23.
   Subjects: $N = 80$; 7, 9, 11, 13 yrs (high and low reading-achievement groups). **Measures:** An anagram test was administered to Ss. Number of correct solutions and average solution time were recorded. **Results:** No sex differences.

Littenberg, R., Tulkin, S. R., and Kagan, J. Cognitive components of separation anxiety. *Developmental Psychology*, 1971, 4, 387–88.
   Subjects: $N = 24$; 11 mos and mothers. **Measures:** After 10 minutes together, the infants watched their mothers leave from an exit in the home that was normally used (1 trial) or rarely used (other trial). For 2 minutes after the mother's exit, the infant was observed for vocalizations, fretting, crying, staring at the exit, and crawling to the exit. **Results:** No sex differences.

Little, K. B. Cultural variations in social schemata. *J. Personality & Social Psychology*, 1968, 10, 1–7.
   Subjects: $N = 432$; 18–21 yrs (college: U.S., Sweden, Greece, Italy, Scotland). **Measures:** Ss placed doll figures (always the same sex as S) in positions appropriate for each of 19 different social interactions. **Results:** (1) No overall sex differences were found in average distance between placement of doll figures. Among Italian and Greek Ss, women placed figures closer together than men did. Among American and Scottish Ss, women placed figures farther apart than men did. (2) Women perceived neutral topics as being discussed at greater distances than men did. Women perceived unpleasant topics as being discussed at closer distances than men did. (3) Women perceived intimate transactions as occurring at closer distances than men did. (4) Women perceived interactions with authority figures or superiors as taking place at greater distances than men did.

Lloyd, B. B. Studies of conservation with Yoruba children of differing ages and experience. *Child Development*, 1971, 42, 415–28.
   Subjects: $N = 80$; 3–8 yrs (Yoruba). **Measures:** 2 types of materials, bricks and sweets, were used to test for conservation of number. **Results:** When bricks were used, boys' performance was superior to that of girls. When sweets were used, no sex differences were found.

Lodge, A., Armington, J. C., Barnet, A. B., Shanks, B. L., and Newcomb, C. N. Newborn infants' electroretinograms and evoked electroencephalographic responses to orange and white light. *Child Development*, 1969, 40, 267–93.
   Subjects: $N = 20$; 1–2 days. **Measures:** Electroretinogram and electroencephalogram data were recorded while Ss viewed a series of orange and white light flashes. Response measures were (1) peak latencies and amplitudes of the x- and b-waves of the ERG, and (2) peak latency and peak-to-trough amplitude of the first positive component of the occipital response. **Results:** No sex differences.

London, P., and Cooper, L. M. Norms of hypnotic susceptibility in children. *Developmental Psychology*, 1969, 1, 113–24.
   Subjects: $N = 240$; 5–16 yrs. **Measures:** Ss were given the Children's Hypnotic Susceptibility Scale. **Results:** No sex differences were found in total susceptibility scores or item difficulty.

Long, A. B., and Looft, W. R. Development of directionality in children. *Developmental Psychology*, 1972, 6, 375–80.
   Subjects: $N = 144$; 6–12 yrs. **Measures:** Each S was given a battery of 125 directionality

items taken from those used by Piaget, Swanson and Benton, Wapner and Cirillo, and some generated by the authors. **Results:** No sex differences.

Long, B. H., and Henderson, E. H. Social schemata of school beginners: some demographic correlates. *Merrill-Palmer Quarterly*, 1970, *16*, 305–24.
Subjects: $N = 192$; 6 yrs (white and black, low and middle SES). **Measures:** A modified version of the preschool Children's Self-Social Constructs Test was administered. Measures assessed were (a) self-esteem: S was presented with a column of circles representing other children and asked to select 1 of the circles to represent himself. Selection of positions closer to the top was assumed to represent a higher level of self-esteem; (b) social interest or dependency: Ss were presented with a diagram in which 3 circles (representing other children) were arranged as the apexes of a triangle. Each S was given a gummed circle (representing himself) to paste anywhere on the sheet of paper. Placement of the gummed circle within, rather than outside, the boundaries of the triangle was assumed to indicate greater social interest or dependency; (c) identification: Ss were presented with a row of circles, with the circle to the extreme left representing either father, mother, teacher, or friends. Each S was asked to select 1 of the remaining circles to represent himself. Fewer circles intervening between self and other was assumed to indicate greater identification with the other; (d) preference for others: Ss were presented with pages on which all possible pairs of 4 stimulus figures appeared (mother, father, teacher, friends). On each page, S was asked to paste a figure representing himself next to 1 of the 2 stimulus persons. The response measure was the number of times each stimulus person was selected; (e) realism size: Ss were presented with an array of circles of 3 sizes. Ss first selected 1 circle to represent father and then 1 circle to represent self. The choice of a smaller circle was assumed to indicate a more realistic conception of one's size; (f) minority identification: Ss were presented with an array of plain circles in a rectangle, accompanied by a plain and a shaded circle to the right. Circles within the rectangle represented other children. Ss were asked to pick 1 of the 2 circles to the right to represent themselves. The selection of the shaded circle was assumed to indicate minority identification. **Results:** (1) There were no sex differences in self-esteem. (2) There were no main sex differences in social interest or dependency. Middle SES girls and lower SES boys had higher scores than their male and female counterparts ($p < .05$). (3) There were no sex differences in identification with mother, teacher, or friends. Boys placed the self closer to the father than girls did ($p = .05$). (4) On the preference-for-others measure, boys placed the self less often with teacher and more often with father than girls did ($p < .005$, $p < .001$). (5) There were no sex differences in realism for size. (6) There were no sex differences in minority identification. Among middle SES blacks, boys chose the shaded circle more often than girls did ($p = .02$).

Long, B. H., Henderson, E. H., and Ziller, R. C. Developmental changes in the self-concept during middle childhood. *Merrill-Palmer Quarterly*, 1967, *13*, 201–15.
Subjects: $N = 312$; 6–13 yrs. **Measures:** (1) Ss were administered the Children's Self-Social Constructs Test, a measure consisting of the following tasks: (a) Ss viewed a large circular area containing an array of smaller circles representing "other children." Each S was asked to select 1 of 2 other circles (one shaded, one not) to represent himself. The choice of the circle different from those representing peers (i.e. shaded) was assumed to indicate a higher degree of individuation. (b) Ss viewed a row of circles representing other children. Each S was asked to select 1 of the circles to represent himself (herself). Positions to the left were assumed to represent a higher level of self-esteem. (c) Ss viewed a diagram in which 1 circle (representing the self) was surrounded by a semicircle of other circles. Other circles were directly above, diagonally above, even with, diagonally below, and directly below the circle representing the self. Ss were asked to select 1 of the 5 other circles to represent certain authority figures (father or teacher). Ss' responses were scored from 1 to 5, with a higher score indicating a lower position for the other person. (d) Each S was presented with 2 gummed circles, 1 representing himself and 1 representing a friend. Ss were asked to place them on a sheet of paper in any way they liked. Distance between circles was measured, with less distance assumed to represent more identification with friends. (e) Ss were presented with a row of circles, with the circle to the extreme left representing an adult other (mother, father, or teacher). Each S was asked to select 1 of the remaining circles to represent himself. The number of circles intervening between self and other was counted, with less distance assumed to indicate more identification with the adult other. (f) Ss were presented with a diagram in which 3 circles (representing parents, teachers, and friends) were arranged as the apexes of an equilateral triangle. Each S was given a gummed circle to represent himself and was asked to paste it anywhere on the sheet of paper. Placement of the

self within rather than outside the triangular area was assumed to reflect a perception of the self as dependent upon, or as a part of, the group of others. (2) Ss were also presented with a list of activities and were asked to indicate whether they would rather do them alone or with a group of friends. **Results:** (1) Individuation: a higher proportion of boys than girls represented the self as "different" from others. (2) Self-esteem: no sex differences. (3) Power of self in relation to father: no sex differences. Power of self in relation to teacher: no sex differences. (4) Identification with friends: no sex differences. (5) (a) Identification with teacher: girls identified more with their teachers than boys did ($p < .05$). Little difference was found between the sexes on this measure in the first grade. Henceforth, the sex difference increased until the sixth grade, where it declined again (possibly because the only male teacher in the sample taught a sixth-grade class). (b) Identification with mother: girls identified more with their mothers than boys did ($p < .05$). (c) Identification with father: no sex differences. (d) Boys did not identify more with their fathers than with their mothers; girls identified more with their mothers than with their fathers ($p < .05$). Boys were less closely identified with their fathers than girls were with their mothers ($p < .05$). (6) Dependency on others: no sex differences. (7) Girls chose to pursue more group activities than boys did ($p < .001$).

Long, B. H., Henderson, E. H., and Ziller, R. C. Self-ratings on the semantic differential: content versus response set. *Child Development*, 1968, *39*, 647–56.
Subjects: $N = 312$; 6–13 yrs (white, rural, middle SES). A random sample of 52 was studied for sex effects. **Measures:** All Ss rated self on 6 pairs of adjective-opposite in 2 scales, evaluative and power. Responses were scored from 1 to 5, with a high score indicating high self-rating in power or value. Scores were summed to provide content scores for each scale. Responses were also scored for extremity in response set. **Results:** (1) Boys rated self higher on the power scale than girls did ($p < .001$). (2) Girls rated self higher on evaluative scale than boys did ($p < .001$). (3) Set scores declined over grade level except for 10-year-old boys and 11-year-old girls (evaluative $p < .05$, set scores $p < .01$). (4) Boys made more extreme responses and fewer qualified responses than girls did ($p < .01$, $p < .05$). (5) 10-year-old girls and 11-year-old boys made relatively less use of extremes and greater use of neutral positions than their opposite sex counterparts did ($p < .05$, $p < .05$).

Long, B. H., Ziller, R. C., Kanisetti, R. V., and Reddy, V. E. Self-description as a function of evaluative and activity ratings among American and Indian adolescents. *Child Development*, 1970, *41*, 1017–24.
Subjects: $N = 200$; 10–14 yrs (U.S., India). **Measures:** Ss rated themselves on 81 adjectives from the Thorndike-Lorge Teachers' Word Book. **Results:** (1) Boys checked more words than girls did ($p < .05$). (2) There was greater concordance between cultures for girls than for boys ($p = .001$).

Longstreth, L. E. Birth order and avoidance of dangerous activities. *Developmental Psychology*, 1970, *2*, 154.
Subjects: $N = 130$; 18–21 yrs (college). **Measures:** Ss retrospectively rated themselves on a 7-point scale on the dangerous activities and rough games they avoided at age 12. **Results:** Boys rated themselves as having been more daring than girls rated themselves ($p < .02$).

Loo, C., and Wenar, C. Activity level and motor inhibition: their relationship to intelligence-test performance in normal children. *Child Development*, 1971, *42*, 967–71.
Subjects: $N = 40$; 5–6 yrs. **Measures:** Ss' classroom activity levels were measured by actometers attached to their dominant wrists and ankles. Inhibition of movement was measured by the Draw a Line Slowly Test and the Walk Slowly Test. The Primary Mental Abilities Test was also administered. Teachers rated the Ss on activity and impulsivity. **Results:** Sex of subject was not significantly correlated with actometer scores, IQ scores, or motor-inhibition scores. Teachers rated more boys than girls as active and impulsive, and as having less inhibiting control.

Looft, W. R. Sex differences in the expression of vocational aspirations by elementary school children. *Developmental Psychology*, 1971, *5*, 366 (brief report).
Subjects: $N = 66$; 6–8 yrs. **Measures:** Each S was asked, "What would you like to be when you grow up?" and "What do you think you *really* will do when you grow up?" The response measure was S's first choice. **Results:** (1) In response to the first question, boys named 18 different occupations, the most frequent being football player and policeman. Other desirable occupations included doctor, dentist, priest, scientist, airline pilot, and astronaut. Girls named 8 different occupations, the most frequent being teacher and nurse. Other desirable occupa-

tions included housewife, mother, airline stewardess, and salesgirl. (2) In response to the second question, more boys than girls changed from their initial response to other vocations.

Looft, W. R., and Charles, D. C. Modification of the life concept in children. *Developmental Psychology*, 1969, *1*, 445 (brief report).
Subjects: $N = 35$; 7–9 yrs. Measures: Before and after viewing an instructional film on the biological nature of life, Ss indicated whether each of 18 familiar phenomena was living or nonliving. Results: No sex differences.

Lott, A. J., and Lott, B. E. Liked and disliked persons as reinforcing stimuli. *J. Personality & Social Psychology*, 1969, *11*, 129–37.
Subjects: $N = 100$; 14 yrs. Measures: On each trial of a visual discrimination learning task, Ss were presented with 2 figures that varied on 3 dimensions: shape, size, and color. Only 1 dimension (size) was relevant. The choice of the large stimulus was correct for half the Ss, while the choice of the small stimulus was correct for the remaining Ss. Following a correct response, Ss were presented with either a card on which the word "right" was printed, a photo of a liked same-sex peer, a photo of a neutrally regarded peer, or a photo of a disliked peer. Ss in a fifth condition were shown a photo of a disliked peer following an incorrect response. Results: There were no sex differences.

Lott, A. J., Bright, M. A., Weinstein, P., and Lott, B. E. Liking for persons as a function of incentive and drive during acquisition. *J. Personality & Social Psychology*, 1970a, *14*, 66–76.
Subjects: $N = 31$; 18–21 yrs (college). Measures: Attitudes toward two different E's were measured by semantic differential, personal feelings, and the like-dislike scales; 1 E had been present when Ss attained high scores on an intelligence test, the other E had been present when Ss performed poorly. For each S, a difference score was obtained for each measure: liking for the E who was present during high achievement minus liking for the E who was present during low achievement. Results: No sex differences.

Lott, A. J., Lott, B. E., and Walsh, M. L. Learning of paired associates relevant to differentially liked persons. *J. Personality & Social Psychology*, 1970b, *16*, 274–83.
Subjects: $N = 52$; 18–21 yrs (college). Measures: Ss learned to associate nonsense syllables with the names of well-liked, neutral, and disliked acquaintances. The performance measure was the number of errors made before reaching the criterion of 2 consecutive errorless trials. Results: No sex differences.

Lott, A. J., Lott, B. E., Reed, T., and Crow, T. Personality-trait descriptions of differentially liked persons. *J. Personality & Social Psychology*, 1970c, *16*, 284–90.
Experiment I: Subjects: $N = 50$; 18–21 yrs (college). Measures: Ss were asked to name 3 persons: a well-liked friend, a disliked acquaintance, and a neutrally regarded acquaintance. Ss were then presented with a list of personality traits. Ss were asked to indicate which of the 3 persons was most appropriately described by each trait. Results: No sex differences.
Experiment II: Subjects: $N = 60$; 18–21 yrs (college). Measures: Same as Experiment I. Results: In describing their friends, women chose adjectives that were higher in "likableness" value than men did ($p < .05$). No other sex differences were found.

Lott, B. E., and Lott, A. J. The relationship of manifest anxiety in children to learning task performance and other variables. *Child Development*, 1968, *39*, 207–20.
Subjects: $N = 233$; 9, 10 yrs (white, black). Measures: Ss were given the Children's Manifest Anxiety Scale. Results: No sex differences were found in either Anxiety-scale or Lie-scale scores.

Loughlin, K. A., and Daehler, M. W. The effects of distraction and added perceptual cues on the delayed reaction of very young children. *Child Development*, 1973, *44*, 384–88.
Subjects: $N = 51$; 2–4 yrs. Measures: Ss performed a delayed reaction task (toy lamb hidden in each of 4 boxes). During the delay, S either remained looking at the boxes or interacted with E. Distraction was provided by placing pictures in front of the boxes. Results: No sex differences.

Lunneborg, P. W., and Rosenwood, L. W. Need affiliation and achievement; declining sex differences. Bureau of Testing, University of Washington, 1972.
Subjects: $N = 465$; 18–21 yrs (college). Measures: Ss answered the following questions: (1) "What would make you happy?" (2) "What makes you sad?" and (3) "What makes you an-

gry?" Ss' responses were scored for *n* affiliation and *n* achievement. **Results:** In response to question 1, women showed more *n* affiliation than men did ($p < .01$).

Luria, Z., and Rebelsky, F. Children's conceptions of events before and after confessions of transgression. *Child Development*, 1969, *40*, 1055–61.
Subjects: $N = 80$; 10–13 yrs. **Measures:** Ss were given 4 transgression stories to read. All 4 ended with the protagonist (always of the same sex as S) confessing the crime to the person transgressed against. After each story, Ss indicated how likely it would be before confessing for the protagonist to feel (a) unhappy, (b) afraid of being found out, (c) afraid of being punished, (d) anxious and worried, (e) sorry, and (f) guilty. Ss also indicated the probability after confessing that the protagonist would be (a) forgiven, (b) praised, (c) punished, (d) scolded, (e) reasoned with, (f) hit, and (g) deprived of something, with the probability of "things getting better" and of "things getting worse." **Results:** No sex differences.

Lynn, D. B., and Lynn, R. The structured doll play test as a projective technique with children. *J. Projective Techniques*, 1959, *23*, 335–44.
Subjects: $N = 49$; 4, 6 yrs. **Measures:** Structured Doll Play Test. **Results:** (1) Among 4-year-old Ss, a higher proportion of boys than girls picked the bottle (immature choice) instead of the cup (mature choice) ($p < .05$). (2) Among 6-year-olds, boys received lower dependency scores than girls; among 4-year-olds, no sex differences were found.

MacArthur, R. Sex differences in field dependence for the Eskimo. *International J. Psychology*, 1967, *2*, 139–40.
Subjects: $N = 167$; 9–15 yrs (western Eskimo). **Measures:** Vernon's Embedded Figures Test. **Results:** No sex differences.

McBain, W. N., Fox, W., Kumura, S., Nakanishi, M., and Tirado, J. Quasi-sensory communication: an investigation using semantic matching and accentuated affect. *J. Personality & Social Psychology*, 1970, *14*, 281–91.
Subjects: $N = 22$; 18–21 yrs (college). **Measures:** 1 subject in each pair of same-sex or opposite-sex Ss concentrated on 1 of 5 symbols, without communicating with his partner. The partner's task was to guess which 1 of the 5 symbols had been concentrated on. **Results:** The guesses of like-sex pairs of Ss were more accurate than those of opposite-sex pairs of Ss. ($p < .001$).

McCall, R. B., and Kagan, J. Attention in the infant: effects of complexity, contour, perimeter, and familiarity. *Child Development*, 1967, *38*, 939–52.
Subjects: $N = 36$; 4 mos. **Measures:** Ss were presented with slides of 9 solid black, random shapes, having 5, 10, or 20 turns and 3 different contour lengths. Response measures were first fixation time, total fixation time, number of fixations, average fixation time, nonfretful vocalization, smiling frequency, resting cardiac level, and magnitude of cardiac deceleration. Each infant's height and weight were also recorded. Information on feeding was obtained from parent interviews. **Results:** Girls were more likely to be nursed than boys. No other sex differences were found.

McCall, R. B., and Kagan, J. Individual differences in the infant's distribution of attention to stimulus discrepancy. *Developmental Psychology*, 1970, *2*, 90–98.
Subjects: $N = 72$; 4 mos. **Measures:** Ss were repeatedly exposed to a standard of 3 objects. Intermittently, either 1, 2, or 3 new objects were substituted for those in the standard set. Fixation times were recorded. **Results:** No sex differences.

McCall, R. B., Hogarty, P. S., Hamilton, J. S., and Vincent, J. M. Habituation rate and the infant's response to visual discrepancies. *Child Development*, 1973, *44*, 280–87.
Subjects: $N = 120$; 12, 18 wks. **Measures:** Ss viewed a stimulus pattern until visual fixation reached habituation criterion. A discrepant stimulus varying in magnitude of discrepancy was then introduced. Rate of habituation and fixation were measured. **Results:** No sex differences.

McCarson, C., and Daves, W. F. Free recall of object names in preschool children as a function of intracategory variation. *Developmental Psychology*, 1971, *4*, 295 (brief reports).
Subjects: $N = 20$; 4, 5 yrs. **Measures:** Each S, tested individually, was shown 48 common objects, comprising 12 different categories. For 6 categories the same object was repeated 4 times; for the other 6 categories, 4 different specimens were used. The objects, randomly arranged

on 2 turntables, were exposed for 2 seconds each. Then E asked S to recall what he saw. **Results:** No sex differences.

McCarthy, J. J., and Kirk, S. A. *The construction, standardization, and statistical characteristics of the Illinois Test of Psycholinguistic Abilities.* Urbana: University of Illinois Press, 1963.

Subjects: $N = 700$; 28–32, 34–38, 40–44, 46–50, 52–56, 58–62, 64–68, 70–74, 76–80, 82–86, 88–92, 94–98, 100–104, 106–110 mos. **Measures:** The Illinois Test of Psycholinguistic Abilities. **Results:** (1) Among 40-44- and 82-86-month-old Ss, girls scored higher than boys in auditory decoding ($p < .05$; $p < .05$). (2) Among 52-56-, 100-104-, and 106-110-month-old Ss, boys scored higher than girls in visual decoding ($p < .05$; $p < .01$; $p < .01$). (3) Among 58-62- and 70-74-month-old Ss, girls scored higher than boys in auditory vocal association ($p < .05$; $p < .05$). The opposite was true among 106-110-month-old Ss ($p < .01$). (4) Among 40-44- and 94-98-month-old Ss, girls scored higher than boys in visual-motor association ($p < .01$; $p < .05$). (5) There were no sex differences on the vocal encoding and the auditory vocal automatic tests. (6) Among 64-66- and 106-110-month-old Ss, boys scored higher than girls in motor encoding ($p < .05$; $p < .05$). (7) Among 88-92-month-old Ss, girls scored higher than boys in auditory-vocal sequencing ($p < .01$). (8) Among 82-86-month-old Ss, girls scored higher than boys in visual motor sequencing ($p < .01$; $p < .01$).

McCarver, R. B. A developmental study of the effect of organizational cues on short-term memory. *Child Development,* 1972, *43,* 1317–25.

Subjects: $N = 160$; 5, 7, 10, 18–21 yrs (college). **Measures:** Ss were shown 8 colored drawings of familiar objects, 1 at a time, for a period of 1 or 2 seconds each. Each picture was turned over and placed in a horizontal row after it was presented. A drawing identical to 1 of the 8 was then given to Ss, with instructions to find its duplicate. The percentage of Ss' first-choice responses that were correct was recorded. **Results:** No sex differences.

McCarver, R. B., and Ellis, N. R. Effect of overt verbal labeling on short-term memory in culturally deprived and nondeprived children. *Developmental Psychology,* 1972, *6,* 38–41.

Subjects: $N = 60$; 5–6 yrs (low, middle SES). **Measures:** Ss completed the Peabody Picture Vocabulary Test, a digit-span test, and a short-term-memory task with or without verbal labeling of stimuli by Ss. **Results:** No sex differences.

Maccoby, E. E., and Feldman, S. S. Mother-attachment and stranger-reactions in the third year of life. *Monographs of the Society for Research in Child Development,* 1972, *37.*

American Study: **Subjects:** $N = 64$; 2 yrs. 35 Ss were retested at 2½ yrs, 38 at 3 yrs. **Measures:** At each testing, Ss were observed in the following sequence of events involving the presence or absence of their mother and/or a stranger in a room with toys: Episode 1: Mo and Ch brought to testing room by E. E leaves. Episode 2: Mo sits in chair, then gets down on floor to play with Ch. Mo returns to chair. Episode 3: Str enters, greets Mo, sits quietly for 1 minute, converses with Mo, then plays with Ch. Mo leaves. Episode 4: Str gradually disengages from play with child. Episode 5: Mo returns, Str leaves. Mo calls to child, waits for a moment, then plays with Ch. Mo leaves. Episode 6: Ch remains alone for 3 minutes. Episode 7: Str enters, stands quietly for a moment, then moves to chair. Episode 8: Mo enters, then talks to Ch. Mo and Ch collect belongings in preparation for leaving. **Results:** (1) No sex differences were found in manipulative play during Episode 2, 3, or 6. During Episodes 4 (at age 2½ only) and 7 (at age 2 only), boys exhibited manipulative play more frequently than girls did. No sex differences were found in duration of longest manipulation of single toy before shifting to another (personal communication). (2) No sex differences were found in activity level during Episode 3, 6, or 7. During Episodes 2 (at age 3 only) and 4 (at age 2 only), boys were more active than girls. Overall, 2-year-old boys had a higher activity level than 2-year-old girls. (3) During Episodes 2 and 3, no sex differences were found in proximity to Mo, total looks at Mo, or total number of speaks, smiles, or shows item to Mo. (4) During Episodes 4 and 7, no sex differences were found in proximity to Str. During Episodes 3, 4, and 7, no sex differences were found in total number of speaks, smiles, or shows item to Str. (5) During Episodes 4, 6, and 7, no sex differences were found in crying. (6) When left alone during Episode 6, more boys than girls banged on the door. (7) No difference was found between 2-year-old boys and girls in the amount of time that elapsed before they made their first approach to Mo during Episode 2. No analysis was made of the data at 2½ and 3 years of age.

Kibbutz Study: **Subjects:** $N = 20$; 2 yrs. **Measures:** Procedures were identical to those followed in the American study. The amount of crying and manipulative play Ss exhibited during

Episodes 4 and 6 and the amount of proximity to mothers displayed during Episode 3 were added together to yield a summary attachment score. Manipulative play was given a negative value in the sum. **Results:** No sex differences.

Maccoby, E. E., and Jacklin, C. N. Stress, activity and proximity seeking: sex differences in the year old child. *Child Development*, 1973, *44*, 34–42.

 EXPERIMENT I: **Subjects:** $N = 40$; 13, 14 mos. **Measures:** Ss were observed in an unfamiliar room with their mothers. The room was marked off into 18-inch squares and contained 6 toys. At the beginning of each of 2 phases, half the Ss were placed in the square adjacent to where their mothers were seated, while the other half were placed 8 feet away. Phase 1 was free-play period lasting 5 minutes. Phase 2 began with exposure to a loud, angry male voice, followed by a free-play period of 4 minutes. **Results:** (1) Boys crossed more squares than girls did (Phase 1, $p < .05$; Phase 2, $p < .05$). Boys showed a decrease in activity from Phase 1 to Phase 2; girls did not ($p < .01$). (2) Boys made more trips to their mothers during Phase 1 than girls did ($p < .05$). (3) Following presentation of the fear stimulus, boys had longer latencies to first movement than girls did ($p < .01$). (4) No sex differences were found in time spent in proximity to or in physical contact with mother, in frequency of looking at mother, or in frequency of crying.

 EXPERIMENT II: **Subjects:** $N = 40$; 13, 14 mos. **Measures:** Same as Experiment I, except that (a) all Ss were placed 8 feet away from their mothers at the beginning of both phases, (b) the angry male voice was presented either at a high or at a moderate level of intensity. **Results:** No sex differences.

McCormick, C. C., Schnobrich, J., and Footlik, S. W. IE Arrow-Dot performance in different adolescent populations. *Perceptual & Motor Skills*, 1966, *22*, 507–10.

 Subjects: $N = 72$; 14–17 yrs (black). **Measures:** The Arrow-Dot subtest of the IES (Impulse, Ego, Superego) Test was administered to Ss (mean IA = 66). **Results:** Girls had lower E scores and higher S scores than boys ($p < .0005$; $p < .0005$). No sex differences were found in I scores.

McCullers, J. C. Associative strength and degree of interference in children's verbal paired-associate learning. *J. Experimental Child Psychology*, 1967, *5*, 58–68.

 Subjects: $N = 144$; 11 yrs. **Measures:** Ss were given a verbal paired-associates learning task. The number of trials Ss needed to reach criterion was recorded. **Results:** No sex differences.

McCullers, J. C. Size-discrimination difficulty and verbal paired-associate learning in children. *Developmental Psychology*, 1969, *1*, 447–48 (brief report).

 EXPERIMENT I: **Subjects:** $N = 120$; 11 yrs. **Measures:** A size-discrimination task and a verbal paired-associates learning task were administered to Ss concurrently. **Results:** No sex differences.

 EXPERIMENT II: **Subjects:** $N = 40$; 9 yrs. **Measures:** Same as Experiment I. **Results:** No sex differences.

McCullers, J. C., and Martin, J. A. A reexamination of the role of incentive in children's discrimination learning. *Child Development*, 1971, *42*, 827–37.

 EXPERIMENT I: **Subjects:** $N = 24$; 9 yrs. **Measures:** Ss rated their preference for 12 objects and then made forced choices between objects having the same value. Ss were allowed to select and keep any objects they wanted. **Results:** Boys selected more objects to keep than girls ($p < .001$).

 EXPERIMENT II: **Subjects:** $N = 72$; 9 yrs. **Measures:** 2 high-incentive (bubblegum, chocolate kiss) and 2 low-incentive (paper clip, slip of paper) objects from Experiment I were selected. Ss rated objects, and made forced choices as in I. Ss performed a discrimination-learning task, with the value of the reinforcing object varied. **Results:** No sex differences.

McDavid, J. W. Imitative behavior in preschool children. *Psychological Monographs: General and Applied*, 1959, *73*.

 EXPERIMENT I: **Subjects:** $N = 32$; 3–5 yrs. **Measures:** Ss were reinforced for imitating the response of either an adult male or an adult female model in a 2-choice discrimination-learning problem. To make the correct response on each trial, Ss had to avoid paying attention to irrelevant environmental cues. **Results:** No main sex differences were found in (a) tendency to imitate on trial 1, (b) total number of imitative responses, or (c) deviation from chance imitation scores (calculated by recording the difference between the number of imitative responses made by Ss in each 4-trial block and the value 2). Among older Ss (above 56 months), girls made more imitative responses than boys did; among younger Ss (45–56 months), boys made more imitative responses than girls did.

EXPERIMENT II: **Subjects:** $N = 26$; 3–5 yrs. **Measures:** Stanford-Binet Intelligence Test, Form L. **Results:** No sex differences.

MacDonald, A. P., Jr. Birth order and religious affiliation. *Developmental Psychology,* 1969, *1,* 628 (brief report).
Subjects: $N = 393$; 18–21 yrs (college). **Measures:** After indicating their religious preference (Catholic, Jewish, Protestant, other, or none), Ss rated their church attendance on a 6-point scale. **Results:** (1) There were no sex differences in church attendance among Ss who indicated no religious preference. (2) Among Ss who did indicate a preference, Catholic women who were only children attended church more frequently than Catholic men who were only children.

MacDonald, A. P., Jr. Anxiety, affiliation, and social isolation. *Developmental Psychology,* 1970, *3,* 242–54.
Subjects: $N = 149$; 18–21 yrs (college). **Measures:** Ss reported to the testing session in small mixed-sex groups. After being told that a series of electric shocks would be given to them later in the experiment, Ss rated their uneasiness on a 100-point scale and indicated their preference to be alone or with others. Ss were then assigned to 1 of 2 conditions without regard to their stated preference. Groups in the affiliation condition were sent to an adjacent room where they remained for 5 minutes. In the isolation condition, Ss remained alone in separate cubicles in the experimental room for an identical period of time. Afterward, Ss in the affiliation condition were returned to the experimental room. Then, the uneasiness scale was readministered and the option to drop out was given. **Results:** (1) On the initial administration of the uneasiness scale, women reported higher levels of anxiety than men ($p < .005$). (2) No sex differences were found in preference to wait alone or with others. (3) On the second administration of the uneasiness scale, no main sex differences were found in change in anxiety scores. Men who preferred waiting alone and women who preferred waiting with others showed more anxiety reduction than men who preferred affiliation and women who preferred isolation ($p < .025$). (4) Firstborn women were more likely to drop out of the experiment than firstborn men ($p < .05$). No sex differences were found among later-borns. (This result can be found in an article by A. P. MacDonald, Jr., entitled "Manifestations of Differential Levels of Socialization by Birth Order," *Developmental Psychology,* 1969, *1,* 485–92.)

McDonald, R. L. Effects of sex, race, and class on self, ideal-self and parental ratings in southern adolescents. *Perceptual & Motor Skills,* 1968, *27,* 15–25.
Subjects: $N = 528$; 17 yrs (white, black). **Measures:** Self, parental, and ideal-self ratings were obtained on the Interpersonal Checklist. **Results:** (1) Self ratings: men had higher dominance and lower love scores than women. (2) Ideal-self ratings: Women had higher love scores than men. (3) Parental ratings: Women described their fathers as higher in love than men did. No sex differences were found in Ss' descriptions of their mothers.

MacFarlane, J. W., Allen, L., and Honzik, M. P. *A developmental study of the behavior problems of normal children between 21 months and 14 years.* Berkeley: University of California Press, 1962.
Subjects: $N = 116$; mothers (children 21 mos–14 yrs). **Measures:** Interviews regarding child's behavior. **Results:** (1) Mothers of boys reported a greater incidence of the following problem behaviors than mothers of girls: diurnal enuresis, excessive emotional dependence, irritability (21 months); temper tantrums (5 years); stealing (7 years); hyperactivity, temper tantrums, lying (8 years); excessive demanding of attention (9 years); lying, excessive demanding of attention, jealousy, competitiveness (11 years); overactivity, lying (12 years); overactivity, selfishness in sharing (13 years). (2) Mothers of girls reported a greater incidence of the following problem behaviors than mothers of boys: excessive modesty, specific fears (3 years); thumb-sucking (4 years); thumb-sucking, physical timidity (5 years); food fussiness, oversensitiveness, mood swings (6 years); excessive emotional dependence, shyness, excessive reserve (7 years); excessive modesty, excessive reserve (8 years); shyness, somberness (9 years); excessive reserve (10 years); shyness (11 years); disturbing dreams, physical timidity (12 years); specific fears (13 years).

McIntyre, A. Sex differences in children's aggression. *Proceedings* of the 80th Annual Convention of the APA, 1972, *7,* 93–94.
Subjects: $N = 27$; 2–4 yrs. **Measures:** Ss were observed at their preschool. Response measures were frequency of verbal and nonverbal activities with peers and/or adults (social activity rate) and frequency of each of 4 classes of aggressive behavior (direct physical aggression, indirect physical aggression, direct verbal aggression, and indirect verbal aggression). **Results:**

(1) More boys than girls had high social activity rates. (2) More boys than girls scored high in physical aggression. No sex differences were found in verbal aggression, direct aggression, or indirect aggression.

McKinney, J. D. Problem solving strategies in impulsive and reflective second graders. *Developmental Psychology*, 1973, *8*, 145 (brief report).
Subjects: $N = 60$; 7 yrs. Measures: Reflective and impulsive Ss (as determined by the Matching Familiar Figures Test) were asked to determine the "correct" stimulus (out of 16) by asking questions answerable by "yes" or "no." Problem-solving strategies were assessed. Results: No sex differences were found in amount of information obtained from questions.

McKitrick, K. G. Bodily activity and perceptual activity. *Perceptual & Motor Skills*, 1965, *20*, 1109–12.
Subjects: $N = 200$; 18–21 yrs (college). Measures: Ss were tested for the autokinetic illusion. Results: Latency to perceiving autokinesis was greater for women than for men.

McMains, M. J., and Liebert, R. M. Influence of discrepancies between successively modeled self-reward criteria on the adoption of a self-imposed standard. *J. Personality & Social Psychology*, 1968, *8*, 166–71.
Subjects: $N = 48$; 9 yrs. Measures: While playing a bowling game, Ss were trained to employ a stringent self-reward standard by a model who subsequently adhered to the standard or deviated from it. Ss then performed in the model's absence. Afterward, Ss were exposed to a second model, who displayed either the same stringent self-reward criterion that the Ss had previously been taught or a more lenient standard. Ss then played the game alone for a second time. The response measure was the number of times Ss did not adhere to the stringent self-reward criterion. Results: (1) No sex differences were found in Game 1. (2) Boys were more lenient than girls in Game 2 ($p < .05$).

McManis, D. L. Pursuit-rotor performance of normal and retarded children in four verbal-incentive conditions. *Child Development*, 1965, *36*, 667–83.
Subjects: $N = 96$; 10–11 yrs (normal intelligence), 12–13 yrs (retardates). Measures: Ss' base levels of pursuit-rotor performance were established under neutral incentive; 4 mixed-ability treatment groups were established: neutral E response, praise, reproof, and competition. Ss performed the task again in presence of a same-sex peer. Task persistence was measured. Results: (1) There were no sex differences in accuracy or response to treatments. (2) Boys were more persistent in continuing tasks than girls ($p < .05$).

McManis, D. L. Marble-sorting rate of elementary school children as a function of verbal-incentive and performance-level pairings. *Perceptual & Motor Skills*, 1966, *23*, 499–507.
Subjects: $N = 240$; 9–11 yrs. Measures: Ss performed alternate trials on a marble-sorting task with same-sex partners whose performance rates in baseline were either similar or different. Each dyad experienced 1 of 3 treatments: (1) S_1 was criticized by E while S_2 was praised; (2) S_1 was criticized while S_2 was told to try as hard as he could to beat his partner's score on the previous trial; (3) S_1 was praised while S_2 was told to be competitive. Response measures were changes in rate of response between baseline and the experimental sessions. Results: Boys showed larger increases in response rates than girls ($p < .05$).

McMichael, R. E., and Grinder, R. E. Children's guilt after transgression: Combined effect of exposure to American culture and ethnic background. *Child Development*, 1966, *37*, 425–31.
Subjects: $N = 114$; 12–13 yrs (rural and urban Japanese Americans, Hawaiian Americans, and Caucasian Americans). Measures: 5 stories describing common transgressions were presented to Ss. After reading each story, Ss indicated how they would feel and behave if they were the protagonist. The multiple-choice questions they responded to assessed remorse, confession, and restitution. Results: Among rural Japanese Americans ($N = 23$), girls scored higher than boys on confession and restitution. No other sex differences were found.

MacMillan, D. L., and Keogh, B. K. Effect of instructional set on twelve-year-old children's perception of interruption. *Developmental Psychology*, 1971a, *4*, 106.
Subjects: $N = 60$; 11 yrs. Measures: Ss were asked to duplicate 6 designs pictured on cards using 9 blocks given to them by E. Ss were allowed to complete 3 of the designs. While working on the other 3, they were interrupted before completion (interruption was attributed either to success or to failure). In a third condition, interruption was defined as a neutral event.

Afterward, Ss were asked to pick 1 design to try again. They were also asked to explain why they did not complete 3 of the designs. **Results:** No sex differences were found in Ss' choice of designs to repeat or in their placement of blame for not completing 3 of the designs.

MacMillan, D. L., and Keogh, B. K. Normal and retarded children's expectancy for failure. *Developmental Psychology*, 1971b, *4*, 343–48.
 Subjects: $N = 120$; 8 yrs (normal, retarded). **Measures:** Ss performed 6 block design tasks; 3 were interrupted before completion. Instructions prior to the task defined interruption as an indication of success, failure, or neutral. After the task, Ss were asked which design they would like to do over and why some tasks had not been completed. **Results:** No sex differences.

McNamara, J. R., and Porterfield, C. L. Levels of information about the human figure and their characteristic relationship to human figure drawing in young disadvantaged children. *Developmental Psychology*, 1969, *1*, 669–72.
 Subjects: $N = 78$; 5–6 yrs (black disadvantaged). **Measures:** Human Figure Drawing Test. **Results:** No sex differences.

McNeel, S. P., McClintock, C. G., and Nuttin, J. M. Effects of sex role in a two person mixed-motive game. *J. Personality & Social Psychology*, 1972, *24*, 372–80.
 Subjects: $N = 144$; 18–21 yrs (college). **Measures:** Ss in like-sex and mixed-sex pairs played a modified version of the Prisoner's Dilemma game. Competitive choices reflected a single motive (relative gain maximization), while the remaining 2 choices reflected either own gain or joint gain considerations. **Results:** (1) Mixed-sex pairs were less competitive than like-sex pairs. No difference was found between male and female pairs. (2) Men in mixed-sex pairs were less competitive than men in like-sex pairs ($p < .02$). No differences were found for women.

Madsen, C. Nurturance and modeling in preschoolers. *Child Development*, 1968, *39*, 221–36.
 Subjects: $N = 40$; 4–5 yrs. **Measures:** Ss were assigned for 6 weeks to male teachers trained to be either nurturant or nonnurturant. During weeks 7 and 8, Ss viewed 2 films; the actor in each film was either their teacher or an unfamiliar adult male. In the aggression film, novel physical and verbal aggressive behaviors toward a Bobo doll were modeled. After watching the film, Ss were taken to an experimental room where they were observed for 5 minutes. Measures were taken of imitative, partially imitative, and nonimitative aggression. Ss were then asked to perform all the behaviors they had observed in the film. Matching responses were praised and rewarded with candy. In the toy-rejection film, the model made disparaging comments about a mechanical dog and pleasurable comments about a robot while playing exclusively with the latter. Ss were allowed to play with the 2 toys at the completion of the film. The time they spent playing with the robot minus the time they spent playing with the dog was recorded. **Results:** (1) Boys exhibited more imitative physical aggression, more non-imitative verbal aggression, and less nonimitative Bobo-directed aggression than girls. Boys who were exposed to the familiar model exhibited more imitative aggression than boys exposed to the unfamiliar model; no such difference was found among girls. No sex differences were found in Ss' display of partially imitative aggression, imitative verbal aggression, or total verbal imitation (aggressive and nonaggressive). In the recall task, no sex differences were found in number of novel aggressive behaviors performed. (2) No difference was found between boys and girls on the measure "time spent on robot minus time spent on dog."

Madsen, C. H., and London, P. Role playing and hypnotic susceptibility in children. *J. Personality & Social Psychology*, 1966, *3*, 13–19.
 Subjects: $N = 42$; 7–11 yrs. **Measures:** Children's Hypnotic Susceptibility Scale, Hypnotic Simulation Test, Dramatic Acting Test. **Results:** No sex differences.

Madsen, M. C., and Shapira, A. Cooperative and competitive behavior of urban Afro-American, Anglo-American, Mexican-American, and Mexican village children. *Developmental Psychology*, 1970, *3*, 16–20.
 Experiment I: Subjects: $N = 144$; 7–9 yrs (Afro-, Anglo-, and Mexican American). **Measures:** Same-sex groups of 4 were tested on Madsen's Cooperation board. Rewards were received first on a group (trials 1–3) and then on an individual basis (trials 4–6). Owing to the nature of the apparatus, cooperation was adaptive. For each group, the change in amount of cooperation between trials 3 and 4 was recorded. **Results:** No sex differences.
 Experiment III: Subjects: $N = 156$; 7–9 yrs (Afro-, Anglo-, and Mexican-American; Mexi-

can). **Measures:** Procedures similar to Experiment I were followed, with 1 exception: throughout the testing session, rewards were received on an individual basis. **Results:** No differences were found in the amount of cooperation exhibited by boys and girls.

Maehr, M. L., and Stallings, W. M. Freedom from external evaluation. *Child Development*, 1972, *43*, 177–85.
> **Subjects:** $N = 154$; 13 yrs. **Measures:** For each of 10 problems, Ss judged which of 4 geometric designs was different from the other 3. In the external evaluation condition, Ss were informed that the task was a test of their ability and that the results would be given to their teachers. In the internal evaluation condition, Ss were told to complete the task in a spirit of fun and interest, since no one but themselves would see their scores. Afterward, Ss' willingness to return to perform a similar task at a later date was assessed. **Results:** (1) No sex differences were found in task performance. (2) Girls indicated a greater willingness to return than boys did ($p < .01$).

Maier, N. R. Male vs. female discussion leaders. *Personnel Psychology*, 1970, *23*, 455–61.
> **Subjects:** $N = 384$; 18–21 yrs (college). **Measures:** Ss participated in the Changing Work Procedure Problem, a role-playing situation in which a foreman attempts to get 3 workers to change their work method. Foremen were given the facts of the problem and were either supplied (Standard Condition) or not supplied (Facts Only Condition) with a rather obvious solution. There were 3 outcomes possible: (1) workers successfully resist the change, (2) leader succeeds in getting his solution adopted, or (3) workers and leader compromise on an alternative solution. **Results:** (1) With males as foremen, differences between the 2 experimental conditions were nonsignificant; with females as foremen, more groups accepted the leader's solution in the Standard Condition than in the Facts Only Condition ($p < .01$). (2) More groups with a male rather than a female as foreman accepted the leader's solution in the Facts Only Condition ($p < .01$). No sex differences were found in the Standard Condition.

Maier, N. R., and Burke, R. J. Response availability as a factor in the problem solving performance of males and females. *J. Personality & Social Psychology*, 1967, *5*, 304–10.
> **EXPERIMENT I: Subjects:** $N = 173$; 18–21 yrs (college). **Measures:** Ss were given the standard version of the horse-trading problem. **Results:** Men chose the correct answer more often than women ($p < .01$). Women chose the incorrect "broke even" answer more often than men ($p < .01$).
> **EXPERIMENT II: Subjects:** $N = 126$; 18–21 yrs (college). **Measures:** Same as Experiment I, except that a rationale was provided for each alternative answer. **Results:** Same as Experiment I.
> **EXPERIMENT III: Subjects:** $N = 114$; 18–21 yrs (college). **Measures:** Same as Experiment I, except that the broke even alternative was eliminated. **Results:** No sex differences.
> **EXPERIMENT IV: Subjects:** $N = 114$; 18–21 yrs (college). **Measures:** Ss were told that a man bought a secondhand car for his wife. Since she didn't like it, he sold it. Ss were asked whether the man lost money, broke even, made a small profit, or made a large profit. No financial figures were given to influence Ss' choices. **Results:** Men chose the lost money alternative more often than women ($p < .01$). Women chose the broke even alternative more often than men ($p < .01$).
> **EXPERIMENT V: Subjects:** $N = 69$; 18–21 yrs (college). **Measures:** Same as Experiment IV, except that the roles of the husband and wife were reversed. **Results:** Men chose the lost money alternative more often than women ($p < .05$). Women chose the broke even alternative more often than men ($p < .01$).
> **EXPERIMENT VI: Subjects:** $N = 88$; 18–21 yrs (college). **Measures:** The horse-trading problem was modified to make the broke even alternative correct. **Results:** No sex differences.

Mallick, S. R., and McCandless, B. R. A study of catharsis of aggression. *J. Personality & Social Psychology*, 1966, *4*, 591–96.
> **EXPERIMENT I: Subjects:** $N = 48$; 8–9 yrs. **Measures:** After being either frustrated or not frustrated by a same-sex confederate, Ss were given the opportunity to administer shocks to the confederate. **Results:** No sex differences.
> **EXPERIMENT II: Subjects:** $N = 60$; 8–9 yrs. **Measures:** Ss were either frustrated or not frustrated by a same-sex confederate (first phase). Ss then either engaged in aggressive play, talked with E, or received a reasonable interpretation of the confederate's behavior (second phase). Afterward, Ss were given the opportunity to either impede (by pressing a "slowing" button) or facilitate (by pushing a "helping" button) the confederate's performance on a block-building task. Ss provided like-dislike ratings of the confederate after the first and second phases. **Results:** (1) No sex differences were found in the number of times Ss pressed the

"slowing" button. (2) After the first phase, boys expressed more dislike for the confederate than girls did, but only in the frustration condition ($p < .05$). After the second phase, no sex differences were found in Ss' ratings.

EXPERIMENT III: **Subjects:** $N = 60$; 8–9 yrs. **Measures:** Same as Experiment I, except that only half of the Ss completed the like-dislike rating scales. **Results:** No sex differences were found in number of times Ss pressed the "slowing" button.

Malouf, R. E., and Dodd, D. H. Role of exposure, imitation, and expansion in the acquisition of an artificial grammatical rule. *Developmental Psychology*, 1972, 7, 195–203.
  Subjects: $N = 84$; 6 yrs. **Measures:** An assessment was made of the effects of various environmental factors (exposure, imitation, and expansion) on Ss' learning of an artificial grammatical rule. **Results:** No sex differences were found in number of errors or number of trials to acquisition.

Manheimer, D. I., and Mellinger, G. D. Personality characteristics of the child accident repeater. *Child Development*, 1967, 38, 491–513.
  Subjects: $N = 8,874$; 4–18 yrs. **Measures:** Each S's history of medically attended injuries was obtained from his medical records. **Results:** Boys' accident rate was higher than that of girls.

Manosevitz, M., Prentice, N. M., and Wilson, F. Individual and family correlates of imaginary companions in preschool children. *Developmental Psychology*, 1973, 8, 72–79.
  Subjects: $N = 222$; 3–5 yrs. **Measures:** Parents completed the Imaginary Companion Questionnaire, designed to provide data about home setting and play activities of Ss. Part II of the questionnaire was answered only by parents whose children had imaginary companions. **Results:** (1) Girls had more imaginary companions than boys did. (2) Boys were more likely to have a male than a female imaginary companion, whereas girls showed only a slight tendency to have same-sex imaginary companions. (3) Parents reported that boys had more fights than girls did.

Markel, N. N., Prebor, L. D., and Brandt, J. F. Biosocial factors in dyadic communication: sex and speaking intensity. *J. Personality & Social Psychology*, 1972, 23, 11–13.
  Subjects: $N = 72$; 18–21 yrs (college). **Measures:** Ss spoke to male and female Es at near and far interpersonal distances. Average speaking intensity was measured. **Results:** (1) Men had a higher speaking intensity than women ($p < .01$). (2) Men Ss had a higher speaking intensity than women Ss when speaking to a woman E. When E was a man, no sex differences were found.

Marks, E. Some situational correlates of recognition-response level. *J. Personality & Social Psychology*, 1967, 6, 102–6.
  Subjects: $N = 722$; 18–21 yrs (college). **Measures:** Ss initially learned the names of 8 line-drawn figures. Ss were then presented with a set of 6 specially constructed test booklets. Pp. 2–5 of each booklet contained drawings that represented parts of 1 of 8 figures learned in the first phase. The drawings ranged from the most incomplete representation of the figures (p. 2) to the complete figures (p. 5). The drawing on p. 2 contained elements common to all 8 figures, the drawing on p. 3 contained elements common to 4 of the figures, and the drawing on p. 4 contained elements common to 2 of the figures. Ss were told to tear off 1 page at a time. When they felt they could identify the figure represented, Ss were instructed to write its name on that page and not tear off any more pages. The response measure was the total number of pages pulled. **Results:** No sex differences.

Marks, E. Personality factors in the performance of a perceptual recognition task under competing incentives. *J. Personality & Social Psychology*, 1968, 8, 69–74.
  Subjects: $N = 760$; 18–21 yrs (college). **Measures:** Ss answered 3 self-report inventories assessing quick and intuitive behavior, lack of forethought, and lack of need for definiteness. Ss also completed 3 self-report scales of concrete thinking, black-white thought processes, and activity level. Scores on the SAT verbal section and the Advanced Vocabulary Test were obtained. **Results:** No sex differences.

Marlatt, G. A. A comparison of vicarious and direct reinforcement control of verbal behavior in an interview setting. *J. Personality & Social Psychology*, 1970, 16, 695–703.
  Subjects: $N = 96$; 18–21 yrs (college). **Measures:** Ss were first exposed to a tape-recorded same-sex model who described personal problems to an interviewer. Ss then discussed their problems in 2 interviews, separated by a 1-week interval. Ss received either positive, negative, or neutral reinforcement from either a male or a female interviewer. The response measures

were number of problems discussed and length of time spent talking. **Results:** (1) No sex differences were found in number of problems discussed. (2) During the first interview, Ss discussed more problems with female interviewers than with male interviewers ($p < .01$). No differences were found during the second interview. (3) Men talked longer than women did in both interviews ($p < .05$). (4) Ss talked more with female interviewers than with male interviewers ($p < .05$ for both interviews).

Marquis, P. C. Experimenter-subject interaction as a function of authoritarianism and response set. *J. Personality & Social Psychology*, 1973, 25, 289–96.
  Subjects: $N = 52$; 18–21 yrs (college). **Measures:** Ss' attitudes on a topic were assessed before and after exposure to a persuasive communication. **Results:** No sex differences were found in attitude change.

Martin, J. C. Competitive and noncompetitive behavior of children in beanbag toss game. Preliminary draft, University of California, 1973.
  Subjects: $N = 51$; 7 yrs. **Measures:** Ss could choose to shoot beanbags at any 1 of 4 targets. Targets farther away were higher in value (i.e. worth more marbles) than the targets close by. In the competitive condition, Ss played in same-sex pairs. At the end of the game, the most successful member of each pair was allowed to keep not only the marbles he had won but also his opponent's winnings. In the noncompetitive condition, Ss played alone. **Results:** (1) Girls threw at the closer target more often than boys did. This difference was greatest between Ss who threw after their opponents did in the competitive condition ($p < .05$). (2) No sex differences were found in number of marbles won.

Martin, M. F., Gelfand, D. M., and Hartmann, D. P. Effect of adult and peer observers on boys' and girls' responses to an aggressive model. *Child Development*, 1971, 42, 1271–75.
  Subjects: $N = 100$; 5–7 yrs. **Measures:** Ss observed a male model displaying aggression toward an inflated plastic doll. Ss were observed for 10 minutes of free play in an identical setting with either a male or female, adult or peer observer, or no observer. Imitative and total aggressive behaviors were rated. Afterward, Ss' free-play activities were observed in an identical setting in the presence of either a male or female, adult or peer observer. In a fifth condition, no observer was present. Aggressive responses were recorded. **Results:** Under all conditions, boys displayed more imitative and total aggression than girls ($p < .001$, $p < .001$).

Marvin, R. S. Attachment- and communicative-behavior in two-, three-, and four-year-old children. Unpublished doctoral dissertation, University of Chicago, 1971.
  Subjects: $N = 48$; 2–4 yrs and mothers. **Measures:** Ss and their mothers were brought to the testing room. After a 3-minute observation period (Episode 1), Ss were exposed to the following situations: entrance of a stranger (Episode 2); departure of Mo (Episode 3); departure of Str, entrance of Mo (Episode 4); departure of Mo (Episode 5); entrance of Str (Episode 6); departure of Str, entrance of Mo (Episode 7). The presence or absence of the following behaviors was noted: crying, smiling, vocalizing, exploratory locomotion, exploratory manipulation, visual exploration, visual orientation to Mo, visual orientation to Str, and visual orientation to objects in the room other than the toys. In addition, the incidence of each of the following classes of behavior toward Mo was rated on a 7-point scale: proximity- or contact-seeking (e.g. approaching and clambering up, reaching, leaning); contact-maintaining (e.g. clinging, embracing, clutching); proximity-avoiding (e.g. ignoring, looking away, turning away); and searching for Mo following her departure (e.g. following Mo to door, trying to open the door, going to Mo's chair). **Results:** (1) Within each of the 3 age groups, no sex differences were found in smiling, vocalizing, locomotor exploration, searches for Mo following her departure, visual orientation to Mo, visual orientation to Str, or visual orientation to some object in the room other than a toy. (2) Among 2-year-old Ss, boys displayed less manipulatory exploration, less visual exploration (mother-absent episodes only), more crying (beginning with Episode 3), and a greater incidence of contact-maintaining behavior (no difference in average amount), whereas girls exhibited more proximity-avoiding behaviors (significant for Episodes 4 and 7 only). No sex difference was found in the frequency of proximity-seeking behaviors. (3) Among 3-year-old Ss, no sex differences were found. (4) Among 4-year-old Ss, girls displayed less manipulatory exploration, less visual exploration (beginning after Episode 3), more crying (beginning with Episode 4), more proximity-seeking behavior, and a greater average amount of contact-maintaining behavior (no difference in incidence). No sex difference was found in the frequency of proximity-avoiding behavior.

Marwell, G., Schmitt, D. R., and Shotola, R. Cooperation and interpersonal risk. *J. Personality & Social Psychology,* 1971, *18,* 9–32.

> Experiment I: Subjects: *N* = 64; 18–21 yrs (college). Measures: Ss could choose to perform an individual or a cooperative task. The basic response for either was pulling a plunger. On the individual task, a single pull of the plunger was reinforced. On the cooperative task, Ss could earn money only by coordinating their responses. The mutual choice of cooperation entailed the risk that either S could take some of the other's earnings by pressing a take button. Each press of the take button transferred 1 cent. Results: Women pressed the take button more often than men did ($p < .001$). On the last few trials, a similar number of male and female pairs cooperated.
> Experiment II: Subjects: *N* = 56; 18–21 yrs (college). Measures: Same as Experiment I, except each press of the take button transferred $1.00. No sex differences were found in the number of times Ss pressed the take button or in the number of pairs who reached steady-state cooperation.
> Experiment III: Subjects: *N* = 22; 18–21 yrs (college). Measures: Same as Experiment II, except ability to take was made available to Ss regardless of task choice. Individual task no longer provided protection. Results: (1) Women pressed the take button more often than men did ($p < .001$). (2) No sex differences were found in number of pairs of Ss who eventually established cooperation.
> Experiment IV: Subjects: *N* = 24; 18–21 yrs (college). Measures: Same as Experiment II, except that Ss were allowed to communicate with each other. Results: No sex differences.
> Experiment V: Subjects: *N* = 20; 18–21 yrs (college). Measures: Same as Experiment II, except that ability to communicate was introduced partway into the experiment. Results: No sex differences.

Mascaro, G. F., and Graves, W. Contrast effects of background factors on the similarity-attraction relationship. *J. Personality & Social Psychology,* 1973, *25,* 346–50.

> Subjects: *N* = 33; 18–21 yrs (college). Measures: After examining an attitude questionnaire completed by a moderately similar stranger, Ss completed the Interpersonal Judgment Scale measure of attraction and a measure of perceived similarity. Results: No sex differences.

Massari, D. J., and Mansfield, R. S. Field dependence and outer-directedness in the problem solving of retardates and normal children. *Child Development,* 1973, *44,* 346–50.

> Subjects: *N* = 104; 21–25 yrs (high and low MA, field-dependent and -independent retardates). Measures: Ss performed a discrimination-learning task with squares that varied in size and color. Results: No sex differences were found in the number of trials Ss needed to reach criterion.

Massari, D. J., Hayweiser, L., and Meyer, W. J. Activity level and intellectual functioning in deprived preschool children. *Developmental Psychology,* 1969, *1,* 286–90.

> Subjects: *N* = 33; 5 yrs (low SES). Measures: Draw-A-Line and Walk-A-Line tests were administered during the first and last weeks of a 6-week preschool program. Ss were instructed to perform both tasks as slowly as possible, and as quickly as possible. In addition, on the Walk-A-Line test, Ss were given a no-instruction condition. Results: No sex differences.

Masters, J. C. Effects of social comparison upon subsequent self-reinforcement behavior in children. *J. Personality & Social Psychology,* 1968, *10,* 391–401.

> Experiment I: Subjects: *N* = 30; 3–5 yrs. Measures: While playing a question game, Ss received either as many tokens as their younger same-sex partners or more or fewer. Ss in 2 control groups played alone. Ss then played a maze game during which they were free to help themselves to rewards (tokens, pennies, and pieces of paper). The response measure was Ss' self-reinforcing behavior during the maze game. Results: (1) Sex of Ss had no main effect on number of tokens taken. In control groups, boys took more tokens than girls; in experimental groups (excluding the equal group), girls took more tokens than boys ($p < .05$). (2) Sex of Ss had no main effect on number of pennies taken. Boys took more pennies than girls in the control and equal conditions; girls took more pennies than boys in the low and high experimental conditions ($p < .05$). (3) Sex of Ss had no main effect on number of pieces of paper taken. In the low and high experimental groups, girls took more pieces of paper than boys ($p < .05$); in control groups, boys took more pieces of paper than girls ($p < .05$).
> Experiment II: Subjects: *N* = 40; 3–5 yrs. Measures: Same as Experiment I, but instead of the maze game, Ss played a second question game without their partners. During this second game each S divided a preset number of tokens between E and himself. In addition,

1 of the 2 control conditions was eliminated. **Results:** Sex of Ss had no effect on the number of tokens Ss took for themselves.

EXPERIMENT III: **Subjects:** $N = 30$; 3–5 yrs. **Measures:** Same as Experiment I, except that Ss played a second question game with their partners, during which the Ss divided a preset number of tokens between themselves and their partners. Both control conditions were eliminated. **Results:** Sex of Ss had no effect on the number of tokens children took for themselves.

Masters, J. C. Social comparison, self-reinforcement, and the value of a reinforcer. *Child Development*, 1969a, *40*, 1027–38.
    Subjects: $N = 59$; 4–5 yrs. **Measures:** Ss played a question-and-answer game, either alone or with a younger same-sex partner. In the 3 experimental conditions, Ss received 9 tokens for their performance, while their partners received either 54, 9, or 3. In the 2 control conditions, 54 tokens were placed in a box either for the other children in the nursery school or for no special purpose. As in the experimental conditions, control Ss received 9 tokens, 1 after each question. To assess how valuable the tokens were to each child, Ss played a game called Store. The main response measure was the number of tokens Ss were willing to trade for a shiny new penny. Afterward, Ss played the same question-and-answer game with E. After each question, Ss were given 4 tokens to dispense in any way they wished between themselves and E. The number of tokens Ss kept for themselves was recorded. **Results:** No sex differences.

Masters, J. C. Word association and the functional definition of words. *Developmental Psychology*, 1969b, *1*, 517–19.
    Subjects: $N = 72$; 4–9 yrs. **Measures:** Ss were given a word association test and a word definition test. The number of syntagmatic associations and functional definitions Ss produced was recorded. **Results:** No sex differences.

Masters, J. C. Effects of social comparison upon children's self-reinforcement and altruism toward competitors and friends. *Developmental Psychology*, 1971, 5, 64–72.
    Subjects: $N = 120$; 4–5 yrs. **Measures:** In 3 of 5 conditions, Ss played a question-and-answer game with a younger same-sex partner; in the 2 control conditions, Ss played alone. Ss always received 9 tokens for their performance. Their partners in the experimental conditions received either more (54), less (3), or the same number. In the social-comparison control condition, 54 tokens were placed in a box "for all the other children in the nursery school." In the no-comparison control condition, 54 tokens were again dropped in a box, but the box was not designated for any special purpose. Afterward, Ss were provided with the opportunity to give as many of their tokens as they wished to their partner and to a friend, both of whom were absent. In the social-comparison control condition, Ss could donate their tokens "to all the other children in the nursery school." Ss then played the question-and-answer game again, this time with E as their partner. After each question, Ss were given 4 tokens to divide between themselves and E. **Results:** No sex differences were found in the number of tokens Ss gave to their partners or to their friends, or in the number of tokens Ss kept for themselves while playing the question-and-answer game with E.

Masters, J. C. Effects of social comparison upon the imitation of neutral and altruistic behaviors by young children. *Child Development*, 1972a, *43*, 131–42.
    Subjects: $N = 80$; 4–5 yrs. **Measures:** Ss played "Paymaster," a question-and-answer game. Each time they answered a question correctly, Ss received 1 token. In 3 of the 5 conditions, Ss played with an adult model (M) who received either more, fewer, or the same number of tokens as Ss. In the 2 remaining conditions, Ss played alone. At the conclusion of the Paymaster game, Ss watched as M played with several toys. Half the children observed a same-sex model and half observed an opposite-sex model. After M departed, Ss played with the toys for 3 minutes. Measures were taken of number of imitative behaviors. **Results:** No sex differences were found. The interaction between sex of S and sex of M did not reach significance.

Masters, J. C. Effects of success, failure, and reward outcome upon contingent and non-contingent self-reinforcement. *Developmental Psychology*, 1972b, 7, 110–18.
    Subjects: $N = 80$; 7–8 yrs. **Measures:** Ss either succeeded or failed (prearranged) on a pursuit rotor task. They received high or low token reward for success. Ss performed either the same or a different task, with as many self-reward tokens available as they "deserved" or as they "wished." **Results:** There were no main sex differences. Boys showed greater self-reinforcement than girls when prior reward had been of low magnitude ($p < .05$).

Masters, J. C. Effects of age and social comparison upon children's noncontingent self-reinforcement and the value of a reinforcer. *Child Development*, 1973, 44, 111–16.
    Subjects: $N = 160$; 4–5 yrs. **Measures:** Same-sex pairs played "Paymaster," a matching task

involving difficult discriminations selected from the Matching Familiar Figures Test; 1 child of pair was the subject, and he received 9 tokens in every condition. Tokens dispensed to partner were either lower than, higher than, or equal to, the number S received. In the control condition, S played by himself and 54 tokens were placed in box for "all the children." Discrepancy in allotment of tokens was either contingent or noncontingent. Ss then completed a maze drawing task for which they reinforced themselves with tokens. Ss were asked to recall distribution of tokens during Paymaster game and were questioned as to how they valued the reinforcer. **Results:** (1) There was no sex effect during social comparison phase. (2) Among younger Ss, girls were more responsive to social comparison manipulation than boys were, as measured by amount of self-reinforcement ($p < .05$). (3) Girls valued tokens less than boys did ($p < .001$).

Masters, J. C., and Christy, M. C. Achievement standards for contingent self-reinforcement: effects of task length and task difficulty. Presented at the meeting of the Society for Research in Child Development, 1973.
   Subjects: $N = 32$; 7 yrs. **Measures:** Ss completed 4 versions (long-easy, long-difficult, short-easy, short-difficult) of a form-discrimination task, a card-sorting task, and an arithmetic task. After completing each task, Ss were allowed to reward themselves with from 0 to 10 tokens. The response measures were the number of tokens taken and the amount of time needed to complete each task. **Results:** (1) No sex differences were found in number of tokens taken. (2) The difference in time taken to complete difficult and easy tasks was greater for boys than for girls ($p < .05$). No main effects were found.

Masters, J. C., and Driscoll, S. A. Children's imitation as a function of the presence or absence of a model and the description of his instrumental behaviors. *Child Development*, 1971, *42*, 161–70.
   EXPERIMENT I: **Subjects:** $N = 48$; 4 yrs. **Measures:** E read Ss a story that described the novel arrangement of 8 toys. In 1 condition, the model in the story (Tarzan) arranged the toys. In a second condition, the model found the toys already arranged. In a third condition, Ss were simply told the model discovered the 8 toys, with no reference to their arrangement. At the end of the story, Tarzan was rewarded by being made "king of the jungle." After listening to the stories, Ss were presented with the same 8 toys and left alone for 3 minutes. The way in which Ss arranged the toys was recorded. **Results:** Boys imitated the novel toy arrangements more than girls did ($p < .05$).
   EXPERIMENT II: **Subjects:** $N = 40$; 4 yrs. **Measures:** Same as Experiment I, except that a fourth condition was added and Tarzan was rewarded with a bag of candy instead of being made king. In the added condition, the novel arrangement of the 8 toys was described, but no mention was made of Tarzan. **Results:** No sex differences.

Masters, J. C., and Mokros, J. R. Effects of incentive magnitude upon discriminative learning and choice preference in young children. *Child Development*, 1973, *44*, 225–31.
   EXPERIMENTS I, II, III, IV: **Subjects:** $N = 234$; 4–5 yrs. **Measures:** Ss performed 2-choice discrimination tasks; high- or low-magnitude incentives were offered in a manner designed to maximize their distracting or satiating effects. **Results:** No sex differences.

Masters, J. C., and Morris, R. J. Effects of contingent and noncontingent reinforcement upon generalized imitation. *Child Development*, 1971, *42*, 385–92.
   Subjects: $N = 56$; 4 yrs. **Measures:** Ss were asked to imitate each of 7 aggressive behaviors performed by a female model. In 1 condition, Ss were rewarded by E after every imitative sequence. In a second condition, no reinforcements were given. In a third condition, a machine dispensed marbles to Ss after every response. In a fourth condition, marbles were given to Ss in a bunch at the beginning of the experiment. Afterward, all Ss were exposed to a male model who exhibited 6 neutral behaviors. The number of imitative behaviors Ss performed following the male model's departure was recorded. **Results:** Boys showed greater imitation of the male model than girls did ($p < .05$).

Masters, J. C., and Peskay, J. Effects of race, socioeconomic status and success or failure upon contingent and noncontingent self-reinforcement in children. *Developmental Psychology*, 1972, *7*, 139–45.
   Subjects: $N = 112$; 7–9 yrs (white and black, low and high SES). **Measures:** Ss received success, failure, or neutral feedback about their performance on trials of game. After the game, Ss could self-reward as deserved (contingent condition) or as wanted (noncontingent condition). Number of reward tokens dispensed was determined. **Results:** No sex differences.

Matheny, A. P., Jr. Heredity and environmental components of competency of children's articulation. Paper presented at the Biennial Meeting of the Society for Research in Child Development. Philadelphia, 1973.
    Subjects: $N = 22$ opposite-sex twin pairs; 3–8 yrs. **Measures:** Templin-Darley Screening Test of Articulation. **Results:** Girls had higher articulation scores than boys ($p < .001$).

Mathews, M. E., and Fozard, J. L. Age differences in judgments of recency for short sequences of pictures. *Developmental Psychology*, 1970, *3*, 208–17.
    Subjects: $N = 128$; 5, 6, 7, 8, 11, 12 yrs. **Measures:** Ss were presented with either 7 or 12 pictures, 1 at a time. Afterward, 2 pictures from the set were shown a second time. Ss were asked to judge which of the 2 pictures had been presented to them more recently. **Results:** No sex differences.

Matlin, M. W. Response competition as a mediating factor in the frequency-affect relationship. *J. Personality & Social Psychology*, 1970, *16*, 536–52.
    Subjects: $N = 39$; 18–21 yrs (college). **Measures:** Ss rated their liking for each of 120 words of different frequencies. **Results:** No sex differences.

Maw, W. H., and Maw, E. W. Differences in preference for investigatory activities by school children who differ in curiosity level. *Psychology in the Schools*, 1965, *2*, 263–66.
    EXPERIMENTS I, II, III: **Subjects:** $N = 914$; 10, 11 yrs. **Measures:** Ss' activity preferences were assessed from their responses to multiple-choice questions. **Results:** In each of the 3 experiments, boys selected outgoing investigatory activities more often than girls did ($p < .05$, $p < .01$, $p < .0005$).

May, R. R. A method for studying the development of gender identity. *Developmental Psychology*, 1971, *5*, 484–87.
    Subjects: $N = 75$; 8, 9, 10 yrs. **Measures:** Ss were asked to write stories about a picture of a male and a female trapeze artist in midair and a picture of a bullfighter alone in the ring. Stories were scored so that more positive scores indicated a more "feminine" pattern (deprivation followed by enhancement) rather than a more "masculine" pattern (enhancement followed by deprivation). **Results:** Girls' mean score was higher than boys' ($p < .0005$).

Meddock, T. D., Parsons, J. A., and Hill, K. T. Effects of an adult's presence and praise on young children's performance. *J. Experimental Child Psychology*, 1971, *12*, 197–211.
    Subjects: $N = 64$; 4–5 yrs. **Measures:** After a baseline minute, Ss performed a nonskill task (marble-dropping) under 4 conditions: supportive or unresponsive E, present or absent E. Performance rate change was assessed. **Results:** Girls had higher baseline response rates, but there were no sex differences in change scores.

Mehrabian, A. Measures of vocabulary and grammatical skills for children up to age six. *Developmental Psychology*, 1970, *2*, 439–46.
    Subjects: $N = 127$; 3–5 yrs. **Measures:** Ss were given a picture vocabulary test, a comprehension of meaningful commands test, a comprehension of meaningless commands test, a sentence-completion test measuring grammatical ability, a test entitled "Judgment of the Grammaticalness of Sentences and Phrases," and a verbal imitation test. **Results:** No sex differences.

Meichenbaum, D., and Goodman, J. Reflection-impulsivity and verbal control of motor behavior. *Child Development*, 1969, *40*, 785–97.
    Subjects: $N = 30$; 5–6 yrs. **Measures:** Ss performed a finger-tapping task and a foot-depression task. Both were designed to assess verbal control of motor behavior. On the first administration of the tapping task, Ss pressed a telegraph key while saying aloud the words "faster" and "slower" for 2 15-second trials each. On the second administration, Ss said the words quietly to themselves. The response measure was the number of taps Ss performed under each of the various conditions. While performing the foot-depression task, Ss were presented with a random sequence of 24 lights (12 blue, 12 yellow). Ss were required to push the toe foot pedal whenever the blue light came on, but not to push it if the yellow light came on. The task was given to Ss twice, first without, then with the instructions to verbalize the meaning of the lights ("push" or "don't push") before responding. The number of accurate responses Ss performed was recorded. Then 2 weeks after the administration of these tasks, Ss were given the Matching Familiar Figures (MFF) test. **Results:** (1) On the first administration of the foot-depression task, girls incorrectly responded to the appearance of the yellow light by pushing the foot pedal more frequently than boys did. (2) On the MFF, girls had lower response latencies than boys.

There were no sex differences in number of recognition errors. (3) No sex differences were found on any other measure.

Meisels, M., and Guardo, C. J. Development of personal space schemata. *Child Development*, 1969, *40*, 1167–78.
> **Subjects:** $N = 431$; 8–15 yrs. **Measures:** Ss were shown silhouette figures representing same-sex and opposite-sex peers. In the first 2 subsections of the task, the stimulus figure was described as (1) a best friend, (2) an acquaintance, (3) a stranger, (4) someone liked very much, (5) someone disliked very much, (6) someone neither liked nor disliked, (7) someone feared. In the latter 2 subsections, the group stimulus figures were described as (1) friends, (2) strangers, (3) feared peers. For each situation, S was asked to place a silhouette figure representing himself in face-to-face relation to the stimulus figure(s). Interfigure distances were recorded. **Results:** (1) Overall, girls employed greater spatial distances between themselves and "a stranger," "someone neither liked nor disliked," "someone disliked very much," "someone feared," "feared peers," and "strangers," while boys used more distance between themselves and "a friend." (2) For "a friend," "an acquaintance," "a stranger," and "strangers," boys used more space at 8 years and sometimes also at 9 and 10 years, while girls generally used more distance at 11, 12, and 13 years. At 14 and 15 years of age, no sex differences were found. (3) For "someone feared," "feared peers," and "strangers," boys maintained smaller distances from opposite-sex peers than from same-sex peers, while girls maintained the same distances from both sexes.

Mendelsohn, G. A., and Griswold, B. B. Assessed creative potential, vocabulary level, and sex as predictors of the use of incidental cues in verbal problem solving. *J. Personality & Social Psychology*, 1966, *4*, 423–31.
> **Subjects:** $N = 223$; 18–21 yrs (college). **Measures:** Vocabulary test of the Institute of Educational Research Intelligence Scale CAVD, Barron-Welsh Art Scale (BWAS), and Remote Associates Test (RAT). **Results:** Women scored higher than men on the BWAS ($p < .05$). No sex differences were found on the vocabulary test or the RAT.

Mendelsohn, G. A., and Griswold, B. B. Anxiety and repression as predictors of the use of incidental cues in problem solving. *J. Personality & Social Psychology*, 1967, *6*, 353–59.
> **Subjects:** $N = 181$; 18–21 yrs (college). **Measures:** Ss memorized a list of 25 words while another list of 25 words was being played on a tape recorder. Ss then attempted to solve 30 anagrams; 10 of the solution words had appeared on the focal (memory) list, and another 10 words had appeared on the peripheral (interference) list. The response measures were numbers of focal, peripheral, and neutral solutions. Ss also completed the first- and second-factor scales of the MMPI, A and R. **Results:** (1) No sex differences were found in R scores. Women had higher A scores than men ($p < .01$). (2) No sex differences were found in number of focal, peripheral, or neutral solutions.

Messé, L. A., Aronoff, J., and Wilson, J. P. Motivation as a mediator of the mechanisms underlying role assignments in small groups. *J. Personality & Social Psychology*, 1972, *24*, 84–90.
> **Subjects:** $N = 72$; 18–21 yrs (college). **Measures:** Ss responded to a 60-item sentence-completion test (SCT) that assessed the degree to which Ss were concerned with satisfying safety and esteem needs. Only Ss high in one motive and low in the other were selected to participate. Ss were run in 24 3-person groups composed of 2 women and 1 man. All members of a group were homogeneously safety- or esteem-oriented. Ss worked a number of tasks both individually and as a group for 2 hours. Videotapes were made of each group. Ss' behavior was scored as to whether they gave procedural suggestions, suggested solutions, gave opinions, gave orientations, drew attention, or asked opinions. Composite leadership scores were then calculated. **Results:** In two-thirds of the safety-oriented groups, men had higher leadership scores than women ($p < .02$).

Messer, S. B., and Lewis, M. Social class and sex differences in the attachment and play behavior of the year-old infant. *Merrill-Palmer Quarterly*, 1972, *18*, 295–306.
> **Subjects:** $N = 25$; 13 mos (low SES) and mothers. **Measures:** Infants were observed in a playroom containing the following toys: a set of blocks, a pail, a lawnmower, a stuffed dog, a plastic cat, a set of quoits, a wooden mallet, a pegboard, and a wooden pull-toy bug. After receiving a signal from E, mothers removed the infants from their laps and placed them on the floor. For the next 15 minutes, mothers passively watched their infants play. The following infant behaviors were recorded: latency to return to Mo, number of returns to Mo, number of seconds in contact with Mo, number of seconds spent vocalizing to Mo, number of seconds

spent looking at Mo, number of looks to Mo, number of activity changes, duration of longest activity, number of squares traversed (the room was marked off into 12 equal squares), number of seconds spent playing with each of the toys, number of seconds spent banging toys, number of seconds spent putting toys into pail, and number of seconds spent playing with nontoys (doorknob, doorstopper, lights, etc.). **Results:** (1) Girls returned to their mothers more quickly and more frequently than boys did ($p < .025$), ($p < .025$). (2) Girls spent more time touching their mothers than boys did ($p < .025$). (3) Girls traversed more squares than boys did ($p < .025$).

Meyer, J. W., and Sobieszek, B. J. The effect of a child's sex on adult interpretations of its behavior. *Developmental Psychology*, 1972, 6, 42–48.
   Subjects: $N = 85$; 18–45 yrs. **Measures:** Each S was shown 2 short videotapes of 2 17-month-old children, with each child sometimes being described as a boy and sometimes as a girl. After viewing each tape, S described the child on a short questionnaire with 24 bipolar items, 17 of which were sex-role-linked. **Results:** (1) Women attributed more qualities to the children than men did ($p < .02$). (2) Men attributed more qualities to the child described as a boy, whereas women attributed more qualities to the child described as a girl ($p < .04$).

Meyer, W. J., and Thompson, G. G. Sex differences in the distribution of teacher approval and disapproval among sixth-grade children. *J. Educational Psychology*, 1956, 47, 385–97.
   Subjects: $N = 78$; 11 yrs. **Measures:** (1) Teacher-pupil interactions were observed for 30 hours in each of 3 classrooms. Each incident in which the teacher expressed either approval or disapproval to a pupil was recorded. (2) Common situations in which pupils receive approval or disapproval from their teacher were described to Ss. For each situation, Ss nominated the 4 pupils in their class whom they viewed as being most likely involved in such an incident. **Results:** (1) Observations: boys received more praise (1 of 3 classrooms) and disapproval (all 3 classrooms) from their teachers than girls did. (2) Peer nominations: both sexes perceived boys as receiving more disapproval from their teachers than girls (2 of 3 classrooms). No differences were found in Ss' perceptions of the frequency of boys' and girls' receiving teacher approval.

Meyers, W. J., and Cantor, G. N. Infants' observing and heart period responses as related to novelty of visual stimuli. *Psychonomic Science*, 1966, 5, 239–40.
   Subjects: $N = 24$; 5 mos. **Measures:** Ss viewed a given stimulus projected on a screen for 4 trials (phase 1). A new stimulus was introduced and the 2 stimuli were each presented 4 times (phase 2). A third stimulus was subsequently added (phase 3) and a fourth (phase 4), each appearing 4 times within a given phase. Cardiovascular responses were recorded for each infant. **Results:** During phases 1 and 2, both sexes exhibited similar heart rate decelerations accompanying stimulus presentation. During the last 2 phases, boys showed increased heart rate decelerations; girls showed decreased heart rate decelerations ($p < .05$).

Meyers, W. J., and Cantor, G. N. Observing and cardiac responses of human infants to visual stimuli. *J. Experimental Child Psychology*, 1967, 5, 16–25.
   Subjects: $N = 44$; 6 mos. **Measures:** Fixation time, heart period change, and latency of heart period change of infants' responses to visual stimuli (ball, clown) were recorded in familiarization and test phases. **Results:** (1) Boys demonstrated longer latencies in the group that viewed the ball; girls demonstrated longer latencies in the group that viewed the clown ($p < .05$). (2) For boys, larger heart period changes occurred in response to the nonfamiliarized stimulus than to the familiarized stimulus; this was not true for girls ($p < .01$).

Mikesell, R. H., Calhoun, L. G., and Lottman, T. J. Instructional set and the Coopersmith Self-Esteem Inventory. *Psychological Reports*, 1970, 26, 317–18.
   Subjects: $N = 21$ boys, 8 girls; 15 yrs. **Measures:** Coopersmith's Self-Esteem Inventory was administered to Ss 3 times. On each administration, Ss received a different instructional set. Ss were requested to either (a) answer honestly, (b) present a favorable impression of themselves, or (c) present an unfavorable impression of themselves. **Results:** No sex differences.

Milburn, T. W., Bell, N., and Koeske, G. F. Effects of censure or praise and evaluative dependence in a free-learning task. *J. Personality & Social Psychology*, 1970, 15, 43–47.
   EXPERIMENT I: **Subjects:** $N = 86$; 18–21 yrs (college). **Measures:** Ss were successively presented with 3 lists of words. Ss were asked to recall as many words as possible from each list. In between lists, Ss received either subtle approval or censure from E. **Results:** Women recalled more words than men did ($p < .01$).
   EXPERIMENT II: **Subjects:** $N = 48$; 18–21 yrs (college). **Measures:** Same lists as Experiment

I. Procedures were changed to minimize contact between S and E. **Results:** Women recalled more words than men did ($p < .01$).

Milgram, N. A., and Wolfgang, W. R. Developmental and experimental factors in making wishes. *Child Development*, 1969, *40*, 763–71.
Subjects: $N = 160$; 6, 9, 12, 15 yrs (white and black, normal and noninstitutionalized retardates). **Measures:** Ss were asked, "If you could make 3 wishes, what 3 wishes would you make?" Wishes were scored on abstract/concrete and adult/child dimensions. **Results:** No sex differences.

Milgram, N. A., Shore, M. F., and Malasky, C. Linguistic and thematic variables in recall of a story by disadvantaged children. *Child Development*, 1971, *42*, 637–40.
Subjects: $N = 99$; 5–7 yrs (white and black, low and middle SES). **Measures:** An illustrated story was read aloud to Ss. Afterward, they were asked to retell the story in their own words. Ss' stories were scored for (a) total number of words, (b) total number of sentences (each new thought expressed was considered a sentence), (c) total number of relevant sentences (sentences were scored according to whether they were part of the story—mere description of the pictures or elaboration of the material was not credited), and (d) presence of each of 22 themes considered essential to the story. **Results:** No sex differences.

Miller, A. G., and Thomas, R. Cooperation and competition among Blackfoot Indian and urban Canadian children. *Child Development*, 1972, *43*, 1104–10.
Experiment I: Subjects: $N = 96$; 7–11 yrs. **Measures:** Ss played the Madsen Cooperation Board. Group and individual awards were administered. Cooperative behavior resulted in high rewards for everyone, whereas competitive behavior resulted in low rewards. **Results:** No sex differences.
Experiment II: Subjects: $N = 96$; 7–11 yrs. **Measures:** Same as Experiment I, except that the inhibition of competitive behavior resulted in individual Ss' being rewarded. **Results:** No sex differences.

Miller, D. J., Cohen, L. B., and Hill, K. T. A methodological investigation of Piaget's theory of object concept development in the sensory-motor period. *J. Experimental Child Psychology*, 1970, *9*, 59–85.
Subjects: $N = 84$; 6, 8, 10, 12, 14, 16, 18 mos. **Measures:** Ss were given 8 of the 16 tasks of the Uzgiris and Hunt "Visual Pursuit and Permanence of Objects" series. 6- and 8-month-olds were tested on Tasks 1–8; 10- and 12-month-olds on Tasks 4–9; and 11-12, and 14-, 16- and 18-month-olds on Tasks 8–9 and 11–16. For 28 Ss, the procedures used by Uzgiris and Hunt were followed as closely as possible (Replication condition); for the remaining 56 Ss, a considerable number of procedural changes were made (Extension condition). **Results:** Among 14-18-month-olds in the Replication condition, girls exhibited a higher level of performance than boys ($p < .05$). No other sex differences were found.

Miller, L. K. Developmental differences in the field of view during tachistoscopic presentation. *Child Development*, 1971, *42*, 1543–51.
Experiment I: Subjects: $N = 36$; 7, 11, 20 yrs. **Measures:** Ss were shown a series of displays of letters that were divided by lines to form 4 quadrants. After Ss' fixation time was assessed, they were asked to name the quadrant containing the target letter for each array. **Results:** No sex differences.
Experiment II: Subjects: $N = 36$; 7, 11, 20 yrs. **Measures:** Same as Experiment I, except that the set of displays eliciting the most marked differences in performance associated with target distance was presented in such conditions as to elicit age differences in overall performance. **Results:** No sex differences.

Miller, P. H. Attention to stimulus dimensions in the conservation of liquid quantity. *Child Development*, 1973, *44*, 129–36.
Subjects: $N = 100$; 5, 8 yrs (white, middle SES). **Measures:** Ss were given a pretraining session to assess their understanding of "same" and "different" concepts. An attention task followed in which relative saliences of height, width, and quantity of liquids were determined. Ss were then given a liquid conservation task. **Results:** No sex differences.

Miller, R. R. No play: a means of conflict resolution. *J. Personality & Social Psychology*, 1967, *6*, 150–56.
Subjects: $N = 120$; 18–21 yrs (college). **Measures:** Same-sex pairs of Ss played a modified version of the Prisoner's Dilemma game in which a third choice with an automatic zero-zero payoff (overriding any choice by the other player) was available. **Results:** No sex differences.

Miller, T. W. Communicative dimensions of mother-child interaction as they affect the self-esteem of the child. Paper read at the 79th APA meeting, Washington, D.C., 1971.
　　Subjects: $N = 203$; 13 yrs and mothers (white and black, urban and suburban). **Measures:** Ss completed Coopersmith's Self-Esteem Inventory. Mothers answered (1) the Parental Response Inventory, which assessed their reactions to positive and negative children's behaviors, and (2) the Relationship Inventory-B, which assessed their affective and empathic reactions in family interactions. **Results:** (1) In the inner-city black sample, mothers showed greater empathy, genuineness, and positive regard toward their daughters than toward their sons. (2) Girls showed higher levels of overall self-esteem than boys did ($p < .05$).

Milton, G. A. Sex differences in problem solving as a function of role appropriateness of the problem content. *Psychological Reports*, 1959, 5, 705–8.
　　Subjects: $N = 48$; 18–21 yrs (college). **Measures:** Ss were given a set of 20 problems, half with content appropriate to the masculine role and half with content appropriate to the feminine role. **Results:** Men solved more problems than women did (for "masculine" problems, $p < .001$; for "feminine" problems, $p < .05$). The difference between the men's and women's scores was less when the problems were stated with content appropriate to the feminine role ($p < .05$).

Minard, J. G. Response-bias interpretation of "perceptual defense"; a selective review and evaluation of recent research. *Psychological Review*, 1965, 72, 74–88.
　　Subjects: $N = 52$; 18–21 yrs (college). **Measures:** Ss were tachistoscopically presented with slides of emotion-arousing and neutral words. Interspersed among these were smudged blank slides. After each presentation, Ss were asked to name the word that had been on the screen. **Results:** (1) Neither sex evidenced response bias. (2) Men identified neutral words more accurately than emotional words; for women, the reverse was true ($p < .01$).

Minard, J. G., Bailey, D. E., and Wertheimer, M. Measurement and conditioning of perceptual defense, response bias, and emotionally biased recognition. *J. Personality & Social Psychology*, 1965, 2, 661–68.
　　Subjects: $N = 52$; 18–21 yrs (college). **Measures:** Ss identified neutral and emotion-arousing words that were tachistoscopically presented at better-than-chance levels of accurate recognition. **Results:** Women showed a greater predominance of emotional word responses among accurate stimulus identifications than men did ($p < .05$). No sex differences were found in response bias.

Minor, M. W. Experimenter-expectancy effect as a function of evaluation apprehension. *J. Personality & Social Psychology*, 1970, 15, 326–32.
　　Subjects: $N = 39$; 18–21 yrs (college). **Measures:** Ss rated the degree of success or failure experienced by individuals in a series of 10 photographs. **Results:** Women rated the pictures more negatively than men did ($p < .03$).

Minton, C., Kagan, J., and Levine, J. A. Maternal control and obedience in the two-year-old. *Child Development*, 1971, 42, 1873–94 (and personal communication).
　　Subjects: $N = 90$; 27 mos (firstborn) and their mothers (low, lower-middle, middle, upper-middle SES). **Measures:** Each mother-child pair was visited at home on 2 separate occasions. Mothers' reactions to (a) requests and (b) violations of maternal standards were recorded. **Results:** (1) Boys interacted with their mothers more than girls did. (2) Boys committed more violations of maternal standards than girls did. More of boys' than girls' violations involved the integrity of household goods. In contrast to girls, boys were more often reprimanded for aggressing toward their mothers. Girls, in contrast, were more often reprimanded for failing to perform a task with competence (significant for upper-middle SES sample, personal communication). Girls were more likely than boys to obey their mothers immediately. (3) No sex difference was found in the rate of occurrence of requests. Requests for help were more frequent for girls than for boys ($p < .10$), whereas requests for information and permission were more frequent for boys than for girls ($p < .10$). (4) No differences were found between mothers of boys and girls in the frequency of occurrence of anticipation sequences (mother anticipates the child's violation of 1 of her standards) or commands, or in their display of the following types of responses to violations: simple prohibitions; mildly negative statements; removal of object; explanation; questioning; distraction; physical punishment. In comparison to mothers of girls, mothers of boys were more likely to move their child from the locus of the violation and less likely to use directive prohibitions. (5) Mothers of girls worried more often about personal danger to their child and less often about danger to household goods than mothers of boys.

Miranda, S. B. Visual abilities and pattern preference of premature infants and full-term neonates. *J. Experimental Child Psychology*, 1970, *10*, 189–205.

> **Subjects:** $N = 54$; 3 days (full term), 22 days (premature with gestation age of 8 mos). **Measures:** Ss were presented with pairs of geometric and facial stimuli. Fixation times were recorded. **Results:** No sex differences.

Mischel, H. N. Professional sex bias and sex-role stereotypes in the U.S. and Israel. Corrected draft, 1972.

> EXPERIMENT I: **Subjects:** $N = 56$; 17–21 yrs. **Measures:** Ss were presented with 1 article from the professional literature of each of 4 occupational fields: law, city planning, primary education, and dietetics. Law and city planning were thought to be strongly associated with men, whereas primary education and dietetics were considered primarily feminine fields. Articles were ascribed to either male or female authors. After reading each article, Ss answered a set of 9 evaluative questions. **Results:** (1) There were no main effects of sex of subject or sex of author. (2) Articles ascribed to male authors in the male fields were rated more favorably than those ascribed to female authors; articles ascribed to female authors in the female fields were rated more favorably than those ascribed to male authors ($p < .01$).
>
> EXPERIMENT II: **Subjects:** $N = 21$; 18–21 yrs. **Measures:** Ss were asked to indicate the degree to which each of 10 occupational fields was associated with men or with women. **Results:** (1) There were no main effects of sex of subject. (2) Law and city planning were perceived as masculine fields, dietetics and primary education as feminine fields ($p < .01$).
>
> EXPERIMENT III: **Subjects:** $N = 52$; 13–20 yrs (Israel). **Measures:** Same as Experiment I. **Results:** No sex differences.
>
> EXPERIMENT IV: **Subjects:** $N = 74$; 14–17, 25–48 yrs (Israel). **Measures:** Same as Experiment II. **Results:** Same as Experiment II ($p < .001$).

Mischel, W., and Grusec, J. Determinant of the rehearsal and transmission of neutral and aversive behaviors. *J. Personality & Social Psychology*, 1966, *3*, 197–205.

> **Subjects:** $N = 56$; 3–5 yrs. **Measures:** Ss were exposed to an adult female model who displayed aversive and neutral behaviors while playing a game. Afterward, in the model's absence, Ss were given the opportunity to demonstrate the game to a confederate. Measures were taken of Ss' rehearsal of the neutral and aversive behaviors in the model's presence, and of Ss' transmission of these behaviors to the confederate. **Results:** No sex differences.

Mischel, W., and Grusec, J. Waiting for rewards and punishments: effects of time and probability on choice. *J. Personality & Social Psychology*, 1967, *5*, 24–31.

> **Subjects:** $N = 96$; 9–10 yrs. **Measures:** Ss chose between smaller immediate and larger delayed rewards and punishments. **Results:** No sex differences.

Mischel, W., and Liebert, R. M. Effects of discrepancies between observed and imposed reward criteria on their acquisition and transmission. *J. Personality & Social Psychology*, 1966, *3*, 45–53.

> **Subjects:** $N = 54$; 9 yrs. **Measures:** Ss alternated turns with an adult female model (M) in a bowling game. Ss were guided to adopt a criterion of self-reward that was either consistent or inconsistent with the self-reward criterion modeled by M. Afterward, half the Ss demonstrated the game to a younger child and then performed alone. The remaining half went through the reverse sequence. The response measures were the scores for which Ss rewarded themselves when performing alone and when demonstrating the game. Measures were also taken of the self-reward criteria Ss imposed on the younger children. **Results:** No sex differences.

Mischel, W., and Liebert, R. M. The role of power in the adoption of self-reward patterns. *Child Development*, 1967, *38*, 673–83.

> **Subjects:** $N = 56$; 7–8 yrs. **Measures:** Ss played a miniature bowling game for which E controlled the scores. Each S practiced games with the male model, who rewarded himself for high scores and guided S to reward himself. However, the model rewarded himself for some lower scores for which he would not allow S to reward himself. In Phase I, Ss were led to believe that the model would possibly give S a free sample game if S performed well. In Phase II, Ss expected no potential reward. Each S performed the game alone in 2 phases. In the second phase, each S in the experimental group was informed that no sample games were available. The response measure was the occurrence or nonoccurrence of self-reward when S performed alone. **Results:** No sex differences.

Mischel, W., and Underwood, B. Instrumental ideation in delay of gratification. Unpublished manuscript, Stanford University, 1973.
Subjects: $N = 80$; 2–5 yrs. Measures: After choosing between 2 rewards, E left Ss alone with instructions that if they waited until he came back, they would be rewarded with their preferred choice. However, they were informed that at any time they could signal him to return and immediately receive the less preferred reward. Results: Girls waited for a longer period of time than boys did ($p < .01$).

Mischel, W., Coates, B., and Raskoff, A. Effect of success and failure on self-gratification. *J. Personality & Social Psychology*, 1968, 10, 381–90.
Experiment I: Subjects: $N = 60$; 7–9 yrs. Measures: After receiving instructions from E to reward themselves for good scores, Ss experienced either repeated success or repeated failure in a miniature bowling game. The response measure was the number of rewards taken. Ss were then given maze designs to solve. While attempting to solve the mazes, Ss were allowed to (noncontingently) help themselves to reward tokens. The response measures were the number of reward tokens taken, number of mazes completed, and amount of time spent working on the mazes. Results: (1) No sex differences were found in the number of rewards or tokens Ss took or in the number of mazes they completed. (2) No main sex differences were found in time spent working on the mazes. Boys who succeeded on the bowling task spent more time on the mazes than boys who failed; for girls, there was no effect ($p < .05$).
Experiment II: Subjects: $N = 120$; 8–9 yrs. Measures: Same as Experiment I, except that Ss obtained either success, failure, or neutral (no-score) outcomes on the bowling game. No rewards were made available for good scores. The bowling game and the maze task were presented either sequentially (as in Experiment I) or concurrently. Ss rewarded themselves under conditions of greater privacy and anonymity while working on the maze designs. Results: (1) No sex differences were found in number of maze tokens taken or in number of mazes completed. Girls spent more time in the maze situation (working on mazes, collecting make tokens) than boys did ($p < .05$). (2) In the concurrent treatment group, no sex differences were found in the amount of time that elapsed before Ss first switched tasks, or in the total number of times Ss changed tasks.

Mischel, W., Grusec, J., and Masters, J. C. Effects of expected delay time on the subjective value of rewards and punishments. *J. Personality & Social Psychology*, 1969, 11, 363–73.
Experiment I: Subjects: $N = 36$; 9–10 yrs. Measures: Ss rated the relative value (attractiveness or unpleasantness) of immediate and delayed rewards and punishments. Results: No sex differences.
Experiment III: Subjects: $N = 30$; 18–21 yrs (college). Measures: Same as Experiment I. Rewards and punishments were changed to make them appropriate for adults. Results: No sex differences.
Experiment IV: Subjects: $N = 51$; 18–21 yrs (college). Measures: Ss indicated their preferences for receiving (a) immediate vs. delayed shocks and (b) shocks requiring less delay vs. shocks requiring more delay. Ss also rated how unpleasant they expected the shocks to feel. Results: No sex differences.

Mischel, W., Mailer, J., and Zeiss, A. Attribution of internal-external control for positive and negative events: developmental and stimulus effects. Unpublished manuscript, 1973.
Experiment I: Subjects: $N = 60$; 4–8 yrs. Measures: The Stanford Preschool Internal-External Scale (SPIES) was administered to Ss 3 times. On 1 occasion, Ss answered for themselves. On the other 2 occasions, Ss answered for a liked and disliked peer. The SPIES consists of 14 forced-choice items; 6 describe positive events and 8 describe negative events. For each item, Ss must decide whether to attribute the cause of the event to external or internal forces. Results: No sex differences.
Experiment II: Subjects: $N = 40$; 18–21 yrs (college). Measures: Same as Experiment I, except that the Stanford College Internal-External Scale (SCIES) was used instead of the SPIES. The format of the SCIES is identical to that of the SPIES except that the items are worded for adults. Results: When an analysis of variance was performed on the overall data, women were found to attribute more responsibility for negative events to themselves than to others ($p < .05$); for men a nonsignificant trend was observed in the opposite direction.

Mitler, M. M., and Harris, L. Dimension preference and performance on a series of concept identification tasks in kindergarten, first grade and third grade. *J. Experimental Child Psychology*, 1969, 7, 374–84.
Subjects: $N = 77$; 5–9 yrs. Measures: Dimension preference (color, form, number) and con-

cept identification were measured by the Wisconsin Card Sorting Test. **Results:** No sex differences.

Mock, R. L., and Tuddenham, R. D. Race and conformity among children. *Developmental Psychology*, 1971, *4*, 349–65.
Subjects: $N = 280$; 9–11 yrs (white, black). **Measures:** Each S made visual-spatial judgments while simultaneously confronted with perceptual stimuli and with supposed information about 4 same-sex peers' judgments on the same stimuli. Information from peers (actually experimenter-controlled) was from 1 to 3 degrees discrepant from normal perception of stimuli. The response measure was the extent to which Ss conformed to the group's judgment. **Results:** Girls were more conforming than boys ($p < .01$).

Modreski, R. A., and Goss, A. E. Young children's initial and changed names for form-color stimuli. *J. Experimental Child Psychology*, 1968, *8*, 402–9.
Subjects: $N = 10$; 3–5 yrs. **Measures:** Ss named stimuli that varied in form and color. **Results:** No sex differences.

Moffatt, G. H. Avoidance conditioning in young children with interruption of a positive stimulus as the aversive event. *J. Experimental Child Psychology*, 1972, *13*, 21–28.
Subjects: $N = 48$; 6 yrs. **Measures:** During a delayed conditioning paradigm, Ss heard recordings of high and low interest value. The interruption of the recordings could be avoided by a hand-pushing response. Half of the Ss could avoid interruption by the pushing response and could escape duration of omission interval by another response. The other half could only avoid interruption but not reinstate the recording. **Results:** (1) There were no sex differences in number of Ss who conditioned or reached extinction. (2) Boys made more avoidance responses than girls did on the first acquisition trial block ($p < .05$).

Monahan, L., Kuhn, D., and Shaver, P. Intrapsychic versus cultural explanations of the "fear of success" motive. *J. Personality & Social Psychology*, 1974, *29*, 60–64.
Subjects: $N = 120$; 10–16 yrs. **Measures:** Ss were asked to make up a story starting with the following sentence: "After first-term finals, Ann (John) finds herself (himself) at the top of her (his) medical school class." Ss' stories were analyzed for positive and negative attitudes expressed toward the actor and toward the achievement. **Results:** There were no sex differences. More Ss responded to the Ann cue than to the John cue with negative attitudes (for boys, $p < .0006$; for girls, $p < .07$).

Monday, L. A., Hout, D. P., and Lutz, S. W. *College Student Profiles: American College Testing Program*. Iowa City: ACT Publications, 1966–67.
Subjects: $N = 238, 145$; 18 yrs. **Measures:** Ss were given the ACT. The high school grades of most of the sample ($N = 225, 402$) were also obtained. **Results:** (1) On the ACT, women had higher English scores, whereas men had higher Mathematics, Natural Science, and Total Composite scores. No sex differences were found in Social Science scores. (2) Women's high school grades were higher than those of men.

Montanelli, D. S. Multiple cue learning in children. *Developmental Psychology*, 1972, *7*, 302–12.
Subjects: $N = 144$; 8, 10, 12, 14 yrs. **Measures:** Ss were given a multiple-cue learning task. By using the color, form, and border of each of 64 geometric stimuli, Ss were asked to judge how far to move a lever across a slot. Each stimulus was presented twice. **Results:** (1) No main sex differences were found in cue utilization. Boys made greatest use of the most valid cue, whereas girls showed greatest use of the cue of intermediate validity. (2) Boys showed a tendency to use the cues of highest and intermediate validity without regard to their physical characteristics, whereas girls tended to use the form cue in conjunction with the cue of highest validity. (3) No sex differences were found in response latencies.

Montanelli, D. S., and Hill, K. T. Children's achievement expectations and performance as a function of two consecutive reinforcement experiences, sex of subject, and sex of experimenter. *J. Personality & Social Psychology*, 1969, *13*, 115–28.
Subjects: $N = 108$; 10 yrs. **Measures:** During each of 2 sessions, Ss received either praise, criticism, or no reaction from either a male or female E while performing a simple operant task (dropping marbles into holes). Ss' achievement expectancies (AEs) were obtained before and after session 1, and after session 2. Ss' response rates were also recorded. **Results:** (1) Boys had higher initial AEs than girls ($p < .05$). Ss with male Es had higher initial AEs than those with female Es ($p < .05$). (2) No sex differences were found in post-session-1 AEs

or in change from initial AEs to post-session-1 AEs. (3) No sex differences were found in pre-session-2 AEs or in change from post-session-1 AEs to pre-session-2 AEs. Ss with male Es had higher pre-session-2 AEs than Ss with female Es. (4) No sex differences were found in Ss' response rates during the baseline period. Ss with male Es had higher base rates than those with female Es ($p < .01$). (5) No sex differences were found in session 1 or session 2 response rates, holding constant Ss' base rates.

Moore, B. S., Underwood, B., and Rosenhan, D. L. Affect and altruism. *Developmental Psychology*, 1973, *8*, 99–104.

> **Subjects:** $N = 42$; 7–8 yrs. **Measures:** Ss were paid 25 pennies for participation in a "hearing" test. After being told to think of something either happy or sad for 40 seconds, Ss were given a 90-second private opportunity to keep or share their pennies. Control Ss either counted slowly or sat quietly during the affective period. **Results:** There was no main effect for sex in the analysis of mean amounts contributed. Girls' median contributions were higher than those of boys ($p < .05$).

Moore, M. Aggression themes in a binocular rivalry situation. *J. Personality & Social Psychology*, 1966, *3*, 685–88.

> **Subjects:** $N = 180$; 8, 10, 12, 14, 16, 18 yrs. **Measures:** By means of a stereoscope, Ss were simultaneously exposed to paired sets of a violent and a nonviolent picture. The response measure was the number of violent pictures seen. **Results:** Boys perceived more violence than girls ($p < .01$).

Moore, T. Language and intelligence: a longitudinal study of the first eight years. Part 1. Patterns of development in boys and girls. *Human Development*, 1967, *10*, 88–106.

> **Subjects:** $N = 76$; tested at ½, 1½, 3, 5, 8 yrs. **Measures:** (1) Griffiths Scale of Infant Development: GQ, Speech Quotient (tested at 6, 18 mos); (2) Stanford-Binet: IQ, Vocabulary (tested at 3, 5, 8 yrs); (3) while tested on the above measures, Ss were rated for (a) comprehension of language (at 3, 5, 8 yrs), (b) length and complexity of sentences (at 3, 5 yrs), (c) enunciation (at 3, 5 yrs), (d) amount of vocalization (at 6 mos), (e) vocal communicativeness (at 18 mos, 3 yrs). **Results:** Among 18-month-old Ss, girls had higher speech quotients than boys ($p < .01$). No other sex differences were found.

Moran, L. J., and Swartz, J. D. Longitudinal study of cognitive dictionaries from ages nine to seventeen. *Developmental Psychology*, 1970, *3*, 21–28.

> **Subjects:** $N = 280$; 9, 12, 15 yrs. **Measures:** An 80-word free association list was administered to Ss, who were retested with same list after 1- and 2-year intervals. Responses were scored as dimension-referent (contrast as in dark-light, or logical coordinate as in apple-orange), perceptual-referent (sensory predicate as in yellow-banana, or abstract predicate as in eagle-bold), concept-referent (synonym or superordinate), paradigmatic (same part of speech), or syntagmatic (summation of noun-verb, noun-adjective, verb-noun, adjective-noun associates). **Results:** No sex differences.

Morf, M. E., and Howitt, R. Rod-and-Frame Test performance as a function of momentary arousal. *Perceptual & Motor Skills*, 1970, *31*, 703–8.

> **Subjects:** $N = 44$; 18–21 yrs (college). **Measures:** The portable model of the Rod-and-Frame Test was administered to Ss. Palmar sweat fingerprints were obtained from each S during the second block of 8 trials. **Results:** No sex differences.

Morf, M. E., Kavanaugh, R. D., and McConville, M. Intratest and sex differences on a portable Rod-and-Frame Test. *Perceptual & Motor Skills*, 1971, *32*, 727–33.

> **Subjects:** $N = 82$; 18–21 yrs (college). **Measures:** Rod-and-Frame Test (portable model). **Results:** No sex differences were found in the initial block of 8 trials. Men were more field-independent than women on trials 9–16 ($p < .05$).

Morin, R. E., Hoving, K. L., and Konick, D. S. Short-term memory in children: keeping track of variables with few or many states. *J. Experimental Child Psychology*, 1970, *10*, 181–88.

> **Subjects:** $N = 48$; 4 yrs. **Measures:** Ss learned the names of 6 familiar objects in each of 4 categories represented by line drawings. E sequentially presented 1 object from each category, after which he asked Ss about the most recent exposure of a particular category ("which animal did you see?"). Stimuli were presented visually to 1 group and aurally to the other. **Results:** No sex differences were found in number of incorrect responses.

Moss, H. A. Sex, age, and state as determinants of mother-infant interaction. *Merrill-Palmer Quarterly*, 1967, *13*, 19–36.

Subjects: $N = 29$; 3 wks (firstborns) and mothers. 25 Ss were retested at 3 mos. Measures: Home observations were made of infant and maternal behaviors. Results: (1) At both observations (a) boys fussed more than girls; (b) boys were more irritable than girls; (c) girls slept more than boys. (2) At 3 weeks of age (but not at 3 months) (a) boys were passively awake more often than girls; (b) boys were observed in the supine position more frequently than girls. (3) At 3 months of age (but not at 3 weeks), mouthing was more frequent in girls than boys. (4) No differences were found between boys and girls in the following behaviors: crying, drowsiness, vocalizations, smiling, eyes on mother, actively awake. (5) At 3 weeks (but not at 3 months), mothers of boys were higher than mothers of girls on the following behaviors: holds infant distant, attends infant, maternal contact (number of holds and attends), stresses musculature, stimulates/arouses infant. (6) No differences were found between mothers of boys and girls on the following behaviors: holds infant close, total number of holds, feeds infant, stimulates feeding, burps infant, affectionate contact, rocks infant, imitates infant, looks at infant, talks to infant, smiles at infant.

Moss, H. A., and Robson, K. S. Maternal influences in early social visual behavior. *Child Development*, 1968, *39*, 401–8.

Subjects: $N = 54$; tested at 1, 3 mos (firstborns) and mothers (18–34 yrs). Measures: (1) 3 home observations were conducted at the end of the infant's first and third months. The frequency with which mother and child simultaneously looked at one another's faces was recorded. (2) At 3 months of age, each infant was presented with geometric and facial stimuli in a laboratory setting. The response measure was the length of the infant's fixation to each stimulus. Results: (1) No sex differences were found during the 3 home observations. (2) In the visual study at 3 months of age, boys looked at both series of stimuli more than girls did (social stimuli, $p < .01$; geometric stimuli, $p < .001$).

Moss, H. A., and Robson, K. S. The relation between the amount of time infants spend at various states and the development of visual behavior. *Child Development*, 1970, *41*, 509–17.

Subjects: $N = 42$; tested at 1, 3 mos (firstborns) and mothers (18–34 yrs). Measures: At both sessions, Ss were observed in their homes. The frequency of fusses and cries and the amount of time Ss spent in each of 2 states (awake and drowsy) were recorded. Results: At 3 months, boys fussed more than girls. No other sex differences were found.

Moyer, K. E., and von Haller, G. B. Experimental study of children's preferences and use of blocks in play. *J. Genetic Psychology*, 1956, *89*, 3–10.

Subjects: $N = 87$; 3–5 yrs. Measures: Ss were exposed to a set of 300 blocks and were then observed by E. Results: No sex differences were found in the amount of time Ss spent playing with the blocks, in the number of structures they built, or in the number of blocks they used.

Moynahan, E. D. The development of knowledge concerning the effect of categorization upon full recall. *Child Development*, 1973, *44*, 238–46.

Subjects: $N = 144$; 6, 8, 10 yrs. Measures: Ss predicted the relative ease of recalling sets of categorized vs. noncategorized stimuli. Recall was measured. Results: No sex differences.

Moynahan, E. D., and Glick, J. Relation between identity conservation and equivalence conservation within four conceptual domains. *Developmental Psychology*, 1972, *6*, 247–51.

Subjects: $N = 96$; 5–6 yrs. Measures: Ss performed identity and equivalence conservation tasks in 4 domains: length, number, weight, and continuous quantity. Results: Boys' identity, equivalence, and total conservation scores were higher than those of girls ($p < .05$; $p < .01$; $p < .05$).

Mueller, E. The maintenance of verbal exchanges between young children. *Child Development*, 1972, *43*, 930–38.

Subjects: $N = 48$; 3–5 yrs. Measures: After being introduced to each other, pairs of Ss were observed in free play in a room equipped with a variety of toys and games. Each S was paired with a child of the same sex. Response measures were frequency of verbal interaction and number of successful and unsuccessful utterances. An utterance was coded as a success if the listener clearly responded to it. If the utterance failed to elicit any response, it was classified as a failure. Results: Boys talked more than girls ($p < .05$). No other sex differences were found.

Mullener, N., and Laird, J. D. Some developmental changes in the organization of self-evaluations. *Developmental Psychology*, 1971, 5, 233–36.
Subjects: $N = 72$; 12, 17, 25–35 yrs. Measures: Ss completed a self-evaluation questionnaire on 40 personal characteristics represented by 5 content areas: achievement traits, intellectual abilities, interpersonal skills, physical skills, and social responsibility. Evaluation scores (sum of ratings for the 8 items in a content area) and variance scores (variance of each S's evaluation scores across content areas) were analyzed. Results: No sex differences.

Mumbauer, C. C., and Gray, S. W. Resistance to temptation in young Negro children. *Child Development*, 1970, 41, 1203–7.
Subjects: $N = 96$; 5 yrs (black, father present or father absent). Measures: Ss played a bean-bag game with a black male or female E; then they played alone when E was gone. The reward was the prize Ss had chosen. Results: No main sex differences were found.

Mumbauer, C. C., and Miller, J. O. Socioeconomic background and cognitive functioning in preschool children. *Child Development*, 1970, 41, 471–80.
Subjects: $N = 64$; 4–5 yrs (low, high SES). Measures: Stanford-Binet IQ test, Paired Associates Learning Task, Kagan's Matching Familiar Figures Test, Motoric Inhibition Test, Children's Embedded Figures Test, and Reactive Object Curiosity Test. Results: No sex differences.

Munroe, R. L., and Munroe, R. H. Effect of environmental experience on spatial ability in an East African society. *J. Social Psychology*, 1971, 83, 15–22.
Subjects: $N = 30$; 3–7 yrs. Measures: Observations were made of Ss' distance from home, and the directed or undirected character of their activities. Results: Overall, no sex differences were found in distance from home. During their free time, boys traveled farther away from home than girls ($p < .01$).

Murray, F. B. Acquisition of conservation through social interaction. *Developmental Psychology*, 1972, 6, 1–6.
Subjects: $N = 108$; 6 yrs. Measures: Ss took a series of conservation tasks (2-dimensional space, number, substance, continuous quantity, weight, and discontinuous quantity). Ss were tested under 3 conditions: alone, in 3-member group (with the stipulation that all members had to agree on answers), and again alone (with additional stimuli, transformations, and tests for concepts of length and area). Results: No sex differences.

Nachamie, S. Machiavellianism in children: the children's Mach scale and the bluffing game. Unpublished doctoral dissertation, Columbia University, 1969.
Subjects: $N = 72$; 11 yrs (Puerto Rican, Chinese, black, white). Measures: Ss completed a modified version of Christie's Likert-type Machiavellianism Scale. 47 Ss with either high or low scores were then paired with a middle Mach child of the same sex. S was given a pair of dice to roll. After each throw, S could either bluff or tell the truth about the outcome. The middle Mach child could then either accept or challenge S's statement. Higher rewards were received for successful bluffs and successful challenges. Results: No sex differences were found in Mach scores or in number of successful bluffs or challenges.

Nakamura, C. Y. Effect of prominence of dissonance associated stimuli during evaluation of the stimuli. *J. Experimental Child Psychology*, 1966, 3, 86–99.
Subjects: $N = 32$; 9 yrs. Measures: Criterion measures of dissonance reduction were established on 4 tasks: 1 making a stimulus that was in the rewarded situation most cognitively salient, the other 3 tasks intended to require greater generalization of stimuli in order for dissonance reduction to be manifested in evaluations of the stimuli. Results: There were no main sex differences. Boys took longer to extinguish on task performance following low reward than high reward treatment; for girls the converse was true.

Nakamura, C. Y. Effects of increasing and decreasing reward magnitude and pre-experimental persistence level on focal and incidental responses. *J. Experimental Child Psychology*, 1969, 7, 514–31.
Subjects: $N = 48$; 5–6 yrs. Measures: Ss' predisposition to persist were rated by teachers. Persistence on a marble game was measured with increasing, decreasing, and random rewards. Results: (1) Low-persistence boys made more lever strokes (release marbles) than high-persistence boys; the converse was true for girls. (2) Under nonreward conditions, boys took more trials to extinction than girls.

Nakamura, C. Y., and Finck, D. Effect of social or task orientation and evaluative or non-evaluative situations on performance. *Child Development*, 1973, *44*, 83–93.

> **Subjects:** $N = 251$; 9–12 yrs. **Measures:** Ss completed the hypothetical situation questionnaire (HSQ), comprising 18 items describing familiar academic situations. Each item is followed by the question "What would you do if you were the child in that situation?" and 4 response choices. On the basis of their answers, Ss were assigned scores on 3 scales: social orientation, task orientation, and self-assurance. Then 204 of the Ss were given a modified version of Pearson and Maddi's Similes Performance Inventory. Ss' task was to learn the correct endings to 30 easy and 30 difficult simile stems. For each set of stems, the number of trials Ss needed to reach the criterion and the total number of errors they made were recorded. **Results:** No sex differences.

Nakamura, C. Y., and Rogers, M. M. Parents' expectations of autonomous behavior and children's autonomy. *Developmental Psychology*, 1969, *1*, 613–17 (and personal communication).

> **Subjects:** $N = 78$; parents of 39 3-year-olds. **Measures:** The Parent's Expectation Inventory was administered to mothers and fathers. Two 10-item subscales measured parents' expectations of 2 types of autonomous behavior in their child—practical and assertive. **Results:** (1) Fathers of girls had higher expectations of assertive autonomy than fathers of boys did. No difference was found between boys' and girls' mothers. (2) Mothers of boys had higher expectations of practical autonomy than mothers of girls did. No difference was found between boys' and girls' fathers. (3) The overall expectations of mothers of boys were greater than those of fathers of boys. No difference was found between the overall expectations of mothers and fathers of girls.

Nash, S. C. Conceptions and concomitants of sex-role stereotyping. Unpublished doctoral dissertation, Columbia University, 1973.

> **Subjects:** $N = 207$; 11, 14 yrs. **Measures:** E administered the group versions of the Embedded Figures Test (GEFT) and the Differential Aptitudes Test, Space Relations (DAT). Demographic data and standardized arithmetic and reading scores were obtained for all Ss. Sex-role preference and theories of sex differences were assessed from Ss' written reports. Ss were given a Stereotypic Questionnaire (99 bipolar items concerning sex-role characteristics) on which they were asked to describe most men, most women, self, and ideal self. **Results:** (1) Among 11-year-old Ss, there were no sex differences on the DAT or the GEFT. Among 14-year-old Ss, boys scored higher than girls on the DAT ($p < .02$) and the GEFT ($p < .01$). There were no main effects of handedness on either spatial reasoning task. (2) There were no sex differences on the standardized arithmetic and reading tests. (3) In both age groups, girls reported they preferred to be boys (11 years, $p < .01$; 14 years, $p < .05$). More 11- than 14-year-old girls preferred to be boys. (4) Among 11-year-old Ss, girls and boys reported it is better to be a boy ($p < .02$). (5) In both age groups, girls rated more bipolar items stereotypic than boys did (11 years, $p < .05$; 14 years, $p < .05$). (6) Ss who preferred to be boys scored higher on the DAT than Ss who preferred to be girls. There were no sex differences on the DAT among Ss who preferred to be boys.

Natsoulas, T. Locus and orientation of the perceiver (ego) under variable, constant, and no perspective instructions. *J. Personality & Social Psychology*, 1966, *3*, 190–96.

> **Subjects:** $N = 96$; 18–21 yrs (college). **Measures:** (1) While S closed his eyes, a letter of the alphabet (either d, b, p, or q) was traced on the side of his head. S's task was to identify which of the 4 letters had been traced. The response measure was the number of times S assumed an internal perspective. (2) Same as Part I, except that S was asked to assume either an external or an internal perspective. The response measure was the number of correct identifications S made. (3) While S closed his eyes, 45- and 90-degree angles were traced on the side of his head. S's task was to draw the traced figures from either an internal or an external perspective. The response measure was the accuracy of S's drawing. **Results:** No sex differences.

Navrat, M. L. Color tint matching by children. *Perceptual & Motor Skills*, 1965, *21*, 215–22.

> **Subjects:** $N = 160$; 3–10 yrs. **Measures:** 9 different tints of the same color were placed in front of Ss. Ss were then given a tint identical to 1 of the 9. S's task was to match it with its duplicate. **Results:** No sex differences were found in the accuracy of Ss' responses.

Nawas, M. M. Change in efficiency of ego functioning and complexity from adolescence to young adulthood. *Developmental Psychology*, 1971, *4*, 412–15.

> **Subjects:** $N = 125$; 26 yrs (originally tested at 18 yrs). **Measures:** The Thematic Apperception Test Ego Sufficiency Scale (measuring ability to cope with emotional issues posed by the ambiguous TAT scenes and figures, and mastery of problems Ss get characters involved in) and the Complexity Scale (number of constructs used in Ss stories, i.e. achievement, affiliation, hostility, etc.) were administered to each S. **Results:** At adolescence, girls' scores for both ego sufficiency and complexity were higher than those of boys. In young adulthood, men's scores exceeded those of women.

Nelsen, E. A., and Rosenbaum, E. Language patterns within the youth subculture: development of slang vocabularies. *Merrill-Palmer Quarterly*, 1972, *18*, 273–85.

> **Subjects:** $N = 1,916$; 12–17 yrs. **Measures:** Same-sex groups of 4 were asked to list as many slang terms as they could that were associated with each of 9 topic areas. **Results:** Boys listed more terms than girls for "money" and "autos and motorbikes." Girls listed more terms than boys for "clothes, styles, and appearance," "boys," "a popular person," and "an unpopular person." No sex differences were found for "cigarettes," "alcohol," or "girls."

Nelson, J. D., Gelfand, D. M., and Hartmann, D. P. Children's aggression following competition and exposure to an aggression model. *Child Development*, 1969, *40*, 1085–97.

> **Subjects:** $N = 96$; 5–7 yrs. **Measures:** Ss observed either an aggressive or a nonaggressive adult model. Subsequent to viewing the model, two-thirds of the Ss either succeeded or failed in competitive games; the remaining Ss engaged in noncompetitive play. All SS were then taken to an experimental room, where they engaged in 10 minutes of free play. The room contained a variety of aggressive and nonaggressive toys, among which were those the aggressive model had used. Displays of imitative and nonimitative aggression were recorded. A total (imitative plus nonimitative) aggression score was then computed. **Results:** (1) After viewing the nonaggressive model, boys were more aggressive than girls. No sex differences were found following exposure to the aggressive model. (2) No sex differences were found in imitative physical aggression scores. Too few displays of imitative verbal aggression were observed to be analyzed.

Nelson, K. E. Accommodation of visual tracking patterns in human infants to object movement patterns. *J. Experimental Child Psychology*, 1971, *12*, 182–96.

> **Subjects:** $N = 80$; 3–9 mos. **Measures:** Ss' visual movements were videotaped while they watched a model train travel around a track and in and out of a tunnel. After criterion was reached (4 or 8 visual movements toward end of tunnel after the train entered), a series of reversal trials (direction reversals made in tunnel) and original direction trials were made. **Results:** No main sex differences.

Nelson, L., and Madsen, M. C. Cooperation and competition in four-year-olds as a function of reward contingency and subculture. *Developmental Psychology*, 1969, *1*, 340–44.

> **Subjects:** $N = 72$; 4 yrs (white and black Head Start programs; white, middle SES nursery school). **Measures:** Same- and opposite-sex pairs of Ss played Madsen's Cooperation Board under 2 conditions: (1) group-reward, in which it was possible for both subjects to get prizes on every trial, and (2) limited-reward, in which it was possible for only 1 subject to get a prize on a trial. **Results:** No sex differences.

Nemeth, C. Effects of free versus constrained behavior on attraction between people. *J. Personality & Social Psychology*, 1970, *15*, 302–11.

> **Subjects:** $N = 120$; 15–17 yrs. **Measures:** After a same-sex confederate either helped or did not help Ss finish a task, Ss completed a questionnaire designed to measure Ss' liking for the confederate and the degree to which Ss felt the confederate liked them. Ss and confederate then participated in a role-playing situation. Ss were asked a standard set of 5 questions by the confederate. The response measure was the amount of time Ss spent talking. Ss then responded to a second questionnaire designed to measure how much they wanted to impress the confederate, and how well they felt they knew him. As Ss were dismissed, Ss were stopped by the confederate and asked to complete a survey. Ss also were asked to take additional surveys for others to complete. The response measures were number of surveys taken (help offered) and number of surveys eventually mailed back (help received). **Results:** No sex differences.

Newson, J., and Newson, E. *Four years old in an urban community.* Harmondworth, England: Pelican Books, 1968 (and personal communication).
Subjects: $N = 700$; 4 yrs and mothers (England). Measures: Maternal interviews. Results: (1) There were no sex-of-child effects on maternal level of restrictions and demands regarding bedtime, table behavior, neatness, physical mobility. (2) There were no sex-of-child effects on maternal intervention in child's quarrels, or encouragement/permission of aggression toward parents. (3) Mothers were more likely to use physical punishment toward boys than toward girls. Fewer boys than girls were "smacked" less than once a week ($p < .03$). (4) There were no sex differences in bed-wetting. (5) More girls than boys were self-reliant in dressing themselves ($p < .001$).

Nisbett, R. E., and Gordon, A. Self-esteem and susceptibility to social influence. *J. Personality & Social Psychology,* 1967, 5, 268–76.
Subjects: $N = 152$; 18–21 yrs (college). Measures: Ss initially completed 2 self-esteem measures and an intelligence test. At a second session, Ss were informed they had done either extremely well or extremely poorly on the intelligence test. Ss then completed both self-esteem tests for a second time and read various persuasive communications, after which Ss indicated their opinions on the topics dealt with in the communications. Results: No sex differences.

Nisbett, R. E., and Gurwitz, S. B. Weight, sex, and the eating behavior of human newborns. *J. Comparative & Physiological Psychology,* 1970, 73, 245–53.
Subjects: $N = 76$; newborn infants. Measures: Special feedings of the hospital's standard formula and a sweetened version of the formula were given to the infants daily. In a second study, sucking the formula was made difficult by decreasing the diameter of the nipple hole. Results: (1) Girls were more responsive than boys to the difference in taste, i.e. relative to boys, girls consumed more sweetened than unsweetened formula ($p < .02$). (2) Girls consumed less formula when sucking was made difficult; boys showed no change ($p < .025$).

Noble, C. E., and Hays, J. R. Discrimination reaction performance as a function of anxiety and sex parameters. *Perceptual & Motor Skills,* 1966, 23, 1267–78.
Subjects: $N = 200$; 18–21 yrs (college). Measures: Ss' task was to learn to snap the correct toggle switch in response to the lighting of a pair of red and green signal lights. Ss had to choose from among 4 switches. When the correct switch was thrown, a white light turned off. Results: Men had faster reaction times than women ($p < .001$).

Northman, J. E., and Gruen, G. E. Relationship between identity and equivalence conservation. *Developmental Psychology,* 1970, 2, 311 (brief report).
Subjects: $N = 60$; 6–9 yrs. Measures: Ss performed identity and equivalence conservation tasks with liquids. Results: (1) There were no sex differences in identity or equivalence conservation among 6-7-year-old Ss. (2) Among 8-9-year-old Ss, boys made more equivalence and identity conservation responses than girls ($p < .01$).

Novak, D. W., and Lerner, M. J. Rejection as a consequence of perceived similarity. *J. Personality & Social Psychology,* 1968, 9, 147–52.
Subjects: $N = 96$; 18–21 yrs (college). Measures: Ss indicated their willingness to interact with same-sex partners who were presented as either similar or dissimilar to themselves, and as either normal or emotionally disturbed. Ss also rated partners' attractiveness and similarity to themselves. Results: (1) No sex differences were found in willingness to interact with partner. (2) Women rated their partners lower in attractiveness than men did ($p < .01$). (3) Women perceived their partners to be less well adjusted than men did ($p < .05$). (4) No main sex differences were found in perceived similarity. Women perceived partners who had been presented as either similar and/or normal to be more similar to themselves than men did; women perceived partners who had been presented as either dissimilar and/or as emotionally disturbed to be less similar than men did.

Nowicki, S., Jr., and Roundtree, J. Correlates of locus of control in secondary school population. *Developmental Psychology,* 1971, 4, 477–78 (brief report).
Subjects: $N = 87$; 17 yrs. Measures: Ss were asked to list the extracurricular activities they were involved in. Results: Girls were more involved in extracurricular activities than boys ($p < .01$).

Nuessle, W. Reflectivity as an influence on focusing behavior of children. *J. Experimental Child Psychology*, 1972, *14*, 265–76.

> **Subjects:** $N = 40$; 10 yrs. **Measures:** To study relationship between developmental differences in hypothesis-testing behavior and problem-solving styles, Ss were presented with 16 simultaneous concept identification problems, for which feedback was given on a prearranged random schedule. E recorded stimulus choice (which allowed determination of which problem-solving hypothesis S used) and 2 response-latency measures. **Results:** (1) Girls had a higher probability of repeating a preceding hypothesis after positive feedback than boys ($p < .05$). (2) Girls took a longer time than boys to complete a problem ($p < .05$). Girls' latency between feedback and the next response was longer than that of boys, but girls were not more effective focusers than boys. (3) There were no sex differences in mean proportion of blank-trial sequences with consistent hypotheses used, probability of repeating preceding hypotheses following negative feedback, or efficiency with which Ss used feedback information to solve problems (focusing behavior).

Nunnally, J. C., Duchnowski, A. J., and Knott, P. D. Association of neutral objects with rewards: effects of massed versus distributed practice, delay of testing, age, and sex. *J. Experimental Child Psychology*, 1967, *5*, 152–63.

> **Subjects:** $N = 144$; 6, 8, 10 yrs. **Measures:** Ss played a conditioning game in which a spin-wheel pointer stopping on 1 nonsense syllable resulted in the winning of 2 pennies, stopping on another syllable meant the loss of 1 penny, and stopping on a third had no consequence. Conditioning effects on the syllables were assessed with 3 response measures: (1) E named each of 3 stick figures "boys" with one of the nonsense syllables, and asked Ss which of the boys would do certain positive, negative, and neutral acts; (2) Ss learned to discriminate among boxes labeled with the different nonsense syllables; and (3) E decided how many times to look at pictures of each of the 3 syllables. Before the experiment, Ss were randomly assigned to 4 levels of practice-massing treatment. **Results:** No sex differences.

Odom, R. D., and Guzman, R. D. Problem solving and the perceptual salience of variability and constancy: a developmental study. *J. Experimental Child Psychology*, 1970, *9*, 156–65.

> **Subjects:** $N = 144$; 5, 11 yrs. **Measures:** Ss performed concept identification tasks in which both constancy and variability were represented on each trial. For half of the Ss, identification of variability was relevant to solution, whereas for the other half, identification of stimulus constancy was relevant to solution. Number of errors to criterion of 10 successive correct identifications was recorded. **Results:** No sex differences.

Odom, R. D., and Guzman, R. D. The development of hierarchies of dimensional salience. *Developmental Psychology*, 1972, *6*, 271–87.

> **Subjects:** $N = 408$; 5–12 yrs. **Measures:** Relative dimensional salience was assessed for choice tasks in which all possible 2-dimensional and 3-dimensional combinations of form, color, number, and position were presented. A final task of identity involved the same dimensions, with definite correct and incorrect choices. Choices and response times were recorded. **Results:** (1) On the 2-dimensional task, boys made more position choices than girls ($p < .05$). (2) On the 3-dimensional task, boys had longer response times on form choices than girls ($p < .01$).

Odom, R. D., and Mumbauer, C. C. Dimensional salience and identification of the relevant dimension in problem solving: a developmental study. *Developmental Psychology*, 1971, *4*, 135–40.

> **Subjects:** $N = 277$; 6–19 yrs. **Measures:** Ss performed a color-form salience task, and were free to choose a comparison stimulus that matched the standard in either form or color. Ss (judged as form-dominant) performed a concept-identification problem with either form or color relevant to the solution. **Results:** No sex differences.

Offenbach, S. I., Baecher, R., and White, M. Stability of first-grade children's dimensional preferences. *Child Development*, 1972, *43*, 689–92.

> **Subjects:** $N = 42$; 6 yrs. **Measures:** Ss chose which of 2 stimuli was most like a third. Projected images varied in color, shape, and size. There was no reinforcement. Lists were administered 3 times in 6 months as a stability measure. **Results:** No sex differences were found in Ss' dimensional preferences.

Ogletree, E. A cross-cultural examination of the creative thinking ability of public and private school pupils in England, Scotland, and Germany. *J. Social Psychology*, 1971, *83*, 301–2.

Subjects: $N = 1,165$; 8–11 yrs (English, Scottish, German). Measures: Ss were given the verbal and figural batteries of the Torrance Tests of Creative Thinking. Results: On the verbal battery, girls were superior to boys. On the figural battery, English and German girls were superior to boys; no sex difference was found in the Scottish sample.

Ohnmacht, Fred W., and Robert F. McMorris. Creativity as a function of field independence and dogmatism. *J. Psychology*, 1971, *79*, 165–68.

Subjects: $N = 74$; 18–21 yrs. Measures: Remote Associations Test. Results: No sex differences.

Okonji, M. O. The differential effects of rural and urban upbringing on the development of cognitive styles. *International J. Psychology*, 1969, *4*, 293–305.

Subjects: $N = 33$; 12 yrs (rural Nigerian). $N = 25$; 21–27 yrs (University of Nigeria, urban upbringing). $N = 65$; adult (rural Nigerian). Measures: Rural adolescents were given the Children's Embedded Figures Test (CEFT). Rural adults completed the CEFT and the Rod-and-Frame Test (RFT). Ss in the university sample took the RFT and the Embedded Figures Test (EFT). Results: (1) Rural boys were more field-independent on the CEFT than rural girls ($p < .02$). (2) Among university Ss, men were more field-independent than women on the RFT, but not on the EFT. (3) Among rural adults, men were more field-independent than women on the CEFT ($p < .01$), but not on the RFT.

Oltman, P. R. A portable Rod-and-Frame apparatus. *Perceptual & Motor Skills*, 1968, *26*, 503–6.

Subjects: $N = 163$; 18–21 yrs (college). Measures: Rod-and-Frame Test (both the portable and the standard model). Results: No sex differences.

Omark, D. R., and Edelman, M. Peer group social interactions from an evolutionary perspective. Paper presented at the Society for Research in Child Development Conference, Philadelphia, 1973.

Subjects: $N = 436$; 4–8 yrs. Measures: Playground observations were recorded by the "nearest neighbor" method (sex, distance, and nature of interaction with nearest neighbor). The "hierarchy" test was given, in which Ss were asked to rank themselves and classmates on "toughness"). In the Draw A Picture Together test (DAPT), each S in a pair was given a distinctive color crayon, and the pair was asked to make a joint picture. The response measures were integration of theme, integration of color (do both colors appear in the same area?), imitation, dominance of outline, and dominance of territory. Results: (1) Boys congregated in larger groups than girls (both maximum and average size of play groups). Girls tended to move in groups of 2 or 3, boys in "swarms." (2) On the DAPT, boys dominated girls with respect to both territory and outline at every grade level except kindergarten (age 5). (3) Among same-sex pairs, little relationship was shown between dominance on the "toughness" hierarchy and dominance in the drawing task. In 2 age groups out of 4 (6 and 8 years old) there was "a slight tendency for the tougher child to dominate" the drawings and to draw the outline of the picture more often.

Omark, D. R., Omark, M., and Edelman, M. Dominance hierarchies in young children. Paper presented at International Congress of Anthropological and Ethnological Sciences, Chicago, 1973.

Subjects: $N = 950$; 4–8 yrs (U.S.), 5–9 yrs (Switzerland), 8–10 yrs (Ethiopia). Measures: Playground observations were made of distance from nearest neighbor, sex of nearest neighbor, and nature of interaction between the subject and his neighbor. Ss were asked "who is tougher" concerning their classmates and themselves. Pictures were used to identify classmates for kindergarten Ss; paper-and-pencil form was used for older children. Results: (1) In all 3 societies, a child's nearest neighbor was most frequently a same-sex child; this trend appeared earlier among boys than girls. (2) Girls were near the teacher more frequently than boys were. (3) Boys were more frequently engaged in physical interaction with an age-mate than girls were. (4) The frequency of aggressive interaction was greater for boys than for girls in all 3 cultures (i.e. hitting or pushing without smiling). (5) Opposite-sex neighbors were farther apart than same-sex neighbors. Boys maintained a greater distance between self and nearest neighbor than girls did (analyzed for American sample only). (6) Boys covered greater distance per unit time than girls did (analyzed for American sample only). (7) In all 3 cultures, boys were higher than girls in the "toughness" hierarchy. (8) Dominance hierarchy was more fully established (more fully agreed upon) between boy-boy dyads than between cross-sex and girl-girl dyads (analyzed for Swiss and American samples only). (9) Boys more often than girls overrated their own position in the dominance hierarchy (analyzed for Swiss and American samples only).

Oskamp, S., and Kleinke, C. Amount of reward as a variable in the Prisoner's Dilemma game. *J. Personality & Social Psychology*, 1970, *16*, 133–40.
Subjects: $N = 100$; 14–17 yrs. **Measures:** Ss played the Prisoner's Dilemma game in same-sex pairs; 5 different pay-off matrices were used. **Results:** (1) Individually, boys were more cooperative than girls ($p < .01$). (2) Girls showed a marked decrease in cooperation between the first and last block of 10 trials; boys' level of cooperation remained constant ($p < .05$).

Osser, H., Wang, M., and Zaid, F. The young child's ability to imitate and comprehend speech: a comparison of two subculture groups. *Child Development*, 1969, *40*, 1063–75.
Subjects: $N = 32$; 4–5 yrs (black, white). **Measures:** Ss imitated sentences read by E and then chose which of 3 simple drawings was described by each sentence. Figures in the drawings were considered racially neutral. Comprehension and imitation errors were recorded. **Results:** No sex differences.

Osterhouse, R. A., and Brock, T. C. Distraction increases yielding to propaganda by inhibiting counterarguing. *J. Personality & Social Psychology*, 1970, *15*, 344–58.
Subjects: $N = 160$; 18–21 yrs (college). **Measures:** After being either distracted or not distracted while listening to a discrepant communication, Ss answered a questionnaire assessing communication acceptance. Ss were then given 3 minutes to express their comments on the issues involved (this was used to obtain an approximate measure of the extent to which Ss had counterargued during communication reception). **Results:** No sex differences.

Ostfeld, B., and Katz, P. A. The effect of threat severity in children of varying socioeconomic levels. *Developmental Psychology*, 1969, *1*, 205–10.
Subjects: $N = 28$; 4–5 yrs (white nursery school, white and black Head Start Program). **Measures:** Ss were presented with 5 crayons and 5 toys, and asked to rank-order each group according to preference. Ss were then asked to color pictures of toys with the color of their choice. During a free-play period, Ss were randomly assigned to low- or high-threat conditions (verbally prohibited from playing with their favorite toy). After free play, Ss were again asked to rank toys and crayons, and color pictures of toys. Finally, Ss were asked which toy they would like to buy. **Results:** No sex differences.

Overton, W. F., and Jordan, R. Stimulus preference and multiplicative classification in children. *Developmental Psychology*, 1971, *5*, 505–10.
Subjects: $N = 120$; 4, 6 yrs. **Measures:** Ss completed a stimulus-preference test of matching problems, each of which could be paired in 2 ways depending on Ss' preferred dimension (color, form, number, size). A 2×2 matrix test was accompanied by a choice of 4 items, 1 of which completed the matrix correctly. **Results:** No sex differences.

Palermo, D. S. Racial comparisons and additional normative data on the children's manifest anxiety scale. *Child Development*, 1959, *30*, 53–57.
Subjects: $N = 470$; 9–11 yrs (white, black). **Measures:** Children's Manifest Anxiety Scale. **Results:** In both racial groups, girls had higher scores than boys on the Anxiety scale ($p < .01$) and on the Lie scale ($p < .05$).

Palermo, D. S. Characteristics of word association responses obtained from children in grades one through four. *Developmental Psychology*, 1971, *5*, 118–23.
Subjects: $N = 100$; 6–9 yrs. **Measures:** Ss gave free-association responses to each of 100 words. The words were taken from the Palermo-Jenkins list. **Results:** Girls gave more popular responses than boys.

Pallak, M. S., Brock, T. C., and Kiesler, C. A. Dissonance arousal and task performance in an incidental verbal learning paradigm. *J. Personality & Social Psychology*, 1967, *7*, 11–20.
Subjects: $N = 39$; 18–21 yrs (college). **Measures:** Before performing a boring task, Ss were either given or not given the option to leave. The task consisted of copying a list of 10 paired associates 20 times. After completing the task, retention of selected paired associates was measured. Ss also indicated how much choice they felt they had in deciding whether to

complete the task or to leave, how interesting and worthwhile the experiment was to them, and how willing they would be to participate in a similar experiment at a later date. **Results:** No sex differences.

Palmer, R. M., and Masling, J. Vocabulary for skin color in Negro and white children. *Developmental Psychology*, 1969, *1*, 396–401.
Subjects: $N = 48$; 8–16 yrs (low SES). **Measures:** A white E asked Ss to describe 16 bubble gum pictures of black and white baseball players. The response measure was number of different color descriptions. After Ss completed this task they were asked to describe 16 blue paint samples in order to determine general verbal fluency for colors. **Results:** No sex differences.

Pancratz, C. N., and Cohen, L. B. Recovery of habituation in infants. *J. Experimental Child Psychology*, 1970, *9*, 208–16.
Subjects: $N = 32$; 15–20 wks. **Measures:** Ss were presented with 10 15-second exposures of 1 of 4 habituation stimuli: a green circle, a blue triangle, a yellow rod, or a red square. Before proceeding to the test phase, half of the Ss were given 20 15-second presentations of a filler stimulus (a black star); for the other Ss, the test phase immediately followed the habituation phase. The test phase consisted of alternate presentations of the familiar stimulus and the novel stimuli (the 3 geometric patterns to which Ss had no previous exposure). **Results:** (1) In the habituation phase, boys showed a response decrement; girls did not ($p < .05$). (2) In the test phase, no main sex differences were found in fixation times to the novel and familiar stimuli.

Paolino, A. F. Sex differences in aggressive content. *J. Projective Techniques & Personality Assessment*, 1964, *28*, 219–26.
Subjects: $N = 84$; 18–21 yrs (college). **Measures:** Ss recorded their dreams as soon as possible after awakening. Later, these reports were analyzed for aggressive content. **Results:** (1) Men involved more of their characters in aggressive actions than women ($p < .01$). (2) Men initiated more aggression in their dreams than women ($p < .01$); no sex differences were found in amount of aggression received. (3) The average intensity of aggression reported by men was higher than the average intensity reported by women ($p < .01$). Men instigated and received more severe aggressive acts than women ($p < .05$, $p < .05$). (4) Men received more aggression from males than women did ($p < .05$); women received more aggression from females than men did ($p < .01$). (5) Men directed more aggression toward male victims than women did ($p < .05$); women directed more aggression toward female victims than men did ($p < .01$). (6) Women received more aggression than men from older people ($p < .01$) and from familiar persons ($p < .01$). Men received more aggression than women from persons whose age was not specified ($p < .01$) and from strangers ($p < .01$).

Papageorgis, D., and McCann, B. M. Effects of characteristic definitions on changes in self perception. *Perceptual & Motor Skills*, 1965, *20*, 717–25.
Subjects: $N = 54$; 18–21 yrs (college). **Measures:** Ss received high hostility scores on a fake group personality test and were then provided with 1 of 3 definitions of hostility (vague, weak, and strong). The vague definition allowed Ss considerable latitude in structuring the meaning of the characteristic on their own; the weak and strong definitions did not. Of these latter 2 definitions, the weak one described hostility in mild, internalized terms, whereas the strong one suggested the definite possibility of overt, disruptive aggressive behavior. Afterward, Ss rated themselves on hostility. **Results:** (1) Men rated themselves more hostile than women did ($p < .01$). (2) Of the male groups, men who received the strong definition rated themselves highest in hostility, whereas men who were provided with the vague definition rated themselves lowest; men who received the weak definition were intermediate. The reverse was true for women ($p < .05$). (3) On a postexperimental questionnaire, men expressed more agreement with their test scores than women did ($p < .01$).

Papousek, H. Experimental studies of appetitional behavior in human newborns and infants. In H. W. Stevenson, E. H. Hess, and H. L. Rheingold, eds., *Early behavior: comparative and developmental approaches*. New York: Wiley, 1967.
Subjects: $N = 130$; birth, 3, 5 mos. **Measures:** Head movements were studied as a conditionable motor complex of infantile appetitional behavior. Conditioning, extinction, discrimination, and reconditioning were studied, using an electric bell and buzzer as the CS and milk as the UCS. Response measures were head-turning and changes in general activity (vocalization, facial response, eye movements, breathing). **Results:** No sex differences.

Parisi, D. Development of syntactic comprehension in preschool children as a function of socioeconomic level. *Developmental Psychology*, 1971, 5, 186–89.
> **Subjects:** $N = 144$; 3–6 yrs. **Measures:** Ss completed a test of Syntactic Comprehension in which they chose 1 of 4 items for each of 20 syntactic contrasts. **Results:** No sex differences.

Parke, R. D. Nurturance, nurturance withdrawal, and resistance to deviation. *Child Development*, 1967, 38, 1101–10.
> **Subjects:** $N = 80$; 6, 7 yrs. **Measures:** In the continuous nurturance condition, E encouraged Ss to draw pictures for 10 minutes. In the nurturance-withdrawal condition, E encouraged Ss to draw pictures for 5 minutes, then ignored Ss for 5 minutes. After the nurturance session, Ss were left alone with 5 attractive but prohibited toys for 15 minutes. E asked Ss to read a book and not touch any toys while E left the room. **Results:** Boys deviated more often than girls.

Parke, R. D., O'Leary, S. E., and West, S. Mother-father-newborn interaction: effects of maternal medication, labor, and sex of infant. Proceedings of the Eightieth Annual Convention, American Psychological Association, 1972.
> **Subjects:** $N = 19$; tested at birth to 2 days (firstborn) and parents. **Measures:** Observations were made of parent-infant interactions in mother's hospital room. The following parental behaviors were recorded: looks, smiles, vocalizes, holds, kisses, touches, rocks, imitates infant, explores infant, feeds, hands infant over to other parent. **Results:** Boy infants were touched by their mothers and fathers more frequently than girl infants.

Parry, M. H. Infants' responses to novelty in familiar and unfamiliar settings. *Child Development*, 1972, 43, 233–37.
> **Subjects:** $N = 48$; 10–12 mos. **Measures:** Infants were observed in a familiar (home) and a nonfamiliar (laboratory) setting while sitting in their mothers' laps. They were familiarized to 1 strange stimulus (wooden disc) and presented with an incongruous stimulus. Fixation time and manipulation were recorded. **Results:** No sex differences.

Parsley, K. M., Powell, M., O'Connor, H. A., and Deutsch, M. Are there really sex differences in achievement? *J. Educational Research*, 1963, 57, 210–12.
> **Subjects:** $N = 5,020$; 7–13 yrs. **Measures:** Ss took the California Reading Achievement Test, the California Arithmetic Test, and the California Test of Mental Maturity; 5 scores were recorded for each S: IQ, Reading Vocabulary, Grade Placement, Reading Comprehension Grade Placement, Arithmetic Reasoning Grade Placement, and Arithmetic Fundamentals Grade Placement. **Results:** No sex differences.

Parten, M. B. Leadership among preschool children. *J. Abnormal & Social Psychology*, 1933a, 27, 430–40.
> **Subjects:** $N = 34$; 4 yrs (nursery school). **Measures:** Ss were observed during their free-play hour. **Results:** No differences were found in the number of boys and girls who directed group activities or who reciprocally directed or shared leadership with another child.

Parten, M. B. Social play among preschool children. *J. Abnormal & Social Psychology*, 1933b, 28, 136–47.
> **Subjects:** $N = 34$; 2–4 yrs (nursery school). **Measures:** Ss were observed during their free-play hour. **Results:** (1) Boys preferred boys as playmates, girls preferred girls. (2) Girls played with dolls more than boys did. (3) Excluding doll play, no sex differences were found in number of times Ss "played house." (4) Boys rode on the kiddie car and played with blocks and trains more often than girls did. (5) Girls strung beads, cut paper, painted, and played on the swings more frequently than boys did.

Parton, D. A., and Geshuri, Y. Learning of aggression as a function of presence of a human model, response intensity, and target of the response. *J. Experimental Child Psychology*, 1971, 11, 491–504.
> **Subjects:** $N = 112$; 4–5 yrs. **Measures:** Half the Ss viewed videotapes of a 6-year-old boy aggressing toward surrogate or nonsurrogate targets. The videotapes shown to the other half of the Ss were the same, except that the model was never visible. Afterward, Ss were asked to perform the behaviors they had observed. For each imitative response, Ss were rewarded with a token. Response measures were frequency and intensity of Ss' imitative responses. After the acquisition test, Ss in the model-present condition were asked to select 1 of 6 amounts of candy to give to the model. **Results:** (1) Mean frequency of imitative responses was higher for boys than for girls ($p < .05$). No sex differences were reported in the intensity

of Ss' aggressive responses. (2) No sex differences were found in the amount of candy Ss wanted to give to the model.

Pascual-Leone, J., and Smith, J. The encoding and decoding of symbols by children: new experimental paradigm and a neo-Piagetian model. *J. Experimental Child Psychology*, 1969, *8*, 328–55.
> **Subjects:** $N = 60$; 5, 7, 9 yrs. **Measures:** Ss were trained to choose between 2 objects on the basis of a verbal or gestural cue given by E. Ss then reproduced E's role in presenting problems and giving cues. **Results:** No sex differences.

Patterson, G. R. Parents as dispensers of aversive stimuli. *J. Personality & Social Psychology*, 1965, *2*, 844–51.
> **Subjects:** $N = 60$; 7–9 yrs. **Measures:** Ss dropped marbles into either of 2 holes. Following a baseline period (to identify the more preferred hole), Ss received social disapproval from either their mother or their father contingent upon the occurrence of the more preferred response. The response measure was the increase in frequency of the less preferred response. **Results:** No sex differences.

Paulson, M. J., Lin, Tien-Teh, and Hanssen, C. Family harmony: an etiological factor in alienation. *Child Development*, 1972, *43*, 591–603.
> **Subjects:** $N = 210$; 18–21 yrs (college). **Measures:** Ss completed a family history data sheet and the Maternal form of the Parental Attitude Research Instrument (Ss were asked to respond as if they were the parent). **Results:** Among establishment Ss with dominant mothers, men had lower factor scores than women. Women more often than men recalled attitudes of their parents associated with greater degree of maternal warmth and love, environment of intimacy, affectional parental closeness, and lessened parental irritability.

Pawlicki, R. E. The influence of contingent and noncontingent social reinforcement upon children in a simple operant task. *Child Development*, 1972, *43*, 1432–38 and personal communication.
> **Subjects:** $N = 170$; 8 yrs. **Measures:** Ss played a marble-drop game. After base rate was established, Ss heard a noncontingent or contingent, supportive or neutral comment. There was a no-treatment condition. **Results:** There were no main sex differences. Contingency of comment and supportiveness of comment influenced performance of boys but not of girls.

Pecan, E. V., and Schvaneveldt, R. W. Probability learning as a function of age, sex, and type of constraint. *Developmental Psychology*, 1970, *2*, 384–88.
> **Subjects:** $N = 40$; 12–15, 35–45 yrs. **Measures:** Ss in 1 of 2 conditions guessed which of 2 colors of poker chips would be drawn next for 200 draws. In the noncontingent condition, chips were in 1 container in 80 : 20 ratio. The contingent condition involved a red container with red and blue chips (ratio of 80 : 20), and a blue container with blue and red (ratio of 80 : 20). After starting with a red chip from the red container, subsequent draws were made from the container of the color matching the previously drawn chip. **Results:** (1) Males reached a higher level of probability learning (predicting the more likely event) than females ($p < .01$). This difference was greatest in later trials ($p < .001$). (2) Females repeated the prediction of an infrequent event (perseverance) as often as they switched to predicting a more frequent event, whereas males were more likely to predict the more frequent event (results held for both conditions). Males tended to repeat the more frequent response (especially when correct) with higher probability than females.

Pedersen, D. M., Shinedling, M. M., and Johnson, D. L. Effects of sex of examiner and subject on children's quantitative test performance. *J. Personality & Social Psychology*, 1968, *10*, 251–54.
> **Subjects:** $N = 24$; 8 yrs (24 undergraduates served as Es). **Measures:** The arithmetic subtest of the WISC was administered 3 times by a male proctor and 3 times by a female proctor. **Results:** (1) No sex differences were found in Ss' scores on the arithmetic subtests. (2) Female Ss tested by female Es did better than male Ss tested by female Es ($p < .05$) and female Ss tested by male Es ($p < .05$). No differences were found between male Ss tested by female Es and male Ss tested by male Es. (3) Owing primarily to the outstanding performance of female Ss when tested by female Es, female Es elicited better performance than male Es ($p < .025$).

Pedersen, F. A., and Bell, R. Q. Sex differences in preschool children without histories of complications of pregnancy and delivery. *Developmental Psychology*, 1970, *3*, 10–15.

Subjects: $N = 55$; 2–3 yrs. **Measures:** Same-sex groups of 5 or 6 were observed in nursery school. (1) During the indoor free-play period, measures were taken of the following behaviors: aggression toward peers, positive social interaction with peers, play with clay and dough, looking and listening, watching peers, manipulation of physical objects. (2) During rest period, Ss were encouraged to lie down on their blankets. Both teachers rested to provide the children with appropriate models. A record was kept of the length of time each child was observed in the following 3 positions: up and about (active nonconformity), sitting down (passive nonconformity), lying down (copies teacher's posture). (3) Rest period was terminated each day by a series of imitation games. The behaviors that Ss imitated were modeled by the teachers. The number of times each child imitated correctly was recorded. (4) Following the imitation games, Ss were tested in the Bell Pull situation. Pairs of Ss were lifted over a gate and sent to pull bells off a nearby rack. The cries of their peers encouraged them to hurry. Occasionally 1 of the 6 bells was attached in such a way that it could not be removed. The persistence (struggling time plus number of tugs) and vigor (strength measured in pounds) exhibited by Ss in attempting to detach the bell were recorded.

In a second experimental situation, desirable toys were surrounded by a fence of light boards and boxes. The rate at which Ss tore down the barrier to get at the toys was recorded. (5) During story and refreshment time, measures were taken of gulping, number of seating changes, amount of solids eaten, and amount of juice consumed. In addition, activity recorders attached to the left foot measured nonfunctional motor responses. (6) During the outdoor free-play period, measures were taken of the following behaviors: smiling, squealing, watching, running, tricycle riding, walking, glider or swing play. Activity recorders attached to the back measured gross motor movements. The amount of time Ss spent in separate activities was also recorded. **Results:** (1) Boys exhibited more walking and more manipulation of physical objects than girls did. Boys were also more aggressive, more active, and more passively nonconforming. (2) Girls exhibited more glider and swing play and more play with clay and dough than boys did. Girls were also more imitative of adult models (copies posture, follows game), ate more solids, and spent more time in single activities before changing.

Pedersen, F. A., and Robson, K. S. Father participation in infancy. *American J. Orthopsychiatry*, 1969, *39*, 466–72.

Subjects: $N = 45$; tested at 8, 9½ mos (firstborn) and their mothers and fathers. **Measures:** The extent and quality of father's involvement with the child was ascertained from interviews with mother. Then 6 measures of paternal behavior were derived: (1) variety and frequency of caretaking activities; (2) investment (emotional involvement with the infant); (3) time spent in play; (4) irritability level (irritability threshold, reactivity to the infant's prolonged fussing or crying); (5) apprehension over infant's well-being; (6) stimulation level of play. When father entered the home after a period of absence, observations were made of the infant's greeting behavior; age of onset and intensity were recorded. **Results:** (1) Fathers were more apprehensive over the well-being of girl infants than boy infants ($p < .01$). No other differences were found between fathers of boys and girls. (2) No sex differences were found in Ss' greeting behavior.

Pederson, D. R. Children's reactions to failure as a function of interresponse interval. *J. Experimental Child Psychology*, 1971, *12*, 51–58.

Subjects: $N = 32$; 7–8 yrs. **Measures:** The time interval between success and failure on a ball-tower task and the signal to pull the lever varied (0.5, 1.0, and 5.0 seconds). Starting and movement speeds were recorded. **Results:** (1) Boys' starting speeds were slower than girls' ($p < .05$). Boys' speeds increased in rough linear fashion as a function of interresponse interval; girls' speeds increased from 0.5 to 1.0 second interresponse, then slightly decreased with the 5.0 second interval ($p < .05$).

Penk, W. Developmental changes in idiodynamic set responses of children's word associations. *Developmental Psychology*, 1971, *5*, 55–63.

Subjects: $N = 100$; 7–11 yrs. **Measures:** Ss were asked to give word associations to 24 words. Ss' responses were classified as either object-referent associates (e.g. scissors-cut; lamp-light), concept-referent associates (e.g. tug-pull; blossom-flower), or dimension-referent associates (e.g. long-short, high-low). Mediational faults (more than 1 response word, no response, delayed response, association identical to stimulus word), reaction times, commonality scores, and Thorndike-Lorge frequency values were also recorded. **Results:** (1) Overall, girls gave more concept-referent and dimension-referent associations than boys. (2) Boys had a higher number of mediational faults than girls. (3) Girls had higher commonality means than boys.

Penney, R. K. Reactive curiosity and manifest anxiety in children. *Child Development,* 1965, *36,* 697–702.
   Subjects: *N* = 108; 9–11 yrs. **Measures:** Children's Manifest Anxiety Scale, Peabody Picture Vocabulary Test. **Results:** Girls received higher manifest anxiety scores than boys ($p < .005$). No sex differences on PPVT.

Peskay, J., and Masters, J. C. Effects of socioeconomic status and the value of a reinforcer upon self-reinforcement by children. *Child Development,* 1961, *42,* 2120–23.
   Subjects: *N* = 80; 6 yrs (low, high SES). **Measures:** Ss played a maze game in which they could self-dispense rewards of high- and low-incentive value in a noncontingent situation. **Results:** No sex differences.

Peters, L. Verbal mediators and cue discrimination in the transition from nonconservation to conservation of number. *Child Development,* 1970, *41,* 707–21.
   Subjects: *N* = 131; 5–6 yrs (low SES). **Measures:** Ss were initially tested on conservation of number, conservation of difference, and conservation of area tasks. Also administered were a language comprehension test designed to evaluate Ss' understanding of several specific aspects of language (e.g. the differences between more and less, same and different, before and after, etc.), and an object sorting task. After receiving training in conservation (control Ss received no training), Ss were retested on the conservation measures. **Results:** No sex differences.

Petersen, A. C. The relationship of androgenicity in males and females to spatial ability and fluent production. Unpublished doctoral dissertation, University of Chicago, 1973.
   Experiment I: Subjects: *N* = 75; 13, 16, 17–18 yrs. **Measures:** 2 cognitive batteries were administered, the Wechsler Bellevue (WB) at ages 13 and 16, and the Primary Mental Abilities (PMA) at ages 17 and 18. The Block Design (WB) and Spatial (PMA) subtests were used as measures of spatial ability; the Digit Symbol (WB) and Word Fluency (PMA) subtests were used as measures of fluency. The physical parameters were: (1) growth during adolescence (age at peak height velocity), (2) measures of androgenicity in body shape (muscle/fat, overall body rating), and (3) ratings of secondary sex characteristics (genital size in males, breast size in females, pubic hair for both sexes). The ratings were assessed from nude photographs of Ss. **Results:** There were no main sex differences. Among 18-year-old, highly androgenized Ss, boys were fluency-dominant and girls were spatially-dominant. Among boys, early maturers tended to be space-dominant at age 18; among girls, the relationship was unclear.

Phares, E. J., Ritchie, D. E., and Davis, W. L. Internal-external control and reaction to threat. *J. Personality & Social Psychology,* 1968, *10,* 402–5.
   Subjects: *N* = 40; 18–21 yrs (college). **Measures:** After completing a series of personality tests, Ss received individualized reports containing both positive and negative information about their personalities. Ss checked those interpretations that made them slightly uncomfortable and rated each interpretation on several scales. Ss also rated how committed they were to deal with the problems suggested in the interpretations and how useful they felt the overall experiment was in shedding light on the process of psychotherapy. At the end of the experiment, Ss recalled as many interpretations as they could. **Results:** No sex differences.

Phillips, R. Syntax and vocabulary of mothers' speech to young children: age and sex comparisons. *Child Development,* 1973, *44,* 182–85.
   Subjects: *N* = 57; 8, 18, 28 mos and mothers. **Measures:** While mother and child engaged in free play, mother's speech was recorded. E then involved mother in casual conversation for 15 minutes. Mother's speech was scored for syntactic complexity, number of verbs, modifiers per utterance, proportion of function words, proportion of content words, number of verb forms, proportion of Old English verbs, proportion of weak verbs, type-token ratio, and concreteness of nouns. **Results:** No sex differences.

Piliavin, I. M., Rodin, J., and Piliavin, J. A. Good samaritanism. *J. Personality & Social Psychology,* 1969, *13,* 289–99.
   Subjects: *N* = 4,450; adults. **Measures:** Either a white or a black male confederate staged a collapse after boarding a New York City subway train. On each trial, an observer noted the race, sex, and location of (a) every rider seated or standing in the immediate area and (b) every person who came to the victim's assistance. **Results:** Men were more likely than women to be the first person to come to the assistance of the victim.

Pilisuk, M., Skolnick, P., and Overstreet, E. Predicting cooperation from the two sexes in a conflict situation. *J. Personality & Social Psychology*, 1968, *10*, 35–43.
  Subjects: N = 176; 18–21 yrs (college). **Measures:** Ss played a modified version of the prisoner's Dilemma game in same-sex pairs or against simulated same-sex or opposite-sex others. **Results:** (1) No sex differences were found in percentage of cooperative responses. (2) Women who played against simulated opposite-sex partners were less cooperative than women who played against simulated same-sex partners ($p < .001$). No such difference was found for men.

Pishkin, V. Concept identification of mnemonic cues as a function of children's sex and age. *J. Educational Psychology*, 1972, *63*, 93–98.
  Subjects: N = 144; 6–9 yrs. **Measures:** Ss indicated which category (yes or no) stimuli should be placed in; 3 types of feedback were provided: right cues, wrong cues, or right-wrong cues. The measure of performance was the number of errors committed by each S. **Results:** (1) Among 8-year-old Ss, girls made fewer errors than boys. (2) 8-year-old girls made fewer errors than 6-year-old girls; 8-year-old boys made more errors than 6-year-old boys ($p < .001$). (3) When provided with either right cues or right-wrong cues, girls made fewer errors than boys; when wrong cues were provided, no sex difference was found ($p < .01$).

Pishkin, V., and Shurley, J. T. Auditory dimensions and irrelevant information in concept identification of males and females. *Perceptual & Motor Skills*, 1965, *20*, 673–83.
  Subjects: N = 120; 25–50 yrs. **Measures:** On each trial of a concept-identification task, Ss classified auditory stimuli into 2 categories. The dimension that was relevant was either the tone's duration (1 or 3 seconds), its frequency (1,000 or 3,000 cps), or its laterality (presented to either the right or the left ear). The number of irrelevant dimensions was varied (0, 1, 2, or 3). **Results:** When laterality was the relevant dimension, men made more errors and required more trials to reach the criterion of 16 correct, consecutive responses than women did. When duration or frequency was the relevant dimension, there were no sex differences in performance.

Pishkin, V., Wolfgang, A., and Rasmussen, E. Age, sex, amount, and type of memory information in concept learning. *J. Experimental Psychology*, 1967, *73*, 121–24.
  Subjects: N = 270; 10–18 yrs. **Measures:** Ss were administered a concept-learning task (the Wisconsin Card Sorting Task). On each trial, the results of either the previous 0, 1, or 2 trials were made available for Ss' inspection. Ss in 1 group were informed only when they had made a correct choice, whereas Ss in a second group were informed only when they had made an incorrect choice. Ss in a third group were told on every trial whether they had made the correct or the incorrect decision. Performance measure was number of errors made. **Results:** (1) Girls made fewer errors than boys when either 0 or 2 previous trials were available to them for inspection ($p < .05$). No sex differences were found in the N = 1 condition. (2) When informed of only their incorrect choices, girls made fewer errors than boys ($p < .05$). No sex differences were found in the other 2 conditions.

Platt, J. J., Eisenman, R., and DeGross, E. Birth order and sex differences in future time perspective. *Developmental Psychology*, 1969, *1*, 70.
  Subjects: N = 132; 18–21 yrs (college). **Measures:** Ss were given 2 instruments to measure the future time perspective (FTP) dimension of extension (described as the length of the future time span that an individual is able to conceptualize) and 2 to measure the FTP dimension of density (described as a measure of the number of events populating an individual's personal future). Ss also completed the Time Metaphors Test, a measure of directionality. Directionality was defined as a sense of moving forward from the present into the future. **Results:** (1) No main sex differences were found on the extension instruments. (2) On 1 of the 2 density instruments, women exhibited greater FTP than men. (3) No main sex differences were found in directionality. Later-born women saw the passage of time in a more active way than other Ss, particularly later-born men ($p < .001$).

Podell, J. E. Ontogeny of the locus and orientation of the perceiver. *Child Development*, 1966, *37*, 993–97.
  Subjects: N = 112; 3, 4, 5, 6, 7, 9, 11 yrs. **Measures:** Laterally asymmetrical figures were traced on S's forehead and occiput. S was asked to indicate what had been drawn by pointing to 1 of 2 given figures. **Results:** No sex differences.

Porges, S. W., Arnold, W. R., Forbes, E. J. Heart rate variability: an index of attentional responsivity in human newborns. *Developmental Psychology*, 1973, *8*, 85–92.

Subjects: $N = 24$; 1–3 days. **Measures:** Ss' heart-rate patterns were recorded in response to a moderately intense (75 decibels) auditory stimulus. **Results:** No sex differences.

Porteus, B. D., and Johnson, R. C. Children's responses to two measures of conscience development and their relation to sociometric nomination. *Child Development,* 1965, *36,* 703–11.
> **Subjects:** $N = 235$; 14 yrs. **Measures:** Ss listened to stories in which a male or a female yielded to temptation. Affective or cognitive measures of moral judgment were required. Ss responded to a sociometric test concerning the characters. Responses were scored as mature or immature. **Results:** (1) Girls responded with more guilt (affective measure) to stories of moral deviations than boys ($p < .01$). (2) Girls scored higher than boys on the cognitive measure ($p < .05$).

Portuges, S. M., and Feshbach, N. D. The influence of sex and socioethnic factors upon imitation of teachers by elementary school children. *Child Development,* 1972, *43,* 981–89.
> **Subjects:** $N = 96$; 8–10 yrs (white, black). **Measures:** Ss viewed 2 films of a white teacher giving a lesson on African geography using either positive or negative verbal teaching techniques and incidental gestures. Ss were then asked to teach a similar lesson to boy and girl life-size dolls (ambiguous as to race). Measures were made of Ss' preference for the teachers and of their dependence-independency status (teacher rating). **Results:** Girls imitated the teacher model more than boys did ($p < .01$). No sex differences were found in teacher preference.

Potter, M. C., and Levy, E. Spatial enumeration without counting. *Child Development,* 1968, *39,* 265–72.
> **Subjects:** $N = 58$; 2–4 yrs. **Measures:** Ss were presented with a booklet consisting of 23 pages. On each page were pasted colored stickers of animals, flowers, geometric shapes, etc. Ss were asked to touch each sticker just once and then to turn to the next page. Repeats and omissions were scored as errors. **Results:** No sex differences were found in the average number of errors in the younger group ($N = 29$, median age 41 months). A significant difference was found in the older group ($N = 29$, median age 47 months) in favor of the girls ($p < .02$).

Pratoomraj, S., and Johnson, R. C. Kinds of questions and types of conservation tasks as related to children's conservation responses. *Child Development,* 1966, *37,* 343–53.
> **Subjects:** $N = 128$; 4–7 yrs. **Measures:** Ss were tested on 5 conservation-of-substance problems. **Results:** No sex differences.

Presbie, R. J., and Coiteux, P. F. Learning to be generous or stingy: imitation of sharing behavior as a function of model generosity and vicarious reinforcement. *Child Development,* 1971, *42,* 1033–38.
> **Subjects:** $N = 64$; 6 yrs. **Measures:** Ss observed either a stingy or a generous male model share marbles with a child who was not present (full-faced photographs of either a boy or a girl served to designate the sharee). After the model distributed the last marbles, Ss either did or did not hear E praise the model or the model praise himself. Ss were then given the opportunity to share marbles with the absent child. **Results:** No sex differences were found in the number of marbles given to the sharee.

Prescott, D. Efficacy-related imagery, education, and politics. Unpublished honors thesis, Harvard University, 1971.
> **Subjects:** $N = 70$; 18 yrs (college). **Measures:** Men were asked to write stories, given the following verbal lead: "After first-term finals, John finds himself at the top of his medical school class." For women, "Anne" was substituted for "John." Ss' stories were scored for fear-of-success imagery. **Results:** More women than men wrote stories high in fear-of-success imagery ($p < .001$).

Prescott, G. A. Sex differences in Metropolitan Readiness test results. *J. Educational Research,* 1955, *48,* 605–10.
> **Subjects:** $N = 14,959$; 6 yrs. **Measures:** Metropolitan Readiness test. **Results:** When a subsample of 800 Ss was randomly drawn from the population and matched according to chronological age, girls had higher scores than boys ($p < .05$).

Preston, R. C. Reading achievement of German and American children. *School and Society,* 1962, *90,* 350–54.
> **Subjects:** $N = 2,391$; 9, 11 yrs (Germany, U.S.). **Measures:** 2 reading comprehension tests

were administered, the Frankfurter Test (translated into English for American Ss) and the comprehension subtest of the Gates Reading Survey (translated into German for the German Ss). Reading speed was measured by interrupting the Gates subtest 10 minutes into the test and having Ss mark the paragraph they were then reading. **Results:** (1) Among American Ss, girls were superior to boys on all 3 measures. (2) Among 9-year-old German Ss, girls read faster than boys. No sex differences were found on the comprehension tests. Among 11-year-old German Ss, boys scored higher than girls on all 3 measures. (3) Based on the 3 test scores, a higher proportion of American boys than girls were classified as "retarded" or "severely retarded" in reading ability (9 of 12 comparisons significant at the .05 level). In 10 of 12 comparisons (4 of which were significant at the .05 level), a higher proportion of German girls than boys scored in the "retarded" and "severely retarded" range.

Pruit, D. G. Reward structures and cooperation: the decomposed Prisoner's Dilemma game. *J. Personality & Social Psychology*, 1967, 7, 21–27.
   Subjects: $N = 100$; 18–21 yrs (college). **Measures:** Same-sex pairs of Ss played either the standard Prisoner's Dilemma game (Game 1), 1 of 3 versions (Game 2, 3, or 4) of the decomposed PD game (in a single play of the DPD, each party receives 2 payoffs—one as a result of his own behavior and one as a result of the other's), or an expanded version (Game 5) of the DPD (created by adding intermediate alternatives to Game 4). **Results:** (1) No sex differences were found in Games 1–4. (2) Since Game 5 is a variant of Game 4, the results of these games were compared. In Game 4, men started at a higher level of cooperation than women, whereas in Game 5, women started at a higher level of cooperation than men ($p < .05$). (3) Women in Game 4 and men in Game 5 showed a greater increase in level of cooperation than men in Game 4 and women in Game 5 ($p < .001$).

Pulaski, M. Play as a function of toy structure and fantasy predisposition. *Child Development*, 1970, 41, 531–37.
   Subjects: $N = 64$; 5–7 yrs. **Measures:** Ss were observed during 4 15-minute play sessions. E presented each set of playthings twice. Ss were asked to make up a story or put on a play. Fantasies were scored according to richness, variability, and flexibility. There was a 5-point scale rating behavior correlates. **Results:** (1) Boys scored higher than girls on enjoyment ($p < .05$) and movement ($p < .05$) in toy play sessions. (2) Among low-fantasy Ss, boys showed greater movement in toy play sessions than girls ($p < .05$). (3) Boys played with more movement than girls in all conditions ($p < .05$). (4) More girls than boys played with opposite-sex toys in the highly structured play session ($p < .05$).

Pytkowicz, A. R., Wagner, N. N., and Sarason, I. G. An experimental study of the reduction of hostility through fantasy. *J. Personality & Social Psychology*, 1967, 5, 295–303.
   Subjects: $N = 120$; 18–21 yrs (college). **Measures:** Ss initially rated the frequency with which they experienced each of 120 daydreams. After either being insulted or not being insulted, Ss then completed the Sarason Hostility Scale (a difference score was derived by subtracting scores Ss achieved at the beginning of the quarter from scores Ss achieved following the experimental conditions) and an attitude questionnaire (Ss' responses scored for aggressive content). **Results:** (1) Men expressed more hostility on the attitude questionnaire than women ($p < .01$). Whereas insulted men expressed more hostility than noninsulted men, no similar difference was found among women ($p < .05$). (2) No main sex differences were found in change scores on the Hostility Scale.

Quay, L. C. Language dialect, reinforcement, and the intelligence-test performance of Negro children. *Child Development*, 1971, 42, 5–15.
   Subjects: $N = 100$; 3–5 yrs (black Head Start program). **Measures:** Stanford-Binet Test of Intelligence Form L-M was administered under the following conditions: (a) Standard English, intangible reinforcement (praise); (b) Standard English, tangible reinforcement (candy); (c) Negro dialect, praise; (d) Negro dialect, candy. **Results:** No sex differences.

Quay, L. C. Negro dialect and Binet performance in severely disadvantaged black four-year-olds. *Child Development*, 1972, 43, 245–50.
   Subjects: $N = 50$; 4 yrs (black, low SES). **Measures:** Stanford-Binet Form L-M was administered to 1 group in Standard English and to another group in Negro dialect. **Results:** No sex differences.

Rabbie, J. M., and Howitz, M. Arousal of ingroup-outgroup bias by a chance win or loss. *J. Personality & Social Psychology*, 1969, 13, 269–77.
   Subjects: $N = 112$; 15 yrs (Holland). **Measures:** Groups of 8 same-sex Ss were randomly

subdivided into 2 groups of 4. As a result of either a toss of a coin, E's decision, or decision of 1 of the group, members of 1 group were rewarded while members of the other group were not. Ss then evaluated own and other groups by rating the personal attributes of both groups' members as well as the attributes of each group as a whole. **Results:** No sex differences.

Rabinowitz, F. M., and DeMyer, S. Stimulus and response alternation in young children. *Developmental Psychology*, 1971, *4*, 43–54.

Subjects: $N = 96$; 4, 5 yrs. **Measures:** Each S chose between 2 toy cars (black or white, light gray or dark gray) by pressing the window of the car he wanted or pushing the button under it. S was allowed to play with the chosen toy between trials. Choice and response latency were recorded for each trial. **Results:** (1) There were no sex differences in stimulus-alternation (alternation of choices by brightness). (2) There were no main sex differences in response-alternation of position. On trial blocks 1–3, 4-year-old girls repeated responses more than 4-year-old boys did, whereas 5-year-old girls alternated responses more than 5-year-old boys did ($p < .05$).

Radin, N. A comparison of maternal behavior with four-year-old boys and girls in lower-class families. Unpublished manuscript, 1973.

Subjects: $N = 52$; 4 yrs (white and black, low SES). **Measures:** (1) Ss took the Peabody Picture Vocabulary Test (PPVT) and the Stanford-Binet Intelligence Scale. While completing the Stanford-Binet, 30 of the Ss were rated on achievement motivation by the psychologists administering the test. (2) Ss were present while interviews were conducted with their mothers. Mothers' behaviors toward their children were recorded and classified as either nurturant or restrictive. (3) Using the Pupil Behavior Inventory, teachers rated Ss on academic motivation. **Results:** (1) No sex differences were found in IQ, PPVT, achievement motivation, or academic motivation scores. (2) Mothers were more restrictive with their sons than with their daughters. No sex differences were found in nurturance or in total number of mother-child interactions.

Raina, M. K. A study of sex differences in creativity in India. *J. Creative Behavior*, 1969, *3*, 111–14.

Subjects: $N = 180$; 13–15 yrs. **Measures:** Verbal and Figural forms of the Torrance Tests of Creative Thinking. **Results:** (1) Boys were more fluent, elaborated more, and had a higher total verbal score than girls. (2) Boys scored higher than girls on all measures of the Figural form.

Ramirez, M., III, Taylor, C., Jr., and Peterson, B. Mexican-American cultural membership and adjustment to school. *Developmental Psychology*, 1971, *4*, 141–48.

Subjects: $N = 600$; 12–17 yrs (Mexican-American, Anglo-American). **Measures:** All Ss completed a 62-item scale assessing attitudes toward teachers and education. 120 Ss completed the School Situations Picture Stories test, and a projective test designed to assess needs for power, achievement, affiliation, and rejection. **Results:** Boys scored higher than girls in need for achievement ($p < .01$). Among Anglo-American Ss, boys had higher need for affiliation than girls; Among Mexican-American Ss, the reverse was true, but to a much lesser degree ($p < .01$).

Rapoport, A., and Chammah, A. M. Sex differences in factors contributing to the level of cooperation in the Prisoner's Dilemma game. *J. Personality & Social Psychology*, 1965, *2*, 831–38.

Subjects: $N = 420$; 18–31 yrs (college). **Measures:** Ss played the Prisoner's Dilemma game in either same-sex or opposite-sex pairs. **Results:** (1) Male pairs were more cooperative than female pairs. No sex differences were found in the frequency of cooperative choices in opposite-sex pairs. (2) No sex differences were found in the percentage of Ss who made the cooperative choice on the first and second trials. More male pairs were exclusively cooperative on the last 25 trials than female pairs. More female pairs were exclusively competitive on the last 25 trials than male pairs.

Ratcliff, R. G., and Tindall, R. C. Interaction of reward, punishment, and sex in a two-choice discrimination task with children. *Developmental Psychology*, 1970, *3*, 150 (brief report).

Subjects: $N = 72$; 9 yrs. **Measures:** Ss performed a 2-choice discrimination task (60 training and 30 extinction trials) with 1 of 3 reinforcement types: (1) token for each correct response, (2) loud tone for each incorrect response, (3) tone or token for each correct or incorrect response, respectively. The number of correct responses in each block of 5 trials was recorded.

Results: When loud tones were administered for incorrect responses, boys learned faster than girls.

Rau, M., Stover, L., and Guerney, B. G., Jr. Relationship of socioeconomic status, sex, and age to aggression of emotionally disturbed children in mothers' presence. *J. Genetic Psychology,* 1970, *116*, 95–100.

> **Subjects:** $N = 79$; 4–10 yrs (emotionally disturbed) and their mothers. **Measures:** Each mother-child pair was observed during a half-hour play session. Frequency and intensity of aggression with toys and toward mother were recorded. **Results:** Boys were more aggressive than girls ($p < .01$).

Rebelsky, F., and Hanks, C. Fathers' verbal interaction with infants in the first three months of life. *Child Development,* 1971, *42*, 63–68.

> **Subjects:** $N = 10$ (7 boys, 3 girls); 2 wks and fathers. **Measures:** At age 2 weeks, 24-hour tape recordings were made approximately every 2 weeks for a 3-month period by attaching a microphone to the infant. Two coders recorded duration, time of day, and activity occurring each time the father vocalized to his child. **Results:** (1) Fathers spent less time vocalizing to their infants during last half than in first half of study. (2) Fathers of female infants verbalized more than fathers of male infants at both 2 weeks and 4 weeks of age. Fathers of male infants vocalized somewhat more than fathers of female infants at 12 weeks of age (statistics not reported). (3) Fathers of female infants verbalized more during caretaking activities than fathers of male infants did. (4) Number of vocalizations during noncaretaking activities remained the same for fathers of male infants, but decreased somewhat for fathers of female infants.

Reese, A. H., and Palmer, F. H. Factors related to change in mental test performance, *Developmental Psychology Monograph,* 1970, *3*.

> **Subjects:** $N = 622$; tested at 6, 12, 17 yrs. **Measures:** Subsamples of Ss were (longitudinally or cross-sectionally) tested on the Stanford-Binet (S-B) and/or the Wechsler-Bellevue (W-B). **Results:** (1) At ages 6 and 12, no sex differences were found on the S-B. At age 17, boys received higher scores than girls. No sex differences were found in the amount of change in scores between the ages of 6 and 12, or 12 and 17. (2) No sex differences were found in W-B Full Scale or Performance IQs. Boys had higher verbal IQs than girls.

Reese, H. W. Attitudes toward the opposite sex in late childhood. *Merrill-Palmer Quarterly,* 1966, *12*, 157–63.

> EXPERIMENT I: **Subjects:** $N = 318$; 10–13 yrs. **Measures:** Ss were asked to rate their liking for each of their classmates on a 5-point scale. **Results:** Among 10-year-old Ss, girls had more favorable attitudes toward the opposite sex than boys did ($p < .001$). Among 11-, 12-, and 13-year-old Ss, boys had more favorable attitudes toward the opposite sex than girls ($p < .05$).
> EXPERIMENT II: **Subjects:** $N = 255$; 10 yrs (75 Ss from Experiment I). **Measures:** Same as Experiment I. **Results:** Overall, no sex differences were found. In the Experiment I sample (as reported above), girls had more favorable attitudes toward the opposite sex than boys did. In the new sample, boys had more favorable attitudes toward the opposite sex than girls did ($p < .001$).
> EXPERIMENT III: **Subjects:** $N = 102$; 10 yrs. **Measures:** Same as Experiment I. Ss rated their classmates 3 times during the year. **Results:** Overall, no sex differences were found. In September, girls were more favorable toward the opposite sex than boys were; in February and June, the reverse was true ($p < .005$).

Reese, H. W. Imagery in children's paired-associate learning. *J. Experimental Child Psychology,* 1970, *9*, 174–78.

> **Subjects:** $N = 71$; 3–5 yrs. **Measures:** Ss in 4 groups performed a paired-associates task, with groups differing by how responses to the stimulus cards were presented: (1) The object on the response card was verbalized, (2) the stimulus and response card objects were verbalized, (3) Ss saw a picture of the stimulus and response objects interacting, with stimulus and response objects verbalized, and (4) Ss heard a sentence describing the interaction between the stimulus and response items, but only saw the response item (though both were verbalized). The process was repeated 2 weeks later. **Results:** No sex differences.

Reese, H. W. Imagery and multiple-list paired-associate learning in young children. *J. Experimental Child Psychology,* 1972, *13*, 310–23.

> **Subjects:** $N = 48$; 2–6 yrs. **Measures:** Ss learned 4 paired-associate lists in a study-test procedure. Recognition was required on test trials, and reinforcement (flashing red bulbs) was given for correct responses. Retention test with no feedback was given after list learning. **Results:** No sex differences.

Regan, J. W. Guilt, perceived injustice, and altruistic behavior. *J. Personality & Social Psychology*, 1971, *18*, 124–32.

Subjects: $N = 81$; 18–21 yrs (college). **Measures:** Ss either were made to feel responsible for ruining an experiment or were only involved as witnesses. No misfortune occurred to Ss in a control group. Half of the Ss were then given an opportunity to reflect on the misfortune and to express their feelings. Afterward, Ss were asked to donate money to a cause only remotely associated with the misfortune. **Results:** No sex differences were found in Ss' donating behavior.

Reppucci, N. D. Parental education, sex differences, and performance on cognitive tasks among two-year-old children. *Developmental Psychology*, 1971, *4*, 248–53.

Subjects: $N = 48$; 2 yrs. **Measures:** E administered an embedded figures task, a 2-choice discrimination-learning task, a vocabulary recognition task, and a vocabulary-naming task. **Results:** No sex differences.

Rettig, S. Group discussion and predicted ethical risk taking. *J. Personality & Social Psychology*, 1966, *3*, 629–33.

Subjects: $N = 160$; 18–21 yrs (college). **Measures:** Ss were presented with a set of descriptions of fictitious situations, each portraying a person (either S himself or a hypothetical other) in a dilemma about whether or not to steal money from a bank. For each situation, Ss predicted whether or not the money would be taken. Half of the Ss made their judgments following group discussion. **Results:** No sex differences.

Rheingold, H. L., and Eckerman, C. O. The infant's free entry into a new environment. *J. Experimental Child Psychology*, 1969, *8*, 271–83.

Subjects: $N = 24$; 9–10 mos and mothers (2 experiments). **Measures:** Ss and their mothers were taken to the smaller of 2 adjacent rooms. Ss were allowed free entry into the larger room, which was marked off into 3-foot squares and contained either 0, 1, or 3 toys. Measures were taken of (1) how quickly Ss entered the larger room, number and duration of entries, number and location of squares entered; (2) onset and duration of contact with mother, manipulation of toys, and manipulation of other objects; (3) number of 10-second periods during which Ss vocalized or fussed. **Results:** No sex differences.

Rheingold, H. L., and Eckerman, C. O. The infant separates himself from his mother. *Science*, 1970, *168*, 78–83.

Subjects: $N = 48$; 1, 1½, 2, 2½, 3, 3½, 4, 4½, 5 yrs and mothers. **Measures:** The distance the child roamed from his mother was observed. **Results:** No sex differences.

Rheingold, H. L., and Samuels, H. R. Maintaining the positive behavior of infants by increased stimulation. *Developmental Psychology*, 1969, 1,520–27.

Subjects: $N = 20$; 10 mos and mothers. **Measures:** Ss were observed in an experimental room for 2 10-minute sessions with their mothers present. During the first observational period, no furniture or toys were present. Measures were taken of the following: latency of fussing, frequency of fussing, frequency of vocalizing, number of lines crossed (the room was marked off with masking tape into squares), latency of touching mother, duration of contact with mother, and duration of object manipulation (drapes, doorstop, Ss' own clothing, etc.). During the second session, 5 toys were made available to half the Ss. For the other 10 children, the room remained unchanged. For each of the measures cited above, Ss' score for the second session was the change in their performance from the first observational period. For experimental Ss, 2 additional measures were recorded: latency and duration of contact with the toys. **Results:** No sex differences.

Rheingold, H. L., Gewirtz, J. L., and Ross, H. W. Social conditioning of vocalizations in the infant. In S. W. Bijou and D. M. Baer, eds., *Child development: readings in experimental analysis*. New York: Meredith Publishing Co., 1967.

Subjects: $N = 21$; 3 mos. **Measures:** Ss were tested on 6 successive days. On days 1, 2, 5, and 6, E leaned over and positioned her head above S's head. S's vocalizations were recorded. On days 3 and 4, procedures were identical except that each vocalization was reinforced by E. E's response consisted of a broad smile, three "tsk" sounds, and a light touch applied to S's abdomen. **Results:** No sex differences were found in number of vocalizations.

Rhine, R. J., Hill, S. J., and Wandruff, S. E. Evaluative responses of preschool children. *Child Development*, 1967, *38*, 1035–42.

Subjects: $N = 50$; 2–5 yrs (nursery school). **Measures:** Ss were shown line drawings of children in activities considered bad, good, or neutral. A female E described the content of each picture as it was shown to Ss. The pictures were then arranged in subsets of 4 containing either

1 good and 3 neutral, 1 bad and 3 neutral, or all neutral pictures. For each of 12 subsets, Ss were asked to point to the picture that showed a good (or bad) activity. The Stanford-Binet picture vocabulary test was also administered to Ss. **Results:** No sex differences.

Ricciuti, H. N. Object grouping and selective ordering behavior in infants 12 to 34 months old. *Merrill-Palmer Quarterly,* 1965, *11,* 129–48.
  Subjects: $N = 48$; 1, 1½, 2 yrs. **Measures:** Ss were given 4 different object-grouping tasks, each consisting of 2 kinds of objects. No specific sorting instructions were given; Ss were simply encouraged to play with the objects. The order in which objects were touched or manipulated (selective ordering) and the degree to which similar objects were spatially constituted as groups (object grouping) were recorded. **Results:** No sex differences.

Rickard, H. C., and Joubert, C. E. Subject-model sexual status and observer performance. *Psychonomic Science,* 1968, *10,* 407–8.
  Subjects: $N = 40$; 18–21 yrs (college). **Measures:** Ss heard prerecorded tapes of words spoken by either a man or a woman. The first 50 words contained no animal names (the critical response class). Each consecutive 50-word set thereafter contained 9, 21, 33, and 47 animal names, respectively. After every fifth word, the tape recorder was stopped and Ss were asked to say the first word that occurred to them. **Results:** No sex of subject or sex of model differences were found in number of animal names emitted. On the last 10 trials, men who heard the adult female responded with more animal names than men who heard the adult male; for women, the reverse was true ($p < .05$).

Rickard, H. C., Ellis, N. E., Barnhart, S., and Holt, M. Subject-model sexual status and verbal imitative performance in kindergarten children. *Developmental Psychology,* 1970, *3,* 405 (brief report).
  Subjects: $N = 40$; 5 yrs. **Measures:** Same as Rickard and Joubert (1968); see preceding item. **Results:** No sex of subject or sex of model differences were found.

Rieber, M. Hypothesis testing in children as a function of age. *Developmental Psychology,* 1969, *1,* 389–95.
  Subjects: $N = 120$; 5, 7, 9 yrs. **Measures:** 3-dimensional, 2-choice discrimination problems were individually administered to Ss. The blank trials technique was used to determine the nature of Ss' strategy from a sequence of 5 responses. Ss were randomly assigned to 4 groups that differed in the dimensions and values reinforced. **Results:** No sex differences.

Riegel, K. F., Riegel, R. M., and Levine, R. S. An analysis of associative behavior and creativity. *J. Personality & Social Psychology,* 1966, *4,* 50–56.
  Subjects: $N = 48$; 18–21 yrs (college). **Measures:** Ss were administered 13 restricted word-association tasks; the same stimuli (35 nouns) were used for all tasks. For each stimulus, a measure was taken of the number of times Ss gave the same response in 2 different tasks. The degree to which each task overlapped with the remaining 12 was then calculated. **Results:** No sex differences were found in task overlap.

Rigg, M. G. The relative variability in intelligence of boys and girls. *J. Genetic Psychology,* 1940, *56,* 211–14.
  Subjects: $N = 10,079$; 8–13 yrs. **Measures:** National Intelligence Test. **Results:** No sex differences were found in variability.

Rileigh, K. K., and Odom, P. B. Perception of rhythm by subjects with normal and deficient hearing. *Developmental Psychology,* 1972, 7, 54–61.
  Subjects: $N = 72$; 10, 15 yrs. **Measures:** Ss saw films of 5- and 10-second black-dot rhythm patterns and reproduced each with a telegraph key; 1 hearing group received white noise through earphones during presentation and reproduction periods. Reproductions were scored for correctness of number of beats reproduced, total duration of patterns, and rhythmic relationships, regardless of errors in total duration. **Results:** (1) There were no sex differences in accuracy of reproducing the number of beats. (2) Boys were more accurate than girls in reproducing the total duration of the sequences. (3) There were no sex differences in accuracy of rhythm reproduction.

Rivenbark, W. H., III. Self-disclosure among adolescents. *Psychological Reports,* 1971, *28,* 35–42.
  Subjects: $N = 149$; 9, 11, 13, 15, 17 yrs. **Measures:** A modified version of Jourard and Lasakow's questionnaire was used to measure self-disclosure. For each of the 40 items on the ques-

tionnaire, Ss rated their self-disclosure to each of 4 target persons: mother, father, best male friend, best female friend. **Results:** (1) Girls disclosed more to their best male friends and to their best female friends than boys did. Girls disclosed more to their best female friends than to their best male friends; boys disclosed more to their best male friends than to their best female friends ($p < .001$). (2) Girls disclosed more to their mothers than boys did to their fathers. No sex differences were found in disclosure to the opposite-sex parent.

Roberge, J. J., and Paulus, D. H. Developmental patterns for children's class and conditional reasoning abilities. *Developmental Psychology*, 1971, *4*, 191–200.
> **Subjects:** $N = 263$; 9, 11, 13, 15 yrs. **Measures:** Paulus Conditional Reasoning Test, Paulus-Roberge Class Reasoning Test. **Results:** No sex differences.

Roberts, G. C., and Black, K. N. The effect of naming and object permanence on toy preferences. *Child Development*, 1972, *43*, 858–68.
> **Subjects:** $N = 40$; 1 yr and mothers. **Measures:** In the first session, Ss were presented with 16 toys, 1 at a time, half named and half unnamed. Immediately afterward Ss were given a series of timed preference choices between named and unnamed toy pairs. In the second session, the object permanence and vocal imitation subscales of the Infant Psychological Development Scale were administered. **Results:** There were no main sex differences. Boys showed more differentiation between named and unnamed toys in the visual mode; girls showed more differentiation in the tactile mode. No sex differences were found on the object permanence scale, or on mothers' reports of the children's language development.

Robson, K. S., Pederson, F. A., and Moss, H. A. Developmental observations of dyadic gazing in relation to the fear of strangers and social approach behavior. *Child Development*, 1969, *40*, 619–27.
> **Subjects:** $N = 45$; tested at 8, 9½ mos. **Measures:** Mother-infant pairs were visited in their home by 2 male observers. At the beginning and end of each visit, one observer approached the infant while the mother held him, picked him up, held him for approximately 1 minute, and then returned him to his mother's lap. Ss' responses were rated on a 13-point fear-of-strangers scale. During the unstructured portions of the visit, the amount of approach behavior the infant initiated toward both observers while unrestrained was recorded. Information regarding which month infants first exhibited a clear-cut avoidance response to an unfamiliar adult was obtained during interviews with mothers. **Results:** (1) No sex differences were found in fear-of-stranger ratings. (2) Boys exhibited more approach behavior toward observers than girls did (level of significance not given). (3) Girls displayed fear-of-stranger responses at an earlier age than boys ($p < .01$).

Roll, S. Reversibility training and stimulus desirability as factors in conservation of number. *Child Development*, 1970, *41*, 501–7.
> **Subjects:** $N = 87$; 5–7 yrs (Colombian). **Measures:** Ss performed 6 conservation-of-number tasks. **Results:** No sex differences.

Rollins, H., and Castel, K. Dimensional preference, pretraining, and attention in children's concept identification. *Child Development*, 1973, *44*, 363–66.
> **Subjects:** $N = 72$; 3–5 yrs. **Measures:** Two-thirds of the Ss were pretrained on a matching task—one-third on their preferred dimension and one-third on their nonpreferred dimension. All Ss performed a concept identification task with the preferred or nonpreferred dimension relevant (form, color). **Results:** No sex differences.

Roodin, M. L., and Gruen, G. E. The role of memory in making transitive judgments. *J. Experimental Child Psychology*, 1970, *10*, 264–75.
> **Subjects:** $N = 72$; 5–7 yrs. **Measures:** Ss made transitivity judgments about stick lengths. Half of the Ss used a memory-aid stick for initial comparisons; the other half did not. The performance measure was the number of transitive responses Ss gave. **Results:** No sex differences.

Rosekrans, M. A., and Hartup, W. W. Imitative influences of consistent and inconsistent response consequences to a model on aggressive behavior in children. *J. Personality & Social Psychology*, 1967, *7*, 429–34.
> **Subjects:** $N = 36$; 3–5 yrs. **Measures:** Ss were exposed to an adult female model who was either consistently rewarded, consistently punished, or inconsistently reinforced (by an adult female E) for performing novel aggressive responses with a number of toys. Ss were then allowed to play with the toys in the presence of E. The response measures were the frequency of each of 3 types of aggressive behavior (imitative, partially imitative, and nonimitative) and the elapsed time before the initial occurrence of each. **Results:** No sex differences.

Rosenberg, B. G., and Sutton-Smith, B. A revised conception of masculine-feminine differences in play activities. *J. Genetic Psychology*, 1960, *96*, 165–70.
    Subjects: $N = 187$; 9, 10, 11 yrs. Measures: Ss were presented with a list of 181 games and were asked to check only those games they had played. Results: (1) Boys chose the following games more frequently than girls did: bandits, bows and arrows, boxing, building forts, cars, cops and robbers, darts, football, hunting, marbles, making model airplanes, shooting, soldiers, spacemen, snowball throwing, toy trains, using tools, and wrestling. (2) Girls chose the following games more frequently than boys did: blindman's buff, building snowmen, cartwheels, Clue, cooking, crack the whip, dancing, doctors, dolls, dressing up, drop the handkerchief, farmer in the dell, follow the leader, fox and geese, hide the thimble, hopscotch, houses, huckle buckle beanstalk, in and out the window, I've got a secret, jacks, jump rope, leap frog, London bridge, Mother may I, mulberry bush, musical chairs, name that tune, pick up sticks, red rover, ring around the rosy, scrapbook making, see saw, sewing, school, Simon says thumbs up, statues, stoop tag, and store.

Rosenberg, B. G., and Sutton-Smith, B. The relationship of ordinal position and sibling sex status to cognitive abilities. *Psychonomic Science*, 1964, *1*, 81–82.
    Subjects: $N = 377$; 19 yrs (college). Measures: American College Entrance Examination. Results: (1) Women had higher language (L) scores than men ($p < .01$). (2) No sex differences were found in quantitative (Q) or total (T) scores. (3) Men had higher Q > L ratios than women ($p < .01$).

Rosenberg, B. G., and Sutton-Smith, B. Sibling association, family size, and cognitive abilities. *J. Genetic Psychology*, 1966, *109*, 271–79.
    Subjects: $N = 600$; 18–20 yrs (college). Measures: American College Entrance Examination. Results: (1) Men had higher quantitative (Q) scores than women ($p < .01$). No sex differences were found in language (L) scores. (2) Women had higher total scores than men ($p < .001$). (3) The Q > L ratio was higher for men than for women ($p < .001$).

Rosenberg, B. G., and Sutton-Smith, B. Sibling age spacing effects upon cognition. *Developmental Psychology*, 1969, *1*, 661–68.
    Subjects: $N = 1,013$; 19 yrs (college). Measures: American College Entrance Examination. Results: (1) Men had higher quantitative (Q) scores than women ($p < .01$). (2) Women had higher language (L) scores ($p < .01$) and total (T) scores ($p < .01$) than men.

Rosenfeld, H. M. Approval-seeking and approval-inducing functions of verbal and non-verbal responses in the dyad. *J. Personality & Social Psychology*, 1966, *4*, 497–605.
    Subjects: $N = 92$; 18–21 yrs (college). Measures: 1 member of each same-sex dyad was secretly instructed to either gain or avoid the approval of his partner. Dyads were then observed in free interaction. Measures were taken of several categories of verbal and nonverbal behavior. Afterward, naïve Ss were asked to rate their partners on a like-dislike scale and to list characteristics of their partners that they liked and disliked. Results: (1) The length of women's speeches was shorter than the length of men's speeches ($p < .05$). (2) The ratio of speech disturbances to total words spoken was higher for men than for women ($p < .05$). (3) Women rated their partners more positively than men did. (4) No sex differences in gestures or number of utterances.

Rosenhan, D., and Messick, S. Affect and expectation. *J. Personality & Social Psychology*, 1966, *3*, 38–44.
    Subjects: $N = 116$; 18–21 yrs (college). Measures: For each of 150 trials, Ss guessed which of 2 stimuli (a smiling or an angry face) would next appear. Ss were exposed to 1 of 2 input ratios: 70% smiling faces / 30% angry faces (SA condition) or 70% angry faces / 30% smiling faces (AS condition). Results: No sex differences were found in proportion of responses to the stimulus with the 70% input.

Rosenhan, D., and White, G. M. Observation and rehearsal as determinants of prosocial behavior. *J. Personality & Social Psychology*, 1967, *5*, 424–31.
    Subjects: $N = 130$; 9–10 yrs. Measures: Ss observed a male model donate half of his winnings (gift certificates) from a bowling game to charity. Ss then played the bowling game twice, once in the presence of the model and once in his absence. Results: No sex differences.

Rosenhan, D., Frederick, F., and Burrowes, A. Preaching and practicing: effects of channel discrepancy on norm internalization. *Child Development*, 1968, *39*, 291–301.
    Subjects: $N = 72$; 8–9 yrs. Measures: Ss played a bowling game with preset scores. A model

explained the game and played the first round of 20 trials with Ss. Ss were randomly assigned to 4 conditions of model behavior: consistent (lenient, strict) and discrepant (child-indulgent, self-indulgent). Extent to which the model verbally instructed and personally exhibited high or low standards of self-reward was varied. Ss played the game alone, and norm violations were scored. **Results:** No sex differences.

Rosenkoetter, L. T. Resistance to temptation: inhibitory and disinhibitory effects of models. *Developmental Psychology*, 1973, *8*, 80–84.
> **Subjects:** $N = 48$; 8–12 yrs. **Measures:** Ss were required to sit where they were unable to see a Woody Woodpecker film after observing either a yielding model (who succumbed to temptation and moved to see the film) or a nonyielding model (who resisted temptation to move). Control Ss observed no models. **Results:** No sex differences.

Rosenkrantz, P. S., and Crockett, W. H. Some factors influencing the assimilation of disparate information in impression formation. *J. Personality & Social Psychology*, 1965, *2*, 397–402.
> **Subjects:** $N = 176$; 18–21 yrs (college). **Measures:** Ss listened as 8 speakers each illustrated 2 traits of a male stimulus person (SP). Of the 8 speakers, 4 described positive traits and 4 described negative traits. Half of the Ss recorded their impressions of the SP after hearing 4 speakers, and again after hearing 8 speakers (using the same measuring instruments on each occasion). The remaining Ss heard all 8 speakers before recording their impressions; 2 measures were derived from Ss' responses to the objective scales: a recency score (number of responses similar in valence to the most recently received set of information) and a change score (number of items on which Ss' final impressions differed from their initial impressions). **Results:** No main sex differences were found.

Rosenthal, T. L., and White, G. M. Initial probability, rehearsal, and constraint in associative class selection. *J. Experimental Child Psychology*, 1972, *13*, 261–74.
> EXPERIMENT I: **Subjects:** $N = 112$; 8 yrs. **Measures:** Ss were presented with 15 stimulus nouns. To the right of each noun were 3 words, 1 of which was a noun, 1 a verb, and 1 a color (e.g. book: page, reads, violet). Ss' task was to pick which of the 3 available responses went best with each stimulus word (baseline phase). Ss then observed an adult model respond to the same stimulus words; afterward, new response sheets were distributed and Ss were asked to imitate the model's choices (imitative phase). Finally, Ss were again asked to express their own preferences to each of the 15 stimulus nouns (preference phase). In each of the last 2 phases, the number of times Ss imitated the model's preferences was recorded. **Results:** No sex differences.
>
> EXPERIMENT II: **Subjects:** $N = 96$; 8 yrs. **Measures:** Same as experiment I, except that after observing the model, Ss received instructions urging them neither to imitate the model nor to pick the responses they felt fit the stimulus words best. **Results:** In the baseline phase, girls chose nouns more often than boys. No other sex differences were found.

Rosenthal, T. L., Alford, G. S., and Rasp, L. M. Concept attainment generalization, and retention through observation and verbal coding. *J. Experimental Child Psychology*, 1972, *13*, 183–94.
> **Subjects:** $N = 80$; 7 yrs. **Measures:** After a baseline was established, modeled clustering of stimulus objects was observed. The model displayed either no verbalizations, low-information verbalizations, or high-information verbalizations about her clustering. The response measure was the number of fully correct clusters Ss produced. **Results:** (1) Boys scored more correct clusters than girls ($p < .04$). (2) Boys' performance surpassed girls during imitation ($p < .025$), but not during generalization.

Roskens, R. W., and Dizney, H. F. A study of unethical academic behavior in high school and college. *J. Educational Research*, 1966, *59*, 231–34.
> **Subjects:** $N = 2,871$; 18, 21 yrs (college). **Measures:** Ss completed a questionnaire on academic cheating. **Results:** (1) Among 21-year-old Ss, men reported more cribbing, less plagiarism and ghost-writing; women reported more plagiarism and ghost-writing, less cribbing. (2) Among 18-year-old Ss, more men than women cheated in high school; more women than men expressed concern about cheating.

Ross, B. M. Probability concepts in deaf and hearing children. *Child Development*, 1966, *37*, 917–27.
> **Subjects:** $N = 140$; 7, 9, 11, 13, 15 yrs (normal, deaf). **Measures:** Ss watched as E placed balls of 2 different colors in a box. Ss then shook the box and predicted the color of the ball

they would draw out. Ss continued predicting and drawing out balls until box was empty. Ss were confronted with 3 types of choice situations: (1) "sure thing" choices occurred when balls of only 1 color remained; (2) "uneven odds" choices occurred whenever there were more balls of 1 color than the other; (3) "even odds" choices occurred when both colors were equally represented. **Results:** (1) Among 13-year-old deaf Ss, boys made more correct predictions when confronted with "uneven odds" than girls did ($p < .05$). (2) No sex differences were found for "even odds" or "sure thing" choices.

Ross, B. M., and Youniss, J. Ordering of nonverbal items in children's recognition memory. *J. Experimental Child Psychology*, 1969, 8, 20–32.
  Subjects: $N = 64$; 6, 10 yrs. **Measures:** Ss' task was to recognize 3 picture items (previously pointed out to them) from an array of 9. Either (1) Ss were instructed to point to the items in the original presentation order, or (2) the ordering of responses was not mentioned. There was either a 10-second delay or no delay between presentation and recognition trials. **Results:** No sex differences.

Ross, H. S., Rheingold, H. L., and Eckerman, C. O. Approach and exploration of a novel alternative by 12-month-old infants. *J. Experimental Child Psychology*, 1972, *13*, 85–93.
  Subjects: $N = 12$; 11–12 mos and mothers. **Measures:** Two 5-minute trials took place. In Trial 1 Ss were placed with their mothers in the "start" room and allowed to enter 1 test room and play with the toy it contained. In Trial 2 the door to the second test room was opened and Ss were allowed to enter either test room. Test rooms and the toys they contained differed in degree of novelty. Response measures were latency to enter test room, time in test room, latency to contact toy, time contacting toy, toy chosen, and vocalizations. **Results:** There were no main effects of sex of Ss on either trial, and no interaction of sex and novelty.

Ross, S. A. A test of generality of the effects of deviant preschool models. *Developmental Psychology*, 1971, *4*, 262–67 (and personal communication).
  Subjects: $N = 48$; 3–5 yrs. **Measures:** Ss were taught how to operate a toy store by a same-age, same-sex model. After the model left, a same-sex peer entered the store and bought 1 toy with play money. Measures were taken of the number of storekeeper behaviors Ss exhibited that were imitative of the mannerisms displayed by the model and of the number of storekeeper behaviors exhibited that were nonimitative. As the customer left the store, the model returned to inform the Ss that they could have 1 toy. Then the model took either 1 or 3 toys for himself and left the room. The number of toys Ss took and any behavioral signs of conflict during toy selection were recorded. **Results:** Boys exhibited more nonimitative storekeeper behaviors (e.g. pointing out the advantage of various toys, asking the customer if the toy was for himself or for a friend, etc.) than girls did ($p < .01$). No sex differences were found in the number of imitative behaviors Ss displayed. (2) Boys were more concerned than girls that the customer select a sex-appropriate toy ($p < .001$). (3) No sex differences were found in the number of behavioral signs of conflict Ss exhibited during toy selection or in the number of Ss who took more than 1 toy.

Rothbart, M. K. Effects of motivation, equity, and compliance on the use of reward and punishment. *J. Personality & Social Psychology*, 1968, 9, 353–62.
  Subjects: $N = 60$; 18–21 yrs (college). **Measures:** Ss were free to administer both promises of monetary reward and threats of monetary punishment as incentives for increasing a confederate's performance. **Results:** No sex differences.

Rothbart, M. K. Birth order and mother-child interaction in an achievement situation. *J. Personality & Social Psychology*, 1971, *17*, 113–20.
  Subjects: $N = 56$; 5 yrs and mothers. **Measures:** *Task 1*: While their mothers received instructions, Ss played with a set of toys in an adjacent room. Afterward, mothers asked their children to name all the toys they had seen. *Task 2*: Mothers were given 2 cartoons. They were then asked to explain to their children what was happening in each cartoon. *Task 3*: Ss were shown a picture of 20 zoo animals. After the picture was turned over, mothers asked their children to name as many animals as they could remember. Observers rated the amount of achievement pressure mothers exerted. Before the task was administered, mothers estimated how well their children would perform. *Task 4*: Mothers were given a simple diagram of the workings of a water tap, along with an extremely complicated written description. Mothers were asked to explain to their children how the tap worked. *Task 5*: Mothers supervised their children's performance on a difficult geometric puzzle. Estimates of how quickly the puzzle would be solved were obtained from each mother. Mothers were requested to clean up the room (with the child's help) before E's return. **Results:** (1) No main differences were found between boys'

and girls' performances on Tasks 1, 3, and 5. (2) No main sex differences were found in the extent to which Ss participated in the clean-up of the room. (3) No main sex differences were found in mothers' estimates of their children's performances (Tasks 3 and 5). On the picture task (Task 5), mothers of firstborn girls gave higher estimates than mothers of second-born girls; a weaker trend in the opposite direction was found among mothers of boys ($p < .05$). (4) No sex differences were found in the complexity of mothers' explanations (Tasks 2 and 4). (5) No main sex differences were found in mothers' structuring of Task 3 or 5. Structuring was defined as the amount of information mothers gave to their children concerning what would happen to them in the task and what would be expected of them. Mothers structured Task 5 more for firstborn girls and second-born boys than for their opposite-sex counterparts ($p < .01$). (6) In Tasks 1, 2, and 4, no sex differences were found in the number of questions mothers asked or in the amount of time they spent in conversation or explanation. (7) No main sex differences were found on the 2 maternal measures of pressure for success in Task 3. More pressure for remembering was exerted on firstborn girls and second-born boys than on their opposite-sex counterparts ($p < .01$). (8) In Tasks 2, 3, and 4, no sex differences were found in mothers' use of praise or criticism. (9) In Tasks 1, 2, 3, and 4, no main sex differences were found in the number of times children were told by their mothers that they were correct or incorrect. Firstborn girls and second-born boys were more likely to be told they were incorrect than their opposite-sex counterparts ($p < .05$). (10) Across all tasks, mothers of girls exhibited more anxious intrusiveness than mothers of boys.

Rothenberg, B. B. Conservation of number among four- and five-year-old children: some methodological considerations. *Child Development*, 1969, *40*, 383–406.
 Subjects: $N = 210$; 4, 5 yrs (low SES). Measures: After a warm-up task, Ss performed a modified conservation of number task. Results: No sex differences.

Rothenberg, B. B. Children's social sensitivity and the relationship to interpersonal competence, intrapersonal comfort, and intellectual level. *Developmental Psychology*, 1970, *2*, 335–50.
 Subjects: $N = 108$; 8, 10 yrs. Measures: After concentrating on 1 of 2 actors in 4 tape-recorded stories depicting 4 common emotions, Ss were asked to describe how an actor felt. Teachers and peers rated Ss on 7 dimensions of interpersonal confidence. Ss completed a self-concept measure, the Peabody Picture Vocabulary Test, Block Designs of the WISC, and a defensiveness measure. Results: No sex differences.

Rothenberg, B. B., and Courtney, R. G. Conservation of number in very young children. *Developmental Psychology*, 1969a, *1*, 493–502.
 Subjects: $N = 117$; 3 yrs (low, middle SES). Measures: On a conservation-of-number task, Ss were tested on the following transformations: collapsing, rotation, expansion, equal addition, and unequal addition. Results: No sex differences.

Rothenberg, B. B., and Courtney, R. G. A developmental study of nonconservation choices in young children. *Merrill-Palmer Quarterly*, 1969b, *15*, 363–73.
 Subjects: $N = 285$; 2–6 yrs (low, middle SES). Measures: On a conservation-of-number task, Ss were tested on the following transformations: equal subtraction, rotation, collapsing, expansion, and addition. Results: No sex differences.

Rothenberg, B. B., and Orost, J. H. The training of conservation of number in young children. *Child Development*, 1969, *40*, 707–26.
 Subjects: $N = 20$; 5–6 yrs (low, middle SES). Measures: Ss were tested on 3 conservation-of-number tasks. Ss received training for 2 sessions, after which they were post-tested. Results: No sex differences.

Rotter, J. B., and Mulry, R. C. Internal versus external control of reinforcement and decision time. *J. Personality & Social Psychology*, 1965, *2*, 598–604.
 Subjects: $N = 120$; 18–21 yrs (college). Measures: Ss performed a difficult matching task in which there were actually no correct matches. Before each trial, Ss rated their probability of success on a 10-point scale. Ss were told they were correct on 75% of the first 8 trials; however, on subsequent trials Ss were consistently told they had made the wrong choice. The response measures were (a) mean decision time, (b) mean expectancy of success for the initial 8 trials, (c) frequency of unusual shifts in expectancies, and (d) number of trials to extinction. Ss were considered extinguished when they stated an expectancy of 0 or 1 on 2 consecutive trials. Results: No sex differences.

Routh, D. K., and Tweney, D. Effects of paradigmatic response training on children's word associations. *J. Experimental Child Psychology*, 1972, *14*, 398–407.
   Subjects: $N = 60$; 5, 10 yrs. **Measures:** Ss performed a free-association task before and after receiving training on paradigmatic associates. **Results:** No sex differences.

Rubenstein, J. Maternal attentiveness and subsequent exploratory behavior in the infant. *Child Development*, 1967, *38*, 1089–1100.
   Subjects: $N = 44$; 6 mos and mothers. **Measures:** Ss were presented with a novel stimulus (Bell Test). The number of seconds Ss spent manipulating (oral and tactile), looking at, and vocalizing to the Bell were recorded. The Bell was then paired with each of 10 novel stimuli (Pairs Test). The number of seconds Ss spent exploring the novel stimuli (looking at, manipulating) minus the number of seconds Ss spent exploring the Bell was recorded. **Results:** No sex differences.

Rubin, K. H. Relationship between egocentric communication and popularity among peers. *Developmental Psychology*, 1972, *7*, 364 (brief report).
   Subjects: $N = 80$; 5, 7, 9, 11 yrs. **Measures:** (1) Ss were asked to name the 3 children with whom they would most like to spend their free time. (2) Ss were also asked to describe each of 10 nonsense figures in such a way that E (who was visually separated from Ss and had 10 identical figures) could identify which figure was being described. The mean number of distinctive features used by Ss to describe each figure was added to a score based on Ss' response to E's inquiries for further information to yield a score of communicative egocentrism. **Results:** No sex differences were found in popularity or in egocentrism scores.

Rubin, Z. Measurement of romantic love. *J. Personality & Social Psychology*, 1970, *16*, 265–73.
   EXPERIMENT I: **Subjects:** $N = 158$ couples; 18–21 yrs (college). **Measures:** Ss completed a love and liking scale first with respect to their dating partner and later with respect to a close, same-sex friend. **Results:** (1) Women liked their dating partner more than they were liked in turn ($p < .01$). No differences were found between men's and women's love for their dating partners. (2) Women loved their same-sex friends more than men did ($p < .01$). No sex differences were found in Ss' liking for their same-sex friends.
   EXPERIMENT II: **Subjects:** $N = 79$ couples; 18–21 yrs (college). **Measures:** Ss were paired with either their boyfriends or their girlfriends or with another person's boyfriend or girlfriend. Before the experiment began, Ss' visual behavior was recorded when E was out of the room. **Results:** Women spent more time looking at the men than men spent looking at the women ($p < .01$).

Ruble, D. N., and Nakamura, C. Y. Task orientation versus social orientation in young children and their attention to relevant social cues. *Child Development*, 1972, *43*, 471–80.
   Subjects: $N = 56$; 7–10 yrs. **Measures:** Ss were given the Gerard rod-and-frame test, 2 object assembly tasks (puzzles) and a concept identification task. Before the object assembly tasks were administered, Ss were assigned to 1 of 2 conditions. In the experimental condition, E assembled and then disassembled puzzle 2, while Ss attempted puzzle 1. Afterward, Ss were given the pieces to puzzle 2 to put together. In the control condition, E simply watched Ss perform. Response measures were number of pieces correctly placed (bonus points were awarded for completing the task quickly) and number of glances away from task. In the concept identification task, Ss had to decide which of 3 squares was correct. The squares varied in color and size. In the first trial block, E repeatedly looked at and leaned very slightly toward the correct choice (always the largest square). In the second trial block, E again directed her attention toward the correct selection, but the largest square was no longer always correct. Rather, the correct answer was randomized over the 3 sizes (small, medium, and large). During the third trial block, no social cue was given. Selection of the small square was always correct. The number of trials Ss needed to reach criterion in each trial block was recorded. **Results:** No sex differences.

Rule, B. G., and Rehill, D. Distraction and self-esteem effects on attitude change. *J. Personality & Social Psychology*, 1970, *15*, 359–65.
   Subjects: $N = 90$; 18–21 yrs (college). **Measures:** Ss read a communication advocating a position opposite theirs. The response measure was amount of attitude change Ss exhibited on a postexperimental scale. **Results:** No sex differences.

Ryan, T. J., and Strawbridge, J. E. Effects of observer condition, instructional set, reward schedule, and sex of subject upon performer and observer. *Developmental Psychology*, 1969, *1*, 474–81.

Subjects: $N = 192$; 5–6 yrs. Measures: Same-sex pairs of Ss were brought to an experimental room to perform a lever-pulling task; 1 member of each pair was randomly designated as Child A and the other as Child B. Child A Ss were assigned to 1 of 2 main conditions: (a) half were rewarded with a marble after each of 40 lever-pulling responses; the other half were rewarded after every other trial. Child B Ss were also assigned to 1 of 2 conditions. Half performed a lever-pulling response immediately after each of Child A's responses and were rewarded for each response (active observer condition). Ss in the other half (passive observer condition) first observed Child A perform all 40 responses; then, in the presence of Child A, they performed 40 responses, each of which was rewarded. Measures were taken of each child's starting speed and movement speed. Results: (1) Starting speeds for Ss designated as Child A: boys with an active observer had higher mean speeds than boys with a passive observer; no effect was found for girls ($p < .05$). (2) Movement speeds of Child A Ss: boys with an active observer had higher mean speeds than girls with an active observer. (3) Starting speeds for Child B Ss: no sex differences. (4) Movement speeds for Child B Ss: in the active observer condition, boys had higher mean speeds than girls; no sex differences were found in the passive observer condition.

Ryan, T. J., and Voorhoeve, A. C. A parametric investigation of reinforcement schedule and sex of S as related to acquisition and extinction of an instrumental response. *J. Experimental Child Psychology*, 1966, *4*, 189–97.

Subjects: $N = 120$; 5 yrs. Measures: Ss were divided into 6 groups according to percent of trials reinforced on a lever-pulling task (100%, 70%, 50%, 30%, 0%). Starting and movement time was measured on 40 acquisition trials. After acquisition, groups split into 2 subgroups; one received 30 extinction trials, the other received 30 more acquisition trials. Results: No sex differences.

Rychlak, J. F., and Lerner, J. J. An expectancy interpretation of manifest anxiety. *J. Personality & Social Psychology*, 1965, *2*, 667–84.

Subjects: $N = 40$; 18–20 yrs (college). Measures: Ss were given 6 performance tests of manual dexterity. Preceding Test 1, Ss stated their expectancy for success. Ss then experienced either success or failure on Tests 1–4. Prior to Test 5, Ss again stated their expectancy for success. Test 5 scores were manipulated so that Ss who previously experienced failure on Tests 1–4 performed well above average on Test 5, whereas Ss who previously experienced success on Tests 1–4 performed well below average on Test 5. Preceding Test 6, Ss stated their expectancy for success for a third time. Results: (1) Preceding Test 1, men had a higher expectancy for success than women. (2) No sex differences were found in the change in expectancy for success between Tests 5 and 6.

Saarni, C. I. Piagetian operations and field independence as factors in children's problem-solving performance. *Child Development*, 1973, *44*, 338–45.

Subjects: $N = 64$; 10–15 yrs. Measures: Ss performed a Rod-and-Frame Test (RFT) and 2 Piagetian tasks, "specific gravity" and "chemical combination." Results: Boys were more field-independent than girls on the RFT. No sex differences were found on the Piagetian tasks.

Sabo, R. A., and Hagen, J. W. Color cues and rehearsal in short-term memory. *Child Development*, 1972, *44*, 77–82.

Subjects: $N = 240$; 8, 10, 12 yrs. Measures: Ss were presented with rows of pictures and were asked to remember the location of the picture designated "central." For half of the trials there was a color cue. Rehearsal and nonrehearsal conditions were established. Results: No sex differences.

Saltz, E., and Soller, E. The development of natural language concepts. *Child Development*, 1972, *43*, 1191–1202.

Subjects: $N = 72$; 5–6, 8–9, 11–12 yrs. Measures: Ss were presented with a concept word (both verbally and in writing) and were asked to match with it as many of 72 picture cards as they thought appropriate. The main categories (concepts) were food, animals, transportation, clothes, toys, and furniture. Results: No sex differences.

Saltzstein, H. D., Diamond, R. M., and Belensky, M. Moral judgment level and conformity behavior. *Developmental Psychology*, 1972, *7*, 327–36.

Subjects: $N = 63$; 12 yrs. Measures: Following Kohlberg's procedure, individual interviews were conducted to assess each child's moral judgment level. Ss then met in same-sex groups of 6 and participated in a modified Asch-type conformity experiment. Ss' task was to decide which of 3 comparison strips was identical in length to a standard. Afterward, Ss filled out a questionnaire. **Results:** (1) In comparison with boys, girls were overrepresented at Stage 3 and underrepresented at Stages 1–2 and Stages 4–5 ($p < .001$). (2a) On critical trials in the conformity experiment (group choice was incorrect), no sex differences were found in the number of Ss who yielded to the group influence; (2b) on neutral trials (group choice was correct) boys made fewer errors than girls; (2c) on the post experimental questionnaire no differences were found in the number of boys and girls who indicated they thought the experiment was "some kind of trick."

Samorajczyk, J. Children's responsiveness to imagination suggestions during school entry. *Developmental Psychology*, 1969, *1*, 211–15.
> **Subjects:** $N = 60$; 6 yrs. **Measures:** The Barber Suggestibility Scale (BSS), a scale composed of 8 "make-believe" suggestions, was individually administered to each S. Ss' responses to each of the 8 suggestions (e.g. lowering their arms in response to the suggestion that their arms were feeling heavier, closing their hands in response to the suggestion that their hands were stuck together, etc.) were recorded. Afterward, Ss who exhibited the suggested effect were asked whether they had really felt the effect. **Results:** No sex differences.

Sampson, E. E., and Hancock, F. T. An examination of the relationship between ordinal position, personality and conformity. *J. Personality & Social Psychology*, 1967, *5*, 398–407.
> **Subjects:** $N = 251$; 15–17 yrs. **Measures:** Ss made estimates of (a) the number of circles on a poster held up before them, and (b) the height of a triangle, once before and once after exposure to fictitious group norms. Ss also completed a shortened version of the Mandler-Sarason Test Anxiety Scale, and the need for achievement, need for autonomy, and need for affiliation measures from Edward's Personal Preference Schedule. **Results:** (1) Boys conformed to the group norms more than girls ($p < .05$), an effect almost entirely attributable to the high level of conformity of firstborn sons. (2) No sex differences were found in test anxiety, n achievement, n autonomy, or n affiliation.

Sander, L. Twenty-four-hour distributions of sleeping and waking over the first month of life in different infant caretaking systems. Paper presented at the meeting of the Society for Research in Child Development, Philadelphia, 1973.
> **Subjects:** $N = 18$; newborns awaiting adoption. **Measures:** Around-the-clock observations were made of 9 infants from days 2 to 25. Data were obtained on the other infants from days 11 to 25. **Results:** Both during the day and night, girls spent more time sleeping than boys did.

Sandidge, S., and Friedland, S. J. Sex role-taking and aggressive behavior in children. Paper presented at the meeting of the Society for Research in Child Development, Philadelphia, 1973.
> **Subjects:** $N = 40$; 9–10 yrs (low SES). **Measures:** Ss were shown schematic cartoons of a boy or a girl speaking aggressively to another child of the same or opposite sex. Ss were asked to respond as they believed the second child would. Each response was scored either as an antisocial aggressive response or as a neutral-prosocial aggressive response. **Results:** There were no sex of S effects. Ss gave more antisocial aggressive responses when they answered for girls than when they answered for boys ($p < .01$).

Santrock, J. W. Paternal absence, sex typing, and identification. *Developmental Psychology*, 1970, *2*, 264–72.
> **Subjects:** $N = 60$; 4–6 yrs (black, low SES), father-absent (FA) or father-present (FP), and mothers. **Measures:** Mothers completed a revised Sears, Maccoby, and Levin maternal interview (MI). The children completed a structured doll-play interview (DPI) that assessed dependency (subordinate learning relationship by child doll toward mother and/or father doll, particularly mother), aggression (offensive action by doll same-sex as S), and masculinity-femininity (sex of picture selected during 12 choice sets). **Results:** Boys were more independent (DPI, $p < .05$), more aggressive (DPI, $p < .05$), and more masculine (DPI, $p < .001$; MI, $p < .001$) than girls.

Santrock, J. W. Relation of type and onset of father absence to cognitive development. *Child Development*, 1972, *43*, 455–69.
> **Subjects:** $N = 286$; 12–17 yrs (father-absent). **Measures:** Ss filled out a questionnaire about their fathers. Ss' third- and sixth-grade Otis Quick Scoring IQ and Stanford Achievement Test Scores were obtained from their school's files. **Results:** (1) Boys had lower sixth-grade IQs

than girls did ($p < .05$). (2) Among Ss whose fathers were absent because of divorce, desertion, or separation, boys had lower sixth grade IQs than girls did ($p < .05$). (3) When father absence due to divorce, desertion, or separation occurred in the 12- to 13-year age period, girls had higher sixth-grade IQ scores than boys did ($p < .05$). (4) Among Ss whose fathers were dead, boys scored lower on the sixth-grade achievement test than girls did ($p < .01$). (5) When father absence due to death occurred in the 3- to 5-year age period, girls had higher sixth-grade achievement scores than boys did ($p < .05$).

Sarason, I. G., and Ganzer, V. J. Anxiety, reinforcement, and experimental instructions in a free verbalization setting. *J. Abnormal & Social Psychology*, 1962, 65, 300–307.
Subjects: $N = 96$; 18–19 yrs (college). Measures: Ss were asked to talk about themselves. After a baseline period of 10 minutes, one group of Ss was reinforced for positive self-references (PSRs), while a second group was reinforced for negative self-references (NSRs). A third group of Ss was not reinforced at all. During baseline and conditioning, measures were taken of number of PSRs, NSRs, ambiguous self-references (ASRs), and references to others (ORs). Results: The differences between baseline and conditions in percentage of PSRs, NSRs, ASRs, and ORs were similar for men and women. The difference in total number of responses was higher for men than for women ($p < .01$).

Sarason, I. G., and Harmatz, M. G. Test anxiety and experimental conditions. *J. Personality & Social Psychology*, 1965, 1, 499–505.
Subjects: $N = 144$; 15 yrs. Measures: Number of correct responses in 2 serial learning tasks. Results: No sex differences.

Sarason, I. G., and Koenig, K. P. Relationships of test anxiety and hostility to description of self and parents. *J. Personality & Social Psychology*, 1965, 2, 617–21.
Subjects: $N = 48$; 18–21 yrs (college). Measures: Ss described themselves in general, themselves in academic situations, their fathers, and their mothers. Ss' descriptions were content-analyzed for positive, negative, and ambiguous evaluations of self and parents. Results: (1) Overall, women made more positive references than men did ($p < .05$). (2) No sex differences were found in self-descriptions. (3) For academic self-descriptions, women made more positive references than men did ($p < .05$). (4) Women made more positive references to mothers than men did ($p < .05$). (5) No sex differences were found in descriptions of fathers.

Sarason, I. G., and Minard, J. Test anxiety, experimental instructions and the Wechsler Adult Intelligence Scale. *J. Educational Psychology*, 1962, 53, 299–302.
Subjects: $N = 96$; 18–21 yrs (college). Measures: Ss completed the Vocabulary, Comprehension, Block Design, and Digit Symbol subtests of the WAIS. Results: Men scored higher than women on the Block Design subtest ($p < .05$).

Sarason, I. G., and Winkel, G. H. Individual differences among subjects and experimenters and subjects' self-descriptions. *J. Personality & Social Psychology*, 1966, 3, 448–57.
Subjects: $N = 48$; 18–21 yrs (college). Measures: Ss were asked to talk about themselves by either same-sex or opposite-sex peer Es. After Ss presented their self-descriptions, E and S rated each other's behavior. Es' behavior was also rated by observers. Results: (1) No sex differences were found in number of positive self-references (PSRs). Male Es elicited more PSRs than female Es did ($p < .05$). (2) Women made more negative self-references (NSRs) than men ($p < .05$). Male Es elicited more NSRs than female Es ($p < .025$). Women made slightly more NSRs than men when E was a female; when E was a male, women made a great many more NSRs than men ($p < .005$). (3) No sex differences were found in number of ambiguous self-references. (4) No sex differences were found in number of positive, ambiguous, or negative references to others or in the number of references to mother, father, or peers. (5) No sex differences were found in the number of statements asking E for further directions. (6) No sex differences were found in number of present-tense, future-tense, or past-tense references. Ss paired with female Es made more past-tense references than Ss paired with male Es ($p < .05$). (7) Men emitted more "ah's" than women ($p < .01$). (8) No sex differences were found in number of incompleted sentences. Women made more incompleted sentences than men when E was a male; men made more incompleted sentences than women when E was a female ($p < .025$). (9) No sex differences were found in number of sentence corrections, serial repetitions of 1 word or more, or stutters. (10) Women laughed more frequently than men ($p < .01$). (11) Women perceived Es to be more pleasant, courteous, encouraging, and interested than men did. Women liked the Es with whom they were paired more than men did ($p < .025$). Ss perceived female Es to be more enthusiastic, more pleasant, more professional, more encouraging, and friendlier than male Es. Men rated male Es as friendlier, more

personal, more relaxed, and more casual than female Es; on these same variables, women rated female Es more favorably than male Es ($p < .05$). (12) Es rated female Ss higher than male Ss on liking of S, S's enthusiasm, S's businesslike air, and body movements. (13) Female Es were rated as looking, smiling and nodding in agreement more frequently than male Es. Female Es were also described as making more hand gestures and placing their hands near their faces more frequently than male Es. Male Es were described as fidgeting and as manipulating objects with their hands more frequently than female Es.

Saravo, A., Bagby, B., and Haskins, K. Transfer effects in children's oddity learning. *Developmental Psychology*, 1970, 2, 273–82.
Subjects: $N = 144$; 3–7 yrs. Measures: Ss were given an oddity-learning pretraining problem, 6 oddity-discrimination problems, and either a reversal-oddity or new set oddity transfer test. Results: Girls learned the pretraining task in fewer trials than boys ($p < .025$). No sex differences were found in subsequent phases of the experiment.

Savell, J. M. Generalization of the effects of prior agreement and disagreement. *J. Personality & Social Psychology*, 1970, 15, 94–100.
Subjects: $N = 96$; 11–12 yrs. Measures: Ss indicated which of 2 pictures they preferred on each of 20 trials. A female E expressed agreement or disagreement with Ss' choice after each trial. Ss were then presented with an additional set of picture pairs; before calling for Ss' preference, E always announced her own choice first. The performance measure was the number of times Ss conformed to E's choice. Results: No sex differences.

Savitsky, J. C., and Izard, C. E. Developmental changes in the use of emotion cues in a concept formation task. *Developmental Psychology*, 1970, 3, 350–57.
Subjects: $N = 50$; 4–8 yrs. Measures: Ss chose the 2 most similar human faces from 96 triads of photographs. Two of each triad contained either common elements of hats or facial expressions of emotion. Results: No main sex differences.

Schaefer, C. E. Imaginary companions and creative adolescents. *Developmental Psychology*, 1969, 1, 747–49.
Subjects: $N = 800$; 15–17 yrs. Measures: Ss were asked the following question: "As a child, did you ever have any imaginary companions?" Results: No sex differences.

Schaffer, H. R., and Parry, M. H. Effects of stimulus movement on infants' wariness of unfamiliar objects. *Developmental Psychology*, 1972, 7, 87 (brief report).
Subjects: $N = 12$; 1 yr. Measures: Ss were exposed for 4 30-second trials to a 10-centimeter-high metal container with flashing lights and bleeps that were either in an approach movement, in a nonapproach movement (along an arc at a standard distance), or stationary. Latency to make contact was recorded. Results: No sex differences.

Schaie, K. W., and Strother, C. R. Cognitive and personality variables in college graduates of advanced age. In G. A. Talland, ed., *Human aging and behavior*. New York: Academic Press, 1968.
Subjects: $N = 50$; 70–88 yrs (retired academics and professionals). Measures: Ss completed the Burgess Attitude Scale. Ss also rated how happy their lives had been and how satisfied they were with their accomplishments. Results: (1) No sex differences were found in feelings of happiness as assessed by the Burgess Attitude Scale. (2) No sex differences were found in Ss' self-ratings.

Schell, D. J. Conceptual behavior in young children: learning to shift dimensional attention. *J. Experimental Child Psychology*, 1971, 12, 72–87.
Subjects: $N = 72$; 4, 5 yrs. Measures: After an initial session to familiarize them with the task, Ss were trained by E to identify the relevant dimensions in a card-sorting task. During training, the relevant dimension was changed several times. A final testing, during which only 1 dimension was relevant, followed the training session. Measures were taken of the number of trials Ss needed to reach criterion. Results: No sex differences.

Schiff, W., and Dytell, R. S. Tactile identification of letters: a comparison of deaf and hearing children's performances. *J. Experimental Child Psychology*, 1971, 11, 150–64.
Subjects: $N = 293$; 7–19 yrs. Measures: Ss were presented with raised capital letters (2 to a page) and were asked to either point out the matching letter from a sheet on which the entire alphabet was printed (hearing and deaf Ss), use the manual alphabet to identify the matching letter (deaf Ss only), or vocally identify the letter (hearing Ss only). Results: No sex differences.

Schneider, F. W. Conforming behavior of black and white children. *J. Personality & Social Psychology*, 1970, *16*, 466–71.
    EXPERIMENT I: **Subjects:** $N = 96$; 12, 13 yrs (white, black). **Measures:** After receiving erroneous judgments from a unanimous peer majority, Ss judged which of 3 geometric figures was largest in area. The performance measure was the number of times Ss conformed to the majority's choice. **Results:** No sex differences.
    EXPERIMENT II: **Subjects:** $N = 192$; 12, 13 yrs (white, black). **Measures:** Ss' attitudes toward the other ethnic group were measured by a modified version of the Miller and Biggs children's social distance scale. **Results:** No sex differences.

Scholnick, E. K. Inference and preference in children's conceptual performance. *Child Development*, 1970, *41*, 449–60.
    Subjects: $N = 108$; 5, 7, 9 yrs. **Measures:** On each administration of a 2-trial concept-identification task, Ss were presented with a pair of geometric stimuli that varied on 1 of 3 dimensions (color, form, or size). Based on information provided to them by E, Ss had to infer which dimension was relevant and which value was correct. **Results:** No sex differences were found in number of errors made.

Scholnick, E. K. Use of labels and cues in children's concept identification. *Child Development*, 1971, *42*, 1849–58.
    Subjects: $N = 96$; 5, 7 yrs. **Measures:** Ss were pretested on discriminative and vocabulary skills. They were given sample inference tasks to assure their knowledge of positive and negative instances of relevant cue location; 3 verbalization treatment groups were conducted: stimulus comparison, conjunctive labels, and repetition of locational cues. In the experimental task, Ss were asked to locate a single relevant cue among 4 choices in a 2-stimulus inference task. **Results:** No sex differences.

Scholnick, E. K., and Osler, S. F. Effect of pretest experience on concept attainment in lower- and middle-class children. *Developmental Psychology*, 1969, *1*, 440–43.
    Subjects: $N = 192$; 8 yrs (low, middle SES). **Measures:** Ss were asked to separate geometric figures into 2 piles. The figures varied on 4 dimensions, only 1 of which was relevant: size (large and small), color (red and blue), form (circle and square), and number (single and double figures). After every correct response, Ss were rewarded with a marble. Measures were taken of the number of trials Ss needed to reach criterion. **Results:** No sex differences.

Schubert, J., and Cropley, A. J. Verbal regulation of behavior and IQ in Canadian Indian and white children. *Developmental Psychology*, 1972, *7*, 295–301.
    Subjects: $N = 211$; 6–15 yrs (central Saskatchewan Indians), 9–14 yrs (white rural and urban Canadians), 11–14 yrs (northern Saskatchewan Indians). **Measures:** Ss were trained in the use of strategies for solving similarities and Block Design problems from the Wechsler Intelligence Scale for Children and were given a test of verbal regulation of behavior. **Results:** No sex differences.

Schwartz, D. W., and Karp, S. A. Field dependence in a geriatric population. *Perceptual & Motor Skills*, 1967, *24*, 495–504.
    Subjects: $N = 120$; 17, 30–39, 58–82 yrs. **Measures:** Body Adjustment Test, Rod-and-Frame Test, Embedded Figures Test. **Results:** Among 17-year-old and 30-39-year-old Ss, men were more field-independent than women on all 3 tests. Among the 58-82-year-old Ss, no sex differences were found.

Schwartz, J. C. Effects of peer familiarity on the behavior of preschoolers in a novel situation. *J. Personality & Social Psychology*, 1972, *24*, 276–84.
    Subjects: $N = 57$; 4 yrs. **Measures:** Ss were placed in a room containing novel and familiar toys, either alone, with a close friend, or with an unfamiliar peer. Ss' free behavior was rated for affect and motility. The amount of time Ss spent near or with each of 4 toys was also recorded. For Ss in the stranger and friend conditions, a record was kept of time spent looking at partner. **Results:** (1) No sex differences were found for any of the measures. (2) Boys fired the gun mounted on the novel copter toy more often than girls did ($p < .01$).

Schwartz, J. C., and Wynn, R. The effects of mothers' presence and previsits on children's emotional reactions to starting nursery school. *Child Development*, 1971, *42*, 871–81.
    Subjects: $N = 108$; 3–5 yrs. **Measures:** On the first day of school, mothers left their children either immediately or 20 minutes after arriving. Each S's separation reaction was rated on a 6-point scale by a student teacher. During the last 20 minutes of free play, S's locus relative

to others ("alone," "with teacher," "with peer") and his activity ("active," "passive," "interactive") were recorded. Ratings were also made of S's motility and comfort in the classroom. S's emotional reaction to school was assessed on the first day and again 1 week later. **Results:** No sex differences.

Schwartz, S. H., and Clausen, G. T. Responsibility, norms, and helping in an emergency. *J. Personality & Social Psychology*, 1970, *16*, 299–310.
> **Subjects:** $N = 179$; 18–21 yrs (college). **Measures:** Ss were exposed to the tape-recorded sounds of a victim (in an adjoining room) experiencing a seizure. Ss were led to believe that either no other bystanders were present (2-person condition) or that 4 other bystanders were present (6-person condition). Half of the Ss assigned to the 6-person condition were informed that 1 of the other bystanders was medically competent (6-person-competent condition). The response measures were the speed and nature of Ss' response to the victim's cries for help. **Results:** (1) No main sex differences were found in speed of helping. In the 2-person groups, women responded more quickly than men ($p < .05$), whereas in the 6-person-competent condition, men responded more quickly than women ($p < .05$). No sex differences were found in the 6-person condition. (2) No main sex differences were found in the proportion of Ss who did not emerge from their rooms to help the victim. (3) Of these Ss who emerged from their rooms, more women than men said (in a postexperimental interview) that rather than help the victim directly, they intended to report the incident to others, or to simply see what was going on ($p < .05$, 1-tailed). No sex differences were found in the proportion of Ss who said they intended to do nothing. (4) In 6-person-competent groups, men were more likely than women to indicate (on a postexperimental questionnaire) that they had thought action might be made easier because others would join them in helping ($p < .05$). Taking the sample as a whole, women were more likely than men to express uncertainty about what steps to take ($p < .05$), to be more concerned that their actions might be deemed inappropriate ($p < .05$), to think about their lack of capability to help ($p < .01$), and to expect others to join them in helping ($p < .01$).

Seitz, V. R. Multidimensional scaling of dimensional preferences; a methodological study. *Child Development*, 1971, *42*, 1701–20.
> **Subjects:** $N = 144$; 4–6 yrs. **Measures:** Ss chose which of 2 stimuli was more like a third. Stimuli varied in color and form. Forced-choice form, forced-choice color, and nonforced-choice trials were pretested. **Results:** No sex differences.

Seitz, V. R., and Weir, M. W. Strength of dimensional preferences as a predicator of nursery-school children's performance on a concept shift task. *J. Experimental Child Psychology*, 1971, *12*, 370–86.
> **Subjects:** $N = 104$; 4–5 yrs. **Measures:** Ss' dimensional preference strengths for color and shape were scaled by a multidimensional comparison technique. Matched for kind and strength of preference, Ss performed a 2-choice simultaneous discrimination task (1–3 weeks later) with either color or form relevant to the solution. They then performed either intra- or extra-dimensional shift problems. Reinforcement was a marble for "correct" responses and nothing for "incorrect" ones. **Results:** No sex differences.

Self, P. A., Horowitz, F. D., and Paden, L. Y. Olfaction in newborn infants. *Developmental Psychology*, 1972, *7*, 349–63.
> **Subjects:** $N = 32$; 1, 2, 3 days. **Measures:** When respiration was stable and activity minimal, Ss were presented with odors of oil of anise, tincture of asafetida, oil of lavender, and tincture of valerian. Responses were recorded by respirometer and visual observation. **Results:** No consistent sex differences were found in olfactory sensitivity.

Selman, R. L. The relation of role-taking to the development of moral judgment in children. *Child Development*, 1971a, *42*, 79–91.
> **Subjects:** $N = 60$; 8, 9, 10 yrs. **Measures:** Ss completed Kohlberg's Moral Judgment Scale and 2 of Flavell's role-taking tasks. **Results:** No sex differences.

Selman, R. L. Taking another's perspective: role-taking development in early childhood. *Child Development*, 1971b, *42*, 1721–34.
> **Subjects:** $N = 60$; 4, 5, 6 yrs. **Measures:** Ss were given 2 role-taking tasks in which they were asked to predict a peer's responses in a situation in which Ss had more information than the peer. In a second task (designed by DeVries), competitive guessing and hiding behavior changed over time as role-taking ability increased. **Results:** There were no sex differences in verbal role-taking skill.

Semler, I. J., and Eron, L. D. Replication report: relationship of aggression in third grade children to certain pupil characteristics. *Psychology in the Schools*, 1967, *4*, 356–58.
> **Subjects:** $N = 863$; 8 yrs. **Measures:** Each child rated every other child in his classroom on a series of items having to do with specific aggressive behaviors (Peer-Rate Index of Aggression). **Results:** Boys were rated higher in aggression than girls ($p < .001$).

Semler, I. J., Eron, L. D., Meyerson, L. J., and Williams, J. F. Relationship of aggression in third grade children to certain pupil characteristics. *Psychology in the Schools*, 1967, *4*, 85–88.
> **Subjects:** $N = 567$; 8 yrs. **Measures:** Each child rated every other child in his classroom on a series of items having to do with specific aggressive behaviors (Peer-Rate Index of Aggression). **Results:** Boys were rated higher in aggression than girls ($p < .001$).

Serbin, L. A., O'Leary, K. D., Kent, R. N., and Tonick, I. J. A comparison of teacher response to the pre-academic and problem behavior of boys and girls. *Child Development*, 1973, *44*, 796–804.
> **Subjects:** 15 female teachers and their pupils (ages 3–5). Number of children in each class ranged from 12 to 17. **Measures:** Teachers' responses to 2 classes of behavior—disruption (ignoring teacher directions, destruction of materials, and aggression toward others) and dependency (crying, proximity to the teacher, and solicitation of teacher attention—were recorded. Also observed were teachers responses to appropriate participation in ongoing classroom activities. **Results:** (1) Boys emitted more aggressive ($p < .02$) and ignoring ($p < .02$) responses than girls. Girls were observed within arm's reach of their teachers more often than boys ($p < .01$). No sex differences were found in frequency of crying or solicitation of teacher attention. (2) Teacher response to disruptive behaviors: (a) teachers were more likely to respond when boys were aggressive than when girls were ($p < .05$); teachers did not respond at different rates to boys' and girls' ignoring responses; (b) boys received more loud reprimands for disruptive behaviors than girls ($p < .02$); no differences were found between boys and girls in frequency of receipt of soft reprimands (audible only to the child and his neighbors) or other forms of negative attention. (3) Teacher response to dependent behaviors: (a) teachers were more likely to respond to boys when they solicited attention than to girls ($p < .01$); rates of praise, hugging, and brief conversation (nondirectional instruction less than 1 sentence in length) in response to solicitation were not different for boys and girls; 3 classes of teacher response to solicitation—extended conversation, brief direction (telling child to do something), and extended direction (detailed instructions or demonstration intended to teach the child how to do something for himself)—were all given at higher rates to boys than to girls ($p < .05$, $p < .02$, $p < .02$); (b) no difference was found in the rate of teacher attention received by boys and girls for being close; girls received more teacher attention when they were near her than when participating in classroom activities farther away; boys did not ($p < .01$); (c) rate of teacher response to crying could not be analyzed because of the low base rates of this behavior. (4) Teacher response to appropriate participation in ongoing classroom activities: (a) teachers responded at higher rates to boys than to girls ($p < .001$); (b) praise, brief directions, and extended directions were given more often to boys than to girls ($p < .01$, $p < .001$, $p < .01$); (c) boys were hugged more frequently than girls ($p < .02$); (d) teachers engaged in extended conversation more often with boys than with girls ($p < .01$). (5) No sex differences were found in the frequency of the following teacher behaviors: brief conversation, touching, and helping. (6) On a postexperimental questionnaire, teachers reported giving more loud reprimands to boys than to girls. They were not aware of responding differentially to boys and girls, or of giving different amounts of positive or instructional attention to either sex.

Sewell, J. B., III, Bowen, P., and Lieberman, L. R. Projective study of college students' attitudes towards marriage. *Perceptual & Motor Skills*, 1966, *23*, 418.
> **Subjects:** $N = 40$; 18–21 yrs (college). **Measures:** Ss were presented with 24 photographs of young men and women, half of whom were judged to be good-looking, the other half of average attractiveness. Ss were told that 6 of the men and 6 of the women were married. Ss' task was to pick out the married persons. **Results:** Women thought that more of the good-looking males were married than men did.

Seyfried, B. A., and Hendrick, C. When do opposites attract? When they are opposite in sex and sex-role attitudes. *J. Personality & Social Psychology*, 1973, *25*, 15–20.
> **Subjects:** $N = 89$; 18–21 yrs (college). **Measures:** Ss completed the Masculine-Feminine Preferences Test (MFPT), a scale designed to measure sex-role attitudes; 29 Ss who had

ambiguous or inverted sex-role preferences on this measure were dropped from the study. Ss then examined two MFPT forms (supposedly completed by strangers) and were asked to evaluate each stranger on several scales; 4 types of stimulus persons were created by E: a masculine male, a masculine female, a feminine male, and a feminine female. **Results:** (1) Men rated strangers with masculine attitudes more similar than strangers with feminine attitudes ($p < .05$). No difference was found in women's ratings. No interaction was found between sex of S and sex of stranger. (2) Men rated masculine males more similar than feminine ($p < .05$). (3) Men's similarity ratings of the masculine female and the feminine female did not differ; nor did women's similarity ratings of the masculine male and the feminine male differ. (4) Men liked the masculine male more than any other stranger (feminine male, $p < .05$; masculine female, $p < .05$; feminine female, N.S.). Men did not differ in their like-dislike ratings of either the feminine female or the masculine female. The feminine male was disliked more than any other stranger. (5) Women liked the masculine male more than any other stranger (masculine female, $p < .05$; feminine male, $p < .05$; feminine female, N.S.). Women did not differ in their like-dislike ratings of the feminine male and the masculine female.

Sgan, M. L. Social reinforcement, socioeconomic status, and susceptibility to experimenter influence. *J. Personality & Social Psychology*, 1967, 5, 202–10.
 Subjects: $N = 72$; 6 yrs (low, middle SES). **Measures:** Ss indicated their preference for 1 member of each of 14 pairs of pictures. The response measure was the number of times Ss changed an initial preference to agree with E's stated preference on a subsequent administration of the task. **Results:** (1) No main sex differences were found. (2) Low SES boys changed less often than low SES girls ($p < .05$), middle SES girls ($p < .05$), and middle SES boys ($p < .02$). The latter 2 groups did not differ from each other.

Shantz, C. U. A developmental study of Piaget's theory of logical multiplication. *Merrill-Palmer Quarterly*, 1967a, *13*, 121–37.
 Subjects: $N = 72$; 7, 9, 11 yrs. **Measures:** Multiplication of classes was assessed by the revised children's Raven's Progressive Matrices Test. Multiplication of asymmetric logical relations was assessed by a specially constructed multiple-relations test. Multiplication of spatial relations was assessed by a modified version of Piaget's landscape test. **Results:** No sex differences.

Shantz, C. U. Effects of redundant and irrelevant information on children's seriation ability. *J. Experimental Child Psychology*, 1967b, 5, 208–22.
 Subjects: $N = 72$; 7, 9, 11 yrs. **Measures:** Ss were presented with a vertical series of 4 geometric figures that systematically varied on at least 2 dimensions (e.g. 1 set of figures decreased in size and increased in color brightness as viewed from top to bottom). Between the third and fourth member of each array was an empty space. Ss' task was to choose from among 12 figures the one that best completed the series. Performance measures were number of correct choices and latency to solution. **Results:** No sex differences.

Shapira, A., and Madsen, M. C. Cooperative and competitive behavior of kibbutz and urban children in Israel. *Child Development*, 1969, *40*, 609–17.
 Experiment I: **Subjects:** $N = 80$; 6–10 yrs (kibbutz, urban). **Measures:** Same-sex groups of 4 were tested on Madsen's Cooperation Board. Prizes were rewarded first on a group and then on an individual basis. In both conditions, cooperation was adaptive. **Results:** No sex differences were found in the group reward condition. In the individual reward condition, no mention was made of a first-order sex difference.
 Experiment II: **Subjects:** $N = 80$; 6–10 yrs (identical to the sample in Experiment I). **Measures:** Same-sex groups of 4 were tested on Madsen's Cooperation Board. Prizes were rewarded only on an individual basis. The board was altered to make competition adaptive. **Results:** Urban boys were more competitive than urban girls (no significance test was reported). No sex differences were found in the kibbutz sample.

Shapiro, A. H. Verbalization during the preparatory interval of a reaction-time task and development of motor control. *Child Development*, 1973, *44*, 137–42.
 Subjects: $N = 96$; 5, 8 yrs. **Measures:** Ss in 1 group were initially pretrained with a metronome to either say or whisper the nonsense word "veb"; Ss in a second group were pretrained to either whisper or count aloud the numbers 1 to 10. Control Ss simply listened to the metronome. All Ss participated in a reaction-time task. On each trial, a buzzer was followed 9 seconds later by a chime that served as the "press" signal for Ss. During the 9-second interval between the buzzer and the chime, Ss repeated the cues they had learned during pretraining. Measures were taken of reaction time and number of errors of anticipation (premature key presses during the interval between the buzzer and the chime). Eye movements

and blinks, gross body movement, and EOG (electroculogram) and EMG (electromograph) frequencies were also recorded. **Results:** Whispering either the numbers 1–10 or the nonsense word "veb" up until presentation of the chime hindered girls' performance on the reaction-time task more than it hindered boys'. No other sex differences were reported.

Shapiro, S. S. Aural paired associates learning in grade-school children. *Child Development*, 1966, *37*, 417–24.
> **Subjects:** $N = 80$; 10–11, 13–14 yrs. **Measures:** Ss were tested on a list of 8 aurally presented paired associates. The number of trials Ss needed to reach the criterion of 1 perfect recitation was recorded. **Results:** No main sex differences.

Sharan (Singer), S., and Weller, L. Classification patterns of underprivileged children in Israel. *Child Development*, 1971, *42*, 581–94.
> **Subjects:** $N = 357$; 6 yrs. **Measures:** (1) Ss were presented with 12 familiar objects. E picked up 1 object from the array and put it aside. Ss' task was to select from among the remaining 11 objects those that had some characteristic in common with the 1 chosen by E. This same procedure was followed with each of the 12 objects. After each sort, Ss were asked to explain their selection. (2) Ss were presented with groups of 2 or 3 objects and asked to explain why the objects within each group were alike or went together. Ss' explanations were scored on 2 major dimensions: style of categorization (categorical, inferential, relational-contextual, or descriptive) and grouping ability. (Ss were credited with a grouping response if they mentioned in their explanations all of the objects and at least 1 reason for grouping them together; Ss were charged with a nongrouping response if they failed to mention each of the objects they had grouped together or if they assigned different attributes to 2 or more objects; Ss' responses were classified as nonscorable if no verbal explanation was given or if their reasons were unclear.) (3) Ss were asked to draw a 5½-inch line as slowly as possible. The number of seconds Ss took to draw the line was recorded. **Results:** (1) Boys gave fewer grouping responses and more nonscorable responses than girls ($p < .01$, $p < .01$). (2) Girls employed the descriptive style of categorizing more frequently than boys ($p < .05$). (3) Boys drew the line more quickly than girls ($p < .01$).

Sharma, K. L. Dominance-deference: a cross cultural study. *J. Social Psychology*, 1969, *79*, 265–66.
> **Subjects:** $N = 293$; 18–20 yrs (Asian Indians). **Measures:** A dominance-deference scale, consisting of 10 dominance and 10 deference items, was administered to Ss, who were asked to select the 10 items that best described themselves. Ss' score was the number of dominance items selected. **Results:** No sex differences.

Shaw, J. I., and Skolnick, P. Attribution of responsibility for a happy accident. *J. Personality & Social Psychology*, 1971, *18*, 380–83.
> **Subjects:** $N = 116$; 18–21 yrs (college). **Measures:** After reviewing background data on a fictitious college male, Ss read about an accident (with a pleasant or unpleasant outcome) in which he was involved. A postexperimental questionnaire was administered. **Results:** (1) No sex differences were found in the amount of responsibility Ss attributed to the fictitious male for the accident. (2) Men more than women perceived the fictitious male as trustworthy ($p < .05$), identified with him ($p < .03$), and said they would have been likely to engage in the behavior (mixing chemicals) that led to the accident ($p < .001$).

Shears, L. M., and Behrens, M. G. Age and sex differences in payoff demands during tetrad game negotiations. *Child Development*, 1969, *40*, 559–68.
> **Subjects:** $N = 316$; 8, 9 yrs. **Measures:** Ss were assigned to groups of 4 children of the same age and sex. Each tetrad played 8 rounds of "Sticks and Chips." At the beginning of each round, sticks of different lengths were distributed to the players. The object of the game was for 2 or more players to join together to build the longest stick. Any pair that included the player with the longest stick could win, as could any triple alliance. Members of the winning coalition shared in a prize of 20 chips. The actual division of the chips was determined during the bargaining process. Players suggested possible payoff divisions to other players until a stable winning alliance was formed. **Results:** When holding the longest stick, boys were less accommodative (more exploitative) than girls (8-year-old Ss, $p < .05$; 9-year-old Ss, $p < .01$). No sex differences were found among Ss who held sticks of shorter lengths.

Shechtman, A. Age patterns in children's psychiatric symptoms. *Child Development*, 1970, *41*, 683–93.
> **Subjects:** $N = 546$; 5–8, 9–11, 12–14, 15–17 yrs (outpatients in a mental clinic). **Measures:** Ss' psychiatric records were assessed for 91 deviant behavior traits. **Results:** (1) Among 5-8-

year-old Ss, girls had a higher mean number of deviant behavior traits than boys. (2) Among 9-14-year-old Ss, more boys than girls were classified as externalizers (directing hostility against environment or others) or internalizers (exhibiting conflicts within self).

Shepard, W. O. Word association and definition in middle childhood. *Developmental Psychology*, 1970, *3*, 412 (brief report).
Subjects: $N = 137$; 9, 11, 13 yrs. Measures: Ss wrote single-word associations to 20 words from the Palermo-Jenkins norms. Ss were also asked to define each word. An association was scored syntagmatic if it was of a different form class or often followed the stimulus word in natural language. A definition was scored simple-functional if Ss gave a way in which the word could be used. Definitions were scored complex-functional if both a synonym and a function were given. Results: (1) Among 9- and 11-year-old Ss, girls gave more syntagmatic responses than boys ($p < .01$). (2) Girls gave more complex definitions than boys ($p < .01$).

Shepard, W. O., and Ascher, L. M. Effects of linguistic rule conformity on free recall in children and adults. *Developmental Psychology*, 1973, *8*, 139 (brief report and personal communication).
Subjects: $N = 96$; 6, 11, 18-21 yrs (college). Measures: Ss heard meaningful, anomalous (syntax preserved by violation of semantic rules), and unstructured 5-word strings read either normally (conversationally) or with uniform word emphasis. The response measure was the total number of words correctly recalled. Results: Girls recalled more words than boys did.

Sher, M. A., and Lansky, L. M. The It Scale for Children: effects of variations in the sex-specificity of the It figure. *Merrill-Palmer Quarterly*, 1968, *14*, 323-30.
Experiment I: Subjects: $N = 32$; 5-6 yrs. Measures: Ss were administered the It Scale for Children (ITSC) with the It figure unconcealed. Results: Boys had higher masculine scores than girls ($p < .05$).
Experiment II: Subjects: $N = 24$; 5-6 yrs. Measures: Ss were administered the ITSC with the It figure concealed. Afterward, Ss were asked to attribute a sex first to the concealed It figure and then to the unconcealed It figure. Results: Boys had higher masculine scores than girls ($p < .005$). Boys tended to call the concealed It a boy; girls tended to call the concealed It a girl ($p < .007$, 1-tailed). Of those Ss who made an own-sex attribution to the concealed It figure, more girls than boys changed their attributions upon seeing the It figures ($p < .025$, 1-tailed).
Experiment III: Subjects: $N = 21$; 5-6 yrs. Measures: After attributing a sex to the unconcealed It figure, Ss responded to the ITSC for an It of that sex. Results: Girls called It a boy more than boys called It a girl ($p < .025$, 1- tailed). No sex differences were found in Ss' ITSC scores.

Sherif, C. W. Social distance as categorization of intergroup interaction. *J. Personality & Social Psychology*, 1973, *25*, 327-34.
Subjects: $N = 315$; 18-21 yrs (white and black college). Measures: Ss judged how advisable it would be for a black student to decide to interact with whites in a series of situations, each described briefly. Ss' attitudes were not directly assessed. Rather, Ss classified the descriptions into as many categories as they felt suitable to differentiate among the situations. The response measure was the number of categories used. Upon completing the task, Ss were to label any categories in which they felt "quite uncomfortable" or "definitely uncomfortable," with the option of labeling any other categories if desired. The number of categories not labeled constituted the latitude of noncommitment. Results: (1) Men used fewer categories than women ($p < .01$). The sex difference was greater in the black sample than in the white sample. (2) Women's latitude of noncommitment was greater than men's ($p < .025$).

Shipman, V. C. Disadvantaged children and their first school experiences. Educational Testing Service Head Start Longitudinal Study, 1971.
Subjects: Total $N = 1,875$; 3-4 yrs (white, black). Only sex differences significant at the $p < .01$ level were reported.
Experiment I: Measures: ($N = 1,371$.) Ss were shown a picture of a girl named Jane and a picture of a boy named Johnnie and asked the following questions: (1) If Jane (Johnnie) really wants to be a boy (girl), can she (he) be? (2) If Jane's (Johnnie's) hair were short (long) like a boy's (girl's), then would she (he) be a boy (girl)? (3) If Jane (Johnnie) wore clothes like a boy (girl), then would she (he) be a boy (girl)? (4) If Jane (Johnnie) played with a boy's (girl's) toys, then would she (he) be a boy (girl)? (5) If Jane (Johnnie) had short (long) hair like a boy's (girl's) and wore clothes like a boy's (girl's) and played

with a boy's (girl's) toys, then would she (he) be a boy (girl)? **Results:** (1) Picture of Jane: No sex differences were found in response to question 1. In response to questions 2–5, boys answered in the negative more frequently than girls. (2) Picture of Johnnie: No sex differences were found in Ss' responses.

EXPERIMENT II: **Measures:** ($N = 1,194$.) For 6 trials Ss were shown a slide of 20 chromatic straight lines. On the seventh trial, a picture of chromatic curved lines was presented. The amount of time Ss looked at each picture was recorded after every trial. The response measures were (a) change in fixation time over trials 1–6, and (b) difference in fixation time between trials 6 and 7. Similar procedures were also followed with slides of chromatic and achromatic schematic representations of a family. After the chromatic slide was shown 6 times, the achromatic slide was presented on the seventh trial. **Results:** No sex differences.

EXPERIMENT III: **Measures:** ($N = 1,448$.) ETS Story Sequence Task I: Ss were given sets of drawings depicting animals in a variety of situations. Afterward, stories about the animals were read. Ss' task was to arrange the drawings according to the order in which the animals in the stories encountered situations. **Results:** No sex differences.

EXPERIMENT IV: **Measures:** ($N = 1,371$.) Brown IDS Self-Concept Referents Test: Each S was shown a picture of himself. He was then asked to rate the child in the photograph on 15 bipolar adjectives. **Results:** No sex differences were found in self-concept scores. Girls smiled at the picture of themselves more often than boys did.

EXPERIMENT V: **Measures:** ($N = 1,438$.) Children's Auditory Discrimination Inventory: Ss were presented with 2 pictures and told the name of each. Then E stated the name of only 1 of the pictures. Ss' task was to point to that picture. **Results:** Girls' performance was superior to that of boys.

EXPERIMENT VI: **Measures:** ($N = 1,395$.) Ss were asked to point once, and only once, to each circle in an array. Measures were taken of the number of omissions and repetitions. **Results:** Girls' performance was superior to boys'.

EXPERIMENT VII: **Measures:** ($N = 1,435$.) Educational Testing Service Matched Pictures Language Comprehension Test: Ss were presented with pairs of pictures. Though both pictures in each pair contained identical stimulus elements, they depicted different relationships between the elements. E then told Ss the names of both pictures without indicating which title went with which picture. Ss' task was to match each title with the correct picture. **Results:** No sex differences.

EXPERIMENT VIII: **Measures:** ($N = 1,411$.) Johns Hopkins Perceptual Test: Ss were asked to indicate which of several geometric shapes was identical to a standard. **Results:** No sex differences.

EXPERIMENT IX: **Measures:** ($N = 1,497$.) Hess and Shipman Toy Sorting Task: After being trained by their mothers, Ss were asked to sort a set of toys into groups as their mothers had shown them. Ss then explained why they sorted the toys as they did. **Results:** No sex differences were found in sorting. Girls cooperated with their mothers during training more than boys did.

EXPERIMENT X: **Measures:** ($N = 1,462$.) Same as Experiment IX, but with blocks. **Results:** No sex differences were found in sorting. Girls cooperated with their mothers during training more than boys did.

EXPERIMENT XI: **Measures:** ($N = 1,198$.) Peabody Picture Vocabulary Test, Forms A and B. **Results:** No sex differences.

EXPERIMENT XII: **Measures:** ($N = 1,403$.) Picture Completion subtest of the Wechsler Preschool and Primary Scale of Intelligence: Ss were asked to name or indicate the missing part in each of 23 pictures. **Results:** No sex differences.

EXPERIMENT XIII: **Measures:** ($N = 1,288$.) The Preschool Embedded Figures Test was administered. Measures were taken of the total number of correct items and of the latency of the first response to each item. **Results:** No sex differences.

EXPERIMENT XIV: **Measures:** ($N = 1,474$.) Ss were given the Preschool Inventory, a measure of achievement in areas regarded as necessary for success in school (e.g. listening-comprehension, writing, form copying, arithmetic). **Results:** Girls achieved higher scores than boys.

EXPERIMENT XV: **Measures:** ($N = 1,445$.) Ss were asked to choose between a toy that they could see and a paper bag that contained either 5 toys or none at all. **Results:** Boys chose the uncertain outcome (the paper bag) more frequently than girls.

EXPERIMENT XVI: **Measures:** ($N = 1,274$.) After placing a set of tiles in front of himself, E asked Ss (who previously had been provided with their own set of tiles) to "put out the same number." Measures were taken of the number of tiles Ss put out. E recorded whether Ss arranged their tiles in a pattern identical to the configuration of E's tiles. **Results:** No sex differences.

EXPERIMENT XVII: **Measures:** ($N = 1,470$.) Ss were asked to turn a crank as fast as they could for 15 seconds and to run as quickly as possible across a distance of 12 feet. **Results:** Boys turned the crank faster than girls. No sex differences were found in running speed.

EXPERIMENT XVIII: **Measures:** ($N = 1,091$.) Sigel Object Categorization Test: Ss were presented with 12 familiar objects. On each of 12 trials, E selected 1 of the objects and asked Ss to choose from among the 11 remaining objects those that shared some common property. After each trial, Ss explained why they selected the objects they did. Measures were taken of the adequacy of Ss' explanations and of the latency of their initial responses on each trial. **Results:** No sex differences.

EXPERIMENT XIX: **Measures:** ($N = 1,129$.) Seguin Form Board: Ss were presented with 10 differently shaped blocks and a large board with recesses corresponding to the various shapes, with instructions to place the blocks in their correct spots as quickly as possible. Measures were taken of the number of seconds it took Ss to complete the task and of the number of errors they made. Any attempt Ss made to put a block into the wrong recess on the board was considered an error. **Results:** No sex differences.

EXPERIMENT XX: **Measures:** ($N = 1,460$.) Form Reproduction Test: Ss were asked to make copies of 6 geometric forms. **Results:** Girls made more accurate copies than boys.

EXPERIMENT XXI: **Measures:** ($N = 1,098$.) Massad Mimicry Test, Part 1: Ss heard a tape-recorded model utter nonsense words. Ss were then asked to pronounce each word aloud. **Results:** Girls reproduced words more accurately than boys.

EXPERIMENT XXII: **Measures:** ($N = 1,060$.) Massad Mimicry Test, Part 2: Ss heard a tape-recorded model utter meaningful words. Ss were then asked to pronounce each word aloud. **Results:** No sex differences.

EXPERIMENT XXIII: **Measures:** ($N = 1,399$.) Ss were given the Matching Familiar Figures Test. Response times and error rates were recorded. **Results:** No sex differences.

EXPERIMENT XXIV: **Measures:** ($N = 1,458$.) Ss were asked to choose between a smaller immediate reward and a larger delayed reward. **Results:** No sex differences.

Shomer, R. W. Differences in attitudinal responses under conditions of implicitly manipulated group salience. *J. Personality & Social Psychology,* 1970, *15,* 125–32.
  Subjects: $N = 200$; 18–21 yrs (college). **Measures:** Ss responded anonymously to a questionnaire assessing attitudes toward feminism and child rearing in 1 of 3 group settings: all Ss of the same sex, half of the Ss from each sex, or all Ss of the same sex except one. **Results:** (1) Women were more pro-feminist than men ($p < .001$). No sex differences were found in attitudes toward child rearing. (2) Group composition had no effect on Ss' responses to the child-rearing items. With respect to feminist items, the effect of group composition was significant only for men ($p < .01$). Men who responded in the presence of a lone female member and a male E achieved the highest pro-feminist scores of any group, male or female. All male groups with a male E achieved the highest anti-feminist scores. Remaining male and female groups fell in between these 2 extremes.

Shomer, R. W., Davis, A. H., and Kelley, H. H. Threats and the development of coordination: further studies of the Deutsch and Krauss trucking game. *J. Personality & Social Psychology,* 1966, *4,* 119–26.
  Subjects: $N = 64$; 18–21 yrs (college). **Measures:** Same-sex pairs of Ss played a non-zero sum game formulated in terms of the interaction between 2 trucking firms. The amount of money Ss earned was directly related to the speed with which they achieved a state of cooperation. In order to provide a means for Ss to communicate with one another, half the dyads were provided with 2 buttons, one marked "threat" and the other marked "fine." By pressing the "threat" button, Ss could inform their partners of their intention to deliver a fine. By pressing the "fine" button Ss could impose a fine on their partners. **Results:** (1) Male dyads earned more money than female dyads ($p < .01$). (2) On the postexperimental questionnaire, more male than female dyads perceived and used the threat response as a signal to cooperate ($p < .01$).

Shortell, J. R., and Biller, H. B. Aggression in children as a function of sex of subject and sex of opponent. *Developmental Psychology,* 1970, *3,* 143–44 (brief report).
  Subjects: $N = 48$; 11 yrs. **Measures:** Ss were told they were competing in a reaction time experiment against a boy or a girl (actually E) in another room, and that on each trial the slower person would receive a loud tone. Each S chose the noise level for the "opponent's" tone (in case opponent lost) before each trial. Ss completed a semantic differential-rating scale about the opponents. **Results:** (1) Boys set higher noise level for the opponent to receive than girls did ($p < .05$). (2) Girl opponents had less aggression directed at them

than boy opponents did ($p < .01$). (3) Male opponents were rated as less aggressive ($p < .01$) than female opponents (this effect was due primarily to the low rating boys gave to male opponents). (4) Male opponents were rated as less socially desirable than female opponents ($p < .01$). Boys rated both male and female opponents about equally, whereas girls rated male opponents as less socially desirable than boys did ($p < .01$).

Shrader, W. K., and Leventhal, T. Birth order of children and parental report of problems. *Child Development*, 1968, 39, 1165–75.
   Subjects: $N = 599$; 6–17 yrs. Measures: Parents of Ss filled out a checklist of 237 items and described their child's "problem" area on an open-ended questionnaire (eating, sleep, elimination, speech, psychosomatics, self-destruction, school, sibling relations, self-feeling, fears, depression, passivity control, irresponsibility, motor behavior, psychosis, parent relations, sex, peer relations, and habits). Results: No sex differences.

Shuck, S. Z., Shuck, A., Hallam, E., Mancini, F., and Wells, R. Sex differences in aggressive behavior subsequent to listening to a radio broadcast of violence. *Psychological Reports*, 1971, 28, 921–26.
   Subjects: $N = 40$; 18–21 yrs (college). Measures: Ss were asked to shock a same-sex confederate every time he or she gave the wrong answer in a learning experiment. Results: Men administered higher levels of shock than women ($p < .001$).

Shultz, T. R., Charness, M., and Berman, S. Effects of age, social class, and suggestion to cluster on free recall. *Developmental Psychology*, 1973, 8, 57–61.
   Subjects: $N = 160$; 6, 10 yrs (low, middle SES). Measures: S looked at either 16 or 20 object drawings (younger Ss saw fewer) belonging to 1 of 4 categories (fruit, vehicle, clothing, furniture). Ss were asked for verbal recall after presentation of stimuli, either with specific labels verbalized or with specific labels and conceptual categories verbalized. Results: There were no sex differences in proportion of items recalled or amount of clustering in recall.

Shure, M. B., Spivack, G., and Jaeger, M. Problem-solving thinking and adjustment among disadvantaged preschool children. *Child Development*, 1971, 42, 1791–1803.
   Subjects: $N = 62$; 4 yrs. Measures: Ss were given a preschool interpersonal problem-solving test. Problems involved children of the same sex playing with toys (same toys in all cases except 1: trucks for boys, dolls for girls). Ss heard stories about children of their own sex. Authority problems were presented in the same manner. Ss were given an awareness-of-consequences test and a causality test. Ss were rated by teachers on adjustment. Results: No sex differences.

Sieber, J. E., and Lanzetta, J. T. Some determinants of individual differences in predecision information-processing behavior. *J. Personality & Social Psychology*, 1966, 4, 561–71.
   Subjects: $N = 60$; 18–21 yrs (college). Measures: Ss were exposed to slides designed to present ambiguous information (this was accomplished through the use of unusual and touched-up pictures). Ss' task was to identify the main objects in each slide. Slides were presented tachistoscopically for .01-second durations. Ss were free to observe each slide as frequently as they wished before making a decision. Prior to performing, Ss were trained either to name many possible solutions to given problems or to notice and evaluate relevant information in stimulus pictures. Control Ss received no prior training. The response measures were (a) number of queries (number of times Ss looked at each slide before making a decision), (b) amount of time taken between queries, (c) number of correct decisions, (d) amount of information given with each decision, and (e) amount of uncertainty Ss expressed about the correctness of their identifications. Results: (1) There were no main sex differences. (2) Men who were trained to name many possible solutions to given problems looked at the slides a greater number of times before making a decision than women who received similar training ($p < .05$).

Siebold, J. R. Children's rating responses as related to amount and recency of stimulus familiarization and stimulus complexity. *J. Experimental Child Psychology*, 1972, 14, 257–64.
   Subjects: $N = 72$; 10, 11 yrs. Measures: Ss rated their like or dislike for simple or complex figures from the Welsh Figure Preference Test during familiarization, concurrent testing, and post-testing phases. Results: No sex differences.

Siegel, A. W. Variables affecting incidental learning in children. *Child Development*, 1968, 39, 957–68.
   Subjects: $N = 96$; 8, 14 yrs. Measures: Ss operated a stimulus display and response console

to perform a learning-discrimination series of 3 tasks. Selected-stimuli drawings and incidental drawings were presented on a screen, and Ss had to choose the "correct" picture in order to receive the marble reward. There were 3 conditions in which the stimuli were presented with a varying number of incidental objects. Number of presentations was varied. Errors, incidental learning, and response latencies were measured. **Results:** No sex differences.

Siegel, A. W., and Kresh, E. Children's ability to operate within a matrix: a developmental study. *Developmental Psychology*, 1971, *4*, 232–39.

Subjects: $N = 80$; 4–8 yrs (black and white). **Measures:** While viewing a covered 3×3 matrix and its uncovered attribute cells (defining matrix rows and columns), Ss chose duplicates of the matrix stimuli according to which cell of the matrix E pointed to. In a different order, Ss guessed the shape and color of the objects in each covered matrix cell. Next, with the matrix cells empty and uncovered, and with the attribute cells filled and uncovered. Ss placed matrix stimuli in their correct positions. Finally Ss identified the common attribute defining members of rows or columns. **Results:** No sex differences.

Siegel, A. W., and McBurney, D. H. Estimation of line length and number: a developmental study. *J. Experimental Child Psychology*, 1970, *10*, 170–80.

Subjects: $N = 96$; 6–13 yrs. **Measures:** Ss were asked to hand-grip a tensiometer apparatus to match line lengths and verbal numbers; i.e. the longer the line or higher the number, the harder the hand grip should be squeezed. **Results:** There were no sex differences in hand grip as a function of line length or number size.

Siegel, A. W., and Stevenson, H. W. Incidental learning: a developmental study. *Child Development*, 1966, *37*, 811–17.

Subjects: $N = 96$; 7–14 yrs. **Measures:** Ss were given successive-discrimination problems in 3 parts: (1) a 3-choice successive discrimination problem, (2) the presentation of each discriminative stimulus embedded in a stimulus complex with 3 other objects, and (3) a test of incidental learning in which incidental object and discriminative stimuli were presented separately. The response measure was the number of times Ss made response to incidental objects that were correct for stimulus complex in which they were embedded. **Results:** There were no sex differences in incidental learning scores for children.

Siegel, A. W., and Vance, B. J. Visual and haptic dimensional preference: a developmental study. *Developmental Psychology*, 1970, *3*, 264–66.

Subjects: $N = 64$; 5, 6, 8 yrs. **Measures:** For 8 trials, Ss felt or saw 3 stimuli differing in size, form, and color in the visual condition, and in size, form, and texture in the haptic condition. Ss made judgments on which 2 of 3 stimuli were the same. Dimension preference was assessed. **Results:** (1) In the visual condition, girls had greater form preference than boys ($p < .05$). There were no sex differences in color preference scores or size preference scores. (2) In the haptic condition, there were no significant sex differences in form, texture, or size preference.

Siegel, L. S. The development of the ability to process information. *J. Experimental Child Psychology*, 1968, *6*, 368–83.

Subjects: $N = 192$; 9, 11 yrs. **Measures:** Ss performed an information-processing task involving digits. **Results:** No sex differences.

Siegel, L. S. The sequence of development of certain number concepts in preschool children. *Developmental Psychology*, 1971, *5*, 357–61.

Subjects: $N = 77$; 3–5 yrs. **Measures:** Ss were given tests of continuous and discrete magnitude discrimination, equivalence, conservation, ordination, seriation, and addition. **Results:** No sex differences.

Siegel, L. S. Development of the concept of seriation. *Developmental Psychology*, 1972, *6*, 135–37.

Subjects: $N = 415$; 3–9 yrs. **Measures:** Ss were asked to choose stimuli of varying relative heights (smallest, middle-sized, next to largest, etc.) from 2-, 3-, or 4-choice stimulus arrays to the criterion of 9 out of 10 consecutive correct responses. **Results:** No sex differences.

Siegel, W., and Van Cara, F. The effects of different types of reinforcement on young children's incidental learning. *Child Development*, 1971, *42*, 1596–1601.

Subjects: $N = 108$; 5, 7, 9 yrs. **Measures:** Ss operated a stimulus-response console involving a 3-part successive discrimination task (original learning, presentation of incidental stimuli, and a test of recognition and recall of incidental stimuli). There were 3 reinforcement conditions: right-blank, wrong-blank, and right-wrong. **Results:** No sex differences.

Siegelman, M. Evaluation of Bronfenbrenner's questionnaire for children concerning parental behavior. *Child Development*, 1965, *36*, 163–74.
    Subjects: $N = 212$; 9, 10, 11 yrs (low SES). **Measures:** Ss completed Bronfenbrenner's Parent Behavior Questionnaire. **Results:** (1) Boys rated their mothers as using more physical punishment and deprivation of privileges than girls did. No sex differences were found in Ss' ratings of (a) their mothers' use of affective reward, affective punishment, social isolation, expressive rejection, prescription, or principled discipline; (b) their mothers' display of nurturance, instrumental companionship, affiliative companionship, protectiveness, power, or indulgence; (c) the extent of their mothers' achievement demands. (2) Boys rated their fathers as using more physical punishment, deprivation of privileges, expressive rejection, and social isolation than girls did. Girls rated their fathers as using more affective reward than boys did. No sex differences were found in Ss' ratings of (a) their fathers' use of affective punishment, prescription, or principled discipline; (b) their fathers' display of nurturance, instrumental companionship, affiliative companionship, protectiveness, power, or indulgence; (c) the extent of their fathers' achievement demands.

Siegenthaler, B. M., and Barr, C. A. Auditory figure-background perception in normal children. *Child Development*, 1967, *38*, 1163–67.
    Subjects: $N = 100$; 4, 5, 7, 9, 11 yrs. **Measures:** Speech reception threshold (SRT) was measured by the Picture Identification test, a test requiring Ss to point to pictures upon demand. Ss were given the test twice, once in the absence of noise and once in the presence of a tape recording of a jumble of voices (40-db). Shifts in SRT due to the effect of masking noises were recorded. **Results:** Among the 11-year-old Ss, boys showed less of an increase in SRT than girls ($p < .02$).

Signori, E. I., and Rempel, R. Research on the picture titles subtest of the IES Test. *Perceptual & Motor Skills*, 1966, *22*, 161–62.
    Subjects: $N = 182$; 18–21 yrs (college). **Measures:** The Picture Titles Subtest of the IES (Impulse, Ego, Superego). Test consists of 12 pictures depicting I, E, and S activity. Ss' task was to give each picture an appropriate title. Responses based on inconsequential details of the pictures were designated defensive (D). **Results:** There were no sex differences in the number of I, E, and S responses. Boys made more D responses than girls ($p < .02$).

Silverman, I. Role-related behavior of subjects in laboratory studies of attitude change. *J. Personality & Social Psychology*, 1968, *8*, 343–48.
    Subjects: $N = 403$; 18–21 yrs (college). **Measures:** After reading a persuasive message, Ss responded to 4 opinion items. The response measure was the amount Ss were persuaded by the message. **Results:** No sex differences.

Silverman, I., Shulman, A. D., and Wiesenthal, D. L. Effects of deceiving and debriefing psychological subjects on performance in later experiments. *J. Personality & Social Psychology*, 1970, *14*, 203–12.
    Subjects: $N = 98$; 18–21 yrs (college). **Measures:** Ss listened to 4 persuasive communications and then rated their agreement or disagreement with each. Ss also completed the Rotter Incomplete Sentence Blank, Gough and Heilbrun's Adjective Check List, and a measure of responsiveness to implicit demands. **Results:** (1) No sex differences were found in persuasibility, responsiveness to implicit demands, or maladjustment scores on the RISB. (2) No sex differences were found in total number of adjectives checked or in percentage of favorable adjectives checked. Two of the 21 subscales yielded sex differences: men showed less counseling readiness ($p < .01$) and more self-control ($p < .01$) than women.

Silverman, I., Shulman, A. D., and Wiesenthal, D. L. The experimenter as a source of variance in psychological research: modeling and sex effects. *J. Personality & Social Psychology*, 1972, *21*, 219–27.
    Subjects: $N = 224$; 18–21 yrs (college). **Measures:** Male and female Es were filmed while administering a person-perception task to confederates. Ss were then shown these films and asked to rate each E on 22 personality traits. **Results:** (1) Women made more ratings in the vain, competent, and vigorous directions than men ($p < .01$). (2) Female Es were judged as more vigorous, competent, and extraverted, and as less warm than male Es.

Silverman, I. W. Incidence of guilt reactions in children. *J. Personality & Social Psychology*, 1967, 7, 338–40.

Subjects: $N = 199$; 11 yrs. **Measures:** Ss were given the opportunity to score their own tests. On the basis of their scoring behavior, Ss were classified as either noncheaters (did not falsify any answers), low cheaters (falsified some answers, but not enough to win a prize), or high cheaters (falsified a sufficient number of answers to win a prize). Ss were then invited to volunteer from 1 to 60 minutes of their time for an experiment scheduled at a later date. The response measure was amount of time Ss volunteered. **Results:** (1) Fewer girls than boys were classified as noncheaters; fewer boys than girls were classified as low cheaters ($p < .01$). No sex difference was found in number of high cheaters. (2) No sex difference was found in the number of minutes volunteered.

Silverman, J., Buchsbaum, M., and Stierlin, H. Sex differences in perceptual differentiation and stimulus intensity control. *J. Personality & Social Psychology*, 1973, 25, 309–18.

EXPERIMENT I: **Subjects:** $N = 30$; 18–22 yrs. **Measures:** The Rod and Frame Test was administered to Ss. They were then given the EEG averaged evoked response measure of perceptual differentiation. Line segments appearing in 1 of 4 positions of tilt to the right of the vertical (0, 6, 19, and 30 degrees) were presented 512 times. Ss were told to judge whether or not each line was vertical with respect to the walls of the room. They were asked not to make any vocal or motor response. Ss' EEG responses were recorded. **Results:** (1) Men had lower RFT error scores than women ($p < .02$) No sex differences were found in averaged evoked-response indexes.

EXPERIMENT II: **Subjects:** $N = 31$; 14–17 yrs (patients with behavior disorders), 13–20 yrs (their siblings). **Measures:** The Rod and Frame Test was administered to Ss. They were then given the EEG averaged evoked response measure of stimulus intensity control. 4 intensities of light flashes were presented to Ss in randomized blocks of 10 of the same intensity for 480 trials. Ss' EEG responses were recorded. The response measure was the rate of increase of averaged evoked-response amplitude in relationship to the intensity of the stimulus. **Results:** (1) Male siblings had lower RFT error scores than female siblings ($p < .05$). No sex differences were found among patients. (2) Male siblings evidenced lower averaged evoked-response slopes than female siblings ($p < .05$). Male patients evidenced higher averaged evoked-response slopes than female patients ($p < .05$).

Simner, M. L. Newborn's response to the cry of another infant. *Developmental Psychology*, 1971, 5, 136–50 (and personal communication).

EXPERIMENT I: **Subjects:** $N = 94$; 2–3 days. **Measures:** Ss were exposed to the taped spontaneous cry of a 5-day-old female infant. The duration of Ss' cries was recorded. **Results:** No sex differences.

EXPERIMENT II: **Subjects:** $N = 25$; 2–3 days (15 Ss from Experiment I). **Measures:** Same as Experiment I. **Results:** No sex differences.

EXPERIMENT IV: **Subjects:** $N = 30$; 2–3 days. **Measures:** At each of 2 testings spaced 24 hours apart, Ss were exposed to the taped spontaneous cry of a 5-day-old female infant. The duration of Ss' cries was recorded. **Results:** No sex differences were found in cry duration scores. Girls' reactions to the female infant's cries were more stable than boys'.

EXPERIMENT IVa: **Subjects:** $N = 100$; 2–3 days. **Measures:** Same as Experiment I. **Results:** No sex differences.

Simon, W. E. Some sociometric evidence for validity of Coopersmith's Self-Esteem Inventory. *Perceptual & Motor Skills*, 1972, 34, 92–94.

Subjects: $N = 129$; 11 yrs. **Measures:** Coopersmith's Self-Esteem Inventory. **Results:** No sex differences.

Sistrunk, F. Negro-white comparisons in social conformity. *J. Social Psychology*, 1971, 85, 77–85.

Subjects: $N = 64$; 16–17 yrs (Upward Bound students, black and white). **Measures:** Ss were presented with a number of statements of fact and asked to indicate their agreement or disagreement with each. Before responding to each item, Ss were informed of the majority judgment of a group of persons who had been questioned previously. The number of times Ss conformed to the inaccurate response of the majority rather than give the correct answer was recorded. **Results:** Among black Ss, girls conformed more frequently than boys did. Among white Ss, no sex differences were found.

Sistrunk, F., and McDavid, J. W. Sex variable in conforming behavior. *J. Personality & Social Psychology*, 1971, *17*, 200–207.

EXPERIMENT I: **Subjects:** $N = 80$; 18–21 yrs (college). **Measures:** On each of 45 statements in a conformity measure constructed to control for the sex relatedness of items, Ss were informed whether the majority of a previous college sample had agreed or disagreed with the statement. The response measure was the number of times Ss conformed to the majority opinion. **Results:** (1) Overall, there were no sex differences in conformity. (2) By item, there were no sex differences in conformity to masculine items; men conformed to neutral and feminine items more than women.

EXPERIMENT II: **Subjects:** $N = 90$; 18–21 yrs (college). **Measures:** Same as Experiment I. **Results:** (1) Overall, no sex differences were found in conformity. (2) Women conformed to masculine items more than men did. There were no sex differences in conformity to neutral or feminine items.

EXPERIMENT III: **Subjects:** $N = 40$; 14–17 yrs. **Measures:** Same as Experiment I. **Results:** (1) There were no main sex differences. (2) Men conformed to feminine items more than women did; women conformed to masculine items more than men did. There were no sex differences in conformity to neutral items.

EXPERIMENT IV: **Subjects:** $N = 60$; 18–21 yrs (college). **Measures:** Same as Experiment I, except that Ss were told the sample on which the normative data were based had been either all male or all female. **Results:** (1) Neither sex of subject nor sex of influence source was significant as a main effect. (2) Women conformed to masculine items more than men. There were no sex differences in conformity to neutral and feminine items.

Sistrunk, F., Clement, D. E., and Guenther, Z. C. Developmental comparisons of conformity across two cultures. *Child Development*, 1971, *42*, 1175–85.

Subjects: $N = 80$; 9–10, 13–14, 17–18, 20–21 yrs (Brazil, U.S.). **Measures:** In an Asch-type conformity experiment, Ss judged which of 3 lines was longest. **Results:** Among Brazilian Ss, girls conformed more at ages 9–10 and 20–21, whereas boys conformed more at ages 13–14 and 17–18 (significance not tested). Among American Ss, no sex differences were found.

Sitkei, E. G., and Meyers, C. E. Comparative structure of intellect in middle- and lower-class four year olds of two ethnic groups. *Developmental Psychology*, 1969, *1*, 592–604.

Subjects: $N = 100$; 3–4 yrs (white and black, low and middle SES). **Measures:** Ss were given the following tests: (1) Peabody Picture Vocabulary; (2) Action-Agent Convergent (Ss must supply the right word to such sentence stems as "What runs——?"); (3) Comprehension (Ss are tested for their understanding of the WISC comprehension items); (4) Picture Description (Ss are asked to describe pictures); (5) Action-Agent Divergent (Ss must give multiple answers to such questions as "What runs——?"); (6) Orpet Utility (Ss must give multiple uses for objects); (7) Monroe Language Classification (Ss are asked to name as many examples as possible of items belonging in a certain category, e.g. animals); (8) ITPA Vocal Encoding (Ss must provide descriptions); (9) Color-Form Matching, and (10) Figure Matching (both require Ss to quickly but accurately discriminate visually presented material); (11) Pre-Raven Matrices (Ss are asked to select the right fill-in for a missing portion of a visual matrix); (12) Design Discrimination (Ss must select the 1 item in a series that differs from the others); (13) Letter Span, and (14) Binet Digits, and (15) ITPA Auditory Vocal Sequencing (Ss are required to memorize sequences of letters or digits); (16) Memory for Sentences (Ss are given the sentences-memory items of the Binet; (17) Paired Pictures, and (18) Picture Memory (after naming objects and pictures, Ss are later asked to recall or identify them); (19) Object Memory, and (20) Visual Sequence Memory (Ss are tested for their memory of objects and nonrepresentational play materials); (21) Cube Test (no explanation given); (22) Picture Description (no explanation given). **Results:** (1) Among lower SES white Ss, girls were superior to boys on the Pre-Raven Matrices, and boys were superior to girls on the Object Memory Test. (2) Among middle SES white Ss, no sex differences were found. (3) Among lower SES black Ss, girls were superior to boys on the Action-Agent Divergent and the ITPA Vocal Encoding tests, and boys were superior to girls on the Picture Memory test. (4) Among middle SES black Ss, girls were superior to boys on the Action-Agent Divergent, Letter Span, and Memory for Sentences tests.

Skolnick, E. K. Effects of stimulus availability in children's inferences. *Child Development*, 1971, *42*, 183–94.

Subjects: $N = 144$; 5, 7 yrs. **Measures:** On each trial of a concept identification task, Ss were either sequentially or simultaneously presented with 2 stimuli. Each pair differed in shape (flower or circle) or color (red or green). On the basis of information provided by E, Ss inferred which dimension was relevant and which value was correct. **Results:** No sex differences.

Skolnick, P. Reactions to personal evaluations: a failure to replicate. *J. Personality & Social Psychology*, 1971, *18*, 62–67.
> **Subjects:** $N = 114$; 18–21 yrs (college). **Measures:** Ss were induced to believe they had failed or succeeded on 2 performance tests; a control group was left uncertain as to how they performed. After receiving positive or negative evaluation from a stooge, Ss rated the stooge on a semantic differential scale. Ss then rated themselves on a similar scale and completed a questionnaire designed to measure self-esteem. **Results:** No sex differences.

Slaby, R. G. Verbal regulation of aggression and altruism in children. Paper presented at the First International Conference on the "Determinants and origins of aggressive behavior." Monte Carlo, 1973.
> EXPERIMENT I: **Subjects:** $N = 60$; 8–9 yrs. **Measures:** 24 groups of 3 words each were read to Ss. After hearing each group, Ss were asked to select 1 of the 3 words and repeat it out loud. Ss were reinforced for selecting either the aggressive, the neutral, or the helpful word in each triad. Afterward, Ss were tested for aggressive behavior on a punching machine. Ss were told another child was in an adjacent room solving arithmetic problems. Every time the other child made a mistake, Ss were asked to deliver a punch to the other child by pressing a button. The buttons were numbered 1 through 10, with number 1 supposedly delivering a soft punch, number 5 a medium punch, and number 10 a hard punch. The measure of aggressive behavior was the sum of Ss' button-press responses. **Results:** (1) No sex differences were found in Ss' performance on the verbal learning task. (2) Boys had higher aggression scores than girls ($p < .05$).
>
> EXPERIMENT II: **Subjects:** $N = 66$; 8–9 yrs. **Measures:** Same as Experiment I, except that following the verbal training procedure, Ss were tested for altruistic behavior rather than aggressive behavior. As in Experiment I, Ss were told another child was in the next room working on a set of arithmetic problems. Every time the child solved a problem correctly, Ss were asked to reward him with pennies (ranging from 1 to 5). For each trial on which Ss rewarded the child with fewer than 5 pennies, they were allowed to keep the extra money. The response measure was the total number of pennies Ss gave the other child. **Results:** (1) No sex differences were found in Ss' performance on the verbal learning task. (2) No sex differences were found in altruism scores.

Slaby, R. G., and Parke, R. D. Effect of resistance to deviation of observing a model's affective reaction to response consequences. *Developmental Psychology*, 1971, *5*, 40–47.
> **Subjects:** $N = 132$; 5–8 yrs. **Measures:** Each S watched a filmed male peer model play with prohibited toys and display either a positive, negative, or neutral emotional affect upon being socially rewarded or punished. Ss were left alone with identical toys for 15 minutes. **Results:** (1) Among Ss who saw the model rewarded and displaying no affect, boys touched the prohibited toys more often and for longer periods than girls. There were no sex differences on same measures when Ss saw the model rewarded and showing positive affect, or rewarded and showing negative affect. (2) There were no sex differences on number or duration of touches when Ss saw model punished, regardless of model's affect upon being punished. (3) There were no sex differences on latency to first touch of prohibited toys, regardless of consequences to model or model affect.

Slobin, D. I. Antonymic phonetic symbolism in three natural languages. *J. Personality & Social Psychology*, 1968, *10*, 301–5.
> **Subjects:** $N = 46$; 18–21 yrs (college). **Measures:** Ss matched English antonym pairs with antonym pairs from Thai and Kanarese. **Results:** No sex differences.

Slovic, P. Risk-taking in children: age and sex differences. *Child Development*, 1966, 37, 169–76.
> **Subjects:** $N = 1,047$; 6–16 yrs. **Measures:** Ss at a county fair performed a switch-pulling game as a measure of risk taking. **Results:** (1) Among 11-, 14-, 15-, and 16-year-old Ss, girls stopped more often than boys. (2) Girls won more candy (per person) than boys as a result of their caution.

Smart, M. S., and Smart, R. C. Self-esteem and social-personal orientation of Indian 12- and 18-year-olds. *Psychological Reports*, 1970, 27, 107–15.
> **Subjects:** $N = 267$; 11–12, 18 yrs. **Measures:** Carlson's measures of self-esteem and social-per-

sonal orientation were administered to Ss. **Results:** Among preadolescent Ss, girls had higher self-esteem scores and were more socially oriented than boys. No sex differences were found among 18-year-old Ss.

Smith, C. R., Williams, L., and Willis, R. H. Race, sex and belief as determinants of friendship acceptance. *J. Personality & Social Psychology*, 1967, 5, 127–37.
> **Experiment I: Subjects:** $N = 119$; 18–21 yrs (college). **Measures:** Ss rated each member of pairs of stimulus persons on friendship potential. Pairs of stimulus persons differed with regard to race, sex, beliefs, or combinations of any 2 of these factors. **Results:** No sex differences.
> **Experiment II: Subjects:** $N = 167$; 18–21 yrs (black college). **Measures:** Same as Experiment I. **Results:** Relative to race, belief congruence was more important for friendship acceptance among women than among men.

Smith, P. K., and Connolly, K. Patterns of play and social interaction in pre-school children. In N. B. Jones, ed., *Ethological Studies of Child Behavior*, London: Cambridge, 1972, pp. 65–95.
> **Subjects:** $N = 40$; 2–4 yrs. **Measures:** Observations were made of Ss' indoor and outdoor free-play activities. **Results:** (1) Girls talked to other children more frequently than boys did. (2) Boys made more play noises (e.g. "brr-brr," "bang") than girls did. (3) No sex differences were found in total number of vocalizations. (4) Girls engaged in sucking activities (putting a digit or a toy in contact with 1 or both lips) more often than boys did. (5) Boys engaged in rough-and-tumble play more frequently than girls did. (6) Boys' overall physical activity level was higher than that of girls.

Smith, R. E., Ascough, J. C., Ettinger, R. F., and Nelson, D. A. Humor, anxiety, and task performance. *J. Personality & Social Psychology*, 1971, 19, 243–46.
> **Subjects:** $N = 215$; 18–21 yrs (college). **Measures:** Ss were given a humorous or nonhumorous form of a course examination under standard classroom conditions. The response measure was Ss' performance on the exam. **Results:** No sex differences.

Smothergill, D. W. Accuracy and variability in the localization of spatial targets at three age levels. *Developmental Psychology*, 1973, 8, 62–66.
> **Subjects:** $N = 60$; 6–7, 9–10, 18–21 yrs (college). **Measures:** S used his left hand to mark on the underside of a pegboard the position of a target on the top of the pegboard, either while the target was present or 5, 15, or 25 seconds after removal. The target was either S's seen or unseen right index finger or a pencil. **Results:** No sex differences.

Smothergill, D. W., and Dusek, J. B. An attentional analysis of observational learning in preschool children." Unpublished manuscript, Syracuse University, 1973.
> **Subjects:** $N = 48$; 4 yrs. **Measures:** Models of the same age as Ss and of either the same or opposite sex were presented with 3 pictures of each trial and asked to guess which of the 3 pictures was preferred by E. For half the Ss (correct group), the model was told on 12 of 15 trials that he had guessed correctly and on 3 of 15 trials that he had guessed incorrectly; for the other half of the Ss (incorrect group), the model was told on 12 of 15 trials that he was incorrect and on the remaining trials that he was correct. Afterward, with duplicate pictures in front of them, Ss attempted to recall the models' choices. **Results:** No main sex differences were found. Girls performed better in the correct than in the incorrect condition; no effect was found for boys ($p < .05$).

Snow, C. E., and Rabinovitch, M. S. Conjunctive and disjunctive thinking in children. *J. Experimental Child Psychology*, 1969, 7, 1–9.
> **Subjects:** $N = 97$; 5–13 yrs. **Measures:** Ss performed conjunctive and disjunctive concept card tasks. Cards were sorted into 2 groups on the basis of some rule, using both positive and negative instances of that rule. **Results:** No sex differences.

Solkoff, N. Race of experimenter as a variable in research with children. *Developmental Psychology*, 1972, 7, 70–75.
> **Subjects:** $N = 224$; 8–11 yrs. **Measures:** Each S was picked up at home by the same black woman and transported to E's office, where each completed the Sarason Test Anxiety Scale for Children and the Wechsler Intelligence Scale for Children (without maze subtest), administered by either a black or white female E. **Results:** (1) Boys had higher scores on the Picture Completion and Object Assembly performance of WISC than girls. Girls scored higher on Coding performance subtest than boys. (2) No sex differences in test anxiety scores.

Solomon, D., and Ali, F. A. Age trends in the perception of verbal reinforcers. *Developmental Psychology*, 1972, 7, 238–43.
> **Subjects:** N = 294; 5, 7, 9, 11, 13, 15, 17, 21–25 yrs (college). **Measures:** Ss listened to a tape recording of a teacher making evaluative comments to children in her class. The comments were positive, neutral, or negative in content, and were said in a pleased, indifferent, or displeased tone of voice. The tape contained all combinations of content and intonation. After hearing each of the teacher's comments, Ss were asked 3 questions: (1) "What did the teacher mean?" (2) "How does the child feel?" and (3) "Does the teacher like or dislike the child?" **Results:** (1) In answer to questions 2 and 3, boys displayed more positive perceptions than girls ($p < .01$, $p < .05$). The sex differences were of greatest magnitude among 5-year-old Ss. (2) In answer to questions 1 and 2, girls showed more responsiveness to changes in intonation than boys ($p < .001$, $p < .05$).

Solomon, O., Houlihan, K. A., and Pareluis, R. J. Intellectual achievement responsibility in Negro and white children. *Psychological Reports*, 1969, 24, 479–83.
> **Subjects:** N = 262; 9, 11 yrs. **Measures:** Ss were given the Intellectual Achievement Responsibility Questionnaire, which yielded 2 subscale scores and a total score. The I+ and I– subscales measured Ss' respective tendencies to see themselves as responsible for the positive and negative reinforcement they received in intellectual academic situations. The total I score measured Ss' acceptance of responsibility for the outcomes of their achievement efforts. **Results:** Among white Ss, girls had higher I+ ($p < .01$) and total I ($p < .01$) scores than boys (high scores in each case represent internal responsibility; low scores represent external responsibility). Among black Ss, no sex differences were found.

Spear, P. S., and Spear, S. A. Social reinforcement, discrimination learning, and retention in children. *Developmental Psychology*, 1972, 7, 220 (extended version of brief report).
> **Subjects:** N = 192; 6–7, 10–11 yrs. **Measures:** Ss performed a series of 2-choice simultaneous discrimination problems with immediate accuracy feedback under 1 of 3 reinforcement conditions: praise, criticism, silence. Retention was tested 8 days later. **Results:** No sex differences.

Speer, D. C. Marital dysfunctionality and two-person non-zero-sum game behavior. *J. Personality & Social Psychology*, 1972, 21, 18–24.
> **Subjects:** N = 120; adult married couples. **Measures:** Prisoner's Dilemma game. **Results:** No sex differences.

Speer, D. C., Briggs, P. F., and Gavolas, R. Concurrent schedules of social reinforcement and dependency behavior among four-year-old children. *J. Experimental Child Psychology*, 1969, 8, 356–65.
> **Subjects:** N = 40; 4 yrs. **Measures:** Ss performed a puzzle-completion task. Responses were coded as dependent or competent and were subjected to different schedules of social reinforcement. **Results:** Girls emitted more dependent responses during extinction than boys did, ($p < .05$). No other sex differences were found.

Spence, J. T. Verbal-discrimination performance as a function of instructions and verbal-reinforcement combination in normal and retarded children. *Child Development*, 1966, 37, 269–81.
> **Subjects:** N = 192; 7–9 yrs (normal), 10–19 yrs (retardates). **Measures:** Ss were given a verbal discrimination task. Ss in the "informed" condition were instructed about the meaning of reinforcers and the meaning of "blank." Ss in the "uninformed" condition received no explanation of reinforcement procedures. Ss were reinforced by "right" after correct choices and nothing after incorrect responses, by "wrong" after incorrect choices and nothing after correct responses, or by "right" or "wrong" after each choice. The task was administered for 16 trials, or until the criterion of 2 successive perfect trials. **Results:** No sex differences.

Spence, J. T. Do material rewards enhance the performance of lower class children? *Child Development*, 1971, 42, 1461–60.
> **Subjects:** N = 64; 5 yrs (black, low SES). **Measures:** Trained or untrained, Ss performed in a conceptual task and received either symbolic (light flash) or material (M&M) reward. Experiments I and II were identical. **Results:** No main sex differences.

Spence, J. T. Verbal and nonverbal rewards and punishments in the discrimination learning of children of varying socioeconomic status. *Developmental Psychology*, 1972, 6, 381–84.

Subjects: $N = 200$; 4–5 yrs (low, middle SES). Measures: Ss performed a 2-choice discrimination-learning task (choosing pictures) under 1 of 4 conditions: nonverbal reward, nonverbal punishment, verbal reward, and verbal punishment. Results: No sex differences.

Spitz, H. H., Goettler, D. R., and Diveley, S. L. A comparison of retardates and normals on the Poggendorff and Oppel-Kundt Illusions. *Developmental Psychology*, 1970, *3*, 48–65.
Subjects: $N = 112$; 9, 15, 35 yrs. Measures: Ss were tested on the Poggendorff and Oppel-Kundt (filled space) illusions. Results: No sex differences.

Spitz, H. H., Goettler, D. R., and Webreck, C. A. Effects of two types of redundancy on visual digit span performance of retardates and varying aged normals. *Developmental Psychology*, 1972, *6*, 92–103.
Experiment I: Subjects: $N = 120$; 9, 13, 20 yrs (normal), 15 yrs (retardates). Measures: Ss viewed a digit series under 3 types of redundancy conditions: repetition, couplet, or nonredundancy. Ss were asked for recall. Results: No sex differences.
Experiment II: Subjects: $N = 90$; 8, 17 yrs (normal), 15 yrs (retardates). Measures: Same as Experiment I, except that repetition redundancy was emphasized by spatial separation, underlining, and punctuation. Results: No sex differences.
Experiment III: Subjects: $N = 22$; adults. Measures: Same as Experiments I and II, except that there was no external organization. Results: No sex differences.
Experiment IV: Subjects: $N = 44$; 14–17 yrs. Measures: Half of the Ss received nonredundant digits plus externally organized repetition redundancy. The other half received redundant digits, plus digits containing externally organized couplet redundancy. Results: No sex differences.

Stabler, J. R., and Johnson, E. E. Instrumental performance as a function of reinforcement schedule, luck versus skill instructions, and sex of child. *J. Experimental Child Psychology*, 1970, *9*, 330–35.
Subjects: $N = 64$; 5 yrs. Measures: Ss pressed telegraph keys to obtain prizes. They received luck or skill instructions, partial or continuous reinforcement. Results: Girls showed more resistance to extinction than boys did.

Stabler, J. R., Johnson, E. E., and Jordan, S. E. The measurement of children's self-concepts as related to racial membership. *Child Development*, 1971, *42*, 2094–97 (brief report).
Subjects: $N = 60$; 5 yrs (white, black). Measures: Ss viewed a black box and a white box and were asked to choose which of the 2 boxes emitted negative or positive self-concept statements. On each trial, the 2 boxes emitted the same statement with equal intensity. Results: No sex differences.

Stafford, R. E. Sex differences in spatial visualization as evidence of sex-linked inheritance. *Perceptual & Motor Skills*, 1961, *13*, 428.
Subjects: $N = 232$; teenagers and their parents. Measures: Identical Blocks Test. Results: In both age groups, males scored higher than females.

Stanes, D. Analytic responses to conceptual style test as a function of instructions. *Child Development*, 1973, *44*, 389–91.
Subjects: $N = 60$; 6 yrs. Measures: Ss were given the Conceptual Styles Test with varied instructions: choose pictures that "are alike," "go together," or "are alike or go together." Results: Boys made more analytic responses than girls.

Stanford Research Institute. Follow-through pupil tests, parent interviews, and teacher questionnaires. Appendix C, 1972.
Subjects: $N =$ approx. 13,000 (total tested); 5, 7 yrs. Measures: Follow-through test batteries were administered to Ss after completion of a Head Start program. Some Ss were tested longitudinally, others were not. Results: Girls performed better than boys on the tests of reading knowledge ($N = 13,155$), language ability ($N = 7,101$), and quantitative ability (New York Alpha, $N = 6,607$). Girls also had higher scores on the Wide Range Achievement Test ($N = 7,301$).

Staub, E. A child in distress: the influence of age and number of witnesses on children's attempts to help. *J. Personality & Social Psychology*, 1970, *14*, 130–40.
Subjects: $N = 232$; 5, 6, 7, 9, 11 yrs. Measures: Ss' responses to the tape-recorded sounds of

a child (in an adjoining room) in severe distress were recorded. Ss were either alone or in same-sex pairs. **Results:** No sex differences were found in helping behavior.

Staub, E. A child in distress: the influence of nurturance and modeling on children's attempts to help. *Developmental Psychology*, 1971a, 5, 124–32.
Subjects: $N = 64$; 5 yrs. **Measures:** After interacting with Ss in either a nurturant or non-nurturant manner, E went into an adjoining room either to help a girl who had fallen down (Ss heard tape-recorded sounds of mild distress) or to check on the girl who was in there (no distress cues). After returning to tell Ss what had happened, E left to do some work. Ss' responses to subsequent sounds of severe distress from the adjoining room were recorded. **Results:** No sex differences were found in Ss' helping responses.

Staub, E. Helping a person in distress: the influence of implicit and explicit "rules" of conduct on children and adults. *J. Personality & Social Psychology*, 1971b, 17, 137–44.
Subjects: $N = 40$; 12 yrs. **Measures:** Ss were exposed to tape-recorded sounds of a young girl in distress in an adjoining room. **Results:** No sex differences were found in Ss' responses to the distress cue.

Staub, E. The use of role playing and induction in children's learning of helping and sharing behavior. *Child Development*, 1971c, 42, 805–16.
Subjects: $N = 75$; 5 yrs. **Measures:** Same-sex pairs participated in the first session, opposite-sex pairs in the second. Experimental treatments included role playing (Ss enacted situations in which 1 needed help and 1 provided help), induction (Ss provided verbal solutions to the same situations as in role playing), role playing with induction, and control (Ss acted scenes unrelated to helping). For the specific post-test, Ss heard distress sounds coming from a room in which they knew a child was alone; Ss' behavior following noises was observed for helping responses. Then E played a game with Ss during which E spilled paper clips; Ss' helping behavior was observed with and without E; 1 of the post-tests was delayed 5–7 days. Sharing behavior was assessed by the number of candies Ss were willing to put aside for a poor child. **Results:** In the role-playing group, girls helped the child in distress more than boys, while boys donated more candies than girls ($p < .01$, $p < .01$). There were no other main sex effects.

Staub, E. Effects of persuasion and modeling on delay of gratification. *Developmental Psychology*, 1972, 6, 166–77.
Subjects: $N = 144$; 12 yrs. **Measures:** After a base-rate delay-of-gratification measure was obtained, Ss were exposed to 1 of 4 experimental treatments aimed at changing delay behaviors: persuasion by a "scientist" who had done research on the topic, modeling of delayed choice behaviors by a scientist, a neutral speech by a scientist describing her research (control), or a recommendation that Ss choose larger, more valuable rewards (same basic speech as in control). An immediate post-test was given on behavior and attitude measures. A delayed post-test was given 2 weeks later. **Results:** (1) Overall, girls chose a larger number of delayed objects than boys ($p < .05$). (2) There were no other main sex effects.

Staub, E., and Sherk, L. Need for approval, children's sharing behavior, and reciprocity in sharing. *Child Development*, 1970, 41, 243–53.
Subjects: $N = 90$; 9 yrs. **Measures:** Ss responded to a questionnaire that assessed their need for approval, friendship choices, and candy preferences. Each S listened to a taped story with a same-sex child in the room. S was given a bag of his favorite candy to eat during the story. Sharing behavior was observed. E asked S and the other child to draw a picture about the story, but only gave a crayon to the other child. Again, sharing behavior was observed. **Results:** Boys shared more candy than girls did ($p < .02$). No sex differences in need for approval.

Stayton, D. J., Hogan, R., and Ainsworth, M. D. S. Infant obedience and maternal behavior: the origins of socialization reconsidered. *Child Development*, 1971, 42, 1057–69.
Subjects: $N = 25$; 9–12 mos and mothers. **Measures:** Mother-infant pairs were observed at 3-week intervals in their homes. The degree of harmony in the interaction between mother and child was rated on 3 scales: sensitivity-insensitivity, acceptance-rejection, and cooperation-interference. Mothers were also scored for frequency of verbal commands, frequency of discipline-oriented physical interventions, and extent of floor freedom permitted the child. There were 27 measures of infant behavior recorded: frequency of compliance to maternal commands and frequency of display of self-inhibiting, self-controlling behaviors. Infants were also given the Griffiths Scale of Mental Development. **Results:** No sex differences.

Stayton, S. E. Sensory organization in retardates and normals. *Developmental Psychology*, 1970a, *2*, 66–70.

Subjects: $N = 112$; 16 yrs (normals, retardates). Measures: Ss were asked to take marbles, 1 at a time, from a box of 5 white and 5 black marbles and place them in test tubes. The sequence in which Ss transferred the marbles was recorded. The retardates' scores on the Stanford-Binet and the normal Ss' scores on the Science Research Associates Test of Educational Ability were obtained. Results: (1) Among normal Ss, boys produced fewer sensory sequences (transferring all 5 marbles of 1 color, then all 5 of the other color) than girls did ($p < .025$). (2) Among retarded Ss, boys produced more sensory sequences ($p < .05$) and fewer alternating sequences ($p < .02$) than girls did. (3) No sex differences were found in normal Ss' ability quotients or in retarded Ss' IQs.

Stayton, S. E. Sensory organization and intelligence: a modification and replication. *Developmental Psychology*, 1970b, *3*, 146.

Subjects: $N = 192$; 17 yrs (retardates). Measures: Equal numbers of black and white beads were placed in front of Ss. Ss were told to pick up the beads 1 at a time and make the best bead chain they could. Results: No sex differences were found in the frequency of sensory sequences (all beads of 1 color strung first, then all beads of the other color) or of alternating sequences (black-white-black-white, etc.).

Steele, L. P., and Horowitz, A. B. "Looking versus remembering: A comparison of the mediational activity of kindergarten children in three retention tasks." Paper presented at the Society for Research in Child Development Conference, Philadelphia, 1973.

Subjects: $N = 72$; 6 yrs. Measures: Ss were told either to look at or to try to remember a series of 12 single-line drawings of common objects. Afterward, retention of the stimuli was tested in 1 of 3 ways. Ss in 1 group were asked to recall the names of as many as possible of the objects. Ss in a second group were asked to choose from among 36 drawings those that they had seen. Ss in a third group listened as E read the names of 36 objects to them. Ss were asked to respond whenever E named an object that had been included in the set of 12 drawings. Results: No sex differences.

Stein, A. H. The influence of social reinforcement on the achievement behavior of fourth grade boys and girls. *Child Development*, 1969, *40*, 727–36.

Subjects: $N = 160$; 9 yrs. Measures: Ss performed a digit-letter coding task under neutral conditions for 3 minutes, then under 1 of 4 treatment conditions (praise, correct, disapproval, alone) for 7 minutes. In the praise condition, E made general praising statements such as "Good" and "Fine." In the correct condition, E emphasized to Ss the accuracy of their responses (e.g. "You're getting them right"). In the disapproval condition, E made general statements of disapproval (e.g. "You're not doing too well"). In the alone condition, Ss completed the task without E present. Changes in response rates from the neutral to the experimental conditions were recorded. Results: (1) Girls had higher response rates in the neutral condition than boys ($p < .01$). (2) No sex differences were found in changes in rates of response. In the disapproval condition, the variance of the girls was larger than that of the boys. (3) Sex of E had no effect on Ss' scores.

Stein, A. H., Pohly, S., Pohly, R., and Mueller, E. The influence of masculine, feminine, and neutral tasks on children's achievement behavior, expectancies of success, and attainment values. *Child Development*, 1971, *42*, 195–207.

Subjects: $N = 96$; 11 yrs. Measures: 3 tasks involving digit-letter coding, copying the letters of foreign alphabets, and drawing lines between the double borders of figures were administered to Ss. Each task was presented as masculine, feminine, or neutral. At the beginning of the experiment, Ss stated the score they expected to receive on each task. Ss were then given 10 minutes to complete all 3 tasks. The amount of time Ss spent on each task was recorded. Afterward, Ss were asked (1) how important was it for them to do well on each task (attainment value), (2) which tasks they liked most and least, and (3) which tasks they considered hardest and easiest. Results: (1) Boys' expectancy and attainment value scores were highest on masculine tasks and lowest on feminine tasks; girls' expectancy and attainment value scores were lower on masculine tasks than on either feminine or neutral tasks ($p < .01$). (2) Attainment value scores were higher with male Es than with female Es ($p < .05$). Expectancy scores on the feminine task were lower with a female E than with a male E ($p < .05$). (3) Boys spent the greatest amount of time on the masculine task, and the least amount of time on the feminine task ($p < .001$). Girls spent about the same amount of time on all 3 tasks. (4) For boys, the difference between the time spent on masculine and feminine tests was greater with male Es than with female Es. Sex of E did not influence the pattern of time scores for girls. (5) Boys liked the masculine tests most and the feminine tests least ($p < .001$); girls liked the tests equally well. Neither sex group attributed differences in difficulty to the 3 tests.

Stein, H. A., and Smithells, J. Age and sex differences in children's sex-role standards about achievement. *Developmental Psychology*, 1969, *1*, 252–59.
    Subjects: $N = 120$; 7, 11, 17 yrs. **Measures:** Ss were successively presented with 42 items representing 6 areas of achievement: athletic, spatial and mechanical, arithmetic, reading, artistic, and social skills. 7 items were included for each area: 6 described specific activities, and 1 was a general item intended to portray the area as a whole. Ss judged whether the activity described in each item was more masculine or more feminine. **Results:** (1) Girls made more feminine choices than boys ($p < .01$). The sex difference was greatest at age 7, intermediate at age 11, and negligible at age 17 ($p < .05$). (2) Among 7-year-old and 11-year-old Ss, boys rated more athletic items as masculine than girls ($p < .01$, $p < .01$). (3) Among 7-year-old Ss, girls rated more reading items as feminine than boys ($p < .01$). (4) No sex differences were found in Ss' rank-orderings.

Stein, K. B., and Lenrow, P. Expressive styles and their measurement. *J. Personality & Social Psychology*, 1970, *16*, 656–64.
    Subjects: $N = 249$; 18–21 yrs (college). **Measures:** Ss rated their degree of interest in activities that were either motoric, ideational, or sensory-perceptual. **Results:** Women showed greater interest in sensory-perceptual activities than men ($p < .01$). Men showed a greater interest in motoric activities than women ($p < .01$). No sex differences were found in Ss' preferences for ideational activities.

Stevenson, A. H., and Lynn, D. B. Preference for high variability in young children. *Psychonomic Science*, 1971, *23*, 143–44.
    Subjects: $N = 88$; 3–7 yrs. **Measures:** Ss' preferences for random shapes of varying number of turns were assessed. **Results:** Boys had a higher preference for variability than girls ($p < .05$).

Stevenson, H. W., and Odom, R. D. Visual reinforcement with children. *J. Experimental Child Psychology*, 1964, *1*, 248–55.
    Subjects: $N = 192$; 6–7, 10–11 yrs. **Measures:** Ss performed a simple bar-pressing task. After their base rates were obtained, visual reinforcers were presented for a period of 6 minutes. 3 types of visual reinforcers were used: colored drawings of animals, line drawings of common objects, and hues. A 4-minute extinction phase was introduced immediately after termination of the reinforcement period. Difference scores were computed by subtracting each child's base rate from his response rate during the reinforcement and extinction periods. **Results:** (1) No sex differences were found in response rates during the baseline period. (2) During the reinforcement period, older boys showed a greater increase in response rate across minutes than older girls did ($p < .001$). (3) During extinction, older boys had higher difference scores than older girls ($p < .025$).

Stevenson, H. W., and Odom, R. D. The relation of anxiety to children's performance on learning and problem-solving tasks. *Child Development*, 1965, *36*, 1003–12.
    Subjects: $N = 318$; 9, 11 yrs. **Measures:** (1) Test Anxiety Scale for Children (A), (2) Defensiveness Scale for Children (D), (3) Anagrams task, (4) Paired associates learning task. (5) On each trial of a concept identification task, Ss were presented with a pair of geometric shapes that varied in size (large or small) and brightness (black or white). Ss' task was to learn which dimension was relevant, size or brightness, and which value within that dimension was correct. **Results:** Among 11-year-old Ss, girls had higher A scores and higher D scores than boys ($p < .01$, $p < .01$). Among 9-year-old Ss, girls had higher D scores than boys ($p < .01$). No other sex differences were found.

Stevenson, H. W., Hill, K. T., Hale, G. A., and Moely, B. E. Adult ratings of children's behavior. *Child Development*, 1966, *37*, 929–41.
    Subjects: $N = 862$; 17–23, above 24 (college). **Measures:** Ss watched a film consisting of 1-minute interviews with each of 20 third-grade children and 20 sixth-grade children. Children were questioned about their activities and interests. Each child was rated by Ss on 7-point bipolar adjective scales. **Results:** (1) Women rated the children in both grades as being more attractive, definite, friendly, colorful, pleasant, mature, and sociable than men did. (2) On the masculine-feminine scale, women's ratings of boys and girls were more extreme than men's ratings. (3) Girls in both grades were rated as being more feminine, interested, jolly, warm, friendly, pleasant, sensitive and sociable than boys. Among third-grade children, girls

were rated as being more calm, mature, colorless, timid, passive, shy, and nonassertive than boys. Among sixth-grade Ss, girls were rated as being more definite, active, agitated, enthusiastic, and bright than boys.

Stevenson, H. W., Hale, G. A., Hill, K. T., and Moely, B. E. Determinants of children's preferences for adults. *Child Development*, 1967, 38, 1–14.
    Subjects: $N = 1,930$; 5–11 yrs (low, middle SES). **Measures:** Ss watched films of marble-dropping game in which men and women portraying supportive and neutral roles reinforced the performance of a child playing the game. After viewing each film, Ss were asked to choose which adult they would prefer to play with. 3 types of films were shown: (1) supportive-neutral: Ss chose between same-sex pair of adults on the basis of their role (supportive or neutral) in the film; (2) male-female: Ss chose between a male and a female adult, both of whom were either supportive or neutral; (3) mixed: Ss chose between a male and a female adult, 1 of whom was supportive and the other neutral. **Results:** For male-female films, all Ss chose the adult of their own sex more frequently than chance (for films in which both adults played a neutral role, $p < .01$; for films in which both adults played a supportive role, no test of significance was reported).

Stevenson, H. W., Hale, G. A., Klein, R. E., and Miller, L. K. Interrelations and correlates in children's learning and problem solving. *Monographs of the Society for Research in Child Development*, 1968a, 33.
    Experiment I: Subjects: $N = 256$; 12–14 yrs. **Measures:** Ss performed the following tasks: anagram, concept of probability regarding faces and pegs, conservation of volume, verbal memory (questions about a story), paired-associates, discrimination learning, and probability-learning and incidental-learning. IQ scores on the Thorndike and Iowa Tests of Basic Skills were obtained. **Results:** (1) Girls performed better than boys on incidental learning tasks and verbal memory (some IQ groups). (2) Among high-IQ Ss, girls performed better than boys on paired-associates (abstract forms). Boys performed better than girls on concept of probability. (3) Among low-IQ Ss, girls performed better than boys on discrimination-learning, verbal memory, and anagrams.
    Experiment II: Subjects: $N = 475$; 8–12 yrs. **Measures:** Similar to Experiment I. **Results:** Girls did better than boys on incidental learning and anagrams.

Stevenson, H. W., Klein, R. E., Hale, G. A., and Miller, L. K. Solution of anagrams: a developmental study. *Child Development*, 1968b, 39, 905–12.
    Subjects $N = 529$; 8–14 yrs. **Measures:** Ss were instructed to make as many English words as possible from a given word ("generation"). **Results:** At all age levels, girls performed at a higher level than boys.

Stevenson, H. W., Friedricks, A. G., and Simpson, W. E. Learning and problem solving by the mentally retarded under three testing conditions. *Developmental Psychology*, 1970, 3, 307–12.
    Subjects: $N = 96$; 14 yrs. **Measures:** Ss performed paired-associates, discrimination-learning, incidental-learning, verbal-memory, and anagram tasks with a male or female E under conditions of group testing, with an individual testing with a neutral E, or with an individual testing with supportive E. **Results:** (1) During individual testing, girls performed at a higher level than boys in incidental learning ($p < .05$). (2) During group testing, girls performed at a higher level than boys on anagrams ($p < .05$). (3) No sex differences in paired associates or discrimination learning.

Stiller, A., Schwartz, H. A., and Cowen, E. L. The social desirability of trait-descriptive terms among high-school students. *Child Development*, 1965, 36, 981–1002.
    Subjects: $N = 465$; 14, 17 yrs (low, high SES). **Measures:** Ss were asked to rate a series of 114 trait-descriptive adjectives along a 7-point scale of social desirability. **Results:** Girls produced more extreme social desirability ratings and were more variable than boys ($p < .001$, $p < .001$).

Stingle, S. F. Age and sex differences in the cooperative and competitive behavior of children. Unpublished doctoral dissertation, Columbia University, 1973.
    Subjects: $N = 126$; 5, 8, 11 yrs. **Measures:** Same-sex or opposite-sex pairs of Ss played an unspecified cooperative-competitive task. The task was structured so that cooperative behavior maximized reward achievement. Measures were taken of latency (time per trial), type of goal achieved (individual reward goal, joint reward goal, no goal), and number of rewards. **Results:**

11-year-old boy pairs were more competitive than all other pairs in terms of latency, but not in terms of rewards achieved.

Stodolsky, S. S. How children find something to do in preschools. Paper submitted for publication, University of Chicago, 1971.
> EXPERIMENT I: **Subjects:** $N = 35$; 3–5 yrs (black, low SES; white and black, middle SES). **Measures:** Observations were made of Ss' free-play activities. **Results:** (1) Among low SES black Ss, average length of activity segments was longer for girls than for boys. Girls were observed more often than boys in 1 activity for the entire length of the observation period (15 minutes). Boys changed activities more often than girls. Boys spent less time in activities than girls (an activity was defined as a stream of behavior at least 1 minute in length, with a focus and a beginning, middle, and end). (2) No sex differences were found among middle SES subjects.
> EXPERIMENT II: **Subjects:** $N = 38$; 4–6 yrs (white and black, middle SES). **Measures:** Same as Experiment I. **Results:** No sex differences.

Stone, L. J., and Hokanson, J. E. Arousal reduction via self-punitive behavior. *J. Personality & Social Psychology*, 1969, *12*, 72–79.
> **Subjects:** $N = 14$; 18–21 yrs (college). **Measures:** Following receipt of a shock, a reward, or neither from a confederate (C), Ss performed 1 of 3 counterresponses: they could deliver a shock or a reward to C or they could shock themselves. During the baseline and extinction phases, C's behavior was random. If Ss pressed the self-shock button following receipt of a shock from C (during the conditioning phase), on the next trial a reward followed from C with a 0.9 probability. Pressing the self-shock button was adaptive in such circumstances, since the self-imposed shock was of a lower magnitude than the shock delivered by C. The response measure was the plethysmographic recovery time on those trials on which Ss received a shock from C. **Results:** No sex differences were found during baseline, conditioning, or extinction. Both sexes showed an increase in the self-shock counterresponse during the conditioning phase.

Stouwie, R. J. Inconsistent verbal instructions and children's resistance to temptation behavior. *Child Development*, 1971, *42*, 1517–31 (and personal communication).
> **Subjects:** $N = 120$; 7, 8 yrs. **Measures:** Ss were placed in a room with 9 toys (previously judged to be of equal attractiveness to boys and girls). Ss were assigned to 1 of 4 conditions. In the first condition both a man and a woman told Ss not to play with the toys. In a second condition the woman told Ss they could play with the toys, and the man prohibited them from doing so. In a third condition the two adults reversed roles. In the fourth condition both adults allowed Ss to play with the toys. Following the adults' departure, Ss were observed for 15 minutes. Measures were taken of latency of S's first deviant response, the number of times he touched the toys, and the amount of time he spent in contact with the toys. **Results:** (1) Boys had shorter latencies than girls. (2) Girls spent less time touching the toys than boys did.

Stouwie, R. J. An experimental study of adult dominance and warmth, conflicting verbal instructions, and children's moral behavior. *Child Development*, 1972, *43*, 959–71 (and personal communication).
> **Subjects:** $N = 112$; 7, 8 yrs. **Measures:** Ss were shown 9 toys previously judged to be equally attractive to boys and girls. Ss were then introduced to an adult male and female, one of whom was dominant, the other warm. After interacting with Ss for 5 minutes, 1 of the adults instructed the Ss not to play with the toys, whereas the other gave Ss permission to do so. Ss were then left alone for 15 minutes. The latency of Ss' first deviant responses, the number of times Ss touched the toys, the total amount of time Ss spent in physical contact with the toys, and the average duration of Ss' deviations were recorded. Weighted scores for each of the last 3 measures were calculated by assigning higher values to toys farthest from Ss. **Results:** (1) No sex differences were found in latency of first deviant response or in number of deviations. (2) Boys had higher weighted duration scores (time spent touching the toys) than girls ($p < .05$). (3) The average duration of boys' deviations was longer than that of girls.

Stouwie, R. J., Hetherington, E. M., and Parke, R. D. Some determinants of children's self-reward criteria. *Developmental Psychology*, 1970, *3*, 313–19.
> **Subjects:** $N = 156$; 8–9 yrs. **Measures:** High and low achievement orientation was determined by the number of seconds Ss used on 5 embedded figures tasks. Ss participated in a bowling game with a male or female adult who set higher standards for Ss' reward than for self-reward. Afterward, Ss played alone. Self-reward standards were assessed. **Results:** (1)

There were no sex differences in achievement orientation. (2) Children who interacted with the female model took fewer rewards than those who interacted with the male model ($p < .05$). (3) There were no sex differences in self-reward standards.

Strain, G. S., Unikel, I. P., and Adams, H. E. Alternation behavior by children from lower socioeconomic status groups. *Developmental Psychology*, 1969, *1*, 131–33.
  Subjects: $N = 48$; 5, 6 yrs (low, middle SES). **Measures:** Ss were successively presented with 5 dishes containing an equal number of 2 different colors of M&M's. Ss were asked to take 1 piece of candy from each dish. Measures were taken of the number of times Ss alternated their choice of colors. **Results:** Among low SES subjects, boys alternated less often than girls ($p < .001$). Among middle SES subjects, no sex differences were found.

Strayer, J., and Ames, E. W. Stimulus orientation and the apparent development lag between perception and performance. *Child Development*, 1972, *43*, 1345–54 (and personal communication).
  Subjects: $N = 40$; 4–5 yrs. **Measures:** All Ss were given a form-board task, a pretraining copying test, programmed discrimination training, and a post-training copying test. Forms to be copied were the same as those presented in the form-board. **Results:** (1) Girls made fewer training errors than boys ($p < .05$), especially on the Rhombus vs. Diamond item ($p < .01$) and on the Left vs. Right Oblique item ($p < .05$). (2) There were no sex differences on form-board errors, latencies, or pretest or post-test copying performance.

Stricker, L. J., Messick, S., and Jackson, D. N. Suspicion of deception: implications for conformity research. *J. Personality & Social Psychology*, 1967, *5*, 379–89.
  Subjects: $N = 190$; 16–17 yrs. **Measures:** After participating in a simulated group version of the Asch situation and responding to questionnaires containing fictitious group norms, Ss completed open-ended questionnaires concerning their perceptions of the purpose and method of each study. Based on their responses, Ss were classified as either suspicious, unsuspicious, or indeterminate. **Results:** Boys were more suspicious than girls about the purpose and method of the simulated group experiment, and about the method of the questionnaire study ($p < .05$). No sex differences were found in Ss' suspicions about the purpose of the questionnaire.

Stricker, L. J., Messick, S., and Jackson, D. N. Conformity, anticonformity, and independence: their dimensionality and generality. *J. Personality & Social Psychology*, 1970, *16*, 494–507.
  Subjects: $N = 190$; 16–18 yrs. **Measures:** Ss both estimated the number of clicks they heard and responded to attitude items in an Asch-type situation. Ss also completed 2 questionnaires (estimating probabilities of events, responding to attitude statements) with the purported average answers for the group provided. Responses from an initial administration of each questionnaire in which Ss answered without knowledge of the ostensible group norms were compared with Ss' responses after exposure to group judgments. Conformity, anticonformity, and independence scores were calculated for each measure. **Results:** No main sex differences were found. Among unsuspicious Ss, girls were less conforming and more independent on the attitude questionnaire, and less anti-conforming on the Asch situations than boys.

Strickland, B. R. Aspiration responses among Negro and white adolescents. *J. Personality & Social Psychology*, 1971, *19*, 315–20.
  Subjects: $N = 120$; 14 yrs (low, middle SES). **Measures:** The Rotter Level of Aspiration Board. **Results:** Among middle SES subjects of both races, boys had higher aspiration levels than girls ($p < .01$). There were no sex differences in frequency of shifts or number of unusual shifts in level of aspiration.

Strickland, B. R. Delay of gratification as a function of race of the experimenter, *J. Personality & Social Psychology*, 1972, *22*, 108–12.
  Subjects: $N = 300$; 11–13 yrs (black, white). **Measures:** For completing a locus-of-control measure, Ss were offered either 1 record as an immediate reward or 3 records if they agreed to wait for E (either a black or white male) to return 3 weeks later. **Results:** No sex differences were found in number of delayed vs. immediate choices.

Stroebe, W., Insko, C. A., Thompson, V. D., and Layton, B. D. Effects of physical attractiveness, attitude similarity, and sex on various aspects of interpersonal attraction. *J. Personality & Social Psychology*, 1971, *18*, 79–91.
  Subjects: $N = 200$; 18–21 yrs (college). **Measures:** Ss' attraction to opposite-sex others of high, medium, or low physical attractiveness, and of similar, moderately similar, or dissimilar

attitudes, was measured in terms of Ss' liking for other, Ss' preference for other as a co-worker, and whether or not Ss would consider other as a dating or a marriage partner. **Results:** (1) There were no main sex effects. (2) On 3 of the 4 variables (working dating, marrying), effects of physical attractiveness were stronger for men than for women. (3) On 2 of the 4 variables (liking, working), women were more influenced by similarity than men were.

Strongman, K. T., and Champness, B. G. Dominance hierarchies and conflict in eye contact. *Acta Psychologica*, 1968, *28*, 376–86.
    Subjects: $N = 10$; 18–21 yrs. **Measures:** Each S was paired with each of the other Ss for a period of 2 minutes. Before meeting their partners, Ss were instructed to use the 2 minutes to "become acquainted." Measures were taken of eye contact, directed gaze, and speech with gaze. **Results:** No sex differences.

Strutl, G. F., Anderson, D. R., and Well, A. D. Developmental trends in the effects of irrelevant information on speeded classification. Paper presented to the Society for Research in Child Development, Philadelphia, 1973.
    Subjects: $N = 54$; 6, 9, 12 yrs. **Measures:** Ss were instructed to sort cards into 2 piles as quickly as possible. In sorting, 1 dimension of the stimuli on the cards was relevant, whereas either 0, 1, or 2 dimensions were irrelevant. Ss were informed which dimension was relevant before beginning. **Results:** Sorting times were lower for girls than for boys, especially at the younger ages.

Stuart, I. R., Breslow, A., Brechner, S., Ilyus, R. B., and Wolpoff, M. The question of constitutional influence on perceptual style. *Perceptual & Motor Skills*, 1965, *20*, 419–20.
    Subjects: $N = 64$; 17–25 yrs. **Measures:** Embedded Figures Test, Short Form. **Results:** No sex differences.

Suchman, R. G. Color-form preference, discriminative accuracy, and learning of deaf and hearing children. *Child Development*, 1966, *37*, 439–51.
    Subjects: $N = 72$; 7–12 yrs. **Measures:** Ss were given 2 tests of color-form preference. Discriminative accuracy was tested within color and form dimensions. Successive discrimination was tested, using form-only problems, color-only problems, and color-form combination problems. **Results:** No sex differences.

Sullivan, E. V., McCullough, G., and Stager, M. A developmental study of the relationship between conceptual, ego, and moral development. *Child Development*, 1970, *41*, 399–411.
    Subjects: $N = 120$; 12, 14, 17 yrs. **Measures:** Hunt and Halverson's Conceptual Level Questionnaire, Kohlberg's Moral Development Test, Loevinger and Wessler's Ego Development Test. **Results:** No sex differences.

Sumners, D. L., and Felker, D. W. Use of the It Scale for Children in assessing sex-role preference in preschool Negro children. *Developmental Psychology*, 1970, *2*, 330–34.
    Subjects: $N = 30$; 5 yrs. **Measures:** The It Scale for Children was administered to Ss twice, once with the It figure as the projective device and once with a picture of a child drawn by Ss as the projective device. **Results:** On both administrations, boys obtained more masculine scores than girls.

Sundberg, N., and Ballinger, T. Nepalese children's cognitive development as revealed by drawings of man, woman, and self. *Child Development*, 1968, *39*, 969–85.
    Subjects: $N = 807$; 6–13 yrs (urban and rural Nepal). **Measures:** Ss were asked to make drawings of man, woman, and self according to directions in the Harris revision of the Goodenough Draw-a-Man Test (translated into Nepali). **Results:** No sex differences.

Suppes, P., and Feldman, S. Young children's comprehension of logical connectives. *J. Experimental Child Psychology*, 1971, *12*, 304–17.
    Subjects: $N = 64$; 4–6 yrs (middle SES, disadvantaged). **Measures:** Ss were given 11 verbal commands to test their comprehension of 3 logical connectives: conjunction, disjunction, and negation. **Results:** No sex differences.

Sutton-Smith, B., and Savasta, M. Sex differences in play and power. Paper presented at the Annual Meeting of the Eastern Psychological Association, Boston, 1972.
    Subjects: $N = 17$; 3–4 yrs. **Measures:** Videotapes were made of Ss' nursery school activities, which either Ss or their peers initiated. **Results:** (1) Boys engaged in more episodes of social

testing and spent more time in such activity than girls did (social testing is an attempt by S to get other players in a game to do what he wanted them to). No sex differences were found in the number of episodes or time spent in exploration, world construction, testing (S asserts something about himself and then does it), contesting (testing against another), imitation (S asserts something about his relationship with another), or sociodrama (imitation involving other children in roles). (2) Behaviors classified as social testing were broken down into those directed at children and at adults. Each of these categories was in turn broken down into 4 subcategories: (a) supplicatory behaviors (S seeks sustenance, aid, etc., from another), (b) inclusive-exclusive behaviors (S attempts to control others by promising inclusion or threatening exclusion), (c) attacks, and (d) dominance behaviors. Within each of these subcategories, Ss' tactics were further classified as to whether a physical, verbal, or strategic modality had been used. By employment of this classification system in a reanalysis of the data, boys were found to attack their peers more; girls were found to exhibit more inclusive-exclusive behaviors. No sex differences were found in supplicatory or dominance behaviors, in the distribution of Ss' tactics across modalities, or in Ss' behavior toward adults.

Sutton-Smith, B., Rosenberg, B. G., and Landy, F. Father-absence effects in families of different sibling compositions. *Child Development*, 1968, *39*, 1213–21.
Subjects: $N = 295$, father absent, plus 760, father present; 19 yrs. Measures: American College Entrance Examination. Results: No sex differences.

Svensson, A. Relative achievement. School performance in relation to intelligence, sex and home environment. Stockholm: Almquist & Wiksell, 1971.
Experiment I: 1961. Subjects: $N = 5,828$; 13 yrs (Swedish elementary school children). $N = 3,077$; 13 yrs (Swedish experimental comprehensive school children). Measures: Ss completed a verbal and a mathematics achievement test and 2 intelligence tests—Opposites (a test of verbal ability) and Number series (a test of mathematical reasoning ability). Results: Boys scored higher than girls on the math achievement test and on Number series, while girls were superior to boys on the verbal achievement test. No sex differences were found on Opposites.
Experiment II: 1966. Subjects: $N = 1,550$; 13 yrs (Swedish elementary school children). $N = 6,144$; 13 yrs (Swedish comprehensive school children). Measures: Identical to Experiment I. Results: (1) Girls' scores were superior to those of the boys on the verbal achievement test. No sex differences were found on Opposites. (2) Among comprehensive school children, boys were superior to girls on the math achievement test and on Number series. No sex differences were found in the elementary school sample.

Swingle, P. G. Exploitative behavior in non-zero-sum games. *J. Personality & Social Psychology*, 1970, *16*, 121–32.
Subjects: $N = 60$; 18–21 yrs (college). Measures: During the first 100 trials of a non-zero-sum game, Ss were exposed to a 90% cooperative same-sex opponent. During the final 50 trials, the opponent's response matched Ss' previous response 90% of the time. The response measure was the percentage of exploitative responses. Results: No sex differences.

Szal, J. A. Sex differences in the cooperative and competitive behaviors of nursery school children. Unpublished master's thesis, Stanford University, 1972.
Subjects: $N = 60$; 4–5 yrs. Measures: Ss in same-sex or opposite-sex pairs played 2 10-trial sessions of a marble-pull game developed by Madsen. The game is designed in such a way that cooperation is adaptive and competition maladaptive to the goal of acquiring marbles. The number of marbles each pair obtained and the amount of sharing each pair exhibited were recorded. In addition, a running account was kept of Ss' actions and verbalizations. Actions were classified as either cooperative (receptive, permissive, submissive, or general— a category designated for those actions considered adaptive to the goal of obtaining marbles but lacking in the defining affect or history of receptive, permissive, or submissive cooperation), competitive (benign, aggressive, or general), or uncooperative. Verbalizations were similarly judged on the dimensions of cooperativeness, competitiveness, or uncooperativeness; in addition, they were categorized according to their grammatical form (narrative, command, suggestion), and their intended target (undirected, directed to other S, directed to E). Results: (1) Pairs of girls were more cooperative than pairs of boys. The measures that yielded differences were number of marbles obtained ($p < .05$), number of marbles shared ($p < .01$), and number of cooperative actions (total, $p < .05$; permissive, $p < .01$). Girl-boy pairs were midway in performance between same-sex pairs. (2) Male pairs were more competitive than female pairs. The measures that yielded differences were number of competitive actions (total, $p < .05$; aggressive, $p < .05$); and number of competitive verbalizations (total, $p < .01$; aggressive, $p < .05$). Opposite-sex pairs were again midway in performance between same-sex pairs.

(3) An examination of the individual performance of Ss in opposite-sex pairs revealed 2 differences: (a) boys exhibited more cooperative actions (total) than girls ($p < .05$), and (b) over sessions, girls increased in competitive verbalizations more than boys ($p < .05$). (4) Boys in opposite-sex pairs shared more marbles than boys in same-sex pairs ($p < .05$). (5) Girls in opposite-sex pairs exhibited more competitive actions (total, $p < .05$; aggressive, $p < .01$) and less cooperative actions (total, $p < .05$) than girls in same-sex pairs.

Taft, R., and Johnston, R. The assimilation of adolescent Polish immigrants and parent-child interaction. *Merrill-Palmer Quarterly*, 1967, *13*, 111–21.
Subjects: $N = 39$; 15–16 yrs (Australia). **Measures:** Ss were asked questions about tensions with their parents in 3 areas of assimilation: food, language, and social relations. **Results:** No sex differences.

Taylor, S. P., and Epstein, S. Aggression as a function of the interaction of the sex of the aggressor and the sex of the victim. *J. Personality*, 1967, *35*, 474–96.
Subjects: $N = 24$; 18–21 yrs (college). **Measures:** Aggression was measured by the magnitude of shock the subject set for his opponent to receive in a reaction-time task. Wins and losses on the task and aggressiveness of the opponent were actually programmed by E. **Results:** (1) There were no sex differences in aggression across conditions. (2) Whereas women were less aggressive in the low provocation condition, they showed a greater increase in aggression with increasing provocation than men did ($p < .001$). (3) All Ss were more aggressive to male than to female opponents ($p < .05$). (4) All Ss demonstrated a greater rise in skin conductance when competing with female rather than male opponents ($p < .05$).

Tedeschi, J. T., Horai, J., Lindskold, S., and Gahagan, J. P. The effects of threat upon prevarication and compliance in social conflict. Proceedings of the 76th Annual Convention of the APA, 1968a, *3*, 399–400.
Subjects: $N = 96$; 18–21 yrs (college). **Measures:** Ss played a modified version of the Prisoner's Dilemma game with a simulated partner (E). On selected trials, E threatened Ss with a loss of points unless they made the cooperative response on the next trial. Ss were required to respond with 1 of 3 available messages. **Results:** (1) Women made the cooperative response more frequently than men ($p < .04$). (2) Women lost less money than men ($p < .04$). (3) After being threatened by E, more men than women made the competitive choice after indicating to E their intention to make the cooperative choice ($p < .003$).

Tedeschi, J., T. Lesnick, S., and Gahagan, J. Feedback and "washout" effects in the Prisoner's Dilemma game. *J. Personality & Social Psychology*, 1968b, *10*, 31–34.
Subjects: $N = 64$; 18–21 yrs (college). **Measures:** Ss played 100 trials of the Prisoner's Dilemma game with a simulated other. **Results:** (1) No sex differences were found in percentage of cooperative responses over 100 trials. (2) On the first 10 trials, women were more cooperative than men ($p < .03$).

Tedeschi, J. T., Hiester, D., and Gahagan, J. P. Matrix values and the behavior of children in the Prisoner's Dilemma game. *Child Development*, 1969a, *40*, 517–27.
Subjects: $N = 96$; 8, 9 yrs. **Measures:** Same-sex pairs of Ss played a modified version of the Prisoner's Dilemma game. **Results:** (1) Girls made more cooperative choices than boys ($p < .01$). Boys made more jointly competitive choices than girls ($p < .01$). No sex differences were found in number of jointly cooperative choices. (2) Girls displayed more trust than boys ($p < .01$). Trust was exhibited when S cooperated on trial ($n + 1$) after both he and his partner made the competitive choice on trial n. (3) Girls were more forgiving than boys ($p < .05$). Forgiveness was exhibited when S cooperated on trial ($n + 1$) after his partner made the competitive choice and he made the cooperative choice on trial n. (4) No sex differences were found in trustworthiness or repentance. Trustworthiness was exhibited when S cooperated on trial ($n + 1$) after both he and his partner made the cooperative choice on trial n. Repentance was exhibited when S cooperated on trial ($n + 1$) after his partner made the cooperative choice and he made the competitive choice on trial n.

Tedeschi, J. T., Lindskold, S., Horai, J., and Gahagan, J. P. Social power and the credibility of promises. *J. Personality & Social Psychology*, 1969b, *13*, 253–61.
Subjects: $N = 200$; 18–21 yrs (college). **Measures:** After every tenth trial of the Prisoner's Dilemma game, Ss received a promise of cooperation from a simulated same-sex partner. Ss replied with 1 of 3 available messages. **Results:** Whereas both sexes were preponderantly truthful, women made the cooperative response more often than men after promising their partners they would ($p < .002$).

Templer, D. I., Ruff, C. F., and Franks, C. M. Death anxiety: age, sex and parental resemblance in diverse populations. *Developmental Psychology,* 1971, *4,* 108 (brief report).
Subjects: $N = 2,559$; 13–21, 17–59, 18–61, 19–85 yrs (students, parents of students, psychiatric patients, low SES hospital aides, high SES apartment dwellers). Measures: Ss completed a 15-item true-false Death Anxiety Scale. Results: Among apartment house residents, adolescents, and parents of adolescents, women had higher Death Anxiety Scale scores than men. No sex differences were found among hospital aides or psychiatric patients.

Ter Vrugt, D., and Pederson, D. R. The effects of vertical rocking frequencies on the arousal level in two-month-old infants. *Child Development,* 1973, 44, 205–9.
Subjects: $N = 64$; 1–2 mos. Measures: Infants were vertically rocked at 1 of 4 frequencies. Observers rated each S's general level of arousal during the baseline, rocking, and post-rocking phases. Results: No sex differences.

Thalhofer, N. N. Responsibility, reparation, and self-protection as reasons for three types of helping. *J. Personality & Social Psychology,* 1971, *19,* 144–51.
Subjects: $N = 192$; 18–21 yrs (college). Measures: After reading about a disturbed boy whose teacher had recommended that he be removed to a more punishment-oriented school, Ss were asked to rate the boy on how much he could continue to benefit from his present school experience. Ss had previously been led to believe either that they alone (unique condition) or that others were reading about the boy (nonunique condition). After rating the boy, Ss were informed that a decision had been made to transfer him. Ss were then given the opportunity to (a) offer either time or money to help the boy (labeled help relevant to dependency), and (b) rerate the boy on the same scale used previously in rating (labeled help relevant to harm, measured by computing the difference between the first and second ratings). Ss were free to assume that their second ratings might have some effect on the transfer decision. Ss were asked if they'd be willing to participate in future studies, and to fill out an additional questionnaire (labeled help irrelevant to harm and dependency). Results: (1) No main sex effects were found. In the nonunique condition, women offered more help relevant to dependency than men did ($p < .05$). (2) In answer to questions concerning their reactions to the study, women more than men liked the boy they read about, thought that one should help another whom one has harmed, and thought that one should help another who is in need ($p < .001, p < .001, p < .001$).

Thelen, M. H. Modeling of verbal reactions to failure. *Developmental Psychology,* 1969, *1,* 297 (brief report).
Subjects: $N = 98$; 10–12 yrs (Catholic school). Measures: Ss watched an audio-video film in which an adult male model performed a card-sorting task. Experimental Ss observed the model make self-blame or rationalization statements after each failure, which had either positive, negative, or no consequences. The control group observed no model. Ss then performed the same card-sorting task, with E asking for comments after each failure trial. Self-blame or rationalization statements similar to model's were recorded. Results: No sex differences.

Thelen, M. H. Long term retention of verbal imitation. *Developmental Psychology,* 1970, 3, 29–31.
Subjects: $N = 38$; 10–12 yrs. Measures: Ss observed a filmed adult male model perform a card-sorting task, failing and making self-blame statements on half of the trials. Ss observed E make either a supportive statement to model (positive consequences of failure) or a critical statement (negative consequences). Ss then performed the identical task. Results: There were no sex differences in number of self-blame statements.

Thelen, M. H., Rennie, D. L., Fryrear, J. L., and McGuire, D. Expectancy to perform and vicarious reward: their effects upon imitation. *Child Development,* 1972, *43,* 699–703.
Subjects: $N = 60$; 6, 7, 8 yrs. Measures: Ss viewed a film about pushing buttons to light up a clown face. Before the film, Ss were manipulated as to expectancy to perform or not to perform. The model in the film was either rewarded or not rewarded. Ss were asked to recall and imitate the model's behavior. Results: No sex differences.

Thoman, E. B., Barnett, C. R., and Leiderman, P. H. Feeding behaviors of newborn infants as a function of parity of the mother. *Child Development,* 1971, *42,* 1471–83.
Subjects: $N = 271$; 12–16 hrs and mothers. Measures: Infants of primiparous and multiparous bottle-feeding and breast-feeding mothers were observed during feeding. Results: No sex differences were found in (1) time spent in feeding and nonfeeding activities, (2) amount of formula consumed, or (3) number of feeding intervals.

Thoman, E. B., Leiderman, P. H., and Olson, J. P. Neonate-mother interaction during breast feeding. *Developmental Psychology*, 1972, *6*, 110–18.

> **Subjects:** $N = 40$; 2 days and mothers. **Measures:** Mothers were observed while breast-feeding their infants. The amount of time mothers devoted to breast-feeding, water feeding, and non-feeding activities was recorded. **Results:** (1) Primiparous mothers spent a greater percentage of the total observation time breast-feeding their sons than their daughters; for multiparous mothers, the reverse was true ($p < .05$). (2) While breast-feeding, primiparous mothers talked to their daughters more than to their sons; multiparous mothers showed no preference ($p < .05$). (3) During nonfeeding activities, no difference was found in the percentage of time mothers talked to their boy and girl infants.

Thomas, L. E. Family correlates of student political activism. *Developmental Psychology*, 1971, *4*, 206–14.

> **Subjects:** $N = 60$; 18–21 yrs (college) and parents (liberal, conservative). **Measures:** Parent and child open-ended interviews were coded for family emotional climate (permissiveness, warmth, conflict, family interaction), family political climate (parental dedication to causes, parental political tutoring), student activism, and conventional political activity. **Results:** (1) There were no sex differences in student activism and student political participation within liberal or conservative groups. (2) Among conservative Ss, parents of girls were less permissive than parents of boys ($p < .05$).

Thompson, N. L., and McCandless, B. R. It score variations by instructional style. *Child Development*, 1970, *41*, 425–36.

> **Subjects:** $N = 72$; 4–5 yrs (white, black). **Measures:** The It Scale for Children (ITSC) was administered to Ss 3 times. 3 sets of instructions were given: (1) Standard (Ss were asked to answer for the It figure who was visible to them throughout the test); (2) Concealed (Ss were asked to answer for a child named "It"; the It figure was kept concealed in an envelope); (3) "It is you" (the It figure was identified as a child of the same-sex as S). **Results:** On each administration of the ITSC, boys' scores were more masculine than girls'.

Thompson, S. K., and Bentler, P. M. The priority of cues in sex discrimination by children and adults. *Developmental Psychology*, 1971, *5*, 181–85 (and personal communication).

> **Subjects:** $N = 240$; 4, 5, 6, over 21 yrs. **Measures:** Ss sorted doll clothes into masculine and feminine types. Ss viewed a nude male or female doll with either long or short hair, and were asked to dress it for party and swimming, identify it as mommy or daddy, and justify their identification. **Results:** (1) There were no sex differences in adults' task performances. (2) Boys had lower scores (dressed dolls more femininely) than girls did ($p < .05$). (3) There were no main sex differences in sex identity classifications. Girls gave more masculine classification to the feminine-bodied short-haired dolls than boys did.

Thompson, S. K., and Bentler, P. M. A developmental study of gender constancy and parent preference. *Archives of Sexual Behavior*, 1973, *65*, 211–15.

> **Subjects:** $N = 144$; 4–6 yrs. **Measures:** Ss were asked the following questions: (1) Are you going to be a mommy or a daddy? (2) Could you be a mommy/daddy if you wanted to be? (For this question, Ss were asked if they could be the opposite of their response to the first question.) (3) Do you like your mommy or daddy best? **Results:** (1) All boys were aware that they would become fathers and (with the exception of 1 6-year-old) all girls were aware that they would become mothers. (2) No sex differences were found in the number of Ss who indicated it was possible for them to become an opposite-sex parent. (3) Girls preferred their mothers more than boys did; boys preferred their fathers more than girls did ($p < .01$).

Thomson, G. H. *An analysis of performance test scores of a representative group of Scottish children.* London: University of London Press, 1940.

> **Subjects:** $N = 873$; 9–11 yrs. **Measures:** Manikin Test, Sequin Form Board, Stutsman Picture Test, Red Riding Hood Test, Healy Picture Completion Test II, Knox Cube Imitation Test, Cube Construction Test, Kohs Block Design. **Results:** No sex differences.

Tisher, R. P. A Piagetian questionnaire applied to pupils in a secondary school. *Child Development*, 1971, *42*, 1633–36 (and personal communication).

> **Subjects:** $N = 232$; 12–14 yrs. **Measures:** A Piagetian questionnaire and interview tasks concerning invisible magnetism, equilibrium in the balance, and combinations of chemicals were administered to each S. **Results:** No sex differences.

Titkin, S., and Hartup, W. Sociometric status and the reinforcing effectiveness of children's peers. *J. Experimental Child Psychology*, 1965, *2*, 306–15.
Subjects: $N = 84$; 7, 10 yrs. **Measures:** A nonskill task (marble dropping) was verbally reinforced by a popular, unpopular, or socially isolated peer. The number of marbles Ss dropped was recorded. Difference scores indicated the effects of peer reinforcement on response rate. **Results:** There were no main sex differences. Among 10-year-old Ss reinforced by unpopular peers, girls showed a substantial increment in marble dropping, whereas boys' rate decreased.

Titley, R. W., and Viney, W. Expression of aggression toward the physically handicapped. *Perceptual & Motor Skills*, 1969, *29*, 51–56.
Subjects: $N = 40$; 17 yrs. **Measures:** Ss were asked to administer a shock to a same-sex or opposite-sex confederate of an intensity just below what they estimated to be the confederate's pain threshold. The confederate appeared to be either physically disabled or normal. **Results:** (1) Men delivered a higher intensity of shock than women ($p < .05$). (2) Men delivered more shock to women than to men; the reverse was true for women ($p < .001$). (3) Men delivered more shock to the physically disabled confederate than to the normal confederate; the reverse was true for women ($p < .001$).

Todd, F. J., and Hammond, K. R. Differential feedback in two multiple-cue probability learning tasks. *Behavioral Science*, 1965, *10*, 429–35.
Subjects: $N = 72$; 18–21 yrs (college). **Measures:** Ss were given a multiple-cue probability learning task. **Results:** No sex differences.

Todd, J., and Nakamura, C. Y. Interactive effects of informational and affective components of social and nonsocial reinforcers on independent and dependent children. *Child Development*, 1970, *41*, 365–76.
Experiment I: Subjects: $N = 54$; 5–7 yrs. **Measures:** 3 marble-sorting tasks were administered to Ss. Half the Ss received feedback only when they performed correctly, while the other half were informed only when they performed incorrectly. In 4 of the 6 conditions, Ss heard E say "correct" or "incorrect" in either a positive or negative tone of voice; feedback in the other 2 conditions consisted simply of exposure to light flashes. The response measure was the number of trials Ss needed to reach criterion. **Results:** No sex differences.
Experiment III: Subjects: $N = 48$; 6–7 yrs. **Measures:** While cutting out designs, Ss received either positive or negative reinforcement from E. Ss in a third condition were exposed to an E who remained silent until Ss completed the task. All Ss were then administered 3 bead-sorting games. Correct responses were reinforced either by E ("correct" said in a neutral tone of voice) or by a light flash. The number of trials Ss needed to reach criterion was recorded. **Results:** Boys reached criterion faster than girls did.

Tolor, A., and Orange, S. An attempt to measure psychological distance in advantaged and disadvantaged children. *Child Development*, 1969, *40*, 407–20.
Subjects: $N = 40$; 5–14 yrs. **Measures:** Using a Psychological Distance Board, Ss had to re-create physical distance between stimulus dyads of simulated persons. Ss also completed the Make-A-Picture-Story test. **Results:** On 3 out of 12 pairings, girls placed the figures farther apart than boys ($p < .05$).

Torrance, E. P. *Rewarding creative behavior.* Englewood Cliffs, N.J.: Prentice-Hall, 1965.
Experiment I: Subjects: $N = 114$; elementary school teachers. **Measures:** Teachers were asked to describe incidents in which they believed they had rewarded creative behavior in their classrooms. **Results:** In 75% of the cases, teachers were able to recall who initiated the rewarded behavior; more boys than girls were mentioned ($p < .01$).
Experiment II: Subjects: $N = 212$; 6–8 yrs. **Measures:** During the administration of the Product Improvement Task, Ss were rated on the degree to which they manipulated each of the 3 toys: a nurse's kit, a fire truck, and a stuffed toy dog. **Results:** Among 7- and 8-year-old Ss, boys were more manipulative than girls.
Experiment III: Subjects: $N = 171$; 11 yrs. **Measures:** Ss completed questionnaires about their reading experiences. **Results:** (1) No sex differences were found in the number of Ss who liked to read. (2) Boys were less likely than girls to go to the library to check out books. (3) Girls indicated that they read more books per month than boys. (4) Boys reported that they owned more books than girls. (5) Boys were more likely than girls to check on the accuracy of a statement they did not believe. (6) Girls enjoyed giving oral book reports in class more than boys. (7) A greater number of girls than boys reported that they sometimes became so absorbed in what they were reading that they were unable to think of other things they should

be doing. (8) Girls indicated they were more likely to become "lost to the world" when beginning a book than boys. (9) Boys expressed a greater preference than girls for books dealing with sports, science, and hobbies, whereas girls expressed a greater preference than boys for fiction, animal stories, fairy tales, classical novels, career stories, drama, poetry, and religion (no tests of significance reported). (10) No sex differences were found in the number of Ss who reported they enjoyed telling others about what they had read or who stated that they sometimes found errors in spelling or grammar while reading.

EXPERIMENT IV: **Subjects:** $N = 75$; 12, 13 yrs (minimum IQ 135). **Measures:** The Ask-and-Guess Test, the Unusual Uses Test, the Product Improvement Task, the Consequences Test, and the figural or nonverbal tests of creative thinking were administered to Ss. Ss also completed make-up arithmetic and social studies problems. **Results:** (1) On the figural tests, boys scored higher than girls on nonverbal fluency ($p < .005$), nonverbal originality ($p < .005$), and nonverbal penetration ($p < .025$). (2) On the Consequences Test, boys scored higher than girls on flexibility ($p < .025$) but not on fluency. (3) Girls performed better than boys on the make-up social studies problems ($p < .005$).

EXPERIMENT V: **Subjects:** $N = 50$; 11 yrs. **Measures:** Parallel Lines Test, Ask-and-Guess Test. **Results:** (1) On the Parallel Lines Test, boys scored higher than girls on originality ($p < .025$), and girls scored higher than boys on elaboration ($p < .01$). No sex differences were found on the fluency or flexibility measures. (2) On the Ask-and-Guess Test, girls scored higher than boys on asking questions ($p < .025$) and on causal hypotheses ($p < .025$). No sex differences were found on consequential hypotheses.

EXPERIMENT VI: **Subjects:** $N = 555$; 6–11 yrs. **Measures:** The Product Improvement Task was administered under competitive and noncompetitive conditions. Ss' responses were scored for fluency, flexibility, and originality. **Results:** (1) Among 8-year-old Ss, boys scored higher in originality (competition condition only) and fluency than girls. (2) Among 9- and 11-year-old Ss, boys had higher originality scores in the competitive condition than girls. (3) Among 10-year-old Ss, girls had higher fluency and flexibility scores than boys.

EXPERIMENT VII: **Subjects:** $N = 320$; 6–11 yrs. **Measures:** The Pictures Construction Task and the Incomplete Figures Task were administered to Ss. During practice sessions preceding each test, half the Ss received positive, constructive evaluation from E. The other half of the Ss received encouragement from E but no evaluation. **Results:** (1) Picture Construction Test: (a) Among 6-year-old Ss, girls had higher originality scores than boys; (b) among 8-year-old Ss, girls had higher elaboration scores than boys; boys had higher originality scores than girls (unevaluated condition only); (c) among 9-year-old Ss, girls had higher elaboration scores than boys (evaluated condition only); (d) among 10-year-old Ss, girls had higher elaboration scores than boys in the unevaluated condition, whereas the reverse was true in the evaluated condition; (e) among 11-year-old Ss, girls had higher elaboration scores than boys (evaluated condition only). (2) Incomplete Figures Test: (a) among 8-year-old Ss, girls had higher originality scores than boys; boys had higher closure scores than girls (unevaluated condition only); (b) among 10-year-old Ss, girls had higher elaboration scores than boys (unevaluated condition only); (c) among 11-year-old Ss, girls had higher elaboration scores and higher closure scores (evaluated condition only) than boys.

Torrance, E. P., and Aliotti, N. C. Sex differences in levels of performance and test-retest reliability on the Torrance Tests of Creative Thinking Ability. *J. Creative Behavior*, 1969, 3, 52–57.

Subjects: $N = 118$; 10 yrs. **Measures:** Ss, responses to Forms A and B of the figural and verbal batteries of the Torrance Tests of Creative Thinking Ability were scored for fluency, flexibility, originality, and elaboration. **Results:** (1) On the figural tests, boys were superior to girls in flexibility (Form A, $p < .05$; Form B, NS) and originality ($p < .01$, $p < .05$). Girls scored higher than boys on elaboration ($p < .001$, $p < .001$). No sex differences were found in fluency. (2) On the verbal tests, girls were superior to boys in fluency ($p < .01$, $p < .002$), flexibility ($p < .01$, $p < .002$), and originality ($p < .01$, $p < .002$).

Touhey, J. C. Comparison of two dimensions of attitude similarity on heterosexual attraction. *J. Personality & Social Psychology*, 1972, 23, 8–10.

Subjects: $N = 250$; 18–21 yrs (college). **Measures:** Men and women in a computer-dating study were matched on the basis of maximal or minimal similarity in either religious or sexual attitudes. Ss' impressions of their dates were assessed on a modified version of Byrne's Interpersonal Judgment Scale. **Results:** (1) Women were more attracted to their dates than men were ($p < .05$). (2) Women were more attracted to men with religiously similar attitudes; men were more attracted to women with sexually similar attitudes ($p < .05$).

Tuddenham, R. D. A study of reputation: children's evaluations of their peers. In G. G. Thompson, F. J. DiVesta, and J. Horrocks, eds., *Social development and personality.* Somerset, N.J.: Wiley, 1971.

Subjects: $N = 1,439$; 6, 8, 10 yrs. Measures: Ss were asked questions about their classmates (in answering each item, Ss were free to name themselves). Results: (1) Among 6-year-old Ss, girls were judged to be more popular, more quiet, and less quarrelsome than boys. (2) Among 8-year-old Ss, girls were judged to be more popular, more quiet, less quarrelsome, and less bossy than boys. Girls were also rated more favorably than boys on the "doesn't get mad—gets mad easily" dimension. (3) Among 10-year-old Ss, girls were judged to be more quiet and tidy than boys; boys were judged to take more chances, to be bigger show-offs, and to be better at games than girls. (4) Girls voted for others more often than boys did. Boys mentioned themselves more frequently than girls did. Girls judged others of the same sex more favorably than boys did. Boys gave more favorable self-evaluations than girls did. No tests of significance were reported.

Tulving, E., and Pearlstone, Z. Availability versus accessibility of information in memory for words. *J. Verbal Learning & Verbal Behavior,* 1966, 5, 381–91 (and personal communication).

Subjects: $N = 929$; 15–17 yrs. Measures: Ss learned lists of words in specific conceptual categories. Immediate recall and cued-recall category name tests followed. Results: Girls showed greater recall than boys.

Turiel, E. A comparative analysis of moral knowledge and moral judgment in males and females. To appear in L. Kohlberg and E. Turiel, eds., *Recent research in moral judgment.* New York: Holt, Rinehart & Winston, 1973.

Subjects: $N = 210$; 11, 14, 17 yrs. Measures: Ss were individually given a moral judgment interview consisting of 5 stories. In 1 form of the interview the stories involved male protagonists, while in the second form the stories involved female protagonists. Each S was assigned a moral maturity score based on Kohlberg's Scale. A few days later, Ss were given a moral knowledge test composed of 30 statements, each describing a transgression committed by either a boy (for male Ss) or a girl (for female Ss). Ss rated the degree of wrongness of each transgression. Results: (1) At ages 11 and 14, girls had higher moral maturity scores than boys; at age 17, boys had higher scores than girls ($p < .05$). (2) No sex differences were found in the moral knowledge test.

Turkewitz, G., Moreau, T., Birch, H. G., and Crystal, D. Relationship between prior head position and lateral difference in responsiveness to somesthetic stimulation in the human neonate. *J. Experimental Child Psychology,* 1967, 5, 548–61.

Subjects: $N = 51$; 1–3 days. Measures: With infants lying on their backs, their heads held in midline position with no lateralized pressure detectable on E's fingers, the touch of a camel's hair brush was applied for 1-second trials to the area around the mouth. Mock presentation consisted of moving brush toward mouth but not making contact. On all trials, direction of first head movement after removal of brush was recorded. Results: No sex differences.

Turnure, C. Response to voice of mother and stranger by babies in the first year. *Developmental Psychology,* 1971, 4, 182–90.

Subjects: $N = 33$; 3, 6, 9 mos. Measures: Ss heard tape recordings (normal, slightly distorted, and grossly distorted) of their mothers' voices. Half of the Ss then heard an additional sequence of auditory stimuli consisting of (a) the voice of an unfamiliar person and (b) more presentations of their mothers' voices (normal and distorted). Movies taken of Ss were scored for limb movement. Results: First phase of the experiment in which all Ss participated: (1) at 3 months, girls showed more limb movements to the slight distortion and to the gross distortion of their mothers' voices than boys did ($p < .05$); (2) at 9 months, girls showed more limb movement to their mothers' normal voices than boys did ($p < .05$); (3) no sex differences were found when mean limb movement during the 15 seconds immediately preceding each stimulus presentation was subtracted from mean limb movement during the stimulus period. No sex differences were found in the second phase of the experiment ($N = 15$).

Turnure, J. E. Children's reactions to distractors in a learning situation. *Developmental Psychology,* 1970, 2, 115–22.

Subjects: $N = 90$; 5–7 yrs. Measures: Ss performed oddity discrimination problems with either visual distraction, auditory distraction, or no distraction. Correct responses and glances away from the task were recorded. Results: No sex differences.

Turnure, J. E. Control of orienting behavior in children under five years of age. *Developmental Psychology*, 1971, *4*, 16–24.
Subjects: $N = 40$; 3, 4 yrs. Measures: Ss performed 2-choice discrimination tasks under conditions of distraction and no distraction. E recorded Ss' glances away from the task. Results: There were no main sex differences. Girls made greater gains in correct responses over trials than boys ($p < .05$).

Tyron, A. F. Thumbsucking and manifest anxiety: a note. *Child Development*, 1968, *39*, 1159–61.
Subjects: $N = 104$; 7–14 yrs (current thumbsuckers and non-thumbsuckers). Measures: Children's Manifest Anxiety Scale. Results: No sex differences.

Unikel, I. P., Strain, G. W., and Adams, H. E. Learning of lower socioeconomic status children as a function of social and tangible reward. *Developmental Psychology*, 1969, *1*, 553–55.
Subjects: $N = 144$; 5–6 yrs (Head Start program). Measures: Ss played a simple discrimination-learning game under 1 of 3 conditions: tangible reward (candy), social reward, and no reward (control). Results: (1) There was no main effect for sex of S. (2) Ss performed better with a female rather than with a male E ($p < .05$).

Unruh, S. G., Gross, M. E., and Zigler, E. Birth order, number of siblings, and social reinforcer effectiveness in children. *Child Development*, 1971, *42*, 1153–63.
Subjects: $N = 144$; 6, 7, 8 yrs. Measures: Ss played a marble game designed to be tedious, so that social reinforcement would become the main determinant of how long Ss played. E either did or did not support Ss' performance. Results: No sex differences.

Vassiliou, V., Georgas, J. G., and Vassiliou, G. Variations in manifest anxiety due to sex, age, and education. *J. Personality & Social Psychology*, 1967, *6*, 194–97.
Subjects: $N = 400$; adults (Greek). Measures: Taylor Manifest Anxiety Scale. Results: Women had higher anxiety scores than men ($p < .01$).

Vaughan, G. M., and White, K. D. Conformity and authoritarianism reexamined. *J. Personality & Social Psychology*, 1966, *3*, 363–66.
Subjects: $N = 312$; 18–21 yrs (college). Measures: Berkowitz and Wolkon's forced-choice version of the authoritarian F scale. Results: No sex differences.

Vaught, G. M. The relationship of role identification and ego strength to sex differences in the Rod-and-Frame Test. *J. Personality*, 1965, *33*, 271–83.
Subjects: $N = 180$; 18–21 yrs (college). Measures: Rod-and-Frame Test. Results: Men were more field-independent than women ($p < .01$).

Vernon, D. T., Foley, J. M., and Schulman, J. L. Effect of mother-child separation and birth order on young children's responses to two potentially stressful experiences. *J. Personality & Social Psychology*, 1967, *5*, 162–74.
Experiment I: Subjects: $N = 32$; 2–5 yrs. Measures: Ss were brought to a hospital for surgery and put through standard admission procedures, with their mother either present or absent. Both before and after admission procedures, Ss were placed in a free-play activity situation. Ss were rated for quality of play, aggression, and mood. Results: No sex differences.
Experiment II: Subjects: $N = 32$; 2–5 yrs. Measures: Prior to anesthesia induction, Ss were placed in a free-play activity situation, with their mothers present. Estimates were made of Ss' mood both during the free-play period and during anesthesia induction. After Ss were released from the hospital, their mothers completed a post-hospital behavior questionnaire. Mothers' descriptions of their child's behavior were scored for (a) general anxiety and regression, (b) separation anxiety, (c) sleep anxiety, (d) eating disturbance, (e) aggression toward authority, and (f) apathy withdrawal. Results: No sex differences.

Very, P. S. Differential factor structures in mathematical abilities. *Genetic Psychology Monographs*, 1967, *75*, 169–207.
Subjects: $N = 355$; 18–21 yrs (college). Measures: A battery of mathematical, verbal, and spatial tests. Results: (1) Women scored higher than men on Logical Reasoning, Number Comparisons, Visual Motor Velocity, Moore-Castore Vocabulary. Moore-Castore Paragraph Reading, and English Placement Vocabulary. (2) Men scored higher than women on Division, Arithmetic Reasoning, Mathematical Aptitude, General Reasoning, Spatial Relations, Cards, Cubes, Spatial Orientation, Judgment, Moore-Castore Arithmetic, and Moore-Castore Algebra.

(3) There were no sex differences in Addition, Subtraction, Arithmetic Computation, Number Arrangement, Ship Destination, Practical Estimation, Math Puzzles, Nonsense Syllogisms, Deductive Reasoning, Letter Concepts, Inductive Reasoning, Picture Concepts, and Letter Reasoning.

Voissem, N. H., and Sistrunk, K. F. Communication schedule and cooperative game behavior. *J. Personality & Social Psychology*, 1971, *19*, 160–67.
Subjects: $N = 96$; 18–21 yrs (college). **Measures:** Same-sex pairs of Ss played the Prisoner's Dilemma game, with or without opportunities for communication. **Results:** No sex differences were found in percentage of cooperative responses.

Vondracek, S. I., and Vondracek, F. W. The manipulation and measurement of self-disclosure in pre-adolescents. *Merrill-Palmer Quarterly*, 1971, *17*, 51–58.
Subjects: $N = 80$; 11 yrs. **Measures:** Ss were asked to disclose things about themselves that ordinarily they would reveal only to a few special people. Ss' statements were scored for degree of intimacy. **Results:** No sex differences.

Wagman, M. Sex differences in types of daydreams. *J. Personality & Social Psychology*, 1967, *7*, 329–32.
Subjects: $N = 206$; 18–21 yrs (college). **Measures:** Ss reported the frequency of their daydreams in 24 content categories. **Results:** Men reported a higher frequency of aggressive, sexual, hostile, and heroic or self-aggrandizing daydreams than women. Women reported a higher frequency of passive, affiliative, narcissistic, oral, physical attractiveness, practical, and planning daydreams than men.

Walberg, H. J. Physics, femininity, and creativity. *Developmental Psychology*, 1969, *1*, 47–54.
Random subsamples of 2,074 students taking a new high school physics course were tested.
EXPERIMENT I: **Subjects:** $N = 1,050$; 16–17 yrs. **Measures:** (1) The Science Process Inventory and the Test on Understanding Science, (2) the Physics Achievement Test, (3) the Pupil Activity Inventory. **Results:** (1) Girls scored higher than boys on the Science Process Inventory and on the Test on Understanding Science. Boys scored higher than girls on the Physics Achievement Test. (2) On the Pupil Activity Inventory, girls indicated greater participation in nature study and applications of science. Boys indicated greater participation in cosmological activities and tinkering activities.
EXPERIMENT II: **Subjects:** $N = 450$; 16–17 yrs. **Measures:** (1) Henmon-Nelson Intelligence Test, Form B, 12 grade level, (2) The Study of Values: Theoretical, Economic, Aesthetic, Social, Political, and Religious, (3) Personality measures of dogmatism, authoritarianism, rigidity, need for achievement, need for order, need for affiliation, and need for change. **Results:** (1) Girls scored higher than boys on the IQ test. (2) Girls scored higher than boys on the Social, Aesthetic, and Religious scales; boys scored higher than girls on the Economic, Political, and Theoretical scales. (3) Girls scored higher than boys on the need for affiliation and need for change measures; boys scored higher than girls on the dogmatism measure.
EXPERIMENT III: **Subjects:** $N = 850$; 16–17 yrs. **Measures:** Using semantic differential scales, Ss rated each of 4 physical science concepts: (1) universe, (2) physics, (3) laboratory experiments, and (4) myself as a physics student. **Results:** (1) Girls rated universe as more friendly and beautiful than boys did. (2) Girls rated physics as less safe than boys did. (3) Boys rated laboratory experiments as less important and more simple than girls did. (4) As physics students, girls saw themselves as less facile and as "more apt to be starting" than boys did.
EXPERIMENT IV: **Subjects:** $N = 455$; 16–17 yrs. **Measures:** Ss indicated their agreement or disagreement with items describing characteristics of the socio-emotional climate of learning in the school classroom. **Results:** (1) Girls rated their classes more satisfying, egalitarian, and diverse in their goals than boys did. Girls also perceived more intimacy among the class members than boys did. (2) Boys felt more friction among class members, perceived greater social differences among their fellow students, felt more constrained about what could be said in class, and saw a greater degree of group subservience than girls did.

Waldrop, M. Longitudinal and cross-sectional analyses of seven-and-a-half-year-old peer behavior. Unpublished manuscript, National Institute of Mental Health, 1972.
Subjects: $N = 62$; 7½ yrs. **Measures:** Mothers were asked to keep a diary of their children's activities for a period of 1 week. To supplement these written reports, mothers were individually interviewed at the end of the week. Objective counts were made of hours with peers, hours with 1 peer, and hours with more than 1 peer. The age and sex of each child's play-

mates were also recorded. **Results:** When with peers, highly social boys had extensive peer relations (i.e. they usually played with groups of boys), whereas highly social girls had intensive peer relations (i.e. they usually played with 1 other girl).

Walker, R. N. Some temperament traits in children as viewed by their peers, their teachers, and themselves. *Monographs of the Society for Research in Child Development*, 1967, 32.
Subjects: $N = 450$; 8–11 yrs. **Measures:** (1) 406 children rated themselves on 96 self-descriptive statements, 16 for each of 6 traits: energetic, surgent, social, stable, fearful, and aggressive. (2) All 450 children were rated by their teachers on each of the 6 traits. **Results:** Teachers viewed boys and boys viewed themselves as more aggressive and energetic and as less stable and fearful than girls.

Wallach, M. A., and Mabli, J. Information versus conformity in the effects of group discussion on risk taking. *J. Personality & Social Psychology*, 1970, 14, 149–56.
Subjects: $N = 108$; 18–21 yrs (college). **Measures:** Based on Ss' responses to Wallach and Kagan's choice-dilemmas battery, 36 3-person groups were formed, composed of either a risky majority and a conservative minority or vice versa. Groups were homogeneous with respect to sex. Effects of group discussion on risk taking were assessed by measuring shifts from initial decisions (on the choice-dilemmas instrument) to group consensus decisions, and from initial decisions to postconsensus person decisions. **Results:** No sex differences.

Wallach, M. A., and Martin, M. L. Effects of social class on children's motoric expression. *Developmental Psychology*, 1970, 3, 106–13.
Subjects: $N = 283$; 6, 7, 9, 11 yrs (low, middle SES). **Measures:** Ss were asked to draw designs on a piece of paper. The amount of area that their drawings covered was used as an index of motoric construction-expansiveness. **Results:** Among middle SES 9-year-old Ss, girls were more expansive than boys. No other sex differences were found.

Walls, R. T., and Cox, J. Disadvantaged and nondisadvantaged children's expectancy in skill and chance outcomes. *Developmental Psychology*, 1971, 4, 299.
Subjects: $N = 80$; 8–9 yrs. **Measures:** Ss placed as many pegs into a board as possible under 1 of 4 treatments, which varied as to Ss' perceptions about and actual existence of amount of chance and skill. Ss then completed the Internal-External Locus of Control Scale for Children and answered questions concerning occupational aspiration. **Results:** (1) There were no sex differences in pegboard task performance. (2) More disadvantaged than nondisadvantaged girls had a general external expectancy on Internal-External Locus of Control measure; the opposite was true for boys. (3) Among disadvantaged Ss, boys displayed a more internal locus, whereas girls displayed a more external locus. (4) Girls expected to hold more prestigious jobs but earn less money than boys.

Walls, R. T., and DiVesta, F. J. Cognitive factors in the conditioning of children's preferences. *Developmental Psychology*, 1970, 2, 318–24.
Subjects: $N = 108$; 6 yrs. **Measures:** Ss matched descriptive adjectives with Greek letter stimuli (as a measure of stimulus preference) before and after conditioning sessions involving 1 or 2 marble reinforcement procedures: reinforced stimuli remaining the same or differing over sessions. **Results:** There were no sex differences in preferences for stimuli on final rating day.

Walster, E. Assignment of responsibility for an accident. *J. Personality & Social Psychology*, 1966, 3, 73–79.
Subjects: $N = 88$; 18–21 yrs (college). **Measures:** Ss rated the degree to which a young man was responsible for an accident. Real and possible consequences of the accident varied. **Results:** (1) There were no main sex differences. (2) Men judged the young man to be more responsible when he seriously injured another person than when he might have done so; women judged the young man to be equally responsible in both conditions ($p < .05$). (3) Women judged the young man to be more responsible ($p < .001$) when he might have seriously injured another person than when he might have demolished his own car. Men did not assign more responsibility to the young man as the possible consequences of the accident increased.

Wapner, S. Age changes in perception of verticality and of the longitudinal body axis under body tilt. *J. Experimental Child Psychology*, 1968, 6, 543–55.
Subjects: $N = 192$; 7–16 yrs. **Measures:** Positions of apparent vertical location of the longitudinal axis of the body and their relation were assessed under erect and 30-degree left and right body tilt. **Results:** (1) The effect of starting position was greater for girls than for boys (apparent vertical). (2) Girls showed a greater shift of apparent body axis than boys. (3) The effect of starting position was greater for girls than for boys (apparent body axis).

Ward, W. C. Creativity in young children. *Child Development*, 1968a, *39*, 736–54.
Subjects: $N = 87$; 4–6 yrs. Measures: 3 measures of creativity were administered to Ss: the Uses test, the Patterns test, and the Instances test. Ss' responses were scored for fluency and originality. Results: No sex differences.

Ward, W. C. Reflection-impulsivity in kindergarten children. *Child Development*, 1968b, *39*, 867–74.
Subjects: $N = 87$; 5 yrs. Measures: (1) Ss were given Forms A and B of the Peabody Picture Vocabulary Test. The items of the PPVT were arranged in order of increasing difficulty, and the test was administered until Ss missed 6 of any 8 consecutive items. The mean response latency of Ss' last 6 errors was used as a measure of reflectiveness. (2) Ss were shown cards with a vertical line drawn down the center of each. On both halves of each card was an array of dots. Ss' task was to decide which half had more dots. The number of errors Ss made and the latencies of their responses to the most difficult items were recorded. (3) Ss were presented with 6 figures and were asked to indicate which of the 6 was identical to a standard. The number of incorrect matches that each S made was recorded. (4) Ss were given 2 tests based on Kagan's Matching Familiar Figures procedure. Response latency and number of errors were recorded. Results: Girls made fewer errors on the dot tests than boys did ($p < .01$). No other sex differences were found.

Ward, W. C. Creativity and environmental cues in nursery school children. *Developmental Psychology*, 1969, *1*, 543–47.
Subjects: $N = 55$; 4 yrs (nursery school). Measures: In a barren experimental room, Ss were individually given the Uses test (name all the uses for a newspaper, knife, cup, and coat hanger) and the Patterns test (interpret 8 simple abstract patterns). 2½ months later, Ss were given the Instances test (name instances of round things, soft things, and red things) under 1 of 2 conditions: in a barren experimental room or in a cue-rich environment containing 38 objects chosen to be relevant to the test. The response measures were fluency (total number of ideas given) and uniqueness (number of ideas given only by 1 child in the sample). Results: No sex differences.

Ward, W. C., and Legant, P. Naming and memory in nursery school children in the absence of rehearsal. *Developmental Psychology*, 1971, *5*, 174–75 (note and extended report).
EXPERIMENT II: Subjects: $N = 20$; 3–4 yrs. Measures: On each of 10 trials, Ss were shown 2 pictures. Ss either verbally named them or remained silent. After a 20-second delay with no opportunity for covert rehearsal, Ss were instructed to choose those 2 pictures from an array of 9. Results: No sex differences.
EXPERIMENT III: Subjects: $N = 29$; 4 yrs. Measures: Same as Experiment II, except that picture stimuli were alternated with color stimuli. Results: No sex differences.

Ward, W. D. Variance of sex-role preference among boys and girls. *Psychological Reports*, 1968, *23*, 467–70.
Subjects: $N = 48$; 4–7 yrs. Measures: Ss were presented with pictures of 15 pairs of toys, 1 masculine and 1 feminine, and were asked to indicate which toy in each pair they would like to play with. The sex-role preference measure was the number of times Ss chose own-sex toy. Results: (1) Girls showed greater group variance than boys ($p < .01$). (2) Boys preferred boys' toys more than girls preferred girls' toys ($p < .01$).

Ward, W. D. Process of sex-role development. *Developmental Psychology*, 1969a, *1*, 1963–68.
Subjects: $N = 32$; 5–8 yrs. Measures: (1) Sex-role preference was assessed by having Ss choose pictures of masculine and feminine toys on the Toy Preference Test (TPT). (2) A Pointer Game (PG) was devised to determine the extent to which boys and girls would imitate or adopt the responses of either a man or a woman. (3) Identification was measured by S's perceived similarity to parent on the Polar Adjectives Test (PAT). Results: (1) On the TPT, boys and girls preferred their own-sex toys (the main effect was accounted for by the older Ss). (2) On the PG, boys imitated the man and girls imitated the woman. (3) Among younger Ss, there was no perceived similarity with either parent on the PAT; among older Ss, both sexes saw themselves as similar to their mother.

Ward, W. D. The withholding and the withdrawing of rewards as related to level of aspiration. *Child Development*, 1969b, *40*, 491–97.
Subjects: $N = 36$; 5, 6, 7 yrs. Measures: Ss tossed a ball on the floor, and tried to make it land on certain lines. The withholding group started the game without tokens, and received tokens

as rewards. The withdrawing group started with 50 tokens, which were taken away whenever S "failed." Level of aspiration was assessed. **Results:** No sex differences.

Ward, W. D., and Furchak, A. F. Resistance to temptation among boys and girls. *Psychological Reports*, 1968, *23*, 511–14.
> **Subjects:** $N = 24$; 5, 7 yrs. **Measures:** E encouraged Ss to play with a collection of uninteresting, broken-down toys, and told them not to play with a group of attractive toys. Afterward, E left Ss alone in the playroom. The length of time Ss refrained from touching the attractive toys was recorded. **Results:** Girls showed greater resistance to temptation than boys ($p < .02$).

Ware, C. K. Cooperation and competition in children: a developmental study of behavior in Prisoner's Dilemma and maximizing differences games. Yale University, 1969.
> **Subjects:** $N = 216$; 6, 9, 12 yrs. **Measures:** Same-sex and opposite-sex pairs of Ss played 1 of 2 games; each was in the form of the Prisoner's Dilemma. **Results:** (1) Girl-girl pairs made more cooperative responses than either boy-boy or girl-boy pairs. (2) No sex differences were found in initial readiness to cooperate. (3) Girls in girl-girl pairs were more likely to cooperate after making a competitive response than Ss in girl-boy or boy-boy pairs. No differences were found among girl-girl, girl-boy, or boy-boy pairs in tendency to cooperate after making a cooperative response.

Warren, V. L., and Cairns, R. B. Social reinforcement satiation: an outcome of frequency of ambiguity? *J. Experimental Child Psychology*, 1972, *13*, 249–60.
> **Subjects:** $N = 100$; 7 yrs. **Measures:** On each trial in a discrimination-learning task, Ss were free to press either of 2 buttons. Every time Ss pressed the "correct" button, E responded with verbal approval (e.g. "right"). The number of times Ss selected the "correct" button was recorded. **Results:** No sex differences.

Wasik, H., and Wasik, J. L. Performance of culturally deprived children on the concept assessment kit—conservation. *Child Development*, 1971, *42*, 1586–90.
> **Subjects:** $N = 117$; 6–9 yrs (white and black, low SES). **Measures:** The Concept Assessment Kit—Conservation was administered to Ss. 8 areas of conservation were measured: 2-dimensional space, number, substance, continuous quantity, weight, discontinuous quantity, area, and length. **Results:** No sex differences were found.

Wasserman, S. A. Values of Mexican-American, Negro, and Anglo blue-collar and white-collar children. *Child Development*, 1971, *42*, 1624–28.
> **Subjects:** $N = 180$; 4 yrs (middle class, working class). **Measures:** Ss were questioned about pictures depicting value conflict situations. The questions pertained to what the persons in the pictures should do. Measures were obtained of Ss' preferences for 4 humanitarian values (helpfulness, cooperation, concern for others, and sharing) and 4 success values (competition, status, expertise-seeking, and task completion). **Results:** No main sex differences were found. Middle SES boys scored higher on humanitarian values (total score) than girls did ($p < .05$).

Watson, J. S. Perception of object orientation in infants. *Merrill-Palmer Quarterly*, 1966, *12*, 73–94.
> Experiment II: **Subjects:** $N = 48$; 7–8, 13–14, 19–20, 25–26 wks and mothers. **Measures:** After being placed in a supine position, S was exposed to 3 orientations each of his mother's (M's) face, of E's face, and of a multicolored cloth mask worn by E. The 3 orientations were a normal (0°) view (E's or M's eyes directly above S's eyes, E's or M's chin directly above S's chin), a sideways (90°) view, and an upside-down (180°) view (E's or M's forehead directly above S's chin, E's or M's chin directly above S's forehead). The response measure was the average time spent smiling to the 0° orientation minus the average time spent smiling to the 90° and 180° orientations. **Results:** No sex differences.
>
> Experiment III: **Subjects:** Same as Experiment II. **Measures:** Ss were simultaneously presented with 2 orientations (0° and 180°) of a schematic face. The response measure was the time spent fixating on the 0° orientation minus the time spent fixating on the 180° orientation. **Results:** No sex differences.

Watson, J. S. Operant conditioning of visual fixation in infants under visual and auditory reinforcement. *Developmental Psychology* 1969, *1*, 408–16.
> Experiment I: **Subjects:** $N = 32$; 14 wks. **Measures:** Visual fixation on 2 blank targets was differentially reinforced with contingent visual (face) and auditory (soft tones) stimuli. The frequency of fixation on the 2 target positions was recorded by an observer blind to the specific target on which fixation was being reinforced and to the modality and duration of the reinforce-

ment. **Results:** There were no main sex differences in baseline fixation rates or learning scores. Learning was better under visual than auditory reinforcement for boys; the opposite was true for girls.

EXPERIMENT II: **Subjects:** $N = 24$; 10 wks. **Measures:** S was given a 10-minute conditioning session that was divided into several periods involving 3 different types of reinforcement: auditory alone, visual alone, and a simultaneous presentation of both visual and auditory. The response measures were the same as for Experiment I. **Results:** No main sex differences. The relation between sex and effective modality of reinforcement found in Experiment I was not replicated.

Weber, D. S. A time perception task. *Perceptual & Motor Skills,* 1965, *21,* 863–66.
Subjects: $N = 72$; 16–25 yrs (college). **Measures:** Ss were asked to identify from among 9 flashing lights the 1 light containing interflash intervals of a fixed duration. **Results:** Men made more correct identifications than women ($p < .05$).

Weener, P. Language structure and the free recall of verbal messages by children. *Developmental Psychology,* 1971, *5,* 237–43.
EXPERIMENT I: **Subjects:** $N = 90$; 5–8 yrs. **Measures:** Ss heard tapes of word strings with 2 levels of syntax and associativity: with syntax/with associativity (e.g. "swift deer jump high fences"), with syntax/without associativity (e.g. "last foxes sail silver gardens"), without syntax/with associativity (associativity sentences word orders reversed), without associativity/without syntax (word order of without-associativity sentences reversed). Ss were asked to recall words without regard to order. **Results:** No sex differences.

EXPERIMENT II: **Subjects:** $N = 69$; 5–8 yrs (same as Experiment I, 4 months later). **Measures:** Additional stimulus items were constructed by adding intonation to all word strings from Experiment I that had syntax. Ss were only tested on these items; scores were compared to without-intonation scores. **Results:** No sex differences.

Wei, J. D., Lavatelli, C. B., and Jones, R. S. Piaget's concept of classification: a comparative study of socially disadvantaged and middle-class young children. *Child Development,* 1971, *42,* 919–27.
Subjects: $N = 80$; 5, 7 yrs. **Measures:** Ss performed 4 Piagetian classification tasks (changing criteria, classification, class inclusion, and matrices). **Results:** No sex differences.

Weinberg, S., and Rabinowitz, J. A sex difference in the Wechsler IQ vocabulary scores as a predictor of strategy in a probability-learning task performed by adolescents. *Developmental Psychology,* 1970, *3,* 218–24.
Subjects: $N = 48$; 12–19 yrs. **Measures:** Ss predicted which of 2 stimuli would be presented in each trial of a series. Unknown to Ss, stimuli had an 8 : 2 ratio. Prediction strategies were analyzed through choices and questioning. Before predictions, Ss completed the Block Design and Vocabulary subtests of the Wechsler Intelligence Scale for Children. **Results:** (1) More boys than girls used a maximizing strategy (predicted the more frequently appearing stimulus); more girls than boys used matching strategy (attempted to match the sequence exactly). (2) There were no sex differences on Block Design and Vocabulary scores.

Weiner, B. Achievement motivation and task recall in competitive situations. *J. Personality & Social Psychology,* 1966, *3,* 693–96.
Subjects: $N = 70$; 18–21 yrs (college). **Measures:** Ss attempted to complete more puzzle tasks than their same-sex or opposite-sex opponents. Recall of incompleted and completed tasks was assessed later. Ss also completed the Achievement Risk-Preference Scale (ARPS). **Results:** (1) There were no main sex differences. (2) Men recalled relatively more incompleted than completed tasks when competing against a woman than when competing against a man ($p < .01$). No similar difference was found for women. (3) Men who obtained high scores on the ARPS recalled relatively more incompleted than completed tasks than men who obtained low scores on the ARPS ($p < .01$). No similar difference was found for women.

Weinheimer, S. Egocentrism and social influence in children. *Child Development,* 1972, *43,* 567–68.
Subjects: $N = 160$; 5–8 yrs. **Measures:** Ss were presented with 9 stimuli. After each was shown, they reported what they had seen to E. E then informed Ss of the responses previously reported by a group of alters (3 male or female adults or peers) who had been seated at the opposite end of the table. The stimuli that were described were placed in the middle of the table so that Ss saw them from a different perspective than that of the alters. Afterward, Ss judged the correctness of their own and alters' responses. Ss' judgments were classified into 3 categories:

reconciling, conforming, and independent. **Results:** (1) Girls conformed more than boys (*p* < .01). Girls conformed more in the presence of male adult alters than boys did in the presence of female adult alters (*p* < .001). (2) Boys were more independent than girls (*p* < .01). (3) No sex differences were found in number of reconciling responses.

Weinraub, M., and Lewis, M. Infant attachment and play behavior: sex of child and sex of parent differences. *Educational Testing Service Research Bulletin*, Princeton, N.J., 1973.

   Subjects: *N* = 18; 2 yrs. **Measures:** Ss were tested in a free-play situation twice, once in the presence of their mothers and once in the presence of their fathers. Parents were instructed to respond to their children, but not to initiate any interaction. The number of seconds Ss spent in sustained toy play and the number of seconds Ss engaged in each of 4 attachment behaviors (touching the parent, proximity to the parent, looking at the parent, and vocalizing to the parent) were recorded. **Results:** (1) No sex-of-child or sex-of-parent differences were found in amount of time spent in sustained play. Girls showed more sustained play in the presence of their mothers than in the presence of their fathers; no such difference was found for boys (*p* < .01). Girls played more than boys in the presence of their mothers (*p* < .01); no sex differences were found in the presence of fathers. (2) No sex differences were found in attachment behaviors.

Weisbroth, S. P. Moral judgment, sex, and parental identification in adults. *Developmental Psychology*, 1970, 2, 396–402.

   Subjects: *N* = 78; 21–39 yrs (college graduates). **Measures:** Ss completed Kohlberg's moral judgment test. **Results:** No sex differences.

Weiss, R. F., Lombardo, J. P., Warren, D. R., and Kelley, K. A. Reinforcing effects of speaking in reply. *J. Personality & Social Psychology*, 1971, 20, 186–99.

   Subjects: *N* = 418; 18–21 yrs (college). **Measures:** After listening to a tape of another person's viewpoint on a topic, Ss were told to press a switch if they wanted to reply to the other person. During the acquisition phase, Ss were allowed to speak either on every trial on which they pressed the switch or on only 50% of the trials. During the extinction phase, no opportunity was given to reply to the other person. The response measure was the elapsed time between the presentation of the signal "Press switch if you wish to comment" and Ss' response. **Results:** No sex differences.

Weizmann, F., Cohen, L. B., and Pratt, R. J. Novelty, familiarity, and the development of infant attention. *Developmental Psychology*, 1971, 4, 149–54.

   Subjects: *N* = 32; tested at 6, 8 wks. **Measures:** Beginning at age 4 weeks, each S was placed in a bassinet and exposed to a stabile 30 minutes a day for a period of a month. At 6 weeks and again at 8 weeks of age, half the Ss were observed for 2 1-minute periods in each of 4 conditions (double observation group); the other half of the Ss were observed only at 8 weeks of age (single observation group). The 4 conditions were (1) familiar bassinet–familiar stabile; (2) familiar bassinet–novel stabile; (3) novel bassinet–familiar stabile; (4) novel bassinet– novel stabile. Fixation times to the stabiles were recorded. **Results:** (1) In the double observation group, boys had longer fixation times than girls; in the single observation group, no sex differences were found. (2) In the familiar bassinet, boys fixated on the novel stabile longer than girls.

Weller, G. M., and Bell, R. Q. Basal skin conductance and neonatal state. *Child Development*, 1965, 36, 647–57.

   Subjects: *N* = 40; 2–4 days. **Measures:** Basal skin conductance, level of arousal, respiration rate, and regularity of respiration (standard deviation of respiration rate data) were recorded between feeding periods. **Results:** Girls had higher skin conductance than boys. No other sex differences were found.

Weller, L., and Sharan (Singer), S. Articulation of the body concept among first-grade Israeli children. *Child Development*, 1971, 42, 1553–59.

   Subjects: *N* = 362; 6 yrs. **Measures:** Ss were asked to draw a human figure. Drawings were scored for degree of articulation of the body concept. **Results:** (1) Among lower SES Ss whose parents were born in Yemen, and among middle SES Ss whose parents were born in Poland, girls showed greater body articulation than boys. (2) No sex differences were found among lower SES Ss whose parents were born in Poland or Iran, or among lower or middle SES Ss whose parents were born in Iraq.

Wenar, C. Executive competence and spontaneous social behavior in one-year-olds. *Child Development*, 1972, *43*, 256–60.

Subjects: $N = 26$; 12–15 mos and mothers. **Measures:** Child's executive competence activity was scored for duration, intensity, and level, as well as for kind and intensity of affect. Spontaneous social response was scored for kind, duration, and intensity. Overall executive competence was scored for persistence. **Results:** No sex differences.

Werden, D., and Ross, L. E. A comparison of the trace and delay classical conditioning performance of normal children. *J. Experimental Child Psychology*, 1972, *14*, 126–32.

Subjects: $N = 48$; 4–6 yrs. **Measures:** Ss were conditioned to pure tones under trace-and-delay conditions for 250 single-cue eyelid-conditioning trials. **Results:** Boys conditioned better than girls ($p < .05$).

Werner, E. E., Honzik, M. P., and Smith, R. S. Prediction of intelligence and achievement at ten years from pediatric and psychological examinations. *Child Development*, 1968, *39*, 1063–75.

Subjects: $N = 639$; tested at 20 mos, 10 yrs. **Measures:** A Perinatal Stress Score, a psychological appraisal, the Cattell Infant Intelligence Scale, and the Doll's Vineland Social Maturity Scale were given at 20 months. The Science Research Associates Primary Mental Abilities Test (PMA), the Wechsler Intelligence Scale (for Ss who scored below mean on the PMA), and a teacher's summary of school achievement were given at age 10. An SES rating was obtained for each family. **Results:** (1) Both pediatricians and psychologists rated a larger proportion of boys than girls "low normal" or "retarded." (2) Among average and below-average SES Ss, girls obtained higher scores than boys on the Cattell Scale. (3) Among below-average SES Ss, girls obtained higher scores than boys on the PMA.

Wheeler, R. J., and Dusek, J. B. The effects of attentional and cognitive factors on children's incidental learning. *Child Development*, 1973, *44*, 253–58.

Subjects: $N = 144$; 5, 8, 10 yrs. **Measures:** Incidental and central learning were tested. Ss viewed paired drawings of animals and household objects, either spatially separated or contiguous, under labeling or nonlabeling conditions. **Results:** Overall, girls had greater recall on central learning than boys. There were no sex differences on incidental learning.

White, G. M. Immediate and deferred effects of model observation and guided and unguided rehearsal on donating and stealing. *J. Personality & Social Psychology*, 1972, *21*, 139–48.

Subjects: $N = 210$; 9–10 yrs. **Measures:** Following exposure to an altruistic model, Ss either did or did not rehearse charitable behavior (placing gift certificates in a charity box) in the model's presence. Immediately afterward, half of the Ss were given the opportunity to donate certificates in the absence of the model (Session I), and then again 2 days later (Session II). The remainings Ss only performed during Session II. The response measure was the number of certificates donated. **Results:** (1) No sex difference was found when the Session I performance of Ss playing immediately was compared with the Session II performance of Ss playing later. (2) When the Session II performances of both groups were examined, girls were found to donate more than boys. (3) When the Session I and Session II performances of Ss playing immediately were compared, girls were found to be more stable givers than boys ($p < .002$). (4) No sex differences were found in the donating behavior of control Ss.

White, K. M. Conceptual style and conceptual ability in kindergarten through the eighth grade. *Child Development*, 1971, *42*, 1652–56.

Subjects: $N = 150$; 5–6, 7, 9, 11, 13 yrs. **Measures:** Ss were presented with 48 drawings of humans, animals, and objects. Ss were asked to make 10 different groups, placing together those drawings with some characteristic in common. Ss were free to place a drawing in more than 1 group. Ss' groupings were classified as either inferential, descriptive, or relational. **Results:** No sex differences.

White, W. F., Anderson, H. E., Jr., and Cryder, H. The emerging self-concept in relation to select variables of secondary school students. *J. Social Psychology*, 1967, *72*, 81–88.

Subjects: $N = 225$; 13–17 yrs. **Measures:** Ss were administered the McKinney Sentence Completion Blank (a self-concept inventory). Ss' responses were classified by 3 judges into the following categories: (a) Sense of Bodily Self, (b) Sense of Continuing Self-Identity, (c) Sense of Self-Esteem, Pride, (d) Sense of Self-Extension, (e) Sense of Self-Image, (f) Sense of Self as a Rational Coper, and (g) Sense of Self as a Propriate Striver. **Results:** Girls made more responses that fell into categories (b), (d), and (g) than boys. Boys made more responses that fell into category (e) than girls.

Whiteman, M. Children's conceptions of psychological causality. *Child Development,* 1967, *38,* 143–55.

Subjects: N = 42; 5–6, 8–9 yrs (black, Puerto Rican). **Measures:** 7 stories were read to Ss. In each, a young girl exhibited 1 of 7 mechanisms of adjustment: displacement, wishful dreaming, projection, repression, regression, rationalization, or denial. After each story, Ss were asked to explain why the young girl acted as she did. Ss were rated on how well they explained the girl's behavior. **Results:** No sex differences.

Whiting, B., and Pope, C. A cross-cultural analysis of sex differences in the behavior of children aged three to eleven. *J. Social Psychology,* 1974, in press. (Further analysis of the data originally appearing in B. B. Whiting, ed., *Six cultures: studies of child rearing.* New York and London: John Wiley & Sons, 1963.)

EXPERIMENT I: **Subjects:** N = 134; 3–11 yrs (Nyansongo, Kenya; Taira, Okinawa; Khalapur, India; Toronj, Philippines; Juxtlahuaca, Mexico; Orchard Town, U.S.A.). **Measures:** Over a period of 2 years (1954–56) each child was observed in natural settings an average of 17 different times. **Results:** Though the data were analyzed separately for each culture, only the overall results of the combined sample are reported here. (1) Among younger (3-6-year-old) Ss, girls sought help more frequently than boys. No sex difference was found among older Ss. (2) Among 7-11-year-old Ss, boys sought attention more frequently than girls. No sex difference was found among younger Ss. (3) Among younger Ss, girls were observed to seek or offer physical contact more often than boys. No sex difference was found among older Ss. (4) No sex differences were found in sociability. (5) No sex differences were found in the frequency with which Ss withdrew from aggressive instigations. Among older Ss, boys more often than girls reacted with counteraggression after being attacked by peers; among younger Ss, no sex differences were found. (6) No overall sex differences were found in compliance to prosocial and egotistically dominant instigations. Among older Ss, girls were more compliant than boys to their mothers' commands and suggestions. (7) No sex differences were found in the proportion of acts that were self-instigated. (8) Among older Ss, girls offered help and support to others more frequently than boys. No sex differences were found among younger Ss. (9) Among 3-6-year-old Ss, girls offered responsible suggestions more frequently than boys. No sex difference was found among older Ss. (10) Among younger Ss, boys were more dominant than girls. No sex difference was found among older Ss. (11) Boys engaged in more rough-and-tumble play than girls. (12) Boys were more verbally aggressive than girls. (13) Assaulting with the intent to injure was not observed frequently enough to make any definitive statement. (14) Among older Ss, girls took care of children under 18 months of age more frequently than boys. (15) Girls interacted with adult women more frequently than boys. Boys interacted with peers more frequently than girls.

EXPERIMENT II: **Subjects:** N = 57; 3–10 yrs (Ngecha, Kenya). **Measures:** Observations were made of Ss for periods of 30 minutes over the course of 2 years. **Results:** (1) Among 3-6-year-olds, boys were more sociable than girls. (2) No sex differences were found in the frequency with which Ss offered help and support to others or in the frequency with which they sought attention from others. (3) There were no sex differences in the number of times Ss engaged in rough-and-tumble play.

Wicker, A. W., and Bushweiler, G. Perceived fairness and pleasantness of social exchange situations: two factorial studies of inequity. *J. Personality & Social Psychology,* 1970, *15,* 63–75.

Subjects: N = 142; 18–21 yrs (college). **Measures:** Ss responded to 18 hypothetical situations derived from all possible combinations of the following statements: (a) I (like, dislike) my co-worker, (b) I believe myself to be (more, equally, less) valuable to my employer than my co-worker, (c) I make (more, the same, less) money per hour (than) my co-worker. Ss were asked to rate the pleasantness and fairness of each situation. **Results:** No main sex differences.

Wilcox, B. M., and Clayton, F. L. Infant visual fixation on motion pictures of the human face. *J. Experimental Child Psychology,* 1968, *6,* 22–32.

Subjects: N = 6 boys, 4 girls; 5 mos. **Measures:** Ss' fixation times to silent motion pictures of a woman's face were recorded. Each S had 60-second exposures to smiling, frowning, and neutral, moving and nonmoving faces. **Results:** No sex differences.

Willerman, L., Broman, S. H., and Fiedler, M. Infant development, preschool IQ, and social class. *Child Development*, 1970, *41*, 69–77.
 Subjects: $N = 3,037$; tested at 8 mos, 4 yrs. **Measures:** Ss were given the Collaborative Research Form of the Bayley Scales of Mental and Motor Development at age 9 months and Form L-M of the Stanford-Binet IQ test at 4 years. **Results:** (1) Girls scored higher than boys on the Motor Scale ($p < .01$). No sex differences were found on the Mental Scale. (2) Girls scored higher than boys on the Stanford-Binet ($p < .001$).

Williams, J. E. Connotations of racial concepts and color names. *J. Personality & Social Psychology*, 1966, *3*, 531–40.
 Subjects: $N = 520$; 18–21 yrs (white and black college). **Measures:** Ss rated race-related color-person concepts (brown, yellow, red, white, black person) and ethnic-national concepts (Asiatic Indian, Oriental, American Indian, Caucasian, and Negro) on 12 scales, 6 of which reflected an evaluation factor, 3 a potency factor, and 3 an activity factor. **Results:** No sex differences.

Williams, J. F., Meyerson, L. J., Eron, L. D., and Semler, I. J. Peer-rated aggression and aggressive responses elicited in an experimental situation. *Child Development*, 1967, *38*, 181–90.
 Subjects: $N = 120$; 8 yrs. **Measures:** Ss whose scores on the Peer-Rate Index of Aggression were either 1 standard deviation above or below their class mean were assigned to same-sex triads. Each triad was asked to turn off a set of lights by pressing buttons situated directly below the lights. Each triad was led to believe it was competing against other teams for a prize and that the team reaching criterion first (i.e. performing the task correctly 3 times in a row) would win. On each of the first 15 trials, each S was informed that both his partners had performed incorrectly. He was then given the opportunity to let his partners know by pressing 1 of 10 buttons, each of which produced a noxious sound in their earphones. Buttons to the right produced louder sounds than buttons to the left. Measures were taken of latency, duration, intensity, and frequency of Ss' responses. **Results:** Among high-aggression Ss, boys delivered more intense sounds than girls did. A similar difference was found between low-aggression boys and girls. No sex differences were found in latency, frequency, or duration.

Williams, R. L., and Byars, H. Negro self-esteem in a transitional society. *Personnel & Guidance Journal*, 1968, *47*, 120–25.
 Subjects: $N = 310$; 14–17 yrs (black, white). **Measures:** Tennessee Self-Concept Scale. **Results:** Among black Ss, boys had lower scores on the Self-Criticism Scale than girls, implying that they were more defensive than girls about their reported self-esteem.

Williams, T. M., and Fleming, J. W. Methodological study of the relationship between associative fluency and intelligence. *Developmental Psychology*, 1969, *1*, 155–62.
 Subjects: $N = 36$; 3–4 yrs. **Measures:** The Peabody Picture Vocabulary test and a verbal and a visual associative task were administered to Ss under both an evaluative and a play atmosphere. On the verbal associative task, Ss were asked to name uses for a common object and to give examples of objects that have some particular characteristic. On the visual associative task, Ss were shown 7 simple, black line drawings. For each item, Ss were asked to name all the things they thought it could be. A total score (number of responses given) and a fluency score (total score minus number of responses that were incomprehensible, obscure, or repetitious) were obtained for each associative task item. **Results:** No sex differences.

Willis, F. N. Initial speaking distance as a function of the speaker's relationship. *Psychonomic Science*, 1966, *5*, 221–22.
 Subjects: $N = 755$; adults. **Measures:** Distances between individuals who were classified as either strangers, acquaintances, friends, or close friends were recorded at the moment conversation began. **Results:** (1) Women were approached more closely than men ($p < .01$). (2) Compared to men, women stood closer to good friends, but farther away from friends ($p < .01$).

Willis, R. H., and Willis, Y. A. Role playing versus deception: an experimental comparison. *J. Personality & Social Psychology*, 1970, *16*, 472–77.
 Subjects: $N = 96$; 18–21 yrs (college). **Measures:** Ss in same-sex pairs ranked 10 stimulus photographs according to aesthetic value. Ss were then informed of the scores earned by their own and partner's rankings, and received a copy of partner's ranking. Ss' subsequent reranking

of the stimuli was compared with partner's initial ranking to yield a net conformity score. **Results:** No sex differences.

Willoughby, R. H. Field-dependence and locus of control. *Perceptual & Motor Skills,* 1967, *24,* 671–72.
Subjects: $N = 76$; 18–21 yrs (college). **Measures:** Hidden Figures Test. **Results:** No sex differences.

Wilson, P. R., and Russell, P. N. Modification of psychophysical judgments as a method of reducing dissonance. *J. Personality & Social Psychology,* 1966, *3,* 710–12.
Subjects: $N = 60$; 18–21 yrs (college). **Measures:** After being blindfolded, Ss lifted a heavy and a light weight the same vertical distance (Ss were unaware of this fact). Afterward, Ss were asked to estimate how high they had lifted each weight. Response measure was the difference between Ss' estimates. **Results:** No sex differences.

Wilson, R. S., and Harpring, E. B. Mental and motor development in infant twins. *Development Psychology,* 1972, *7,* 277–87.
Subjects: $N = 261$ pairs of twins; tested at 3, 6, 9, 12, 18, 24 mos. **Measures:** Bayley Scales of Infant Development. **Results:** At 9 months, girls scored higher than boys on the motor scale ($p < .05$). At 18 months, girls scored higher than boys on the mental scale ($p < .05$).

Wilson, R. S., Brown, A. M., and Matheny, A. P. Emergence and persistence of behavioral differences in twins. *Child Development,* 1971, *42,* 1381–98.
Subjects: $N = 232$ pairs of same-sex twins; 3–72 mos and mothers. **Measures:** Interviews were conducted with mothers on a regular basis. For each of 17 behavioral variables, mothers were asked whether both twins displayed the behavior to an equal degree (concordance), or whether 1 twin exhibited the behavior to a greater degree than the other (discordance). **Results:** A higher proportion of female twins than male twins were reported concordant in quality of vocalization at 24, 36, and 72 months of age.

Wilson, W., and Insko, C. Recency effects in face-to-face interaction. *J. Personality & Social Psychology,* 1968, *9,* 21–23.
Subjects: $N = 158$; 18–21 yrs (college). **Measures:** After playing a modified version of the Prisoner's Dilemma game with a confederate of the same sex, Ss rated the confederate on the following traits: generosity, cooperativeness, fairness, willingness to accommodate, willingness to compromise, greed, kindness, and meanness. The response measure was the sum of the ratings on these traits. **Results:** No sex differences.

Winitz, H. Language skills of male and female kindergarten children. *J. Speech & Hearing Research,* 1959, *2,* 377–86.
Subjects: $N = 150$; 5 yrs. **Measures:** The Wechsler Intelligence Scale for Children, Ammons Full-Range Vocabulary Test, and the Templin Screening Test of Articulation were administered. Verbal responses elicited from Ss after the presentation of the Children's Apperception Test Cards were scored for length of responses, number of words in the 5 longest responses, number of 1-word responses, standard deviation, number of different words, and structural complexity. 4 measures of word fluency were also obtained: Ss were asked to name as many children's names, as many adults' names, as many names of things, and as many words that rhymed with certain sounds as they could think of. **Results:** (1) Girls had higher WISC Performance Scale IQs than boys ($p < .02$). No sex differences were found in WISC Full Scale IQ or WISC Verbal Scale IQ. (2) No sex differences were found in vocabulary and articulation tests. (3) For the verbal response measures, the 5 longest responses ($p < .01$) and the standard deviation ($p < .05$) were both higher for girls than for boys. (4) Girls named more children's names than boys did ($p < .01$). No sex differences were found on the other 3 word fluency measures.

Winkel, G. H., and Sarason, G. Subject, experimenter, and situational variables in research on anxiety. *J. Abnormal & Social Psychology,* 1964, *68,* 601–8.
Subjects: $N = 144$; 18–21 yrs (college). **Measures:** Ss who were either high or low in test anxiety were presented with 12 nonsense words for 15 trials in a word-anticipation task. After completing the task, Ss were informed by E that they had performed either extremely well or extremely poorly. Ss were then given a second list of 12 nonsense words for 15 trials. The 24 male Es who administered the tasks were either high or low in anxiety (as assessed by the Test Anxiety Scale). **Results:** (1) Women made more correct anticipations than men (List 1, $p < .05$; List 2, $p < .01$). (2) Women performed better under low-anxiety Es than under high-anxiety Es, whereas the reverse was true for men (List 1, $p < .01$; List 2, $p < .05$).

Wispé, L. G., and Freshley, H. B. Race, sex, and sympathetic helping behavior. *J. Personality & Social Psychology*, 1971, *17*, 59–65.

EXPERIMENT I: **Subjects:** $N = 176$; adults (white, black). **Measures:** S's responses to a black or white female accomplice who dropped a bag of groceries in front of S as S left a supermarket were classified as either helping or nonhelping. **Results:** More black men helped the female accomplice than black women did ($p < .02$). No sex difference was found in the white sample.

EXPERIMENT II: **Subjects:** $N = 48$; adults (observed Ss in Experiment I refuse to help female accomplice). **Measures:** Helping behavior of observers. **Results:** More men helped the female accomplice than women did ($p < .05$).

Witkin, H. A., Goodenough, D. R., and Karp, S. A. Stability of cognitive style from childhood to young adulthood. *J. Personality & Social Psychology*, 1967, *7*, 291–300.

Subjects: $N = 515$; 8, 10–13, 15, 17, 18–21 yrs (cross-sectional study). $N = 47$; tested at 8, 13 yrs. $N = 51$, tested at 10, 14, 17 yrs. **Measures:** Series 3 of the Rod-and-Frame Test was administered to all Ss. Ss in the cross-sectional study were also given the Embedded Figures Test (EFT) and the Body Adjustment Test (BAT) of the Tilting-Room-Tilting-Chair Test. **Results:** (1) In the cross-sectional study, boys were more field-independent on the RFT and EFT than girls. No sex differences were found on the BAT. (2) In the 5-year longitudinal study, boys were more field-independent than girls at both ages. In the 7-year longitudinal study, no sex differences were found.

Witkin, H. A., Birnbaum, J., Lomonaco, S., Lehr, S., and Herman, J. L. Cognitive patterning in congenitally totally blind children. *Child Development*, 1968, *39*, 768–86.

Subjects: $N = 53$; 12–19 yrs (blind, sighted). **Measures:** Ss completed a tactile embedded figures test, an auditory embedded figures test, 2 analytic-ability problem-solving tasks (the tactile block design task and the tactile matchsticks task), a clay-modeling body-concept test, and the verbal section of the Wechsler intelligence scales. **Results:** Girls performed better than boys on the tactile matchsticks task. No sex differences were found on the other tests.

Wittig, M. A., and Weir, M. W. The role of reinforcement procedure in children's probability learning as a function of age and number of response alternatives. *J. Experimental Child Psychology*, 1971, *12*, 228–39.

Subjects: $N = 80$; 4–5 yrs. **Measures:** Ss performed either a 2- or a 4-choice probability-learning task under either contingent or noncontingent reinforcement procedures. On each trial, Ss were told to guess which of 2 (or 4) buttons would light up by pressing that button. The buttons were arranged in a horizontal row. **Results:** (1) No sex differences were found in the number of times Ss chose the higher probability alternative. (2) On the 2-choice task, there were no sex differences in the frequency with which Ss exhibited either of the following simple response patterns: left button–right button–left button or right button–left button–right button. (3) On the 4-choice task, boys in the contingent reinforcement condition emitted more left-to-right or right-to-left sequences of responses than did their female counterparts ($p < .01$). No sex differences were found in the noncontingent reinforcement condition.

Wohlford, P. Extension of personal time, affective states, and expectation of personal death. *J. Personality & Social Psychology*, 1966, *3*, 559–66.

Subjects: $N = 147$; 18–21 yrs (college). **Measures:** Before providing descriptions of a future event (either a pleasant or unpleasant experience or their death), Ss completed a personal association test. For each association, Ss were requested to give temporal referents. Dates were converted to scale scores to yield measures of extension (the length of the time span encompassed by Ss' cognition), protension (Ss' extension of personal time into the future), and retrotension (Ss' extension of personal time into the past). **Results:** Women had higher retrotension scores than men ($p < .01$). No sex differences were found in protension and extension scores.

Wohlford, P., Santrock, J. W., Berger, S. E., and Liberman, D. Older brothers' influence on sex-typed, aggressive, and dependent behavior in father-absent children. *Developmental Psychology*, 1971, *4*, 124–34.

Subjects: $N = 66$; 4–6 yrs (black, low SES, father-absent). **Measures:** Ss responded to forced-choice picture pairs of male- or female-typed activities, people or scenes, doll-play situations that elicited aggressive responses, and doll-play situations that were scored for dependency. Mothers were interviewed on Ss' masculinity-femininity, aggression, and dependency. **Results:** (1) Boys' sex-typed behavior was more masculine than girls' on the forced-choice masculinity-femininity measures ($p < .001$). (2) There were no sex differences in maternal report of masculinity-femininity. (3) Boys displayed more intense aggression (i.e. hitting as opposed to threatening to hit) in the doll-play interview than girls ($p < .03$). Boys were also higher on frequency of doll-play interview aggression ($p = .02$), but no sex difference was found on the mother-interview report of aggression. (4) There were no sex differences in dependency on either doll-play or maternal interview measures.

Wohlwill, J. F. Texture of the stimulus field and age as variables in the perception of relative distance in photographic slides. *J. Experimental Child Psychology*, 1965, 2, 163–77.
   Subjects: $N = 96$; 6, 9, 13, 16 yrs. **Measures:** Photographic slides of stimulus fields were taken at an angle to convey the impression of depth. The fields varied in texture density and in the regularity of patterning of their texture elements. Each field featured a toy cow in the foreground and a toy horse in the background; a toy fence was placed at varying distances in between. Ss' task was to judge which of the two stimuli, the cow or the horse, was closer to the fence. **Results:** No sex differences.

Wolf, T. M. Effects of live modeled sex-inappropriate play behavior in a naturalistic setting. *Developmental Psychology*, 1973, 9, 120–23.
   Subjects: $N = 60$; 7–11 yrs. **Measures:** Ss viewed a male or female peer model play with a toy judged to be sex-inappropriate for the child observer (for boys, a toy oven; for girls, a truck). Following exposure to the model, Ss were observed in free play for 5 minutes. Latency to touch the inappropriate toy and total time spent playing with it were recorded. Ss were then asked whether they liked or disliked the model. **Results:** (1) No main sex differences were found on either the latency or duration measure. Boys played with the oven longer following exposure to a boy than to a girl model. Girls played with the truck more quickly following exposure to a girl than to a boy model. (2) Boys and girls did not differ in their liking of the models. Boys liked same-sex models more than opposite-sex models; no difference was found for girls.

Wolf, T. M. Response consequences to televised modeled sex-inappropriate play behavior. Submitted for publication, *Developmental Psychology*, 1974.
   Subjects: $N = 140$; 5–9 yrs. **Measures:** Each S viewed a videotape of a boy or girl model playing with a toy judged to be sex-inappropriate for S (a doll for boys, a fire engine for girls). Models were either praised, criticized, or not reinforced while playing with the toy. After completion of the filmed sequence, Ss were observed in free play for 5 minutes. Latency to touch the sex-inappropriate toy and total time spent playing with it were recorded. Ss were then asked to exhibit as many of the unusual responses performed by the model as possible. During both the free play and recall phase, measures were taken of the number of different unusual responses displayed by each child. Liking for the model was also assessed. **Results:** (1) Girls touched the inappropriate toy longer and more readily than boys did. Both sexes played with the toy longer after being exposed to a same-sex model than after viewing an opposite-sex model. (2) During the recall task, boys displayed more unusual responses than girls. No sex differences were found during the free play phase. (3) Girls liked the model more than boys did. The same-sex model was liked more by girls than the opposite-sex model; no difference was found for boys.

Wolfensberger, W. P., Miller, M. B., Foshee, J. G., and Cromwell, R. L. Rorschach correlates of activity level in high school children. *J. Consulting Psychology*, 1962, 26, 269–72.
   Subjects: $N = 100$; 13–17 yrs. **Measures:** While Ss listened to music, their activity level was measured with a ballistograph. **Results:** 44 Ss who had either the highest or the lowest activity levels were selected to participate in a second study. Of these 44 Ss, more boys than girls were hyperkinetic ($p < .01$).

Wolff, P. The role of stimulus-correlated activity in children's recognition of nonsense forms. *J. Experimental Child Psychology*, 1972, 14, 427–41.
   EXPERIMENT I: **Subjects:** $N = 67$; 4–7 yrs. **Measures:** Ss performed a task involving a visual recognition of nonsense forms with voluntary haptic activity. **Results:** No sex differences.
   EXPERIMENT II: **Subjects:** $N = 30$; 4–5 yrs. **Measures:** Same as Experiment I, except that Ss were trained in haptic activity. **Results:** No sex differences.

Wolff, P., and Wolff, E. A. Correlational analysis of motor and verbal activity in young children. *Child Development*, 1972, 43, 1407–11.
   Subjects: $N = 55$; 4–5 yrs. **Measures:** Teachers rated their pupils on gross motor activity, fine motor activity, manual dexterity, verbal output, and verbal skill. **Results:** No sex differences.

Wolman, R. N., Lewis, C., and King, M. The development of the language of emotions: conditions of emotional arousal. *Child Development,* 1971, *42,* 1288–93.

Subjects: $N = 256$; grade school. Measures: Ss were interviewed about their feelings and emotions: hunger, thirst, sadness, sleepiness, happiness, anger, fear, and nervousness. If Ss indicated they had experienced an emotion, they were asked, "When do you get it?" Ss' responses were classified as either internal (e.g. "I get hungry when my stomach feels empty") or external (e.g. "I get hungry when it is time for lunch"). Results: Among older Ss (age range not given), boys reported that the conditions eliciting their emotions occurred more frequently within themselves and less frequently outside themselves than girls did (level of significance not reported).

Woodruff, D. S., and Burren, J. E. Age changes and cohort differences in personality. *Developmental Psychology,* 1972, *6,* 252–59 (and personal communication).

Subjects: $N = 77$; 16, 18–21 yrs (college). $N = 85$; 43–46 yrs (previously tested at 18–21 yrs). Measures: The California Test of Personality was administered to Ss; 43-46-year-old Ss were tested twice: (1) In the self-condition, Ss described themselves. (2) In the retrospective condition, Ss answered the test as they thought they had responded in 1944. Results: (1) No main sex differences were found among 16- or 18-21-year-old Ss. (2) No main sex differences were found in the 1944 scores of the 43-46-year-old sample, nor were there any sex differences in their 1969 scores in either the self or retrospective condition.

Woods, M. G. The unsupervised child of the working mother. *Developmental Psychology,* 1972, *6,* 14–25.

Subjects: $N = 108$; 10 yrs (black). Measures: Ss indicated whether or not they were supervised by adults during the critical periods of the school day (breakfast, lunch hour, and after school until dinner). Results: More girls than boys reported a lack of supervision ($p < .02$).

Worchel, S., and Brehm, J. W. Effect of threat to attitudinal freedom as a function of agreement with the communicator. *J. Personality & Social Psychology,* 1970, *14,* 18–22.

Subjects: $N = 73$; 18–21 yrs (college). Measures: S filled out attitude questionnaires before and after reading a persuasive speech. Speeches were either for or against S's position, and were designed to either threaten or not threaten S's freedom to decide for himself. The response variable was the amount of change in attitude either toward or away from S's advocated position. Results: No sex differences.

Wright, D. Social reinforcement and maze learning in children. *Child Development,* 1968, *39,* 177–83.

Subjects: $N = 80$; 10, 11 yrs. Measures: Ss attempted to solve a maze task twice. Social reinforcement was given in 3 conditions: positive, negative, and mixed. The control group received no reinforcement. The measure of learning was the number of trials to criterion. Results: Boys were better at learning the maze task than girls ($p < .05$). This effect appears due to the presence of girls in the control group; girls in the experimental groups tended to do slightly better than boys.

Wyer, R. S., Jr. Self-acceptance, discrepancy between parents' perceptions of their children, and goal-seeking effectiveness. *J. Personality & Social Psychology,* 1965, *2,* 311–16.

Subjects: $N = 889$; 18 yrs and parents. Measures: Ss rated (their acceptance of) themselves on each of 24 adjectives. Using the same set of adjectives, parents recorded their feelings about their children. Results: (1) No sex differences were found in self-acceptance. (2) Mothers' acceptance ratings of their daughters were higher than their ratings of their sons. No sex differences were found in fathers' acceptance ratings.

Wyer, R. S., Jr. Effects of incentive to perform well, group attraction, and group acceptance on conformity in a judgmental task. *J. Personality & Social Psychology,* 1966, *4,* 21–26.

Subjects: $N = 80$; 14–17 yrs. Measures: Ss estimated the number of dots presented on slides. Judgments were made both before and after exposure to fictitious group norms. The response measure was the degree of conformity. Results: No sex differences.

Wyer, R. S., Jr. Behavioral correlates of academic achievement: conformity under achievement- and affiliation-incentive conditions. *J. Personality & Social Psychology,* 1967, *6,* 255–63.

EXPERIMENT I: Subjects: $N = 2,000$; 18 yrs (college). Measures: Ss' scores on the American College Testing Service Entrance Examination (ACTS) and their first-term freshman grade-point averages (GPA) were obtained. **Results:** No sex differences.

EXPERIMENT II: **Subjects:** $N = 128$; 18 yrs (same as Experiment I). **Measures:** Ss selected from the larger sample were either high-high, high-low, low-high, or low-low in performance (GPA) and aptitude (ACTS). Before and after exposure to fictitious group norms, Ss (in groups of 7–10) estimated the number of dots on each of 10 slides. Ss were tested under 2 conditions: achievement-incentive (Ss were told that their performance would reflect their achievement potential) and affiliative-incentive (group attractiveness was made salient while the importance of the task was deemphasized). The response measure was the degree to which Ss conformed to the fictitious group norms. **Results:** (1) There were no main sex differences. (2) Conformity scores for men were higher in the affiliative-incentive condition than in the achievement-incentive condition; conformity scores for women showed the reverse trend ($p < .05$).

Wyer, R. S., Jr. Effects of task reinforcement, social reinforcement, and task difficulty on perseverance in achievement-related activity. *J. Personality & Social Psychology*, 1968, *8*, 269–76.

Subjects: $N = 70$; 3–6 yrs. **Measures:** Ss were asked to perform an objectively easy or difficult task. The response measure was Ss' perseverance on the task. Ss were then shown a series of 5 games, 1 of which was described as easy for other children to perform and the other as difficult. Ss' relative preferences for the easy and difficult games were recorded. **Results:** No sex differences.

Wylie, R. C., and Hutchins, E. B. Schoolwork ability estimates and aspirations as a function of socioeconomic level, race, and sex. *Psychological Reports*, 1967, Monographic Supplement 3-V21.

Subjects: $N = 3,422$; 12–17 yrs. **Measures:** 11 groups of senior high school students (ranging in size from 39 to 448) and 6 groups of junior high school students (ranging in size from 34 to 149) were asked (1) whether they thought they were in the top or bottom half of their homerooms in ability to do schoolwork; (2) whether they felt they had the ability to do college work; (3) whether they were interested in going to college; (4) whether they were planning to go to college; (5) whether their parents had encouraged them to attend college; (6) whether their same-sex close friends would admire them for trying to do well in their schoolwork; and (7) if they thought their grade averages for the year were in the top half of their homerooms. Ss were also questioned about their grade aspirations and career plans. **Results:** Following each result below are 2 numbers. The first gives the fraction of subgroups that exhibited the stated sex difference. The second gives the number of subgroups in which this difference was significant. (1) More boys than girls placed themselves in the top half of their homerooms in ability: junior high school (JHS), 6/6, 0; senior high school (SHS), no trend emerged. (2) More boys than girls felt they had the ability to do college work: JHS, 6/6, 0; SHS, no trend emerged. (3) More boys than girls wanted to go to college: JHS, 6/6, 1; SHS, 7/8, 3. (4) More boys than girls planned to go to college: SHS, 3/3, 3. (5) More boys than girls reported that their parents had encouraged them to attend college: JHS, 5/5, 1; SHS, 11/11, 6. (6) More girls than boys indicated that their friends would admire them if they tried to do their best in their schoolwork: JHS, 5/6, 1; SHS, 3/3, 3. (7) More girls than boys judged that their grade average for the year was in the top half of their homerooms: JHS, no trend emerged; SHS, 6/6, 3. (8) More girls than boys had high career aspirations: JHS, 5/6, 1. More boys than girls had high career aspirations: SHS, 7/11, 4. (9) More girls than boys aspired to high grades: JHS, no trend emerged; SHS, 6/6, 3.

Yamamoto, K. Development of ability to ask questions under specific testing conditions. *J. Genetic Psychology*, 1962, *101*, 83–90.

Subjects: $N = 780$; 6–17 yrs. **Measures:** Ask and Guess Test. **Results:** (1) Among 9-year-old Ss, girls asked twice as many "Be?" questions as boys ($p < .01$). (2) Among 10-year-old Ss, girls asked 3 times as many "Where?" questions as boys. Boys asked twice as many "Be?" questions as girls ($p < .01$). (3) Among 12-year-old Ss, boys asked 3 times as many "What?" questions as girls ($p < .01$).

Yando, R. M., and Kagan, J. The effect of teacher tempo on the child. *Child Development*, 1968, *39*, 27–34.

Subjects: $N = 160$; 6 yrs. **Measures:** The Matching Familiar Figures Test was administered to Ss twice—once in the fall and once in the spring. **Results:** At the initial testing, no sex differences were found in response time. At the spring testing, boys and girls exhibited similar changes in scores.

Yando, R. M., and Zigler, E. Outerdirectedness in the problem-solving of institutionalized and noninstitutionalized normal and retarded children. *Developmental Psychology*, 1971, 4, 277–88.

Subjects: $N = 192$; 5–6, 9–10 yrs. Measures: Ss performed a 3-choice discrimination-learning task and an imitation task. On each trial of the discrimination task, Ss received a marble after choosing the largest of 3 squares. On each trial of the imitation task, Ss either watched E make a design, viewed a slide of a design projected onto a screen, or did both. Ss were then given the opportunity to make any design they wanted to. Results: (1) No main sex differences were found in the number of errors on the discrimination-learning task. (2) Both sexes exhibited a similar degree of imitation of the model's and of the projector's designs.

Yando, R. M., Zigler, E., and Gates, M. The influence of Negro and white teachers rated as effective or noneffective on the performance of Negro and white lower-class children. *Developmental Psychology*, 1971, 5, 290–99.

Subjects: $N = 144$; 8 yrs. Measures: (1) Ss were given 3 tasks assessing social approach and avoidance tendencies; 2 of these required Ss to place free forms on a large felt panel. After each trial, the distance of Ss' placement from E's end of the panel was recorded. The third task offered Ss the choice of looking through 1 of 4 Viewmasters that varied in distance from E. A record was kept of Ss' choice of Viewmasters. Ss also completed the Peabody Picture Vocabulary Test and a curiosity measure. All 5 tests were administered by black or white female teachers who were judged by a school psychologist to be either highly effective or noneffective. Both classroom teachers and teacher Es rated each child on (a) his classroom achievement (or in the case of the teacher E, his "probable" achievement), (b) the amount of fear he displayed in his interaction with adults, and (c) the frequency with which he displayed positive and negative attention-seeking behaviors. Results: (1) No main sex differences were found on the social approach and avoidance tasks. On trial 1 of 1 of the 2 placing tasks, girls placed the felt forms closer to white Es than boys did. (2) Among Ss in the white sample, boys obtained higher scores on the PPVT than girls did. No sex difference was found in the black sample. (3) Among Ss in the black sample, boys showed less curiosity than girls. No difference was found between white boys and girls. (4) Teacher Es rated girls as more fearful than boys. No other sex differences were found in their ratings. (5) Among white Ss, boys were rated by their classroom teachers as displaying more positive and negative attention-seeking behavior than girls; among black Ss, no sex differences were found. No differences were found between teachers' fearfulness or achievement ratings of black or white boys and girls.

Yang, R. K., and Douthitt, T. C. Newborn responses to threshold tactile stimulation. *Child Development*, 1974, in press.

Subjects: $N = 43$; 2 days. Measures: Air puffs of increasing intensities were presented to Ss' abdomens until a motor response occurred. Changes in heart rate were recorded. Results: No sex differences.

Yarrow, L. J., Rubenstein, J. L., and Pedersen, F. A. Dimensions of early stimulation: differential effects on infant development. Paper presented at the meeting of the Society for Research in Child Development, 1971 (and personal communication).

Subjects: $N = 41$; tested at 5, 6 mos (black) and their primary caretakers. Measures: At 5 months of age, 2 home observations were made of infants and their primary caretakers. Infants were scored for frequency of positive vocalization, frequency of fussing and crying, and amount of time spent in focused exploration of their environment. Caretakers were scored for proximity to infant, level and variety of social stimulation, contingency of response to the infant's positive vocalizations, and contingency of response to the infant's distress calls. Measures were also taken of the variety, complexity, and responsiveness of the objects available to the infant. During the fifth month, a research form of the Bayley Tests of Infant Development was also administered. The Bayley yields a Mental Developmental Index, a Psychomotor Index, and 8 more differentiated clusters: Social Responsiveness, Language Development, Fine Motor, Gross Motor, Goal Orientation, Reaching and Grasping, Secondary Circular Reaction, and Object Permanence. A ninth cluster, Problem Solving, was developed from 4 supplementary items administered after the Bayley. At 6 months of age, Ss were given a structured situational test designed to assess exploratory behavior and preference for novel stimuli. Ss were first presented with a novel toy (a bell) for 10 minutes. Durations of manipulating, looking, and vocalizing to the bell were recorded. Then a series of 10 new toys were presented 1 at a time. Each was paired with the bell. Two measures were taken: (1) time spent looking at the novel toy minus time spent looking at the bell, and (2) time spent manipulating the novel toy minus time spent manipulating the bell. **Results:** (1) Boys received higher levels and a greater variety of social stimulation than girls did ($p < .05$, $p < .01$). Boys' gross motor responses were encouraged more than girls' ($p < .05$). (2) Boys scored higher than girls on Goal Orientation and Object Permanence ($p < .05$). (3) Girls looked at the bell more than boys did ($p < .05$).

Yarrow, M. R., and Scott, P. M. Imitation of nurturant and non-nurturant models. *J. Personality & Social Psychology*, 1972, *23*, 259–70.
> **Subjects:** $N = 118$; 3–5 yrs. **Measures:** Ss participated in small mixed-sex play groups under the supervision of either a nurturant or nonnurturant female caretaker, who performed a variety of neutral, nurturant, and nonnurturant behaviors. Imitative displays of the models' behavior were recorded. **Results:** No sex differences.

Yarrow, M. R., Waxler, C. Z., and Scott, P. M. Child effects on adult behavior. *Developmental Psychology*, 1971, *5*, 300–311.
> **Subjects:** $N = 118$; 3–5 yrs. **Measures:** Child-woman and child-peer interactions were observed in a nursery school setting for 4 30-minute play sessions. Ss were in play groups of 6–8 members with either a high- or low-nurturant adult caretaker. **Results:** There were no sex differences in frequency of bids for adult attention.

Yee, A. H., and Runkel, P. J. Simplicial structures of middle-class and lower-class pupils' attitudes toward teachers. *Developmental Psychology*, 1969, *1*, 646–52.
> **Subjects:** $N = 209$; 9–12 yrs (low, middle SES). All classes had male teachers. **Measures:** The About My Teacher Inventory was administered to Ss to assess their attitudes toward their teachers on 5 dimensions: affective (e.g. Is your teacher fun to be with?), cognitive (e.g. Does your teacher explain your lesson clearly?), disciplinary (e.g. Does your teacher succeed in keeping the pupils under control?), innovative (e.g. Does your class go on field trips that help you understand what you are studying?), and motivational (e.g. Does your teacher make you feel like learning a lot on your own?). **Results:** No sex differences.

Yelen, D. R. Identification: the acquisition of evaluative connotations. *J. Personality & Social Psychology*, 1969, *12*, 328–32.
> **Subjects:** $N = 96$; 18–21 yrs (college). **Measures:** 1 member (model) of each same-sex pair of Ss was conditioned to associate either positive or negative connotations with nonsense syllables. Afterward, the model (M) and his partner (P) rated the nonsense syllables on semantic scales. M responded first by saying 1 of the scale numbers aloud. P then indicated his choice. Each time that P imitated M's rating, he was reinforced by E. Imitation was defined as a rating on the same side of the scale as the M's rating. Before and after the imitation trials, P was presented with the nonsense syllables followed by pairs of bipolar evaluative words. For each item, P indicated which of the 2 words had a meaning most similar to that of the nonsense syllable. **Results:** (1) No sex differences were found on the pre-imitation test. (2) No sex differences were found in models' ratings. (3) Women imitated model's ratings more than men did ($p < .05$). (4) On the post-imitation test, women acquired more reinforced evaluative connotations than men did ($p < .05$).

Youniss, J., and Murray, J. P. Transitive inference with nontransitive solutions controlled. *Developmental Psychology*, 1970, *2*, 169–75.
> **Subjects:** $N = 64$; 5, 8 yrs. **Measures:** Ss performed 20 transitivity judgments of stick lengths in 3 paradigms. **Results:** No sex differences.

Youssef, Z. I. The role of race, sex, hostility, and verbal stimulus in inflicting punishment. *Psychonomic Science*, 1968, *12*, 285–86.
> **Subjects:** $N = 120$; 18–21 yrs (college). **Measures:** Ss administered shocks to either a black or white, male or female confederate. Ss also completed a scale composed of items from Cook and Medley's Hostility Scale and Siegel's Manifest Hostility Scale. **Results:** (1) Men inflicted more intense shocks than women ($p < .05$). (2) Male confederates received higher levels of shock than female confederates ($p < .05$). (3) Men scored higher than women on the hostility scale ($p < .01$).

Zander, A., and van Egmond, E. Relationship of intelligence and social power to the interpersonal behavior of children. *J. Educational Psychology*, 1958, *49*, 257–68.
> **Subjects:** $N = 418$; 7, 10 yrs. **Measures:** Ss were randomly assigned to 4-person groups. Every group worked on 4 tasks, each of which required a group decision as a first step toward completion of the task. The number of times Ss exhibited the following behaviors was recorded: (a) attempts to influence others; (b) successful influence attempts; (c) un-

successful influence attempts; (d) demanding influence attempts; (e) suggestions; (f) evaluation of another child's behavior (positive or negative); (g) aggressive acts; and (h) affect-laden acts (friendly and unfriendly). **Results:** (1) Boys engaged in the following behaviors more often than girls: attempt to influence others, successful influence attempts, unsuccessful influence attempts, demanding influence attempts, and aggressive acts. (2) No other sex differences were found.

Zander, A., Fuller, R., and Armstrong, W. Attributed pride or shame in group and self. *J. Personality & Social Psychology*, 1972, *23*, 346–52.
> **Subjects:** $N = 88$; 18–21 yrs (college). **Measures:** S rated the amount of pride or shame he would have in his group or himself, after his group had earned each of 5 gradated scores on an unspecified task. **Results:** (1) Men had higher pride-in-self ratings than women ($p < .02$). (2) No sex differences were found in pride-in-group ratings.

Zelazo, P. R. Smiling to social stimuli: eliciting and conditioning effects. *Developmental Psychology*, 1971, *4*, 32–42.
> EXPERIMENT I: **Subjects:** $N = 20$; 3 mos. **Measures:** After base-rate smiling to unresponsive E was recorded, E responded contingently to S's smiles by smiling back and talking while touching S's abdomen. Number of contingently stimulated smiles (when E was not interacting with S), elicited smiles (during interaction time), and total smiling were recorded. **Results:** No sex differences.
>
> EXPERIMENT II: **Subjects:** $N = 30$; 3 mos. **Measures:** After base-rate smiling data were recorded, E administered social stimulation under contingent (same as Experiment I), noncontingent (social stimulation administered at random without regard to occurrence of infant smiling), or unresponsive control conditions. All smiling during 3-second periods was recorded as 1 smile. **Results:** No sex differences.

Zern, D. The "mental step" hypothesis in solving verbal problems: effects of variations in question-phrasing on a grade school population. *Developmental Psychology*, 1971, *4*, 103–4 (brief report).
> **Subjects:** $N = 69$; 7, 9–12 yrs. **Measures:** Ss answered 72 questions, each of which was similar in form to the following: "The answer was 27. Is it or is it not true that the answer was not an even number?" Measures were taken of the number of errors that Ss made and the latencies of their responses. **Results:** No sex differences.

Zern, D., and Taylor, A. L. Rhythmic behavior in the hierarchy of responses of preschool children. *Merrill-Palmer Quarterly*, 1973, *19*, 137–45.
> **Subjects:** $N = 41$; 2–4 yrs (nursery school). **Measures:** Classroom observers noted S's rhythmicities, i.e. rhythmical repetitive body movements, exclusive of goal-directed behavior. **Results:** No sex differences were found in frequency of oral or non-oral rhythmicities.

Zigler, E. Motivational aspects of change in culturally deprived nursery school children. *Child Development*, 1968, *39*, 1–14.
> **Subjects:** $N = 52$; 3–4 yrs (white, black). **Measures:** Stanford-Binet IQ Test. **Results:** No sex differences.

Zigler, E., and Balla, D. Developmental course of responsiveness to social reinforcement in normal children and institutionalized retarded children. *Developmental Psychology*, 1972, *6*, 66–73.
> **Subjects:** $N = 50$; mental ages 8, 11 yrs. **Measures:** Ss performed a monotonous task (Marble-in-the-Hole Game), receiving predetermined verbal and nonverbal reinforcement. The Zigler Social Deprivation Scale was used to assess preinstitutional social histories of retarded Ss; 4 measures of maintenance of contact with family and friends were collected. Length of institutionalization, percentage of life institutionalized, and age at time of institutionalization were obtained. **Results:** No sex differences (data of youngest mental-age group were not analyzed).

Zigler, E., and Yando, R. Outer directedness and imitative behavior of institutionalized and noninstitutionalized younger and older children. *Child Development*, 1972, *43*, 413–25.
> **Subjects:** $N = 192$; 7, 11 yrs. **Measures:** Before each trial in a marble-sorting task, Ss observed either a female E or a marble dispenser drop a marble into 1 of 4 quadrants of a wooden bowl. Measures were taken of the number of times Ss displayed imitative behavior (i.e. chose a marble of the same color and dropped it into the same quadrant as did E or the machine). **Results:** No sex differences.

Zigler, E., Levine, J., and Gould, L. Cognitive challenge as a factor in children's humor appreciation. *J. Personality & Social Psychology*, 1967, *6*, 332–36.
Subjects: $N = 60$; 8, 10, and 12 yrs. Measures: After exposure to cartoons varying in level of difficulty, Ss rated the cartoons for humor. A measure of comprehension was obtained by asking Ss what they found particularly funny about each cartoon. Spontaneous mirth responses were recorded. Results: No sex differences.

Zigler, E., Abelson, W. D., and Seitz, V. Motivational factors in the performance of economically disadvantaged children on the Peabody Picture Vocabulary List. *Child Development*, 1973, *44*, 294–303.
EXPERIMENT I: Subjects: $N = 82$; 4–5 yrs. Measures: Peabody Picture Vocabulary Test (Form B). Results: No sex differences.
EXPERIMENT II: Subjects: $N = 96$; 3–5 yrs. Measures: Same as Experiment I, with new E. Whether E played with S before testing varied. Results: No sex differences.

Zillmann, D., and Cantor, J. R. Directionality of transitory dominance as a communication variable affecting humor appreciation. *J. Personality & Social Psychology*, 1972, *24*, 191–98.
Subjects: $N = 40$; 18–21 yrs (college). Measures: Ss were presented with cartoons and jokes involving expressions of interpersonal hostility and aggressiveness. Ss rated each communication for its humorous content and novelty. Results: No sex differences.

Zimmerman, B. J. Effects of modeling and reinforcement on the acquisition and generalization of question-asking behavior. *Child Development*, 1972, *43*, 892–907.
Subjects: $N = 36$; 7 yrs (Mexican-American). Measures: In the first phase of the study, Ss were asked to pose questions to their teachers about pictures shown to them. During the second phase, two-thirds of the Ss were praised for asking questions; the remaining 12 Ss received no reinforcement. Of the 24 Ss who received praise, 12 were additionally exposed to a model who exhibited question-asking behavior. During Phases 3 and 4, procedures identical to Phases 1 and 2 were followed. Results: There were no main sex differences. During Phase 4, boys asked more questions than girls; no sex differences were found during the other 3 phases ($p < .05$).

Zimmerman, B. J., and Bell, J. A. Observer verbalization and abstraction in vicarious rule learning, generalization, and retention. *Developmental Psychology*, 1972, *7*, 227–31.
Subjects: $N = 84$; 9–12 yrs. Measures: Ss in 3 conditions (verbal description, passive observation, irrelevant verbalization) observed a model's task performance exemplifying either an associative or a conceptual rule. Ss then performed the task. Results: No sex differences.

Ziv, A. Sex differences in performance as a function of praise and blame. *J. Genetic Psychology*, 1972, *120*, 111–19.
Subjects: $N = 240$; 13 yrs. Measures: The Raven Matrix was administered to all Ss at the beginning and at the end of a 4-hour testing session. Ss received either positive, negative, or neutral reinforcement from either a male or female E prior to the second administration of the matrix. Results: (1) There were no main sex differences. (2) Boys' scores increased when E was a male; girls' scores increased when E was a female ($p < .05$).

Zurich, M., and Ledwith, B. E. Self-concepts of visually handicapped and sighted children. *Perceptual & Motor Skills*, 1965, *21*, 771–74.
Subjects: $N = 58$; 8–9 yrs (visually handicapped, sighted). Measures: Lipsitt's self-concept scale. Results: (1) Among visually handicapped Ss, girls rated themselves higher than boys did on the adjectives friendly, happy, likable, trusted, cooperative, and cheerful. Boys rated themselves higher than girls did on the adjective polite. (2) Among sighted Ss, girls rated themselves higher than boys did on the adjectives good, courteous, obedient, and clean. Boys rated themselves higher than girls did on the adjectives happy, kind, honest, likable, trusted, and proud.

Zussman, J. U. Sex differences in parental discipline techniques. Manuscript in preparation, Stanford University, 1973.
Subjects: $N = 44$; 10 yrs and mothers. Measures: Ss were questioned about their parents' disciplinary techniques. Interviews were also conducted with mothers. Results: (1) Parents practiced love withdrawal (e.g. isolation, acting hurt or upset) more frequently with boys than with girls (mothers' reports, $p < .05$; Ss' reports, $p < .01$). (2) Parents used teaching techniques (e.g. reasoning, discussion, role-taking) more often with girls than with boys

(mothers' reports, $p < .05$; Ss' reports, NS). (3) No sex differences were found in parental use of power-assertive techniques (e.g. spanking, withdrawal of privileges).

Zussman, J. U., and Reimer, D. G. An exploration of two processes of empathy. Unpublished manuscript, Stanford University, 1973.

> **Subjects:** $N = 64$; 9, 10 yrs. **Measures:** After watching 2 puppet monologues, Ss were asked to recall as much of each monologue as they could. **Results:** No sex differences.

Zytkoskee, A., Strickland, B. R., and Watson, J. Delay of gratification and internal versus external control among adolescents of low socioeconomic status. *Developmental Psychology*, 1971, *4*, 93–98.

> **Subjects:** $N = 132$; 14–17 yrs (white, black). **Measures:** Ss completed the Bialer Locus of Control Scale and a delay-of-reward measure. **Results:** No sex differences.
> No sex differences.

Index

Personal names are indexed only if we have directly quoted the people in question or their works, or cited a personal communication from them, or discussed one or more of their works at length.
All published works cited or listed in the text appear in either the Annotated Bibliography or the References Cited section.

M

F